## The Essential
# GLUTEN-FREE
# RESTAURANT GUIDE
### **6**th Edition

---

# Symbols Summary

 **Gluten-free menu is available on site.** See the Section 2 User's Guide for more information about what constitutes a gluten-free menu.

 **Gluten-free specialty items, such as bread, beer, pasta, etc., are available.** Always call ahead to confirm the availability of gluten-free specialty items. Restaurants may sell out and deliveries can arrive late.

**100%** **This is a 100% gluten-free establishment.** No gluten on site

 **This is a chain restaurant, and you can find its gluten-free information in Section 3.** More on this in the Section 3 User's Guide.

**No Icon.** None of the above apply. See the restaurant's description for information about its gluten-free accommodations.

---

**B** = Breakfast      **L** = Lunch      **D** = Dinner      **S** = Snack

**¢** = under $10      **$** = $10 to $15      **$$** = $15 to $25      **$$$** = $21 to $29      **$$$$** = $30+

THE ESSENTIAL GLUTEN-FREE RESTAURANT GUIDE, 6TH EDITION
Copyright © 2013 by Triumph Dining

Published by Triumph Dining
1409 Chapin Avenue
Mezzanine
Burlingame, CA 94010

Find us on the web at: www.triumphdining.com
Find free gluten-free news and updates at: www.triumphdining.com/blog

ISBN 978-1-938104-06-0

Printed in the United States of America

# CONTENTS

## SECTION 1: HOW TO GET A GF MEAL ANYWHERE.........13

Chapter 1 - Conveying Information Effectively .. 13
Chapter 2 - Building Short-Term Relationships .. 17
Chapter 3 - Building Long-Term Relationships... 19
Chapter 4 - A Few Final Words of Advice....... 21

## SECTION 2: RESTAURANT LISTINGS BY STATE .............25

User's Guide................................25
Dining out checklist ......................29
Alabama ...................................30
Alaska .....................................35
Arizona ....................................39
    Phoenix.............................39
    Scottsdale..........................42
    Tucson .............................45
    All Other Cities....................48
Arkansas ...................................53
    Little Rock..........................53
    All Other Cities....................54
California ...................................56
    Los Angeles ........................56
    San Diego ..........................59
    San Francisco.......................62
    All Other Cities....................65
Colorado...................................100
    Boulder ............................100
    Colorado Springs ...................104
    Denver..............................106
    Fort Collins.........................111
    All Other Cities....................113
Connecticut ................................122
Delaware...................................130
District of Columbia........................137

**Florida**  . . . . . . . . . . . . . . . . . . . . . . . . . . . . . . . . . **142**
    Boca Raton . . . . . . . . . . . . . . . . . . . . . . . . 142
    Jacksonville . . . . . . . . . . . . . . . . . . . . . . 143
    Naples . . . . . . . . . . . . . . . . . . . . . . . . . . 145
    Orlando . . . . . . . . . . . . . . . . . . . . . . . . . 146
    Sarasota . . . . . . . . . . . . . . . . . . . . . . . . . 149
    Tampa . . . . . . . . . . . . . . . . . . . . . . . . . . 150
    All Other Cities . . . . . . . . . . . . . . . . . . . . 152
**Georgia**  . . . . . . . . . . . . . . . . . . . . . . . . . . . . . . . . . **166**
    Atlanta . . . . . . . . . . . . . . . . . . . . . . . . . 166
    All Other Cities . . . . . . . . . . . . . . . . . . . . 173
**Hawaii**  . . . . . . . . . . . . . . . . . . . . . . . . . . . . . . . . . **182**
    Honolulu . . . . . . . . . . . . . . . . . . . . . . . . 182
    All Other Cities . . . . . . . . . . . . . . . . . . . . 185
**Idaho**  . . . . . . . . . . . . . . . . . . . . . . . . . . . . . . . . . **192**
**Illinois**  . . . . . . . . . . . . . . . . . . . . . . . . . . . . . . . . . **196**
    Chicago . . . . . . . . . . . . . . . . . . . . . . . . 196
    All Other Cities . . . . . . . . . . . . . . . . . . . . 205
**Indiana**  . . . . . . . . . . . . . . . . . . . . . . . . . . . . . . . . . **217**
    Indianapolis  . . . . . . . . . . . . . . . . . . . . . 217
    All Other Cities . . . . . . . . . . . . . . . . . . . . 221
**Iowa**  . . . . . . . . . . . . . . . . . . . . . . . . . . . . . . . . . **227**
**Kansas**  . . . . . . . . . . . . . . . . . . . . . . . . . . . . . . . . . **232**
**Kentucky** . . . . . . . . . . . . . . . . . . . . . . . . . . . . . . . **240**
    Louisville . . . . . . . . . . . . . . . . . . . . . . . 240
    All Other Cities . . . . . . . . . . . . . . . . . . . . .243
**Louisiana** . . . . . . . . . . . . . . . . . . . . . . . . . . . . . . . **245**
**Maine**  . . . . . . . . . . . . . . . . . . . . . . . . . . . . . . . . . **248**
**Maryland** . . . . . . . . . . . . . . . . . . . . . . . . . . . . . . . **253**
    Baltimore  . . . . . . . . . . . . . . . . . . . . . . .253
    All Other Cities . . . . . . . . . . . . . . . . . . . . .255
**Massachusetts** . . . . . . . . . . . . . . . . . . . . . . . . . . . **261**
    Boston . . . . . . . . . . . . . . . . . . . . . . . . . 261
    Cambridge . . . . . . . . . . . . . . . . . . . . . . .265
    All Other Cities . . . . . . . . . . . . . . . . . . . . .267
**Michigan**  . . . . . . . . . . . . . . . . . . . . . . . . . . . . . . **280**

Minnesota . . . . . . . . . . . . . . . . . . . . . . . . . . . . . . . . .288
    Minneapolis . . . . . . . . . . . . . . . . . . . . . . 288
    Rochester . . . . . . . . . . . . . . . . . . . . . . . . 290
    All Other Cities . . . . . . . . . . . . . . . . . . . .292
Mississippi . . . . . . . . . . . . . . . . . . . . . . . . . . . . . .298
Missouri . . . . . . . . . . . . . . . . . . . . . . . . . . . . . . . .302
    Kansas City . . . . . . . . . . . . . . . . . . . . . . . 302
    Saint Louis . . . . . . . . . . . . . . . . . . . . . 304
    All Other Cities . . . . . . . . . . . . . . . . . . . . 306
Montana . . . . . . . . . . . . . . . . . . . . . . . . . . . . . . . . .311
    Bozeman . . . . . . . . . . . . . . . . . . . . . . . . . 311
    All Other Cities . . . . . . . . . . . . . . . . . . . . 312
Nebraska . . . . . . . . . . . . . . . . . . . . . . . . . . . . . . . 314
    Omaha . . . . . . . . . . . . . . . . . . . . . . . . . . .314
    All Other Cities . . . . . . . . . . . . . . . . . . . . 317
Nevada . . . . . . . . . . . . . . . . . . . . . . . . . . . . . . . . 319
    Las Vegas . . . . . . . . . . . . . . . . . . . . . . . .319
    All Other Cities . . . . . . . . . . . . . . . . . . . .323
New Hampshire . . . . . . . . . . . . . . . . . . . . . . . . . . . .324
New Jersey . . . . . . . . . . . . . . . . . . . . . . . . . . . . . . 331
New Mexico . . . . . . . . . . . . . . . . . . . . . . . . . . . . . 341
    Albuquerque . . . . . . . . . . . . . . . . . . . . . .341
    All Other Cities . . . . . . . . . . . . . . . . . . . . 343
New York . . . . . . . . . . . . . . . . . . . . . . . . . . . . . . . .345
    New York . . . . . . . . . . . . . . . . . . . . . . . . 345
    Rochester . . . . . . . . . . . . . . . . . . . . . . . .353
    All Other Cities . . . . . . . . . . . . . . . . . . . . 354
North Carolina . . . . . . . . . . . . . . . . . . . . . . . . . . . .370
    Asheville . . . . . . . . . . . . . . . . . . . . . . . . 370
    Charlotte . . . . . . . . . . . . . . . . . . . . . . . . 371
    Raleigh/Durham . . . . . . . . . . . . . . . . . . . .374
    All Other Cities . . . . . . . . . . . . . . . . . . . .375
North Dakota . . . . . . . . . . . . . . . . . . . . . . . . . . . . 381
Ohio     . . . . . . . . . . . . . . . . . . . . . . . . . . . . . . . .383
    Cincinnati . . . . . . . . . . . . . . . . . . . . . . . 383
    Columbus . . . . . . . . . . . . . . . . . . . . . . . 384
    All Other Cities . . . . . . . . . . . . . . . . . . . .387

NATURALLY FLAVORED
**HONEY NUT.**
JUST ONE OF
SIX AMAZING
**GLUTEN**
# FREE
FLAVORS.

Six flavors. Gluten free. Delicious news.

www.facebook.com/Chex

Wheat Chex® and Multi-Bran Chex® are *not* gluten free.

**Oklahoma** . . . . . . . . . . . . . . . . . . . . . . . . . . . . . . . .**394**
    Oklahoma City. . . . . . . . . . . . . . . . . . . . .394
    Tulsa . . . . . . . . . . . . . . . . . . . . . . . . . . . . . .397
    All Other Cities. . . . . . . . . . . . . . . . . . . . 398

**Oregon** . . . . . . . . . . . . . . . . . . . . . . . . . . . . . . . **400**
    Eugene. . . . . . . . . . . . . . . . . . . . . . . . . . . 400
    Portland. . . . . . . . . . . . . . . . . . . . . . . . . . .401
    All Other Cities. . . . . . . . . . . . . . . . . . . . 405

**Pennsylvania**. . . . . . . . . . . . . . . . . . . . . . . . . . .**410**
    Philadelphia . . . . . . . . . . . . . . . . . . . . . .410
    Pittsburgh . . . . . . . . . . . . . . . . . . . . . . . . 414
    All Other Cities. . . . . . . . . . . . . . . . . . . . 416

**Rhode Island**. . . . . . . . . . . . . . . . . . . . . . . . . . .**426**
    Providence . . . . . . . . . . . . . . . . . . . . . . . 426
    All Other Cities. . . . . . . . . . . . . . . . . . . . .427

**South Carolina**. . . . . . . . . . . . . . . . . . . . . . . . . .**429**
**South Dakota** . . . . . . . . . . . . . . . . . . . . . . . . . . .**446**
**Tennessee**. . . . . . . . . . . . . . . . . . . . . . . . . . . . . . .**449**
    Knoxville . . . . . . . . . . . . . . . . . . . . . . . . . 449
    Nashville . . . . . . . . . . . . . . . . . . . . . . . . . 451
    All Other Cities. . . . . . . . . . . . . . . . . . . . 453

**Texas** . . . . . . . . . . . . . . . . . . . . . . . . . . . . . . . . .**459**
    Austin. . . . . . . . . . . . . . . . . . . . . . . . . . . . 459
    Dallas . . . . . . . . . . . . . . . . . . . . . . . . . . . 464
    Houston. . . . . . . . . . . . . . . . . . . . . . . . . . 468
    San Antonio . . . . . . . . . . . . . . . . . . . . . .472
    All Other Cities. . . . . . . . . . . . . . . . . . . . .475

**Utah** . . . . . . . . . . . . . . . . . . . . . . . . . . . . . . . . .**487**
    Salt Lake City. . . . . . . . . . . . . . . . . . . . . .487
    All Other Cities. . . . . . . . . . . . . . . . . . . . 489

**Vermont** . . . . . . . . . . . . . . . . . . . . . . . . . . . . . . .**495**
**Virginia** . . . . . . . . . . . . . . . . . . . . . . . . . . . . . . .**505**
    Arlington/Alexandria . . . . . . . . . . . . . . . 505
    Richmond . . . . . . . . . . . . . . . . . . . . . . . . 508
    Virginia Beach . . . . . . . . . . . . . . . . . . . . 509
    All Other Cities. . . . . . . . . . . . . . . . . . . . .510

# A CRAFT BEER THAT JUST HAPPENS TO BE GLUTEN-FREE.

As beer fans and celiacs, we made it our mission to give beer back to the over two million people who are intolerant to gluten. But it had to be a craft beer that can be enjoyed by all. The result is Bard's Beer, America's first gluten-free sorghum beer and the only beer brewed with 100% malted sorghum.

*Discuss it over a Bard's*

bardsbeer.com 1.877.440.2337 • Please enjoy responsibly.

**Washington**. . . . . . . . . . . . . . . . . . . . . . . . . . . . . . . . . . **521**
    Seattle . . . . . . . . . . . . . . . . . . . . . . . . . . . . . . 521
    All Other Cities. . . . . . . . . . . . . . . . . . . . .524
**West Virgina** . . . . . . . . . . . . . . . . . . . . . . . . . . . . . . . .**533**
**Wisconsin** . . . . . . . . . . . . . . . . . . . . . . . . . . . . . . . . . .**535**
    Madison. . . . . . . . . . . . . . . . . . . . . . . . . . . . .535
    All Other Cities. . . . . . . . . . . . . . . . . . . . .537
**Wyoming** . . . . . . . . . . . . . . . . . . . . . . . . . . . . . . . . . .**543**

**SECTION 3: CHAIN RESTAURANTS** . . . . . . . . . . . . . . . . . . . . . . . . **546**

# Section 1: How to Get a GF Meal Anywhere

## Chapter 1 Conveying Information Effectively

If you remember only two pieces of information from this guide, it should be these:
1. The first fundamental building block of successful gluten-free dining is the ability to share your dietary information in a clear, efficient manner.
2. The second is developing beneficial short and long-term relationships with restaurant staff.

Almost everything you will ever do to improve your gluten-free dining out experience will flow from these two skill sets. The next two chapters will start you on the path to building these essential skills.

### Build the Right Knowledge Base

It seems obvious enough that in order to share knowledge, you must first possess it. And, when it comes to gluten-free dining, you are your own first line of defense. You should make educated decisions about what you are and are not willing to try so that you can avoid inadvertently stepping into dangerous territory, or missing out on perfectly safe, enticing dining options.

This is why you should be vigilant about collecting information on different cuisines, restaurant dishes, ingredients, and common cooking techniques. It's important to think about each cuisine (e.g. Mexican, Chinese, American, etc.) separately because each one has different ingredients and cooking methods and, hence, different potential problems for Celiacs.

Read cookbooks, watch cooking shows, research common restaurant dishes, talk with knowledgeable people, and ask questions. Initially, this may require a big time commitment and a lot of work, but it becomes easier as you start to pick things up, and it's worth the investment. Knowing the details about a particular cuisine makes every other part of the dining out experience significantly easier.

Some of our customers use Triumph Dining Cards as reference materials for building knowledge about particular cuisines. They find that the cards help them understand what information to convey and the best way to organize it for a particular type of restaurant. Our Triumph Dining Cards offer a clean framework for thinking about a restaurant's kitchen – the cards present information in three broad sections, covering (a) foods we cannot ever eat, (b) foods that are possibilities but require additional research (such as reading a label), and (c) foods that are okay for us to eat. Each section goes into enough specific detail on individual items in the restaurant's kitchen that the cards are an effective learning tool to help you identify likely safe options and potential pitfalls of a particular cuisine.

The challenge, of course, is effectively sharing this information in a restaurant setting. To accomplish this, it is necessary to focus on sharing the right information in a clear and concise manner. This involves boiling down the information into its most important and basic components and presenting them in a way that a chef can understand and use.

## Communicate Effectively

Unfortunately, saying "no wheat, rye, barley, or oats" just isn't enough to get a safe meal in a restaurant. It takes most Celiacs months to understand the nuances of what that really means; we can't expect a chef to make sense of it the first time he or she hears it. We need to give the chef enough information to really understand our needs. That means not leaving the chef to just guess where wheat, rye, barley, and oats might lurk. Give obvious examples like bread and pasta to start him or her on the right track, and then reinforce the nuances of the diet by explicitly mentioning hidden sources of gluten, like soy sauce.

Be careful, though, not to overwhelm the kitchen with irrelevant information that will impair the staff's ability to grasp the big picture and successfully accommodate you. For example, items you might want to bring up in an Indian restaurant are different from those you might mention in an Italian restaurant. Loading up an Indian kitchen with information about pasta or croutons (neither of which are typically found in Indian cuisine) or not cooking vegetables in pasta water, can lead to confusion. You might even distract the kitchen from the important task at hand – making you gluten-free Indian food. We need to strike a useful balance!

## Strike a Useful Balance

The best way to do this is to pare your information down to only those instructions that are relevant to the restaurant you are currently visiting. Then, structure it in an order that's easy to follow and understand. For example, start with a quick general statement (e.g. "I can't eat wheat…") and follow it up with a few obvious items that are prohibited (e.g. egg rolls and buns in a Chinese restaurant) to give a little context and help the kitchen staff comprehend the basic concepts of the gluten-free diet. Then, lead into the potentially big problem areas that are less obvious (e.g. sticking with our Chinese restaurant example, mention soy sauce and cross-contamination). Next, depending on the circumstances, you may want to provide some examples of foods you can eat to give the chef some starting points for preparing a safe dish.

At different restaurants, you should expect to provide different instructions, customized for the type and style of cuisine served. It's a good idea to practice your instructions and develop a personal style that feels comfortable for you.

## Look for Evidence of Thorough Understanding

The gluten-free diet has received a lot of mainstream media attention in the last few years. As a result we're seeing more and more restaurant employees who seem to "get it." Mention "no wheat, rye, barley or oats" to these staffers and you may immediately hear, "Oh, you're gluten-free" or "You have Celiac disease - I know how to handle that."

Staff awareness is the first step toward better restaurant accommodations and that initial sign of recognition can be very comforting. In fact, it might even make some diners comfortable enough just to hand over the reins and let the staffer take over. But, that willingness is likely a little premature, and here's why:

- As you know, there's a huge difference between knowing generally what "gluten-free" means and understanding all the nuances of the diet. It took us months to learn all the details of eating safely, so we know that level of granularity can't be communicated in the mainstream newspapers, magazines, and internet articles from which most people learn about Celiac disease.
- It's not reasonable to require that these well-intentioned servers should be familiar with all the ins and outs of the gluten-free diet, like hidden sources of gluten and the dangers of cross-contamination. Before allowing them to prepare your meal, it's essential that you make sure the restaurant staff is on the right page.

## Don't Make Assumptions

There's a lot of conflicting information on the gluten-free diet out there, even among dieticians, support groups, and other experts in the field. Some people believe blue cheese is gluten-free; others believe it's a danger. Some say distilled vinegar is safe while others choose to steer clear. Don't expect a chef to guess what your definition of gluten-free is.

And don't expect the chef to be 100% up-to-date on the latest research (we've seen the old rumor that spelt is gluten-free circulating again. Being a form of wheat, it is obviously not). In an ideal world, the food service industry would be required to attend trainings on and stay informed about all food sensitivity issues. But, for now at least, keeping up-to-date is your job, not the chef's.

Now, it's impractical (and even a little rude) to lecture a server for half an hour on all the nuances of the gluten-free diet. But it is within bounds to go over a few key items just to make sure that they are fully on the same page with you. If the server says "oh you're gluten-free," we usually say something along the lines of "Great! I'm so glad you've heard about it. What a relief!" Then, we ask some basic cross-contamination questions, such as whether anything breaded is prepared on the same surface as what we want to order.

As we do this, we are as concerned about the content of the actual answer as we are with the general tone and ease with which the staffer provides it. Get a feel for how educated this restaurant is. Does the server immediately grasp the underlying reasons for your concern? Does it sound like he's been trained on this, and/or that she knows the kitchen has safe, standard operating procedures in effect?

If this spot check produces good results, it gives us a strong level of comfort. If it doesn't, we fall back on some of the other communication techniques described in this Guide to make sure we convey the essentials of safe, gluten-free dining.

We advise doing this little verbal spot check at every restaurant you visit, no matter how highly recommended it comes.

## Use a Dining Card

We don't want to present the illusion that communicating effectively to restaurant staff is easy. It can be a very challenging task. A lot of information needs to be conveyed effectively in very little time. For that and other reasons, we recommend using a good dining card to supplement your verbal instructions.

A good dining card provides the kitchen with a written record of your conversation. They can reference it when preparing your meal, in case they forget or confuse any of the information you've provided them. It is also a good crutch for your verbal instructions – it serves as a visual cue to help you remember everything you want to share and gives you a safety net in case you forget to mention something.

Finally, when you're dealing with ethnic restaurants, a carefully translated dining card can help you bridge the language barrier. For example, in most Thai restaurants, an English explanation of our diet only goes so far. But, with well-written Thai instructions, we can get most dishes on the menu prepared gluten-free.

It's important, however, not to choose just any dining card. Make sure the translation is one you can trust. And just as important, make sure you know what the card says.

## Don't Say 'Gluten' ... at First

Some words are simple: They have only one meaning, and that meaning is clear. Unfortunately for us, gluten is not one of those words. Often, it means different things to different people.

Obviously, for Celiacs, "gluten" refers to the protein specifically found in wheat, rye, and barley. However, for chefs, "gluten" can be a much more expansive term that refers to plant proteins found in many cereal grains, even some that are safe for a gluten-free diet (including rice and corn). Common terms like "glutinous rice," which is also safe for a gluten-free diet, add further confusion. Without appropriate context, a chef may interpret a "gluten-free" meal to be free of flour, rice, corn, and other starches.

That's why we recommend spelling out "no wheat, rye, barley or oats" and avoiding the word "gluten" the first time you explain the diet to a new restaurant. It reduces the chance of a mix-up.

Now, that's not to say you'll never use the word "gluten" in a restaurant again. Providing information on the diet and appropriate terminology is an essential part of building long-term relationships and educating restaurants. The point here is simply that on your first visit to a new restaurant, the word "gluten" can do more harm than good.

## Consider Using the Word "Allergy"

We all know that Celiac disease is not an allergy. And it should never be a goal to spread misinformation. That said, some restaurants have reportedly approached "gluten-free" as if it were a version of the Atkins Diet or a voluntary, fad diet. In short, they didn't afford certain patrons the attention Celiac disease requires.

We've learned over the years that the word "allergy" means business in the restaurant world. It can often trigger special attention from the manager and special operating procedures in the kitchen. Depending on the circumstances, categorizing your gluten-free needs as an allergy may increase your chances of receiving a safe meal.

Now, we can't think of a good reason why the word "allergy" should carry more weight than "medically restricted diet" or "food intolerance," but we're not interested in splitting semantic hairs. Our goal is simply to give you the tools necessary to get a gluten-free meal. It's ultimately your decision whether you're comfortable using the word "allergy," but we do at least want you to be aware of the option, should you have trouble getting the attention you deserve in a restaurant.

## Talk to the Right Person

Finally, underlying this whole approach is one key assumption that we'd like to acknowledge: Your instructions, verbal or written, are only as good as the eyes or ears taking them in. Most Celiacs know that one of the easiest ways to get sick in any restaurant is to tell the wrong person about your special needs. Have you ever had a waiter who seemed too rushed to invest in understanding your instructions or just didn't seem to get it? Or, maybe you felt like she was playing a risky version of the old telephone game, selectively giving the kitchen only the bits and pieces she felt were important?

If you encounter situations like this, the most carefully prepared, expertly delivered instructions may not help you. It is absolutely essential to your success that you seek out and engage the right person early in your restaurant visit. Make sure your instructions are heard by someone who has the power, ability, and motivation to get you a gluten-free meal. Depending on the circumstances, this might be the manager, the maître d', or the owner. We'll switch gears in the next chapter to develop a framework for identifying and reaching the right person, along with other techniques central to building successful relationships.

# Chapter 2 Building Short-Term Relationships

There are things you can do every time you're in a restaurant that will improve the service you receive right then and there, and these techniques build strong short-term relationships. There are other things you can do to build powerful long-term relationships. You might use these techniques now or in the near future, and they will pay dividends on every subsequent trip to a restaurant.

Consistently successful gluten-free dining requires the development of both short and long-term relationships.

## Find the Right Restaurant

The first technique is deceptively simple: choose the right restaurant. There are a lot of factors to consider when picking a restaurant. First, some cuisines are better choices for Celiacs than others. For example, Indian and Thai cuisines often present dozens of options for the gluten-free diet, while the local pizzeria might not have any suitable options and could present a very high risk of cross-contamination.

Second, some restaurant business models create a better environment for Celiacs than others. For example, restaurants that focus on high-quality food, service, and providing fresh ingredients will be far more likely to offer you special treatment than restaurants geared toward high-speed table turning, low prices, and using pre-prepared items.

Finally, owner-operated restaurants are more likely to be Celiac-friendly than bigger chains and franchises (although there are some exceptions). At many large chains, dishes are prepared off-site with heavily-processed ingredients, making modifications very difficult. Furthermore, since the restaurant kitchen staff members receive dishes partially prepared, they are not always familiar with the composition of the dishes. On the other hand, owner-operated restaurants are far more likely to prepare dishes from scratch and therefore be more knowledgeable about the ingredients.

You should keep a close eye on these factors, along with other signals in the restaurant's environment. But the bottom line is that you should always trust your gut (no pun intended). If something about the restaurant feels off, or you aren't getting enough conscientious attention from the restaurant staff, choose another restaurant. We have walked out of restaurants when we've felt at risk, and you should feel empowered to do the same. There are plenty of other places that would be happy to have your business.

The timing of your restaurant visit is also very important. Restaurants have obvious peak hours (usually lunch and dinner rushes) during which they strain their resources just to accommodate all their customers. As a first-time customer, your objective is to convince the restaurant to invest in a short-term relationship with you, to find and prepare a gluten-free meal. This requires substantially more time and effort than accommodating a non-Celiac customer. If at all possible, your first visit to a new restaurant should be during non-peak hours (either well before or well after the peak rush), because the restaurant staff will be far better equipped and more likely to help you.

## Notify the Restaurant Beforehand

It's usually best to make reservations, letting the restaurant know in advance about your special dietary needs. (But don't worry - not having a reservation isn't the end of the world.) And when making a reservation, be sure to speak with the right person.

Surprisingly, the person answering the phone sometimes has very limited knowledge of how the restaurant actually operates. The restaurant could have the best gluten-free service in the country, and the reservationist may never know! Don't get discouraged. If you sense confusion from the first person you're speaking with, ask for the manager or, even better, the chef, to make sure the restaurant can accommodate you and to find out what protocol they would like you to follow.

## The Maitre D' = Your Best Friend

When you enter the restaurant, the first thing you should do (even before you sit down) is identify yourself as a special needs customer to the maître d'. The last thing you want is to make a busy restaurant staff feel ambushed.

The maître d' is a wonderful person to have on your side because she often serves as the restaurant's traffic cop. An experienced maître d' knows every server and line cook, can speak to the kitchen on your behalf, and can determine which waiters are most capable of handling special needs. By talking with the maître d' immediately upon arrival, you can substantially reduce the chances that you'll receive bad or disinterested service.

When we talk to the host on our first visit to a particular restaurant, we usually say something along the lines of the following: "Hi. We're the Smith's. We've heard great things about your restaurant, and we'd really like to eat here tonight. We have a restricted diet and can't eat wheat and a few other things. This card has instructions on what we can and cannot eat." - We hand him a dining card - "Will you be able to help us tonight?"

Throughout hundreds of restaurant meals, we've only been turned away twice. But, we actually found that helpful. It's better to know you can't be accommodated as soon as you walk in the door, as opposed to after you've sat down and ordered drinks.

In addition to determining whether a restaurant can accommodate you, talking to the maître d' immediately and honestly does one other extremely important thing: It humanizes you. The maître d' may see hundreds of people a night, and it's very easy for him to start viewing everyone who comes in the door as just another customer, a source of revenue. When you ask for his help and he pledges it to you, you've formed a bond. Call it empathy, sympathy, or whatever you like – the chances are very good that your maître d' will go that extra mile to make sure you eat safely.

If you're in a group and feel self-conscious about your diet, let the maître d' seat you without mentioning your special needs. Then, excuse yourself from your group, return to the maître d', and explain your situation privately. That should be enough to get you appropriate treatment, without drawing the group's attention to your special diet.

## Make It Easy

Once you have a table, there are a few more things you can do to strengthen your immediate relationship with the restaurant staff. Keep in mind that the typical restaurant staff is usually busy, in a rush, and often stressed. Anything you can do to make their jobs easier will be greatly appreciated and result in better service.

For example, it's rarely enough to tell the waiter what you can't eat. Instead, be proactive. You know more about the gluten-free diet than she does, so don't make her guess the menu options that might be suitable for you. Scout the menu for choices that are likely to be gluten-free and present them to the waiter as items for further investigation. If you do this, you allow the waiter to use his valuable time to interface with the kitchen and to confirm that your choice is a safe one.

It's also important to be considerate and show appreciation when the restaurant staff goes the extra mile to accommodate you. Think back to the last time you went out of your way to help someone. Why did you do it? What made it worthwhile? A restaurant's staff sees a lot of demanding and disgruntled customers in the course of an evening. Your smiling face and kind words will make you stand out from the crowd; you will be remembered and rewarded!

## Double Check

Finally, when your meal is served, always confirm with the server that it was prepared gluten-free. Good restaurants will typically do this as a matter of course. If they don't, be proactive and ask. This simple step should provide confirmation that your special needs were not lost in the shuffle, and it will reduce the chances of an unpleasant surprise partway through your meal.

# Chapter 3  Building Long-Term Relationships

The real rewards in gluten-free dining come when you move beyond the transactional nature of a first-time restaurant visit and begin establishing long-term relationships with restaurants.

Over time, as you develop a relationship with a particular restaurant, you have the opportunity to open doors to even more specialized service. We have heard of and experienced many situations in which restaurants have learned to make their Celiac "regulars" anything they want from scratch. Other Celiacs have inspired restaurants to stock gluten-free soy sauce or even create dedicated gluten-free menus! Every relationship with a restaurant will be different, but the sky is the limit when you start using the following tools to build mutually rewarding, long-term relationships.

## Help Yourself by Helping Them

The key to building successful long-term relationships is to align the needs of the restaurant and its staff with your own. In other words, encourage an environment where helping you and providing for your needs meets their needs.

The first component of developing this environment is to understand the needs and interests of the restaurant and its staff. Every situation is different, but you can make some basic generalizations that will be more or less accurate the vast majority of the time.

For example, it's a safe bet that the restaurant's owner and manager are looking to build a strong business and satisfy customers. Likewise, the restaurant's employees are probably interested in generous tips and a pleasant work environment.

But also keep your eyes and ears open for less obvious information (and ways you can react to it). For example, maybe the restaurant is trying to increase traffic on slow evenings (offer to refer your friends) or build a business hosting events (arrange a support group dinner). Understanding the restaurant's interests will allow you to target your efforts and improve your effectiveness.

## Reward Extra Service with an Extra Tip

The first and easiest strategy is to tip generously for good service. We generally tip 20-25% when someone handles our needs well, though we'll go higher if we receive exceptional service. We do this because waiting on Celiac patrons requires far more effort and involvement than serving typical diners. In giving you more thorough care, your server is spending less time attending to the needs of other tables. So if you tip like everyone else, the waiter could make less money for investing more time in you. That can actually create a disincentive for the waiter to spend extra time serving you well! If you reward his extra effort, however, you can actually incentivize him to go all out and be extra vigilant about your needs during future visits.

## Make Yourself a Familiar Figure

The strategy of tipping generously can be complemented by returning to the restaurant often. Frequent visits have two impacts. First, working with you regularly helps the staff learn the specific needs of your diet. Second, regular visits increase your value as a customer. And the more valuable you are as a customer, the greater the restaurant's incentive to invest in providing a variety of suitable, delicious gluten-free options.

If you receive great service from a particular staff member, get that person's name. When you return to the restaurant, request to be seated in that server's section. You'll build loyalty and the server's gluten-free knowledge base. And if you follow the previous suggestion, the server will know she can earn a generous tip by taking care of your dietary needs. If she knows she's working toward a reward, she'll be attentive every time.

## The Most Powerful Strategy: A Sincere Thank You

Believe it or not, the most effective tool for building long-term relationships is simply saying "thank you." Everyone likes to be appreciated and acknowledged for doing a good job.

Thanking the server directly is a great start. You can also take it to the next level by mentioning responsive staff to management.

Restaurant managers usually hear from customers when something goes wrong. Because they mostly hear complaints from customers, your compliments are a welcome breath of fresh air. They will make you stand out (in a good way) with management and help cement the long-term relationship you're building.

## Bring Your Friends

The next step in building a long-term relationship is to help grow the restaurant's business by referring your friends. Often, this goes hand-in-hand with a sincere "thank you."

For example, when we talk to the manager of a restaurant, we typically start by thanking him – both for the quality of his restaurant's food and the special care his staff showed in handling our dietary needs (assuming that's accurate). Then we ask him if he gets many gluten-free customers and if he'd like to serve more in the future.

The managers we've spoken with are almost always happy to have more gluten-free business, so we tell the manager that we'll mention his restaurant to other Celiacs and in this Restaurant Guide. You should also feel free to use this Guide as a tool to reward Celiac-friendly restaurants. Just e-mail us if you'd like us to look into adding a restaurant to the next edition.

The key to this technique is recognizing that restaurants are businesses; restaurant owners worry about paying their bills and earning a profit. When you visit a restaurant regularly, you become a valuable customer. When you start sending your friends, you become an extremely valuable customer! The more you contribute to their bottom line, the more the restaurant will invest in catering to your special needs.

Remember that while referring additional Celiacs is great for our community, the friends you bring don't need to have Celiac disease to contribute to the restaurant's bottom line and make management happy. Just don't forget to mention your efforts to the manager, so that you get credit for any bump in business!

As you employ these strategies, you will notice that your relationships with restaurants will strengthen substantially over time. You may find that as you tip generously, visit frequently, thank the management, and send your friends, restaurants will become substantially more accommodating of your needs. And that's an amazing progress.

## Just Ask

The most effective way to get something, whether you want to try a new dish or to get gluten-free soy sauce stocked, is to ask for it. It's really that simple! You'll be amazed at what you can get just by asking. Gluten-free restaurant dining is no exception. Use the techniques in this book to identify what makes you a valuable customer (the frequency of your visits, your plan to continue visiting regularly, your friend referrals, etc.) and ask if there's someone on staff who can work with you to find more menu options or even to create a dedicated gluten-free menu. Once you've established a good relationship, you'll most likely find that many of the restaurants you visit will be happy to go that extra mile to accommodate your needs.

# Chapter 4  A Few Final Words of Advice

We've covered a lot of ground in this section. We've discussed techniques to convey information on the gluten-free diet effectively, and strategies to develop productive short and long-term relationships. Now, we'll cover final, crucial concepts that will help you put these techniques to work.

## Attitude is Everything

All of the strategies covered in this Guide work best when delivered politely. Our attitudes are often reflected right back at us. Come in ready for battle, and you'll likely get one – your waiter, sensing your mood, will probably become defensive. Instead, come in smiling. It's hard for people, even overworked, stressed restaurant staff, to ignore genuine kindness. Be sure to ask for people's names, and use them often. Don't give orders, but ask for help.

Be careful that your instructions don't turn into a 10-minute lecture. People may zone out or, worse, become resentful. Instead, engage your server in a dialogue by involving him in your dining selections; make him your ally. The more involved he feels in the process, the more likely he is to go that extra mile for you.

## Patience is a Virtue

The Celiac diet is complex, so don't expect the restaurant staff to catch on immediately. Don't be discouraged if your waiter asks you questions seemingly out of left field, like, "Is salt okay? How about vegetables?" Is the waiter displaying genuine curiosity? Does she seem to be catching on (even if slowly)? If so, be patient and hold your temper. If she's doing her best to learn how to serve you, try not to flare up at a few innocent, if misdirected, questions.

## Give the Benefit of the Doubt

If someone who has been helpful so far makes a mistake – for example, if your salad comes with croutons – please give your server the benefit of the doubt. We've never been to a restaurant that intentionally tries to make its customers sick. Keep in mind the chaotic nature of restaurants, and please do not hurl accusations or insults.

The best way to handle this type of situation is to calmly point out the problem and reiterate that you can become ill without proper care. That is usually enough to correct any missteps. Making a scene, especially before trying to remedy the problem in a civil manner, is a no-win situation all around. Remember that these restaurants are not obligated to serve gluten-free food. Please treat them with the respect and dignity they deserve, so that they will continue serving other Celiacs in the future.

## Where to Start

We've now covered numerous strategies for successful gluten-free dining and how to apply them. We hope you've realized that gluten-free dining doesn't have to be scary or intimidating if you take the right approach and use the tools in this book.

The several thousand restaurants listed in this guide provide good, low-risk starting points for your gluten-free dining experiences. You can follow the paths of success enjoyed by other Celiacs by visiting restaurants with strong track records.

But, remember that before these restaurants were listed in this guide, a Celiac had to eat there for the first time, share information about our diet, and build that initial relationship. Now you too are equipped to do exactly that.

For every restaurant in this guide, there are hundreds more that may have no experience at all with gluten-free dining. This guide is designed to open doors for you, not shut them. So please visit the restaurants listed here, but don't necessarily rule out those that aren't in this guide. Some unlisted restaurants may present fantastic, unrealized opportunities. It's up to you to identify them. Use these tools to seek out more gluten-free opportunities to dine out, and make them successful.

# Section 2: Restaurant Listings by State

## User's Guide

In this section, there are over 5,000 restaurant locations listed alphabetically by state, with independent sub-categories for over forty of the nation's biggest and most Celiac-friendly cities. Each restaurant (or restaurant chain) was considered for inclusion in this guide based on recommendations from other Celiacs and thorough research by our editors. To determine its ability to accommodate gluten-free diners, we evaluated each restaurant for the availability of its gluten-free specialty items, the extensiveness of its gluten-free menu, and its staff's knowledge of the gluten-free diet. We used stories and suggestions from hundreds of Celiac diners, a variety of restaurant resources, and our own culinary savvy – in addition to information provided by the restaurants themselves – to come up with this broad listing of gluten-free aware restaurants.

Unfortunately, there's no such thing as worry-free gluten-free dining. By its nature, ordering a gluten-free meal will almost always take more time and effort than ordering a "regular" one. It requires constant vigilance, no matter how Celiac-friendly the restaurant may be. Our Guide is designed to help make this process as easy as possible for you.

The objective of this guide is to provide the tools you need to make safe dining choices. Not every Celiac will feel at ease frequenting every type of restaurant we've chosen to list (e.g., some people avoid *Pizza* parlors because there is a stronger possibility of cross-contamination). Everyone has his/her own level of comfort, and we advise you to find your own and stick to it. We provide information about as wide a range of restaurants as possible, not to suggest that you could or should frequent these places, but to aid you in making that decision for yourself. This Guide is about enabling you to make safe, healthy choices. It is not about making them for you.

Please keep in mind that we are not recommending or endorsing any of the restaurants in this book. We have merely aggregated information for your convenience. Because the restaurant industry is constantly and rapidly changing, you should always independently verify the information presented in this Guide.

### Overview of the Types of Restaurants Listed

The restaurants listed in this section of the guide can be broadly categorized into the following groups:

<u>Non-chain (independent) restaurants</u>
- Type 1: With gluten-free menus or specialty items
- Type 2: Without gluten-free menus or specialty items

<u>Chain restaurants</u>
- Type 1: With gluten-free specialty items or gluten-free menus/lists
- Type 2: Without gluten-free menus or lists

## Non-Chain (Independent) Restaurants

By "non-chain" or "independent," we mean owner-operated restaurants. Generally speaking, these restaurants are more Celiac-friendly than large chain restaurants, where individualized service is harder to find. We've included two different types of non-chain restaurants in this guide:

### Type 1: Non-Chain Restaurants with Gluten-Free Menus or Gluten-Free Specialty Items

In our book, a gluten-free menu has three qualities:

1) A gluten-free menu is printed. It's not in the chef's head or on the manager's computer.
2) A gluten-free menu is available to customers. This means that it is not an internal list hanging in the kitchen or in a service area; rather, it is something you can take to your table with you and choose a meal from.
3) A gluten-free menu, obviously, must list gluten-free items. It might be a separate menu or section on the menu listing only gluten-free items, or, alternatively, it can be a regular menu that clearly indicates gluten-free items (e.g. with an asterisk, a "GF," or another symbol).

A gluten-free specialty item is something that is not commonly gluten-free (like bread, pasta, pizza crust, or beer), but can be gluten-free if prepared specially.

Restaurants that have gluten-free menus or gluten-free specialty items are flagged with star-shaped icons. We've confirmed the availability of all gluten-free menus by phone, fax, or e-mail. We have not, however, independently verified the gluten-free status of the items on those menus.

In addition to flagging restaurants with gluten-free menus, we've tried to list some gluten-free menu items in the notes section, which is meant only to give you an idea of the type of cuisine served. **Never order directly from the notes section.** Many of the items listed can be prepared gluten-free only with the proper modifications, which the restaurant can make only if they know you are on a gluten-free diet!

Additionally, never assume that a gluten-free menu or gluten-free specialty items guarantee a gluten-free meal. Always show your dining card and carefully explain the gluten-free diet to your server. Please, don't make any assumptions when it comes to your health.

And don't forget: If you're going out for a gluten-free specialty item like pizza or pasta, be sure to call the restaurant ahead of time to make sure the item is in stock. Sometimes restaurants run out of these products.

### Type 2: Non-Chain Restaurants without Gluten-Free Menus

In this section, we included some non-chain restaurants without gluten-free menus. These restaurants were selected based on recommendations from other Celiacs, as well as follow-up research that included conversations with restaurant management and staff. In the notes section, you will find important references to those conversations.

On occasion, the notes section also includes a few menu items that, according to the restaurant staff, are or can be modified to be gluten-free. These short lists are intended to give you an idea about what kind of food the restaurant serves. They are not designed to be comprehensive, and it is not appropriate or safe to order from these lists. When dining out at one of these establishments, please work with the restaurant staff to find a dish that's right for you. **Again, never order directly from the notes section of this guide.** Many of the items listed can be prepared gluten-free only with the proper modifications, which the restaurant can make only if they know you are on a gluten-free diet!

It's important to remember that these restaurants are listed because other Celiacs have safely enjoyed eating at them in the past, and they seemed aware during our conversations with management and staff. Many of them do not have any formally listed gluten-free offerings, and it's possible that certain employees at these restaurants have little to no experience with Celiac disease or the gluten-free diet.

As at any restaurant, even those with gluten-free menus, you should approach your dining experience with a certain amount of caution: Use your dining card, explain your diet carefully, and specify exactly how you'd like your food to be handled. Use your judgment, and if you're not entirely comfortable with the level of service being provided, leave the premises. Then, be sure to let us know, so we can revisit that restaurant's entry with extra caution when we prepare the next edition of this guide.

In addition to owner-operated, "non-chain" restaurants, this section also contains two types of chain restaurants:

## Type 1: Chain Restaurants with Gluten-Free Menus or Lists

In this section, we've included some or all locations of select chain restaurants that have gluten-free menus at each location, or gluten-free lists not present at each location but readily available from the corporate office or franchisor.

Next to Type 1 chain restaurants, you will see an icon of an open book. This means that you can find information on these restaurants in Section III of this guide. Please be sure to read the Section III User's Guide before reviewing any of the information included there. Gluten-free options are typically available at all locations, but may, in certain circumstances, be unavailable. Call a specific restaurant location ahead of time to confirm the availability of gluten-free items.

Note: Section III also contains many additional chain restaurants for which locations are not listed in Section II. For more information about these restaurants and their gluten-free offerings, please see Section III.

## Type 2: Chain Restaurants without Gluten-Free Lists

Finally, this section includes listings for certain chain restaurants, such as Roy's, that do not have gluten-free lists, but do have on-site management that is generally regarded as very helpful, knowledgeable, and attentive. Each of these restaurants should be able to work with your dietary needs on an individual, local level.

## Some Commonly-Used Terms

GF Aware. The term "GF aware" appears occasionally in the restaurant notes section. That term simply means that our contact with the restaurant suggested that the managers and staff are familiar with the term "gluten-free" and the gluten-free diet. The term "GF aware" can indicate a range of knowledge, from "they have heard of the diet" to "they are formally trained on the requirements of the diet." You may still have to explain the details and nuances of the diet, but hopefully, you'll encounter staff members who have at least a baseline of knowledge on which to build.

Along the same lines, all the information presented here is "straight from the horse's mouth." We contacted every non-chain restaurant recommended for this guide and asked about gluten-free accommodations. In the following pages, we've reported their responses. We could not, however, quiz each restaurant to test the full extent and depth of the staff's knowledge. That's why it's important for you to remain vigilant and always ask questions.

## Lunch vs. Dinner

The specific information provided in each restaurant's listing pertains to dinner, unless dinner is not served at that particular restaurant. Price categories apply to dinner entrées only; they do not include appetizers, drinks, etc. If dinner is not served at a particular restaurant, the price category refers to lunch or whatever meal is served.

Often, the dynamics of a restaurant change vastly between lunch and dinner. Lunch menus typically consist of lower-priced options like sandwiches, and many restaurants focus primarily on fast service. This makes it harder for restaurants to offer specialized attention.

Accordingly, the gluten-free options available at a restaurant may be very different for lunch and for dinner. For this reason, we recommend calling to get more information before visiting a restaurant for lunch.

## A Few Final Notes

The restaurant business changes quickly and seems to be in a constant state of flux – even more so now, during an economic recession. New restaurants open while old ones close, owners sell businesses, chefs come and go, menus are updated, dish ingredients are modified, corporate policies change, managers leave, employees turn over or change shifts, etc. Any one of these (or other) factors could result in a one-time unpleasant dining experience at an otherwise reliable restaurant; they can also flat out ruin a formerly accommodating restaurant.

That's why it's important that you always individually verify the information presented in this Restaurant Guide (think of it as a starting point, not a definitive resource) and confirm that a restaurant can accommodate your needs before each visit. Remain vigilant, ask questions, make suggestions, and keep an eye on how the restaurant is handling your requests. If you're uncomfortable at any point, ask the manager to intervene. If that doesn't work, find another restaurant. It's not worth risking your health.

*Finally, we would love to hear from you about your dining experiences – good or bad – at restaurants listed in this guide or new restaurants we haven't yet discovered. Future editions of this guide will be only as good as the feedback we receive from you, so if you'd like to see a restaurant added to these listings (or one removed), e-mail us or visit our website (www. TriumphDining.com) to let us know.*

# Restaurant Listings

## Stop!

Before you visit any restaurant listed in this guide, review this Summary Checklist and the User's Guides in Sections 2 and 3.

### Before You Leave the House

- ☑ Research the restaurant. Is it a buffet, sandwich shop, or other type of cuisine that increases the risk of cross-contamination? If so, will you feel safe eating there?
- ☑ If dining at a chain restaurant, call the corporate office to request the most recent gluten-free menu or list. (See Section III for contact information.)
- ☑ Regardless of the type of restaurant, call the location you plan to visit in advance. Does the restaurant still have a gluten-free menu? (If not, can they accommodate you tonight?)
- ☑ Also, confirm that gluten-free specialty items are in stock. (E.g., if you're going for the gluten-free pasta, do they have it tonight?)

### When You Get There

- ☑ Introduce yourself to the maitre d', and mention your dietary needs.
- ☑ Ask for the gluten-free menu, if applicable.
- ☑ Never make any assumptions. Present your dining card, even if they have a gluten-free menu. Ask a few questions. Confirm that they understand the diet, even if they have a gluten-free menu.
- ☑ Also, review and use the tips and strategies for safe restaurant dining presented in the previous sections of this book.
- ☑ And remember, there is no way any restaurant (or restaurant guide) can guarantee a gluten-free meal. Always independently verify information and be vigilant when eating out. A bit of caution goes a long way in getting a safe and delicious gluten-free meal.

# ALABAMA

## 32 Degrees Yogurt Bar 📖
Birmingham ▪ (205) 871-7328
229 Country Club Pk
Cullman ▪ (256) 734-0110
1930 Marktplatz
Madison ▪ (256) 864-9430
7690 Hwy 72 W
Montgomery ▪ (334) 272-4773
7030 Eastchase Pkwy
Oxford ▪ (256) 835-6559
252 Oxford Exchange Blvd

## Amsterdam Café $$LD
Auburn ▪ (334) 826-8181
410 S Gay St ▪ Seafood ▪ Restaurant notes
that they are "comfortable" accommodating
GF diners. In the kitchen, servers and
cooks have a list of which menu items can
be modified to be GF. Ask for a manager,
who will indicate GF menu options. ▪
www.amsterdamcafeauburn.com

## Au Bon Pain 📖
Auburn ▪ (334) 844-1284
255 Duncan Dr
Mobile ▪ (251) 435-7222
5 Mobile Infirmary Cir

## Berkeley Bob's Coffee House ¢S
Cullman ▪ (256) 775-2944
304 1st Ave SE ▪ Café ▪ Owner Bob reports
that although he has stopped regularly
stocking GF bread, he can provide it with
advance notice. They also serve GF salads.
Bob adds that GF diners need only talk to
him, and he will "work something out." ▪
www.berkeleybob.com

## Bonefish Grill ✪📖
Hoover ▪ (205) 985-9545
3430 Galleria Cir
Mobile ▪ (251) 633-7196
6955 Airport Blvd
Huntsville ▪ (256) 883-0643
4800 Whitesburg Dr S Ste 33

Montgomery ▪ (334) 396-1770
7020 Eastchase Pkwy

## Cactus Flower Café $LD
Dothan ▪ (334) 984-0717
5412 Montgomery Hwy
Gulf Shores ▪ (251) 948-4642
3800 Gulf Shores Pkwy ▪ Mexican ▪ GF
list includes tacos, tostadas, enchiladas,
huevos rancheros, nachos, and more. Some
items may be available only with certain
toppings, or may require modification to
become GF. Alert a server upon arrival
to help navigate the menu. Manager Lee
notes that items for GF customers are
fried separately in a skillet to avoid CC. ▪
cactusflowercafe.net

## Cafe Dupont ★$$$$LD
Birmingham ▪ (205) 322-1282
113 20th St N ▪ Southern ▪ The restaurant
reports that they accommodate GF
customers "all the time," with most
modifications involving "excluding some
sort of starch" from a dish. Alert server
upon arrival to learn more about GF
options. ▪ www.cafedupont.net

## California Dreaming Restaurant and Bar ✪📖
Spanish Fort ▪ (251) 626-9942
30500 State Hwy 181

## Cantina Laredo 📖
Huntsville ▪ (256) 327-8580
6782 Old Madison Pike

## Carino's Italian ✪📖
Hoover ▪ (205) 560-0505
4330 Creekside Ave

## Carrabba's Italian Grill ✪📖
Birmingham ▪ (205) 980-1016
4503 Riverview Pkwy
Huntsville ▪ (256) 288-1333
2801 Memorial Pkwy SW
Mobile ▪ (251) 342-3662
3917 Airport Blvd
Montgomery ▪ (334) 271-7500
1510 Eastern Blvd

### Ellen's Creative Cakes ✪★$$$$$
*Huntsville* ▪ *(256) 217-1517*
*603 Jordan Ln* ▪ *Bakery* ▪ Non-dedicated bakery offering a variety of GF cakes. Flavors include carrot, hummingbird, and chocolate, and each is available in a range of sizes. Owner Ellen suggests placing an order in advance, but she notes that she usually has some GF cake stored in the freezer for fast pickup. ▪ *www.ellenscreativecakes.com*

### Elli Bistro ★$$LD
*Gulf Shores* ▪ *(251) 948-4710*
*3800 Gulf Shores Pkwy* ▪ *American* ▪ No GF menu but willing to accommodate considering a majority of the menu can be made GF. Upon request, the chef will come out and take any special requests to ensure CC will not occur. ▪ *www.ellibistro.com*

### Firebirds Wood Fired Grill ✪⌂
*Hoover* ▪ *(205) 733-2002*
*191 Main St*

### Flat Top Grill ⌂
*Birmingham* ▪ *(205) 994-3113*
*250 Summit Blvd*

### Fleming's Prime Steakhouse & Wine Bar ✪⌂
*Vestavia* ▪ *(205) 262-9463*
*103 Summit Blvd*

### Fox and Hound Pub & Grille ⌂
*Birmingham* ▪ *(205) 968-3823*
*3425 Colonnade Pkwy*

### Genghis Grill ⌂
*Hoover* ▪ *(205) 538-2347*
*4730 Chace Cir*
*Montgomery* ▪ *(334) 277-5766*
*7216 E Chase Pkwy*

### Hangout, The ★$$BLD
*Gulf Shores* ▪ *(251) 948-3030*
*101 E Beach Blvd* ▪ *American* ▪ Restaurant reports that many menu items can be modified to be GF, including sandwiches without buns and seafood dishes. Confirm the timeliness of this information before dining in. Alert a server upon arrival. ▪ *www.thehangoutal.com*

### Hope's Cheesecake ★$$$$
*Gulf Shores* ▪ *(888) 968-4673*
*210 E 20th Ave* ▪ *Dessert* ▪ The raspberry cheesecake can be altered to be GF upon request. ▪ *www.hopescheesecake.com*

### Jason's Deli ✪⌂
*Huntsville* ▪ *(256) 883-7300*
*4800 Whitesburg Sr S*
*Huntsville* ▪ *(256) 971-5325*
*1395 Enterprise Wy*
*Tuscaloosa* ▪ *(205) 752-6192*
*2300 McFarland Blvd E*
*Birmingham* ▪ *(205) 987-8740*
*3032 John Hawkins Pkwy*
*Birmingham* ▪ *(205) 995-4933*
*4700 US 280*
*Birmingham* ▪ *(205) 877-8477*
*583 Brookwood Village*
*Montgomery* ▪ *(334) 409-9890*
*1520 Eastern Blvd*
*Mobile* ▪ *(251) 281-0801*
*3756 Airport Blvd*

### Jersey Mike's ⌂
*Birmingham* ▪ *(205) 980-1866*
*4673 Hwy 280 E*
*Huntsville* ▪ *(256) 382-0873*
*6290 University Dr*
*Birmingham* ▪ *(205) 661-0771*
*1873 Gadsden Hwy*
*Opelika* ▪ *(334) 705-7827*
*2336 Tiger Town Pkwy*
*Hoover* ▪ *(205) 987-7115*
*1851 Montgomery Hwy*

### Jim 'n Nick's Bar-B-Q ✪★⌂
*Birmingham* ▪ *(205) 320-1060*
*1908 11th Ave S*
*Alabaster* ▪ *(205) 605-0170*
*295 Alabaster Blvd*
*Gardendale* ▪ *(205) 608-3315*
*915 Odum Rd*
*Homewood* ▪ *(205) 942-3336*
*220 Oxmoor Rd*
*Hoover* ▪ *(205) 733-1300*
*1810 Montgomery Hwy*
*Birmingham* ▪ *(205) 661-3100*
*1660 Gadsen Hwy*
*Jasper* ▪ *(205) 221-2271*

1804 Hwy 78 E
Montgomery ▪ (334) 213-0046
6415 Atlanta Hwy
Prattville ▪ (334) 290-1000
2550 Cobb's Ford Rd
Tuscaloosa ▪ (205) 469-2060
305 21st Ave
Birmingham ▪ (205) 991-1306
2831 Greystone Commercial Blvd

### Jimmy's                              ★ $$LD
Opelika ▪ (334) 745-2155
104 S 8th St ▪ American ▪ Owner and Chef
Jim reports that they will prepare GF meals
at "any time." He notes that many dishes,
including the fresh fish, the beef tenderloin,
and the lobster, are GF, while other items can
be modified to be GF. Confirm the timeliness
of this information before dining in. GF pasta
is available. ▪ www.jimmysopelika.com

### Joe's Crab Shack                      ✪▢
Hoover ▪ (205) 981-2999
20 Meadow View Dr

### Johnny Brusco's New York
### Style Pizza                           ★▢
Auburn ▪ (334) 826-0055
2408 E University Dr
Auburn ▪ (334) 826-0545
2415 Moores Mill Rd
Jasper ▪ (205) 221-9700
1705 Hwy 78 E
Vestavia Hilla ▪ (205) 637-5270
2516 Rocky Ridge Rd

### Lone Star Steakhouse & Saloon         ✪▢
Huntsville ▪ (256) 837-0010
5901 University Dr NW
Oxford ▪ (256) 831-7441
171 Colonial Dr
Trussville ▪ (205) 661-9339
4720 Norrel Dr

### Lulu's Buffet                         ✪SLD
Gulf Shores ▪ (251) 967-5858
200 E 25th Ave ▪ American ▪ Lulu's
offers a GF menu with items such as
smoked tuna dip, chicken fingers, various salad options, mahi tacos and more. ▪
www.lulubuffett.com

### Maestro 2300                          $$$LD
Auburn ▪ (334) 821-4448
2300 Moores Mill Rd ▪ Mediterranean ▪
The restaurant reports that there are "lots
of options" for GF diners. In addition to
naturally GF items, they can "adjust" many
dishes to meet the needs of GF diners. Examples include roasted red pepper involt-
ini, beef carpaccio, and most proteins and
seafood dishes. Ask for a manager upon
arrival, and they will be able to help select a
GF meal. ▪ www.maestro2300.com

### Manna Grocery & Deli                  ₵L
Tuscaloosa ▪ (205) 752-9955
2300 McFarland Blvd E ▪ Deli ▪ Manager Mike reports that the deli can
accommodate GF diners and that the
staff is "knowledgeable about the ingredients" in their food. He recommends
asking for a manager upon arrival. ▪
www.mannagrocery.com

### Melting Pot, The                      ✪▢
Birmingham ▪ (205) 981-8001
611 Doug Baker Blvd
Huntsville ▪ (256) 327-8888
340 Bridge St Town Centre

### Moonlight Bistro, The                 ★SLD
Mentone ▪ (256) 634-4560
6080 Hwy 117 ▪ American ▪ The restaurant reports that the chili, trout, sirloin,
and BBQ pork are naturally GF and the
chefs are willing to alter other items to
make them GF. Confirm the timeliness
of this information before dining in. ▪
www.themoonlightbistro.com

### Mr. Chen's                            ★₵LD
Birmingham ▪ (205) 824-8283
1917 Hoover Ct
Tuscaloosa ▪ (205) 343-6889
514 14th St ▪ Chinese ▪ The manager states that while they do not have
a GF menu, they are "very happy"
to modify dishes on the menu to accommodate the needs of GF diners. ▪
www.mrchenschinesecooking.com

### Mughal Indian Cuisine   $LD
*Birmingham* ▪ *(205) 408-1008*
*5426 Hwy 280* ▪ *Indian* ▪ No GF
menu, however servers will notify
chef and the staff will accommodate. ▪
*www.mughalindiancuisine.com*

### O'Charley's   📖
*Montgomery* ▪ *(334) 271-7500*
*1510 Eastern Blvd*
*Huntsville* ▪ *(256) 837-3431*
*6152 University Dr NW*
*Mobile* ▪ *(251) 344-0200*
*3649 Airport Blvd*
*Birmingham* ▪ *(205) 942-8001*
*109 Wildwood Pkwy*
*Alabaster* ▪ *(205) 621-7453*
*285 S Colonial Promenade*
*Daphne* ▪ *(251) 447-0744*
*6840 US Hwy 90*
*Decatur* ▪ *(256) 355-0505*
*2148 Beltline Rd SW*
*Dothan* ▪ *(334) 673-1956*
*3320 Montgomery Hwy*
*Foley* ▪ *(251) 943-3181*
*3060 S McKenzie St*
*Fultondale* ▪ *(205) 849-6401*
*1709 Fulton Rd*
*Mobile* ▪ *(251) 633-9710*
*725 Schillinger Rd S*
*Opelika* ▪ *(334) 749-0719*
*2501 Gateway Dr*
*Oxford* ▪ *(256) 831-8305*
*4 Recreation Dr*
*Prattville* ▪ *(334) 285-2990*
*2301 Cobbs Ford Rd*
*Tuscaloosa* ▪ *(205) 556-5143*
*3799 McFarland Blvd E*

### Organic Harvest Café   ✪★¢L
*Hoover* ▪ *(205) 978-0318*
*1580 Montgomery Hwy* ▪ *Café* ▪ Offers
GF brown rice tortilla as bread substitute,
in addition to various soup, salad, and
smoothie options. ▪ *orgharvest.info/cafe/*

### P.F. Chang's China Bistro   ✪★📖
*Huntsville* ▪ *(256) 327-8320*
*305 The Bridge St Ste 101*

*Vestavia* ▪ *(205) 967-0040*
*233 Summit Blvd*

### Papa Dubi's   $LD
*Guntersville* ▪ *(256) 894-7878*
*3931 Brashers Chapel Rd* ▪ *Cajun &
Creole* ▪ Owner Dan reports that the
restaurant does not serve GF diners on
a regular basis. He suggests alerting the
server upon arrival, and asking the server
to get him or his son, Patrick, who is the
kitchen manager. Dan notes that grilled
chicken, fish, shrimp, and salads are among
the items that can be modified to be GF.
Confirm the timeliness of this information
before dining in.

### Pho Que Huong Vietnamese   ★¢LD
*Birmingham* ▪ *(205) 942-5400*
*430 Green Springs Hwy* ▪ *Vietnamese* ▪
The restaurant reports that there are many
naturally GF dining options such as rice
noodle bowls and soups. Additionally, chef is
willing to alter other dishes on the menu to
make them GF. Alert the server upon arrival.

### Red Brick Pizza   ✪★📖
*Enterprise* ▪ *(334) 475-2156*
*847 Boll Weevil*

### Rojo   ✪$LD
*Birmingham* ▪ *(205) 328-4733*
*2921 Highland Ave S* ▪ *Latin American* ▪
GF menu includes salads, burgers without
buns, burritos, tacos, and paella. Alert
server upon arrival so they can prepare
the necessary procedures to avoid CC. ▪
*rojo.birminghammenus.com*

### Romano's Macaroni Grill   ✪★📖
*Huntsville* ▪ *(256) 722-4770*
*5901 University Dr NW*
*Vestavia* ▪ *(205) 298-7998*
*241 Summit Blvd*
*Mobile* ▪ *(251) 450-4556*
*3250 Aiport Blvd*

### Ruth's Chris Steak House   ✪📖
*Huntsville* ▪ *(256) 539-3930*
*800 Monroe St*
*Birmingham* ▪ *(205) 879-9995*

*2300 Woodcrest Pl*
*Mobile* ▪ *(251) 476-0516*
*2058 Airport Blvd*

**Sebastien's Restaurant**                    ★$$D
*Albertville* ▪ *(256) 660-1222*
*330 Hwy 75 N* ▪ *French* ▪ Manager said
they are willing to accommodate any cus-
tomer needs and that many GF customers
eat at the restaurant everyday. Confirm the
timeliness of this information before din-
ing in ▪ *www.sebastiens.com/menu.html*

**Shane's Rib Shack**                         ✪☐
*Mobile* ▪ *(351) 447-2116*
*6401 Airport Blvd*
*Birmingham* ▪ *(205) 874-6888*
*2673 Valleydale Rd*
*Huntsville* ▪ *(256) 715-9899*
*4800 Whitesburg Dr*

**Singleton's Barbeque**                      ★₵LD
*Florence* ▪ *(252) 760-0802*
*4220 Huntsville Rd* ▪ *Barbeque* ▪ The
restaurant reports that most items can be
prepared GF upon customer request. Alert
the server upon arrival.

**Sunflower Café**                        ✪★$LD
*Fairhope* ▪ *(251) 929-0055*
*320 Eastern Shore Shopping Ctr* ▪ *Or-*
*ganic* ▪ GF items are marked on the menu
and include hummus, sunflower salad,
grilled wild ahi sandwich, and lemongrass
stir fry. GF bread and pizza are available. ▪
*www.va-fairhopehealthfoods.com*

**Surin of Thailand**                         ☐
*Birmingham* ▪ *(205) 871-4531*
*64 Church St*
*Huntsville* ▪ *(256) 213-9866*
*975 Airport Rd*
*Tuscaloosa* ▪ *(205) 752-7970*
*1402 University Blvd*

**Sweet Cece's**                              ☐
*Huntsville* ▪ *(256) 270-7574*
*326 N Sutton Rd*
*Tuscaloosa* ▪ *(205) 561-6458*
*2217 University Blvd*
*Huntsville* ▪ *(256) 585-3837*
*8 Parade St* ▪ *Dessert* ▪ All frozen yogurt,

with the exceptions of Cake Batter, Cookies
n' Cream, Red Velvet Cake, and Heath Bar,
are GF. ▪ *www.sweetceces.com*

**Tin Drum AsiaCafé**                         ✪☐
*Birmingham* ▪ *(205) 968-8083*
*214 Summit Blvd*

**Urban Cookhouse**                           ★₵LD
*Birmingham* ▪ *(205) 879-0883*
*2846 18th St S*
*Birmingham* ▪ *(205) 969-6700*
*250 Summit Blvd* ▪ *American* ▪ The
manager reports that they are "more
than willing" to accommodate GF cus-
tomers. Items such as meats, rice and
vegetables are naturally GF, and oth-
ers can be altered to become GF. ▪
*urbancookhouse.com/menus/lunch-dinner/*

**Veranda on Highland**                       ★$$$D
*Birmingham* ▪ *(205) 939-5551*
*2220 Highland Ave S* ▪ *Southern* ▪
Restaurant reports that GF diners can
be accommodated with "no problem."
Alert a server upon arrival and they will
talk to the chef who will then list items
on the menu that can be made GF. ▪
*www.verandaonhighland.com*

**Village Tavern**                            ✪☐
*Birmingham* ▪ *(205) 970-1640*
*101 Summit Blvd*

**Zazu Gastropub**                            ★$$LD
*Auburn* ▪ *(334) 887-0206*
*149 E Magnolia Ave* ▪ *American* ▪ The
head chef reports that they are "always will-
ing to accommodate" GF customers. All
salads and most dinner entrées are GF, and
other items can be modified upon request.
▪ *www.zazuauburn.com*

**Zen Restaurant**                            ★$$LD
*Orange Bch* ▪ *(251) 981-2988*
*25775 Perdido Bch Blvd* ▪ *Fusion* ▪ Restaurant reports that most items can be GF if
made without soy sauce. They recommend
alerting the server so that information can
be relayed to the chef to ensure no CC oc-
curs. ▪ *www.zenorangebeach.com*

# ALASKA

## Acai Alaska                                   ¢BL
Anchorage ■ (907) 333-2224
750 W Dimond Blvd ■ American ■ GF items
include any of the acai bowls. Most toppings
are GF including a flax granola. Sandwiches
are also served, be sure to ask server about
GF options. ■ www.acaiak.commenu

## Bistro Red Beet                            ★ $LD
Wasilla ■ (907) 376-1400
5031 E Mayflower Ln ■ American ■ Owner
and Chef Sally reports that "except on pasta
or meat pie days," the restaurant is entirely
GF. Confirm the timeliness of this information before dining in. GF list usually includes
breads, cookies, brownies, muffins, and more.
■ redbeetbistro.com

## Boston's Restaurant & Sports Bar
❂★📖
Anchorage ■ (907) 770-1270
2830 C St
Fairbanks ■ (907) 458-9222
1243 Old Steese Hwy

## Café Orca and Gallery                    ★ $LD
Whittier ■ (907) 472-2549
Whittier Boat Harbor Loop ■ Café ■ GF
bread is available for burgers and sandwiches. ■ alaskacafeorca.com

## Flying Squirrel Bakery Café             ★ $S
Talkeetna ■ (907) 733-6887
Mile 11 Talkeetna Spur ■ Bakery & Café
■ Choices of GF black brownies and GF
quiches are available on request. Also the
bakery makes GF bread the first Friday of
every month. ■ flyingsquirrelcafe.com

## Ginger                                  ❂$$$LD
Anchorage ■ (907) 929-3680
425 W 5th Ave ■ Pacific Rim ■ GF menu
includes appetizers, salads and soups as
well as entrées such as ribeye steak, filet
mignon, sesame crusted ahi, vegan curry
and beef curry. ■ www.gingeralaska.com

## Glacier Brewhouse                      ❂$$$LD
Anchorage ■ (907) 274-2739
737 W 5th Ave ■ American ■ GF menu
includes appetizers, salads, soups, sandwiches on GF bread, roasted chicken, pork,
king crab legs, grilled ribeye, flat iron steak,
BBQ baby back ribs, and prime rib, as well
as dessert. GF bread and beer are available.
■ www.glacierbrewhouse.com

## Grape Tap                                   $$D
Wasilla ■ (907) 376-8466
322 N Boundary St ■ Modern American
■ GF appetizers, entrées and desserts
available. The restaurant recommends
alerting a hostess upon arrival so she can
inform the kitchen of the GF request ahead
of time. ■ www.thegrapetap.com

## Gustavus Inn at Glacier Bay          ★ $$$
Gustavus ■ (907) 697-2254
1 Mile Gustavus Rd ■ American ■ Owner
Dave reports that they are "comfortable
with GF diets." He adds that he makes
his own GF bread and that all dinners
are "adaptable." They will also send a GF
sack lunch with guests when they go on
"excursions." Noting GF upon making a
reservation is strongly recommended. ■
www.gustavusinn.com

## Hangar on the Warf                     ★ $$LD
Juneau ■ (907) 586-5018
2 Marine Wy ■ American ■ GF pasta is
available. At lunch time between 11am-
2pm the restaurant serves lentil meatloaf. ■
www.hangaronthewharf.com

## Hott Stixx                                  $$D
Anchorage ■ (907) 563-8888
1921 W Dimond Blvd ■ Modern American
■ Hostess reports that kitchen is very
accommodating of GF diners. Any
entrée item can be made GF and GF
pasta is available upon special request. ■
www.hottstixx.com

## Ivory Jacks Restaurant                  ★ $LD
Goldstream Valley ■ (907) 455-6666
2581 Goldstream Rd ■ American ■
GF pizza, bread, hamburger buns, and

beer are available, as are GF brownies and cookies for dessert. Owner Joni reports that she has GF family members, so she is very GF aware. ▪ *www.mosquitonet.com~ivoryjacks/ij*

### Jack Sprat Restaurant    ✪$$$LD
*Girdwood* ▪ *(907) 783-5225*
*165 Olympic Mountain Loop* ▪ *American* ▪ GF menu available upon request. GF items include hummus plate, bacon wrapped dates, scallop ceviche, pork rib, halibut, organic chicken, ribeye steak and vegetable curry. Confirm the timeliness of this information before dining in. ▪ *www.jacksprat.net*

### Julia's Solstice Café    ✪$BLD
*Fairbanks* ▪ *(907) 388-2583*
*206 Driveway St* ▪ *Café* ▪ Julia's Café offers a wide variety of GF baked goods such as granola, muffins, cookies, cakes, pies, and brownies. ▪ *www.rosiecreekorganicfoods.com*

### Kincaid Grill    $$$$D
*Anchorage* ▪ *(907) 243-0507*
*6700 Jewel Lake Rd* ▪ *Modern American* ▪ Note GF when making reservations. Upon arrival server will alert chef of GF needs and the chef will come out and list the items on the menu that can be made GF. ▪ *www.kincaidgrill.com*

### Lahn Pad Thai    $LD
*Anchorage* ▪ *(907) 272-8424*
*2101 Abbott Rd* ▪ *Thai* ▪ Most dishes can be made GF. Alert server upon arrival.

### Lavelle's Bistro    $D
*Fairbanks* ▪ *(907) 450-0555*
*575 1st Ave* ▪ *American* ▪ GF diners can be accommodated. Alert server upon arrival and they will have chef list items on the menu that can be made GF. ▪ *www.lavellesbistro.com*

### Ling & Louie's Asian Bar & Grill    ✪★📖
*Anchorage* ▪ *(907) 338-5464*
*3801 Old Seward Hwy*

### Lone Star Steakhouse & Saloon    ✪📖
*Anchorage* ▪ *(907) 562-7827*
*4810 C St*

### Ludvig's Bistro    $$$D
*Sitka* ▪ *(907) 966-3663*
*256 Katlian St* ▪ *Mediterranean* ▪ Items that are GF or can be modified to be GF include king salmon with risotto, paella, caesar salad with scallops, skewered lamb kebabs, and lamb meatballs with pine nuts and herbs. Alert a server upon arrival. Reservations noting GF are recommended. ▪ *www.ludvigsbistro.com*

### Marx Brothers Café    $$$$LD
*Anchorage* ▪ *(907) 278-2133*
*627 W 3rd Ave* ▪ *Modern American* ▪ Owner Jack recommends reservations noting GF. He explains that when a GF reservation is made, the chef will "figure something out" and advise the server on how to accommodate the GF diner. ▪ *www.marxcafe.com*

### Middleway Café    ★✿$
*Anchorage* ▪ *(907) 272-6433*
*1200 W Northern Lights Blvd* ▪ *Bakery & Café* ▪ The café reports that they offer GF sandwich wraps, salads, and soups. They recommend calling on a specific day for further details or speaking with a server upon arrival. ▪ *www.middlewaycafe.com*

### Moose's Tooth    ★✪$LD
*Anchorage* ▪ *(907) 258-2537*
*3300 Old Seward Hwy* ▪ *American* ▪ GF pizza crust is available in addition to a small GF section located on the menu in the restaurant. ▪ *www.moosestooth.net*

### Muse    $$BLD
*Anchorage* ▪ *(907) 929-9210*
*625 C St* ▪ *American* ▪ Muse does not offer a GF menu, however several salads are available GF and cooks are willing to accommodate GF guests and adapt regular menu items to suit their needs. ▪ *www.anchoragemuseum.org*

### Organic Oasis ✪$$LD
*Anchorage ▪ (907) 277-7882*
*2610 Spenard Rd ▪ American ▪* GF items
are marked on the menu and include
chicken nachos, buffalo grass fed ribeye,
Alaskan seasonal fish platter, and more.
They also have a kids menu, and various
soups and salads. Alert the server upon
arrival. ▪ *organicoasis.com*

### Orso $$LD
*Anchorage ▪ (907) 222-3232*
*737 W 5th Ave ▪ Modern American ▪* The
restaurant reports that they can "absolutely" accommodate GF diners. Most servers
are aware of GF menu modifications, and
less-experienced servers will ask the chef.
Reservations noting GF are recommended,
as is alerting the server upon arrival. ▪
*www.orsoalaska.com*

### Pie in the Sky Bakery and Café ★¢S
*Juneau ▪ (907) 523-9135*
*223 Seward St ▪ Bakery & Café ▪* GF
bread is available, as well as an "ever-
changing selection" of other items. The
café recommends calling ahead to see
what is available on the day of your visit. ▪
*www.pieintheskybakeryandcafe.com*

### Prospectors Pizzeria & Alehouse ★$LD
*Denali ▪ (907) 683-7437*
*Milepost 238.9 Parks Hwy ▪ Pizza ▪*
Prospectors Pizzeria has GF crust available
in addition to various GF salad and soup
options. ▪ *prospectorspizza.com*

### Roadhouse Café & Bakery ★¢BLD
*Talkeetna ▪ (907) 733-1351*
*13550 E Main St ▪ Bakery & Café ▪* Road-
house Café offers GF brownies and flavored
muffins in addition to various soup and
salad options which are naturally GF. ▪
*www.talkeetnaroadhouse.com*

### Rookery Café, The ¢BLD
*Juneau ▪ (907) 463-3013*
*111 Seward St ▪ Bakery ▪* GF cookies and cakes available daily. ▪
*www.therookerycafe.com*

### Sacks Café & Restaurant $$$LD
*Anchorage ▪ (907) 274-4022*
*328 G St ▪ Modern American ▪* Menu
changes regularly. Call beforehand to see
what GF options are available for either
lunch or dinner. ▪ *www.sackscafe.com*

### Sea Bean, The ★$BLD
*Seward ▪ (907) 224-6623*
*225 4th Ave ▪ American ▪* GF bakery
items include chocolate chip cookie tarts,
coconut chocolate cupcake tarts and Mt.
Marathon bars. GF bread is also available
for sandwiches. ▪ *www.seabeancafe.com*

### Seven Glaciers Restaurant ✪$$$$D
*Girdwood ▪ (907) 754-2237*
*1000 Arlberg Ave ▪ American ▪* GF
menu includes entrées such as pan
roasted Alaskan halibut, grilled Alaskan
salmon, and a grilled New York steak. ▪
*www.alyeskaresort.com*

### Simon and Seafort's Saloon & Grill ✪$$$LD
*Anchorage ▪ (907) 274-3502*
*420 L St ▪ Seafood & Steakhouse ▪* GF
menu available. Some items include clams,
mussels, oysters, crab legs, seafood louie,
halibut, salmon, tiger prawns, lobster tail,
sirloin and prime rib. Dessert includes
vanilla burnt cream and a fruit sorbet. ▪
*www.simonandseaforts.com*

### Sipping Streams Tea House ★¢BL
*Fairbanks ▪ (907) 457-1660*
*3535 College Rd ▪ Teahouse ▪* The
tea house reports that all of their tea
drinks are GF. GF food items include
GF crepes, salads, soups, cookies and
rice cakes. Alert server upon arrival. ▪
*www.sippingstreams.com*

### Snow City Café ★$BL
*Anchorage ▪ (907) 272-2489*
*1034 W 4th Ave ▪ American ▪* The restaurant reports that several menu items,
including five varieties of eggs benedict,
tofu or chicken stir fry, and omelets, can
be modified to be GF. The eggs benedict
will come with brown rice or corn torti-

llas instead of the english muffin. Fruit smoothies and milkshakes are available, as are GF cookies and brownies. Confirm the timeliness of this information before dining in. ▪ *www.snowcitycafe.com*

### Southside Bistro                    $$$LD
*Anchorage* ▪ *(907) 348-0088*
*1320 Huffman Park Dr* ▪ *American* ▪ Note GF when making reservations and alert server upon arrival. ▪ *www.southsidebistro.com*

### Spenard Roadhouse        ✪★$LD
*Anchorage* ▪ *(907) 770-7623*
*1049 W Northern Lights Blvd* ▪ *American* ▪ GF menu includes blackened tiger prawn curry noodles, grilled Alaskan salmon, summer quinoa and GF jambalaya. ▪ *www.spenardroadhouse.com*

### Starfire                          $$LD
*Skagway* ▪ *(907) 983-3663*
*4th Ave & Spring* ▪ *Fusion* ▪ Owner Jeffrey reports that the restaurant serves many GF diners. All servers are educated on the GF diet and can indicate GF items. Servers will flag all GF orders to help prevent CC. He also notes that there is an internal list of GF items, which includes lemongrass coconut soup, tom yum soup, curries, waterfall beef salad, spicy rockfish with vegetables, the big fat burrito, and more. Confirm the timeliness of this information before dining in.

### Take 5 Coffee Lounge          ★¢BLD
*Fairbanks* ▪ *(907) 456-1610*
*1755 Westwood Wy* ▪ *Coffee Shop* ▪ The shop offers a variety of GF baked goods, including almond cake and "House Friends" GF bread ▪ *www.take5coffeelounge.blogspot.com*

### Taproot                         ★$D
*Anchorage* ▪ *(907) 345-0282*
*3300 Spenard Rd* ▪ *American* ▪ GF beer available. GF food options include salads, wings and fish tacos without the tortilla. ▪ *taprootalaska.com*

### Terra Bella                      ✪★¢S
*Anchorage* ▪ *(907) 562-2259*
*601 E Dimond Blvd* ▪ *Bakery* ▪ GF bread, cookies, cake, muffins, and brownies are available. Any sandwich can be prepared on GF bread, and soups are usually GF. President Linda reports that the bistro quiche from the regular menu is GF. Confirm the timeliness of this information before dining in. ▪ *www.terrabellacoffee.com*

### Thai Kitchen                     ★$LD
*Anchorage* ▪ *(907) 561-0082*
*3405 E Tudor Rd* ▪ *Thai* ▪ GF accommodations can be made. GF soy sauce is available and the yellow curry being served does not contain gluten, however stay clear of the green and red curry. Alert the server upon arrival. ▪ *thaikitchenak.com*

### Tracy's King Crab Shack        $$$LD
*Juneau* ▪ *(907) 723-1811*
*356 S Franklin St* ▪ *Seafood* ▪ GF items include crab, shrimp, scallops and a crab bisque. ▪ *www.kingcrabshack.com*

### Turkey Red                      $$BLD
*Palmer* ▪ *(907) 746-5544*
*550 S Alaska St* ▪ *Mediterranean* ▪ The restaurant reports that most of their salads and soups are GF, as well as burgers without buns. Confirm the timeliness of this information before dining in. ▪ *www.turkeyredak.com*

### Twisted Fish Company
### Alaskan Grill                  ★$$$LD
*Juneau* ▪ *(907) 463-5033*
*550 S Franklin St* ▪ *Seafood & Steakhouse* ▪ GF pasta is available in addition to various seafood options such as Alaskan salmon, halibut, prawns and king crab. ▪ *twistedfish.hangaronthewharf.com*

### Wasabi's                        $$$$D
*Homer* ▪ *(907) 226-3663*
*59217 E End Rd* ▪ *Sushi* ▪ The restaurant reports that they do not have a GF menu, but notes that if GF diners call ahead and make a reservation, the chef will "come

up with a few dishes to choose from." ▪
*www.wasabisrestaurant.com/sushi.html*

# ARIZONA

## PHOENIX

### Barrio Café                                    $$LD
*Phoenix* ▪ *(602) 636-0240*
*2814 N 16th St* ▪ *Mexican* ▪ GF options
include appetizers (minus tostada chips),
salads, soups, most of the meat, chicken,
and fish dishes, and all of the tacos and
enchiladas. Confirm the timeliness
of this information before dining in▪
*www.barriocafe.com*

### BJ's Restaurant and Brewhouse ✪★☐
*Phoenix* ▪ *(480) 538-0555*
*21001 N Tatum Blvd*

### Bombay Spice Grill & Wine          ✪$LD
*Phoenix* ▪ *(602) 795-0020*
*10810 N Tatum Blvd* ▪ *Indian* ▪ Extensive
GF menu includes mango chicken salad,
kebab skewers, tikka skewers, biryani,
chicken keema, curries, and more. ▪
*www.bombayspice.com*

### Café Boa                                    ★$$LD
*Phoenix* ▪ *(408) 893-3331*
*5063 E Elliot Rd* ▪ *Italian* ▪ Manager Kevin
reports that the restaurant takes food allergies and dietary restrictions very seriously
and is very informed about CC concerns.
GF pastas and salads available and listed in
the online menu. ▪ *www.caffeboa.com*

### Café Rio Mexican Grill               ☐
*Phoenix* ▪ *(602) 425-5380*
*2131 E Camelback Rd*

### Capital Grille, The                   ✪☐
*Phoenix* ▪ *(602) 952-8900*
*2502 E Camelback Rd*

### Feast                                  ✪★$$BLD
*Tucson* ▪ *(520) 326-9363*
*3719 E Speedway Blvd* ▪ *Modern
American* ▪ Items that can be prepared GF
are marked on the regular menu. Items
included are red potato salad, pumpkin
seed crusted beets, grilled onglet, and
black bottom black top coconut bavarois.
▪ *www.eatatfeast.com*

### First Watch - The Daytime Café   ✪☐
*Phoenix* ▪ *(602) 265-2092*
*61 W Thomas Rd*
*Phoenix* ▪ *(602) 943-3232*
*9645 N Black Canyon Hwy*

### Genghis Grill                          ☐
*Phoenix* ▪ *(602) 765-2695*
*4722 E Cactus Rd*

### Giuseppe's on 28th                 ★$LD
*Phoenix* ▪ *(602) 381-1237*
*2824 E Indian School Rd* ▪ *Italian* ▪ GF
pasta is available. Owner Richard reports
that several menu items can be prepared
GF and they can usually accommodate
GF diners. He recommends reservations
noting GF and mentioning the
word "allergy" to the server. ▪
*www.giuseppeson28th.com*

### Gluten-Free Creations
### Bakery & Café                          ¢$
*Phoenix* ▪ *(602) 522-0659*
*2940 E Thomas Rd* ▪ *Bakery & Café* ▪
Dedicated GF bakery offering a wide
variety of products, all of which are
made from scratch. GF bread, hamburger
buns, pasta, and pizza crust are available.
GF baked goods include cookies, pies,
cakes, donuts, brownies, and more.
Many items are offered in bulk, including
bagels, donuts, and GF baking flours.
Café offers full GF menu including
sandwiches, burgers, and brunch items. ▪
*www.glutenfreecreations.com*

**Green Vegetarian**  ✪⊄LD
*Phoenix ▪ (602) 258-1870*
*2022 N 7th St ▪ Vegetarian* ▪ The Green Vegetarian has a GF in store menu including apple and spinach salad, a roasted veggie bowl and Italian enchiladas. GF cupcakes are also available. ▪ *greenvegetarian.com*

**Hard Rock Café**  ✪▭
*Phoenix ▪ (602) 261-7625*
*3 S 2nd St*

**Havana Café**  $$LD
*Phoenix ▪ (602) 952-1991*
*4225 E Camelback Rd ▪ Cuban* ▪ The restaurant reports that over 50% of menu items are naturally GF and most other can be prepared GF. Ask a server for details when dining in. ▪ *www.havanacafe-az.com*

**Hillstone Restaurants**  ▭
*Phoenix ▪ (602) 957-9700*
*2650 E Camelback Rd*

**In-N-Out Burger**  ▭
*Phoenix ▪ (800) 786-1000*
*9585 W Camelback Rd*
*Phoenix ▪ (800) 786-1000*
*2770 W Peoria Ave*
*Phoenix ▪ (800) 786-1000*
*34850 N Valley Pkwy*
*Phoenix ▪ (800) 786-1000*
*19407 N 27th Ave*
*Phoenix ▪ (800) 786-1000*
*12413 N Tatum*
*Phoenix ▪ (800) 786-1000*
*21001 N Tatum Blvd*

**Islands Fine Burgers & Drinks**  ▭
*Phoenix ▪ (480) 513-7231*
*21001 N Tatum Blvd*
*Phoenix ▪ (602) 494-4434*
*12811 N Tatum Blvd*

**Jason's Deli**  ✪▭
*Phoenix ▪ (602) 870-8611*
*10217 N Metro Pkwy W*

**Jersey Mike's**  ▭
*Phoenix ▪ (602) 569-6453*
*4550 E Bell Rd*

*Phoenix ▪ (480) 753-6453*
*4605 E Chandler Blvd*
*Phoenix ▪ (623) 582-6453*
*2501 W Happy Valley Rd*
*Phoenix ▪ (602) 265-1135*
*18 E Camelback Rd*
*Phoenix ▪ (602) 253-6738*
*1515 North 7th Ave*
*Phoenix ▪ (602) 268-7411*
*2415 E Baseline Rd*
*Phoenix ▪ (602) 866-6930*
*245 E Bell Rd*
*Phoenix ▪ (602) 867-5039*
*4603 E Cactus Rd*

**Joe's Crab Shack**  ✪▭
*Tempe ▪ (480) 345-0972*
*1606 W Baseline*

**Kincaid's**  ▭
*Phoenix ▪ (602) 340-0000*
*2 S 3rd St*

**La Fontanella**  ★$$D
*Phoenix ▪ (602) 955-1213*
*4231 E Indian School Rd ▪ Italian* ▪ GF pasta is available. Other items on the menu can be modified to be GF. Alert the server upon arrival. ▪ *lafontanellaphx.com*

**Lone Star Steakhouse & Saloon**  ✪▭
*Phoenix ▪ (602) 265-7827*
*1743 E Camelback Rd*

**Loving Hut**  ▭
*Phoenix ▪ (602) 264-3480*
*3239 E Indian School Rd*

**Luci's Healthy Marketplace**  ✪★⊄BLD
*Phoenix ▪ (602) 773-1339*
*1590 E Bethany Home Rd ▪ American* ▪ Manager reports that they have a "wide variety" of GF options, including soups, salads, and sandwiches. GF bread is available, as well as GF pancake and waffle options for breakfast. ▪ *www.lucishealthymarketplace.com*

**Malee's Thai Bistro**  ✪⊄LD
*Scottsdale ▪ (480) 947-6042*
*7131 E Main St ▪ Thai* ▪ GF menu is available in-house. The restaurant recommends

avoiding fried foods, as the chance of CC is high, but adds that most other dishes can be prepared GF. GF soy sauce is available and several other sauces can be prepared GF as well. ▪ *www.maleesthaibistro.com*

### NYPD Pizza                                ★ $LD
*Phoenix* ▪ *(602) 343-6973*
*556 W McDowell Rd* ▪ *Pizza* ▪ GF pizza is available at the listed locations only. The restaurant also notes that their Broadway bruschetta and spinach artichoke dip are available GF. ▪ *www.aznypdpizza.com*

### Old Spaghetti Factory, The          ✪★📖
*Phoenix* ▪ *(602) 257-0380*
*1418 N Central Ave*

### P.F. Chang's China Bistro          ✪★📖
*Phoenix* ▪ *(623) 707-4495*
*2420 W Happy Valley Rd*

### Pei Wei Asian Diner                    ✪📖
*Phoenix* ▪ *(602) 308-0410*
*701 W Mcdowell Rd*
*Phoenix* ▪ *(602) 956-2300*
*4340 E Indian School Rd*
*Phoenix* ▪ *(602) 707-2800*
*267 E Bell Rd*
*Phoenix* ▪ *(602) 707-0049*
*742 E Glendale Ave*

### Pomegranate Café                      ✪$BL
*Phoenix* ▪ *(480) 706-7472*
*4025 E Chandler Blvd Suite 28* ▪ *Vegetarian* ▪ GF foods and alternatives are marked on the available menu items making it easy to see what they have. Everything is vegan. Be sure to ask about all the options. ▪ *www.pomegranatecafe.com*

### Pugzie's Restaurant                    ★ ₵L
*Phoenix* ▪ *(602) 277-6017*
*4700 N 16th St* ▪ *Deli* ▪ GF bread is available. The restaurant reports that they only use GF mayo and mustard, and all salad dressings are GF. Other GF items like soups are also available. The restaurant recommends that GF diners ask for Lynn if they have any additional questions. ▪ *www.pugzies.com*

### Romano's Macaroni Grill          ✪★📖
*Phoenix* ▪ *(480) 538-8755*
*21001 N Tatum Blvd*
*Phoenix* ▪ *(623) 580-8681*
*2949 W Agua Fria Fwy*

### Rosati's Pizza                            ★📖
*Phoenix* ▪ *(602) 996-1110*
*4010 E Bell Rd*
*Phoenix* ▪ *(602) 276-8200*
*2320 E Baseline Rd*
*Phoenix* ▪ *(602) 978-0007*
*2737 W Thunderbird Rd*
*Phoenix* ▪ *(623) 581-1112*
*602 W Union Hills Dr*

### Ruffino Italian Cuisine          ★ $$$LD
*Phoenix* ▪ *(480) 893-8544*
*4902 E Warner Rd* ▪ *Italian* ▪ Owner Steve reports that all servers are "generally familiar" with the GF diet, and they serve GF diners frequently. They can modify many dishes, such as the chicken piccata, to be GF. GF pasta is always available but it takes longer to prepare because it is cooked on order. Confirm the timeliness of this information before dining in. Alert a server upon arrival. ▪ *www.ruffinoaz.com*

### Ruth's Chris Steak House          ✪📖
*Phoenix* ▪ *(602) 957-9600*
*2201 E Camelback Rd*

### Shane's Rib Shack                      ✪📖
*Phoenix* ▪ *(623) 581-3704*
*2501 W Happy Valley Rd*

### Spinato's Pizzeria                  ✪★ $LD
*Phoenix* ▪ *(602) 867-1010*
*1614 E Bell Rd*
*Phoenix* ▪ *(602) 277-0088*
*1219 E Glendale Ave*
*Phoenix* ▪ *(480) 961-0208*
*4848 E Chandler Blvd* ▪ *Pizza* ▪ GF menu includes pizza with a variety of toppings, salads, and more. GF pizza crust is brought in from a 100% GF bakery. ▪ *www.spinatospizza.com*

**True Food Kitchen**   ✪★📖
*Phoenix ▪ (602) 774-3488*
*2502 E Camelback Rd*

**Tryst Café**   ✪$BLD
*Phoenix ▪ (480) 585-7978*
*21050 N Tatum Blvd #108 ▪ American ▪*
According to employee a menu is available in the restaurant with starred GF food options for breakfast, lunch, an dinner. Options include huevos rancheros, grilled flat iron steak, and salmon. ▪ *trystcafeaz.com*

**Uno Chicago Grill**   ✪★📖
*Phoenix ▪ (602) 253-3355*
*455 N 3rd St*

**White Chocolate Grill, The**   ✪$$LD
*Phoenix ▪ (480) 563-3377*
*7000 E Mayo Blvd ▪ Modern American*
▪ GF menu includes grilled artichokes and tomato gin soup, among other things, as appetizers. As entrées, it lists a bunless cheeseburger, BBQ baby back ribs, center cut filet, New York strip, balsamic ribeye and more. For dessert, it offers a silky chocolate soufflé cake ▪ *www.whitechocolategrill.com*

**Yard House**   ✪📖
*Phoenix ▪ (480) 563-9273*
*21001 N Tatum Blvd*

**Z'Tejas Southwestern Grill**   ✪★📖
*Phoenix ▪ (480) 948-9010*
*10625 N Tatum Blvd*

**Zinburger**   ₵LD
*Phoenix ▪ (602) 424-9500*
*2502 E Camelback Rd ▪ American ▪*
Manager Doug of the Tucson location and Manager Mike of the Phoenix location report that they are very accustomed to serving GF diners. Alert a server upon arrival. All staff members are trained on the GF diet, and Doug reports that they accommodate GF diners "on a daily basis." There is a dedicated GF fryer, and all fries except for the zucchini fries are GF. Confirm the timeliness of this information before dining in. ▪ *www.foxrc.com*

**Zpizza**   ✪📖
*Phoenix ▪ (602) 234-3289*
*53 W Thomas Rd*
*Phoenix ▪ (602) 254-4145*
*111 W Monroe St*

## ARIZONA

## SCOTTSDALE

**Blanco Tacos & Tequila**   $LD
*Scottsdale ▪ (480) 305-6692*
*6166 N Scottsdale Rd ▪ Mexican ▪* Manager Lindsey at the Scottsdale location and Manager Max at the Tucson location both report that they accommodate GF diners "very often." They note that with the exceptions of flour tortillas and enchilada sauce, most dishes are GF. Alert a server, who will indicate GF menu items. ▪ *www.foxrc.com*

**Buca di Beppo**   ✪📖
*Scottsdale ▪ (480) 949-6622*
*3828 N Scottsdale Rd*

**Cantina Laredo**   📖
*Scottsdale ▪ (480) 951-3807*
*7361 E Frank Lloyd Wright Blvd*

**Capital Grille, The**   ✪📖
*Scottsdale ▪ (480) 348-1700*
*16489 N Scottsdale Rd*

**Carrabba's Italian Grill**   ✪📖
*Scottsdale ▪ (480) 948-8881*
*17007 N Scottsdale Rd*

**Charleston's Restaurant**   ✪📖
*Scottsdale ▪ (480) 563-7666*
*17001 N Scottsdale Rd*

**Culinary Dropout**   $$LD
*Scottsdale ▪ (480) 970-1700*
*7135 E Camelback Rd ▪ Modern American*
▪ Executive Chef Clint reports that there is "plenty of stuff" on the menu that he can prepare GF. Examples include salmon,

pork ribs, coq au vin, and bistro steak.
Confirm the timeliness of this information before dining in. Alert a server upon
arrival. Clint notes that they serve GF
diners "a couple times a week," and that the
servers are trained to ask him if they have
questions about GF items on the menu. ▪
www.foxrc.com

### Don & Charlie's                    ✪$$$D
Scottsdale ▪ (480) 990-0900
7501 E Camelback Rd ▪ American ▪
GF menu includes salads, BBQ ribs,
chicken, and steaks. The restaurant takes
GF cooking "very seriously," and everything is separated in the kitchen. ▪
www.donandcharlies.com

### du Jour Restaurant                    ★$$L
Scottsdale ▪ (480) 603-1066
10585 N 114th St ▪ Modern American ▪ GF
bread and chocolate decadence cake are
available with advance notice. Manager
Matthew reports that the GF diet "has
been talked about to death" in class, so all
servers and chefs are very familiar with it.
He specifies that reservations noting GF
are required, as is alerting the server upon
arrival. Operated by the Arizona Culinary
Institute, the restaurant offers a fine dining
experience prepared by the student test
kitchen. ▪ www.arizonaculinary.com

### Eddie V's                    ✪📖
Scottsdale ▪ (480) 730-4800
15323 N Scottsdale Rd

### First Watch - The Daytime Café    ✪📖
Scottsdale ▪ (480) 248-9602
16455 N Scottsdale Rd

### Fleming's Prime
### Steakhouse & Wine Bar           ✪📖
Scottsdale ▪ (480) 538-8000
20753 N Pima Rd
Scottsdale ▪ (480) 596-8265
6333 N Scottsdale Rd

### Fogo De Chao                    ★📖
Scottsdale ▪ (480) 609-8866
6300 N Scottsdale Rd

### Genghis Grill                    📖
Scottsdale ▪ (480) 991-4745
7401 E Frank Lloyd Wright Blvd

### Gluten-Free Creations
### Bakery & Café                    ⊂S
Scottsdale ▪ (480) 990-2253
7607 E McDowell Rd ▪ Bakery & Café
▪ Dedicated GF bakery offering a wide
variety of products, all of which are made
from scratch. GF bread, hamburger
buns, pasta, and pizza crust are available.
GF baked goods include cookies, pies,
cakes, donuts, brownies, and more.
Many items are offered in bulk, including
bagels, donuts, and GF baking flours.
Café offers full GF menu including
sandwiches, burgers, and brunch items. ▪
www.glutenfreecreations.com

### Greene House, The                $$$LD
Scottsdale ▪ (480) 889-9494
15024 N Scottsdale Rd ▪ Modern American ▪ GF diners can be accommodated. Be
sure to alert the server upon arrival, and
the server will forward requests on to the
chef. ▪ www.foxrc.com

### Havana Café                    $$LD
Scottsdale ▪ (480) 991-1496
6245 E Bell Rd ▪ Cuban ▪ The restaurant
reports that over 50% of menu items
are naturally GF and most other can be
prepared GF. Ask a server for details when
dining in. ▪ www.havanacafe-az.com

### In-N-Out Burger                    📖
Scottsdale ▪ (800) 786-1000
7467 Frank L Wright

### Jason's Deli                    ✪📖
Scottsdale ▪ (480) 443-3811
10605 N Scottsdale Rd

### Jersey Mike's                    📖
Scottsdale ▪ (480) 661-1345
15807 E Frank Lloyd Wright
Scottsdale ▪ (480) 922-6453
10392 N Scottsdale Rd

**Ling & Louie's Asian Bar & Grill** ✪★🕮
*Scottsdale* ▪ *(480) 767-5464*
*9397 E Shea Blvd*

**Los Sombreros**
**Mexican Restaurant** $$D
*Scottsdale* ▪ *(480) 994-1799*
*2534 N Scottsdale Rd* ▪ *Mexican* ▪ Owner
Azucena reports that nearly the entire
menu is GF, and servers are trained to
indicate non-GF items. Alert a server upon
arrival. Azucena adds that they serve GF
diners "every day." ▪ *www.lossombreros.com*

**Maggiano's Little Italy** ★🕮
*Scottsdale* ▪ *(480) 333-4100*
*16405 N Scottsdale Rd*

**Marco's Italian Bistro** ✪★$$D
*Scottsdale* ▪ *(480) 767-3933*
*10855 N Frank Lloyd Wright Blvd* ▪
*Italian* ▪ GF menu is available online
and in restaurant. Owner Marco reports
that other dishes can also be made GF
upon request. GF pasta is available. ▪
*www.marcosbistro.com*

**Melting Pot, The** ✪🕮
*Scottsdale* ▪ *(480) 607-1799*
*8260 N Hayden Rd*

**Modern Steak** $$$$LD
*Scottsdale* ▪ *(480) 423-7000*
*7014 E Camelback Rd* ▪ *Steakhouse*
▪ Restaurant notes that GF diners are
"regularly" accommodated. Several menu
items are naturally GF. Upon request, the
chef is happy to come discuss GF options
and modifications at the table. Reservations noting GF are highly recommended. ▪
*www.foxrc.com*

**Morton's Steakhouse** ✪🕮
*Scottsdale* ▪ *(480) 951-4440*
*15233 N Kierland Blvd*

**Nourish** ✪$$LD
*Scottsdale* ▪ *(480) 684-2233*
*7147 E Highland Ave* ▪ *American* ▪
The restaurants reports that all of their
dishes are 100% GF. Items include
teriyaki wild rice bowl, wild salmon with

pineapple mango salsa, glazed roasted 1/2
chicken and a variety of GF desserts. ▪
*nourish123.com*

**NYPD Pizza** ★$LD
*Scottsdale* ▪ *(480) 451-6973*
*14884 N Pima Rd*
*Scottsdale* ▪ *(480) 609-8666*
*10433 N Scottsdale Rd* ▪ *Pizza* ▪ GF pizza
is available at the listed locations only. The
restaurant also notes that their Broadway
bruschetta and spinach artichoke dip are
available GF. ▪ *www.aznypdpizza.com*

**O'Charley's** 🕮
*Scottsdale* ▪ *(480) 948-8881*
*17007 N Scottsdale Rd*

**Old Town Tortilla Factory** ✪$$D
*Scottsdale* ▪ *(480) 945-4567*
*6910 E Main St* ▪ *Southwest* ▪ In
store menu has 15-20 GF options.
Please alert server of GF needs. ▪
*www.oldtowntortillafactory.com*

**Olive & Ivy** ★$$$LD
*Scottsdale* ▪ *(480) 751-2200*
*7135 E Camelback Rd* ▪ *Mediterranean* ▪
GF options are marked on the menu and
include bacon wrapped dates, Atlantic
salmon, bacon wrapped pork tenderloin,
spicy shrimp risotto, filet of beef, and
natural chicken. Alert the server upon
arrival. Reservations noting GF are
recommended. ▪ *www.foxrc.com*

**P.F. Chang's China Bistro** ✪★🕮
*Scottsdale* ▪ *(480) 949-2610*
*7135 E Camelback Rd Ste 101*
*Scottsdale* ▪ *(480) 367-2999*
*7132 E Greenway Pkwy*

**Pei Wei Asian Diner** ✪🕮
*Scottsdale* ▪ *(480) 365-6000*
*8787 N Scottsdale Rd*
*Scottsdale* ▪ *(480) 365-6002*
*20851 N Scottsdale Rd*
*Scottsdale* ▪ *(480) 488-8630*
*32607 N Scottsdale Rd*
*Scottsdale* ▪ *(480) 308-9898*
*8700 E Raintree Dr*

**Romano's Macaroni Grill**    ✪★📖
*Scottsdale* ▪ *(480) 595-6676*
*7245 E Gold Dust Ave*

**Rosati's Pizza**    ★📖
*Scottsdale* ▪ *(480) 513-2552*
*10989 E Dynamite Blvd*
*Scottadale* ▪ *(480) 429-9777*
*1495 N Hayden Rd*

**Ruth's Chris Steak House**    ✪📖
*Scottsdale* ▪ *(480) 991-5988*
*7001 N Scottsdale Rd*

**Spinato's Pizzeria**    ✪★$LD
*Scottsdale* ▪ *(480) 391-2347*
*11108 N Frank Lloyd Wright Blvd* ▪ *Pizza*
▪ GF menu includes pizza with a variety of
toppings, salads, and more. GF pizza crust
is brought in from a 100% GF bakery. ▪
*www.spinatospizza.com*

**Takeda Thai**    ★$LD
*Scottsdale* ▪ *(480) 483-5006*
*10271 N Scottsdale Rd* ▪ *Thai* ▪ The restaurant reports that all items on the menu can
be altered to be GF. Confirm the timeliness
of this information before dining in, and
alert the manager upon arrival to address
CC concerns. ▪ *www.takedathai.com*

**True Food Kitchen**    ✪★📖
*Scottsdale* ▪ *(480) 265-4500*
*15191 N Scottsdale Rd, #100*

**Village Tavern**    ✪📖
*Scottsdale* ▪ *(480) 951-6445*
*8787 N Scottsdale Rd*

**Yard House**    ✪📖
*Scottsdale* ▪ *(480) 675-9273*
*7014 E Camelback Rd*

**Z'Tejas Southwestern Grill**    ✪★📖
*Scottsdale* ▪ *(480) 946-4171*
*7014 E Camelback Rd*

# ARIZONA

## TUCSON

**Bamboo Club Asian Bistro, The**✪★$$LD
*Tucson* ▪ *(520) 514-9665*
*5870 E Broadway* ▪ *Asian* ▪ Manager
reports a wide range of GF options,
including edamame, GF noodles,
and sweet and sour chicken. Ask a
server for a list of the items available. ▪
*www.rimrestaurants.com*

**BJ's Restaurant and Brewhouse** ✪★📖
*Tucson* ▪ *(520) 512-0330*
*5510 E Broadway Blvd*
*Tucson* ▪ *(520) 690-1900*
*4270 N Oracle Rd*

**Blanco Tacos & Tequila**    $LD
*Tucson* ▪ *(520) 232-1007*
*2905 E Skyline Dr* ▪ *Mexican* ▪ Manager
Lindsey at the Scottsdale location and
Manager Max at the Tucson location both
report that they accommodate GF diners
"very often." They note that with the excep-
tions of flour tortillas and enchilada sauce,
most dishes are GF. Alert a server, who will
indicate GF menu items. ▪ *www.foxrc.com*

**Bluefin Seafood Bistro**    $$$LD
*Tucson* ▪ *(520) 531-8500*
*7053 N Oracle Rd* ▪ *Seafood* ▪ The restaurant reports that all servers are trained
to accommodate GF diners, and they do
so "all the time." They note that GF diners
have many menu choices, including many
naturally GF items, which can be explained
by any server. ▪ *www.bluefintucson.com*

**Bob's Steak & Chop House**    📖
*Tucson* ▪ *(520) 877-2377*
*2727 W Club Dr*

**Create Café & Catering**    ✪¢BLD
*Tucson* ▪ *(520) 298-3421*
*4660 E Camp Lowell* ▪ *American* ▪
Dedicated GF menu available. Items
include sandwiches, burgers, breakfast and
a kids menu. ▪ *www.createcafe.com*

## El Charro Café                           ✪$LD
*Tucson ▪ (520) 622-1922*
*311 N Court Ave*
*Tucson ▪ (520) 745-1922*
*6310 E Broadway Blvd*
*Tucson ▪ (520) 514-1922*
*6910 E Sunrise Dr ▪ Mexican ▪* GF items
are marked on the menu and include
ceviche, enchiladas, tacos, chiles rellenos,
tamales, chicken mole, and more. Each restaurant has separate fryers and dedicated
prep areas to minimize the chances of CC.
Alert the server upon arrival and be sure
to order corn tortillas where applicable. ▪
*www.elcharrocafe.com*

## Firebirds Wood Fired Grill          ✪🕮
*Tucson ▪ (520) 577-0747*
*2985 E Skyline Dr*

## Fleming's Prime Steakhouse & Wine
## Bar                                      ✪🕮
*Tucson ▪ (520) 529-5017*
*6360 N Campbell Ave*

## Fox and Hound Pub & Grille          🕮
*Tucson ▪ (520) 575-1980*
*7625 N LaCholla Blvd*

## Frogs Organic Bakery           ✪★¢BL
*Tucson ▪ (520) 229-2124*
*7109 N Oracle Rd ▪ Bakery & Café ▪* All
GF items are noted on the main menu.
Items include soups, salads and omelettes. ▪
*www.frogsorganicbakery.com*

## Genghis Grill                           🕮
*Tucson ▪ (520) 887-0012*
*4386 N Oracle Rd*

## Gourmet Girls Go Gluten Free         ¢BL
*Tucson ▪ (520) 408-9000*
*5845 N Oracle Rd ▪ Bakery & Café ▪*
Everything is GF and baked fresh daily. ▪
*www.gourmetgirlsglutenfree.com*

## Guadalajara Grill                   ★$BLD
*Tucson ▪ (520) 323-1022*
*1220 E Prince Rd ▪ Mexican ▪* Hostess
Maria reports that they accommodate GF
diners weekly but not daily. She notes that
most of the sauces and salsas are GF. Corn

tortillas are available. Alert a server, who
will ask the manager or kitchen staff for assistance. ▪ *guadalajaraoriginalgrill.com*

## In-N-Out Burger                         🕮
*Tucson ▪ (800) 786-1000*
*4620 N Oracle Rd*
*Tucson ▪ (800) 786-1000*
*7111 E Broadway Blvd*
*Tucson ▪ (800) 786-1000*
*3711 Broadway Blvd*
*Tucson ▪ (800) 786-1000*
*1978 E Ajo Wy*

## Jason's Deli                          ✪🕮
*Tucson ▪ (520) 407-1100*
*4545 N Oracle Rd*
*Tucson ▪ (520) 790-7000*
*6061 E Broadway Blvd*

## Joe's Crab Shack                     ✪🕮
*Tucson ▪ (520) 751-0050*
*410 n Wilmot Rd*

## Jonathan's Cork                    ✪$$$D
*Tucson ▪ (520) 296-1631*
*6320 E Tanque Verde Rd ▪ American ▪*
Owner Jonathan reports that they accommodate GF diners every day. He notes that
reservations noting GF are "helpful," but
alerting the server is sufficient. GF items
are indicated with asterisks on the menu
and include blackened chicken, Alaskan
king crab, bison filet, and lobster tail. ▪
*www.jonathanscork.com*

## Kingfisher Grill                      $$$LD
*Tucson ▪ (520) 323-7739*
*2564 E Grant Rd ▪ Seafood ▪* Menu can
be modified to adhere to GF requests.
Recommend alerting the server, who
will discuss GF options with the chef. ▪
*www.kingfishertucson.com*

## Lodge on the Desert          ✪★$$$BLD
*Tucson ▪ (520) 320-2000*
*306 N Alvernon Wy ▪ American ▪*
GF menu available upon request.
Manager states the staff is currently working on their CC policy. ▪
*www.lodgeonthedesert.com/dining_room.php*

### Lovin' Spoonfuls ✪★⊄BLD
*Tucson ▪ (520) 325-7766*
*2990 N Campbell Ave ▪ Vegetarian ▪* GF
menu includes breakfast, lunch, and dinner
items, and all sauces are made with GF
thickeners. Confirm the timeliness of this
information before dining in. GF options
include pancakes, waffles, sandwiches, and
more. ▪ *www.lovinspoonfuls.com*

### My Big Fat Greek Restaurant ✪▥
*Tucson ▪ (520) 722-6000*
*7131 E Broadway*

### Old Pueblo Grille ✪$$LD
*Tucson ▪ (520) 326-6000*
*60 N Alvernon Wy ▪ Southwest ▪* Restaurant has a dedicated GF lunch and dinner
menu. From starters to desserts, they have
it all. ▪ *www.metrorestaurants.com*

### P.F. Chang's China Bistro ✪★▥
*Tucson ▪ (520) 615-8788*
*1805 E River Rd Ste 100*

### Pei Wei Asian Diner ✪▥
*Tucson ▪ (520) 884-7413*
*845 E University Blvd*
*Tucson ▪ (520) 514-7004*
*5285 E Broadway Blvd*
*Tucson ▪ (520) 297-3238*
*633 W Ina Rd*

### Renee's Organic Oven ✪★$$LD
*Tucson ▪ (520) 886-0484*
*7065 E Tanque Verde Rd*
*Tucson ▪ (520) 886-0484*
*7065 E Tanque Verde Rd ▪ Pizza ▪* GF
pizza (only available in 10" size), cake, and
beer are available. GF menu also includes
other items like spinach and artichoke dip,
hummus tostada, and a variety of salads.
For dessert, GF cakes and brownies are
available. ▪ *www.reneesorganicoven.com*

### Romano's Macaroni Grill ✪★▥
*Tucson ▪ (520) 790-0177*
*5100 E Broadway Blvd*
*Tucson ▪ (520) 544-4655*
*2265 W Ina Rd*

### Rosati's Pizza ★▥
*Tucson ▪ (520) 531-1100*
*2944 W Ina Rd*
*Tucson ▪ (520) 622-2200*
*1838 E 6th St*

### Sir Veza's Taco Garage ✪⊄LD
*Tucson ▪ (520) 323-8226*
*4699 E Speedway Blvd*
*Tucson ▪ (520) 888-8226*
*220 W Wetmore ▪ Tex-Mex ▪* GF menu
includes guacamole, salads, tamale pie,
wings, burgers without buns, chicken
lettuce wraps, tacos, seafood, and more. ▪
*www.sirvezas.com*

### Tucson Tamale Company ⊄BLD
*Tucson ▪ (520) 305-4760*
*2545 E Broadway Blvd ▪ Mexican ▪* All
the tamales that are made are 100% GF. ▪
*www.tucsontamalecompany.com*

### Wildflower ★$$$LD
*Tucson ▪ (520) 219-4230*
*7037 N Oracle Rd ▪ Modern American*
▪ Hostess Lauren reports that they
accommodate GF diners "a lot." GF options
include grilled whole artichokes, steelhead
salmon, red wine braised short ribs and
chicken street tacos. She notes that "everyone
is aware" of the GF diet, so alert a server upon
arrival. Servers are trained to know what
modifications must be made to make meals
GF. ▪ *www.foxrc.com*

### Zinburger ⊄LD
*Tucson ▪ (520) 299-7799*
*1865 E River Rd*
*Tucson ▪ (520) 298-2020*
*6390 E Grant Rd ▪ American ▪* Manager
Doug of the Tucson location and Manager
Mike of the Phoenix location report that they
are very accustomed to serving GF diners.
Alert a server upon arrival. All staff members
are trained on the GF diet, and Doug reports
that they accommodate GF diners "on a daily
basis." There is a dedicated GF fryer, and
all fries except for the zucchini fries are GF.
Confirm the timeliness of this information
before dining in. ▪ *www.foxrc.com*

# ARIZONA

## ALL OTHER CITIES

### 24 Carrots                                    ★ ¢BL
*Chandler* ▪ (480) 753-4411
*6140 W Chandler Blvd Suite 2* ▪ *Vegetarian* ▪ GF menu items available upon request. Alert a server and they will provide a list. ▪ *www.24carrotsjuice.com*

### Abuelo's                                         ✪▢
*Chandler* ▪ (480) 855-0960
*3440 W Chandler Blvd*
*Peoria* ▪ (623) 878-8282
*16092 N Arrowhead Fountains Center Dr*

### Alberto Italian Restaurant         ★ $$D
*Cave Creek* ▪ (480) 488-5800
*7171 E Cave Creek Rd* ▪ *Italian* ▪ GF pasta is available upon request. Alert a server upon arrival.

### Beaver Street Brewery              ✪ $$LD
*Flagstaff* ▪ (928) 779-0079
*11 S Beaver St* ▪ *Fusion* ▪ GF menu includes steamed mussels in curry sauce, pork chops, salmon, jambalaya, hummus, pizza and sandwiches or burgers without buns. Alert a server upon arrival and ask for the GF menu (menu only available in restaurant at this time). ▪ *www.beaverstreetbrewery.com*

### BJ's Restaurant and Brewhouse  ✪★▢
*Chandler* ▪ (480) 917-0631
*3155 W Chandler Blvd*
*Mesa* ▪ (480) 324-1675
*6622 E Superstition Springs Blvd*
*Peoria* ▪ (623) 772-6470
*9748 W Northern Ave*

### Boston's Restaurant & Sports Bar
✪★▢
*Tempe* ▪ (480) 517-1500
*400 W University Dr*
*Marana* ▪ (520) 572-1555
*5825 W Arizona Pavilions Dr*

### Brandy's Bakery & Restaurant     $$BL
*Flagstaff* ▪ (928) 779-2187
*1500 E Cedar Ave* ▪ *American* ▪ Restaurant reports that most of their menu items can be prepared GF. Be sure to alert server upon arrival and they will list some options. Early morning GF pastries are available but quickly sell out, according to the restaurant. ▪ *www.brandysrestaurant.com*

### Buca di Beppo                              ✪▢
*Chandler* ▪ (480) 785-7272
*7111 W Ray Rd*
*Mesa* ▪ (480) 507-9463
*1730 S Val Vista Dr*
*Peoria* ▪ (623) 412-9463
*16091 N Arrowhead Fountains Ctr Dr*

### Café Rio Mexican Grill                    ▢
*Gilbert* ▪ (480) 751-2000
*1939 E Baseline Rd*

### Cantina Laredo                               ▢
*Gilbert* ▪ (480) 782-6777
*2150 E Williams Field Rd*

### Carrabba's Italian Grill                  ✪▢
*Avondale* ▪ (623) 936-0597
*9920 W Mcdowell Rd*
*Chandler* ▪ (480) 785-8586
*1060 N 54th St*
*Gilbert* ▪ (480) 726-7455
*2709 S Market St*
*Glendale* ▪ (602) 863-6444
*5646 W Bell Rd*
*Mesa* ▪ (480) 654-9099
*1740 S Clearview Ave*
*Oro Valley* ▪ (520) 742-7442
*7635 N Oracle Rd*
*Surprise* ▪ (623) 214-3299
*14043 W Bell Rd*

### Cartwright's Sonoran Ranch House  $$$D
*Cave Creek* ▪ (480) 488-8031
*6710 E Cave Creek Rd* ▪ *Southwest* ▪ The restaurant reports that they serve GF customers "frequently" and adds that accommodations can be made for any item on the menu. Be sure to alert server upon arrival. ▪ *www.cartwrightssonoranranchhouse.com*

## Charleston's Restaurant    ✪📖
*Chandler* ▪ *(480) 961-9434*
*1040 N 54th St*
*Mesa* ▪ *(480) 635-9500*
*1623 S Stapley Dr*

## Cookies From Home    ★¢S
*Tempe* ▪ *(480) 894-1944*
*1605 W University Dr* ▪ *Bakery* ▪ Non-dedicated bakery offering GF cookies. GF gift items and sets available online as well. Baked in a separate facility and cooked on dedicated baking sheets and ovens then sent to the bakery. ▪ *www.cookiesfromhome.com*

## Cottage Place Restaurant, The    $$$$D
*Flagstaff* ▪ *(928) 774-8431*
*126 W Cottage Ave* ▪ *Modern American* ▪ The restaurant accommodates GF diners "quite often." Most menu items can be modified to be GF. Alert the server. Reservations noting GF are recommended. ▪ *www.cottageplace.com*

## Cowboy Club    $$LD
*Sedona* ▪ *(928) 282-4200*
*241 N State Route 89A* ▪ *Steakhouse* ▪ The kitchen is aware of GF meal preparation. Chicken, sirloin steaks, burgers without buns, mashed potatoes, salmon, and shrimp can be prepared GF. Alert a server upon arrival. The same GF options are also available at the Silver Saddle room. ▪ *www.cowboyclub.com*

## Dhaba, The    ✪$LD
*Tempe* ▪ *(480) 557-8800*
*1872 E Apache Blvd* ▪ *Indian* ▪ The Dhaba has an online menu showing GF options. Restaurant is supported by Gluten Intolerance group and have a very strong policy against CC. ▪ *www.the-dhaba.com*

## Diablo Burger    ★¢LD
*Flagstaff* ▪ *(928) 774-3274*
*120 N Leroux St* ▪ *American* ▪ Manager Eli reports that any burger can be served on a GF bun and with GF french fries. Alert the server upon arrival. ▪ *www.diabloburger.com*

## Dragoon Market and Café    ★¢S
*Dragoon* ▪ *(520) 248-9218*
*Dragoon Marketplace* ▪ *Bakery* ▪ GF bread is available by the loaf. Baker Debbie reports that she is "developing" some other products, including chocolate chip cookies and lemon bars. They set up a kiosk in Dragoon Marketplace on Saturdays and Sundays, but recommend calling for the most current information about where they are located. ▪ *www.dragoonmarketplace.mysite.com*

## El Charro Café    ✪$LD
*Oro Valley* ▪ *(520) 229-1922*
*7725 N Oracle Rd*
*Sahuarita* ▪ *(520) 325-1922*
*15920 S Rancho Sahuarita Blvd* ▪ *Mexican* ▪ GF items are marked on the menu and include ceviche, enchiladas, tacos, chiles rellenos, tamales, chicken mole, and more. Each restaurant has separate fryers and dedicated prep areas to minimize the chances of CC. Alert the server upon arrival and be sure to order corn tortillas where applicable. ▪ *www.elcharrocafe.com*

## Firebirds Wood Fired Grill    ✪📖
*Peoria* ▪ *(623) 773-0500*
*16067 N Arrowhead Fountains Ctr Dr*
*Chandler* ▪ *(480) 814-8003*
*3435 W Chandler Blvd*

## Fleming's Prime Steakhouse & Wine Bar    ✪📖
*Chandler* ▪ *(480) 940-1900*
*905 N 54th St*
*Peoria* ▪ *(623) 772-9463*
*9712 W Northern Ave*

## Fox and Hound Pub & Grille    📖
*Gilbert* ▪ *(480) 507-2343*
*1017 E Baseline Rd*
*Peoria* ▪ *(623) 486-0779*
*8320 W Mariners Wy*

## Genghis Grill    📖
*Glendale* ▪ *(623) 334-2695*
*7350 W Bell Rd*

*Chandler* ▪ *(480) 785-2695*
*900 N 54th St*
*Tempe* ▪ *(480) 777-2695*
*2000 E Rio Salado Pkwy*

## Green Vegetarian    ✪⊄LD
*Tempe* ▪ *(480) 941-9003*
*2240 N Scottsdale Rd #8* ▪ *Vegetarian*
▪ The Green Vegetarian has a GF in store
menu including apple and spinach salad,
a roasted veggie bowl and Italian enchiladas. GF cupcakes are also available. ▪
*greenvegetarian.com*

## Heartline Café    ✪$$$D
*Sedona* ▪ *(928) 282-0785*
*1610 W State Route 89A* ▪ *American* ▪ GF
items are indicated on the menu with an
asterisk. Options include grilled marinated
vegetables, pulled pork & polenta, grilled
wild salmon, blackened ribeye steak,
and more. Confirm the timeliness of this
information before dining in. Alert a server
upon arrival. ▪ *www.heartlinecafe.com*

## In-N-Out Burger    📖
*Avondale* ▪ *(800) 786-1000*
*1525 Dysart Rd*
*Casa Grande* ▪ *(800) 786-1000*
*873 N Promenade Pkwy*
*Chandler* ▪ *(800) 786-1000*
*2910 E German Rd*
*Chandler* ▪ *(800) 786-1000*
*7050 W. Ray Rd*
*Chandler* ▪ *(800) 786-1000*
*2790 W Chandler Blvd*
*Gilbert* ▪ *(800) 786-1000*
*2449 S Market St*
*Kingman* ▪ *(800) 786-1000*
*1770 Beverly Ave*
*Lake Havasu* ▪ *(800) 786-1000*
*81-101 London Bridge*
*Marana* ▪ *(800) 786-1000*
*8180 Cortaro Rd*
*Mesa* ▪ *(800) 786-1000*
*1342 S Alma School Rd*
*Mesa* ▪ *(800) 786-1000*
*1650 S Stapley Rd*
*Mesa* ▪ *(800) 786-1000*
*1859 S Signal Butte Rd*

*Oro Valley* ▪ *(800) 786-1000*
*11545 N Oracle Rd*
*Peoria* ▪ *(800) 786-1000*
*8285 W Bell Rd*
*Prescott* ▪ *(800) 786-1000*
*3040 HWY 69*
*Tempe* ▪ *(800) 786-1000*
*920 E Playa Del Norte Dr*
*Yuma* ▪ *(800) 786-1000*
*1940 E 16th St*

## Islands Fine Burgers & Drinks    📖
*Avondale* ▪ *(623) 907-1214*
*10055 W McDowell Rd*

## Jason's Deli    ✪📖
*Chandler* ▪ *(480) 705-9266*
*7230 W Ray Rd*
*Gilbert* ▪ *(480) 813-1358*
*1065 E Baseline Rd*
*Glendale* ▪ *(623) 412-7940*
*17275 N 79th Ave*
*Chandler* ▪ *(480) 812-2892*
*3491 W Frye Rd*

## Jersey Mike's    📖
*Tempe* ▪ *(480) 966-6453*
*555 N Scottsdale Rd*
*Chandler* ▪ *(480) 782-6453*
*2780 W Chandler Blvd*
*Glendale* ▪ *(623) 776-7827*
*7410 W Bell Rd*
*Chandler* ▪ *(480) 857-8184*
*1085 W Queen Creek Rd*
*Gilbert* ▪ *(480) 632-6453*
*891 E Baseline Rd*
*Mesa* ▪ *(480) 497-6453*
*1939 S Val Vista Dr*
*Laveen* ▪ *(602) 237-8703*
*5130 W Baseline Rd*

## Joe's Crab Shack    ✪📖
*Tempe* ▪ *(480) 730-0303*
*1604 E Southern Ave*

## La Stalla Cucina Rustica    $$$LD
*Chandler* ▪ *(480) 855-9990*
*68 W Buffalo St* ▪ *Italian* ▪ The restaurant
reports that although they no longer have
GF pasta, they do offer several GF entrées,
like grilled salmon and grilled chicken in

cream sauce. Confirm the timeliness of this information before dining in. Staff recommends alerting the server upon arrival, and asking for a manager "if necessary." ▪ www.lastallacr.com

### Landmark Restaurant, The    ✪$$LD
Mesa ▪ (480) 962-4652
809 W Main St ▪ American ▪ GF menu includes prime rib, Atlantic salmon, artichoke chicken, and more. All entrées come with a side, which includes mashed potatoes, candied carrots, sweet potatoes, or baked potato. Staff recommends alerting the server upon arrival and specifying that the meal must be GF. ▪ www.landmarkrestaurant.com

### Ling & Louie's Asian Bar & Grill ✪★▢
Chandler ▪ (520) 796-7281
5040 Wild Horse Pass Blvd

### Loving Hut    ▢
Glendale ▪ (602) 978-0393
3515 W Union Hills Dr

### Macy's European Coffeehouse    ★¢$
Flagstaff ▪ (928) 774-2243
14 S Beaver St ▪ Café ▪ GF baked goods are sometimes available. Potential GF items include cheesecake bars and flourless chocolate tortes. Several entrées are naturally GF but not made everyday. Call ahead of time to confirm availability of GF options. ▪ www.macyscoffee.net

### Margaritaville    ✪★▢
Glendale ▪ (623) 772-0011
6751 N Sunset Blvd

### Melting Pot, The    ✪▢
Glendale ▪ (623) 444-4946
19420 N 59th Ave Ste B113

### Mountain Oasis    $LD
Flagstaff ▪ (928) 214-9270
11 E Aspen Ave ▪ Global ▪ Veteran Server Mary Jane reports that GF requests are "really common." Alert a server upon arrival. She notes that the staff has a "cheat sheet" that they can look at if they are unsure which items

are GF. Spring rolls, hummus, and the coconut curry salmon are examples of GF items. Confirm the timeliness of this information before dining in. ▪ www.themenuplease.com/mountainoasis

### My Big Fat Greek Restaurant    ✪▢
Sierra Vista ▪ (520) 459-1306
4177 Hwy 90

### NYPD Pizza    ★$LD
Avondale ▪ (623) 536-6973
1619 N Dysart Rd
Chandler ▪ (480) 722-0898
2580 W Chandler Blvd
Gilbert ▪ (480) 782-6973
2743 S Market St
Glendale ▪ (623) 561-6973
8280 W Union Hills Dr
Surprise ▪ (623) 544-6915
13980 W Bell Rd
Tempe ▪ (480) 705-6973
9845 S Priest Dr ▪ Pizza ▪ GF pizza is available at the listed locations only. The restaurant also notes that their Broadway bruschetta and spinach artichoke dip are available GF. ▪ www.aznypdpizza.com

### O'Charley's    ▢
Surprise ▪ (623) 214-3299
14043 W Bell Rd
Gilbert ▪ (480) 726-7455
2709 S Market St
Oro Valley ▪ (520) 742-7442
7635 N Oracle Rd
Glendale ▪ (602) 863-6444
5646 W Bell Rd
Mesa ▪ (480) 654-9099
1740 S Clearview

### Oaxaca Restaurant    ✪$BLD
Sedona ▪ (928) 282-4179
321 N Hwy 89A ▪ Mexican ▪ GF items marked on the menu include the red rock salad, nachos, tacos, and the Oaxaca posole (chicken stew), among other things. They have dedicated utensils for GF items to prevent CC. ▪ www.oaxacarestaurant.com

**Old Spaghetti Factory, The**     ✪★📖
Chandler ▪ (480) 786-5705
3155 W Chandler Blvd

**P.F. Chang's China Bistro**     ✪★📖
Chandler ▪ (480) 899-0472
3255 W Chandler Blvd
Goodyear ▪ (623) 536-3222
14681 W Mcdowell Rd
Mesa ▪ (480) 218-4900
6610 E Superstition Springs Blvd
Peoria ▪ (623) 412-3335
16170 N 83rd Ave
Tempe ▪ (480) 731-4600
740 S Mill Ave Ste 140

**Pei Wei Asian Diner**     ✪📖
Avondale ▪ (623) 535-9830
1619 N Dysart Rd
Chandler ▪ (480) 940-3800
7131 W Ray Rd
Chandler ▪ (480) 812-2230
1085 W Queen Creek Rd
Gilbert ▪ (480) 926-9749
1084 S Gilbert Rd
Glendale ▪ (623) 825-9949
20022 N 67th Ave
Mesa ▪ (480) 539-4454
3426 E Baseline Rd
Surprise ▪ (623) 546-6868
14155 W Bell Rd
Tempe ▪ (480) 333-0014
1825 E Guadalupe Rd

**Romano's Macaroni Grill**     ✪★📖
Mesa ▪ (480) 632-2699
1705 S Stapley Dr
Goodyear ▪ (623) 547-0299
1828 N Litchfield Rd

**Rosati's Pizza**     ★📖
Arcadia ▪ (602) 381-0009
4041 Thomas Rd
Anthem ▪ (623) 551-8545
3668 W Anthem Wy
Cave Creek ▪ (480) 538-5380
28325 N Tatum Blvd
Chandler ▪ (480) 883-0333
3120 S Gilbert Rd
Fountain Hills ▪ (480) 836-8400

12605 N Saguaro Blvd
Gilbert ▪ (480) 633-3000
53 N Val Vista Dr
Gold Canyon ▪ (780) 983-7400
6900 E Hwy 60
Lake Havasu City ▪ (928) 855-8665
91 London Bridge Rd
Mesa ▪ (480) 854-0444
3654 N Power Rd
Mesa ▪ (480) 838-7448
2057 S Alma School Rd
Mesa ▪ (480) 324-0777
1309 N Greenfield Rd
Peoria ▪ (623) 878-8558
10651 W Olive Ave

**Shane's Rib Shack**     ✪📖
Glendale ▪ (623) 877-7427
9404 W Westgate Blvd

**Spinato's Pizzeria**     ✪★$LD
Tempe ▪ (480) 967-0020
227 S Smith Rd ▪ Pizza ▪ GF menu includes pizza with a variety of toppings, salads, and more. GF pizza crust is brought in from a 100% GF bakery. ▪ www.spinatospizza.com

**Tonto Bar & Grill**     ✪★$$$LD
Cave Creek ▪ (480) 488-0698
5736 E Rancho Manana Blvd ▪ Modern American ▪ GF menu available. Items include tortilla-crusted crab cakes, orange grilled BBQ salmon, root beer braised beef short ribs, and skillet seared scallops. GF bread is available for burgers and sandwiches. Menu may alter seasonally, so be sure to call for the most current GF menu options. ▪ www.tontobarandgrill.com

**Troia's**     ★$$$D
Sedona ▪ (928) 282-0123
1885 W Highway 89A ▪ Italian ▪ GF pizza and rice pasta are available. Manager Douglas reports that they also stock GF flour to use for breaded items such as chicken parmesan. Douglas adds that the staff is "very conscious" of customers with "allergies." Alert the server upon arrival. ▪ www.troias.com

### Tsom Vegetarian Flavors   ⊄LD
*Tempe* ▪ *(480) 377-2833*
*933 E University Dr, #115* ▪ *Vegetarian*
▪ The restaurant reports that 95% of the
menu is naturally GF and the chances of
CC are "extremely slim". Confirm the timeliness of this information before dining in.
▪ *www.tsomveggie.com*

### Yard House   ✪📖
*Glendale* ▪ *(623) 872-3900*
*9401 W Westgate Blvd*

### Z'Tejas Southwestern Grill   ✪★📖
*Chandler* ▪ *(480) 893-7550*
*7221 W Ray Rd*
*Tempe* ▪ *(480) 377-1170*
*20 W 6th St*

# ARKANSAS

## LITTLE ROCK

### American Pie Pizza   ★⊄LD
*N Little Rock* ▪ *(501) 758-8800*
*9709 Maumelle Blvd*
*N Little Rock* ▪ *(501) 753-0081*
*4830 N Hills Blvd* ▪ *Pizza* ▪ All locations
carry GF pizza. GF pizza cooked on its
own pan and is prepared separately. ▪
*www.americanpiepizza.net*

### Bonefish Grill   ✪📖
*Little Rock* ▪ *(501) 228-0356*
*11525 Cantrell Rd Ste 901*

### Boston's Restaurant & Sports Bar
✪★📖
*Little Rock* ▪ *(501) 235-2000*
*3201 Bankhead Dr*

### Brave New Restaurant   $$$LD
*Little Rock* ▪ *(501) 663-2677*
*2300 Cottondale Ln* ▪ *Modern American*
▪ Manager Akku reports that GF diners
are welcome and notes that accommodating GF is "not a problem." He adds

that they frequently get GF customers
and advises communicating clearly with
the server regarding GF requests. He
adds that the seasoning salt is not GF. ▪
*www.bravenewrestaurant.com*

### Café Bossa Nova   ★$$LD
*Little Rock* ▪ *(501) 614-6682*
*2701 Kavanaugh Blvd,* ▪ *Brazilian* ▪
Brazilian-style GF cheese bread available
in addition to various GF entrées which
are marked on the in restaurant menu. ▪
*www.cafebossanova.com*

### Cantina Laredo   📖
*Little Rock* ▪ *(501) 280-0407*
*207 N University Ave*

### Carino's Italian   ✪📖
*Little Rock* ▪ *(501) 225-3434*
*11600 Pleasant Ridge Rd*
*North Little Rock* ▪ *(501) 758-8226*
*4221 Warden Rd*

### Dempsey Bakery   ⊄LD
*Little Rock* ▪ *(501) 375-2257*
*323 Cross St* ▪ *Bakery* ▪ 100% GF bakery
offering items such as breads, pizzas, pies,
cup cakes, cookies, and specialty holiday
items. ▪ *www.dempseybakery.com*

### Fox and Hound Pub & Grille   📖
*N Little Rock* ▪ *(501) 753-8300*
*2800 Lakewood Village Dr*

### Genghis Grill   📖
*Little Rock* ▪ *(501) 223-2695*
*12318 Chenal Pkwy*

### Izzy's Restaurant   ✪⊄LD
*Little Rock* ▪ *(501) 868-4311*
*5601 Ranch Dr* ▪ *Café* ▪ GF menu includes
appetizers like beef or veggie tamales,
cheese dip with chips, and guacamole with
chips. It also features a wide variety of
soups and salads. ▪ *www.izzyslittlerock.com*

### Jason's Deli   ✪📖
*North Little Rock* ▪ *(501) 945-7700*
*4209 E McCain Blvd*
*Little Rock* ▪ *(501) 954-8700*
*301 N Shackleford Rd*

## Lilly's Dim Sum, Then Some   ✪★$LD
*Little Rock* ▪ (501) 716-2700
*11121 N Rodney Parham Rd* ▪ *Asian* ▪ The pan-Asian GF menu features Vietnamese spring rolls and Korean bibim bop with grilled steak. For dessert, there is coconut crème brûlée. Co-owner Kathy reports that all staff members are trained on the GF diet and on CC avoidance. GF soy sauce is available. Confirm the timeliness of this information before dining in. ▪ *www.lillysdimsum.com*

## Lone Star Steakhouse & Saloon   ✪📖
*Little Rock* ▪ (501) 227-8898
*10901 N Rodney Parham Rd*

## P.F. Chang's China Bistro   ✪★📖
*Little Rock* ▪ (501) 225-4424
*317 S Shackleford Rd*

## Pei Wei Asian Diner   ✪📖
*Little Rock* ▪ (501) 280-9423
*205 N University Ave*

## Pizza Café, The   ★$LD
*Little Rock* ▪ (501) 664-6133
*1517 Rebsamen Park Rd* ▪ *Pizza* ▪ GF pizza is available. ▪ *pizzacafe.wetpaint.com*

## Romano's Macaroni Grill   ✪★📖
*Little Rock* ▪ (501) 221-3150
*11100 W Markham St*

## Shorty Smalls   📖
*W Little Rock* ▪ (501) 224-3344
*1100 Rodney Parham*

## Trio's   $$$LD
*Little Rock* ▪ (501) 221-3330
*8201 Cantrell Rd* ▪ *Fusion* ▪ Restaurant reports that GF diners can "definitely" be accommodated. Naturally GF menu items include chicken enchiladas, some salmon dishes, and halibut, as well as the flourless chocolate mousse cake and crème brûlée for dessert. Confirm the timeliness of this information before dining in. Restaurant reports that other menu items can be modified to be GF. ▪ *www.triosrestaurant.com*

## US Pizza Company Salad Express   ★$L
*Little Rock* ▪ (501) 374-5561
*402 Louisiana St* ▪ *Pizza* ▪ GF pizza is available. The restaurant reports that the kitchen keeps GF pizza separate from other foods, and that GF pizza is cut with separate utensils on a clean cutting board. ▪ *www.uspizzaco.net*

## Ya Ya's Euro Bistro   ✪$$$LD
*Little Rock* ▪ (501) 821-1144
*17711 Chenal Pkwy* ▪ *Bistro* ▪ Manager Matt reports that the restaurant serves GF diners with "increasing" frequency. He notes that the restaurant has a strict protocol for flagging orders with "allergies." Ask server to confer with a chef or manager about the best GF options, as not all servers are fully educated in the GF diet. ▪ *www.yayasar.com*

# ARKANSAS

## ALL OTHER CITIES

## Abu's Gyros & More   ¢LD
*Russellville* ▪ (479) 968-2007
*605 N Arkansas Ave* ▪ *Mediterranean* ▪ The restaurant reports that many menu items can be made GF. Alert the server upon arrival and they "will be happy to accommodate your needs."

## Abuelo's   ✪📖
*Rogers* ▪ (479) 621-0428
*4005 W Walnut*

## American Pie Pizza   ★¢LD
*Little Rock* ▪ (501) 225-1900
*10912 Colonel Glenn Rd* ▪ *Pizza* ▪ All locations carry GF pizza. GF pizza cooked on its own pan and is prepared separately. ▪ *www.americanpiepizza.net*

## Au Bon Pain   📖
*Fayetteville* ▪ (479) 575-3232
*435 N Garland*

## Autumn Breeze Restaurant   ✪ ★ $$LD
*Eureka Springs* ▪ *(479) 253-7734*
*190 Huntsville Rd* ▪ *American* ▪ GF
menu features items such as oysters,
filet mignon, NY strip steak, lobster, crab, and various dessert items. ▪
*www.autumnbreezerestaurant.com*

## Bliss Cupcake Café   ★ ¢S
*Fayetteville* ▪ *(479) 575-0575*
*112 W Center St*
*Fayetteville* ▪ *(479) 966-4186*
*637 E Joyce Blvd* ▪ *Bakery* ▪ GF cupcakes
include blueberry, chocolate milkshake,
red velvet, very vanilla, peanut butter
brownie, strawberry bliss, lavender honey,
choc nilla, lemon, strawberry lemonade
and the elvis. ▪ *www.blisscupcakecafe.com*

## Bonefish Grill   ✪ 📖
*Rogers* ▪ *(479) 273-0916*
*3201 Market St Ste 100*

## Bordinos   ✪ ★ $$$LD
*Fayetteville* ▪ *(479) 527-6795*
*310 W Dickson St* ▪ *Modern American* ▪
GF menu includes salmon, duck breast,
beef tenderloin, and various salads. GF
pasta is available. ▪ *www.bordinos.com*

## Brewski's Draft Emporium   ★ ¢S
*Fayetteville* ▪ *(479) 973-6969*
*408 W Dickson St* ▪ *Pub Food* ▪ GF beer is
available.

## Bush's Pizza   ★ $LD
*Bull Shoals* ▪ *(870) 445-4100*
*803 Central Ave* ▪ *Pizza* ▪ GF pizza available in 10" size with any toppings offered
on regular pizza. ▪ *bushspizza.webs.com*

## Café Amore   $$D
*Eureka Springs* ▪ *(479) 253-7192*
*2070 E Van Buren* ▪ *Italian* ▪ Café Amore
offers a GF non breaded chicken parmesan dish served with vegetables. ▪
*www.cafeamorearkansas.com/menu.html*

## Carino's Italian   ✪ 📖
*Rogers* ▪ *(479) 633-0544*
*535 N 46th St*

## Carrabba's Italian Grill   ✪ 📖
*Rogers* ▪ *(479) 273-2962*
*3300 Pinnacle Hills Pky*

## Devito's Restaurant   $$LD
*Harrison* ▪ *(870) 741-8832*
*350 Devitos Loop* ▪ *Italian* ▪ Restaurant
reports that they have "quite a few" menu
items available for their GF diners. One of
their popular GF entrées is the trout. Alert
the server upon arrival and they will point
out the other GF items that are on the
menu. ▪ *www.devitosrestaurant.com*

## Garden Bistro   $$LD
*Eureka Springs* ▪ *(479) 253-1281*
*119 N Main St* ▪ *Modern American* ▪
Restaurant reports that they are willing to
accommodate GF diners and offer naturally GF entrées such as fish, chicken, steak,
stuffed mushrooms, and artichoke dip. ▪
*eurekagardenbistro.com*

## Genghis Grill   📖
*Rogers* ▪ *(479) 717-2695*
*2011 Promenade Blvd*

## Green Room, The   ★ ¢S
*Fayetteville* ▪ *(479) 251-7665*
*326 N W Ave* ▪ *Pub Food* ▪ GF beer is available. This billiard hall doesn't serve food.

## Greenhouse Grille   ★ $LD
*Fayetteville* ▪ *(479) 444-8909*
*481 S School Ave* ▪ *Fusion* ▪ Owner Jeremy
reports that all soups and salads are GF. He
adds that other menu items, such as the
free range chicken breast and grilled vegetable kabobs, are either naturally GF or can
be prepared GF. Confirm the timeliness of
this information before dining in. GF beer
is available. ▪ *www.greenhousegrille.com*

## Herman's Ribhouse   ★ $$$LD
*Fayetteville* ▪ *(479) 442-9671*
*2901 N College Ave* ▪ *Steakhouse* ▪
The restaurant reports that they have
"a variety of GF options" on the menu,
and requests that GF customers ask their
server to go over the menu with them. ▪
*hermansribhouse.com/menu.php*

**Hog Haus Brewing Co.**    ✿$$$LD
*Fayetteville* ▪ *(479) 521-2739*
*430 W Dickson St* ▪ *Fusion* ▪ GF menu
includes appetizers, salads, bunless burgers,
and entrées. Examples are jalapeno pepper
shrimp, sirloin salad, grilled tuna, and
gouda baked salmon. For dessert, there is a
root beer float. ▪ *www.hoghaus.com*

**HuHot Mongolian Grill**    📖
*Fayetteville* ▪ *(479) 445-6688*
*637 E Joyce Blvd*

**Jason's Deli**    ✿📖
*Fayetteville* ▪ *(479) 442-5500*
*745 E Joyce Blvd*

**Johnny Brusco's New York
Style Pizza**    ★📖
*Bentonville* ▪ *(479) 268-6748*
*700 SE Walton Blvd*

**Jose's Southwest Grille**    ✿$LD
*Springdale* ▪ *(479) 750-9055*
*5240 Sunset Ave* ▪ *Mexican* ▪ A GF menu
is available in the restaurant upon customer
request. ▪ *www.oleforjoses.com*

**Local Flavor Café**    $$BLD
*Eureka Springs* ▪ *(479) 253-9522*
*71 S Main St* ▪ *American* ▪ The
restaurant reports that they are willing to
accommodate GF diners and have several
menu items that can be prepared GF. These
include grilled salmon, fish tacos, and
shrimp diablo. Alert the server upon arrival.
▪ *www.localflavorcafe.net*

**Mama Fu's Asian House**    ✿📖
*Bentonville* ▪ *(479) 254-8381*
*700 SE Walton Blvd*

**O'Charley's**    📖
*Jonesboro* ▪ *(870) 933-7102*
*2312 E Parker Rd*

**Ozark Natural Foods**    ★✿S
*Fayetteville* ▪ *(479) 521-7558*
*1554 N College Ave* ▪ *Deli* ▪ Supervisor
Rachel reports that GF brownies, cookies,
pizza dough, and birthday cakes are available. She recommends calling ahead to discuss GF options and place a special order.

Deli is located in the Ozark Natural Foods
Market. ▪ *www.ozarknaturalfoods.com*

**P.F. Chang's China Bistro**    ✿★📖
*Rogers* ▪ *(479) 621-0491*
*2203 Promenade Blvd Ste 13100*

**Ruth's Chris Steak House**    ✿📖
*Rogers* ▪ *(479) 633-8331*
*3529 Pinnacle Hills Pkwy*

**Shorty Smalls**    📖
*Jonesboro* ▪ *(870) 336-2658*
*3000 E Highland Ave*

**Truly Asian Restaurant**    ✿★$LD
*Jonesboro* ▪ *(870) 275-6000*
*2704 Alexander Dr* ▪ *Asian* ▪ Truly Asian
offers a GF menu featuring items such
as GF fried rice, sautéed tofu and scal-
lions, sautéed garlic chicken and shrimp. ▪
*www.trulyasianrestaurant.com/menu.php*

**UGO's Pizzeria**    ★$LD
*Harrison* ▪ *(870) 204-6244*
*125 W Rush Ave* ▪ *Italian* ▪ GF pizza available daily with almost 90% of the toppings
being naturally GF. The pizza is cooked and
prepared in a completely separate area in
order to minimize CC.

# CALIFORNIA

## LOS ANGELES

**American Girl Place**    ★$$$LD
*Los Angeles* ▪ *(877) 247-5223*
*189 The Grove Dr* ▪ *American* ▪ GF pizza
and pasta are usually available. Restaurant
recommends making reservations at least
a few days in advance, especially during
summer. They suggest noting GF in reser-
vations so that they have time to prepare
for GF diners. Restaurant is family friendly,
though it is geared towards young girls.

## BabyCakes NYC ★ ℂⓈ
*Los Angeles* ▪ *(213) 623-5555*
*130 E 6th St*
*Los Angeles* ▪ *(855) 462-2292*
*236 N Larchmont Blvd* ▪ *Bakery* ▪ Non-dedicated GF bakery offering only very few non-GF products. GF items include cupcakes, muffins, crumb cakes, brownies, scones, pies, and more. Bakery reports that GF products are "always" in stock. ▪ *www.babycakesnyc.com*

## BJ's Restaurant and Brewhouse ✪★▢
*Los Angeles* ▪ *(310) 432-0470*
*10250 Santa Monica Blvd*

## Bombay Bite ✪Ⓢ㎙
*Los Angeles* ▪ *(310) 824-1046*
*1051 Gayley Ave* ▪ *Indian* ▪ GF items on the menu include tandoori vegetables, chicken wings, tandoori chicken, chicken tikka, malai kabab, sheekh kabab, lamb tikka, rack of lamb, tandoori salmon and tandoori shrimp. Other items on menu can be altered for GF customers. Confirm the timeliness of this information before dining in. Alert server upon arrival. ▪ *www.bombaybite.com*

## Border Grill ✪$$$㎙
*Los Angeles* ▪ *(213) 486-5171*
*445 S Figueroa St* ▪ *Mexican* ▪ General manager Julie at the Los Angeles location notes that they have "high sanitation practices" when it comes to preparing special dietary orders. Their extensive GF menu includes plantain empanadas, ceviche, chicken poblano enchiladas, chile relleno, chicken mole verde, and more. ▪ *www.bordergrill.com*

## Breakaway Bakery ℂⓈ
*Los Angeles* ▪ *(310) 968-9380*
*5264 W Pico Blvd* ▪ *Bakery* ▪ According to the owner, "each delicious selection is GF and is the result of much love and attention to detail." Call beforehand in order to confirm availability of items because not all items are baked daily. ▪ *www.breakawaybakery.com*

## Capital Grille, The ✪▢
*Los Angeles* ▪ *(310) 358-0650*
*8614 Beverly Blvd*

## Chili Addiction ★ℂ㎙
*Los Angeles* ▪ *(323) 203-1793*
*408 N La Cienega Blvd* ▪ *American* ▪ Several GF options available such as their GF chili mac, GF mac and cheese, and ice cream brownies. GF buns are available for substitution. Owner has Celiac disease so the issue of CC is very important to them. They have a strict policy in order to prevent CC. ▪ *www.chiliaddiction.com*

## Cru Restaurant $㎙
*Los Angeles* ▪ *(323) 667-1551*
*1521 Griffith Park Blvd* ▪ *Vegan* ▪ The Cru is 100% GF and has a menu featuring items such as bruschetta, vegetable lasagna, pad thai, pesto wrap and more. A variety of desserts are also offered such as dark chocolate truffle cake, blueberry cheesecake with crème fraiche, key lime pie and more. ▪ *www.crusilverlake.com*

## Deano's Gourmet Pizza ★$$㎙
*Los Angeles* ▪ *(323) 935-6373*
*6333 W 3rd St* ▪ *Pizza* ▪ GF pizza and pasta available. GF pizzas can be prepared with any toppings. Restaurant reports a "99.9% GF rule," which means that while they are very careful with GF preparations, there is always a risk of CC. ▪ *www.deanospizzala.com*

## EVO Kitchen ✪★$㎙
*Los Angeles* ▪ *(323) 375-3390*
*7950 W Sunset Blvd #104* ▪ *American* ▪ GF options are marked with a plus sign on regular menu. GF options include salmon filet, California cobb salad, pizzas, and chocolate cake. ▪ *evokitchenla.com*

## Fleming's Prime
## Steakhouse & Wine Bar ✪▢
*Los Angeles* ▪ *(213) 745-9911*
*800 W Olympic Blvd*

## Freebirds on the Fly    ✪📖
*Los Angeles* ▪ *(213) 746-1212*
*3335 S Figueroa St*

## Fugetsu-Do Confections    ★¢$
*Los Angeles* ▪ *(213) 625-8595*
*315 E 1st St* ▪ *Asian* ▪ GF mochi cake is available. Mochi is made with rice and bean base. ▪ *www.fugetsu-do.com*

## Hugo's Tacos    ¢BLD
*Los Angeles* ▪ *(323) 664-9400*
*3300 Glendale Blvd* ▪ *Mexican* ▪ Restaurants report that much of their food is naturally GF. They use corn tortillas and do not dredge meats in flour. Manager David at the Glendale Blvd location recommends speaking to a manager about which items are GF. Both locations are taco stands with no indoor seating. For a sit-down meal, see Hugo's, the mother restaurant. ▪ *www.hugostacos.com*

## In-N-Out Burger    📖
*Los Angeles* ▪ *(800) 786-1000*
*922 Gayley*
*Los Angeles* ▪ *(800) 786-1000*
*3640 Cahuenga Blvd*
*Los Angeles* ▪ *(800) 786-1000*
*9149 S Sepulveda Blvd*
*Los Angeles* ▪ *(800) 786-1000*
*9245 W Venice Blvd*

## Jersey Mike's    📖
*Los Angeles* ▪ *(310) 208-3900*
*1020 Glendon Ave*
*Los Angeles* ▪ *(310) 268-1500*
*12003 Wilshire Blvd*

## Locali Deli & Market    ★¢BLD
*Los Angeles* ▪ *(323) 466-1360*
*5825 Franklin Ave* ▪ *American* ▪ No GF menu but there are several GF options. GF bread and quinoa bowls are available daily as well as several wraps. ▪ *www.localiyours.com*

## Maggiano's Little Italy    ★📖
*Los Angeles* ▪ *(323) 965-9665*
*189 The Grove Dr Ste Z80*

## Maria's Italian Kitchen    ✪★$LD
*Los Angeles* ▪ *(213) 623-4777*
*615 S Flower St* ▪ *Italian* ▪ GF pasta and pizza are available, along with all their salads that come with several GF dressings. ▪ *www.mariasdowntownla.com*

## Morton's Steakhouse    ✪📖
*Los Angeles* ▪ *(310) 246-1501*
*435 S LaCienega Blvd*
*Los Angeles* ▪ *(213) 553-4566*
*735 S Figueroa St*

## Napa Valley Grille    ✪$$$LD
*Los Angeles* ▪ *(310) 824-3322*
*1100 Glendon Ave* ▪ *Modern American* ▪ Manager Alicia of the Bloomington location reports that they always have GF options, but notes that the menu changes frequently. She advises alerting both the server and the manager upon arrival. Manager Tracy of the Los Angeles location adds that reservations noting GF are recommended but not required. ▪ *www.napavalleygrille.com*

## P.F. Chang's China Bistro    ✪★📖
*Los Angeles* ▪ *(310) 854-6467*
*121 N La Cienega Blvd # 117*

## Palomino    📖
*Los Angeles* ▪ *(310) 208-1960*
*10877 Wilshire Blvd*

## Pei Wei Asian Diner    ✪📖
*Los Angeles* ▪ *(323) 762-1275*
*8000 Sunset Blvd*

## Pizzeria Il Fico    ★$$LD
*Los Angeles* ▪ *(310) 271-3426*
*310 S Robertson Blvd* ▪ *Italian* ▪ GF pizza and pasta are available. In order to minimize the risk of CC, all GF items are cooked using different utensils. ▪ *www.pizzeriailfico.com*

## Real Food Daily    ★$LD
*Los Angeles* ▪ *(310) 289-9910*
*414 N La Cienega Blvd* ▪ *Organic* ▪ GF items are marked on the menu and include a corn meal crust pizza, enchiladas, GF pancakes, GF waffles, and hemp milk-

shakes. Additional items may be GF as well- ask a server for details. The restaurant notes that the staff is very familiar with GF dining. Alert a server upon arrival. When a GF request is rung in by a server, a special note is sent to the kitchen. ▪ *www.realfood.com*

### Rosa Mexicano    ✪📖
*Los Angeles* ▪ *(213) 746-0001*
*800 W Olympic Blvd*

### San Gennarro Café    ★$$LD
*Los Angeles* ▪ *(310) 476-9696*
*140 S Barrington Pl* ▪ *Italian* ▪ GF pasta, personal pizza and chicken dishes are available. Reservations noting GF are recommended but not required. ▪ *www.sangennarocafe.com*

### Tossed    ✪📖
*Los Angeles* ▪ *(213) 612-4322*
*700 Wilshire Blvd*

### Truxton's American Bistro    ★$LD
*Los Angeles* ▪ *(310) 417-8789*
*8611 Truxton Ave* ▪ *American* ▪ GF pizza is available. ▪ *www.truxtonsamericanbistro.com*

### Veggie Grill, The    ✪★📖
*Los Angeles* ▪ *(323) 822-7575*
*8000 W Sunset Blvd*

### Yard House    ✪📖
*Los Angeles* ▪ *(213) 745-9273*
*800 W Olympic Blvd*

### Zpizza    ✪📖
*Los Angeles* ▪ *(323) 466-6969*
*123 N Larchmont*

# CALIFORNIA
## SAN DIEGO

### Andres Restaurant    $LD
*San Diego* ▪ *(619) 275-4114*
*1235 Morena Blvd* ▪ *Cuban* ▪ The restaurant reports that most menu items are naturally GF or can be modified to be GF. A manager will be able to point out which menu items to avoid and ensure that the meal is prepared safely. ▪ *www.andresrestaurantsd.com*

### Barolo Ristorante Italiano    $$LD
*San Diego* ▪ *(858) 622-1202*
*8935 Towne Centre Dr* ▪ *Italian* ▪ Alert a server that your meal must be GF and they will recommend the best options that the chef is willing to prepare. Typical options include risotto, grilled fish, and grilled chicken. The kitchen staff are "well aware" of GF meal preparation and use separate utensils to avoid CC. ▪ *www.barolos.com*

### Buca di Beppo    ✪📖
*San Diego* ▪ *(858) 536-2822*
*10749 Westview Pkwy*
*San Diego* ▪ *(619) 233-7272*
*705 6th Ave*

### Capriccio's Italian Restaurant    ★$LD
*San Diego* ▪ *(858) 578-2741*
*9349 Mira Mesa Blvd* ▪ *Italian* ▪ GF pizza and pasta are available in addition to GF bread crumbs which are used to make breaded chicken entrées. ▪ *www.capricciositalianrestaurant.com*

### Casa de Luz    ✪$BLD
*San Diego* ▪ *(619) 501-1200*
*2920 University Ave* ▪ *Organic* ▪ Menu changes daily and is almost always 100% GF. Call ahead to confirm GF status of the daily menu. ▪ *www.casadeluz.org*

### Corvette Diner    ✪¢LD
*San Diego* ▪ *(619) 542-1476*
*2965 Historic Decatur Rd* ▪ *American* ▪ GF menu available in-house. Options

include burgers and sandwiches without buns, French fries, baked potato skins, and more. Confirm the timeliness of this information before dining in. ▪ www.cohnrestaurants.com

### Cozymel's Coastel Mex   ✪📖
San Diego ▪ (858) 658-0480
4303 La Jolla Village Dr

### Cupcakes Squared   ★ ₵₷
San Diego ▪ (619) 226-3485
3772 Voltaire St ▪ Bakery ▪ GF cupcakes and squares are available. Requests for specific flavors can be accommodated if placed a few days in advance. The bakery reports that any flavor can be modified to be GF. ▪ www.cupcakessquared.com

### Cups Organic   ✪★₵₷
La Jolla ▪ (858) 459-2877
7857 Girard Ave ▪ Bakery ▪ Non-dedicated GF bakery offering a wide variety of GF cupcake flavors. At least 3 GF options are available daily, but special orders must be made at least 2 days in advance for a specific flavor. ▪ cupslj.comflavors/

### Eddie V's   ✪📖
La Jolla ▪ (858) 459-5500
1270 Prospect St

### Fish Market, The   $$LD
San Diego ▪ (619) 232-3474
750 N Harbor Dr ▪ Seafood ▪ Shrimp, oysters, and fish can be made GF by eliminating the sauce. Confirm the timeliness of this information before dining in. Managers at all locations note that although they are happy to accommodate GF diners, the kitchens are not GF environments, so CC may occur. Speaking with a manager upon arrival is recommended. ▪ www.thefishmarket.com

### Fleming's Prime Steakhouse & Wine Bar   ✪📖
San Diego ▪ (619) 237-1155
380 K St At 4th Ave
San Diego ▪ (858) 535-0078
8970 University Center Ln

### Hard Rock Café   ✪📖
San Diego ▪ (619) 615-7625
801 4th Ave

### In-N-Out Burger   📖
San Diego ▪ (800) 786-1000
3102 Sports Arena
San Diego ▪ (800) 786-1000
9410 Mira Mesa Blvd
San Diego ▪ (800) 786-1000
4375 Kearny Mesa Rd
San Diego ▪ (800) 786-1000
2005 Camino Del Estate

### Jersey Mike's   📖
San Diego ▪ (858) 484-0222
13173-6 Black Mountain Rd
San Diego ▪ (619) 291-1122
8590 Rio San Diego Dr
San Diego ▪ (858) 578-0588
10764 Westview Pkwy
San Diego ▪ (619) 221-0200
3670 Rosecrans St
San Diego ▪ (858) 675-1411
15805 Bernardo Center Dr
San Diego ▪ (619) 229-0820
6083 El Cajon Blvd
San Diego ▪ (619) 255-5555
3975 5th Ave
San Diego ▪ (858) 452-2211
4353 La Jolla Village Dr

### Joe's Crab Shack   ✪📖
San Diego ▪ (619) 233-7391
525 E Harbor Dr
San Diego ▪ (619) 574-8617
7610 Hazard Circle Dr
San Diego ▪ (858) 274-3474
4325 Ocean Blvd

### Jsix   $$$BLD
San Diego ▪ (619) 531-8744
616 J St ▪ American ▪ Restaurant reports that many menu items are naturally GF or can be prepared GF. Examples include smoked duck and endive salad, fennel-crusted albacore tuna, local Carlsbad mussels, and grilled New York steak. Inform your server that your meal must be GF so they can alert the kitchen. ▪ www.jsixrestaurant.com

### Long Island Mike's Pizza　★ $LD
*San Diego* ▪ (858) 569-7499
*5250 Murphy Canyon Rd* ▪ *Pizza* ▪ GF pizza is available with any toppings. Confirm the timeliness of this information before dining in, and double check with server that all toppings are GF. ▪ *www.longislandmikespizza.com*

### Loving Hut　📖
*San Diego* ▪ (619) 683-9490
*1905 El Cajon Blvd*
*San Diego* ▪ (858) 578-8885
*9928 Mira Mesa Blvd*

### Melting Pot, The　✪📖
*San Diego* ▪ (858) 638-1700
*8980 University Center Ln*
*San Diego* ▪ (619) 234-5554
*901 5th Ave*

### Morton's Steakhouse　✪📖
*San Diego* ▪ (619) 696-3369
*285 J St*

### Old Spaghetti Factory, The　✪★📖
*San Diego* ▪ (619) 233-4323
*275 5th Ave*

### P.F. Chang's China Bistro　✪★📖
*San Diego* ▪ (619) 260-8484
*7077 Friars Rd*
*San Diego* ▪ (858) 458-9007
*4540 La Jolla Village Dr*

### Pei Wei Asian Diner　✪📖
*San Diego* ▪ (858) 207-2730
*10562 Craftsman Wy*
*San Diego* ▪ (619) 321-6670
*1025 Camino De La Reina*

### Prado at Balboa Park, The　$$$LD
*San Diego* ▪ (619) 557-9441
*1549 El Prado* ▪ *Global* ▪ The restaurant reports that GF modifications can be made to certain dishes on the menu. Any of the sandwiches and burgers can be made without bread. Note GF when making reservations and remind waiter of GF request. ▪ *www.cohnrestaurants.com*

### Ritual Tavern　✪★ $D
*San Diego* ▪ (619) 283-1720
*4095 30th St* ▪ *American* ▪ GF items marked on the menu include shepherd's pie, seafood bouillabaisse, herb & ale marinated chicken, and hanger steak. Some items may require modification to become GF, so be sure to discuss with the server. GF beer is available. ▪ *www.ritualtavern.com*

### Ruth's Chris Steak House　✪📖
*San Diego* ▪ (619) 233-1422
*1355 N Harbor Dr*
*San Diego* ▪ (858) 755-1454
*11582 El Camino Real*

### Sammy's Woodfired Pizza　✪📖
*San Diego* ▪ (858) 695-0900
*10785 Scripps Poway Pkwy*
*San Diego* ▪ (858) 259-6600
*12925 El Camino Real*
*San Diego* ▪ (619) 298-8222
*1620 Camino De La Reina*
*San Diego* ▪ (619) 222-3111
*2401 Truxton Rd*
*San Diego* ▪ (619) 230-8888
*770 4th Ave*
*San Diego* ▪ (858) 404-9898
*8650 Genesee Ave*

### Terra American Bistro　✪$$LD
*San Diego* ▪ (619) 293-7088
*7091 El Cajon Blvd* ▪ *American* ▪ The restaurant reports that several items on the menu can be prepared GF, including the black mussels, fish tacos, flat iron steak, and some of the salads. Alert a server, who will notify the kitchen. Confirm the timeliness of this information before dining in. ▪ *www.terrasd.com*

### Tony Roma's　📖
*San Diego* ▪ (858) 272-7427
*4110 Mission Blvd*

### Trails Neighborhood Eatery, The
✪★ ¢BL
*San Diego* ▪ (619) 667-2233
*7389 Jackson Dr* ▪ *American* ▪ GF menu includes GF pancakes and an assortment of omelettes for breakfast, and a variety of salads and sandwiches (served on GF bread)

for lunch. The restaurant reports that they use a separate toaster for GF bread and a separate grill for GF pancakes. GF beer and cider are also available. ▪ *thetrailseatery.com*

### True Food Kitchen                     ✪★📖
*San Diego* ▪ *(619) 810-2929*
*7007 Friars Rd*

### Urban Solace                          ✪$$LD
*San Diego* ▪ *(619) 295-6464*
*3823 30th St* ▪ *Modern American* ▪ GF menu includes pan-seared salmon, the half chicken, steak, a broiled portabella sandwich without bread, and more. ▪ *www.urbansolace.net*

### Yard House                            ✪📖
*San Diego* ▪ *(619) 233-9273*
*1023 4th Ave*

# CALIFORNIA

## SAN FRANCISCO

### Amici's East Coast Pizzeria          ★$$$LD
*San Francisco* ▪ *(415) 885-4500*
*2200 Lombard St* ▪ *Pizza* ▪ GF pizza and beer are available at the listed locations only. ▪ *www.amicis.com*

### Betelnut Pejiu Wu                      ✪$LD
*San Francisco* ▪ *(415) 929-8855*
*2030 Union St* ▪ *Asian* ▪ GF menu available. ▪ *www.betelnutrestaurant.com*

### Bob's Steak & Chop House             📖
*San Francisco* ▪ *(415) 273-3085*
*500 California St*

### Bubba Gump Shrimp Co.                 ✪📖
*San Francisco* ▪ *(415) 781-4867*
*Pier 39*

### Buca di Beppo                         ✪📖
*San Francisco* ▪ *(415) 543-7673*
*855 Howard St*

### Cups and Cakes Bakery                ★¢S
*San Francisco* ▪ *(415) 437-2877*
*451 9th St* ▪ *Bakery* ▪ Non-dedicated bakery with over 80 flavors of cupcakes, all of which can be made GF. They also offer an 7-inch "XXL Cupcake" and a 6-inch mini cake, both of which can be made GF. ▪ *cupsandcakesbakery.com*

### Dosa                                   $$$LD
*San Francisco* ▪ *(415) 642-3672*
*995 Valencia St*
*San Francisco* ▪ *(415) 441-3672*
*1700 Fillmore St* ▪ *Indian* ▪ "Dietary needs" tab online lists items made without wheat. Examples include corn & curry leaf soup, caramelized onion uttapam, and lamb pepper fry. Confirm the timeliness of this information before dining in. ▪ *www.dosasf.com*

### Eagle Pizzeria                        ★$LD
*San Francisco* ▪ *(415) 566-3113*
*1712 Taraval St* ▪ *Pizza* ▪ GF pizza is available in the 12-inch size for an additional $5. ▪ *www.eaglepizzeria.com*

### Extreme Pizza                         ★$$LD
*San Francisco* ▪ *(415) 929-8234*
*1980 Union St*
*San Francisco* ▪ *(415) 929-9900*
*1730 Fillmore St*
*San Francisco* ▪ *(415) 701-9000*
*1062 Folsom St* ▪ *Pizza* ▪ GF pizza is available at the listed locations, and corporate office manager Simone reports that other locations worldwide will be "following suit shortly." She also notes that GF pizzas are prepared in separate areas and cooked on dedicated trays using separate utensils and toppings. If you wish to visit an Extreme Pizza location not listed in this guide, call ahead to find out if they carry GF pizza. ▪ *www.extremepizza.com*

### Gracias Madre                         $LD
*San Francisco* ▪ *(415) 683-1346*
*2211 Mission St* ▪ *Mexican* ▪ Restaurant reports that GF diners can be accommodated and only 2 items on the menu contain

gluten, both of which are pre-prepared to minimize CC risks. Confirm the timeliness of this information before dining in. ▪ www.gracias-madre.com

### Greens Restaurant     $$$LD
San Francisco ▪ (415) 771-6222
Fort Mason Bldg A ▪ Vegetarian ▪ The restaurant reports that all of the servers are "very knowledgeable" about the GF diet. Alert the server, who will notify the kitchen. They also recommend reservations noting GF, as this will allow the restaurant to prepare more thoroughly. ▪ www.greensrestaurant.com

### Hard Rock Café     ✪▭
San Francisco ▪ (415) 956-2013
39 Pier #256

### Herbivore the Earthly Grill    ✪★¢BLD
San Francisco ▪ (415) 826-5657
983 Valencia St
San Francisco ▪ (415) 885-7133
531 Divisadero St ▪ Vegan ▪ GF items are marked on the menu include quinoa tabbouleh, pad thai, chicken fried rice, and more. GF pasta is available. Staff cautions that there are items containing gluten in the kitchen and advises GF guests to "make informed choices." ▪ www.herbivorerestaurant.com

### Hillstone Restaurants     ▭
San Francisco ▪ (415) 392-9280
1800 Montgomery St

### Hot Spud     ¢LD
San Francisco ▪ (415) 399-1065
2640 Mason St ▪ American ▪ The restaurant reports that most items on their menu are GF, including their signature hot potatoes. ▪ www.hotspudsf.com

### Ike's Place     ★¢LD
San Francisco ▪ (415) 553-6888
3489 16th St ▪ Deli ▪ GF bread is available for sandwiches. The restaurant reports than certain sauces and vegan meats contain gluten. Ask a server which choices are GF. ▪ www.ilikeikesplace.com

### In-N-Out Burger     ▭
San Francisco ▪ (800) 786-1000
333 Jefferson

### Joe's Crab Shack     ✪▭
San Francisco ▪ (415) 673-2266
245 Jefferson St

### Kara's Cupcakes     ★¢S
San Francisco ▪ (415) 563-2223
3249 Scott St
San Francisco ▪ (415) 563-2223
900 N Pt ▪ Bakery ▪ GF cupcakes are available in sweet vanilla, chocolate velvet, and vanilla or chocolate coconut. Mini cupcakes are available by preorder, and 6-inch cakes are available at the Palo Alto and San Jose locations. The Palo Alto location also hosts cupcake decorating parties upon request. The Scott St location bakes all GF goods, some of which get delivered to North Point. ▪ www.karascupcakes.com

### Kuleto's     $$$BLD
San Francisco ▪ (415) 397-7720
221 Powell St ▪ Italian ▪ Alert the server, who will indicate GF options. Reservations noting GF are recommended. It is best to call in advance, as GF items are not always available. ▪ www.kuletos.com

### Loving Hut     ▭
San Francisco ▪ (415) 362-2199
1365 Stockton St
San Francisco ▪ (415) 975-3888
845 Market St
San Francisco ▪ (415) 731-1957
524 Irving St

### Mariposa     ¢S
San Francisco ▪ (510) 595-0955
1 Ferry Building ▪ Dedicated GF bakery offering biscottis, brownies, coffee cake, cupcakes, squares, bagels, crostini, pizza crust, cinnamon rolls, breads and rolls as well as a small pecan pie. ▪ www.mariposabaking.com

### Morton's Steakhouse     ✪▭
San Francisco ▪ (415) 986-5830
400 Post St

## One Market Restaurant $$$$LD
San Francisco ▪ (415) 777-5577
1 Market St ▪ Fusion ▪ Restaurant reports
that they can "certainly accommodate
any dietary needs" and that serving a GF
diner "would not be a problem." Reservations noting GF are recommended. ▪
www.onemarket.com

## Palomino  📖
San Francisco ▪ (415) 512-7400
345 Spear St

## Pica Pica Maize Kitchen  ★ ¢BLD
San Francisco ▪ (415) 400-5453
401 Valencia St ▪ Latin American ▪ The
restaurant offers a mix-and-match style
of GF cuisine. Diners choose one of three
cornbreads and a filling. Empanadas
are also served. GF beer is available. ▪
www.picapicakitchen.com

## Plant Café Organic, The  ✪$$LD
San Francisco ▪ (415) 984-1973
The Embarcadero
San Francisco ▪ (415) 693-9730
101 California St
San Francisco ▪ (415) 931-2777
3352 Steiner St ▪ Organic ▪
www.theplantcafe.com

## Ruth's Chris Steak House  ✪📖
San Francisco ▪ (415) 673-0557
1601 Van Ness Ave

## San Francisco Soup Company  ✪BLD
San Francisco ▪ (415) 397-7687
50 Post St
San Francisco ▪ (415) 495-4765
1 Market St
San Francisco ▪ (415) 512-0472
845 Market St
San Francisco ▪ (415) 512-7687
301 Howard St
San Francisco ▪ (415) 566-7687
3251 20th Ave
San Francisco ▪ (415) 644-1321
142 2nd St
San Francisco ▪ (415) 834-0472
221 Montgomery St
San Francisco ▪ (415) 904-7660

50 Fremont St
San Francisco ▪ (415) 986-3634
1 California St
San Francisco ▪ (415) 989-7687
315 California St
San Francisco ▪ (415) 788-7687
275 Battery St
San Francisco ▪ (415) 781-7687
580 California St
San Francisco ▪ (650) 821-7687
SFO Terminal 3
San Francisco ▪ (415) 537-7687
135 4th St ▪ American ▪ Soups rotate daily.
Check the website for a given day's GF
offerings. Most locations also have GF options marked on the board. Some locations,
including those in airports, do not have GF
options marked on the board, but they will
have a chart of GF options upon request. All
GF soups made before soups containing gluten. Hours vary by location. Burlingame location is called Urban Bistro but same menu
and policies apply. ▪ www.sfsoupco.com

## Slanted Door, The  $$$$LD
San Francisco ▪ (415) 861-8032
1 Ferry Building ▪ Asian Fusion ▪ The
restaurant reports that most items on the
menu can be "adjusted to suit the needs of
GF guests." Alert the server upon arrival. ▪
slanteddoor.com

## Underdog- the Organic
## Sausage Joint  ★ ¢LD
San Francisco ▪ (415) 665-8881
1634 Irving St ▪ Organic ▪ GF meat
sausages wrapped in corn tortillas are
available. Avoid the veggie and vegan
sausages, gluten is present. Restaurant
reports that they have GF pies and pastries.
▪ underdogorganic.com

## Zadin  ✪★$$D
San Francisco ▪ (415) 626-2260
4039 18th St ▪ Vietnamese ▪ GF items
indicated on menu. Items include fish rolls,
imperial rolls, mixed green salad, salt and
pepper calamari, beef noodle soup, sate
beef noodle soup, chicken noodle soup,
sate chicken noodle soup, land and sea

noodle soup, shaken beef, spicy tofu and eggplant, green curry scallops and pan fried pho noodles. ▪ *www.zadinsf.com*

---

# CALIFORNIA

## ALL OTHER CITIES

### 118 Degrees　　　　　　　★ $BLD
*Costa Mesa* ▪ *(714) 754-0718*
*2981 Bristol St* ▪ *Raw* ▪ Team member Alexis reports that almost the entire menu is GF or "can be made GF for you." Alert the server that your meal must be GF and they will make a note to omit any non-GF items. ▪ *www.shop118degrees.com*

### 2Good2B Bakery & Café　　　　¢BLD
*Encinitas* ▪ *(760) 942-4663*
*204 N El Camino Real* ▪ *Bakery & Café* ▪ Dedicated GF restaurant featuring items such as a turkey & roasted red pepper press, a BLT and GF pizzas in addition to their baked breads. ▪ *www.2good2b.com*

### Aladino's Pizza　　　　　　★ ¢LD
*Antioch* ▪ *(925) 757-6363*
*1324 Sunset Dr* ▪ *Pizza* ▪ 12-inch GF pizzas are available with any toppings. ▪ *www.aladinospizza.net*

### All of the Above Bakery　　　¢S
*Temecula* ▪ *(951) 693-4000*
*28120 Jefferson Ave* ▪ *Bakery* ▪ A 100% GF bakery offering menu items such as chicken noodle soup, stuffed chicken popovers, peppermint cookies, oatmeal, magic chocolate cake, and various flavored muffins. ▪ *allaftheabovebakery.com*

### Amia Bakery　　　　　　✪★¢S
*Fremont* ▪ *(510) 793-8808*
*39095 Fremont Hub* ▪ *Bakery* ▪ Non-dedicated GF bakery offering GF cakes and cupcakes in select flavors, including

chocolate and vanilla for full-size cakes and caramel, lemon, PB&J, and chocolate chip. Confirm the timeliness of this information before dining in. ▪ *www.amiabakery.com*

### Amici's East Coast Pizzeria　★ $$$LD
*Mountain View* ▪ *(650) 961-6666*
*790 Castro St*
*San Jose* ▪ *(408) 289-9000*
*225 W Santa Clara St*
*Vacaville* ▪ *(707) 451-7777*
*1679 E Monte Vista Ave*
*Dublin* ▪ *(925) 875-1600*
*4640 Tassajara Rd*
*Cupertino* ▪ *(408) 252-3333*
*10310 S De Anza Blvd*
*La Jolla* ▪ *(858) 729-9988*
*811 Prospect St*
*Menlo Park* ▪ *(650) 329-8888*
*880 Santa Cruz Ave*
*Redwood Shores* ▪ *(650) 654-3333*
*226 Redwood Shores Pkwy*
*San Rafael* ▪ *(415) 455-9777*
*1242 Fourth St* ▪ *Pizza* ▪ GF pizza and beer are available at the listed locations only. ▪ *www.amicis.com*

### Argyle Steakhouse　　　　✪$$$$BLD
*Carlsbad* ▪ *(760) 603-6908*
*7447 Batiquitos Dr* ▪ *American* ▪ GF menu lists a range of options, from fish and shellfish to meats like wagyu beef. It also details which salads, "enhancers," and sides are GF. Located inside the Four Seasons Resort. ▪ *www.argylesteakhouse.com*

### Ariel's Grotto　　　　　　$$$$BLD
*Anaheim* ▪ *(714) 781-3463*
*1313 S Harbor Blvd* ▪ *American* ▪ The restaurant reports that they can accommodate GF diners and recommends that GF guests ask to speak with the manager or chef to find out the current GF offerings. Located at Disney's California Adventure. ▪ *disneyland.disney.go.com*

### Asian Box　　　　　　　¢LD
*Palo Alto* ▪ *(650) 391-9305*
*855 El Camino Real* ▪ *Asian* ▪ 100% GF establishment serving customizable box

meals. Guests are able to choose their base (rice, noodles, or vegetables), protein, toppings, and sauces in whatever combination they wish. ▪ *asianboxpaloalto.com*

### Astaria ✪$LD
San Mateo ▪ (650) 344-9444
50 E 3rd Ave ▪ *American* ▪ GF items are indicated with an asterisk on the menu and include pork tendeloin, mushroom madeira risotto, grilled Scottish salmon, and more. The manager reports that they serve GF customers every day and they are "more than happy to accommodate" their customers' needs. ▪ *astariasm.com*

### Aubrey Rose Tea Room ★$$$$
La Mesa ▪ (619) 461-4832
8362 La Mesa Blvd ▪ *Teahouse* ▪ Two of their tea menus, the Lady Anne and the Queen Victoria, are available GF. GF versions of all items in these menus are usually available. The tea room advises making a reservation noting GF a few days in advance to ensure availability. ▪ *www.theaubreyrosetearoom.com*

### Aunti Gluten's Bakery ¢$
Pleasonton ▪ (925) 639-9977
4290 Stanley Blvd ▪ *Bakery* ▪ Dedicated GF bakery offering cakes, cupcakes, cookies, breads, trail mix, and more. ▪ *www.auntiglutens.com*

### Award Wieners ★¢LD
Anaheim ▪ (714) 781-3463
1313 S Harbor Blvd ▪ *American* ▪ GF hot dog buns are available. The restaurant reports that their John Morrell brand hot dogs are GF. Confirm the timeliness of this information before dining in. Located inside Disney's California Adventure. ▪ *disneyland.disney.go.com*

### Beverly Hills Thai ★$LD
Beverly Hills ▪ (310) 288-4321
9036 Burton Wy ▪ *Thai* ▪ Owner PJ reports that they are "very conscious" of the GF diet. She explains that they have one regular customer who is "very sensitive," and who taught them how to prepare GF meals.

Alert a server upon arrival. The servers are aware of the GF diet and will alert the kitchen to use a fresh wok. GF soy sauce is available. ▪ *www.beverlyhillsthai.com*

### Big Kitchen Café $BL
San Diego ▪ (619) 234-5789
3003 Grape St ▪ *American* ▪ According to manager they have various vegetable options in addition to several scrambles which can be prepared GF upon customer request. ▪ *www.bigkitchencafe.com*

### Big Thunder Ranch Barbecue $$LD
Anaheim ▪ (714) 781-3463
1313 S Harbor Blvd ▪ *Barbeque* ▪ The restaurant reports that they can accommodate GF diners and recommends that GF guests ask to speak with the manager or chef to find out the current GF offerings. Located in Disneyland Park. ▪ *disneyland.disney.go.com*

### BJ's Restaurant and Brewhouse ✪★📖
Anaheim Hills ▪ (714) 787-3580
8188 E Santa Ana Canyon Rd
Arcadia ▪ (626) 462-1494
400 E Huntington Ave
Bakersfield ▪ (661) 241-5115
10750 Stockdale Hwy
Brea ▪ (714) 990-2095
600 Brea Mall Dr
Brentwood ▪ (925) 809-1950
2365 Sand Creek Rd
Burbank ▪ (818) 557-0881
107 S 1st St
Carlsbad ▪ (760) 579-4440
5613 Paseo Del Norte
Cerritos ▪ (562) 467-0850
11101 183rd St
Chino Hills ▪ (909) 993-5960
4585 Chino Hills Pkwy
Chula Vista ▪ (619) 591-2490
555 Broadway
City of Industry ▪ (626) 363-9460
17615 Castleton St
Concord ▪ (925) 849-1090
385 Sun Valley Mall
Corona ▪ (951) 271-3610
2520 Tuscany St

**Culver City** ▪ (310) 574-5170
6000 Sepulveda Blvd
**Cupertino** ▪ (408) 865-6970
10690 N De Anza Blvd
**Downey** ▪ (562) 231-0820
121 Stonewood St
**Dublin** ▪ (925) 452-1155
3620 Fallon Rd
**Elk Grove** ▪ (916) 753-1500
9237 Laguna Springs Dr
**Escondido** ▪ (760) 466-0700
204 E Via Rancho Pkwy
**Folsom** ▪ (916) 404-2000
27301 E Bidwell St
**Fresno** ▪ (559) 570-1900
715 E Shaw
**Glendale** ▪ (818) 844-0160
101 N Brand Blvd
**Huntington Beach** ▪ (714) 374-2224
200 Main St
**Huntington Beach** ▪ (714) 842-9242
16060 Beach Blvd
**Irvine** ▪ (714) 665-8595
13130 Jamboree Rd
**Laguna Beach** ▪ (949) 494-3802
280 S Coast Hwy
**Laguna Hills** ▪ (949) 900-2670
24032 El Toro Rd
**La Jolla** ▪ (858) 455-0662
8873 Villa La Jolla Dr
**La Mesa** ▪ (619) 589-7222
5500 Grossmont Center Dr
**Long Beach** ▪ (562) 439-8181
5258 E Second St
**Menifee** ▪ (951) 566-9935
30208 Haun Rd
**Modesto** ▪ (209) 846-6940
3401 Dale Rd
**Montebello** ▪ (323) 201-5290
1716 Montebello Town Center
**Moreno Valley** ▪ (951) 571-9370
22920 Centerpoint Dr
**Newark** ▪ (510) 456-3750
5699 Mowry Ave
**Newport Beach** ▪ (949) 675-7560
106 Main St
**Oxnard** ▪ (805) 485-1124
461 W Esplanade Dr

**Palmdale** ▪ (661) 538-9040
1325 Rancho Vista Blvd
**Pasadena** ▪ (626) 204-0845
234 E Colorado Blvd
**Rancho Cucomonga** ▪ (909) 581-6750
11520 4th St
**Rancho Santa Margarita** ▪ (949) 835-1890
22022 El Paseo
**Roseville** ▪ (916) 580-2100
1200 Roseville Pkwy
**Sacramento** ▪ (916) 570-1327
3531 N Fwy Blvd
**Sacramento** ▪ (916) 570-1920
1689 Arden Wy
**Salinas** ▪ (831) 737-1690
1730 N Main St
**San Bernardino** ▪ (909) 380-7100
1045 E Harriman Pl
**San Bruno** ▪ (650) 243-4530
1150 El Camino Real
**San Jose** ▪ (408) 284-4260
925 Blossom Hill Rd
**San Mateo** ▪ (650) 931-2990
2206 Bridgepointe Pkwy
**San Rafael** ▪ (415) 755-6250
5800 Northgate Mall
**Santa Rosa** ▪ (707) 303-1980
334 Coddingtown Center
**Stockton** ▪ (209) 373-4660
5733 Pacific Ave
**Temecula** ▪ (951) 252-8370
26500 Ynez Rd
**Torrance** ▪ (310) 802-6440
3525 W Carson St
**Vacaville** ▪ (707) 359-2200
190 Nut Tree Pkwy
**Valencia** ▪ (661) 288-1299
24320 Town Center Dr
**West Covina** ▪ (626) 858-0054
2917 Eastland Center Dr
**Westlake Village** ▪ (805) 497-9393
3955 E Thousand Oaks Blvd
**Westwood** ▪ (310) 209-7475
939 Broxton Ave
**Woodland Hills** ▪ (818) 340-1748
6424 Canoga Ave

**Blue Bayou**                                    $$$**LD**
*Anaheim* ■ *(714) 781-3463*
*1313 S Harbor Blvd* ■ *Cajun & Creole* ■ GF
items include five pepper roast NY steak,
blackened cajun spiced salmon, Tesoro
Island chicken, portobello mushroom
with macque choux, broiled filet mi-
gnon, and bayou surf & turf (available
after 4 PM). Confirm the timeliness
of this information before dining in.
Located at Disneyland Park inside the
Pirates of the Caribbean attraction. ■
*disneyland.disney.go.com*

**Boardwalk Pizza & Pasta**            ★ **SLD**
*Anaheim*
*1313 S Harbor Blvd* ■ *Pizza* ■ GF salads
include field greens salad, caesar salad,
and Italian salad, all with no breadsticks
or croutons. GF pizza options include
cheese, pepperoni, or BBQ chicken. GF
rice noodles with marinara sauce are also
available. Confirm the timeliness of this
information before dining in. Located
inside Disney's California Adventure. ■
*disneyland.disney.go.com*

**Bobby G's Pizzeria**                      ★ **SLD**
*Berkeley* ■ *(510) 665-8866*
*2072 University Ave* ■ *Pizza* ■ GF pizza is
available with any topping in the 12-inch
size only. GF pizzas are prepared on sepa-
rate trays. ■ *www.bobbygspizzeria.com*

**Border Grill**                          ✪$$$**LD**
*Santa Monica* ■ *(310) 451-1655*
*1445 4th St* ■ *Mexican* ■ General manager
Julie at the Los Angeles location notes
that they have "high sanitation practices" when it comes to preparing special
dietary orders. Their extensive GF menu
includes plantain empanadas, ceviche,
chicken poblano enchiladas, chile relleno, chicken mole verde, and more. ■
*www.bordergrill.com*

**Borrelli's Pizza**                    ✪★$$**LD**
*Encinitas* ■ *(760) 436-1501*
*285 N El Camino Real* ■ *Pizza* ■ GF menu
available. Includes GF pizza with various

toppings to choose from, specialty salads,
and GF pasta including spaghetti, penne
rigate, penne with alfredo sauce and
baked ziti. The restaurant reports that they
have a GF prep area but cannot guaran-
tee no CC due to the common kitchen. ■
*www.borrellispizza.net*

**Boskos Trattoria**                      ✪$$**LD**
*Calistoga* ■ *(707) 942-9088*
*1364 Lincoln Ave* ■ *Italian* ■ Staff reports
that almost all items on the menu can
be prepared GF. Naturally GF items are
noted on the menu as well. GF meals are
prepared in a shared kitchen, but are kept
completely separate from NON GF items.
■ *www.boskos.com*

**Boston's Restaurant & Sports Bar**
✪★📖
*Rancho Cucamonga* ■ *(909) 758-9115*
*11260 4th St*
*Long Beach* ■ *(562) 436-1300*
*90 Aquarium Wy*

**Bottle Inn, The**                      ★$$$**LD**
*Hermosa Beach* ■ *(310) 376-9595*
*26 22nd St* ■ *Italian* ■ GF brown rice pasta
is available. Alert server upon arrival. ■
*www.thebottleinn.com*

**Brick Oven Restaurant**                ★**SLD**
*Poway* ■ *(858) 274-2568*
*12222 Poway Rd* ■ *Pizza* ■ GF pizza is avail-
able in the 12-inch size. Ask a staff mem-
ber to indicate which toppings to avoid. ■
*www.858brickoven.com*

**Bubba Gump Shrimp Co.**              ✪📖
*Anaheim* ■ *(714) 635-4867*
*321 W Katella Ave*
*Long Beach* ■ *(562) 437-2434*
*87 Aquarium Wy*
*Monterey* ■ *(831) 373-1884*
*720 Cannery Row*
*Santa Monica* ■ *(310) 393-0458*
*301 Santa Monica Pier*
*Universal City* ■ *(818) 753-4867*
*1000 Universal Studios Blvd*

## Buca di Beppo    ✪📖

*Brea* ▪ *(714) 529-6262*
*1609 E Imperial Hwy*
*Campbell* ▪ *(408) 377-7722*
*1875 S Bascom Ave*
*Carlsbad* ▪ *(760) 479-2533*
*1921 Calle Barcelona*
*Claremont* ▪ *(909) 399-3287*
*505 W Foothill Blvd*
*Encino* ▪ *(818) 995-3288*
*17500 Ventura Blvd*
*Garden Grove* ▪ *(714) 740-2822*
*11757 Harbor Blvd*
*Huntington Beach* ▪ *(714) 891-4666*
*7979 Center Ave*
*Irvine* ▪ *(714) 665-0800*
*13390 Jamboree Rd*
*Palo Alto* ▪ *(650) 329-0665*
*643 Emerson St*
*Pasadena* ▪ *(626) 792-7272*
*80 W Green St*
*Redondo Beach* ▪ *(310) 540-3246*
*1670 S Pacific Coast Hwy*
*Roseville* ▪ *(916) 771-9463*
*1212 Galleria Blvd*
*Sacramento* ▪ *(916) 922-6673*
*1249 Howe Ave*
*San Jose* ▪ *(408) 226-1444*
*925 Blossom Hill Rd*
*Santa Monica* ▪ *(310) 587-2782*
*1442 2nd St*
*Thousand Oaks* ▪ *(805) 449-3688*
*205 N Moorpark Rd*
*Universal City* ▪ *(818) 509-9463*
*1000 Universal Studios Blvd*
*Santa Clarita* ▪ *(661) 253-1900*
*26940 Theater Dr*

## Buckhorn Steak and Roadhouse    $$$D

*Winters* ▪ *(530) 795-4503*
*2 Main St* ▪ *Steakhouse* ▪ The restaurant reports that GF diners can just "pick what they want" from the menu, and the chef will most likely be able to accommodate them. Staff notes that nearly the entire menu is naturally GF, and that GF diners are "pretty common." ▪ *www.buckhornsteakhouse.com*

## Cafe Delfini    ★$$$$D

*Santa Monica* ▪ *(310) 459-8823*
*145 W Channel Rd* ▪ *Italian* ▪ GF Tinkyada pasta is available. ▪ *www.caffedelfini.com*

## Caffe Riace    ★$$LD

*Palo Alto* ▪ *(650) 328-0407*
*200 Sheridan Ave* ▪ *Italian* ▪ GF pasta is available. ▪ *www.cafferiace.com*

## Café Carolina    ★$LD

*Encino* ▪ *(818) 881-8600*
*17934 Ventura Blvd* ▪ *Italian* ▪ GF pasta and pizza are available. Owner Giuseppe notes that there are also several GF meat entrées, like the chicken, the fish, and the filet mignon. Confirm the timeliness of this information before dining in. Alert a server upon arrival. The servers "know very well" which items are GF. ▪ *www.organiccafecarolina.com*

## Café Fina    ★$$LD

*Monterey* ▪ *(831) 372-5200*
*47 Fisherman's Wharf* ▪ *Seafood* ▪ GF pasta is available with countless sauce options in addition to various sides such as soup and salad. ▪ *www.cafefina.com*

## Café Gratitude    ✪★$BLD

*Berkeley* ▪ *(510) 725-4418*
*1730 Shattuck Ave*
*San Rafael* ▪ *(415) 578-4928*
*2200 4th St*
*Santa Cruz* ▪ *(831) 427-9583*
*103 Lincoln St* ▪ *Vegan* ▪ 90% of menu is GF. Sandwiches cannot be made GF but all other items on the menu are naturally GF. ▪ *www.cafegratitude.com*

## Café Orleans    ★$$LD

*Anaheim* ▪ *(714) 781-3463*
*1313 S Harbor Blvd* ▪ *Cajun & Creole* ▪ GF items include house salad, Crescent City salad with salmon or chicken, N'awlins vegetable ragout, kids chicken breast, and kids seared salmon fillet. GF rice noodles are available upon request with kids entrées. Confirm the timeliness of this information before dining in. Located inside Disneyland Park. ▪ *disneyland.disney.go.com*

## Café Rio Mexican Grill    📖
*Lake Forest* ▪ *(949) 334-9292*
*24312 Rockfield Blvd*
*Manhattan Beach* ▪ *(424) 456-3800*
*1800 Rosecrans Ave*
*Costa Mesa* ▪ *(949) 335-6800*
*253 17th St*
*Tustin* ▪ *(657) 622-3000*
*1140 Irvine Blvd*
*Oxnard* ▪ *(805) 288-3250*
*1831 N Rose Ave*
*Lakewood* ▪ *(562) 616-6700*
*5021 Lakewood Blvd*
*Redlands* ▪ *(909) 801-6900*
*27510 W Lugonia Ave*

## California Café Los Gatos    ★ $LD
*Los Gatos* ▪ *(408) 354-8118*
*50 University Ave Suite 260* ▪ *Fusion* ▪ Chef
JR reports that he is "willing to accommodate
all diners in anyway he can". He adds that
options for GF diners include salmon with
purple potatoes, various meat entrées, and
rice noodle pasta. They also have gelato and
sorbet for dessert. ▪ *www.californiacafe.com*

## California Café Palo Alto    ✪$LD
*Palo Alto* ▪ *(650) 325-2233*
*700 Welch Rd* ▪ *Fusion* ▪ The restaurant
reports that their menu changes often, so
it is best to make a reservation noting GF
to ensure that GF options will be available.
Sample GF menu includes arugula & peach
salad, vegetarian risotto, seared scallops,
and grilled beef kabob. Manager Lisa reports that their team is "exceedingly aware
of the importance of preventing any cross-
contamination" ▪ *www.californiacafe.com*

## Capital Grille, The    ✪📖
*Costa Mesa* ▪ *(714) 432-1140*
*3333 Bristol St*

## Carino's Italian    ✪📖
*Antioch* ▪ *(925) 522-8252*
*5799 Lone Tree Wy*
*Chino* ▪ *(909) 902-1800*
*3801 Grand Ave*
*Downey* ▪ *(562) 803-0108*
*12036 Lakewood Blvd*

*El Centro* ▪ *(760) 337-9588*
*3203 S Dogwood Rd*
*Fairfield* ▪ *(707) 438-1801*
*1640 Gateway Blvd*
*Gilroy* ▪ *(408) 842-3130*
*6805 Camino Arroyo*
*Mira Loma* ▪ *(951) 360-9850*
*12447 Limonite Ave*
*Modesto* ▪ *(209) 578-9432*
*3401 Dale Rd*
*Palmdale* ▪ *(661) 947-9700*
*1173 W Rancho Vista Blvd*
*Rancho Cucamonga* ▪ *(909) 646-9985*
*12240 Foothill Blvd*
*Sacramento* ▪ *(916) 419-4049*
*3860 Truxel Rd*
*Victorville* ▪ *(760) 949-8700*
*11920 Amargosa Rd*
*West Covina* ▪ *(626) 966-9878*
*147 N Barranca St*
*Whittier* ▪ *(562) 947-3020*
*15600 Whittier Blvd*

## Carnation Café    ★ $$BLD
*Anaheim* ▪ *(714) 781-3463*
*1313 S Harbor Blvd* ▪ *American* ▪ GF items
available for all three meals. Breakfast items
include scrambled eggs, breakfast potatoes,
bacon, ham, and fresh fruit. Lunch and
dinner items include pan-seared boneless
chicken breast and sandwiches on GF buns.
Confirm the timeliness of this information
before dining in. Located inside Disneyland Park. ▪ *disneyland.disney.go.com*

## Casa de Pico    ✪$LD
*La Mesa* ▪ *(619) 463-3267*
*5500 Grossmont Ctr Dr* ▪ *Mexican* ▪ The
restaurant reports they have an entire GF
menu featuring items such as a Mexican
chopped salad, chicken and avocado pepita
salad, grilled salmon, chile verde, pico enchiladas, chicken & avocado tacos, and fiesta fajitas. Confirm the timeliness of this information before dining in. ▪ *www.casadepico.com*

## Casa Orinda    $$$D
*Orinda* ▪ *(925) 254-2981*
*20 Bryant Wy* ▪ *American* ▪ The restaurant
reports that they can accommodate GF

diners. Alert server upon arrival and they will help select a meal and confer with the chef if necessary. ■ *www.casaorinda.net*

### Cascal Restaurant ✪$$$LD
*Mountain View* ■ *(650) 940-9500*
*400 Castro St* ■ *Latin American* ■ Allergy menu denotes regular menu items that are GF as well as items that may be "adjusted" to remove non-GF ingredients. Reservations noting GF are recommended but not required. ■ *www.cascalrestaurant.com*

### Chez Panisse Restaurant & Café $$$LD
*Berkeley* ■ *(510) 548-5525*
*1517 Shattuck Ave* ■ *Modern American* ■ The restaurant reports that GF diners are welcome, and recommends reservations noting GF. The upstairs restaurant has a fixed menu, but they will specially accommodate GF diners. The downstairs café serves a la carte items only, so GF diners should discuss GF options with the servers. ■ *www.chezpanisse.com*

### China Chef ✪$LD
*La Jolla* ■ *(858) 454-7597*
*623 Pearl St* ■ *Chinese* ■ Most of the items on China Chef's menu can be made GF upon customer request. ■ *www.lajollachinachef.com*

### Cicero's Pizzeria ✪★¢LD
*Lake Forest* ■ *(949) 855-3114*
*24531 Trabuco Rd* ■ *Italian* ■ Cicero's offers a GF menu including entrées such as lasagna, chicken primavera pasta, penne carbonara, and GF pizza crust. ■ *www.ciceroslakeforest.com*

### Claire's on Cedros ★$BL
*Solana Beach* ■ *(858) 259-8597*
*246 N Cedros Ave* ■ *American* ■ GF bread is available. It can be used to make French toast for breakfast or substituted into any sandwich for lunch. GF muffins, cookies, brownies, and more are also available. ■ *www.clairesoncedros.com*

### Cocina Cucamonga $LD
*Anaheim*
*1313 S Harbor Blvd* ■ *Mexican* ■ GF items include a half chicken, carne asada, three way veggies, six way veggies, kid's chicken, Mexican rice, veggie salad, and refried beans. The restaurant also notes that their corn tortillas, guacamole, pico de gallo, and sour cream are GF. Confirm the timeliness of this information before dining in. Located inside Disney's California Adventure. ■ *disneyland.disney.go.com*

### Cosi ✪📖
*Temecula* ■ *(951) 296-6208*
*41493 Margarita Rd Suite G-109*
*Costa Mesa* ■ *(714) 957-6191*
*901 S Coast Dr*

### Country Gourmet American Bistro ✪★$BLD
*Sunnyvale* ■ *(408) 733-9446*
*1314 S Mary Ave* ■ *American* ■ Extensive GF menu includes breakfast, lunch and dinner items. The restaurant reports that they make "every effort" to avoid CC, and recommends specifying that your meal must be GF when ordering any item from the menu. GF cornbread and brownies are available. ■ *country-gourmet.com*

### Cozymel's Coastel Mex ✪📖
*El Segundo* ■ *(310) 606-5505*
*2171 Rosecrans Ave*

### Creekside Brewing Company $$LD
*San Luis Obispo* ■ *(805) 542-9804*
*1040 Broad St* ■ *American* ■ Creekside offers a GF black bean chili dish for dinner and a GF veggie tostada for lunch. ■ *www.creeksidebrewing.com*

### Crepes Café ★¢BLD
*Menlo Park* ■ *(650) 473-0506*
*1195 Merrill St* ■ *French* ■ GF buckwheat crepes are available. Restaurant can make any crepe dish on the menu with the GF shell. ■ *www.crepescafe.com*

**Cups** ★ ₵S
*La Jolla* ▪ *(858) 459-2877*
*7857 Girard Ave* ▪ *Bakery* ▪ Bakery reports that one GF cupcake is available daily. Special orders of two dozen cupcakes or more require advance notice of two days. GF flavors include limone ricotta, chocolate decadence, chocolate and vanilla, and carrot with almonds and pecans. ▪ *www.cupslj.com*

**Cyrus Restaurant** $$$$D
*Healdsburg* ▪ *(707) 433-3311*
*29 North St* ▪ *American* ▪ The chef reports that accommodating GF guests is "no problem" and adds that they serve GF diners "all the time." He notes that many menu items can be modified to be GF. Reservations noting GF are recommended, and advance notice of one week is preferred. ▪ *www.cyrusrestaurant.com*

**Del Mar Rendezvous** ✪$$LD
*Del Mar* ▪ *(858) 755-2669*
*1555 Camino Del Mar* ▪ *Chinese* ▪ Del Mar has an entire GF menu which can be found on their website. It includes items such as chicken lettuce wraps, Chow fun, curry chicken, shrimp with lobster sauce, and shrimp & scallop sauté. ▪ *www.delmarrendezvous.com*

**Dharma's** ✪★$BLD
*Capitola* ▪ *(831) 462-1717*
*4250 Capitola Rd* ▪ *Vegetarian* ▪ Extensive GF menu includes curries, burritos, pizza, sandwiches, pasta, salads, soups, and a variety of breakfast items. GF pizza, pasta, and bread are available. Staff recommends calling ahead to confirm that specialty items are available. ▪ *www.dharmaland.com*

**Disney's California Adventure** ₵S
*Anaheim* ▪ *(714) 781-4565*
*1313 S Disneyland Dr* ▪ *American* ▪ Items reported to be GF throughout the park include fountain Minute Maid lemonade, light lemonade, and frozen lemonade, fresh fruit, turkey legs, cotton candy, popcorn, and kettle corn. Confirm the timeliness of this information before visiting. For information on specific restaurants within the park, see their individual listings. ▪ *disneyland.disney.go.com*

**Disneyland** ₵S
*Anaheim* ▪ *(714) 781-4565*
*1313 S Harbor Blvd* ▪ *American* ▪ Items reported to be GF throughout the park include fountain Minute Maid lemonade, light lemonade, and frozen lemonade, fresh fruit, turkey legs, cotton candy, popcorn, and kettle corn. Confirm the timeliness of this information before visiting. For information on specific restaurants within the park, see their individual listings. ▪ *disneyland.disney.go.com*

**Dosa Republic, The** $LD
*San Mateo* ▪ *(650) 458-3672*
*2299 S El Camino Real* ▪ *Indian* ▪ Most items on the menu are naturally GF, including the wide variety of dosas (Indian crepes) for which the restaurant is named. Alert the server that the meal must be GF so they can tell the kitchen to prepare accordingly. ▪ *www.thedosarepublic.com*

**Doughboy's Pizzeria** ✪★$LD
*Grover Beach* ▪ *(805) 474-8888*
*1800 Grand Ave* ▪ *Pizza* ▪ GF pizza and beer are available. GF menu includes appetizers and salads as well as a wide selection of pizza choices. The restaurant reports that they are "very careful not to have cross-contamination" and notes that work areas are kept separate. ▪ *www.doughboyspizzeria.net*

**Dragonfly** $$$LD
*Truckee* ▪ *(530) 587-0557*
*10118 Donner Pass Rd* ▪ *Asian Fusion* ▪ Chef Billy says they "deal with Celiac all the time" and that GF diners are welcome. He adds that all servers are GF aware and all GF items are made to order. Reservations noting GF are highly recommended. ▪ *www.dragonflycuisine.com*

## Earth Bistro                          ★ ⟲LD
*Temecula* ▪ **(951) 506-8888**
*40695 Winchester Rd* ▪ *American*
▪ GF pizza is available as well as GF
buns for burgers and sandwiches. ▪
*www.myearthbistro.com*

## Extreme Pizza                        ★ $$LD
*San Bruno* ▪ **(650) 873-6336**
*851 Cherry Ave*
*Berkeley* ▪ **(510) 486-0770**
*2352 Shattuck Ave*
*Point Richmond* ▪ **(510) 620-1800**
*151 Park Pl*
*San Ramon* ▪ **(925) 244-1000**
*164 Sunset Dr*
*Hercules* ▪ **(510) 964-9990**
*3700 San Pablo Ave*
*Walnut Creek* ▪ **(925) 930-6100**
*1630 Cypress St*
*Alamo* ▪ **(925) 838-1122**
*3227 Danville Blvd*
*Brentwood* ▪ **(925) 513-3001**
*3120 Balfour Rd*
*Dublin* ▪ **(925) 833-2400**
*6599 Dublin Blvd*
*San Rafael* ▪ **(415) 454-6111**
*703 4th St*
*Berkeley* ▪ **(510) 420-0770**
*3204 College Ave*
*Petaluma* ▪ **(707) 763-8100**
*3100 Lakeville Hwy*
*Novato* ▪ **(415) 898-6575**
*104 Vintage Wy* ▪ *Pizza* ▪ GF pizza is
available at the listed locations, and
corporate office manager Simone reports
that other locations worldwide will be
"following suit shortly." She also notes
that GF pizzas are prepared in separate
areas and cooked on dedicated trays
using separate utensils and toppings.
If you wish to visit an Extreme Pizza
location not listed in this guide, call
ahead to find out if they carry GF pizza. ▪
*www.extremepizza.com*

## Farm Stand                          ✪$$LD
*El Segundo* ▪ **(310) 640-3276**
*422 Main St* ▪ *Global* ▪ Hostess Aurora
reports that GF items on the menu are
denoted with an asterisk. For dessert,
coconut flan is available. Aurora also
notes that it is essential to notify a server
of GF requests, so that the server can tell
the kitchen to take extra precautions. ▪
*www.farmstand.us*

## Fat Mike's Pizza                     ★$LD
*Elk Grove* ▪ **(916) 686-8543**
*8970 Grant Line Rd* ▪ *Pizza* ▪ GF pizza is
available in the 8-inch or 12-inch size. ▪
*www.fatmikespizza.com*

## Fire + Ice                           ★📖
*S Lake Tahoe* ▪ **(530) 542-6650**
*4100 Lake Tahoe Blvd*
*Anaheim* ▪ **(714) 808-9757**
*321 W Katella Ave*

## Firefly Bistro                       $$$D
*South Pasadena* ▪ **(626) 441-2443**
*1009 El Centro St* ▪ *Fusion* ▪ Manager
Gina reports that there are "plenty of options" for GF diners. She notes that all servers are "absolutely" familiar with the GF
diet, and they are able to ask the kitchen
if they have questions about ingredients. ▪
*www.eatatfirefly.com*

## Firefly Grill & Wine Bar             $$$D
*Encinitas* ▪ **(760) 635-1066**
*251 N El Camino Real* ▪ *American* ▪ The
restaurant reports that most of the menu
is "already GF" as they do not use any
flours to thicken sauces or soups. Consult with your server to find out what
modifications, if any, are required for a
dish to be GF. Confirm the timeliness
of this information before dining in. ▪
*www.fireflygrillandwinebar.com*

## Fish Hopper Seafood & Steaks    ✪$$$LD
*Monterey* ▪ **(831) 372-8543**
*700 Cannery Row* ▪ *Seafood & Steak-*
*house* ▪ GF menu includes bacon
wrapped scallops, spicy shrimp ceviche,
seafood cioppino, sesame crusted ahi

tuna, seafood paella, and more. Confirm the timeliness of this information before dining in, and be sure to alert the server that your meal must be GF. ▪ *www.fishhopper.com*

### Fish Market, The    $$LD
*Palo Alto* ▪ (650) 493-8862
*3150 El Camino Real*
*Santa Clara* ▪ (408) 246-3474
*3775 El Camino Real*
*Solana Beach* ▪ (858) 755-2277
*640 Via De La Valle*
*San Mateo* ▪ (650) 349-3474
*1855 S Norfolk St*
*San Jose* ▪ (408) 269-3474
*1007 Blossom Hill Rd* ▪ *Seafood* ▪ Shrimp, oysters, and fish can be made GF by eliminating the sauce. Confirm the timeliness of this information before dining in. Managers at all locations note that although they are happy to accommodate GF diners, the kitchens are not GF environments, so CC may occur. Speaking with a manager upon arrival is recommended. ▪ *www.thefishmarket.com*

### Fit 2B Thai    ✪★₵LD
*Thousand Oaks* ▪ (805) 496-2501
*593 N Moorpark Rd* ▪ *Thai* ▪ GF items are marked on the menu, and GF soy sauce is available. The restaurant recommends alerting the server, who will use a special button to notify the kitchen of the GF order. The restaurant notes that the GF items are not standard, so be sure to specify GF when placing your order. ▪ *www.fit2b-thai.com*

### Flaherty's Seafood    $$$LD
*Carmel* ▪ (831) 625-1500
*6th Ave & Dolores* ▪ *Seafood* ▪ Kenneth states that they are "very familiar" with the GF diet and they "understand about Celiac and cross-contamination." Their menu has "many items" that are GF. Alert the server upon arrival. ▪ *www.flahertysseafood.com*

### Fleming's Prime Steakhouse & Wine Bar    ✪📖
*El Segundo* ▪ (310) 643-6911
*2301 Rosecrans Ave*
*Fresno* ▪ (559) 222-5823
*639 E Shaw Ave*
*Palo Alto* ▪ (650) 329-8457
*180 El Camino Real*
*Rancho Mirage* ▪ (760) 776-6685
*71800 Highway 111*
*Woodland Hills* ▪ (818) 346-1005
*6373 Topanga Canyon Blvd*
*Rancho Cucamonga* ▪ (909) 463-0416
*7905 Monet Ave*
*Walnut Creek* ▪ (925) 287-0297
*1685 Mt Diablo Blvd*
*Newport Beach* ▪ (949) 720-9633
*455 Newport Ctr Dr*

### Flore Vegan Cuisine    ✪★$BLD
*Silverlake* ▪ (323) 953-0611
*3818 W Sunset Blvd* ▪ *Vegan* ▪ GF items are marked on the menu and include griddle cakes, a tofu scramble, crispy kale, edamame, grapefruit and fennel salad, portobello tacos, and more. GF pancakes are available. Some items may require modification to become GF, so be sure to alert the server. ▪ *www.florevegan.com*

### Fogo De Chao    ★📖
*Beverly Hills* ▪ (310) 289-7755
*133 N La Cienega Blvd*

### Fontana's Italian    ★$$LD
*Cupertino* ▪ (408) 725-0188
*20840 Stevens Creek Blvd* ▪ *Italian* ▪ GF pasta is available. Alert server upon arrival. ▪ *www.fontanasitalian.com*

### Freebirds on the Fly    ✪📖
*Agoura Hills* ▪ (818) 874-9171
*29125 Canwood St*
*Clovis* ▪ (559) 324-0808
*1755 Herndon Ave*
*Elk Grove* ▪ (916) 683-2201
*8235 Laguna Blvd*
*Fresno* ▪ (559) 275-5780
*2784 W Shaw Ave*

*Folsom* ▪ *(916) 984-6972*
*310 Palladio Pkwy*
*Foster City* ▪ *(650) 525-1593*
*1000 Metro Ctr Blvd*
*Granada Hills* ▪ *(818) 368-8239*
*17947 W Chatsworth St*
*Huntington Beach* ▪ *(714) 841-7639*
*18541 Beach Blvd*
*Marina Del Rey* ▪ *(310) 306-9600*
*4025 Del Rey Ave*
*Modesto* ▪ *(209) 521-6400*
*1707 McHenry Ave*
*Modesto* ▪ *(209) 545-0200*
*3601 Pelandale Ave*
*Orange* ▪ *(714) 628-0651*
*1632 E Katella Ave*
*Redondo Beach* ▪ *(310) 214-4850*
*1509 Hawthorne Blvd*
*Roseville* ▪ *(916) 791-1233*
*10305 Fairway Dr*
*Sacramento* ▪ *(916) 928-0700*
*2281 Del Paso Rd*
*San Jose* ▪ *(408) 293-0103*
*1205 The Alameda*
*Simi Valley* ▪ *(805) 581-1689*
*2490 Sycamore Dr*
*Temecula* ▪ *(951) 719-3146*
*40408 Winchester Rd*
*Tracy* ▪ *(209) 835-6000*
*1920 W 11th St*
*Turlock* ▪ *(209) 632-1157*
*3202 Countryside Dr*
*Vacaville* ▪ *(707) 446-0106*
*112 Nut Tree Pkwy*
*Ventura* ▪ *(805) 477-0174*
*5752 Telephone Rd*

## French Garden Restaurant & Bistro
★ $$$**LD**

*Sebastopol* ▪ *(707) 824-2030*
*8050 Bodega Ave* ▪ *Bistro* ▪ Staff reports
that the chef is very accommodating when
it comes to preparing GF meals. A server
will be able to advise which menu op-
tions may be prepared GF. The restaurant
adds that their kitchen is "really good
about" keeping GF items safe from CC. ▪
*frenchgardenrestaurant.com*

## Fresco Café & Bakery          ★ $**BLD**

*Santa Barbara* ▪ *(805) 967-6037*
*3987 State St* ▪ *Café* ▪ GF bread and GF
quinoa pasta are available. The restaurant
also has a "create your own meal" option
in which diners can customize their own
GF dish. Team member Kyle recommends
alerting a server upon arrival. As with
all specialty items, call ahead to confirm
availability. ▪ *www.frescosb.com*

## Fresh Brothers          ✪ ★ $**LD**

*Manhattan Beach* ▪ *(310) 546-4444*
*2008 N Sepulveda Blvd*
*Redondo Beach* ▪ *(310) 374-5678*
*407 N Pacific Coast Hwy*
*Marina Del Rey* ▪ *(310) 823-3800*
*4722 1/2 Admiralty Wy*
*Thousand Oaks* ▪ *(805) 777-8448*
*180 Promenade Wy*
*Beverly Hills* ▪ *(310) 860-9400*
*250 S Beverly Dr*
*Calabasas* ▪ *(818) 225-7555*
*4751 Commons Wy*
*Brentwood* ▪ *(310) 826-0777*
*11740 San Vicente Blvd*
*Santa Monica* ▪ *(310) 656-6888*
*1447 Lincoln Blvd* ▪ *Pizza* ▪ GF menu lists
several specialty pizzas as well as a list
of GF toppings to create a custom pizza.
A variety of salads are also available, as
well as boneless chicken bites and buf-
falo wings. The restaurant reports that
their kitchen staff have been trained
through the NFCA "GREAT" program
and have an extensive CC policy. ▪
*www.freshbrothers.com*

## Freshies          ★ $**LD**

*S Lake Tahoe* ▪ *(530) 542-3630*
*3330 Lake Tahoe Blvd* ▪ *American* ▪ GF
tamari is available. The restaurant reports
that they are accustomed to GF diners, and
that 90% of menu items are naturally GF.
Alert a server, who will indicate GF op-
tions. ▪ *www.freshiestahoe.com*

### Fritto Misto                          ★ $LD
*Santa Monica* ▪ *(310) 458-2829*
*601 Colorado Ave*
*Hermosa Beach* ▪ *(310) 318-6098*
*316 Pier Ave* ▪ *Italian* ▪ GF rice pasta is available, or diners can substitute veggies in any dish with a pasta side. ▪ *www.usmenuguide.com*

### Garlic Jim's                          ✪★📖
*Redondo Beach* ▪ *(310) 543-5500*
*1876 S Pacific Coast Hwy*

### Gather                                ✪$$BLD
*Berkeley* ▪ *(510) 809-0400*
*2200 Oxford St* ▪ *Modern American* ▪ The restaurant reports that most items on their menu are GF, and manager Jodi notes that they are "more than happy" to try to make other dishes GF as well. Alert the server upon arrival. ▪ *www.gatherrestaurant.com*

### Gladstone's                           ✪$$$$LD
*Pacific Palisades* ▪ *(310) 454-3474*
*17300 Pacific Coast Hwy* ▪ *Seafood* ▪ Dedicated GF menu with many options. Chef Dean reports that in order to minimize CC, GF dishes are cooked in separate areas on the grill and dedicated GF utensils are used. ▪ *www.sbe.comgladstones*

### Gluten Not Included                   ⊄$
*Escondido* ▪ *(760) 432-6100*
*2250 S Escondido Blvd* ▪ *Bakery & Café* ▪ Dedicated GF bakery offering a wide selection of bread products, including croutons and bread crumbs. GF desserts such as cupcakes, brownies, cookies, macaroons, and muffins are also available. ▪ *www.gnibakery.com*

### Golden Vine Winery Trattoria          ★$$LD
*Anaheim*
*1313 S Harbor Blvd* ▪ *Italian* ▪ GF options include caprese salad, shrimp picatta, Italian iceberg wedge, and garlic & herb roasted chicken. The restaurant recommends asking to speak with the manager or chef, as some items may require modification to become GF. GF pasta is available. Confirm the timeliness of this information before dining in. Located inside Disney's California Adventure. ▪ *disneyland.disney.go.com*

### Good Habit                            ✪★⊄L
*Thousand Oaks* ▪ *(805) 494-4922*
*1625 E Thousand Oaks Blvd* ▪ *Bakery & Café* ▪ The entire menu is available GF and includes soups, salads, sandwiches, burgers, and tacos. GF bread is available for all sandwiches, as well as GF cookies and granola. ▪ *www.goodhabit.com*

### Goofy's Kitchen                       ★$$$$BLD
*Anaheim* ▪ *(714) 956-6755*
*1150 Magic Wy* ▪ *American* ▪ GF pancakes and waffles are available for breakfast. GF pizza and pasta are available. Other GF items include bacon & eggs, NY roast, and baked potato. Confirm the timeliness of this information before dining in. Reservations noting GF are recommended. Located inside the Disneyland Hotel. ▪ *disneyland.disney.go.com*

### Green Elephant Gourmet               ✪$LD
*Palo Alto* ▪ *(650) 494-7391*
*3950 Middlefield Rd* ▪ *Asian* ▪ GF menu available. Alert the server upon arrival. ▪ *www.greenelephantgourmet.com*

### Hard Rock Café                        ✪📖
*Universal City* ▪ *(818) 622-7625*
*1000 Universal Studios Blvd*
*Hollywood* ▪ *(323) 464-7625*
*6801 Hollywood Blvd*

### Healthy Creations                     ✪★⊄BLD
*Encinitas* ▪ *(760) 479-0500*
*376 N El Camino Real* ▪ *Organic* ▪ Baker Mary reports that everything in the bakery case is GF, but the options change frequently. She also notes that though the menu changes monthly, there are always a number of GF options. GF pasta, biscuits, and baked goods are available. ▪ *www.healthycreations.com*

### Herbivore the Earthly Grill     ✪★₵**BLD**
*Berkeley* ▪ *(510) 665-1675*
*2451 Shattuck Ave* ▪ *Vegan* ▪ GF items
are marked on the menu include quinoa
tabbouleh, pad thai, chicken fried rice,
and more. GF pasta is available. Staff
cautions that there are items containing
gluten in the kitchen and advises GF
guests to "make informed choices." ▪
*www.herbivorerestaurant.com*

### Hillstone Restaurants     📖
*Santa Monica* ▪ *(310) 576-7558*
*202 Wilshire Blvd*

### Hostaria del Piccolo     ★$$**LD**
*Santa Monica* ▪ *(310) 393-6633*
*606 Broadway* ▪ *Italian* ▪ GF
pasta and pizza are available. ▪
*www.hostariadelpiccolo.com*

### Hugo's     ✪$**BLD**
*West Hollywood* ▪ *(323) 654-3993*
*8401 Santa Monica Blvd*
*Studio City* ▪ *(818) 761-8985*
*12851 Riverside Dr*
*Agoura Hills* ▪ *(818) 707-0300*
*5046 Cornell Rd* ▪ *Fusion* ▪ GF menu
includes salads with GF dressings, egg
frittatas, tamales, tacos on corn tortillas,
Asian stir fry, tikka masala vegetable patties,
black bean chili, portabello stew, shepherd's
pie, lentil and rice dishes, and more. ▪
*www.hugosrestaurant.com*

### Hugo's Tacos     ₵**BLD**
*Studio City* ▪ *(818) 762-7771*
*4749 Coldwater Canyon Ave* ▪ *Mexican*
▪ Restaurants report that much of their
food is naturally GF. They use corn tortillas
and do not dredge meats in flour. Manager
David at the Glendale Blvd location recommends speaking to a manager about which
items are GF. Both locations are taco stands
with no indoor seating. For a sit-down
meal, see Hugo's, the mother restaurant. ▪
*www.hugostacos.com*

### Hungry Bear Restaurant     ★$**LD**
*Anaheim*
*1313 S Harbor Blvd* ▪ *American* ▪ GF
hamburger buns are available. GF diners
should request that their fries be cooked
in the "fries only" fryer. The watermelon
chicken salad is also GF. Confirm the
timeliness of this information before dining in. Located inside Disneyland Park. ▪
*disneyland.disney.go.com*

### Hurley's     ✪★$$$**LD**
*Yountville* ▪ *(707) 944-2345*
*6518 Washington St* ▪ *American* ▪ Restaurant has an extensive GF menu featuring
items such as oakwood grilled Atlantic salmon, rosemary & maple roasted
chicken, and grilled Moroccan beef skewers. Staff reports that a separate preparation area is used for GF items, but advises
caution since the kitchen is shared. ▪
*www.hurleysrestaurant.com*

### Ike's Quarter Café     ★$**BLD**
*Nevada City* ▪ *(530) 265-6138*
*401 Commercial St* ▪ *American* ▪ The
restaurant offers a variety of GF breakfast items such as omelets and scrambles,
in addition to entrées such as blackened
catfish, chicken and beef, all of which must
be requested to be served without a bun. ▪
*www.ikesquartercafe.com*

### In-N-Out Burger     📖
*Millbrae* ▪ *(800) 786-1000*
*11 Rollins Rd*
*Anaheim* ▪ *(800) 786-1000*
*600 S Brookhurst*
*Anaheim Hills* ▪ *(800) 786-1000*
*5646 E La Palma*
*Arcadia* ▪ *(800) 786-1000*
*420 N Santa Ana*
*Arroyo Grande* ▪ *(800) 786-1000*
*1170 W Branch St*
*Atascadero* ▪ *(800) 786-1000*
*6000 San Anselmo Rd*
*Auburn* ▪ *(800) 786-1000*
*130 Grass Valley Hwy*
*Azusa* ▪ *(800) 786-1000*
*324 S Azusa*

Bakersfield ▪ (800) 786-1000
2310 Panama Ln
Bakersfield ▪ (800) 786-1000
5100 Stockdale Hwy
Balwin Park ▪ (800) 786-1000
13850 Francisquito Ave
Barstow ▪ (800) 786-1000
2821 Lenwood Rd
Brentwood ▪ (800) 786-1000
5581 Lone Tree Wy
Buena Park ▪ (800) 786-1000
7926 Valley View
Burbank ▪ (800) 786-1000
761 First St
Carmarillo ▪ (800) 786-1000
1316 Ventura Blvd
Canoga Park ▪ (800) 786-1000
6841 N Topanga Canyon
Carlsbad ▪ (800) 786-1000
5950 Avenida Encinas
Carmel Mountain ▪ (800) 786-1000
11880 Carmel Mt Rd
Chico ▪ (800) 786-1000
2050 Business Ln
Chino ▪ (800) 786-1000
3927 Grand Ave
Chula Vista ▪ (800) 786-1000
1725 Eastlake Pkwy
City of Industry ▪ (800) 786-1000
21620 E Valley Blvd
City of Industry ▪ (800) 786-1000
17849 E Colima Rd
Clovis ▪ (800) 786-1000
382 N Clovis Ave
Corona ▪ (800) 786-1000
450 Auto Center Dr
Corona ▪ (800) 786-1000
2305 Compton Ave
Costa Mesa ▪ (800) 786-1000
3211 Harbor Blvd
Costa Mesa ▪ (800) 786-1000
594 W 19th St
Covina ▪ (800) 786-1000
1371 Grand Ave
Daly City ▪ (800) 786-1000
260 Washington St
Davis ▪ (800) 786-1000
1020 Olive Dr

Diamond Bar ▪ (800) 786-1000
21133 Golden Springs
Downey ▪ (800) 786-1000
8767 Firestone Blvd
El Cajon ▪ (800) 786-1000
1541 N Magnolia Ave
El Centro ▪ (800) 786-1000
2390 S 4th St
Elk Grove ▪ (800) 786-1000
9188 E Stockton Blvd
Escondido ▪ (800) 786-1000
1260 W Valley Pkwy
Fairfield ▪ (800) 786-1000
1364 Holiday Ln
Folsom ▪ (800) 786-1000
225 Placerville Rd
Fontana ▪ (800) 786-1000
9855 Sierra Ave
Foothill Ranch ▪ (800) 786-1000
26482 Towne Centre
Fremont ▪ (800) 786-1000
43349 Pac. Commons
Fresno ▪ (800) 786-1000
5106 W Shaw St
Fresno ▪ (800) 786-1000
8010 N Blackstone
Fresno ▪ (800) 786-1000
2657 S Second St
Fresno ▪ (800) 786-1000
4302 N Blackstone Ave
Fullerton ▪ (800) 786-1000
1180 S Harbor Blvd
Garden Grove ▪ (800) 786-1000
9032 Trask Ave
Gilroy ▪ (800) 786-1000
641 Leavesley Rd
Glendale ▪ (800) 786-1000
119 S Brand Blvd
Glendale ▪ (800) 786-1000
310 N Harvey Blvd
Glendora ▪ (800) 786-1000
1261 S Lone Hill
Goleta ▪ (800) 786-1000
4865 Calle Real
Hacienda Heights ▪ (800) 786-1000
14620 E Gale
Hemet ▪ (800) 786-1000
2885 W Florida Ave

**Hesperia** ▪ (800) 786-1000
17069 Bear Valley Rd
**Hesperia** ▪ (800) 786-1000
13074 Main St
**Highland** ▪ (800) 786-1000
28009 Greenspot Rd
**Hollywood** ▪ (800) 786-1000
7009 Sunset Blvd
**Huntington Beach** ▪ (800) 786-1000
18062 Beach Blvd
**Huntington Park** ▪ (800) 786-1000
6000 Pacific Blvd
**Indio** ▪ (800) 786-1000
82043 Hwy 111
**Inglewood** ▪ (800) 786-1000
3411 W Century Blvd
**Irvine** ▪ (800) 786-1000
4115 Campus Dr
**Kettleman City** ▪ (800) 786-1000
33464 Bernard Dr
**Laguna Hills** ▪ (800) 786-1000
24001 Avenida de la Carlota
**Laguna Niguel** ▪ (800) 786-1000
27380 La Paz Rd
**La Habra** ▪ (800) 786-1000
2030 E Lambert Rd
**Lake Elsinore** ▪ (800) 786-1000
331 Railroad Canyon
**Lakewood** ▪ (800) 786-1000
5820 Bellflower Blvd
**La Mirada** ▪ (800) 786-1000
14341 Firestone Blvd
**Lancaster** ▪ (800) 786-1000
2021 W Ave I
**La Puente** ▪ (800) 786-1000
15259 E Amar Rd
**La Verne** ▪ (800) 786-1000
2098 Foothill Blvd
**Lebec** ▪ (800) 786-1000
5926 Dennis McCarthy
**Lemon Grove** ▪ (800) 786-1000
7160 Broadway
**Livermore** ▪ (800) 786-1000
1881 N Livermore Ave
**Lodi** ▪ (800) 786-1000
2625 W Kettleman Ln
**Long Beach** ▪ (800) 786-1000
6391 E Pacific Coast Hwy

**Long Beach** ▪ (800) 786-1000
4600 Los Coyotes Diagonal
**Long Beach** ▪ (800) 786-1000
7691 Carson St
**Manteca** ▪ (800) 786-1000
1490 Yosemite Ave
**Marina Del Rey** ▪ (800) 786-1000
13425 Washington Blvd
**Menifee** ▪ (800) 786-1000
30296 Haun Rd
**Merced** ▪ (800) 786-1000
1579 ML King Jr Wy
**Mill Valley** ▪ (800) 786-1000
798 Redwood Hwy
**Milpitas** ▪ (800) 786-1000
50 Ranch Dr
**Modesto** ▪ (800) 786-1000
3900 Pelandale Ave
**Moorpark** ▪ (800) 786-1000
856 Los Angeles Ave
**Moreno Valley** ▪ (800) 786-1000
23035 Hemlock
**Morgan Hill** ▪ (800) 786-1000
895 Cochrane Rd
**Mountain View** ▪ (800) 786-1000
1159 Rengstorff
**Murrieta** ▪ (800) 786-1000
39697 Avenida Acacias
**Napa** ▪ (800) 786-1000
820 Imola Ave
**National City** ▪ (800) 786-1000
500 Mille of Cars Wy
**Natomas** ▪ (800) 786-1000
2900 Del Paso Rd
**Newbury Park** ▪ (800) 786-1000
1550 Newbury Rd
**Newhall** ▪ (800) 786-1000
25220 N The Old Rd
**North Hollywood** ▪ (800) 786-1000
5864 Lankershim
**Norco** ▪ (800) 786-1000
1810 Hamner
**Northridge** ▪ (800) 786-1000
8830 Tampa Ave
**Northridge** ▪ (800) 786-1000
9858 Balboa Blvd
**Norwalk** ▪ (800) 786-1000
14330 Pioneer Blvd

Oakland ▪ (800) 786-1000
8300 Oakport St
Oceanside ▪ (800) 786-1000
4605 Frazee
Ontario ▪ (800) 786-1000
2235 Mountain
Ontario ▪ (800) 786-1000
4310 E Ontario Mills Pkwy
Ontario ▪ (800) 786-1000
1891 E G St
Orange ▪ (800) 786-1000
2585 N Tunstin St
Orange ▪ (800) 786-1000
3501 E Chapman
Oxnard ▪ (800) 786-1000
381 W Esplanade
Pacific Beach ▪ (800) 786-1000
2910 Damon Ave
Palmdale ▪ (800) 786-1000
142 E Palmdale Blvd
Panorama City ▪ (800) 786-1000
13651 Roscoe Blvd
Pasadena ▪ (800) 786-1000
2114 E Foothill
Petaluma ▪ (800) 786-1000
1010 Lakeville Hwy
Pico Rivera ▪ (800) 786-1000
9070 Whittier Blvd
Pinole ▪ (800) 786-1000
1417 Fitzgerald Dr
Pittsburg ▪ (800) 786-1000
4550 Delta Gateway B
Placentia ▪ (800) 786-1000
825 W Chapman
Placerville ▪ (800) 786-1000
3055 Forni Rd
Pleasant Hill ▪ (800) 786-1000
570 Contra Costa Blvd
Pleasanton ▪ (800) 786-1000
6015 Johnson Dr
Pomona ▪ (800) 786-1000
1851 Indian Hill
Pomona ▪ (800) 786-1000
2505 Garey Ave
Porter Ranch ▪ (800) 786-1000
19901 Rinaldi St
Poway ▪ (800) 786-1000
12890 Gregg Ct

Rancho Cordova ▪ (800) 786-1000
2475 Sunrise Blvd
Rancho Cucamonga ▪ (800) 786-1000
8955 Foothill Blvd
Rancho Cucamonga ▪ (800) 786-1000
12599 Foothill Blvd
Redding ▪ (800) 786-1000
1275 Dana Dr
Redondo Beach ▪ (800) 786-1000
3801 Inglewood Ave
Redwood City ▪ (800) 786-1000
949 Veterans Blvd
Riverside ▪ (800) 786-1000
7467 Indiana Ave
Riverside ▪ (800) 786-1000
6634 Clay
Rohnert Park ▪ (800) 786-1000
5145 Redwood Dr
Rosemead ▪ (800) 786-1000
4242 N Rosemead Blvd
Roseville ▪ (800) 786-1000
1803 Taylor
Roseville ▪ (800) 786-1000
10309 Fairway Dr
Sacramento ▪ (800) 786-1000
2001 Alta Arden Expwy
Sacramento ▪ (800) 786-1000
4600 Madison Ave
Sacramento ▪ (800) 786-1000
3501 Truxel Rd
Salinas ▪ (800) 786-1000
151 Kern St
San Bernardino ▪ (800) 786-1000
795 W 5th St
San Bernardino ▪ (800) 786-1000
1065 Harriman Pl
San Carlos ▪ (800) 786-1000
445 Industrial Rd
San Fernando ▪ (800) 786-1000
11455 Laurel Canyon Blvd
San Jose ▪ (800) 786-1000
2950 E Capitol Expwy
San Jose ▪ (800) 786-1000
5611 Santa Teresa
San Jose ▪ (800) 786-1000
550 Newhall Dr
San Juan Capistrano ▪ (800) 786-1000
28782 Camino Capistrano

*San Leandro* ■ (800) 786-1000
15575 Hesperian Blvd
*San Marcos* ■ (800) 786-1000
583 Grande Ave
*San Pedro* ■ (800) 786-1000
1090 N Western Ave
*San Ramon* ■ (800) 786-1000
2270 San Ramon Valley
*Santa Ana* ■ (800) 786-1000
3361 S Bristol
*Santa Ana* ■ (800) 786-1000
815 N Bristol
*Santa Clara* ■ (800) 786-1000
3001 Mission College
*Santa Clarita* ■ (800) 786-1000
26401 Bouquet Canyon Rd
*Santa Clarita* ■ (800) 786-1000
28368 Sand Canyon Rd
*Santa Fe Springs* ■ (800) 786-1000
10525 Carmenita
*Santa Maria* ■ (800) 786-1000
1330 S Bradley Rd
*Santa Nella* ■ (800) 786-1000
28900 Henry Miller Rd
*Santa Rosa* ■ (800) 786-1000
2131 County Center Dr
*Santee* ■ (800) 786-1000
9414 Mission Gorge Rd
*Seal Beach* ■ (800) 786-1000
12365 Seal Beach Blvd
*Sherman Oaks* ■ (800) 786-1000
4444 Van Nuys Blvd
*Signal Hill* ■ (800) 786-1000
799 E Spring St
*Simi Valley* ■ (800) 786-1000
2600 Stearns
*Stockton* ■ (800) 786-1000
2727 W March Ln
*Sunnyvale* ■ (800) 786-1000
604 E El Camino Real
*Temecula* ■ (800) 786-1000
30697 Temecula Pkwy
*Temecula* ■ (800) 786-1000
27700 Jefferson Ave
*Temple City* ■ (800) 786-1000
10601 Lower Azusa Rd
*Thousand Palms* ■ (800) 786-1000
72265 Varner Rd

*Torrance* ■ (800) 786-1000
730 W Carson
*Torrance* ■ (800) 786-1000
20150 Hawthorne Blvd
*Torrance* ■ (800) 786-1000
24445 Crenshaw Blvd
*Tracy* ■ (800) 786-1000
575 Clover Rd
*Tujunga* ■ (800) 786-1000
6225 Foothill Blvd
*Turlock* ■ (800) 786-1000
3071 Countryside Dr
*Tustin* ■ (800) 786-1000
2895 Park Ave
*Tustin* ■ (800) 786-1000
3020 El Camino Real
*Union City* ■ (800) 786-1000
32060 Union Landing
*Upland* ■ (800) 786-1000
1837 Foothill Blvd
*Vacaville* ■ (800) 786-1000
170 Nut Tree Pkwy
*Van Nuys* ■ (800) 786-1000
7930 Van Nuys Blvd
*Van Nuys* ■ (800) 786-1000
7220 N Balboa
*Ventura* ■ (800) 786-1000
2070 Harbor Blvd
*Victorville* ■ (800) 786-1000
15290 Civic Dr
*Visalia* ■ (800) 786-1000
1933 S Mooney Blvd
*Vista* ■ (800) 786-1000
2010 Hacienda Dr
*West Covina* ■ (800) 786-1000
15610 San Bernardino
*West Covina* ■ (800) 786-1000
2940 E Garvey Ave
*Westminster* ■ (800) 786-1000
6292 Westminster Blvd
*West Sacramento* ■ (800) 786-1000
780 Ikea Ct
*Woodland* ■ (800) 786-1000
2011 Bronze Star Dr
*Woodland Hills* ■ (800) 786-1000
19920 Ventura Blvd
*Yuba City* ■ (800) 786-1000
1375 Sunsweet Blvd

## Islands Fine Burgers & Drinks    📖

*Brea* ▪ *(714) 256-1666*
*250 S State College Blvd*
*Agoura Hills* ▪ *(818) 879-8550*
*29271 Agoura Rd*
*Anaheim Hills* ▪ *(714) 974-5709*
*105 S Festival Dr*

## Jason's Deli    ⭐📖

*Riverside* ▪ *(951) 697-7666*
*2555 Canyon Springs Pkwy*

## Java Man Coffee House    ★ℭBL

*Hermosa Beach* ▪ *(310) 379-7209*
*157 Pier Ave* ▪ *Coffee Shop* ▪ GF
muffins are available occasion-
ally. Call ahead to confirm availability. ▪
*www.javamancoffeehouse.com*

## Jersey Mike's    📖

*Ojai* ▪ *(805) 640-9070*
*423 E Ojai Ave*
*Oxnard* ▪ *(805) 985-3900*
*1231 S Victoria Ave*
*Ventura* ▪ *(805) 644-9040*
*1145 S Victoria Ave*
*Oxnard* ▪ *(805) 981-1966*
*2041 N Oxnard Blvd*
*Camarillo* ▪ *(805) 482-7040*
*370 N Lantana*
*Camarillo* ▪ *(805) 484-5525*
*5800 Santa Rosa Rd*
*Newbury Park* ▪ *(805) 498-8500*
*1610-2 Newbury Rd*
*Westlake Village* ▪ *(805) 777-7167*
*3825 E Thousand Oaks Blvd*
*Simi Valley* ▪ *(805) 579-7827*
*2790 Cochran St*
*Castaic* ▪ *(661) 295-9967*
*31765 Castaic Rd*
*Valencia* ▪ *(661) 775-6288*
*23872 Copper Hill Dr*
*Canyon Country* ▪ *(661) 252-5010*
*18635 Soledad Canyon Rd*
*Huntington Beach* ▪ *(714) 963-7400*
*10035 Adams Ave*
*Lake Forest* ▪ *(949) 273-5007*
*45 Auto Center Dr*
*La Canada* ▪ *(818) 790-5050*
*711 Foothill Blvd*

*Saugus* ▪ *(661) 296-1910*
*26510 Bouquet Canyon Rd*
*Costa Mesa* ▪ *(949) 515-9888*
*2300 Harbor Blvd*
*Pacific Beach* ▪ *(858) 224-1880*
*1975 Garnet Ave*
*Tarzana* ▪ *(818) 343-0371*
*19458 Ventura Blvd*
*Burbank* ▪ *(818) 524-2002*
*875 N San Fernando Blvd*
*Laguna Woods* ▪ *(949) 273-6557*
*24365-A El Toro Rd*
*Santa Maria* ▪ *(805) 347-0097*
*2358 S Bradley Rd*
*Irvine* ▪ *(949) 955-2400*
*16525-G Von Karman Ave*
*Moorpark* ▪ *(805) 517-1574*
*144 W Los Angeles Ave*
*Northridge* ▪ *(818) 886-5800*
*19350 C Nordhoff St*
*Arroyo Grande* ▪ *(805) 489-5747*
*1540 E Grand Ave*
*Lake Forest* ▪ *(949) 770-0270*
*23572 El Toro Rd*
*Palmdale* ▪ *(661) 267-1515*
*39604 10th St W*
*Long Beach* ▪ *(562) 491-1800*
*One World Trade Center*
*Hawthorne* ▪ *(310) 643-7272*
*5342 Rosecrans Ave*
*Bakersfield* ▪ *(661) 588-2711*
*4715 Coffee Rd*
*Brea* ▪ *(714) 674-4999*
*955 E Birch St*
*Beverly Hills* ▪ *(310) 288-0288*
*279 S Beverly Hills Dr*
*West Hollywood* ▪ *(323) 850-1111*
*7100 Santa Monica Blvd*
*Mission Viejo* ▪ *(949) 206-8598*
*25280-C Marguerite Pkwy*
*Granada Hills* ▪ *(818) 923-5080*
*18131 Chatsworth St*
*Chatsworth* ▪ *(818) 727-7827*
*9840E Topanga Canyon Blvd*
*Stevenson Ranch* ▪ *(661) 253-1600*
*25660 The Old Rd*
*Monrovia* ▪ *(626) 359-1333*
*444 W Huntington Dr*

*Calabasas* ▪ *(818) 880-2600*
*26799 Agoura Rd*
*Thousand Oaks* ▪ *(805) 497-7800*
*605 E Janss Rd*
*Woodland Hills* ▪ *(818) 225-7070*
*22649 Ventura Blvd*
*Orange* ▪ *(714) 289-9300*
*1545 E Katella Ave*
*Solana Beach* ▪ *(858) 259-9111*
*915 Lomas Santa Fe Dr*
*San Marcos* ▪ *(760) 471-2211*
*595 Grand Ave*
*Pasadena* ▪ *(626) 584-7000*
*122 S Lake Ave*
*San Diego* ▪ *(858) 279-6453*
*7420 Clairemont Mesa Blvd*
*Torrance* ▪ *(310) 530-5888*
*2463 Crenshaw Blvd*
*Norco* ▪ *(951) 279-6453*
*1411 Hamner Ave*
*Hollywood* ▪ *(323) 461-6161*
*1517 Vine St*
*Bakersfield* ▪ *(661) 716-2711*
*5120 Stockdale Hwy*
*Rancho Cucomonga* ▪ *(909) 944-3400*
*8880 Foothill Blvd*
*Fountain Valley* ▪ *(714) 965-9888*
*18120 Brookhurst St*
*West Covina* ▪ *(626) 938-7000*
*2536 E Workman Ave*
*Encinitas* ▪ *(760) 634-6800*
*1070 N El Camino Real*
*la Jolla* ▪ *(858) 200-9888*
*7836 Herschel Ave*
*Murrieta* ▪ *(951) 696-5111*
*25359 Madison Ave*
*Glendora* ▪ *(626) 335-5888*
*865 W Route 66*
*Escondido* ▪ *(760) 747-7427*
*1829 S Centre City Pkwy*
*Glendale* ▪ *(818) 241-4888*
*813 Americana Wy*
*Oxnard* ▪ *(805) 486-3333*
*2721 S Rose Ave*
*Upland* ▪ *(909) 931-0773*
*1945 N Campus Ave*
*Goleta* ▪ *(805) 685-1122*
*7034 Marketplace Dr*

*Arcadia* ▪ *(626) 445-5007*
*400 S Baldwin Ave*
*La Verne* ▪ *(909) 593-1977*
*2212 Foothill Blvd*
*Orange* ▪ *(714) 245-0100*
*763 S Main St*
*Tustin* ▪ *(714) 505-1515*
*13681 Newport Ave*
*Marina del Rey* ▪ *(310) 822-9500*
*4020 Lincoln Blvd*
*Eastvale* ▪ *(951) 360-6453*
*12569 Limonite Ave*
*Orange* ▪ *(714) 744-1500*
*3428 E Chapman Ave*
*South Pasadena* ▪ *(626) 403-0400*
*462 Fair Oaks Ave*
*Huntington Beach* ▪ *(714) 891-1222*
*6041 Bolsa Ave*
*Long Beach* ▪ *(562) 494-1888*
*1831 Ximeno Ave*
*Westminister* ▪ *(714) 843-9911*
*16470 Beach Blvd*

## Joe's Crab Shack                    ✪📖

*Newport Beach* ▪ *(949) 650-1818*
*2607 Pacific Coast Hwy*
*Oceanside* ▪ *(760) 722-1345*
*314 Harbor Dr*
*Ventura* ▪ *(805) 643-3725*
*567 San Jon Rd*
*Long Beach* ▪ *(562) 594-6551*
*6550 Marina Dr*
*Redondo Beach* ▪ *(310) 406-1999*
*230 Portofino Wy*
*Garden Grove* ▪ *(714) 703-0505*
*12011 Harbor Blvd*
*Industry* ▪ *(626) 839-4116*
*1420 S Azusa Ave*
*Sacramento* ▪ *(916) 553-4249*
*1210 Front St*
*Rancho Cucomonga* ▪ *(909) 463-6599*
*12327 Foothill Blvd*

## Jolly Holiday Bakery Café          ★ $BLD
*Anaheim*

*1313 S Harbor Blvd* ▪ *American* ▪ GF buns
are available for sandwiches. The following sandwiches are listed as GF: turkey,
caprese, tuna salad, waldorf salad, angus

roast beef, and pastrami reuben. The tomato soup, jolly holiday salad, and angus roast beef salad are also GF if ordered without breadsticks. Confirm the timeliness of this information before dining in. Located inside Disneyland Park. ▪ *disneyland.disney.go.com*

### Jules Thin Crust Pizza        ★ $$LD
*Danville* ▪ *(925) 743-2790*
*820 Sycamore Valley Rd* ▪ *Pizza* ▪ GF pizza is available with any toppings. The restaurant reports that their staff has been "fully trained" on GF procedures, and notes that all their GF items are prepared with dedicated utensils and prep surfaces to avoid CC. ▪ *www.julesthincrust.com*

### Julian Bakery        ★ CS
*La Jolla* ▪ *(858) 454-1198*
*5621 La Jolla Blvd* ▪ *Bakery* ▪ Non-dedicated bakery offering GF "Purity Bread." It is baked on Mondays, Tuesdays, and Thursdays, and can be purchased at the storefront or ordered online. ▪ *www.julianbakery.com*

### Kaati Fresh        ✪ ★ CLD
*San Jose* ▪ *(408) 577-1400*
*680 River Oaks Pkwy* ▪ *Indian* ▪ The restaurant reports that everything on the menu can be altered to be GF upon request. Alert the server upon arrival. ▪ *www.kaatifresh.com*

### Kara's Cupcakes        ★ CS
*Burlingame* ▪ *(650) 342-2253*
*1309 Burlingame Ave*
*Napa* ▪ *(707) 258-2253*
*610 1st St*
*Palo Alto* ▪ *(650) 326-2253*
*855 El Camino Real*
*San Jose* ▪ *(408) 260-2222*
*3055 Olin Ave*
*Walnut Creek* ▪ *(925) 933-2222*
*1388 N Main St* ▪ *Bakery* ▪ GF cupcakes are available in sweet vanilla, chocolate velvet, and vanilla or chocolate coconut. Mini cupcakes are available by preorder, and 6-inch cakes are available at the Palo Alto

and San Jose locations. The Palo Alto location also hosts cupcake decorating parties upon request. The Scott St location bakes all GF goods, some of which get delivered to North Point. ▪ *www.karascupcakes.com*

### Ki's Restaurant        ✪ ★ $BLD
*Cardiff* ▪ *(760) 436-5236*
*2591 S Coast Hwy 101* ▪ *American* ▪ The restaurant reports that their menu is constantly changing, but adds that they always have soups, salads, or meat entrées that are GF. ▪ *kisrestaurant.com*

### Kincaid's        📖
*Burlingame* ▪ *(650) 342-9844*
*60 Bay Vw Pl*
*Oakland* ▪ *(510) 835-8600*
*1 Franklin St*
*Redondo Beach* ▪ *(310) 318-6080*
*500 Fishermans Wharf*

### Kitti's Place        $LD
*Sausalito* ▪ *(415) 331-0390*
*3001 Bridgeway* ▪ *Asian Fusion* ▪ The restaurant reports that most dishes are naturally GF, and everything is made to order. Alert server upon arrival. ▪ *www.kittisplace.com*

### La Biscotteria        ★ CS
*Redwood City* ▪ *(650) 366-4888*
*2747 El Camino Real* ▪ *Bakery* ▪ Non-dedicated bakery offering GF amaretti cookies and GF "torrone" or candy nougat. ▪ *www.labiscotteria.com*

### La Farfalla Café        CLD
*Escondido* ▪ *(760) 741-0835*
*155 S Orange St* ▪ *Mediterranean* ▪ The restaurant reports that almost any entrée can be made GF. Their house-made salad dressings and soups are also GF. Alert the server upon arrival to discuss GF options. ▪ *www.lafarfallacafe.com*

### La Mirage Café & Grill        ✪ $LD
*San Diego* ▪ *(619) 294-4444*
*815 F St* ▪ *Mediterranean* ▪ GF items are marked on the menu and include lentil soup, salmon filet, shish

kebab, and more. Be sure to alert your server of your dietary needs. ▪ *www.themediterraneancuisine.com*

### Lawry's The Prime Rib    $$$$D
*Beverly Hills* ▪ *(310) 652-2827*
*100 N La Cienega Blvd* ▪ *Steakhouse*
▪ Manager Christopher at Beverly Hills strongly recommends speaking to a manager prior to dining at any Lawry's restaurant to "ensure that they are aware of your situation and able to help you navigate through their individual menus." He notes that plain prime rib (no gravy, no au jus) and lobster among items that are typically GF, but again stresses the importance of notifying the server and manager on duty so they can ensure safe preparation. ▪ *www.lawrysonline.com*

### Lette Macarons    ¢S
*Beverly Hills* ▪ *(310) 275-0023*
*9466 Charleville Blvd* ▪ *Bakery* ▪ The bakery reports that all of their macarons are naturally GF, but cautions that other, non-GF items are prepared in the bakery. Calling ahead for large or specialized orders is recommended. ▪ *www.lettemacarons.com*

### Linnaea's Café    ¢BLD
*San Luis Obispo* ▪ *(805) 541-5888*
*1110 Garden St* ▪ *Café* ▪ The restaurant reports that all soups and salads are GF and come with a wide variety of toppings and lettuce combinations. ▪ *linnaeas.com*

### Local Habit    ✪¢LD
*San Diego* ▪ *(619) 795-4770*
*3827 5th Ave* ▪ *American* ▪ The menu at Local Habit is coded with a "GF" next to the items which do not contain gluten. Options include various GF pizzas, sides, salads, sandwiches, and desserts. ▪ *www.mylocalhabit.com*

### Lombardi's Pasta Familia    ★$D
*Paso Robles* ▪ *(805) 237-7786*
*836 11th St* ▪ *Italian* ▪ GF pizza and pasta are available. Call beforehand to confirm availability because the restaurant reports that they sometimes run out of these items. ▪ *www.lombardispaso.com*

### Lone Star Steakhouse & Saloon    ✪📖
*Corona* ▪ *(951) 278-4117*
*955 Montecito Dr*
*Laguna Hills* ▪ *(949) 951-8687*
*24231 Avenida De La Carlota*
*Lake Elsinore* ▪ *(951) 674-4158*
*18601 Dexter Ave*
*Tustin* ▪ *(714) 508-8996*
*1222 Irvine Blvd*

### Lotus Asia's Best    ★¢LD
*San Luis Obispo* ▪ *(805) 439-1188*
*1819 Osos St* ▪ *Asian* ▪ GF rice noodles are available for substitution into applicable dishes. Owner suggests calling beforehand to confirm availability of items and so they can better prepare for a GF diner. ▪ *lotusasiasbest.com*

### Lotus Cuisine of India    $LD
*San Rafael* ▪ *(415) 456-5808*
*704 4th St* ▪ *Indian* ▪ Manager Amba reports that many of their customers are GF, and notes that many items on the menu can be prepared GF upon request. Alert the server upon arrival. ▪ *www.lotusrestaurant.com*

### Loving Hut    📖
*Alhambra* ▪ *(626) 289-2684*
*621 W Main St*
*Brea* ▪ *(714) 990-2261*
*1065 Brea Mall*
*Claremont* ▪ *(909) 621-1668*
*175 N Indian Hill Blvd*
*Elk Grove* ▪ *(916) 478-9590*
*8355 Elk Grove Blvd*
*Fresno* ▪ *(559) 237-4052*
*1495 N Van Ness Ave*
*Huntington Beach* ▪ *(714) 962-6449*
*19891 Brookhurst St*
*Milpitas* ▪ *(408) 943-0250*
*516 Barber Ln*
*Orange* ▪ *(714) 464-0544*
*237 S Tustin St*
*Ladera Ranch* ▪ *(949) 365-1077*
*27522 Antonio Pkwy*
*Palo Alto* ▪ *(650) 321-5588*
*165 University Ave*
*Sacramento* ▪ *(916) 451-6842*

3500 Stockton Blvd
San Jose ▪ (408) 229-2795
925 Blossom Hill Rd
Upland ▪ (909) 982-3882
903 W Foothill Blvd

## Lucky Fortune Cookery                    $LD
Anaheim
1313 S Harbor Blvd ▪ Asian ▪ GF options
include chicken, beef, or tofu with rice and
vegetables. The sauce must be substituted
with yuzu. Confirm the timeliness of this
information before dining in. Located
inside Disney's California Adventure. ▪
disneyland.disney.go.com

## LYFE Kitchen                    ✪★¢BLD
Palo Alto ▪ (650) 325-5933
167 N Hamilton Ave ▪ American ▪ GF
menu includes farmer's market frittata,
Greek yogurt parfait, sweet corn chowder,
chopped napa cabbage salad, grilled chick-
en, fish tacos, a variety of flatbread pizzas,
and more. GF bread, burger buns, and
pizza are available. ▪ www.lyfekitchen.com

## Maggiano's Little Italy                    ★▥
Costa Mesa ▪ (714) 546-9550
3333 Bristol St
San Jose ▪ (408) 423-8973
3055 Olin Ave
Woodland Hills ▪ (818) 887-3777
6100 Topanga Canyon Blvd

## Malabar                    ✪$$$BLD
Sacramento ▪ (916) 574-9074
2960 Del Paso Rd ▪ American ▪ GF menu
includes lemon garlic brick chicken,
rib-eye steak, and jumbo scallops &
risotto carbonara. Manager recommends
calling beforehand to confirm availability and timeliness of this information. ▪
www.malabaramericancooking.com

## Mamma's Brick Oven                    ★$LD
South Pasadena ▪ (626) 799-1344
710 Fair Oaks Ave
Pasadena ▪ (626) 405-9877
311 S Rosemead Blvd ▪ Pizza ▪ GF pizza
crust is available in the 10" and 14". ▪
www.mammasbrickoven.com

## Mariposa                    ¢S
Oakland ▪ (510) 595-0955
5427 Telegraph Ave ▪ Bakery ▪

## Melting Pot, The                    ✪▥
Brea ▪ (714) 671-6000
375 W Birch St Ste 1
Irvine ▪ (949) 955-3242
2646 Dupont Dr
Larkspur ▪ (415) 461-6358
125 E Sir Francis Drake Blvd
Pasadena ▪ (626) 792-1941
88 W Colorado Blvd
Sacramento ▪ (916) 443-2347
814 15th St
San Clemente ▪ (949) 661-1966
647 Camino De Los Mares
San Mateo ▪ (650) 342-6358
2 N B St
Temecula ▪ (951) 693-2222
39738 Winchester Rd
Torrance ▪ (310) 316-7500
21525 Hawthorne Blvd
Westlake Village ▪ (805) 370-8802
3685 E Thousand Oaks Blvd

## Miner Moe's Pizza                    ★$LD
Nevada City ▪ (530) 265-0284
102 Argall Wy ▪ Pizza ▪ GF pizza is available in 12-inch size. ▪
www.minermoespizza.com

## Mission Pizza & Pub                    ★$$LD
Fremont ▪ (510) 651-6858
1572 Washington Blvd ▪ Pizza ▪ GF pizza
available in small size only. BBQ chicken
and artichokes are not GF, but all other
toppings are. Red garlic, regular red and
pesto sauce are GF. Confirm the timeliness
of this information before dining in. Pizza
is prepared with its own utensils and cut-
lery and cooked in a common oven but on
a separate sheet. ▪ www.missionpizza.com

## Moody's Bistro                    $$$LD
Truckee ▪ (530) 587-8688
10007 Bridge St ▪ Modern American ▪ The
restaurant reports that most of the menu is
naturally GF, and GF diners can be accommodated. Note GF when making reserva-

tions and remind the server, who will alert the chef and point out GF options on the menu. ▪ *www.moodysbistro.com*

### Morton's Steakhouse                    ✪⬜
*Anaheim* ▪ *(714) 621-0101*
*1895 S Harbor Blvd*
*Burbank* ▪ *(818) 238-0424*
*3400 W Olive Ave*
*Palm Desert* ▪ *(760) 340-6865*
*74-880 Country Club Dr*
*Sacramento* ▪ *(916) 442-5091*
*621 Capitol Mall*
*San Jose* ▪ *(408) 947-7000*
*177 Park Ave*
*Santa Ana* ▪ *(714) 444-4834*
*1641 W Sunflower Ave*
*Woodland Hills* ▪ *(818) 703-7272*
*6250 Canoga Ave*

### Mountain Room Restaurant      ✪$$$$D
*Yosemite National Park* ▪ *(209) 372-1274*
*Yosemite Lodge At The Falls* ▪ *Modern American* ▪ GF menu includes soups, salads, trout, lamb, grass fed beef stew, pomegranate chipotle chicken, the catch of the day, and the ribeye steak. Servers and the kitchen staff are aware of the GF diet and can accommodate it. Upon arrival, alert the hostess, who will remind the servers and the kitchen staff. ▪ *www.yosemitepark.com*

### Mustard Seed                           $$$LD
*Davis* ▪ *(530) 758-5750*
*222 D St* ▪ *Modern American* ▪ Owner Robin reports that GF diners are welcome and notes that there are naturally GF menu items. GF items include pork chops, duck breasts, and shrimp risotto. Reservations noting GF are recommended. ▪ *www.mustardseeddavis.com*

### Napa Rose                             $$$$D
*Anaheim* ▪ *(714) 956-6755*
*1600 S Disneyland Dr* ▪ *American* ▪ GF items include grilled steak, grilled fish, and chicken quesadilla with corn tortilla. The restaurant also notes that all sauces are GF. Confirm the timeliness of this information before dining in. Located at the Grand

Californian Hotel inside the Disneyland Resort. ▪ *disneyland.disney.go.com*

### Natural Food Works Farmer's Kitchen
### Café                                   ᶜBLD
*Davis* ▪ *(530) 756-1862*
*624 4th St* ▪ *Bakery & Café* ▪ Dedicated GF bakery and café offering GF breads, buns, bread crumbs, pie crusts, a variety of pastas, and pastries. The café serves GF lunches and dinners, but the menu changes regularly. The daily menu can be viewed online. ▪ *www.naturalfoodworks.com*

### Newport/Naples Rib Company ✪★$$$D
*Long Beach* ▪ *(562) 439-7427*
*5800 E 2nd St*
*Costa Mesa* ▪ *(949) 631-2110*
*2196 Harbor Blvd* ▪ *Barbeque* ▪ GF menu is available at both locations and includes baby back ribs, BBQ chicken, hamburgers on a GF bun, and filet mignon. GF buns are available. ▪ *www.ribcompany.com*

### Novo Restaurant & Lounge        ✪$$$LD
*San Luis Obispo* ▪ *(805) 543-3986*
*726 Higuera St* ▪ *Global* ▪ Menu specifies what items can be made GF on request. Brunch items include huevos rancheros and a shrimp, goat cheese and avocado scramble. Lunch offers a variety of salads and sandwiches that are wrapped with lettuce instead of a bun. Dinner includes tandoori spiced prawns, local rabbit and chorizo paella, stuffed quail, duck mole, roast duck breast and a few curry dishes. Be sure to notify server that you are eating GF and they will be happy to accommodate. ▪ *www.novorestaurant.com*

### Old California
### Coffee House & Eatery              ★ᶜBLD
*San Marcos* ▪ *(760) 744-2112*
*1080 San Marcos Blvd* ▪ *Café* ▪ GF bread is available for their breakfast sandwiches in addition to various omelet, fruit, and soup options. ▪ *www.oldcalcoffee.com*

### Old Spaghetti Factory, The       ✪★⬜
*Concord* ▪ *(925) 687-5030*
*1955 Mount Diablo St*

*Duarte* ▪ (626) 358-2115
1431 Buena Vista St
*Elk Grove* ▪ (916) 478-2400
7727 Laguna Blvd
*Fresno* ▪ (559) 222-1066
1610 E Shaw Ave
*Fullerton* ▪ (714) 526-6801
110 E Santa Fe Ave
*Newport Beach* ▪ (949) 675-8654
2110 Newport Blvd
*Rancho Cordova* ▪ (916) 985-0822
12401 Folsom Blvd
*Rancho Cucamonga* ▪ (909) 980-3585
11896 Foothill Blvd
*Redlands* ▪ (909) 798-7774
1635 Industrial Park Ave
*Riverside* ▪ (951) 784-4417
3191 Mission Inn Ave
*Roseville* ▪ (916) 773-3950
731 Sunrise Ave
*Sacramento* ▪ (916) 443-2862
1910 J St
*San Jose* ▪ (408) 288-7488
51 N San Pedro St
*San Marcos* ▪ (760) 471-0155
111 N Twin Oaks Valley Rd
*Stockton* ▪ (209) 473-3695
2702 W March Ln
*Rancho Mirage* ▪ (760) 341-5600
71743 Hwy 111
*Redwood City* ▪ (650) 216-9713
2107 Broadway St

**P.F. Chang's China Bistro**          ✪★📖
*Anaheim* ▪ (714) 507-2021
321 W Katella Ave Ste 120
*Bakersfield* ▪ (661) 664-8100
10700 Stockdale Hwy
*Burbank* ▪ (818) 391-1070
201 E Magnolia Blvd Ste 281
*Carlsbad* ▪ (760) 795-0595
5621 Paseo Del Norte
*Chino Hills* ▪ (909) 590-8250
3445 Grand Ave
*Chula Vista* ▪ (619) 421-2080
2015 Birch Rd Ste 1401
*Corte Madera* ▪ (415) 413-9890
301 Corte Madera Town Ctr Spc A
*El Segundo* ▪ (310) 607-9062

2041 Rosecrans Ave Ste 120
*Emeryville* ▪ (510) 879-0990
5633 Bay St
*Fremont* ▪ (510) 657-1400
43316 Christy St
*Fresno* ▪ (559) 438-0814
7894 N Blackstone Ave
*Irvine* ▪ (949) 453-1211
61 Fortune Dr
*Long Beach* ▪ (562) 308-1025
340 S Pine Ave
*Mission Viejo* ▪ (949) 364-6661
800 The Shops At Mission Viejo
*Monterey* ▪ (831) 375-0143
1200 Del Monte Ctr
*Newport Beach* ▪ (949) 759-9007
1145 Newport Center Dr
*Palo Alto* ▪ (650) 330-1782
900 Stanford Shopping Ctr Bldg W
*Pasadena* ▪ (626) 356-9760
260 E Colorado Blvd Ste 201
*Pleasanton* ▪ (925) 224-9916
1330 Stoneridge Mall Rd
*Rancho Cucamonga* ▪ (909) 463-4095
7870 Monticello Ave
*Rancho Mirage* ▪ (760) 776-4912
71800 Highway 111 Ste C104
*Riverside* ▪ (951) 689-4020
3475 Galleria At Tyler
*Roseville* ▪ (916) 788-2800
1180 Galleria Blvd
*Sacramento* ▪ (916) 288-0970
1530 J St Ste 100
*San Jose* ▪ (408) 961-5250
98 S 2nd St
*San Jose* ▪ (408) 960-2940
925 Blossom Hill Rd Ste 1515
*Santa Monica* ▪ (310) 395-1912
326 Wilshire Blvd
*Sherman Oaks* ▪ (818) 784-1694
15301 Ventura Blvd Ste P22
*Sunnyvale* ▪ (408) 991-9078
390 W El Camino Real
*Temecula* ▪ (951) 296-6700
40762 Winchester Rd Ste 400
*Thousand Oaks* ▪ (805) 277-5915
2250 Thousand Oaks Blvd
*Torrance* ▪ (310) 793-0590

3525 W Carson St Ste 166
**Walnut Creek** ▪ (925) 979-9070
1205 Broadway Plz
**Woodland Hills** ▪ (818) 340-0491
21821 Oxnard St

## Palermo Ristorante Italiano ★ $$D
**Elk Grove** ▪ (916) 686-1582
9632 Emerald Oak Dr ▪ Italian ▪ GF
pizza and pasta are available. Owner and
Chef Giovanni reports that the restaurant serves GF diners regularly. Servers are educated on the GF diet, but if
they have questions, they will ask him. ▪
www.palermo-ristorante.com

## Palm Greens Cafe ★ $BL
**Palm Springs** ▪ (760) 864-9900
611 S Palm Canyon Dr ▪ Vegetarian ▪ GF
items marked are on regular menu and
include pancakes, rice wraps, salads with
GF salad dressings, vegan tempeh reuben,
vegan B.L.A.T (bacon, lettuce, avocado,
and tomato) brownies, muffins, cookies,
and more. ▪ www.palmgreenscafe.com

## Pampas $$$LD
**Palo Alto** ▪ (650) 327-1323
529 Alma St ▪ Brazilian ▪ Chef Nikki
reports that the staff is trained to "be aware
of food allergies and how to avoid cross-
contamination." She adds that all items on
their buffet are labeled with potential allergens and each has its own serving utensil.
She also notes that all meats on the Rodizio
menu are GF, and she only marinates with
GF soy sauce to avoid CC. GF cheese bread
made with cassava starch is available. ▪
www.pampaspaloalto.com

## Paradise Garden Grill $LD
**Anaheim**
1313 S Harbor Blvd ▪ Mediterranean ▪ GF
items include beef skewer, chicken skewer,
vegetable skewer, Moroccan chili, tandoori
spiced yogurt, tzatziki, cucumber salad,
and Greek salad. Confirm the timeliness of
this information before dining in. Located
inside Disney's California Adventure. ▪
disneyland.disney.go.com

## PCH Grill ★ $$BD
**Anaheim** ▪ (714) 781-3463
1717 S Disneyland Dr ▪ American ▪ For
breakfast, GF pancakes are available, as
well as bacon, eggs, and fresh fruit. GF
dinner items include NY steak, roasted half
chicken, BBQ ribs, GF pizza, GF pasta, and
a hamburger on a GF bun. Any salad can
be made GF by requesting no croutons.
Confirm the timeliness of this information
before dining in. Located at the Paradise
Pier Hotel in the Disneyland Resort. ▪
disneyland.disney.go.com

## Pei Wei Asian Diner ✪ 📖
**Brea** ▪ (714) 989-5570
985 E Birch St
**Encinitas** ▪ (760) 635-2888
1560 Leucadia Blvd
**Huntington Beach** ▪ (714) 230-2050
7621 Edinger Ave
**Lake Forest** ▪ (949) 860-2001
23632 El Toro Rd
**Newport Beach** ▪ (949) 629-1000
1302 Bison Ave
**Pasadena** ▪ (626) 325-9020
3455 E Foothill Blvd
**San Marcos** ▪ (760) 304-7010
113 S Las Posas Rd
**Santa Clarita** ▪ (661) 600-0132
24250 Valencia Blvd
**Seal Beach** ▪ (562) 668-5090
12235 Seal Beach Blvd
**Torrance** ▪ (310) 517-9366
2777 Pacific Coast Hwy
**Tustin** ▪ (714) 259-1125
2695 Park Ave
**Laguna Niguel** ▪ (949) 249-0130
27321 La Paz Rd
**Orange County** ▪ (949) 252-6125
J W Aprt Term C

## Peking Wok ★ $$LD
**Bonsall** ▪ (760) 724-8078
5256 S Mission Rd ▪ Chinese ▪ Restaurant
notes that everything on the menu can be
prepared and modified to be GF and can
be made with GF soy sauce. Alert a server
upon arrival. ▪ www.pekingwokbonsall.com

## Pennini's Ristorante Italiano    ★$$LD
Moraga ▪ (925) 376-1515
1375 Moraga Wy ▪ Pizza ▪ GF pizza is
available in the medium size. The restaurant reports that "precautions are
taken" to make sure there is no CC. ▪
www.penninis.com

## Piatti Ristorante & Bar    ★$$LD
Mill Valley ▪ (415) 380-2525
625 Redwood Hwy
Danville ▪ (925) 838-2082
100 Sycamore Valley Rd W
Sacramento ▪ (916) 649-8885
571 Pavilions Ln
Santa Clara ▪ (408) 330-9212
3905 Rivermark Plz
La Jolla ▪ (858) 454-1589
2182 Avenida De La Playa
Danville ▪ (925) 838-2082
100 Sycamore Valley Rd W
Santa Clara ▪ (408) 330-9212
3905 Rivermark Plaza
La Jolla ▪ (858) 454-1589
2182 Avenida De La Playa
Mill Valley ▪ (415) 380-2525
625 Redwood Hwy
Sacramento ▪ (916) 649-8885
571 Pavilions Ln ▪ Italian ▪ GF pasta is
available. The restaurant reports that staff
is trained on GF preparation and GF diners
are accommodated "all the time." They note
that the risotto is GF and that many menu
items can be modified to be GF. Alert a
server upon arrival. ▪ www.piatti.com

## Pica Pica Maize Kitchen    ★¢BLD
Napa ▪ (707) 251-3757
610 1st St ▪ Latin American ▪ The restaurant offers a mix-and-match style of
GF cuisine. Diners choose one of three
cornbreads and a filling. Empanadas
are also served. GF beer is available. ▪
www.picapicakitchen.com

## Pizza Cookery, The    ✿★$$LD
Woodland Hills ▪ (818) 887-4770
6209 Topanga Canyon Blvd ▪ Pizza ▪
GF menu is available and includes pizzas,

pastas such as penne alfredo and veggie
lasagna, sandwiches on GF herbed focaccia bread, breadsticks, and desserts. Call
ahead, as sometimes only certain pizza
sizes are available. GF beer is also available.
▪ www.pizzacookery.com

## Pizza Guru    ★$LD
Santa Barbara ▪ (805) 563-3250
3534 State St ▪ Pizza ▪ Pizza Guru offers
a wide variety of GF pasta options in addition to their GF pizza crust which can
be topped with a variety of choices and
combinations. ▪ www.pizzaguru.com

## Pizza Pirate, The    ★$LD
Benicia ▪ (707) 745-1667
72 Solano Sq ▪ Pizza ▪ GF pizza is available
in the personal and small sizes. GF beer is
also available. ▪ www.mypizzapirate.com

## Pizza Rustica    ★$$$LD
Oakland ▪ (510) 654-1601
5422 College Ave
Oakland ▪ (510) 339-7878
6106 La Salle Ave ▪ Pizza ▪ GF pizza crust
is available in the 12" size. Salads and soups
are GF, just be sure to indicate no croutons
or bread. ▪ www.caferustica.com

## PizzaSalad    ✿★$LD
Thousand Oaks ▪ (805) 371-7878
1655 E Thousand Oaks Blvd ▪ Pizza ▪ GF
pizza is available, as well as GF salads and
desserts. The kitchen is certified by the
NFCA. ▪ www.pizzasalad.com

## Planet Raw    $LD
Santa Monica ▪ (310) 587-1552
609 Broadway St ▪ Raw ▪ Restaurant serving entirely GF and raw cuisine. Sample
menu items include green curry pasta,
pumpkin veggie taco, and truffle cream
linguini. GF "pasta" is made with zucchini
or kelp. ▪ www.planetraw.com

## Plant Café Organic, The    ✿$$LD
San Francisco ▪ (650) 821-9290
San Francisco International Airport,
Terminal 2 ▪ Organic ▪ GF menu includes
soup, shiitake spring rolls, seared scal-

lops with cilantro aioli, griddled calamari, ginger miso quinoa, Thai green curry, daily fish specials, and more. While the Pier 3 and Steiner St locations are sit-down restaurants open for lunch and dinner, the California St location closes at 3pm and serves only breakfast and lunch. The GF menu at the California St location is slightly more limited. ▪ *www.theplantcafe.com*

### Plaza Inn                                    ★ $$BLD
*Anaheim*
*1313 S Harbor Blvd* ▪ *American* ▪ GF breakfast selections include omelets, bacon, sausage, ham, hash browns, and fresh fruit. GF waffles are available as well. For lunch and dinner, the only GF option listed is the baked chicken. Confirm the timeliness of this information before dining in. Located inside Disneyland Park. ▪ *disneyland.disney.go.com*

### Pleasure Pizza                              ★ ¢LD
*Santa Cruz* ▪ *(831) 475-4999*
*4000 Portola Dr* ▪ *Pizza* ▪ GF pizza and bread available upon request. ▪ *pleasurepizzasc.com*

### Prima Ristorante                            $$$LD
*Walnut Creek* ▪ *(925) 935-7780*
*1522 N Main St* ▪ *Italian* ▪ Hostess Heather reports that the chef "can always accommodate GF guests" and the kitchen is "very careful" when preparing GF orders. Consult the server, who will recommend the most suitable menu options. ▪ *www.primaristorante.com*

### Rancho del Zocalo Restaurante              $LD
*Anaheim* ▪ *(714) 781-4000*
*1313 S Harbor Blvd* ▪ *Mexican* ▪ GF options include vegetable tacos, plain chicken tacos, 50/50 cheese quesadillas, cheese enchiladas with carne asada, fire roasted chicken, and tostada salad with no shell. The restaurant also notes that the rice, beans, shredded lettuce, 50/50 cheese, pico de gallo, guacamole, and sour cream are GF. Be sure to request CORN TORTILLAS with all items. Confirm the

timeliness of this information before dining in. Located inside Disneyland Park. ▪ *disneyland.disney.go.com*

### Ravens' Restaurant                    ✪★ $$$BD
*Mendocino* ▪ *(707) 937-5615*
*44850 Comptche Ukiah Rd* ▪ *Vegetarian* ▪ Most of the menu is GF, and non-GF items are clearly marked. Selections include tamari-maple glazed tofu, grilled mushroom salad, spicy peanut curry, and tamales. Be sure to alert your server of your needs. Located in the Stanford Inn by the Sea. ▪ *www.ravensrestaurant.com*

### Real Food Daily                            ★ $LD
*Santa Monica* ▪ *(310) 451-7544*
*514 Santa Monica Blvd*
*Pasadena* ▪ *(626) 844-8900*
*899 E Del Mar Blvd* ▪ *Organic* ▪ GF items are marked on the menu and include a corn meal crust pizza, enchiladas, GF pancakes, GF waffles, and hemp milkshakes. Additional items may be GF as well- ask a server for details. The restaurant notes that the staff is very familiar with GF dining. Alert a server upon arrival. When a GF request is rung in by a server, a special note is sent to the kitchen. ▪ *www.realfood.com*

### Red - A Restaurant & Bar                  $$$$LD
*City Of Industry* ▪ *(626) 854-2509*
*1 Industry Hills Pkwy* ▪ *Fusion* ▪ Items on the menu can be modified to be GF. Reservations noting GF are recommended, as is alerting the server upon arrival. ▪ *www.redrestaurant.net*

### Red Brick Pizza                          ✪★ 📖
*Brea* ▪ *(714) 256-2828*
*215 W Birch St*
*Rolling Hills Estates* ▪ *(310) 544-4040*
*550 Deep Valley Dr*
*Irvine* ▪ *(949) 725-0018*
*6721 Quail Hill Pkwy*
*Foothill Ranch* ▪ *(949) 707-7499*
*27412 Portola Pkwy*
*Buena Park* ▪ *(714) 736-9999*
*7550 Orangethrope*
*Fontana* ▪ *(909) 355-3637*

16155 Sierra Lakes Pkwy
Temecula ▪ (951) 693-4438
32195 State Hwy 79
Del Rey Oaks ▪ (831) 899-4566
459 Canyon Del Rey Rd
Millbrae ▪ (650) 259-9654
979 Broadway
San Mateo ▪ (650) 347-3333
200 S B St
Paso Robles ▪ (805) 238-7711
1145 24th St
Bakersfield ▪ (661) 829-1010
9500 Brimhall Rd
Ventura ▪ (805) 658-2828
4990 Telephone Rd

### Redd Rockett's Pizza Port          ★ $LD
Anaheim ▪ (714) 781-4000
1313 S Harbor Blvd ▪ Pizza ▪ GF options
include rice noodles with marinara or
tomato basil sauce, romaine lettuce with
chicken breast and fat free raspberry dressing, "starfield of greens" with basil vinaigrette, and GF cheese or pepperoni pizza.
Confirm the timeliness of this information
before dining in. Located inside Disneyland Park. ▪ disneyland.disney.go.com

### Rick and Ann's Restaurant          ★ $BLD
Berkeley ▪ (510) 649-8538
2922 Domingo Ave ▪ American ▪ GF items
include sandwiches and burgers which can
be made with GF buns, bagels, muffins,
salads and the chicken pot pie, which can
be made with mashed potatoes instead of
the breading. ▪ www.rickandanns.com

### Ricky's House of Pizza          ★ $LD
Santa Maria ▪ (805) 310-4940
4869 S Bradley Rd ▪ Pizza ▪ Ricky's
offers GF pizza crust which is available with any topping combination. ▪
www.rickyspizza.com

### Rising Hearts Bakery          ¢$
Culver City ▪ (310) 815-1800
10836 1/2 Washington Blvd ▪ Bakery ▪ GF
breads, muffins, brownies, and cakes are
made fresh daily. Their products can also
be found in nearby local stores as well. Call

beforehand to confirm availability of items.
▪ risingheartsbakery.com

### River Belle Terrace          ★ $BLD
Anaheim
1313 S Harbor Blvd ▪ Southern ▪ GF buns
are available for sandwiches. The only
sandwich noted as GF is the Mississippi
turkey breast, but GF diners can ask their
server for other options. Confirm the
timeliness of this information before dining in. Located inside Disneyland Park. ▪
disneyland.disney.go.com

### Robin's Restaurant          ✪$$LD
Cambria ▪ (805) 927-5007
4095 Burton Dr ▪ Global ▪ GF items
are marked on the menu and include
lemon-thyme roasted chicken, lobster
enchiladas, tofu pad thai, several curries,
and more. Owner Shanny reports that
all servers are trained on the GF diet, so
they can discuss specific GF options. ▪
www.robinsrestaurant.com

### Romano's Macaroni Grill          ✪★📖
Aliso Viejo ▪ (949) 425-0180
26641 Aliso Creek Rd
Anaheim ▪ (714) 637-6643
8150 E Santa Ana Canyon Rd
Bakersfield ▪ (661) 588-2277
8850 Rosedale Hwy
Cerritos ▪ (562) 916-7722
12875 Towne Center Dr
Chula Vista ▪ (619) 656-0966
2015 Birch Rd
City of Industry ▪ (626) 581-8051
17603 Colima Rd
Corona ▪ (951) 278-0999
3591 Grand Oaks
El Cerrito ▪ (510) 524-9336
8000 El Cerrito
El Segundo ▪ (310) 643-0812
2321 Rosecrans Ave
Elk Grove ▪ (916) 478-2878
8295 Laguna Blvd
Escondido ▪ (760) 741-6309
202 E Via Rancho Pkwy
Folsom ▪ (916) 984-9401
2739 E Bidwell St

**Fresno** ▪ (559) 436-6690
7650 N Blackstone Ave
**Huntington Beach** ▪ (714) 901-4481
7901 Edinger Ave
**Irvine** ▪ (714) 508-7990
13652 Jamboree Rd
**Milpitas** ▪ (408) 935-9875
110 Ranch Dr
**Montclair** ▪ (909) 621-2604
4955 S Montclair Plaza Ln
**Northridge** ▪ (818) 725-2620
19400 Plummer St
**Oceanside** ▪ (796) 722-9905
2655 Vista Wy
**Redlands** ▪ (909) 798-4142
27490 W Lugonia Ave
**Roseville** ▪ (916) 773-6399
2010 Douglas Blvd
**San Mateo** ▪ (650) 638-3580
31 Hillsdale Blvd W
**Seal Beach** ▪ (562) 598-5979
12380 Seal Beach Blvd
**Simi Valley** ▪ (805) 306-1303
2920 Tapo Canyon Rd
**Stevenson Ranch** ▪ (661) 284-1850
25720 The Old Rd
**Stockton** ▪ (209) 951-7064
5420 Pacific Ave
**Temecula** ▪ (951) 296-0700
41221 Margarita Rd
**Torrance** ▪ (310) 534-1001
25352 Crenshaw Blvd
**Ventura** ▪ (805) 447-9925
4880 Telephone Rd
**Westlake Village** ▪ (805) 370-1133
4000 E Thousand Oaks Blvd

### Romeo Cucina ★ $$LD
**Laguna Beach** ▪ (949) 497-6627
249 Broadway St
**Laguna Niguel** ▪ (949) 831-4131
28241 Crown Valley Pkwy ▪ Italian ▪ GF
pasta is available. ▪ www.romeocucina.com

### Rosa Mexicano ✪ 📖
**West Hollywood** ▪ (310) 657-4991
8570 Sunset Blvd

### Rosati's Pizza ★ 📖
**Roseville** ▪ (916) 797-7492
5140 Foothills Blvd
**Temecula** ▪ (951) 587-2500
30680 Rancho California Rd

### Rosti Tuscan Kitchen ✪ $$LD
**Calabasas** ▪ (818) 591-2211
23663 Calabasas Rd
**Santa Monica** ▪ (310) 393-3236
931 Montana Ave
**Encino** ▪ (818) 995-7179
16350 Ventura Blvd ▪ Italian ▪ GF pasta
and pizza available. GF pasta is cooked in
separate pots and water to minimize CC.
Pizza is cooked in the same oven but dedicated GF trays are used to hold the pizza. ▪
www.rostituscankitchen.com

### Ruth's Chris Steak House ✪ 📖
**Anaheim** ▪ (714) 750-5466
2041 S Habor Blvd
**Beverly Hills** ▪ (310) 859-8744
224 S Beverly Dr
**Fresno** ▪ (559) 490-0358
7844 N Blackstone Ave
**Irvine** ▪ (949) 252-8848
2961 Michelson Dr
**Palm Desert** ▪ (760) 779-1998
74740 Hwy 111
**Pasadena** ▪ (626) 583-8122
369 E Colorado Blvd
**Roseville** ▪ (916) 780-6910
1185 Galleria Blvd
**Sacramento** ▪ (916) 286-2702
501 Pavillions Ln
**Walnut Creek** ▪ (925) 977-3477
1553 Olympic Blvd
**Woodland Hills** ▪ (818) 227-9505
6100 Topanga Canyon Blvd

### Salt Creek Grille ✪ $$LD
**Dana Point** ▪ (949) 661-7799
32802 Pacific Coast Hwy
**El Segundo** ▪ (310) 335-9288
2015 E Park Pl
**Valencia** ▪ (661) 222-9999
24415 Town Center Dr ▪ American ▪ Corporate executive chef Scott reports that there
are "several GF items" available, and they

have "specific protocols" in place to prevent CC, including using clean utensils and prep items when preparing a GF order. Scott recommends alerting the server of any dietary restrictions upon arrival. Since the Valencia location is franchised, he recommends calling ahead to ensure that they have GF options available. ▪ www.saltcreekgrille.com

### Sam's Anchor Café                          $$$LD
*Tiburon* ▪ (415) 435-4527
*27 Main St* ▪ *Seafood* ▪ The restaurant reports that they can "alter many items" to be GF, and advises GF guests to alert their server upon arrival. ▪ www.samscafe.com

### Sammy's Woodfired Pizza             ✪📖
*Carlsbad* ▪ (760) 438-1212
*5970 Avenida Encinas*
*La Jolla* ▪ (858) 456-5222
*702 Pearl St*
*La Mesa* ▪ (619) 460-8555
*8555 Fletcher Pkwy*
*Palm Desert* ▪ (760) 836-0500
*73595 El Paseo Rd*
*San Marcos* ▪ (760) 591-4222
*121 S Las Posas Rd*
*El Segundo* ▪ (310) 335-9999
*780 S Sepulveda Blvd*
*Studio City* ▪ (818) 762-3330
*12050 Ventura Blvd*

### San Francisco Soup Company       ✪BLD
*E Palo Alto* ▪ (650) 322-7687
*1950 University Ave*
*Oakland* ▪ (510) 763-7687
*1300 Clay St*
*Berkeley* ▪ (510) 848-7687
*2512 Bancroft Wy*
*Burlingame* ▪ (650) 347-7687
*270 Lorton Ave* ▪ *American* ▪ Soups rotate daily. Check the website for a given day's GF offerings. Most locations also have GF options marked on the board. Some locations, including those in airports, do not have GF options marked on the board, but they will have a chart of GF options upon request. All GF soups made before soups containing gluten. Hours vary by location. Burl-

ingame location is called Urban Bistro but same menu and policies apply. ▪ www.sfsoupco.com

### Scott's Seafood                      ✪$$$$LD
*Folsom* ▪ (916) 989-6711
*9611 Greenback Ln*
*Sacramento* ▪ (916) 379-5959
*4800 Riverside Blvd* ▪ *Seafood* ▪ Staff reports that a GF menu is available in house and all GF items are cooked separately to avoid CC. It is "a big red flag" when a GF order goes to the kitchen. GF menu items include grilled wild prawn skewers, cioppino, and halibut, and Brittany from the Folsom location adds that they will "try to make adjustments" to other dishes. Confirm the timeliness of this information before dining in. ▪ www.scottsseafood.net

### Sensitive Sweets                          $$
*Fountain Valley* ▪ (714) 968-9169
*17431 Brookhurst St* ▪ *Bakery* ▪ Dedicated GF and nut free bakery. GF muffins, cupcakes, cookies, and breads baked fresh daily. Boxed packages of mixes are also available to buy in stores. ▪ www.sensitivesweets.com

### Sid's Smokehouse                     ★$$LD
*Aptos* ▪ (831) 662-2227
*10110 Soquel Dr* ▪ *Barbeque* ▪ GF pizza is available. ▪ www.sidssmokehouse.com

### Skosh Monahan's                  ✪★$$LD
*Costa Mesa* ▪ (949) 548-0099
*2000 Newport Blvd* ▪ *Steakhouse* ▪ GF menu includes a wide variety of options including seared sesame ahi, corned beef & cabbage, Irish lamb stew, several burgers and hot dogs, and more. GF donuts and crème brûlée are available for desserts. Confirm the timeliness of this information before dining in. ▪ www.skoshmonahans.com

### Slice Pizzeria and Ristorante, The
★$$LD
*Rancho Mirage* ▪ (760) 202-3122
*72775 Dinah Shore Dr* ▪ *Pizza* ▪ GF pasta is available and cooked separate from other pasta. ▪ www.theslicepizza.com

### Sojourner Café   ★ $LD
*Santa Barbara* ▪ (805) 965-7922
*134 E Canon Perdido St* ▪ *American* ▪
GF items are marked on the menu and
include polenta royale, baked potato
supreme, rice & veggies, tacos, tostadas,
and more. GF pasta is available, and
is made to order and put in a separate
steamer. Restaurant has an allergen button on the order screen that alerts the
kitchen. Alert a server upon arrival. ▪
*www.sojournercafe.com*

### Solomon's Bakery & Deli   ★ ¢BL
*Laguna Hills* ▪ (949) 586-4718
*23020 Lake Forest Dr* ▪ *Bakery & Café*
▪ GF bread is available and can be used to
make any of the sandwiches on the deli
menu. ▪ *www.solomonsbakery.com*

### Sorrento's Italian Restaurant and Pizza
★ $$LD
*Walnut Creek* ▪ (925) 938-3366
*2064 Treat Blvd* ▪ *Pizza* ▪ GF pizza is avail-
able. ▪ *www.sorrentowalnutcreek.com*

### Spot, The   $LD
*Hermosa Beach* ▪ (310) 376-2355
*110 2nd St* ▪ *Mexican* ▪ The restaurant
reports that the staff is knowledgeable
about the GF diet and that there are
naturally GF menu items. GF diners can
view the chef's cookbooks to scan the
ingredients. Staff recommends alerting
the server, who will alert the kitchen. ▪
*www.worldfamousspot.com*

### Steakhouse 55   ★ $$$BD
*Anaheim* ▪ (714) 956-6402
*1150 Magic Wy* ▪ *Steakhouse* ▪ For breakfast, GF pancakes are available, as well as
bacon, eggs, roast potatoes, and fresh fruit.
GF dinner options include grilled steaks,
grilled salmon, grilled chicken, grilled pork
porterhouse, lobster, baked potato, shrimp
cocktail, and grilled asparagus. Confirm
the timeliness of this information before
dining in. Located at the Disneyland Hotel.
▪ *disneyland.disney.go.com*

### Stellar Brew and Deli   ★ $BLD
*Mammoth Lakes* ▪ (760) 924-3559
*3280 Main St* ▪ *Café* ▪ GF bread, tortillas,
and rolls are available.

### Steve's Pizza   ★ $LD
*Rancho Cordova* ▪ (916) 851-0749
*3191 Zinfandel Dr*
*Elk Grove* ▪ (916) 683-2200
*9135 W Stockton Blvd*
*Woodland* ▪ (530) 666-2100
*714 Main St*
*Roseville* ▪ (916) 787-4311
*5080 Foothills Blvd*
*El Dorado Hills* ▪ (916) 939-2100
*3941 Park Dr*
*Fair Oaks* ▪ (916) 961-1800
*11711 Fair Oaks Blvd* ▪ *Pizza* ▪ GF pizza is
available at all locations. Some locations
also carry GF brownies. Their pre-prepared
GF pizza dough is cooked in separate
pans and a different pizza cutter is used. ▪
*www.stevespizza.com*

### Stone Brewing World Bistro & Gardens   $$LD
*Escondido* ▪ (760) 471-4999
*1999 Citracado Pkwy* ▪ *American* ▪
The restaurant reports that they have
a GF menu in house and use separate
prep areas to make GF entrées. ▪
*www.stoneworldbistro.com*

### Storytellers Café   ★ $$$BLD
*Anaheim* ▪ (714) 635-2300
*1600 S Disneyland Dr* ▪ *American* ▪ For
breakfast, GF pancakes and waffles are
available, as well as bacon, eggs, hash
browns, and fresh fruit. GF lunch & dinner
options include grilled NY steak sandwich
(GF bun), roast New York, grilled salmon,
hamburger (GF bun), hot dog (GF bun),
GF pizza, French fries, baked potato,
and salad with oil & vinegar. Confirm
the timeliness of this information before
dining in. The restaurant also recommends
asking to speak with the chef about GF
options. Located at the Grand Californian
Hotel in the Disneyland Resort. ▪
*disneyland.disney.go.com*

## Studio $$$$D
*Laguna Beach* ▪ (949) 715-6420
*30801 S Coast Hwy* ▪ *Fusion* ▪ According to an employee, they always have GF options available. She recommends calling ahead of time so the necessary arrangements can be made to accommodate a GF diner. ▪ *www.studiolagunabeach.com*

## Sun Café Organic Cuisine $LD
*Studio City* ▪ (818) 308-7420
*3711 W Cahuenga Blvd* ▪ *American* ▪ The restaurant reports that most of their regular menu is GF. ▪ *www.suncafe.com*

## Table Café ¢LD
*Larkspur* ▪ (415) 461-6787
*1167 Magnolia Ave* ▪ *Global* ▪ GF dosas, a savory Indian pancake, are available except for the lamb. Dosas are naturally GF, and all soups and salads are GF. Alert the server upon arrival. ▪ *www.table-cafe.com*

## Tabu Grill $$$$D
*Laguna Beach* ▪ (949) 494-7743
*2892 S Coast Hwy* ▪ *Asian Fusion* ▪ Sous-chef Norberto reports that they can make a vegetable stir fry with black Thai rice for GF diners. For dessert, they offer flourless chocolate cake. He notes that future menus will "definitely" offer more GF options, as they have been accommodating "a lot more" GF diners "lately." ▪ *www.tabugrill.com*

## Tangaroa Terrace $BLD
*Anaheim* ▪ (714) 778-6600
*1150 Magic Wy* ▪ *Hawaiian* ▪ GF breakfast items include tofu & egg white bake, breakfast potatoes, bacon, and eggs. For lunch and dinner, GF options include angus burger with no bun, green papaya slaw, jasmine rice, grilled salmon, and fish tacos. Confirm the timeliness of this information before dining in. Located at the Disneyland Hotel. ▪ *disneyland.disney.go.com*

## Tantalum $$BD
*Long Beach* ▪ (562) 431-1414
*6272 E Pacific Coast Hwy* ▪ *Fusion* ▪ They do not have a specific GF menu, however the chef and staff are "more than willing" to accommodate GF diners and alter dishes "in any reasonable manner" that would make them GF. ▪ *www.tantalumrestaurant.com*

## Taste Pilots' Grill ★$LD
*Anaheim* ▪ (714) 781-3462
*1313 S Harbor Blvd* ▪ *American* ▪ GF items include a grilled chicken salad with no cucumber sticks and a hamburger or grilled chicken sandwich with GF bun. Request that the chicken be grilled in a fresh pan and request that fries be cooked in the "fries only" fryer. Confirm the timeliness of this information before dining in. Located inside Disney's California Adventure. ▪ *disneyland.disney.go.com*

## Tiki Juice Bar ¢S
*Anaheim* ▪ (714) 781-3463
*1313 S Harbor Blvd* ▪ *American* ▪ GF items include pineapple spears and the Dole Whip frozen drink. Confirm the timeliness of this information before dining in. Located inside Disneyland Park. ▪ *disneyland.disney.go.com*

## Tillie Gort's Café ★$BLD
*Pacific Grove* ▪ (831) 373-0335
*111 Central Ave* ▪ *American* ▪ GF options include a variety of salads and soups, veggie stir-fry, and vegetarian curry made with coconut milk. Sandwiches can be made on corn tortillas and wheat free pasta is available for another $3.50. Confirm the timeliness of this information before dining in. ▪ *www.tilliegortscafe.com*

## Today's Pizza & Salad ✪$LD
*Encinitas* ▪ (760) 753-6425
*481 Santa Fe Dr* ▪ *Pizza* ▪ Today's pizza offers 15 GF pizza options in addition to GF salad, pasta, dessert, and beer. ▪ *www.todayspizzaandsalad.com*

## Tomato Joe's Pizza ★$LD
*Santa Clarita* ▪ (661) 263-8646
*27732 McBean Pkwy* ▪ *Pizza* ▪ GF pizza is available with most toppings. Ask a server for details. ▪ *tomatojoespizza.com*

### Tomorrowland Terrace   ★ $BLD
*Anaheim*
*1313 S Harbor Blvd* ▪ *American* ▪
GF options include scrambled eggs, bacon, and potatoes for breakfast, and hamburger, cheeseburger, and grilled chicken breast sandwich for lunch or dinner. GF buns are available for burgers and sandwiches. Confirm the timeliness of this information before dining in. Located inside Disneyand Park. ▪ *disneyland.disney.go.com*

### Tony Roma's   📖
*Anaheim* ▪ *(714) 520-0200*
*1640 S Harbor Blvd*
*Carson* ▪ *(310) 329-5723*
*20720 S Avalon Blvd*
*Universal City* ▪ *(818) 763-7674*
*1000 Universal Studios Blvd*
*Encino* ▪ *(818) 461-8400*
*16575 Ventura Blvd*
*Fullerton* ▪ *(714) 871-4000*
*1300 S Harbor Blvd*
*Palm Desert* ▪ *(760) 568-9911*
*73155 Hwy 111*
*San Jose* ▪ *(408) 253-4900*
*4233 Moorpark Ave*
*San Marcos* ▪ *(760) 736-4343*
*1020 W San Marcos Blvd*
*Torrance* ▪ *(310) 326-7427*
*24301 Crenshaw Blvd*
*Union City* ▪ *(510) 324-7427*
*32135 Union Landing Blvd*

### Tra Vigne   $$$LD
*Saint Helena* ▪ *(707) 963-4444*
*1050 Charter Oak Ave* ▪ *Italian* ▪ Upon arrival, alert the hostess, who will notify the server. The server will then go over GF options in detail. Reservations noting GF should be made in advance and are highly recommended. ▪ *www.travignerestaurant.com*

### Trader Sam's Enchanted Tiki Bar   $LD
*Anaheim* ▪ *(714) 778-6600*
*1150 Magic Wy* ▪ *Asian Fusion* ▪ GF items include fish tacos and green papaya slaw. Confirm the timeliness of this information before dining in. Located at the Disneyland Hotel. ▪ *disneyland.disney.go.com*

### True Food Kitchen   ✪★📖
*Santa Monica* ▪ *(310) 593-8300*
*395 Santa Monica Pl*

### Uno Chicago Grill   ✪★📖
*Antioch* ▪ *(925) 522-8554*
*4827 Lone Tree Wy*
*Modesto* ▪ *(209) 521-8667*
*1533 Oakdale Rd*

### Va de Vi   ✪$LD
*Walnut Creek* ▪ *(925) 979-0100*
*1511 Mt Diablo Blvd* ▪ *Bistro* ▪ GF menu includes carrot ginger soup, roasted butternut squash, beer sirloin, seared scallops, and more. Chocolate soufflé is available for dessert. ▪ *www.va-de-vi-bistro.com*

### Veg-N-Out   ⦉LD
*San Diego* ▪ *(619) 546-8411*
*3442 30th St* ▪ *Vegetarian* ▪ GF items are marked on the menu with a 'GF' symbol. Options include a variety of sandwiches and burgers, sweet potato medallions, Thai tofu, homemade chili, and more. Ingredients that are not GF are clearly marked so that they can be omitted upon ordering. Be sure to alert the server that the meal must be GF. ▪ *www.vegnout.com*

### Veggie Grill, The   ✪★📖
*Irvine* ▪ *(949) 509-0003*
*4213 Campus Dr*
*Irvine* ▪ *(949) 727-9900*
*81 Fortune Dr*
*El Segundo* ▪ *(310) 535-0025*
*720 S Allied Wy*
*Hollywood* ▪ *(323) 962-3354*
*6374 Sunset Blvd*
*Los Angeles* ▪ *(323) 933-3997*
*110 S Fairfax Ave*
*Westwood* ▪ *(310) 209-6070*
*10916 Lindbrook Dr*
*Santa Monica* ▪ *(310) 829-1155*
*2025 Wilshire Blvd*

*Long Beach* ▪ (562) 430-4986
*6451 E Pacific Coast Hwy*
*San Jose* ▪ (408) 296-6473
*3055 Olin Ave*

### Via Italia Trattoria                                    ★ $$LD
*Encinitas* ▪ (760) 479-9757
*569 S Pacific Coast Hwy 101* ▪ *Italian* ▪
GF pasta and salad options are available. ▪
*www.viaitaliapizzeria.com*

### Vic Stewarts                                            $$$$D
*Walnut Creek* ▪ (925) 943-5666
*850 S Broadway* ▪ *Steakhouse* ▪ Accommodations for GF diners can be made.
Alert the server, who will ensure that the
kitchen is aware of GF requests. Reservations noting GF are recommended. ▪
*www.vicstewarts.com*

### Village Haus                                            ★ $LD
*Anaheim*
*1313 S Harbor Blvd* ▪ *American* ▪ GF options include the apple cheddar salad, as
well as the angus pastrami burger, hamburger, and cheeseburger, all with GF
buns. For French fries, request that they be
cooked in the "fries only" fryer. Confirm
the timeliness of this information before
dining in. Located inside Disneyland Park.
▪ *disneyland.disney.go.com*

### Vintage Tea Leaf                                        ★ $$$L
*Long Beach* ▪ (562) 435-5589
*969 E Broadway* ▪ *Teahouse* ▪ GF
scones are available. The tea shop reports that they are "GF friendly" and are
"happy to accommodate dietary needs." ▪
*www.vintagetealeaf.com*

### Wente Vineyards Restaurant                             $$$LD
*Livermore* ▪ (925) 456-2450
*5050 Arroyo Rd* ▪ *Modern American* ▪
The menu changes frequently, but hostess
Joy reports that they can "always accommodate" GF diners. A GF meal is "not an
uncommon request" and the kitchen staff
is "pretty well versed" in dealing with GF
orders. ▪ *www.wentevineyards.com*

### White Water Snacks                                     ★ ¢LD
*Anaheim*
*1600 S Disneyland Dr* ▪ *American* ▪
GF pizza, hamburger buns, and hot
dog buns are available. Confirm the
timeliness of this information before
dining in. Located at the Grand California Hotel in the Disneyland Resort. ▪
*disneyland.disney.go.com*

### Wild Goat Bistro                                       ★ $$LD
*Petaluma* ▪ (707) 658-1156
*6 Petaluma Blvd N* ▪ *American* ▪
Team member Nancy reports that
nearly the entire menu is GF. Rice
flour is used for anything dredged
in flour and GF bread and pasta are
available, as well as a selection of GF
desserts and beer. GF food is prepared
in separate areas using different
cooking surfaces and utensils. Nancy
reports that they "have never had any
complaints about cross-contamination." ▪
*www.wildgoatbistro.com*

### Willi's Seafood and Raw Bar                            ✪ $LD
*Healdsburg* ▪ (707) 433-9191
*403 Healdsburg Ave* ▪ *Seafood* ▪ GF
menu includes ceviche, chicken skewers, BBQ bacon wrapped scallops, pan
roasted shrimp, several salads, and more. ▪
*www.willisseafood.net*

### Willow Street Wood-Fired Pizza ✪ ★ $LD
*Los Gatos* ▪ (408) 354-5566
*20 S Santa Cruz Ave*
*San Jose* ▪ (408) 971-7080
*1072 Willow St*
*San Jose* ▪ (408) 871-0400
*1554 Saratoga Ave* ▪ *Pizza* ▪ GF items are
marked on the menu and include grilled
salmon with mango salsa, grilled chicken
breast with vegetables, several salads, and
fresh Manila clams. GF pizza and pasta
are available. Menu indicates which pasta
and pizza options can be prepared GF. ▪
*www.willowstreet.com*

### Wilson Creek Winery                                    ✪ ★ $$$L
*Temecula* ▪ (951) 699-9463

35960 Rancho California Rd ▪ Fusion ▪ GF menu includes ratatouille vegetable, Cornish hen, Argentine steak, pork porterhouse, and several salads. GF beer is available. ▪ *www.wilsoncreekwinery.com*

### Wolfgang Puck's Chinois    $$$$LD
*Santa Monica* ▪ (310) 392-9025
*2709 Main St* ▪ *Chinese* ▪ Manager Natalia reports that they can accommodate GF diners, but it is not something they do frequently. Alert server, who will consult with the chef. Reservations noting GF are strongly recommended. ▪ *www.wolfgangpuck.com*

### Yard House    ✪📖
*Brea* ▪ (714) 529-9273
*160 S Brea Blvd*
*Chino Hills* ▪ (909) 631-2200
*13881 Peyton Dr*
*Costa Mesa* ▪ (949) 642-0090
*1875 Newport Blvd*
*Irvine* ▪ (949) 753-9373
*71 Fortune Dr*
*Long Beach* ▪ (562) 628-0455
*401 Shoreline Village Dr*
*Newport Beach* ▪ (949) 640-9273
*849 Newport Center Dr*
*Pasadena* ▪ (626) 577-9273
*330 E Colorado Blvd Ste 230*
*Rancho Cucamonga* ▪ (909) 646-7116
*12473 N MainSt*
*Riverside* ▪ (951) 688-9273
*3775 Tyler St Ste 1A*
*Temecula* ▪ (951) 296-3116
*40770 Winchester Rd Ste 750*
*Rancho Mirage* ▪ (760) 779-1415
*71800 Highway 111*
*Fresno* ▪ (559) 261-2165
*90 El Camino*
*Northridge* ▪ (818) 721-0085
*9301 Tampa Ave*
*Palmdale* ▪ (661) 274-9271
*1247 Rancho Vista Blvd*
*Roseville* ▪ (916) 780-9273
*1166 Roseville Pkwy*
*San Jose* ▪ (408) 241-9273
*300 Santana Row*

### Z'Tejas Southwestern Grill    ✪★📖
*Costa Mesa* ▪ (714) 979-7469
*3333 Bristol St*

### Zest Bakery    cS
*San Carlos* ▪ (650) 241-9378
*1224 Arroyo Ave* ▪ *Bakery & Café* ▪ Their GF menu changes daily based on what is fresh that day. Call ahead for availability. All items are GF and are marked DF (dairy-free) EF (egg-free) when applicable. ▪ *www.zestbakery.com*

### Zpizza    ✪📖
*Aliso Viejo* ▪ (949) 425-0102
*26921 Aliso Crk Rd*
*Anaheim Hills* ▪ (714) 998-4171
*5745 E Santa Ana Cyn Rd*
*Brea* ▪ (714) 257-3000
*421 S Associated Rd*
*Burbank* ▪ (818) 840-8300
*116 E Palm Ave*
*Claremont* ▪ (909) 621-7555
*520 W 1st St*
*Danville* ▪ (925) 362-4010
*95 Railroad Ave*
*El Segundo* ▪ (310) 648-7919
*829 N. Douglas St*
*Fremont* ▪ (510) 360-9900
*46703 Mission Blvd*
*Glendora* ▪ (909) 599-4500
*1365 E Gladstone St*
*Huntington Beach* ▪ (714) 968-8844
*10035 Adams Ave*
*Huntington Beach* ▪ (714) 536-3444
*9035 Golden W Ave*
*Irvine* ▪ (949) 797-9044
*17655 Harvard*
*La Habra* ▪ (714) 738-4249
*1202 S Idaho*
*Ladera Ranch* ▪ (949) 347-8999
*25672 Crown Valley Pkwy*
*Laguna Niguel* ▪ (949) 481-3948
*32371 Golden Lantern*
*Livermore* ▪ (925) 447-5000
*922 Larkspur Dr*
*Long Beach* ▪ (562) 987-4500
*4612 E 2nd St*
*Long Beach* ▪ (562) 498-0778

5718 E 7th St
*Mammoth Lakes* ▪ (760) 934-5800
26 Old Mammoth Rd
*Newport Beach* ▪ (949) 715-1117
7956 E Pacific Coast Hwy
*Newport Beach* ▪ (949) 760-3100
2549 Eastbluff Dr
*Newport Beach* ▪ (949) 219-9939
1616 San Miguel Dr
*Newport Beach* ▪ (949) 723-0707
3423 Via Lido
*Newport Beach* ▪ (949) 722-1330
1124 Irvine Ave
*Porter Ranch* ▪ (818) 363-2600
19300 Rinaldi St
*Palm Desert* ▪ (760) 568-5405
73607 Highway 111
*Petaluma* ▪ (707) 658-2895
615 E Washington St
*Roseville* ▪ (916) 786-9797
3984 Douglas Blvd
*San Clemente* ▪ (949) 498-3505
1021 Avenida Pico
*San Diego* ▪ (858) 675-9300
11975 Carmel Mtn Rd
*La Jolla* ▪ (858) 450-0660
8657 Villa La Jolla Dr
*San Diego* ▪ (619) 272-0022
5175 Linda Vista Rd
*San Diego* ▪ (858) 689-9449
10006 Scripps Ranch Blvd
*San Francisco* ▪ (415) 995-5552
883 Mission St
*San Juan Capistrano* ▪ (949) 429-8888
32341 Camino Capistrano
*San Ramon* ▪ (925) 328-0525
3141-D Crow Canyon Pl
*Santa Ana* ▪ (714) 564-9166
121 E Memory Ln
*Santa Ana* ▪ (714) 437-1111
3941 S Bristol
*Seal Beach* ▪ (562) 596-9300
148 Main St
*Seal Beach* ▪ (562) 493-3440
12430 Seal Beach Blvd
*Tustin* ▪ (714) 734-9749
12932 Newport Ave
*Upland* ▪ (909) 949-1939

1943-C N Campus Ave
*Valencia* ▪ (661) 259-5000
27015 McBean Pkwy
*West Hollywood* ▪ (310) 360-1414
8869 Santa Monica Blvd
*Thousand Oaks* ▪ (818) 991-4999
5776 Lindero Canyon Rd

# COLORADO

## BOULDER

### Abo's Pizza                              ★📖
*Boulder* ▪ (303) 494-1274
637 S Broadway St
*Boulder* ▪ (303) 443-3199
1124 13th St
*Boulder* ▪ (303) 443-1921
2761 Iris Ave

### Aji                                      ✪$$LD
*Boulder* ▪ (303) 442-3464
1601 Pearl St ▪ *Latin American* ▪ GF
menu includes ceviche, soups, salads, and
a variety of meat and seafood entrées.
Items marked with an asterisk contain
ingredients that are "fried in the presence
of gluten", but the restaurant reports that
these items can be removed in most cases.
Inquire with the server for further details. ▪
*www.ajirestaurant.com*

### Amante Coffee                           ★¢S
*Boulder* ▪ (303) 448-9999
4580 Broadway St
*Boulder* ▪ (303) 546-9999
1035 Walnut St ▪ *Coffee Shop* ▪ Menu
fluctuates daily. GF quickbreads and burritos available. Call ahead to confirm availability. ▪ *www.amantecoffee.com*

### Antica Roma                             ★$$LD
*Boulder* ▪ (303) 449-1787
1308 Pearl St ▪ *Italian* ▪ GF pasta is available. ▪ *www.anticaroma.com*

### Beau Jo's Colorado Style Pizza ✪★$LD
*Boulder* ■ *(303) 554-5312*
*2690 Baseline Rd* ■ *Pizza* ■ GF pizza is
available at all locations. GF menu includes
GF appetizers, pizzas, and sandwiches and
notes which pizza sauces and toppings are
safe for GF diners. ■ *www.beaujos.com*

### BJ's Restaurant and Brewhouse ✪★📖
*Boulder* ■ *(303) 440-5200*
*1690 28th St*

### Black Cat Restaurant $$$D
*Boulder* ■ *(303) 444-5500*
*1964 13th St* ■ *Organic* ■ Menu changes
daily. Call ahead to see what types of
GF options are available on the menu. ■
*www.blackcatboulder.com*

### Blackjack ✪★
*Boulder* ■ *(303) 530-2600*
*6545 Gunpark Dr*
*Boulder* ■ *(303) 442-6677*
*3023 Walnut St* ■ *Pizza* ■ *odbj.com*
GF pizza is available in 10" and 12" size.

### Brasserie Ten Ten ✪★$LD
*Boulder* ■ *(303) 998-1010*
*1011 Walnut St* ■ *French* ■ GF options
marked on the menu include a variety of
omelettes, salade nicoise, moules au pistou,
coq au vin and steak frites. The server will
know whether the item is naturally GF or
substitutions must be made. GF pasta is
available. ■ *www.brasserietenten.com*

### Brewing Market ★₵$
*Boulder* ■ *(303) 499-1345*
*2610 Baseline Rd*
*Boulder* ■ *(303) 444-4858*
*2525 Arapahoe Ave*
*Boulder* ■ *(303) 443-2098*
*1918 13th St* ■ *Coffee Shop* ■ GF quickbreads and other pastries available. Items
vary by location ■ *brewingmarketcoffee.com*

### Buff Restaurant, The ✪★$BL
*Boulder* ■ *(303) 442-9150*
*1725 28th St* ■ *American* ■ The majority of
items on the menu are marked as GF or
GF optional. Dishes include a variety of

omelettes and skillets, French toast, griddle
cakes, huevos rancheros, grilled sandwiches,
and burgers, among other things. Alert the
server upon arrival and specify that your
order must be GF. ■ *www.buffrestaurant.com*

### Caffé Sole ★₵$
*Boulder* ■ *(303) 499-2985*
*637 S Broadway St* ■ *Coffee Shop* ■ GF
paninis, cakes and boba bars are available.
They offer cake in strudel, chocolate, and
pumpkin flavors. ■ *www.caffesole.com*

### Cantina Laredo 📖
*Boulder* ■ *(303) 444-2260*
*1680 29th St*

### Carelli's Ristorante Italiano ✪★$$LD
*Boulder* ■ *(303) 938-9300*
*645 30th St* ■ *Italian* ■ GF bread, pizza
and pasta are available. GF menu includes
grilled chicken parmigiana, pollo del vesuvio, steak pizzaiola, diver scallops cacciatore, and more. The restaurant reports that
the chef is GF and therefore understands
the precautions that must be taken with GF
meals. ■ *www.carellis.com*

### Casa Alvarez ✪$LD
*Boulder* ■ *(303) 546-0630*
*3161 Walnut St* ■ *Mexican* ■ GF menu
includes GF corn tortilla quesadillas, soups
& salads, huevos rancheros, enchiladas,
and a variety of seafood dishes and house
specialties. Vanilla ice cream sundae or
banana split are available for dessert. ■
*www.casaalvarezcolorado.com*

### Centro Latin Kitchen & Refreshment Palace $$LD
*Boulder* ■ *(303) 442-7771*
*950 Pearl St* ■ *Latin American* ■ Most
items on the menu are naturally GF
and items that are not can be modified to be made GF. Alert a server upon
arrival and they will list GF options. ■
*www.centrolatinkitchen.com*

### Dagabi Cucina ★$$D
Boulder ▪ (303) 786-9004
3970 N Broadway St ▪ Spanish ▪
GF pizza and pasta are available. ▪
www.dagabicucina.com

### Folsom Street Coffee Co. ★₵$
Boulder ▪ (303) 440-8808
1795 Folsom St ▪ Café ▪ GF specialty
items are available, but the options change
often. GF wraps are also available daily. ▪
www.folsomstreetcoffee.com

### Garbanzo 📖
Boulder ▪ (720) 974-6600
1905 29th St

### It's All Good Gluten Free ₵$
Boulder ▪ (303) 494-2253
3622 Walnut St ▪ Bakery ▪ Dedicated
GF bakery. Includes cookies, brownies, macaroons, cinnamon buns, and
apple turnovers. Bakery also makes GF
pies, tarts and cakes as well as quiche. ▪
www.itsallgoodglutenfree.com

### Kitchen, The ★$$$LD
Boulder ▪ (303) 544-5973
1039 Pearl St ▪ Global ▪ GF bread is available for sandwiches. Restaurant reports
that there are "always several options" for
GF diners. Many items are naturally GF,
and other items can be modified to be GF.
They add that they take dietary restrictions
seriously and always try to accommodate
them. Alert the server upon arrival. ▪
www.thekitchencafe.com

### Laudisio Restaurant ✪★$$$LD
Boulder ▪ (303) 442-1300
1710 29th St ▪ Italian ▪ GF pasta and pizza
crusts are available upon request. GF items
are marked on the menu and include risottos, polenta, calamari steak, long farm pork
loin, and more. All GF pastas are made in
a separate boiling pot from the pastas containing gluten. ▪ www.laudisio.com

### Leaf Vegetarian Restaurant $LD
Boulder ▪ (303) 442-1485
2010 16th St ▪ Vegetarian ▪ Chelsea
reports that the deviled eggs, Jamaican jerk tempeh, and all four salads are
GF. Confirm the timeliness of this information before dining in. The menu
changes frequently so call ahead or ask a
server for the most current GF options. ▪
www.leafvegetarianrestaurant.com

### Mateo ★$$LD
Boulder ▪ (303) 443-7766
1837 Pearl St ▪ French ▪ Restaurant
states that almost everything on their
menu is naturally GF or can be made
to be GF. A few of the available items
include risotto, salads and trout. ▪
www.mateorestaurant.com

### MED Mediterranean Restaurant ✪$LD
Boulder ▪ (303) 444-5335
1002 Walnut St ▪ Mediterranean ▪ GF
items marked on the menu. The server will
indicate whether the item is naturally GF
or whether substitutions must be made. ▪
www.themedboulder.com

### Milo's Pizza and Po Boys ★$LD
Boulder ▪ (720) 565-3665
2655 Broadway ▪ Pizza ▪ GF pizza is available. ▪ www.milosboulder.com

### Modmarket ✪$BLD
Boulder ▪ (303) 440-0476
1600 28th St ▪ American ▪ The restaurant
reports that everything on the menu is either naturally GF or can be modified to be
GF. The manager said they "make their best
efforts" to avoid CC by using separate prep
areas and utensils. ▪ www.modmarket.com

### Nick-N-Willy's ★📖
Boulder ▪ (303) 444-9898
801 Pearl St
Boulder ▪ (303) 499-9898
4800 Baseline Rd

### O! Pizza ★$$LD
Boulder ▪ (303) 444-9100
3980 Broadway St ▪ Pizza ▪ GF pizza
is available in the 12-inch size and
can be made with any toppings. ▪
www.o-pizza.com

### Organic Dish, The　　　✪★$**LD**
*Boulder* ▪ *(303) 736-9930*
*2690 28th St* ▪ *Take-&-Bake* ▪ "Do-it-yourself" style meals consist of prepared foods that must be cooked at home. GF menu changes monthly, but examples of GF options include turkey kielbasa with lentils and tofu with mushrooms and peas over egg noodles. The GF menu specifies whether an item is naturally GF or must be modified to be GF. GF pasta is available. ▪ *www.theorganicdish.com*

### Page Two　　　　　　　★₵S
*Boulder* ▪ *(303) 530-3339*
*6565 Gunpark Dr* ▪ *Café* ▪ Rudi's GF bread is available for all sandwiches. They also carry a variety of GF baked goods, including breads, muffins, and bars. ▪ *www.pagetwocafe.com*

### Pasta Jays　　　　　　　　★
*Boulder* ▪ *(303) 444-5800*
*1001 Pearl St* ▪ *Italian* ▪ GF pizza is available in the small size, as well as GF pasta. Staff reports that GF pizzas are prepared in a separate area and cooked on a separate stone to reduce the chance of CC. Selection changes daily so be sure to call ahead to confirm availability. ▪ *www.pastajays.com*

### Pei Wei Asian Diner　　　✪▢
*Boulder* ▪ *(720) 479-5570*
*1675 29th St*

### Pekoe Sip House　　　　★₵S
*Boulder* ▪ *(303) 444-5953*
*1225 Alpine Ave*
*Boulder* ▪ *(303) 444-4207*
*2500 30th St*
*Boulder* ▪ *(303) 444-4535*
*1125 18th St* ▪ *Teahouse* ▪ GF quickbread and burritos are available. ▪ *www.pekoesiphouse.com*

### Radda Trattoria　　　　★$**LD**
*Boulder* ▪ *(303) 442-6100*
*1265 Alpine Ave* ▪ *Italian* ▪ GF pizza is available. The restaurant reports that plenty of protein-based dishes can be modified to be GF. Confirm the timeliness of this in-formation before dining in. Alert a server, who will punch in a note to notify the kitchen. ▪ *www.raddatrattoria.com*

### Restaurant 4580　　　✪★$$**LD**
*Boulder* ▪ *(303) 448-1500*
*4580 Broadway # D-1* ▪ *American* ▪ GF selections are marked on the menu and include bacon wrapped dates, seared scallops, slow braised short ribs, and stuffed acorn squash. Staff reports that they are "very prepared for highly Celiac guests". GF bread is available. Confirm the timeliness of this information before dining in. ▪ *www.restaurant4580.com*

### Salt Bistro　　　　　　$$$**LD**
*Boulder* ▪ *(303) 444-7258*
*1047 Pearl St* ▪ *Modern American* ▪ Restaurant reports that GF diners can "certainly" be accommodated. They note that several menu items are naturally GF, and the kitchen is very flexible when it comes to modifying dishes for dietary requests. Alert a server, who will discuss GF options in detail. ▪ *www.saltboulderbistro.com*

### San Francisco Soup Company　✪**BLD**
*Boulder* ▪ *(303) 440-3632*
*1600 28th St* ▪ *American* ▪ Soups rotate daily. Check the website for a given day's GF offerings. Most locations also have GF options marked on the board. Some locations, including those in airports, do not have GF options marked on the board, but they will have a chart of GF options upon request. All GF soups made before soups containing gluten. Hours vary by location. Burlingame location is called Urban Bistro but same menu and policies apply. ▪ *www.sfsoupco.com*

### Sink, The　　　　　　　★₵**LD**
*Boulder* ▪ *(303) 444-7465*
*1165 13th St* ▪ *American* ▪ GF pizza is available. ▪ *www.thesink.com*

### Smiling Moose Deli　　　　✪▢
*Boulder* ▪ *(720) 565-3354*
*1685 29th St*

**Sushi Tora**                                    ★¢LD
Boulder ▪ (303) 444-2280
2014 10th St ▪ Sushi ▪ GF menu available. ▪
www.sushitora.net

**Taj Indian Cuisine**                            $LD
Boulder ▪ (303) 494-5216
2630 Baseline Rd ▪ Indian ▪ GF options
available. Alert server upon arrival. ▪
www.tajcolorado.com

**Ted's Montana Grill**                          ✪▢
Boulder ▪ (303) 449-5546
1701 Pearl St

**Tokyo Joe's**                                  ✪▢
Boulder ▪ (303) 443-1555
2525 Arapahoe Ave

**Turley's**                                    ✪$BLD
Boulder ▪ (303) 442-2800
2805 Pearl St ▪ American ▪ Separate
GF menu includes breakfast items such
as pancakes, omelettes and applewood
smoked salmon hash. Burger buns are
replaced with Gillian's rice buns, rice buns
can also be substituted for any bread item
on the menu. GF entrées include cioppino,
pesto stuffed chicken and blackened mahi
mahi. ▪ www.turleysrestaurant.com

**Vic's Again**                                  ★¢S
Boulder ▪ (303) 440-2918
3305 30th St ▪ Coffee Shop ▪ GF granola bars and breads are available. The
restaurant recommends calling ahead for
GF bread, as it occasionally sells out. ▪
www.vicsespresso.com

**West End Tavern**                              $$LD
Boulder ▪ (303) 444-3535
926 Pearl St ▪ Modern American ▪
GF items include ribs, sockeye salmon
salad, picnic eggs, buffalo wings, chicken
guacamole and any burger or sandwich
without the bread. Confirm the timeliness
of this information before dining in. ▪
www.thewestendtavern.com

**Zolo Grill**                                   $$LD
Boulder ▪ (303) 449-0444
2525 Arapahoe Ave ▪ Mexican ▪ The restaurant reports that most menu items are
GF. They note that although they discon-
tinued their GF menu because of liability
issues, they still have many GF ingredients. Staff notes that the servers are "very
well-versed" in GF dining. Approximately
75% of their menu "is" or "can be" GF. ▪
www.zologrill.com

**Zpizza**                                       ✪▢
Boulder ▪ (303) 545-5222
1695 29th St

## COLORADO

## COLORADO SPRINGS

**Biaggi's**                                     ✪★▢
Colorado Springs ▪ (719) 262-9500
1805 Briargate Pkwy

**BJ's Restaurant and Brewhouse** ✪★▢
Colorado Springs ▪ (719) 268-0505
5150 N Nevada Ave

**Bonefish Grill**                               ✪▢
Colorado Springs ▪ (719) 598-0826
5102 N Nevada Ave

**Borriello Brothers Pizza**            ★$$LD
Colorado Springs ▪ (719) 884-2020
5490 Powers Center Pt
Colorado Springs ▪ (719) 520-5600
3240 Centennial Blvd
Colorado Springs ▪ (719) 633-5452
229 S 8th St
Colorado Springs ▪ (719) 574-5050
4750 Barnes Rd
Colorado Springs ▪ (719) 578-9361
215 E Platte Ave ▪ Pizza ▪ GF pizza is
available. Crusts are pre-prepared and
baked in a separate oven to prevent CC. ▪
www.borriellobrothers.com

### Carino's Italian   ✪📖
*Colorado Springs* ▪ *(719) 622-8041*
*3015 New Center Pt*

### Carrabba's Italian Grill   ✪📖
*Colorado Springs* ▪ *(719) 527-1126*
*2815 Geyser Dr*
*Colorado Springs* ▪ *(719) 264-0401*
*7120 Campus Dr*

### Fox and Hound Pub & Grille   📖
*Colorado Springs* ▪ *(719) 570-0500*
*3101 New Ctr Pt Dr*

### Garbanzo   📖
*Fort Collins* ▪ *(970) 449-5020*
*100 W Troutman*
*Colorado Springs* ▪ *(719) 219-1600*
*1685 Briargate Pkwy*

### Gertrude's Restaurant   ★$$$BLD
*Colorado Springs* ▪ *(719) 471-0887*
*2625 W Colorado Ave* ▪ *American* ▪ All items on the menu can be made GF except the pasta dishes. Alert a server upon arrival and they will list of GF options. ▪ *www.gertrudesrestaurant.com*

### HuHot Mongolian Grill   📖
*Colorado Springs* ▪ *(719) 598-4044*
*1190 N Academy Blvd*
*Colorado Springs* ▪ *(719) 574-6647*
*5843 Constitution Ave*

### Jason's Deli   ✪📖
*Colorado Springs* ▪ *(719) 302-0234*
*7455 N Academy Blvd*

### Joe's Crab Shack   ✪📖
*Colorado Springs* ▪ *(719) 380-7620*
*805 Citadel Dr*

### Jose Muldoons   ✪₵LD
*Colorado Springs* ▪ *(719) 636-2311*
*222 N Tejon St*
*Colorado Springs* ▪ *(719) 574-5673*
*5710 S Carefree Cir* ▪ *Mexican* ▪ GF menu available in-house includes chili con queso, nachos grande, chicken mango salad, and fajitas, along with several other options. GF meals are prepared in a separate area according to the staff. ▪ *www.josemuldoons.com*

### Melting Pot, The   ✪📖
*Colorado Springs* ▪ *(719) 385-0300*
*30 E Pikes Peak Ave Ste A*

### My Big Fat Greek Restaurant   ✪📖
*Colorado Springs* ▪ *(719) 260-7300*
*7605 N Academy Blvd*

### Nosh   $$LD
*Colorado Springs* ▪ *(719) 635-6674*
*121 S Tejon St* ▪ *Modern American* ▪ Several items on the menu are or can be modified to be GF. Depending on your level of sensitivity, options may be more or less limited. Ask your server for details. ▪ *www.nosh121.com*

### Olive Branch, The   ✪★$BLD
*Colorado Springs* ▪ *(719) 475-1199*
*23 S Tejon St* ▪ *American* ▪ Extensive GF menu includes breakfast, lunch, and dinner selections. Selections include various omlettes, belgian waffles, lasagna, green chicken enchiladas, pasta marinara, mahi mahi and more. Staff reports that GF meals are prepared in a separate area. GF bread, pasta, and desserts are available. ▪ *www.theolivebranchrest.com*

### Outside the Breadbox   ★₵S
*Colorado Springs* ▪ *(719) 633-3434*
*2027 W Colorado Ave* ▪ *Bakery* ▪ Dedicated GF bakery offering breads, crackers, hamburger buns, cookies, pizza crust, pies, and more. GF items are baked on site every day. The bakery recommends calling 48 hours in advance for special orders. ▪ *www.outsidethebreadbox.com*

### P.F. Chang's China Bistro   ✪★📖
*Colorado Springs* ▪ *(719) 593-8580*
*1725 Briargate Pkwy*

### Panino's   ✪★$LD
*Colorado Springs* ▪ *(719) 635-1188*
*1721 S 8th St*
*Colorado Springs* ▪ *(719) 635-7452*
*604 N Tejon St* ▪ *Italian* ▪ Any panino can be made GF by baking it in a boat without the dough, and serving with romaine lettuce. Call the restaurant or visit to inquire about other GF options. ▪ *www.paninos.com*

**Pei Wei Asian Diner**   ✪📖
*Colorado Springs* ▪ *(719) 260-9922*
*7148 N Academy Blvd*

**Romano's Macaroni Grill**   ✪★📖
*Colorado Springs* ▪ *(719) 540-9833*
*2510 Tenderfoot Hill St*

**Sonterra Southwest Grill**   ✪$$$LD
*Colorado Springs* ▪ *(719) 471-9222*
*28 S Tejon St* ▪ *Southwest* ▪ They have
extensive GF menus for lunch and din-
ner. GF menus include prime rib, pork
chops, spinach enchiladas, sea bass,
house made flan, and bananas foster. ▪
*www.rockymtnrg.com/sonterragrill*

**Tapateria**   ✪LD
*Colorado Springs* ▪ *(719) 471-8272*
*2607 W Colorado Ave* ▪ *Spanish* ▪ Dedi-
cated GF establishment featuring tradi-
tional Spanish-style tapas as well as some
new creations. GF bread is baked for the
restaurant by Outside the Breadbox. Two
GF beers are also available. Staff cautions
that while they do offer a GF menu, CC
is still a remote possibility due to several
non-GF beers served at the establishment.
▪ *www.tapateria.com*

**Ted's Montana Grill**   ✪📖
*Colorado Sprgs* ▪ *(719) 598-6195*
*1685 Briargate Pkwy*

**Uchenna Ethiopian Restaurant**   ✪$LD
*Colorado Springs* ▪ *(719) 634-5070*
*2501 W Colorado Ave #108* ▪ *Ethio-
pian* ▪ Items on both the Ethiopian and
Mediterranean menus are marked as GF,
and include doro wat (a popular Ethio-
pian dish made with chicken and spices),
chicken tibs, lamb with basmati rice, and
a variety of salads. Traditional Ethio-
pian injera bread is also naturally GF. ▪
*uchennaalive.com*

**Zio's**   ✪📖
*Colorado Springs* ▪ *(719) 593-9999*
*6650 Corporate Dr*

# COLORADO

## DENVER

**5 Star Burgers**   ★LD
*Denver* ▪ *(303) 623-0085*
*555 Broadway* ▪ *American* ▪ GF buns are
available for burgers and sandwiches. ▪
*www.5starburgers.com*

**Abo's Pizza**   ★📖
*Denver* ▪ *(303) 722-3434*
*303 S Downing St*

**Abrusci's Italiano Ristorante**   ✪★$LD
*Denver* ▪ *(303) 462-0513*
*300 Fillmore St* ▪ *Italian* ▪ There are sepa-
rate GF menus for lunch and dinner. Both
are extensive, and both include a variety
of pastas and entrées. GF bread, pasta, and
beer are available. The Wheat Ridge loca-
tion also has a dedicated fryer for GF items.
▪ *www.abruscis.com*

**Aquarium Restaurant**   $$LD
*Denver* ▪ *(303) 561-4450*
*700 Water St* ▪ *Seafood* ▪ Alert manager who will alert chef. Chef will
come to the table and recommend
some dishes that can be made GF. ▪
*www.aquariumrestaurants.com*

**Avenue Grill**   ★$$$LD
*Denver* ▪ *(303) 861-2820*
*630 E 17th Ave* ▪ *American* ▪ The res-
taurant reports that many GF options
are available. Items include cioppino
dish, filet without the sauce, and tempeh.
GF bread is available for sandwiches. ▪
*www.avenuegrill.com*

**Beau Jo's Colorado Style Pizza**   ✪★$LD
*Denver* ▪ *(303) 758-1519*
*2710 S Colorado Blvd* ▪ *Pizza* ▪ GF pizza is
available at all locations. GF menu includes
GF appetizers, pizzas, and sandwiches and
notes which pizza sauces and toppings are
safe for GF diners. ▪ *www.beaujos.com*

### Bistro Vendôme   $$$D

*Denver* ▪ *(303) 825-3232*
*1420 Larimer St* ▪ *French* ▪ Server who has
Celiac reports that GF customers can enjoy
"almost half of the menu" and accommodations can be made. Alert a server upon
arrival and they will list the GF options. ▪
*www.bistrovendome.com*

### Blue Bonnet Mexican Café   ✪₵LD

*Denver* ▪ *(303) 778-0147*
*457 S Broadway* ▪ *Mexican* ▪ GF menu
items include tacos, chimichangas,
enchiladas, tamales, and more. All are
prepared with white corn tortillas. For
dessert, they offer homemade flan and
coconut custard. President Gary asks that
guests pay careful attention to the GF
menu, where all necessary substitutions
and instructions are printed. GF dishes
are prepared in a separate prep area. ▪
*www.bluebonnetrestaurant.com*

### Bubba Gump Shrimp Co.   ✪📖

*Denver* ▪ *(303) 623-4867*
*1437 California St*

### Café Colore   ★$LD

*Denver* ▪ *(303) 534-6844*
*1512 Larimer St* ▪ *Italian* ▪ GF pizza and
pasta available. The restaurant reports
that all pizza and pasta dishes can be
prepared GF. As with all specialty items,
call ahead to confirm availability. ▪
*www.cafecoloredenver.com*

### Capital Grille, The   ✪📖

*Denver* ▪ *(303) 539-2500*
*1450 Larimer St*

### City O'City   ✪$LD

*Denver* ▪ *(303) 831-6443*
*206 E 13th Ave* ▪ *Vegetarian* ▪ Extensive
GF menu includes warm steel cut oats,
power waffle, tortilla soup, minestrone
genovese and a variety of GF baked goods.
While they do not have dedicated utensils
and fryers for their GF items, manager
said they are more than happy to work
with their customers to fit their needs. ▪
*www.cityocitydenver.com*

### Deby's Gluten Free Bakery & Café   ₵BLD

*Denver* ▪ *(303) 283-4060*
*2369 S Trenton Wy* ▪ *Bakery* ▪ Dedicated
GF facility offering a wide variety of
baked goods and "take-&-bake" style
meals. Items include burritos, ravioli,
cinnamon rolls, and a variety of breads
and muffins. They also offer soups,
pizzas, chicken wings, cookies, pies,
brownies, and more. Products are
available at the storefront or from several
retailers around Colorado and beyond. ▪
*www.debysglutenfree.com*

### Earls Kitchen & Bar   ✪$LD

*Denver* ▪ *(303) 595-3275*
*1600 Glenarm Pl*
*Denver* ▪ *(303) 320-3275*
*201 Columbine St* ▪ *Global* ▪ Each
location has a "Gluten Aware" menu with
a variety of salads, entrées, and sides
available. Marketing coordinator Melissa
reports that all chefs are trained to "be
aware of allergy needs" and will "happily
accommodate" dietary restrictions. Alert
server upon arrival. ▪ *www.earls.ca*

### East Side Kosher Deli   ★$$BLD

*Denver* ▪ *(303) 322-9862*
*499 S Elm St* ▪ *Deli* ▪ GF options available. GF bread is available for sandwiches
and burgers for $1 extra. Mexican food
can be made with corn tortillas instead of
flour. Other options include grilled salmon
fillet, steak, lamb chop, BBQ ribs, baked
potatoes, brisket and grilled chicken. ▪
*www.eastsidekosherdeli.com*

### Fogo De Chao   ★📖

*Denver* ▪ *(303) 623-9600*
*1513 Wynkoop St*

### Fresh Fish Company   ✪$$$LD

*Denver* ▪ *(303) 740-9556*
*7800 E Hampden Ave* ▪ *Seafood* ▪
Manager Sina reports that the chef has
put together a list of non-GF items. This
list is available on the printable menu on
their website. Sina notes that all unlisted
items, including the majority of the fish

entrées, are GF. Confirm the timeliness of this information before dining in. ▪ *www.thefreshfishco.com*

### Gaia Bistro + Rustic Bakery      ★ ¢ BLD
*Denver* ▪ *(303) 777-5699*
*1551 S Pearl St* ▪ *Café* ▪ Organic crepes can be made GF upon request as well as sandwiches. Dessert includes a flourless chocolate cake with 3 berry sauce. Alert server upon arrival. ▪ *www.gaiabistro.com*

### Garbanzo      📖
*Denver* ▪ *(303) 433-9990*
*3453 W 32nd Ave*

### Gluten Escape, The      ✪ ¢ S
*Denver* ▪ *(303) 694-9999*
*4403 S Tamarac Pkwy #103* ▪ *Bakery* ▪ Everything on the menu is 100% GF, such as their brownies, cakes, muffins and challah bread. ▪ *www.theglutenescape.com*

### Hacienda Colorado      ✪ $$ LD
*Denver* ▪ *(303) 756-5700*
*4100 E Mexico Ave* ▪ *Mexican* ▪ GF menu available. Items include various appetizers, salads and tacos, poblano de pollo, camarones baja, salmon del mar, fajitas, enchiladas. GF flourless chocolate brownie is available for dessert. The restaurant cautions that items on the GF menu may be exposed to gluten in the kitchen. Alert a server upon arrival. ▪ *www.haciendacolorado.com*

### Hard Rock Café      ✪ 📖
*Denver* ▪ *(303) 623-3191*
*500 16th St Mall*

### Highland's Garden Café      $$ LD
*Denver* ▪ *(303) 458-5920*
*3927 W 32nd Ave* ▪ *Modern American* ▪ Menu changes frequently. The restaurant recommends calling ahead of time to find out what GF items will be on menu. ▪ *www.highlandsgardencafe.com*

### Hillstone Restaurants      📖
*Denver* ▪ *(303) 333-4688*
*303 Josephine St*

### Hops and Pie      ★ $ LD
*Denver* ▪ *(303) 477-7000*
*3920 Tennyson St* ▪ *Pizza* ▪ GF pizza and hard cider are available. ▪ *www.hopsandpie.com*

### Jason's Deli      ✪ 📖
*Denver* ▪ *(303) 243-5599*
*702 16th St*

### Jax Fish House      $$$ D
*Denver* ▪ *(303) 292-5767*
*1539 17th St* ▪ *Seafood* ▪ The restaurant reports that GF diners can be accommodated and many menu items can be altered to be GF. Alert a server upon arrival and they will go over GF options on the menu and speak to the chef. ▪ *www.jaxfishhousedenver.com*

### Jersey Mike's      📖
*Denver* ▪ *(303) 825-1744*
*555 Broadway*

### Jim 'n Nick's Bar-B-Q      ✪ ★ 📖
*Denver* ▪ *(303) 371-1566*
*8264 E 49th Ave*

### Kitchen, The      ★ $$$ LD
*Denver* ▪ *(303) 623-3127*
*1530 16th St* ▪ *Global* ▪ GF bread is available for sandwiches. Restaurant reports that there are "always several options" for GF diners. Many items are naturally GF, and other items can be modified to be GF. They add that they take dietary restrictions seriously and always try to accommodate them. Alert the server upon arrival. ▪ *www.thekitchencafe.com*

### Lala's Wine Bar & Pizzeria      ✪ $ LD
*Denver* ▪ *(303) 861-9463*
*410 E 7th Ave* ▪ *Italian* ▪ Extensive GF menu includes caprese salad, sandwiches on GF flatbreads, pizza, eggplant parma, and more. Manager Erin is GF and wrote the GF menu with help from the head chef. ▪ *www.lalaswinebar.com*

### Ling & Louie's Asian Bar & Grill  ✪ ★ 📖
*Denver* ▪ *(303) 371-4644*
*8354 Northfield Blvd*

## Lola                              $$$D

Denver ▪ (720) 570-8686
1575 Boulder St ▪ Mexican ▪ The restaurant reports that several items on menu can be made GF. Alert a server upon arrival and they will go over the options. ▪ www.loladenver.com

## Mad Greens Inspired Eats          ✿L

Denver ▪ (720) 468-4173
1600 Stout St
Denver ▪ (720) 496-4158
1200 Acoma St
Denver ▪ (303) 333-1842
222 Columbine St
Denver ▪ (303) 756-1222
2073 S Colorado Blvd ▪ Deli ▪ Online interactive allergy menu allows you to filter the menu based on what you can and cannot eat. GF selections include three bean chili, Dionysos salad, and southwestern grilled chicken. Confirm the timeliness of this information before dining in. ▪ www.madgreens.com

## Maggiano's Little Italy            ★▢

Denver ▪ (303) 260-7707
500 16th St Ste 150

## Mercury Café                      ★$$D

Denver ▪ (303) 294-9258
2199 California St ▪ Organic ▪ Many items on the menu can be made GF upon request. Alert a server upon arrival. All servers are educated about the GF diet. GF pasta is available. ▪ www.mercurycafe.com

## Mici Italian                       $$LD

Denver ▪ (303) 629-6424
1531 Stout St
Denver ▪ (303) 355-6424
2373 Central Park Blvd
Denver ▪ (303) 322-6424
3030 E 2nd Ave ▪ Italian ▪ GF pizza is available. ▪ www.miciitalian.com

## Morton's Steakhouse               ✪▢

Denver ▪ (303) 825-3353
1710 Wynkoop St

## Ninth Door, The                    ✪$D

Denver ▪ (303) 292-2229
1808 Blake St ▪ Spanish ▪ GF items indicated on menu. Items include pan seared serrano ham dish, chilled grilled shrimp and avocado salad, smoked salmon wrapped with grilled asparagus, and many more. ▪ www.theninthdoor.com

## Old Spaghetti Factory, The         ✪★▢

Denver ▪ (303) 295-1864
1215 18th St

## P.F. Chang's China Bistro          ✪★▢

Denver ▪ (303) 260-7222
1415 15th St

## Panzano                            ✪★$$$BLD

Denver ▪ (303) 296-3525
909 17th St ▪ Italian ▪ There are separate GF menus for each meal. GF bread, muffins, and beer are available. Manager Jason adds that they make GF desserts every day, and can make special GF cakes with advance notice. Their head chef has Celiac so they are currently trying to expand their GF menu, to cater to more customers with Celiac. ▪ www.panzano-denver.com

## Papou's Pizzeria                    ★

Denver ▪ (303) 388-3211
5075 Leetsdale Dr ▪ Pizza ▪ GF pizza is available in the 10 inch size. ▪ papouspizza.com

## Pei Wei Asian Diner                 ✪▢

Denver ▪ (720) 532-5999
200 Quebec St
Denver ▪ (303) 942-3445
3970 Buchtel Blvd

## Piatti Ristorante & Bar            ★$$LD

Denver ▪ (303) 321-1919
190 Saint Paul St
Denver ▪ (303) 321-1919
190 Saint Paul St ▪ Italian ▪ GF pasta is available. The restaurant reports that staff is trained on GF preparation and GF diners are accommodated "all the time." They note that the risotto is GF and that many menu

items can be modified to be GF. Alert a server upon arrival. ▪ *www.piatti.com*

**Pizza Fusion**                           ★ 📖
*Denver* ▪ *(303) 830-0223*
*571 E Colfax Ave*

**Rodizio Grill**                          ★ 📖
*Denver* ▪ *(303) 294-9277*
*1801 Wynkoop St*

**Saucy Noodle**                      ✪ ★ $**LD**
*Denver* ▪ *(303) 733-6977*
*727 S University Blvd* ▪ *Italian* ▪ GF pizza and pasta are available. GF menu lists all GF pasta and pizza options as well as appetizers, salads, and entrées such as chicken cacciatore, shrimp scampi, and baked polenta. ▪ *www.saucynoodle.com*

**Smiling Moose Deli**                    ✪ 📖
*Denver* ▪ *(303) 297-3354*
*1517 Wynkoop*

**Steuben's**                           ✪ $$**LD**
*Denver* ▪ *(303) 830-1001*
*523 E 17th Ave* ▪ *American* ▪ GF menu includes habanero fried corn, shrimp & grits, tomato soup, skirt steak, grilled salmon, and a variety of "breadless" sandwiches. The restaurant notes that they always ask about the severity of a gluten intolerance in order to alert the kitchen. ▪ *www.steubens.com*

**Sushi Den**                       ✪ ★ $$**LD**
*Denver* ▪ *(303) 777-0826*
*1487 S Pearl St* ▪ *Sushi* ▪ GF options indicated on menu. Items include yellow beefsteak tomato gazpacho, miso soup, fresh halibut, waygu NY strip steak, and steamed vegetables, as well as a variety of sushi. Alert server upon arrival. ▪ *www.sushiden.net*

**Sushi Sasa**                         ★ $$**LD**
*Denver* ▪ *(303) 433-7272*
*2401 15th St* ▪ *Sushi* ▪ GF options indicated on menu. Items include a variety of soups and salads, saffron snow crab stuffed salmon, Chilean sea bass, and angus choice tenderloin, as well as a variety of sushi and sushi rolls. All vegetarian

dishes are either naturally GF or can be made GF. GF rice noodles are available. ▪ *www.sushisasadenver.com*

**Ted's Montana Grill**                   ✪ 📖
*Denver* ▪ *(303) 893-0654*
*1401 Larimer St*

**Texas De Brazil Churrascaria**        ★ 📖
*Denver* ▪ *(720) 374-2100*
*8390 Northfield Blvd*

**Tokyo Joe's**                          ✪ 📖
*Denver* ▪ *(303) 825-0321*
*1001 16th St*
*Denver* ▪ *(303) 722-7666*
*1700 E Evans Ave*
*Denver* ▪ *(720) 213-0580*
*2320 S Parker Rd*
*Denver* ▪ *(303) 830-7277*
*1360 Grant St*

**True Food Kitchen**                   ✪ ★ 📖
*Denver* ▪ *(720) 509-7661*
*2800 E 2nd Ave*

**Uno Chicago Grill**                   ✪ ★ 📖
*Denver* ▪ *(303) 371-1555*
*16375 E 40th Ave*

**Vesta Dipping Grill**               ✪ $$$**D**
*Denver* ▪ *(303) 296-1970*
*1822 Blake St* ▪ *Modern American* ▪ GF menu includes duck breast, grilled flat iron steak, venison, jalapeno grilled tofu, scallops, and braised short ribs. The menu also indicates which dipping sauces are GF. The restaurant reports that they host GF diners "all the time." Menu changes seasonally, so GF options may vary. Call for the most current information. ▪ *www.vestagrill.com*

**Village Tavern**                        ✪ 📖
*Denver* ▪ *(720) 887-6900*
*100 W Flatiron Crossing Dr*

**Walter's Pizzeria**                    ★ $**LD**
*Denver* ▪ *(303) 864-9000*
*1906 Pearl St* ▪ *Pizza* ▪ GF pizza is available. ▪ *www.walterspizzeria.com*

### Watercourse Bakery ★ ⊄S

Denver ▪ (303) 318-9843
214 E 13th Ave ▪ Bakery ▪ Non-dedicated bakery offering a wide variety of GF baked goods, including cookies, pies, bars, muffins, scones, and breads. The bakery has no store front, as its primary purpose is to provide baked goods to local restaurants, but they accept special orders by phone. ▪ www.watercoursefoods.com

### Watercourse Foods ✪$BLD

Denver ▪ (303) 832-7313
837 E 17th Ave ▪ Vegetarian ▪ GF items indicated on the menu include the macro plate, mesquite tofu, polenta Florentine, enchiladas, tacos, Thai stir fry, blackened tofu and a variety of salads. GF bread is available for any sandwich. The restaurant also has a display case with GF bakery items including cupcakes, cookies, muffins, crème brûlée, pies and cakes. ▪ www.watercoursefoods.com

### Yard House ✪⊞

Denver ▪ (303) 572-9273
1555 Court Pl

## COLORADO

### FORT COLLINS

### Austin's American Grill ✪$LD

Fort Collins ▪ (970) 267-6532
2815 E Harmony Rd
Fort Collins ▪ (970) 224-9691
100 W Mountain Ave ▪ American ▪ GF menu available. Items include salads, sandwiches made with GF bread, rotisserie chicken, short smoked wild salmon and two different types of steak. Crème brûlée is available for dessert. Confirm the timeliness of this information before dining in. ▪ www.austinsamericangrill.com

### Beau Jo's Colorado Style Pizza ✪★$LD

Fort Collins ▪ (970) 498-8898
100 N College Ave ▪ Pizza ▪ GF pizza is available at all locations. GF menu includes GF appetizers, pizzas, and sandwiches and notes which pizza sauces and toppings are safe for GF diners. ▪ www.beaujos.com

### Café Rio Mexican Grill ⊞

Fort Collins ▪ (970) 530-2700
4414 S College Ave

### Carrabba's Italian Grill ✪⊞

Fort Collins ▪ (970) 225-6800
1212 Oakridge Dr

### Cozzola's Pizza ★$LD

Fort Collins ▪ (970) 229-5771
1112 Oakridge Dr ▪ Pizza ▪ GF pizza is available. ▪ cozzolaspizza.com

### Cuppy's Coffee ★⊄BL

Fort Collins ▪ (970) 232-9778
353 W Drake Rd ▪ Café ▪ GF bread available for sandwiches. ▪ www.cuppyscoffeefc.com

### Enzio's Italian Kitchen ✪★$LD

Fort Collins ▪ (970) 484-8466
126 W Mountain Ave ▪ Italian ▪ GF menu includes appetizers, salads, chicken, and several meat and seafood dishes. GF pasta and pizza are available. For dessert, there is chocolate torte, sorbet, and spumoni. ▪ www.enzios.com

### Happy Lucky's Teahouse and Treasures ★⊄S

Fort Collins ▪ (970) 689-3417
236 Walnut St ▪ Teahouse ▪ GF brownies and two types of coffee cake available. ▪ www.happyluckys.com

### HuHot Mongolian Grill ⊞

Fort Collins ▪ (970) 416-0555
249 S College Ave
Fort Collins ▪ (970) 568-8136
2720 Council Tree Ave

### Ingredient Restaurant ✪★⊞

Fort Collins ▪ (970) 672-8475
101 S College Ave

**J. Gumbo's**　　　　　　★☐
*Fort Collins* ▪ *(970) 672-8375*
*2842 Council Tree Ave*

**Jason's Deli**　　　　　　✪☐
*Fort Collins* ▪ *(970) 204-9203*
*1538 E Harmony Rd*

**Jersey Mike's**　　　　　　☐
*Fort Collins* ▪ *(970) 226-6453*
*4709 S Timberline Rd*

**Mad Greens Inspired Eats**　　¢L
*Fort Collins* ▪ *(970) 224-2434*
*616 S College Ave* ▪ *Deli* ▪ Online
interactive allergy menu allows you to
filter the menu based on what you can
and cannot eat. GF selections include
three bean chili, Dionysos salad, and
southwestern grilled chicken. Confirm
the timeliness of this information before
dining in. ▪ *www.madgreens.com*

**Melting Pot, The**　　　　✪☐
*Fort Collins* ▪ *(970) 207-0100*
*334 E Mountain Ave*

**Moot House, The**　　　✪★$$$LD
*Fort Collins* ▪ *(970) 226-2121*
*2626 S College Ave* ▪ *American* ▪ GF
menu available. Items include escargot,
green chile burger, prime rib, black angus
top sirloin, beef tenderloin, Colorado
lamb T-Bones, steak & grilled shrimp,
salmon florentine and Alaskan king crab
legs. GF hamburger buns are available. ▪
*www.themoothouse.com*

**Mugs Coffee Lounge**　　　★¢BLD
*Fort Collins* ▪ *(970) 472-6847*
*261 S College Ave*
*Fort Collins* ▪ *(970) 226-6847*
*306 W Laurel St* ▪ *Café* ▪ GF sweet breads,
bagels and flatbreads available and can be
used to make sandwiches or wraps. Call
ahead to confirm availability of GF items. ▪
*www.mugscoffeelounge.com*

**Nyala Ethiopian Cuisine**　　$LD
*Fort Collins* ▪ *(970) 223-6734*
*2900 Harvard St* ▪ *Ethiopian* ▪ The res-
taurant reports that all items on the menu

are naturally GF. Confirm the timeliness
of this information before dining in. ▪
*www.nyalafc.com*

**Panino's**　　　　　✪★$LD
*Fort Collins* ▪ *(970) 498-8292*
*310 W Prospect Rd* ▪ *Italian* ▪ Any panino
can be made GF by baking it in a boat
without the dough, and serving with
romaine lettuce. Call the restaurant or
visit to inquire about other GF options. ▪
*www.paninos.com*

**Rodizio Grill**　　　　　★☐
*Fort Collins* ▪ *(970) 482-3103*
*200 Jefferson St*

**Romano's Macaroni Grill**　✪★☐
*Fort Collins* ▪ *(970) 206-9249*
*4627 S Timberline Rd*

**Suehiro Japanese Restaurant**　✪$LD
*Fort Collins* ▪ *(970) 482-3734*
*223 Linden St*
*Fort Collins* ▪ *(970) 672-8185*
*4431 Corbett Dr* ▪ *Japanese* ▪ GF
menu available at both locations. ▪
*www.suehirofc.com*

**Tasty Harmony**　　　　★$LD
*Fort Collins* ▪ *(970) 689-3234*
*130 S Mason St* ▪ *Vegetarian* ▪ GF items
include the stir fry, falafels, polenta
dish, fajitas, nachos, raw hummus, royal
Hawaiian, raw enchiladas, and salads.
The restaurant also reports that any
of the daily plates can be made GF. ▪
*www.tastyharmony.com*

**Tokyo Joe's**　　　　　✪☐
*Fort Collins* ▪ *(970) 449-6991*
*100 W Troutman Pkwy*
*Fort Collins* ▪ *(970) 682-2317*
*2519 S Shields St*

**Uncle's Pizzeria**　　　★$$LD
*Fort Collins* ▪ *(970) 224-7100*
*120 W Olive St* ▪ *Pizza* ▪ GF pizza is
available. The restaurant recommends
calling ahead, as GF pizza crusts are made
in-house and may not always be available.
They also have a blackboard of entrées,

some of which are GF. Advance notice of 24 hours is required for large GF orders. ▪ *www.unclespizzeria.com*

# COLORADO

## ALL OTHER CITIES

### 240 Union                                    $$$**LD**
*Lakewood* ▪ (303) 989-3562
*240 Union Blvd* ▪ *Modern American*
▪ The restaurant reports that GF accommodations can be made for any dish on the menu. Alert server upon arrival who will alert the chef of GF needs. ▪ *www.240union.com*

### 5 Star Burgers                              ★ ¢**LD**
*Centennial* ▪ (303) 795-8181
*2330 E Arapahoe Rd* ▪ *American* ▪ GF buns are available for burgers and sandwiches. ▪ *www.5starburgers.com*

### 7 West Pizzeria & Pub                        ★
*Longmont* ▪ (303) 678-9378
*526 Main St* ▪ *Pizza* ▪ GF menu includes beef kabobs, steak & scallops, fish tacos, bourbon mushroom strip steak, and more. For dessert, there is vanilla crème brûlée, and a chocolate dish called "Sin-Viche." ▪ *www.7westpizza.com*

### Abo's Pizza                                  ★ 📖
*Louisville* ▪ (303) 604-9896
*1355 S Boulder Rd*
*Superior* ▪ (720) 304-6000
*502 Center Dr*
*Longmont* ▪ (303) 678-0111
*1834 N Main St*
*Erie* ▪ (303) 828-9777
*720 Austin Ave*
*Centennial* ▪ (303) 468-4700
*7475 E Arapahoe Rd*
*Broomfield* ▪ (303) 438-8383
*799 US Hwy 287*

*Highlands Ranch* ▪ (303) 470-9999
*2229 Wildcat Reserve Pkwy*
*Niwot* ▪ (303) 652-0830
*7960 Niwot Rd*
*Northglenn* ▪ (303) 450-2267
*2145 E 120th Ave*

### Abrusci's Italiano Ristorante       ✪ ★ $**LD**
*Wheat Ridge* ▪ (303) 232-2424
*3244 Youngfield St* ▪ *Italian* ▪ There are separate GF menus for lunch and dinner. Both are extensive, and both include a variety of pastas and entrées. GF bread, pasta, and beer are available. They also have a dedicated GF fryer. ▪ *www.abruscis.com*

### Amicas                                       ★ $**LD**
*Salida* ▪ (719) 539-5219
*136 E 2nd St* ▪ *Pizza* ▪ GF pizza and bread for sandwiches are available. ▪ *www.amicassalida.com*

### Angelina's Fine Italian Dining      $$$**LD**
*Littleton* ▪ (303) 932-7708
*8100 W Crestline Ave* ▪ *Italian* ▪ Most items on the menu can be made GF except the lasagna, eggplant, gnocchi, meatballs, stuffed shells, manicotti and cavatelli. Alert server upon arrival. ▪ *www.angelinas-italian.com*

### Angelo's Pizza                              ★ $**LD**
*Pueblo* ▪ (719) 544-8588
*105 E Riverwalk*
*Pueblo* ▪ (719) 547-4388
*74 N Component Dr* ▪ *Pizza* ▪ GF pizza is available. ▪ *menusfirst.com/pueblo/angelosunion.htm*

### Arte Pizzeria                               ★
*Loveland* ▪ (970) 669-9000
*1467 W Eisenhower Blvd* ▪ *Pizza* ▪ GF pizza is available. ▪ *artepizzeria.com*

### Bacco Trattoria                             ★ $**LD**
*Littleton* ▪ (303) 979-2665
*10125 W San Juan Wy*
*Boulder* ▪ (303) 442-3899
*1200 Yarmouth Ave* ▪ *Italian* ▪ GF pasta and pizza are available. The restaurant recommends calling ahead to confirm availability. ▪ *www.baccodenver.com*

**Beau Jo's Colorado Style Pizza** ✪ ★ $LD
*Evergreen* ▪ (303) 670-2744
*28186 Hwy 74*
*Idaho Springs* ▪ (303) 567-4376
*1517 Miner St*
*Arvada* ▪ (303) 420-8376
*7525 W 53rd Ave*
*Steamboat Springs* ▪ (970) 870-6401
*704 Lincoln Ave* ▪ Pizza ▪ GF pizza
is available at all locations. GF menu
includes GF appetizers, pizzas, and
sandwiches and notes which pizza sauces
and toppings are safe for GF diners. ▪
*www.beaujos.com*

**Biaggi's** ✪ ★ 📖
*Loveland* ▪ (970) 663-0100
*5929 Sky Pond Dr*

**Big Bill's Pizza** ★ $LD
*Centennial* ▪ (303) 741-9245
*8243 S Holly St* ▪ Pizza ▪ GF pizza is available. ▪ *www.bigbillsnypizza.com*

**BJ's Restaurant and Brewhouse** ✪ ★ 📖
*Aurora* ▪ (303) 366-3550
*14442 E Cedar Ave*
*Westminster* ▪ (303) 389-6444
*10446 Town Center Dr*

**Blackjack** ✪ ★
*Longmont* ▪ (303) 776-1900
*1102 Francis St*
*Louisville* ▪ (303) 665-0400
*1075 E S Boulder Rd* ▪ Pizza ▪ GF pizza is
available in 10" and 12" size. ▪ *odbj.com*

**Bonefish Grill** ✪ 📖
*Westminster* ▪ (303) 423-3474
*10438 Town Center Dr*
*Greenwood Village* ▪ (303) 741-3474
*4948 S Yosemite St*
*Littleton* ▪ (303) 948-3474
*8100 W Crestline Ave Unit F*
*Johnstown* ▪ (970) 663-3474
*4920 Thompson Pkwy*

**Borriello Brothers Pizza** ★ $$LD
*Monument* ▪ (719) 484-0011
*15910 Jackson Creek Pkwy*
*Fountain* ▪ (719) 393-0071

*5180 Fontaine Blvd*
*Fort Carson* ▪ (719) 884-2020
*6371 Specker Ave Bldg 1532 "The Hub"*
*Lakewood* ▪ (720) 420-2600
*120 S Wadsworth Blvd* ▪ Pizza ▪ GF pizza
is available. Crusts are pre-prepared and
baked in a separate oven to prevent CC. ▪
*www.borriellobrothers.com*

**Boston's Restaurant & Sports Bar**
✪ ★ 📖
*Grand Junction* ▪ (970) 256-7654
*2404 Patterson Rd*

**Boulevard Pizza** ★
*Castle Rock* ▪ (303) 660-6458
*78 E Allen St* ▪ Pizza ▪ GF pizza is available.
▪ *blvdpizza.com*

**Brewing Market** ★ ¢S
*Longmont* ▪ (303) 651-7716
*1520 S Hover St*
*Lafayette* ▪ (720) 890-3993
*2770 Dagny Wy* ▪ Coffee Shop ▪
GF quickbreads and other pastries
available. Items vary by location. ▪
*brewingmarketcoffee.com*

**Bubba Gump Shrimp Co.** ✪ 📖
*Breckenridge* ▪ (970) 547-9000
*231 S Main St*

**Buca di Beppo** ✪ 📖
*Broomfield* ▪ (303) 464-7673
*615 Flatiron Marketplace Dr*

**Bundt Shoppe, The** ★ $$
*Castle Rock* ▪ (303) 422-8638
*7437 Village Square Dr* ▪ Bakery ▪ GF
bundt cakes available. GF bundt flavors include chocolate chocolate chip,
red velvet, raspberry chocolate, banana
chocolate chip, pumpkin with chocolate
bits, key lime, orange creamsicle and
spiced orange. Some flavors might not
be available year round, so be sure to
call ahead to determine availability. ▪
*www.thebundtshoppe.com*

## Cabin Restaurant & Lounge, The
✪ ★ $$$**D**
*Steamboat Springs* ▪ *(970) 871-5550*
*2300 Mount Werner Cir* ▪ *Steakhouse*
▪ GF items marked on the menu. Items
include summer corn bisque, filet mi-
gnon, smoked gold canyon Colorado pork
rib chop, rocky mountain red trout, and
Colorado top sirloin. GF pasta and bread
for sandwiches and burgers is available
upon request. ▪ *www.steamboatgrand.com*

## Café 13
★ ¢**BL**
*Golden* ▪ *(303) 278-2225*
*1301 Arapahoe St* ▪ *Café* ▪ GF brown rice
tortillas are available for breakfast entrées
or wraps. They also offer three different
types of GF bread, including chocolate
zucchini bread and lemon poppyseed bread
as well as a GF hoagie for sandwiches. ▪
*www.cafe13golden.com*

## Café Profusion
$**LD**
*Dillon* ▪ *(970) 513-8336*
*119 E La Bonte St* ▪ *Indian* ▪ Dedicated
GF restaurant offering a variety of curries,
coriander orange roast pork, pomegran-
ate braised baby back ribs, tomato basil
lemongrass soup, mango salad, and more. ▪
*www.cafeprofusion.com*

## Café Rio Mexican Grill
📖
*Glendale* ▪ *(720) 389-3400*
*610 S Colorado Blvd*
*Grand Junction* ▪ *(970) 208-1800*
*2412 F Rd*

## Camp Robber Creative Cuisine
✪$$**LD**
*Montrose* ▪ *(970) 240-1590*
*1515 Ogden Rd* ▪ *American* ▪ Gluten Intolerance Group (GIG) accredited restaurant
featuring a large GF menu with items like
grilled chicken spinach salad, St. Louis
ribs, and grilled salmon with sundried
tomato cream sauce. Some dishes require
modification to become GF, so be sure to
alert your server. ▪ *www.camprobber.com*

## Carino's Italian
✪📖
*Grand Junction* ▪ *(970) 255-0560*
*2480 Highway 6 And 50*
*Greeley* ▪ *(970) 506-4200*
*2473 W 28th St*
*Lakewood* ▪ *(720) 963-1866*
*389 S Wadsworth Blvd*
*Longmont* ▪ *(303) 485-8077*
*2033 Ken Pratt Blvd*
*Loveland* ▪ *(970) 203-9900*
*1455 Rocky Mountain Ave*
*Parker* ▪ *(303) 841-7103*
*9355 Crown Crest Blvd*
*Pueblo* ▪ *(719) 542-1745*
*5700 N Elizabeth St*

## Carrabba's Italian Grill
✪📖
*Aurora* ▪ *(303) 338-8600*
*2088 S Abilene St*
*Louisville* ▪ *(303) 926-4411*
*575 S Mccaslin Blvd*
*Westminster* ▪ *(303) 940-5620*
*7401 W 92nd Ave*

## Colterra Food and Wine
★ $$$**LD**
*Niwot* ▪ *(303) 652-0777*
*210 Franklin St* ▪ *European* ▪ Restaurant
reports that all items on the menu can be
made GF upon request. GF bread is avail-
able for sandwiches. ▪ *www.colterra.com*

## Coquette's Bistro & Bakery
$**BLD**
*Manitou Springs* ▪ *(719) 685-2420*
*915 Manitou Ave* ▪ *French* ▪ Dedicated GF
restaurant and bakery offering appetizers,
salads, savory & sweet crepes, and a variety
of entrées. Entrées include pan seared
duck breast, flat iron steak, poached
salmon, chicken piccata, chicken pot pie,
and burgers. ▪ *www.coquettecreperie.com*

## Del Frisco's Double Eagle Steak House 📖
*Greenwood Village* ▪ *(303) 796-0100*
*8100 E Orchard Rd*

## Dillon Dam Brewery
✪$$**LD**
*Dillon* ▪ *(970) 262-7777*
*100 Little Dam St* ▪ *American* ▪ Server
JJ reports that they are very GF aware.
Menu items that can be modified to be GF
include beef, buffalo, and veggie burg-

ers without buns, along with salads and grilled mushroom entrées. Confirm the timeliness of this information before dining in. Alert a server, who will notify the chef. ▪ *www.dambrewery.com*

### Double D's Sourdough Pizza ✪★$$LD
*Broomfield* ▪ *(303) 665-5006*
*535 Zang St Suite A*
*Westminster* ▪ *(303) 410-0002*
*5160 W 120th Ave Suite K* ▪ *Pizza* ▪ GF menu available. Items include various salads, hot wings, and ribs. GF pizza is also available in the 12" size with an extensive list of topping choices. ▪ *www.doubledspizza.com*

### Earls Kitchen & Bar ✪$LD
*Lone Tree* ▪ *(303) 792-3275*
*8335 Park Meadows Center Dr* ▪ *Global* ▪ Each location has a "Gluten Aware" menu with a variety of salads, entrées, and sides available. Marketing coordinator Melissa reports that all chefs are trained to "be aware of allergy needs" and will "happily accommodate" dietary restrictions. Alert server upon arrival. ▪ *www.earls.ca*

### East Coast Pizza ★$LD
*Pueblo* ▪ *(719) 583-9000*
*1638 W US Hwy 50* ▪ *Pizza* ▪ GF pizza is available. ▪ *eastcoastpizzapueblo.com*

### Ed's Cantina & Grill ✪¢BLD
*Estes Park* ▪ *(970) 586-2919*
*390 E Elkhorn Ave* ▪ *Mexican* ▪ GF menu available. Items include chicken avocado salad, strawberry spinach salad, caesar salad, enchiladas, fajitas, pozole, fajita taco salad, and tamales. The restaurant recommends avoiding fried items such as tacos and nachos, as a common fryer is used for all items. Alert a server upon arrival. ▪ *www.edscantina.com*

### Ernie's Bar & Pizza ★$LD
*Denver* ▪ *(303) 955-5580*
*2915 W 44th Ave* ▪ *Pizza* ▪ GF pizza is available, as well as GF bread. The restaurant reports that most sandwiches are "GF capable" and all pizza toppings EXCEPT meatballs are GF. Confirm the timeliness

of this information before dining in. ▪ *www.erniesdenver.com*

### Fanelli's Amici's ★$LD
*Wheat Ridge* ▪ *(303) 455-5585*
*4300 Wadsworth Blvd* ▪ *Italian* ▪ GF pasta is available. ▪ *www.fanellisamicis.com*

### Fire Bowl Café ✪📖
*Englewood* ▪ *(303) 799-1690*
*11435 E Briarwood Ave*

### Fleming's Prime Steakhouse & Wine Bar ✪📖
*Englewood* ▪ *(303) 768-0827*
*191 Inverness Dr W*

### Fox and Hound Pub & Grille 📖
*Lone Tree* ▪ *(720) 875-9161*
*9239 Park Meadows Dr*
*Westminster* ▪ *(303) 464-7366*
*4750 W 120th Ave*

### Garbanzo 📖
*Greenwood Village* ▪ *(303) 694-7777*
*8547 E Arapahoe Rd*
*Aurora* ▪ *(303) 627-4444*
*6750 S Cornerstar Wy*
*Littleton* ▪ *(303) 932-8888*
*8246 W Bowles Ave*
*Englewood* ▪ *(303) 705-9700*
*8225 S Chester St*
*Glendale* ▪ *(303) 757-5900*
*630 S Colorado Blvd*
*Highlands Ranch* ▪ *(303) 471-6100*
*1100 Sergeant Jon Stiles Dr*
*Lakewood* ▪ *(720) 214-7100*
*14700 W Colfax Ave*
*Englewood* ▪ *(303) 705-9700*
*8225 S Chester St*
*Lone Tree* ▪ *(303) 397-1910*
*9996 Commons St*

### Garlic Jim's ✪★📖
*Highlands Ranch* ▪ *(303) 346-5467*
*3982 Red Cedar Dr*

### Genghis Grill 📖
*Grand Junction* ▪ *(970) 241-5020*
*2474-C Hwy 6*
*Centennial* ▪ *(303) 792-5426*
*9617 E County Line*

## Granny's Gluten-Free Zone          ☾S

*Loveland* ▪ *(970) 669-9986*
*3419 W Eisenhower Blvd* ▪ *Bakery* ▪
Dedicated GF grocery store with a wide
variety of GF baked goods, including
breads, pizza crusts, muffins, cinnamon
buns, cookies, and more. Baked goods
are brought onto the premises from other
bakeries. ▪ *www.grannysglutenfree.com*

## Hacienda Colorado          ✪$$LD

*Englewood* ▪ *(303) 858-8588*
*10500 Bierstadt Wy*
*Westminster* ▪ *(303) 460-0111*
*10422 Town Center Dr*
*Lakewood* ▪ *(303) 932-0272*
*5056 S Wadsworth Wy* ▪ *Mexican* ▪ GF
menu available. Items include various
appetizers, salads and tacos, poblano de
pollo, camarones baja, salmon del mar,
fajitas, enchiladas. GF flourless chocolate brownie is available for dessert. The
restaurant cautions that items on the GF
menu may be exposed to gluten in the
kitchen. Alert a server upon arrival. ▪
*www.haciendacolorado.com*

## Hearthstone          ✪$$$$D

*Breckenridge* ▪ *(970) 453-1148*
*130 S Ridge St* ▪ *American* ▪ GF menu includes elk, filet mignon and plank salmon.
▪ *www.hearthstonerestaurant.biz*

## Highlands Pizza Company          ★☾LD

*Aspen* ▪ *(970) 920-3747*
*133 Prospector Rd* ▪ *Pizza* ▪ GF "Signature Thin Crust" pizza is available. ▪
*www.highlandspizzaco.com*

## Indochine Cuisine          ✪★$L

*Parker* ▪ *(720) 851-8559*
*19751 E MainSt* ▪ *Asian* ▪ Items that can
be prepared GF are indicated on the
menu and include pad thai, tom yum
soup, a variety of curries, clay pot catfish,
and much more. Chef Yume reports that
the kitchen is not certified GF, but they
have taken many steps to prevent CC. ▪
*www.indochine-cuisine.com*

## Jason's Deli          ✪📖

*Broomfield* ▪ *(303) 465-2882*
*549 Flatiron Blvd*
*Greenwood Village* ▪ *(720) 489-8900*
*5302 DTC Blvd*
*Lakewood* ▪ *(303) 986-1111*
*204 Union Blvd*
*Englewood* ▪ *(303) 708-1448*
*9525 E County Line Rd*
*Aurora* ▪ *(303) 991-2311*
*5440 S Parker Rd*

## Jersey Mike's          📖

*Edgewater* ▪ *(303) 232-2785*
*2255 Sheridan Blvd*
*Westminister* ▪ *(303) 252-1337*
*12003 N Pecos St*
*Greenwood Village* ▪ *(303) 740-9100*
*5137 S Yosemite St*
*Parker* ▪ *(720) 851-9740*
*18366 E Lincoln Ave*
*Aurora* ▪ *(720) 381-0919*
*3571 S Tower Rd*
*Highlands Ranch* ▪ *(303) 683-3066*
*9362 S Colorado Blvd*

## Jim 'n Nick's Bar-B-Q          ✪★📖

*Aurora* ▪ *(720) 274-5300*
*24153 E Prospect Ave*

## Joe's Crab Shack          ✪📖

*Aurora* ▪ *(303) 306-7070*
*14025 E Evans Ave*
*Westminster* ▪ *(303) 657-0776*
*8911 N Yates St*
*Parker* ▪ *(303) 840-4201*
*19320 Cottonwood Dr*

## Juicy Lucy's Steakhouse          $$LD

*Glenwood Springs* ▪ *(970) 945-4619*
*308 7th St* ▪ *Seafood & Steakhouse* ▪ GF
items include steamed artichoke, mussels,
oysters on half shells, top sirloin, New York
steak, lamb chops, herbed chicken, salmon
filet, fish of the day, filet mignon, porterhouse T-bone steak, and steamed king crab
legs, as well as crème brûlée and a root
beer float for dessert. Confirm the timeliness of this information before dining in. ▪
*www.juicylucyssteakhouse.com*

## Kenosha Steakhouse   ✪$$$LD
*Breckenridge* ▪ *(970) 453-7313*
*301 S Main St* ▪ *Steakhouse* ▪ GF items
are marked on menu. Some items include
a hickory smoked rib basket, Colorado
buffalo chili cheese dip, summit nachos,
wings, Asian barbecue salmon, stuffed
squash and tomatoes, a variety of steaks,
and burgers and sandwiches with no bun. ▪
*www.kenoshasteakhouse.com*

## Larkspur Restaurant   $$$$LD
*Vail* ▪ *(970) 754-8050*
*458 Vail Valley Dr* ▪ *Modern American*
▪ GF items are marked with asterisks,
and the restaurant reports that most
other menu items can be modified
to be GF. Alert server upon arrival. ▪
*www.larkspurvail.com*

## Lefty's Gourmet Pizza and Ice Cream
★$$LD
*Niwot* ▪ *(303) 652-3100*
*364 2nd Ave* ▪ *Italian* ▪ GF pizzas are avail-
able in the 12-inch size. GF "lasagna," made
with cabbage instead of pasta, is also avail-
able. ▪ *www.leftysgourmetpizza.com*

## Lil' Ricci's NY Pizzeria   ★
*Highlands Ranch* ▪ *(303) 471-0070*
*44 W Centennial*
*Golden* ▪ *(303) 215-1618*
*16950 W Colfax Ave*
*Parker* ▪ *(303) 220-7422*
*16526 Keystone Blvd* ▪ *Pizza* ▪ GF pizza is
available. Other GF items include Ricci's
wings, dinner salad, and lemon chicken.
Confirm the timeliness of this information
before dining in. ▪ *www.lilriccispizza.com*

## Local Joe's Pizza   ★
*Edwards* ▪ *(970) 926-4444*
*280 Main St*
*Vail* ▪ *(970) 476-2222*
*1000 Lions Ridge Loop* ▪ *Pizza* ▪ GF pizza
is available. ▪ *localjoespizza.com*

## Lone Star Steakhouse & Saloon   ✪📖
*Arvada* ▪ *(303) 420-7827*
*7450 W 52nd Ave*
*Brighton* ▪ *(303) 655-9433*

*305 Pavilions Pl*
*Golden* ▪ *(303) 237-5727*
*11905 W 6th Ave*
*Littleton* ▪ *(303) 932-1718*
*4817 S Wadsworth Blvd*
*Loveland* ▪ *(970) 203-9464*
*5330 Stone Creek Cir*
*Thornton* ▪ *(303) 252-0770*
*237 E 120th Ave*

## Loveland Coffee Company   ★ϹS
*Loveland* ▪ *(970) 278-1221*
*620 E 29th St* ▪ *Coffee Shop* ▪ GF brown-
ies, breakfast burritos, breads and more. ▪
*www.lovelandcoffeeco.com*

## Mad Greens Inspired Eats   Ϲ
*Centennial* ▪ *(303) 662-8119*
*8283 S Akron St*
*Boulder* ▪ *(720) 496-4157*
*1805 29th St*
*Lakewood* ▪ *(720) 496-4139*
*150 S Union Blvd*
*Fort Collins* ▪ *(970) 372-6216*
*2120 E Harmony Rd*
*Greenwood Village* ▪ *(720) 259-4441*
*4948 S Yosemite St*
*Longmont* ▪ *(303) 702-4440*
*2341 Clover Basin Dr* ▪ *Deli* ▪ Online interac-
tive allergy menu allows you to filter the
menu based on what you can and cannot eat.
GF selections include three bean chili, Dio-
nysos salad, and southwestern grilled chick-
en. Confirm the timeliness of this informa-
tion before dining in. ▪ *www.madgreens.com*

## Maggiano's Little Italy   ★📖
*Englewood* ▪ *(303) 858-1405*
*7401 S Clinton St*

## Mama Rose's   ★$$D
*Estes Park* ▪ *(970) 586-3330*
*338 E Elkhorn Ave* ▪ *Italian* ▪ GF rice
pasta or shredded zucchini is available
for substitution into any pasta dish except
lasagna or ravioli. Restaurant reports that
they accommodate GF diners "all the time,"
and the servers are well-educated on the
GF diet. Servers can indicate GF options. ▪
*www.mamarosesrestaurant.com*

### Mambo Italiano       ★ $$D
*Steamboat Springs* ▪ *(970) 870-0500*
*521 Lincoln Ave* ▪ *Italian* ▪ Kitchen staffer
Vince reports that the everyone is educated on the GF diet. He adds that they
had a "GF 101" training course, so any
server will be able to indicate GF items
on the menu. GF pasta is usually available, but Vince notes that sometimes their
supplier is inconsistent, so call ahead to
confirm the availability of this item. ▪
*www.mambos.com*

### Melting Pot, The       ✪ 📖
*Littleton* ▪ *(303) 794-5666*
*2707 W Main St*
*Louisville* ▪ *(303) 666-7777*
*732 Main St*

### Mi Casa Mexican Restaurant       ✪ $$LD
*Breckenridge* ▪ *(970) 453-2071*
*600 S Park Ave* ▪ *Mexican* ▪ GF menu
includes soups, enchiladas, fajitas, fish
tacos, and pork tamales. Tostitos corn
chips are available upon request. The
restaurant notes that the servers are
trained to punch GF requests into the
computer and alert the kitchen manager. ▪
*www.micasamexicanrestaurant.com*

### Modmarket       ✪ $BLD
*Glendale* ▪ *(303) 757-1772*
*1000 S Colorado Blvd*
*Greenwood Village* ▪ *(303) 220-9961*
*8575 E Arapahoe Rd* ▪ *American* ▪ The
restaurant reports that everything on the
menu is either naturally GF or can be
modified to be GF. The manager said they
"make their best efforts" to avoid CC by
using separate prep areas and utensils. ▪
*www.modmarket.com*

### Morning Glory Farm Fresh Café   ★ ₵BLD
*Lafayette* ▪ *(303) 604-6351*
*1377 Forest Park Circle Suite 101* ▪
*American* ▪ A variety of GF options on
the breakfast, lunch and dinner menus.
Options include blueberry pancakes,
fried egg sandwich, lentil walnut pate,

glory meatloaf and more. Many items on
the menu are GF and all GF options are
indicated on menu, as well as GF desserts. ▪
*www.morningglorycafe.org*

### Nick-N-Willy's       ★ 📖
*Loveland* ▪ *(970) 613-1007*
*1433 Denver Ave*
*Broomfield* ▪ *(303) 465-6000*
*3700 W 144th Ave*
*Silverthorne* ▪ *(970) 262-1111*
*277 Summit Pl*
*Grand Junction* ▪ *(970) 245-6425*
*683 Horizon Dr*
*Arvada* ▪ *(303) 467-2700*
*15200 W 64th Ave*
*Castle Pines* ▪ *(303) 660-8090*
*7284 Lagae Rd*

### Nicolo's Pizza       ✪ ★ $LD
*Longmont* ▪ *(303) 651-2335*
*1631 Pace St*
*Castle Rock* ▪ *(303) 688-9800*
*848 Ridge Rd*
*Highlands Ranch* ▪ *(303) 791-9800*
*9346 S University Blvd*
*Lakewood* ▪ *(303) 969-9000*
*7847 W Jewell Ave* ▪ *Pizza* ▪ GF pizza
is available at the listed locations only. ▪
*www.nicolospizza.com*

### Old Stone Church Restaurant   ✪ $$$LD
*Castle Rock* ▪ *(303) 688-9000*
*210 3rd St* ▪ *Fusion* ▪ GF items are marked
on the menu and include blackened tuna,
pulled pork lettuce wraps, grilled Australian seabass, grilled pork tenderloin,
commander's pasta, grilled brie cheese,
shirimp enichiladas and more. Some items
may require modification to become GF.
Be sure to alert your server of your dietary
needs. ▪ *www.oscrestaurant.com*

### Original Pizza       ★
*Broomfield* ▪ *(303) 469-9117*
*1300 W Midway Blvd* ▪ *Pizza* ▪ GF pizza is
available. ▪ *www.originalpizza.us*

### P.F. Chang's China Bistro       ✪ ★ 📖
*Aurora* ▪ *(303) 627-5450*
*23902 E Prospect Ave*

Broomfield ■ (720) 887-6200
1 Flatiron Cir Ste 500 Bldg 5
Lakewood ■ (303) 922-5800
7210 W Alameda Ave
Littleton ■ (303) 790-7744
8315 Park Meadows Center Dr
Loveland ■ (970) 622-9313
5915 Sky Pond Dr

### Pasta Jays                                  ★
Lone Tree ■ (303) 799-1800
9226 Park Meadows Dr ■ Italian ■ GF pizza
is available in the small size, as well as GF
pasta. Staff reports that GF pizzas are prepared in a separate area and cooked on a separate stone to reduce the chance of CC. Selection changes daily so be sure to call ahead to
confirm availability. ■ www.pastajays.com

### Pei Wei Asian Diner                        ✪▢
Highlands Ranch ■ (303) 346-4329
9352 S Colorado Blvd
Lakewood ■ (303) 215-1933
14255 W Colfax Ave

### Pietra's Pizzeria                          ★$LD
Wheat Ridge ■ (303) 421-4100
9045 W 44th Ave ■ Pizza ■ GF pizza is
available. ■ www.pietraspizza.com

### Poppy's Pizza & Grill                      ★$$LD
Estes Park ■ (970) 586-8282
342 E Elkhorn Ave ■ Pizza ■ The restaurant reports that GF diners can order
pizza with zucchini crust. They also note
that the kitchen can modify most regular
menu items to be GF. The staff is reportedly "well-educated" on the GF diet. Alert
a server, who will notify the kitchen. ■
www.poppyspizzaandgrill.com

### Posh Pastries Gourmet Bakery              ✪★₵$
Parker ■ (303) 840-1251
10471 S Parker Rd ■ Bakery ■ Non-
dedicated bakery offering a variety of
GF baked goods, including GF quiches,
pies, angel food cakes, and petits fours.
Orders for specific items should be
placed at least 48 hours in advance. ■
www.poshpastriesbakery.com

### Rheinlander Bakery                         ★₵$
Arvada ■ (303) 467-1810
5721 Olde Wadsworth Blvd ■ Bakery
■ Non-dedicated bakery offering an
entire line of GF products, including cakes, cupcakes, and pastries. They
also sell GF cake mixes to take home. ■
www.rheinlanderbakery.com

### Romano's Macaroni Grill                    ✪★▢
Aurora ■ (303) 364-0249
14241 E Alameda Ave
Broomfield ■ (303) 439-9333
10411 Town Center
Greenwood Village ■ (303) 220-7866
7979 E Arapahoe Rd
Lakewood ■ (303) 215-1519
14245 W Colfax Ave
Littleton ■ (303) 904-9495
8156 W Bowles Ave

### Rosati's Pizza                             ★▢
Westminster ■ (303) 464-7477
9960 Wadsworth Pkwy
Westminster ■ (303) 920-3636
12910 N Zuni St

### Sansone's Bistro                           ✪$$$D
Greenwood Village ■ (303) 794-4026
5969 S University Blvd ■ European ■ GF
menu available. Items include mussels
Provence, French brie, beef carpaccio, sautéed escargot, trout or chicken vera cruz,
stuffed eggplant, South African style lamb
chops, veal liver, grilled NY steak, crispy
duck and veal or chicken anjou. All items
indicate changes that make the dish GF. ■
www.sansonesbistro.com

### Santeramo's                                ★$LD
Greeley ■ (970) 353-4844
1229 10th Ave ■ Italian ■ GF pizza is available. ■ www.santeramos.com

### Smiling Moose Deli                         ✪▢
Edwards ■ (970) 926-2400
1170 Edwards Village Blvd
Silverthorne ■ (970) 513-1414
273 Summit Pl
Frisco ■ (970) 668-3420
842 Summit Blvd

*Westminster* ▪ *(303) 254-7779*
*1005 W 120th Ave*
*Louisville* ▪ *(303) 604-9960*
*459 S McCaslin Blvd*
*Arvada* ▪ *(303) 467-3354*
*5324 Wadsworth Blvd*
*Centennial* ▪ *(303) 790-4877*
*11001 E Arapahoe Pl*
*Erie* ▪ *(303) 665-3354*
*3336 Arapahoe Pl*
*Evergreen* ▪ *(303) 526-0374*
*29017 Hotel Wy*

### Stage Coach Inn    ✪★$$$LD
*Manitou Springs* ▪ *(719) 685-9400*
*702 Manitou Ave* ▪ *American* ▪ GF menu
includes black bean chili, BBQ baby back
ribs, sirloin steak, roasted turkey, and
more. GF buns for burgers and sandwiches are available. GF beer is available. ▪
*www.stagecoachinn.com*

### Sun Rose Café    ✪★$BLD
*Longmont* ▪ *(303) 651-3533*
*379 Main St* ▪ *Café* ▪ Extensive GF breakfast and lunch menus include a variety of
omelets and scrambles, paninis made on
GF flat bread, and deli sandwiches made
on GF hoagie rolls, as well as several salad
selections. GF items are prepared in a separate area in the kitchen, and staff reports
that they are "very careful" about CC. ▪
*www.sunrosecafe.com*

### Tavern, The    $LD
*Estes Park* ▪ *(970) 586-5958*
*2625 Marys Lake Rd* ▪ *American* ▪ Noting
GF when making reservations is recommended so that the kitchen staff can prepare in advance. Many items on the menu
can be prepared GF. Alert the server upon
arrival. ▪ *www.maryslakelodge.com*

### Ted's Montana Grill    ✪📖
*Aurora* ▪ *(720) 374-7220*
*16495 E 40th Cir*
*Aurora* ▪ *(720) 870-4470*
*6105 S Main St*
*Lakewood* ▪ *(303) 922-7770*
*330 S Teller St*

*Westminster* ▪ *(303) 410-8337*
*11950 Bradburn Blvd*
*Greenwood Village* ▪ *(303) 771-3038*
*5370 Greenwood Pza Blvd*
*Littleton* ▪ *(720) 283-2303*
*7301 S Santa Fe Dr*

### Tokyo Joe's    ✪📖
*Aurora* ▪ *(303) 627-5485*
*23955 E Plaza Ave*
*Aurora* ▪ *(720) 214-2455*
*6775 S Cornerstar Wy*
*Centennial* ▪ *(303) 656-4392*
*6879 S Vine St*
*Centennial* ▪ *(720) 873-6641*
*8225 S Chester St*
*Centennial* ▪ *(303) 721-8886*
*8727 E Dry Creek Rd*
*Englewood* ▪ *(303) 806-0112*
*901 W Hampden Ave*
*Glendale* ▪ *(303) 524-3462*
*1000 S Colorado Blvd*
*Greenwood Village* ▪ *(303) 804-0988*
*4950 S Yosemite St*
*Highlands Ranch* ▪ *(303) 683-8217*
*6642 Timberline Rd*
*Highlands Ranch* ▪ *(303) 791-9222*
*9131 S Broadway*
*Lakewood* ▪ *(303) 273-5363*
*14227 W Colfax Ave*
*Lakewood* ▪ *(303) 988-1176*
*145 Union Blvd*
*Littleton* ▪ *(303) 904-9201*
*8501 W Bowles Ave*
*Louisville* ▪ *(303) 926-7100*
*1116 W Dillon Rd*
*Westminster* ▪ *(303) 255-4828*
*1005 W 120th Ave*
*Aurora* ▪ *(720) 121-3058*
*2320 S Parker Rd*
*Arvada* ▪ *(303) 928-8725*
*8770 Wadsworth Blvd*
*Greenwood Village* ▪ *(303) 220-2877*
*6380 S Fiddlers Green Cir*
*Aurora* ▪ *(720) 974-9364*
*13950 E Mississippi Ave*

**True Food Kitchen**                    ✪★⌂
*Newport Beach* ▪ *(949) 644-2400*
*451 Newport Center Dr*

**Union - An American Bistro**      ★$$LD
*Castle Rock* ▪ *(303) 688-8159*
*3 S Wilcox St* ▪ *American* ▪ Although nothing is noted online, the staff states they will make any accommodation necessary to serve their customers. Alert a staff member upon arrival and they will list everything that is either GF naturally or can be prepared so. ▪ *unionamericanbistro.com*

**Via Toscana**                          ✪★$$D
*Louisville* ▪ *(303) 604-6960*
*356 S McCaslin Blvd* ▪ *Italian* ▪ GF menu available. Items include scampi toscana, chicken marsala, cioppino, trout rubino, wild mushroom risotto, king salmon, pork loin milanese, and veal saltimbocca. Alert server that you are eating GF so accommodations can be made for menu. ▪ *www.viatoscana.com*

**White Chocolate Grill, The**      ✪$$LD
*Lone Tree* ▪ *(303) 799-4841*
*8421 Park Meadows Center Dr* ▪ *Modern American* ▪ GF menu includes grilled artichokes and tomato gin soup, among other things, as appetizers. As entrées, it lists a bunless cheeseburger, BBQ baby back ribs, center cut filet, New York strip, balsamic ribeye and more. For dessert, it offers a silky chocolate soufflé cake ▪ *www.whitechocolategrill.com*

**Yard House**                          ✪⌂
*Lakewood* ▪ *(303) 278-9273*
*14500 W Colfax Ave Unit 341*
*Lone Tree* ▪ *(303) 790-7453*
*8437 Park Meadows Center Dr*

**Zpizza**                              ✪⌂
*Greenwood Village* ▪ *(303) 221-0015*
*4940 S Yosemite St*

# CONNECTICUT

**Abate Apizza and Seafood Restaurant**
★$LD
*New Haven* ▪ *(203) 776-4334*
*129 Wooster St* ▪ *Pizza* ▪ Small size GF pizza, calzones and beer are available in addition to various meat and seafood options. ▪ *abate-restaurant.com*

**Amore Baking Company**              ★¢S
*Fairfield* ▪ *(203) 292-8475*
*1215 Post Rd* ▪ *Bakery* ▪ A small selection of GF specialty breads and cookies are available. ▪ *amorebakingco.com*

**Apizza Pie**                          ★$$LD
*Norwalk* ▪ *(203) 642-3262*
*4 New Canaan Ave* ▪ *Pizza* ▪ GF pizza, pastas, and paninis are available. Owner Mike notes that the kitchen is very GF aware.

**Au Bon Pain**                          ⌂
*Hartford* ▪ *(860) 728-8793*
*185 Asylum St*
*Hartford* ▪ *(860) 241-8260*
*80 Seymour St*
*Hartford* ▪ *(860) 241-8980*
*114 Woodland St*
*Farmington* ▪ *(860) 521-5319*
*500 Westfarms Mall*
*New Haven* ▪ *(203) 865-5554*
*One Broadway*

**Bartaco**                              ✪$LD
*Stamford* ▪ *(203) 323-8226*
*222 Summer St*
*W Hartford* ▪ *(860) 586-8226*
*971 Farmington Ave* ▪ *Mexican* ▪ Director of marketing Ria reports that they are "90% GF" and use separate fryers as well as gloves when preparing GF items. The menu features a variety of specialty tacos, including lamb barbacoa, portobello with queso fresco, and Thai shrimp, as well as salads, rice bowls, tamales, ceviche, and more. The 3 non-GF

items are clearly marked on the menu. Alert server upon arrival. ■ *www.bartaco.com*

### Basil's Pizza & Catering　★$$LD
*Shelton* ■ *(203) 926-6848*
*725 Bridgeport Ave* ■ *Pizza* ■ GF pizza only available in 9". GF pizza is baked on a raised screen and does not touch the oven surface where non-GF pizza is baked. Confirm the timeliness of this information before dining in. ■ *www.basilspizzaandcatering.com*

### Bella Napoli　★$$LD
*Milford* ■ *(203) 877-1102*
*864 Boston Post Rd*
*Stratford* ■ *(203) 375-7700*
*1112 Barnum Ave* ■ *Pizza* ■ GF pizza is available in the small size. ■ *www.bellanapolionline.com*

### Bertucci's　✪▭
*Avon* ■ *(860) 676-1177*
*380 W Main St*
*Danbury* ■ *(203) 739-0500*
*98 Newtown Rd*
*Darien* ■ *(203) 655-4299*
*54 Post Rd*
*Glastonbury* ■ *(860) 633-2225*
*2882 Main St*
*Manchester* ■ *(860) 648-0730*
*194 Buckland Hills Dr*
*Newington* ■ *(860) 666-1949*
*2929 Berlin Tpke*
*Orange* ■ *(203) 799-6828*
*550 Boston Post Rd*
*Shelton* ■ *(203) 926-6058*
*768 Bridgeport Ave*
*Waterbury* ■ *(203) 755-6224*
*495 Union St*
*West Hartford* ■ *(860) 231-9571*
*330 N Main St*
*Westport* ■ *(203) 454-1559*
*833 Post Rd E*
*Southington* ■ *(860) 621-8626*
*20 Spring St*

### Bloodroot Vegetarian Restaurant　$$LD
*Bridgeport* ■ *(203) 576-9168*
*85 Ferris St* ■ *Vegetarian* ■ The restaurant reports that GF options are "mostly rice dishes" and are all marked on the regular menu. ■ *www.bloodroot.com*

### Bobby's Apizza Restaurant　★$$LD
*North Branford* ■ *(203) 484-0773*
*1179 Foxon Rd* ■ *Pizza* ■ GF pizza is available in the small size only.

### Boston's Restaurant & Sports Bar　✪★▭
*Manchester* ■ *(860) 648-4490*
*1436 Pleasant Valley Rd*

### Burtons Grill　✪★▭
*South Windsor* ■ *(860) 432-4575*
*100 Evergreen Wy*

### Café Romeo　✪★$$BLD
*New Haven* ■ *(203) 865-2233*
*534 Orange St* ■ *Café* ■ GF menu includes pasta salad, pizzas, prosciutto salad, prosciutto frittata, sausage frittata, tofu scramble, three bean salad, soups and more. ■ *www.cafe-romeo.com*

### Capital Grille, The　✪▭
*Stamford* ■ *(203) 967-0000*
*230 Tresser Blvd*

### Carl Anthony Trattoria　★$$LD
*Monroe* ■ *(203) 268-8486*
*477 Main St* ■ *Italian* ■ GF pizza and pasta are available. Restaurant notes that the staff was recently trained on accommodating GF diners. ■ *www.carlanthonys.com*

### Carrabba's Italian Grill　✪▭
*Manchester* ■ *(860) 643-4100*
*31 Redstone Rd*

### Chuck and Augie's Restaurant　✪★$LD
*Storrs Mansfield* ■ *(860) 486-5633*
*2110 Hillside Rd* ■ *American* ■ GF menu includes sandwiches and paninis on GF bread, nachos, artichoke dip, Caribbean and honey dijon chicken salads with GF dressings, shrimp scampi with GF pasta, and more. GF bread, hamburger buns, pasta, soy sauce, and brownies are available. Strict CC policy in place. Located in the student union building on the campus of the University of Connecticut. ■ *www.chuckandaugies.uconn.edu*

## Claire's Corner Copia ✪★⊄BLD
*New Haven* ▪ (203) 562-3888
*1000 Chapel St* ▪ *Vegetarian* ▪ GF menu includes stir fries and curries over brown rice, huevos rancheros, enchiladas, and quesadillas. Directions for ordering dishes GF are included on the GF menu. Owner Claire says "we have you covered" and reports that they "serve Celiac customers all the time." GF bread and desserts are always available. Be sure to alert a server that your meal must be GF. ▪ *www.clairescornercopia.com*

## Cosi ✪📖
*West Hartford* ▪ (860) 521-8495
*970 Farmington Ave*
*Avon* ▪ (860) 678-8989
*385 W Main St*
*Stamford* ▪ (203) 595-9350
*1209 High Ridge Rd*
*Stamford* ▪ (203) 324-8981
*230 Tresser Blvd*
*Greenwich* ▪ (203) 861-2373
*129 W Putnam Ave*

## Cugino's Restaurant ★$$$LD
*Farmington* ▪ (860) 678-9366
*1053 Farmington Ave* ▪ *Italian* ▪ The restaurant reports that the staff and chef are willing to accommodate GF diners. GF pasta is available and can be substituted into most pasta dishes. ▪ *www.cuginosrestaurantfarmington.com*

## Davinci's Pizza ★$$LD
*Norwalk* ▪ (203) 853-1111
*60 Connecticut Ave* ▪ *Pizza* ▪ GF pizza crust is available upon request. ▪ *davincispizzanorwalk.com*

## Dee's One Smart Cookie ⊄S
*Glastonbury* ▪ (860) 633-8000
*398 Hebron Ave* ▪ *Bakery* ▪ Dedicated GF bakery offering muffins, bars, whoopie pies, tarts, and truffles, as well as frozen pasta, pizza, and flatbreads. Owner Dee reports that special orders can be accommodated with advance notice of one week. ▪ *www.deesonesmartcookie.com*

## Divine Treasures ★$$$$$
*Manchester* ▪ (860) 643-2552
*404 Middle Turnpike W* ▪ *Dessert* ▪ A variety of GF cookies, chocolates, and other dessert items are available. Call ahead to confirm availability. ▪ *www.dtchocolates.com*

## Edge of the Woods ★⊄S
*New Haven* ▪ (203) 787-1055
*379 Whalley Ave* ▪ *Bakery* ▪ GF chocolate crème bars and slices of GF almond buckwheat cake are almost always available at the bakery. Entire GF cakes can be ordered 48 hours in advance. ▪ *www.eotwm.com*

## Eggs Up Grill ✪★⊄BL
*Portland* ▪ (860) 342-4968
*1462 Portland Cobalt Rd* ▪ *European* ▪ Extensive GF breakfast menu includes omelets, egg sandwiches on GF rolls, GF muffins, fresh fruit, and more. GF bread can be used for sandwiches at lunch. ▪ *eggsup.icuinternet.com*

## Elephant Trail, The ★$LD
*Avon* ▪ (860) 677-0065
*39 E Main St* ▪ *Thai* ▪ GF soy sauce is available. Restaurant reports that nearly all dishes can be modified to be GF. ▪ *www.theelephanttrail.com*

## Elizabeth's Bar & Restaurant $$D
*Rocky Hill* ▪ (860) 721-6932
*825 Cromwell Ave* ▪ *Italian* ▪ The restaurant reports that nearly all entrées can be prepared GF aside from the sandwiches, and even those can be prepared without the bread. Alert the server upon arrival. ▪ *www.lizrestaurant.com*

## Engine No 6 Pizza Co ★$LD
*Norwich* ▪ (860) 887-3887
*195 W Thames St* ▪ *Pizza* ▪ GF pizza, pasta, lasagna, calzones, and breadsticks are available. The restaurant reports that they have extensive procedures to mitigate CC, including using a dedicated mixer, baking on dedicated screens, and using separate utensils and surfaces for GF pizzas. ▪ *www.engineno6pizza.com*

## Famous Pizza ★ $LD
*Bethel* ■ *(203) 797-1550*
*1 PT Barnum Sq* ■ *Pizza* ■ GF pizza is available. Thursdays are "Gluten-Free Thursdays," and customers can buy GF pizzas at a discounted price. Confirm the timeliness of this information before dining in. ■ *www.famouspizzabethel.com*

## Fitzgerald's Pizza ✪★ $LD
*Simsbury* ■ *(860) 658-1210*
*710 Hopmeadow St* ■ *Pizza* ■ GF pizza is available in 14" only. Restaurant recommends ordering 20-25 minutes in advance for preparation. They note that all toppings except the chicken, eggplant, and meatballs are GF. Located within Fitzgerald's Foods. ■ *www.fitzgeraldsfoods.com*

## Flatbread Pizza Company ★▢
*Canton* ■ *(860) 693-3314*
*110 Albany Tpke*

## Fleming's Prime Steakhouse & Wine Bar ✪▢
*Wt Hartford* ■ *(860) 676-9463*
*44 S Main St*

## Foodworks ★ ¢BLD
*Guilford* ■ *(203) 458-9778*
*450 Boston Post Rd*
*Old Saybrook* ■ *(860) 395-0770*
*17 Main St*
*Monroe* ■ *(203) 452-9500*
*477 Main St* ■ *Deli* ■ GF bread is available for sandwiches at the Guilford location. Muffins and other baked goods, as well as frozen foods, are available at both locations. The Guilford location has a deli and bakery that supplies the Old Saybrook location with GF goods. ■ *www.food-works.org*

## Fountain of Youth ★ ¢S
*Westport* ■ *(203) 259-9378*
*1789 Post Rd E* ■ *Bakery* ■ The bakery carries a wide selection of GF baked goods, including cookies, cupcakes, and specialty breads. ■ *www.fountainofyouthwholefoods.com*

## Fratelli Market ✪★ $S
*Stamford* ■ *(203) 322-1632*
*17 Cedar Heights Rd* ■ *Take-&-Bake* ■ Fresh GF pastas, raviolis, tortellinis, gnocchi, pizza, microwave meals, croutons, cake mixes, bagels and more are available. ■ *www.fratellimarketct.com*

## Fresh City ★▢
*Windson Locks* ■ *(860) 292-1580*
*Term A Schopoester Rd*

## Georgie's Diner ✪★ $BLD
*West Haven* ■ *(203) 933-1000*
*427 Elm St* ■ *American* ■ Extensive GF menu features breakfast, lunch, and dinner options. Examples include eggs benedict, French toast, a variety of burgers and sandwiches, Waldorf salad, grilled tuna, pork chops, and more. GF pancakes, pasta, bread, and rolls are available. ■ *www.georgies-diner.com*

## Giove's Pizza Kitchen ★ $LD
*Fairfield* ■ *(203) 254-3772*
*246 Post Rd*
*Shelton* ■ *(203) 225-6000*
*494 Bridgeport Ave* ■ *Pizza* ■ GF pizza is available at listed locations only, upon request. ■ *www.giovespizzakitchen.com*

## Grants Restaurant & Bar $$$LD
*West Hartford* ■ *(860) 236-1930*
*977 Farmington Ave* ■ *Modern American* ■ Manager Grant reports that the executive chef has Celiac, so the restaurant is "fully aware" of GF "issues." Almost every item on the regular menu can be modified to be GF. He recommends making reservations noting GF and reminding a server upon arrival. ■ *www.billygrant.com*

## Hard Rock Café ✪▢
*Mashantucket* ■ *(860) 312-7625*
*350 Trolley Line Blvd*

## Illiano's Restaurant-Pizzeria ✪★ $$LD
*Middletown* ■ *(860) 343-9244*
*534 Washington St*
*Meriden* ■ *(203) 634-4000*
*510 W Main St*

*New London* ▪ (860) 447-9390
*929 Bank St*
*Norwich* ▪ (860) 889-6163
*257 W Town St*
*Waterford* ▪ (860) 437-1999
*709 Broad St Ext*
*Niantic* ▪ (860) 739-7017
*228 Flanders Rd*
*Colchester* ▪ (860) 537-4434
*119 S Main St*
*Old Lyme* ▪ (860) 434-1110
*163 Boston Post Rd*
*Meriden* ▪ (203) 634-4000
*510 W Main St*
*Middletown* ▪ (860) 346-5656
*404 S Main St* ▪ *Italian* ▪ GF pizza and GF Redbridge beer are available. Manager Cruse reports that there is a wide variety of GF toppings. The pizza is prepared in a completely separate room but the pizzas are baked in the same oven with a screen. ▪ *www.illianospizza.com*

### It's Only Natural ✪★$$LD
*Middletown* ▪ (860) 346-9210
*386 Main St* ▪ *Vegetarian* ▪ GF menu includes pizzas, vegetarian burgers, bread and buns for sandwiches and rice plates. GF pizza, bread, and hamburger buns are available. ▪ *www.ionrestaurant.com*

### Izzi B's Allergen-Free Cupcakes $$$
*Norwalk* ▪ (203) 810-4378
*22 Knight St* ▪ *Bakery* ▪ Dedicated GF cupcake and cake bakery offering flavors such as chocolate chip, cinnamon French toast, and golden yellow. Hours are by appointment only, and special orders can be picked up, hand delivered, or shipped. ▪ *www.ibcakes.com*

### Jean-Louis $$$$LD
*Greenwich* ▪ (203) 622-8450
*61 Lewis St* ▪ *French* ▪ Owner and Chef Jean-Louis Gerin recommends reservations noting GF. Chefs and managers are trained on the GF diet, and they will be happy to accommodate their guests. A possible meal consists of the endive and caviar salad, the red snapper steamed with ginger, and the chocolate mousse. ▪ *www.restaurantjeanlouis.com*

### Jersey Mike's 📖
*Branford* ▪ (203) 481-8050
*845 W Main St*

### Jessica Tuesday's ★CBL
*Putnam* ▪ (860) 928-5118
*35 Main St* ▪ *American* ▪ The restaurant reports that many of their soups are GF, and they also carry GF rolls which can be used for any sandwich on the menu. Confirm the timeliness of this information before dining in. ▪ *jessicatuesdays.com*

### Joe's Pizzeria ★$$LD
*New Canaan* ▪ (203) 966-2226
*23 Locust Ave* ▪ *Pizza* ▪ GF pizzas and pastas are available.

### John's Best Pizza & Grille ★$LD
*Westport* ▪ (203) 227-7247
*361 Post Rd W* ▪ *Italian* ▪ GF pizza, pasta, cookies, and beer are available. Manager Isho notes that GF diners are "a regular occurrence" at the restaurant. ▪ *johnsbestpizzawestport.vpweb.com*

### Jordan's Restaurant & Pizza ★$LD
*Westport* ▪ (203) 259-2299
*1759 Post Rd E*
*Norwalk* ▪ (203) 852-0003
*252 Flax Hill Rd*
*Norwalk* ▪ (203) 846-9557
*369 Westport Ave* ▪ *Mediterranean* ▪ GF pizza is available in the 10" size. ▪ *www.jordansrestaurants.com*

### La Piastra ✪★$LD
*Cromwell* ▪ (860) 632-7528
*25 Shunpike Rd* ▪ *Italian* ▪ Sample GF menu includes salads, soups, pasta, ravioli, and a variety of entrées. GF cookies and truffles are available for dessert. Owner Lauren notes that the shop also offers several GF specials each month. Meals are available for carry-out only. ▪ *www.lapiastra.com*

### La Rosticceria　　　　✪★₵$
*Guilford* ■ *(203) 458-8885*
*500 Village Walk* ■ *Deli* ■ GF soups and salads such as legume brown rice and tofu casserole, steak salad, and chicken salad are available. GF carrot cupcakes with cream cheese frosting are also available. ■ *www.guilfordtakeout.com*

### Luigi's Apizza　　　　★$LD
*North Haven* ■ *(203) 234-9666*
*323 Washington Ave* ■ *Pizza* ■ GF pizza and beer are available. ■ *www.luigisapizza.com*

### Lyman Orchards Apple Barrel　★₵BL
*Middlefield* ■ *(860) 349-1793*
*Rtes 147 & 157* ■ *American* ■ The "eatery" serves breakfast on Saturdays and Sundays only. GF breakfast includes a wide variety of omelets. Confirm the timeliness of this information before dining in. Chef George suggests asking for him upon arrival or calling in advance to give him or the chef on duty time to prepare. GF cookies are available from the bakery. ■ *www.lymanorchards.com*

### Mangetout Organic Café　✪★₵BL
*New London* ■ *(860) 444-2066*
*140 State St* ■ *Café* ■ GF items are marked on the menu and include frittatas, salads, and sandwiches & wraps without the bread. For dessert, there is chocolate tofu pudding, GF cookies, and GF crisp bars. Confirm the timeliness of this information before dining in. ■ *www.mangetoutorganic.com*

### Margaritaville　　　　✪★📖
*Uncasville* ■ *(860) 862-2626*
*1 Mohegan Sun Blvd*

### Mario's Brick Oven Pizza　★$LD
*Waterbury* ■ *(203) 575-0485*
*1650 Watertown Ave* ■ *Pizza* ■ GF pizza crust is available upon request. Separate preparation area and cooking surface is used in order to prevent Cross Contamination. ■ *www.mariosbrickovenpizza.com*

### Max A Mia　　　　✪★$$$L
*Avon* ■ *(860) 677-6299*
*70 E Main St* ■ *Italian* ■ GF menu includes mussels with chorizo sausage, monkfish marsala, veal piccata, wood-fired half chicken, and more. GF pasta is available, and GF pasta options are listed on the GF menu. ■ *www.maxrestaurantgroup.com*

### Max Amore　　　　✪★$$$LD
*Glastonbury* ■ *(860) 659-2819*
*140 Glastonbury Blvd* ■ *Italian* ■ GF menu includes salads with GF croutons, seared sea scallops, breadless chicken parmagiana, wood grilled NY strip, and more. GF pizza, pasta, and bread are available. ■ *www.maxrestaurantgroup.com*

### Max Burger　　　　★$$LD
*West Hartford* ■ *(860) 232-3300*
*124 Lasalle Rd* ■ *Deli* ■ GF beer and hamburger buns are available. Restaurant reports that all servers are trained in the GF diet. ■ *www.maxrestaurantgroup.comburger/*

### Max Downtown　　　　✪$$$$LD
*Hartford* ■ *(860) 522-2530*
*185 Asylum St* ■ *Modern American* ■ GF menu includes zinfandel marinated skirt steak, pan seared sea scallops & shrimp, roasted chicken, a variety of "chophouse classics," and more. Menu specifies which chophouse sauces are GF. For dessert, there is flourless chocolate cake, crème brûlée, and ice cream or sorbet. GF dinner rolls, beer, and cider are available. ■ *www.maxrestaurantgroup.com*

### Max's Oyster Bar　　　✪$$$LD
*W Hartford* ■ *(860) 236-6299*
*964 Farmington Ave* ■ *Seafood* ■ GF menu includes shellfish, sashimi plates, grilled fish with brown rice and root vegetables, steak, and lobster. ■ *www.maxrestaurantgroup.com*

### Melting Pot, The　　　　✪📖
*Darien* ■ *(203) 656-4774*
*14 Grove St*

**Mitchell's Fish Market**          ✪📖
*Stamford* ▪ *(203) 323-3474*
*230 Tresser Blvd*

**Morton's Steakhouse**             ✪📖
*Hartford* ▪ *(860) 724-0044*
*30 State House Sq*
*Stamford* ▪ *(203) 324-3939*
*377 N State St*

**Naples Pizza**                    ★$LD
*Farmington* ▪ *(860) 674-8876*
*838 Farmington Ave* ▪ *Pizza* ▪ GF pizza
is available, limited to the small size only.
Restaurant reports that requests for GF
pizza are "common" and that all GF pizzas
are cooked carefully in order to prevent
CC. ▪ *www.naplespizzact.com*

**Nature's Grocer**                 ✪¢BLD
*Vernon* ▪ *(860) 870-0020*
*81 East St* ▪ *Bakery & Café* ▪ All products
baked on the premises are GF. Non-GF
items like wraps, which are brought in
from outside, are prepared on separate
surfaces. GF muffins, cookies, brownies,
and more are available. GF cakes are
available for order. Café also houses a
grocery store with many GF options. ▪
*www.naturesgrocervernon.com*

**New Morning Natural and Organic** ★¢S
*Woodbury* ▪ *(203) 263-4868*
*738 Main St S* ▪ *Bakery & Café* ▪ GF
scones, brownies, and blondies are
sometimes available at the deli. Restaurant
notes that if customers buy a loaf of GF
bread in the store, the deli will make a
sandwich on it at a discounted price. ▪
*www.newmorn.com*

**Ninety Nine**                     ✪📖
*Dayville* ▪ *(860) 774-3399*
*1068 Killingly Commons Dr*
*Glastonbury* ▪ *(860) 652-9699*
*3025 Main St*
*Cromwell* ▪ *(860) 632-2099*
*36 Shunpike Rd*
*Bristol* ▪ *(860) 314-9900*
*827 Pine St*
*Wallingford* ▪ *(203) 284-9989*

*914 N Colony Rd*
*Enfield* ▪ *(860) 741-7499*
*54 Hazard Ave*
*Torrington* ▪ *(860) 489-1299*
*1 S Main St*
*Vernon* ▪ *(860) 872-1199*
*295 Hartford Tpke*
*Norwich* ▪ *(860) 892-1299*
*5 Salem Tpke*
*Groton* ▪ *(860) 449-9900*
*117 Long Hill Rd*
*Stratford* ▪ *(203) 378-9997*
*411 Barnum Ave Cutoff*

**Olde World Apizza**               ★$LD
*North Haven* ▪ *(203) 287-8820*
*1957 Whitney Ave* ▪ *Pizza* ▪ GF pizza
is available in the small size with
most toppings. Some toppings may
contain gluten, so be sure to ask your
server which toppings are safe. ▪
*www.oldeworldapizza.com*

**P.F. Chang's China Bistro**       ✪★📖
*Farmington* ▪ *(860) 561-0097*
*322 Westfarms Mall Spc F226*
*Stamford* ▪ *(203) 363-0434*
*230 Tresser Blvd Ste H007*

**Palmieri's Pizza**                ★$LD
*Putnam* ▪ *(860) 928-1010*
*235 Kennedy Dr* ▪ *Pizza* ▪ GF pizza is available in the 12-inch size. GF wraps are also
available. ▪ *palmierispizza.com*

**Paperback Café,**
**Coffee House & Eatery**           ✪★¢B
*Old Saybrook* ▪ *(860) 388-9718*
*210 Main St* ▪ *American* ▪ GF menu
includes an open cranberry chicken
sandwich on a GF english muffin, an open
tuna sandwich on a GF english muffin,
mixed vegetables with marinara and
parmesan over GF toast, pesto pizza, GF
deli sandwiches, and more.

**Penny Lane Pub**                  $$$LD
*Old Saybrook* ▪ *(860) 388-9646*
*150 Main St* ▪ *American* ▪ Restaurant
notes that it can accommodate GF diners.
They note that salads, some fish dishes,

and vegetable sides are naturally GF, as well as burgers ordered without the bun. Some other menu items can be modified to be GF. Alert a server upon arrival. ■ *www.pennylanepub.net*

### Piccolo Pizza & Jazzeria ✪★$$LD
*Ridgefield* ■ (203) 438-8200
*24 Prospect St* ■ *Pizza* ■ GF pizza is available in the 12-inch size, and rice pasta is available for substitution into any of the regular pasta dishes. ■ *www.piccolopizzeria.com*

### Pizza Pie, A ✪★$$LD
*Norwalk* ■ (203) 642-3260
*4 New Canaan Ave* ■ *Italian* ■ GF menu includes spinach and cheese ravioli, pizzas with any toppings (except meatballs) and several paninis. Restaurant notes that they serve GF customers regularly. GF pizza, bread, and pastas are also available. Be sure to mention GF when placing an order.

### Pizzetta ★$LD
*Mystic* ■ (860) 536-4443
*7 Water St* ■ *Pizza* ■ GF pizza and beer are available. The restaurant reports that separate prep items are used for GF pizzas. ■ *www.pizzettamystic.com*

### Port Coffeehouse ★¢BL
*Bridgeport* ■ (203) 345-8885
*2889 Fairfield Ave* ■ *Coffee Shop* ■ GF baked goods, including cookies, cupcakes, and specialty breads, are available. ■ *www.portcoffeehouse.com*

### Quattro Pazzi ★$$$LD
*Fairfield* ■ (203) 259-7417
*1599 Post Rd*
*Stamford* ■ (203) 324-7000
*269 Bedford St*
*Norwalk* ■ (203) 855-1800
*165 Fillow St* ■ *Italian* ■ An assortment of GF pastas including cavatelli, penne, fettuccine, and farfalle are available daily. As with all specialty items, call head to confirm availability. ■ *www.quattropazzi.com*

### Rizzuto's ★$$LD
*Bethel* ■ (203) 790-4444
*6 Stony Hill Rd*
*West Hartford* ■ (860) 232-5000
*111 Memorial Rd*
*Westport* ■ (203) 221-1002
*540 Riverside Ave*
*Stamford* ■ (203) 324-5900
*1980 W Main St* ■ *Italian* ■ GF pasta and pizza are available. *www.rizzutos.com*

### Rodizio Grill ★🕮
*Stamford* ■ (203) 964-9177
*5 Broad St*

### Rowayton Pizza ★$$LD
*Rowayton* ■ (203) 853-7555
*104 Rowayton Ave* ■ *Pizza* ■ GF items are available upon request.

### Ruth's Chris Steak House ✪🕮
*Newington* ■ (860) 666-2202
*2513 Berlin Tpke*

### Shoreline Diner & Vegetarian Enclave ✪★$$BLD
*Guilford* ■ (203) 458-7380
*345 Boston Post Rd* ■ *Global* ■ Extensive GF menu includes breakfast, lunch, and dinner items. Examples include buckwheat pancakes, omelettes, sandwiches, burgers, curried chickpea & quinoa pilaf, NY steak, grilled salmon filet, and more. GF pasta, sandwich buns, and bread are available. For dessert, they offer GF cheesecake, caramel flan, rice pudding, and ice cream sundaes. ■ *www.shorelinediner.com*

### Sweet Harmony Café & Bakery ¢L
*Middletown* ■ (860) 344-9646
*158 Broad St* ■ *Bakery & Café* ■ The restaurant reports that all salads are GF and they "try to have a GF dessert on hand" every day. Additionally, the staff recommends asking the server for other GF options that may be available, as the menu changes frequently. ■ *www.sweetharmonycafebakery.com*

## Sweet Spot, The    ★ ⊂S
*New Milford* ▪ *(860) 799-7170*
*60 Railroad St* ▪ *Bakery* ▪ Non-dedicated bakery that "keeps at least one GF item available" daily. The bakery reports that almost any item can be made GF by special order, but cautions that their baking environment is not GF. ▪ *thesweetspotct.com*

## Ted's Montana Grill    ✪ 📖
*S Windsor* ▪ *(860) 648-1100*
*500 Evergreen Wy*

## Tivoli Pizza & Trattoria    ★ $$LD
*Danbury* ▪ *(203) 748-4821*
*79 Newtown Rd* ▪ *Pizza* ▪ GF pasta and pizza is available. Pizza dough is bought pre-made and cooked in the same oven with the other NON GF pizzas. ▪ *www.tivolipizzatrattoria.com*

## Toozy Patza Pizza & Jazzeria    ✪★ $$LD
*Wilton* ▪ *(203) 544-9500*
*991 Danbury Rd* ▪ *Pizza* ▪ GF pizza is available in the 12-inch size, and rice pasta is available for substitution into any of the regular pasta dishes. ▪ *www.toozypatzapizza.com*

## Toscana Restaurant    ★ $$$LD
*Ridgefield* ▪ *(203) 894-8995*
*43 Danbury Rd* ▪ *Italian* ▪ GF pasta is available. The restaurant also notes that chicken or steak can be prepared GF. Reservations noting GF are recommended. Alert server upon arrival. ▪ *www.toscanaridgefield.com*

## Trumbull Kitchen    ✪ $$LD
*Hartford* ▪ *(860) 493-7412*
*150 Trumbull St* ▪ *Asian Fusion* ▪ GF menu includes seafood pad thai, herb cured chicken, sautéed scallops, and Vietnamese grilled pork chop, among other things. ▪ *www.maxrestaurantgroup.com*

## Uno Chicago Grill    ✪★ 📖
*Danbury* ▪ *(203) 778-1100*
*7 Backus Ave*

## Vito's By the Park    ★ $$$LD
*Hartford* ▪ *(860) 244-2200*
*26 Trumbull St* ▪ *Italian* ▪ GF pasta and pizza are available daily on request. The GF pasta is cooked in a separate pot of water and the GF pizza is cooked on a dedicated pan in the oven to help prevent CC. ▪ *www.vitosbythepark.com*

## Wilton Pizza & Jazzeria    ✪★ $$LD
*Wilton* ▪ *(203) 762-0007*
*202 Town Green* ▪ *Pizza* ▪ GF pizza is available in the 12-inch size, and rice pasta is available for substitution into any of the regular pasta dishes. ▪ *www.wiltonpizza.com*

## Wood-n-Tap Bar and Grill    ✪★ $$LD
*Farmington* ▪ *(860) 773-6736*
*1274 Farmington Ave*
*Hartford* ▪ *(860) 232-8277*
*99 Sisson Ave*
*Southington* ▪ *(860) 329-0032*
*420 Queen St*
*Rocky Hill* ▪ *(860) 571-9444*
*12 Town Line Rd*
*Vernon* ▪ *(860) 872-6700*
*236 Hartford Tpke*
*Orange* ▪ *(203) 799-9663*
*311 Boston Post Rd*
*Wallingford* ▪ *(203) 265-9663*
*970 N Colony Rd* ▪ *American* ▪ GF menu includes chop house steak salad, Atlantic salmon, Santa Fe chicken, a variety of burgers served on GF buns, GF pizza, and more. GF hamburger buns, dessert, and beer are available. ▪ *www.woodntap.com*

# DELAWARE

## Abbott's Grill    $$LD
*Milford* ▪ *(302) 491-6736*
*249 NE Front St* ▪ *American* ▪ No GF menu but many items on the regular menu are either naturally GF or can be modified. Alert server, who will list the available GF

options for that night. The restaurant also recommends pointing out to server that it is an "allergy" as opposed to a preference so the kitchen can take the necessary precautions. ▪ www.abbottsgrillde.com

### Addy Sea Bed & Breakfast $$B
*Bethany Beach* ▪ *(302) 539-3707*
*99 Ocean View Pkwy* ▪ *American* ▪ Make reservations 1-2 days ahead stating that you would like GF options for breakfast and staff will buy GF flour to accommodate your stay. ▪ www.addysea.com

### Back Porch Café, The $$$LD
*Rehoboth Beach* ▪ *(302) 227-3674*
*59 Rehoboth Ave* ▪ *Modern American* ▪ Many GF options available on menu. Alert server upon arrival and note GF when making reservations. ▪ www.backporchcafe.com

### Bella's Cookies ★ CS
*Milton* ▪ *(302) 684-8152*
*18572 Cool Spring Rd* ▪ *Bakery* ▪ Non-dedicated GF bakery offering GF cookies and occasionally GF bread. GF cookie varieties include chocolate crème filled sandwich cookies, champion chunk cookies, and coconut macaroons. ▪ www.bellascookies.com

### Bertucci's ✪ 📖
*Christiana* ▪ *(302) 286-6600*
*201 W Main St*
*Wilmington* ▪ *(302) 529-0800*
*3596 Concord Pike*

### Bethany Blues $$LD
*Bethany Beach* ▪ *(302) 537-1500*
*6 N Pennsylvania Ave*
*Lewes* ▪ *(302) 644-2500*
*18385 Coastal Hwy* ▪ *Barbeque* ▪ Managers at both locations report that they are familiar with the GF diet and can accommodate GF diners. Ask for a manager upon arrival. Certain BBQ items, steaks, and fresh fish items are among the dishes that can be prepared GF. Confirm the timeliness of this information before dining in. ▪ www.bethanyblues.com

### Big Fish Grill ✪ $$$LD
*Rehoboth Beach* ▪ *(302) 227-3474*
*20298 Coastal Hwy* ▪ *Seafood* ▪ GF menu includes fresh goat cheese salad, Greek salad, the fish of the day, Black Angus filet, pork chops, and grilled shrimp. The restaurant recommends noting that your request is for an "allergy" as opposed to a preference so the kitchen staff can take further precautions to minimize CC. ▪ www.bigfishgrill.com

### Big Fish Grill on the Riverfront ✪ $$$LD
*Wilmington* ▪ *(302) 652-3474*
*720 Justison St* ▪ *Seafood* ▪ GF menu includes grilled charcoal shrimp, goat cheese salad, chopped salad, sirloin steak and shrimp, grilled shrimp, grilled pork chops, filet mignon, a variety of grilled or blackened fish, baked spiced apples, succotash, and sweet potato mashers. ▪ www.bigfishriverfront.com

### Blue Water Grill $$LD
*Millsboro* ▪ *(302) 934-5160*
*226 Main St* ▪ *American* ▪ No GF menu but several items are naturally GF such as their steamed items and steaks. The server will list the GF options available that night. The restaurant recommends mentioning the word "allergy" to the server. ▪ www.bluewatergrillmillsboro.com

### Bugaboo Creek Steak House ✪ 📖
*Newark* ▪ *(302) 283-0615*
*1323 New Churchmans Rd*

### Café Azafrán $$$BLD
*Lewes* ▪ *(302) 644-4446*
*109 W Market St*
*Rehoboth Beach* ▪ *(302) 227-8100*
*18 Baltimore Ave* ▪ *Mediterranean* ▪ Chef Richard states that most items are either naturally GF or can be made GF. Just alert a server and they will discuss the options with the customer after discussing it with him. The Lewes location does not offer GF options for dinner but offers GF salads and GF ratatouille for lunch. ▪ www.cafeazafran.com

## Café On 26, The    $$$BLD
*Ocean View* ▪ (302) 539-2233
*84 Atlantic Ave* ▪ *American* ▪ Café on 26
offers every item on their menu in a GF
version. Additionally, separate prep surfaces and utensils are used to prepare GF
items. ▪ *www.thecafeon26.com*

## Café Tamburelli's    ★$LD
*Greenwood* ▪ (302) 349-9700
*3 W Market St* ▪ *Italian* ▪ GF pizza is
available, and is baked on a separate tray. ▪
*www.cafetamburelli.com*

## Cake Break    ★¢S
*Rehoboth Beach* ▪ (302) 260-9264
*7 S 1st St* ▪ *Bakery* ▪ GF cupcakes available
but the flavors vary on a daily basis. Confirm the timeliness of this information before dining in. Owner Deb says she tries to
keep the GF cupcakes completely separated
from gluten but gluten in the air is always a
possibility. ▪ *www.cakebreakrehoboth.com*

## Capers & Lemons Restaurant    $$$LD
*Wilmington* ▪ (302) 256-0524
*301 Little Falls Dr* ▪ *American* ▪ No GF
menu available, however, there a lot of GF
options for diners. Manager Michael is
GF himself so he is well informed about
what is GF and what is not. He states that
while they have plenty of GF options,
the kitchen does not have a CC policy, so
diners should be aware that they cannot guarantee anything to be 100% GF. ▪
*www.platinumdininggroup.com*

## Captain Pete's Mediterranean Cove    $$D
*Fenwick Island* ▪ (302) 537-5900
*700 Coastal Hwy* ▪ *Greek* ▪ Owner Helen
reports that GF diners are welcome and
that some menu items can be modified to
be GF. She notes that everything is made to
order. Greek salads, rice dishes, and baked
potatoes are some examples of GF options.
Confirm the timeliness of this information
before dining in.

## Cheeseburger in Paradise    ✪★▢
*Newark* ▪ (302) 368-9060
*40 Geoffrey Dr*

## China Express    ¢LD
*Bethany Beach* ▪ (302) 537-9956
*33260 Coastal Hwy* ▪ *Chinese* ▪ Owner Xi
says they can make "anything GF for their
customers." Just alert an employee and
Xi will personally come out to describe
the options for you. They can make their
General Tso's chicken, sesame chicken,
and noodles GF.

## Corner Grille    ★¢BL
*Rehoboth Beach* ▪ (302) 227-7653
*11 S First St* ▪ *Greek* ▪ Limited GF options
include home fries, hummus, and salad.
Confirm the timeliness of this information
before dining in.

## Cosi    ✪▢
*Greenville* ▪ (302) 655-2226
*3828 Kennett Pike*
*Wilmington* ▪ (302) 652-8800
*125 S W St*
*Newark* ▪ (302) 737-6665
*111 E Main St*

## Crabby Dicks    ✪$LD
*Rehoboth Beach* ▪ (302) 645-9132
*18831 Coastal Hwy*
*Delaware City* ▪ (302) 832-5100
*30 Clinton St* ▪ *Seafood* ▪ GF menu
items include salads, crab cakes, and
oyster tapas. Inform the server of any
dietary restrictions and the server will
alert kitchen staff. Confirm the timeliness
of this information before dining in. ▪
*crabby-dicks.com*

## Cultured Pearl Restaurant & Sushi Bar    ★$$$D
*Rehoboth Beach* ▪ (302) 227-8493
*301 Rehoboth Ave* ▪ *Asian* ▪ GF soy sauce
is available on request. Most sushi and
sashimi are naturally GF with a few exceptions for the tempura. Confirm the timeliness of this information before dining in. ▪
*www.culturedpearl.us*

**Domaine Hudson**  $$$**LD**
*Wilmington* ▪ *(302) 655-9463*
*1314 N Washington St* ▪ *Modern American* ▪ Restaurant states that all servers are well versed in GF options.There are many naturally GF items on the menu, as well as items that can be prepared GF upon request. These items include seared scallops, cioppino, grilled pork chop, and fire roasted gazpacho. Alert the server upon arrival. ▪ *www.domainehudson.com*

**Don Pablo's**  ✪📖
*Newark* ▪ *(302) 737-3984*
*600 Center Blvd*

**Dover Newsstand and Café**  ¢**BL**
*Dover* ▪ *(302) 678-8999*
*25 W Loockerman St* ▪ *Café* ▪ Several GF desserts and snacks available daily. According to staff "some days we have chocolate chip cookies, Kind's Bar, or Larabar's. It changes daily" All GF items are prepared with clean prep items according to kitchen staff. ▪ *www.dovernewsstand.com*

**Firebirds Wood Fired Grill**  ✪📖
*Newark* ▪ *(302) 366-7577*
*1225 Churchmans Rd*

**Fresh Thymes Café**  ★¢**BL**
*Wilmington* ▪ *(302) 656-2026*
*1836 Lovering Ave* ▪ *American* ▪ GF options are available upon request. ▪ *www.facebook.com/freshthymes*

**Georgia House Restaurant**  ✪**LD**
*Milford* ▪ *(302) 422-6763*
*18 S Walnut St*
*Millsboro* ▪ *(302) 934-6737*
*119 Main St*
*Selbyville* ▪ *(302) 436-6474*
*2 E Church St*
*Laurel* ▪ *(302) 875-0555*
*300 Delaware Ave* ▪ *American* ▪
*www.eatgh.com*

**Georgia House Restaurant**  ✪**LD**
*Milford* ▪ *(302) 422-6763*
*18 S Walnut St*
*Millsboro* ▪ *(302) 934-6737*

*119 Main St*
*Selbyville* ▪ *(302) 436-6474*
*2 E Church St*
*Laurel* ▪ *(302) 875-0555*
*300 Delaware Ave* ▪ *American* ▪ Small GF menu available in stores that includes Cajun catfish, shrimp salad, and several side dishes. No strict CC policy is enforced in the kitchen but according to chef, all utensils are cleaned before use in general. ▪ *www.eatgh.com*

**Greene Turtle Sports Bar & Grill, The** ✪📖
*Lewes* ▪ *(302) 644-6840*
*17388 N Village Main Blvd Unit 21*
*Rehoboth Beach* ▪ *(302) 226-2000*
*101 S Boardwalk*

**Harry's Savoy Grill**  ✪$$$**LD**
*Wilmington* ▪ *(302) 475-3000*
*2020 Naamans Rd* ▪ *American* ▪ Company General Manager Kelly notes that all chefs are trained to prepare GF meals, and all floor staff members are trained to serve GF diners. GF menu includes herb-seared ahi tuna tataki, clams casino, pan seared Maine lobster, and black angus sirloin. Confirm the timeliness of this information before dining in. ▪ *www.harrys-savoy.com*

**Harry's Seafood Grill**  ✪$$$**LD**
*Wilmington* ▪ *(302) 777-1500*
*101 S Market St*
*Wilmington* ▪ *(302) 777-1500*
*101 S Market St* ▪ *Seafood* ▪ Company General Manager Kelly notes that all chefs are trained to prepare GF meals, and all floor staff members are trained to serve GF diners. GF menu includes steamed littleneck clams, cajun seared rainbow trout, and scarlet snapper ceviche. ▪ *www.harrysseafoodgrill.com*

**Hobos Restaurant & Bar**  ★$$$**LD**
*Rehoboth Beach* ▪ *(302) 226-2226*
*56 Baltimore Ave* ▪ *Global* ▪ GF bread can be used for sandwiches, corn tortillas can be substituted for quesadillas, and several GF soups are available. Chef Gretchen

said that CC is always an issue but they do their best to reduce that possibility. ▪ www.myhobos.com

## Home Grown Café   ✪$$**LD**
Newark ▪ (302) 266-6993
126 E Main St ▪ American ▪ GF menu covers everything from soups, sandwiches, and appetizers, to entrées and salads. Alert the manager upon arrival to address CC concerns. ▪ www.homegrowncafe.com

## Irish Eyes Pub & Restaurant   $**LD**
Lewes ▪ (302) 645-6888
213 Anglers Rd
Rehoboth Beach ▪ (302) 227-5758
52 Rehoboth Ave ▪ Irish ▪ GF options include several seafood entrées and salads. Only the two listed locations reported GF options. Alert a manager upon arrival to address CC concerns. ▪ www.irisheyespub.com

## Iron Hill Brewery & Restaurant   ✪★📖
Newark ▪ (302) 266-9000
147 E Main St
Wilmington ▪ (302) 472-2739
620 Justison St

## J.B. Dawson's Restaurant & Bar ✪★$$**LD**
Newark ▪ (302) 369-4000
315 Christiana Mall ▪ American ▪ Extensive GF menu includes a variety of starters, soups, salads, burgers, and sandwiches, as well as pastas, fish dishes, meat dishes, and sides. Several GF desserts are available. GF beer, sandwich buns, and pasta are available. Necessary modifications are noted on the menu for applicable dishes. Director of Kitchens Steven notes that once a diner informs the server that they have Celiac, the floor manager and kitchen manager are immediately notified and oversee the preparation process from start to finish. ▪ www.jbdawsons.com

## Jake's Seafood House   $$**LD**
Rehoboth Beach ▪ (302) 227-6237
29 Baltimore Ave
Rehoboth Beach ▪ (302) 644-7711
19178 Coastal Hwy ▪ Seafood ▪ All menu items are grilled on the same grill and fried in the same fryers. All prep items are cleaned whenever possible to minimize CC. Most fish dishes are naturally GF along with some salads. ▪ www.jakesseafoodhouse.com

## JD's Filling Station   ✪$**BLD**
Lewes ▪ (302) 644-8400
329 Savannah Rd ▪ American ▪ Sirloin fajita, fish fajita, and lobster quesadilla are several GF options available daily. All GF dishes are prepared separately according to kitchen staff. ▪ www.jdsfillingstation.com

## Joe's Crab Shack   ✪📖
Willmington ▪ (302) 777-1803
600 S Madison St

## Kid Shelleen's   ✪$$**LD**
Wilmington ▪ (302) 658-4600
1801 W 14th St ▪ American ▪ Hot crab and artichoke dip, roasted turkey cobb, char grilled filet mignon, and fire roasted Cajun ribeye are all items on the GF menu. Restaurant states that they "serve diners with food allergies every day" and "do their best to accommodate." ▪ www.harrys-savoy.comkidshelleens.asp

## Klondike Kate's   ✪$$**LD**
Newark ▪ (302) 737-6100
158 E Main St ▪ American ▪ GF menu includes blackened tuna, grilled chicken, pesto salmon, stuffed shrimp, and more. The menu also notes any modifications necessary to make a dish GF. Confirm the timeliness of this information before dining in. ▪ www.klondikekates.com

## Kool Bean Bistro, The   ★$$$**BLD**
Ocean View ▪ (302) 541-5377
111 Atlantic Ave ▪ Modern American ▪ Manager Nancy reports that the restaurant has several regular GF customers. She notes that several items on the menu are

naturally GF. GF pasta is also available but only during the nights. Confirm the timeliness of this information before dining in. She also cautions that GF diners should be prepared to educate servers on the GF diet. Upon arrival, alert a server and ask for a manager. ■ *www.koolbeanbistro.com*

### Lone Star Steakhouse & Saloon ☺▥

*Dover* ■ *(302) 736-5836*
*365 N Dupont Hwy*
*New Castle* ■ *(302) 322-3854*
*113 S Dupont Hwy*
*Wilmington* ■ *(302) 478-7616*
*307 Rocky Run Pkwy*

### Melting Pot, The ☺▥

*Wilmington* ■ *(302) 652-6358*
*1601 Concord Pike*

### Mixx ☺$$D

*Rehoboth Beach* ■ *(302) 226-8700*
*26 Baltimore Ave* ■ *Fusion* ■ Items that are GF are marked on the regular menu with a GF sign. Dishes include deviled short ribs, seared scallops, and filet mignon caprese. Alert the server upon arrival and be sure to emphasize that your meal must be GF. ■ *www.mixxrehoboth.com*

### NAGE Bistro and Wine Bar $$$BLD

*Rehoboth Beach* ■ *(302) 226-2037*
*19730 Coastal Hwy* ■ *American* ■ General manager Mark at the Rehoboth location reports that they can "certainly create dishes" for GF diners, and are "able to provide GF options every night of the year." ■ *www.nagerestaurant.com*

### Papa's Pastry Shop ★₵S

*Wilmington* ■ *(302) 777-0877*
*600 N Union St* ■ *Bakery* ■ GF 8" pizza is available. GF pastry options include banana cake, scones, cupcakes, crème brûlée, pies, quiches, and more. For round cakes and special request items, the manager recommends calling at least 48 hours in advance. She also notes that they prepare all GF products "as carefully as can be" but cautions that they are not a 100% GF environment. ■ *www.papaspastry.com*

### Perucci's Classic Italian Restaurant ★$$LD

*Millville* ■ *(302) 829-8727*
*35507 Atlantic Ave* ■ *Italian* ■ GF pasta available. ■ *peruccis.com*

### Piccolina Toscana $$$LD

*Wilmington* ■ *(302) 654-8001*
*1412 N Dupont St* ■ *Italian* ■ Several GF options available daily. Capellini, salads, salmon, and cape sante are naturally GF. The kitchen has dedicated utensils and prep surfaces for all dishes that must be prepared GF to minimize CC. ■ *www.piccolinatoscana.com*

### Pig & Fish Restaurant Co $$LD

*Rehoboth Beach* ■ *(302) 227-7770*
*236 Rehoboth Ave* ■ *American* ■ According to the restaurant, they have several customers who have Celiac so they are knowledgeable about their GF items. Most items on their regular menu are naturally GF or can be easily be prepared GF. Alert the server upon arrival. ■ *www.thepigandfish.com*

### Pizza by Elizabeths ★$$LD

*Greenville* ■ *(302) 654-4478*
*3801 Kennett Pike* ■ *Pizza* ■ GF pizza, beer, and dessert available daily. Call ahead to confirm availability of items. GF pizza is baked on a dedicated screen. ■ *www.pizzabyelizabeths.com*

### Port $$D

*Dewey Beach* ■ *(302) 227-0669*
*1205 Hwy 1* ■ *American* ■ GF items include chicken, shrimp or vegetarian pad thai, salads, salmon, flounder and steaks. Alert a server upon arrival. ■ *www.portdewey.com*

### Potstickers Asian Grill & Sushi Bar ✪$LD

*Newark* ■ *(302) 731-0188*
*1247 Churchmans Rd* ■ *Asian Fusion* ■ Ginger salmon, Singapore curry, Thai spicy beef with basil and kaffir lime leaves are several dishes listed on their GF menu. Kitchen staff states they serve GF diners every week, so they are well informed in this area. All GF dishes are cooked with clean utensils on dedicated prep surfaces. ■ *www.potstickersasiangrill.com*

### Ristorante Attilio                                          ★ $$LD
*Wilmington* ■ *(302) 428-0909*
*1900 Lancaster Ave* ■ *Italian* ■ GF
pasta is available upon request. ■
*www.ristoranteattilio.com*

### Roma Italian Restaurant                                     ★ $$LD
*Dover* ■ *(302) 678-1041*
*3 President Dr* ■ *Italian* ■ GF pasta is available on request along with a few other GF
dishes as well. Manager Ken said that there
is a select few options available daily, just
inform server. ■ *www.romadover.com*

### Romano's Macaroni Grill                                     ✪★ 📖
*Wilmington* ■ *(302) 479-1800*
*4157 Concord Pike*

### Soffritto Italian Grill                                     ✪$$$LD
*Newark* ■ *(302) 455-1101*
*1130 Kirkwood Hwy* ■ *Italian* ■ GF menu
includes salads, chicken marsala, grilled
salmon, filet mignon, and more. Management reports that the staff is knowledgeable
about the GF diet and avoiding CC, and
recommends calling with any concerns. ■
*www.soffrittogrill.com*

### Soybean Asian Grille                                        $$LD
*Wilmington* ■ *(302) 636-0800*
*4702 Limestone Rd* ■ *Asian Fusion* ■ The
restaurant reports that most items on the
menu can be prepared GF. Alert a server
upon arrival and they can help select GF
options. ■ *www.soybeanasiangrille.com*

### Stanley's Tavern                                            ✪$$LD
*Wilmington* ■ *(302) 475-1887*
*2038 Foulk Rd* ■ *American* ■ GF menu
includes buffalo wings, baby back ribs,
char grilled ahi tuna, and baked apple.
The restaurant reports that they accommodate "several GF customers a week." ■
*www.stanleys-tavern.com*

### Stoney Lonen                                                $$D
*Rehoboth Beach* ■ *(302) 227-2664*
*208 2nd St* ■ *Pub Food* ■ No GF menu but
several items can be modified to be GF,
such as their fresh fish and steak dishes.

Confirm the timeliness of this information
before dining in. ■ *www.stoneylonen.com*

### Summer House Saloon                                         ✪$$$LD
*Rehoboth Beach* ■ *(302) 227-3895*
*228 Rehoboth Ave* ■ *American* ■ Limited
GF menu, which only includes a caesar
salad, chopped salad, fresh beefsteak
tomato salad, and fresh fish of the day. ■
*www.summerhousesaloon.com*

### Tutto Fresco                                                ★ $$LD
*Wilmington* ■ *(302) 762-9094*
*514 Philadelphia Pike* ■ *Italian* ■ GF
spaghetti noodles are available for all pasta
dishes. ■ *tuttofrescode.com*

### Two Stones Pub                                              $$LD
*Newark* ■ *(302) 294-1890*
*2 Chesmar Plaza*
*Wilmington* ■ *(302) 439-3231*
*2502 Foulk Rd* ■ *American* ■ GF options
are marked on the regular menu and
include chargrilled Cuban pork tenderloin,
jumbo lump crab cakes, and pub nachos.
Corn tortillas are available for the tacos on
request. All kitchen equipment is sanitized
before use but prep areas are shared with
non GF items. ■ *www.twostonespub.com*

### Ulysses American Gastropub                                  ✪$$BLD
*Wilmington* ■ *(302) 691-3456*
*1716 Marsh Rd* ■ *Pub Food* ■ Extensive GF
menu that includes onion and tomato gratin, beer brined chicken wings, shrimp and
grits, and pan roasted duck breast. Manager Chris says they "try very hard" to eliminate the risk of CC by using completely
separate prep areas. ■ *ulyssesgastropub.com*

### Uno Chicago Grill                                           ✪★ 📖
*Dover* ■ *(302) 674-5055*
*1255 N Dupont Hwy*

### Walter's Steakhouse                                         $$$D
*Wilmington* ■ *(302) 652-6780*
*802 N Union St* ■ *Steakhouse* ■ GF items
include prime rib, filet, New York strip,
rack of lamb, porterhouse, and most seafood dishes, as well as some desserts. Alert
a server upon arrival and they will discuss
GF options. ■ *www.walters-steakhouse.com*

# DISTRICT OF COLUMBIA

## 1789 Restaurant $$$$D
*Washington* ■ *(202) 965-1789*
*1226 36th St NW* ■ *French* ■ The restaurant reports that they accommodate GF diners "all the time." Staff recommends noting GF when making a reservation, as this gives the kitchen time to prepare. ■ *www.1789restaurant.com*

## Au Bon Pain 📖
*Washington* ■ *(202) 393-8809*
*406 10th St NW*
*Washington* ■ *(202) 289-7809*
*1100 13th St NW*
*Washington* ■ *(202) 842-1179*
*1101 Vermont Ave*
*Washington* ■ *(202) 842-2467*
*1401 I St NW*
*Washington* ■ *(202) 887-9331*
*1701 Pennsylvania Ave NW*
*Washington* ■ *(202) 331-4190*
*1724 L St NW*
*Washington* ■ *(202) 296-8696*
*1801 L St NW*
*Washington* ■ *(202) 833-0120*
*1850 M St NW*
*Washington* ■ *(202) 828-5601*
*2100 Penn Ave NW*
*Washington* ■ *(202) 638-8060*
*601 Indiana Ave*
*Washington* ■ *(202) 639-0846*
*700 13th St NW*
*Washington* ■ *(202) 789-1397*
*800 N Capitol St*
*Washington* ■ *(202) 887-9215*
*2000 Pennsylvania Ave*
*Washington* ■ *(202) 887-9721*
*1850 K St*
*Washington* ■ *(202) 479-6863*
*470 L'Enfant Plaza E SW*
*Washington* ■ *(202) 898-0619*
*1325 Second St NE*
*Washington* ■ *(202) 289-7265*
*1300 Pennsylvania Ave NW*
*Washington* ■ *(202) 244-3758*
*5255 Loughboro Rd*
*Washington* ■ *(202) 898-0299*
*50 Massachusetts Ave*
*Washington* ■ *(202) 783-9601*
*1299 Pennsylvania Ave NW*

## Austin Grill ✪$LD
*Washington* ■ *(202) 393-3776*
*750 E St NW* ■ *Tex-Mex* ■ GF menu includes grilled salmon salad, carnitas fajitas, huevos rancheros, grilled vegetable enchiladas, and more. Regional manager Robert stresses the importance of noting GF when placing an order so that the server can notify the manager and start the appropriate procedures for GF preparation. ■ *www.austingrill.com*

## B. Smith's $$$LD
*Washington* ■ *(202) 289-6188*
*50 Massachusetts Ave NE* ■ *Modern American* ■ Manager Mike reports that they have "some items" which are GF or can be prepared GF. He recommends making reservations noting GF and alerting a server upon arrival. He notes that "the server will be knowledgeable," and also that they have an internal GF list which servers can consult. Some items that can be prepared GF include their BBQ ribs, seared scallops, and grilled catfish. ■ *www.bsmith.com*

## Bertucci's ✪📖
*Washington* ■ *(202) 463-7733*
*1218 Connecticut Ave NW*
*Washington* ■ *(202) 296-2600*
*2000 Pennsylvania Ave NW*

## Birch & Barley ★$$$D
*Washington* ■ *(202) 567-2576*
*1337 14th St NW* ■ *Modern American* ■ Managerial Assistant Lindsay reports that nearly all menu items can be prepared GF, and GF flatbreads can be made upon request. Several different GF beers are available. Lindsay recommends making

reservations noting GF and to avoid ordering fried items because all items, gluten or GF, are prepared in the same fryer. ▪ *www.birchandbarley.com*

### Brasserie Beck    $$$$**LD**
*Washington* ▪ *(202) 408-1717*
*1101 K St NW* ▪ *European* ▪ The restaurant reports that they can "certainly accommodate" GF diners, and notes that several menu items are naturally GF. Alert a server, who will notify the chef. If necessary, the chef will come to the table to help choose a GF meal. ▪ *www.beckdc.com*

### Buca di Beppo    ✿📖
*Washington* ▪ *(202) 232-8466*
*1825 Connecticut Ave NW*

### Busboys and Poets    ✿$$**BLD**
*Washington* ▪ *(202) 387-7638*
*2021 14th St NW*
*Washington* ▪ *(202) 789-2227*
*1025 5th St NW* ▪ *American* ▪ Offer countless GF options for all three meals of the day including but not limited to nachos, pizza, salmon, pan fried chicken, and pan seared basil tofu. ▪ *www.busboysandpoets.com*

### CakeLove    ★📖
*Washington* ▪ *(202) 588-7100*
*1506 U St NW*

### Capital Grille, The    ✿📖
*Washington* ▪ *(202) 737-6200*
*601 Pennsylvania Ave NW*

### Carmine's Restaurant    ✿★$$$**LD**
*Washington* ▪ *(202) 552-4300*
*425 7th St NW* ▪ *Italian* ▪ GF pasta is available. An "allergy menu" with a GF section can be requested. GF items include all porterhouse steaks, chicken contadina, lobster fra diavolo, and more. Several GF desserts are available, including chocolate torte, fresh fruit, or tartufo. Alert a server upon arrival. ▪ *www.carminesnyc.com*

### Cava Mezze    ✿$**LD**
*Washington* ▪ *(202) 543-9090*
*527 8th St SE* ▪ *Greek* ▪ Restaurant reports

frequently accommodating GF diners. Alert a server upon arrival. Many menu items are naturally GF, such as salads, dips, omelets and saffron risotto. Confirm the timeliness of this information before dining in. They have a GF list of menu items online and instores. ▪ *www.cavamezze.com*

### Ceiba    $$$**LD**
*Washington* ▪ *(202) 393-3983*
*701 14th St NW* ▪ *Latin American* ▪ The restaurant reports that GF items include red snapper vera cruz with tomato sofrito, jumbo shrimp in pineapple salsa, and slow braised pork shank, among others. Confirm the timeliness of this information before dining in. Staff recommends alerting the server upon arrival and, if necessary, asking for a manager. ▪ *www.ceibarestaurant.com*

### Chef Geoff's    ✿$$$**LD**
*Washington* ▪ *(202) 237-7800*
*3201 New Mexico Ave NW*
*Washington* ▪ *(202) 464-4461*
*1301 Pennsylvania Ave NW* ▪ *American* ▪ Manager Benjamin reports that every location is very happy to adjust their menu to fit the needs of their gluten intolerant customers. He notes that if customers have a specific dish they want prepared GF, they should call ahead a day ahead of time to inform the chef. ▪ *www.chefgeoff.com*

### Chop't    📖
*Washington* ▪ *(202) 347-3225*
*730 7th St NW*
*Washington* ▪ *(202) 783-0007*
*618 12th St NW*
*Washington* ▪ *(202) 327-2255*
*1300 Connecticut Ave NW*
*Washington* ▪ *(202) 955-0665*
*1105 1/2 19th St NW*
*Washington* ▪ *(202) 688-0333*
*1629 K St NW*
*Washington* ▪ *(202) 499-2393*
*1730 Pennsylvania Ave*
*Washington* ▪ *(202) 688-0330*
*50 Massachusetts Ave NE*

### ChurchKey ★$LD
*Washington* ▪ *(202) 567-2576*
*1337 14th St NW* ▪ *Modern American* ▪
Managerial Assistant Lindsay reports that
GF flatbreads are available upon request,
but she notes that many other menu items
cannot be prepared GF. A selection of GF
beers is available. ▪ *www.churchkeydc.com*

### Clyde's 📖
*Washington* ▪ *(202) 333-9180*
*3236 M St NW*
*Washington* ▪ *(202) 349-3700*
*707 7th St NW*

### Comet Ping Pong & Pizza ★$LD
*Washington* ▪ *(202) 364-0404*
*5037 Connecticut Ave NW* ▪
*Pizza* ▪ GF pizza is available. ▪
*www.cometpingpong.com*

### Commissary DC ★$BLD
*Washington* ▪ *(202) 299-0018*
*1443 P St NW* ▪ *Modern American* ▪ Manager Josh reports that they accommodate
GF diners "fairly easily." He notes that it
is restaurant policy to ask arriving guests
if they have any dietary restrictions, and
that there is an "extensive allergen list" for
servers to check which menu items are GF.
▪ *www.commissarydc.com*

### Cosi ✪📖
*Washington* ▪ *(202) 296-9341*
*1350 Connecticut Ave*
*Washington* ▪ *(202) 628-0602*
*1001 Pennsylvania Ave NW*
*Washington* ▪ *(202) 408-1119*
*1275 K St NW*
*Washingotn* ▪ *(202) 332-6364*
*1647 20th St NW*
*Washington* ▪ *(202) 639-8999*
*1501 K St NW*
*Washington* ▪ *(202) 289-5888*
*1333 H St NW*
*Washington* ▪ *(202) 546-3345*
*301 Pennsylvania Ave SE*
*Washington* ▪ *(202) 347-0307*
*601 Penn Ave NW*
*Washington* ▪ *(202) 537-9306*

*5252 Wisconsin Ave NW*
*Washington* ▪ *(202) 638-7101*
*1700 Pennsylvania Ave*
*Washington* ▪ *(202) 824-0730*
*700 11th St NW*
*Washington* ▪ *(202) 687-3136*
*1300 36th St NW*
*Washington* ▪ *(703) 415-0088*
*Ronald Reagan Washington National*
*Airport Terminal*

### DC Coast Restaurant $$$LD
*Washington* ▪ *(202) 216-5988*
*1401 K St NW* ▪ *Seafood* ▪ Staff reports that
they serve GF diners "all the time," and that
all team members are trained on the GF
diet. Alert a server upon arrival. The chef
notes that calling ahead is "helpful," but not
necessary. ▪ *www.dccoast.com*

### Dino ✪$$$D
*Washington* ▪ *(202) 686-2966*
*3435 Connecticut Ave NW* ▪ *Italian* ▪ GF
items marked on the menu include polenta
with sage and garlic mushrooms, veggie
antipasto, and two types of risotto. For
dessert, they offer roasted fruit and gelato.
Confirm the timeliness of this information
before dining in. Owner and chef Dean
recommends speaking to a manager to
ensure a GF meal. ▪ *www.dino-dc.com*

### Ella's Wood Fired Pizza ★$LD
*Washington* ▪ *(202) 638-3434*
*901 F St NW* ▪ *Pizza* ▪ Any pizza is available on GF crust. For dessert, they offer
double chocolate pudding or a selection of ice creams and sorbets. Located
a short walk from the National Mall. ▪
*www.ellaspizza.com*

### Fogo De Chao ★📖
*Washington* ▪ *(202) 347-4668*
*1101 Pennsylvania Ave NW*

### Founding Farmers $$BLD
*Washington* ▪ *(202) 822-8783*
*1924 Pennsylvania Ave NW* ▪ *American*
▪ The restaurant reports that they take
GF requests "very seriously." They recom-
mend making reservations noting GF and

asking for a manager upon arrival. GF options include rotisserie chicken, all fish entrées, and steak. Confirm the timeliness of this information before dining in. ▪ *www.wearefoundingfarmers.com*

### FUEL Pizza ✪★📖
*Washington* ▪ *(202) 659-3835*
*1606 K St NW*
*Washington* ▪ *(202) 547-3835*
*600 F St NW*

### Greene Turtle Sports Bar & Grill, The ✪📖
*Washington* ▪ *(202) 637-8889*
*601 F St NW*

### Grillfish $$LD
*Washington* ▪ *(202) 331-7310*
*1200 New Hampshire Ave NW* ▪ *Seafood* ▪ Staff reports that they serve GF diners "all the time," and adds that the servers are "very familiar" with the GF diet. All of the grilled fish dishes and the steaks are naturally GF. Confirm the timeliness of this information before dining in. ▪ *www.grillfishdc.com*

### Hard Rock Café ✪📖
*Washington* ▪ *(202) 737-7625*
*999 E St NW*

### Heights, The $$LD
*Washington* ▪ *(202) 797-7227*
*3115 14th St NW* ▪ *Modern American* ▪ Manager Ben reports that the restaurant "makes an effort to modify" menu items according to the needs of GF customers. He notes that the dinner menu is probably the easiest to modify to be GF. Alert a server, who will notify a manager. ▪ *www.theheightsdc.com*

### Hello Cupcake ★¢S
*Washington* ▪ *(202) 861-2253*
*1361 Connecticut Ave NW*
*Washington* ▪ *(202) 544-2210*
*705 8th St SE* ▪ *Bakery* ▪ GF cupcakes are available. A different GF cupcake selection is available every day. Owner Penny reports that GF cupcakes are made first

to avoid CC. She recommends placing special orders 48 hours in advance. ▪ *www.hellocupcakeonline.com*

### Jaleo DC ✪$$$LD
*Washington* ▪ *(202) 628-7949*
*480 7th St NW* ▪ *Spanish* ▪ The restaurant reports that GF menu items include paellas, grilled hangar steak, duck confit, traditional chorizo tapas, and more. Confirm the timeliness of this information before dining in. Speaking to a manager upon arrival is recommended. ▪ *www.jaleo.com*

### Kavanagh's Pizza Pub ★$LD
*Washington* ▪ *(202) 337-3132*
*2400 Wisconsin Ave NW* ▪ *Pizza* ▪ GF pizza is available in the 10-inch size and can be prepared with any available toppings except meatballs, which are not GF. Co-owner Lee recommends ordering GF pizza with extra sauce. GF beer is also available. ▪ *www.kavanaghspizzapub.com*

### Legal Sea Foods ✪📖
*Washington* ▪ *(202) 347-0007*
*704 7th St NW*

### Logan Tavern $LD
*Washington* ▪ *(202) 332-3710*
*1423 P St NW* ▪ *Modern American* ▪ Manager Tony reports that the restaurant serves GF diners "all the time." Alert a server, who will ask the kitchen manager or restaurant manager if he or she is unsure of what ingredients are in a certain dish. He also advises GF diners to avoid grilled and fried foods because there are a lot of bread in those areas. ▪ *www.logantavern.com*

### Maggiano's Little Italy ★📖
*Washington* ▪ *(202) 966-5500*
*5333 Wisconsin Ave NW*

### Melting Pot, The ✪📖
*Washington* ▪ *(202) 857-0777*
*1220 19th St NW*

### Mitsitam Native Foods Café ✪$L
*Washington* ▪ *(202) 633-7038*
*4th St & Independence Ave SW* ▪ *American* ▪ Executive Chef Richard reports that

there are "signs" on all of the GF items. He notes that staff members are trained on the GF diet, so ask any one of them to confirm whether or not an item is GF. The café is located inside the Smithsonian National Museum of the American Indian. ■ *www.mitsitamcafe.com*

### Morton's Steakhouse    ✪ 📖
*Washington* ■ (202) 955-5997
*1050 Connecticut Ave*
*Washington* ■ (202) 342-6258
*3251 Prospect St NW*

### NAGE Bistro and Wine Bar    $$$**BLD**
*Washington* ■ (202) 448-8005
*1600 Rhode Island Ave NW* ■ *American* ■ General manager Mark at the Rehoboth location reports that they can "certainly create dishes" for GF diners, and are "able to provide GF options every night of the year." ■ *www.nagerestaurant.com*

### Old Ebbitt Grill    $$**BLD**
*Washington* ■ (202) 347-4800
*675 15th St NW* ■ *American* ■ Manager Christian reports that the restaurant gets "hundreds of allergy requests" every day, many of which come from GF diners. He suggests making a reservation noting GF and alerting the server upon arrival. All servers are familiar with the GF diet and will notify the chef. Most menu items, including fish and meats, can be modified to be GF. ■ *www.ebbitt.com*

### Oyamel Cocina Mexicana    ✪$**LD**
*Washington* ■ (202) 628-1005
*401 7th St NW* ■ *Mexican* ■ GF items are marked on the menu and include ceviche, queso fundido, grilled cactus, seared scallops, braised lamb chalupas, a wide variety of tacos, and more. Confirm the timeliness of this information before dining in. Alert the server upon arrival to ensure a GF meal. ■ *www.oyamel.com*

### Pete's New Haven Style Apizza    ★ ¢**LD**
*Washington* ■ (202) 332-7383
*1400 Irving St NW*
*Washington* ■ (202) 332-7383

*4940 Wisconsin Ave NW* ■ *Pizza* ■ GF pizza is available, as are GF pasta and GF beer. Customers can add toppings of their choice to the GF pizza. The restaurant reports that they "take special dietary needs very seriously," and recommends asking for a manager, chef, or owner when placing a GF order. ■ *www.petesapizza.com*

### Pi Pizzeria    ★ $$**LD**
*Washington* ■ (202) 393-5484
*912 F St NW* ■ *Pizza* ■ GF thin crust pizza available. The manager reports that GF pizza is cooked in a separate area, but cautions that there is still a risk of CC due to the large amount of flour in the kitchen. ■ *www.restaurantpi.com*

### Prêt A Manger    📖
*Washington* ■ (202) 393-0533
*1399 New York Ave*
*Washington* ■ (202) 464-2791
*1155 F St*
*Washington* ■ (202) 559-8000
*1432 K St NW*
*Washington* ■ (202) 403-2992
*1825 Eye St NW*
*Washington* ■ (202) 689-1982
*1828 L St*
*Washington* ■ (202) 289-0186
*50 Massachusetts Ave*

### Red Velvet Cupcakery    ★ ¢$
*Washington* ■ (202) 347-7895
*501 7th St NW* ■ *Bakery* ■ The Red Velvet Cupcakery offers GF "Black and White Velvet" cupcakes in GF options. ■ *www.redvelvetcupcakery.com*

### Restaurant Nora    $$$$**D**
*Washington* ■ (202) 462-5143
*2132 Florida Ave NW* ■ *American* ■ The restaurant reports that many menu items are naturally GF. The chef notes that with advance notice of at least half a day, the kitchen can put together several GF options. He recommends making reservations noting GF and asking for a manager or chef upon arrival. ■ *www.noras.com*

## Ruth's Chris Steak House    ✪▢

*Washington* ▪ (202) 797-0033
*1801 Connecticut Ave NW*
*Washington* ▪ (202) 393-4488
*724 9th St NW*

## Scion Restaurant    ✪$$LD

*Washington* ▪ (202) 833-8899
*2100 P St NW* ▪ *American* ▪ GF menu includes jade vegan curry, wasabi caesar salad, smoked salmon, steak frites, spicy yogurt chicken, pan seared rockfish, and seafood marinara. ▪ *www.scionrestaurant.com*

## Smith & Wollensky    ▢

*Washington* ▪ (202) 466-1100
*1112 19th St NW*

## Sticky Fingers Sweets & Eats    ★¢BLD

*Washington* ▪ (202) 299-9700
*1370 Park Rd NW* ▪ *Bakery & Café* ▪ Sticky Fingers offers GF cupcakes, cakes, and cookies in addition to a sandwich wrap served on a GF tortilla wrap. ▪ *stickyfingersbakery.com*

## Uno Chicago Grill    ✪★▢

*Washington* ▪ (202) 842-0438
*50 Mass Ave NE*

## Zaytinya    ✪¢LD

*Washington* ▪ (202) 638-0800
*701 9th St NW* ▪ *Mediterranean* ▪ GF menu includes a variety of mezze, or small plates. Examples are Syrian lamb and beef sausage, Ottoman style roasted eggplant, and goat cheese wrapped in grape leaves. ▪ *www.zaytinya.com*

## Zengo    ✪$$LD

*Washington* ▪ (202) 393-2929
*781 7th St NW* ▪ *Fusion* ▪ GF menu includes a variety of sushi, small plates, and large plates. Examples are tuna tataki salad and chicken tandoori. For dessert, they offer GF tofu cheesecake and dulce de leche pudding. Reservations noting GF are recommended. ▪ *www.modernmexican.com*

## Zpizza    ✪▢

*Washington DC* ▪ (202) 347-8472
*806 H St NW*

# FLORIDA
## BOCA RATON

## Abe & Louie's    $$$$LD

*Boca Raton* ▪ (561) 447-0024
*2200 W Glades Rd* ▪ *Steakhouse* ▪ They have plenty of GF items and accommodate GF diners frequently, ask you server for details. ▪ *www.abeandlouies.com*

## Bonefish Grill    ✪▢

*Boca Raton* ▪ (561) 483-4949
*21065 Powerline Rd Ste C-15*

## Capital Grille, The    ✪▢

*Boca Raton* ▪ (561) 368-1077
*6000 Glades Rd*

## Carrabba's Italian Grill    ✪▢

*Boca Raton* ▪ (561) 544-8838
*6909 SW 18th St*

## Duffy's Sports Grill    ✪▢

*Boca Raton* ▪ (561) 869-0552
*21212 Saint Andrews Blvd*

## First Watch - The Daytime Café    ✪▢

*Boca Raton* ▪ (561) 544-8875
*21210 Saint Andrews Blvd*

## Jersey Mike's    ▢

*Boca Raton* ▪ (561) 479-0003
*8903 Glades Rd*
*Boca Raton* ▪ (561) 391-7827
*7050 W Palmetto Park Rd*
*Boca Raton* ▪ (561) 443-0868
*1200 Yamato Rd*
*Orange Park* ▪ (904) 272-0037
*410 Blanding Blvd*

## Legal Sea Foods    ✪▢

*Boca Raton* ▪ (561) 447-2112
*6000 Glades Rd*

## Maggiano's Little Italy    ★▢

*Boca Raton* ▪ (561) 361-8244
*21090 Saint Andrews Blvd*

## Melting Pot, The    ✪▢

*Boca Raton* ▪ (561) 997-7472
*5455 N Federal Hwy*

## New York Prime ✪★$$$D
*Boca Raton* ▪ *(561) 998-3881*
2350 Executive Center Dr ▪ Steakhouse ▪
All steak and chicken entrées are GF. Most
fish entrées are too, with the exception of
anything covered with flour/bread. If a customer likes something on the menu that is
usually not GF, the restaurant is willing to
alter the recipe if possible. Alert the server
upon arrival. ▪ *www.newyorkprime.com*

## P.F. Chang's China Bistro ✪★📖
*Boca Raton* ▪ *(561) 393-3722*
1400 Glades Rd

## Pei Wei Asian Diner ✪📖
*Boca Raton* ▪ *(561) 322-1001*
7152 Beracasa Wy
*Boca Raton* ▪ *(561) 226-0290*
1914 NE 5th Ave

## Romano's Macaroni Grill ✪★📖
*Boca Raton* ▪ *(561) 997-5492*
2004 NW Executive Center Cir

## Ruth's Chris Steak House ✪📖
*Boca Raton* ▪ *(561) 392-6746*
255 NE Mizner Blvd

## Shane's Rib Shack ✪📖
*Boca Raton* ▪ *(561) 392-7002*
2240 NW 19th St

## Smokey Bones 📖
*Boca Raton* ▪ *(561) 852-7870*
21733 SR 7

## Stir Crazy ★📖
*Boca Raton* ▪ *(561) 338-7500*
6000 Glades Rd

## Tossed ✪📖
*Boca Raton* ▪ *(561) 544-3144*
6000 Glades Rd

## Yard House ✪📖
*Boca Raton* ▪ *(561) 417-6124*
201 Plaza Real

# FLORIDA

## JACKSONVILLE

## BJ's Restaurant and Brewhouse ✪★📖
*Jacksonville* ▪ *(904) 998-0460*
4907 Gate Pkwy

## Blue Fish, The $$$LD
*Jacksonville* ▪ *(904) 387-0700*
3551 Saint Johns Ave ▪ Seafood ▪ The restaurant reports that they can accommodate
GF diners, and recommends asking the
server for current GF options upon arrival.
▪ *bluefishjax.com*

## Bonefish Grill ✪📖
*Jacksonville* ▪ *(904) 370-1070*
10950 San Jose Blvd

## Boston's Restaurant & Sports Bar ✪★📖
*Jacksonville* ▪ *(904) 751-7499*
13070 City Station Dr

## Brick Restaurant $$LD
*Jacksonville* ▪ *(904) 387-0606*
3585 Saint Johns Ave ▪ Modern American
▪ The restaurant reports that they often
accommodate GF diners, and recommends
any of the steak or fish on the menu, which
can almost always be prepared GF. Confirm the timeliness of this information before dining in. Alert a server upon arrival. ▪
*www.brickofavondale.com*

## Buca di Beppo ✪📖
*Jacksonville* ▪ *(904) 363-9090*
10334 Southside Blvd

## Cantina Laredo 📖
*Jacksonville* ▪ *(904) 997-6110*
10282 Bistro Dr

## Capital Grille, The ✪📖
*Jacksonville* ▪ *(904) 997-9233*
5197 Big Island Dr

## Carrabba's Italian Grill ✪📖
*Jacksonville* ▪ *(904) 363-2254*
8137 Point Meadows Wy

*Jacksonville* ▪ *(904) 726-9000*
*9840 Atlantic Blvd*
*Jacksonville* ▪ *(904) 262-8280*
*9965 San Jose Blvd*

### Eleven South Bistro & Bar     $$$LD
*Jacksonville Beach* ▪ *(904) 241-1112*
216 11th Ave S ▪ American ▪ The restaurant reports that they do not have a GF menu but they can make "almost any dish" GF. Alert the server upon arrival. ▪ *www.elevensouth.com*

### First Watch - The Daytime Café     ✪📖
*Jacksonville* ▪ *(904) 223-0909*
*13470 Beach Blvd*
*Jacksonville* ▪ *(904) 268-8331*
*11111 San Jose Blvd*

### Jason's Deli     ✪📖
*Jacksonville* ▪ *(904) 620-0707*
*4375 Southside Blvd*

### Jersey Mike's     📖
*Jacksonville* ▪ *(904) 387-0007*
*4621 Roosevelt Blvd*
*Jacksonville* ▪ *(904) 399-5006*
*1615 Hendricks Ave*
*Jacksonville* ▪ *(904) 337-0159*
*9700 Deer Lake Ct*

### Joe's Crab Shack     ✪📖
*Jacksonville* ▪ *(904) 249-6160*
*6 Beach Blvd*

### Lemongrass     $$LD
*Jacksonville* ▪ *(904) 645-9911*
9846 Old Baymeadows Rd ▪ Thai ▪ The restaurant reports that they can accommodate GF diners. Reservations noting GF are recommended. Alert a server upon arrival.

### Maggiano's Little Italy     ★📖
*Jacksonville* ▪ *(904) 380-4360*
*10367 Midtown Pkwy*

### Mama Fu's Asian House     ✪📖
*Jacksonville* ▪ *(904) 260-1727*
*11105 San Jose Blvd*

### Marker 32     $$$LD
*Jacksonville* ▪ *(904) 223-1534*
14594 Beach Blvd ▪ American ▪ No GF menu but can accommodate GF diners. ▪ *www.marker32.com*

### Melting Pot, The     ✪📖
*Jacksonville* ▪ *(904) 642-4900*
*7860 Gate Pkwy*

### Miller's Ale House Restaurants     ✪★📖
*Jacksonville* ▪ *(904) 821-5687*
*3238 Hodges Blvd*
*Jacksonville* ▪ *(904) 720-0551*
*9541 Regency Sq Blvd*
*Jacksonville* ▪ *(904) 565-2882*
*9711 Deer Lake Ct*
*Jacksonville* ▪ *(904) 292-0003*
*11112 San Jose Blvd*

### Mitchell's Fish Market     ✪📖
*Jacksonville* ▪ *(904) 645-3474*
*5205 Big Island Dr*

### O'Charley's     📖
*Jacksonville* ▪ *(904) 726-0740*
*410 Commerce Center Dr*

### Ocean 60     $$$D
*Atlantic Beach* ▪ *(904) 247-0060*
60 Ocean Blvd ▪ Global ▪ The restaurant reports that they can make "almost anything on the menu" GF. Reservations noting GF are recommended. Alert the server upon arrival. ▪ *www.ocean60.com*

### P.F. Chang's China Bistro     ✪★📖
*Jacksonville* ▪ *(904) 641-3392*
*10281 Midtown Pkwy Ste 137*

### Pei Wei Asian Diner     ✪📖
*Jacksonville* ▪ *(904) 645-9320*
*4849 Town Ctr Pwy*

### Ruth's Chris Steak House     ✪📖
*Jacksonville* ▪ *(904) 396-6200*
*1201 Riverplace Blvd*

### Shane's Rib Shack     ✪📖
*Jacksonville* ▪ *(904) 992-0130*
*13546-1 Beach Blvd*

### Sticky Fingers Smokehouse     ✪📖
*Jacksonville* ▪ *(904) 493-7427*
*8129 Point Meadows Wy*
*Jacksonville* ▪ *(904) 309-7427*
*13150 City Station Dr*

## Sweet Cece's    📖
*Jacksonville* ■ *(904) 647-6890*
*3267 Hodges Blvd* ■ *Dessert* ■ All frozen yogurt, with the exceptions of Cake Batter, Cookies n' Cream, Red Velvet Cake, and Heath Bar, are GF. ■ *www.sweetceces.com*

## Sweet Pete's    ★₵S
*Jacksonville* ■ *(904) 376-7161*
*1922 Pearl St* ■ *Ice Cream* ■ Sweet Pete's is a GF certified candy shop that sells a wide variety of delicious GF and vegan sweets. ■ *www.sweetpete.net*

## Ted's Montana Grill    ✪📖
*Jacksonville* ■ *(904) 771-1964*
*8635 Blanding Blvd*
*Jacksonville* ■ *(904) 998-0010*
*10281 Midtown Pkwy*

## Tommy's Brick Oven Pizza    ✪★₵LD
*Jacksonville* ■ *(904) 565-1999*
*4160 Southside Blvd* ■ *Pizza* ■ GF pizzas are available in the 12-inch size and can be prepared with any toppings. GF beer is available, and there is always at least one GF soup. For dessert, they offer GF cheesecake and brownies. ■ *www.tbopizza.com*

# FLORIDA

## NAPLES

## Aurelio's Pizza    ★📖
*Naples* ■ *(239) 403-8882*
*2048 Tamiami Trl*

## Bistro 821    ✪$$$D
*Naples* ■ *(239) 261-5821*
*821 5th Ave S* ■ *Bistro* ■ GF menu includes jumbo prawns, seafood paella, sea bass, ribeye steak, and risottos. Owner Michelle reports that several GF customers are accommodated "on a regular basis." She also notes that everything is made to order. ■ *www.bistro821.com*

## Bonefish Grill    ✪📖
*Naples* ■ *(239) 417-1212*
*1500 5th Ave S Unit 112*

## Boston's Restaurant & Sports Bar    ✪★📖
*Naples* ■ *(239) 692-9294*
*4270 Tamiami Trl E*

## BrickTop's    ✪📖
*Naples* ■ *(239) 596-9112*
*5555 Tamiami Trl N*

## Buca di Beppo    ✪📖
*Naples* ■ *(239) 596-6662*
*8860 Tamiami Trl N*

## Café Luna    ✪$$LD
*Naples* ■ *(239) 213-2212*
*467 5th Ave S* ■ *Italian* ■ GF menu is available on request, just inform server ahead of time to ensure timeliness of meal. ■ *www.cafelunanaples.com*

## Capital Grille, The    ✪📖
*Naples* ■ *(239) 254-0604*
*9005 Mercato Dr*

## Carrabba's Italian Grill    ✪📖
*Naples* ■ *(239) 774-2965*
*12631 Tamiami Trl E*
*Naples* ■ *(239) 643-7727*
*4320 Tamiami Trl N*

## Chops City Grill    ✪$$$$D
*Naples* ■ *(239) 262-4677*
*837 5th Ave S* ■ *Seafood & Steakhouse* ■ GF menu at both locations includes shrimp cocktail, clams on the half shell, beef satay, sushi, tuna, salads, NY strip steak, grilled chicken breast, and more. ■ *www.chopscitygrill.com*

## First Watch - The Daytime Café    ✪📖
*Naples* ■ *(239) 566-7395*
*1000 Immokalee Rd*
*Naples* ■ *(239) 213-1709*
*13030 Livingston Rd*
*Naples* ■ *(239) 434-0005*
*225 Banyan Blvd*
*Naples* ■ *(239) 304-0746*
*7163 Radio Rd*

**Fleming's Prime
Steakhouse & Wine Bar**    ✪▢
*Naples* ▪ *(239) 598-2424*
*8985 Tamiami Trl N*

**For Goodness Sake Café**    ★ ₵L
*Naples* ▪ *(239) 597-0120*
*2464 Vanderbilt Beach Rd* ▪ *Café* ▪
GF bread and wraps are available for
sandwiches. A variety of GF desserts is
available. Call ahead to confirm availability, especially at the Bonita Springs
location. Located within the For Goodness Sake Natural Marketplace. ▪
*www.forgoodnesssake123.com*

**Melting Pot, The**    ✪▢
*Naples* ▪ *(239) 732-6666*
*2950 Tamiami Trl N*

**Miller's Ale House Restaurants**    ✪★▢
*Naples* ▪ *(239) 591-0125*
*6320 Hollywood Blvd*

**Noodles Italian Café & Sushi Bar**
✪★$$$LD
*Naples* ▪ *(239) 592-0050*
*1585 Pine Ridge Rd* ▪ *American* ▪ GF
menu includes chicken & artichoke hearts,
shrimp rustica, cioppino, and tomato basil
soup. Owner Patty reports that the kitchen
has "no problem" preparing GF meals and
that the kitchen takes many precautions to
help prevent CC. GF rice pasta is available.
▪ *www.noodlescafe.com*

**P.F. Chang's China Bistro**    ✪★▢
*Naples* ▪ *(239) 596-2174*
*10840 Tamiami Trl N*

**Pazzo! Cucina Italiana**    ✪★$$$$D
*Naples* ▪ *(239) 434-8494*
*853 5th Ave S* ▪ *Italian* ▪ GF menu in-
cludes salads, pasta dishes, grilled steak
and fish, and more. GF pasta is available. ▪
*www.pazzoitaliancafe.com*

**Pei Wei Asian Diner**    ✪▢
*Naples* ▪ *(239) 596-5515*
*2355 Vanderbilt Beach Rd*

**Real Seafood Co.**    $$$LD
*Naples* ▪ *(239) 591-3232*
*8960 Fontana Del Sol Wy* ▪ *Seafood*
▪ No GF menu but every server carries
around a GF option card that highlights
special entrées for that night. Reservations noting GF are recommended. ▪
*www.realseafoodcorestaurant.com*

# FLORIDA

## ORLANDO

**Au Bon Pain**    ▢
*Orlando* ▪ *(407) 825-7851*
*9202 Jeff Fuqua Blvd*

**B-Line Diner**    ✪$$BLD
*Orlando* ▪ *(407) 345-4460*
*9801 International Dr* ▪ *American* ▪
Chef Corey reports that the restaurant is
experienced in accommodating GF diners.
GF items are marked on the regular menu
and include mojo chicken paillard, coco-
nut poached local fish, and sweet potato
fries. Located inside the Peabody Hotel. ▪
*www.peabodyorlando.com/dining/B-Line/*

**BJ's Restaurant and Brewhouse**    ✪★▢
*Orlando* ▪ *(407) 352-0225*
*4151 Conroy Rd*

**Bonefish Grill**    ✪▢
*Orlando* ▪ *(407) 355-7707*
*7830 W Sand Lake Rd*
*Orlando* ▪ *(407) 816-6355*
*5463 Orlando Gateway Village Cir*
*Orlando* ▪ *(321) 677-0025*
*6730 Central Florida Pkwy*

**Bubba Gump Shrimp Co.**    ✪▢
*Orlando* ▪ *(407) 903-0044*
*6000 Universal Blvd*

**Buca di Beppo**    ✪▢
*Orlando* ▪ *(407) 859-7844*
*8001 S Orange Blossom Trl*

**Cantina Laredo**                     📖
Orlando ▪ (407) 345-0186
8000 Via Dellagio Wy

**Capital Grille, The**              ✪📖
Orlando ▪ (407) 370-4392
9101 International Dr

**Carrabba's Italian Grill**        ✪📖
Orlando ▪ (407) 888-2727
1001 Sand Lake Rd
Orlando ▪ (407) 355-7277
5701 Vineland Rd
Orlando ▪ (407) 938-0015
8702 Vineland Ave

**Ceviche**                            📖
Orlando ▪ (321) 281-8140
125 W Church St

**Chatham's Place Restaurant**    $$$$D
Orlando ▪ (407) 345-2992
7575 Dr Phillips Blvd ▪ Modern American ▪ Chef Tony reports that the restaurant serves GF diners often, and notes that all fish entrées, beef dishes, and the rack of lamb can be prepared GF. Confirm the timeliness of this information before dining in. Alert a server upon arrival, who can indicate GF items. ▪ www.chathamsplace.com

**Dandelion Communitea Café**    ✪◊S
Orlando ▪ (407) 362-1864
618 N Thornton Ave ▪ Organic ▪ GF menu options include quinoa pilaf, Polynesian bananas and spring greens, along with several GF sides like hummus, tabouli, queso, and black bean dip. GF dessert options are also available. Restaurant reports that one of the founders is GF, so they are very conscious about GF options. ▪ dandelioncommunitea.com

**Don Pablo's**                     ✪📖
Orlando ▪ (407) 354-1345
8717 International Dr

**First Watch - The Daytime Café**  ✪📖
Orlando ▪ (407) 363-5622
7500 W Sand Lake Rd # A101

Orlando ▪ (407) 823-8146
3402 Technological Ave

**Fleming's Prime Steakhouse & Wine Bar**                               ✪📖
Orlando ▪ (407) 352-5706
8030 Via Dellagio Way Bldg F

**Fogo De Chao**                     ★📖
Orlando ▪ (407) 370-0711
8282 Int Dr

**Hard Rock Café**                   ✪📖
Orlando ▪ (407) 351-7625
6050 Universal Blvd

**Hillstone Restaurants**             📖
Winter Park ▪ (407) 740-4005
215 S Orlando Ave

**Jason's Deli**                     ✪📖
Orlando ▪ (407) 898-9806
2915 E Colonial Dr
Orlando ▪ (407) 425-3562
25 W Crystal Lake St

**Jersey Mike's**                     📖
Orlando ▪ (407) 445-6453
6700 Conroy Rd
Orlando ▪ (407) 384-1200
12420 Lake Underhill Rd
Orlando ▪ (407) 286-1336
3402 Technological Ave
Orlando ▪ (407) 506-1334
3042 W Sand Lake Rd
Orlando ▪ (407) 412-5935
2100 Edgewater Dr
Orlando ▪ (407) 440-6492
13651 Hunters Oak Dr
Orlando ▪ (407) 730-4400
54 W Church St

**Joe's Crab Shack**                 ✪📖
Orlando ▪ (407) 658-9299
4601 S Semoran Blvd
Orlando ▪ (407) 465-1895
12124 S Apopka Vineland Rd
Orlando ▪ (407) 352-2928
8400 International Dr

**Lone Star Steakhouse & Saloon**  ✪📖
Orlando ▪ (407) 827-8225
8850 Vineland Ave

**Loving Hut**  📖
Orlando ▪ (407) 894-5673
2101 E Colonial Dr

**Maggiano's Little Italy**  ★📖
Orlando ▪ (407) 241-8650
9101 International Dr Ste 2400

**Margaritaville**  ✪★📖
Orlando ▪ (407) 224-2155
6000 Universal Blvd

**Melting Pot, The**  ✪📖
Orlando ▪ (407) 903-1100
7549 W Sand Lake Rd

**Miller's Ale House Restaurants**  ✪★📖
Orlando ▪ (407) 856-7045
6141 S Semoran Blvd
Orlando ▪ (407) 736-0333
641 N Alafaya Trl
Orlando ▪ (407) 240-4080
1667 Florida Mall Ave
Orlando ▪ (407) 295-0838
7379 W Colonial Dr
Orlando ▪ (407) 852-9151
13536 John Young Pkwy
Orlando ▪ (407) 370-6688
8963 Intl Dr
Orlando ▪ (407) 248-0000
5573 S Kirkman Rd
Orlando ▪ (407) 239-1800
12371 Winter Garden Vineland Rd

**Morton's Steakhouse**  ✪📖
Orlando ▪ (407) 248-3485
7600 Dr Phillips Blvd

**Napa**  ✪$$$$BLD
Orlando ▪ (407) 352-4000
9801 Int Dr ▪ American ▪ GF items are
marked on the regular menu and include
eggplant & quinoa, Alaskan halibut, beef
filet, grilled spring lamb loin, and more. ▪
www.peabodyorlando.com/dining/napa/

**O'Charley's**  📖
Orlando ▪ (407) 354-0010
8081 Turkey Lake Rd

**P.F. Chang's China Bistro**  ✪★📖
Orlando ▪ (407) 345-2888
4200 Conroy Rd

**Pei Wei Asian Diner**  ✪📖
Orlando ▪ (407) 563-8777
3011 E Colonial Dr
Orlando ▪ (407) 241-3301
8015 Turkey Lake Rd
Orlando ▪ (407) 563-9905
3402 Technological Ave

**Prato**  ★$$$LD
Winter Park ▪ (407) 262-0050
124 N Park Ave ▪ Italian ▪ GF pasta is
available. The restaurant also reports
that they can modify most menu items
for GF diners. Ask server for details. ▪
www.prato-wp.com

**Raphsodic Bakery**  ★¢S
Orlando ▪ (407) 704-8615
710 N Mills Ave ▪ Bakery ▪ GF cupcakes,
cookies, biscotti, and other sweets are avail-
able daily. ▪ www.raphsodic.com

**Romano's Macaroni Grill**  ✪★📖
Orlando ▪ (407) 658-0109
315 N Alafaya Trl
Orlando ▪ (407) 239-6676
12148 S Apopka Vineland Rd
Orlando ▪ (407) 851-1334
Orlando International Airport

**Rusty Spoon, The**  $$$LD
Orlando ▪ (407) 401-8811
55 W Church St ▪ American ▪ Most
menu items can be modified to be GF. ▪
www.therustyspoon.com

**Ruth's Chris Steak House**  ✪📖
Orlando ▪ (407) 226-3900
7501 W Sand Lake Rd

**Smokey Bones**  📖
Orlando ▪ (407) 894-1511
3400 E Colonial Dr
Orlando ▪ (407) 249-2009
303 N Alafaya Tr

**Texas De Brazil Churrascaria**  ★📖
Orlando ▪ (407) 355-0355
International Dr

### Tony Roma's                    📖
*Orlando* ▪ *(407) 857-7244*
*7015 S Semoran Blvd*
*Orlando* ▪ *(407) 248-0094*
*8560 International Dr*

### Uno Chicago Grill          ✪★📖
*Orlando* ▪ *(407) 827-1212*
*12553 State Road 535*
*Orlando* ▪ *(407) 351-8667*
*8250 International Dr*

### Yellow Dog Eats                $LD
*Orlando* ▪ *(407) 296-0609*
*1236 Hempel Ave* ▪ *Southern* ▪ GF items
are marked on the in-store menu. ▪
*yellowdogeats.com*

## FLORIDA

## SARASOTA

### Bonefish Grill                 ✪📖
*Sarasota* ▪ *(941) 924-9090*
*3971 S Tamiami Trl*
*Sarasota* ▪ *(941) 360-3171*
*8101 Cooper Creek Blvd University Park*

### Café Baci                     ★$$LD
*Sarasota* ▪ *(941) 921-4848*
*4001 S Tamiami Trl* ▪ *Italian* ▪ Manager
Roberto reports that the restaurant does not
serve GF diners often. Alert a server upon
arrival. Roberto notes that servers should
know what can be modified to be GF, and if
they have a question, he is available for consult. Grilled fish, veal, or chicken are a few
possible GF options as well as a GF pasta.
Confirm the timeliness of this information
before dining in. ▪ *www.cafebaci.net*

### Carrabba's Italian Grill      ✪📖
*Sarasota* ▪ *(941) 925-7407*
*1940 Stickney Point Rd*
*Sarasota* ▪ *(941) 359-1050*
*2875 University Pkwy*

### Ceviche                       📖
*Sarasota* ▪ *(941) 952-1036*
*1216 1st St*

### Columbia Restaurant           ✪$$LD
*Sarasota* ▪ *(941) 388-3987*
*411 St Armands Cir* ▪ *Cuban* ▪ There
is a printed list of GF menu items at
all locations. GF options include the
beefsteak tomato salad, the paella, and the
queso fundido, among other things. For
dessert, they offer flan and crema catalana.
▪ *www.columbiarestaurant.com*

### First Watch - The Daytime Café   ✪📖
*Sarasota* ▪ *(941) 954-1395*
*1395 Main St*
*Sarasota* ▪ *(941) 923-6754*
*8383 S Tamiami Trl*
*Sarasota* ▪ *(941) 894-3765*
*3706 Cattlemen Rd*

### Fleming's Prime Steakhouse & Wine
### Bar                           ✪📖
*Sarasota* ▪ *(941) 358-9463*
*2001 Siesta Dr*

### Island Gluten Free Bakery      ★¢$
*Sarasota* ▪ *(941) 923-0200*
*1220 Old Stickney Point Rd* ▪ *Bakery* ▪
Dedicated GF bakery offering GF bread,
hamburger buns, pizza crust, cookies,
muffins, scones, brownies, pies, carrot
cakes, and some frozen meals to go. A GF
lunch menu is also available and includes
sandwiches and pizza. The bakery recommends calling in advance for special
orders. ▪ *www.islandgfbakery.com*

### Jason's Deli                   ✪📖
*Sarasota* ▪ *(941) 351-5999*
*5231 University Pkwy*

### Lee Roy Selmon's               ✪★$$LD
*Sarasota* ▪ *(941) 360-3287*
*8253 Cooper Creek Blvd* ▪ *American* ▪ GF
menu includes grilled shrimp salad, burgers without buns, backyard BBQ chicken,
pulled pork, and more. Selmon's Super
Sundae is available for dessert. GF beer is
also available. Jennifer at customer service

recommends alerting a manager upon arrival. ▪ *www.leeroyselmons.com*

### Melting Pot, The ✪📖
*Sarasota* ▪ *(941) 365-2628*
*1949 Ringling Blvd*

### Morel Restaurant $$$D
*Sarasota* ▪ *(941) 927-8716*
*3809 S Tuttle Ave* ▪ *American* ▪ Owner Paula reports that they serve GF diners "all the time." She adds that everything is made to order, so the GF diet is easy to accommodate. She cautions that sauces contain gluten, so GF diners should ask for "no sauce" or request that the chef make a special GF sauce. Alert server upon arrival. ▪ *www.morelrestaurant.com*

### Ophelia's on the Bay $$$D
*Sarasota* ▪ *(941) 349-2212*
*9105 Midnight Pass Rd* ▪ *Modern American* ▪ Restaurant reports that all meals are made from scratch so accommodating GF diners is no trouble at all. Menu changes daily but GF options are always available. GF desserts are also available. Be sure to alert server upon arrival or note GF when making reservations. ▪ *www.opheliasonthebay.net*

### Ruth's Chris Steak House ✪📖
*Sarasota* ▪ *(941) 924-9442*
*6700 S Tamiami Trl*

# FLORIDA

## TAMPA

### Ballyhoo Grill $LD
*Tampa* ▪ *(813) 792-1500*
*7604 Ehrlich Rd* ▪ *Seafood & Steakhouse* ▪ The restaurant reports that they make everything from scratch, so almost anything can be prepared GF. The manager cautions that each diner should explain his or her dietary restrictions because staff may not be "fully educated" on the

GF diet. Alert the server upon arrival. ▪ *www.ballyhootampa.com*

### Bonefish Grill ✪📖
*Tampa* ▪ *(813) 876-3535*
*3665 Henderson Blvd*
*Tampa* ▪ *(813) 969-1619*
*13262 N Dale Mabry Hwy*

### Boston's Restaurant & Sports Bar ✪★📖
*Tampa* ▪ *(813) 901-9590*
*9316 Anderson Rd*

### Capital Grille, The ✪📖
*Tampa* ▪ *(813) 830-9433*
*2223 N Westshore Blvd*

### Carrabba's Italian Grill ✪📖
*Tampa* ▪ *(813) 265-9844*
*11435 N Dale Mabry Hwy*
*Tampa* ▪ *(813) 920-3239*
*11950 Sheldon Rd*
*Tampa* ▪ *(813) 396-4061*
*5503 W Spruce St.*
*Tampa* ▪ *(813) 875-4411*
*700 N Dale Mabry Hwy*

### Ceviche 📖
*Tampa* ▪ *(813) 250-0203*
*2500 W Azeele St*

### Columbia Café ✪$LD
*Tampa* ▪ *(813) 229-5511*
*801 Old Water St* ▪ *Spanish* ▪ The printed list of GF items includes the beefsteak tomato salad and the chicken with yellow rice, as well as the half and half combo with a soup and a salad. Chef Scott advises alerting a server, who will find out what modifications must be made to GF meals. ▪ *www.columbiarestaurant.com*

### Columbia Restaurant ✪$$LD
*Tampa* ▪ *(813) 248-4961*
*2117 E 7th Ave*
*Tampa* ▪ *(813) 229-5511*
*801 Old Water St*
*Tampa* ▪ *(813) 221-4900*
*4100 George J Bean Pkwy* ▪ *Cuban* ▪ There is a printed list of GF menu items at all locations. GF options include the

beefsteak tomato salad, the paella, and the queso fundido, among other things. For dessert, they offer flan and crema catalana. ▪ *www.columbiarestaurant.com*

### First Watch - The Daytime Café   ✪☐
*Tampa* ▪ *(813) 961-4947*
*13186 N Dale Mabry Hwy*
*Tampa* ▪ *(813) 975-1718*
*2726 E Fowler Ave*
*Tampa* ▪ *(813) 307-9006*
*520 Tampa St*
*Tampa* ▪ *(813) 350-3447*
*3712 Henderson Blvd*

### Fleming's Prime
### Steakhouse & Wine Bar   ✪☐
*Tampa* ▪ *(813) 874-9463*
*4322 W Boy Scout Blvd*

### Genghis Grill   ☐
*Tampa* ▪ *(813) 265-2695*
*3805 Northdale Blvd*

### Gourmet Pizza Company   ★$LD
*Tampa* ▪ *(813) 258-1999*
*610 S Armenia Ave* ▪ *Pizza* ▪ GF pizza, flatbread, and breadsticks are available. ▪ *www.gourmetpizza-company.com*

### Hard Rock Café   ✪☐
*Tampa* ▪ *(813) 627-7757*
*5223 N Orient Rd*

### J. Christopher's   ¢BL
*Tampa* ▪ *(813) 908-7023*
*14366 N Dale Mabry Hwy* ▪ *Modern American* ▪ Owner Bill reports that GF diners are "very welcome." He reports that many egg white omelets, chicken dishes, and vegetable dishes are GF. Confirm the timeliness of this information before dining in. He recommends asking a server to indicate GF menu items. ▪ *www.jchristophers.com*

### Jason's Deli   ✪☐
*Tampa* ▪ *(813) 903-0017*
*2702 E Fowler Ave*
*Tampa* ▪ *(813) 341-3354*
*11921 N Dale Mabry hwy*

### Jersey Mike's   ☐
*Tampa* ▪ *(813) 269-0191*
*14839 N Dale Mabry Hwy*
*Tampa* ▪ *(813) 910-1118*
*14925 Bruce B Downs Blvd*
*Tampa* ▪ *(813) 289-1900*
*1155 S Dale Mabry Hwy*
*Tampa* ▪ *(813) 251-1240*
*2121 W Kennedy Blvd*

### Lee Roy Selmon's   ✪★$$LD
*Tampa* ▪ *(813) 977-3287*
*17508 Dona Michelle Dr*
*Tampa* ▪ *(813) 871-3287*
*4302 W Boy Scout Blvd* ▪ *American* ▪ GF menu includes grilled shrimp salad, burgers without buns, backyard BBQ chicken, pulled pork, and more. Selmon's Super Sundae is available for dessert. GF beer is also available. Jennifer at customer service recommends alerting a manager upon arrival. ▪ *www.leeroyselmons.com*

### Loving Hut   ☐
*Tampa* ▪ *(813) 977-7888*
*1905 E Fletcher Ave*

### Maggiano's Little Italy   ★☐
*Tampa* ▪ *(813) 288-9000*
*203 Westshore Plz*

### Melting Pot, The   ✪☐
*Tampa* ▪ *(813) 962-6936*
*13164 N Dale Mabry Hwy*

### Miller's Ale House Restaurants   ✪★☐
*Tampa* ▪ *(813) 969-0020*
*14803 N Dale Mabry Hwy*

### Mise En Place   $$$$LD
*Tampa* ▪ *(813) 254-5373*
*442 W Kennedy Blvd* ▪ *American* ▪ Menu changes frequently but they can make most of their menu items GF. ▪ *miseonline.com*

### Mitchell's Fish Market   ✪☐
*Tampa* ▪ *(813) 289-3663*
*204 Westshore Plz*

### P.F. Chang's China Bistro   ✪★☐
*Tampa* ▪ *(813) 289-8400*
*219 Westshore Plz*

**Pei Wei Asian Diner**   ✪⌂
*Tampa ▪ (813) 207-1190*
*217 S Dale Mabry Hwy*
*Tampa ▪ (813) 960-2031*
*12927 N Dale Mabry Hwy*

**Pizza Fusion**   ★⌂
*Tampa ▪ (813) 463-1600*
*777 N Ashley Dr*
*Tampa ▪ (813) 792-1516*
*9556 W Linebaugh Ave*

**Rigatoni's Tuscan Oven Restaurant**
✪$$LD
*Tampa ▪ (813) 879-7000*
*3437 W Kennedy Blvd ▪ Italian ▪* GF menu
includes Tuscan chicken pomodoro, sea-
food paella, and pizza in a bowl. Manager
Sunia notes that "several" GF diners come
to the restaurant each week, and recom-
mends making reservations noting GF. ▪
*www.rigatonisonline.com*

**Romano's Macaroni Grill**   ✪★⌂
*Tampa ▪ (813) 977-7798*
*17641 Bruce B Downs Blvd*
*Tampa ▪ (813) 264-6676*
*14904 N Dale Mabry Hwy*
*Tampa ▪ (813) 873-2878*
*1580 N Dale Mabry Hwy*

**Ruth's Chris Steak House**   ✪⌂
*Tampa ▪ (813) 282-1118*
*1700 N Westshore Blvd*

**Smokey Bones**   ⌂
*Tampa ▪ (813) 920-9434*
*8020 Citrus Park Dr*

**Stacy's Gluten Free Goodies**   ⊂S
*Tampa ▪ (813) 477-4247*
*10335 Cross Creek Blvd ▪ Bakery ▪*
Manager said that everything baked
here is "100% GF and 100% delicious." ▪
*gluten-free-goodies.com*

**Texas De Brazil Churrascaria**   ★⌂
*Tampa ▪ (813) 871-1400*
*4112 W Boy Scout Blvd*

## FLORIDA

### ALL OTHER CITIES

**32 Degrees Yogurt Bar**   ⌂
*Destin ▪ (850) 837-0020*
*10562 Emerald Coast Pkwy*
*Pensacola ▪ (850) 471-2000*
*5046 Bayou Blvd*

**5 Napkin Burger**   $LD
*Miami ▪ (305) 538-2277*
*455 Lincoln Rd ▪ American ▪* GF
rolls are available for any burger. ▪
*5napkinburger.com*

**Abuelo's**   ✪⌂
*Kissimmee ▪ (407) 870-0901*
*2431 W Osceola Pkwy*
*Lakeland ▪ (863) 686-7500*
*3700 Lakeside Village Blvd*

**Au Bon Pain**   ⌂
*Miami ▪ (305) 416-3357*
*800 Brickell Ave*
*Miami ▪ (305) 347-6495*
*100 SE 2nd St*
*Miami ▪ (305) 273-7031*
*8950 N Kendall Dr*
*Miami ▪ (305) 326-6131*
*900 NW 17th St*
*Miami ▪ (305) 375-0332*
*1001 Brickell Bay Dr*
*Miami ▪ (305) 670-6642*
*9155 S Dadeland Blvd*
*Coral Gables ▪ (786) 308-3000*
*5000 University Dr*
*Doral ▪ (305) 436-3890*
*2315 NW 107th Ave*
*Miami ▪ (305) 325-9595*
*1351 NW 12th St*
*Melbourne ▪ (321) 952-6994*
*1350 S Hickory St*
*Miami ▪ (305) 545-9999*
*1611 NW 12th Ave*
*Miami ▪ (786) 456-7826*
*1500 NW 12th Ave*
*Miami ▪ (305) 228-5440*

11750 SW 40th St
**Pembroke Pines** ▪ **(954) 441-0093**
703 N Flamingo Rd
**Miami** ▪ **(305) 264-4111**
777 Northwest 72nd Ave
**Miami** ▪ **(305) 854-7313**
3659 S Miami Ave
**Miami** ▪ **(305) 871-3003**
Miami Int'l Airport-Concourse G
**Miami** ▪ **(305) 668-0151**
6200 SW 73 St
**Hollywood** ▪ **(954) 322-7769**
3501 Johnson St
**Miami** ▪ **(305) 377-1772**
200 S Biscayne Blvd
**Miami** ▪ **(305) 383-3050**
15955 SW 96th St
**Miami** ▪ **(305) 243-4197**
1475 NW 12th St

### Aurelio's Pizza                    ★▣
**Ft Myers** ▪ **(239) 274-8446**
9909 Gulf Coast Main St

### BabyCakes NYC                    ★⊄S
**Lake Buena Vista** ▪ **(407) 938-9044**
1674 E Buena Vista Dr ▪ Bakery ▪ Non-dedicated GF bakery offering only very few non-GF products. GF items include cupcakes, muffins, crumb cakes, brownies, scones, pies, and more. Bakery reports that GF products are "always" in stock. ▪ www.babycakesnyc.com

### Ballyhoo Grill                    $$**LD**
**Gainesville** ▪ **(352) 373-0059**
3700 W University Ave ▪ Seafood ▪ Manager Mike reports that they have served several GF diners. Alert a server upon arrival. Mike notes that many servers have been working at the restaurant for years, but he still recommends requesting that the server speak to a manager about GF options. ▪ www.ballyhoogrill.com

### Belly Hugs                    ⊄S
**Hollywood** ▪ **(954) 322-8291**
6678 Stirling Rd ▪ Bakery ▪ Dedicated GF bakery offering a variety of breads, cakes,

cupcakes, cookies, mini pound cakes, muffins, pizza, and more. ▪ www.bellyhugs.com

### Better Than Sex Desserts                    ★$S
**Key West** ▪ **(305) 296-8102**
926 Simonton St ▪ Dessert ▪ Dark Chocolate truffle with raspberry sorbet is the only GF item available. ▪ www.betterthansexkw.com

### BJ's Restaurant and Brewhouse ✪★▣
**Citrus Park** ▪ **(813) 852-1910**
8002 Citrus Park Town Ctr
**Clearwater** ▪ **(727) 726-8855**
27001 US Hwy 19 N
**Daytona Beach** ▪ **(386) 226-2005**
2514 W Intl Speedway Blvd
**Doral** ▪ **(305) 463-9750**
1401 NW 107th Ave
**Gainesville** ▪ **(352) 331-8070**
6611 W Newberry Rd
**Kissimmee** ▪ **(407) 932-5245**
2421 W Osceola Pkwy
**Miami** ▪ **(305) 251-7550**
8888 SW 136th St
**Pembroke Pines** ▪ **(954) 430-3545**
12100 Pines Blvd
**Pinellas Park** ▪ **(727) 525-4640**
3800 Park Blvd

### Bonefish Grill                    ✪▣
**Bonita Springs** ▪ **(239) 390-9208**
26381 S Tamiami Trl Ste 104
**Fort Myers** ▪ **(239) 489-1240**
14261 S Tamiami Trl Ste 1
**Cape Coral** ▪ **(239) 574-1018**
900 SW Pine Island Rd
**Miami** ▪ **(305) 487-6430**
14220 SW 8th St Unit 11
**Gainesville** ▪ **(352) 377-8383**
3237 SW 35th Blvd
**The Villages** ▪ **(352) 674-9292**
3580 Wedgewood Ln
**Ocala** ▪ **(352) 873-3846**
4701 SW College Rd Unit 1A
**Ormond Beach** ▪ **(386) 615-7889**
814 S Atlantic Ave
**Longwood** ▪ **(407) 331-0131**
1761 W State Road 434
**Winter Garden** ▪ **(407) 654-6093**

3279 Daniels Rd Ste P-108
Kissimmee ▪ (407) 931-1790
2699 W Osceola Pkwy
Boynton Beach ▪ (561) 732-1310
1880 N Congress Ave
Palm Beach Gardens ▪ (561) 799-2965
11650 US Highway 1
Lake Worth ▪ (561) 965-2663
9897 Lake Worth Rd
St Petersburg ▪ (727) 344-8600
2408 Tyrone Blvd N
Trinity ▪ (727) 372-7540
10750 State Road 54
Belleair Bluffs ▪ (727) 518-1230
2939 W Bay Dr
St Petersburg ▪ (727) 521-3434
5062 4th St N
Clearwater ▪ (727) 726-1315
2519 N Mcmullen Booth Rd
Stuart ▪ (772) 288-4388
2283 S Federal Hwy
Brandon ▪ (813) 571-5553
1015 Providence Rd
Wesley Chapel ▪ (813) 907-8202
1640 Bruce B Downs Blvd
Panama City Beach ▪ (850) 249-0428
11535 Hutchinson Blvd
Tallahassee ▪ (850) 297-0460
3491 Thomasville Rd
Pensacola ▪ (850) 471-2324
5025 N 12Th Ave
Destin ▪ (850) 650-3161
4447 Commons Dr E
Panama City ▪ (850) 747-9331
641 W 23rd St
Lakeland ▪ (863) 701-9480
225 W Pipkin Rd
Jacksonville Beach ▪ (904) 247-4234
2400 3rd St S Ste 302B
University Park ▪ (941) 360-3171
8101 Cooper Creek Blvd
Bradenton ▪ (941) 795-8020
7456 Cortez Rd W
Weston ▪ (954) 389-9273
4545 Weston Rd
Plantation ▪ (954) 472-3592
10197 W Sunrise Blvd
Ft Lauderdale ▪ (954) 492-3266

6282 N Federal Hwy
Coral Springs ▪ (954) 509-0405
1455 N University Dr
Kissimmee ▪ (321) 677-0103
7801 W Irlo Bronson Memorial Hwy
Kendall ▪ (786) 293-5713
12520 SW 120th St
Meritt Island ▪ (321) 453-3011
795 E Merritt Island Causeway
Venice ▪ (941) 493-4180
1681 US Hwy 41 Bypass S

## Bubba Gump Shrimp Co.          ✪📖
Daytona Beach ▪ (386) 947-8433
250 N Atlantic Ave
Ft Lauderdale ▪ (954) 463-0777
429 S Fort Lauderdale Beach Blvd
Madeira Beach ▪ (727) 397-4867
185 Boardwalk Pl W
Miami ▪ (305) 379-8866
401 Biscayne Blvd
Destin ▪ (850) 650-1881
14059 Emerald Coast Pky
Jupiter ▪ (561) 744-1300
1065 N Hwy A1A

## Bubble Room                           $$LD
Captiva ▪ (239) 472-5558
15001 Captiva Dr ▪ American ▪ Manager
Julie notes that GF diners come in "all the
time." She reports that several steak dishes,
vegetables, sides, and seafood dishes can be
modified to be GF. Confirm the timeliness
of this information before dining in. Upon
arrival, alert a server and ask for the manager. ▪ www.bubbleroomrestaurant.com

## Buca di Beppo                         ✪📖
Brandon ▪ (813) 681-8462
11105 Causeway Blvd
Davie ▪ (954) 577-3287
3355 S University Dr
Maitland ▪ (407) 622-7663
1351 S Orlando Ave
Wellington ▪ (561) 790-3287
2025 Wellington Green Dr
Tallahassee ▪ (850) 300-0058
1500 Apalachee Pkwy

### Cactus Flower Café                    $LD
*Pensacola* ▪ *(850) 432-8100*
*3425 N 12th Ave*
*Pensacola* ▪ *(850) 458-3833*
*3309 Gulf Beach Hwy*
*Navarre* ▪ *(850) 936-4111*
*8725 Ortega Park Dr* ▪ *Mexican* ▪ GF list includes tacos, tostadas, enchiladas, huevos rancheros, nachos, and more. Some items may be available only with certain toppings, or may require modification to become GF. Alert a server upon arrival to help navigate the menu. Manager Lee notes that items for GF customers are fried separately in a skillet to avoid CC. ▪ *cactusflowercafe.net*

### Café 118                              $$LD
*Winter Park* ▪ *(407) 389-2233*
*153 E Morse Blvd* ▪ *Vegan* ▪ Owner Joseph reports that nearly the entire menu is GF, with the exception of two desserts that contain oat flour. Confirm the timeliness of this information before dining in. He adds that all staff members are trained on the GF diet, so GF diners need only alert a server upon arrival. ▪ *www.cafe118.com*

### Café Margaux                      ★ $$$LD
*Cocoa* ▪ *(321) 639-8343*
*220 N Brevard Ave* ▪ *Modern American* ▪ The restaurant strongly recommends reservations two days in advance noting GF because they will be able to prepare more options, like GF rice pasta, and because they use a "team service" system, so it's best if servers are alerted in advance. ▪ *www.cafemargaux.com*

### Cantina Laredo                        📖
*Fort Myers* ▪ *(239) 415-4424*
*5200 Big Pine Wy*
*Hallandale Beach* ▪ *(954) 457-7662*
*501 Silks Run*
*Palm Beach Gardens* ▪ *(561) 622-1223*
*4635 PGA Blvd*
*Sandestin* ▪ *(850) 654-5649*
*585 Grand Blvd*
*Wesley Chapel* ▪ *(813) 907-3068*
*2000 Piazza Ave*

### Capital Grille, The                   ✪📖
*Fort Lauderdale* ▪ *(954) 446-2000*
*2430 E Sunrise Blvd*
*Miami* ▪ *(305) 374-4500*
*444 Brickell Ave*
*Palm Beach Gardens* ▪ *(561) 630-4994*
*11365 Legacy Ave*

### Carino's Italian                      ✪📖
*Doral* ▪ *(305) 403-7919*
*8240 NW 36th St*

### Carrabba's Italian Grill              ✪📖
*Altamonte Springs* ▪ *(407) 788-4222*
*931 N State Road 434*
*Bonita Springs* ▪ *(239) 949-0981*
*27220 Bay Landing Dr*
*Boynton Beach* ▪ *(561) 734-5152*
*1999 N Congress Ave*
*Bradenton* ▪ *(941) 755-7712*
*2106 Cortez Rd W*
*Brandon* ▪ *(813) 657-8166*
*801 Providence Rd*
*Brooksville* ▪ *(352) 597-9805*
*12607 Cortez Blvd*
*Cape Coral* ▪ *(239) 574-2797*
*762 SW Pine Island Rd*
*Clearwater* ▪ *(727) 712-0844*
*19919 US Highway 19 N*
*Clermont* ▪ *(352) 394-8602*
*2240 E Highway 50*
*Coral Springs* ▪ *(954) 345-4600*
*2501 N University Dr*
*Daytona Beach* ▪ *(386) 255-3344*
*2200 W International Speedway Blvd*
*Delray Beach* ▪ *(561) 266-9393*
*335 E Linton Blvd*
*Fort Myers* ▪ *(239) 690-2426*
*10075 Gulf Center Dr*
*Fort Myers* ▪ *(239) 433-0877*
*12990 S Cleveland Ave*
*Gainesville* ▪ *(352) 692-0083*
*3021 SW 34th St*
*Hialeah* ▪ *(305) 816-9131*
*18600 NW 87th Ave*
*Jacksonville Beach* ▪ *(904) 249-5550*
*9 3rd St N*
*Kissimmee* ▪ *(407) 390-9600*
*7890 W Irlo Bronson Hwy*

*Lakeland* ▪ (863) 646-2518
*4829 S Florida Ave*
*Lutz* ▪ (813) 926-8212
*16525 Pointe Village Dr*
*Melbourne* ▪ (321) 253-0991
*7620 N Wickham Rd*
*Merritt Island* ▪ (321) 453-7045
*60 Palmetto Ave*
*Miami Beach* ▪ (305) 673-3525
*3921 Collins Ave*
*North Palm Beach* ▪ (561) 630-7386
*11201 US Highway 1*
*Ocala* ▪ (352) 867-0240
*2370 SW College Rd*
*Orange Park* ▪ (904) 278-1077
*1750 Wells Rd*
*Palm Bay* ▪ (321) 956-1900
*1575 Palm Bay Rd NE*
*Palm Harbor* ▪ (727) 787-8910
*33983 US Highway 19 N*
*Panama City Beach* ▪ (850) 230-4522
*13820 Panama City Beach Pkwy*
*Pensacola* ▪ (850) 438-0073
*311 N 9th Ave*
*Plant City* ▪ (813) 752-0760
*1205 Townsgate Ct*
*Plantation* ▪ (954) 423-2214
*1003 S University Dr*
*Pompano Beach* ▪ (954) 782-2688
*1299 S Federal Hwy*
*Port Charlotte* ▪ (941) 743-5299
*1811 Tamiami Trl*
*Port Richey* ▪ (727) 869-4886
*10110 US Highway 19*
*Port St Lucie* ▪ (772) 344-5897
*1900 SW Fountainview Blvd*
*Royal Palm Beach* ▪ (561) 793-9980
*11141 Southern Blvd*
*Sandestin* ▪ (850) 837-1140
*10562 Emerald Coast Pkwy W*
*South Miami* ▪ (305) 661-2426
*5829 SW 73rd St*
*St Augustine* ▪ (904) 819-9093
*155 State Road 312 W*
*St Petersburg* ▪ (727) 897-9375
*1951 4th St N*
*St Petersburg* ▪ (727) 384-1818
*3530 Tyrone Blvd N*

*Stuart* ▪ (772) 223-6377
*2700 SE Federal Hwy*
*Temple Terrace* ▪ (813) 989-3898
*5515 E Fowler Ave*
*The Villages* ▪ (352) 430-1304
*650 N US Highway 441*
*University Park* ▪ (941) 355-4116
*5425 University Pkwy*
*Vero Beach* ▪ (772) 299-5999
*1285 US Highway 1*
*West Palm Beach* ▪ (561) 615-8900
*2224 Palm Beach Lakes Blvd*
*Winter Springs* ▪ (407) 696-6600
*5820 Red Bug Lake Rd*
*Tallahassee* ▪ (850) 297-1100
*2799 Capital Cir NE*
*Winter Haven* ▪ (863) 293-6635
*700 Third St SW*
*Jacksonville Beach* ▪ (904) 249-5550
*9 N 3rd St*
*Citrus Park* ▪ (813) 920-3239
*11902 Sheldon Rd*

## Ceviche                                        📖

*St Petersburg* ▪ (727) 209-2299
*10 Beach Dr*
*Clearwater* ▪ (727) 799-3082
*2930 Gulf to Bay Blvd*

## Cheeseburger in Paradise          ✪★📖

*Miramar Beach* ▪ (850) 837-0197
*10562 US Highway 98 W*
*Ft Myers* ▪ (239) 481-4386
*5050 Daniels Pwy*

## Chef Brooke's Natural Café          ✪℄LD

*Fort Myers* ▪ (239) 332-2433
*1850 Boyscout Dr* ▪ American ▪ The restaurant reports that almost everything on the menu is GF or can be easily modified. Some items include curry, tuna, fish tacos, and a variety of smoothies and GF baked goods. ▪ *chefbrookeonline.com*

## China Grill at Hilton Ft. Lauderdale
## Marina                                  ✪$$$$BD

*Fort Lauderdale* ▪ (954) 759-9950
*1881 SE 17th St* ▪ Asian Fusion ▪ Manager Gary notes that they serve GF diners with "no problem at all." He suggests noting

GF in reservations, and then confirming with the server upon arrival. Gary notes that a variety of menu items can be modified to be GF. Servers are trained to speak with the chef about these options. ▪ *www.chinagrillmgt.com*

### Chops City Grill                    ✪$$$$D
*Bonita Springs* ▪ *(239) 992-4677*
*8200 Health Ctr Blvd* ▪ *Seafood & Steakhouse* ▪ GF menu at both locations includes shrimp cocktail, clams on the half shell, beef satay, sushi, tuna, salads, NY strip steak, grilled chicken breast, and more. ▪ *www.chopscitygrill.com*

### Columbia Restaurant              ✪$$LD
*St Augustine* ▪ *(904) 824-3341*
*98 St George St*
*St Petersburg* ▪ *(727) 822-8000*
*800 2nd Ave NE*
*Clearwater* ▪ *(727) 596-8400*
*1241 Gulf Blvd*
*Celebration* ▪ *(407) 566-1505*
*649 Front St* ▪ *Cuban* ▪ There is a printed list of GF menu items at all locations. GF options include the beefsteak tomato salad, the paella, and the queso fundido, among other things. For dessert, they offer flan and crema catalana. ▪ *www.columbiarestaurant.com*

### Doc Ford's                               $$$LD
*Sanibel* ▪ *(239) 472-8311*
*973 Rabbit Rd* ▪ *Seafood* ▪ Manager Jean reports that they serve GF diners "all the time." She recommends alerting a server upon arrival. Servers should know what food is GF, but they will ask the chef if they have questions. She notes that many fish dishes can be modified to be GF. Confirm the timeliness of this information before dining in. ▪ *www.docfordssanibel.com*

### Don Pablo's                           ✪▢
*Sanford* ▪ *(407) 328-1885*
*100 Towne Center Blvd*
*Sarasota* ▪ *(941) 312-6994*
*5911 Fruitville Rd*

### Duffy's Sports Grill              ✪▢
*Boynton Beach* ▪ *(561) 963-3234*
*4746 N Congress Ave*
*Boynton Beach* ▪ *(561) 752-4949*
*6545 Boynton Beach Blvd*
*Deerfield Beach* ▪ *(954) 429-8820*
*401 N Federal Hwy*
*Delray Beach* ▪ *(561) 276-3332*
*1750 S Federal Hwy*
*Ft Lauderdale* ▪ *(954) 713-6363*
*1804 Cordova Rd*
*West Palm Beach* ▪ *(561) 642-6388*
*6864 Forest Hill Blvd*
*Jensen Beach* ▪ *(772) 692-9123*
*4179 NW Federal Hwy*
*Jupiter* ▪ *(561) 743-4405*
*185 E Indiantown Rd*
*Jupiter* ▪ *(561) 741-8900*
*6791 W Indiantown Rd*
*North Palm Beach* ▪ *(561) 721-2650*
*11588 US Hwy 1*
*Palm Beach Gardens* ▪ *(561) 493-8381*
*4280 Northlake Blvd*
*Plantation* ▪ *(954) 473-0477*
*811 S University Dr*
*Port St Lucie* ▪ *(772) 924-3565*
*1608 NW Courtyard Cir*
*Port St Lucie* ▪ *(772) 873-8150*
*790 SW Saint Lucie W Blvd*
*West Palm Beach* ▪ *(561) 792-4045*
*11935 Southern Blvd*
*Stuart* ▪ *(772) 221-4899*
*1 SW Osceola St*
*Stuart* ▪ *(772) 781-1388*
*6431 SE Federal Hwy*
*West Palm Beach* ▪ *(561) 478-8852*
*6845 Okeechobee Blvd*
*West Palm Beach* ▪ *(561) 688-1820*
*721 Village Blvd*
*North Miami Beach* ▪ *(305) 760-2124*
*3969 NE 163rd St*
*Coconut Creek* ▪ *(954) 422-9789*
*4800 W Hillsboro Blvd*
*West Palm Beach* ▪ *(561) 249-1682*
*225 Clematis St*
*Melbourne* ▪ *(321) 725-2840*
*1700 Evans Rd*

### EthosVegan Kitchen ✪★$LD
*Winter Park* ▪ *(407) 228-3899*
*601 S. New York Ave* ▪ *Vegetarian* ▪ GF
items marked on the menu include
edamame, several soups and sandwiches,
and all of the side dishes. Rice wrap
is available for the sandwiches, for
those who want to try their new
sandwiches but are GF. Co-owner
Laina cautions that the Sunday brunch
menu has "very limited" GF options. ▪
*www.ethosvegankitchen.com*

### Fiorella Italian Restaurant ✪★$$$LD
*Lake Worth* ▪ *(561) 963-4999*
*7008 Charleston Shores Blvd* ▪ *Italian* ▪
Extensive GF menu includes pasta dishes
with GF spaghetti or penne, seafood, salads, veal, chicken, and more. GF pasta is
available. ▪ *www.fiorellarestaurant.com*

### First Watch - The Daytime Café ✪▥
*Altamonte Springs* ▪ *(407) 682-2315*
*249 W State Road 436*
*Bonita Springs* ▪ *(239) 390-0554*
*26381 S Tamiami Trl Ste 140*
*Bradenton* ▪ *(941) 792-6071*
*7118 Cortez Rd W*
*Clearwater* ▪ *(727) 712-8769*
*2569 Countryside Blvd*
*Fort Myers* ▪ *(239) 437-0020*
*13211 Mcgregor Blvd*
*Fort Myers* ▪ *(239) 461-9765*
*2059 Altamont Ave*
*Fort Myers* ▪ *(239) 274-5551*
*7091 College Pkwy*
*Jupiter* ▪ *(561) 746-5960*
*6240 W Indiantown Rd*
*Lakewood Ranch* ▪ *(941) 907-6657*
*8306 Market St*
*Longwood* ▪ *(407) 774-1830*
*2425 W State Road 434*
*Maitland* ▪ *(407) 740-7437*
*1221 S Orlando Ave*
*Palm Harbor* ▪ *(727) 789-3447*
*35146 US Highway 19 N*
*Stuart* ▪ *(772) 220-4076*
*2125 SE Federal Hwy*
*Sunrise* ▪ *(954) 846-1313*

*12594 W Sunrise Blvd*
*Wesley Chapel* ▪ *(813) 929-3947*
*1648 Bruce B Downs Blvd*
*Winter Garden* ▪ *(407) 654-2826*
*3017 Daniels Rd*
*Lady Lake* ▪ *(352) 633-1520*
*1568 Bella Cruz Dr*
*Bradenton* ▪ *(941) 907-6657*
*8306 Market St*
*Panama City Beach* ▪ *(850) 234-5700*
*11160 Panama City Beach Pkwy*
*Ocala* ▪ *(352) 291-2344*
*3411 SW 36th Terrace*
*Jacksonville Beach* ▪ *(904) 834-3789*
*544 Marsh Landing Pkwy*

### Fleming's Prime Steakhouse & Wine Bar ✪▥
*Coral Gables* ▪ *(305) 569-7995*
*2525 Ponce De Leon Blvd*
*Winter Park* ▪ *(407) 699-9463*
*933 N Orlando Ave*
*Sandestin* ▪ *(850) 269-0830*
*600 Grand Blvd*

### Fogo De Chao ★▥
*Miami Beach* ▪ *(305) 672-0011*
*836 1st St*

### For Goodness Sake Café ★¢L
*Bonita Springs* ▪ *(239) 992-5838*
*9118 Bonita Beach Rd SE* ▪ *Café* ▪
GF bread and wraps are available for
sandwiches. A variety of GF desserts is
available. Call ahead to confirm availability, especially at the Bonita Springs
location. Located within the For Goodness Sake Natural Marketplace. ▪
*www.forgoodnesssake123.com*

### Frida's Café & Bakery ✪★¢BLD
*Largo* ▪ *(727) 587-7077*
*9700 Ulmerton Rd* ▪ *Bakery & Café* ▪ GF
breads and sweets are made fresh daily. ▪
*www.fridascafe.com*

### Genghis Grill ▥
*Brandon* ▪ *(813) 662-2695*
*910 Providence Rd*
*Gainesville* ▪ *(352) 375-4444*
*3208 SW Archer Rd*

*Homestead* ▪ *(305) 246-2690*
*2580 NE 10th Ct*
*Tallahassee* ▪ *(850) 422-4444*
*1400 Village Square Blvd*
*Panama City* ▪ *(850) 785-4444*
*741 W 23rd St*
*Pembroke Pines* ▪ *(954) 606-5426*
*12598 Pines Blvd*
*Tallahassee* ▪ *(850) 656-4444*
*830 E Lafayette St*

## Hard Rock Café                        ✪📖
*Destin* ▪ *(850) 654-3310*
*4260 Legendary Dr*
*Hollywood* ▪ *(954) 315-9112*
*1 Seminole Wy*
*Key West* ▪ *(305) 293-0230*
*313 Duval St*
*Miami* ▪ *(305) 377-3110*
*401 Biscayne Blvd*

## Harry's Continental Kitchen    ✪$$$BLD
*Longboat Key* ▪ *(941) 383-0777*
*5600 Gulf of Mexico Dr.* ▪ *European* ▪
Owner and Chef Harry reports that they
are pleased to now offer a GF menu. Possible GF options include grilled grouper,
seafood cobb, braised baby ossobuco alla
Milanese - veal with risotto, and chili
braised short ribs. Confirm the timeliness
of this information before dining in. He
recommends showing a dining card upon
arrival. ▪ *www.harryskitchen.com*

## Hillstone Restaurants            📖
*Coral Gables* ▪ *(305) 529-0141*
*201 Miracle Mile*

## Horse and Hounds Restaurant    $$LD
*Ocala* ▪ *(352) 690-6100*
*4620 E Silver Springs Blvd*
*Ocala* ▪ *(352) 620-2500*
*6998 N US Highway 27* ▪ *American* ▪
Managers at both locations report that
although GF diners are not frequent,
they can be accommodated. Manager
Jay at the Silver Springs location recommends alerting a server, who will sum-
mon a manager to go over options with
GF customers. Lisa at the Highway 27

location notes that an allergy button is
used to input orders from customers with
any type of food "allergy," including GF.
This button alerts the kitchen staff that
the food must be prepared separately. ▪
*www.horseandhoundsrestaurant.com*

## Iam Pasta Café                        ★⟨LD
*Winter Haven* ▪ *(863) 508-7433*
*7220 Cypress Gardens Blvd* ▪ *Italian* ▪
GF bread, pasta, and pizza crust available. GF spaghetti, linguini, and macaroni and cheese pasta made fresh daily.
The crust is made on request so calling
a day in advance is recommended. ▪
*www.iampastacafe.com*

## Jason's Deli                          ✪📖
*Port Charlotte* ▪ *(941) 235-3354*
*1100 El Jobean Rd*
*Melbourne* ▪ *(321) 733-6075*
*1509 W New Haven Ave*
*Altamonte Springs* ▪ *(407) 830-0699*
*303 E Altamonte Dr*
*Cape Coral* ▪ *(239) 458-8700*
*2311 Santa Barbara Blvd*
*Fort Myers* ▪ *(239) 590-9994*
*13550 Reflections Pkwy*
*Naples* ▪ *(239) 593-9499*
*2700 Immokalee Rd*
*Jacksonville Beach* ▪ *(904) 246-7585*
*2230 3rd St S*
*Clearwater* ▪ *(727) 793-0446*
*25801 US Hwy 19 N*
*Pembroke Pines* ▪ *(954) 438-1280*
*14531 SW 5th St*
*Boynton Beach* ▪ *(561) 738-1820*
*870 N Congress Ave*
*Wellington* ▪ *(561) 333-1263*
*2565 S State Rd*
*Gainesville* ▪ *(352) 333-6923*
*6791 W Newberry Rd*
*Tallahassee* ▪ *(850) 402-0135*
*2335 Apalachee Pkwy*

## Jersey Mike's                         📖
*Winter Park* ▪ *(407) 960-2881*
*1150 S Orlando Ave*
*Pensacola* ▪ *(850) 471-2228*
*1620 Airport Blvd*

*Port Saint Lucie* ▪ *(772) 878-4033*
*262 SW Port St. Lucie Blvd*
*Destin* ▪ *(850) 269-2925*
*817 Harbor Blvd*
*Sarasota* ▪ *(941) 921-8111*
*3820 S Tuttle Ave*
*University Park* ▪ *(941) 359-1500*
*8210 Tourist Center Dr*
*Brandon* ▪ *(813) 662-0099*
*10951 Causeway Blvd*
*Fort Meyers* ▪ *(239) 274-8877*
*12377 S Cleveland Ave*
*Fort Meyers* ▪ *(239) 931-7827*
*6810 Shoppes at Plantation Dr*
*Bonita Springs* ▪ *(239) 495-3588*
*8951 Bonita Beach Rd*
*Lake Mary* ▪ *(407) 936-7827*
*819 Rinehart Rd*
*Vero Beach* ▪ *(772) 978-0884*
*628 21st St*
*Stuart* ▪ *(772) 220-0880*
*3321 S Federal Hwy*
*Jupiter* ▪ *(561) 747-7272*
*6390 W Indiantown Rd*
*West Palm Beach* ▪ *(561) 689-8082*
*931 Village Blvd*
*Boynton Beach* ▪ *(561) 738-5615*
*2260 Woolbright Rd*
*Delray Beach* ▪ *(561) 330-9060*
*1554 S Federal Hwy*
*Delray Beach* ▪ *(561) 276-8949*
*455C NE 5th Ave*
*Okeechobee* ▪ *(863) 467-8100*
*611 W S Park St*
*Altamonte Springs* ▪ *(407) 293-1715*
*851 S State Rd 434*
*Altamonte Springs* ▪ *(407) 637-2975*
*175 E Altamonte Dr*
*Oldsmar* ▪ *(813) 854-6453*
*3860 Tampa Rd*
*Daytona Beach* ▪ *(386) 257-9119*
*1808 W International Speedway Blvd*
*Melbourne* ▪ *(321) 473-8996*
*1515 Palm Bay Rd*
*Port Orange* ▪ *(386) 310-4820*
*3843 S Nova Rd*
*Tallahassee* ▪ *(850) 765-0712*
*1801 W Tennessee St*

*Melbourne* ▪ *(321) 622-8813*
*1070 N Wickham Rd*
*Tallahassee* ▪ *(850) 320-6210*
*1355 Market St*
*Bradenton* ▪ *(941) 748-7827*
*4020 14th St W*
*Ormond Beach* ▪ *(386) 265-1933*
*1474 W Granada Blvd*
*Melbourne* ▪ *(321) 821-4483*
*90 W Hibiscus Blvd*
*Winter Park* ▪ *(407) 671-0053*
*4004 N Goldenrod Rd*
*Gainesville* ▪ *(352) 672-6606*
*2015 NW 43rd St*
*Maitland* ▪ *(407) 790-4839*
*246 N Orlando Ave*
*St. Petersburg* ▪ *(727) 826-0755*
*10304 Roosevelt Blvd N*
*Jupiter* ▪ *(561) 622-6883*
*5500 N Military Trl*
*Tallahassee* ▪ *(850) 727-5358*
*3122 Mahan Dr*

## Jim 'n Nick's Bar-B-Q                    ✪★📖

*Niceville* ▪ *(850) 729-7200*
*1052 E John Simms Pkwy*
*Destin* ▪ *(850) 424-5895*
*14073 Emerald Coast Pkwy*

## Joe's Crab Shack                         ✪📖

*Naples* ▪ *(239) 793-7700*
*1355 Fifth Ave S*
*Fort Meyers* ▪ *(239) 332-1881*
*2024 W First St*
*Lauderhill* ▪ *(954) 749-2722*
*4402 N University Dr*
*Destin* ▪ *(850) 650-1882*
*14055 Emerald Coast pkwy*
*Clearwater* ▪ *(727) 799-8530*
*2730 Gulf to Bay Blvd*
*Sanford* ▪ *(407) 323-0934*
*4659 W 1st St*
*Celebration* ▪ *(321) 939-6880*
*10 Blake Blvd*
*Kissimmee* ▪ *(407) 787-0041*
*7903 Irlo Bronson Memorial Hwy*
*Daytona Beach* ▪ *(386) 238-4050*
*1200 Main St*

## Le Bistro                    ✪★$$D
*Lighthouse Point* ▪ *(954) 946-9240*
*4626 N Federal Hwy* ▪ *French* ▪ GF items
are marked on the menu and include lamb
osso bucco, shrimp risotto, steak frites,
and wild mushroom soup, among other
things. GF beer is also available, as are GF
desserts like crème brûlée and fresh fruit. ▪
*www.lebistrorestaurant.com*

## Lee Roy Selmon's              ✪★$$LD
*Fort Myers* ▪ *(239) 690-3287*
*5056 Daniels Pkwy*
*St Petersburg* ▪ *(727) 347-5774*
*2424 Tyrone Blvd N*
*Bradenton* ▪ *(941) 798-3287*
*6510 Cortez Rd W*
*Palm Harbor* ▪ *(727) 216-6566*
*34200 US Highway 19 N*
*Brandon* ▪ *(813) 654-5454*
*11310 Causeway Blvd* ▪ *American* ▪ GF
menu includes grilled shrimp salad, burgers without buns, backyard BBQ chicken,
pulled pork, and more. Selmon's Super
Sundae is available for dessert. GF beer is
also available. Jennifer at customer service
recommends alerting a manager upon arrival. ▪ *www.leeroyselmons.com*

## Loving Hut                    📖
*Cape Coral* ▪ *(239) 424-8433*
*1918 Del Prado Blvd S*
*Naples* ▪ *(239) 254-9490*
*975 Pine Ridge Rd*

## Mama Fu's Asian House          ✪📖
*Hollywood* ▪ *(954) 983-5500*
*3257 Hollywood Blvd*

## Mantanzas Innlet Restaurant     ✪$$LD
*St Augustine* ▪ *(904) 461-6824*
*8805 A1A S* ▪ *Seafood* ▪ Most of their
seafood items are naturally GF as well
as their sandwiches without the bread. ▪
*www.matanzas.biz*

## Margaritaville                 ✪★📖
*Key West* ▪ *(305) 292-1435*
*500 Duval St*
*Panama City Beach* ▪ *(850) 235-7870*
*16230 Front Beach Rd*

## Michael's Genuine Food & Drink   $$$LD
*Miami* ▪ *(305) 573-5550*
*130 NE 40th St* ▪ *American* ▪ The restaurant reports that "some pre-made
GF options" are available, and adds that
most dishes can be prepared GF upon
request. Alert server upon arrival. ▪
*www.michaelsgenuine.com/miami*

## Miller's Ale House Restaurants   ✪★📖
*Boca Raton* ▪ *(561) 988-9142*
*1200 Yamato Rd*
*Boca Raton* ▪ *(561) 487-2989*
*9244 W Glades Rd*
*Boynton Beach* ▪ *(561) 735-0591*
*2212 N Congress Ave*
*Brandon* ▪ *(813) 643-0511*
*1817 W Brandon Blvd*
*Coral Gables* ▪ *(305) 444-3600*
*101 Miracle Mile*
*Coral Springs* ▪ *(954) 825-0574*
*1915 N University Dr*
*Davie* ▪ *(954) 236-0062*
*2080 S University Dr*
*Daytona* ▪ *(954) 236-0062*
*2610 W Intl Speedway Blvd*
*Destin* ▪ *(850) 837-0694*
*34906 Emerald Coast Pkwy*
*Miami* ▪ *(305) 629-9442*
*3271 NW 87th Ave*
*Ft Myers* ▪ *(239) 461-9334*
*10065 Gulf Ctr Dr*
*Fort Lauderdale* ▪ *(954) 565-5747*
*2861 N Federal Hwy*
*Ft Myers* ▪ *(239) 931-4160*
*4400 Kernel Cir*
*Gainesville* ▪ *(352) 371-0818*
*3950 SW Archer Rd*
*Palm Beach Gardens* ▪ *(561) 691-1915*
*9800 Alt A1A*
*Hollywood* ▪ *(954) 925-7275*
*3215 Oakwood Blvd*
*Jensen Beach* ▪ *(772) 692-3611*
*3611 NW Fed Hwy*
*Jupiter* ▪ *(561) 746-6720*
*126 Ctr St*
*Miami* ▪ *(305) 595-7448*
*11625 N Kendall Dr*
*Lakeland* ▪ *(863) 709-9262*

5650 S Florida Ave
*Palmetto* ▪ (305) 259-8844
13603 S Dixie Hwy
*Miami Lakes* ▪ (305) 231-8585
15251 NW 67th Ave
*N Miami* ▪ (305) 945-6878
3227 NE 163rd St
*Ocala* ▪ (352) 620-8989
305 SE 17th St
*Orange Park* ▪ (904) 278-4600
1756 Wells Rd
*Altamonte Sprgs* ▪ (407) 331-6611
477 E Altamonte Dr
*Kissimmee* ▪ (407) 238-4499
8123 Irlo Bronson Mem Hwy
*Sanford* ▪ (407) 328-7037
50 Town Ctr Cir
*Winter Park* ▪ (407) 671-1011
101 University Park Dr
*Oviedo* ▪ (407) 365-6331
321 Mitchell Hammock Rd
*Pensacola* ▪ (850) 505-2670
5906 N Davis Hwy
*Pembroke Pines* ▪ (954) 438-0111
11795 Pines Blvd
*Sarasota* ▪ (941) 378-8888
3800 Kenny Dr
*St. Petersburg* ▪ (727) 217-9206
7901 Martin Luther King St N
*Tallahassee* ▪ (850) 222-0364
722 Appalachee Pkwy

**Mitchell's Fish Market**                    ✪ 📖
*Sandestin* ▪ (850) 650-2484
500 Grand Blvd
*Winter Park* ▪ (407) 339-3474
460 N Orlando Ave

**Morton's Steakhouse**                       ✪ 📖
*Boca Raton* ▪ (561) 392-7724
5050 Town Ctr Cir
*Coral Gables* ▪ (305) 442-1662
2333 Ponce de Leon Blvd
*Fort Lauderdale* ▪ (954) 467-9720
500 E Broward Blvd
*Miami* ▪ (305) 400-9990
1200 Brickell Ave
*N Miami* ▪ (305) 945-3131
17399 Biscayne Blvd

*W Palm Beach* ▪ (561) 835-9664
777 S Flagler Dr

**O'Charley's**                                📖
*Panama City* ▪ (850) 784-8110
311 E 23rd St
*Orange Park* ▪ (904) 264-2673
1609 County Rd 220
*Pensacola* ▪ (850) 484-8936
6233 N Davis Hwy

**Ozona Pizza**                               ★ $LD
*Ozona* ▪ (727) 786-9662
404 Orange St ▪ Pizza ▪ GF pizza and
other GF desserts are available daily. ▪
*www.ozonapizza.com*

**P.F. Chang's China Bistro**               ✪★📖
*Aventura* ▪ (305) 957-1966
17455 Biscayne Blvd
*Fort Myers* ▪ (239) 590-9197
10081 Gulf Center Dr
*Ft Lauderdale* ▪ (954) 565-5877
2418 E Sunrise Blvd
*Miami* ▪ (305) 358-0732
901 S Miami Ave Ste 104
*Miami* ▪ (305) 234-2338
8888 SW 136th St Ste 100
*Palm Beach Gardens* ▪ (561) 691-1610
3101 Pga Blvd Ste F142
*Sandestin* ▪ (850) 269-1806
640 Grand Blvd
*Sunrise* ▪ (954) 845-1113
1740 Sawgrass Mills Cir
*Winter Park* ▪ (407) 622-0188
436 N Orlando Ave

**Pampas Churrascaria**                    ★ $$$$BLD
*West Palm Beach* ▪ (561) 444-2147
651 Okeechobee Blvd ▪ Brazilian ▪ General Manager Paul at the Las Vegas location
reports that all meats and seafood are GF,
and most items in the side/salad bar area
are as well. GF bread is available. Paul adds
that the Florida location will have the same
GF options. Call either location before visting to ensure that GF options are available.
▪ *www.pampasusa.com*

**Pei Wei Asian Diner**　⊙📖
*Boynton Beach* ▪ (561) 364-1830
*1750 N Congress Ave*
*Kissimmee* ▪ (407) 846-0829
*2501 W Osceola Pkwy*
*Miami* ▪ (305) 386-8510
*13616 N Kendall Dr*
*Miami Lakes* ▪ (305) 817-8320
*15519 NW 67th Ave*
*Pembroke Pines* ▪ (954) 499-8820
*11049 Pines Blvd*
*Plantation* ▪ (954) 308-3720
*522 N Pine Island Rd*
*St Petersburg* ▪ (727) 347-1351
*1402 66th St N*
*Stuart* ▪ (772) 219-0466
*2101 SE Federal Hwy*
*University Park* ▪ (941) 359-8570
*8511 Cooper Creek Blvd*
*Wellington* ▪ (561) 753-6260
*10610 Bay 10 Forest Hill Blvd*
*Weston* ▪ (954) 308-7330
*4517 Weston Rd*
*Altamonte Springs* ▪ (407) 834-0752
*355 E Altamonte Dr*
*Fort Lauderdale* ▪ (954) 565-5881
*1730 N Federal Hwy*
*Fort Lauderdale* ▪ (954) 767-0873
*1515 SE 17th St*
*Miami* ▪ (305) 935-2230
*18801 Biscayne Blvd*

**Pizza Fusion**　★📖
*Fort Lauderdale* ▪ (954) 358-5353
*1013 N Federal Hwy*
*Fort Myers* ▪ (239) 337-7979
*12901 McGregor Blvd*
*Miami Beach* ▪ (305) 672-7778
*1115 5th St*
*Weston* ▪ (954) 641-5353
*2378 Weston Rd*

**Prime One Twelve**　$$$$**LD**
*Miami Beach* ▪ (305) 532-8112
*112 Ocean Dr* ▪ *Steakhouse* ▪ The restaurant reports that they keep a list of items that contain gluten, and can prepare most dishes without these

items. Alert the server upon arrival. ▪
*www.mylesrestaurantgroup.com*

**Red Brick Pizza**　⊙★📖
*Naples* ▪ (239) 514-3900
*6355 Naples Blvd*
*Panama City Beach* ▪ (850) 236-1413
*801 Pier Park Dr*
*Destin* ▪ (850) 424-5990
*4144 Legendary Dr*

**Rodizio Grill**　★📖
*Pensacola* ▪ (850) 466-2113
*605 E Gregory St*

**Romano's Macaroni Grill**　⊙★📖
*Altamonte Springs* ▪ (407) 682-2577
*884 W State Road 436*
*Brandon* ▪ (813) 685-6530
*132 Brandon Town Center Dr*
*Clearwater* ▪ (727) 726-6676
*28795 US Hwy 19 N*
*Doral* ▪ (305) 477-6676
*8700 NW 18th Terrace*
*Fort Meyers* ▪ (239) 433-7786
*13721 S Tamiami Trl*
*Gainesville* ▪ (352) 331-0638
*6401 W Newberry Rd*
*Kissimmee* ▪ (407) 933-6995
*3286 N John Young Pkwy*
*Kissimmee* ▪ (407) 396-6155
*5320 W Irlo Bronson Hwy*
*Lake Mary* ▪ (407) 333-4547
*835 Currency Cir*
*Miami* ▪ (305) 270-0621
*12100 SW 88th St*
*Oviedo* ▪ (407) 365-4405
*7123 Red Bug Lake Rd*
*Pembroke Pines* ▪ (954) 704-2331
*13620 Pines Blvd*
*Pensacola* ▪ (850) 479-2491
*5100 N 9th Ave*
*Plantation* ▪ (954) 473-5770
*100 N University Dr*
*Saint Petersburg* ▪ (727) 343-0050
*2302 Tyrone Blvd N*
*Tallhassee* ▪ (850) 877-1706
*1498 Apalachee Pkwy*

*Wellington* ▪ (561) 792-2248
*2535 S State Rd 7*
*Winter Garden* ▪ (407) 654-0351
*3143 Daniels Rd*

### Rookery Grill, The                         ★ $BLD
*Marco Island* ▪ (239) 394-2511
*400 S Collier Blvd* ▪ *American* ▪ GF bread
and wraps are available. Manager Kathleen
reports that the entire menu is "geared
toward people with allergies," so the chef
can create many GF options. Located in
the Marco Island Resort and Spa. Dinner
served only on Fridays and Saturdays. ▪
*www.marcoislandmarriott.com/rookery.html*

### Ruth's Chris Steak House              ✪ 📖
*Bonita Springs* ▪ (239) 948-8888
*23151 Village Shops Wy*
*Coral Gables* ▪ (305) 461-8360
*2320 Salzedo St*
*Destin* ▪ (850) 337-5108
*15000 Emerald Coast Pkwy*
*Fort Lauderdale* ▪ (954) 565-2338
*2525 N Federal Hwy*
*Lake Mary* ▪ (407) 804-8220
*80 Colonial Center Pkwy*
*North Palm Beach* ▪ (561) 863-0660
*661 US Hwy 1*
*Ponte Vedra Beach* ▪ (904) 285-0014
*814 A1A N*
*West Palm Beach* ▪ (561) 514-3544
*651 Okeechobee Blvd*
*Winter Park* ▪ (407) 622-2444
*610 N Orlando Ave*

### Seasons 52-Palm Beach Gardens
✪$$$LD
*Palm Beach Gardens* ▪ (561) 625-5852
*11611 Ellison Wilson Rd* ▪ *Modern American*
▪ GF menu is available. Manager Kimmy
reports that GF diners are accommodated
"on a regular basis." Alert a server upon
arrival. Reservations noting GF are recom-
mended. ▪ *www.seasons52.com*

### Serendipity Café                          ¢BL
*Dunedin* ▪ (727) 483-9233
*664 Main St* ▪ *American* ▪ Everything on
the menu is 100% GF and 100% freshly

made. Items on the menu include kale
salad, French toast, buffalo chicken under
wrap, and Gramma's loaded pizza. ▪
*myserendipitycafe.com*

### Shane's Rib Shack                        ✪📖
*Boynton Beach* ▪ (561) 735-0742
*950 N Congress Ave*
*Gulf Breeze* ▪ (850) 934-7427
*3707 Gulf Breeze Pkwy*
*Lakeland* ▪ (863) 686-7427
*1529 Town Center Dr*
*Royal Palm Beach* ▪ (561) 333-7427
*11051 Southern Blvd*
*Tallahassee* ▪ (850) 309-7427
*1424 W Tennessee St*
*Ocala* ▪ (352) 304-5255
*2602 SW 19th Ave Rd*
*Panama City Beach* ▪ (850) 249-8111
*10100 Hutchison Blvd*

### Smith & Wollensky                        📖
*Miami Beach* ▪ (305) 673-2800
*1 Washington Ave*

### Smokey Bones                             📖
*Clearwater* ▪ (727) 712-1930
*2693 Gulf to Bay Blvd*
*Brandon* ▪ (813) 655-3400
*136 Brandon Town Center Dr*
*Lakeland* ▪ (863) 815-8870
*3901 US Hwy 98 N*
*Kissimmee* ▪ (407) 397-7102
*2911 Vineland Rd*
*Sanford* ▪ (407) 688-8227
*1000 WP Ball Blvd*
*Casselberry* ▪ (407) 673-4901
*1490 State Rd 436*
*Melbourne* ▪ (321) 951-9777
*1510 W New Haven*
*Wellington* ▪ (561) 383-8240
*10260 Forest Hill Blvd*
*Plantation* ▪ (954) 474-3833
*809 S University Dr*

### Soul Vegetarian Restaurant              ✪¢LD
*Tallahassee* ▪ (850) 893-8208
*1205 S Adams St* ▪ *Vegetarian* ▪ GF menu
available online and in the restaurant.
Around 90% of the food served is GF, and

a list of items to avoid is also included on the GF list. Alert the server upon arrival. ▪ *soulvegtallahassee.com*

### Stir Crazy                                    ★📖
*Estero* ▪ *(239) 498-6430*
*23106 Fashion Dr*
*Pembroke Pines* ▪ *(954) 919-4900*
*I-75 & Pines Blvd*

### Sugarcane Raw Bar Grill            $$**LD**
*Miami* ▪ *(786) 369-0353*
*3250 NE 1st Ave* ▪ *Fusion* ▪ The restaurant reports that they can accommodate GF diners and requests that GF guests inform their server upon arrival. ▪ *www.sugarcanerawbargrill.com*

### Ted's Montana Grill                  ✪📖
*Estero* ▪ *(239) 947-9318*
*8017 Pza Del Lago Dr*
*Tallahassee* ▪ *(850) 561-8337*
*1954 Village Green Wy*

### Texas De Brazil Churrascaria       ★📖
*Miami Beach* ▪ *(305) 695-7702*
*300 Alton Rd*
*Miami* ▪ *(305) 599-7729*
*11401 NW 12th St*
*Fort Lauderdale* ▪ *(954) 400-5630*
*2457 E Sunrise Blvd*
*Hallandale Beach* ▪ *(954) 843-7600*
*800 Silks Run*

### That Deli                          ✪★¢**LD**
*Lake Mary* ▪ *(321) 363-1394*
*3801 W Lake Mary Blvd* ▪ *Deli* ▪ GF bread is available for sandwiches. Other GF items, such as soups and salads, are marked on the menu. Upon request, sandwiches can be prepared in a separate area to lower the risk of CC. ▪ *thatdelifl.com*

### Tony Roma's                          📖
*Aventura* ▪ *(305) 936-9190*
*19501 Biscayne Blvd*
*Jensen Beach* ▪ *(772) 225-6327*
*3750 NE Indian River Dr*
*Miami* ▪ *(305) 994-7511*
*3300 NW 87th Ave*
*Miami* ▪ *(305) 513-4337*

*1455 NW 107 Ave*
*Sunrise* ▪ *(954) 851-0759*
*12801 W Sunrise Blvd*
*Wellington* ▪ *(561) 790-3888*
*10300 W Forest Hill Blvd*

### Tony's Sushi Japanese Steakhouse ★ $$**LD**
*Ocala* ▪ *(352) 237-3151*
*3405 SW College Rd* ▪ *Japanese* ▪ Manager Jane reports that there are a number of naturally GF menu items. She notes that all servers are GF aware and that GF soy sauce is available for substitution. Alert a server and speak to a manager upon arrival. ▪ *www.tonysushi.com*

### Uno Chicago Grill                  ✪★📖
*Kissimmee* ▪ *(407) 396-2755*
*5350 W Irlo Bronson Memorial Hwy*
*Melbourne* ▪ *(321) 255-1400*
*8260 N Wickham Rd*
*Winter Garden* ▪ *(407) 877-6510*
*3167 Daniels Rd*

### Vertoris Pizza House              ✪★$**LD**
*Bradenton* ▪ *(941) 751-0333*
*6830 14th St W* ▪ *Pizza* ▪ Extensive GF menu includes pizza, pasta, chicken tenders, eggplant parmesan, sandwiches, and more. Several GF desserts are available, including GF flourless chocolate cake, cheesecake, and tiramisu. GF beer is also available. ▪ *www.vertorispizza.com*

### Village Tavern                       ✪📖
*Boynton Beach* ▪ *(561) 853-0280*
*1880 N Congress Ave Suite 170*
*Pembroke Pines* ▪ *(954) 874-1001*
*14555 SW 2nd St*

### Yakko-San                           ★$**LD**
*North Miami Beach* ▪ *(305) 947-0064*
*3881 NE 163 St* ▪ *Japanese* ▪ The restaurant reports that their rice and fish are GF. GF soy sauce is available. Staff recommends that GF guests ask that their meal be prepared with the GF soy sauce and not order anything with teriyaki. Alert the server upon arrival. ▪ *www.yakko-san.com*

## Yard House                            ✪📖
Coral Gables ▪ (305) 447-9273
320 San Lorenzo Ave
Palm Beach Gardens ▪ (561) 691-6901
11701 Lake Victoria Gardens Ave
Hallandale Beach ▪ (954) 454-9950
601 Silks Run

# GEORGIA

## ATLANTA

### 5 Seasons Brewing                    ✪$$LD
Atlanta ▪ (404) 875-3232
1000 Marietta St ▪ Modern American ▪
Manager Jamie at the Alpharetta location
and reservationist Kat at the Sandy Springs
location report that GF diners are welcome,
and they accommodate GF diners often.
They advise making reservations noting
GF and alerting the server upon arrival. GF
items are marked on the regular menu and
they can modify many others to fit your
dietary needs. ▪ www.5seasonsbrewing.com

### Aja                                 ★$$$LD
Atlanta ▪ (404) 231-0001
3500 Lenox Rd NE ▪ Asian Fusion ▪ GF soy
sauce is sometimes available. Restaurant reports that they serve GF diners "at least once
a day." Alert a server upon arrival. Servers
are trained to speak with the chef, who will
recommend a few GF items. Almost any
curry dish is GF. ▪ www.h2sr.com

### Bacchanalia                         $$LD
Atlanta ▪ (404) 365-0410
1198 Howell Mill Rd ▪ American ▪ The
restaurant reports that the chefs have "no
problem" accommodating GF diners and
adds that several dishes can be modified
to be GF. Alert the server upon arrival. ▪
starprovisions.com

### Blue Moon Pizza                     ★$$LD
Atlanta ▪ (404) 814-1515
325 E Paces Ferry Rd ▪ Pizza ▪ GF menu
includes any pizza made with GF crust,
cheesy bread, bruschetta, a variety of
salads, and more. A GF brownie is available for dessert. The restaurant has an
extensive CC policy, which is detailed
under the gluten-free tab on their website.
▪ www.bluemoonpizzaatl.com

### Blue Ridge Grill                    ✪$$$$LD
Atlanta ▪ (404) 233-5030
1261 W Paces Ferry Rd NW ▪ Modern
American ▪ GF menu includes iron skillet
mussels, tuna tartare, wild Scottish salmon,
beet and goat cheese salad, Georgia trout,
and more. Alert a server upon arrival. ▪
www.blueridgegrill.com

### Bocado                              $$$LD
Atlanta ▪ (404) 815-1399
887 Howell Mill Rd ▪ Modern American
▪ Restaurant reports that "quite a few" of
their menu items are GF, and others can
be "reworked" to become GF. Alert your
server and they will go over the menu with
you. ▪ bocadoatlanta.com

### Bone's Restaurant                   $$$$LD
Atlanta ▪ (404) 237-2663
3130 Piedmont Rd NE ▪ Seafood & Steakhouse ▪ The chef notes that the kitchen
takes GF requests "extremely seriously",
and that they make every effort to make the
GF dining experience "as normal as possible." He reports that most steak and seafood dishes are naturally GF. Confirm the
timeliness of this information before dining in. Alert a server, who will confer with
the kitchen. ▪ www.bonesrestaurant.com

### Bonefish Grill                      ✪📖
Altanta ▪ (404) 235-4024
1540 Ave Pl

### BrickTop's                         ✪📖
Atlanta ▪ (404) 841-2212
3280 Peachtree Rd NE

### Brookhaven Bistro ¢BL
*Atlanta* ▪ *(404) 846-2233*
*4274 Peachtree Rd NE* ▪ *Café* ▪ Owner
and Chef Chip reports that GF items are
marked on the menu board but not on
the printed menus. He notes that with the
exception of sandwiches and wraps, almost
all items in the deli case are GF. Confirm
the timeliness of this information before
dining in. ▪ *www.brookhavenbistro.com*

### Buckhead Pizza Co. ★$LD
*Atlanta* ▪ *(404) 869-0678*
*3324 Peachtree Rd NE*
*Atlanta* ▪ *(770) 405-0722*
*One Galleria Pkwy SE* ▪ *Pizza* ▪ GF pizza
is available in the personal size only. GF
desserts like carrot cakes and brownies
are available at the Atlanta location only. ▪
*www.buckheadpizzaco.com*

### Canoe $$$LD
*Atlanta* ▪ *(770) 432-2663*
*4199 Paces Ferry Rd SE* ▪ *Modern Ameri-*
*can* ▪ The restaurant reports that they are
"able to address any dietary need" their
customers have. Several menu items are
GF, though not advertised as such. Alert a
server, who will point out available GF options. ▪ *www.canoeatl.com*

### Cantina Taqueria & Tequila Bar $$LD
*Atlanta* ▪ *(404) 892-9292*
*3280 Peachtree Rd NW* ▪ *Mexican* ▪ Manager Katie reports that salads, fajitas with
chicken and vegetables, chicken wraps, and
corn tortillas are options for GF diners. Confirm the timeliness of this information before
dining in. Upon arrival, alert a server and ask
for a manager or chef. ▪ *www.h2sr.com*

### Capital Grille, The ✪▢
*Atlanta* ▪ *(404) 262-1162*
*255 E Paces Ferry Rd*
*Atlanta* ▪ *(770) 730-8447*
*94 Perimeter Ctr W*

### Cardamom Hill $$$LD
*Atlanta* ▪ *(404) 549-7012*
*1700 Northside Dr* ▪ *Indian* ▪ The restaurants reports several GF options, including GF fried chicken, biryani, short ribs,
and a daily salad. Confirm the timeliness
of the information before dining in. ▪
*cardamomhill.net*

### Carrabba's Italian Grill ✪▢
*Atlanta* ▪ *(770) 804-0467*
*1210 Ashford Crossing*
*Atlanta* ▪ *(770) 437-1444*
*2999 Cumberland Blvd SE*

### Coast $D
*Atlanta* ▪ *(404) 869-0777*
*111 W Paces Ferry Rd NW* ▪ *Seafood* ▪
Manager Chet reports that GF diners are
welcome. He notes that the fish is freshly
prepared and can be made to be GF. Confirm the timeliness of this information
before dining in. He notes that GF diners
should alert a server and ask for a manager.
▪ *www.h2sr.com*

### Davio's Northern Italian Steakhouse ✪▢
*Atlanta* ▪ *(404) 844-4810*
*3500 Peachtree Rd NE*

### Doc Chey's Noodle House ★¢LD
*Atlanta* ▪ *(404) 378-8188*
*1556 N Decatur Rd*
*Atlanta* ▪ *(404) 888-0777*
*1424 N Highland Ave*
*Atlanta* ▪ *(404) 688-4238*
*563 Memorial Dr* ▪ *Asian* ▪ GF menu
includes Thai fried rice, Indian curry,
tomato ginger noodles, and Vietnamese
prawn salad. GF rice noodles and various
other items are also available. Manager
Tyler recommends alerting a server, who
can assure that all GF meals are prepared
properly. ▪ *www.doccheys.com*

### Don Pablo's ✪▢
*Atlanta* ▪ *(770) 955-5929*
*3131 Cobb Pkwy SE*

### Ecco ✪$$$D
*Atlanta* ▪ *(404) 347-9555*
*40 7th St NE* ▪ *Mediterranean* ▪ GF menu
available on request. Examples of GF
entrées include braised beef short ribs and

roasted monk fish, among others. Confirm the timeliness of this information before dining in. ▪ *www.ecco-atlanta.com*

### Eclipse di Luna                    ✪$LD
*Atlanta* ▪ *(678) 205-5862*
*4505 Ashford Dunwoody Rd NE*
*Atlanta* ▪ *(404) 846-0449*
*764 Miami Cir NE* ▪ *Spanish* ▪ GF menus are available at both locations. GF menu items include tomato mozzarella, mussels and chorizo, halibut, carne asada, beef skewers, and roasted scallops. Alert the manager upon arrival to address CC concerns. ▪ *www.eclipsediluna.com*

### Empire State South                    $$$$LD
*Atlanta* ▪ *(404) 541-1105*
*999 Peachtree St* ▪ *Southern* ▪ The restaurant reports that they can "easily work around any food allergy." Alert a server, who will specify GF options and notify the kitchen. ▪ *empirestatesouth.com*

### Figo Pasta                    ✪★◖LD
*Atlanta* ▪ *(404) 351-3700*
*1210 Howell Mill Rd NW*
*Atlanta* ▪ *(770) 698-0505*
*1140 Hammond Dr NE*
*Atlanta* ▪ *(404) 351-9667*
*1170 Collier Rd NW*
*Atlanta* ▪ *(404) 586-9250*
*1220 Caroline St NE*
*Atlanta* ▪ *(770) 434-4444*
*2941 Paces Ferry Rd NE* ▪ *Italian* ▪ GF pasta is available. GF items are marked on the menu and include caprese salad, baked eggplant with tomato sauce, and any pasta dish made with GF fusilli pasta. ▪ *www.figopasta.com*

### Fleming's Prime Steakhouse & Wine Bar                    ✪📖
*Atlanta* ▪ *(770) 698-8112*
*4501 Olde Perimeter Wy*

### Fogo De Chao                    ★📖
*Atlanta* ▪ *(404) 266-9988*
*3101 Piedmont Rd*

### Fresh 2 Order                    ✪$LD
*Atlanta* ▪ *(404) 503-9999*
*3344 Peachtree Rd NE*
*Atlanta* ▪ *(678) 564-1400*
*1260 Cumberland Mall SE*
*Atlanta* ▪ *(404) 593-2333*
*860 Peachtree St NE*
*Atlanta* ▪ *(404) 567-8646*
*6125 Roswell Rd NE*
*Atlanta* ▪ *(678) 564-1400*
*1727 Clifton Rd*
*Atlanta* ▪ *(404) 530-6600*
*6000 N Term Pkwy B A1A* ▪ *Café* ▪ GF menu includes a variety of salads, as well as brown sugar roasted pork loin, salmon entrée without sauce or seasoning, and un-marinated grilled chicken breast. The GF menu also notes which salad dressings, add-ons, sauces, and sides are GF. Area director Craig recommends asking for a manager upon arrival. ▪ *www.fresh2order.com*

### Garrison's Broiler & Tap                    ★$$$LD
*Atlanta* ▪ *(770) 436-0102*
*4300 Paces Ferry Rd SE* ▪ *American* ▪ Manager Les reports that GF diners should alert a server upon arrival. Servers will go directly to the chef, and, if necessary, a manager will come to the table. He also says that they have a celiac waitress so they are extremely well-informed about GF options. Les notes that the steaks, burgers without buns, and salmon with no sauce are GF. Confirm the timeliness of this information before dining in. ▪ *www.garrisonsatlanta.com*

### Goldfish                    $$LD
*Atlanta* ▪ *(770) 671-0100*
*4400 Ashford Dunwoody Rd NE* ▪ *Global* ▪ Manager Brett reports that they serve GF diners "all the time." He recommends that GF customers alert their servers, who can point out suitable entrées. Servers know the menu "very well," but they always double check with chefs when dealing with GF. Located in Perimeter Mall. ▪ *h2sr.com/goldfish/*

## Hard Rock Café ✪📖
*Atlanta ▪ (404) 688-7625*
*215 Peachtree St NE*

## Imperial Fez $$$$D
*Atlanta ▪ (404) 351-0870*
*2285 Peachtree Rd NE ▪ Middle Eastern*
▪ GF accommodations can be made. The restaurant reports that all entrée items can be made GF upon request. Alert server upon arrival and they will inform chef. ▪ *www.imperialfez.com*

## Jason's Deli ✪📖
*Atlanta ▪ (404) 231-3333*
*3330 Piedmont Rd NE*
*Atlanta ▪ (770) 671-1555*
*4705 Ashford Dunwoody Rd*
*Atlanta ▪ (770) 432-4414*
*1109 Cumberland Mall*
*Atlanta ▪ (404) 843-8212*
*5975 Roswell Rd*
*Atlanta ▪ (404) 853-3760*
*230 10th St NE*
*Atlanta ▪ (404) 344-4844*
*3755 Carmia Dr SW*

## Jersey Mike's 📖
*Atlanta ▪ (404) 349-5707*
*6035 Bakers Ferry Rd*
*Atlanta ▪ (678) 279-9990*
*2014 Powers Ferry Rd*
*Atlanta ▪ (404) 605-7001*
*2020 Howell Mill Rd*
*Atlanta ▪ (404) 846-3380*
*3740 Roswell Rd*
*Atlanta ▪ (404) 252-9898*
*227 Sandy Springs Place NE*
*Atlanta ▪ (404) 846-4060*
*3895 Peachtree Rd North E*
*Atlanta ▪ (404) 321-0080*
*2470 Briarcliff Rd*
*Atlanta ▪ (770) 451-2023*
*2036 Johnson Ferry Rd*
*Atlanta ▪ (770) 457-0539*
*3489A Chamblee Tucker Rd*
*Atlanta ▪ (404) 724-0760*
*1000 Northside Dr NW*

## Joey D's Oak Room $$$LD
*Atlanta ▪ (770) 512-7063*
*1015 Crown Pointe Pkwy ▪ American*
▪ Staff states there are a variety of GF and GF optional items on their menu, although they are not listed online. When dining in, be sure to alert the server to any dietary needs and they will provide a list of GF items available. ▪ *www.centraarchy.comjoey-ds-oak-room/*

## Johnny Brusco's New York Style Pizza ★📖
*Atlanta ▪ (404) 874-8304*
*1810 Cheshire Bridge Rd*
*Atlanta ▪ (404) 603-8043*
*1465 Chattahoochee Ave*
*Atlanta ▪ (678) 973-0634*
*5495 Cascade Rd*

## La Tavola Trattoria ✪$$$D
*Atlanta ▪ (404) 873-5430*
*992 Virginia Ave NE ▪ Italian* ▪ GF menu includes beet and watercress salad, zucchini salad, shrimp risotto, roasted trout, market fish, flat iron steak, grilled lamb chops with polenta and asparagus, and more. ▪ *www.latavolatrattoria.com*

## Legal Sea Foods ✪📖
*Atlanta ▪ (678) 500-3700*
*275 Baker St NW*

## Maggiano's Little Italy ★📖
*Atlanta ▪ (770) 799-1580*
*1601 Cumberland Mall SE*
*Atlanta ▪ (404) 816-9650*
*3368 Peachtree Rd NE*
*Atlanta ▪ (770) 804-3313*
*4400 Ashford Dunwoody Rd NE*

## Melting Pot, The ✪📖
*Atlanta ▪ (404) 389-0099*
*754 Peachtree St NE*

## MetroFresh ✪$BLD
*Atlanta ▪ (404) 724-0151*
*931 Monroe Dr*
*Atlanta ▪ (404) 474-9589*
*1345 Piedmont Ave ▪ American* ▪ Manager Diane reports that the menu and its

marked GF items change daily, but there are always several GF options to choose from. Examples of GF items are mixed field greens with fruit and goat cheese, roasted beet and plum salad, seared trout with spinach, and chilled sweet corn. ▪ *www.metrofreshatl.com*

### Metrotainment Bakery    ★ $$$$$
*Atlanta* ▪ *(404) 873-6307*
*1119 Logan Cir NW* ▪ *Bakery* ▪ GF cake options include chocolate cake with fudge frosting and mini chocolate chips, yellow cake with vanilla buttercream, and yellow cake with chocolate buttercream. Manager Keith reports that customers must call at least 48 hours in advance to place an order. Also, because it is not a dedicated GF bakery, they cannot guarantee no CC. ▪ *www.metrobakery.com*

### Miller Union    $$$LD
*Atlanta* ▪ *(678) 733-8550*
*999 Brady Ave NW* ▪ *Modern American* ▪ Owner Neal reports that the entire menu is GF "apart from 2 or 3 things". A server will be able to direct you to the appropriate menu items. ▪ *www.millerunion.com*

### Morton's Steakhouse    ✪📖
*Atlanta* ▪ *(404) 577-4366*
*303 Peachtree Ctr Ave*

### Nan Thai Fine Dining    $$$LD
*Atlanta* ▪ *(404) 870-9933*
*1350 Spring St NW* ▪ *Thai* ▪ Manager Yai recommends making reservations noting GF and requesting dishes that require soy sauce in advance, as they are willing to make modifications if possible. Yai reports that it is necessary to alert a server, who will "make sure with the chef." ▪ *www.nanfinedining.com*

### New York Prime    ✪★$$$D
*Atlanta* ▪ *(404) 846-0644*
*3424 Peachtree Rd NE* ▪ *Steakhouse* ▪ All steak and chicken entrées are GF. Most fish entrées are too, with the exception of anything covered with flour/bread. If a customer likes something on the menu that is usually not GF, the restaurant is willing to alter the recipe if possible. Alert the server upon arrival. ▪ *www.newyorkprime.com*

### Noche    ✪D
*Atlanta* ▪ *(770) 777-9555*
*3719 Old Alabama Rd*
*Atlanta* ▪ *(404) 815-9155*
*1000 Virginia Ave NE*
*Atlanta* ▪ *(770) 432-3277*
*2850 Paces Ferry Rd SE*
*Atlanta* ▪ *(404) 364-9448*
*705 Town Blvd NE* ▪ *Spanish* ▪ All locations note that they accommodate GF diners on a regular basis. Menu items that can be modified to be GF. Note GF when making reservations. ▪ *www.h2sr.com*

### P.F. Chang's China Bistro    ✪★📖
*Atlanta* ▪ *(770) 352-0500*
*500 Ashwood Pkwy*
*Atlanta* ▪ *(770) 803-5800*
*1624 Cumberland Mall SE Ste Ls108*

### Paolo's Gelato Italiano    ✪S
*Atlanta* ▪ *(404) 607-0044*
*1025 Virginia Ave NE* ▪ *Ice Cream* ▪ All gelatos are GF. ▪ *www.paolosgelato.com*

### Pure Taqueria    ✪✪LD
*Atlanta* ▪ *(404) 522-7873*
*300 N Highland Ave* ▪ *Latin American* ▪ GF menu includes ceviche, fajitas with corn tortillas, duck confit, pescado veracruz, grilled shrimp, and more. The restaurant reports that all salsas, rice, and beans are GF, and adds that GF chips are available. Since there is a common fryer for all items, they recommend avoiding fried foods. Confirm the timeliness of this information before dining in. ▪ *www.puretaqueria.com*

### Quinones at Bacchanalia    $$$$D
*Atlanta* ▪ *(404) 365-0410*
*1198 Howell Mill Rd NW* ▪ *American* ▪ Restaurant reports that all meals are made from scratch, so the chef can accommodate any needs or special requests. Reservations noting GF are required. ▪ *www.starprovisions.com*

## R. Thomas' Deluxe Grill    ★ $BLD
*Atlanta* ▪ *(404) 881-0246*
*1812 Peachtree St NW* ▪ *American* ▪
Veteran Server Nina reports that the
only non-GF items that do not have
GF alternatives are the toast and the
sandwich buns. Confirm the timeliness
of this information before dining in. ▪
*www.rthomasdeluxegrill.net*

## Real Chow Baby, The    ★ $LD
*Atlanta* ▪ *(404) 815-4900*
*1016 Howell Mill Rd NW*
*Atlanta* ▪ *(404) 671-4202*
*782 Ponce de Leon Ave NE* ▪ *Asian* ▪ Manager Ben at Howell Mill reports that both
locations have a list of GF sauces, which
customers can carry through the buffet
line. Both locations have rice noodles,
meats, and vegetables that are GF. GF
customers should put white sticks in their
bowls to indicate GF to the stir fry cook. ▪
*www.therealchowbaby.com*

## Restaurant Eugene    $$$$D
*Atlanta* ▪ *(404) 355-0321*
*2277 Peachtree Rd NE* ▪ *Modern American* ▪ Restaurant reports that the menu
changes frequently, and most menu items
are naturally GF. They also note that all
dishes are made from scratch. Reservations
noting GF are recommended. Alert a server
upon arrival. ▪ *www.restauranteugene.com*

## Ruth's Chris Steak House    ✪▣
*Atlanta* ▪ *(404) 365-0660*
*3285 Peachtree Rd NE*
*Atlanta* ▪ *(404) 223-6500*
*267 Marietta St*
*Atlanta* ▪ *(404) 255-0035*
*5788 Roswell Rd NW*

## Saba    ✪★₵LD
*Atlanta* ▪ *(404) 377-7786*
*1451 Oxford Rd NE* ▪ *Italian* ▪ GF menu
includes a variety of appetizers, salads, pastas, and side orders. Owner
Shane reports that the entire staff is GF
aware. GF pasta and beer are available. ▪
*www.saba-restaurant.com*

## Shane's Rib Shack    ✪▣
*Atlanta* ▪ *(404) 525-7427*
*1221 Caroline St NE*
*Atlanta* ▪ *(770) 399-9010*
*123 Perimeter Ctr W*
*Atlanta* ▪ *(770) 951-7211*
*3155 Cobb Pkwy*
*Atlanta* ▪ *(404) 231-1742*
*3247 Roswell Rd NE*

## Shed at Glenwood, The    $$$D
*Atlanta* ▪ *(404) 835-4363*
*475 Bill Kennedy Way SE* ▪ *American* ▪ GF
items include roast beef salad, pan seared
free range chicken, and grilled all natural
ribeye. Owner Cindy reports that most
items can be modified to be GF. It is best to
alert the server of your dietary restrictions.
▪ *www.theshedatglenwood.com*

## Shout    ★ $$$LD
*Atlanta* ▪ *(404) 846-2000*
*1197 Peachtree St* ▪ *Modern American* ▪
Manager Amanda reports that GF diners
will typically eat a vegetable plate with
roasted chicken or other simple fare.
She also notes that several menu items
can be modified to be GF, depending on
the availability of ingredients. Reservations noting GF are recommended. ▪
*h2sr.com/shout/*

## SOHO Restaurant    ✪$$$LD
*Atlanta* ▪ *(770) 801-0069*
*4300 Paces Ferry Rd SE* ▪ *Modern
American* ▪ GF menu includes chicken
soup with tortilla chips, mussels, blackened grouper, and beef short ribs.
Restaurant reports that they get "a fair
amount" of GF diners every month. ▪
*www.sohoatlanta.com*

## South City Kitchen    ✪$$$LD
*Atlanta* ▪ *(404) 873-7358*
*1144 Crescent Ave NE* ▪ *Southern* ▪
GF menu includes Georgia mountain trout, molasses brined pork chop,
Atlantic salmon, steak, and more. ▪
*www.southcitykitchen.com*

**Strip**                              $$$**LD**
*Atlanta* ▪ *(404) 385-2005*
*245 18th St NW* ▪ *Seafood & Steakhouse*
▪ Sous-chef James reports that GF diners
"definitely have some options." He notes
that they are accustomed to accommodat-
ing "all types of food allergies." Alert a
server upon arrival. Servers are trained
to go "directly" to the chef and follow a
specific protocol. ▪ *www.h2sr.com*

**Surin of Thailand**                         📖
*Atlanta* ▪ *(404) 892-7789*
*810 N Highland Ave*

**Ted's Montana Grill**                    ✪📖
*Atlanta* ▪ *(770) 863-0041*
*1000 Cumberland Mall*
*Atlanta* ▪ *(404) 521-9796*
*133 Luckie St NW*
*Atlanta* ▪ *(404) 355-3897*
*1874 Peachtree Rd*
*Atlanta* ▪ *(678) 581-7890*
*2500 Cobb Pl Ln*

**Tin Drum AsiaCafé**                      ✪📖
*Atlanta* ▪ *(404) 303-0910*
*4367 Roswell Rd*
*Atlanta* ▪ *(404) 373-8887*
*1561 N Decatur Rd NE*
*Atlanta* ▪ *(404) 688-3182*
*84 Peachtree St NW*
*Atlanta* ▪ *(404) 745-3068*
*265 18th St*
*Atlanta* ▪ *(770) 393-3006*
*4530 Olde Perimeter Wy*
*Atlanta* ▪ *(404) 881-1368*
*88 5th St*
*Atlanta* ▪ *(404) 846-8689*
*2561 Piedmont RD NE*
*Atlanta* ▪ *(404) 565-2266*
*1197 Peachtree St*

**Twist**                              ★$$**LD**
*Atlanta* ▪ *(404) 869-1191*
*3500 Peachtree Rd NE* ▪ *Global* ▪ The
restaurant reports that several menu items
are naturally GF. GF options include pork
ribs, beef short steak, garlic and pepper

shrimp satay, paella, and scallops. Confirm
the timeliness of this information before
dining in. Ask the server to indicate GF
menu items. ▪ *h2sr.com/twist/*

**Urban Pl8**                          ✪$$**LD**
*Atlanta* ▪ *(404) 367-0317*
*1082 Huff Rd* ▪ *Modern American* ▪
Urban Pl8 has an in restaurant menu with
asterisks showing which items are GF and
which are not. ▪ *www.urbanpl8.com*

**Village Tavern**                        ✪📖
*Alpharetta* ▪ *(770) 777-6490*
*11555 Rainwater Dr*

**Wisteria Restaurant**                  ✪$$**D**
*Atlanta* ▪ *(404) 525-3363*
*471 N Highland Ave* ▪ *American* ▪
GF menu includes pork tenderloin,
shrimp and grits, almond crusted trout,
lamb shank, beef tenderloin and oysters.
*www.wisteria-atlanta.com*

**Woodfire Grill**                      $$$$**D**
*Atlanta* ▪ *(404) 347-9055*
*1782 Cheshire Bridge Rd NE* ▪ *Modern*
*American* ▪ Manager notes that most menu
items can be modified to be GF. For a
primetime meal, make reservations noting
GF at least a couple of weeks in advance. ▪
*www.woodfiregrill.com*

**World Peace Café**                ✪★¢**BLD**
*Sandy Springs* ▪ *(404) 256-2100*
*220 Hammond Dr* ▪ *Vegetarian* ▪ GF
items are labeled on the in house menu
and include a variety of frittatas and
omelettes, a breakfast wrap made with
corn tortilla, several salads, and more.
GF bread is available for sandwiches.
Breakfast served on weekends only. ▪
*worldpeacecafeatlanta.com*

**Yard House**                            ✪📖
*Atlanta* ▪ *(404) 815-8990*
*261 19th St NW*

**Yeah! Burger**                        ★¢**LD**
*Atlanta* ▪ *(404) 437-7845*
*1017 N Highland Ave*
*Atlanta* ▪ *(404) 496-4393*

1168 Howell Mill Rd ▪ *American* ▪ Yeah Burger has a regular menu which is marked to show customers which GF items are available. ▪ *www.yeahburger.com*

## GEORGIA

### ALL OTHER CITIES

#### 32 Degrees Yogurt Bar 📖
*Carrollton* ▪ *(770) 214-8489*
*1109 S Park St*

#### 5 Seasons Brewing ✪$$LD
*Sandy Springs* ▪ *(404) 255-5911*
*5600 Roswell Rd*
*Alpharetta* ▪ *(770) 521-5551*
*3655 Old Milton Pkwy* ▪ *Modern American* ▪ Manager Jamie at the Alpharetta location and reservationist Kat at the Sandy Springs location report that GF diners are welcome, and they accommodate GF diners often. They advise making reservations noting GF and alerting the server upon arrival. GF items are marked on the regular menu and they can modify many others to fit your dietary needs. ▪ *www.5seasonsbrewing.com*

#### Aqua Blue $$$D
*Roswell* ▪ *(770) 643-8886*
*1564 Holcomb Bridge Rd* ▪ *Global* ▪ Though they do not have a GF menu, the restaurant reports that they have "accommodated many GF customers in the past" and "have always been able to do something for them." Alert server upon arrival. ▪ *www.aquablueatl.com*

#### Aqua Terra Bistro $LD
*Buford* ▪ *(770) 271-3000*
*55 E Main St* ▪ *Bistro* ▪ Restaurant reports that many items are naturally GF

or can be modified to be GF, as the chef does not use flour in many sauces. Servers are GF aware and will accommodate. ▪ *www.aquaterrabistro.com*

#### Aurelio's Pizza ★📖
*Marietta* ▪ *(770) 578-6606*
*1255 Johnson Ferry Rd*

#### Belly's Pizza ★$LD
*Roswell* ▪ *(770) 594-8118*
*550 W Crossville Rd* ▪ *Pizza* ▪ GF pizza and beer are available. Restaurant reports that all specialty pizzas can be prepared GF, and recommends alerting the server upon arrival. ▪ *www.bellyspizza.com*

#### Big Shanty Smokehouse ¢LD
*Kennesaw* ▪ *(770) 499-7444*
*3393 Cherokee St* ▪ *Barbeque* ▪ The restaurant reports that most of the menu is naturally GF. The owner has Celiac and all employees are very familiar with procedures to prevent CC. Alert the server upon arrival. ▪ *bigshantybbq.com*

#### Blue Moon Pizza ★$$LD
*Marietta* ▪ *(770) 984-2444*
*2359 Windy Hill Rd SE*
*Smyrna* ▪ *(770) 436-4446*
*4600 W Village Pl SE*
*Sandy Springs* ▪ *(404) 236-7200*
*5610 Glenridge Dr* ▪ *Pizza* ▪ GF menu includes any pizza made with GF crust, cheesy bread, bruschetta, a variety of salads, and more. A GF brownie is available for dessert. The restaurant has an extensive CC policy, which is detailed under the gluten-free tab on their website. ▪ *www.bluemoonpizzaatl.com*

#### Bonefish Grill ✪📖
*Macon* ▪ *(478) 477-5256*
*5080 Riverside Dr Ste 506*
*Snellville* ▪ *(678) 344-8945*
*1350 Highway 124 N*
*Buford* ▪ *(678) 546-8240*
*3420 Buford Dr Bldg C Ste 590*
*Augusta* ▪ *(706) 737-2929*
*2911 Washington Rd*
*Alpharetta* ▪ *(770) 475-6668*

11705 Jones Bridge Rd
*Saint Simons Island* ▪ (912) 634-0246
202 Retreat Vlg # 3
*Savannah* ▪ (912) 691-2575
5500 Abercorn St Ste 44
*Columbus* ▪ (706) 321-2015
6783-2 Veterans Pkwy

### Brookwood Grill                       ✪$$LD
*Roswell* ▪ (770) 587-0102
880 Holcomb Bridge Rd ▪ American ▪ A
GF menu is available in-house and includes
a selection of salads and meat or seafood
entrées, including marinated chicken
breast & NY strip steak. Be sure to consult
with the server to ensure a GF meal. ▪
*www.brookwoodgrill.com*

### Buca di Beppo                       ✪📖
*Alpharetta* ▪ (770) 643-9463
2335 Mansell Rd
*Augusta* ▪ (706) 733-5475
3450 Wrightsboro Rd
*Macon* ▪ (478) 471-1246
5080 Riverside Dr

### Buckhead Pizza Co.                    ★$LD
*Cumming* ▪ (770) 781-0304
415 Peachtree Pkwy ▪ Pizza ▪ GF pizza
is available in the personal size only. GF
desserts like carrot cakes and brownies
are available at the Atlanta location only. ▪
*www.buckheadpizzaco.com*

### Café Life                          ★¢LD
*Marietta* ▪ (770) 977-9583
1453 Roswell Rd ▪ Vegetarian ▪ GF bread
is available for sandwiches, and select
entrées are GF. Located inside Life Grocery.
▪ *www.lifegrocery.com*

### California Dreaming Restaurant and
### Bar                               ✪📖
*Augusta* ▪ (706) 860-6206
3241 Washington Rd
*Duluth* ▪ (770) 813-9240
1630 Cross Pointe Wy
*Kennesaw* ▪ (770) 428-2055
745 Chastain Rd NW

### Carino's Italian                    ✪📖
*Albany* ▪ (229) 439-1022
3007 Kensington Ct
*Columbus* ▪ (706) 317-3343
3033 Manchester Expy
*East Point* ▪ (404) 494-3000
3330 Camp Creek Pkwy
*Lawrenceville* ▪ (678) 847-6300
1802 N Brown Rd
*Warner Robins* ▪ (478) 929-1800
2707 Watson Blvd

### Carrabba's Italian Grill            ✪📖
*Athens* ▪ (706) 546-9938
3194 Atlanta Hwy
*Augusta* ▪ (706) 733-0123
2832 Washington Rd
*Columbus* ▪ (706) 494-8144
5555 Whittlesey Blvd
*Douglasville* ▪ (770) 947-0330
2700 Chapel Hill Rd
*Duluth* ▪ (770) 497-4959
2030 Sugarloaf Cir
*Kennesaw* ▪ (770) 499-0338
1160 Ernest W Barrett Pkwy NW
*Macon* ▪ (478) 474-5115
3913 River Place Dr
*Morrow* ▪ (770) 968-3233
1887 Mount Zion Rd
*Peachtree City* ▪ (770) 631-1057
500 Commerce Dr
*Savannah* ▪ (912) 961-7073
10408 Abercorn St
*Cumming* ▪ (770) 292-9104
420 Peachtree Pkwy

### Corleone's                         ★$$LD
*Savannah* ▪ (912) 232-2720
44 Martin Luther King Blvd ▪ Italian ▪ GF
pasta is available. ▪ *www.corleones.tv/*

### Crab Shack, The                      $$LD
*Tybee Island* ▪ (912) 786-9857
40 Estill Hammock Rd ▪ Seafood ▪
Restaurant reports that most servers are
familiar with GF, but cannot guarantee
CC will not occur. Lisa notes that they can

prepare a GF meal. She suggests previewing the menu online before coming in. ▪ *www.thecrabshack.com*

**East West Bistro**                    $LD
*Athens ▪ (706) 546-9378*
*351 E Broad St ▪ Global ▪* No GF menu but the restaurant reports that GF dishes include Hawaiian tuna tataki, a vegetable bowl over GF noodles, grilled chicken, salmon filet, a hamburger patty with seasonal vegetables, and misto salad. ▪ *www.eastwestbistro.com*

**Fatz Eatz & Drinkz**                    📖
*Athens ▪ (706) 425-8780*
*4115 Lexington Rd*
*Blairsville ▪ (706) 781-1643*
*206 Hwy 515 E*
*Evans ▪ (706) 650-2421*
*464 N Belair Rd*
*Jasper ▪ (706) 692-0003*
*800 Noah Dr*
*Pooler ▪ (912) 748-2557*
*400 Pooler Pkwy*
*Warner Robins ▪ (478) 971-1090*
*2715 Watson Blvd*
*Winder ▪ (770) 867-3344*
*442 Atlanta Hwy NW*

**Figo Pasta**                    ✪★🖍📖
*Alpharetta ▪ (770) 569-1007*
*5950 N Point Pkwy*
*Decatur ▪ (404) 377-2121*
*627 E College Ave ▪ Italian ▪* GF pasta is available. GF items are marked on the menu and include caprese salad, baked eggplant with tomato sauce, and any pasta dish made with GF fusilli pasta. ▪ *www.figopasta.com*

**Fox and Hound Pub & Grille**          📖
*Kennesaw ▪ (770) 794-4444*
*2500 Cobb Pl Ln*

**Fresh 2 Order**                    ✪$LD
*Duluth ▪ (678) 720-9333*
*10900 Medlock Bridge Rd ▪ Café ▪* GF menu includes a variety of salads, as well as brown sugar roasted pork loin, salmon entrée without sauce or seasoning, and un-marinated grilled chicken breast. The GF menu also notes which salad dressings, add-ons, sauces, and sides are GF. Area director Craig recommends asking for a manager upon arrival. ▪ *www.fresh2order.com*

**Fuego Mundo South American Wood-Fire Grill**                    ✪$LD
*Sandy Springs ▪ (404) 256-4330*
*5590 Roswell Rd ▪ Latin American ▪* GF items are marked with asterisks on the menu. All breads are stored and prepared in different areas to prevent CC. ▪ *fuegomundo.com*

**Genghis Grill**                    📖
*Buford ▪ (678) 733-5426*
*1825 Mall of Georgia Blvd*
*Sandy Springs ▪ (678) 587-0050*
*1165 Perimeter Center W*

**Gluten Free Cutie**                    🖍$
*Roswell ▪ (770) 518-7858*
*45 Park Sq Ct ▪ Bakery ▪* GF Cutie is a 100% dedicated GF bakery offering items such as cupcakes, cake pops, puddings, and cakes. ▪ *glutenfreecutie.com*

**Good Grub Subs**                    ★🖍LD
*Alpharetta ▪ (678) 701-5644*
*5905 Atlanta Hwy ▪ Deli ▪* Good Grub Subs has every sub on their normal menu available in a GF version. Separate preparation stations are used along with dedicated oven trays and utensils. ▪ *www.goodgrubsubs.com*

**Harbor Inn Seafood Restaurant**     ★📖
*Augusta ▪ (706) 729-0187*
*3404 Wrightsboro Rd*

**Jason's Deli**                    ✪📖
*Alpharetta ▪ (770) 619-2300*
*3070 Windward Plaza*
*Norcross ▪ (770) 368-9440*
*5131 Peachtree Pkwy*
*Alpharetta ▪ (770) 664-5002*
*7300 N Pint Pkwy*
*Columbus ▪ (706) 494-8857*
*5555 Whittlesey Blvd*

*Athens* ▪ (706) 425-4950
140 Alps Rd
*Tucker* ▪ (770) 493-4020
4073 Lavista Rd
*Duluth* ▪ (678) 957-1973
11720 Medlock Bridge Rd
*Kennesaw* ▪ (678) 398-4000
945 Ernest W Barrett Pkwy

**Jersey Mike's**  📖
*Acworth* ▪ (770) 966-1923
3330 N Cobb Pkwy
*Newnan* ▪ (770) 251-2260
90 Glenda Trace
*Peachtree City* ▪ (770) 631-4136
2729 Highway 54 W
*Smyrna* ▪ (404) 799-8977
4715 S Atlanta Rd
*Marietta* ▪ (770) 578-3973
2960 Shallowford Rd
*Roswell* ▪ (770) 992-1605
665 Holcomb Bridge Rd
*Dunwoody* ▪ (770) 394-1999
2458 Jett Ferry Rd
*Alpharetta* ▪ (678) 366-3866
4075 Old Milton Pkwy
*Canton* ▪ (678) 493-0006
149 Reinhardt College Pkwy
*Duluth* ▪ (678) 957-9845
3780 Old Norcross Rd
*Lawrenceville Georgia-z* ▪
(678) 847-6688
1820 N Brown Rd
*Suwanee* ▪ (678) 482-2188
3463 Lawrenceville-Suwanee Rd
*Shellville* ▪ (678) 344-4482
2050 Highway 124
*Loganville* ▪ (770) 554-7474
4018 Atlanta Hwy
*Monroe* ▪ (770) 266-1055
2120 W Spring St
*Holy Springs* ▪ (770) 926-7775
5341 Old Highway 5
*Kennesaw* ▪ (770) 426-8010
840 Ernest W Barrett Pkwy NW
*Savannah* ▪ (912) 898-3540
111 Jazie Dr
*Savannah* ▪ (912) 355-3077
7400 Abercom St

*Dalton* ▪ (706) 529-7827
1367 W Walnut Ave
*Grovetown* ▪ (706) 650-1806
4010 Gateway Blvd
*Columbus* ▪ (706) 221-7349
1640 Rollins Wy
*Peachtree Corners* ▪ (770) 417-1417
6050 Peachtree Pkwy

**Jim 'n Nick's Bar-B-Q**  ✪★📖
*Conyers* ▪ (770) 785-4453
2275 GA Hwy 20
*Hiram* ▪ (770) 439-2662
5153 Jimmy Lee Smith Pkwy
*Smyrna* ▪ (678) 556-0011
4574 S Cobb Dr
*Cumming* ▪ (678) 845-1565
3130 Ronald Reagan Blvd
*Suwanee* ▪ (770) 255-1717
1103 Old Peachtree Rd

**Joe's Crab Shack**  ✪📖
*Morrow* ▪ (770) 472-0024
1965 Mt Zion Rd
*Kennesaw* ▪ (770) 429-7703
2501 Cobb Place Blvd
*Duluth* ▪ (770) 381-6333
1590 Pleasant Hill Rd
*Lilburn* ▪ (770) 736-2900
4300 Stone Mountain Hwy
*Douglasville* ▪ (770) 947-5990
2868 Chapel Hill Rd

**Johnny Brusco's**
**New York Style Pizza**  ★📖
*Acworth* ▪ (770) 529-5300
3541 Cobb Pkwy NW
*Alpharetta* ▪ (678) 867-6773
869 N Main St
*Alpharetta* ▪ (770) 777-8000
11875 Jones Bridge Rd
*Athens* ▪ (706) 354-1515
1040 Gaines School Rd
*Hickory Flat* ▪ (770) 704-6776
6124 Hickory Flat Hwy
*Canton* ▪ (770) 945-7131
559 Riverstone Pkwy
*Carrollton* ▪ (770) 830-5955
1670 US Hwy 27 S
*Cartersville* ▪ (678) 721-0520

244 N Dixie Ave
*Columbus* ▪ *(706) 507-5050*
6770 Veterans Pkwy
*Conyers* ▪ *(770) 922-1000*
2455 Salem Rd
*Cornelia* ▪ *(706) 776-2200*
700 Historical 441 Hwy
*Covington* ▪ *(678) 342-4343*
10176 Carlin Dr
*Cumming* ▪ *(678) 947-4260*
3490 Keith Bridge Rd
*Dacula* ▪ *(678) 377-2434*
720 Dacula Rd
*Dallas* ▪ *(770) 445-9500*
49 Hosiery Mill Rd
*Dawsonville* ▪ *(706) 216-1224*
355 Quill Dr
*Douglasville* ▪ *(678) 214-8486*
2911 Chapel Hill Rd
*Dublin* ▪ *(478) 272-8966*
2301 Bellevue Rd
*Fayetteville* ▪ *(770) 461-4225*
230 N Glynn St
*Gainesville* ▪ *(678) 989-5050*
104 Carrington Park Dr
*Grayson* ▪ *(770) 962-9181*
2023 Grayson Hwy
*Hapeville* ▪ *(404) 766-3727*
834 Virginia Ave
*Hiram* ▪ *(770) 439-0109*
5140 Jimmy Lee Smith Pkwy
*Jasper* ▪ *(706) 253-0800*
744 Noah Dr
*Jefferson* ▪ *(706) 367-1314*
940 Lee St
*Alpharetta* ▪ *(770) 777-9799*
9950 Jones Brigdge Rd
*Kennesaw* ▪ *(678) 355-0825*
3940 Cherokee St
*Kennesaw* ▪ *(678) 996-0911*
1615 Ridenour Blvd
*Lawrenceville* ▪ *(678) 985-8288*
3157 Sugarloaf Pkwy
*Lithia Springs* ▪ *(770) 745-5555*
230 Thornton Rd
*Macon* ▪ *(478) 405-3232*
6255 Zebulon Rd
*Marietta* ▪ *(678) 797-0505*

2970 Canton Rd
*Marietta* ▪ *(770) 425-8333*
3718 Dallas Hwy
*Marietta* ▪ *(678) 560-2228*
4880 Lower Roswell Rd
*McDonough* ▪ *(770) 954-4225*
24 Old Jackson Rd
*Newnan* ▪ *(770) 252-3495*
1111 Lower Fayetteville Rd
*Norcross* ▪ *(678) 966-0868*
5005 Peachtree Pkwy
*Peachtree City* ▪ *(770) 486-5480*
494 Crosstown Dr
*Rockmart* ▪ *(770) 684-7700*
1735 Nathan Dean Pkwy
*Rome* ▪ *(706) 232-6555*
233 Broad St
*Sandy Springs* ▪ *(770) 804-3322*
7887A Roswell Rd
*Smyrna* ▪ *(770) 431-0600*
1435 Highlands Ridge Rd
*Smyrna* ▪ *(770) 438-0300*
2651 Cumberland Blvd
*Snellville* ▪ *(770) 978-8180*
3035 Centerville Hwy
*Flowery Branch* ▪ *(770) 965-0429*
7363 Spout Spring Rd
*Stockbridge* ▪ *(678) 289-1449*
608 Eagles Landing Pkwy
*Suwanee* ▪ *(770) 932-1998*
1165 A Peachtree Industrial Blvd
*Villa Rica* ▪ *(678) 840-5111*
2000 Mirror Lake Blvd
*Bonaire* ▪ *(478) 988-0220*
778 Hwy 96
*West Point* ▪ *(706) 645-2010*
712 3rd Ave
*Winder* ▪ *(770) 867-0401*
133 W Athens St
*Woodstock* ▪ *(770) 928-9494*
1105 Parkside Ln

### Lavender Asian Bistro                ✪ ★ $LD
*Lawrenceville* ▪ *(770) 982-3887*
1195 Scenic Hwy ▪ Asian ▪ GF menu is for
dining in only and includes pad thai, green
curry, and Mongolian beef, among many

other items. For take-out, ask about GF options. Hostess Ria reports that over half of the take-out menu is naturally GF. GF soy sauce is available for dining in and take-out. ▪ *www.lavenderasianbistro.com*

## Lemon Grass                                    $LD
*Marietta* ▪ (770) 973-7478
*2145 Roswell Rd* ▪ *Thai* ▪ Manager Ginger reports that all of the curry dishes and the pad thai are naturally GF. Confirm the timeliness of this information before dining in. She also notes that the chef, who is her brother, is willing to create dishes for GF customers who want something special. Ginger recommends asking for her upon arrival so that she can help choose a GF meal. ▪ *www.lemongrassmarietta.com*

## Life Grocery and Café              ✪$BLD
*Marietta* ▪ (770) 977-9583
*1453 Roswell Rd* ▪ *American* ▪ Server Julie reports that although the menu changes daily, a selection of WF and GF food is served at the hot and cold bars. She also notes that GF items are indicated in menu descriptions. Examples of past GF items include cake, salads, and vegetable stir-fry. Upon arrival, ask for the chef, or ask the server for GF details. ▪ *www.lifegrocery.com*

## Loving Hut                                      📖
*Norcross* ▪ (678) 421-9191
*6385 Spalding Dr*
*Kennesaw* ▪ (770) 429-0666
*2700 Town Center Dr*

## Melting Pot, The                          ✪📖
*Duluth* ▪ (770) 623-1290
*3610 Satellite Blvd*
*Kennesaw* ▪ (770) 425-1411
*2500 Cobb Place Ln NW Ste 800*
*Roswell* ▪ (770) 518-4100
*1055 Mansell Rd*
*Savannah* ▪ (912) 349-5676
*232 E Broughton St*

## Miller's Ale House Restaurants   ✪★📖
*Alpharetta* ▪ (678) 277-2581
*10750 Davis Dr*

## O'Charley's                                      📖
*Buford* ▪ (770) 271-0534
*3217 Buford Dr*
*Acworth* ▪ (678) 574-7378
*3285 Cobb Pkwy NW*
*Augusta* ▪ (706) 739-0855
*276 Robert C Daniel Jr Pkwy*
*Hiram* ▪ (770) 222-0822
*4790 Jimmy Lee Smith Pkwy*
*Austell* ▪ (770) 941-0253
*4130 Austell Rd*
*Kennesaw* ▪ (770) 792-7866
*705 Town Park Ln*
*Lawrenceville* ▪ (770) 237-3788
*830 Lawrenceville-Suwanee Rd*
*Macon* ▪ (478) 477-2050
*3740 Bloomfield Rd*
*Marietta* ▪ (770) 579-2690
*3550 Sandy Plains Rd*
*McDonough* ▪ (770) 954-9871
*1842 Jonesboro Rd*
*Newnan* ▪ (770) 252-8584
*545 Bullsboro Dr*
*Snellville* ▪ (770) 736-3231
*2049 Scenic Hwy N*
*Stockbridge* ▪ (770) 389-4095
*3511 Hwy 138 SE*
*Tucker* ▪ (770) 491-6245
*2039 Crescent Centre Blvd*
*Villa Rica* ▪ (770) 456-4245
*921 S Carrol Rd*
*Woodstock* ▪ (770) 592-7501
*10009 Hwy 92*
*Canton* ▪ (770) 720-6161
*1409 Riverstone Pkwy*
*Carrollton* ▪ (770) 832-2125
*1591 S Hwy 27*
*Centerville* ▪ (478) 971-1145
*2990 Watson Blvd*
*Columbus* ▪ (706) 324-2929
*1528 Bradley Park Dr*
*Cumming* ▪ (770) 888-3880
*920 Buford Rd*
*Conyers* ▪ (770) 922-2280
*1289 Dogwood Dr*
*Dalton* ▪ (706) 226-5057
*1520 W Walnut Ave*
*Fayetteville* ▪ (770) 716-3731

1350 Hwy 85 N
*Douglasville* ▪ (770) 920-4646
2320 The Landing Dr
*Gainesville* ▪ (770) 534-2455
1711 Brown's Bridge
*Ft. Oglethorpe* ▪ (706) 861-5520
2542 Battlefield Pkwy
*Griffin* ▪ (770) 233-8156
1512 W McIntosh Rd

### Oar House Inc., The       ★$$$LD
*Dahlonega* ▪ (706) 864-9938
3072 Highway 52 E ▪ *American* ▪ Menu items that can be modified to be GF mainly include the seafood and steak. Reservations noting GF are highly recommended. ▪ *www.theoarhouse.com*

### Olde Pink House, The       ✪$$$LD
*Savannah* ▪ (912) 232-4286
23 Abercorn St ▪ *Southern* ▪ Manager Kristen reports that they have a GF menu and serve GF diners "all the time." She notes that nearly all of the seafood dishes, including the jumbo sea scallops and the fish of the day, are naturally GF. Confirm the timeliness of this information before dining in. She recommends alerting a server, who will notify the chef.

### P.F. Chang's China Bistro       ✪★📖
*Alpharetta* ▪ (770) 992-3070
7925 N Point Pkwy
*Augusta* ▪ (706) 733-0161
3450 Wrightsboro Rd Ste D215
*Buford* ▪ (678) 546-9005
3333 Buford Dr Ste Va03

### Pappasito's Cantina       📖
*Marietta* ▪ (770) 541-6100
2788 Windy Hill Rd SE

### Pepperoni's       ✪★$LD
*Duluth* ▪ (770) 232-0224
2750 Buford Hwy ▪ *Italian* ▪ GF pizza, pasta, chicken nuggets, and brownies are available. Alert a manager upon arrival to address CC concerns. ▪ *www.pepperonisduluth.com*

### Pure Taqueria       ✪⊄LD
*Alpharetta* ▪ (678) 240-0023
103 Roswell St
*Woodstock* ▪ (770) 952-7873
405 Chambers St
*Duluth* ▪ (770) 609-2630
3108 Main St
*Roswell* ▪ (770) 817-7873
1143 Alpharetta St ▪ *Latin American* ▪ GF menu includes ceviche, fajitas with corn tortillas, duck confit, pescado veracruz, grilled shrimp, and more. The restaurant reports that all salsas, rice, and beans are GF, and adds that GF chips are available. Since there is a common fryer for all items, they recommend avoiding fried foods. Confirm the timeliness of this information before dining in. ▪ *www.puretaqueria.com*

### Ray's Killer Creek       $$$$LD
*Alpharetta* ▪ (770) 649-0064
1700 Mansell Rd ▪ *American* ▪ Chef Daniel reports that they do not serve GF diners very often, but there are many options for GF diners. He recommends reservations noting GF, so the server is made aware in advance. Servers are fairly educated on the GF diet, but still Daniel suggests asking the server to speak to him about modifying food to be GF. ▪ *www.raysrestaurants.com*

### Ritters Restaurant       $$LD
*Marietta* ▪ (770) 973-1230
4719 Lower Roswell Rd ▪ *Southern* ▪ The restaurant reports that GF requests are not a problem. They can substitute GF rice flour for regular flour. Confirm the timeliness of this information before dining in. ▪ *www.rittersrestaurant.net*

### Romano's Macaroni Grill       ✪★📖
*Alpharetta* ▪ (770) 360-6302
5045 Windward Pkwy
*Augusta* ▪ (706) 736-3029
275 Robert C Daniel Jr Pkwy
*Buford* ▪ (678) 714-0049
3207 Buford Dr
*Dunwoody* ▪ (770) 394-6676
4788 Ashford Dunwoody Rd

*Marietta* ▪ *(678) 581-5624*
*3625 Dallas Hwy SW*
*Savannah* ▪ *(912) 692-1488*
*7804 Abercorn St*
*Snellville* ▪ *(770) 985-8022*
*1350 Scenic Hwy N*

### RosaMia Ristorante Italiano ✪$$LD

*Johns Creek* ▪ *(770) 772-6456*
*11730 A Jones Bridge Rd* ▪ *Italian* ▪
GF items are marked on the menu and
include seared sole, chicken marsala, veal
piccata, and more. GF pasta is available, as
well as spicy torta cioccolato for dessert.
Some dishes may require modification to
become GF, so be sure to alert the server. ▪
*www.rosamiaitalian.com*

### Ruth's Chris Steak House ✪📖

*Kennesaw* ▪ *(770) 420-1985*
*620 Chastain Rd NW*
*Savannah* ▪ *(912) 721-4800*
*111 W Bay St*

### Saba ✪★◁LD

*Decatur* ▪ *(404) 377-9266*
*350 Mead Rd* ▪ *Italian* ▪ GF menu
includes a variety of appetizers, salads, pastas, and side orders. Owner
Shane reports that the entire staff is GF
aware. GF pasta and beer are available. ▪
*www.saba-restaurant.com*

### Sally's Bakery ◁S

*Sandy Springs* ▪ *(404) 847-0211*
*5920 Roswell Rd NE*
*Alpharetta* ▪ *(470) 226-7965*
*4390 Kimball Bridge Rd* ▪ *Bakery* ▪
Dedicated GF bakery offering a variety
of breads, cookies, english muffins, and
"take-&-bake" pizzas. Establishment
recommends placing orders for specific items at least one day in advance. ▪
*www.sallysglutenfreebakery.com*

### Seasons 52 ✪$$LD

*Dunwoody* ▪ *(770) 671-0052*
*90 Perimeter Ctr W* ▪ *Modern American*
▪ GF menu lists regular menu options that
are naturally GF or can be modified to be
GF. Manager Jay reports that items are easy

to modify, as all dishes are made fresh to
order. Reservations noting GF are recommended. ▪ *www.seasons52.com*

### Shane's Rib Shack ✪📖

*Alpharetta* ▪ *(678) 297-2041*
*270 Rucker Rd*
*Alpharetta* ▪ *(770) 569-1988*
*4180 Old Milton Pkwy*
*Athens* ▪ *(706) 548-4650*
*196 N Milledge Ave*
*Brunswick* ▪ *(912) 264-4227*
*315 Village At Glynn Pl*
*Canton* ▪ *(678) 880-1141*
*135 Reinhardt College Pkwy*
*Canton* ▪ *(770) 720-8835*
*2864 E Cherokee Dr*
*Carrollton* ▪ *(770) 830-7427*
*1141 Bankhead Hwy*
*Conyers* ▪ *(770) 483-4363*
*2890 Highway 212 SW*
*Covington* ▪ *(770) 786-2101*
*11162 Highway 142 N*
*Dacula* ▪ *(678) 546-8150*
*3465 Braselton Hwy*
*Eatonton* ▪ *(706) 485-3003*
*106 Harmony Xing*
*Ellijay* ▪ *(706) 635-7427*
*289 Highland Xing*
*Evans* ▪ *(706) 855-8227*
*4446 Washington Rd*
*Flowery Branch* ▪ *(770) 965-0123*
*5877 Spout Springs Rd*
*Hinesville* ▪ *(912) 877-7675*
*300 W General Screven Wy*
*Kennesaw* ▪ *(770) 420-3344*
*400 Ernest W Barrett Pkwy NW*
*Lawrenceville* ▪ *(770) 962-1870*
*4835 Sugarloaf Pkwy*
*Locust Grove* ▪ *(678) 583-8186*
*4980 Bill Gardner Pkwy*
*Loganville* ▪ *(770) 554-8200*
*4743 Atlanta Hwy*
*Macon* ▪ *(478) 257-6038*
*3267 Vineville Ave*
*Marietta* ▪ *(678) 290-0053*
*3894 Due W Rd NW Ste 280*
*Mcdonough* ▪ *(770) 898-7878*
*2136 Highway 155 N*

*Mcdonough* ▪ *(678) 583-0011*
*2788 Highway 81 E*
*Mcdonough* ▪ *(678) 583-1998*
*579 Jonesboro Rd*
*Newnan* ▪ *(770) 683-6416*
*55 Newnan Crossing Byp*
*Norcross* ▪ *(770) 416-6606*
*5770 Peachtree Industrial Blvd*
*Peachtree City* ▪ *(678) 364-9700*
*1261 N Peachtree Pkwy*
*Rome* ▪ *(706) 291-6062*
*315 Riverside Pkwy NE*
*Savannah* ▪ *(912) 354-3744*
*6730 Waters Ave*
*Smyrna* ▪ *(678) 213-2640*
*300 Village Green Cir SE*
*Snellville* ▪ *(770) 985-3733*
*4017 Annistown Rd*
*St Simons Island* ▪ *(912) 268-2272*
*70 Retreat Vlg*
*Statesboro* ▪ *(912) 681-4227*
*1100 Brampton Ave*
*Suwanee* ▪ *(770) 886-6657*
*2609 Peachtree Pkwy*
*Suwanee* ▪ *(770) 945-1117*
*3131 Lawrenceville Suwanee Rd*
*Winder* ▪ *(770) 307-1339*
*108 E May St*
*Roswell* ▪ *(678) 297-2041*
*270 Rucker Rd*
*Barnesville* ▪ *(678) 359-1402*
*534 College Dr*
*Bethlehem* ▪ *(770) 307-0071*
*916 Loganville Hwy*
*Brunswick* ▪ *(912) 264-4227*
*315 Village at Glynn Pl*
*Canton* ▪ *(770) 517-8655*
*4504 Old Hwy 5*
*Canton* ▪ *(770) 720-8835*
*2864 E Cherokee Dr*
*Douglasville* ▪ *(770) 947-4105*
*2750 Chapel Hill Rd*
*Jefferson* ▪ *(706) 367-0351*
*388 Hwy 82 S*
*Pooler* ▪ *(912) 748-8711*
*441 Pooler Pkwy*
*Warner Robins* ▪ *(478) 988-0020*
*670 Lake Joy Rd*

### Shell House Restaurant    $$D

*Savannah* ▪ *(912) 927-3280*
*8 Gateway Blvd E* ▪ *Seafood* ▪ Manager Nathan reports that they can accommodate GF diners. He notes that several chicken and seafood dishes can be modified to be GF. Confirm the timeliness of this information before dining in. Upon arrival, ask to speak with a chef or manager, who will discuss GF options. ▪ *www.shellhousesav.com*

### Smokey Bones    📖

*Columbus* ▪ *(706) 320-0021*
*5555 Whittlesey Blvd*
*Peachtree City* ▪ *(678) 364-8460*
*100 Market Place Blvd*
*Lithonia* ▪ *(770) 484-0020*
*2930 Stonecrest Cir*

### South City Kitchen    ✪$$$LD

*Smyrna* ▪ *(770) 435-0700*
*1675 Cumberland Pkwy SE* ▪ *Southern* ▪ GF menu includes Georgia mountain trout, molasses brined pork chop, Atlantic salmon, steak, and more. ▪ *www.southcitykitchen.com*

### Sticky Fingers Smokehouse    ✪📖

*Savannah* ▪ *(912) 925-7427*
*7921 Abercorn St*
*Augusta* ▪ *(706) 733-7427*
*277 Robert C Daniel Pkwy*
*Macon* ▪ *(478) 324-7427*
*5080 Riverside Dr*

### Sweet Carolina Cupcakes    ★✪S

*Savannah* ▪ *(912) 234-6380*
*38 Whitaker St* ▪ *Dessert* ▪ GF & vegan cupcakes made every Monday and Thursday. ▪ *sweetcarolinacupcakes.com*

### Tam's Backstage    $$LD

*Cumming* ▪ *(678) 455-8310*
*215 Ingram Ave* ▪ *American* ▪ Manager Vicki reports that all veggies, grilled chicken breast, shrimp, and fish dishes can be modified to be GF. Almost 90% of the menu is naturally GF. Confirm the timeliness of this information before dining in. ▪ *www.tamsbackstage.com*

## Ted's Montana Grill ✪📖
*Buford* ▪ *(678) 546-3631*
*1680 Mall of Georgia Blvd*
*Cumming* ▪ *(678) 947-3530*
*410 Peachtree Pkwy*
*Decatur* ▪ *(404) 378-1123*
*201 W Ponce de Leon*
*Lawrenceville* ▪ *(770) 979-6202*
*1250 Scenic Hwy*
*Marietta* ▪ *(770) 578-8337*
*640 Johnson Ferry Rd*
*Marietta* ▪ *(678) 594-7242*
*3625 Dallas Hwy SW*
*Norcross* ▪ *(678) 405-0305*
*5165 Peachtree Pkwy*
*Peachtree City* ▪ *(678) 829-0272*
*314 City Cir*

## Tin Drum AsiaCafé ✪📖
*Augusta* ▪ *(706) 736-6095*
*1149 Agerton Ln*
*Cumming* ▪ *(678) 965-5915*
*410 Peachtree Pkwy*

## Union Restaurant, The $$LD
*Milton* ▪ *(770) 569-7767*
*14275 Providence Rd* ▪ *American* ▪ GF
items marked on regular menu include
oven roasted chicken, steak frites, cobb
salad, farmer's beef shortribs, filet mignon, shrimp and grits, and more. ▪
*www.theunionrestaurant.com*

## Vinny's ✪$$$$LD
*Alpharetta* ▪ *(770) 772-4644*
*5355 Windward Pkwy* ▪ *Modern*
*American* ▪ GF menu consists of regular menu items that can be modified to
be GF. It includes rack of lamb, Atlantic salmon, sautéed trout, mussels, and
several soups and salads. Hostess Pam
reports that chefs are very GF aware. ▪
*www.knowwheretogogh.com/vinnys.html*

## Zpizza ✪📖
*Alpharetta* ▪ *(678) 205-4471*
*5315 Windward Pkwy*
*Duluth* ▪ *(770) 817-0526*
*11720 Medlock Bridge Rd*

# HAWAII

## HONOLULU

## Alan Wong's $$$$D
*Honolulu* ▪ *(808) 949-2526*
*1857 S King St* ▪ *American* ▪ The restaurant reports that their culinary
team "is excellent in accommodating
any dietary restrictions." They strongly
recommend reservations noting GF, and
also add that it is helpful to know in
advance what GF customers would like
to order. Alert the server upon arrival. ▪
*www.alanwongs.com*

## Auntie Pasto's ★$$LD
*Honolulu* ▪ *(808) 523-8855*
*1099 S Beretania St* ▪ *Italian* ▪ GF spaghetti or penne is available. GF pizza is
available in 10" size only at the Waipahu
location. ▪ *www.auntiepastos.com*

## Bubba Gump Shrimp Co. ✪📖
*Honolulu* ▪ *(808) 949-4867*
*1450 Ala Moana Blvd*

## Buca di Beppo ✪📖
*Honolulu* ▪ *(808) 591-0800*
*1030 Auahi St*

## Cake Works ★¢S
*Honolulu* ▪ *(808) 946-4333*
*2820 S King St* ▪ *Bakery* ▪ Non-dedicated GF bakery offering GF French
macaroons made with almond flour
and "chocolate extravagance", a flourless
chocolate cake with a hint of orange. ▪
*www.cakeworkshi.com*

## Da Kitchen $BL
*Honolulu* ▪ *(808) 957-0099*
*925 Isenberg St* ▪ *Hawaiian* ▪ GF items
include two pork dishes as well as rice. ▪
*www.da-kitchen.com*

## Down to Earth ★¢BLD
*Honolulu* ▪ *(808) 947-7678*
*2525 S King St* ▪ *Deli* ▪ GF cookies and
cake available. ▪ *www.downtoearth.org*

## Duke's Canoe Club                    $$$BLD
*Honolulu ▪ (808) 922-2268*
*2335 Kalakaua Ave ▪ Hawaiian ▪* GF diners can be accommodated. Be sure to alert server upon arrival and manager will speak to guests about what items on the menu can be made GF. ▪ *www.dukeswaikiki.com*

## Formaggio Wine Bar                   $D
*Honolulu ▪ (808) 739-7719*
*2919 Kapiolani Blvd ▪ American ▪* Limited GF options include salads with no croutons, smoked salmon carpaccio, and grilled vegetable napoleon. Confirm the timeliness of this information before dining in. ▪ *formaggio808.com*

## G.I. Cakes                           ★$$$
*Honolulu ▪ (808) 845-8629*
*255 Sand Island Access Rd ▪ Bakery ▪* Non-dedicated GF bakery offering GF cakes, brownies, and other baked goods. Call ahead to ensure availability. ▪ *www.gi-cakes.com*

## Hard Rock Café                       ✪▢
*Honolulu ▪ (808) 955-7383*
*280 Beachwalk*

## Hula Grill Waikiki                   ✪$$$$
*Honolulu ▪ (808) 923-4852*
*2335 Kalakaua Ave ▪ American ▪* GF menu includes island-style soup, Hawaiian ceviche, sashimi, grilled Hawaiian fish, coconut seafood chowder, tandoori style fish, bone-in New York steak, and lemon ginger roasted chicken. For dessert, there is coconut crème brûlée. ▪ *www.hulagrillwaikiki.com*

## India Café                           $LD
*Honolulu ▪ (808) 262-1800*
*600 Kailua Rd*
*Honolulu ▪ (808) 423-3330*
*4725 Bougainville Dr*
*Honolulu ▪ (808) 216-7477*
*2560 McCarthy Mall ▪ Indian ▪* The restaurant reports that their vegetables, rice, and dosai are GF. Confirm the timeliness of this information before dining in. Be sure to alert a server that your meal must be GF so they can notify the kitchen. ▪ *www.indiacafehawaii.com*

## Indigo Restaurant & Bar             $$$LD
*Honolulu ▪ (808) 521-2900*
*1121 Nuuanu Ave ▪ American ▪* Restaurant reports that the lunch buffet can accommodate GF diners with several salads or other vegetables. For dinner, GF options are limited, as most meals are pre-prepared and pre-seasoned. Alert the server and ask for the manager. Reservations noting GF are strongly recommended. ▪ *www.indigo-hawaii.com*

## Islands Fine Burgers & Drinks       ▢
*Honolulu ▪ (808) 943-6670*
*1450 Ala Moana Blvd*

## Kincaid's                           ▢
*Honolulu ▪ (808) 591-2005*
*1050 Ala Moana Blvd*

## Loving Hut                          ▢
*Honolulu ▪ (808) 373-6465*
*1614 S King St*
*Honolulu ▪ (808) 626-5626*
*1102 Pensacola St*

## Margaritaville                      ✪★▢
*Honolulu ▪ (808) 791-1200*
*2300 Kalakaua Ave*

## Morton's Steakhouse                 ✪▢
*Honolulu ▪ (808) 949-1300*
*1450 Ala Moana Blvd*

## Old Spaghetti Factory, The          ✪★▢
*Honolulu ▪ (808) 591-2513*
*1050 Ala Moana Blvd*

## Romano's Macaroni Grill             ✪★▢
*Honolulu ▪ (808) 356-8300*
*1450 Ala Moana Blvd*

## Ruffage Natural Foods               $BLD
*Honolulu ▪ (808) 922-2042*
*2443 Kuhio Ave ▪ Vegetarian ▪* The restaurant reports that "a few items" are GF, including the veggie chili with brown rice, the totally vegan special, and most of the salads. Confirm the timeliness of this information before dining in.

## Rumfire                                    ✪$$LD
*Honolulu* ▪ (808) 922-4422
*2255 Kalakaua Ave* ▪ *Pacific Rim* ▪ Restaurant states there is a full GF menu in-house for their GF diners. Ask a server upon arrival. Located inside the Sheraton Waikiki Hotel. ▪ *www.rumfirewaikiki.com*

## Ruth's Chris Steak House          ✪☐
*Honolulu* ▪ (808) 599-3860
*500 Ala Moana Blvd*

## Sansei Seafood
## Restaurant & Sushi Bar            ★$$D
*Honolulu* ▪ (808) 931-6286
*2552 Kalakaua Ave* ▪ *Seafood* ▪ GF tamari sauce is available. The restaurant reports that "the staff is aware of how to handle dietary restrictions" and they are "happy to accommodate the needs" of GF diners. ▪ *sanseihawaii.com*

## Seaside Bar & Grill               $BLD
*Honolulu* ▪ (808) 922-8227
*2256 Kuhio Ave* ▪ *American* ▪ GF entrées such as lobster and steak are available. Alert the server upon arrival.

## Side Street Inn                   $LD
*Honolulu* ▪ (808) 591-0253
*1225 Hopaka St*
*Honolulu* ▪ (808) 739-3939
*614 Kapahulu Ave* ▪ *American* ▪ The restaurant reports that some of their menu items can be prepared GF, and recommends asking a server for details. No GF menu. ▪ *sidestreetinn.com*

## Spalding House Café               ★$L
*Honolulu* ▪ (808) 237-5225
*2411 Makiki Heights Dr* ▪ *American* ▪ Manager Susan says there "definitely are GF dishes available." She reports that all salads are GF and they offer quinoa as well. She recommends making reservations noting GF so the chef can prepare a special menu. Located inside the Honolulu Museum of Art. ▪ *honolulumuseum.org/*

## To Thai For                       $LD
*Honolulu* ▪ (808) 734-3443
*3571 Waialae Ave, Suite 101* ▪ *Thai* ▪ The restaurant reports that since everything is made to order, most menu items can be prepared GF by avoiding ingredients with gluten in them. Alert a server upon arrival and be sure to specify GF when placing your order. ▪ *www.itstothaifor.com*

## Tony Roma's                       ☐
*Honolulu* ▪ (808) 942-2121
*1972 Kalakaua*

## Uncle Bo's                        $$$LD
*Honolulu* ▪ (808) 735-8311
*559 Kapahulu Ave* ▪ *Asian Fusion* ▪ The restaurant reports that they do not have a menu or list of GF items, but notes that the servers and chefs are "very accommodating" and will be able to "come up with something" for GF diners. ▪ *unclebosrestaurant.com*

## Veggie Star Natural Foods         ★$BLD
*Honolulu* ▪ (808) 922-9568
*417 Nahua St* ▪ *Vegetarian* ▪ GF bread is available for sandwiches. The restaurant reports that many items are GF or can be prepared GF, including sandwiches, veggie burritos, chili, and salads. Confirm the timeliness of this information before dining in. Alert a server, who will go over GF options.

## Yard House                        ✪☐
*Honolulu* ▪ (808) 923-9273
*226 Lewers St*

## Yoshiya                           ★$BLD
*Honolulu* ▪ (808) 922-8877
*2255 Kalakaua Ave* ▪ *Japanese* ▪ Restaurant states they do not have anything on the menu that is classified as GF. They cook with a lot of flour and most of their ingredients come from Japan. Team member Ramon reports that they do have steak entrées that will work for GF diners. Be sure to alert the server upon arrival of any dietary needs so they can review the ingredients of any item you would like. ▪ *www.yoshiyahawaii.com/en/*

**Zpizza**　　　　　　　　　　☉🕮
*Honolulu* ▪ *(808) 596-0066*
*1200 Ala Moana Blvd*

# HAWAII

## ALL OTHER CITIES

**808 Deli**　　　　　　　　　★ ¢BL
*Kihei* ▪ *(808) 879-1111*
*2511 S Kihei Rd* ▪ *Deli* ▪ Sandwiches are
available on GF bread for $1 more. The
deli reports that all salads are also GF. ▪
*www.808deli.com*

**Amigo's Authentic Mexican Food**　$BLD
*Kihei* ▪ *(808) 879-9952*
*41 E Lipoa St*
*Kahului* ▪ *(808) 872-9595*
*333 Dairy Rd*
*Lahaina* ▪ *(808) 661-0210*
*658 Front St* ▪ *Mexican* ▪ Anything on the
menu can be made GF with the exception of the burritos and quesadillas. ▪
*amigosmaui.com*

**Auntie Pasto's**　　　　　　★ $$LD
*Waipahu* ▪ *(808) 680-0005*
*94-673 Kupuohi St* ▪ *Italian* ▪ GF spaghetti
or penne is available. GF pizza is available
in 10" size only at the Waipahu location. ▪
*www.auntiepastos.com*

**Bamboo**　　　　　　　　　$$LD
*Hawi* ▪ *(808) 889-5555*
*Akoni Pule Hwy 270* ▪ *Hawaiian* ▪ Team
member Joan reports that they have a
"nice selection" of GF items on their menu.
GF diners are "good to go" with them. ▪
*bamboorestaurant.info/*

**Bianelli's Gourmet Pizzeria**　　★ $LD
*Kailua-Kona* ▪ *(808) 322-0377*
*78-6831 Alii Dr* ▪ *Pizza* ▪ GF 9" pizza and
pasta available. ▪ *www.bianellis.com*

**Big Island Grill**　　　　　★ $BLD
*Kailua Kona* ▪ *(808) 326-1153*
*75-5702 Kuakini Hwy* ▪ *Hawaiian* ▪
Manager reports that they serve GF diners
"regularly." They have GF stir fries, roast
pork without gravy, and grilled chicken.
Confirm the timeliness of this information
before dining in. Alert a server, who can
help choose an appropriate meal.

**Bistro Casanova**　　　　　$$$LD
*Kahului* ▪ *(808) 873-3650*
*33 Lono Ave* ▪ *Mediterranean* ▪ GF quinoa
pasta is available as well as steaks, fish,
paella, salads and eggplant parmesan. ▪
*www.bistrocasanova.com*

**Blue Dragon Restaurant**　　$$$D
*Kamuela* ▪ *(808) 882-7771*
*61-3616 Kawaihae Rd* ▪ *Hawaiian* ▪ GF
menu includes 'from big island' house salad, hamakua mushroom polenta, organic
hearts of romaine, up beet salad and daily
fresh fish. ▪ *www.bluedragonrestaurant.com*

**Brown's Beach House Restaurant**　$$$D
*Kohala Coast* ▪ *(808) 887-7368*
*1 N Kaniku Dr* ▪ *Pacific Rim* ▪ Their "Lifestyles
Menu" contains a GF section that includes
organic watercress & tomato salad, kumo-
moto oysters, spicy shrimp corn tostada, and
curry lemongrass chicken skewers. For des-
sert, warm chocolate mochi is available. Chef
de cuisine Skye reports that they can also
modify many other items to be GF, and that
the staff is "experienced in the preparation of
GF foods." Located at the Fairmont Orchid
Hotel. ▪ *www.fairmont.com/orchid-hawaii/*

**Bubba Gump Shrimp Co.**　　☉🕮
*Kailua Kona* ▪ *(808) 331-8442*
*75-5776 Alii Dr*
*Lahaina* ▪ *(808) 661-3111*
*889 Front St*

**Caffe Coco**　　　　　　　★ $$LD
*Wailua* ▪ *(808) 822-7990*
*4-369 Kuhio Hwy* ▪ *Global* ▪ GF pasta and
wraps are available. The restaurant reports
that they are "more than willing to substitute" ingredients in their other dishes to

accommodate the needs of GF diners. ▪ *www.restauranteur.com/caffecoco/*

### Da Kitchen $BL
*Kahului* ▪ *(808) 871-7782*
*425 Koloa St*
*Kihei* ▪ *(808) 875-7782*
*2439 S Kihei Rd* ▪ *Hawaiian* ▪ GF items include two pork dishes as well as rice. ▪ *www.da-kitchen.com*

### Dixie Grill ★$LD
*Aiea* ▪ *(808) 485-2722*
*99-016 Kamehameha Hwy* ▪ *Barbeque* ▪ GF beer available. ▪ *www.dixiegrill.com*

### Dondero's Italian Restaurant ✪$$$$BLD
*Koloa* ▪ *(808) 240-6456*
*1571 Poipu Rd* ▪ *Global* ▪ GF items are marked on the menu and include ahi tuna carpaccio, grilled shrimp, wild mushroom risotto, osso bucco, seafood cioppino, chestnut braised pork shoulder, and more. Confirm the timeliness of this information before dining in, and be sure to alert the server that your meal must be GF. Located at the Grand Hyatt Kauai. ▪ *kauai.hyatt.com*

### Down to Earth ★¢BLD
*Kahului* ▪ *(808) 877-2661*
*305 Dairy Rd*
*Kailua* ▪ *(808) 262-3838*
*201 Hamakua Dr*
*Aiea* ▪ *(808) 488-1375*
*98-129 Kaonohi St*
*Kapolei* ▪ *(808) 675-2300*
*4460 Kapolei Pkwy* ▪ *Deli* ▪ GF cookies and cake available. ▪ *www.downtoearth.org*

### Eastside, The $$D
*Kapaa* ▪ *(808) 823-9500*
*4-1380 Kuhio Hwy* ▪ *Asian Fusion* ▪ GF options available on request. Alert the server upon arrival. ▪ *www.theeastsidekauai.com*

### Feast at Lele, The $$$$D
*Lahaina* ▪ *(808) 667-5353*
*505 Front St* ▪ *Hawaiian* ▪ No GF menu but GF options are available upon request. Alert the server upon arrival. ▪ *www.feastatlele.com*

### Fish Hopper Seafood & Steaks ✪$$$LD
*Kailua-Kona* ▪ *(808) 326-2002*
*75-5683 Alii Dr* ▪ *Seafood & Steakhouse* ▪ GF menu includes a variety of meat and seafood items, all with no sauce. The restaurant reports that the only GF sauce is the citrus lemon sauce. GF guests can request this sauce for their meal or ask the chef what other GF seasonings can be used. The restaurant also adds that mashed potatoes, rice, Molokai potatoes, and baked potatoes are all safe sides. Confirm the timeliness of this information before dining in. ▪ *www.fishhopper.com*

### Five Palms Beach Grill $$$$BLD
*Kihei* ▪ *(808) 879-2607*
*2960 S Kihei Rd* ▪ *American* ▪ GF menu available. Items include scallops, seared ahi, Chinese style ribs, rack of rib, beef tenderloin, salads, fresh fish and a few dessert items.

### Flatbread Pizza Company ★📖
*Paia* ▪ *(808) 579-8989*
*89 Hana Hwy*

### Gannon's Restaurant $$$$BLD
*Wailea* ▪ *(808) 875-8080*
*100 Wailea Golf Club Dr* ▪ *Hawaiian* ▪ GF options include crab dishes, salads, ahi tuna, sea scallops, filet, ribeye, pork chops and grilled vegetables. ▪ *www.gannonsrestaurant.com*

### Gaylord's at Kilohana $$$LD
*Lihue* ▪ *(808) 245-9593*
*3-2087 Kaumualii Hwy* ▪ *American* ▪ The restaurant has an internal list of items that can be prepared GF. Alert a server, who will go over the list with guests to help choose a satisfactory meal option. ▪ *www.gaylordskauai.com*

### Hali'imaile General Store $$$$LD
*Makawao* ▪ *(808) 572-2666*
*900 Hali'imaile Rd* ▪ *Hawaiian* ▪ The restaurant reports that many items on the menu can be modified to be GF. Alert server upon arrival. ▪ *bevgannonrestaurants.com/haliimaile/*

## Hard Rock Café    ✪📖
*Lahaina* ▪ (808) 667-7400
*900 Front St*

## Hawaiian Moons Natural Foods
## Grocery & Deli    $BLD
*Kihei* ▪ (808) 875-4356
*2411 S Kihei Rd* ▪ *Deli* ▪ GF options available. Tell server that you are GF and they will give you a selection of items. ▪ *www.hawaiianmoons.com*

## Huggo's On the Rocks    ★$LD
*Kailua-Kona* ▪ (808) 329-1493
*75-5828 Kahakai Rd* ▪ *Hawaiian* ▪ GF buns are available for most burgers and sandwiches. Executive chef Ken reports that GF diners should notify the restaurant ahead of time so the kitchen can have time to prepare. ▪ *huggosontherocks.com*

## Hukilau Lanai    ✪★$$$D
*Kapaa* ▪ (808) 822-0600
*520 Aleka Loop* ▪ *American* ▪ GF menu includes bbq ribs, ahi poke, mahi mahi, Hawaiian snapper, prime rib, macadamia crusted chicken, pork tenderloin, filet mignon, opah and steak. GF bread is also available. GF kids menu as well as catering and banquet menu also available. ▪ *www.hukilaukauai.com*

## Hula Grill Kaanapali    ✪$$LD
*Lahaina* ▪ (808) 667-6636
*2435 Kaanapali Pkwy* ▪ *Hawaiian* ▪ "Allergy Free" menu features a GF section with items such as sashimi, coconut seafood chowder, macadamia nut crusted island fish, prime NY steak, wood grilled asparagus, and more. ▪ *www.hulagrillkaanapali.com*

## Jackie Rey's Ohana Grill    $$LD
*Kailua-Kona* ▪ (808) 327-0209
*75-5995 Kuakini Hwy* ▪ *Hawaiian* ▪ GF items include salad, tacos, pork chops, jalapeno crusted ahi tuna, wild mushroom risotto, New York steak with no sauce and seared scallops. Confirm the timeliness of this information before dining in. Alert the server upon arrival. ▪ *jackiereys.com*

## Java Kai    ★¢BLD
*Kapaa* ▪ (808) 823-6887
*4-1384 Kuhio Hwy* ▪ *Café* ▪ GF muffins are available. The café reports that most items can be made with a GF English muffin or tortilla. Ask a cashier, who will go over GF options. ▪ *www.javakaihawaii.com*

## Joy's Place    ★¢BL
*Kihei* ▪ (808) 879-9258
*1993 S Kihei Rd* ▪ *American* ▪ Restaurant offers a GF rice wrapper as alternative to bread for their sandwiches. ▪ *www.joysplacemaui.com*

## Kahului Ale House    ✪$LD
*Kahului* ▪ (808) 877-9001
*355 E Kamehameha Ave* ▪ *American* ▪ GF items indicated on menu. Items include house smoked bbq ribs, steamed edamame, loaded nachos, potato skins, spinach artichoke dip, chips and salsa, salad selections without the wontons, sesame seared mahi mahi, prime cut steak, bbq ribs, chicken enchiladas and cheese enchiladas. ▪ *www.kahuluialehouse.com*

## Kalaheo Café & Coffee Co.    ★$$BLD
*Kalaheo* ▪ (808) 332-5858
*2-2560 Kaumualii Hwy* ▪ *American* ▪ GF bread is available and can be substituted anywhere regular bread is used. Alert a server upon arrival and they will go over the GF options. ▪ *kalaheo.com*

## Kauai Pasta    ★$$LD
*Kapaa* ▪ (808) 822-7447
*4-939B Kuhio Hwy*
*Lihue* ▪ (808) 245-2227
*3-3142 Kuhio Hwy* ▪ *Italian* ▪ GF brown rice pasta is available. The restaurant notes that several other menu items may be prepared GF as well. Alert a server upon arrival. ▪ *www.kauaipasta.com*

## Keei Café    $$LD
*Kealakekua* ▪ (808) 322-9992
*79-7511 Mamalahoa Hwy* ▪ *Hawaiian* ▪ The restaurant reports that they are able to modify many items for GF diners. GF

items include fish, chicken, pork, sautéed vegetables, steamed rice and mashed potatoes. ▪ www.keeicafe.net

### Keoki's Paradise                           ✪$$$LD
*Koloa* ▪ (808) 742-7534
*2360 Kiahuna Plantation Dr* ▪ *Hawaiian* ▪ GF menus available for the dining room as well as the bar. GF items include sashimi, smoked marlin, half roasted chicken, shrimp and lobster tail, pork chops, filet mignon, top sirloin and prime cut steak. Alert a server upon arrival. ▪ www.keokisparadise.com

### Kilauea Bakery & Pau Hana Pizza ★$BLD
*Kilauea* ▪ (808) 828-2020
*2484 Keneke St* ▪ *Bakery & Café* ▪ GF pizza is available. The bakery offers a wide variety of GF baked goods, including bread, cookies, bagels, muffins, and macaroons. ▪ kilaueabakery.wordpress.com

### Kilauea Lodge Restaurant        ★$$$BLD
*Volcano Village* ▪ (808) 967-7366
*19-3948 Old Volcano Rd* ▪ *Global* ▪ GF pasta is available. The restaurant notes that many fish, chicken, and beef dishes can be prepared GF, and some sauces can be changed to be GF. Alert a server, who will go over the options or notify a manager. ▪ www.kilaualodge.com

### Kimo's                                       $$$LD
*Lahaina* ▪ (808) 661-4811
*845 Front St* ▪ *Hawaiian* ▪ GF items include sashimi, shrimp cocktail, smoked marlin, shrimp, tropical smoked fish, seared ahi, lobster tail and sirloin steak. ▪ www.kimosmaui.com

### Ko at the Fairmont                    ✪$$$$LD
*Kihei* ▪ (808) 875-2210
*4100 Wailea Alanui* ▪ *Hawaiian* ▪ Restaurant reports they have a GF in-house menu for all guests. When making your reservation let the concierge know and they will provide you with the GF menu. Located inside The Fairmont Kea Lani Hotel. ▪ korestaurant.com

### Lahaina Coolers                    ★$$$BLD
*Lahaina* ▪ (808) 661-7082
*180 Dickenson St* ▪ *Fusion* ▪ General manager Josh reports that the majority of the staff is knowledgeable of GF dietary needs. The pork chop, the NY strip, and the black garlic fish are naturally GF. For dessert, GF diners can order the chocolate taco. Confirm the timeliness of this information before dining in. ▪ www.lahainacoolers.com

### Lahaina Grill                            $$$$D
*Lahaina* ▪ (808) 667-5117
*127 Lahainaluna Rd* ▪ *American* ▪ The restaurant reports that many items on the menu can be modified for GF diners. Note GF when making reservations and be sure to alert server upon arrival. ▪ www.lahainagrill.com

### Lotus Café                                 ✪$LD
*Kailua-Kona* ▪ (808) 327-3270
*73-5617 Maiau St* ▪ *Asian* ▪ Lotus Café offers a wide variety of GF options such as chicken enchiladas, smoothies and milk shakes, salads, nachos, stir fries, and ice cream. ▪ thelotuscafe.com

### Luibueno's
### Mexican and Latin Cuisine        $$LD
*Haleiwa* ▪ (808) 637-7717
*66-165 Kamehameha Hwy* ▪ *Mexican* ▪ The restaurant reports that they "do not advertise" any GF options but "can certainly accommodate" GF requests. They recommend consulting a server, who will go over the most suitable options on the menu. ▪ luibueno.com

### LuLu's Lahaina Surf Club & Grill    $BLD
*Lahaina* ▪ (808) 661-0808
*1221 Honoapiilani Hwy* ▪ *Hawaiian* ▪ Events director Desiree reports that the chef is willing to work with diners to alter or create a dish that suits their needs. Calling ahead is recommended so the chef can have time to prepare. Confirm the timeliness of this information before dining in. ▪ www.luluslahaina.com/menus.html

## Mala Ocean Tavern                    $$LD

*Lahaina* ▪ *(808) 667-9394*
*1307 Front St* ▪ *Hawaiian* ▪ The restaurant reports that many items on the menu can be modified to be GF. Alert server upon arrival and they will list the GF items available or ask the chef if necessary. ▪ *www.malaoceantavern.com*

## Mala Wailea                    ✪$$$BD

*Wailea* ▪ *(808) 875-9394*
*3700 Wailea Alanui Dr* ▪ *Hawaiian* ▪ GF menu items include jumbo black tiger shrimp cocktail, sashimi grade Hawaiian ahi, salads, garlic cheese flatbread, margherita pizza, one pound steamed manila clams, Balinese stir fry with fresh island fish, all natural angus fillet mignon, roasted Australian lamb chops, Asian seafood pasta as well as a variety of side dishes. ▪ *malawailea.com*

## Mama's Fish House                    $$$$LD

*Paia* ▪ *(808) 579-8488*
*799 Poho Pl* ▪ *American* ▪ Note GF when making reservations. Upon arrival, chef and manager will guide customer through menu items that can be prepared GF. ▪ *www.mamasfishhouse.com*

## Mana Foods                    ★$BLD

*Paia* ▪ *(808) 579-8078*
*49 Baldwin Ave* ▪ *Hawaiian* ▪ GF deli items are available, ask server which items are GF and they will be happy to list them. For the bakery, GF items are indicated on the name card. ▪ *www.manafoodsmaui.com*

## Manta & Pavilion Wine Bar                    ✪$$$$BD

*Kohala Coast* ▪ *(808) 882-7222*
*62-100 Mauna Kea Beach Dr* ▪ *Hawaiian* ▪ GF items are marked on the regular menu, which changes often. Sample items include potato & leek soup, pork porterhouse, chicken "two ways", mahi mahi, cioppino, and more. Be sure to alert the server that your meal must be GF. Located inside the Mauna Kea Beach Hotel. ▪ *www.princeresortshawaii.com*

## Maui Brick Oven                    $LD

*Kihei* ▪ *(808) 875-7896*
*1215 S Kihei Rd* ▪ *American* ▪ Dedicated GF restaurant offering a wide variety of lunch and dinner selections. This includes chicken parmesan, fish & chips, teriyaki chicken skewers, and more. GF pizza and pasta are available. ▪ *mauibrickoven.com*

## Maui Specialty Bakery                    ★$$

*Lahaina* ▪ *(808) 662-0033*
*878 Front St* ▪ *Bakery* ▪ The bakery reports that "just about anything" in their regular line of products can be made GF. Baked goods offered include cakes, cookies, pies, macaroons, and more. ▪ *www.mauispecialtybakery.com*

## Melting Pot, The                    ✪📖

*Lahaina* ▪ *(808) 661-6181*
*325 Keawe St*

## Merriman's                    $$$$D

*Kamuela* ▪ *(808) 885-6822*
*65-1227 Opelo Rd*
*Lahaina* ▪ *(808) 669-6400*
*1 Bay Club Pl*
*Koloa* ▪ *(808) 742-8385*
*2829 Ala Kalani Kaumaka St* ▪ *Hawaiian* ▪ All three locations have indicated GF items on their menu. All three locations report that the chefs are very accommodating of GF diners. They serve GF diners on a regular basis and recommend making reservations noting GF. ▪ *www.merrimanshawaii.com*

## Monkeypod Kitchen                    $$LD

*Wailea* ▪ *(808) 891-2322*
*10 Wailea Gateway Pl* ▪ *American* ▪ The restaurant reports that GF items on the menu include vegan Portuguese soup, fish tacos, bulgogi pork tacos, and ahi Nicoise. They also note that most salads are GF and the fish special is typically GF. Alert a server upon arrival and they will go over GF options. ▪ *monkeypodkitchen.com*

### Nasturtium Café                          $BLD
*Kealakekua ▪ (808) 322-5083*
*74-7491 Mamalahoa Hwy ▪ American ▪* GF
accommodations can be made to any item
on the menu. Alert a server upon arrival. ▪
*nasturtium-natural-cafe.weebly.com*

### Old Lahaina Luau                        $$LD
*Maui ▪ (800) 248-5828*
*1251 Front St ▪ Hawaiian ▪* Staff reports
that some items on the buffet are GF, and a
copy of the buffet ingredients list is available upon request. There is also a GF meal
option: grilled lemon thyme chicken. A
list of GF choices is also available upon request. Reservations noting GF are strongly
recommended. ▪ *www.oldlahainaluau.com*

### Ono Bar & Grill                         $BLD
*Lahaina ▪ (808) 667-2525*
*2365 Ka'anapali Pkwy ▪ Hawaiian ▪*
Alert the server upon arrival and they
will provide all the GF options available.
There is no menu online but all the servers
know exactly what is GF and what is not. ▪
*www.westinmaui.com/dining/ono/*

### Pacific'O                               $$$$LD
*Lahaina ▪ (808) 667-4341*
*505 Front St ▪ Hawaiian ▪* The restaurant
reports that GF items are not on the menu.
But, their chefs are "able to easily accommodate" any special dietary needs. Alert
a server, who will communicate with the
chefs. ▪ *www.pacificomaui.com*

### Pah Ke's Chinese Restaurant            $LD
*Kaneohe ▪ (808) 235-4505*
*46-018 Kamehameha Hwy ▪ Chinese ▪*
Owner/Chef Raymond says he is always
willing to accommodate GF diners. The
soy sauce he cooks with and serves with
is GF. Call a day or two ahead and let him
know what you need and he will be "more
than glad to honor your requests". He also
mentioned that even if a customer wants
something they do not usually serve GF, he
will "make it happen". ▪ *www.pahke.com*

### Papalani Gelato                         ⊘S
*Koloa ▪ (808) 742-2663*
*2360 Kiahuna Plantation Dr ▪ Dessert*
▪ GF chocolates as well as 200 of the 300
flavors are GF. GF choices are indicated on
the flavor cards. ▪ *www.papalanigelato.com*

### Papaya's Natural Foods & Café  ★$BLD
*Kapaa ▪ (808) 823-0190*
*4-831 Kuhio Hwy ▪ American ▪* GF muffins are available. The café also reports
that GF diners can make use of the salad
bar, and they can make their taro burgers GF by wrapping them in lettuce. ▪
*papayasnaturalfoods.com*

### Penne Pasta Café                        ★$$LD
*Lahaina ▪ (808) 661-6633*
*180 Dickenson St ▪ Italian ▪* GF 10"
thin crust pizza and pasta available. ▪
*www.pennepastacafe.com*

### Postcards Café                          ✪$$$D
*Hanalei ▪ (808) 826-1191*
*5-5075 Kuhio Hwy ▪ American ▪* GF items
are marked on the menu and include baked
portobello mushroom, fennel crusted
lobster tail, grilled or blackened island fish,
Thai coconut rice noodles, and more. GF
chocolate silk pie is available for dessert.
Alert a server upon arrival. Confirm the
timeliness of this information before dining in. ▪ *www.postcardscafe.com*

### Rainbow Living Foods                    $BL
*Kapaa ▪ (808) 821-9759*
*4-1384 Kuhio Hwy ▪ Vegan ▪* Dedicated
GF restaurant serving a variety of raw
and vegan appetizers, entrées, and salads,
as well as smoothies, shakes, and sweets.
Examples of menu items include sprouted
buckwheat pizza, kale avocado salad, rainbow veggie wrap, and chia seed pudding.
Wedding, birthday, and other occasion
cakes are available by special order. ▪
*rainbowlivingfood.com*

### Romano's Macaroni Grill                 ✪★📖
*Waikoloa ▪ (808) 443-5515*
*201 Waikoloa Beach Dr*

### Ruth's Chris Steak House ☻📖
*Kohala Coast* ▪ *(808) 887-0800*
*68-1330 Mauna Lani Dr*
*Lahaina* ▪ *(808) 661-8815*
*900 Front St*
*Waikiki* ▪ *(808) 440-7910*
*226 Lewers St*
*Wailea* ▪ *(808) 847-8880*
*3750 Wailea Alanui*

### Saigon Café, A          $$LD
*Wailuku* ▪ *(808) 243-9560*
*1792 Main St* ▪ *Vietnamese* ▪ GF options
available. Alert server upon arrival. ▪
*www.yelp.com/biz/a-saigon-cafe-wailuku*

### Sansei Seafood Restaurant & Sushi Bar          ★$$D
*Lahaina* ▪ *(808) 669-6286*
*600 Office Rd*
*Kihei* ▪ *(808) 879-0004*
*1881 S Kihei Rd*
*Waikoloa* ▪ *(808) 886-6286*
*201 Waikoloa Bch Dr* ▪ *Seafood* ▪ GF
tamari sauce is available. The restaurant
reports that "the staff is aware of how to
handle dietary restrictions" and they are
"happy to accommodate the needs" of GF
diners. ▪ *sanseihawaii.com*

### Scotty's Beachside BBQ          $$$BLD
*Kapaa* ▪ *(808) 823-8480*
*4-1546 Kuhio Hwy* ▪ *Barbeque* ▪ Many
items on the menu can be modified to be
GF. The chicken, mahi mahi, and the luau
plum sauce all CONTAIN GLUTEN; however, particular sauces that contain gluten
can be substituted for something else. Alert
server upon arrival and they will be able to
list GF options. ▪ *www.scottysbbq.com*

### South Kona Fruit Stand          ⊄S
*Honaunau* ▪ *(808) 328-8547*
*84-4770 Mamalahoa Hwy* ▪ *Coffee Shop*
▪ GF baked goods including carrot cake,
banana bread, cookies and brownies.
Smoothies and juice drinks are also GF. ▪
*www.southkonafruitstand.com*

### Stella Blues Café          $$BLD
*Kihei* ▪ *(808) 874-3779*

*1279 S Kihei Rd* ▪ *American* ▪ Restaurant
states they have a variety of GF menu items
available. Alert the server upon arrival
and they will provide a list of options. ▪
*stellablues.com*

### Sushi Rock          ☻$$LD
*Kapaau* ▪ *(808) 889-5900*
*55-3435 Akoni Pule Hwy* ▪ *Sushi* ▪ Restaurant reports they have an in-house GF
menu available for GF diners. GF menu
includes appetizers, hand rolls, entrées
and desserts. Alert the server upon arrival
and they will provide the GF menu. ▪
*www.sushirockrestaurant.net/menu.html*

### Sweet Marie's Restaurant & Bakery ⊄BL
*Lihue* ▪ *(808) 823-0227*
*3-3204 Kuhio Hwy* ▪ *Bakery* ▪ Dedicated
GF bakery & restaurant offering a variety of
GF baked goods, including cakes, cookies,
muffins, brownies, and more. Lunch menu
selections include pizza, lasagna, polenta,
meatloaf, pork ribs, and baked chicken. ▪
*www.sweetmarieskauai.com*

### Taqueria Cruz          ⊄LD
*Kihei* ▪ *(808) 875-2910*
*2395 S Kihei Rd* ▪ *Mexican* ▪ The restaurant
reports that most menu items are GF. A
server can direct guests to the appropriate
menu options.

### Tony Roma's          📖
*Aiea* ▪ *(808) 487-9911*
*98-150 Kaonohi St*

### Ululani's Hawaiian Shave Ice          ⊄S
*Lahaina* ▪
*790 Front St*
*Lahaina* ▪ *(360) 606-2745*
*819 Front St*
*Kahului* ▪
*333 Dairy Rd*
*Kihei* ▪
*61 S Kihei Rd* ▪ *Hawaiian* ▪ All items are
GF. ▪ *ululanisshaveice.com*

### Verde New Mexican Restaurant ☻★$LD
*Kapa'a* ▪ *(808) 821-1400*

4-1101 *Kuhio Hwy* ▪ *Mexican* ▪ Owner and Chef Joshua reports that all staff members are trained on the GF diet, and they serve GF diners every day. He advises alerting the server and mentioning the word "allergy." GF options include tacos, enchiladas, and all salsas in the salsa bar. Confirm the timeliness of this information before dining in. ▪ *www.verdehawaii.com*

### Yum Cha Asian Eatery    ✪$$$D

*Koloa* ▪ *(808) 240-6456*
*1571 Poipu Rd* ▪ *Asian* ▪ "GF optional" items are marked on the regular menu. Selections include Indonesian chicken satay, green papaya salad, tom yum soup, pad thai, wagyu szechuan beef, whole island fish, and more. Be sure to alert the server that your meal must be GF, as most items require modification. Located at the Grand Hyatt Kauai. ▪ *kauai.hyatt.com*

### Zpizza    ✪📖

*Kailua* ▪ *(808) 230-8400*
*151 Hekili St*

# IDAHO

### 1313 Club    ★¢BLD

*Wallace* ▪ *(208) 752-9391*
*608 Bank St* ▪ *Modern American* ▪ Manager Dean reports that they welcome GF diners and can work with the kitchen to make GF meals. He notes that they have some regular GF customers. GF beer is available. ▪ *www.1313club.com*

### Angell's Bar & Grill    $$$LD

*Boise* ▪ *(208) 342-4900*
*999 Main St* ▪ *Modern American* ▪ Pam, a server, says that all salads and most meats can be GF on request. All servers are informed about the restaurant's GF options. Alert the manager upon arrival to address CC concerns. ▪ *www.angellsbarandgrill.com*

### Antonio's Italian Café    ✪$LD

*Lewiston* ▪ *(208) 746-6262*
*1407 Main St* ▪ *Italian* ▪ GF 12" four cheese pizza available. Additional charges for added toppings. ▪ *www.antonioslewiston.comMenu.html*

### Babs' Pizzeria    ★$LD

*Sandpoint* ▪ *(208) 265-7992*
*1319 Hwy 2* ▪ *Pizza* ▪ GF pizza and pasta available upon request ▪ *www.babspizzeria.com*

### Bangkok Cuisine    $LD

*Sandpoint* ▪ *(208) 265-4149*
*202 N 2nd Ave* ▪ *Thai* ▪ Owner Pat reports that "almost everything" except curries can be modified to be GF. She advises alerting a server upon arrival and notes that all servers should be familiar with GF.

### Barbacoa    $$$LD

*Boise* ▪ *(208) 338-5000*
*276 Bobwhite Ct* ▪ *Spanish* ▪ Ask chef to prepare almost any menu item GF. ▪ *www.barbacoa-boise.com*

### Bistro Rouge at Pend d'Oreille Winery    ✪★$LD

*Sandpoint* ▪ *(208) 265-8545*
*220 Cedar St* ▪ *American* ▪ GF pizza is available. ▪ *powine.combistro-rouge-cafe/*

### Boise Fry Co.    ¢LD

*Boise* ▪ *(208) 495-3858*
*111 S Broadway Ave*
*Boise* ▪ *(208) 965-1551*
*3083 S Bown Wy* ▪ *American* ▪ GF french fries are available. Owner Blake reports that most of the sauces are also GF, and that they are "currently working" on a GF hamburger bun, which will be available soon. ▪ *www.boisefrycompany.com*

### Bonefish Grill    ✪📖

*Boise* ▪ *(208) 433-1234*
*855 W Broad St Ste 260*

### Bonsai Bistro & Sushi Bar    ✪★$LD

*Coeur d'Alene* ▪ *(208) 765-4321*
*101 E Sherman Ave* ▪ *Asian Fusion* ▪ GF menu includes General Tso's chicken,

Mongolian beef, and honey cashew crispy prawns, among other items. GF beer and soy sauce are available. For dessert, they offer white chocolate coconut crème brûlée or homemade green tea ice cream. ■ *www.bonsaibistro.com*

### Brakeman American Grill, The    ★$LD
Victor ■ (208) 787-2020
27 N Main St ■ American ■ GF buns are available upon request for an extra $2. ■ *brakemangrill.com*

### Café Rio Mexican Grill    📖
Ammon ■ (208) 821-3636
2537 S 25 E
Twin Falls ■ (208) 944-3333
835 Blue Lakes Blvd N
Boise ■ (208) 287-9400
8233 W Franklin Rd
Pocatello ■ (208) 425-5300
285 E Alameda Rd
Coeur d'Alene ■ (208) 620-4000
560 W Kathleen Ave

### Café Vicino    $$$LD
Boise ■ (208) 472-1463
808 W Fort St ■ Italian ■ GF items marked on regular menu. Options include risotto, steak salad, cider-brined pork chops, pan-roasted duck breast and more. ■ *www.cafevicino.com*

### Carino's Italian    ✪📖
Ammon ■ (208) 523-4411
2833 S 25th E
Boise ■ (208) 373-4968
1700 S Entertainment Ave
Meridian ■ (208) 888-7801
3551 E Fairview Ave
Twin Falls ■ (208) 734-4833
1921 Blue Lakes Blvd N

### Cellar, The    ✪$$$D
Idaho Falls ■ (208) 525-9300
3520 E 17th St ■ American ■ GF menu includes small plates, soups, salads, meats, seafood and desserts. Dishes include shrimp cocktails, pan-fried Mahi Mahi fish tacos, Northwest crab cakes, chardonnay poached salmon, crème brûlée, and choco-late ganache cake and more. GF beer is also available. ■ *www.thecellar.biz*

### Cottonwood Grille    ✪$$$LD
Boise ■ (208) 333-9800
913 W River St ■ American ■ GF menu includes appetizers and salads, as well as a wide variety of seafood, meat, poultry, and game dishes. Crème brûlée, raspberry brûlée, ice cream, and sorbet are available for dessert. ■ *www.cottonwoodgrille.com*

### Desperado's    ★$LD
Ketchum ■ (208) 726-3068
211 4TH St ■ Mexican ■ GF tacos, en-chiladas, and burritos are available. All items can be made with corn tortillas. ■ *www.despossv.com/default.aspx*

### Dover Bay Cafe    ✪$LD
Dover ■ (208) 265-6467
651 Lakeshore Ave ■ American ■ GF items include New York steak, half chicken, udon soup, gnocchi, mahi mahi tacos, pad thai, ribs and burger with no bun. Alert the server upon arrival. Please note, this restaurant is only open for dinner during the winter. ■ *www.doverbaycafe.com*

### Fork    $$LD
Boise ■ (208) 287-1700
199 N 8th St ■ American ■ Asterisks on menu indicating GF. Options include house chips, slow cooked Idaho venison chili, seared lollipop lamb chops and more. ■ *boisefork.com*

### Forty-One South    $$LD
Sagle ■ (208) 265-2000
41 Lakeshore Dr ■ American ■ GF items include all salads, most fish and steak dishes. Alert server upon arrival and they will list off items on the menu that are GF. ■ *www.41southsandpoint.com/menus.html*

### Globus Restaurant    $$D
Ketchum ■ (208) 726-1301
291 6th St E ■ Thai ■ GF items indicated on menu. Items include black pepper calamari, kobe beef skewers, cucumber salad, organic mixed greens, warm spinach

and braised mushroom salad, sesame crusted Hawaiian ahi tuna, organic chicken breast, apple cider and tamari marinated pork tenderloin and green Thai curry. ■ *www.globus-restaurant.com*

**Goodwood Barbecue Company**   $LD
*Boise* ■ *(208) 658-7173*
*7849 W Spectrum St*
*Meridian* ■ *(208) 884-1021*
*1140 N Eagle Rd* ■ *Barbeque* ■ Most menu items except for sandwiches are GF, manager will assist with GF orders. ■ *goodwoodbbq.com*

**Ivano's Ristorante**   ✪★$$LD
*Sandpoint* ■ *(208) 263-0211*
*102 S 1st Ave, #101* ■ *Italian* ■ GF menu available. Includes a variety of appetizers, entrées and desserts. All dishes are prepared with rice pasta including penne, linguine and risotto and all sauces are prepared with rice or potato flour. ■ *ivanos-sandpoint.com/gluten-free.html*

**Jalapeno's**   $LD
*Boise* ■ *(208) 375-2077*
*8799 Franklin Rd*
*Nampa* ■ *(208) 442-6355*
*1921 Caldwell Blvd* ■ *Mexican* ■ Owner Laeticia reports that the kitchen is trained and GF aware. She notes that several items can be modified to be GF, but customers should stay away from fried items because they do not have dedicated fryers. Calling ahead to note GF is recommended. ■ *www.jalapenosidaho.com*

**Jenny's Lunch Line**   ✪$L
*Boise* ■ *(208) 433-0092*
*106 N 6th St* ■ *American* ■ All items on their menu are labeled GF or vegan/ dairy free. Many things are naturally GF or can modified to be GF. ■ *www.jennyslunchline.com*

**Joe's Crab Shack**   ✪📖
*Boise* ■ *(208) 336-9370*
*2288 N Garden St*

**Leku Ona**   $$$LD
*Boise* ■ *(208) 345-6665*
*117 S 6th St* ■ *Spanish* ■ Head Chef Ramone recommends calling ahead and asking for him so he can arrange a meal beforehand. Alert a server and ask him or her to communicate with the kitchen about the pre-arranged GF meal. ■ *www.lekuonaid.com*

**Ling & Louie's Asian Bar & Grill**   ✪★📖
*Meridian* ■ *(208) 888-5000*
*3210 E Louise Dr*

**Little Olive Restaurant**   ★$LD
*Sandpoint* ■ *(208) 597-7499*
*124 S 2nd Ave* ■ *Greek* ■ The manager said they offer a wide variety of food for those who have a GF lifestyle. Ask a server for alternatives. ■ *www.littleolivefood.com/menu.html*

**Louie's Pizza & Italian Restaurant**   ★$LD
*Meridian* ■ *(208) 884-5200*
*2500 E Fairview Ave* ■ *Italian* ■ GF pasta and pizza are available. Manager Chris notes that GF requests are common. The GF pizza is baked on a screen so it never touches the oven. The GF pasta is cooked in separate water as well. ■ *www.louiespizza.com*

**Mai Thai**   $LD
*Boise* ■ *(208) 344-8424*
*750 W Idaho St* ■ *Thai* ■ No GF menu but manager said almost anything on the menu can be "converted into GF". Their tom yum soup, pad thai, noodle delight, all curries, and mango sticky rice are naturally GF. Confirm the timeliness of this information before dining in. ■ *www.maithaigroup.com*

**Maxie's Pizza & Pasta**   ✪★$LD
*Kimberly* ■ *(208) 423-5880*
*626 Main St N* ■ *Pizza* ■ All new 10" GF pizza crust is available with a wide variety of toppings. ■ *www.maxiespizzapasta-kimberly.com*

**McGrath's Fish House**   ✪📖
*Boise* ■ *(208) 375-6300*
*1749 S Cole Rd*

### Melting Pot, The    ✪📖
Boise ▪ (208) 383-0900
200 N 6th St

### MickDuff's Brewing Company    ★$LD
Sandpoint ▪ (208) 255-4351
312 N 1st Ave ▪ American ▪ They
have a GF tortilla for their wraps
that is available upon request. ▪
www.mickduffs.com/food.htm

### Moon's Kitchen Café    ★¢BL
Boise ▪ (208) 385-0472
712 W Idaho St ▪ American ▪ GF bread
is available. The owner also states that
their GF cheesecake and GF fish fillet
are very popular among his customers. ▪
www.moonskitchen.com/index.htm

### Old Spaghetti Factory, The    ✪★📖
Boise ▪ (208) 336-2900
610 W Idaho St

### P.F. Chang's China Bistro    ✪★📖
Boise ▪ (208) 342-8100
391 S 8th St

### Pizza Pie Café    ✪★$LD
Rexburg ▪ (208) 359-1123
240 N 2nd E
Ammon ▪ (208) 522-5873
3160 E 17th St
Pocatello ▪ (208) 237-8740
4141 Poleline Rd ▪ Pizza ▪ GF pizza and pasta are available. Any pizza can be made with
GF crust; however, pasta sauce options are
somewhat limited. ▪ www.pizzapiecafe.co/

### Pizzalchik    ★$LD
Boise ▪ (208) 853-7757
7330 W State St ▪ Pizza ▪ GF pizza is
available. As with all specialty items,
call ahead to confirm availability. ▪
www.pizzalchik.com

### Salmon River Brewery    ✪★$D
McCall ▪ (208) 634-4772
300 W Colorado St ▪ American ▪ GF
items on the menu include "Somebody
Stop Me", chicken wings (without sauce),
black and blue elk burger (with no bun),
western elk burger (with no bun), double
smoked bacon brat (with no roll), German
brat (with no roll), chicken sandwich (with
no bun), garden salad, cobb salad, hot dog
and just a brat (with no roll). All items are
served with GF kettle chips or GF multi-
grain chips. ▪ www.salmonriverbrewery.com

### Sangria Grille    ✪$$LD
Moscow ▪ (208) 882-2693
2124 W Pullman Rd ▪ Latin American ▪
Server Elisa states that there are many GF
options. She warns against ordering fried
items because there are no dedicated fryers
but she says that all other prep items are
clean and sanitized before cooking GF
dishes. ▪ www.sangriagrille.com

### Second Avenue Pizza    ★$LD
Sandpoint ▪ (208) 263-9321
215 S 2nd Ave ▪ Pizza ▪ GF pizza is available in the small size. GF bottled beer is
also available. All GF pizza is prepared in
a separate area and cooked on a screen. ▪
www.secondavenuepizza.com

### Smoky Mountain Pizzeria Grill    ✪★$LD
Boise ▪ (208) 387-2727
1805 W State St
Boise ▪ (208) 429-0011
415 E Parkcenter Blvd
Eagle ▪ (208) 939-0212
127 E State St
Meridian ▪ (208) 884-1067
980 E Fairview Ave
Nampa ▪ (208) 461-7333
2007 N Cassia
Mountain Home ▪ (208) 587-2840
1465 American Legion Blvd
Ketchum ▪ (208) 622-5625
200 Sun Valley Rd
Moscow ▪ (208) 892-8000
1838 W Pullman Rd ▪ Pizza ▪ GF pizza is
available in the 10.5 inch size, as well as
GF penne pasta and several grilled meat
and fish items. Food & beverage director
Tom reports that they have procedures
in place to prevent CC, and recommends
consulting with a manager upon arrival to
ensure that your meal is handled safely. ▪
www.smokymountainpizza.com

## Snow Eagle Brewing and Grill    ★ $LD
*Idaho Falls* ▪ (208) 557-0455
*455 River Pkwy* ▪ *American* ▪ GF pizza is available. ▪ *www.snoweaglebrewing.com*

## Sushi Bar, The    $D
*McCall* ▪ (208) 634-7874
*414 Railroad Ave* ▪ *Sushi* ▪ Soy wrap or GF options available on request ▪ *www.sushibarmccall.com/menu.html*

## Taj Mahal    $LD
*Boise* ▪ (208) 473-7200
*150 N 8th St* ▪ *Indian* ▪ According to manager, they have "tons of GF options and we can modify any dish to suit the needs of their customers." ▪ *www.tajmahalofboise.com*

## Valentino's Pizza    ✪★ $LD
*Coeur d'Alene* ▪ (208) 772-0220
*219 W Canfield* ▪ *Pizza* ▪ Valentino's has GF crust, however, it is only available in medium size. Very strict CC policies in place. There is a separate preparation area and set of utensils. All employees attend a GF informational seminar upon hiring. ▪ *valstakenbake.com*

## Wing Nutz    $LD
*Nampa* ▪ (208) 468-9464
*1228 N Galleria Dr* ▪ *American* ▪ The restaurant reports that their wings are neither breaded nor deep fried, making them naturally GF. However, some sauces may contain gluten, so the restaurant recommends asking the server to check ingredients upon dining in. ▪ *www.bakedwingsarebetter.com*

## Wraptor    ★ ¢LD
*McCall* ▪ (208) 634-5599
*616 N Third St* ▪ *Deli* ▪ Anything that has a tortilla can be made in a bowl. Some sauces do contain gluten but most items on the menu can be modified to be GF. ▪ *www.wraptormccall.com*

# ILLINOIS

## CHICAGO

## Adobo Grill    ✪$$LD
*Chicago* ▪ (312) 266-7999
*1610 N Wells St* ▪ *Mexican* ▪ GF menu available but varies slightly by location. Examples of GF menu items are enchiladas, grilled half chicken in tamarind, and sautéed tilapia. GF desserts include tamal de chocolate and vanilla flan with caramel sauce. ▪ *www.adobogrill.com*

## Alinea Restaurant    $$$$D
*Chicago* ▪ (312) 867-0110
*1723 N Halsted St* ▪ *American* ▪ Reservationist Emily reports that they serve GF diners "all the time." She notes that customers will always be asked about food allergies and special diets when making a reservation, and she recommends noting GF at this time. Most items on both prix fixe menus can be easily modified to be GF.

## Au Bon Pain    📖
*Chicago* ▪ (312) 427-4925
*122 S Michigan Ave*
*Chicago* ▪ (312) 419-3837
*161 N Clark St*
*Chicago* ▪ (312) 578-0120
*181 W Madison Ave*
*Chicago* ▪ (312) 419-7571
*200 W Adams*
*Chicago* ▪ (312) 616-9249
*200 E Randolph St*
*Chicago* ▪ (312) 419-1054
*108 N State St*
*Chicago* ▪ (773) 880-4606
*200 E Superior*
*Chicago* ▪ (312) 755-9779
*222 W Merchandise Mart*
*Chicago* ▪ (312) 926-2268
*251 E Huron St*
*Chicago* ▪ (312) 926-6641
*201 E Huron Ave*
*Chicago* ▪ (312) 563-3758
*1653 W Congress Pkwy*

Chicago ▪ (312) 563-4442
1725 W Harrison St
Chicago ▪ (312) 563-3757
1700 W Van Buren
Chicago ▪ (312) 750-9129
125 S Wacker Dr
Chicago ▪ (773) 293-8871
5145 N California
Chicago ▪ (312) 207-1819
222 S Riverside Plaza
Chicago ▪ (773) 702-2748
5841 S Maryland Ave

## Aurelio's Pizza                            ★🕮
Chicago Heights ▪ (708) 481-5040
1545 S Western Ave
Chicago ▪ (312) 994-2000
506 W Harrison St

## Basil Leaf Café                      ★ $$LD
Chicago ▪ (773) 348-7243
2465 N Clark St ▪ Italian ▪ GF linguine and
penne pastas are available as well as their
salads. ▪ www.basilleaf.com

## Between Boutique Café & Lounge ★ $D
Chicago ▪ (773) 292-0585
1324 N Milwaukee Ave ▪ Latin American
▪ Manager Carl reports serving GF diners
regularly and notes that they can "absolutely" be accommodated. Most items are
not breaded, and the ceviche is a popular
GF order. Confirm the timeliness of this
information before dining in. Alert a server
upon arrival. Servers generally know which
menu items are or can be modified to be
GF, but they are trained to ask the chef if
they are unsure. ▪ www.betweenchicago.com

## Big Bowl Restaurant                    ✪$LD
Chicago ▪ (312) 951-1888
60 E Ohio St
Chicago ▪ (312) 640-8888
6 E Cedar St ▪ Asian ▪ GF menu includes Thai chicken lettuce wraps as an
appetizer, various pad thai dishes and
chicken kung pao as entrées, and two GF
desserts, including the trio of tastes. ▪
www.bigbowl.com

## Big Jones                              $$LD
Chicago ▪ (773) 275-5725
5347 N Clark St ▪ Modern American
▪ Restaurant reports that most menu
items can be modified to be GF, including sauces, entrées, and sides. They also
note that the corn bread is naturally GF.
All staff members are trained on GF dining, so just alert a server upon arrival. ▪
www.bigjoneschicago.com

## Bistrot Zinc                          $$$LD
Chicago ▪ (312) 337-1131
1131 N State St ▪ French ▪ Restaurant
owner Casey reports that GF diners are
welcome and advises customers to be
specific about dietary needs. Ask for the
manager upon arrival so that someone
will go over menu options with you. ▪
www.bistrotzinc.com

## BOKA                                   $$$D
Chicago ▪ (312) 337-6070
1729 N Halsted St ▪ Fusion ▪ Manager
Tim reports that they accommodate GF
diners on a "very regular basis," and all
staff members are thoroughly trained on
the GF diet. He adds that all menu items
are either naturally GF or can be modified
to be GF. Alert a server, who will indicate which dishes must be modified, and
which modifications must be made. ▪
www.bokachicago.com

## Bombay Spice Grill & Wine            ✪$LD
Chicago ▪ (312) 477-7657
450 N Clark St ▪ Indian ▪ Extensive GF
menu includes mango chicken salad,
kebab skewers, tikka skewers, biryani,
chicken keema, curries, and more. ▪
www.bombayspice.com

## Boundary, The                          $LD
Chicago ▪ (773) 278-1919
1932 W Division St ▪ Global ▪ Restaurant
reports that GF diners are "welcome."
Restaurant notes that most menu items can
be modified to be GF. Upon arrival, alert a
server and ask to speak with a manager. ▪
www.boundarychicago.com

## Bristol, The                                              $$D
*Chicago* ▪ *(773) 862-5555*
*2152 N Damen Ave* ▪ *Fusion* ▪ GF items
include trout, steak, chicken, salads,
cheese boards, sable fish, prawns and beef
tartare. Alert the server upon arrival. ▪
*www.thebristolchicago.com*

## Bubba Gump Shrimp Co.                          ✪ ▢
*Chicago* ▪ *(312) 252-4867*
*700 E Grand Ave*

## Buca di Beppo                                       ✪ ▢
*Chicago* ▪ *(312) 396-0001*
*521 N Rush St*

## Café Absinthe                                           $$$D
*Chicago* ▪ *(773) 278-4488*
*1954 W North Ave* ▪ *Modern American*
▪ Restaurant reports that they receive
GF requests "all the time." They note that
menu items that can be modified to be
GF include the ahi tuna tartar, foie gras,
endive and apple salad, Alaskan halibut,
sea scallops, and salmon. Alert a server
upon arrival, and ask for manager. Reservations noting GF are recommended. ▪
*www.cafe-absinthe.com*

## Café Ba Ba Reeba!                              ✪ ★ $$LD
*Chicago* ▪ *(773) 935-5000*
*2024 N Halsted St* ▪ *Spanish* ▪ GF menu
includes paellas, tapas, seared ahi tuna
salad, mixed greens salad with beets
and goat cheese, chicken skewers, and
more. GF beer, bread, and desserts such
as GF profiteroles are also available. ▪
*www.cafebabareeba.com*

## Cantina Laredo                                          ▢
*Chicago* ▪ *(312) 955-0014*
*508 N State St*

## Capital Grille, The                                  ✪ ▢
*Chicago* ▪ *(312) 337-9400*
*633 N Saint Clair St*

## Carnivale                                                 $$$LD
*Chicago* ▪ *(312) 850-5005*
*702 W Fulton St* ▪ *Latin American* ▪ Restaurant reports that with advance notice,

preferably a day or two beforehand, they
can accommodate GF diners. They note
that several dishes on the menu are naturally GF or can be modified to be GF. GF
diners should make a reservation, and then
upon arrival, talk to the server about GF
options. ▪ *www.carnivalechicago.com*

## Chicago Diner, The                           ✪ ★ $BLD
*Chicago* ▪ *(773) 935-6696*
*3411 N Halsted St*
*Chicago* ▪ *(773) 252-3211*
*2333 N Milwaukee Ave* ▪ *Vegetarian* ▪ Extensive GF menu includes nachos, a variety
of salads, avocado tostadas, quesadillas,
stir fry, and more. Restaurant notes that
fried items are prepared in the same fryer
as non-GF items. For dessert, they offer GF
cheesecake in various flavors. Confirm the
timeliness of this information before dining in. ▪ *www.veggiediner.com*

## Chicago's Pizza                                    ★ $$LD
*Chicago* ▪ *(773) 477-2777*
*3114 N Lincoln Ave*
*Chicago* ▪ *(773) 348-1700*
*1919 W Montrose Ave*
*Chicago* ▪ *(773) 427-0100*
*4520 W Irving Park Rd* ▪ *Pizza* ▪
House made GF pizza is available
in 3 different styles and any size. ▪
*www.chicagos-pizza.com*

## Club Lucky                                      ✪ ★ $$$LD
*Chicago* ▪ *(773) 227-2300*
*1824 W Wabansia Ave* ▪ *Italian* ▪ GF pasta
is available. Restaurant notes that salads,
fish dishes, Italian sausage, and most
meat dishes can be modified to be GF.
Confirm the timeliness of this information before dining in. Reservations noting
GF are recommended. Upon arrival, alert
a server, who will notify the kitchen. ▪
*www.clubluckychicago.com*

## Cookie Bar                                            ★ ¢S
*Chicago* ▪ *(773) 348-0300*
*2475 N Lincoln Ave* ▪ *Dessert* ▪ Multiple
flavors of GF cookies available daily. ▪
*www.cookiebaronline.com*

## Cosi                    ✪📖
*Chicago* ▪ *(312) 223-1061*
*116 S Michigan Ave*
*Chicago* ▪ *(312) 321-1990*
*55 E Grand Ave*
*Chicago* ▪ *(312) 782-4755*
*230 W Monroe St*
*Chicago* ▪ *(312) 368-4400*
*203 N LaSalle St*
*Chicago* ▪ *(312) 938-3200*
*233 N Michigan Ave*
*Chicago* ▪ *(312) 727-0290*
*33 N Dearborn St*
*Chicago* ▪ *(312) 422-1002*
*230 W Washington St*
*Chicago* ▪ *(773) 472-2674*
*2200 N Clark*

## Del Frisco's Double Eagle Steak House
📖
*Chicago* ▪ *(312) 888-2499*
*58 E Oak St*

## Dunlays on Clark              $$LD
*Chicago* ▪ *(773) 883-6000*
*2600 N Clark St* ▪ *Modern American* ▪
GF items are available on the menu. The
restaurant recommends avoiding fried
items because of high risk of CC. Alert
the server upon arrival. The restaurant
recommends stressing the severity of the
"allergy" to ensure proper preparation. ▪
*www.dunlaysonclark.com*

## Everest                    $$$$D
*Chicago* ▪ *(312) 663-8920*
*440 S Lasalle St 40th Floor* ▪ *French* ▪
Kitchen manager reports that the restaurant serves GF diners regularly and
does everything they can do to accommodate their guests. Reservations noting
GF must be made 48 hours in advance. ▪
*www.everestrestaurant.com*

## Feast Restaurant + Bar       ✪$$LD
*Chicago* ▪ *(773) 772-7100*
*1616 N Damen Ave* ▪ *American* ▪ GF menu
includes chicken tortilla soup, coconut
curry chicken quesadilla, pork chops,
blackened fish tacos, sautéed whitefish, a

dark chocolate flourless truffle cake and
more. GF brunch is available Fridays-
Sundays from 9am-3pm and GF lunch is
served Monday-Thursdays from 11am-
3pm. ▪ *feastrestaurant.com*

## Flat Top Grill               📖
*Chicago* ▪ *(312) 726-8400*
*30 S Wabash*
*Chicago* ▪ *(773) 665-8100*
*3200 Southport Ave*
*Chicago* ▪ *(312) 787-7676*
*319 W North Ave*
*Chicago* ▪ *(312) 829-4800*
*1000 W Washington Blvd*

## Fleming's Prime
## Steakhouse & Wine Bar        ✪📖
*Chicago* ▪ *(312) 329-9463*
*25 E Ohio St*

## Fogo De Chao                 ★📖
*Chicago* ▪ *(312) 932-9330*
*661 N LaSalle Blvd*

## Frankie's Pizzeria & Scaloppine  ✪$LD
*Chicago* ▪ *(312) 266-2500*
*900 N Michigan Ave* ▪ *Pizza* ▪ GF menu
includes calamari, chicken roma, crispy
brick chicken, and the risotto of the day.
GF desserts include chocolate meringue
cookies. The restaurant has two dining
rooms serving different items, so confirm
that GF items are available in a particular dining room before being seated. ▪
*www.frankiesscaloppine.com*

## Geja's Café                  $$$$D
*Chicago* ▪ *(773) 281-9101*
*340 W Armitage Ave* ▪ *European* ▪
Manager Adam reports that they serve GF
diners "all the time." He notes that six of
eight fondue dipping sauces are GF, and
none of the seafood or meats are dredged
in any sort of flour. Confirm the timeliness
of this information before dining in. Adam
recommends noting GF in reservations.
Restaurant has an internal list of GF items
that is available to customers upon request.
▪ *www.gejascafe.com*

## Green Zebra                                              $BD
Chicago ▪ (312) 243-7100
1460 W Chicago Ave ▪ Vegetarian ▪ Team
member Jerome reports that "plenty of
items" on the menu are naturally GF or can
be prepared GF. He recommends reservations noting GF so the kitchen staff can
properly prepare. Alert the server upon
arrival. ▪ www.greenzebrachicago.com

## Handlebar                                               $BD
Chicago ▪ (773) 384-9546
2311 W North Ave ▪ American ▪ Owner
Josh reports that there are extensive GF
options. He notes that GF diners come in
"on a regular basis." GF items include black
bean maduro, ground nut stew, tostadas,
and several sides. Confirm the timeliness
of this information before dining in. Alert
a server, who will talk to the kitchen. ▪
www.handlebarchicago.com

## Hard Rock Café                                          ✪📖
Chicago ▪ (312) 943-2252
63 W Ontario

## Ina's                                                  ★$BL
Chicago ▪ (312) 226-8227
1235 W Randolph St ▪ American ▪ Manager Seana reports that they have GF items
at every meal, but she advises speaking to
a manager before ordering. GF items are
marked on the regular menu. GF fried
chicken night is the second Wednesday of
every month. GF beer, bread, pasta, and
cake available. ▪ www.breakfastqueen.com

## Jason's Deli                                            ✪📖
Chicago ▪ (312) 850-0547
1258 S Canal St
Chicago ▪ (312) 750-1318
195 N Dearborn St

## Jersey Mike's                                           📖
Chicago ▪ (312) 263-0830
200 W Monroe St
Chicago ▪ (312) 923-0950
203 E Ohio St
Chicago ▪ (773) 360-8726
3152 N Broadway

## Jin Ju                                                  $$D
Chicago ▪ (773) 334-6377
5203 N Clark St ▪ Asian ▪ Rice-based
dishes with mixed vegetables, spicy chick-
en, and spicy squid can be modified to be
GF. It is imperative to alert a server and to
be prepared to explain GF to the server.
Restaurant recommends asking for the chef
or manager.

## Joe's Seafood,
## Prime Steak, and Stone Crab    ✪$$$$LD
Chicago ▪ (312) 379-5637
60 E Grand Ave ▪ American ▪ Full GF
menu includes items such as salmon au
poivre, bacon-wrapped sea scallops, ribeye
steak, stone crabs, and a variety of salads
and sides. GF desserts include vanilla ice
cream, orange sherbet, and fresh berries with whipped cream. The restaurant
reports that they safely handle GF orders
"every day" and have "procedures in place"
against CC. ▪ www.joes.net

## Karyn's Cooked                                          ★$LD
Chicago ▪ (312) 587-1050
738 N Wells St ▪ Vegan ▪ GF items marked
on the menu include stuffed eggplant,
grilled polenta, and green enchiladas. GF
desserts are available. Alert a server, even if
ordering a GF item. ▪ www.karynraw.com

## Karyn's Raw Café                                        ✪$BLD
Chicago ▪ (312) 255-1590
1901 N Halsted ▪ Raw ▪ GF items are
marked on the menu and include various salads, chili, various soups, stuffed
eggplant, and much more. Alert the server
upon arrival. ▪ www.karynraw.com

## L20                                                     ✪★$$$$D
Chicago ▪ (773) 868-0002
2300 N Lincoln Park W ▪ Seafood ▪
Restaurant reports that many menu items
are naturally GF, as it is a seafood restaurant. The menu changes every day, so
with reservations, the chef can take GF
requests into consideration. Reservations
noting GF are highly recommended. ▪
www.l2orestaurant.com

## Lawry's The Prime Rib                $$$$D
*Chicago* ▪ *(312) 787-5000*
*100 E Ontario St* ▪ *Steakhouse* ▪ Manager
Christopher at Beverly Hills strongly recommends speaking to a manager prior to
dining at any Lawry's restaurant to "ensure
that they are aware of your situation and
able to help you navigate through their individual menus." He notes that plain prime
rib (no gravy, no au jus) and lobster among
items that are typically GF, but again stresses the importance of notifying the server
and manager on duty so they can ensure
safe preparation. ▪ *www.lawrysonline.com*

## Loving Hut                          📖
*Chicago* ▪ *(773) 275-8797*
*5812 N Broadway*

## Luxbar                              $$LD
*Chicago* ▪ *(312) 642-3400*
*18 E Bellevue* ▪ *American* ▪ Manager
Michael reports that there are "plenty of
items" on the menu that can be modified to
be GF because almost everything is made
from scratch. Alert a server upon arrival.
"Most servers" are GF aware, and all servers are trained to "let the chef know" as
soon as they are alerted of a GF diner. ▪
*www.luxbar.com*

## M Henry Chow for Now                CBL
*Chicago* ▪ *(773) 561-1600*
*5707 N Clark St* ▪ *Modern American* ▪
GF menu includes a variety of breakfast
and lunch options, including omelettes,
house potatoes, sesame crusted yellowfin
on mixed greens, azteca black bean bowl,
and more. The restaurant also reports that
many other items on the regular menu
can be modified to be GF. They also add
that they are "in the process of keeping a GF bread in stock all the time." ▪
*www.mhenry.net*

## Maggiano's Little Italy              ★📖
*Chicago* ▪ *(312) 644-7700*
*516 N Clark St*

## Mana Food Bar                       ✪$D
*Chicago* ▪ *(773) 342-1742*
*1742 W Division St* ▪ *Global* ▪ GF menu
available. Items included are hot dishes
such as chili and saag paneer and cold
dishes like endive salad and hummus. ▪
*www.manafoodbar.com*

## Marcello's,
## A Father and Son Restaurant         ✪★$LD
*Chicago* ▪ *(773) 252-2620*
*2475 N Milwaukee Ave*
*Chicago* ▪ *(312) 654-2550*
*645 W North Ave* ▪ *Pizza* ▪ GF pizza,
pasta, brownies, and apple or berry dessert
pizza are available as well as a GF beer. ▪
*www.marcellos.com*

## Margaritaville                      ✪★📖
*Chicago* ▪ *(312) 496-3840*
*700 E Grand Ave*

## Melting Pot, The                    ✪📖
*Chicago* ▪ *(312) 573-0011*
*609 N Dearborn St*

## Mercat a la Planxa                  $$$$BLD
*Chicago* ▪ *(312) 765-0524*
*638 S Michigan Ave* ▪ *Spanish* ▪ According
to the restaurant, they have several regular
customers who have Celiac and they have
"no problem" accommodating their dietary
needs. Reservations noting GF are advised
so they can thoroughly prepare beforehand. ▪ *www.mercatchicago.com*

## Mity Nice Bar & Grill               ✪$LD
*Chicago* ▪ *(312) 335-4745*
*835 N Michigan Ave* ▪ *American* ▪ Ask the
host or server for a GF menu upon arrival.
The restaurant reports that GF foods are
cooked separately from other foods. ▪
*www.mitynicechicago.com*

## Morton's Steakhouse                 ✪📖
*Chicago* ▪ *(312) 266-4820*
*1050 N State St*
*Chicago* ▪ *(312) 201-0410*
*65 E Wacker Pl*

**Nacional 27** ★$$$D
Chicago ▪ (312) 664-2747
325 W Huron St ▪ Latin American ▪ The restaurant reports that GF options are available, and that many menu items are naturally GF. GF items on the menu include the tequila-marinated chicken, several tapas, ahi tuna, and gaucho barbeque items. Alert a server, who will discuss details more extensively. ▪ nacional27chicago.com

**Naf Naf Grill** $LD
Chicago ▪ (312) 251-9000
309 W Washington ▪ Middle Eastern ▪ Most menu items are naturally GF except for their pita, schnitzel, and taboule. ▪ www.nafnafgrill.com

**Naha** ★$$$$LD
Chicago ▪ (312) 321-6242
500 N Clark St ▪ Fusion ▪ The restaurant reports that many items on the menu can be modified to be GF. They recommend noting GF when making reservations so that the chef can create GF dishes and ideas ahead of time. Alert server upon arrival. ▪ www.naha-chicago.com

**North Pond** $$$$D
Chicago ▪ (773) 477-5845
2610 N Cannon Dr ▪ Fusion ▪ Restaurant reports that GF diners can be accommodated "without a problem." Reservations noting GF are highly recommended, so that the server can be informed in advance. GF options will be discussed with chef. ▪ www.northpondrestaurant.com

**Opart Thai** ¢LD
Chicago ▪ (773) 989-8517
4658 N Western Ave
Chicago ▪ (312) 567-9898
1906 S State St ▪ Thai ▪ Pad Thai, all curries and several other menu options are GF. ▪ www.opartthai.com

**Osteria Via Stato** ✪$$D
Chicago ▪ (312) 642-8450
620 N State St ▪ Italian ▪ GF menu available. Reservations noting GF are recommended. ▪ www.osteriaviastato.com

**P.F. Chang's China Bistro** ✪★📖
Chicago ▪ (312) 828-9977
530 N Wabash Ave

**Pasta D'Arte Trattoria Italiana** ★$$LD
Chicago ▪ (773) 763-1181
6311 N Milwaukee Ave ▪ Italian ▪ GF pasta is available. Examples of GF meals include risotto pescatora, pasta bolognese, and sirloin beef stuffed with garlic, parmigiano, and parsley. Confirm the timeliness of this information before dining in. All staff members are trained in the GF diet, and the restaurant reports that they are "very conscious of allergies and medical conditions." They recommend discussing dietary needs with the server. ▪ www.pastadarte.com

**Pei Wei Asian Diner** ✪📖
Chicago ▪ (773) 687-0290
2709 N Elston Ave
Chicago ▪ (312) 660-3100
227 E Ontario St

**Pelago Ristorante** ★$$$LD
Chicago ▪ (312) 280-0700
201 E Delaware Pl ▪ Italian ▪ The risotto entrée is GF and upon request the chef is able to make other dishes on the menu GF. ▪ www.pelagorestaurant.com

**Petterino's** ✪$$$LD
Chicago ▪ (312) 422-0150
150 N Dearborn St ▪ Seafood & Steakhouse ▪ GF menu includes midwest corn chowder, prime skirt steak, Atlantic salmon, grilled chicken breast, and more. It also denotes which side dishes are GF and indicates necessary changes to make dishes GF. Sundaes and crème brûlée are available for dessert. Alert a server, who will notify the chef and ensure proper meal preparation. ▪ www.petterinos.com

**Prêt A Manger** 📖
Chicago ▪ (312) 546-8270
211 W Adams St
Chicago ▪ (847) 491-9471
1701 Sherman Ave
Chicago ▪ (312) 660-9494
100 N LaSalle

Chicago ▪ (312) 819-3298
225 N Michigan Ave
Chicago ▪ (312) 260-4301
73 W Monroe
Chicago ▪ (312) 416-9263
1 S State St
Chicago ▪ (312) 873-0416
108 S Michigan Ave

### R.J. Grunts        $LD
Chicago ▪ (773) 929-5363
2056 N Lincoln Park W ▪ American ▪
Manager Andrea reports that GF diners are
welcome and advises alerting a server upon
arrival, as the restaurant has an allergy pro-
cedure which covers GF. She says they can
accommodate GF diners, though they may
have to "improvise" some of the selections.
Their extensive salad bar also caters to GF
diners. ▪ www.rjgruntschicago.com

### Ranalli's of Andersonville    ✪★$LD
Chicago ▪ (773) 334-1300
1512 W Berwyn Ave ▪ Italian ▪ GF menu
includes garlic bread, cheese bread, pizza
bread, and bruschetta for appetizers, as well
as GF croutons and dressings for salads,
sandwiches with GF buns, GF spaghetti
or penne, GF lasagna, and GF pizza. ▪
www.ranallispizza.com

### Reza's Restaurant        $$$LD
Chicago ▪ (773) 561-1898
5255 N Clark St
Chicago ▪ (312) 664-4500
432 W Ontario St
Chicago ▪ (773) 244-0300
2423 N Clark St ▪ Middle Eastern ▪ Managers at all locations report serving GF diners often since 90% of their menu can be
GF. All recommend asking for a manager
upon arrival. Although many servers are
educated on the GF diet, the managers will
know more about which items are GF. ▪
www.rezasrestaurant.com

### Romano's Macaroni Grill    ✪★📖
Chicago ▪ (773) 686-6180
O'Hare International Airport

### Rosati's Pizza        ★📖
Chicago ▪ (773) 792-2585
5544 N Milwaukee Ave
Chicago ▪ (773) 334-3333
4863 N Broadway St
Chicago ▪ (312) 755-9955
126 W Grand Ave

### Ruth's Chris Steak House    ✪📖
Chicago ▪ (312) 321-2725
431 N Dearborn St

### Scoozi!        ✪$$$D
Chicago ▪ (312) 943-5900
41 W Huron St ▪ Italian ▪ GF menu includes mussels arrabbiata, grilled chicken
diavola, balsamic glazed short rib, herb
roasted salmon, and more. GF pasta is
available. GF menu changes seasonally, so
call ahead for the most current options. ▪
www.leye.com/restaurants/directory/scoozi

### Senza Chicago        $$$$BLD
Chicago ▪ (773) 770-3527
2873 N Broadway ▪ American ▪ Everything on the menu is 100% GF. Menu items
include parsnip apple soup, "everything"
gnocchi, foie gras, NY strip and more. ▪
www.senzachicago.com

### Shaw's Crab House        ✪$$$$LD
Chicago ▪ (312) 527-2722
21 E Hubbard St ▪ Seafood ▪ GF
menu includes griddle garlic shrimp,
seared scallops, halibut, salmon, strip
steak, crab, lobster, sushi, and more.
Crème brûlée is available for dessert. ▪
www.shawscrabhouse.com

### Sit Down Café & Sushi Bar, The    ✪¢LD
Chicago ▪ (773) 324-3700
1312 E 53rd St ▪ Global ▪ Extensive
GF menu includes prosciutto rolls,
pizza, and sandwiches on GF bread,
as well as maki and sashimi rolls. ▪
www.thesitdown53.com

### Smith & Wollensky        📖
Chicago ▪ (312) 670-9900
318 N State St

**South Branch**                                                $$$$**LD**
Chicago ▪ (312) 546-6177
*100 S Wacker Dr* ▪ *American* ▪ GF
items clearly marked on regular menu. ▪
*www.southbranchchicago.com*

**Swirlz Cupcakes**                                                ★¢**S**
Chicago ▪ (773) 404-2253
*705 W Belden Ave* ▪ *Bakery* ▪ Non-
dedicated bakery offering GF cupcakes
in flavors that change daily. Possible GF
flavors include red velvet, carrot, chocolate grasshopper mint, and chocolate
chip. Call ahead to find out which flavors
are available on a given day. There is
also a schedule online showing which
GF options are available each day. ▪
*www.swirlzcupcakes.com*

**Takashi**                                                      $$$$**D**
Chicago ▪ (773) 772-6170
*1952 N Damen Ave* ▪ *Japanese* ▪ The
restaurant reports that they are "very
accommodating" to GF diners and have
many dishes that can be modified to be
GF. They recommend reservations noting
GF, so the chef prepare ahead of time. ▪
*www.takashichicago.com*

**Tavern on Rush**                                            $$$$**SBLD**
Chicago ▪ (312) 664-9600
*1031 N Rush St* ▪ *Steakhouse* ▪ Menu
items that can be modified to be GF
include all steaks, several salads, grilled
vegetables, and most seafood dishes. GF
pizza and pasta is also available. Confirm
the timeliness of this information before
dining in. Ask the server to get a manager
or chef, who will come out and discuss GF
options. ▪ *www.tavernonrush.com*

**Taxim**                                                        $$$**D**
Chicago ▪ (773) 252-1558
*1558 N Milwaukee Ave* ▪ *Greek* ▪ Restau-
rant notes that GF diners should request
all meals to come without bread and
discuss GF options with a server. Some
options include heirloom tomato salad,
hummus with vegetables, grape leaves,
pork loin, lamb sausage, octopus, grilled

peppers, braised lamb shank, roasted
chicken, pork skewers and sea bass. ▪
*www.taximchicago.com*

**Texas De Brazil Churrascaria**                    ★📖
Chicago ▪ (312) 670-1006
*51 E Ohio St*

**Topolobampo**                                              $$$$**LD**
Chicago ▪ (312) 661-1434
*445 N Clark St* ▪ *Mexican* ▪ Restaurant
notes that they serve GF diners "quite
often," and they advise alerting the server
upon arrival. Servers must go "directly"
to the chef when they are notified of a GF
diner. ▪ *www.fronterakitchens.com*

**Tru Restaurant**                                          $$$$**D**
Chicago ▪ (312) 202-0001
*676 N Saint Clair St* ▪ *French* ▪ Chef
Anthony reports that serving GF din-
ers is "fairly common." He adds that
almost the entire menu is naturally GF
or can be modified to be GF. He rec-
ommends making reservations noting
GF and alerting the server when he or
she asks about dietary restrictions. ▪
*www.trurestaurant.com*

**Uno Chicago Grill**                                   ✪★📖
Chicago ▪ (312) 321-1000
*29 E Ohio St*
Chicago ▪ (312) 943-4041
*49 E Ontario St*
Chicago ▪ (312) 943-2400
*619 N Wabash Ave*

**Vinci Restaurant**                                   ✪★$$$**D**
Chicago ▪ (312) 266-1199
*1732 N Halsted St* ▪ *Italian* ▪ GF menu
includes appetizers, pasta dishes, meat
courses, and desserts. Examples are
carpaccio, duck, and veal saltimbocca.
GF pasta is available. For dessert, they
offer panna cotta and crème brûlée. ▪
*www.vincichicago.com*

**Weber Grill Restaurant**                            ✪$**LD**
Chicago ▪ (312) 467-9696
*539 N State St* ▪ *American* ▪ Extensive GF
menu includes filet mignon, plank grilled

bourbon salmon, citrus pesto tuna, grilled seasonal vegetable kabobs, and more. Starters include wood roasted mussels and baked onion soup. Confirm the timeliness of this information before dining in. The restaurant reports that a manager oversees all GF orders to ensure they are prepared correctly. ▪ *www.webergrillrestaurant.com*

### Wildfire Restaurant ✪★⌑
Chicago ▪ (312) 787-9000
159 W Erie

### Zad Restaurant ✪$LD
Chicago ▪ (773) 404-3473
3211 N Broadway St ▪ Middle Eastern ▪ GF menu consists only of side dishes such as vegetables, rice, yogurt and feta cheese for entrées such as salads. ▪ *www.zadchicago.com*

# ILLINOIS

## ALL OTHER CITIES

### Antico Posto ✪★$$LD
Oak Brook ▪ (630) 586-9200
118 Oakbrook Ctr ▪ Italian ▪ GF menu includes salads, grilled chicken limone, and oven roasted pork chops. GF pasta is also available. Located in the Oakbrook Center Mall. ▪ *www.antico-posto.com*

### Apple's Bakery ★CS
Peoria ▪ (309) 693-3522
8412 N Knoxville Ave ▪ Bakery ▪ Non-dedicated bakery offering a wide selection of GF products. Pies, cookies, brownies, and breads are available, as well as cakes, cupcakes, and muffins. There is a separate, dedicated GF kitchen where only GF items are prepared. GF baked goods are prepared Monday through Wednesday, but they are sometimes available on other days. ▪ *www.applesbakery.com*

### Au Bon Pain ⌑
Park Ridge ▪ (847) 692-2352
1775 Dempster St
Lake Forest ▪ (847) 535-6855
660 N Westmoreland Rd

### Aurelio's Pizza ★⌑
Mokena ▪ (708) 478-0022
19836 Wolf Rd
Frankfort ▪ (815) 469-2196
310 W Lincoln Hwy
New Lenox ▪ (815) 485-8100
320 W Maple St
Addison ▪ (630) 889-9560
1455 W Lake St
Bourbonnais ▪ (815) 935-1212
1600 N Convent St
Downers Grove ▪ (630) 810-0078
940 Warren Ave
Geneva ▪ (630) 262-8440
330 W State St
Crete ▪ (708) 672-4000
1372 Main St
Frankfort ▪ (815) 469-2196
9901 W Lincoln Hwy
Homewood ▪ (708) 798-8050
18162 Harwood Ave
Joliet ▪ (815) 741-1400
3101 W Jefferson
LaGrange ▪ (708) 579-0900
11 Calendar Ct
Lockport ▪ (815) 588-4422
16529 W 159th St
Macomb ▪ (309) 833-5577
221 N Randolph St
Mokena ▪ (708) 478-0022
19836 Wolf Rd
Morris ▪ (815) 941-9878
1501 Creek Rd
Naperville ▪ (630) 369-0077
931 W 75th St
Naperville ▪ (630) 922-3600
1975 Springbrook Sq Dr
New Lenox ▪ (815) 485-8100
320 W Maple St
Villa Park ▪ (630) 758-0100
100 E Roosevelt Rd
Palos Hghts ▪ (708) 389-5170
6543 W 127th St

*Plainfield* ▪ (815) 254-3500
*14421 Wallin Dr*
*Richton Park* ▪ (708) 481-4400
*3740 Sauk Trl*
*South Holland* ▪ (708) 333-0310
*601 E 170th St*
*Tinley Park* ▪ (708) 429-4600
*15901 Oak Park Ave*
*Woodridge* ▪ (630) 968-0077
*6430 Main St*

## Barraco's Pizzeria                                          ★ $LD

*Crestwood* ▪ (708) 385-2002
*13445 S Cicero*
*Evergreen Park* ▪ (708) 424-8182
*3701 W 95th St*
*Orland Hills* ▪ (708) 873-2540
*8915 W 159th St*
*Orland Park* ▪ (708) 478-1500
*18040 S Wolf Rd* ▪ Pizza ▪ GF 10" pizza
is available at the listed locations only.
Call ahead to confirm availability. ▪
*www.barracos.com*

## Biaggi's                                                 ✪★📖

*Algonquin* ▪ (847) 658-5040
*1524 S Randall Rd*
*Bloomington* ▪ (309) 661-8322
*1501 N Veterans Pkwy*
*Champaign* ▪ (217) 356-4300
*2235 S Neil St*
*Deer Park* ▪ (847) 438-1850
*20560 N Rand Rd*
*Naperville* ▪ (630) 428-8500
*2752 Show Place Dr*
*Deerfield* ▪ (847) 607-2300
*711 Deerfield Rd*
*Peoria* ▪ (309) 686-8114
*2601 W Lake Ave*

## Big Bowl Restaurant                                        ✪$LD

*Schaumburg* ▪ (847) 517-8881
*1950 E Higgins Rd*
*Lincolnshire* ▪ (847) 808-8880
*215 Parkway Dr* ▪ Asian ▪ GF menu
includes Thai chicken lettuce wraps as
an appetizer, various pad thai dishes and
chicken kung pao as entrées, and two GF
desserts, including the trio of tastes. ▪
*www.bigbowl.com*

## Blind Faith Café                                   ✪★$$BLD

*Evanston* ▪ (847) 328-6875
*525 Dempster St* ▪ Bakery & Café ▪ GF
items are marked on the menu and include
maple glazed squash, black bean tostadas, teriyaki fried rice bowl, Thai peanut
noodles, and more. Several GF bakery
items available. Confirm the timeliness
of this information before dining in. ▪
*www.blindfaithcafe.com*

## Bonefish Grill                                             ✪📖

*Schaumburg* ▪ (847) 534-0679
*180 S Roselle Rd*
*Algonquin* ▪ (847) 658-9268
*1604 S Randall Rd*
*Skokie* ▪ (847) 674-4634
*9310 Skokie Blvd*

## Boston's Restaurant & Sports Bar
✪★📖

*Tinley Park* ▪ (815) 464-9844
*7216 W 191ST St*

## Buca di Beppo                                            ✪📖

*Lombard* ▪ (630) 932-7673
*90 Yorktown Ctr*
*Orland Park* ▪ (708) 349-6262
*15350 S 94th Ave*
*Wheeling* ▪ (847) 808-9898
*604 N Milwaukee Ave*
*Champaign* ▪ (217) 378-8731
*200 N Neil St*

## Cab's Wine Bar Bistro                            ✪★$$$D

*Glen Ellyn* ▪ (630) 942-9463
*430 N Main St* ▪ Global ▪ Manager reports
that many meat and seafood dishes can
be modified to be GF. Confirm the timeliness of this information before dining in. ▪
*www.cabsbistro.com*

## Capital Grille, The                                        ✪📖

*Lombard* ▪ (630) 627-9800
*87 Yorktown Ctr*
*Rosemont* ▪ (847) 671-8125
*5340 N River Rd*

## Capri Restaurant                                         ★ ¢LD

*Rockford* ▪ (815) 965-6341

313 E State St ▪ Italian ▪ GF pasta is available, and cheese lasagna can be prepared with advance notice of 24 hours. Other possible GF options include chicken marsala, chicken parmesan and broiled cod. ▪ www.caprirockford.com

### Carlos O'Kelly's    ✪

Bloomington ▪ (309) 662-9747
2105 Veterans Pkwy
Decatur ▪ (217) 877-0967
2930 N Main St
Moline ▪ (309) 762-3785
41st Ave Dr
Peoria ▪ (309) 682-0606
714 W Lake Ave

### Carrabba's Italian Grill    ✪📖

Naperville ▪ (630) 355-3234
944 S Route 59
Woodridge ▪ (630) 427-0900
1001 75th St

### Cellar Bistro, The    ✪$$BLD

Wheaton ▪ (630) 653-6299
132 N Hale St ▪ American ▪ The Cellar has both a GF lunch and dinner menu available online and in the restaurant. ▪ thecellarbistro.com

### Chama Gaucha
### Brazilian Steakhouse    $$$LD

Downers Grove ▪ (630) 324-6002
3008 Finley Rd ▪ Steakhouse ▪ Chama Gaucha offers a variety of GF entrées including filet mignon, ribeye, chicken, and pork ribs. ▪ chamagaucha.com

### Cheeseburger in Paradise    ✪★📖

Algonquin ▪ (847) 658-9627
1608 S Randall Rd
Downers Grove ▪ (630) 953-7095
2970 Finley Rd

### City Park Grill    ✪★$$LD

Highland Park ▪ (847) 432-9111
1791 St Johns Ave ▪ American
GF menu includes cobb salad, roasted chicken, sautéed tilapia, and baby back ribs. GF sandwich buns and pastas are available.

Confirm the timeliness of this information before dining in. www.thecityparkgrill.com

### Claddagh Irish Pub    📖

Geneva ▪ (630) 208-0337
1702 Commons Dr

### Cooper's Hawk
### Winery & Restaurants    ✪★📖

Arlington Hghts ▪ (847) 981-0900
798 W Algonquin Rd
Burr Ridge ▪ (630) 887-0123
510 Village Ctr Dr
Naperville ▪ (630) 245-8000
1740 Freedom Dr
Orland Pk ▪ (708) 633-0200
15690 S Harlem Ave
S Barrington ▪ (847) 836-9463
100 W Higgins Rd
Wheeling ▪ (847) 215-1200
583 N Milwaukee Ave

### Cosi    ✪📖

Hinsdale ▪ (630) 654-5033
25 E Hinsdale Ave
Lincolnshire ▪ (847) 415-2674
910 N Milwaukee Ave
Evanston ▪ (847) 328-2050
1740 Sherman Ave
Glenview ▪ (847) 832-6926
2100 Patriot Blvd

### Cozymel's Coastel Mex    ✪📖

Wheaton ▪ (630) 871-1030
311 E Loop Rd

### Da Luciano    ✪★$$D

River Grove ▪ (708) 453-1000
8343 W Grand Ave ▪ Italian ▪ Extensive GF menu includes chicken Vesuvio, chicken parmigiana, eggplant parmagiana, mozzarella wedges, and various sauces. GF pizza, pasta, and bread are available. Tiramisu, cannoli, and cupcakes are available for dessert. ▪ www.dalucianos.com

### Deerfields Bakery    ✪★₡S

Deerfield ▪ (847) 520-0068
813 N Waukegan Rd
Schaumburg ▪ (847) 520-0068
25 S Roselle Rd

*Buffalo Grove* ▪ (847) 520-0068
*201 N Buffalo Grove Rd* ▪ *Bakery* ▪ GF
menu includes cookies, cakes, brownies,
baguettes, and stuffing. GF menus are available in stores and online. Calling ahead for
specific or large orders is recommended. ▪
*www.deerfieldbakery.com*

### Di Pescara                                    ★ $$$**LD**
*Northbrook* ▪ (847) 498-4321
*2124 Northbrook Ct* ▪ *Italian* ▪ GF pasta
is available. The restaurant reports that
they are able to modify several dishes to
be GF. Alert a server upon arrival. Reservations noting GF are recommended. ▪
*www.di-pescara.com*

### Enzo and Lucia's Ristorante         ★ $$$**LD**
*Long Grove* ▪ (847) 478-8825
*343 Old McHenry Rd* ▪ *Italian* ▪ GF
pasta is available. Restaurant also has a
wide variety of appetizers, salads, and
entrées that can be modified to be GF. ▪
*www.enzoandlucia.com*

### Firehouse Pizza                            ★ $**LD**
*Peoria* ▪ (309) 693-9111
*8879 N Knoxville Ave*
*Champaign* ▪ (217) 607-1308
*510 E John St*
*East Peoria* ▪ (309) 698-9111
*240 S Main St*
*Washington* ▪ (309) 444-2911
*1320 Washington Rd*
*Normal* ▪ (309) 808-1597
*107 E Beaufort St*
*Quincy* ▪ (217) 214-2911
*340 S 36th St*
*Morton* ▪ (309) 291-0911
*201 S Main St* ▪ *Pizza* ▪ GF pizza is
available and is prepared on parch-
ment paper using a different GF pizza
sauce. Corn chips are used to prepare
the nachos, making them GF too. ▪
*www.firehousepizza911.com*

### Flat Top Grill                                    📖
*Normal* ▪ (309) 454-1300
*307 Veterans Pkwy*
*Champaign* ▪ (217) 344-3200

*607 S 6th St*
*Evanston* ▪ (847) 570-0100
*707 Church St*
*Lombard* ▪ (630) 652-3700
*305 Yorktown Ctr*
*Naperville* ▪ (630) 428-8400
*218 S Washington St*
*Oak Park* ▪ (708) 358-8200
*726 Lake St*
*Peoria* ▪ (309) 693-9966
*5201 W War Memorial Dr*

### Fleming's Prime
### Steakhouse & Wine Bar                  ✪📖
*Lincolnshire* ▪ (847) 793-0333
*960 Milwaukee Ave*

### Fox and Hound Pub & Grille            📖
*Arlington Hghts* ▪ (847) 590-9019
*910-918 W Dundee Rd*
*Aurora* ▪ (630) 236-9183
*4320 E New York Ave*
*Bloomingdale* ▪ (630) 295-9626
*370-420 W Army Trail Rd*
*Schaumburg* ▪ (847) 884-6821
*1416 N Roselle Rd*

### Gaetano's                                      ★ $$**D**
*Forest Park* ▪ (708) 366-4010
*7636 Madison St* ▪ *Italian* ▪ GF pasta is
available. Alert a server, who will inform
the kitchen. The kitchen staff members
are all trained to prepare GF meals. ▪
*gaetanosforestpark.com*

### Genghis Grill                                    📖
*Wheaton* ▪ (630) 665-3600
*106 N Hale St*

### Glen Prairie                                  ✪ $$$**BLD**
*Glen Ellyn* ▪ (630) 613-1250
*1250 Roosevelt Rd* ▪ *Modern American* ▪
GF items are marked on the menu and include grilled flat iron steak, seared sea scallops, and wild mushroom risotto. Restaurant
notes that servers use a different notation
when sending GF orders to the kitchen. ▪
*www.glenprairie.com*

**Godfather's Pizza** ★📖
*Springfield* ▪ *(217) 726-2000*
*1754 Wabash Ave*
*E Moline* ▪ *(309) 792-3706*
*1347 Ave of the Cities*

**Golden Chef, The** ★$LD
*Wheeling* ▪ *(847) 537-7100*
*600 S Milwaukee Ave* ▪ *Chinese* ▪ Owner
Esther reports that she is a nutritionist
and is "very familiar" with the GF diet.
She suggests asking for her upon arrival. GF soy sauce is available, and Esther
notes that most items can be made GF. ▪
*www.goldenchefwheeling.com*

**Graziano's Restaurant** ✪★$LD
*Niles* ▪ *(847) 647-4096*
*5960 W Touhy Ave* ▪ *Italian* ▪ The regular
menu mentions the modifications necessary to make items GF. For example, the
grilled chicken avocado wrap can be made
GF by substituting a lettuce wrap. GF pasta
is available, and the menu lists GF sauces. ▪
*www.grazianosrestaurant.com*

**Greco's** ★$$LD
*Willow Springs* ▪ *(708) 839-0333*
*8850 S Archer Ave* ▪ *Italian* ▪ GF pasta is
available. The restaurant also notes that
many of their regular entrées are GF or can
easily be prepared GF. They recommend
calling ahead to confirm availability of GF
pasta. ▪ *www.grecos.ws*

**Guardi's Pizza** ★$D
*Tinley Park* ▪ *(708) 429-1166*
*16711 S. 80th Ave* ▪ *Pizza* ▪ GF pizza is
available in the 10-inch size. Any top-
pings can be added to the GF crust. ▪
*www.guardispizza.com*

**Happy Joe's Pizza & Ice Cream** 📖
*Aledo* ▪ *(309) 582-5636*
*Se 314 3rd St*
*Coal Valley* ▪ *(309) 799-3171*
*320 W 1st Ave*
*Colona* ▪ *(309) 792-3335*
*223 1st St*
*East Dubuque* ▪ *(815) 747-3300*
*222 Sinsinawa*

*East Moline* ▪ *(309) 755-4576*
*4020 Kennedy Dr*
*Galena* ▪ *(815) 777-1830*
*9919 Route 20*
*Galesburg* ▪ *(309) 344-3121*
*1964 N Henderson*
*Geneseo* ▪ *(309) 945-1616*
*925 S Oakwood Ave*
*Kewanee* ▪ *(309) 853-4407*
*515 Tenney St*
*Milan* ▪ *(309) 787-6126*
*909 W 4th St*
*Moline* ▪ *(309) 764-3388*
*2041 16th St*
*Morrison* ▪ *(815) 772-7840*
*109 W Main St*
*Rock Island* ▪ *(309) 788-8777*
*1412 30th St*

**J. Gumbo's** ★📖
*Urbana* ▪ *(217) 337-4840*
*700 S Gregory St*

**Jason's Deli** ✪📖
*Oak Lawn* ▪ *(708) 233-0368*
*6260 W 95th St*
*Naperville* ▪ *(630) 955-1179*
*1739 Freedom Dr*
*Park Ridge* ▪ *(847) 823-0210*
*608 W Touhy Ave*
*Palatine* ▪ *(847) 963-1796*
*1417 N Rand Rd*
*Oak Brook* ▪ *(630) 928-1497*
*2060 York Rd*
*Schaumburg* ▪ *(847) 240-0516*
*1530 McConnor Pkwy*
*Vernon Hills* ▪ *(847) 680-1869*
*545 Lakeview Pkwy*

**Jersey Mike's** 📖
*Elk Grove* ▪ *(847) 258-4605*
*178 Biesterfield Rd*
*Niles* ▪ *(847) 588-2828*
*5691 W Touhy Ave*
*Naperville* ▪ *(630) 364-2982*
*2555 W 75th St*
*Vernon Hills* ▪ *(847) 362-6453*
*1640 N Milwaukee Ave*
*Gurnee* ▪ *(847) 855-0601*
*7105 Grand Ave*

Schaumburg ▪ (847) 517-7000
601 Martingale Rd
Aurora ▪ (630) 499-5110
1147 N Eola Rd
Mount Prospect ▪ (847) 253-3900
106 E Kensington Rd
Lake in the Hills ▪ (847) 658-0808
285 N Randall Rd
Geneva ▪ (630) 845-9000
1770 S Randall Rd
Niles ▪ (847) 583-8300
8484 W Golf Rd
Elmhurst ▪ (630) 832-9700
297 N York Rd
Glenview ▪ (847) 998-0800
2149 Willow Rd
Wheaton ▪ (630) 681-1200
3 Danada Square E
Arlington Heights ▪ (224) 735-3437
115 W Rand Rd
Lisle ▪ (630) 964-2588
1032 Maple Ave
Plainfield ▪ (815) 254-3432
13400 S Route 59
St. Charles ▪ (630) 443-1300
2540 E Main St
Schaumburg ▪ (847) 884-4646
2568 W Schaumburg Rd
Crystal Lake ▪ (815) 356-0808
5006 Northwest Hwy
Orland Park ▪ (708) 226-6077
15625 S La Grange Rd
Boilingbrook ▪ (630) 226-6855
214 N Weber Rd
Rockford ▪ (815) 226-0118
6284 E State St
Shiloh ▪ (618) 622-8934
3284 Green Mount Crossing Dr
Oswego ▪ (630) 554-2993
2428 Route 34
Chicago ▪ (312) 251-0900
120 N Wells St
Lombard ▪ (630) 576-2007
2820 S Highland Ave
Machesney Park ▪ (815) 633-4200
1513 W Lane Rd
Glen Ellyn ▪ (630) 793-9610
711 E Roosevelt Rd

Romeoville ▪ (815) 267-7970
412 S Weber Rd

### Joe's Crab Shack                                    ✪▢
Schaumburg ▪ (847) 517-1212
2000 E Golf Rd
Fairview Heights ▪ (618) 398-9993
51 Ludwig Dr
Peoria ▪ (309) 671-2223
110 SW Water St
Gurnee ▪ (847) 662-4801
5626 Northridge Dr

### Kama Bistro                                    ✪★$$LD
La Grange ▪ (708) 352-3300
8 W Burlington Ave ▪ Indian ▪ A large
portion of the menu is naturally GF. GF
items are indicated on the menu and include tandoori lamb chops, vindaloo, saag
masala, and goan fish curry. GF beer is also
available. ▪ www.kamabistro.com

### Little Joe's
### Famous Pizza & Restaurant                       ★$LD
Tinley Park ▪ (708) 532-2240
7976 W 167th St
New Lenox ▪ (815) 463-1099
1300 N Cedar Rd ▪ Pizza ▪ GF pasta, pizza, and beer are available. ▪
www.littlejoesfamouspizza.com

### Lone Star Steakhouse & Saloon                   ✪▢
Bloomington ▪ (309) 663-7827
903 IAA Dr
Carbondale ▪ (618) 529-2556
1160 E Main St
Crestwood ▪ (708) 239-0900
4949 Cal-Sag Rd
Effingham ▪ (217) 342-7078
1507 Hampton Dr
Elgin ▪ (847) 931-7837
155 S Randall Rd
Gurnee ▪ (847) 855-8182
6210 Grand Ave
Hodgkins ▪ (708) 485-7840
9340 Joliet Rd
Joliet ▪ (815) 436-7600
2705 Plainfield Rd
Mt. Vernon ▪ (618) 244-7827
333 Potomac Blvd #A

*Rockford* ■ *(815) 226-1122*
*6690 E State St*
*Bourbonnais* ■ *(815) 939-1355*
*1605 N State Route 50*

**Luigi's House**                    ★ $$$**LD**
*Aurora* ■ *(630) 375-6400*
*778 N Rt 59* ■ *Italian* ■ GF pasta is available.
■ *www.portillos.com/luigis/*

**Maggiano's Little Italy**              ★□
*Naperville* ■ *(630) 536-2270*
*1847 Freedom Dr*
*Oak Brook* ■ *(630) 368-0300*
*240 Oakbrook Ctr*
*Schaumburg* ■ *(847) 240-5600*
*1901 E Woodfield Rd*
*Skokie* ■ *(847) 933-9555*
*4999 Old Orchard Ctr Ste A28*

**Marcello's,**
**A Father and Son Restaurant**      ✪★$**LD**
*Northbrook* ■ *(847) 498-1500*
*1911 Cherry Ln* ■ *Pizza* ■ GF pizza, pasta,
brownies, and apple or berry dessert
pizza are available as well as a GF beer. ■
*www.marcellos.com*

**Melting Pot, The**                   ✪□
*Buffalo Grove* ■ *(847) 342-6022*
*1205 W Dundee Rd*
*Downers Grove* ■ *(630) 737-0810*
*1205 Butterfield Rd*
*Naperville* ■ *(630) 717-8301*
*4931 S Route 59*
*Schaumburg* ■ *(847) 843-8970*
*255 W Golf Rd*

**Miller's Ale House Restaurants** ✪★□
*Lombard* ■ *(630) 241-3371*
*455 E Butterfield Rd*

**Mississippi Half Step, The**        ✪$$**LD**
*Grafton* ■ *(618) 786-2722*
*420 E Main St* ■ *American* ■ GF menu
is the regular menu with highlights and
notes about GF items and necessary
modifications. Manager Carla recommends alerting a server upon arrival. ■
*www.mississippihalfstep.com*

**Mitchell's Fish Market**             ✪□
*Glenview* ■ *(847) 729-3663*
*2601 Navy Blvd*

**Monical's Pizza Restaurant**         ★□
*Centralia* ■ *(618) 533-2755*
*1310 N Elm St*
*Champaign* ■ *(217) 356-4243*
*103 W Kirby Ave*
*Champaign* ■ *(217) 359-3514*
*205 N Mattis Ave*
*Charleston* ■ *(217) 348-7515*
*909 18th St*
*Chillicothe* ■ *(309) 274-6721*
*322 S Plaza Park*
*Danville* ■ *(217) 443-3490*
*1511 N Bowman Ave Rd*
*Danville* ■ *(217) 446-3111*
*3542 N Vermilion St*
*Decatur* ■ *(217) 864-2060*
*2230 S Mount Zion Rd*
*Decatur* ■ *(217) 423-2333*
*348 W 1st Dr*
*Decatur* ■ *(217) 875-7340*
*4333 N Prospect St*
*Gibson City* ■ *(217) 784-4623*
*314 E 1st St*
*Gilman* ■ *(815) 265-7272*
*625 US Highway 24 W*
*Hoopeston* ■ *(217) 283-7781*
*618 W Orange St*
*Kankakee* ■ *(815) 928-8043*
*1155 W Court St*
*Mahomet* ■ *(217) 586-4242*
*114 S Lombard St*
*Manteno* ■ *(815) 468-7409*
*199 Southcreek Dr*
*Mattoon* ■ *(217) 234-6442*
*815 Broadway Ave*
*Monticello* ■ *(217) 762-8484*
*707 W Bridge St*
*Morton* ■ *(309) 284-0709*
*1067 W Jackson St*
*Normal* ■ *(309) 454-7999*
*1219 S Main St*
*Olney* ■ *(618) 395-3359*
*509 N W St*
*Paris* ■ *(217) 465-7684*
*607 E Jasper St*

Paxton ▪ (217) 379-4835
500 W Ottawa Rd
Pekin ▪ (309) 347-7761
111 S Parkway Dr
Peoria ▪ (309) 691-6477
4100 W Willow Knolls Dr
Peoria ▪ (309) 688-0747
4408 N Knoxville Ave
Pontiac ▪ (815) 844-2660
311 US Route 66
Princeton ▪ (815) 872-0090
302 S Main St
Rantoul ▪ (217) 893-1252
320 E Champaign Ave
Robinson ▪ (618) 544-3228
1703 W Main St
Saint Joseph ▪ (217) 469-7777
703 N 3rd St
Shelbyville ▪ (217) 774-4100
1900 W Main St
Springfield ▪ (217) 546-7258
2640 Prairie Crossing Dr
Sullivan ▪ (217) 728-2373
402 S Hamilton St
Tilton ▪ (217) 443-5545
1628 Georgetown Rd
Tuscola ▪ (217) 253-4749
900 S Court St
Urbana ▪ (217) 367-5781
2720 Philo Rd
Villa Grove ▪ (217) 832-2361
102 N Sycamore St
Washington ▪ (309) 444-7500
6 Cherry Tree Shopping Ctr
Watseka ▪ (815) 432-3714
1004 E Walnut St
Watseka ▪ (815) 432-3320
750 W Walnut St
Bourbonnais ▪ (815) 932-9100
597 William Latham Dr
Canton ▪ (309) 647-1127
135 N 5th Ave
Bloomington ▪ (309) 662-8502
718 S Eldorado Rd
Fairbury ▪ (815) 692-4302
600 W Oak St
Bloomington ▪ (309) 662-6933

2103 N Veterans Pwy
Arcola ▪ (217) 268-4141
528 E Sprinfield
Clinton ▪ (217) 935-2919
1044 Jemima St
El Paso ▪ (309) 527-3663
RR 1 Box 32A
Tolono ▪ (217) 485-5711
102 W Vine St

## Moon Wok                                    $LD
Glenview ▪ (847) 813-6300
1615 Milwaukee Ave ▪ Asian ▪ Moon wok
offers a variety of GF options such as curry
and Mongolian beef, however these items
are not marked on the menu and should
be requested upon ordering to avoid CC. ▪
moonwokglenview.com

## Morton's Steakhouse                         ✪📖
Northbrook ▪ (847) 205-5111
699 Skokie Blvd
Rosemont ▪ (847) 678-5155
9525 W Bryn Mawr Ave
Schaumburg ▪ (847) 413-8771
1470 McConnor Pkwy

## Munch                                       ✪$BLD
Oak Park ▪ (708) 848-4226
104 N Marion St ▪ Vegetarian ▪ Munch
has an online menu marked with GF options. ▪ munchrestaurant.net

## Myron & Phil                             ✪★$$$D
Lincolnwood ▪ (847) 677-6663
3900 W Devon Ave ▪ Steakhouse
▪ All steak, salmon, and white fish
entrees are GF. Manager reports that
some chicken dishes can also be made
GF, but they require advance notice in
order to prepare them without gluten
ingredients. Alert the server upon arrival.
▪ www.myronandphil.com

## Naf Naf Grill                                $LD
Aurora ▪ (630) 499-1700
4430 Fox Valley Center Dr
Niles ▪ (847) 588-1500
5716 W Touhy Ave
Naperville ▪ (630) 904-7200

*1739 Freedom Dr ▪ Middle Eastern ▪*
Most menu items are naturally GF except
for their pita, schnitzel, and taboule. ▪
*www.nafnafgrill.com*

### Nick's Pizza & Pub                    ★ SLD
*Elgin ▪ (847) 531-5550*
*990 S Randall Rd*
*Crystal Lake ▪ (815) 356-5550*
*856 Pyott Rd ▪ Pizza ▪* GF pizza is available. ▪ *www.nickspizzapub.com*

### Nick-N-Willy's                          ★ 📖
*Peoria ▪ (309) 691-2345*
*4700 N University St*
*Peoria ▪ (309) 692-2345*
*9031 N Allen Rd*

### Nirvana Wine & Grillerie          ✪★ $$LD
*Vernon Hills ▪ (847) 918-7828*
*701 N Milwaukee Ave ▪ Global ▪* Certain
menu items are marked "GFA," which
stands for "GF alternative available."
Restaurant explains that many of these
items are naturally GF, while others are
readily modified to be GF. GF crackers and pasta are available. For dessert,
they offer flourless chocolate cake. ▪
*www.findmynirvana.com*

### Nuovo Italia Ristorante            ★ $$$LD
*Addison ▪ (630) 832-2131*
*32 E Lake St*
*St Charles ▪ (630) 584-4040*
*18 N 4th St ▪ Italian ▪* GF pasta available.
Most fish dishes, which are not breaded,
can easily be prepared GF. Flourless
chocolate cake available as a dessert option.
Reservations for parties of 4 or more are
recommended. ▪ *www.nuovaitalia.net*

### O'Charley's                              📖
*Champaign ▪ (217) 355-3901*
*730 W Town Center Blvd*
*Forsyth ▪ (217) 872-1672*
*927 S State Route 51*
*Marion ▪ (618) 993-1555*
*2808 W DeYoung St*
*O'Fallon ▪ (618) 622-0405*
*1313 Central Park Dr*

*Springfield ▪ (217) 787-2809*
*4241 Conestoga Dr*

### Omango                                   ﹤LD
*Aurora ▪ (630) 449-5100*
*1056 N Rt 59 ▪ Indian ▪* All of their curries
are GF as well as their some of their dosas.
Alert a server that you are GF before ordering. ▪ *www.eatomango.com*

### OMG It's Gluten Free                     ﹤BLD
*Frankfort ▪ (815) 469-4900*
*19810 S Harlem Ave ▪ Bakery & Café*
▪ Dedicated GF bakery offering pizza,
lasagna, quiche, sandwiches, and more.
They also offer a wide variety of baked
goods such as breads, cookies, muffins,
brownies, scones, and sweet rolls. Meals
are available for dining in or carrying out. ▪
*www.omgitsglutenfree.com*

### One World                          ★ $BLD
*Peoria ▪ (309) 672-1522*
*1245 W Main St ▪ American ▪* GF items
marked on regular menu, with GF
bread substitutes available as well as
other modified menu items. GF items
include Thai noodle salad, pizzas, Hun-
garian stuffed peppers and more. ▪
*www.oneworld-cafe.com*

### Orchard's Restaurant                    $$LD
*Aurora ▪ (630) 907-0600*
*2411 W Illinois Ave ▪ American ▪* Chef
can make most menu items GF. ▪
*orchardvalleygolf.com*

### Osteria Ottimo                    ✪★ $$LD
*Orland Park ▪ (708) 403-3366*
*16111 S La Grange Rd ▪ Italian ▪* GF pasta
is available. The restaurant reports that
any meat dish can also be prepared GF. ▪
*www.osteriaottimo.com*

### P.F. Chang's China Bistro          ✪★ 📖
*Lombard ▪ (630) 652-9977*
*2361 Fountain Square Dr*
*Northbrook ▪ (847) 509-8844*
*1819 Lake Cook Rd*
*Orland Park ▪ (708) 675-3970*
*14135 S La Grange Rd*

**Schaumburg** ▪ (847) 610-8000
5 Woodfield Mall Spc D313

### Pasta House Co., The                ✪★📖
Edwardsville ▪ (618) 655-9955
1097 S State Route 157
Fairview Heights ▪ (618) 222-7144
4660 N Illinois St

### Pei Wei Asian Diner                ✪📖
Hindale ▪ (630) 288-6635
7135 S Kingery Hwy
Mt Prospect ▪ (847) 704-4095
1021 N Elmhurst Rd

### Pinstripes                ✪★$LD
Northbrook ▪ (847) 480-2323
1150 Willow Rd
South Barrington ▪ (847) 844-9300
100 W Higgins Rd
Oak Brook ▪ (630) 575-8000
7 Oakbrook Center Mall ▪ Bistro ▪ GF
menu includes soups and salads, as well as
a wide variety of sandwiches, pizzas, and
pastas. It also includes entrées such as beef
tenderloin and grilled salmon. GF pasta
and pizza are available with advance notice
of 24 hours. For dessert, they offer flourless
chocolate cake, lemon crème brûlée, and
cheesecake. ▪ www.pinstripes.com

### Pizza Ranch                ✪📖
Roscoe ▪ (815) 623-3800
4797 Bluestem Rd

### Reza's Restaurant                $$$LD
Oak Brook ▪ (630) 424-9900
40 N Tower Rd ▪ Middle Eastern ▪ Managers at all locations report serving GF diners
often since 90% of their menu can be GF.
All recommend asking for a manager
upon arrival. Although many servers are
educated on the GF diet, the managers will
know more about which items are GF. ▪
www.rezasrestaurant.com

### Richard's on Main                $$LD
Peoria ▪ (309) 674-8007
311 Main St ▪ American ▪ All of their
salads are GF as well as their breadless sandwiches and plenty of entrées. ▪
www.richardsonmain.com

### Roberto's                ★$$$D
Elmhurst ▪ (630) 279-8486
483 S Spring Rd ▪ Italian ▪ Manager
says that almost 80% of the entrées can
be modified to be GF and that GF pasta
and pizza is available. All GF dishes are
prepared using dedicated GF utensils. ▪
www.robertosristorante.net

### Romano's Macaroni Grill                ✪★📖
Hoffman Estates ▪ (847) 882-6676
2575 W Higgins Rd
Wheaton ▪ (630) 668-9366
21 Blanchard Cir

### Rosati's Pizza                ★📖
Antioch ▪ (847) 395-5500
1140 Main St
Aurora ▪ (630) 851-8100
2990 Ogden Ave
Aurora ▪ (630) 892-2662
310 W Indian Trl
Barrington ▪ (847) 382-2700
712 S Northwest Hwy
Batavia ▪ (630) 879-2992
334 E Wilson St
Bloomington ▪ (309) 661-6575
203 N Prospect Rd
Carol Stream ▪ (630) 653-9009
161 Hiawatha Dr
Carol Stream ▪ (630) 690-9494
881 E Geneva Rd
Carpentersville ▪ (847) 844-3400
117 Nort Kennedy Dr
Cary ▪ (847) 516-3800
395 Cary Algonquin Rd
Crest Hill ▪ (815) 744-0800
1490 Cedar Wood Dr
Darien ▪ (630) 960-2520
8137 S Cass Ave
Deerfield ▪ (847) 541-5558
20590 Milwaukee Ave
Elburn ▪ (630) 365-0005
860 N Main St
Elgin ▪ (847) 741-5400
2 Tyler Creek Plz
Gilberts ▪ (847) 783-0808
50 Industrial Dr

Glenview ▪ (847) 296-0260
1708 Milwaukee Ave
Grayslake ▪ (847) 543-8800
1866 E Belvidere Rd
Hampshire ▪ (847) 683-1111
826 Centennial Dr
Harvard ▪ (815) 943-8100
360 S Division St
Homer Glen ▪ (708) 301-0400
14218 S Bell Rd
Huntley ▪ (847) 669-6500
10896 N IL Route 47
Lakemoor ▪ (847) 540-6600
700 E IL Route 120
Libertyville ▪ (847) 816-9500
1043 N Milwaukee Ave
Lockport ▪ (815) 588-2000
1047 E 9th St
Lombard ▪ (630) 620-1700
701 E Roosevelt Rd
Loves Park ▪ (815) 636-0600
6104 E Riverside Blvd
Manhattan ▪ (815) 478-7000
530 W North St
Marengo ▪ (815) 568-1888
20001 Telegraph St
McHenry ▪ (815) 344-6667
4802 W Elm St
Mokena ▪ (708) 479-9400
19608 La Grange Rd
Montgomery ▪ (630) 264-4410
2083 Orchard Rd
Morris ▪ (815) 942-6000
223 E US Route 6
Mount Prospect ▪ (847) 437-2112
1629 S Busse Rd
Mt. Greenwood ▪ (773) 239-4900
3150 W 111th St
Naperville ▪ (630) 428-0400
1935 95th St
Naperville ▪ (630) 305-3500
406 W 5th Ave
New Lenox ▪ (815) 485-1000
108 W Illinois Hwy
Niles ▪ (847) 825-5855
8166 N Milwaukee Ave
Normal ▪ (309) 888-4949
1720 Bradford Ln

Northbrook ▪ (847) 498-4080
2833 Dundee Rd
Oswego ▪ (630) 551-1150
2751 Route 34
Plainfield ▪ (815) 254-4500
15925 S Route 59
River Grove ▪ (708) 456-2000
8342 W Grand Ave
Rockford ▪ (815) 395-5300
2221 S Perryville Rd
Romeoville ▪ (815) 293-2600
463 N Weber Rd
Rosemont ▪ (847) 298-2100
7112 Manheim Rd
Sandwich ▪ (815) 786-1500
710 E Railroad St
Schaumburg ▪ (847) 891-5151
1770 W Wise Rd
Schererville ▪ (219) 864-1114
5504 W Lincoln Hwy
Shorewood ▪ (815) 725-8686
707 W Jefferson St
Sleepy Hollow ▪ (847) 426-5000
1027 W Main St
South Elgrin ▪ (847) 697-8667
1165 W Spring St
Sugar Grove ▪ (630) 466-9992
495 N State Route 47
Urbana ▪ (217) 328-2334
701 S Gregory St
Vernon Hills ▪ (847) 362-6999
101 E Townline Rd
Warrenville ▪ (630) 393-9393
2S610 State Route 59
Wauconda ▪ (847) 526-4343
531 W Liberty St
West Chicago ▪ (630) 876-0606
177 N Neltnor Blvd
Westmont ▪ (630) 789-1970
838 E Ogden Ave
Wheaton ▪ (630) 682-3442
1287 Butterfield Rd
Woodstock ▪ (815) 338-3600
1652 S Eastwood Dr
Yorkville ▪ (630) 553-5533
1985 Marketview Dr

## Rose's Wheat Free Bakery                ⊆S
Evanston ▪ (847) 859-2723

*2901 Central St* ▪ *Bakery* ▪ Certified GF bakery offering a variety of GF breads, pizza crusts, granola, muffins, cookies, and brownies. ▪ *www.rosesbakery.com*

### Ruth's Chris Steak House ✪▢
*Northbrook* ▪ *(847) 498-6889*
*933 Skokie Blvd*
*South Barrington* ▪ *(847) 551-3730*
*100 W Higgins Rd*

### Shaw's Crab House ✪$$$$LD
*Schaumburg* ▪ *(847) 517-2722*
*1900 E Higgins Rd* ▪ *Seafood* ▪ GF menu includes griddle garlic shrimp, seared scallops, halibut, salmon, strip steak, crab, lobster, sushi, and more. Crème brûlée is available for dessert. ▪ *www.shawscrabhouse.com*

### Silo, The ★$LD
*Lake Bluff* ▪ *(847) 234-6660*
*625 Rockland Rd* ▪ *Pizza* ▪ The Silo brings GF crust in from a 100% GF bakery and uses dedicated surfaces, utensils and cooking surfaces to prevent CC. ▪ *www.silopizza.com*

### Singapore Grill ★$$LD
*Loves Park* ▪ *(815) 636-1888*
*6390 E Riverside Blvd* ▪ *Asian* ▪ 80% of the menu can be made GF. Alert server upon arrival. ▪ *www.singaporegrill.com*

### Smokey Bones ▢
*Springfield* ▪ *(217) 528-6410*
*2660 S Dirksen Pkwy*
*Fairview Heights* ▪ *(618) 624-1052*
*6118 N Illinois St*

### Stashu's Deli & Pizza ★$LD
*Moline* ▪ *(309) 797-9449*
*4200 44th Ave* ▪ *Pizza* ▪ GF pizza is available with advance notice of at least thirty minutes. Several calzones are also GF.

### Stir Crazy ★▢
*Oak Brook* ▪ *(630) 575-0155*
*105 Oakbrook Ctr*
*Schaumburg* ▪ *(847) 330-1200*
*5 Woodfield Mall*
*Warrenville* ▪ *(630) 393-4700*
*28252 Diehl Rd*

*Northbrook* ▪ *(847) 562-4800*
*1186 Northbrook Ct*

### Sushi Gawa $LD
*Peoria* ▪ *(309) 679-9300*
*2601 W Lake Ave* ▪ *Japanese* ▪ Sushi is naturally GF, just stay away from the sauces, especially soy sauce.

### Sweet Ali's Gluten Free Bakery ¢$
*Hinsdale* ▪ *(630) 908-7175*
*13 W 1st St* ▪ *Bakery* ▪ Dedicated GF bakery offering bread, muffins, cookies, cake, brownies, pizza, quiches, and more. ▪ *www.sweetalis.com*

### Sweet Cece's ▢
*Peoria* ▪ *(309) 692-4212*
*5901 N Prospect Rd*
*Peoria* ▪ *(309) 966-2539*
*1200 W Main St*

### Ted's Montana Grill ✪▢
*Bolingbrook* ▪ *(630) 783-2493*
*623 E Boughton Rd*
*Glenview* ▪ *(847) 729-1117*
*1811 Tower Dr*
*Naperville* ▪ *(630) 848-2255*
*39 W Jefferson Ave*

### Texas De Brazil Churrascaria ★▢
*Schaumburg* ▪ *(847) 413-1600*
*5 Woodfield Mall*

### Trattoria 225 ✪★$$D
*Oak Park* ▪ *(708) 358-8555*
*225 Harrison St* ▪ *Italian* ▪ According to their website, every dish and entrée on the menu can be cooked using GF ingredients. ▪ *www.trattoria225.com*

### Uno Chicago Grill ✪★▢
*Gurnee* ▪ *(847) 856-0000*
*6593 Grand Ave*
*Schaumburg* ▪ *(847) 413-0200*
*1160 N Plaza Dr*

### Va Pensiero ✪★$$$D
*Evanston* ▪ *(847) 475-7779*
*1566 Oak Ave* ▪ *Italian* ▪ Most entrees are GF, including the pork belly and duck. Alert the server upon arrival and they will

provide you with all of the available options. ▪ *www.va-p.com*

## Walker Brothers ★ ¢**BLD**
*Lake Zurich* ▪ *(847) 550-0006*
*767 S Rand Rd*
*Lincolnshire* ▪ *(847) 634-2220*
*200 Marriott Dr*
*Arlington Heights* ▪ *(847) 392-6600*
*825 W Dundee Rd*
*Highland Park* ▪ *(847) 432-0660*
*620 Central Ave*
*Glenview* ▪ *(847) 724-0220*
*1615 Waukegan Rd*
*Wilmette* ▪ *(847) 251-6000*
*153 Green Bay Rd* ▪ *American* ▪ GF pancakes are available, and can be prepared with blueberries or other fruit upon request. Team member Kevin recommend speaking with a manager to "discuss concerns and requirements" upon dining in. ▪ *www.walkerbros.net*

## Weber Grill Restaurant ✪$**LD**
*Lombard* ▪ *(630) 953-8880*
*2331 Fountain Sq*
*Schaumburg* ▪ *(847) 413-0800*
*1010 N Meacham Rd* ▪ *American* ▪ Extensive GF menu includes filet mignon, plank grilled bourbon salmon, citrus pesto tuna, grilled seasonal vegetable kabobs, and more. Starters include wood roasted mussels and baked onion soup. Confirm the timeliness of this information before dining in. The restaurant reports that a manager oversees all GF orders to ensure they are prepared correctly. ▪ *www.webergrillrestaurant.com*

## White Chocolate Grill, The ✪$$**LD**
*Naperville* ▪ *(630) 505-8300*
*1803 Freedom Dr* ▪ *Modern American* ▪ GF menu includes grilled artichokes and tomato gin soup, among other things, as appetizers. As entrées, it lists a bunless cheeseburger, BBQ baby back ribs, center cut filet, New York strip, balsamic ribeye and more. For dessert, it offers a silky chocolate soufflé cake ▪ *www.whitechocolategrill.com*

## Wildfire Restaurant ✪★📖
*Oak Brook* ▪ *(630) 586-9000*
*232 Oakbrook Ctr*
*Lincolnshire* ▪ *(847) 279-7900*
*235 Parkway Dr*
*Schaumburg* ▪ *(847) 995-0100*
*1250 E Higgins Rd*
*Glenview* ▪ *(847) 657-6363*
*1300 Patriot Blvd*

## Yard House ✪📖
*Glenview* ▪ *(847) 729-9273*
*1880 Tower Dr*

# INDIANA

## INDIANAPOLIS

## A2Z Café ★ ¢**BL**
*Indianapolis* ▪ *(317) 569-9349*
*4705 E 96th St* ▪ *American* ▪ GF options are indicated on breakfast and lunch menu. All omelets can be made to be GF. Several GF pasta dishes are available, including salmon linguini and penne gorgonzola. All of their entrée salads can be made GF as well. Inform your server that you are ordering GF. ▪ *www.a2zcafe.com*

## Adobo Grill ✪$$**LD**
*Indianapolis* ▪ *(317) 822-9990*
*110 E Washington St* ▪ *Mexican* ▪ GF menu available but varies slightly by location. Examples of GF menu items are enchiladas, grilled half chicken in tamarind, and sautéed tilapia. GF desserts include tamal de chocolate and vanilla flan with caramel sauce. ▪ *www.adobogrill.com*

## Au Bon Pain 📖
*Indianapolis* ▪ *(317) 226-9300*
*26 Monument Cir*
*Indianapolis* ▪ *(317) 238-7684*
*7800 Col. H. Wier Cool Memorial Dr*
*Indianapolis* ▪ *(317) 926-5840*
*1701 Senate Ave*

**Bakery at Geist, The**                    ★$$
*Indianapolis* ▪ *(317) 723-3879*
*8150 Oaklandon Rd* ▪ *Bakery* ▪ The bakery carries a line of GF breads which are baked in a 100% GF facility and brought in for distribution. ▪ *www.thebakeryatgeist.com*

**Barcelona Tapas Restaurant**          ✪$LD
*Indianapolis* ▪ *(317) 638-8272*
*201 N Delaware St* ▪ *Spanish* ▪ GF menu available from the regular menu items with modifications to make them GF. Examples include black bean soup, curried chicken salad, paprika roasted Spanish almonds, and paella Valencia. For dessert, there is crème brûlée, flan, and a Spanish fruit & nut platter. Alert a server upon arrival and they will bring the GF menu. This information applies to the listed location only. ▪ *www.barcelonatapas.com*

**Bonefish Grill**                       ✪▢
*Indianapolis* ▪ *(317) 863-3474*
*4501 E 82nd St*

**Buca di Beppo**                        ✪▢
*Indianapolis* ▪ *(317) 632-2822*
*35 N Illinois St*
*Indianapolis* ▪ *(317) 842-8666*
*6045 E 86th St*

**Bucceto's Smiling Teeth**              ★▢
*Indianapolis* ▪ *(317) 875-9223*
*1508 W 86th St*
*Indianapolis* ▪ *(317) 842-2356*
*11693 Fall Creek Rd*
*Indianapolis* ▪ *(317) 823-0027*
*7829 Sunnyside Rd*

**Capital Grille, The**                  ✪▢
*Indianapolis* ▪ *(317) 423-8790*
*40 W Washington St*

**Charleston's Restaurant**              ✪▢
*Indianapolis* ▪ *(317) 841-0442*
*6815 E 82nd St*

**Cheeseburger in Paradise**            ✪★▢
*Indianapolis* ▪ *(317) 883-4386*
*4670 Southport Crossings Dr*

**Claddagh Irish Pub**                     ▢
*Indianapolis* ▪ *(317) 822-6274*

*234 S Meridian St*
*Indianapolis* ▪ *(317) 569-3663*
*3835 E 96th St*

**Cooper's Hawk**
**Winery & Restaurants**                 ✪★▢
*Indianapolis* ▪ *(317) 574-9463*
*3815 E 96th St*

**Don Pablo's**                          ✪▢
*Indianapolis* ▪ *(317) 888-0363*
*8150 US 31 S*

**Fleming's Prime**
**Steakhouse & Wine Bar**                ✪▢
*Indianapolis* ▪ *(317) 466-0175*
*8487 Union Chapel Rd*

**Fogo De Chao**                          ★▢
*Indianapolis* ▪ *(317) 638-4000*
*117 E Washington St*

**Fox and Hound Pub & Grille**             ▢
*Indianapolis* ▪ *(317) 913-1264*
*4901 E 82nd St*

**Greek Islands Restaurant, The**     ✪$$LD
*Indianapolis* ▪ *(317) 636-0700*
*906 S Meridian St* ▪ *Greek* ▪ GF menu includes chicken souvlaki, tilapia, dolmades with tzatziki sauce, and more. Rice pudding is available for dessert. Chef Angela reports that they are very aware of GF, as a family friend has Celiac. She adds that all staff members are trained on the GF diet. ▪ *www.greekislandsrestaurant.com*

**Grindstone Charleys**                  ✪$LD
*Indianapolis* ▪ *(317) 481-1870*
*5822 Crawfordsville Rd*
*Indianapolis* ▪ *(317) 243-8760*
*5383 W Rockville Rd* ▪ *American* ▪ GF menu includes salads, barbecue cheddar chicken, and bourbon steak. Confirm the timeliness of this information before dining in, and alert the server upon arrival. ▪ *www.grindstonesrestaurantandpub.com*

**Hard Rock Café**                       ✪▢
*Indianapolis* ▪ *(317) 636-2550*
*49 S Meridian*

**Jasmine Thai Restaurant**              $LD
*Indianapolis* ▪ *(317) 848-8950*
*4825 E 96th St* ▪ *Thai* ▪ Employee Jasmine
reports that "pretty much everything" on
their menu is GF excluding their yellow
curry. Alert the server upon arrival so that
necessary precautions can be taken to prevent CC. ▪ *www.jasminethaiindy.com/home*

**Jason's Deli**                         ✪📖
*Indianapolis* ▪ *(317) 578-0543*
*4130 E 82nd St*

**Jersey Mike's**                        📖
*Indianapolis* ▪ *(317) 347-6453*
*6985 W 38th St*
*Indianapolis* ▪ *(317) 347-6456*
*7125 Georgetown Rd*
*Indianapolis* ▪ *(317) 595-9993*
*5025 E 82nd St*

**Joe's Crab Shack**                     ✪📖
*Indianapolis* ▪ *(317) 888-8099*
*7303 US Hwy 31 S*
*Indianapolis* ▪ *(317) 849-4133*
*8250 Dean Rd*

**Maggiano's Little Italy**              ★📖
*Indianapolis* ▪ *(317) 814-0700*
*3550 E 86th St*

**Melting Pot, The**                     ✪📖
*Indianapolis* ▪ *(317) 841-3601*
*5650 E 86th St Ste A*

**Monical's Pizza Restaurant**           ★📖
*Indianapolis* ▪ *(317) 255-3663*
*2635 E 62nd St*
*Indianapolis* ▪ *(317) 870-7722*
*6010 W 86th St*

**Morton's Steakhouse**                  ✪📖
*Indianapolis* ▪ *(317) 229-4700*
*41 E Washington St*

**O'Charley's**                          📖
*Indianapolis* ▪ *(317) 872-4930*
*3851 Vincennes Rd*
*Indianapolis* ▪ *(317) 254-8238*
*6111 N Keystone Ave*
*Indianapolis* ▪ *(317) 782-0818*
*6930 S Emerson Ave*
*Indianapolis* ▪ *(317) 577-8120*

*7640 N Shadeland Ave*
*Indianapolis* ▪ *(317) 898-1582*
*10289 E Washington St*

**Old Spaghetti Factory, The**           ✪★📖
*Indianapolis* ▪ *(317) 635-6325*
*210 S Meridian St*

**P.F. Chang's China Bistro**            ✪★📖
*Indianapolis* ▪ *(317) 974-5747*
*49 W Maryland St Ste 226*
*Indianapolis* ▪ *(317) 815-8773*
*8601 Keystone Xing*

**Palomino**                             📖
*Indianapolis* ▪ *(317) 974-0400*
*49 W Maryland St*

**Papa Roux**                            ¢LD
*Indianapolis* ▪ *(317) 603-9861*
*8950 E 10th St*
*Indianapolis* ▪ *(317) 603-9861*
*222 E Market St* ▪ *Cajun & Creole* ▪ Restaurant reports that some menu items are
available GF, but some may be prepared
with a flour roux and may not be appropriate for GF customers. A server will be
able to advise which options are safe. ▪
*www.paparouxindy.com*

**Pei Wei Asian Diner**                  ✪📖
*Indianapolis* ▪ *(317) 205-9380*
*6159 N Keystone Ave*

**Puccini's Smiling Teeth**              ✪★📖
*Indianapolis* ▪ *(317) 823-0027*
*7829 Sunnyside Rd*
*Indianapolis* ▪ *(317) 842-4028*
*3944 E 82nd St*
*Indianapolis* ▪ *(317) 842-2356*
*11695 Fall Creek Rd*
*Indianapolis* ▪ *(317) 875-9223*
*1508 W 86th St*

**Romano's Macaroni Grill**             ✪★📖
*Indianapolis* ▪ *(317) 337-0014*
*5720 W 86th St*

**Ruth's Chris Steak House**             ✪📖
*Indianapolis* ▪ *(317) 633-1313*
*45 S Illinois St*
*Indianapolis* ▪ *(317) 844-1155*
*9445 Threel Rd*

## Scotty's Brewhouse ✪★$LD
*Indianapolis* ▪ (317) 571-0808
*1 Virginia Ave*
*Indianapolis* ▪ (317) 574-0101
*3905 E 96th St*
*Indianapolis* ▪ (317) 215-7722
*4530 Southport Crossing Dr* ▪ *American*
▪ GF menu includes nachos, salads, and burgers & sandwiches on GF buns. GF salad dressings and sides are also listed. For dessert, GF chocolate chip cookies are available, as well as a "baby monster" sundae made with the GF cookies. General manager Scott reports that servers are trained to alert a manager if a customer needs a GF meal, and the manager will oversee production of the order. Separate utensils and plates are used for GF meals. ▪ *www.scottysbrewhouse.com*

## Stir Crazy ★▥
*Indianapolis* ▪ (317) 845-5600
*6020 E 82nd St*

## Sweet Tooth Bakery ★$$$
*Indianapolis* ▪ (317) 632-5451
*610 Massachusetts Ave* ▪ *Bakery* ▪ Non-dedicated GF bakery offering a variety of GF items, including cakes and cupcakes. The bakery recommends calling ahead to ensure that GF items are available. Special orders are also accepted. ▪ *www.sweettoothindy.com*

## Ted's Montana Grill ✪▥
*Indianapolis* ▪ (317) 875-8337
*5910 W 86th St*

## Thai Café ★$LD
*Indianapolis* ▪ (317) 722-1008
*1041 Broad Ripple Ave* ▪ *Thai* ▪ Server Antel reports that many dishes, like pad thai and drunken noodles, can be prepared GF. Confirm the timeliness of this information before dining in. GF soy sauce is available. Alert a server, who will indicate GF options. ▪ *www.indythaicafe.com*

## Thr3e Wise Men Brewing Co. ★$LD
*Indianapolis* ▪ (317) 255-5151
*1021 Broad Ripple Ave* ▪ *American* ▪ GF beer and hard cider are available. ▪ *www.thr3ewisemen.com*

## Tulip Noir Café ✪¢BL
*Indianapolis* ▪ (317) 848-5252
*1224 W 86th St* ▪ *Deli* ▪ The manager reports that the menu changes daily but there are always GF options available. Thursdays are their dedicated GF baking days. GF bread and wraps are available. ▪ *tulipnoircafe.com*

## Uno Chicago Grill ✪★▥
*Indianapolis* ▪ (317) 791-8667
*4740 E Southport Rd*

## Weber Grill Restaurant ✪$LD
*Indianapolis* ▪ (317) 636-7600
*10 N Illinois St* ▪ *American* ▪ Extensive GF menu includes filet mignon, plank grilled bourbon salmon, citrus pesto tuna, grilled seasonal vegetable kabobs, and more. Starters include wood roasted mussels and baked onion soup. Confirm the timeliness of this information before dining in. The restaurant reports that a manager oversees all GF orders to ensure they are prepared correctly. ▪ *www.webergrillrestaurant.com*

## Yats ¢LD
*Indianapolis* ▪ (317) 253-8817
*5463 N College Ave*
*Indianapolis* ▪ (317) 686-6380
*659 Massachusetts Ave*
*Fishers* ▪ (317) 585-1792
*8352 E 96th St*
*Greenwood* ▪ (317) 865-9971
*1280 US 31 N*
*Carmel* ▪ (317) 581-1881
*12545 Old Meridian St* ▪ *Cajun & Creole*
▪ Restaurants note that several chilis and stews on the menu are naturally GF. Both locations recommend alerting the server or cashier, so he or she can indicate GF options. ▪ *www.yatscajuncreole.com*

# INDIANA

## ALL OTHER CITIES

### 523 Tap and Grill    $$$**LD**
*Elkhart* ▪ *(574) 523-1523*
*523 S Main St* ▪ *American* ▪ An employee stated their restaurant menu has GF marked by items that do not contain gluten. Also, she said their chef and staff are very cautious of GF cooking practices and take the necessary precautions to ensure CC does not occur. ▪ *www.523tapandgrill.commenu.html*

### 800° Pizza Woodfired    ★$**LD**
*Fort Wayne* ▪ *(260) 490-0111*
*10020 Lima Rd* ▪ *Pizza* ▪ GF pizza is available. ▪ *800degrees.net*

### Abuelo's    ✪📖
*Carmel* ▪ *(317) 815-8175*
*14480 Lowes Wy*
*Merrillville* ▪ *(219) 769-6181*
*8255 Georgia St*
*Traders Point* ▪ *(317) 876-0250*
*5910 W 86th St*

### Antonio's Restaurant    ★$D
*Elkhart* ▪ *(574) 295-8424*
*1105 Goshen Ave* ▪ *Italian* ▪ GF pasta is available daily, and GF pizza is available on weekends only. ▪ *www.antoniositalian.com/antonios/*

### Archie & Clyde's    ★$**LD**
*Newburgh* ▪ *(812) 490-7778*
*8320 Bell Oaks Dr* ▪ *Pizza* ▪ GF pizza is available in the 12" size. ▪ *www.archieandclydes.com*

### Asparagus    ★$$**LD**
*Merrillville* ▪ *(219) 794-0000*
*7876 Broadway* ▪ *Asian Fusion* ▪ GF soy sauce, rice paper, and noodles are available so many items are naturally GF or can easily be made GF. Alert a server and they will suggest the available options for that night. ▪ *www.asparagusrestaurant.com*

### Au Bon Pain    📖
*South Bend* ▪ *(574) 631-9939*
*125 Hesburgh Library*

### Aurelio's Pizza    ★📖
*Beecher* ▪ *(708) 946-9603*
*436 Dixie Hwy*
*Griffith* ▪ *(219) 838-3700*
*112 E Ridge Rd*
*Hammond* ▪ *(219) 932-1470*
*4226 Calumet Ave*
*Crown Point* ▪ *(219) 662-9900*
*1900 N Main St*
*LaPorte* ▪ *(219) 324-9950*
*2330 N Hwy 35*
*Lowell* ▪ *(219) 696-1711*
*166 Deanna Dr*
*Munster* ▪ *(219) 836-2336*
*Munster*
*Portage* ▪ *(219) 763-7788*
*6500 US Rte 6*
*Schererville* ▪ *(219) 322-2590*
*1412 Lincoln Hwy*
*Valparaiso* ▪ *(219) 462-9700*
*265 Morthland Dr*
*Winfield* ▪ *(219) 661-2900*
*10762 Randolph St*

### B. Antonio's Pizza    ★$**LD**
*Fort Wayne* ▪ *(260) 485-2400*
*5417 Meijer Dr*
*Fort Wayne* ▪ *(260) 490-9222*
*10011 Lima Rd* ▪ *Pizza* ▪ GF pizza crust available ▪ *www.bantonios.com/menus.php*

### Beefree Gluten Free Bakery    ★$$
*Carmel* ▪ *(317) 844-8310*
*200 S Rangeline Rd* ▪ *Bakery* ▪ BeeFree bakery is a 100% GF facility distributing items such as GF cereal, flour, cookies, brownies, and pizza crust. ▪ *www.beefreegf.com*

### Biaggi's    ✪★📖
*Evansville* ▪ *(812) 421-0800*
*6401 E Lloyd Expwy*
*Fort Wayne* ▪ *(260) 459-6700*
*4010 W Jefferson Blvd*
*Carmel* ▪ *(317) 818-1777*
*14299 Clay Terrace Blvd*

**BJ's Restaurant and Brewhouse** ✪★📖
*Greenwood* ▪ *(317) 881-3500*
*1251 US 31 N*

**Bloomingfoods Deli**                    ★ ¢**BLD**
*Bloomington* ▪ *(812) 336-5400*
*3220 E 3rd St*
*Bloomington* ▪ *(812) 333-7312*
*316 W 6th St*
*Bloomington* ▪ *(812) 336-5300*
*419 E Kirkwood Ave* ▪ *Deli* ▪ GF bread is
available for sandwiches, and there are
often GF bakery items. Many "grab-and-
go" items are GF. All GF items are labeled
with an orange "gluten-free" sticker. Located inside the Bloomingfoods Market. ▪
*www.bloomingfoods.coop*

**Bonefish Grill**                    ✪📖
*Greenwood* ▪ *(317) 884-3992*
*1001 N State Rd 135*
*Mishawaka* ▪ *(574) 259-2663*
*620 W Edison Rd Ste 100*
*Evansville* ▪ *(812) 401-3474*
*6401 E Lloyd Expwy*

**Boston's Restaurant & Sports Bar**
✪★📖
*Schererville* ▪ *(219) 864-1377*
*625 W US Hwy 30*
*Newburgh* ▪ *(812) 853-3400*
*3911 Venetian Dr*

**Bristol Bar & Grille**                    ✪$$**LD**
*Jeffersonville* ▪ *(812) 218-1995*
*700 W Riverside Dr* ▪ *American* ▪ Cus-
tomer service agent Emilie reports that all
locations offer GF menu choices. She rec-
ommends alerting a manager upon arrival.
▪ *www.bristolbarandgrille.com*

**Buca di Beppo**                    ✪📖
*Greenwood* ▪ *(317) 884-2822*
*659 US 31 N*

**Bucceto's Smiling Teeth**                    ★📖
*Bloomington* ▪ *(812) 331-1234*
*115 S SR 46 Bypass*
*Bloomington* ▪ *(812) 323-0123*
*350 S Liberty Dr*
*W Lafayette* ▪ *(765) 746-5000*

*300 Brown St*
*Indianapolis* ▪ *(317) 842-4028*
*3944 E 82nd St*
*Indianapolis* ▪ *(317) 580-0087*
*13674 N Meridian St*
*Fishers* ▪ *(317) 579-0572*
*8993 E 116th St*
*Columbus* ▪ *(812) 348-7600*
*318 Washington St*

**Carino's Italian**                    ✪📖
*Columbus* ▪ *(812) 372-2266*
*870 Creekview Dr*
*Greenwood* ▪ *(317) 885-5735*
*920 US 31 N*
*Muncie* ▪ *(765) 284-3196*
*1101 W Mcgalliard R*

**Carlos O'Kelly's**                    ✪
*Fort Wayne* ▪ *(260) 483-0080*
*549 Coliseum Blvd E*
*Fort Wayne* ▪ *(260) 459-6777*
*5735 Falls Dr*

**Carrabba's Italian Grill**                    ✪📖
*Carmel* ▪ *(317) 575-2200*
*1235 Keystone Wy*
*Mishawaka* ▪ *(574) 247-9460*
*210 W Day Rd*
*Southport* ▪ *(317) 881-4008*
*4690 Southport Crossing Dr*

**Cerulean Restaurant**                    $$**LD**
*Winona Lake* ▪ *(574) 269-1226*
*1101 E Canal St* ▪ *Mediterranean* ▪ No
GF menu but all servers are aware of all
GF options. The kitchen can also make
modifications depending on the customers' requests. Some items that are naturally
GF are the BBQ tenderloin pork bento
box, maple leaf duck breast bento box,
and peanut ginger chicken bento box. ▪
*www.ceruleanrestaurant.comhome/*

**Charleston's Restaurant**                    ✪📖
*Carmel* ▪ *(317) 846-5965*
*14636 US Hwy 31*

### Cheeseburger in Paradise ✪★📖
*Fishers* ▪ (317) 585-0247
*9770 Crosspoint Blvd*
*Evansville* ▪ (812) 475-1074
*8301 Eagle Lake Dr*
*Terre Haute* ▪ (812) 234-3020
*3830 S US Hwy 41*

### Christos New City Grill $BLD
*West Lafayette* ▪ (765) 497-3164
*1018 Sagamore Pkwy W*
*Lafayette* ▪ (765) 474-6618
*3291 Teal Rd* ▪ *American* ▪ The restaurant recommends asking for the manager upon arrival, who will put GF orders through directly to the chef. Limited options include salads, sandwiches without bread, and more. Confirm the timeliness of this information before dining in. ▪ *www.christosgrill.com*

### Claddagh Irish Pub 📖
*Indianapolis* ▪ (317) 838-9917
*2539 Futura Park Wy*

### Columbus Avenue Pizza ★$LD
*Anderson* ▪ (765) 274-0164
*5436 Columbus Ave* ▪ *Pizza* ▪ GF pizza crust is available. ▪ *www.columbusavenuepizza.com*

### Cooking Greek ✪￠LD
*Carmel* ▪ (317) 657-8084
*12955 Old Meridian St* ▪ *Greek* ▪ Restaurant reports that most menu items can be prepared GF, but may require advance notice. GF wraps are available for sandwiches at an additional cost. The restaurant also offers a "gluten-free/wheat-free delivery service" in which they can prepare a week's worth of meals and deliver them to your home. ▪ *cookinggreekindy.com*

### Cooper's Hawk Winery & Restaurants ✪★📖
*Merrillville* ▪ (847) 836-9463
*2120 Southlake Mall*

### Don Pablo's ✪📖
*Indianapolis* ▪ (317) 576-0819
*3824 E 82nd St*

*Carmel* ▪ (317) 571-8040
*14758 US Hwy 31*
*Lafayette* ▪ (765) 449-0511
*50 N Creasey Ln*
*Merrillville* ▪ (219) 947-5253
*2831 E 80th Ave*

### Fig Tree Café, The ★￠LD
*Lebanon* ▪ (765) 482-3574
*109 N Meridian St* ▪ *Café* ▪ All of the sandwiches can be made GF. All the soups are already GF. ▪ *thefigtreecafe.wordpress.com*

### Flat Top Grill 📖
*Fort Wayne* ▪ (260) 432-4100
*4150 W Jefferson Blvd*
*Mishawaka* ▪ (574) 307-7442
*6501 N Grape Rd*

### Fox and Hound Pub & Grille 📖
*Carmel* ▪ (317) 844-0075
*14490 Lowes Wy*
*Evansville* ▪ (812) 473-5721
*5416 E Indiana St*

### Grindstone Charleys ✪$LD
*Kokomo* ▪ (765) 453-9125
*3830 S Lafountain St*
*Lafayette* ▪ (765) 449-8692
*3442 State Rd 26 E* ▪ *American* ▪ GF menu includes salads, barbecue cheddar chicken, and bourbon steak. Confirm the timeliness of this information before dining in, and alert the server upon arrival. ▪ *www.grindstonesrestaurantandpub.com*

### Hamilton Restaurant, The $$LD
*Noblesville* ▪ (317) 770-4545
*933 Conner St* ▪ *American* ▪ Owner Vanita reports that the restaurant has "several GF customers" who have helped educate the restaurant on GF options. She reports that the restaurant makes its own dressings and all food is cooked to order, so GF requests are easily accommodated. ▪ *www.hamiltonrestaurant.com*

### HuHot Mongolian Grill 📖
*Lafayette* ▪ (765) 447-8903
*100 S Creasy Ln*
*Bloomington* ▪ (812) 339-7882
*2550 E 3rd St*

**J. Gumbo's**   ★ 🕮
*Evansville* ▪ *(812) 473-2951*
*1211 N Tutor Ln*
*Terre Haute* ▪ *(812) 917-2010*
*428 Wabash Ave*

**Jason's Deli**   ✪🕮
*Carmel* ▪ *(317) 569-1473*
*12405 N Meridian St*

**JD's Crepe Company**   ★ ℂ**BLD**
*Valparaiso* ▪ *(219) 242-8611*
*3125 N Calumet Ave* ▪ *French* ▪ All items
on the regular menu can be made GF.
They have GF crepes available daily. Just
alert staff and they will clean all prep and
cooking areas before making the customer's crepe. ▪ *jdcrepecompany.com*

**Jersey Mike's**   🕮
*South Bend* ▪ *(574) 246-0136*
*111 S St. Joseph St*
*Mishawaka* ▪ *(574) 247-0056*
*5718 N Main St*

**Joe's Crab Shack**   ✪🕮
*Merrillville* ▪ *(219) 942-4554*
*2757 E 80th Ave*

**Kincaid's**   🕮
*Carmel* ▪ *(317) 575-9005*
*14159 Clay Terr Blvd*

**Lil' Charlie's**   $**LD**
*Batesville* ▪ *(812) 934-6392*
*504 E Pearl St* ▪ *American* ▪ Kitchen is
willing to modify dishes to suit the preferences of the customers, but GF options are
generally limited to grilled chicken and
steamed vegetables. Alert the server upon
arrival. ▪ *www.lilcharlies.com/menu.asp*

**Lone Star Steakhouse & Saloon**   ✪🕮
*Anderson* ▪ *(765) 640-6550*
*1721 E 60th St*

**Mark Dine and Tap, The**   $$$$**BLD**
*S Bend* ▪ *(574) 204-2767*
*1234 Eddy St* ▪ *American* ▪ The restaurant reports that many items on
the menu can be modified to be
GF. Alert the server upon arrival. ▪
*thecleanplateclubrestaurants.com/mark/*

**Measuring Cup, The**   ℂ$
*Fishers* ▪ *(317) 590-8112*
*Fishers Farmers Market* ▪ *Bakery* ▪ Dedicated GF bakery offering a wide variety of
breads, breakfast items, cookies, cinnamon rolls, cakes, and cupcakes. The menu
changes every Sunday, and the bakers bring
their products to farmers markets in the
area every Saturday. Check the website for
current farmers market information. Baker
Chris notes that customers can place special orders for items not listed on the menu.
▪ *www.gfmeasuringcup.com*

**Melting Pot, The**   ✪🕮
*Greenwood* ▪ *(317) 889-0777*
*1259 N State Road 135*

**Mitchell's Fish Market**   ✪🕮
*Carmel* ▪ *(317) 848-3474*
*14311 Clay Terrace Blvd*

**Monical's Pizza Restaurant**   ★🕮
*Delphi* ▪ *(765) 564-6670*
*1022 S Washington St*
*Kentland* ▪ *(219) 474-9330*
*402 N 7th St*
*Lafayette* ▪ *(765) 448-6066*
*3500 State Road 38 E*
*West Lafayette* ▪ *(765) 464-2885*
*3457 Bethel Dr*
*Fishers* ▪ *(317) 770-8400*
*14099 Mundy Dr*
*Greencastle* ▪ *(765) 301-4404*
*29 Putnam Plz*
*Greenwood* ▪ *(317) 881-1177*
*1675 W Smith Valley Rd*
*Monticello* ▪ *(574) 583-3550*
*912 S Main St*
*Terre Haute* ▪ *(812) 235-4700*
*3712 S US 41*
*Avon* ▪ *(317) 271-2727*
*9271 US 36*
*Linton* ▪ *(812) 847-2900*
*1600 A St NE*

**Morton's Steakhouse**   ✪🕮
*Naperville* ▪ *(630) 577-1372*
*1751 Freedom Dr*

## O'Charley's 📖
*Noblesville* ▪ *(317) 774-9488*
*16725 Mercantile Blvd*
*Avon* ▪ *(317) 209-9245*
*10416 E Us Hwy 36*
*Camby* ▪ *(317) 856-4332*
*8380 Windfall Ln*
*Bloomington* ▪ *(812) 333-6687*
*360 N Jacob Dr*
*Clarksville* ▪ *(812) 284-9646*
*1440 Vaxter Ave*
*Corydon* ▪ *(812) 738-5201*
*160 Pacer St NW*
*Evansville* ▪ *(812) 479-6632*
*7301 E Indiana St*
*Evansville* ▪ *(812) 424-3348*
*5125 Pearl Dr*
*Ft. Wayne* ▪ *(260) 436-9400*
*1220 S Illinois Rd*
*Greenfield* ▪ *(317) 462-9240*
*1993 N State St*
*Fishers* ▪ *(317) 841-3065*
*11655 Fishers Corner Blvd*
*Lafayette* ▪ *(765) 446-9466*
*2413 Sagamore Pkwy S*

## Pikk's Tavern ✪$$$LD
*Valparaiso* ▪ *(219) 476-7455*
*62 W Lincolnway* ▪ **American** ▪ GF menu
includes items such as tuna tartar, caprese
salad, filet mignon, pork chop, and plank
salmon. The GF menu also notes which
side dishes and sauces are GF. GF pasta is
available. ▪ *www.pikkstavern.com*

## Puccini's Smiling Teeth ✪★📖
*Bloomington* ▪ *(812) 323-0123*
*350 S Liberty Dr*
*Bloomington* ▪ *(812) 331-1234*
*115 S State Road 46*
*Carmel* ▪ *(317) 580-0087*
*13674 N Meridian St*
*Columbus* ▪ *(812) 348-7600*
*318 E Washington St*
*Fishers* ▪ *(317) 579-0572*
*8993 E 116th St*
*West Lafayette* ▪ *(765) 746-5000*
*300 Brown St*

## Red Cup Café & Deli ★¢BL
*Chesterton* ▪ *(219) 929-1804*
*115 Broadway* ▪ **Deli** ▪ GF bread and muffins available. GF bread can be used for all
sandwiches. Server Emma suggests ordering sandwiches by phone ahead of time due
to them taking 20 minutes to make. They
are really careful with the preparations. ▪
*www.redcupcafeanddeli.com*

## Romano's Macaroni Grill ✪★📖
*Carmel* ▪ *(317) 582-1637*
*2375 E 116th St*

## Rosati's Pizza ★📖
*Hobart* ▪ *(219) 942-5678*
*1411 S Lake Park Ave*

## Ruth's Chris Steak House ✪📖
*Granger* ▪ *(574) 968-9700*
*902 E University Dr*

## Salvatori's ★¢LD
*New Haven* ▪ *(260) 748-2057*
*12244 McKenzie Dr*
*Fort Wayne* ▪ *(260) 625-5600*
*10337 Illinois Rd* ▪ **Italian** ▪ GF pasta
and pizza crust available on request. All
GF items are cooked using dedicated
utensils and prep areas to prevent CC. ▪
*salvatorispizzeriaprimo.com*

## Scotty's Brewhouse ✪★$LD
*Muncie* ▪ *(765) 747-5151*
*1700 W University Ave*
*Bloomington* ▪ *(812) 331-7171*
*302 N Walnut St*
*West Lafayette* ▪ *(765) 746-3131*
*352 E State St* ▪ **American** ▪ GF menu
includes nachos, salads, and burgers &
sandwiches on GF buns. GF salad dressings
and sides are also listed. For dessert, GF
chocolate chip cookies are available, as well
as a "baby monster" sundae made with the
GF cookies. General manager Scott reports
that servers are trained to alert a manager if
a customer needs a GF meal, and the manager will oversee production of the order.
Separate utensils and plates are used for GF
meals. ▪ *www.scottysbrewhouse.com*

## Scotty's Burger Joint ★ $LD
*Columbus* ▪ *(812) 373-5151*
*310 Washington St* ▪ *American* ▪ GF buns are available for burgers. General manager Scott reports that servers are trained to alert a manager if a customer needs a GF meal, and the manager will oversee production of the order. Separate utensils and plates are used for GF meals. ▪ *www.scottysburgerjoint.com*

## Scotty's Lakehouse ★ $LD
*Fishers* ▪ *(317) 577-2900*
*10158 Brooks School Rd* ▪ *American* ▪ GF buns are available for burgers. The restaurant reports that their baked chips and salsa are also GF. General manager Scott reports that servers are trained to alert a manager if a customer needs a GF meal, and the manager will oversee production of the order. Separate utensils and plates are used for GF meals. ▪ *scottyslakehouse.com*

## Smiling Moose Deli ✪📖
*Evansville* ▪ *(812) 477-3354*
*724 N Burkhardt Rd*

## Smokey Bones 📖
*Fort Wayne* ▪ *(260) 436-6233*
*1203 Apple Glen Blvd*
*Greenwood* ▪ *(317) 859-6499*
*780 US Hwy 31 N*

## Stir Crazy ★📖
*Greenwood* ▪ *(317) 888-6200*
*1251 US Hwy 31 N*

## Sweet Cece's 📖
*Evansville* ▪ *(812) 867-6228*
*12414 US 41 N*
*Evansville* ▪ *(812) 477-5276*
*4827 Davis Lant Dr*
*Evansville* ▪ *(812) 401-5232*
*5625 Pearl Dr*

## Ted's Montana Grill ✪📖
*Carmel* ▪ *(317) 569-8300*
*14490 Clay Terrace Blvd*

## Theo's Steaks and Seafood $$$LD
*Highland* ▪ *(219) 838-8000*
*9144 Indianapolis Blvd* ▪ *Steakhouse* ▪ The restaurant reports that all steaks, seafood, chicken, and salads can be prepared GF, and adds that the grill is cleaned before all GF orders to minimize the chances of CC. ▪ *www.theoshighland.com*

## Third Coast Spice Café ★¢BLD
*Chesterton* ▪ *(219) 926-5858*
*761 Indian Boundary Rd* ▪ *Café* ▪ GF bread is available for toast in the morning or sandwiches at lunchtime. ▪ *www.thirdcoastspice.com*

## Tre Bicchieri $$$LD
*Columbus* ▪ *(812) 372-1962*
*425 Washington St* ▪ *Italian* ▪ As per manager Ike, everything can be GF modified. All chefs are extremely knowledgeable about taking CC precautions. GF brown rice is available. ▪ *www.trebicchieri-columbus.com*

## Uptown Kitchen ✪★$BLD
*Granger* ▪ *(574) 968-3030*
*303 Florence Ave* ▪ *American* ▪ GF pizza, bread, chocolate chip banana French toast, sandwiches, and various cakes are available on their GF menu. ▪ *theuptownkitchen.com*

## Valley Kitchen & Bar $$D
*Valparaiso* ▪ *(219) 531-8888*
*55 Franklin St* ▪ *American* ▪ Restaurant reports they do not have a GF menu but there are "definitely options" for GF diners. Alert the server upon arrival and they will point out the options available. ▪ *eatvalley.com*

## Zing Pizzeria ★$LD
*Chesterton* ▪ *(219) 728-6686*
*442 Sand Creek Dr N* ▪ *Pizza* ▪ GF pizza is available. ▪ *www.zingpizzeria.com*

# IOWA

## Atlas World Grill ✪★$$LD
*Iowa City* ■ *(319) 341-7700*
127 Iowa Ave ■ American ■ Owner reports
that they have many regular guests who
are GF. He notes that the Thai salad, the
Jamaican chicken, and the salmon are
naturally GF. Confirm the timeliness of
this information before dining in. Alert
a server, who will notify a manager. ■
*www.atlasworldgrill.com*

## Au Bon Pain 📖
*Indianola* ■ *(515) 491-0790*
701 N C St

## Aunt Maude's $$$LD
*Ames* ■ *(515) 233-4136*
547 Main St ■ Modern American ■ Manager Dave reports that accommodating
GF diners is "not a problem" and advises
alerting a server upon arrival. The server
will alert the chef and the chef will personally come out to help build a meal
that suits the customer's preferences. ■
*www.auntmaudesames.com*

## Biaggi's ✪★📖
*Cedar Rapids* ■ *(319) 393-6593*
320 Collins Rd NE
*Davenport* ■ *(563) 344-2103*
5195 Utica Ridge Rd
*West Des Moines* ■ *(515) 221-9900*
5990 University Ave

## Blackstone ✪$$$LD
*Iowa City* ■ *(319) 338-1770*
503 Westbury Dr ■ American ■ GF menu
includes ahi tuna salad, burgers without
buns, three berry chicken salad, salmon,
steak, and more. ■ *www.blackstone-ic.com*

## Bonefish Grill ✪📖
*West Des Moines* ■ *(515) 267-0064*
650 S Prairie View Dr Ste 100

## Bourbon Street ✪$$D
*Cedar Falls* ■ *(319) 266-5285*
314 Main St ■ American ■ Limited GF
menu includes sirloin steak, pork tenderloin medallions, grilled chicken,
grilled salmon lafayette, and blackened
yellowfin tuna. All GF items are served
with a side of steamed asparagus and
baked potato. Confirm the timeliness
of this information before dining in. ■
*www.barmuda.com/bourbonstreet*

## Brown Bottle, The ✪$$$LD
*North Liberty* ■ *(319) 626-3900*
125 E Zeller St
*Iowa City* ■ *(319) 351-6704*
115 E Washington St ■ Italian ■ Limited GF menu includes a chef's salad,
shrimp scampi salad, chicken parmesan,
chicken florentine, salmon, and prime
rib. Alert the server upon arrival. ■
*www.iowacitybrownbottle.com*

## Café, The ✪$$BLD
*Ames* ■ *(515) 292-0100*
2616 Northridge Pkwy ■ American ■ GF
menu includes fish tacos with corn tortillas, Korean steak & egg, market salad,
salmon, and all sandwiches in lettuce cups
instead of with bread. Alert a server upon
arrival. ■ *www.thecafeames.com*

## Carlos O'Kelly's ✪
*Ames* ■ *(515) 232-1500*
631 Lincoln Wy
*Burlington* ■ *(319) 753-9800*
321 N Roosevelt
*Cedar Falls* ■ *(319) 277-1121*
6507 University Ave
*Cedar Rapids* ■ *(319) 396-6222*
2635 Edgewood Rd SW
*Des Moines* ■ *(515) 334-3331*
4371 Merle Hay Rd
*Dubuque* ■ *(563) 583-0088*
1355 Associates Dr
*Iowa City* ■ *(319) 354-5800*
1411 Waterfront Dr
*Marion* ■ *(319) 373-1451*
3320 Armar Dr
*Mason City* ■ *(641) 423-9332*

3331 4th St SW
Sioux City ▪ (712) 252-4703
5738 Sunnybrook Dr
Waterloo ▪ (319) 236-8730
1331 Flammang Dr
West Des Moines ▪ (515) 225-4321
4055 Westown Pkwy

**Club Car, The**                          ★ $LD
Clive ▪ (515) 226-1729
13435 University Ave ▪ American ▪ GF
menu includes BBQ shrimp kabobs, baked
salmon, a variety of steaks, and more. GF
pizza and pasta are available. The restaurant reports that they "make every effort"
to prevent CC. ▪ clubcardining.com

**Coach's Pizza**                          ★ $$LD
West Des Moines ▪ (515) 223-2233
560 S Prairie View Dr ▪ Pizza ▪ GF pizza is
available. Manager reports that the kitchen
staff is "supposed to be extremely GF-
aware." ▪ www.coachspizza.com

**Court Avenue Restaurant & Brewing
Company**                                  ✪$$LD
Des Moines ▪ (515) 282-2739
309 Court Ave ▪ American ▪ GF menu
includes blackened salmon, lemon scallop salad, chicken marsala, currant pork
medallions, and more. Appetizers include
wings and a shrimp andouille dish. ▪
www.courtavebrew.com

**Crust Italian Kitchen + Bar**             ✪$LD
Dubuque ▪ (563) 582-6889
299 Main St ▪ Italian ▪ GF pizza and pasta
are available. ▪ www.crustdubuque.com

**Cu Restaurant**                           ✪¢LD
Waterloo ▪ (319) 274-8888
320 E 4th St ▪ American ▪ GF lunch and
dinner menus include shrimp cocktail,
grilled salmon, stuffed duck, and maple
pork medallions. ▪ www.curestaurant.com

**Devotay**                                ✪$$$$LD
Iowa City ▪ (319) 354-1001
117 N Linn St ▪ Spanish ▪ Restaurant
reports that 80% of their menu items are

GF. Be sure to alert server upon arrival. ▪
www.devotay.net

**Fair Grounds Coffee House**               ★ ¢BL
Iowa City ▪ (319) 338-2024
345 S Dubuque St ▪ Bakery & Café ▪
Non-dedicated bakery offering a variety
of GF baked goods, including cupcakes,
muffins, scones, cookies, blondies, and
biscotti. GF cakes are available by preorder only, and they require 2-3 days notice.
▪ www.fairgroundscoffeehouse.com

**Felix and Oscars**                        ★ $LD
Des Moines ▪ (515) 278-8887
4050 Merle Hay Rd
West Des Moines ▪ (515) 457-1000
4801 Westown Pkwy ▪ Italian ▪ GF pizza,
pasta, and bread are available. Restaurant
reports that GF pizza can be made with
any toppings. Confirm the timeliness
of this information before dining in. ▪
www.felixandoscars.com

**Ferrari's Ristorante**                    ✪$$LD
Cedar Falls ▪ (319) 277-1385
1521 Technology Pkwy ▪ American ▪
GF menu includes seared scallop salad,
Tuscan salad, pan-seared chicken breast,
peppercorn encrusted flatiron steak,
NY strip steak, and more. Ice cream
or fresh fruit is available for dessert. ▪
www.barmuda.com/ferraris

**Fia's Pizza Company**                     ✪$LD
Des Moines ▪ (515) 287-6666
3801 SW 9th St ▪ Pizza ▪ GF pizza,
breadsticks, cheesebread, and cinnamon
sticks available. Confirm the timeliness
of this information before dining in. ▪
www.fiaspizzariaco.com

**Fleming's Prime
Steakhouse & Wine Bar**                     ✪📖
W Des Moines ▪ (515) 457-2916
150 S Jordan Creek Pkwy

**Genghis Grill**                           📖
Cedar Rapids ▪ (319) 373-5426
5001 1st Ave

Cedar Rapids ■ (319) 390-5426
2230 Edgewood Rd SW

### Godfather's Pizza ★

Iowa City ■ (319) 354-3312
531 Hwy 1 W
Mason City ■ (641) 424-5133
1703 4th St SE
Ankeny ■ (515) 964-5233
802 N Ankeny Blvd
Des Moines ■ (515) 277-6344
4119 University
Spencer ■ (712) 262-7742
113 Grand Ave
Urbandale ■ (515) 278-8100
8801 Hickman Rd
Le Mars ■ (712) 546-4159
625 Hawkeye Ave SW
W Des Moines ■ (515) 226-8880
5919 Ashworth Rd
Cedar Falls ■ (319) 277-7777
1621 W 1st St_
Waterloo ■ (319) 235-7104
3811 University Ave
Waterloo ■ (319) 233-3000
1946 Schukei Rd
Cedar Rapids ■ (319) 363-2127
3647 1/2 1st Ave SE
Cedar Rapids ■ (319) 364-8187
2201 16th Ave SW
Hampton ■ (641) 456-3355
805 Central Ave W
Webster City ■ (515) 832-3625
817 2nd St
Maquoketa ■ (563) 652-5200
916 W Platt
Waverly ■ (319) 352-6626
1016 W Bremer
Marshalltown ■ (641) 752-4444
50 Lafrentz Ln
Davenport ■ (563) 386-6110
902 W Kimberly Rd
Denison ■ (712) 263-9313
2506 4th Ave S

### Ground Round ✪

Dubuque ■ (563) 556-3540
50 John F Kennedy Rd

### Happy Joe's Pizza & Ice Cream

Anamosa ■ (319) 462-4200
100 Chamber Dr
Bettendorf ■ (563) 359-5457
2430 Spruce Hills Dr
Burlington ■ (319) 753-1665
1011 Lawrence Dr
Cascade ■ (563) 852-3300
1301 1st Ave E
Cedar Rapids ■ (319) 393-0017
5070 Lindale Dr NE
Cedar Rapids ■ (319) 396-0626
3310 Williams Blvd SW
Clinton ■ (563) 242-3121
408 S 1st St
Coralville Temp ■ (319) 351-6900
102 Second Ave
Davenport ■ (563) 324-5656
1414 W Locust St
Davenport ■ (563) 386-1766
201 W 50th St
Davenport ■ (563) 324-0477
2630 Rockingham Rd
Decorah ■ (563) 382-2118
105 E Water St
DeWitt ■ (563) 659-9173
1407 11th St
Dubuque ■ (563) 556-0823
1094 University Dr
Dubuque ■ (563) 556-0820
855 Century Dr
Dryersville ■ (563) 875-7263
1213 12th Ave
Eldridge ■ (563) 285-8673
350 E Le Claire Rd
LeClaire ■ (563) 289-3305
119 N Cody Rd
Maquoketa ■ (563) 652-6721
603 Myatt Dr
Monticello ■ (319) 465-5477
601 S Main
Muscatine ■ (563) 263-5233
203 Lake Park Blvd
Muscatine ■ (563) 263-1320
927 Grandview
Ottumwa ■ (641) 682-4565
315 Church St

*Pella* ▪ *(641) 628-4600*
*718 Broadway*
*Tipton* ▪ *(563) 886-3141*
*310 Cedar St*
*Urbandale* ▪ *(515) 270-0695*
*8056 Douglas Ave*
*Walcott* ▪ *(563) 284-5055*
*755 W Iowa 80 Rd*

## Hickory Park Restaurant Co.    ✪₵LD
*Ames* ▪ *(515) 232-8940*
*1404 S Duff Ave* ▪ *Barbeque* ▪ GF menu
includes a variety burgers without buns,
grilled franks, taco salad, and smoked
meats. The menu notes modifications
needed for dishes to become GF. A GF
kids and ice cream menu is also available. ▪
*www.hickoryparkames.com*

## HuHot Mongolian Grill    📖
*Cedar Falls* ▪ *(379) 553-1100*
*6301 University Ave*
*Coralville* ▪ *(319) 385-9100*
*917 25th Ave*
*Council Bluffs* ▪ *(712) 309-0100*
*3120 Manawa Centre Dr*
*Ankeny* ▪ *(515) 963-7860*
*2310 SE Delaware Ave*
*West Des Moines* ▪ *(515) 457-9090*
*4100 University Ave*
*Dubuque* ▪ *(563) 513-3121*
*555 John F Kennedy Rd*
*Sioux City* ▪ *(712) 224-3400*
*4229 S Lakeport*

## Jason's Deli    ✪📖
*West Des Moines* ▪ *(515) 222-9797*
*3910 University Ave*

## Joe's Crab Shack    ✪📖
*West Des Moines* ▪ *(515) 226-9966*
*130 S Jordan Creek Pkwy*

## King and I Thai Cuisine    $LD
*West Des Moines* ▪ *(515) 440-2075*
*1821 22nd St* ▪ *Thai* ▪ The restaurant notes
that "anything" can be made GF but adds
that many items, like the curries, are naturally GF. Confirm the timeliness of this information before dining in. Alert a server,

who will ensure that the kitchen prepares a
GF meal. ▪ *www.king-and-i-thaicuisine.com*

## Lone Star Steakhouse & Saloon    ✪📖
*Cedar Rapids* ▪ *(319) 393-9648*
*4545 1st Ave SE*
*Waterloo* ▪ *(319) 232-3233*
*4045 Hammond Ave*
*West Des Moines* ▪ *(515) 223-9606*
*1801 22nd St*

## Mama's Deli & Catering    ✪₵LD
*Iowa City* ▪ *(319) 341-0700*
*125 E Washington St* ▪ *Deli* ▪ Serves GF
soups and sandwiches. Confirm the timeliness of this information before dining in. ▪
*mamasdeliandcatering.com*

## Minerva's    ✪📖
*Sioux City* ▪ *(712) 277-0800*
*2945 Hamilton Blvd*
*Okoboji* ▪ *(712) 332-5296*
*1405 Hwy 71*

## Motley Cow Café    $$LD
*Iowa City* ▪ *(319) 688-9177*
*160 N Linn St* ▪ *American* ▪ Restaurant reports that they have "quite a few"
regular diners with dietary restrictions
including GF diners. She notes that chefs
are very accommodating. Servers are
GF aware. Alert a server upon arrival. ▪
*www.motleycowcafe.com*

## Nick-N-Willy's    ★📖
*West Des Moines* ▪ *(515) 223-5700*
*165 S Jordan Creek Pkwy*

## Olde Main
## Brewing Company & Restaurant    ✪$LD
*Ames* ▪ *(515) 232-0553*
*316 Main St* ▪ *American* ▪ GF menu
includes an angus filet, a fresh salmon
filet roasted on a maple plank, and the
southwestern steak salad. General Manager Jamie reports that they are happy to
accommodate GF diners any time of day. ▪
*www.oldemainbrewing.com*

## Other Place, The                          ★ $$LD
Clive ▪ (515) 225-9494
12401 University Ave
Clear Lake ▪ (641) 357-8118
200 Hwy 18 W
Evansdale ▪ (319) 232-3536
3904 Lafayette Rd
Cedar Falls ▪ (319) 277-9720
2214 College St
Waterloo ▪ (319) 287-9400
360 E Ridgeway Ave
Waverly ▪ (319) 352-4742
821 W Bremer
Cedar Falls ▪ (319) 268-1655
4214 University Ave ▪ Pizza ▪ GF
pizza crust available upon request. ▪
theotherplace.com

## P.F. Chang's China Bistro              ✪★📖
West Des Moines ▪ (515) 457-7772
110 S Jordan Creek Pkwy

## Pacgliai's Pizza                          ✪$D
Grinnell ▪ (641) 236-5331
816 5th Ave
Johnston ▪ (515) 253-9800
5312 Merle Hay Rd ▪ Pizza ▪ GF 10"
pizza crust is available at both locations. ▪
www.pagliais.com

## Pizza Ranch                              ✪📖
Algona ▪ (515) 295-6995
1325 Hwy 169 N
Altoona ▪ (515) 967-8800
465 Center Pl SW
Ames ▪ (515) 232-1999
1404 Boston Ave
Boone ▪ (515) 432-2222
1703 S Story St
Carroll ▪ (712) 792-3456
425 Hwy 30 W
Council Bluffs ▪ (712) 256-7701
3505 Metro Dr
Harlan ▪ (712) 755-2262
613 Court St
Cedar Falls ▪ (319) 266-2555
4302 University Ave
Charles City ▪ (641) 228-4100
1000 Blundt Pkwy
Creston ▪ (641) 782-7337

520 Livingston
Decorah ▪ (563) 382-8744
212 College Dr
Dubuque ▪ (563) 556-4488
2020 Radford Rd
Emmetsburg ▪ (712) 852-2222
2120 11th St
Fairfield ▪ (641) 472-0123
1103 W Burlington
Garner ▪ (641) 923-7262
405 State St
Hull ▪ (712) 439-1853
1015 Main St
Independence ▪ (319) 334-9000
1900 1st St W
Indianola ▪ (515) 961-7492
1709 N Jefferson Wy
Iowa City ▪ (319) 337-6800
1610 Sycamore St
Lake Mills ▪ (641) 592-3400
210 W Main
Le Mars ▪ (712) 546-7272
11 Central Ave
Manchester ▪ (563) 927-4600
1100 W Main
Marcus ▪ (712) 376-2168
109 N Main
Marion ▪ (319) 447-2624
1055 Linden Dr
Oelwein ▪ (319) 283-5858
125 1st Ave SE
George ▪ (712) 475-2865
108 E Michigan Ave
Hawarden ▪ (712) 551-2455
723 Central Ave
Marshalltown ▪ (641) 753-7711
2305 S Ctr St
Monticello ▪ (319) 465-6000
505 E Oak St
Mt Pleasant ▪ (319) 986-2222
708 N Grand Ave
Newton ▪ (641) 792-3447
1500 W 18th St S
North Liberty ▪ (319) 626-7999
395 Beaver Kreek Ctr
Orange City ▪ (712) 737-3711
1505 8th St SE
Pella ▪ (641) 628-8844

508 Main St
Pocahontas ▪ (712) 335-4555
211 N Main
Rock Rapids ▪ (712) 472-3258
205 S Union St
Rock Valley ▪ (712) 476-9930
1513 14th St
Rockwell City ▪ (712) 297-5800
102 Warner
Sanborn ▪ (712) 729-5402
107 W 7th St
Sergeant Bluff ▪ (712) 943-7499
204 1st St
Sheldon ▪ (712) 324-4800
104 N Runger
Sibley ▪ (712) 754-4196
316 9th St
Sigourney ▪ (641) 622-9990
416 W Jackson St
Sioux Center ▪ (712) 722-3988
251 N Main _
Spencer ▪ (712) 262-6262
528 N Grand Ave
Story City ▪ (515) 733-4111
1513 Broad St
Vinton ▪ (319) 472-4000
219 W 4th St
Washington ▪ (319) 653-5553
201 S Wiley Ave
Waukee ▪ (515) 978-6603
448 SE University
Waverly ▪ (319) 352-2222
2020 W Bremer
Ankeny ▪ (515) 964-9990
201 SE Oralabor Rd
Grinnell ▪ (641) 260-8020
613 W St S

### Romano's Macaroni Grill            ✪★📖
West Des Moines ▪ (515) 267-8400
4502 University Ave

### Sam & Louie's New York Pizzeria    ★📖
Council Bluffs ▪ (712) 256-7712
1851 Madison Suite
Carroll ▪ (712) 792-6477
425 W Hwy 30
Urbandale ▪ (515) 537-8361
8561 Hickman Rd

### Shane's Rib Shack                  ✪📖
Clive ▪ (515) 327-7427
12695 University Ave

### Sweets Minus Wheat                 ¢S
Norwalk ▪ (515) 493-9824
Main St ▪ Bakery ▪ Dedicated GF bakery that specializes in cinnamon rolls,
cupcakes, brownies, and cheesecakes. ▪
sweetsminuswheat.com

### Tony Roma's                        📖
Dubuque ▪ (563) 690-3249
350 Bell St

### Valentino's                       ★📖
Ames ▪ (515) 233-2111
823 Wheeler St

# KANSAS

### 4 Olives Wine Bar                  ✪★$$D
Manhattan ▪ (785) 539-1295
3033 Anderson Ave ▪ Modern American
▪ GF menu includes sweet pea and shrimp
risotto, sesame-crusted seared ahi tuna,
and more. For dessert, they offer a flourless chocolate torte and crème brûlée. GF
pasta, soy sauce, and beer are available. ▪
www.4olives.biz

### Abuelo's                          ✪📖
Wichita ▪ (316) 634-2230
1413 N Waterfront Pkwy

### Ane Mae's Coffee House            ★¢BL
Independence ▪ (620) 331-4487
112 N 10th St ▪ Café ▪ GF bread is available
for sandwiches. ▪ www.anemaes.net

### Bambino's                         ★$LD
Lawrence ▪ (785) 832-8800
1540 Wakarusa Dr ▪ Italian ▪ GF
pasta is available upon request. ▪
bambinoslawrence.com

## Blue Planet Café ★ ¢BL

*Topeka* ■ *(785) 783-8883*
*110 SE 8th Ave* ■ *Bakery & Café* ■ The restaurant reports that the soup is always GF, and that other GF options may be available depending on the day. There are always "one or two GF options" in the pastry case. Call ahead on the day of your visit to find out what other items are being served. ■ *blueplanettopeka.com*

## Bonefish Grill ✿▢

*Wichita* ■ *(316) 315-0299*
*10250 E 13th St N # 102*
*Leawood* ■ *(913) 239-8856*
*5021 W 135th St*

## BRGR Kitchen & Bar ✿★¢LD

*Prairie Village* ■ *(913) 825-2747*
*4038 W 83rd St* ■ *American* ■ GF buns available for all burgers and sandwiches. GF menu also includes chile fondue, chicken wings, several kinds of fries, soups, roasted cheesy corn, and a variety of salads. Confirm the timeliness of this information before dining in. ■ *www.brgrkitchen.com*

## Bristol Seafood Grill ✿$$$LD

*Leawood* ■ *(913) 663-5777*
*5400 W 119th St* ■ *Seafood* ■ GF menu is available online and in-house. Items include shrimp cocktail, seafood of the day, steaks, cioppino, mesquite grilled chicken, and more. A variety of ice creams and sorbets are available for dessert. ■ *www.bristolseafoodgrill.com*

## Brobecks Barbeque $LD

*Overland Park* ■ *(913) 901-9700*
*4615 Indian Creek Pkwy* ■ *Barbeque* ■ The restaurant reports that their GF options include their sliced meats, pulled pork, chicken dinner, salads, coleslaw, ribs. Confirm the timeliness of this information before dining in. ■ *www.brobecksbbq.com*

## Café Chilingo ✿★¢L

*Leavenworth* ■ *(913) 758-1715*
*227 Cherokee St* ■ *American* ■ GF pasta and hotdog buns are available. ■ *www.cafechilingo.com*

## Café on the Route $LD

*Baxter Springs* ■ *(620) 856-5646*
*1101 Military Ave* ■ *American* ■ The restaurant reports that they can accommodate the needs of any customer and that many dishes can be modified to be GF. Alert the server upon arrival. ■ *www.cafeontheroute.com*

## Carino's Italian ✿▢

*Kansas City* ■ *(913) 299-8253*
*1706 Village W Pkwy*
*Topeka* ■ *(785) 215-8400*
*6130 SW 6th Ave*
*Wichita* ■ *(316) 636-4411*
*3213 N Toben St*

## Carlo's $$LD

*Lenexa* ■ *(913) 825-5200*
*14944 W 87th St Pkwy* ■ *Italian* ■ The restaurant reports that certain menu items can be prepared GF, and suggests asking a server for details upon arrival. ■ *home.roadrunner.com~coparoomkc/*

## Carlos O'Kelly's ✿

*Hays* ■ *(785) 628-9900*
*4107 Vine St*
*Hutchinson* ■ *(620) 665-9885*
*909 E 30th Ave*
*Lawrence* ■ *(785) 832-0550*
*707 W 23rd St*
*Manhattan* ■ *(785) 537-4688*
*330 S Manhattan Ave*
*Salina* ■ *(785) 826-1501*
*2259 S 9th*
*Topeka* ■ *(785) 266-3457*
*3425 S Kansas Ave*
*Wichita* ■ *(316) 689-8800*
*7703 E Douglas Ave*
*Wichita* ■ *(316) 636-4343*
*3025 N Rock Rd*
*Wichita* ■ *(316) 554-1700*
*4872 S Broadway St*
*Wichita* ■ *(316) 721-5885*
*527 S Ridge Cir*

## Carrabba's Italian Grill ✿▢

*Overland Park* ■ *(913) 385-7811*
*10586 Metcalf Ln*

*Wichita* ▪ (316) 315-0777
*3409 N Rock Rd*

## Caspian Bistro                                    ✪★$LD
*Overland Park* ▪ (913) 901-9911
*8973 Metcalf Ave* ▪ *Middle Eastern* ▪
Extensive GF menu includes a wide variety
of kabobs made with chicken, lamb, beef,
and vegetables, as well as salads, stews, and
appetizers. GF bread, beer, and cookies are
available. ▪ *www.caspianbistro-ks.com*

## Chatters Grill                                       ★$LD
*Pittsburg* ▪ (620) 232-7277
*2401 S Rouse* ▪ *American* ▪ GF pasta is
available as well as GF bread for sandwiches. ▪ *chattersgrill.com*

## Cheeseburger in Paradise                    ✪★📖
*Kansas City* ▪ (913) 334-4500
*1705 Village W Pkwy*

## Chiusano's Brick Oven Pizzeria       ★$LD
*Kansas City* ▪ (913) 299-8787
*1713 Village W Pkwy* ▪ *Pizza* ▪ GF pizza is
available with any toppings in the 9-inch
size only. ▪ *www.chiusanospizza.com*

## Coach's Bar & Grill                             ★$LD
*Overland Park* ▪ (913) 897-7070
*9908 W 135th St* ▪ *American* ▪ GF buns are
available for sandwiches at both locations.
The Kansas City location also reports GF
beer and cider. ▪ *www.coach-s.com*

## Cup of Jo-Nes                                    ★¢BLD
*Dodge City* ▪ (620) 789-5282
*909 W Wyatt Earp Blvd* ▪ *Coffee Shop* ▪
GF bread is available for all sandwiches. GF
brownies and muffins are also available.

## Delish Café                                        ✪★¢L
*Wichita* ▪ (316) 683-6078
*2929 E Central Ave* ▪ *Café* ▪ GF lunch
boxes are available. Lunch boxes are made
with sandwiches, wraps or salads. 24-48
hours noticed needed for all orders. ▪
*www.foodforthoughtwichita.com*

## Della Voce                                        ★$$$D
*Manhattan* ▪ (785) 532-9000
*405 Poyntz Ave* ▪ *Italian* ▪ Owner Noah
reports that GF pasta is available as well as

"a plethora" of modified entrées. He adds
that his wife has Celiac so he takes CC very
seriously. Alert a server upon arrival. ▪
*dellavoce.com*

## Edokko Japanese Restaurant      ✪★$$LD
*Lenexa* ▪ (913) 888-8878
*8615 Hauser St* ▪ *Japanese* ▪ Most items
on their menu are GF or can be made so.
The soy paper and seaweed paper used for
rolls are both GF. Stay clear of the tempura
or anything with panko bread crumbs. GF
soy sauce is available in house but not for
to-go orders. ▪ *www.edokkokc.com*

## El Porton Café                                   ✪$LD
*Overland Park* ▪ (913) 381-8060
*4671 Indian Creek Pkwy* ▪ *Latin American*
▪ All of the arepas on the menu are GF. Ask
a staff member upon arrival for any other
suggestions they may have.

## El Salvadoreño                                   ¢BLD
*Overland Park* ▪ (913) 871-6165
*7926 Santa Fe Dr* ▪ *Latin American* ▪ The
restaurant reports that most of their menu
is GF. A server will be able to point out
which options to avoid.

## First Watch - The Daytime Café     ✪📖
*Fairway* ▪ (913) 236-7600
*2800 W 53rd St*
*Lawrence* ▪ (785) 842-7999
*2540 Iowa St*
*Olathe* ▪ (913) 390-6072
*15289 W 119th St*
*Overland Park* ▪ (913) 696-1119
*12040 Blue Valley Pkwy*
*Overland Park* ▪ (913) 383-2904
*7305 W 95th St*
*Overland Park* ▪ (913) 339-6686
*9916 College Blvd*
*Prairie Village* ▪ (913) 649-8875
*4117 W 83rd St*
*Shawnee* ▪ (913) 631-0888
*11112 W 63rd St*
*Overland Park* ▪ (913) 681-3447
*7301 W 151st St*

### Fortune Wok ✪★$LD
*Shawnee Mission* ■ *(913) 239-8646*
*11236 W 135th St*
*Overland Park* ■ *(913) 681-8863*
*14537 Metcalf Ave* ■ **Chinese** ■ Separate GF menu available. Includes sweet and sour beef and chicken, lemon shrimp and chicken, chicken and pork fried rice, chicken chow fun noodles and chicken and shrimp lettuce wraps. GF soy sauce is also available. ■ *www.fortunewokkc.com*

### Fox and Hound Pub & Grille 📖
*Wichita* ■ *(316) 634-2123*
*1421 Waterfront Pkwy*
*Overland Park* ■ *(913) 649-1700*
*10428 Metcalf*

### Freebirds on the Fly ✪📖
*Mission* ■ *(913) 236-9830*
*6029 Metcalf Ave*

### Frida's Contemporary Mexican Cuisine $$LD
*Overland Park* ■ *(913) 897-0606*
*7200 W 121st St* ■ **Mexican** ■ The restaurant reports that almost the entire menu is GF. A server will be able to point out which items to avoid. Confirm the timeliness of this information before dining in. ■ *fridasmexicancuisine.com*

### Genghis Grill 📖
*Wichita* ■ *(316) 682-2695*
*111 Rock Rd*
*Wichita* ■ *(316) 729-4745*
*8448 W Central*

### Godfather's Pizza ★📖
*Topeka* ■ *(785) 273-0313*
*5300 SW 17th St*
*Wichita* ■ *(316) 522-7111*
*4840 S Broadway*
*Overland Pk* ■ *(913) 897-0505*
*12561 Antioch Rd*

### Great Day Café ★¢BLD
*Overland Park* ■ *(913) 642-9090*
*7921 Santa Fe Dr* ■ **American** ■ GF bread is available for all sandwiches. ■ *www.great-day-cafe.com*

### Green Mill Restaurant and Bar ✪📖
*Overland Park* ■ *(913) 492-1111*
*8787 Reeder Rd*
*Wichita* ■ *(316) 687-6455*
*Kellog & Rock Rd*

### Heavy's BBQ $LD
*Concordia* ■ *(785) 262-4132*
*103 W 7th St* ■ **Barbeque** ■ The restaurant reports that their dry rub and all of their sauces are GF, making most of their barbequed items GF. Alert the server upon arrival and they will advise which options are best. ■ *www.heavysbbqnck.com*

### Hot Basil Thai Cuisine $LD
*Overland Park* ■ *(913) 451-3713*
*7528 119th St* ■ **Thai** ■ Many items are either naturally GF or can be modified to be GF such as their curries and fried rice. ■ *www.hotbasilkc.com*

### HuHot Mongolian Grill 📖
*Manhattan* ■ *(785) 320-7320*
*Manhattan Town Center Mall*
*Topeka* ■ *(785) 271-8190*
*5900 SW Huntoon Rd*
*Wichita* ■ *(316) 558-3630*
*2035 N Rock Rd*

### Ingredient Restaurant ✪★📖
*Lawrence* ■ *(785) 832-0100*
*947 Massachusetts*
*Leawood* ■ *(913) 948-6800*
*11563 Ash St*

### Jack Stack Barbecue $LD
*Overland Park* ■ *(913) 385-7427*
*9520 Metcalf Ave* ■ **Barbeque** ■ Director of operations Rod reports that a list of GF items is available at each restaurant. He recommends letting your server know of any "allergies" as soon as you are seated. The server will inform management and provide guests with the GF list. Rod also notes that they follow "strict guidelines" when preparing GF orders and "handle guests with allergens every day." ■ *www.jackstackbbq.com*

**Jason's Deli** ✪📖
*Olathe* ▪ *(913) 825-4422*
*16535 W 119th St*
*Wichita* ▪ *(316) 721-4993*
*7447 W 21st St N*
*Lawrence* ▪ *(785) 842-5600*
*3140 Iowa St*
*Topeka* ▪ *(785) 478-4144*
*6121 SW 12th St*
*Overland Park* ▪ *(913) 498-2255*
*12010 Metcalf Ave*
*Wichita* ▪ *(316) 636-4447*
*2000 N Rock Rd*

**Jersey Mike's** 📖
*Topeka* ▪ *(785) 273-7827*
*2121 SW Wanamaker Rd*
*Topeka* ▪ *(785) 357-7827*
*718 S Kansas Ave*
*Olathe* ▪ *(913) 254-7756*
*15018 S Black Bob Rd*

**Joe's Crab Shack** ✪📖
*Olathe* ▪ *(913) 393-2929*
*11965 S Strang Line Rd*

**Johnny Brusco's New York Style Pizza** ★📖
*Olathe* ▪ *(913) 897-1188*
*10540 S Ridgeview Rd*
*Overland Park* ▪ *(913) 897-8160*
*11228 W 135th St*
*Overland Park* ▪ *(913) 648-6146*
*8909 W 95th St*

**La Bodega** ✪$$LD
*Leawood* ▪ *(913) 428-8272*
*4311 W 119th St* ▪ *Spanish* ▪ GF items are
marked on the menu and include roasted
red peppers stuffed with ahi tuna, pancetta-
wrapped dates stuffed with chorizo, and
pork skewers. ▪ *www.labodegakc.com*

**La Parrilla** $LD
*Olathe* ▪ *(913) 829-0450*
*11977 S Strang Line Rd*
*Lawrence* ▪ *(785) 841-1100*
*814 Massachusetts St* ▪ *Latin American*
▪ The restaurant reports that "just about
everything" on the menu is GF. Examples
include rice bowls and enchiladas. Alert

a server, who will go over the GF options
with you. ▪ *www.laparrillaks.com*

**Lone Star Steakhouse & Saloon** ✪📖
*Garden City* ▪ *(620) 271-0055*
*2306 E Kansas Ave*
*Hutchinson* ▪ *(620) 665-0808*
*1419 E 11Th St*
*Kansas City* ▪ *(913) 334-9995*
*1501 Village W Pkwy*

**Lotus Leaf Café & Creperie** ✪★¢LD
*Wichita* ▪ *(316) 295-4133*
*613 W Douglas Ave* ▪ *American* ▪ GF
options are marked on the regular menu
and include rubbed kale salad, portabella
"pizza", tarragon chicken crepe, and sweet
potato crepe. Flourless chocolate torte and
raw cheesecake are available for dessert. ▪
*www.lotusleafwichita.com*

**Mariscos** ✪$$BLD
*Lawrence* ▪ *(785) 312-9057*
*4821 W 6th St* ▪ *American* ▪ GF menu and
a special GF Sunday menu available. GF
menu includes smoked golden trout salad,
porterhouse chop, truffle mac and cheese
and more. GF Sunday menu is similar but
includes breakfast items such as classic
eggs benedict, whole grain and maple
carrot pancakes, roast prime rib and three
cheese omelet and a breakfast wrap. ▪
*www.mariscosrestaurant.com*

**Martinelli's Little Italy** ✪★$$LD
*Salina* ▪ *(785) 826-9190*
*158 S Santa Fe Ave* ▪ *Italian* ▪ GF menu
available upon request. Selections in-
clude GF pizza, GF pasta, and modified
entrées. Alert the server upon arrival. ▪
*www.martinellisonline.com*

**Mestizo** ✪$$$LD
*Leawood* ▪ *(913) 752-9025*
*5270 W 116th St* ▪ *Mexican* ▪ GF menu
available in-house includes items such as
jicama, cucumber & mango salad, plata-
nos rellenos, several types of tacos, ceviche, and market fish mojo de ajo. Confirm
the timeliness of this information before
dining in. ▪ *www.mestizoleawood.com*

## Morningstar's NY Pizza ✪★$LD
*Lawrence* ■ *(785) 856-6973*
*4931 6th St* ■ *Pizza* ■ GF pizza is available in the 12-inch size only. It can be ordered with any toppings, but the restaurant recommends avoiding the meatballs, as they contain bread. GF pizzas are cooked on a separate screen and sliced with a separate cutter. GF spaghetti is also available upon request.■ *morningstarsnypizza.com*

## Mulligan's Pub ★¢LD
*Wichita* ■ *(316) 636-2220*
*8343 E 32nd St N* ■ *Pub Food* ■ GF pizza is available. ■ *www.mulliganswichita.com*

## Newport Grill ✪$$$LD
*Wichita* ■ *(316) 636-9555*
*1900 N Rock Rd* ■ *Seafood & Steakhouse* ■ GF options include beef rumaki, jumbo lump crab cake, lobster cobb salad, seared ahi tuna, and black and blue filet. The restaurant cautions that while they take precautions, GF items are prepared in a kitchen that contains gluten. ■ *www.newportgrillwichita.com*

## Old Shawnee Pizza ★$LD
*Shawnee* ■ *(913) 631-5737*
*6000 Rogers Dr*
*Kansas City* ■ *(913) 677-1844*
*2422 S 34th St* ■ *Pizza* ■ GF pizza is available. The Shawnee location carries several sizes but the Kansas City location only carries mini size. As with all specialty items, call ahead to confirm availability. ■ *www.theshawneepizza.com*

## Old Town Pizza ★$$LD
*Overland Park* ■ *(913) 897-9242*
*14850 Metcalf Ave* ■ *Pizza* ■ GF pizza is available in 6" and 12". Options include Mexican, chicken alfredo and Southwest BBQ chicken pizzas. Additional toppings are listed on the website. Crust is made in a separate facility and delivered to restaurant. ■ *www.kcoldtownpizza.com*

## Other Place, The ★$$LD
*Olathe* ■ *(913) 791-9500*
*16590 W 135th*
*Overland Park* ■ *(913) 652-9494*
*7324 W 80th* ■ *Pizza* ■ GF pizza crust available upon request. ■ *theotherplace.com*

## P.F. Chang's China Bistro ✪★📖
*Wichita* ■ *(316) 634-2211*
*1401 Waterfront Pkwy*

## Panda Kitchen ¢LD
*Hillsboro* ■ *(620) 947-2080*
*107 W Grand Ave* ■ *Chinese* ■ The restaurant reports that their stir frys can be made GF, but adds that they do not carry GF soy sauce. Alert the server upon arrival.

## Paulo & Bill ✪$$$LD
*Shawnee* ■ *(913) 962-9900*
*16501 Midland Dr* ■ *American* ■ Naturally GF dishes are marked on the menu. These dishes include tilapia salad, grilled chicken breast, steak Diane, pecan crusted salmon, and more. Confirm the timeliness of this information before dining in. ■ *www.pauloandbill.com*

## Pei Wei Asian Diner ✪📖
*Olathe* ■ *(913) 254-7283*
*15141 W 119th St*
*Overland Park* ■ *(913) 693-9777*
*9222 Metcalf Ave*
*Wichita* ■ *(316) 729-7285*
*2441 N Maize Rd*

## Pig In! Pig Out! BBQ ¢LD
*Wichita* ■ *(316) 263-7474*
*1003 E 13th St* ■ *Barbeque* ■ According to the restaurant, everything on the menu is GF EXCEPT for the potato salad, pasta salad, and bread. Confirm the timeliness of this information before dining in. ■ *www.piginpigoutbbq.com*

## Pizza Ranch ✪📖
*Emporia* ■ *(620) 343-8646*
*3000 W 18th Ave*

**Pizza Shoppe**                                              ★ 📖
*Shawnee* ▪ *(913) 422-9600*
*22014 W 66th St*
*Overland Park* ▪ *(913) 341-1491*
*8915 Santa Fe Dr*
*Olathe* ▪ *(913) 397-7117*
*12750 Pflumm Rd*
*Olathe* ▪ *(913) 393-1234*
*1805 S Ridgeview Rd*
*Olathe* ▪ *(913) 764-4555*
*736 W Park St*
*Overland Park* ▪ *(913) 402-4442*
*7908 W 151st St*

**Pizza West**                                                   $LD
*Shawnee* ▪ *(913) 422-9010*
*5436 Roberts St* ▪ *Pizza* ▪ The restaurant
reports that while they do not carry GF
pizza, guests can bring in their own GF
crusts and they will make any pizza with it.
▪ *www.gopizzawest.com*

**Purple Swirl Frozen Yogurt**                                  ¢$
*Manhattan* ▪ *(785) 320-2766*
*1346 Westloop Pl* ▪ *Ice Cream* ▪ Nutrition chart indicates which flavors contain
wheat. ▪ *www.purpleswirlmanhattan.com*

**Romano's Macaroni Grill**                                  ✪★📖
*Overland Park* ▪ *(913) 341-4333*
*9292 Metcalf Ave*

**Rosati's Pizza**                                            ★📖
*Overland Park* ▪ *(913) 696-0400*
*9928 College Blvd*

**RowHouse Restaurant**                                    ★$$$$D
*Topeka* ▪ *(785) 235-1700*
*515 SW Van Buren St* ▪ *American* ▪ GF
beer is available. Although the menu
changes weekly, flourless chocolate cake
and crème brûlée are often available. ▪
*www.rowhouserestaurant.net*

**Rub Bar-B-Que, The**                                        ¢LD
*Olathe* ▪ *(913) 894-1820*
*10512 S Ridgeview Rd* ▪ *Barbeque* ▪ Team
member Dan reports that most menu items
are GF, and suggests asking a server for
more specific options upon arrival. The rub
they use on their meats does not contain

gluten, so any plain meats will be GF. ▪
*www.therubbarbque.com*

**Salty Iguana, The**                                        ✪$BLD
*Lawrence* ▪ *(785) 312-8100*
*4931 W 6th St*
*Olathe* ▪ *(913) 310-9003*
*10478 S Ridgeview Rd*
*Overland Park* ▪ *(913) 402-0200*
*8420 W 135th St*
*Prairie Village* ▪ *(913) 381-3888*
*8228 Mission Rd* ▪ *Mexican* ▪ GF menu
available online and in-house. Some items
included are smokin' nachos, Mexican chili
with corn tortillas, tacos, and enchiladas.
The GF menu also indicates modifications
that must be made to make dishes GF.
Be sure to alert the server upon arrival. ▪
*www.saltyiguana.net*

**Sammy's Pizza and Pub**                                    ★$LD
*Leawood* ▪ *(913) 491-0901*
*13164 State Line Rd* ▪ *Pizza* ▪ GF pizza is
available with any toppings for $3 extra. ▪
*www.sammyspizzaandpub.com*

**Shorty Smalls**                                            📖
*Wichita* ▪ *(316) 773-0900*
*12111 W Maple St*

**Smoke Hoss**                                               ★$BLD
*Meade* ▪ *(620) 873-5101*
*808 W Carthage* ▪ *American* ▪ All items
can be served on a GF corn tortilla, lettuce
wrap, or GF bread. ▪ *www.smokehoss.com*

**Smokey Racks BBQ**                                         ¢LD
*Pittsburg* ▪ *(620) 875-3045*
*912 W 4th St* ▪ *Barbeque* ▪ Restaurant reports that most of their sauces are naturally
GF and their meats are served directly off
the grill. Alert the server upon arrival.

**Spencer Browne's Coffee House**
★ ¢BLD
*Liberal* ▪ *(620) 626-5556*
*7 Village Plaza* ▪ *Café* ▪ GF bread is available for any sandwich. Options include
breakfast sandwiches, hot paninis and bistro
sandwiches. Alert the server upon arrival.

## Spin Pizza ★$$LD
*Olathe* ▪ (913) 764-7746
*14230 W 119th St*
*Lenexa* ▪ (913) 438-7746
*9474 Renner Blvd*
*Overland Park* ▪ (913) 451-7746
*6541 W 119th St* ▪ *Pizza* ▪ All of their pizzas are available GF except those with meatballs. GF salads are also available, just ask for no croutons as they are not GF. Procedures to prevent CC are in place and include using separate prep surfaces and utensils and baking on separate pans. However, the restaurant cautions that they are not a GF environment. ▪ *www.spinpizza.com*

## Story $$$LD
*Prairie Village* ▪ (913) 236-9955
*3931 W 69th Terr* ▪ *American* ▪ Team member Jeremy reports that some menu items can be altered to be GF, and they are also willing to work with guests to come up with a custom dish that will meet their needs. ▪ *www.storykc.com*

## Sweet Designs Cakery ★$S
*Pittsburg* ▪ (620) 231-2253
*311 N Broadway St* ▪ *Bakery* ▪ Non-dedicated GF bakery that bakes GF cakes, cupcakes, cookies, and cheesecakes. Separate utensils are used in the preparation of all GF items. Special orders should be made 2 weeks in advance. ▪ *sweetdesignscakery.com*

## Sweet Perfection Bakery ★¢S
*Olathe* ▪ (913) 523-6908
*1497 E 151st St* ▪ *Bakery* ▪ Non-dedicated GF bakery offering GF cakes, cookies, cream pies, cupcakes, and brownies by special order. ▪ *sweetperfection4u.com*

## Tucson's $$LD
*Salina* ▪ (785) 820-9595
*2750 S 9th St* ▪ *Steakhouse* ▪ The restaurant reports that all of their steaks are GF if ordered without seasoning, and notes that they are "currently working on" a GF menu. Alert the server upon arrival. ▪ *www.tucsonssteakhouse.com*

## TupTim Thai $LD
*Topeka* ▪ (785) 266-2299
*2949 S Kansas Ave* ▪ *Thai* ▪ The restaurant reports that most dishes can be made GF by omitting certain ingredients. Consult with your server about any specific dish and they will ask the kitchen what modifications need to be made. No GF menu. ▪ *www.tuptimthaitopeka.com*

## Unforked ✪$LD
*Overland Park* ▪ (913) 661-9887
*7337 W 119th St* ▪ *American* ▪ GF items marked on the regular menu include burgers on GF buns and tacos. ▪ *www.unforked.com*

## Urban Table ★$LD
*Prairie Village* ▪ (913) 948-6900
*8232 Mission Rd* ▪ *Modern American* ▪ GF bread is available. The restaurant reports that almost any item on the menu can be made GF using the GF bread. Consult your server, who will point out the best options. ▪ *www.urbantablekc.com*

## Via's Pizzeria ★$LD
*Topeka* ▪ (785) 215-8421
*738 SW Gage Blvd* ▪ *Pizza* ▪ GF pizza is available in 8" and 10" sizes, as well as GF beer. ▪ *www.viaspizzeria.com*

## When Pigs Fly Barbecue ¢LD
*Wichita* ▪ (316) 295-2150
*7011 W Central Ave* ▪ *Barbeque* ▪ Manager states that "everything is literally GF except for the bread." He also notes that GF customers come in daily. Confirm the timeliness of this information before dining in. ▪ *whenpigsflywichita.com*

## Wichita Pizza Company ★$LD
*Wichita* ▪ (316) 425-1900
*1520 S Webb Rd* ▪ *Pizza* ▪ GF pizza is available. ▪ *www.wichitapizzacompany.com*

### Wilders on Main Bistro    ✪$$BLD
*Hutchinson* ▪ (620) 259-6559
*2609 N Main St* ▪ *American* ▪ GF items
marked on the regular menu include
risotto, roasted chicken, and grilled
salmon. Confirm the timeliness of
this information before dining in. ▪
*www.wildersonmain.com*

### Yard House    ✪📖
*Kansas City* ▪ (913) 788-4500
*1863 Village W Pkwy*

### Zio's    ✪📖
*Olathe* ▪ (913) 782-2225
*11981 S Strang Line Rd*

# KENTUCKY

## LOUISVILLE

### 32 Degrees Yogurt Bar    📖
*Louisville* ▪ (502) 423-0371
*4005 Summit Plaza Dr*

### Annie May's Sweet Café    $BLD
*Louisville* ▪ (502) 384-2667
*3100 Frankfort Ave* ▪ *Bakery & Café* ▪
Dedicated GF bakery & café serving a
variety of baked goods, breakfast items,
sandwiches, ice cream, and more. GF box
lunches are also available for pickup or
delivery. ▪ *www.anniemayssweetcafe.com*

### Avalon    ★$$LD
*Louisville* ▪ (502) 454-5336
*1314 Bardstown Rd* ▪ *American* ▪ Chef
Larry reports that several menu items, such
as Thai meatballs, pork tacos, and deviled
eggs, are naturally GF. Confirm the timeliness of this information before dining in.
He recommends reservations noting GF,
and adds that all staff members are "pretty
comfortable" with the GF diet. GF pasta is
available for substitution for any pasta dish.
▪ *www.avalonfresh.com*

### Bazo's Fresh Mexican Grill    ★₵LD
*Louisville* ▪ (502) 899-9600
*4014 Dutchmans Ln*
*Louisville* ▪ (502) 899-9746
*1907-C S Fourth St*
*Louisville* ▪ (502) 805-1818
*428 W Market St* ▪ *Mexican* ▪ Restaurant
reports that most of the menu is GF or can
easily be modified to be GF. Most items
made with flour tortillas can be substituted
with corn. Alert a server, who can point out
which items to avoid. ▪ *www.bazosgrill.com*

### BJ's Restaurant and Brewhouse ✪★📖
*Louisville* ▪ (502) 326-3850
*7900 Shelbyville Rd*

### Bonefish Grill    ✪📖
*Louisville* ▪ (502) 412-4666
*657 S Hurstbourne Pkwy*

### Bristol Bar & Grille    ✪$$LD
*Louisville* ▪ (502) 456-1702
*1321 Bardstown Rd*
*Louisville* ▪ (502) 582-1995
*614 W Main St*
*Louisville* ▪ (502) 426-0627
*300 N Hurstbourne Pwy* ▪ *American* ▪
Customer service agent Emilie reports that
all locations offer GF menu choices. She
recommends alerting a manager upon arrival. ▪ *www.bristolbarandgrille.com*

### Buca di Beppo    ✪📖
*Louisville* ▪ (502) 493-2426
*2051 S Hurstbourne Pkwy*

### Bucceto's Smiling Teeth    ★📖
*Lousville* ▪ (502) 721-0170
*4600 Shelbyville Rd*

### Carrabba's Italian Grill    ✪📖
*Louisville* ▪ (502) 412-2218
*617 S Hurstbourne Pkwy*

### Equus Restaurant    ★$$$D
*Louisville* ▪ (502) 897-9721
*122 Sears Ave* ▪ *American* ▪ Manager
Elizabeth reports that GF diners are
"absolutely" welcome, and the kitchen
staff is "well aware" of GF restrictions.
GF pasta is available. Most menu items

can be modified to be GF, so calling in advance with specifications is advised. ▪ www.equusrestaurant.com

## Genghis Grill    📖
Louisville ▪ (502) 426-4945
4002 Towne Center Dr

## Hard Rock Café    ✪📖
Louisville ▪ (502) 568-2202
424 S 4th St

## Hometown Pizza    ✪★$LD
Louisville ▪ (502) 245-4555
11804 Shelbyville Rd
Louisville ▪ (502) 363-4880
4041 Preston Hwy ▪ Pizza ▪ GF small pizza is available. Restaurant reports that GF pizza crusts are individually wrapped and prepared using dedicated utensils. ▪ www.hometownpizza.com

## J. Gumbo's    ★📖
Louisville ▪ (502) 896-4046
2109 Frankfort Ave
Louisville ▪ (502) 425-0096
531 Lyndon Ln
Louisville ▪ (502) 589-9255
416 S 4th St
Louisville ▪ (502) 493-4720
8603 Citadel Wy
Louisville ▪ (502) 690-8080
3017 Poplar Level Rd

## Jason's Deli    ✪📖
Louisville ▪ (502) 412-4101
410 N Hurstbourne Pkwy
Louisville ▪ (502) 896-0150
4600 Shelbyville Rd
Louisville ▪ (502) 493-4130
1975 S Hurstbourne Pkwy

## Jersey Mike's    📖
Louisville ▪ (502) 499-9830
9156 Taylorsville Rd
Louisville ▪ (502) 244-1991
10266 Shelbyville Rd
Louisville ▪ (502) 425-1025
10521 Fischer Park Dr

## Joe's Crab Shack    ✪📖
Louisville ▪ (502) 568-1171
131 River Rd

## Johnny Brusco's New York Style Pizza    ★📖
Louisville ▪ (502) 749-8400
10600 Meeting St

## Limestone Restaurant    $$$LD
Louisville ▪ (502) 426-7477
10001 Forest Green Blvd ▪ Southern ▪ Manager Monty reports that they serve GF guests "pretty frequently," and even some of their regular customers are GF. He notes that all staff members are trained on the GF diet, and servers can indicate GF menu items. Reservations noting GF are recommended. Call ahead to confirm timeliness of information. ▪ www.limestonerestaurant.com

## Lynn's Paradise Café    $BLD
Louisville ▪ (502) 583-3447
984 Barret Ave ▪ American ▪ Chef Jeremy reports that they serve GF diners "really frequently." He adds that "most of the dishes" can be prepared GF, and he recommends that GF diners come in during less busy hours. Alert a server upon arrival. ▪ www.lynnsparadisecafe.com

## Martini's Italian Bistro    ✪★$LD
Louisville ▪ (502) 394-9797
4021 Summit Plaza Dr ▪ Italian ▪ GF pizza and pasta are available. GF pasta can be used as substitution in most pasta dishes. The restaurant also notes that they can work with customers to create other GF options from the menu. ▪ www.martinilouisville.com

## Melting Pot, The    ✪📖
Louisville ▪ (502) 491-3125
2045 S Hurstbourne Pkwy

## Mitchell's Fish Market    ✪📖
Louisville ▪ (502) 412-1818
4031 Summit Plaza Dr

## Morton's Steakhouse  ✪📖
*Louisville* ▪ *(502) 584-0421*
*626 W Main St*

## North End Café  ✪★$$$BLD
*Louisville* ▪ *(502) 896-8770*
*1722 Frankfort Ave*
*Louisville* ▪ *(502) 690-4161*
*2116 Bardstown Rd* ▪ *Spanish* ▪ GF menu available in house includes items such as scallops & grits, grilled flat iron steak, curry satay, and more. GF cornmeal pancakes are available for breakfast. Confirm the timeliness of this information before dining in. ▪ *www.northendcafe.com*

## O'Charley's  📖
*Louisville* ▪ *(502) 339-2264*
*10641 Fischer Park Rd*
*Louisville* ▪ *(502) 491-8372*
*1901 S Hurstbourne Ln*
*Louisville* ▪ *(502) 968-8996*
*4801 Outer Loop*
*Louisville* ▪ *(502) 899-9430*
*962 Breckenridge Ln*

## Old Spaghetti Factory, The  ✪★📖
*Louisville* ▪ *(502) 581-1070*
*235 W Market St*

## P.F. Chang's China Bistro  ✪★📖
*Louisville* ▪ *(502) 327-7707*
*9120 Shelbyville Rd*

## Porcini  $$$D
*Louisville* ▪ *(502) 894-8686*
*2730 Frankfort Ave* ▪ *Italian* ▪ All the "pranzo" items on the menu are or can be made GF. ▪ *www.porcinilouisville.com*

## Proof on Main  $$BLD
*Louisville* ▪ *(502) 217-6360*
*702 W Main St* ▪ *Modern American* ▪ Manager Carter reports that all staff members are "very familiar" with special diets, and they are particularly trained on the GF diet. He recommends reservations noting GF so that the server is notified in advance. The only things that cannot be made GF are their fried items because they do not have dedicated fryers. ▪ *www.proofonmain.com*

## Puccini's Smiling Teeth  ✪★📖
*Louisville* ▪ *(502) 721-0170*
*4600 Shelbyville Rd #101*

## Ramsi's Café on the World  ★$$LD
*Louisville* ▪ *(502) 451-0700*
*1293 Bardstown Rd* ▪ *Global* ▪ Restaurant reports that they accommodate special diets "on a daily basis." In store menu items that are GF are marked with a sign. Server Craig says making a reservation in advance is preferred. Confirm the timeliness of this information before dining in. All staff members are trained on the GF diet. Alert a server, who will notify the kitchen. GF bread is also available. ▪ *www.ramsiscafe.com*

## Romano's Macaroni Grill  ✪★📖
*Louisville* ▪ *(502) 423-9220*
*401 S Hurstbourne Pkwy*

## Ruth's Chris Steak House  ✪📖
*Louisville* ▪ *(502) 479-0026*
*6100 Dutchmans Ln*

## Shane's Rib Shack  ✪📖
*Louisville* ▪ *(502) 429-3907*
*2420 Lime Kiln Ln Ste G*

## Smokey Bones  📖
*Louisville* ▪ *(502) 491-7570*
*2525 Hurstbourne Gem Ln*

## Sweet Surrender Dessert Café  ✪★₡S
*Louisville* ▪ *(502) 899-2008*
*1804 Frankfort Ave* ▪ *Dessert* ▪ Non-dedicated bakery offering several GF items, including mocha concord cake, cheesecake with pecan crust, peanut butter chocolate chip cookies and more. Restaurant recommends giving advance notice of 48 hours. ▪ *www.sweetsurrenderdessertcafe.com*

## Winston's Restaurant  $$$LD
*Louisville* ▪ *(502) 456-0980*
*3101 Bardstown Rd* ▪ *Modern American* ▪ Manager Kevin reports that the restaurant is "more than able" to accommodate GF diners. He adds that the chef is very GF

aware. Reservations noting GF are highly recommended. According to manager, precautions are taken" to help minimize CC chances. ▪ *www.sullivan.edu/winstons*

### Yang Kee Noodle　　　　✪★₵LD
*Louisville* ▪ *(502) 426-0800*
*7900 Shelbyville Rd* ▪ *Asian* ▪ GF menu online lists items that can be prepared GF. These include lettuce wraps, classic pad thai, kung pow, and more. GF soy sauce is also available. Be sure to specify that when ordering from the GF menu, as modifications are required to make the dishes GF. ▪ *www.yangkeenoodle.com*

# KENTUCKY

## ALL OTHER CITIES

### Abuelo's　　　　　　　　✪📖
*Crestview Hills* ▪ *(859) 344-1344*
*2833 Dixie Hwy*
*Lexington* ▪ *(859) 971-0922*
*3395 Nicholasville Rd*

### Argentine Bistro　　　　✪$$LD
*Crestview Hills* ▪ *(859) 426-1042*
*2875 Town Center Blvd* ▪ *American* ▪ GF items include chimichurri chicken, fennel dusted salmon, honey & thyme marinated pork loin, ropa vieja, and more. Confirm the timeliness of this information before dining in. ▪ *www.argentinebistro.com*

### Bella Notte　　　　　✪★$LD
*Lexington* ▪ *(859) 245-1789*
*3715 Nicholasville Rd* ▪ *Italian* ▪ GF menu includes spicy tomato basil soup, salmon oreganato, the petite Black Angus sampler, and other items. GF pasta is available, and there are a variety of pasta dishes on the GF menu. For dessert, they offer crème brûlée and vanilla cream custard. ▪ *www.bellalexington.com*

### Bonefish Grill　　　　　✪📖
*Lexington* ▪ *(859) 233-3474*
*2341 Sir Barton Wy*
*Crescent Springs* ▪ *(859) 426-8666*
*588 Buttermilk Pike*

### Bristol Bar & Grille　　　✪$$LD
*Prospect* ▪ *(502) 292-2585*
*6051 Timber Ridge Dr* ▪ *American* ▪ Customer service agent Emilie reports that all locations offer GF menu choices. She recommends alerting a manager upon arrival. ▪ *www.bristolbarandgrille.com*

### Bucceto's Smiling Teeth　　★📖
*Lexington* ▪ *(859) 223-1588*
*3801 Dylan Pl*
*Lexington* ▪ *(859) 223-1588*
*833 Chevy Chase Pl*
*Lexington* ▪ *(859) 219-0101*
*3191 Beaumont Ctre Cir*

### Captain's Quarters　　　✪$$LD
*Prospect* ▪ *(502) 228-1651*
*5700 Captains Quarters Rd* ▪ *American* ▪ Manager Matt reports that the restaurant accommodates GF diners "at least once a day." He notes that almost every menu item can be modified to be GF. But there is a separate GF menu available on request. Reservations noting GF are recommended and once informed, the kitchen staff will used all new utensils to help minimize CC. ▪ *www.cqriverside.com*

### Carino's Italian　　　　　✪📖
*Frankfort* ▪ *(502) 223-4401*
*1303 US Highway 127 S*
*Lexington* ▪ *(859) 245-0091*
*135 Rojay Dr*
*Lexington* ▪ *(859) 264-1049*
*2333 Sir Barton Wy*

### Carrabba's Italian Grill　　✪📖
*Crestview Hills* ▪ *(859) 344-6163*
*2899 Dixie Hwy*
*Lexington* ▪ *(859) 264-8395*
*1881 Plaudit Pl*

## Claddagh Irish Pub 📖
Newport ▪ (859) 581-8888
1 Levee Wy

## Cosi ✪📖
Lexington ▪ (859) 263-1045
1890 Star Shoot Pkwy
Lexington ▪ (859) 263-1045
640 Convention Ctr
Lexington ▪ (859) 313-6333
One Saint Joseph Dr

## Don Pablo's ✪📖
Newport ▪ (859) 261-7100
401 Riverboat Row

## First Watch - The Daytime Café ✪📖
Covington ▪ (859) 491-0869
50 E Rivercenter Blvd
Crestview Hills ▪ (859) 341-0222
2762 Town Center Blvd
Lexington ▪ (859) 899-3447
3071 Richmond Rd

## Hometown Pizza ✪★$LD
Bedford ▪ (502) 255-9933
18 Alexander Ave
Bloomfield ▪ (502) 252-7208
205 Taylorsville Rd
Carrollton ▪ (502) 732-4256
2352 US Highway 227
Crestwood ▪ (502) 241-0111
6900 Potts Rd
Eminence ▪ (502) 845-5006
210 E Broadway St
Hodgenville ▪ (270) 358-8844
105 Lincoln Dr
La Grange ▪ (502) 222-4444
105 E Adams St
Mount Washington ▪ (502) 538-6633
11230 Highway 44 E
Owenton ▪ (502) 484-4444
80-199 Main St
Shelbyville ▪ (502) 633-7900
1745 Midland Trl
Taylorsville ▪ (502) 477-1111
91 Settlers Center Rd
Warsaw ▪ (859) 567-4451
204 Riverside Dr
Coxs Creek ▪ (502) 348-2233

109 Blakenrod Blvd ▪ Pizza ▪ GF small pizza is available. Restaurant reports that GF pizza crusts are individually wrapped and prepared using dedicated utensils. ▪ www.hometownpizza.com

## I Ching Asian Café ✪★₵LD
Lexington ▪ (859) 543-2742
2312 Sir Barton Wy ▪ Asian ▪ GF menu includes crispy shrimp & calamari, drunken noodles, Singapore tomato curry, sweet and sour chicken or shrimp, and more. GF soy sauce is available on request. Most items are prepared with dedicated GF utensils, but be sure to alert server upon arrival. ▪ www.ichingcafe.com

## J. Gumbo's ★📖
Cold Spring ▪ (859) 360-2695
58 Martha Layne Collins Blvd
Somerset ▪ (740) 368-9494
95 S Main St

## Jersey Mike's 📖
Hopkinsville ▪ (270) 886-2060
2413 Ft. Campbell Blvd
Florence ▪ (859) 746-1222
310 Mt Zion Rd
Newport ▪ (859) 581-5551
86 B Carothers Rd
Oak Grove ▪ (270) 640-3905
16472 Fort Campbell Blvd

## Joe's Crab Shack ✪📖
Bellevue ▪ (859) 581-6333
25 Fairfield Ave

## LaRosa's Pizzeria ★📖
Alexandria ▪ (513) 347-1111
8031 Alexandria Pike

## Melting Pot, The ✪📖
Lexington ▪ (859) 254-6358
152 W Tiverton Wy

## Mitchell's Fish Market ✪★📖
Newport ▪ (859) 291-7454
1 Levee Wy

## Molly Shannon's Irish Pub ✪★$LD
Bowling Green ▪ (270) 781-1473
871 Broadway Ave ▪ Irish ▪ Saturday

brunch is available. All pizzas are available with GF crust. ▪ *www.mollyshannons.com*

### O'Charley's    📖
*Ashalnd* ▪ *(606) 326-0159*
*461 Riverhill Dr*
*Bowling Green* ▪ *(270) 781-0806*
*2717 Scottsville Rd*
*Cold Spring* ▪ *(859) 442-9270*
*100 Cross Roads Dr*
*Danville* ▪ *(859) 936-8040*
*1560 Hustonville Rd*
*Elizabethtown* ▪ *(270) 763-9075*
*1629 N Dixie Hwy*
*Florence* ▪ *(859) 525-6622*
*7414 Turfway Rd*
*Frankfort* ▪ *(502) 223-3282*
*325 Leonard Wood Rd*
*Georgetown* ▪ *(502) 868-9165*
*100 Osbourne Wy*
*Hopkinsville* ▪ *(270) 885-3035*
*4223 Fort Campbell Blvd*
*Lexington* ▪ *(859) 278-6984*
*2099 Harrodsburg Rd*
*Lexington* ▪ *(859) 266-8640*
*2895 Richmond Rd*
*Lexington* ▪ *(859) 278-4164*
*2270 Nicholasville Rd*
*Owensboro* ▪ *(270) 686-8780*
*5205 Frederica St*
*Paducah* ▪ *(270) 442-7770*
*3916 Hinkleville Rd*
*Richmond* ▪ *(859) 624-8868*
*815 Eastern Bypass*
*Shively* ▪ *(502) 447-9203*
*4404 Dixie Hwy*

### P.F. Chang's China Bistro    ✪★📖
*Lexington* ▪ *(859) 271-1165*
*3405 Nicholasville Rd*

### Pasta House Co., The    ✪★📖
*Paducah* ▪ *(270) 575-1997*
*451 Jordan Dr*

### Puccini's Smiling Teeth    ✪★📖
*Lexington* ▪ *(859) 269-0404*
*833 Chevy Chase Pl*
*Lexington* ▪ *(859) 219-0101*
*3191 Beaumont Centre Circle #110*

### Smokey Bones    📖
*Bowling Green* ▪ *(270) 782-1888*
*2450 Scottsville Rd*
*Florence* ▪ *(859) 371-5425*
*7848 Mall Rd*

### Sweet Cece's    📖
*Bowling Green* ▪ *(270) 782-5520*
*760 Campbell Ln*
*Paducah* ▪ *(270) 415-0409*
*2929 James Sanders Blvd*

### Ted's Montana Grill    ✪📖
*Lexington* ▪ *(859) 263-5228*
*2304 Sir Barton Wy*

### Village Pub, The    ★₵S
*Covington* ▪ *(859) 431-5552*
*619 Main St* ▪ *Pub Food* ▪ GF beer is available. Manager Kurt notes that "numerous" diners order the GF beer. ▪ *www.mainstrassevillagepub.com*

# LOUISIANA

### Adobe Cantina and Salsa    ✪★$LD
*Hammond* ▪ *(985) 419-0027*
*1905 W Thomas St, Seville Plaza* ▪ *Mexican* ▪ Manager reports that they can accommodate GF diners. Some fish and steak dishes are naturally GF, while others can be modified to be GF. Confirm the timeliness of this information before dining in. Located in Seville Plaza. ▪ *www.carretarestaurant.com*

### Bayona    ★$$$LD
*New Orleans* ▪ *(504) 525-4455*
*430 Dauphine St* ▪ *American* ▪ The restaurant reports that while there is no GF menu, they do accommodate GF requests regularly. ▪ *www.bayona.com*

## BJ's Restaurant and Brewhouse ✪★📖
*Baton Rouge* ■ *(225) 766-4300*
*6401 Bluebonnet Blvd*

## Bonefish Grill ✪📖
*Baton Rouge* ■ *(225) 216-1191*
*7415 Corporate Blvd*
*Lafayette* ■ *(337) 981-0714*
*1912 Kaliste Saloom Rd*
*Metairie* ■ *(504) 780-9964*
*4848 Veterans Memorial Blvd*

## Bubba Gump Shrimp Co. ✪📖
*New Orleans* ■ *(504) 522-5800*
*429 Decatur St*

## Café Amelie ★$$LD
*New Orleans* ■ *(504) 412-8965*
*912 Royal St* ■ *American* ■ Owner states
the kitchen is "more than happy to make
any changes" to serve GF diners. Alert the
server upon arrival. ■ *www.cafeamelie.com*

## Cantina Laredo 📖
*Shreveport* ■ *(318) 798-6363*
*6535 Youree Dr*

## Carino's Italian ✪📖
*Lafayette* ■ *(337) 988-7535*
*4321 Ambassador Caffery Pkwy*
*Lake Charles* ■ *(337) 474-4741*
*2638 Derek Dr*
*Alexandria* ■ *(318) 767-5942*
*3213 N Macarthur Dr*

## Carrabba's Italian Grill ✪📖
*Baton Rouge* ■ *(225) 925-9999*
*7275 Corporate Blvd*
*Lafayette* ■ *(337) 981-6669*
*2010 Kaliste Saloom Rd*
*Shreveport* ■ *(318) 798-6504*
*1706 E 70th St*

## Chophouse New Orleans ✪★$$$D
*New Orleans* ■ *(504) 522-7902*
*322 Magazine St* ■ *Steakhouse* ■ All steak
and chicken entrées are GF. Most fish
entrées are GF as well, but ask the server
before ordering to make sure no flour is
used to prepare it. Confirm the timeliness
of this information before dining in. ■
*www.chophousenola.com*

## Commander's Palace ★$$$$LD
*New Orleans* ■ *(504) 899-8221*
*1403 Washington Ave* ■ *American* ■ The
restaurant reports that GF diners come
in regularly. All meals are made to order,
so GF requests are not difficult to accommodate. Reservations noting GF are
recommended, so that the kitchen can
prepare in advance. Upon arrival, alert a
server or ask to speak with a manager. ■
*www.commanderspalace.com*

## Coquette Bistro and Wine Bar ★$$$LD
*New Orleans* ■ *(504) 265-0421*
*2800 Magazine St* ■ *European* ■ Menu
changes daily, so there will not always
be a GF option on the regular menu,
but the restaurant staff reports that the
kitchen is really good about accommodating diners with dietary restrictions
and that they will always do their best to
work something out for their guests. ■
*www.coquette-nola.comeat.html*

## Dante's Kitchen ★$$$LD
*New Orleans* ■ *(504) 861-3121*
*736 Dante St* ■ *American* ■ No GF menu
available but manager states they are
more than willing to accommodate all
customers and their dietary needs. ■
*danteskitchen.com*

## Deanie's Seafood ✪$$LD
*New Orleans* ■ *(504) 581-1316*
*841 Iberville St*
*Metairie* ■ *(504) 831-4141*
*1713 Lake Ave* ■ *Seafood* ■ GF menu
includes items like broiled crawfish tails,
shrimp remoulade, grilled chicken breast,
broiled catfish dinner, and more. For dessert, they offer a nectar soda float and an
ice cream sundae. ■ *www.deanies.com*

## Fleming's Prime Steakhouse & Wine Bar ✪📖
*Baton Rouge* ■ *(225) 925-2710*
*7321 Corporate Blvd*

## Fox and Hound Pub & Grille 📖
*Baton Rouge* ■ *(225) 926-1444*
*5246 Corporate Blvd*

New Orleans · (504) 731-6000
1200 S Clearview Pkwy

**Genghis Grill** &#128214;
Shreveport · (318) 532-6604
7435 Youree Dr

**Hard Rock Café** &#9733;&#128214;
New Orleans · (504) 529-5617
125 Bourbon St

**Jason's Deli** &#9733;&#128214;
Lafayette · (337) 216-0194
149 Arnould Blvd
Baton Rouge · (225) 293-9099
6725 Siegen Ln
Baton Rouge · (225) 926-7788
2531 Citiplace Ct
Shreveport · (318) 861-6952
5808 Line Ave
Lake Charles · (337) 214-4096
3527 Ryan St

**Jersey Mike's** &#128214;
Shreveport · (318) 797-1470
7435 Youree Dr

**Joe's Crab Shack** &#9733;&#128214;
Baton Rouge · (225) 292-0802
7620 Andrea Dr
Bossier City · (318) 549-2332
635 Boardwalk Blvd

**La Thai** $$LD
New Orleans · (504) 899-8886
4938 Prytania St · Thai · The restaurant reports that many items can be made GF and suggests that guests ask a server to go over the menu with them. · www.lathaiuptown.com

**Lone Star Steakhouse & Saloon** &#9733;&#128214;
Baton Rouge · (225) 754-7827
1920 O'Neal Ln

**Margaritaville** &#9733;★&#128214;
New Orleans · (504) 592-2565
1104 Decatur St

**Mark Twain's Pizza Landing** ★$$LD
Metairie · (504) 832-8032
2035 Metairie Rd · Pizza · GF pizza is available with up to four top-

pings. Ask your server which toppings are GF. GF beer is also available. · www.marktwainspizza.com

**Meals From the Heart Café** ★¢BL
New Orleans · (504) 525-1953
1100 N Peters St · Café · GF pancakes & bread are available. GF options marked on the menu include omelets, sandwiches (made with GF bread), salads, and okra gumbo with brown rice. Confirm the timeliness of this information before dining in.

**Melting Pot, The** &#9733;&#128214;
Baton Rouge · (225) 928-5677
5294 Corporate Blvd
New Orleans · (504) 525-3225
1820 Saint Charles Ave

**Morton's Steakhouse** &#9733;&#128214;
New Orleans · (504) 566-0221
365 Canal St

**O'Charley's** &#128214;
Monroe · (318) 651-2034
4101 Pecanland Mall Dr
Lake Charles · (337) 478-9927
1780 W Prien Lake Rd
Lafayette · (337) 988-4563
4301 Ambassador Caffery Pkwy

**P.F. Chang's China Bistro** &#9733;★&#128214;
Baton Rouge · (225) 216-9044
7341 Corporate Blvd
Metairie · (504) 828-5288
3301 Veterans Memorial Blvd Ste 63

**Palace Café** &#9733;$$LD
New Orleans · (504) 523-1661
605 Canal St · Modern American · Extensive GF menu includes shrimp rémoulade, rotisserie chicken aux champignons, grilled gulf fish, crispy braised pork shank, a variety of salads, and more. · www.palacecafe.com

**Pei Wei Asian Diner** &#9733;&#128214;
Metairie · (504) 455-6280
4852 Veterans Mem Blvd

**Phil's Grill** &#9733;$LD
Metairie · (504) 324-9080
3020 Severn Ave

**Harahan** ▪ **(504) 305-1705**
*1640 Hickory Ave* ▪ *American* ▪ The Build
Your Own Burger menu has GF options
noted next to each specific item. GF
burgers can be served on a bed of lettuce, cabbage or spinach and guests can
choose from a variety of GF toppings. ▪
*www.phils-grill.com*

### Red Fish Grill                                    $$$LD
*New Orleans* ▪ *(504) 598-1200*
*115 Bourbon St* ▪ *American* ▪ The restaurant reports that while they do not have
a GF menu, they can create "flour-free"
items for customers with special dietary needs. Ask the server for details. ▪
*www.redfishgrill.com*

### Romano's Macaroni Grill            ✪★📖
*Mandeville* ▪ *(985) 727-1998*
*3410 Highway 190*
*Shreveport* ▪ *(318) 795-0491*
*7031 Youree Dr*

### Ruth's Chris Steak House            ✪📖
*Baton Rouge* ▪ *(225) 925-0163*
*4836 Constitution Ave*
*Lafayette* ▪ *(337) 237-6123*
*620 W Pinhook Rd*
*Metairie* ▪ *(504) 888-3600*
*3633 Veterans Blvd*
*New Orleans* ▪ *(504) 587-7099*
*525 Fulton St*

### Shane's Rib Shack                    ✪📖
*Marrero* ▪ *(504) 341-2226*
*1855 Barataria Blvd*

### Texas De Brazil Churrascaria         ★📖
*Baton Rouge* ▪ *(225) 766-5353*
*10155 Perkins Rowe*

### Truly Free Bakery and Deli          ₵BLD
*Baton Rouge* ▪ *(225) 383-3344*
*4321 Perkins Rd*
*Baton Rouge* ▪ *(225) 383-3344*
*4321 Perkins* ▪ *Bakery & Café* ▪ Dedicated GF bakery and deli offering a
wide variety of sandwiches, wraps, pizzas, burgers, soups, salads, and more. ▪
*www.trulyfreebakery.comdeli.php*

### Velvet Cactus, The                   ✪SLD
*New Orleans* ▪ *(504) 301-2083*
*6300 Argonne Blvd* ▪ *Mexican* ▪ GF
menu available in-house includes items
such as ceviche, a variety of salads, fajitas,
and tacos. Be sure to alert the server
when ordering from the GF menu so that
the kitchen can prepare accordingly. ▪
*www.thevelvetcactus.com*

# MAINE

### 40 Paper Italian Bistro & Bar      ✪★$$D
*Camden* ▪ *(207) 230-0111*
*40 Washington St* ▪ *Italian* ▪ GF and GF
optional items are marked on the regular menu, which changes often. Sample
items include kale & sausage soup, grilled
calamari, grilled hanger steak, grilled quail,
and more. GF pasta is available and can be
substituted into any pasta dish. Alert the
server upon arrival. ▪ *40paper.com*

### 98 Provence                        $$$$BL
*Ogunquit* ▪ *(207) 646-9898*
*262 Shore Rd* ▪ *French* ▪ Owner and Chef
Pierre reports that he is "very understanding" of GF diners, and the restaurant serves
them "more and more." He recommends
making reservations noting GF and alerting the server upon arrival. This should be
sufficient, as "everybody is aware" of the GF
diet. ▪ *www.98provence.com*

### AJ's Wood Grill Pizza              ★SLD
*Kittery* ▪ *(207) 439-9700*
*68 Wallingford Square* ▪ *Pizza* ▪ GF pizza,
sandwiches, desserts, and beer are available. GF pizza toppings are marked on
the menu. Several salads are also available
with GF dressing. Ask a server for details. ▪
*www.ajswoodgrillpizza.com*

## Bam Bam Bakery $S
*Portland* ▪ *(207) 899-4100*
*267 Commercial St* ▪ *Bakery* ▪ Bam
Bam Bakery offers 100% GF cupcakes, cakes, breads, and pies. ▪
*www.bambambakery.com*

## Bandaloop $$$D
*Kennebunkport* ▪ *(207) 967-4994*
*2 Dock Sq* ▪ *Modern American* ▪ Alert a
server upon arrival, as all staff members are
trained to handle special dietary needs. ▪
*www.bandaloop.biz*

## Becky's Diner $BLD
*Portland* ▪ *(207) 773-7070*
*390 Commercial St* ▪ *American* ▪ GF
bread is available for burgers and sandwiches. ▪ *www.beckysdiner.com*

## Bibo's Madd Apple Café $LD
*Portland* ▪ *(207) 774-9698*
*23 Forest Ave* ▪ *American* ▪ Owner Bill
reports that the restaurant serves GF diners
"all the time." He reports that the dinner
menu is 90% naturally GF because most
starches used are potatoes or risotto. ▪
*www.bibosportland.com*

## Bugaboo Creek Steak House ✪📖
*S Portland* ▪ *(207) 773-5400*
*264 Gorham Rd*
*Bangor* ▪ *(207) 945-5515*
*24 Bangor Mall Blvd*

## Café This Way ✪$$BD
*Bar Harbor* ▪ *(207) 288-4483*
*14-1/2 Mt. Desert St* ▪ *American* ▪ Items
that are naturally GF or can be made GF
upon request are indicated on menu. Items
include blackened scallops, fried brussels
sprouts, prosciutto wrapped asparagus,
tuna tartare, marinated cheese curds,
smoked duck breast pate, Brazilian flavored
shrimp, scallops or mussels, grilled tuna,
pork flat iron, steamed Maine lobster,
Spanish style chicken, grilled lamb sirloin, bento plate, southwest shepherd's pie
and Moroccan flavored stuffed butternut
squash. ▪ *www.cafethisway.com*

## David's $$$LD
*Portland* ▪ *(207) 773-4340*
*22 Monument Sq* ▪ *Modern American* ▪
The restaurant reports that there are "a ton"
of GF options. The manager adds that they
accommodate GF diners "all the time," and
recommends reservations noting GF. ▪
*www.davidsrestaurant.com*

## DiMillo's on the Water ✪$$$LD
*Portland* ▪ *(207) 772-2216*
*25 Long Wharf* ▪ *Seafood* ▪ GF menu
includes steamed Maine clams, jumbo
shrimp, spinach salad, lobsters steamed
in the shell, grilled salmon, scallops with
no crumbs, and the Tuscan ribeye. ▪
*www.dimillos.com*

## Duffy's Tavern & Grill ✪★$LD
*Kennebunk* ▪ *(207) 985-0050*
*4 Main St* ▪ *American* ▪ GF menu includes
shrimp scampi, grilled chicken sandwich
on GF bread, GF chicken parmesan, and
more. GF pizza, bread, beer and cider are
available. The restaurant recommends
consulting the manager before placing an
order. ▪ *www.duffyskennebunk.com*

## Federal Jack's Restaurant & Pub ✪$$LD
*Kennebunk* ▪ *(207) 967-4322*
*8 Western Ave* ▪ *American* ▪ Extensive
GF menu includes mussels, clam chowder,
variety of salads, sandwiches & burgers
served on GF buns, GF pizza, haddock
dinner, chicken scaloppini, and vegetable
stir fry. Flourless chocolate cake, crème
caramel, fondue, and floats are available for
dessert. ▪ *www.federaljacks.com*

## Flatbread Pizza Company ★📖
*Portland* ▪ *(207) 772-8777*
*72 Commercial St*

## Francesca's Restaurant $LD
*Hallowell* ▪ *(207) 622-1110*
*234 Water St* ▪ *Italian* ▪ Francesca's offers
various GF meat dishes including chicken
parmesan, and countless GF pasta options.
▪ *francescas-restaurant.com*

## Frontier Café ☼$LD
*Brunswick* ▪ (207) 725-5222
*14 Maine St* ▪ *Global* ▪ Restaurant reports that its menu has several naturally GF options, such as the fish tacos, steak frites, and curried mussels. Items that are naturally GF are indicated by a "G". ▪ *www.explorefrontier.com*

## Green Elephant Vegetarian Bistro $LD
*Portland* ▪ (207) 347-3111
*608 Congress St* ▪ *Vegetarian* ▪ Features a regular menu displaying GF options in each category. Some options include coconut soup, hot and sour soup, peanut curry, soy nuggets, and panang curry with vegetables. ▪ *greenelephantmaine.com*

## Ground Round ☼📖
*Hallowell* ▪ (207) 623-0022
*215 Whitten Rd*
*Bangor* ▪ (207) 942-5621
*248 Odlin Rd*

## Gypsy Sweethearts $$$D
*Ogunquit* ▪ (207) 646-7021
*30 Shore Rd* ▪ *American* ▪ GF/GF modifiable items are marked with an asterisk on the regular menu. Chef David reports that they serve GF diners often. He recommends alerting the host upon arrival, and he or she will alert the server. David notes that several menu items are naturally GF, including the sea scallop appetizer, grilled portabello tops, chili rellenos, pork shanks, and more. Confirm the timeliness of this information before dining in. ▪ *www.gypsysweethearts.com*

## Julie's Ristorante & Provisto ☼★$LD
*Ogunquit* ▪ (207) 641-2522
*369 Main St* ▪ *Italian* ▪ GF pizza and pasta are available, as are GF chicken parmigiana, paninis, gnocchi, and ravioli. For dessert, there are GF cookies, muffins, and dessert bars. GF specialties change seasonally. GF gift baskets are available with advance notice. ▪ *www.juliesristorante.com*

## Kamasouptra ★⊄LD
*Portland* ▪ (207) 415-6692
*28 Monument Sq*
*South Portland* ▪ (207) 774-7687
*364 Maine Mall Rd* ▪ *American* ▪ Soup menu changes frequently, but there are always several GF soup options daily. Examples include loaded potato, curried root vegetable & lentil, and maple roasted butternut squash. Daily soup menu is available online with GF soups marked. GF cookies are also available. ▪ *kamasouptra.com*

## Kosta's Restaurant & Bar ☼$$LD
*Brewer* ▪ (207) 989-8811
*429 Wilson St* ▪ *Greek* ▪ The restaurant reports that GF menu items are "displayed in the restaurant." Alert the server upon arrival and they can discuss GF options. ▪ *kostasrestaurantandbar.com*

## Leonardo's Fresh Quality Pizza ★$LD
*Portland* ▪ (207) 775-4444
*415 Forest Ave* ▪ *Pizza* ▪ GF pizza is available in size medium only with an additional charge of $3. ▪ *www.leonardosonline.com*

## Local Sprouts Café $BLD
*Portland* ▪ (207) 899-3529
*649 Congress St* ▪ *Bakery & Café*
▪ GF bread is available in addition to a variety of GF dishes and entrées. ▪ *www.localsprouts.coop*

## Maine Diner ★$$BLD
*Wells* ▪ (207) 646-4441
*2265 Post Rd* ▪ *Seafood* ▪ GF bread is available for all entrées and sandwiches for an additional charge of $.50 cents. ▪ *www.mainediner.com*

## McKays Public House ☼$$$D
*Bar Harbor* ▪ (207) 288-2002
*231 Maine St* ▪ *Seafood & Steakhouse* ▪ GF menu available on request. Alert the server upon arrival. ▪ *www.mckayspublichouse.com*

### Mesa Verde ✪SLD
*Portland* ▪ *(207) 774-6089*
*618 Congress St* ▪ *Mexican* ▪ GF
menu includes nachos, tacos, tostadas,
enchiladas, fajitas, homemade
tamales, steak rancheros, and pollo
con mole. Confirm the timeliness of
this information before dining in. ▪
*www.mesaverdeportlandmaine.com*

### Morning Dew Natural Foods ★CS
*Bridgton* ▪ *(207) 647-4003*
*19 Sandy Creek Rd* ▪ *Deli* ▪ Manager
Judy reports that GF sandwiches are
available at the deli. They also carry rice
flour wraps as another form of substitution. The deli is located within a larger
grocery store, where they offer GF pasta,
donuts, bagels, cake mixes, and more. ▪
*www.morningdewnatural.com*

### Ninety Nine ✪📖
*Auburn* ▪ *(207) 784-9499*
*650 Center St*
*Augusta* ▪ *(207) 623-0999*
*281 Civic Center Dr*
*Bangor* ▪ *(207) 973-1999*
*8 Bangor Mall Blvd*
*Biddeford* ▪ *(207) 283-9999*
*444 Alfred St*
*Topsham* ▪ *(207) 725-4999*
*Topsham Fair Mall Rd*

### Pat's Pizza ★SLD
*Hermon* ▪ *(207) 848-8223*
*1640 Outer Hammond St*
*Hampden* ▪ *(207) 947-6488*
*662 Main Rd N*
*Auburn* ▪ *(207) 784-8221*
*85 Center St*
*Augusta* ▪ *(207) 623-1748*
*292 State St*
*Bethel* ▪ *(207) 824-3637*
*37 Mayville Rd*
*Ellsworth* ▪ *(207) 667-6011*
*396 High St*
*Lincoln* ▪ *(207) 794-2211*
*205 Main St*
*Orono* ▪ *(207) 866-2111*
*11 Mill St*

*Portland* ▪ *(207) 699-4455*
*30 Market St*
*Presque Isle* ▪ *(207) 764-0367*
*9 North St*
*Sanford* ▪ *(207) 324-7500*
*505 Main St*
*Scarborough* ▪ *(207) 883-8441*
*209 US Rte 1*
*Windham* ▪ *(207) 892-1700*
*844 Roosevelt Trl*
*Yarmouth* ▪ *(207) 846-3701*
*791 US Rte 1* ▪ *Pizza* ▪ GF pizza is available.
Pizza is prepared separately but cooked in a
common oven. ▪ *www.patspizza.com*

### Pom's Thai Taste ⊂LD
*Portland* ▪ *(207) 772-7999*
*571 Congress St* ▪ *Thai* ▪ The restaurant
reports that a variety of GF options is
available, and recommends asking a server
to go over the options. Alert the server
upon arrival. ▪ *www.thaitastemaine.com*

### Portland Pie Company ★SLD
*Westbrook* ▪ *(207) 591-6248*
*869 Main St*
*Scarborough* ▪ *(207) 510-6999*
*400 Expedition Dr*
*Portland* ▪ *(207) 772-1231*
*51 York St* ▪ *Pizza* ▪ *www.portlandpie.com*

### Ricetta's Brick Oven Pizza ✪★SLD
*Falmouth* ▪ *(207) 781-3100*
*240 US Route 1* ▪ *Pizza* ▪ GF pizza and
pasta are available. GF menu lists all pizza
and pasta options as well as a variety of salads. GF cupcakes are available for dessert. ▪
*www.ricettas.com*

### Romano's Macaroni Grill ✪★📖
*South Portland* ▪ *(207) 780-6620*
*415 Philbrook Ave*

### Roost Café & Bistro ✪SBLD
*Cape Neddick* ▪ *(207) 363-0266*
*1300 US Rt 1* ▪ *Café* ▪ GF breads, biscuits,
cookies, and other baked goods are available. The extensive GF menu covers all
three meals and includes selections like

eggs benedict with GF biscuits, Cuban black bean soup, seared scallops, and New Zealand lamb lollies. As with all specialty items, call ahead to confirm availability. ▪ *www.roostcafeandbistro.com*

### Sea Dog Brewing Company   ✪★$BLD
**South Portland** ▪ (207) 871-7000
*125 Western Ave*
**Bangor** ▪ (207) 947-8009
*26 Front St*
**Topsham** ▪ (207) 725-0162
*1 Main St* ▪ **American** ▪ GF menu includes a variety of salads with GF dressing, 10 inch GF pizza, chicken breast, salmon fillet, hanger steak, and sea scallops, as well as GF sides including saffron short grain rice and buttermilk whipped potatoes. For dessert, there is crème brûlée, ice cream, or fruit & fondue. ▪ *seadogbrewing.com*

### Sea Grass Bistro   ✪$$$D
**Yarmouth** ▪ (207) 846-3885
*305 US Route 1* ▪ **Bistro** ▪ The restaurant reports that the menu changes every three weeks, but GF options will always be available and marked on the menu. Confirm the timeliness of this information before dining in. ▪ *www.seagrassbistro.com*

### Sebago Brewing Company   ✪$$LD
**Gorham** ▪ (207) 839-2337
*29 Elm St*
**Kennebunk** ▪ (207) 985-9855
*65 Portland Rd*
**Scarborough** ▪ (207) 874-2337
*201 Southborough Dr*
**Portland** ▪ (207) 775-2337
*211 Fore St* ▪ **American** ▪ GF menu available at all four locations. GF food is prepared separately from other foods containing gluten. GF menu includes bayou shrimp, variety of salads and soups, bunless burgers, Hawaiian chicken, mushroom and sage risotto and also includes a kids menu. ▪ *www.sebagobrewing.com*

### Silly's   ✪★₵LD
**Portland** ▪ (207) 772-0360
*40 Washington Ave* ▪ **American** ▪ All wraps can be made GF by substituting the wrap with a chick pea flour pancake as well as any pizza. Other GF options include brownies, pork and lamb sausage, and veggie burgers. There is also a dedicated GF fryer. ▪ *www.sillys.com*

### Slates Restaurant   $$LD
**Hallowell** ▪ (207) 622-9575
*167 Water St* ▪ **Seafood** ▪ Owner Wendy reports that they frequently accommodate GF diners. She adds that they can easily prepare a GF meal, as everything is made to order. Wendy notes that since there is an open kitchen, GF diners can speak directly to the cooks. ▪ *www.slatesrestaurant.com*

### Soakology Foot Sanctuary & Teahouse   ★₵S
**Portland** ▪ (207) 879-7625
*30 City Ctr* ▪ **Teahouse** ▪ GF peanut butter cookies and biscotti are available. ▪ *www.soakology.com*

### Soup For You   ₵LD
**Farmington** ▪ (207) 779-0799
*222 Broadway* ▪ **American** ▪ GF soups are available. Manager Eddie reports that GF soups change every day, but there are always a couple of GF options. GF soup options include chilled tropical gazpacho, BBQ 3 bean chicken chili, and dilled potato and white bean soup. Confirm the timeliness of this information before dining in. ▪ *www.yelp.com/biz/soup-for-you-farmington*

### Stripers Waterfront Seafood Restaurant   $$$LD
**Kennebunkport** ▪ (207) 967-5333
*127 Ocean Ave* ▪ **Seafood** ▪ Manager Niels reports that the restaurant serves GF diners on a regular basis. He notes that many items are GF, and servers know which items can be modified to be GF. ▪ *www.thebreakwaterinn.com*

## Thistle Inn, The                   $$$D
*Boothbay Harbor* ▪ (207) 633-3541
55 Oak St ▪ *Modern American* ▪ The
restaurant reports that most meat and
seafood dishes are GF or can easily be
made GF. They note that they are "always
willing to rearrange" dishes to be suitable
for GF diners. Confirm the timeliness
of this information before dining in. ▪
*www.thethistleinn.com*

## Uno Chicago Grill              ✪★🕮
*Bangor* ▪ (207) 947-5000
725 Stillwater Ave
*South Portland* ▪ (207) 780-8667
280 Maine Mall Rd

## Wild Willy's Burgers                ★¢LD
*York* ▪ (207) 363-9924
765 US Route 1
*South Portland* ▪ (207) 822-9999
449 Westbrook St ▪ *American* ▪ GF buns
are available and can be used to make
almost any burger or sandwich GF. GF
menus are available at all locations, and options differ slightly from restaurant to restaurant. The restaurant reports that all staff
have been "trained in cross-contamination
issues." ▪ *www.wildwillysburgers.com*

# MARYLAND

## BALTIMORE

## Au Bon Pain                           🕮
*Baltimore* ▪ (410) 727-9827
10 N Calvert St
*Baltimore* ▪ (410) 837-9814
1 South St
*Baltimore* ▪ (410) 455-2817
1000 Hilltop Circle Commons Building
*Baltimore* ▪ (410) 685-1976
22 S Green St
*Baltimore* ▪ (410) 244-1937
110 S Paca St

## B&O American Brasserie       $$$BLD
*Baltimore* ▪ (443) 692-6172
2 N Charles St ▪ *American* ▪ GF options
available. Notify the restaurants of your
dietary needs when you make your reservation so they can best prepare for your
arrival. ▪ *www.bandorestaurant.com*

## Bertucci's                          ✪🕮
*Baltimore* ▪ (410) 931-0900
8130 Corporate Dr

## Black Olive, The                $$$$LD
*Baltimore* ▪ (410) 276-7141
814 S Bond St ▪ *Greek* ▪ Many of their
regular menu items are GF and even
more can be modified to be GF. Notify
your server of your dietary needs upon
arrival and they will gladly assist you. ▪
*www.theblackolive.com/restaurant/*

## Blue Hill Tavern                  $$$LD
*Baltimore* ▪ (443) 388-9363
938 S Conkling St ▪ *American* ▪ Manager Jessica reports that GF diners are
becoming "very popular." She adds that
servers have a "verbal list" of GF options that they can recite. It includes the
NY strip, chicken, and black cod, among
other meats, with substituted sides. ▪
*www.bluehilltavern.com*

## Bubba Gump Shrimp Co.           ✪🕮
*Baltimore* ▪ (410) 244-0838
301 Light St

## Capital Grille, The               ✪🕮
*Baltimore* ▪ (443) 703-4064
500 E Pratt St

## Carrabba's Italian Grill           ✪🕮
*Baltimore* ▪ (410) 661-5444
7600 Belair Rd

## Cosi                                ✪🕮
*Baltimore* ▪ (410) 545-0550
100 S Charles St

## Don Pablo's                        ✪🕮
*Baltimore* ▪ (410) 931-7966
8161 Honeygo Blvd

**Donna's Restaurant** $$LD
*Baltimore* ▪ *(410) 532-7611*
*5100 Falls Rd*
*Baltimore* ▪ *(410) 889-3410*
*3101 St Paul St* ▪ *Mediterranean* ▪ The
restaurant reports that most of their entrées
can be modified to be GF. Confirm the
timeliness of this information before din-
ing in. ▪ *www.donnas.com*

**Fleming's Prime Steakhouse & Wine
Bar** ✪📖
*Baltimore* ▪ *(410) 332-1666*
*720 Aliceanna St*

**Fogo De Chao** ★📖
*Baltimore* ▪ *(410) 528-9292*
*600 E Pratt St*

**Gertrude's** ✪$$$LD
*Baltimore* ▪ *(410) 889-3399*
*10 Art Museum Dr* ▪ *American* ▪ Manager
Paul notes that the staff is "pretty familiar" with the GF diet. GF items include
portobella crab imperial, vegetable curry,
and most steaks. Located in the Baltimore
Museum of Art.

**Grano Pasta Bar** ★$LD
*Baltimore* ▪ *(443) 869-3429*
*1031 W 36th St* ▪ *Italian* ▪ GF pasta is available. Ask a server which sauces are GF. ▪
*www.granopastabar.com*

**Greene Turtle Sports Bar & Grill, The**
✪📖
*Baltimore* ▪ *(410) 528-8606*
*1606 Whetstone Wy*
*Baltimore* ▪ *(410) 342-4222*
*718-722 S Broadway*

**Hard Rock Café** ✪📖
*Baltimore* ▪ *(410) 347-7625*
*601 E Pratt St*

**Helmand, The** $$LD
*Baltimore* ▪ *(410) 752-0311*
*806 N Charles St* ▪ *Middle Eastern* ▪ Res-
taurant reports that all items on the menu
are naturally GF with the exception of four
dishes. Alert a server upon arrival and they
will go over the menu. ▪ *www.helmand.com*

**Liquid Earth** ★$$LD
*Baltimore* ▪ *(410) 276-6606*
*1626 Aliceanna St* ▪ *American* ▪ GF
bread is available for substitution into
all sandwiches. Restaurant also notes
that most items on its raw menu are
naturally GF. Alert server upon arrival. ▪
*www.liquidearth.com*

**Meet 27 American Bistro** $$D
*Baltimore* ▪ *(410) 585-8121*
*127 W 27th St* ▪ *American* ▪ The restaurant
reports than many items on the menu can
be modified to be GF. Alert server upon
arrival and they will go over the options. ▪
*www.meet27.com*

**Morton's Steakhouse** ✪📖
*Baltimore* ▪ *(410) 547-8255*
*300 S Charles St*

**P.F. Chang's China Bistro** ✪★📖
*Baltimore* ▪ *(410) 649-2750*
*600 E Pratt St Ste 101*

**Pei Wei Asian Diner** ✪📖
*Baltimore* ▪ *(410) 435-3290*
*6302 York Rd*

**Ruth's Chris Steak House** ✪📖
*Baltimore* ▪ *(410) 783-0033*
*600 Water St*
*Baltimore* ▪ *(410) 230-0033*
*711 Eastern Ave*

**Sammy's Trattoria** ★$$$LD
*Baltimore* ▪ *(410) 837-9999*
*1200 N Charles St* ▪ *Italian* ▪ GF pasta is
available. ▪ *www.sammystrattoria.com*

**Sascha's** ✪$$LD
*Baltimore* ▪ *(410) 539-8880*
*527 N Charles St* ▪ *American* ▪ GF options
are marked with a asterisk on the regular
menu. Options include shrimp and grits,
jerk chicken satay, and free range chicken.
Manager advises reservations noting GF, so
that the servers and chefs will be alerted in
advance. ▪ *www.saschas.com*

### Sweet 27                                          ⊄**BLD**
*Baltimore* ▪ *(410) 464-7211*
123 W 27th St ▪ Café ▪ GF treats include
cakes, cupcakes, cookies, brownies, muffins, and pies. Breakfast, lunch, and dinner
selections include omelets, pancakes, pizza,
tacos, and a variety of meat and seafood
dishes, as well as vegetarian entrées. ▪
*www.glutenfreedesserts.com*

### Uno Chicago Grill                        ✪★▣
*Baltimore* ▪ *(410) 625-5900*
201 E Pratt St

### Woodberry Kitchen                  ✪★$$$**D**
*Baltimore* ▪ *(410) 464-8000*
2010 Clipper Park Rd ▪ American ▪ GF
menu includes deviled eggs, smoked
rockfish, rice & beans, chicken breast, and
more. The owner is GF, so all staff members
are very educated on the GF diet. GF bread
is available. ▪ *www.woodberrykitchen.com*

# MARYLAND

## ALL OTHER CITIES

### Au Bon Pain                                        ▣
*Suitland* ▪ *(301) 516-7338*
4600 Silverhill Rd
*Bethesda* ▪ *(301) 451-7709*
10 Center Dr

### Austin Grill                                      ✪$**LD**
*Silver Spring* ▪ *(240) 247-8969*
919 Ellsworth Dr ▪ Tex-Mex ▪ GF menu
includes grilled salmon salad, carnitas
fajitas, huevos rancheros, grilled vegetable
enchiladas, and more. Regional manager
Robert stresses the importance of noting GF when placing an order so that the
server can notify the manager and start the
appropriate procedures for GF preparation.
▪ *www.austingrill.com*

### Bean Hollow                                     ★⊄**S**
*Ellicott City* ▪ *(410) 465-0233*

8059 Main St ▪ Coffee Shop ▪ Restaurant
reports that GF diners can order salads
without croutons. GF cookies are also
available. ▪ *beanhollowcoffee.com*

### Bertucci's                                        ✪▣
*Annapolis* ▪ *(410) 266-5800*
2207 Forest Dr
*Bel Air* ▪ *(410) 569-4600*
12 Bel Air S Pkwy
*Columbia* ▪ *(410) 312-4800*
9081 Snowden River Pkwy
*No. Bethesda* ▪ *(301) 230-3160*
11301 Rockville Pike
*Timonium* ▪ *(410) 561-7000*
1818 York Rd

### Boloco                                             ★▣
*Bethesda* ▪ *(301) 986-6962*
4930 Elm St

### Bonefish Grill                                   ✪▣
*Gaithersburg* ▪ *(240) 631-2401*
82 Market St
*Frederick* ▪ *(301) 668-1522*
1305 W 7th St Ste 37
*Brandywine* ▪ *(301) 782-7604*
15910 Crain Hwy Bldg F
*Bel Air* ▪ *(410) 420-9113*
696 Bel Air Rd
*Glen Burnie* ▪ *(410) 553-0299*
6711 Governor Ritchie Hwy Ste 201
*Owings Mills* ▪ *(410) 654-5500*
10906 Boulevard Cir
*Gambrills* ▪ *(410) 991-8192*
2381 Brandermill Blvd
*Annapolis* ▪ *(410) 571-8263*
1915 Towne Centre Blvd

### Boston's Restaurant & Sports Bar
✪★▣
*Waldorf* ▪ *(301) 396-4988*
10440 O'Donnell Pl

### Broadway Pizza                              ★⊄**LD**
*Potomac* ▪ *(301) 299-3553*
7965 Tuckerman Ln ▪ Pizza ▪ GF pizza is
available in the 9-inch size. " The GF pizzas
are made with special care to minimize
CC but wheat flour is used in our kitchen."

Toppings include fresh vegetables, chicken, and lamb. ▪ *www.broadwaypizzaonline.com*

### Buca di Beppo ✪▦
*Gaithersburg* ▪ *(301) 947-7346*
*122 Kentlands Blvd*

### Bugaboo Creek Steak House ✪▦
*Gaithersburg* ▪ *(301) 548-9200*
*15710 Shady Grove Rd*

### Busboys and Poets ✪$$**BLD**
*Hyattsville* ▪ *(301) 779-2787*
*5331 Baltimore Ave* ▪ *American* ▪ Offer countless GF options for all three meals of the day including but not limited to nachos, pizza, salmon, pan fried chicken, and pan seared basil tofu. ▪ *www.busboysandpoets.com*

### Café Rio Mexican Grill ▦
*Olney* ▪ *(301) 232-5500*
*3140 Olney Sandy Spring Rd*
*Waldorf* ▪ *(301) 861-5700*
*3082 Festival Wy*

### CakeLove ★▦
*Fort Washington* ▪ *(301) 686-0340*
*160 National Plaza*
*Silver Spring* ▪ *(301) 565-2253*
*8512 Fenton St*

### Capital Grille, The ✪▦
*Chevy Chase* ▪ *(301) 718-7812*
*5310 Western Ave*

### Carini's Pizza & Subs ★$$**LD**
*Stevensville* ▪ *(410) 604-2501*
*356 Romancoke Rd (Rt 8)* ▪ *Pizza* ▪ GF pizza and pasta are available. ▪ *carinispizzaandsubs.com*

### Carrabba's Italian Grill ✪▦
*Bowie* ▪ *(301) 809-0500*
*16431 Governor Bridge Rd*
*Frederick* ▪ *(301) 694-6200*
*1315 W Patrick St*
*Germantown* ▪ *(240) 686-1100*
*19935 Century Blvd*
*Hunt Valley* ▪ *(410) 785-9400*
*130 Shawan Rd*
*Ocean City* ▪ *(410) 213-0037*
*12728 Ocean Gtwy*

*Pasadena* ▪ *(410) 863-5960*
*8030 Ritchie Hwy*
*Waldorf* ▪ *(301) 645-0094*
*3754 Crain Hwy*
*Ellicott City* ▪ *(410) 461-5200*
*4430 Long Gate Pkwy*

### Cava Mezze ✪$**LD**
*Rockville* ▪ *(301) 309-9090*
*9713 Traville Gateway Dr* ▪ *Greek* ▪ Restaurant reports frequently accommodating GF diners. Alert a server upon arrival. Many menu items are naturally GF, such as salads, dips, omelets and saffron risotto. Confirm the timeliness of this information before dining in. They have a GF list of menu items online and instores. ▪ *www.cavamezze.com*

### Cheeseburger in Paradise ✪★▦
*California* ▪ *(301) 863-0489*
*23415 Three Notch Rd*
*Pasadena* ▪ *(410) 761-1003*
*8026 Ritchie Hwy*

### Chef Geoff's ✪$$$**LD**
*Rockville* ▪ *(240) 621-3090*
*12256 Rockville Pike* ▪ *American* ▪ Manager Benjamin reports that every location is very happy to adjust their menu to fit the needs of their gluten intolerant customers. He notes that if customers have a specific dish they want prepared GF, they should call a day ahead of time to inform the chef. ▪ *www.chefgeoff.com*

### Chop House, The ✪$$$$**D**
*Annapolis* ▪ *(410) 224-4344*
*1915 Towne Centre Blvd* ▪ *Steakhouse* ▪ District manager Sue reports that all locations offer GF items, which are marked on the regular menu. She notes that GF diners should always alert a manager about GF requirements. ▪ *www.thechophouserestaurant.com*

### Chop't ▦
*Bethesda* ▪ *(240) 752-9942*
*10307 Old Georgetown Rd*

## Clustered Spires Pastry Shop    ★ ⊄S
*Frederick* ▪ *(301) 662-7446*
*285 Montevue Ln* ▪ *Bakery* ▪ Non-dedicated bakery offering a variety of GF products by pre-order. GF breads, pastries, cakes, danishes, cinnamon rolls, muffins, and tarts are available. All utensils used for dietary restriction foods are triple-washed prior to use. Owner Karen recommends notifying the bakery at least 48 hours in advance for pick-up orders. ▪ *www.clusteredspiresbakery.com*

## Clyde's    📖
*Chevy Chase* ▪ *(301) 951-9600*
*5441 Wisconsin Ave*
*Columbia* ▪ *(410) 730-2829*
*10221 Wincopin Cir*
*Rockville* ▪ *(301) 294-0200*
*2 Preserve Pkwy*

## Comus Inn at Sugarloaf Mountain, The
$$$LD
*Dickerson* ▪ *(301) 349-5100*
*23900 Old Hundred Rd* ▪ *Modern American* ▪ The chef reports that the restaurant serves GF diners often. He recommends alerting the server, who will speak to him about GF options. He also suggests that if GF diners know what they would like when they make their reservation, he is happy to accommodate those requests. ▪ *www.thecomusinn.com*

## Cosi    ⊙📖
*Bethesda* ▪ *(301) 652-6098*
*7251 Woodmont Ave*
*Owings Mills* ▪ *(410) 654-9182*
*9177 Reisterstown Rd*
*Gaithersburg* ▪ *(301) 926-8764*
*177 Kentlands Blvd*
*Rockville* ▪ *(301) 251-1408*
*201 N Washington St*
*Columbia* ▪ *(410) 953-6311*
*6181 Old Dobbin Ln*

## Dogfish Head Alehouse    ⊙$$LD
*Gaithersburg* ▪ *(301) 963-4847*
*800 W Diamond Ave* ▪ *American* ▪ Full GF menu includes several salads, burgers and sandwiches without buns, NY strip, wood-grilled salmon, and more. Modifications necessary to make dishes GF are also noted on the menu. Alert server upon arrival. ▪ *www.dogfishalehouse.com*

## Don Pablo's    ⊙📖
*Columbia* ▪ *(410) 290-1618*
*6191 Columbia Crossing Cir*
*Laurel* ▪ *(301) 725-1993*
*14600 Laurel Pl*
*Owings Mills* ▪ *(410) 902-0300*
*One Restaurant Park Dr*

## First Watch - The Daytime Café    ⊙📖
*Pikesville* ▪ *(410) 602-1595*
*1431 Reisterstown Rd*
*Rockville* ▪ *(301) 762-0621*
*100 Gibbs St*

## Flying Avocado, The    ★ ⊄BL
*Owings Mills* ▪ *(443) 471-2600*
*10210 S Dolfield Rd* ▪ *Organic* ▪ GF wraps and breads are available. ▪ *www.flyingavocado.com*

## Founding Farmers    $$BLD
*Potomac* ▪ *(301) 340-8783*
*12505 Park Potomac Ave* ▪ *American* ▪ The restaurant reports that they take GF requests "very seriously." They recommend making reservations noting GF and asking for a manager upon arrival. GF options include rotisserie chicken, all fish entrées, and steak. Confirm the timeliness of this information before dining in. ▪ *www.wearefoundingfarmers.com*

## Fox and Hound Pub & Grille    📖
*Germantown* ▪ *(301) 515-8880*
*20021 Century Blvd*

## Freedom Bakery    $BL
*Severna Park* ▪ *(410) 975-0261*
*568 Ritchie Hwy* ▪ *Bakery & Café* ▪ Dedicated GF bakery serving sandwiches, pancakes, waffles, cookies, omelets, salads, and breads. The bakery reports that GF birthday cakes are available with advance notice of at least 48 hours. ▪ *www.thefreedombakery.com*

## Genghis Grill  📖
*Waldorf* ▪ *(301) 396-3966*
*2928 Festival Wy*

## Glory Days Grill  ✪📖
*Bowie* ▪ *(301) 805-5299*
*15505 Annapolis Rd*
*Eldersburg* ▪ *(410) 552-5160*
*1348 Liberty Rd*
*Frederick* ▪ *(301) 696-1112*
*1305 W 7th St*
*Glen Burnie* ▪ *(443) 749-4376*
*7939 Ritchie Hwy*
*Towson* ▪ *(443) 901-0270*
*1220 W Joppa Rd*

## Grapeseed  $$$D
*Bethesda* ▪ *(301) 986-9592*
*4865 Cordell Ave* ▪ *Modern American*
▪ Manager Patrick reports that GF diners are "accommodated regularly" and recommends reservations noting GF. He reports the sautéed calamari and the slow-roasted pork-belly can be prepared GF, among other things. Confirm the timeliness of this information before dining in. ▪ *www.grapeseedbistro.com*

## Great Sage  ✪★$LD
*Clarksville* ▪ *(443) 535-9400*
*5809 Clarksville Square Dr* ▪ *Vegetarian*
▪ GF items marked on the menu include Vietnamese spring rolls, green lentil & pumpkin burger, Indian red lentil curry, raw zucchini al pesto, and more. GF cornbread available. For dessert, they offer raw chocolate almond tart, carrot cake, and more. Menu changes seasonally, so actual GF options may vary. ▪ *www.great-sage.com*

## Greene Turtle
## Sports Bar & Grill, The  ✪📖
*Aberdeen* ▪ *(410) 942-4020*
*1113 Beards Hill Rd*
*Columbia* ▪ *(410) 312-5255*
*8872 Mcgaw Rd*
*Edgewater* ▪ *(410) 956-1144*
*3213 Solomons Island Rd Ste A*
*Frederick* ▪ *(301) 698-1979*
*50 Citizens Wy*

*Germantown* ▪ *(240) 686-1800*
*19961 Century Blvd*
*Hagerstown* ▪ *(301) 745-8800*
*12818 Shank Farm Way Ste A*
*Hanover* ▪ *(410) 799-5001*
*7556 Teague Rd*
*La Plata* ▪ *(301) 392-9119*
*6 Saint Marys Ave*
*Ocean City* ▪ *(410) 213-1500*
*9616 Stephen Decatur Hwy*
*Prince Frederick* ▪ *(410) 414-5030*
*98 Solomons Island Rd S*
*Salisbury* ▪ *(410) 860-9991*
*2618 N Salisbury Blvd*
*Towson* ▪ *(410) 825-3980*
*408 York Rd*
*Westminster* ▪ *(410) 871-1524*
*830 Market St*
*Annapolis* ▪ *(410) 266-7474*
*177 Jennifer Rd*
*Hunt Valley* ▪ *(410) 771-0555*
*118 Shawan Rd*
*Mt. Airy* ▪ *(301) 829-9229*
*1604 Ridgeside Ct*
*Olney* ▪ *(305) 570-3043*
*18101 Town Center Dr*
*Owings Mills* ▪ *(443) 501-3822*
*2 Restaurant Park Dr*
*Pasadena* ▪ *(410) 437-0075*
*20 Magothy Beach Rd*
*Gambrills* ▪ *(410) 451-7544*
*2383 Brandermill Blvd*
*Glen Burke* ▪ *(410) 691-9802*
*1000 Friendship St, Terminal D*

## Grump's Café  ★¢BLD
*Annapolis* ▪ *(410) 267-0229*
*117 Hillsmere Dr* ▪ *Café* ▪ Several GF options including most of their salads and steaks. GF granola is offered on the breakfast menu. GF bread is usually available. Confirm availability before dining in. ▪ *www.grumpscafe.com*

## Harbor House Restaurant  $$$D
*Chestertown* ▪ *(410) 778-0669*
*23145 Buck Neck Rd* ▪ *American* ▪ Menu changes daily. Contact restaurant for GF options. ▪ *www.harborhousewcm.com*

### Italian Market, The　　　★$LD
*Annapolis* ▪ *(410) 224-1330*
*126 Defense Hwy* ▪ *Italian* ▪ GF pizza is
available. Restaurant reports that all pizzas
are cooked in the same oven and without
screens. ▪ *www.theitalianmarket.com*

### Jaleo Bethesda　　　✪$$$$LD
*Bethesda* ▪ *(301) 913-0003*
*7271 Woodmont Ave* ▪ *Spanish* ▪ GF menu
includes paellas, a grilled hangar steak tapas,
a duck confit tapas, and a traditional chorizo
tapas, and more. The restaurant recommends speaking to a manager upon arrival.
Confirm the timeliness of this information
before dining in. ▪ *www.jaleo.com*

### Jason's Deli　　　✪▥
*College Park* ▪ *(301) 779-3924*
*7356 Baltimore Ave*
*Lutherville-Timonium* ▪ *(410) 560-4975*
*2159 York Rd*
*Columbia* ▪ *(410) 309-5980*
*8874 McGaw Rd*

### Jersey Mike's　　　▥
*Gaithersburg* ▪ *(301) 977-4842*
*249 Kentlands Blvd*
*Laurel* ▪ *(301) 490-6969*
*13600 Baltimore Ave*
*Germantown* ▪ *(301) 540-6777*
*21040-F Frederick Rd*
*Frederick* ▪ *(240) 439-6095*
*5599 Spectrum Dr*
*Hagerstown* ▪ *(301) 393-9495*
*18015 Garland Groh Blvd*
*Bowie* ▪ *(301) 262-0505*
*6844 Race Track Rd*

### Joe's Crab Shack　　　✪▥
*Gaithersburg* ▪ *(301) 947-4377*
*221 Rio Blvd*
*Greenbelt* ▪ *(301) 313-0396*
*6002 Greenbelt Rd*
*Abingdon* ▪ *(410) 569-8343*
*3414 Merchant Blvd*
*Cockeysville* ▪ *(410) 771-1259*
*50 Shawan Rd*
*Hanover* ▪ *(410) 799-2155*
*7051 Arundel Mills Blvd*

### Legal Sea Foods　　　✪▥
*Bethesda* ▪ *(301) 469-5900*
*7101 Democracy Blvd*

### Lilit Café　　　✪★$BLD
*Bethesda* ▪ *(301) 654-5454*
*7921 Old Georgetown Rd* ▪ *Café* ▪
Extensive GF menu includes breakfast,
sandwiches, appetizers, entrées, and baked
goods. GF bread, pizza, beer, and soy sauce
are available. For dessert, GF tarts, cupcakes, cookies, and cakes are available. ▪
*www.lilitcafe.com*

### Lures Bar and Grille　　　$$LD
*Crownsville* ▪ *(410) 923-1606*
*1397 Generals Hwy* ▪ *American* ▪ They can
modify several dishes to be GF. In any case,
the manager notes that servers will always
discuss with a manager or chef before placing GF orders. ▪ *www.luresbarandgrille.com*

### Melting Pot, The　　　✪▥
*Annapolis* ▪ *(410) 266-8004*
*2348 Solomons Island Rd*
*Columbia* ▪ *(410) 740-9988*
*10451 Twin Rivers Rd Ste 130*
*Gaithersburg* ▪ *(301) 519-3638*
*9021 Gaither Rd*
*Towson* ▪ *(410) 821-6358*
*418 York Rd # 420*

### Miller's Ale House Restaurants　✪★▥
*Rockville* ▪ *(301) 770-8535*
*1471 Rockville Pke*

### Monocacy Crossing　　　✪$$$LD
*Frederick* ▪ *(301) 846-4204*
*4424A Urbana Pike* ▪ *American* ▪
The restaurant reports that they serve
GF diners "very often." If GF is noted
upon arrival, the server will bring a
copy of the menu with GF items highlighted and go over the menu in detail. ▪
*www.monocacycrossing.com*

### Morton's Steakhouse　　　✪▥
*Bethesda* ▪ *(301) 657-2650*
*7400 Wisconsin Ave*

**Not Your Average Joe's**  ✪📖
*Gaithersburg* ■ *(240) 477-1040*
*245 Kentlands Blvd*

**P.F. Chang's China Bistro**  ✪★📖
*Annapolis* ■ *(410) 573-2990*
*307 Sail Pl*
*Columbia* ■ *(410) 730-5344*
*10300 Little Patuxent Pkwy Ste 3020*
*Kensington* ■ *(301) 230-6933*
*11301 Rockville Pike Spc 1-4.1*
*Nottingham* ■ *(410) 931-2433*
*8342 Honeygo Blvd*
*Towson* ■ *(410) 372-5250*
*825 Dulaney Valley Rd Ste 1161*

**Pei Wei Asian Diner**  ✪📖
*Columbia* ■ *(410) 423-2550*
*6478 Dobbin Center Wy*
*Annapolis* ■ *(410) 573-5060*
*1901 Towne Centre*

**Piccola Roma**  $$$LD
*Annapolis* ■ *(410) 268-7898*
*200 Main St* ■ *Italian* ■ The restaurant
reports that several dishes can be modified
to be GF, including the eggplant par-
migiana and chicken in cream sauce. ■
*www.piccolaromaannapolis.com*

**Planet Pizza and Subs**  ★ SLD
*Rockville* ■ *(301) 762-9400*
*819 Hungerford Dr* ■ *Pizza* ■ GF
pizza is available but it is baked in
the same oven with the other pizza. ■
*www.planetpizzaandsubs.com*

**Roma's Café**  $$$LD
*Cockeysville* ■ *(410) 628-6565*
*10515 York Rd* ■ *Italian* ■ Manager recommends reservations noting GF so the
kitchen staff can prepare to cook food
separately, but notes that there is only a
limited list of GF options they can properly prepare. Alert server upon arrival. ■
*www.romascafe.com*

**Romano's Macaroni Grill**  ✪★📖
*Annapolis* ■ *(410) 573-1717*
*178 Jennifer Rd*
*Columbia* ■ *(410) 872-0626*

*6181 Columbia Crossing Cir*
*Frederick* ■ *(301) 624-1026*
*5201 Buckeystown Pike*
*Gaithersburg* ■ *(301) 963-5003*
*211 Rio Blvd*
*Silver Spring* ■ *(301) 562-2806*
*931 Ellsworth Dr*
*Lutherville Timonium* ■ *(410) 628-7112*
*9701 Beaver Dam Rd*

**Rosa Mexicano**  ✪📖
*National Harbor* ■ *(301) 567-1005*
*153 Waterfront St*

**Roscoe's Neapolitan Pizzeria**  ★ $$LD
*Takoma Park* ■ *(301) 920-0804*
*7040 Carroll Ave* ■ *Italian* ■ GF pizza is
available and baked in the same oven as
NON GF pizzas. ■ *www.roscoespizzeria.com*

**Ruth's Chris Steak House**  ✪📖
*Annapolis* ■ *(410) 990-0033*
*301 Seven Ave*
*Berlin* ■ *(888) 632-4747*
*11501 Maid at Arms Wy*
*Bethesda* ■ *(301) 652-7877*
*7315 Wisconsin Ave*
*Pikesville* ■ *(410) 837-0033*
*1777 Reisterstown Rd*

**Scossa Restaurant & Lounge**  ★ $$$LD
*Easton* ■ *(410) 822-2202*
*8 N Washington St* ■ *Italian* ■ GF pasta
available for substitution. Dedicated utensils are used to cook all dishes indicated as
GF by server. ■ *www.scossarestaurant.com*

**Shane's Rib Shack**  ✪📖
*Laurel* ■ *(301) 725-2020*
*13600 Baltimore Ave*

**Smokey Bones**  📖
*Bowie* ■ *(301) 809-6755*
*15209 Major Lansdale Blvd*

**Soretti Ethiopian Cuisine**  ✪SLD
*Burtonsville* ■ *(240) 390-0044*
*15510 Old Columbia Pike* ■ *Ethiopian* ■
Soretti Ethiopian offers 95% of their menu
in a GF version. Menu items include grilled
meat wraps, salads, and sides such as lentil
and cabbage soup. ■ *www.soretti.com*

## Toppings Pizza Company ✪★$LD
*Frederick* ▪ *(301) 668-2040*
*5330 New Design Rd* ▪ *Pizza* ▪ GF pizza is available. ▪ *www.toppingspizza.com*

## Tower Oaks Lodge $$LD
*Rockville* ▪ *(301) 294-0200*
*2 Preserve Pkwy* ▪ *American* ▪ Restaurant notes that most steak, fish, or pork chops can be prepared GF. Most salads are GF and they can make the hamburgers without buns. No dedicated fryers so avoid fried items. Confirm the timeliness of this information before dining in. Alert a server, as servers are trained to communicate GF requests to the chefs and managers. ▪ *www.clydes.comtower*

## U Food Grill 📖
*Aberdeen* ▪ *(443) 345-4663*
*6010 Frankford St*
*Aberdeen* ▪ *(443) 345-1542*
*2401 Chesapeake Ave*

## Uno Chicago Grill ✪★📖
*Bowie* ▪ *(301) 352-5320*
*4001 Town Center Blvd*
*Columbia* ▪ *(410) 964-9945*
*10300 Little Patuxent Pkwy*
*Frederick* ▪ *(301) 668-2512*
*5449 Urbana Pike*
*Fruitland* ▪ *(410) 334-6565*
*100 E Cedar Ln*
*Hagerstown* ▪ *(240) 420-1919*
*17734 Garland Groh Blvd*
*Oakland* ▪ *(301) 387-4866*
*19746 Garrett Hwy*
*Ellicott City* ▪ *(410) 480-1400*
*4470 Long Gate Pkwy*

## Watermans Seafood Co. $$$LD
*Ocean City* ▪ *(410) 213-1020*
*12505 Ocean Gtwy* ▪ *Seafood* ▪ Restaurant reports that any fish on the menu can be prepared GF and recommends that GF diners order broiled fish. Confirm the timeliness of this information before dining in. ▪ *www.watermansseafoodcompany.com*

## Wild Orchid, The $$$LD
*Annapolis* ▪ *(410) 268-8009*
*200 Westgate Cir* ▪ *Modern American* ▪ Manager advises making reservations noting GF and alerting the server upon arrival. Many menu items can be modified to be GF. Crème brûlée and other custom-made options are available with an advance notice of 2 days. ▪ *www.thewildorchidcafe.com*

## Zpizza ✪📖
*Silver Spring* ▪ *(301) 495-5536*
*815 Ellsworth Dr*

# MASSACHUSETTS
## BOSTON

## 5 Napkin Burger $LD
*Boston* ▪ *(617) 375-2277*
*105 Huntington Ave* ▪ *American* ▪ GF rolls are available for any burger. ▪ *5napkinburger.com*

## Abe & Louie's $$$$LD
*Boston* ▪ *(617) 536-6300*
*793 Boylston St* ▪ *Steakhouse* ▪ They have plenty of GF items and accommodate GF diners frequently, ask you server for details. ▪ *www.abeandlouies.com*

## Au Bon Pain 📖
*Boston* ▪ *(617) 248-9441*
*101 Merrimac St*
*Boston* ▪ *(617) 859-2858*
*431 Boylston St*
*Boston* ▪ *(617) 723-8483*
*53 State St*
*Boston* ▪ *(617) 439-9301*
*27 Drydock Building 114*
*Boston* ▪ *(617) 739-6860*
*75 Francis St*
*Boston* ▪ *(617) 723-1278*
*209 Cambridge St*
*Boston* ▪ *(617) 734-0451*
*300 Longwood Ave*
*Boston* ▪ *(617) 542-0412*
*300 Congress St*

Boston ▪ (617) 247-9467
100 Huntington Ave
Boston ▪ (617) 345-9638
One Drydock Ave
Boston ▪ (617) 421-3950
133 Brookline Ave
Boston ▪ (617) 561-6020
Logan Int'l Airport- Terminal A, Level 2
Boston ▪ (617) 567-3782
Logan Intl Airport, Kiosk C, 300 Terminal C
Boston ▪ (617) 569-5547
Logan Int'l Airport, Terminal B, US Airways 2nd Fl
Boston ▪ (617) 578-0711
369 Huntington Ave
Boston ▪ (617) 439-0116
One International Pl
Boston ▪ (617) 338-8948
26 Park Plaza
Boston ▪ (617) 421-9593
800 Boylston St
Boston ▪ (617) 345-0427
Two Atlantic Ave

## Bertucci's                                    ✿📖
Boston ▪ (617) 739-2492          •
1 Blackfan Cir
Boston ▪ (617) 227-7889
22 Merchants Row
Boston ▪ (617) 236-1030
533 Commonwealth Ave

## Boloco                                        ★📖
Boston ▪ (617) 357-9727
133 Federal St
Boston ▪ (617) 369-9087
1080 Boylston St
Boston ▪ (617) 357-9013
50 Congress St
Boston ▪ (617) 262-2200
247 Newbury St
Boston ▪ (617) 536-6814
359-369 Huntington Ave
Boston ▪ (617) 232-2166
283 Longwood Ave
Boston ▪ (617) 422-0162
125 Pearl St
Boston ▪ (617) 357-9727
133 Federal St

Boston ▪ (617) 778-6772
2 Park Plaza
Boston ▪ (617) 778-6750
27 School St
Boston ▪ (617) 266-2200
2 Park Plaza
Boston ▪ (857) 284-7488
284 Congress St

## Brasserie Jo                             ★$$$BLD
Boston ▪ (617) 425-3240
120 Huntington Ave ▪ French ▪ They do not have a set GF menu but there are a variety of entrees that are GF. Alert the manager upon arrival and they will go over the options. Located in The Colonnade Hotel. ▪ www.brasseriejoboston.com

## Capital Grille, The                          ✿📖
Boston ▪ (617) 262-8900
359 Newbury St

## Cosi                                         ✿📖
Boston ▪ (617) 292-3314
133 Federal St
Boston ▪ (617) 723-4447
53 State St
Boston ▪ (617) 426-0593
14 Milk St
Boston ▪ (617) 951-9999
2 S Station
Boston ▪ (617) 720-2674
245 Summer St
Boston ▪ (617) 567-6600
Logan Airport- Air Canada 1 Harborside Dr
Boston ▪ (617) 569-0540
Logan Airport- American Airlines 1 Harborside Dr
Boston ▪ (617) 292-2674
125 High St

## Davio's Northern Italian Steakhouse
✿📖
Boston ▪ (617) 357-4810
75 Arlington St

## Del Frisco's Double Eagle Steak House
📖
Boston ▪ (617) 951-1368
250 Northern Ave

## Elephant Walk, The          ✪$$LD
Boston ▪ (617) 247-1500
*900 Beacon St ▪ Fusion ▪* GF menu includes shrimp curry, grilled flat iron steak, quinoa gratin with vegetables, and more. Most soups and salads are GF. GF desserts like chocolate truffle cake and sorbet are also available. Be sure to alert server that you are ordering from the GF menu. Hands-on GF cooking classes are offered. ▪ *www.elephantwalk.com*

## Equal Exchange Café          ★ ¢BLD
Boston ▪ (617) 372-8777
*226 Causeway St ▪ Café ▪* GF baked goods such as muffins and cookies are available every day. Sometimes they serve other GF items as well. Ask a server which items are GF on a specific day. ▪ *www.equalexchangecafe.com*

## Finale Dessert Company       ✪ ★ $$
Boston ▪ (617) 423-3184
*1 Columbus Ave ▪ Dessert ▪* GF desserts include the flourless dark chocolate decadence cake, the original cheesecake, coconut cream tarts, and a variety of puddings. Confirm the timeliness of this information before dining in. Servers are familiar with GF desserts and will be able to indicate GF items. They also have a GF menu for their lunch and dinner service. ▪ *www.finaledesserts.com*

## Fire + Ice                   ★📖
Boston ▪ (617) 482-3473
*205 Berkeley St*

## Fleming's Prime Steakhouse & Wine Bar          ✪📖
Boston ▪ (617) 292-0808
*217 Stuart St*

## Fogo De Chao                 ★📖
Boston ▪ (617) 585-6300
*200 Dartmouth St*

## Franklin Café, The           ✪$$D
Boston ▪ (617) 350-0010
*278 Shawmut Ave ▪ Modern American ▪* Franklin Café offers a GF dinner menu offering items such as black pepper seared ahi tuna, pan roaster organic chicken, and garlic grilled calamari. ▪ *www.franklincafe.com*

## Fresh City                   ★📖
Boston ▪ (617) 424-7926
*201 Brookline Ave*
Boston ▪ (617) 443-0962
*2 Seaport Ln*
Boston ▪ (617) 561-4700
*Term A*

## Gaslight Brasserie           $$$LD
Boston ▪ (617) 422-0224
*560 Harrison Ave ▪ French ▪* Alert server when ordering that you are GF. Most menu items can be made GF. ▪ *www.gaslight560.com*

## Grill 23 & Bar               $$$$D
Boston ▪ (617) 542-2255
*161 Berkeley St ▪ Modern American ▪* Manager Jason notes that restaurant staff is knowledgeable about gluten. He recommends noting GF in reservations and bringing a GF dining card. The menu varies, but chefs can usually modify seafood and steak dishes to be GF. Confirm the timeliness of this information before dining in. ▪ *www.grill23.com*

## Hamersley's Bistro           $$$$D
Boston ▪ (617) 423-2700
*553 Tremont St ▪ Modern American ▪* The restaurant reports that waiters are "very knowledgeable" about the GF diet. Many dishes can be modified to be GF. Dessert options include crème brûlée, lemon semifreddo, meringue, and chocolate mousse. The manager notes that when it comes to GF diners, "the more advance notice, the better." ▪ *www.hamersleysbistro.com*

## Hard Rock Café               ✪📖
Boston ▪ (617) 424-7625
*22-24 Clinton St*

**Helmand Restaurant**    $$LD
Boston ▪ (617) 492-4646
143 First St ▪ Middle Eastern ▪ The res-
taurant reports that most of their menu is
naturally GF, and recommends asking for a
manager to go over the menu when dining
in. ▪ www.helmandrestaurant.com

**Hillstone Restaurants**    📖
Boston ▪ (617) 573-9777
60 State St

**Legal Sea Foods**    ✪📖
Boston ▪ (617) 266-7775
100 Huntington Ave
Boston ▪ (617) 330-7430
225 Northern Ave
Boston ▪ (617) 742-5300
255 State St
Boston ▪ (617) 426-4444
26 Park Plz
Boston ▪ (617) 266-6800
800 Boylston St
Boston ▪ (617) 568-1888
1 Harborside Dr - Term A
Boston ▪ (617) 568-2811
1 Harborside Dr - Term B
Boston ▪ (617) 568-2800
1 Harborside Dr - Term C
Boston ▪ (617) 477-2900
270 Northern Ave

**Maggiano's Little Italy**    ★📖
Boston ▪ (617) 542-3456
4 Columbus Ave

**Melting Pot, The**    ✪📖
Boston ▪ (617) 357-7007
76 Arlington St

**Morton's Steakhouse**    ✪📖
Boston ▪ (617) 526-0410
2 Seaport Ln

**Myers + Chang**    ✪$LD
Boston ▪ (617) 542-5200
1145 Washington St ▪ Asian ▪ Myers +
Chang offers a GF lunch and dinner menu
containing items such as dim sum, pan
roasted salmon and various rice noodle stir
fries. ▪ www.myersandchang.com

**Nebo Ristorante and Enoteca**    ✪★$$D
Boston ▪ (617) 723-6326
90 N Washington St ▪ Italian ▪ Extensive
GF menu includes variations of almost
all the dishes on the regular menu. Selections include zucchini lasagna, cioppino, a
variety of pasta and pizza dishes, and more.
Several GF dessert selections are also available. ▪ www.neborestaurant.com

**P.F. Chang's China Bistro**    ✪★📖
Boston ▪ (617) 573-0821
8 Park Plz Spc D-6
Boston ▪ (617) 378-9961
Prudential Tower

**Papa Razzi**    ★📖
Boston ▪ (617) 536-9200
159 Newbury St

**Prêt A Manger**    📖
Boston ▪ (617) 204-9280
185 Franklin Str
Boston ▪ (617) 236-0634
507 Boylston St

**Ruth's Chris Steak House**    ✪📖
Boston ▪ (617) 742-8401
45 School St

**Scampo**    ✪★$$BLD
Boston ▪ (617) 536-2100
215 Charles St ▪ Italian ▪ Scampo offers an
online and in restaurant GF menu featur-
ing items such as tandoori fired sea scal-
lops, countless GF spaghetti sauce options,
various meats and fingerling potatoes. ▪
www.scampoboston.com

**Skipjack's**    $$$LD
Boston ▪ (617) 536-3500
199 Clarendon St ▪ Seafood ▪ All locations
report that there are several naturally GF
menu items, as well as a variety of others
that can be modified to be GF. They have
GF lists that can be printed upon request.
Alert a server, who will notify the chef.
Hours and GF options vary by location. ▪
www.skipjacks.com

### Smith & Wollensky  📖
Boston ▪ (617) 423-1112
101 Arlington St
Boston ▪ (617) 778-2200
294 Congress St

### Stephanie's on Newbury  $$$LD
Boston ▪ (617) 236-0990
190 Newbury St ▪ Modern American
▪ Team member Anna reports that
the restaurant accommodates GF diners "every day." She advises alerting the
server, who will notify the chef and
manager. She also notes that the chefs are
happy to speak directly to GF diners. ▪
www.stephaniesonnewbury.com

### Tossed  ✪📖
Boston ▪ (617) 424-8677
800 Boylston St

### Tremont 647  $$$D
Boston ▪ (617) 266-4600
647 Tremont St ▪ American ▪ GF items
are available on the menu except Tuesday nights. The restaurant notes that
the kitchen always accommodates
dietary restrictions and will work with
GF diners to come up with GF options.
Reservations noting GF are recommended. Alert the server upon arrival. ▪
www.tremont647.com

### Tu Y Yo  $$LD
Boston ▪ (617) 623-5411
858 Broadway St ▪ Mexican ▪ Many of
their regular menu items are GF, confirm with your server before ordering. ▪
tuyyo2.com

### U Food Grill  📖
Boston ▪ (617) 561-8899
1 Harborside Dr, Terminal B
Boston ▪ (617) 567-2214
1 Harborside Dr, Terminal C
Boston ▪ (617) 451-0043
530 Washington St
Boston ▪ (857) 254-0082
201 Brookline Ave

### Union Oyster House  $$$LD
Boston ▪ (617) 227-2750

41 Union St ▪ Seafood ▪ The restaurant
notes that accommodating GF diners
should not be a problem, and that broiled
lobster, filets, and scallops are available
GF. Fried items are not GF. Confirm the
timeliness of this information before dining in. Reservations noting GF are recommended. ▪ www.unionoysterhouse.com

### Uno Chicago Grill  ✪★📖
Boston ▪ (617) 424-1697
280 Huntington Ave
Boston ▪ (617) 262-4911
645 Beacon St
Boston ▪ (617) 267-8554
731 Boylston St

### Wagamama  $LD
Boston ▪ (617) 742-9242
1 Faneuil Hall Sq
Boston ▪ (617) 778-2344
800 Boylston St ▪ Asian ▪ GF items
include cha han, yasai cha han, yaki soba,
yasai yaki soba, chicken kare, yasai kare,
moyashi soba, edamame and grilled asparagus. ▪ www.wagamama.us

### Yard House  ✪📖
Boston ▪ (617) 236-4083
126 Brookline Ave

# MASSACHUSETTS
## CAMBRIDGE

### Au Bon Pain  📖
Cambridge ▪ (617) 354-4144
1100 Massachusetts
Cambridge ▪ (617) 492-0884
684 Massachusetts Ave
Cambridge ▪ (617) 225-0347
47 Commercial Ave
Cambridge ▪ (617) 497-9797
1360 Massachusetts Ave
Cambridge ▪ (617) 492-0734
124 Mount Auburn St

*Cambridge* ▪ *(617) 491-9751*
*238 Main St*
*Cambridge* ▪ *(617) 494-9726*
*3 Cambridge Center*

### Bertucci's　✪ 📖
*Cambridge* ▪ *(617) 864-4748*
*21 Brattle St*
*Cambridge* ▪ *(617) 876-2200*
*5 Cambridgepark Dr*
*Cambridge* ▪ *(617) 661-8356*
*799 Main St*

### Blue Room　$$$D
*Cambridge* ▪ *(617) 494-9034*
*1 Kendall Sq* ▪ *Modern American* ▪ Restaurant reports that many items on the menu are naturally GF or can be modified to be GF. Alert a server upon arrival. ▪ *www.theblueroom.net*

### Boloco　★📖
*Cambridge* ▪ *(617) 354-5838*
*71 Mt Auburn St*

### Casablanca　$$$LD
*Cambridge* ▪ *(617) 876-0999*
*40 Brattle St* ▪ *Mediterranean* ▪ Manager advises alerting a server upon arrival. Many dishes, such as the tuna tapas and certain dips, can be modified to be GF. Confirm the timeliness of this information before dining in. ▪ *www.casablanca-restaurant.com*

### Cosi　✪📖
*Cambridge* ▪ *(617) 868-5810*
*290 Main St*

### Elephant Walk, The　✪$$LD
*Cambridge* ▪ *(617) 492-6900*
*2067 Massachusetts Ave* ▪ *Fusion* ▪ GF menu includes shrimp curry, grilled flat iron steak, quinoa gratin with vegetables, and more. Most soups and salads are GF. GF desserts like chocolate truffle cake and sorbet are also available. Be sure to alert server that you are ordering from the GF menu. Hands-on GF cooking classes are offered. ▪ *www.elephantwalk.com*

### EVOO Restaurant　$$$D
*Cambridge* ▪ *(617) 661-3866*
*350 3rd St* ▪ *Modern American* ▪ Server Tim reports that they accommodate GF diners "all the time." He notes that the smoked rabbit confit salad and the beef tenderloin are naturally GF, while other items such as the oysters can be modified to be GF. Confirm the timeliness of this information before dining in. Tim also recommends making a reservation noting GF a day in advance. ▪ *www.evoorestaurant.com*

### Finale Dessert Company　✪★$$
*Cambridge* ▪ *(617) 441-9797*
*30 Dunster St* ▪ *Dessert* ▪ GF desserts include the flourless dark chocolate decadence cake, the original cheesecake, coconut cream tarts, and a variety of puddings. Confirm the timeliness of this information before dining in. Servers are familiar with GF desserts and will be able to indicate GF items. They also have a GF menu for their lunch and dinner service. ▪ *www.finaledesserts.com*

### Fire + Ice　★📖
*Cambridge* ▪ *(617) 547-9007*
*50 Church St*

### John Harvard's Brew House　$$LD
*Cambridge* ▪ *(617) 868-3585*
*33 Dunster St* ▪ *American* ▪ Manager Eric reports that the restaurant serves GF diners "sometimes." He notes that most salads can be made GF, but cautions that dressings are not made on site and may contain gluten. He also recommends ordering chicken or steak dishes without seasoning, as the seasoning is not GF. Confirm the timeliness of this information before dining in. ▪ *www.johnharvards.com*

### Legal Sea Foods　✪📖
*Cambridge* ▪ *(617) 491-9400*
*20 University Rd*
*Cambridge* ▪ *(617) 864-3400*
*5 Cambridge Ctr*

## Lord Hobo                      $$D
*Cambridge* ▪ *(617) 250-8454*
*92 Hampshire St* ▪ *Bistro* ▪ GF options
available on menu. Some items include
polenta fries, lamb belly, duck, oxtail stew,
antipasti plate and trout. Alert server upon
arrival and they will list GF options. ▪
*lordhobo.com*

## P.F. Chang's China Bistro       ✪★▥
*Cambridge* ▪ *(617) 250-9965*
*100 Cambridgeside Pl Ste C101*

## Rialto                      ✪★$$$$D
*Cambridge* ▪ *(617) 661-5050*
*1 Bennett St* ▪ *Mediterranean* ▪ GF
menu available. Alert server upon arrival.
Servers are well versed on menu items
and ingredients and they will be able
to pick out GF items from the menu. ▪
*www.rialto-restaurant.com*

## Stone Hearth Pizza Co.          ✪★$LD
*Cambridge* ▪ *(617) 492-1111*
*1782 Massachusetts Ave* ▪ *Pizza* ▪ GF pizza,
pasta, and beer are available. GF pizza options are marked on the menu, along with
other GF options such as appetizers and
salads. For dessert, they offer hot fudge
sundaes and ice cream floats. The restaurant reports that their CC policies include
using separate utensils and cookware for GF
items and stretching all pizzas on rice flour
to minimize the chance of airborne wheat
particles. ▪ *www.stonehearthpizza.com*

## Uno Chicago Grill               ✪★▥
*Cambridge* ▪ *(617) 497-1530*
*22 Jfk St*

## Wagamama                       $LD
*Cambridge* ▪ *(617) 499-0930*
*57 JFK St* ▪ *Asian* ▪ GF items include cha
han, yasai cha han, yaki soba, yasai yaki
soba, chicken kare, yasai kare, moyashi
soba, edamame and grilled asparagus. ▪
*www.wagamama.us*

# MASSACHUSETTS
## ALL OTHER CITIES

## Alice's Diner               ✪★¢BL
*Fall River* ▪ *(508) 675-9210*
*2663 S Main St* ▪ *American* ▪ GF breakfast
menu includes waffles, pancakes, French
toast, three egg omelet, crepes, and more.
GF lunch menu includes Portuguese
steak, hamburger plate, meatloaf, golden
fried chicken tenders, sandwiches, pizza,
soups, and a variety of seafood specials. ▪
*www.alicesdiner.com*

## Angelo's Pizzeria & Ristorante   ★$$$LD
*Stoneham* ▪ *(781) 438-8598*
*239 Main St* ▪ *Italian* ▪ GF pasta, pizza,
and beer are available. Owner Angelo
notes that accommodating GF requests
is "no problem." Menu items that can
be modified to be GF include eggplant
dishes, chicken, veal, and several seafood
dishes. Upon arrival, alert the server,
who will talk to the kitchen. Reservations noting GF are recommended. ▪
*www.angeloristorante.com*

## Atria                        $$$$D
*Edgartown* ▪ *(508) 627-5850*
*137 Main St* ▪ *Modern American* ▪ Restaurant reports they are able to accommodate
GF diners and have several naturally GF
options as well as some selections that
can be "specialized" to be GF. Reservations noting GF are recommended.
Ask server for current GF options. ▪
*www.atriamv.com*

## Au Bon Pain                     ▥
*Burlington* ▪ *(781) 272-6660*
*1310 Burlington Mall*
*Somerville* ▪ *(617) 623-9601*
*18-48 Holland St*
*Natick* ▪ *(508) 651-0919*
*1245 Worcester St*
*Peabody* ▪ *(978) 531-4849*
*210 Andover St*

*Pembroke* ▪ *(781) 826-9729*
*156 Church St*
*Braintree* ▪ *(781) 356-4497*
*250 Granite St*
*Dedham* ▪ *(781) 329-0758*
*950 Providence Hwy*

## Baku's                                    ✪$LD
*Amherst* ▪ *(413) 253-7202*
*197 N Pleasant St* ▪ African ▪ All menu
items are GF, including appetizers, soups,
and entrées. Examples of entrées are
the sautéed shrimp with onions, curry
chicken, and Nigerian stew. Confirm the
timeliness of this information before dining in. ▪ *www.bakusafricanrestaurant.com*

## Belmont Vegetarian Restaurant    ☾LD
*Worcester* ▪ *(508) 798-8898*
*157 Belmont St* ▪ Vegetarian ▪ Server
will inform you of your GF options upon
request. ▪ *belmontvegetarian.com*

## Bertucci's                              ✪📖
*Amherst* ▪ *(413) 549-1900*
*51 E Pleasant St*
*Andover* ▪ *(978) 470-3939*
*90 Main St*
*Beverly* ▪ *(978) 927-6866*
*27 Enon St*
*Braintree* ▪ *(781) 849-3066*
*412 Franklin St*
*Brockton* ▪ *(508) 584-3080*
*1285 Belmont St*
*Canton* ▪ *(781) 828-9901*
*95 Washington St*
*Chelmsford* ▪ *(978) 250-8800*
*14 Littleton Rd*
*Framingham* ▪ *(508) 879-9161*
*150 Worcester Rd*
*Hingham* ▪ *(781) 740-4405*
*90 Derby St*
*Holliston* ▪ *(508) 429-4571*
*414 Washington St*
*Lexington* ▪ *(781) 860-9000*
*1777 Massachusetts Ave*
*Longmeadow* ▪ *(413) 567-4900*
*674 Bliss Rd*
*Mansfield* ▪ *(508) 261-2371*
*280 School St*

*Marlborough* ▪ *(508) 485-3636*
*601 Donald Lynch Blvd*
*Medford* ▪ *(781) 396-9933*
*4054 Mystic Valley Pkwy*
*Needham* ▪ *(781) 449-3777*
*1257 Highland Ave*
*Newton* ▪ *(617) 244-4900*
*275 Centre St*
*North Andover* ▪ *(978) 685-4498*
*435 Andover St*
*North Attleboro* ▪ *(508) 699-2491*
*999 S Washington St*
*Norwood* ▪ *(781) 762-4155*
*1405 Boston Providence Tpke Ste 1-5*
*Peabody* ▪ *(978) 535-0969*
*15 Newbury St*
*Plymouth* ▪ *(508) 747-1187*
*6 Plaza Wy*
*Randolph* ▪ *(781) 986-8333*
*55 Mazzeo Dr*
*Reading* ▪ *(781) 942-2001*
*45 Walkers Brook Dr*
*Swampscott* ▪ *(781) 581-6588*
*450 Paradise Rd*
*Taunton* ▪ *(508) 880-0222*
*2 Galleria Mall Dr*
*Waltham* ▪ *(781) 684-0650*
*475 Winter St*
*Wellesley* ▪ *(781) 239-0990*
*380 Washington St*
*West Springfield* ▪ *(413) 788-9900*
*847 Riverdale St*
*Westborough* ▪ *(508) 898-3074*
*160 Turnpike Rd Rte 9*
*Woburn* ▪ *(781) 933-1440*
*17 Commerce Wy*
*Wayland* ▪ *(508) 276-8235*
*14 Elissa Ave*

## Beth's Special Teas Bakery & Café  ★☾S
*Sandwich* ▪ *(508) 888-7716*
*16 Jarves St* ▪ Bakery & Café ▪ A rotating selection of GF baked goods is
available, including muffins and cookies. GF lunch options are available as
well. Examples of typical GF menu items
include crustless quiche and salads. ▪
*www.capecodteashop.com*

## Blue Ginger　　　　✿★$$$$**LD**
*Wellesley* ▪ *(781) 283-5790*
*583 Washington St* ▪ *Asian Fusion* ▪ GF
menu includes items such as sake-miso
marinated sablefish, pan seared scallops with ponzu broccoli rabe, and tea
smoked tofu with sautéed farm greens.
Note GF when making reservations, and
alert the server upon arrival. GF fish sauce
and GF tamari soy sauce are available. ▪
*www.ming.com/blueginger*

## Boloco　　　　★📖
*Brighton* ▪ *(617) 739-0340*
*1940 Beacon St*
*Natick* ▪ *(508) 907-7286*
*1265 Worcester St*
*Medford* ▪ *(617) 848-3714*
*340 Boston Ave*
*Wellesley* ▪ *(781) 489-6071*
*102 Central St*

## Box Office Café, The　　　✿★₵**BLD**
*South Chatham* ▪ *(508) 430-5211*
*2642 Main St* ▪ *American* ▪ The Box Office Café offers GF pizza crust and beer
in addition to GF flat bread which any of
their deluxe sandwiches can be made on. ▪
*www.theboxofficecafe.com*

## Boynton Restaurant & Spirits, The ★ $**LD**
*Worcester* ▪ *(508) 756-5432*
*117 Highland St* ▪ *Italian* ▪ GF pizza and
chocolate mousse cake are available. ▪
*www.boyntonrestaurant.com*

## British Beer Company
## Restaurant and Pub, The　　✿★📖
*Walpole* ▪ *(508) 668-9909*
*85 Providence Hwy*
*Sandwich* ▪ *(508) 833-9590*
*46 Route 6A*
*Plymouth* ▪ *(508) 747-1776*
*6 Middle St*
*Pembroke* ▪ *(781) 829-6999*
*15 Columbia Rd*
*Hyannis* ▪ *(508) 771-1776*
*412 Main St*
*Framingham* ▪ *(508) 879-1776*
*120 Worcester Rd*

*Falmouth* ▪ *(508) 540-9600*
*263 Grand Ave*
*Plymouth* ▪ *(508) 888-9756*
*2294 State Rd*
*Franklin* ▪ *(508) 440-5190*
*280 Franklin Village Dr*
*Westford* ▪ *(978) 577-6034*
*149 Littleton Rd*

## Buca di Beppo　　　　✿📖
*Shrewsbury* ▪ *(508) 792-1737*
*7 Boston Tpke*

## Bugaboo Creek Steak House　　✿📖
*Braintree* ▪ *(781) 848-0002*
*551 John Mahar Hwy*
*Methuen* ▪ *(978) 794-9713*
*90 Pleasant Valley St*
*Milford* ▪ *(508) 478-2888*
*124 Medway Rd*

## Bullfinchs Restaurant　　　✿$$$**D**
*Sudbury* ▪ *(978) 443-4094*
*730 Boston Post Rd* ▪ *American* ▪ GF
menu includes filet mignon, grilled chicken,
roasted trout, and a few other items. The
restaurant reports that they are "more than
happy" to modify any dish to fit the needs of
their customers. ▪ *www.bullfinchs.com*

## Burtons Grill　　　　✿★📖
*North Andover* ▪ *(978) 688-5600*
*145 Turnpike St*
*Hingham* ▪ *(781) 749-1007*
*94 Derby St*
*Burlington* ▪ *(781) 221-2281*
*43 Middlesex Tpke*
*Peabody* ▪ *(978) 977-0600*
*210 Andover St*
*Westford* ▪ *(978) 692-1220*
*1 Cornerstone Sq*

## BZ's Mexican Pizzeria　　　★₵**LD**
*Dennisport* ▪ *(508) 394-6247*
*682 Main St* ▪ *Pizza* ▪ GF pizza is available. Restaurant reports that most toppings
are usually GF, but recommends asking a
server for the most current information.
Pizzas are available for dining in, take out,
or delivery. ▪ *www.bzspizza.com*

**Capital Grille, The**  ✪📖
*Burlington* ▪ *(781) 505-4130*
*10 Wayside Rd*
*Chestnut Hill* ▪ *(617) 928-1400*
*250 Boylston St*

**Carrabba's Italian Grill**  ✪📖
*Peabody* ▪ *(978) 535-3600*
*1A Newbury St*
*Tyngsboro* ▪ *(978) 649-8388*
*386 Middlesex Rd*
*W Springfield* ▪ *(413) 733-3960*
*955 Riverdale St*

**Charley's**  ★$$LD
*Chestnut Hill* ▪ *(617) 964-1200*
*199 Boylston St* ▪ *American* ▪ GF
pasta and pizza are available. ▪
*www.charleys-restaurant.com*

**Chianti Café**  ★$$$D
*Beverly* ▪ *(978) 921-2233*
*285 Cabot St* ▪ *Italian* ▪ Zucchilini, a
pasta made from zucchini, is available.
Restaurant reports that many menu items
can be modified to be GF. Alert server
upon arrival and they will notify chef. ▪
*chiantibeverly.com*

**China Sky**  ★$$LD
*Winchester* ▪ *(781) 729-6899*
*27 Converse Pl* ▪ *Chinese* ▪ The restau-
rant reports that GF is the most frequent
"allergy" request. GF soy sauce is available.
Reservations noting GF are recommended.
▪ *www.chinaskywinchester.com*

**Chloe: An American Bistro**  ✪$$$LD
*Hudson* ▪ *(978) 568-1500*
*23 Main St* ▪ *American* ▪ Owner Matthew
reports that GF diners come in "all the
time." Items that may be prepared GF are
denoted with a symbol on the menu, and
include sautéed lemon sole, mushroom
risotto, steak frites, and seared Atlantic salmon. Matthew also notes that the
kitchen is "very GF aware." Reservations
noting GF are recommended. Alert server
upon arrival. ▪ *www.chloebistro.com*

**City Feed and Supply**  ★¢BLD
*Jamaica Plain* ▪ *(617) 524-1700*
*672 Centre St*
*Jamaica Plain* ▪ *(617) 524-1657*
*66A Boylston St* ▪ *Deli* ▪ GF bread is available for any sandwich at both locations.
The Centre Street location also reports GF
baked goods, but notes that they run out
quickly. ▪ *www.cityfeedandsupply.com*

**Coffee Obsession**  ★¢S
*Falmouth* ▪ *(508) 540-2233*
*110 Palmer Ave*
*Woods Hole* ▪ *(508) 540-8130*
*38 Water St* ▪ *Coffee Shop* ▪ GF banana bread and banana muffins are
"almost always" available at both locations. Call ahead to confirm availability. ▪
*www.coffeeobsession.com*

**Cosi**  ✪📖
*Mansfield* ▪ *(508) 261-8740*
*280 School St*
*Wareham* ▪ *(508) 295-1035*
*2421 Cranberry Hwy*

**Crown Bakery & Café, The**  ★¢S
*Worcester* ▪ *(508) 852-0746*
*133 Gold Star Blvd* ▪ *Bakery & Café* ▪
Non-dedicated GF bakery offering GF
baked goods like chocolate triangles, jelly
rolls, cake, and more. GF options change
daily, but Manager Jeanie reports that they
will "always have something" that is GF. ▪
*www.thecrownbakery.com*

**David's Tavern on Brown Square**  $$D
*Newburyport* ▪ *(978) 462-8077*
*11 Brown Sq* ▪ *Global* ▪ Owner and Chef
Steve reports that they accommodate
"almost any allergy." There are many grilled
steak dishes, like filet mignon, steak tips,
and prime rib, on the menu, and they
can all be prepared GF. He adds that the
restaurant serves GF diners "quite often,"
so the staff is familiar with the GF diet. ▪
*www.davidstavern.com*

### Davio's Northern Italian Steakhouse ✪📖
*Foxborough* ▪ *(508) 339-4810*
*236 Patriot Pl*

### Eastside Grill        $$D
*Northampton* ▪ *(413) 586-3347*
*19 Strong Ave* ▪ *Modern American* ▪
Owner Deborah reports that the staff is
very knowledgeable about which menu
items are or can be modified to be GF. ▪
*www.eastsidegrill.com*

### Elephant Walk, The     ✪$$LD
*Waltham* ▪ *(781) 899-2244*
*663 Main St* ▪ *Fusion* ▪ GF menu includes
shrimp curry, grilled flat iron steak, quinoa
gratin with vegetables, and more. Most
soups and salads are GF. GF desserts like
chocolate truffle cake and sorbet are also
available. Be sure to alert server that you
are ordering from the GF menu. Hands-
on GF cooking classes are offered. ▪
*www.elephantwalk.com*

### Evo         ✪★ $$BLD
*Worcester* ▪ *(508) 459-4240*
*234 Chandler St* ▪ *Modern American* ▪
Extensive regular menu marked with GF
options including spinach dip, Italian
French toast, steak, swordfish, baby spinach salad, and several wraps. GF sandwich
breads and burger buns are available. ▪
*www.evodining.com*

### Fireplace, The      ✪$$$LD
*Brookline* ▪ *(617) 975-1900*
*1634 Beacon St* ▪ *Modern American* ▪ GF
brunch, lunch, dinner, and dessert menus
available. GF menu items include butternut
squash bisque, crispy duck in port cherry
sauce, and cedar plank salmon. GF desserts
include assorted cupcakes and a chocolate
brownie sundae. ▪ *www.fireplacerest.com*

### Fitzwilly's        $LD
*Northampton* ▪ *(413) 584-8666*
*23 Main St* ▪ *American* ▪ Manager Matt
reports that GF diners are "very easily"
accommodated. Menu items that can be
modified to be GF include chicken breast
with pico de gallo, seared tuna, and spinach
and artichoke hearts. Confirm the timeliness of this information before dining in. ▪
*www.fitzwillys.com*

### Five Bites Cupcakes     ★₵$
*Wellesley* ▪ *(781) 235-5755*
*141 Linden St* ▪ *Bakery* ▪ Manager Cathy
reports that GF cupcakes are available Wednesday afternoons through
Saturday. GF flavors are vanilla, strawberry, and snickerdoodle. Cathy advises
that GF cupcakes sometimes sell out,
so call ahead to have some set aside. ▪
*www.fivebitescupcakes.com*

### Flatbread Pizza Company    ★📖
*Amesbury* ▪ *(978) 834-9800*
*5 Market Sq*
*Bedford* ▪ *(781) 275-8200*
*213 Burlington Rd*
*Somerville* ▪ *(617) 776-0552*
*45 Day St*
*Edgartown* ▪ *(508) 693-1137*
*17 Airport Rd*

### Flavours       ✪★$$LD
*Pittsfield* ▪ *(413) 443-3188*
*75 North St* ▪ *Asian* ▪ Flavours has a
regular menu marked with GF options.
Options include pad thai noodles, spicy
Malaysian chicken curry, grilled teryaki
ahi tuna, spicy vegetable panang curry
and more. Additionally all of the entrées
offered can be cooked GF, just be sure
to notify your server while ordering. ▪
*www.flavoursintheberkshires.com*

### Flora        $$$D
*Arlington* ▪ *(781) 641-1664*
*190 Massachusetts Ave* ▪ *Modern American* ▪ Chef Keith reports that the restaurant gets GF requests "all the time." He
notes that several dishes are naturally GF,
and many other dishes can be modified
to be GF. Alert the server, who will write
up a special GF ticket and confer with
the kitchen. ▪ *www.florarestaurant.com*

### Franklin Café, The     ✪$$D
*Gloucester* ▪ *(978) 283-7888*
*118 Main St* ▪ *Modern American* ▪ Frank-

lin Café offers a GF dinner menu offering items such as black pepper seared ahi tuna, pan roaster organic chicken, and garlic grilled calamari. ▪ www.franklincafe.com

### Fresh City                                    ★ 📖
*Burlington* ▪ *(781) 273-0500*
*2 Wayside Rd*
*Charlton* ▪ *(508) 248-6788*
*I-90 W*
*Natick* ▪ *(508) 875-5750*
*1400 Worcester Rd*
*Newton* ▪ *(617) 244-7071*
*241 Needham St*
*Woburn* ▪ *(781) 932-1120*
*4-5 Cummings Pk*
*Framingham* ▪ *(508) 788-5114*
*I-90 W*
*Westborough* ▪ *(508) 616-0079*
*I-90 W*
*Lee* ▪ *(413) 243-3268*
*I-90 E*

### Garden at the Cellar                          $$LD
*Boston* ▪ *(617) 230-5880*
*991 Massachusetts Ave* ▪ *American* ▪ Almost all of their menu can be modified to be GF. ▪ www.gardenatthecellar.com

### Gibbet Hill Grill                             ✪$$$D
*Groton* ▪ *(978) 448-2900*
*61 Lowell Rd* ▪ *American* ▪ GF menu includes shepherd's pie, pan-roasted duck, sautéed halibut, sirloin steak tips, and several sides. The restaurant reports that the GF menu is an adaptation of the regular menu, and the chefs went over it "with a fine-tooth comb." They also report that GF diners are "always welcome." ▪ www.gibbethill.com

### Glutenus Minimus                             ⊄BLD
*Belmont* ▪ *(617) 484-3550*
*697 Belmont St* ▪ *Bakery* ▪ Dedicated GF bakery offering a wide selection of baked goods, including cookies, cakes, cupcakes, muffins, and holiday specials. They also offer "take-&-bake" mixes for cookies, breads, and pizza crust. ▪ www.glutenusminimus.com

### Greg's Pizza                                  ★$$LD
*Wilmington* ▪ *(978) 658-3063*
*296 Shawsheen Ave* ▪ *Pizza* ▪ GF pizza is available. Note GF when placing an order.

### Greta's Great Grains                          ★⊄S
*Newburyport* ▪ *(978) 465-1709*
*24 Pleasant St* ▪ *Bakery* ▪ Non-dedicated bakery offering GF muffins, cakes, brownies, cookies, and more. Owner Greta reports that "basic items" are always available, but call ahead to ask what other items they have on a given day. ▪ www.gretasgreatgrains.com

### Grog, The                                     ✪★$$LD
*Newburyport* ▪ *(978) 465-8008*
*13 Middle St* ▪ *Global* ▪ Full GF menu includes seared ahi tuna, Greek spinach salad, steak chimichurri, pan-seared flounder, and more. Chocolate mousse and crème brûlée are available for dessert. GF hamburger buns, beer, and cider are also available. Confirm the timeliness of this information before dining in. ▪ www.thegrog.com

### Hillside Organic Pizza                        ★$$LD
*Hadley* ▪ *(413) 585-0003*
*173 Russell St*
*S Deerfield* ▪ *(413) 665-5533*
*265 Greenfield Rd*
*Bernardston* ▪ *(413) 648-0500*
*77 Church St* ▪ *Pizza* ▪ GF pizza, cupcakes, and whoopie pies are available. The Hadley location also carries GF bread for sandwiches. GF safe pizza toppings are specified on the menu, and the restaurant reports that they "make every effort" to avoid CC. ▪ www.hillsidepizza.com

### India House                                   ✪$$LD
*Northampton* ▪ *(413) 586-6344*
*45 State St* ▪ *Indian* ▪ All special entrées can be cooked GF, and their regular menu is marked to show which sides and appetizers are GF. ▪ www.indiahousenorthampton.com

## J. Gumbo's ★📖
*Amherst* ▪ *(413) 835-0681*
*19 N Pleasant St*

## Jersey Mike's 📖
*Raynham* ▪ *(508) 823-1006*
*325 New State Hwy Route 44*

## John Harvard's Brew House $$LD
*Hancock* ▪ *(413) 738-5500*
*37 Corey Rd*
*Framingham* ▪ *(508) 875-2337*
*1 Worcester Rd* ▪ *American* ▪ Manager
Eric reports that the restaurant serves GF
diners "sometimes." He notes that most
salads can be made GF, but cautions that
dressings are not made on site and may
contain gluten. He also recommends
ordering chicken or steak dishes without
seasoning, as the seasoning is not GF.
Confirm the timeliness of this information
before dining in. ▪ *www.johnharvards.com*

## Kickass Cupcakes ★¢S
*Somerville* ▪ *(617) 628-2877*
*378 Highland Ave* ▪ *Bakery* ▪ A daily assortment of GF cupcakes are available. Possible flavors include vanilla with vanilla or
chocolate frosting and mojito. Special GF
orders can be accommodated with advance
notice of two days. It is recommended
to call prior to coming into the bakery. ▪
*www.kickasscupcakes.com*

## Landing, The ✪$$$LD
*Marblehead* ▪ *(781) 639-1266*
*81 Front St* ▪ *Modern American* ▪ Restaurant reports that an entire GF menu is
available in the restaurant with a wide variety of entrées. Alert server upon arrival. ▪
*www.thelandingrestaurant.com*

## Legal Sea Foods ✪📖
*Braintree* ▪ *(781) 356-3070*
*250 Granite St*
*Burlington* ▪ *(781) 270-9700*
*75 Middlesex Tpke*
*Chestnut Hill* ▪ *(617) 277-0404*
*43 Boylston St*
*Framingham* ▪ *(508) 766-0600*
*50-60 Worcester Rd*

*Dedham* ▪ *(781) 234-6500*
*950 Providence Hwy*
*Peabody* ▪ *(978) 532-4500*
*210 Andover Str*

## Loving Hut 📖
*Worcester* ▪ *(508) 831-1322*
*56 Hamilton St*
*Worcester* ▪ *(508) 459-0367*
*415 Chandler St*

## Lunchbox Deli ★¢LD
*Norwood* ▪ *(781) 769-9500*
*859 Providence Hwy* ▪ *Deli* ▪ The
Lunchbox Deli offers GF bread on
all deli sandwiches, in addition to
various GF soup and salad options. ▪
*www.lunchboxdelinorwood.com*

## Max Burger ★$$LD
*Longmeadow* ▪ *(413) 798-0101*
*684 Bliss Rd* ▪ *Deli* ▪ GF beer and hamburger buns are available. Restaurant reports
that all servers are trained in the GF diet. ▪
*www.maxrestaurantgroup.com/burger*

## Max's Tavern ✪★$$$LD
*Springfield* ▪ *(413) 746-6299*
*1000 W Columbus Ave* ▪ *Modern American* ▪ GF menu is located online and includes shrimp, oysters, chicken wings, strip
steak, salmon, and a chop salad. Restaurant
reports that they host GF diners "every
once in a while." GF pasta is available. ▪
*www.maxrestaurantgroup.com*

## Melting Pot, The ✪📖
*Bedford* ▪ *(781) 791-0529*
*213 Burlington Rd*
*Framingham* ▪ *(508) 875-3115*
*92 Worcester Rd*

## Mezza Luna ✪$$$LD
*Cape Cod* ▪ *(508) 759-4667*
*253 Main St Buzzards Bay* ▪ *Italian* ▪
GF lunch and dinner menus are available. Selections include veal scallopini,
chicken cacciatore, broiled haddock,
filet mignon, and more. Be sure to specify that you are ordering from the GF
menu to "ensure proper preparation." ▪
*www.mezzalunarestaurant.com*

**Miller's Ale House Restaurants** ✪★📖
*Watertown* ▪ *(617) 926-2500*
*617 Arsenal St*

**Nadim's Mediterranean Grill** $$LD
*Springfield* ▪ *(413) 737-7373*
*1390 Main St*
*East Longmeadow* ▪ *(413) 525-1150*
*60 Shaker Rd* ▪ *Middle Eastern* ▪
The majority of the menu is GF. ▪
*www.nadims.com*

**Naked Fish** ✪$$$LD
*Waltham* ▪ *(781) 684-0500*
*455 Totten Pond Rd* ▪ *Seafood* ▪ Items
that CONTAIN gluten are denoted on the
menu. GF guests can choose from options
not marked with CG symbol. Alert a server
upon arrival to ensure proper preparation
of GF items. ▪ *www.nakedfish.com*

**Naked Oyster Restaurant** ✪$$$LD
*Hyannis* ▪ *(508) 778-6500*
*410 Main St* ▪ *Modern American* ▪ Res-
taurant reports that they are a "gluten
free-friendly" restaurant. Several GF en-
trées and appetizers are available for both
lunch and dinner. Examples include oyster
stew, pan seared fish tacos, grilled Thai
shrimp, and pistachio Scottish salmon. ▪
*www.nakedoyster.com*

**Nana's Pizza** ★$LD
*Everett* ▪ *(617) 389-6262*
*416 Main St* ▪ *Pizza* ▪ GF pizza is
available. Other GF options include
soups, salads, and chicken wings. ▪
*www.nanaseverett.com*

**Nancy Chang's** ✪★$LD
*Worcester* ▪ *(508) 752-8899*
*372 Chandler St* ▪ *Asian* ▪ GF menu
includes Thai beef salad, chicken & mango
curry, scallion ginger salmon, and yung
chow fried rice. GF soy sauce is available. ▪
*www.nancychang.com*

**Ninety Nine** ✪📖
*Andover* ▪ *(978) 475-8033*
*464 Lowell St*
*Auburn* ▪ *(508) 832-0999*

*793 Southbridge St*
*Billerica* ▪ *(978) 663-3999*
*160 Lexington Rd*
*Billerica* ▪ *(978) 667-9789*
*672 Boston Rd*
*Braintree* ▪ *(781) 849-9902*
*South Shore Plaza*
*Ashland* ▪ *(508) 820-0999*
*23 Pond St*
*Canton* ▪ *(781) 821-8999*
*362 Turnpike St*
*Centerville* ▪ *(508) 790-8995*
*1600 Falmouth Rd*
*Charlestown* ▪ *(617) 242-8999*
*29-31 Austin St*
*Chicopee* ▪ *(413) 593-9909*
*555 Memorial Dr*
*Danvers* ▪ *(978) 762-8994*
*60 Commonwealth Ave*
*East Longmeadow* ▪ *(413) 525-9900*
*390 N Main St*
*South Easton* ▪ *(508) 238-2999*
*99 Belmont St*
*Fairheaven* ▪ *(508) 992-9951*
*34 Sconticut Neck Rd*
*Fall River* ▪ *(508) 673-8999*
*404 Pleasant St*
*Falmouth* ▪ *(508) 457-9930*
*30 Davis Straits*
*Fitchburg* ▪ *(978) 343-0099*
*275 Summer St*
*Foxboro* ▪ *(508) 543-1199*
*4 Fisher St*
*Haverhill* ▪ *(978) 372-8303*
*786 River St*
*Hingham* ▪ *(781) 740-8599*
*428 Lincoln St*
*Holyoke* ▪ *(413) 532-9918*
*50 Holyoke St*
*Hudson* ▪ *(978) 562-9918*
*255 Washington St*
*Lowell* ▪ *(978) 458-9199*
*850 Chelmsford St*
*Lynnfield* ▪ *(781) 599-8119*
*317 Salem St*
*Marlboro* ▪ *(508) 480-8899*
*32 Boston Post Rd W*
*Mashpee* ▪ *(508) 477-9000*

8 Ryans Wy
*Milford* ▪ (508) 634-1999
196B E Main St
*North Andover* ▪ (978) 686-9999
267 Chickering Rd
*North Attleboro* ▪ (508) 399-9990
1510 S Washington St
*North Dartmouth* ▪ (508) 999-0099
161 Faunce Corner Rd
*Pembroke* ▪ (781) 829-9912
166 Church St
*Pittsfield* ▪ (413) 236-0980
699 Merrill Rd
*Plymouth* ▪ (508) 732-9932
21 Home Depot Dr
*Quincy* ▪ (617) 472-5000
59 Newport Ave
*Revere* ▪ (781) 289-9991
121 VFW Pkwy
*Rockland* ▪ (781) 871-4178
2 Accord Pk
*Salem* ▪ (978) 740-8999
15 Bridge St
*Saugus* ▪ (781) 233-1999
181 Broadway
*Seekonk* ▪ (508) 336-9899
821 Fall River Ave
*Sommerville* ▪ (617) 629-0599
20 Cummings St
*Springfield* ▪ (413) 731-9999
1371 Liberty St
*Springfield* ▪ (413) 273-8999
1655 Boston Rd
*Stoneham* ▪ (781) 279-0399
10 Main St
*Taunton* ▪ (508) 821-9922
158 Dean St
*Tewksbury* ▪ (978) 863-9099
401 Main St
*Walpole* ▪ (508) 668-6017
55 Boston Providence Tpke
*Waltham* ▪ (781) 893-4999
110 South St
*Wareham* ▪ (508) 295-9909
3013 Cranberry Hwy
*West Concord* ▪ (978) 369-0300
13 Commonwealth Ave
*West Springfield* ▪ (413) 585-1995

Riverdae Center
*West Yarmouth* ▪ (508) 862-9990
14 Berry Ave
*Westford* ▪ (978) 589-9948
333 Littleton St
*Weymouth* ▪ (781) 340-9000
1094 Main St
*Wilmington* ▪ (978) 657-9694
144 Lowell St
*Woburn* ▪ (781) 933-8999
160 Olympia Ave
*Woburn* ▪ (781) 935-7210
291 Mishawum Rd
*Woburn* ▪ (781) 938-8999
194 Cambridge Rd
*Worcester* ▪ (508) 363-3999
50 Southwest Cutoff
*Worcester* ▪ (508) 792-9997
11 E Central St
*Worcestor* ▪ (508) 852-2999
900 W Boylston St

## Not Your Average Joe's ✪📖

*Acton* ▪ (978) 635-0101
305 Main St
*Arlington* ▪ (781) 643-1666
645 Massachusetts Ave
*Beverly* ▪ (978) 927-8950
45 Enon St
*Burlington* ▪ (781) 505-1303
4 Wayside Rd
*Dartmouth* ▪ (508) 992-5637
61 State Rd
*Hyannis* ▪ (508) 778-1424
793 Iyannough Rd
*Medford* ▪ (781) 393-9681
501 Fellsway
*Newburyport* ▪ (978) 462-3808
1 Market Sq
*Norwell* ▪ (781) 616-6160
111 Pond St
*Randolph* ▪ (781) 961-7200
16 Mazzeo Dr
*Watertown* ▪ (617) 926-9229
55 Main St
*Westborough* ▪ (508) 986-2350
291 Turnpike Rd
*Methuen* ▪ (978) 974-0015
90 Pleasant Valley St

*Needham* ▪ *(781) 453-9300*
*109 Chapel St*
*Seekonk* ▪ *(508) 343-5637*
*1125 Fall River Ave*

## O'Connors Restaurant and Bar    $$LD
*Worcester* ▪ *(508) 853-0789*
*1160 W Boylston St* ▪ *Irish* ▪ The restaurant reports that many items on the
menu are GF or can easily be modified.
The menu specifically requests that guests
with Celiac disease notify their server. ▪
*www.oconnorsrestaurant.com*

## Old Jailhouse Tavern    ✪$$$LD
*Orleans* ▪ *(508) 255-5245*
*28 West Rd* ▪ *American* ▪ GF menu includes mussels marinara, salads with GF
dressing, oysters, clams, soups, steaks, and
more. ▪ *www.jailhousetavern.com*

## One Eleven Chophouse    ✪★$$$D
*Worcester* ▪ *(508) 799-4111*
*111 Shrewsbury St* ▪ *American* ▪ GF menu
includes crab & avocado cocktail, bacon &
spinach salad, grilled black pepper encrusted NY sirloin, swordfish, and more.
Dessert options include GF cheesecake
with strawberries, chocolate mousse, and
raspberry crème brûlée. GF beer is also
available. ▪ *www.111chophouse.com*

## One Love Café    $LD
*Worcester* ▪ *(508) 753-8663*
*800 Main St* ▪ *American* ▪ Owner reports
that a majority of their menu is GF. ▪
*www.sherwoodhosting.com~onelove/*

## P.F. Chang's China Bistro    ✪★📖
*Dedham* ▪ *(781) 461-6060*
*410 Legacy Pl*
*Natick* ▪ *(508) 651-7724*
*1245 Worcester St Ste 4008*
*Peabody* ▪ *(978) 326-2410*
*210 Andover St*

## Papa Razzi    ★📖
*Burlington* ▪ *(781) 229-0100*
*2 Wall St*
*Chestnut Hill* ▪ *(617) 527-6600*
*199 Boylston St*
*Framingham* ▪ *(508) 848-2300*

*155 Worcester Rd*
*Wellesley* ▪ *(781) 235-4747*
*16 Washington St*
*Concord* ▪ *(978) 371-0030*
*768 Elm St*

## Patsy's Pizzeria    ★
*East Longmeadow* ▪ *(413) 739-0275*
*600 N Main St* ▪ *Pizza* ▪ GF pizza, pasta,
and beer are available. ▪ *patsysel.com*

## Pho Saigon    ⊄LD
*Springfield* ▪ *(413) 781-4488*
*398 Dickinson St* ▪ *Vietnamese* ▪ Pho
is GF because they use rice noodles and
bones in their stock.

## Plum Island Grille    ✪$$$LD
*Newbury* ▪ *(978) 463-2290*
*2 Sunset Blvd* ▪ *Mediterranean* ▪ Owner
and Executive Chef Francis reports that
GF diners are "always welcome," and he
adds that all staff members are "very well
trained" on the GF diet. Items that are GF
are marked on the regular menu. Confirm
the timeliness of this information before
dining in. ▪ *www.plumislandgrille.com*

## Prana Café    ✪$BLD
*Newton* ▪ *(617) 527-7726*
*292 Centre St* ▪ *Raw* ▪ GF menu includes
flax cracker nachos, kelp noodle salad,
zucchini lasagna, chard leaf-wrapped
burrito, pesto primavera, Southwest taco
salad and more. ▪ *eatatprana.com*

## Rancho Chico Mexican Restaurant
✪$LD
*Plainville* ▪ *(508) 643-2534*
*52 Washington St* ▪ *Mexican* ▪ Limited GF
menu includes nachos, fajitas, enchiladas,
and salads.

## Rani Indian Bistro    $LD
*Brookline* ▪ *(617) 734-0400*
*1353 Beacon St* ▪ *Indian* ▪ Host Arjab
reports that "most of the entrées" are
naturally GF. He adds that GF diners can
choose from chicken, lamb, vegetarian,
or seafood dishes, but should be cautious
with appetizers, as many are not GF. Con-

firm the timeliness of this information before dining in. ■ *www.ranibistro.com*

## Rawbert's Organic Garden Café ★$BLD
*Beverly* ■ (978) 922-0004
*294 Cabot St* ■ *Raw* ■ Chef Robert reports that there are over one hundred GF menu options, which means that almost the entire menu is GF. GF bread and pizza are available. For dessert, they offer GF apple pie, blueberry pie, various cheesecakes, homemade chocolates, brownies, and cookies. ■ *www.organicgardencafe.com*

## Redbones Barbecue $$LD
*Somerville* ■ (617) 628-2200
*55 Chester St* ■ *Barbeque* ■ Redbones BBQ offers an extensive list of GF items which are listed on their general info tab on their website. Some of the items on it include salmon, chicken, and steaks, along with sides such as coleslaw and baked potatoes. ■ *redbones.com*

## Romano's Macaroni Grill ✪★▥
*Burlington* ■ (781) 273-5180
*50 S Ave*
*Reading* ■ (781) 944-0575
*48 Walkers Brook Dr*

## Scarlet Oak Tavern $$$LD
*Hingham* ■ (781) 749-8200
*1217 Main St* ■ *Seafood & Steakhouse* ■ Extensive GF menu includes sweet corn risotto, roasted beet salad, grilled BBQ shrimp, potato-crusted haddock, grilled hanger steak, and more. The menu also denotes which steak and seafood sauces are GF. ■ *www.scarletoaktavern.com*

## Scottish Bakehouse ✪★CS
*Vineyard Haven* ■ (508) 693-6633
*977 State Rd* ■ *Bakery* ■ A large assortment of GF baked goods is available, including macaroons, brownies, cookies, cakes, and pies. GF options are available every day, but for a specific item the bakery recommends placing a special order 48 hours in advance. The bakery also has a regular GF menu with lunch and dinner items that change frequently. ■ *scottishbakehousemv.com*

## Siena Italian Grill and Bar ✪★$$$LD
*Mashpee* ■ (508) 477-5929
*17 Steeple St* ■ *Italian* ■ GF menu includes salmon with honey dijon glaze, pan-seared jumbo scallops with citrus-basil pesto, and more. For dessert, they offer flourless chocolate cake. GF penne pasta available on request. ■ *www.siena.us*

## Skipjack's $$$LD
*Foxborough* ■ (508) 543-2200
*226 Patriot Pl* ■ *Seafood* ■ All locations report that there are several naturally GF menu items, as well as a variety of others that can be modified to be GF. They have GF lists that can be printed upon request. Alert a server, who will notify the chef. Hours and GF options vary by location. ■ *www.skipjacks.com*

## Smokey Bones ▥
*Tyngsboro* ■ (978) 649-5410
*431 Middlesex Rd*
*Stoughton* ■ (781) 297-5225
*301 Technology Center Dr*
*Taunton* ■ (508) 884-9566
*1023 County Rd*

## Sole Proprietor, The ✪★$$$LD
*Worcester* ■ (508) 798-3474
*118 Highland St* ■ *Seafood* ■ GF menu includes appetizers, sushi, lunch and dinner fish markets, as well as a variety of other entrées. Desserts on the GF menu include flan, chocolate terrine, cheesecake, and more. GF pasta, soy sauce, and beer are available. ■ *www.thesole.com*

## Spoleto ✪★$$$D
*Northampton* ■ (413) 586-6313
*50 Main St*
*Northampton* ■ (413) 586-6313
*1 Bridge St*
*East Longmeadow* ■ (413) 525-0055
*84 Center Sq* ■ *Italian* ■ GF rice pasta is available. The restaurant also reports a full GF menu in house, which lists available GF sauces and sides. Alert the server upon arrival. ■ *www.fundining.com*

### Stone Hearth Pizza Co.    ✪★$LD
*Belmont* ▪ (617) 484-1700
*57 Leonard St*
*Needham* ▪ (781) 433-0600
*974 Great Plain Ave*
*Allston* ▪ (617) 903-4680
*182 Western Ave* ▪ *Pizza* ▪ GF pizza, pasta, and beer are available. GF pizza options are marked on the menu, along with other GF options such as appetizers and salads. For dessert, they offer hot fudge sundaes and ice cream floats. The restaurant reports that their CC policies include using separate utensils and cookware for GF items and stretching all pizzas on rice flour to minimize the chance of airborne wheat particles. ▪ *www.stonehearthpizza.com*

### Tavolino    ✪★$$LD
*Foxborough* ▪ (508) 543-6543
*274 Patriot Pl*
*Westborough* ▪ (508) 366-8600
*33 E Main St* ▪ *Italian* ▪ Both locations have an extensive GF menu that includes pizzas, salads, antipasti, and carpaccio. GF pizza and pastas are available. ▪ *www.tavolinorestaurant.us*

### Ted's Montana Grill    ✪📖
*Westborough* ▪ (508) 366-5050
*400 Union St*

### Ten Center    $$$LD
*Newburyport* ▪ (978) 462-6652
*10 Center St* ▪ *Italian* ▪ Manager Stacy reports that the restaurant serves GF diners "more often than you would think." She notes that the restaurant staff recently attended an allergy training program that addressed the GF diet. She recommends reservations noting GF. The Atlantic cod with parsnips and bok choy can be prepared GF. Confirm the timeliness of this information before dining in. ▪ *www.tencenterstreet.com*

### Theodore's Blues, Booze & BBQ    $LD
*Springfield* ▪ (413) 736-6000
*201 Worthington St* ▪ *Barbeque* ▪ GF options include, ribs, grilled chicken, and multiple barbeque sauces. ▪ *theobbq.com*

### Tokyo    $$LD
*Springfield* ▪ (413) 782-3333
*415 Cooley St*
*West Springfield* ▪ (413) 788-7788
*1152 Riverdale St.* ▪ *Asian* ▪ Manager reports that all hibachi without soy sauce is GF as well as a majority of their sushi rolls. The soy sauce is NOT GF, so be sure to request items prepared without it. ▪ *www.tokyoasiancuisine.com*

### True Grounds    ★⊄S
*Somerville* ▪ (617) 591-9559
*717 Broadway* ▪ *Café* ▪ GF baked goods are available daily from a local Somerville baker. Call ahead to confirm availability. ▪ *www.truegrounds.com*

### Tu Y Yo    $$LD
*Needham* ▪ (781) 453-1000
*66 Chestnut St* ▪ *Mexican* ▪ Many of their regular menu items are GF, confirm with your server before ordering. ▪ *tuyyo2.com*

### Tuscan Grill    $$D
*Waltham* ▪ (781) 891-5486
*361 Moody St* ▪ *Italian* ▪ Chef Brian reports that nearly everything on the menu is GF. He notes that there is no "hidden gluten" on the menu, so an educated GF diner should have no trouble choosing a dish. Confirm that selections are GF by asking your server. ▪ *www.tuscangrillwaltham.com*

### Twist Bakery & Café    ⊄BLD
*Millis* ▪ (508) 376-1163
*30 Milliston Rd* ▪ *Bakery & Café* ▪ Dedicated GF bakery and café offering a wide variety of breads, pies, cakes, and other desserts, as well as sandwiches, salads, soups and breakfast items. ▪ *www.twist-bakery.com*

### Typical Sicilian Ristorante    ✪$$LD
*Springfield* ▪ (413) 739-7100
*497 Belmont Ave* ▪ *Italian* ▪ GF menu includes spicy garlic mussels, cioppino, chicken marsala, veal saltimbocca, and more. GF flour is used in place of regular

flour where applicable. Manager recommends calling ahead and notifying chefs so necessary precautions can be taken to avoid CC. ▪ *www.typicalsicilian.com*

### U Food Grill                                  📖
*Watertown* ▪ *(617) 923-7676*
*222 Arsenal St*

### Uno Chicago Grill                        ✪★📖
*Holyoke* ▪ *(413) 534-3000*
*50 Holyoke St*
*Attleboro* ▪ *(508) 399-6999*
*221 Washington St*
*Bellingham* ▪ *(508) 966-3300*
*205 Hartford Ave*
*Burlington* ▪ *(781) 229-1300*
*75 Middlesex Tpke Ste 1095*
*Dedham* ▪ *(781) 320-0356*
*270 Providence Hwy*
*Framingham* ▪ *(508) 620-1816*
*70 Worcester Rd*
*Hanover* ▪ *(781) 826-4453*
*1799 Washington St*
*Haverhill* ▪ *(978) 556-9595*
*30 Cushing Ave*
*Leominster* ▪ *(978) 466-7808*
*905 Merriam Ave*
*Millbury* ▪ *(508) 581-7866*
*70 Worcester Providence Tpke*
*Newton* ▪ *(617) 964-2296*
*287 Washington St*
*Springfield* ▪ *(413) 543-6600*
*1722 Boston Rd*
*Springfield* ▪ *(413) 733-1300*
*820 Hall Of Fame Ave*
*Sturbridge* ▪ *(508) 347-6420*
*100 Charlton Rd*
*Swampscott* ▪ *(781) 595-8667*
*970 Paradise Rd*
*Taunton* ▪ *(508) 828-9900*
*904 County St*
*Waltham* ▪ *(781) 487-7177*
*155 Bear Hill Rd*
*Westborough* ▪ *(508) 616-0300*
*225 Turnpike Rd*
*Woburn* ▪ *(781) 937-6016*
*300 Mishawum Rd*
*Wrentham* ▪ *(508) 384-3129*

*1048 South St*
*Braintree* ▪ *(781) 849-8667*
*250 Granite St*
*Worcester* ▪ *(508) 421-9300*
*25 Major Taylor Blvd*
*Revere* ▪ *(781) 289-2330*
*210 Squire Rd*
*Hyannis* ▪ *(508) 775-3111*
*574 Iyannough Route 132 Rd*

### Washington Square Tavern, The ✪★$$D
*Brookline* ▪ *(617) 232-8989*
*714 Washington St* ▪ *Modern American* ▪ GF menu is a list of all regular items that are naturally GF. Typically, this menu includes salads, steaks, burgers without buns, lamb, and chicken dishes. GF beer is available. ▪ *www.washingtonsquaretavern.com*

### Wicked Restaurant & Wine Bar ✪★$$LD
*Mashpee* ▪ *(508) 477-7422*
*680 Falmouth Rd*
*Dedham* ▪ *(781) 326-9100*
*660 Legacy Pl* ▪ *American* ▪ GF menu includes strawberry, goat cheese and arugula salad, sandwiches and burgers on GF buns, lemon poached cod, and more. GF pizza and beer are available. Corinna at the Dedham location reports that "many precautions are taken" against CC. Be sure to alert your server of your dietary needs. ▪ *wickedrestaurant.com*

### Wild Willy's Burgers                  ★¢LD
*Worcester* ▪ *(508) 459-2088*
*317 W Boylston St*
*Watertown* ▪ *(617) 926-9700*
*46 Arsenal St*
*Quincy* ▪ *(617) 472-9453*
*588 Washington St* ▪ *American* ▪ GF buns are available and can be used to make almost any burger or sandwich GF. GF menus are available at all locations, and options differ slightly from restaurant to restaurant. The restaurant reports that all staff have been "trained in cross-contamination issues." ▪ *www.wildwillysburgers.com*

## Woodman's                                ⊘$$LD
*Essex* ▪ *(800) 649-1773*
*121 Main St* ▪ *Seafood* ▪ The few non-GF menu items are marked. GF options include fried plates and family style boxes. Examples are fried clams, fried scallops, boiled lobster, steamed clams, and clam chowder. All menu items are GF excluding the clamcakes, onion rings & sandwiches. ▪ *www.woodmans.com*

## Yard House                               ⊘📖
*Dedham* ▪ *(781) 326-4644*
*950 Providence Hwy*

# MICHIGAN

## Abuelo's                                 ⊘📖
*Sterling Heights* ▪ *(586) 532-7318*
*44350 Schoenherr*

## Amical                                   ⊘$$LD
*Traverse City* ▪ *(231) 941-8888*
*229 E Front St* ▪ *French* ▪ GF menu includes broiled salmon and the bourbon glazed pork chop, among other things. For dessert, they offer raspberry crème brûlée, caramel apples, flourless black bottom cake, and coffee custard. General Manager Jeffrey reports that the staff is "fully trained" on the GF diet. The menu is constantly changing so calling ahead of time to confirm timeliness of information is recommended. ▪ *www.amical.com*

## Amici's Pizza & Living Room      ★$$D
*Berkley* ▪ *(248) 544-4100*
*3249 12 Mile Rd*
*Birmingham* ▪ *(248) 723-2900*
*1160 Grant St* ▪ *Pizza* ▪ GF pizza is available and can be prepared with any toppings. Manager Dave confirmed that GF pizza crusts are made daily on-site. ▪ *www.amicispizza.com*

## Apache Trout Grill                       ⊘$$LD
*Traverse City* ▪ *(231) 947-7079*
*13671 S W Bay Shore Dr* ▪ *Seafood & Steakhouse* ▪ The new GF menu includes blackened or grilled walleye, mahi mahi, whitefish, salmon, bacon wrapped shrimp, and nine layer dip. General Manager reports that in addition, almost any steak, any fish, or any BBQ item can be prepared GF. ▪ *www.apachetroutgrill.com*

## Au Bon Pain                              📖
*Detroit* ▪ *(313) 393-2271*
*100 Renaissance Ctr*

## Bacco Ristorante                         $$$$LD
*Southfield* ▪ *(248) 356-6600*
*29410 Northwestern Hwy* ▪ *Italian* ▪ House made GF pasta available. ▪ *www.baccoristorante.com*

## Bavarian Inn at Frankenmuth        ⊘★$LD
*Frankenmuth* ▪ *(989) 652-7200*
*713 S Main St* ▪ *European* ▪ GF menu includes pan-seared chicken fillet, NY strip steak, smoked pork loin, burger and even GF wines and beers. GF dessert menu includes a cream cheese brownie triangle, chocolate chip cookies, and a variety of take-home products which are available with advance notice of 3 days.. ▪ *www.bavarianinnlodge.com*

## Beggar's Banquet                         $$LD
*East Lansing* ▪ *(517) 351-4573*
*218 Abbott Rd* ▪ *American* ▪ GF items are marked on their regular menu. ▪ *www.beggarsbanquet.com*

## Beverly Hills Grill                      $$$BLD
*Beverly Hills* ▪ *(248) 642-2355*
*31471 Southfield Rd* ▪ *American* ▪ Pride themselves on modifying the menu to anyone's liking, including GF orders. ▪ *www.beverlyhillsgrill.com*

**Bistro Bella Vita** ✪$$$LD
*Grand Rapids* ▪ *(616) 222-4600*
*44 Grandville Ave SW* ▪ *Italian* ▪ Bella
Vita has a full GF menu located on their
website featuring items such as rigatoni
bolognese, four cheese ravioli, various
pizza options, along with meat and sea-
food items. ▪ *bistrobellavita.com*

**Boathouse Restaurant** $$$LD
*Traverse City* ▪ *(231) 223-4030*
*14039 Peninsula Dr* ▪ *French* ▪ Executive
Chef Eric reports that they serve GF meals
"from sun up to sun down." He adds that he
is able and happy to prepare meals for GF
diners. GF desserts include crème brûlée
and the chocolate truffle plate. Confirm the
timeliness of this information before dining in. ▪ *www.boathouseonwestbay.com*

**Bonefish Grill** ✪📖
*Novi* ▪ *(248) 347-1635*
*43304 W 11 Mile Rd*
*Grand Rapids* ▪ *(616) 949-7861*
*1100 E Paris Ave SE Ste 5*

**Boone's Long Lake Inn** ✪$$$LD
*Traverse City* ▪ *(231) 946-3991*
*7208 Secor Rd* ▪ *Seafood & Steakhouse*
▪ GF menu lists regular menu items that
can be prepared GF. It includes various
steak, pork, chicken, and seafood entrées,
as well as shrimp and crab appetizers. ▪
*www.booneslli.com*

**Boston's Restaurant & Sports Bar**
✪★📖
*Shelby Township* ▪ *(586) 247-4992*
*15133 Hall Rd*

**Buca di Beppo** ✪📖
*Livonia* ▪ *(734) 462-6442*
*38888 6 Mile Rd*
*Utica* ▪ *(586) 803-9463*
*12575 Hall Rd*

**Buddy's Pizza** ★$LD
*Auburn Hills* ▪ *(248) 276-9040*
*2612 N Squirrel Rd*
*Dearborn* ▪ *(313) 562-5900*
*22148 Michigan Ave*

*Detroit* ▪ *(313) 892-9001*
*17125 Conant St*
*Farmington Hills* ▪ *(248) 855-4600*
*31646 NW Hwy*
*Grosse Pointe Woods* ▪ *(313) 884-7400*
*19163 Mack Ave*
*Livonia* ▪ *(734) 261-3550*
*33605 Plymouth Rd*
*Warren* ▪ *(586) 574-9200*
*8100 Old 13 Mile Rd*
*Bloomfield Hills* ▪ *(248) 645-0300*
*3637 W Maple Rd*
*Royal Oak* ▪ *(248) 549-8000*
*32218 Woodward Ave* ▪ *Pizza* ▪ GF pizza
is available. The restaurant reports that
they developed their GF crust in conjunc-
tion with a nutritionist and the Tri-County
Celiac Foundation. A GF menu is available
that details which toppings and specialty
pizzas are GF. ▪ *www.buddyspizza.com*

**Cacao Tree Café** ✪★₵LD
*Royal Oak* ▪ *(248) 336-9043*
*204 W 4th St* ▪ *Raw* ▪ The café reports
that almost everything is GF. There is
only one sandwich they offer that is NOT
GF. GF items include desserts as well. ▪
*www.cacaotreecafe.com*

**Café Cortina** ★$$$LD
*Farmington Hills* ▪ *(248) 474-3033*
*30715 W Ten Mile Rd* ▪ *Italian* ▪ One GF
pasta per week as well as several appetizers
and fish dishes. Menu changes weekly. ▪
*cafecortina.com*

**Capital Grille, The** ✪📖
*Troy* ▪ *(248) 649-5300*
*2800 W Big Beaver Rd*

**Carino's Italian** ✪📖
*Allen Park* ▪ *(313) 274-5551*
*23075 Outer Dr*
*Brighton* ▪ *(810) 494-5050*
*9475 Village Place Blvd*
*Commerce Township* ▪ *(248) 926-5300*
*500 Loop Rd*
*Grand Rapids* ▪ *(616) 363-7100*
*2183 E Beltline Ave NE*
*Holland* ▪ *(616) 738-5200*

3015 W Shore Dr
Norton Shores ▪ (231) 798-6363
5607 Harvey St

**Carrabba's Italian Grill** ✪📖
Canton ▪ (734) 844-7400
1900 N Haggerty Rd
Grand Rapids ▪ (616) 940-9865
4061 28th St SE
Grandville ▪ (616) 261-3020
3441 Century Center St SW
Lansing ▪ (517) 323-8055
6540 W Saginaw Hwy
Novi ▪ (248) 735-0400
43455 W Oaks Dr
Portage ▪ (269) 381-0607
5690 S Westnedge Ave
Southgate ▪ (734) 284-5339
14805 Dix Toledo Rd
Sterling Heights ▪ (586) 323-2652
44695 Schoenherr Rd

**Celiac Specialties** ₵S
Rochester Hills ▪ (586) 598-8180
1928 Star Batt Dr
Farmington ▪ (248) 702-6255
31126 Haggerty Rd ▪ Bakery ▪ Dedicated
GF bakery offering pizza, sandwich bread,
pasta, gravies, buns, donuts, granola, cakes,
and more. Advance notice of one day is
required for cake orders. Calling ahead to
confirm the availability of any specific item
is recommended. ▪ www.celiacspecialties.com

**Charlotte Gluten-Free Bakery** ₵S
Grand Rapids ▪ (616) 957-3706
2481 32nd St SE ▪ Bakery ▪ Dedicated GF
bakery offering pizza crust, buttermilk
scones, biscotti, cookies, brownies, muffins, and seasonal pies, as well as breads
and rolls. The bakery recommends calling
a week in advance for special orders. ▪
www.charlotteglutenfreebakery.com

**Cheeseburger in Paradise** ✪★📖
Sterling Heights ▪ (586) 532-9826
13883 Lakeside Cir

**Chop House, The** ✪$$$$D
Grand Rapids ▪ (616) 451-6131
190 Monroe Ave NW

Ann Arbor ▪ (734) 669-9977
322 S Main St ▪ Steakhouse ▪ District
manager Sue reports that all locations offer
GF items, which are marked on the regular
menu. She notes that GF diners should
always alert a manager about GF requirements. ▪ www.thechophouserestaurant.com

**Claddagh Irish Pub** 📖
Lansing ▪ (517) 484-2523
2900 Towne Center Blvd
Livonia ▪ (734) 542-8141
17800 Haggerty Rd

**Clara's** $$LD
Battle Creek ▪ (269) 963-0966
44 McCamly St N
Lansing ▪ (517) 372-7120
637 E. Michigan Ave ▪ American ▪ The
restaurant reports that they will "work with
customers to make almost any item on
the menu GF." Alert server upon arrival. ▪
www.claras.com

**Cosi** ✪📖
Southfield ▪ (248) 213-2700
28674 Telegraph Rd
Farmington Hills ▪ (248) 489-9126
37652 Twelve Mile Rd
Birmingham ▪ (248) 203-9200
101 N Old Woodward Ave
East Lansing ▪ (517) 332-6500
301 E Grand River Ave

**Don Pablo's** ✪📖
Battle Creek ▪ (269) 979-1004
5805 Beckley Rd
Flint ▪ (810) 235-2262
G-3145 Miller Rd
Shelby Township ▪ (586) 247-4651
14181 Hall Rd

**Earle, The** ✪★$$$D
Ann Arbor ▪ (734) 994-0211
121 W Washington St ▪ Modern American
▪ GF items include stuffed mushroom
caps, beef tenderloin, spicy shrimp, French
goat cheese, antipasto, salads, filet, lamb
chops, sea scallops, boneless chicken,
and duck. GF pasta is also available. ▪
www.theearle.com

## Edward's Café & Caterer ★ $$BLD
*Northville* ▪ (248) 344-1550
*115 E Main St* ▪ *Bakery & Café* ▪ Several
naturally GF items are available daily.
Their tomato basil soup, all salads, and
their crème brûlée are a few options. ▪
*www.edwardscaterer.com*

## Efros Brothers Pizza ★ ₵LD
*Troy* ▪ (248) 879-2900
*5925 John R Rd* ▪ *Pizza* ▪ Efros Brothers
now offers an extensive selection of GF
items, all of which are brought in from a
GF facility and topped and cooked in the
restaurant. ▪ *efrosbrotherspizza.com*

## El Dorado Cadillac Grill ₵LD
*Cadillac* ▪ (231) 779-3663
*7839 E 46 1/2 Rd* ▪ *American* ▪ Reservationist Michelle reports that they only offer
mainly salads and soups as GF options.
Located at the Gold Eldorado course. ▪
*www.golfeldorado.com*

## Emil's Bar and Restaurant
*Lansing* ▪ (517) 482-4430
*2012 E Michigan Ave* ▪ *Italian* ▪ Chef
reports that GF options include steak, fish,
and pork and they accommodate GF diners.

## English Inn $$$LD
*Eaton Rapids* ▪ (517) 663-2500
*677 S Michigan Rd* ▪ *American* ▪ Hostess
reports "the chef can always make anything
GF" ▪ *www.englishinn.com/restaurant.shtml*

## Erbelli's ★ $LD
*Portage* ▪ (269) 327-0200
*8342 Portage Rd*
*Kalamazoo* ▪ (269) 375-0408
*6214 Stadium Dr* ▪ *Italian* ▪ GF pizza is available in 10" size. Both locations report that
servers are trained on GF. ▪ *www.erbellis.com*

## Feed Your Karma $$
*Lansing* ▪ (517) 899-8814
*2655 E Grand River Ave* ▪ *Bakery* ▪
Specializes in baking GF cakes. Requires advance notice of at least one
week. No store front but delivers. ▪
*www.feed-your-karma.com*

## Firefly ✪$$$LD
*Traverse City* ▪ (231) 932-1310
*310 Cass St* ▪ *Global* ▪ Firefly offers a full
GF menu for brunch, lunch and dinner.
Items offered include roasted organic
chicken, grilled red wine poached octopus,
pan roasted halibut, and a bunless 1/2lb
hamburger. ▪ *www.tcfirefly.com*

## Flat Top Grill 📖
*Ann Arbor* ▪ (734) 531-0230
*3275 Washtenaw Ave*
*Rochester Hills* ▪ (248) 375-8800
*176 N Adams Rd*

## Fleming's Prime
## Steakhouse & Wine Bar ✪📖
*Birmingham* ▪ (248) 723-0134
*323 N Old Woodward Ave*
*Livonia* ▪ (734) 542-9463
*17400 Haggerty Rd*

## Fox and Hound Pub & Grille 📖
*Canton* ▪ (734) 844-1137
*1777 N Canton Ctr Rd*
*Dearborn* ▪ (313) 277-3212
*22091 Michigan Ave*
*Troy* ▪ (248) 435-3044
*195 W Maple Rd*

## Frankenmuth
## Bavarian Inn Restaurant ✪★$LD
*Frankenmuth* ▪ (989) 652-9941
*713 S Main St* ▪ *American* ▪ GF menu
includes broiled chicken and grilled
New York strip, as well as cream cheese
brownies and carrot cake for dessert.
GF beer is also available. Special orders should be given a 3 day notice. ▪
*www.bavarianinn.com*

## Gaia Café ₵BLD
*Grand Rapids* ▪ (616) 454-6233
*209 Diamond Ave SE* ▪ *Vegetarian* ▪ No
GF menu but they can modify many different items to suit a GF diet.

## Gilly's                                        ✪$$$D
*Grand Rapids* ▪ *(616) 356-2000*
*20 Monroe Ave NW* ▪ *Seafood* ▪ GF items
highlighted on the menu include oysters,
pear and apple salad, Alaskan crab legs,
and filet of beef. The restaurant reports that
they have GF diners come in "all the time."
▪ *www.thebob.com*

## Gluten Free Sensations                           ⊘S
*Three Rivers* ▪ *(269) 273-4090*
*53238 US131 Hwy* ▪ *Bakery* ▪ Dedicated
GF bakery offering a few items for pur-
chase at the storefront. Owner Loretta
notes that GF breads, pastas, cereals, and
bars are available. She cautions that they
sell primarily to larger retail outlets, so
the selection in the store is minimal. ▪
*www.glutenfreesensations.com*

## Godfather's Pizza                              ★▢
*Kalamazoo* ▪ *(269) 342-6500*
*3815 E Cork*

## Green Well, The                               $$LD
*Grand Rapids* ▪ *(616) 808-3566*
*924 Cherry St* ▪ *Global* ▪ The restaurant
reports that nearly 90% of the menu can be
prepared GF. They also recommend notifying the server that your needs result from
an "allergy" as opposed to a preference. ▪
*www.thegreenwell.com*

## Ground Round                                  ✪▢
*Jackson* ▪ *(517) 782-3330*
*1051 Boardman Rd*
*Woodhaven* ▪ *(734) 362-8730*
*22301 Allen Rd*

## Hard Rock Café                                ✪▢
*Detroit* ▪ *(313) 964-7625*
*45 Monroe St*
*New Buffalo* ▪ *(866) 494-6371*
*11111 Wilson Rd*

## Inn Season Café                              ✪★$LD
*Royal Oak* ▪ *(248) 547-7916*
*500 E 4th St* ▪ *Vegetarian* ▪ GF items are
marked on the menu and include cashew
ginger stir fry, enchiladas coloradito, shiitake mushroom sauté, a variety of salads, and

more. GF brown rice tortillas are available.
Some items require substitution to become
GF, so be sure to alert the server upon ar-
rival. ▪ *www.theinnseasoncafe.com*

## Italian Oven Restaurant, The        ✪★$$LD
*Mt Pleasant* ▪ *(989) 773-6836*
*2336 S Mission St* ▪ *Italian* ▪ GF pizza
available. Other entrées that are GF
include chicken parmesan, chicken
marsala, and lemon pepper chicken.
Chocolate chip sandwich and ice
cream brownie available for dessert. ▪
*www.labellemgt.com/italian-oven.cfm*

## Jefferson Market & Cakery            ★$$$$$
*Ann Arbor* ▪ *(734) 665-6666*
*609 W Jefferson St* ▪ *Bakery* ▪ Chocolate flourless cake and cinnamon walnut
bread available on certain days of the week.
Confirm availability before dining in. ▪
*www.jeffersonmarketandcakery.com*

## Jersey Mike's                                 ▢
*Pittsfield* ▪ *(734) 477-9930*
*3650 Carpenter Rd*
*Shelby Township* ▪ *(586) 997-1571*
*12161 23 Mile Rd*
*Rochester Hills* ▪ *(248) 293-5260*
*2670 S Rochester Rd*

## Joe's Crab Shack                             ✪▢
*Sterling Heights* ▪ *(586) 274-4153*
*33879 Van Dyke*
*Ann Arbor* ▪ *(734) 662-7091*
*3020 Lohr Rd*
*Auburn Hills* ▪ *(248) 393-7319*
*4975 S Baldwin*

## Judson's Steak House                       ✪$$$D
*Grand Rapids* ▪ *(616) 356-2000*
*20 Monroe Ave NW* ▪ *Steakhouse* ▪ GF
items indicated on menu include ocean to
plate oysters, simple greens salad, hanger
steak, bay of fundy salmon, natural angus
delmonico, choice filet of beef, stuffed filet,
prime New York strip, cold water lobster
tail, day boat scallops and wild Alaskan
halibut. ▪ *www.thebob.com*

## Lone Star Steakhouse & Saloon ✪📖
*Battle Creek* ■ *(269) 968-6900*
*50 Knapp Dr*
*Dundee* ■ *(734) 529-8270*
*123 Whitetail Dr*
*Jackson* ■ *(517) 768-0884*
*3510 O'Neil Dr*
*Mt Pleasant* ■ *(989) 773-7827*
*5768 E Pickard St*

## Maggiano's Little Italy ★📖
*Troy* ■ *(248) 205-1060*
*2089 W Big Beaver Rd*

## Marie Catribs ★$$BLD
*Grand Rapids* ■ *(616) 454-4020*
*1001-1003 Lake Dr SE # 1003* ■ Bakery &
Café ■ GF brownies, chocolate raspberry
brownies, cakes, puddings, pies, tarts, and
4 types of GF bread for sandwiches are
available. ■ *www.mariecatribs.com*

## Melting Pot, The ✪📖
*Ann Arbor* ■ *(734) 622-0055*
*309 S Main St*
*Grand Rapids* ■ *(616) 365-0055*
*2090 Celebration Dr NE*
*Novi* ■ *(248) 347-6358*
*26425 Novi Rd*
*Troy* ■ *(248) 362-2221*
*888 W Big Beaver Rd*

## Minerva's ✪📖
*Traverse City* ■ *(231) 946-5093*
*300 E State St*

## Mitchell's Fish Market ✪📖
*Birmingham* ■ *(248) 646-3663*
*117 Willits St*
*Lansing* ■ *(517) 482-3474*
*2975 Preyde Blvd*
*Livonia* ■ *(734) 464-3663*
*17600 Haggerty Rd*
*Rochester Hills* ■ *(248) 340-5900*
*370 N Adams Rd*

## Morton's Steakhouse ✪📖
*Troy* ■ *(248) 404-9845*
*888 W Big Beaver Rd*

## Mountain Town Station ✪$$LD
*Mount Pleasant* ■ *(989) 775-2337*
*506 W Broadway St* ■ *American* ■ GF
menu includes nachos, hummus, lobster
tail, chicken parmesan, and filet mignon.
No dedicated fryers so fried foods should
be avoided. ■ *www.mountaintown.com*

## New Aladdin's Restaurant $$LD
*Lansing* ■ *(517) 333-8710*
*300 N Clippert St* ■ *Middle Eastern* ■ The
restaurant reports that "a large portion" of
their menu is either naturally GF or can be
prepared GF.

## P.F. Chang's China Bistro ✪★📖
*Clinton Township* ■ *(586) 263-0860*
*17390 Hall Rd Unit R-103*
*Dearborn* ■ *(313) 429-2030*
*18900 Michigan Ave Spc R-101*
*Lansing* ■ *(517) 267-3833*
*2425 Lake Lansing Rd*
*Northville* ■ *(248) 675-0066*
*17905 Haggerty Rd*
*Troy* ■ *(248) 816-8000*
*2801 W Big Beaver Rd Ste D112*

## Panini Press, The ★◁LD
*Berkley* ■ *(248) 547-7377*
*28983 Woodward Ave* ■ *Deli* ■ Manager
Brad reports that any sandwich can be
made on GF bread. Sandwiches that can
be modified to be GF include the tomato
mozzarella, roast beef and bell peppers,
and tuna and cheddar. The sandwich is
prepared using a separate cutting board,
separate press, and dedicated utensils. ■
*www.thepaninipress.com*

## Pearl's New Orleans Kitchen ✪$$LD
*Elk Rapids* ■ *(231) 264-0530*
*617 Ames St* ■ *Cajun & Creole* ■ Celiac friendly menu offers shrimp creole,
blackened pork loin, and andouille,
hoppin john and grits. Manager notes
that many GF diners come to the restaurant. Although they are very carefully with preparing GF dishes, manager notes that there are chances of CC. ■
*www.magnumhospitality.com/pearls*

## Pei Wei Asian Diner          ✪📖
*Novi* ▪ *(248) 675-0040*
*43170 Grand River Ave*
*Rochester* ▪ *(248) 601-1380*
*1206 Walton Blvd*
*Royal Oak* ▪ *(248) 837-2420*
*30278 Woodward Ave*
*Sterling Heights* ▪ *(586) 566-0362*
*13937 Lakeside Circle*
*Troy* ▪ *(248) 824-1085*
*730 E Big Beaver Rd*
*Warren* ▪ *(586) 834-4020*
*5753 E 12 Mile Rd*

## Piece O' Cake, A          ★₵S
*East Lansing* ▪ *(517) 333-6881*
*4966 Northwind Dr* ▪ *Bakery* ▪ Non-dedicated bakery offering GF graham crackers, bread, pizza, cookies, pies, cakes, and more. GF items are baked on Tuesdays only. ▪ *www.apieceocake.com*

## Pita House, The          $LD
*Grand Rapids* ▪ *(616) 454-1171*
*1450 Wealthy St*
*Kentwood* ▪ *(616) 940-3029*
*3730 28th St*
*Grandville* ▪ *(616) 261-4302*
*4533 Ivanrest Ave* ▪ *Mediterranean* ▪ The restaurant reports that most of their meat, rice, and sides are GF. Alert the server upon arrival and they will go over the options. ▪ *www.thepitahouse.net*

## Pizza Ranch          ✪📖
*Muskegon* ▪ *(231) 739-3300*
*1848 E Sherman Blvd*
*Hudsonville* ▪ *(616) 669-7030*
*3492 Chicago Dr*

## Rattlesnake Club          ✪$$LD
*Detroit* ▪ *(313) 567-4400*
*300 River Pl Dr* ▪ *American* ▪ The menu changes often, but GF options are always available and marked on the menu. Sample items include toasted red quinoa, rack of lamb, duck breast, and mixed grill platter. ▪ *rattlesnakedetroit.com*

## Real Seafood Co.          ✪★$$$LD
*Ann Arbor* ▪ *(734) 769-7738*
*341 S Main St* ▪ *Seafood* ▪ GF menu, which is not available online, includes roasted Atlantic salmon, escargot, clams, and broiled scallops. The restaurant notes that GF diners are accommodated "at least once a day," so the kitchen is very aware of the GF diet. ▪ *www.realseafoodcorestaurant.com*

## Red Mesa Grill          ✪★$LD
*Traverse City* ▪ *(231) 938-2773*
*1544 US Highway 31 N*
*Boyne City* ▪ *(231) 582-0049*
*117 Water St* ▪ *Latin American* ▪ GF options include Costa Rican garlic steak, Sonoma tuna, enchiladas, and fajitas. For dessert, they offer cinnamon ice cream only available at Traverse City location. Ask the server for a "Celiac Safe Menu" to see all GF options. GF soy sauce is available. ▪ *www.magnumhospitality.com/redmesa*

## Rochester Chop House          $$$LD
*Rochester* ▪ *(248) 651-2266*
*306 S Main St* ▪ *Steakhouse* ▪ Most meat dishes are GF. Alert server you are GF before ordering. ▪ *kruseandmuerrestaurants.com*

## Romano's Macaroni Grill          ✪★📖
*Ann Arbor* ▪ *(734) 663-4433*
*3010 S State St*
*Auburn Hills* ▪ *(248) 373-7507*
*2111 N Squirrel Rd*
*Grand Rapids* ▪ *(616) 949-8430*
*5525 28th St SE*
*Livonia* ▪ *(734) 462-6676*
*39300 7 Mile Rd*
*Shelby Township* ▪ *(586) 532-1625*
*14331 Hall Rd*

## Ruth's Chris Steak House          ✪📖
*Grand Rapids* ▪ *(616) 776-6426*
*187 Monroe Ave NW*
*Troy* ▪ *(248) 269-8424*
*755 W Big Beaver Rd*

## San Chez Bistro ✪cBLD
*Grand Rapids* ■ *(616) 774-8272*
*38 W Fulton St* ■ *Global* ■ Extensive GF menu features a variety of tapas, including baked goat cheese and tomato with garlic GF bread, beef tenderloin, and seafood paella. ■ *www.sanchezbistro.com*

## Seva ✪★$LD
*Ann Arbor* ■ *(734) 662-1111*
*314 E Liberty St*
*Detroit* ■ *(313) 974-6661*
*66 E Forest* ■ *Vegetarian* ■ Extensive GF menu includes a variety of alcoholic drinks, salads, and appetizers like baked artichoke-spinach dip, nachos and sweet potato fries. Entrée examples are pasta with soy sausage and cilantro-peanut stir fry. GF brunch options are also available. GF tamari sauce, crackers, pasta and chocolate cake are available. ■ *www.sevarestaurant.com*

## Silvio's Organic
## Ristorante & Pizzeria ★$LD
*Ann Arbor* ■ *(734) 214-6666*
*715 N University Ave* ■ *Pizza* ■ GF pasta and pizza are available. Pizza is available in the 6-inch and 14-inch sizes, while pasta is available for substitution into any pasta dish. GF pizza is prepared a completely separate prep area while GF pasta is cooked using separate pots. ■ *www.silviosorganicpizza.com*

## Smokey Bones 📖
*Grand Rapids* ■ *(616) 956-5398*
*4875 28th St SE*
*Lansing* ■ *(517) 316-9973*
*2401 Lake Lansing Rd*

## Stadium Market ★$LD
*Ann Arbor* ■ *(734) 761-9650*
*1423 E Stadium Blvd* ■ *Pizza* ■ GF pizza, two kinds of beer, bread for sandwiches, kebobs, and cheese bread are available. Restaurant is takeout only.

## Stillwater Grill ✪$$$LD
*Okemos* ■ *(517) 349-1500*
*3544 Meridian Crossing Dr*
*Brighton* ■ *(810) 225-1800*
*503 W. Grand River* ■ *Seafood & Steakhouse* ■ When making reservations, alert staff that you are GF. ■ *www.stillwatergrill.com*

## Stir Crazy ★📖
*Auburn Hills* ■ *(248) 454-0400*
*4248 Baldwin Rd*

## Sugar Kisses Bakery ✪★c$
*Berkley* ■ *(248) 542-5622*
*2688 Coolidge Hwy* ■ *Bakery* ■ A self-described "wheat-free pastry shop," they offer many GF products, which are marked on the menu. GF options include bread, cookies, cakes, pies, muffins, brownies, and more. ■ *www.sugarkissesbakery.com*

## Sweet Lorraine's ✪$$BLD
*Livonia* ■ *(734) 953-7480*
*17100 N Laurel Park Dr*
*Southfield* ■ *(248) 559-5985*
*29101 Greenfield Rd* ■ *American* ■ Chef Paul at the Livonia location reports that all servers and chefs are GF aware. Manager Lisa at the Southfield location reports that they have an internal GF menu that the server or hostess will give to GF diners. Most menu items can be modified to be GF, including maple-cured salmon, pot roast, and several vegetarian entrées. Southfield location does not serve breakfast. ■ *www.sweetlorraines.com*

## Texas De Brazil Churrascaria ★📖
*Detroit* ■ *(313) 964-4333*
*1000 Woodward Ave*

## Tuscan Bistro ✪$$LD
*Traverse City* ■ *(231) 922-7795*
*12930 S W Bay Shore Dr* ■ *Italian* ■ Limited GF menu includes maple lemon glazed salmon, chicken with ground sweet sausage, and sautéed Michigan whitefish. ■ *www.tuscanbistrotc.com*

## Uno Chicago Grill                    ✪★📖
*Bay City* ▪ (989) 684-8667
*2795 Wilder Rd*
*Birch Run* ▪ (989) 624-8667
*8975 Market Place Dr*
*Sterling Heights* ▪ (586) 991-0912
*44805 Mound Rd*

## Vinsetta Garage                      ★$LD
*Berkley* ▪ (248) 548-7711
*27799 Woodward Ave* ▪ *American* ▪ GF
burger buns, pizza, and beer are available. ▪
*vinsettagarage.com*

## Vitale's Italian Restaurant          ★$$LD
*Grand Rapids* ▪ (616) 458-8368
*834 Leonard St NE* ▪ *Italian* ▪ Manager
reports that they have a GF pizza and can
order GF pasta if given a couple days notice. GF dark chocolate truffle cake is also
available. They also have a few items on the
regular menu that are GF without modification. ▪ *www.theoriginalvitales.com*

## Wiches                               ★¢LD
*Oxford* ▪ (248) 572-4790
*40 N Washington St* ▪ *Deli* ▪ Wiches
has an extensive menu, all of which can
be made GF aside from several sauces
and spreads for pizzas and sandwiches. ▪
*www.wichesrestaurant.com*

## Willy O's Pizza & Grill              ★$LD
*South Haven* ▪ (269) 637-3400
*08960 M 140* ▪ *Pizza* ▪ GF pizza, including specialty blueberry pineapple pizza,
is available. All GF pizzas are baked in a
separate oven and prepared in a dedicated
GF area. ▪ *www.willyos.com*

## Winchester, The                      $LD
*Grand Rapids* ▪ (616) 451-4969
*648 Wealthy St SE* ▪ *American* ▪ About
10 menu items are GF or can be modified
to be GF. Notify your server upon arrival
for stricter CC policies on your order. ▪
*www.winchestergr.com*

## Zingerman's Roadhouse                 $$$BLD
*Ann Arbor* ▪ (734) 663-3663
*2501 Jackson Ave* ▪ *American* ▪ Sea
island sweet potato fries, garden salad, and the BBQ pork sandwich are
the only items that are GF options. ▪
*www.zingermansroadhouse.com*

# MINNESOTA

## MINNEAPOLIS

## Amore Victoria                       ★$$LD
*Minneapolis* ▪ (612) 823-0250
*1601 W Lake St* ▪ *Italian* ▪ GF pasta is
available. The restaurant recommends
that GF guests alert their server as soon
as they arrive and that they will "do
their best to accommodate" GF diners. ▪
*www.amorevictoria.com*

## Au Bon Pain                          📖
*Minneapolis* ▪ (612) 341-4420
*225 S 6th St*
*Minneapolis* ▪ (612) 259-0101
*40 S 7th St*
*Minneapolis* ▪ (612) 343-5252
*733 Marquette Ave*

## Buca di Beppo                        ✪📖
*Minneapolis* ▪ (612) 288-0138
*1204 Harmon Pl*

## Capital Grille, The                  ✪📖
*Minneapolis* ▪ (612) 692-9000
*801 Hennepin Ave*

## Chiang Mai Thai                      ✪$LD
*Minneapolis* ▪ (612) 827-1606
*3001 Hennepin Ave S* ▪ *Thai* ▪ The generous selection of GF menu items includes
chicken satay, hot & sour soup, pad thai,
several curries and stir fries, and more. Be
sure to specify GF when placing your order,
as some items may require modification to
become GF. ▪ *www.chiangmaithai.com*

### Christos Greek Restaurant    ✪★$LD
*Minneapolis* ▪ *(612) 871-2111*
*2632 Nicollet Ave S* ▪ *Greek* ▪ Minneapolis
and Minnetoka locations report that they
are familiar with the GF diet, as they have
a GF menu. GF options include all kebabs,
rice pilaf, most soups and salads. They also
use a dill vinagrette for dressing. The Saint
Paul location can accommodate GF diners
as well, but calling ahead is recommended,
as they are mainly run as a buffet. Confirm
the timeliness of this information before
dining in. ▪ *www.christos.com*

### Common Roots    ✪$BLD
*Minneapolis* ▪ *(612) 871-2360*
*2558 Lyndale Ave S* ▪ *Café* ▪ GF menu
offers breakfast, lunch, and dinner items.
Examples include sweet potato hash, breakfast enchiladas, fish tacos, chicken confit,
pad thai, and more. Be sure to notify your
server that you are ordering from the GF
menu. ▪ *www.commonrootscafe.com*

### Cosi    ✪📖
*Minneapolis* ▪ *(612) 332-5700*
*710 Marquette Ave*

### Ecopolitan    ★$BLD
*Minneapolis* ▪ *(612) 874-7336*
*2409 Lyndale Ave S* ▪ *Raw* ▪ The restaurant reports that everything on the menu is
GF, including GF raw pizza with a buckwheat crust and GF raw pasta made with
zucchini or carrots. Confirm the timeliness of this information before dining in. ▪
*www.ecopolitan.com*

### Fogo De Chao    ★📖
*Minneapolis* ▪ *(612) 338-1344*
*645 Hennepin Ave*

### French Meadow Bakery & Café
✪★$$BLD
*Minneapolis* ▪ *(612) 870-7855*
*2610 Lyndale Ave S* ▪ *Bakery & Café* ▪
Menu indicates which items are GF. Items
include soups, salads, GF oatmeal and
granola, blueberry corn pancakes, huevos
rancheros, Cajun hash browns, seared
tilapia and "signature" crab cakes. Tell the

waiter that you are GF when ordering.
May be cooked in separate skillets and
all areas are wiped down and sanitized. ▪
*www.frenchmeadowcafe.com*

### Galactic Pizza    ★$$LD
*Minneapolis* ▪ *(612) 824-9100*
*2917 Lyndale Ave S* ▪ *Pizza* ▪ All specialty
pizzas can be made GF except for the
Thailander and the Alamo. Build your
own pizza is also available in GF 10". ▪
*galacticpizza.com*

### Green Mill Restaurant and Bar    ✪📖
*Minneapolis* ▪ *(612) 374-2131*
*2626 Hennepin*

### Manny's Quality Steaks    $$$$D
*Minneapolis* ▪ *(612) 339-9900*
*825 Marquette Ave S* ▪ *Steakhouse* ▪ The
restaurant recommends making reservations noting GF to give them a "heads-up."
Once guests arrive, a server will go over
the menu with them to help point out
naturally GF options or items that can
easily be made GF. Located in the Foshay
Tower at the corner of 9th and Marquette. ▪
*www.mannyssteakhouse.com*

### Melting Pot, The    ✪📖
*Minneapolis* ▪ *(612) 338-9900*
*80 S 9th St*

### Midori's Floating World Café    ★$$LD
*Minneapolis* ▪ *(612) 721-3011*
*2629 E Lake St* ▪ *Japanese* ▪ Owner
Midori reports that several menu items,
like the grilled fish dinner, tofu, and many
sushi items, can be prepared GF. She notes
that most servers are GF aware. WF tamari
sauce is available. Confirm the timeliness
of this information before dining in. ▪
*www.floatingworldcafe.com*

### Old Spaghetti Factory, The    ✪★📖
*Minneapolis* ▪ *(612) 341-0949*
*233 Park Ave*

### Pei Wei Asian Diner    ✪📖
*Minneapolis* ▪ *(612) 355-4673*
*MSP Int Arpt Term 1*

### Pinstripes ✪★$LD
*Edina* ▪ *(952) 835-6440*
*3849 Gallagher Dr* ▪ *Bistro* ▪ GF menu
includes soups and salads, as well as a wide
variety of sandwiches, pizzas, and pastas. It
also includes entrées such as beef tenderloin and grilled salmon. GF pasta and
pizza are available with advance notice of
24 hours. For dessert, they offer flourless
chocolate cake, lemon crème brûlée, and
cheesecake. ▪ *www.pinstripes.com*

### Pizza Luce ✪★$LD
*Minneapolis* ▪ *(612) 333-7359*
*119 N 4th St*
*Minneapolis* ▪ *(612) 332-2535*
*2200 E Franklin Ave*
*Minneapolis* ▪ *(612) 827-5978*
*3200 Lyndale Ave S* ▪ *Pizza* ▪ Items
marked "GFR" on the menu can be
prepared GF upon request. These include
appetizers, salads, pasta and pizza. Alert
server upon arrival. ▪ *www.pizzaluce.com*

### Rice Paper ✪$$LD
*Edina* ▪ *(952) 288-2888*
*3948 W. 50th St* ▪ *Vietnamese* ▪ GF
& dairy-free menu is available online
and includes items like Vietnamese
noodle salad, pad thai, tamarind rice
trio, plantation chicken, and more. ▪
*www.ricepaperrestaurant.com*

### Romano's Macaroni Grill ✪★▭
*Minneapolis* ▪ *(952) 844-0084*
*7651 France Ave S*

### Ruth's Chris Steak House ✪▭
*Minneapolis* ▪ *(612) 672-9000*
*920 2nd Ave S*

### Signature Café and Catering ★$$LD
*Minneapolis* ▪ *(612) 378-0237*
*130 Southeast Warwick St* ▪ *Modern
American* ▪ The restaurant offers a 100%
GF menu every Tuesday night. The kitchen
is sanitized in the afternoon and no non-
GF prep is done after that time. The owner
also reports that most of the regular menu
is already GF or can be prepared GF, and

GF diners are welcome every day. GF pasta
is available. ▪ *www.signaturecafe.net*

### Wedge Natural Foods Co-op ✪★¢BLD
*Minneapolis* ▪ *(612) 871-3993*
*2105 Lyndale Ave S* ▪ *Bakery & Café*
▪ GF bread and soy sauce are available
for deli items like sandwiches and Thai
red curry mushrooms. GF cookies, pies,
cakes, cupcakes, muffins, and brownies
are some of the GF desserts available. ▪
*www.wedge.coop*

### Zelo ✪$$LD
*Minneapolis* ▪ *(612) 333-7000*
*831 Nicollet Mall S* ▪ *Italian* ▪ GF items are
marked on the menu and include salmon
with local vegetable ragu, scallops & local
sweet corn, filet mignon, dry aged ribeye,
and more. ▪ *www.zelomn.com*

## MINNESOTA

## ROCHESTER

### 300 First ✪$$D
*Rochester* ▪ *(507) 281-2451*
*300 1st Ave NW* ▪ *Modern American* ▪
Items with "GF preparation available" are
marked on the menu. These include filet
mignon, cedar plank Atlantic salmon,
brick baked chicken, a variety of salads, and more. Restaurant reports that
GF diners come in "all the time." Alert
a server, who will notify the kitchen. ▪
*www.cccrmg.com/300first.htm*

### Backroom Deli, The ★¢BLD
*Rochester* ▪ *(507) 289-9061*
*1001 6th St NW* ▪ *Vegan* ▪ GF brown rice
wraps are available. The deli reports that
most of the salads are also GF. Confirm the
timeliness of this information before dining
in. Ask at the counter about the daily GF
soup option. ▪ *www.rochestergoodfood.com*

### Bread Baker Company, The    ★ ⊄S
*Rochester* ▪ *(507) 289-7052*
*16 17th St NW* ▪ *Bakery* ▪ Non-dedicated
bakery offering a variety of GF baked
goods like pizza crusts, breads, muffins,
and cookies. GF products are made once
a week on GF bake days, and then frozen
for weeklong availability. Calling ahead is
recommended, as some things sell out. ▪
*www.breadbakercompany.com*

### Canadian Honker    ✪★ $BLD
*Rochester* ▪ *(507) 282-6572*
*1203 2nd St SW* ▪ *American* ▪ Limited GF
menu includes egg breakfasts with hash-
browns and sausage, Hawaiian cod, bacon
cheeseburger, chicken parmesan sandwich
and cobb salad. GF rolls are available for
sandwiches. ▪ *www.canadianhonker.com*

### City Café Mixed Grille & Bar    ✪★ $$LD
*Rochester* ▪ *(507) 289-1949*
*216 1st Ave SW* ▪ *American* ▪ GF menu
includes scallops, tuna, maple roasted
chicken breast, filet mignon, flank steak,
fresh fish, and chocolate or vanilla crème
brûlée for dessert. ▪ *www.city-cafe.com*

### El Carambas    ✪★ ⊄LD
*Rochester* ▪ *(507) 281-3104*
*1503 12th St SE* ▪ *Mexican* ▪ Manager
Eddie reports that many menu items can
be modified to be GF. Enchiladas, fajitas,
tacos, and tamales are some examples.
Confirm the timeliness of this information
before dining in. There is an internal list
of GF items that chefs, servers, and diners
can all refer to. He offers a short tour of the
restaurant for GF diners who want to see
the kitchen's setup. ▪ *elcarambas.com*

### Fiesta Café    ✪★ $$LD
*Rochester* ▪ *(507) 288-1116*
*1645 Broadway Ave N* ▪ *Mexican* ▪ GF
menu includes fajitas, enchiladas, tortilla
soup, and seafood. Other items on the
regular menu can also be modified to be
GF. Restaurant recommends asking for
manager Victorino, who can discuss GF
options. ▪ *www.fiestacafeandbar.com*

### Godfather's Pizza    ★ 🕮
*Rochester* ▪ *(507) 288-7515*
*1611 NW 16th St*

### Green Mill Restaurant and Bar    ◐🕮
*Rochester* ▪ *(507) 282-4222*
*2723 Commerce Dr NW*

### Paradise Pete's    ✪★ $$LD
*Rochester* ▪ *(507) 287-8700*
*14 17th Ave NW* ▪ *American* ▪ GF pasta,
bread, and sandwich rolls are available. Extensive GF menu includes a variety of sandwiches, salads, and pastas as well grilled
meats and seafood, soups, small plates, and
more. GF cheesecake, yellow cake, and ice
cream are available for dessert. Confirm
the timeliness of this information before
dining in. ▪ *www.paradisepetes.com*

### Redwood Room, The    ✪$$D
*Rochester* ▪ *(507) 281-2978*
*300 1st Ave NW* ▪ *Modern American* ▪
GF menu includes roasted salmon, creamy
Cajun sauté, apple cider pork, and tuna.
For dessert, there is usually crème brûlée. ▪
*www.cccrmg.com/redwoodroom.htm*

### Roscoe's Barbeque    ⊄LD
*Rochester* ▪ *(507) 285-0501*
*603 4th St SE*
*Rochester* ▪ *(507) 281-4622*
*3456 E Circle Dr NE* ▪ *Barbeque* ▪ The
restaurant reports that much of the menu
is GF, including the BBQ sauce for the
meats, the baked beans, and the potato
salad. Confirm the timeliness of this information before dining in. They recommend staying away from fried foods as
there is a common fryer. Alert a server
upon arrival, who will alert the kitchen. ▪
*www.roscoesbbq.com*

### Twigs Tavern & Grille    ✪★ $LD
*Rochester* ▪ *(507) 288-0206*
*401 6th St SW* ▪ *American* ▪ Owner Michelle has Celiac and reports that almost
the entire menu can be prepared GF. A
separate GF menu denotes the exact items,
which include sandwiches, burgers, rice

bowls, small plates, meat and fish entrées, and more. The kitchen has separate appliances, utensils, prep areas, cook tops, fryers, and storage space for GF items. GF guests even get their own salt & pepper shakers, and all staff has been trained in the "safe and proper handling of GF foods." ▪ *twigstavernandgrille.com*

### Valentino's                    ★📖
*Rochester* ▪ (507) 281-2100
*130 Elton Hills Dr*

### Victoria's Italian Cuisine    ✪★$$LD
*Rochester* ▪ (507) 280-6232
*7 1st Ave SW* ▪ *Italian* ▪ GF pasta, rolls, and pizza are available. Full GF lunch and dinner menus are online and include several GF pasta dishes, chicken marsala, veal vesuvio, and more. Salted caramel almond cheesecake and raspberry crème brûlée are available for dessert. Confirm the timeliness of this information before dining in. ▪ *www.victoriasmn.com*

### Zpizza                    ✪📖
*Rochester* ▪ (507) 424-0440
*111 S Broadway*

## MINNESOTA

## ALL OTHER CITIES

### Aurelio's Pizza                    ★📖
*Roseville* ▪ (651) 636-1730
*2827 Hamline Ave*

### Bello Cucina Italian Restaurant    ★$LD
*Fergus Falls* ▪ (218) 998-2221
*106 W Lincoln Ave*
*Morris* ▪ (320) 585-7000
*506 Atlantic Ave*
*St Joseph* ▪ (320) 363-4534
*15 E Minnesota St Suite 101* ▪ *Italian* ▪ GF pasta is available. Restaurant reports that GF diners can also eat salads and other modified dishes. They note that calling ahead is advised, since GF pasta takes longer to cook. ▪ *www.bellocucina.com*

### Biaggi's                    ✪★📖
*Eden Prairie* ▪ (952) 942-8555
*8251 Flying Cloud Dr*
*Maple Grove* ▪ (763) 416-2225
*12051 Elm Creek Blvd N*

### Big Bowl Restaurant            ✪$LD
*Minnetonka* ▪ (952) 797-9888
*12649 Wayzata Blvd*
*Roseville* ▪ (651) 636-7173
*1705 Highway 36 W*
*Edina* ▪ (952) 928-7888
*3669 Galleria* ▪ *Asian* ▪ GF menu includes Thai chicken lettuce wraps as an appetizer, various pad thai dishes and chicken kung pao as entrées, and two GF desserts, including the trio of tastes. ▪ *www.bigbowl.com*

### Bittersweet Bakery            $$
*Eagan* ▪ (651) 686-0112
*2105 Cliff Rd* ▪ *Bakery* ▪ Dedicated GF bakery with a variety of breads, bars, cakes, cupcakes, and "take-&-bake" pizzas. All GF products are made fresh daily. ▪ *www.bittersweetgf.com*

### Black Woods                ★$$LD
*Duluth* ▪ (218) 724-1612
*2525 London Rd*
*Proctor* ▪ (218) 628-0628
*195 Highway 2*
*Two Harbors* ▪ (218) 834-3846
*612 7th Ave*
*Duluth* ▪ (218) 740-0436
*231 E Superior St* ▪ *American* ▪ GF Menu available for lunch and dinner. Items include salmon, top sirloin and ribeye steak, chicken and rib combo platter, baby back ribs, rotisserie chicken, salads and pasta. Let the waiter know that you are GF and they will do their best to prepare your meal GF. ▪ *www.blackwoods.com*

## Boston's Restaurant & Sports Bar

✪★📖

*Coon Rapids* ▪ *(763) 421-2100*
*12794 Riverdale Blvd NW*
*Faribault* ▪ *(507) 331-3255*
*125 1st Ave NE*

## Bubba Gump Shrimp Co.

✪📖

*Bloomington* ▪ *(952) 853-6600*
*396 S Ave*

## Buca di Beppo

✪📖

*Burnsville* ▪ *(952) 892-7272*
*14300 Burnhaven Dr*
*Eden Prairie* ▪ *(952) 934-9463*
*7711 Mitchell Rd*
*Maple Grove* ▪ *(763) 494-3466*
*12650 Elm Creek Blvd N*
*Saint Paul* ▪ *(651) 772-4388*
*2728 Gannon Rd*

## Carlos O'Kelly's

✪

*Rochester* ▪ *(507) 282-2590*
*4825 Hwy 52 N*

## Chianti Grill

✪★$$LD

*Roseville* ▪ *(651) 644-2808*
*2050 Snelling Ave*
*Burnsville* ▪ *(952) 892-7555*
*14296 Plymouth Ave* ▪ *Italian* ▪ Separate
GF menu available. Appetizers include crab
claws and stuffed mushroom caps. Entrées
include bacon wrapped scallops, sirloin
and ribeye steak as well as GF pasta dishes
including GF penne toscana and lobster and
shrimp spaghetti. GF items in kitchen are
prepared separate from items containing
gluten and have dedicated GF preparation
pots and utensils. ▪ *www.chiantigrill.com*

## Christos Greek Restaurant

✪★$LD

*Saint Paul* ▪ *(651) 224-6000*
*214 4th St E*
*Minnetonka* ▪ *(952) 912-1000*
*15600 Highway 7* ▪ *Greek* ▪ Minneapo-
lis and Minnetoka locations report that
they are familiar with the GF diet, as they
have a GF menu. GF options include all
kebabs, rice pilaf, most soups and salads.
They also use a dill vinaigrette for dress-
ing. The Saint Paul location can accom-

modate GF diners as well, but calling
ahead is recommended, as they are mainly
run as a buffet. Confirm the timeliness
of this information before dining in. ▪
*www.christos.com*

## Ciao Bella

✪$LD

*Bloomington* ▪ *(952) 841-1000*
*3501 Minnesota Dr* ▪ *Italian* ▪ GF menu
available in-house includes brick roasted
chicken, herb grilled organic salmon, NY
steak, pork chops, and more. GF desserts
are available. ▪ *www.ciaobellamn.com*

## Ciatti's Ristorante

✪★$$$LD

*Saint Cloud* ▪ *(320) 257-7900*
*2635 W Division St* ▪ *Italian* ▪ GF pasta
and pizza are available. GF menu includes
antipasti, insalate, pasta, entrées, bunless burgers, and pizza. The restaurant
reports that their staff is trained of GF
foods and that chefs "switch pans and
utensils" when preparing GF items. ▪
*www.ciattisristorante.com*

## Claddagh Irish Pub

📖

*Maple Grove* ▪ *(763) 773-7400*
*7890 Main St N*

## Classic Pizza

★$LD

*Woodbury* ▪ *(651) 735-6700*
*1850 Weir Dr* ▪ *Pizza* ▪ GF pizza is available. ▪ *www.classicpizzaofwoodbury.com*

## Crumb Gourmet Deli

✪★¢LD

*Eden Prairie* ▪ *(952) 934-1717*
*7910 Mitchell Rd* ▪ *Deli* ▪ GF bread is available. GF soups, cookies, and salads are also
available. A separate toaster, cutting board,
and knives are used for preparing GF products. ▪ *www.crumbgourmetdeli.com*

## D. Fong's Chinese Cuisine

✪¢LD

*Savage* ▪ *(952) 894-0800*
*4321 Egan Dr* ▪ *Chinese* ▪ Be sure to
specify gluten "allergy" when ordering. GF
items include chicken vegetable soup, egg
drop soup, shrimp and chicken almond
ding, shrimp and chicken with vegetables,
shrimp or chicken egg foo young and
mandarin chicken, beef or shrimp. Chow

mein can be made GF by substituting rice in place of the noodles. ▪ *www.dfongs.com*

## Don Pablo's ☉📖
*Eden Prairie* ▪ (952) 943-2877
*11347 Viking Dr*
*Maple Grove* ▪ (763) 416-6024
*7887 Elm Creek Blvd*
*Richfield* ▪ (612) 861-9686
*980 W 78th St*
*Roseville* ▪ (651) 639-3916
*2700 Lincoln Dr*

## Doolittles Woodfire Grill ✪★$$LD
*Alexandria* ▪ (320) 759-0885
*4409 Hwy 29 S*
*Egan* ▪ (651) 452-6627
*2140 Cliff Rd*
*Golden Valley* ▪ (763) 542-1931
*550 Winnetka Ave N* ▪ *Fusion* ▪ GF menu includes scallops with red curry sauce, spit-roasted chicken, smoked hanger steak, raspberry & fresh pear salad, and more. Crème brûlée and Italian custard are available for dessert. Alexandria location also carries GF beer and vodka. Confirm the timeliness of this information before dining in. ▪ *www.doolittlesrestaurants.com*

## Duluth Grill ✪★$BLD
*Duluth* ▪ (218) 726-1150
*118 S 27th Ave W* ▪ *American* ▪ GF menu includes smoked salmon wrap, veggie mac and cheese, spicy Thai pasta, chicken quesadilla, pesto pasta and bison stuffed Anaheim peppers. Manager notes that the kitchen is not entirely GF, but they do the best they can to separate GF foods from regular menu items during preparation. GF bread is available. ▪ *www.duluthgrill.com*

## Fiesta Café ✪★$$LD
*Red Wing* ▪ (651) 385-8939
*291 N Service Dr* ▪ *Mexican* ▪ GF menu includes fajitas, enchiladas, tortilla soup, and seafood. Other items on the regular menu can also be modified to be GF. Restaurant recommends asking for manager Victorino, who can discuss GF options. ▪ *www.fiestacafeandbar.com*

## Genghis Grill 📖
*Eagan* ▪ (651) 452-2363
*1304 Town Center Dr*

## Godfather's Pizza ★📖
*Albert Lea* ▪ (507) 373-1447
*509 E Main St*
*Mankato* ▪ (507) 388-7765
*1521 Tullemore St*
*Fairmont* ▪ (507) 238-4337
*1153 Hwy 15 S*
*Red Wing* ▪ (651) 388-1138
*2000 Old W Main St*
*Golden Valley* ▪ (763) 542-9780
*8040 Olson Mem Hwy*
*Waseca* ▪ (507) 835-8135
*1500 Hwy 13 N*
*Brooklyn Pk* ▪ (763) 560-2667
*7450 Unity Ave N*
*St Cloud* ▪ (320) 253-7441
*27th & Division*
*Burnsville* ▪ (952) 435-9558
*850 W County Rd*

## Good Earth $BLD
*Roseville* ▪ (651) 636-0956
*1901 Highway 36 W*
*Edina* ▪ (952) 925-1001
*3460 Galleria* ▪ *Modern American* ▪ Both locations report that they are "absolutely able" to accommodate GF diners and have many naturally GF items on the menu. They note that servers can usually indicate possible GF menu items and will ask a manager if they are unsure. ▪ *www.goodearthmn.com*

## Green Mill Restaurant and Bar ☉📖
*Blaine* ▪ (763) 792-9400
*4355 Pheasant Ridge Dr*
*Bloomington* ▪ (952) 884-9898
*1201 W 94th St*
*Duluth* ▪ (218) 727-7000
*340 Lake Ave*
*Albert Lea* ▪ (507) 373-8866
*2218 E Main St*
*Bemidji* ▪ (218) 444-1875
*1025 Paul Bunyan Dr S*
*Eagan* ▪ (651) 686-7000
*1940 Rahncliff Ct*

*Eden Prairie* ▪ (952) 944-3000
*8266 Commonwealth Dr*
*Firmont* ▪ (507) 238-4700
*Junction I-90 and US Hwy 15*
*Hastings* ▪ (651) 438-9191
*909 Vermillion St*
*Lakeville* ▪ (952) 435-8100
*17733 Kenwood Trl*
*Plymouth* ▪ (763) 553-9000
*2705 Annapolis Ln*
*Roseville* ▪ (651) 633-2100
*145 Rosedale Center*
*Woodbury* ▪ (651) 735-1000
*6025 Hudson Rd*
*Shoreview* ▪ (651) 482-1600
*1000 Gramise Rd*
*St. Cloud* ▪ (320) 259-6455
*100 4th Ave S*
*St. Paul* ▪ (651) 698-0353
*57 S Hamline*
*Willmar* ▪ (320) 231-2301
*2100 E. Highway 12*
*Winona* ▪ (507) 452-5400
*1025 Hwy 61 E*

## Ground Round   ✪☐

*Bemidji* ▪ (218) 444-3201
*2200 Paul Bunyan Dr NW*
*Duluth* ▪ (218) 723-1776
*2102 Maple Grove Rd*
*Grand Rapids* ▪ (218) 327-8655
*1001 S Pokegama Ave*
*Saint Cloud* ▪ (320) 252-7321
*2621 W Division St*
*Winona* ▪ (507) 452-3390
*405 Highway 14*
*Worthington* ▪ (507) 376-3043
*1290 Ryans Rd*

## Happy Joe's Pizza & Ice Cream   ☐

*Crookston* ▪ (218) 281-5141
*705 E Robert St*
*New Ulm* ▪ (507) 359-9811
*1700 N Broadway*

## Hubbell House, The   ✪$$$**LD**

*Mantorville* ▪ (507) 635-2331
*502 N Main St* ▪ *American* ▪ The restaurant has separate GF menus for
"noon" and "evening." Noon menu includes several salads and meat entrées,
while evening menu is more extensive and includes salads, steaks, pork
chops, lamb chops, seafood, and more. ▪
*www.hubbellhouserestaurant.com*

## HuHot Mongolian Grill   ☐

*Rochester* ▪ (507) 206-4422
*102 Apache Mall*

## Indian Zayka   $**LD**

*Eagan* ▪ (651) 688-8686
*1260 Town Center Dr* ▪ *Indian* ▪ The
restaurant reports that they have "many
GF options" and recommends alerting a
server upon arrival. The server will go over
GF menu options and alert the kitchen. ▪
*zaykamn.com*

## Jason's Deli   ✪☐

*Eden Prairie* ▪ (952) 944-7200
*11995 Singletree Ln*
*Edina* ▪ (952) 358-9900
*7565 France Ave S*

## Jensen's Supper Club   $$$**D**

*Eagan* ▪ (651) 688-7969
*3840 Sibley Memorial Hwy* ▪ *Seafood &*
*Steakhouse* ▪ The restaurant reports that
they have a "special sheet" of GF items in-
house. If a guest requests GF, a server will
go over this sheet with them to select a safe
meal option. ▪ *www.jenssupperclub.com*

## Jersey Mike's   ☐

*St. Anthony Village* ▪ (612) 362-7827
*2704 Hwy 88*
*Mankato* ▪ (507) 625-8454
*1924 Adams St*
*Coon Rapids* ▪ (763) 427-3333
*3473 River Rapids Dr NW*

## Joe's Crab Shack   ✪☐

*Roseville* ▪ (651) 636-4151
*2704 Snelling Ave N*

## Kincaid's   ☐

*Bloomington* ▪ (952) 921-2255
*8400 Normandale Lake Blvd*
*St Paul* ▪ (651) 602-9000
*380 St Peter St*

**Leonardo's Pizzeria**                ★ $$**LD**
*Mahtomedi* ▪ *(651) 777-1200*
*3150 Century Ave N* ▪ *Pizza* ▪ GF pizza is
available. ▪ *www.leonardospizzeria.net*

**Liffey, The**                        ✪★ $**BLD**
*Saint Paul* ▪ *(651) 556-1420*
*175 W 7th St* ▪ *Irish* ▪ GF menu is available
daily from 11 AM-10 PM and includes qui-
noa salad, sausage & mash, curried chick-
en, chili glazed salmon, and more. GF beer
and cider are available. ▪ *www.theliffey.com*

**Mad Jacks Sports Café**              ✪ $$**LD**
*Vadnais Heights* ▪ *(651) 287-3900*
*935 County Road E* ▪ *American* ▪ Restaurant claims to be "proud owners of the larg-
est GF menu in the U.S." GF menu includes
various appetizers, soups, salads, entrées,
burgers and sandwiches served on a GF
bun. GF pasta and pizza are available. Be
sure to alert server of GF needs when placing an order. ▪ *www.madjacksportscafe.com*

**Napa Valley Grille**                 ✪ $$$**LD**
*Bloomington* ▪ *(952) 858-9934*
*60 E Broadway* ▪ *Modern American* ▪
Manager Alicia of the Bloomington location
reports that they always have GF options,
but notes that the menu changes frequently.
She advises alerting both the server and the
manager upon arrival. Manager Tracy of
the Los Angeles location adds that reserva-
tions noting GF are recommended but not
required. ▪ *www.napavalleygrille.com*

**Nick-N-Willy's**                     ★ 📖
*Bloomington* ▪ *(952) 881-6699*
*3806 W Old Shakopee Rd*

**P.F. Chang's China Bistro**          ✪★ 📖
*Edina* ▪ *(952) 926-1713*
*2700 Southdale Ctr*
*Maple Grove* ▪ *(763) 493-9377*
*12071 Elm Creek Blvd N*

**Panino's**                           ✪★ $**LD**
*North Oaks* ▪ *(651) 486-0296*
*857 Village Center Dr* ▪ *Italian* ▪ Any
panino can be made GF by baking it in a
boat without the dough, and serving with

romaine lettuce. Call the restaurant or
visit to inquire about other GF options. ▪
*www.paninos.com*

**Park Tavern Bowl**                   ★ $**LD**
*St Louis Park* ▪ *(952) 929-6810*
*3401 Louisiana Ave S* ▪ *American* ▪ GF
pizza available. ▪ *www.parktavern.net*

**Pazzaluna Urban Italian Restaurant
and Bar**                              $$$**LD**
*Saint Paul* ▪ *(651) 223-7000*
*360 Saint Peter St* ▪ *Italian* ▪ A sheet
of GF items is available in-house, and
includes several salad options, ribeye steak,
seared scallops, and more. The restaurant
reports that most items can be "tweaked
slightly" to become GF and that they are
always willing to accommodate dietary
restrictions. ▪ *www.pazzaluna.com*

**Pei Wei Asian Diner**                ✪ 📖
*Eden Prairie* ▪ *(952) 656-1000*
*12561 Castlemoor Dr*
*St Louis Park* ▪ *(952) 656-9480*
*5330 Cedar Lake Rd S*
*Woodbury* ▪ *(651) 286-3990*
*8300 Tamarack Vlg*

**Pizza Luce**                         ✪★ $**LD**
*Saint Paul* ▪ *(651) 288-0186*
*1183 Selby Ave*
*Duluth* ▪ *(218) 727-7400*
*11 E Superior St*
*Hopkins* ▪ *(952) 767-0854*
*210 N Blake Rd*
*Richfield* ▪ *(612) 767-8603*
*800 W 66th St* ▪ *Pizza* ▪ Items marked
"GFR" on the menu can be prepared GF
upon request. These include appetizers,
salads, pasta and pizza. Alert server upon
arrival. ▪ *www.pizzaluce.com*

**Pizza Ranch**                        ✪ 📖
*Albert Lea* ▪ *(507) 377-2166*
*2430 N Bridge Ave*
*Alexandria* ▪ *(320) 762-4010*
*1522 Broadway St*
*Austin* ▪ *(507) 396-2677*
*1300 18th Ave NW*
*Baxter* ▪ *(218) 454-3290*

14643 Edgewood
**Delano** ▪ (763) 972-3910
1338 Babcock Blvd E
**Dilworth** ▪ (218) 287-6001
1504 Ctr Ave W
**Elk River** ▪ (763) 441-3000
19141 Freeport St NW
**Fairmont** ▪ (507) 235-8822
1101 N State St
**Glencoe** ▪ (320) 864-5321
2408 9th St E
**Hibbing** ▪ (218) 262-0085
2502 E Beltline
**Jackson** ▪ (507) 847-5555
206 3rd St
**Lakeville** ▪ (952) 898-3333
16995 Kenyon Ave
**Le Sueur** ▪ (507) 665-2222
124 N 2nd St
**Litchfield** ▪ (320) 693-9393
201 N Sibley Ave
**Luverne** ▪ (507) 283-2379
110 E Main
**Mankato** ▪ (507) 386-7077
1551 Tullamore St
**Marshall** ▪ (507) 537-0000
1420 Boyer Dr
**Montevideo** ▪ (320) 269-6738
1504 E Hwy 7
**Monticello** ▪ (763) 295-6500
1220 Highway 25
**New Prague** ▪ (952) 758-9440
1102 1st St NE
**New Ulm** ▪ (507) 354-7772
1927 S Broadway
**Norwood Young America** ▪ (952) 467-4010
425 Merger St
**Pipestone** ▪ (507) 562-2222
108 W Main St
**Redwood Falls** ▪ (507) 644-5936
1360 E Bridge St
**Slayton** ▪ (507) 836-8856
2306 Broadway
**Stewartville** ▪ (507) 533-0117
1580 2nd Ave NW
**Waconia** ▪ (952) 442-3321
224 W 1st St
**Wadena** ▪ (218) 631-2145

106 S Jefferson
**Waite Park** ▪ (320) 203-8646
110 2nd St S
**Waseca** ▪ (507) 833-9080
212 17th Ave NE
**Willmar** ▪ (320) 222-3663
1612 Lakeland Dr
**Worthington** ▪ (507) 376-3711
1132 Oxford St
**Shakopee** ▪ (952) 233-2122
1266 Vierling Dr

### Porterhouse Steaks & Seafood　$$$D
**Little Canada** ▪ (651) 483-9248
235 Little Canada Rd E
**Lakeville** ▪ (952) 469-2995
11211 205th St W ▪ Seafood & Steakhouse
▪ Both locations report "lots of options"
for GF diners, as most of the menu is
steaks and seafood. Alert a server upon
arrival and they will go over the options. ▪
*www.porterhousesteakandseafood.com*

### Rhombus Guys Pizza　✪▥
**Mentor** ▪ (218) 637-2198
110 Garfield Ave N ▪ GF pizza available in
8" size only.

### Rodizio Grill　★▥
**Maple Grove** ▪ (763) 657-1133
12197 Elm Creek Blvd

### Romano's Macaroni Grill　✪★▥
**Hopkins** ▪ (952) 417-9880
11390 Wayzata Blvd
**Saint Paul** ▪ (651) 633-2148
502 Rosedale Ctr

### Supatra's Thai Cuisine　✪$LD
**Saint Paul** ▪ (651) 222-5859
967 W 7th St ▪ Thai ▪ A wide variety of GF
items are marked on the menu, including
chicken satay, tom kha gai soup, pad thai,
a variety of curries and stir-frys, and more.
Some items may require modification
to be GF, so be sure to alert the server. ▪
*www.supatra.com*

### Tasty Asia Take-out　✪★$LD
**Wyoming** ▪ (651) 462-1200
26685 Faxton Ave ▪ Asian ▪ GF soy sauce

is available. GF menu includes hot and spicy chicken with lemongrass, chicken curry, beef with broccoli, spring rolls, fried rice, and more. For dessert, there is flourless chocolate cake and flan. Be sure to specify GF when placing your order. ▪ *www.tastyasia.com*

### Timber Lodge Steakhouse ✪$$D
*Bloomington* ▪ *(952) 881-5509*
*7989 Southtown Ctr*
*Duluth* ▪ *(218) 722-2624*
*325 Lake Ave S*
*Owatonna* ▪ *(507) 444-0303*
*4455 W Frontage Rd* ▪ *Steakhouse* ▪ GF menu includes prime rib, rainbow trout, walleye filet, Atlantic salmon, and more. ▪ *www.timberlodgesteakhouse.com*

### Tony Roma's 📖
*Bloomington* ▪ *(952) 854-7940*
*60 E Broadway*

### Tucci Benucch $$LD
*Bloomington* ▪ *(952) 853-0200*
*114 W Market* ▪ *Italian* ▪ The manager reports that a variety of menu items can be prepared GF, including all salads, chicken marsala, chicken sostanza, salmon risotto, pan fried walleye, and NY strip steak. Confirm the timeliness of this information before dining in. Alert a server, who will start the "allergy process" that includes a allergy button on the computer and a pink slip that is filled out for the kitchen. ▪ *www.tucci-benucch.com*

### Twin City Grill ✪★$$$LD
*Bloomington* ▪ *(952) 854-0200*
*130 N Garden - 1st Floor* ▪ *Seafood & Steakhouse* ▪ Extensive GF menu includes bacon-wrapped scallops, roasted garlic chicken, blackened ahi tuna, NY strip steak, sandwiches and burgers on GF buns, and more. Vanilla ice cream sundae or crème brûlée is available for dessert. GF beer and cider are also available. Located in the Mall of America. ▪ *twincitygrillrestaurant.com*

### Wildfire Restaurant ✪★📖
*Eden Prarie* ▪ *(952) 914-9100*
*Flying Cloud Dr*

### Zpizza ✪📖
*Roseville* ▪ *(651) 633-3131*
*1607 County Rd*

## MISSISSIPPI

### 1818 at Monmouth Plantation $$$D
*Natchez* ▪ *(601) 442-5852*
*36 Melrose Ave* ▪ *Southern* ▪ The restaurant reports that they have "plenty of options" for GF diners and that a CC policy is in place in the kitchen. Reservations noting GF are strongly recommended. Alert a server upon arrival. ▪ *www.monmouthplantation.com*

### 206 Front $$LD
*Hattiesburg* ▪ *(601) 545-5677*
*206 W Front St* ▪ *Fusion* ▪ GF accommodations can be made on only specific dishes. Alert a server upon arrival and they will list items that can be made GF. ▪ *www.206front.com*

### 208 South Lamar $$$D
*Oxford* ▪ *(662) 234-0005*
*208 S Lamar Blvd* ▪ *American* ▪ GF items include steak, vegetable plate, tuna and a variety of salads. ▪ *208southlamar.com*

### 32 Degrees Yogurt Bar 📖
*Hattiesburg* ▪ *(601) 268-1223*
*6136 Hwy 98*
*Gulfport* ▪ *(228) 831-1600*
*15206 Crossroads Pkwy*

### Amerigo Italian Restaurant ✪$$LD
*Ridgeland* ▪ *(601) 977-0563*
*6592 Old Canton Rd* ▪ *Italian* ▪ GF menu features a variety of salads such as tomato and mozzarella, as well as GF entrées

such as flame grilled salmon acuto, prime sirloin, and wild mushroom pasta. ■ *amerigo.net*

### Anthony's Good Food Market $$D
*West Point* ■ (662) 494-0316
*116 W Main St* ■ *American* ■ Owner Ray reports that he himself has Celiac so "any accommodations can be made to the menu" for GF customers. Alert a server upon arrival and they will go talk to Ray about items that can be made GF. ■ *www.anthonysgoodfoodmarket.com*

### Back Bay Seafood Restaurant $$LD
*Gulfport* ■ (228) 248-0505
*1458 Magnolia St* ■ *Seafood* ■ Hostess reports that any item on their menu can be made GF. Be sure to alert server upon arrival and they will inform the chef. ■ *www.backbayseafoodrestaurant.com*

### Biaggi's ✪★📖
*Ridgeland* ■ (601) 354-6600
*970 Highland Colony Pkwy*

### Bonefish Grill ✪📖
*Biloxi* ■ (228) 388-0009
*2600 Beach Blvd Ste 76*
*Madison* ■ (601) 607-3334
*201 Colony Wy*

### Café Anchuca $$$LD
*Vicksburg* ■ (601) 661-0111
*1010 First E St* ■ *Southern* ■ The restaurant does their best to accommodate GF diners, be sure to alert server upon arrival. ■ *www.anchuca.com/cafe.shtml*

### Campbell's Bakery ★¢S
*Jackson* ■ (601) 362-4628
*3013 N State St* ■ *Bakery* ■ Campbell's Bakery has a GF Friday where they prepare a batch of GF cupcakes and baked goods in the morning in order to avoid CC.

### Castle Restaurant & Pub, The $$$BLD
*Natchez* ■ (601) 446-8500
*84 Homochitto St* ■ *American* ■ GF accommodations can be made for any item on the menu. ■ *www.dunleith.com*

### Central Station Grill $$LD
*Starkville* ■ (662) 323-6062
*200 S Montgomery St* ■ *American* ■ GF items include grilled chicken and grilled fish, salads, fish dishes, shrimp, crawfish, filet mignon and ribeye. GF seasoning is also available for any dish. ■ *eatwithus.com/grill*

### Cerami's Italian Restaurant $$D
*Brandon* ■ (601) 919-2829
*5417 Lakeland Dr* ■ *Italian* ■ GF pasta is available and can be substituted in most pasta dishes. Alissa Cerami reports that most grilled items are GF as well, and that steamed or sautéed veggies can be substituted for non-GF sides. ■ *www.ceramis.net*

### China Royal ¢LD
*Columbus* ■ (662) 328-2699
*1613 Main St*
*Oxford* ■ (662) 513-4999
*1938 University Ave* ■ *Chinese* ■ Many menu items can be made or are naturally GF. Alert a server upon arrival and they will list items that can be made GF.

### Crystal Grill $LD
*Greenwood* ■ (662) 453-6530
*423 Carrollton Ave* ■ *American* ■ GF items include any fish and shrimp dishes as well as steak platters. ■ *crystalgrillms.com*

### Eslava's Grille $$LD
*Jackson* ■ (601) 932-4070
*2481 Lakeland Dr* ■ *Mediterranean* ■ The restaurant reports that many items on the menu are naturally GF or can be prepared GF. Alert server upon arrival.

### Famous Joe's
### Cajun Cafe & Oyster Bar $LD
*Biloxi* ■ (228) 354-8000
*14391 Hwy 15* ■ *Cajun & Creole* ■ GF items include a seafood platter, shrimp platter, oyster platter, fish platter, hamburger steak, blackened steak and blackened fish.

### Fox and Hound Pub & Grille 📖
*Southaven* ■ (662) 536-2200
*6565 Towne Ctr Xing*

## Fox's Pizza Den ★$LD
*Hattiesburg* ▪ (601) 264-3690
*5266 Old Hwy 11*
*Petal* ▪ (601) 602-4279
*100 Eastbrook Dr* ▪ *Pizza* ▪ According
to a Fox's Pizza Den employee, GF crust
is available and is stored and prepared in
separate areas in order to prevent CC. ▪
*www.foxspizza.com*

## Genghis Grill 📖
*Flowood* ▪ (601) 633-2000
*121 Market St*

## Hard Rock Café ✪📖
*Biloxi* ▪ (228) 276-5233
*777 Beach Blvd*

## Harvey's $$LD
*Columbus* ▪ (662) 327-1639
*200 Main St*
*Starkville* ▪ (662) 323-1669
*406 Hwy 12*
*Tupelo* ▪ (662) 842-6763
*424 S Gloster St* ▪ *American* ▪ GF options include grilled chicken salad,
grilled chicken and filet mignon. ▪
*eatwithus.com/harveys*

## High Noon Café ¢B
*Jackson* ▪ (601) 366-1513
*2807 Old Canton Rd* ▪ *Vegetarian* ▪
Production manager Bryan reports that they
have a variety of GF items available, including
the "harmony bowl", which consists of mixed
vegetables and tofu served over long grain
rice, several soups, and a salad bar. He adds
that they are happy to serve any menu item
over long grain rice "in order to mitigate the
glutenous hurdle." He cautions that all items
are prepared in a common environment,
but assures diners that they will "accommodate their needs to the best of their ability."
Located inside of Rainbow Natural Grocery
Cooperative. ▪ *rainbowcoop.org/cafe.htm*

## J. Broussard's ★$$D
*Columbus* ▪ (662) 243-1480
*210 5th St S* ▪ *Seafood & Steakhouse* ▪
Chef Beth reports that many of the items
on the menu are naturally GF, and several

others can be prepared with "special rice
flour" that she keeps on hand. The chef
also advises to alert the server of dietary
restrictions. GF hard cider is available. ▪
*jbroussards.com*

## Jason's Deli ✪📖
*Jackson* ▪ (601) 206-9191
*1067 E County Line Rd*

## Jutamas Thai Restaurant $LD
*Hattiesburg* ▪ (601) 584-8583
*910 Timothy Ln* ▪ *Thai* ▪ Any item on the
menu can be made GF. Alert server upon
arrival. ▪ *www.hattiesburgthai.com*

## Lone Star Steakhouse & Saloon ✪📖
*Pearl* ▪ (601) 664-1733
*442 Riverwind Dr*

## Los Lobos Mexican Restaurant $LD
*Wesson* ▪ (601) 643-1327
*2051 Hwy 51 S* ▪ *Mexican* ▪ GF items available. Alert server upon arrival and they will
be able to list options.

## Lusco's $D
*Greenwood* ▪ (662) 453-5365
*722 Carrollton Ave* ▪ *Ameri-*
*can* ▪ GF items include any fish,
steak, crab and shrimp dishes. ▪
*www.greenwoodms.org/menu_pdfs/luscos.pdf*

## Margaritaville ✪★📖
*Biloxi* ▪ (228) 267-7777
*160 5th St*

## Mayflower Café, The $$LD
*Jackson* ▪ (601) 355-4122
*123 W Capitol St* ▪ *Café* ▪ GF options
include salads, steaks, pork chops, baked
potatoes, broiled fish, scallops, shrimp and
oysters.

## O'Charley's 📖
*Gulfport* ▪ (228) 328-1350
*10510 Hwy 49*
*Hattiesburg* ▪ (601) 268-1193
*4640 Hardy St*
*Meridian* ▪ (601) 482-6505
*539 Bonita Lakes Dr*
*Olive Branch* ▪ (662) 893-2334

7880 Craft-Goodman Frontage Rd
**Pearl** ▪ (601) 932-6575
430 Riverwind Dr
**Southhaven** ▪ (662) 349-6663
357 Goodman Rd W
**Tupelo** ▪ (662) 840-4730
3876 N Gloster St

### P.F. Chang's China Bistro ✪★▥
*Ridgeland* ▪ (601) 605-4282
910 Highland Colony Pkwy

### Pita Pit, The ¢BLD
*Oxford* ▪ (662) 238-3535
319 N Lamar Blvd ▪ Deli ▪ The restaurant reports that most pita wraps can be made into a salad with any of several GF sauces. Ask server for details. ▪ *www.pitapitoxford.com*

### Ravine $$$D
*Oxford* ▪ (662) 234-4555
53 CR-321 ▪ Modern American ▪ GF options include salad, pork chops and chicken. ▪ *oxfordravine.com*

### Ruth's Chris Steak House ✪▥
*Biloxi* ▪ (228) 374-2137
777 Beach Blvd
*Ridgeland* ▪ (601) 853-2734
1000 Highland Colony Pkwy

### Sal & Phil's $LD
*Ridgeland* ▪ (601) 957-1188
6600 Old Canton Rd ▪ Seafood ▪ Restaurant reports that they can make any of their fish items GF. Be sure to call ahead or have the server note GF when taking order.

### Salute Italian Restaurant $$LD
*Gulfport* ▪ (228) 864-2500
1712 15th S ▪ Italian ▪ Several items on the menu can be made GF, including the veggie medley, chicken steak and risotto. ▪ *www.saluteitalian.com*

### Surin of Thailand ▥
*Hattiesburg* ▪ (601) 296-9686
6101 US Hwy 49 S

### Sweet Cece's ▥
*Greenville* ▪ (662) 332-5205
1831 S Dr. Martin Luther King Blvd ▪ Dessert ▪ All frozen yogurt, with the exceptions of Cake Batter, Cookies n' Cream, Red Velvet Cake, and Heath Bar, are GF. ▪ *www.sweetceces.com*

### Tabella ✪★$LD
*Hattiesburg* ▪ (601) 255-5488
3720-A Hardy St ▪ Italian ▪ GF menu items include scampi, soups and salads, GF pasta and pasta sauce, fontina chicken, chicken marsala, chicken picatta, chicken parmesan, veal parmesan, veal marsala, grilled salmon, pesto chicken, roma chicken, vegetables and sides and dessert. GF kids menu also available. ▪ *tabellapronto.com*

### Table 100 $$$LD
*Flowood* ▪ (601) 420-4202
100 Ridge Wy ▪ Bistro ▪ GF menu items include tuna, pork belly, salads, angus fillet, salmon fillet, vegetable plate and chicken breast. ▪ *www.tableonehundred.com*

### Thai Siam $LD
*Starkville* ▪ (662) 320-7117
303 Dr Martin Luther King Jr Dr E ▪ Thai ▪ GF items include stir fry, fried rice, pad chashew, pad fried rice and pad thai. ▪ *www.yelp.com/biz/thai-siam-starkville*

### Uptown Grocery ¢LD
*Natchez* ▪ (601) 445-9111
531 S Canal St ▪ American ▪ GF items include salad, red beans and rice as well as gumbo. Thursdays soup of the day is not GF. Alert server. ▪ *uptowngrocery.com*

### Veranda Restaurant, The $$LD
*Starkville* ▪ (662) 323-1231
208 Lincoln Green ▪ American ▪ The restaurant reports that several items on the menu can be modified to be GF. Alert the server upon arrival. ▪ *www.verandastarkville.com*

**Walnut Circle Grill**                    $$LD
*Hattiesburg* ▪ *(601) 544-2202*
*115 Walnut St* ▪ *Southern* ▪ The restaurant
reports that any of the steaks can be made
GF. GF diners should request no onions
on their steaks, as the ingredients contain
gluten. ▪ *www.walnutcirclegrill.com*

**Weidmann's**                             $$LD
*Meridian* ▪ *(601) 581-5770*
*210 22nd Ave* ▪ *American* ▪ GF items
include any vegetable dishes, grilled
fish, grilled chicken and steaks. ▪
*www.weidmanns1870.com*

**Woody's Tupelo Steakhouse**            $$$$D
*Tupelo* ▪ *(662) 840-0460*
*619 N Gloster* ▪ *Steakhouse* ▪ Any item on
the menu that is not breaded or fried can
be made GF. Alert a server upon arrival. ▪
*www.woodyssteak.com*

# MISSOURI

## KANSAS CITY

**Abuelo's**                               ✪⬚
*Kansas Ciry* ▪ *(816) 584-8557*
*8541 NW Prairie View Rd*

**American Restaurant, The**               $$$D
*Kansas City* ▪ *(816) 545-8001*
*200 E 25th St* ▪ *Modern American* ▪
Maitre Demetra reports that they can
accommodate GF diners. She advises
making reservations noting GF and giving
the staff at least one day's notice. GF will
be noted on your reservation, but men-
tion it to your server upon arrival. All
staff are trained in "allergy" procedures. ▪
*www.theamericankc.com*

**Beer Kitchen**                          ✪★$LD
*Kansas City* ▪ *(816) 389-4180*
*435 Westport Rd* ▪ *American* ▪ Hostess
Gemma reports that a GF menu is avail-
able in-house and that they are able to

"substitute or modify most items on the
menu" to fit the needs of GF guests. GF
sandwich buns and pasta are available. ▪
*www.beerkitchenkc.com*

**Blue Bird Bistro**                     ★$$BLD
*Kansas City* ▪ *(816) 221-7559*
*1700 Summit St* ▪ *American* ▪ Manager
Beth reports that there are some GF items
on the menu, and they accommodate GF
diners regularly. Calling ahead is recommended for prep time and item availablility.
▪ *www.bluebirdbistro.com*

**Bonefish Grill**                         ✪⬚
*Kansas City* ▪ *(816) 746-8179*
*6334 N Lucerne Ave*

**Bristol Seafood Grill**                ✪$$$LD
*Kansas City* ▪ *(816) 448-6007*
*51 E 14th St* ▪ *Seafood* ▪ GF menu is
available online and in-house. Items
include shrimp cocktail, seafood of the
day, steaks, cioppino, mesquite grilled
chicken, and more. A variety of ice creams
and sorbets are available for dessert. ▪
*www.bristolseafoodgrill.com*

**Buca di Beppo**                          ✪⬚
*Kansas City* ▪ *(816) 931-6548*
*310 W 47th St*

**Capital Grille, The**                    ✪⬚
*Kansas City* ▪ *(816) 531-8345*
*4740 Jefferson St*

**Classic Cup Café**                     $$$BLD
*Kansas City* ▪ *(816) 753-1840*
*301 W 47th St* ▪ *Bistro* ▪ The restaurant
reports that they accommodate GF diners "at least once a week." Reservations
noting GF can be made a day ahead if
preferred. Alert the server upon arrival. ▪
*www.classiccup.com*

**Coach's Bar & Grill**                   ★$LD
*Kansas City* ▪ *(816) 941-2286*
*414 W 103rd St* ▪ *American* ▪ GF buns are
available for sandwiches at both locations.
The Kansas City location also reports GF
beer and cider. ▪ *www.coach-s.com*

### Eden Alley Café  ✪◗LD
*Kansas City* ▪ *(816) 561-5415*
*707 W 47th St* ▪ *Vegetarian* ▪ GF items
marked on the menu include salads, baby
falafels, tacos, egg salad, and roasted sweet
potatoes. Meals are specified in parentheses on the menu and are available
for carry out, delivery, and dining in. ▪
*www.edenalley.com*

### First Watch - The Daytime Café  ✪📖
*Kansas City* ▪ *(816) 931-1054*
*1022 Westport Rd*

### Fogo De Chao  ★📖
*Kansas City* ▪ *(816) 931-7700*
*222 W 47th St*

### Freebirds on the Fly  ✪📖
*Kansas City* ▪ *(816) 531-5407*
*554 Westport Rd*

### Grand Street Café  ✪★$$$LD
*Kansas City* ▪ *(816) 561-8000*
*4740 Grand Ave* ▪ *Modern American* ▪
GF pasta and bread are available. In-house
GF menu includes items like prime rib
tacos, bone-in pork chop, oven roasted
chicken, seared scallops, and more. ▪
*www.grandstreetcafe.com*

### Ingredient Restaurant  ✪★📖
*Kansas City* ▪ *(816) 994-3350*
*1111 Main St*
*Kansas City* ▪ *(816) 994-3393*
*4807 Jefferson St*

### Jack Stack Barbecue  $LD
*Kansas City* ▪ *(816) 942-9141*
*13441 Holmes Rd*
*Kansas City* ▪ *(816) 472-7427*
*101 W 22 St*
*Kansas City* ▪ *(816) 531-7427*
*4747 Wyandotte St* ▪ *Barbeque* ▪ Director of operations Rod reports that a list
of GF items is available at each restaurant. He recommends letting your server
know of any "allergies" as soon as you are
seated. The server will inform management and provide guests with the GF list.
Rod also notes that they follow "strict

guidelines" when preparing GF orders and
"handle guests with allergens every day." ▪
*www.jackstackbbq.com*

### Jason's Deli  ✪📖
*Kansas City* ▪ *(816) 842-6655*
*1100 S Main St*
*Kansas City* ▪ *(816) 994-8891*
*9026 NW Skyview Ave*

### La Bodega  ✪$$LD
*Kansas City* ▪ *(816) 472-8272*
*703 Southwest Blvd* ▪ *Spanish* ▪ GF items
are marked on the menu and include roasted red peppers stuffed with ahi tuna, pan-
cetta-wrapped dates stuffed with chorizo,
and pork skewers. ▪ *www.labodegakc.com*

### Lone Star Steakhouse & Saloon  ✪📖
*Kansas City* ▪ *(816) 505-1771*
*6501 NW Barry Rd*

### LuLu's Thai Noodle Shop  ✪★◗LD
*Kansas City* ▪ *(816) 474-8424*
*2030 Central St* ▪ *Thai* ▪ GF soy sauce is
available.GF menu includes pad thai, basil
fried rice, and shrimp satay, among other
things. ▪ *www.lulusnoodles.com*

### Melting Pot, The  ✪📖
*Kansas City* ▪ *(816) 931-6358*
*450 Ward Pkwy*

### Milano  ✪★$$LD
*Kansas City* ▪ *(816) 398-4825*
*2450 Grand Blvd* ▪ *Italian* ▪ GF pasta
and pizza are available. GF menu includes
spinach salad, salmon filet, risotto, and
flat iron steak, as well as several pasta and
pizza dishes. Reservations noting GF are
recommended. Alert a server upon arrival.
▪ *www.milanokc.com*

### One More Cup  ★◗S
*Kansas City* ▪ *(816) 994-3644*
*7408 Wornall Rd* ▪ *Coffee Shop* ▪ The
coffee shop offers GF, allergen-free baked
goods from Kneaded Specialties & Be
Free Bakers, including cakes, cookies,
brownies, doughnuts, muffins, and more. ▪
*www.onemorecupkc.com*

## P.F. Chang's China Bistro        ✪★📖
*Kansas City* ▪ *(816) 931-9988*
*102 W 47th St*

## Pizza Shoppe        ★📖
*Kansas City* ▪ *(816) 741-6111*
*7687 NW Prairie View Rd*
*Kansas City* ▪ *(816) 420-0111*
*9329 N Oak Traffic Wy*
*Kansas City* ▪ *(816) 942-0900*
*13612 Washington Ave*

## Rosati's Pizza        ★📖
*Kansas City* ▪ *(816) 605-1672*
*9321 N Oak Trafficway*

## Ruth's Chris Steak House        ✪📖
*Kansas City* ▪ *(816) 531-4800*
*700 W 47th St*

## Spin Pizza        ★$$LD
*Kansas City* ▪ *(816) 561-7746*
*4950 Main St* ▪ *Pizza* ▪ All of their pizzas are available GF except those with
meatballs. GF salads are also available,
just ask for no croutons as they are not
GF. Procedures to prevent CC are in place
and include using separate prep surfaces and utensils and baking on separate
pans. However, the restaurant cautions
that they are not a GF environment. ▪
*www.spinpizza.com*

## Waldo Pizza        ✪★$LD
*Kansas City* ▪ *(816) 363-5242*
*7433 Broadway St* ▪ *Pizza* ▪ GF bread and
pizza are available. Extensive GF menu
includes appetizers, salads, pizzas, and
sandwiches. A wide variety of GF desserts
are also available, including cupcakes,
flourless chocolate cake, butterscotch
pudding, lemonade cake, and cookies. ▪
*www.waldopizza.net*

# MISSOURI
## ST. LOUIS

## Atlas Restaurant        $$$D
*St. Louis* ▪ *(314) 367-6800*
*5513 Pershing Ave* ▪ *Modern American*
▪ Manager Andrew reports that there are
"quite a few options" on the menu that
can be prepared GF, but notes that some
may require modifications. He recommends reservations noting GF and says
to ask for a manager upon arrival. ▪
*www.atlasrestaurantstl.com*

## Au Bon Pain        📖
*St Louis* ▪ *(314) 977-1611*
*20 N Grand St*

## Big Sky Café        ✪$$D
*St. Louis* ▪ *(314) 962-5757*
*47 S Old Orchard Ave* ▪ *Modern American* ▪ GF items are marked on the menu
and include pan-roasted rainbow trout,
rosemary & red wine braised pot roast,
roasted garlic mashed potatoes, spinach
salad with dried cherries, and more.
Some items are "GF optional" and require
modification, so be sure to alert a server
upon arrival. Confirm the timeliness
of this information before dining in. ▪
*www.allgreatrestaurants.com*

## Cardwell's at the Plaza        $$$$LD
*St. Louis* ▪ *(314) 997-8885*
*94 Plaza Frontenac* ▪ *Modern American* ▪ Hostess Tammy reports that the
restaurant frequently serves GF diners.
She recommends alerting a server, who
will notify the kitchen and discuss GF
options with the chef. She notes that
because the menu changes frequently, it
is difficult to tell what types of dishes will
be available, but the chefs can "always
come up with something" for GF diners.
▪ *www.cardwellsattheplaza.com*

### Clark Street Grill ★ $$$**BLD**
*St. Louis* ▪ *(314) 552-5850*
*811 Spruce St* ▪ *Modern American* ▪
Manager Lauren reports that although the
restaurant does not serve GF diners "on
a regular basis," they will make GF items
from scratch. She recommends reservations noting GF so that the restaurant
can make sure to have a chef available to
speak with the GF customer upon arrival.
Located inside The Westin St. Louis hotel. ▪
*www.clarkstreetgrill.com*

### Eleven Eleven Mississippi ✪$$**LD**
*St. Louis* ▪ *(314) 241-9999*
*1111 Mississippi Ave* ▪ *Bistro* ▪ GF menu is
available in-house and includes items such
as grilled salmon, roasted half chicken, pan
roasted grouper, and bacon wrapped pork
tenderloin. Alert a server upon arrival.
Confirm the timeliness of this information
before dining in. ▪ *www.1111-m.com*

### First Watch - The Daytime Café ✪▥
*St. Louis* ▪ *(314) 293-1024*
*5646 Telegraph Rd*

### Fitz's American Grill and Bottling
### Works $**LD**
*St. Louis* ▪ *(314) 726-9555*
*6605 Delmar Blvd* ▪ *American* ▪ The staff
reports that GF diners should ask to speak
with a manager, who will "discuss various options for eliminating gluten" from
menu items. Burgers without buns are a
popular GF item. Confirm the timeliness
of this information before dining in. ▪
*www.fitzsrootbeer.com*

### Fleming's Prime
### Steakhouse & Wine Bar ✪▥
*St Louis* ▪ *(314) 567-7610*
*1855 S Lindbergh Blvd*

### Happy Joe's Pizza & Ice Cream ▥
*St. Louis* ▪ *(314) 961-4074*
*7918 Watson Rd*

### Hard Rock Café ✪▥
*St Louis* ▪ *(314) 621-7625*
*1820 Market St*

### Herbie's ✪★$$**LD**
*St. Louis* ▪ *(314) 769-9595*
*405 N Euclid Ave* ▪ *American* ▪ GF menu
includes raspberry duck, spinach and artichoke dip, vegetable lasagna, and shrimp &
grits. GF pizza is available. Alert the server,
who will direct GF requests to the kitchen.
Reservations noting GF are recommended.
▪ *www.herbies.com*

### HuHot Mongolian Grill ▥
*St. Louis* ▪ *(314) 392-9696*
*12675 Olive Blvd*

### Nachomama's ✪⊄**LD**
*St. Louis* ▪ *(314) 961-9110*
*9643 Manchester Rd* ▪ *Mexican* ▪ GF
items marked on the menu include chalupas, fajitas, enchiladas, tamales, rotisserie chicken, nachos, and more. Be sure
to mention GF when placing an order,
and ask for corn tortillas if applicable. ▪
*www.nachomamas-stl.com*

### O'Charley's ▥
*St. Louis* ▪ *(314) 845-8200*
*4130 Rusty Rd*

### Old Spaghetti Factory, The ✪★▥
*St. Louis* ▪ *(314) 621-0276*
*727 N 1st St*

### P.F. Chang's China Bistro ✪★▥
*St. Louis* ▪ *(314) 862-2624*
*25 The Blvd St. Louis*

### Pasta House Co., The ✪★▥
*St. Louis* ▪ *(314) 894-9161*
*6214 S Lindbergh Blvd*
*St. Louis* ▪ *(314) 432-6750*
*700 N New Ballas Rd*
*St. Louis* ▪ *(314) 638-1240*
*9012 Gravois Rd*
*St. Louis* ▪ *(314) 423-8880*
*1701 Lambert Int'l Blvd*

### Pei Wei Asian Diner ✪▥
*St. Louis* ▪ *(314) 656-5980*
*8885 Ladue Rd*

## Pi Pizzeria ★ $SLD
*St Louis* ▪ (314) 727-6633
*6144 Delmar Blvd*
*St Louis* ▪ (314) 367-4300
*400 N Euclid Ave*
*St Louis* ▪ (314) 588-7600
*610 Washington Ave* ▪ *Pizza* ▪ GF thin crust pizza available. The manager reports that GF pizza is cooked in a separate area, but cautions that there is still a risk of CC due to the large amount of flour in the kitchen. ▪ *www.restaurantpi.com*

## Romano's Macaroni Grill ✪★📖
*St Louis* ▪ (314) 918-8264
*8590 Eager Rd*
*St Louis* ▪ (314) 487-9070
*4125 Lemay Ferry Rd*
*St Louis* ▪ (314) 989-9891
*10453 Olive Blvd*

## Rooster Crepe.Sandwich.Cafe ★ ¢BL
*St. Louis* ▪ (314) 241-8118
*1104 Locust St* ▪ *French* ▪ GF crepes are available. ▪ *www.roosterstl.com*

## Ruth's Chris Steak House ✪📖
*St. Louis* ▪ (314) 259-3200
*315 Chestnut St*

## Tony's $$$$D
*St. Louis* ▪ (314) 231-7007
*410 Market St* ▪ *Italian* ▪ Chef Vince Jr. reports that there are many GF options on the menu and "only a few things" are not available GF. He recommends asking for him upon arrival so he can help select a suitable meal option. ▪ *www.tonysstlouis.com*

## Truffles $$$LD
*St. Louis* ▪ (314) 567-9100
*9202 Clayton Rd* ▪ *Modern American* ▪ The restaurant reports that many items can be prepared GF with "certain modifications". Most meat, poultry, and seafood dishes can be made GF with substitutions. Reservations noting GF are recommended but not required. Alert a server, who will indicate GF menu items. ▪ *www.trufflesinladue.com*

## Winslow's ★ $$BLD
*St. Louis* ▪ (314) 725-7559
*7213 Delmar Blvd* ▪ *American* ▪ GF bread is available, both in the kitchen and for sale. The restaurant reports that staff is GF aware but is not highly educated in this area and that GF is "not the focus of the restaurant." Alert server upon arrival. ▪ *www.winslowshome.com*

# MISSOURI
## ALL OTHER CITIES

## 44 Stone Public House ✪★ $LD
*Columbia* ▪ (573) 443-2726
*3910 Peachtree Dr* ▪ *Global* ▪ Restaurant reports there are a variety of GF items on their menu. A few of them are the roasted chicken, the veggie curry (minus the pita bread) and the tikka masala soup. Confirm the timeliness of this information before dining in. Alert the server upon arrival. ▪ *44stonepub.com*

## 5 Star Burgers ★ ¢LD
*Clayton* ▪ (314) 720-4350
*8125 Maryland Ave* ▪ *American* ▪ GF buns are available for burgers and sandwiches. ▪ *www.5starburgers.com*

## Andrea's Gluten Free ¢S
*Chesterfield* ▪ (636) 536-9953
*759 Spirit Of St. Louis Blvd* ▪ *Bakery* ▪ Dedicated GF bakery offering bread, pizza, hamburger buns, biscuits and more. For dessert, they make cookies, cakes, pies, muffins, and cupcakes, among other things. Products are available for pickup at the storefront location or for ordering online. ▪ *www.andreasglutenfree.com*

### Annie Gunn's                    $$$LD
*Chesterfield* ▪ **(636) 532-7684**
*16806 Chesterfield Airport Rd* ▪ *American*
▪ Hostess Kelsey reports that they "can
definitely accommodate" GF requests. She
recommends alerting a server, who will go
over the menu and help select GF options.
▪ *www.smokehousemarket.com*

### Barcelona Tapas Restaurant    ✪SLD
*St. Louis* ▪ **(314) 863-9909**
*34 N Central* ▪ *Spanish* ▪ GF menu available from the regular menu items with
modifications to make them GF. Examples
include black bean soup, curried chicken
salad, paprika roasted Spanish almonds,
and paella Valencia. For dessert, there is
crème brûlée, flan, and a Spanish fruit &
nut platter. Alert a server upon arrival and
they will bring the GF menu. This information applies to the listed location only. ▪
*www.barcelonatapas.com*

### BrickTop's                       ✪📖
*Frontenac* ▪ **(314) 567-6300**
*10342 Clayton Rd*

### Bristol Seafood Grill          ✪$$$LD
*Creve Coeur* ▪ **(314) 567-0272**
*11801 Olive Blvd*
*O'Fallon* ▪ **(636) 625-6350**
*2314 Technology Dr* ▪ *Seafood* ▪ GF menu
is available online and in-house. Items
include shrimp cocktail, seafood of the
day, steaks, cioppino, mesquite grilled
chicken, and more. A variety of ice creams
and sorbets are available for dessert. ▪
*www.bristolseafoodgrill.com*

### Café Napoli                      $$$LD
*Clayton* ▪ **(314) 863-5731**
*7754 Forsyth Blvd* ▪ *Italian* ▪ The restaurant reports that they are "prepared to
make anything GF" and have been trained
accordingly. Alert a server upon arrival
and they will help select GF options. ▪
*www.cafenapoli.com*

### Cantina Laredo                    📖
*Branson* ▪ **(417) 334-6062**
*1001 Branson Landing Blvd*

### Carino's Italian                 ✪📖
*Joplin* ▪ **(417) 206-9090**
*137 N Rangeline Rd*

### Carlos O'Kelly's                  ✪
*Springfield* ▪ **(417) 890-0220**
*4100 S Campbell Ave*
*St. Joseph* ▪ **(816) 232-6010**
*3818 Frederick Ave*

### Carrabba's Italian Grill        ✪📖
*Independence* ▪ **(816) 795-9944**
*19900 E Valley View Pkwy*

### Corner Pub & Grill, The        ✪★¢LD
*Kirkwood* ▪ **(636) 225-1300**
*13645 Big Bend Rd*
*Chesterfield* ▪ **(636) 230-3400**
*15824 Fountains Plaza Dr* ▪ *Pub Food*
▪ "Hanna's" GF menu includes BBQ
chicken wings, steak kabobs, chicken and
rice, sandwiches & burgers on GF buns,
and more. Both locations have a dedicated GF fryer. The menu is named after
Owner Brant's daughter, who is GF. ▪
*www.cornerpubandgrill.com*

### Espinos Mexican Bar & Grill      $LD
*Chesterfield* ▪ **(636) 519-0044**
*17409 Chesterfield Airport Rd* ▪ *Mexican*
▪ The manager reports that as long as GF
diners alert their servers, they can "always
be accommodated." GF corn tortillas
can be substituted for flour tortillas. ▪
*www.espinosmexicanbargrill.com*

### First Watch - The Daytime Café   ✪📖
*Chesterfield* ▪ **(636) 530-1401**
*120 Hilltown Village Ctr*
*Clayton* ▪ **(314) 863-7330**
*8001 Forsyth Blvd*
*Creve Coeur* ▪ **(314) 994-7171**
*742 N New Ballas Rd*
*Des Peres* ▪ **(314) 966-3913**
*13323 Manchester Rd*
*Independence* ▪ **(816) 795-0814**
*19321 E US Highway 40*
*Kirkwood* ▪ **(314) 909-7271**
*491 S Kirkwood Rd*

*North Kansas City* ■ *(816) 842-7300*
*409 Armour Rd*
*Saint Peters* ■ *(636) 970-0050*
*312 Mid Rivers Ctr*
*Webster Groves* ■ *(314) 968-9984*
*220 W Lockwood Ave*
*Westport* ■ *(816) 931-1054*
*1022 Westport Rd*
*Oakville* ■ *(314) 293-1024*
*5646 Telegraph Rd*

**Fox and Hound Pub & Grille**   📖
*Springfield* ■ *(417) 890-6289*
*2035 E Independence St*
*Chesterfield* ■ *(636) 536-0802*
*17416 Chesterfield Arpt Rd*

**Freebirds on the Fly**   ✪📖
*Lee's Summit* ■ *(816) 554-4864*
*860 NW Blue Pkwy*

**Genghis Grill**   📖
*Ellisville* ■ *(636) 527-2714*
*15819 Fountain Plaza Dr*

**Godfather's Pizza**   ★📖
*Liberty* ■ *(816) 792-1000*
*322 S 291 Hwy*
*Nixa* ■ *(417) 725-4933*
*1890 Deffer Dr*
*Ozark* ■ *(417) 581-9292*
*510 E South St*
*St Joseph* ■ *(816) 233-4430*
*1329 S Belt Hwy*
*Poplar Bluff* ■ *(573) 686-1420*
*791 N Westwood*
*Blue Springs* ■ *(816) 229-5455*
*705 Hwy I-70*

**Ground Round**   ✪📖
*St Joseph* ■ *(816) 671-1906*
*123 S 6th*

**HuHot Mongolian Grill**   📖
*Columbia* ■ *(573) 874-2000*
*3802 Buttonwood Dr*
*Springfield* ■ *(417) 882-0300*
*2825 S Glenstone*

**Ingredient Restaurant**   ✪★📖
*Columbia* ■ *(573) 442-1502*
*304 S 9th St*

**Jason's Deli**   ✪📖
*Lee's Summit* ■ *(816) 246-6400*
*1690 NW Chipman Rd*
*Chesterfield* ■ *(636) 536-6868*
*17245 Chesterfield Airport Rd*

**Jersey Mike's**   📖
*Webster Groves* ■ *(314) 961-3303*
*8567 Watson Rd*

**Joe's Crab Shack**   ✪📖
*St. Peters* ■ *(636) 397-0733*
*5856 Suemandy Dr*
*Independence* ■ *(816) 795-5533*
*20001 E Jackson Dr*
*Branson* ■ *(417) 337-7373*
*717 Branson Landing*

**Kneaded Specialties**   ★₡Ş
*Lees Summit* ■ *(816) 525-8989*
*301 NW Central St Unit 301-H* ■ *Bakery* ■
Specialty GF bakery and CSA recognized.
GF bread, buns, pastries, muffins, cakes,
cookies and brownies. Special order cakes
should be ordered two weeks in advance. ■
*www.kneadedspecialties.com*

**Lone Star Steakhouse & Saloon**   ✪📖
*Branson* ■ *(417) 336-5030*
*201 S Wildwood Dr*
*Bridgeton* ■ *(314) 770-1255*
*11969 Saint Charles Rock Rd*
*Columbia* ■ *(573) 814-1225*
*3220 Vandiver Dr*

**Maggiano's Little Italy**   ★📖
*Richmond Heights* ■ *(314) 824-2402*
*#2 The Blvd St. Louis*

**Melting Pot, The**   ✪📖
*Town And Country* ■ *(636) 207-6358*
*294 Lamp And Lantern Vlg*
*University City* ■ *(314) 725-4141*
*6683 Delmar Blvd*

**Morton's Steakhouse**   ✪📖
*Clayton* ■ *(314) 725-4008*
*7822 Bonhomme Ave*

### New Day Gluten Free ¢**BLD**
*Ellisville* ▪ *(636) 527-5000*
*15622 Manchester Rd* ▪ *Bakery & Café*
▪ Dedicated GF facility. Offers various
pastries, breads and savory items. GF
items include red velvet cupcakes, iced
chocolate brownies and pumpkin bread
as well chicken florentine pasta, macaroni
and cheese, pizza crust and garlic bread. ▪
*newdayglutenfree.comcafe/*

### O'Charley's 📖
*Fenton* ▪ *(636) 326-5106*
*190 Gravois Bluff Cir*
*Florissant* ▪ *(314) 839-4449*
*13971 New Halls Ferry Rd*
*Cape Girardeau* ▪ *(573) 332-0390*
*3093 William St*
*Kirkwood* ▪ *(314) 822-1066*
*1242 S Kirkwood Rd*
*O'Fallon* ▪ *(636) 379-9700*
*2204 Hwy K*
*St. Peters* ▪ *(363) 928-2000*
*3995 Veterans Memorial Pkwy*

### Oceano Bistro ✪$$$**LD**
*Clayton* ▪ *(314) 721-9400*
*44 N Brentwood Dr*
*Chesterfield* ▪ *(636) 536-9404*
*16125 Chesterfield Pkwy W* ▪ *Seafood* ▪
GF options include lemon crab risotto,
grilled jumbo sea scallops, steamed shellfish soffrito, sautéed warm water sea bass.
GF non-seafood options include apple
cider pork chops, pan roasted half chicken
and a grilled choice beef tenderloin. ▪
*www.oceanobistro.com*

### Old Spaghetti Factory, The ✪★📖
*Chesterfield* ▪ *(636) 536-9522*
*17384 Chesterfield Airport Rd*

### P.F. Chang's China Bistro ✪★📖
*Chesterfield* ▪ *(636) 532-0215*
*1295 Chesterfield Pkwy E*

### Pasta House Co., The ✪★📖
*Arnold* ▪ *(636) 296-3330*
*921 Arnold Commons Dr*
*Brentwood* ▪ *(314) 292-5000*
*2539 S Brentwood Blvd*

*Cape Girardeau* ▪ *(573) 335-4450*
*2046 William St*
*Ellisville* ▪ *(636) 227-1970*
*15601 Manchester Rd*
*Farmington* ▪ *(573) 760-0026*
*931 Valley Creek Dr*
*Florissant* ▪ *(314) 838-7300*
*11202 W Florissant Ave*
*High Ridge* ▪ *(636) 677-2711*
*4517 Hwy 30*
*Kirkwood* ▪ *(314) 909-0054*
*11240 Manchester Rd*
*O'Fallon* ▪ *(636) 978-0060*
*2558 Hwy K*
*University City* ▪ *(314) 991-2022*
*8213 Delmar Blvd*
*Saint Peters* ▪ *(636) 441-4366*
*4095 Veterans Memorial Pkwy*
*Springfield* ▪ *(417) 883-5678*
*4109 S National Ave*
*Union* ▪ *(636) 583-4900*
*101 E Independence Dr*
*Ballwin* ▪ *(636) 230-6200*
*14007 Manchester Rd*

### Paul Manno's $$$$**D**
*Chesterfield* ▪ *(314) 878-1274*
*75 Forum Shopping Ctr* ▪ *Italian* ▪ The
restaurant reports that the wait staff is
"GF aware," and many menu items can be
"altered" to be GF. GF diners are welcome
to bring their own pasta, which will be prepared in a separate pot. Confirm the timeliness of this information before dining in.

### Pei Wei Asian Diner ✪📖
*Creve Coeur* ▪ *(314) 656-2004*
*11430 Olive Blvd*

### Pi Pizzeria ★$$**LD**
*Kirkwood* ▪ *(314) 966-8080*
*10935 Manchester Rd*
*Chesterfield* ▪ *(636) 527-5070*
*14870 Clayton Rd* ▪ *Pizza* ▪ GF thin crust
pizza available. The manager reports that
GF pizza is cooked in a separate area, but
cautions that there is still a risk of CC due
to the large amount of flour in the kitchen.
▪ *www.restaurantpi.com*

## Pizza Shoppe ★📖
*St. Joseph* ▪ *(816) 233-8484*
*2229-C N Belt Hwy*
*Belton* ▪ *(816) 331-5555*
*17041 Bel-Ray Blvd*
*Blue Springs* ▪ *(816) 220-8848*
*1402 NW Hwy 7*
*Liberty* ▪ *(816) 407-1011*
*8584 N Church Rd*
*Kearney* ▪ *(816) 903-3544*
*921 W 92 Hwy*
*Lee's Summit* ▪ *(816) 537-7111*
*3504 SW Market St*
*Platte City* ▪ *(816) 858-5333*
*2437 NW Prairie View Rd*
*Savannah* ▪ *(816) 324-3434*
*410 Court St*
*Smithville* ▪ *(816) 532-1101*
*14121 Earthworks Dr*

## PJ's Country Bakery ★⊘S
*Joplin* ▪ *(417) 781-5854*
*3500 Apricot Dr* ▪ *Bakery* ▪ Non-dedicated bakery offering many varieties of GF bread (sourdough, cinnamon raisin, fruit breads, and more), as well as GF dinner rolls, hamburger buns, pasta, muffins, cakes, and brownies. Owner PJ reports that GF items are baked on Mondays only, usually by order. Place an order during the week or stop in on Tuesday to see if there are any leftover GF items.

## R&M Dream Cakes & Dave's BBQ ★⊘S
*Washington* ▪ *(636) 239-2255*
*901 W 14th St* ▪ *American* ▪ Offers GF cakes. Owner's daughter has Celiac so she bakes the GF cakes. BBQ has GF options including all the meat products, the potato salad and the baked beans. GF bread is offered for an additional price.

## Remy's Kitchen & Wine Bar ⊘$$LD
*St. Louis* ▪ *(314) 726-5757*
*222 S Bemiston Ave* ▪ *Mediterranean* ▪ GF items are marked on the menu and include clam risotto with saffron, stuffed grapevine leaves, bronzed mahi mahi, grilled beef tenderloin, and more. Some items may require modification to become GF, so be sure to alert the server when placing an order. ▪ *www.remyskitchen.net*

## Romano's Macaroni Grill ⊘★📖
*Chesterfield* ▪ *(636) 523-2227*
*963 Chesterfield Ctr*
*Columbia* ▪ *(573) 234-1330*
*305 N Stadium Blvd*
*Saint Peters* ▪ *(636) 278-4664*
*121 Costco Wy*

## Rome, The ⊘★$LD
*Columbia* ▪ *(573) 876-2703*
*114 S. 9th St* ▪ *Italian* ▪ GF menu includes GF red bridge beer, grilled chicken parmigiana, penne pesto, baked 5 cheese mac, pizza as well as GF brownie sundaes and spumoni. Inform server that you are eating GF. They have a GF Tuesday night event which includes a rotating chefs choice dish with customer requests. GF items are prepared separate from other items. ▪ *dinerome.com*

## Rosati's Pizza ★📖
*Springfield* ▪ *(417) 877-2008*
*3049 S Fremont Ave*

## Ruth's Chris Steak House ⊘📖
*Clayton* ▪ *(314) 783-9900*
*1 N Brentwood Blvd*

## Salty Iguana, The ⊘$BLD
*Independence* ▪ *(816) 350-8003*
*17717 E 40 Hwy* ▪ *Mexican* ▪ GF menu available online and in-house. Some items included are smokin' nachos, Mexican chili with corn tortillas, tacos, and enchiladas. The GF menu also indicates modifications that must be made to make dishes GF. Be sure to alert the server upon arrival. ▪ *www.saltyiguana.net*

## Schlafly Bottleworks ⊘★$$LD
*Maplewood* ▪ *(314) 241-2337*
*7260 Southwest Ave* ▪ *American* ▪ GF pasta and beer are available. Kitchen Manager Josh reports that "plenty of GF diners" come in. Alert a server, who will notify the chef. ▪ *schlafly.com/bottleworks/*

### Spin Pizza                          ★ $$LD
*Lees Summit* ▪ *(816) 246-7746*
*1808 NW Chipman Rd* ▪ *Pizza* ▪ All of
their pizzas are available GF except those
with meatballs. GF salads are also available,
just ask for no croutons as they are not GF.
Procedures to prevent CC are in place and
include using separate prep surfaces and
utensils and baking on separate pans. However, the restaurant cautions that they are
not a GF environment. ▪ *www.spinpizza.com*

### Stir Crazy                          ★ 📖
*Creve Coeur* ▪ *(314) 569-9300*
*10598 Old Olive St Rd*

### Sunset 44                           $$LD
*Kirkwood* ▪ *(314) 965-6644*
*118 W Adams Ave* ▪ *Modern American* ▪
The restaurant reports that GF diners are welcome, and that while they do not have a GF
menu, they serve GF guests frequently. The
hostess notes that GF diners "usually order
seafood or chicken with steamed veggies."
Alert a server upon arrival and they will help
navigate the menu. ▪ *www.sunset44.com*

### Tony Roma's                         📖
*Hazelwood* ▪ *(314) 227-5307*
*5555 St. Louis Mills Blvd*

### Waldo Pizza                         ✪ ★ $LD
*Lee's Summit* ▪ *(816) 875-2121*
*1543 NE Douglas St* ▪ *Pizza* ▪ GF bread
and pizza are available. Extensive GF menu
includes appetizers, salads, pizzas, and
sandwiches. A wide variety of GF desserts are
also available, including cupcakes, flourless
chocolate cake, butterscotch pudding, lemonade cake, and cookies. ▪ *www.waldopizza.net*

### Wild Horse Grill                     $$$LD
*Chesterfield* ▪ *(636) 532-8750*
*101 Chesterfield Towne Ctr* ▪ *American*
▪ Owner Tony reports that they are a
"scratch kitchen" with everything made
in-house, so GF requests can easily be accommodated. He recommends alerting the
server "in advance" so that they can help
select GF options and notify the kitchen. ▪
*www.wildhorsegrill.com*

### Zio's                               ✪ 📖
*Independence* ▪ *(816) 350-1011*
*3901 S Bolger Rd*
*Springfield* ▪ *(417) 889-1919*
*1249 E Kingsley St*

## MONTANA

## BOZEMAN

### BarBQ 3                             $LD
*Bozeman* ▪ *(406) 587-8789*
*215 N 7th Ave* ▪ *Barbeque* ▪ Both locations carry the same GF list of options.
Items include all meats, french fries,
broccoli salad and garlic mash potatoes. ▪
*www.bar3bbq.com*

### Carino's Italian                    ✪ 📖
*Bozeman* ▪ *(406) 556-1332*
*2159 Burke St*

### Colombo's Pizza & Pasta             ✪ $LD
*Bozeman* ▪ *(406) 587-5544*
*1003 W College St* ▪ *Pizza* ▪ GF menu
includes GF pizza crust and pasta sauces
such as pesto, meat sauce, and marinara. ▪
*www.colombospizzaandpasta.com*

### Daily Coffee Bar & Bakery, The       ★ $S
*Bozeman* ▪ *(406) 585-8612*
*1013 W College St*
*Bozeman* ▪ *(406) 585-4574*
*1203 N Rouse Ave* ▪ *Bakery* ▪ GF items in
bakery change each day. Usually the café is
filled with GF brownies, biscottis, cookies,
cakes and krispies. Call ahead and see what
GF options are in the café for that day. ▪
*www.tdcbar.com*

### Emerson Grill, The                   ★ $$$LD
*Bozeman* ▪ *(406) 586-5247*
*207 W Olive St* ▪ *Italian* ▪ All fish and
meat dishes can be made GF as well
as the risotto. GF pasta is available. ▪
*www.emersongrill.com*

### John Bozeman's Bistro                    $$$LD
*Bozeman* ■ *(406) 587-4100*
*125 W Main St* ■ *American* ■ All staff is
trained to handle GF, as they have many
customers who are GF. They offer an entrée
called the Superfood Platter, a combination
of side dishes, that is always 100% GF. All
main course items on menu can be made
GF. ■ *www.johnbozemansbistro.com*

### Montana Ale Works             ✪★$D
*Bozeman* ■ *(406) 587-7700*
*611 E Main St* ■ *American* ■ GF items available. Ask server about dishes that can be
prepared GF. ■ *www.montanaaleworks.com*

### Naked Noodle                      ★¢LD
*Bozeman* ■ *(406) 585-4501*
*27 S Willson* ■ *Global* ■ GF items indicated
on the menu include Tokyo bowl, pad
thai, authentic Thai green curry, 4 cheese
mac and cheese, lo mein and more. ■
*www.nakednoodle.com*

### Nova Café, The                    ★¢BL
*Bozeman* ■ *(406) 587-3973*
*312 E Main St* ■ *Café* ■ GF pastries differ
each day. GF white, brown, and three seed
bread is available for sandwiches. The restaurant reports that almost anything on the
menu can be made GF. Alert server upon
arrival. ■ *www.thenovacafe.com*

### Over the Tapas                   ✪$$LD
*Bozeman* ■ *(406) 556-8282*
*19 S Willson Ave* ■ *Spanish* ■ GF
items are marked on the dinner menu
only, but they are available all day. ■
*www.bozemantapas.com*

### Smiling Moose Deli                 ✪▥
*Bozeman* ■ *(406) 585-2922*
*2631 W Main*

### Sweet Chili Asian Bistro          ✪$LD
*Bozeman* ■ *(406) 582-1188*
*101 E Main St* ■ *Asian* ■ Any dish on the
menu can be made GF including entrées such as cashew chicken, Mongolian
beef, garlic shrimp, and tiger prawns. ■
*www.sweetchilibozeman.com*

### Sweet Pea Bakery                 ✪★¢S
*Bozeman* ■ *(406) 586-8200*
*2622 W Main St* ■ *Bakery* ■ GF bakery
items available which include New York
style cheesecake, key lime torte, flourless
chocolate torte, flourless chocolate espresso
torte, fresh fruit tart, bourbon-pecan tart,
frangipane tart and banana cream tart. ■
*www.sweetpeabakery.net*

### Ted's Montana Grill               ✪▥
*Bozeman* ■ *(406) 587-6000*
*105 W Main St*

### Vera Fare Café                     ¢BL
*Bozeman* ■ *(406) 922-0888*
*2251 W. Kagy* ■ *Bakery & Café* ■ The first
entirely GF restaurant in Bozeman and
offers delicious baked goods in addition to waffles, fajitas, and rice bowls. ■
*bozemanmtrestaurants.com*

## MONTANA

### ALL OTHER CITIES

### BarBQ 3                            $LD
*Belgrade* ■ *(406) 388-9182*
*100 S Broadway* ■ *Barbeque* ■ Both
locations carry the same GF list of options. Items include all meats, french fries,
broccoli salad and garlic mash potatoes. ■
*www.bar3bbq.com*

### Bert and Ernie's                   $$LD
*Helena* ■ *(406) 443-5680*
*361 N Last Chance Gulch* ■ *Fusion* ■ The
restaurant reports that many items on the
menu can be modified to be GF. Alert a
server upon arrival and ask them to notify
the chef. ■ *www.bertanderniesofhelena.com*

### Biga Pizza                        ★$LD
*Missoula* ■ *(406) 728-2579*
*241 W Main St* ■ *Pizza* ■ GF 12" pizza is
available with advance notice of at least 24
hours. ■ *www.bigapizza.com*

## Boston's Restaurant & Sports Bar
✪★📖
*Great Falls* ▪ *(406) 761-2788*
*1101 7th St S*

## Café Rio Mexican Grill    📖
*Great Falls* ▪ *(406) 791-5000*
*900 10th Ave S*
*Billings* ▪ *(406) 373-7000*
*2816 King Ave*

## Captain Jack's Restaurant   ★ ¢**BL**
*Helena* ▪ *(406) 442-5995*
*2850 Skyway Dr* ▪ American ▪ GF bread
and buns for sandwiches are available.
Alert the server upon arrival and they will
list items that can be modified to be GF. ▪
*www.captainjacksrestaurant.com*

## Carino's Italian    ✪📖
*Billings* ▪ *(406) 652-9661*
*3042 King Ave W*
*Missoula* ▪ *(406) 541-7900*
*3630 N Reserve St*

## Depot Bar & Restaurant   $$$**D**
*Missoula* ▪ *(406) 728-7007*
*201 Railroad St W* ▪ American ▪ The
restaurant reports that the steak, seafood, prime rib and vegetable dishes are
all GF. Confirm the timeliness of this
information before dining in. Alert a
server upon arrival for further details. ▪
*www.depotmissoula.com*

## Fat Cat Pizzeria   ✪★$**LD**
*Missoula* ▪ *(406) 728-6606*
*1502 Dearborn Ave* ▪ Pizza ▪ GF menu
includes salmon, Cajun steak, gorgonzola
smothered sirloin, surf and turf, sirloin
steak, chicken parmesan, shrimp scampi,
and more. GF desserts include a four tier
lemon pound cake, Italian peach bake, and
a classic chocolate sundae. GF pizza and
pasta are available. The restaurant uses
completely separate preparation area to
prevent CC. ▪ *www.fatcatpizzeria.com*

## HuHot Mongolian Grill   📖
*Billings* ▪ *(406) 656-8822*
*1806 King Ave W*
*Kalispell* ▪ *(406) 755-0757*
*130 Hutton Ranch Rd*
*Missoula* ▪ *(406) 829-8888*
*3521 Brooks St*

## Jersey Boy's Pizzeria   ★$**LD**
*Whitefish* ▪ *(406) 862-2212*
*550 E 1st St* ▪ Pizza ▪ Jersey Boy's offers
GF pizza crust upon customer request. ▪
*www.jerseyboyspizzeria.net*

## Montana City Grill   $$$**D**
*Montana City* ▪ *(406) 449-8890*
*1 Jackson Creek Rd* ▪ American ▪ Restaurant reports that most meat dishes can be
made GF. Alert the server upon arrival. ▪
*www.montanacitygrill.com*

## Mustard Seed Asian Café   ✪★$**LD**
*Missoula* ▪ *(406) 542-7333*
*2901 Brooks St* ▪ Asian ▪ The Missoula
location has a GF menu, and the Spokane
location expects to have one soon. Missoula's GF menu includes several halibut
dishes, the Singapore beef, and a few tilapia
entrées. GF soy sauce is available at both
locations. ▪ *www.mustardseedweb.com*

## Naked Noodle   ★¢**LD**
*Whitefish* ▪ *(406) 862-6253*
*10 Baker St* ▪ Global ▪ GF items indicated
on the menu include Tokyo bowl, pad
thai, authentic Thai green curry, 4 cheese
mac and cheese, lo mein and more. ▪
*www.nakednoodle.com*

## Pizza Ranch   ✪📖
*Champlin* ▪ *(763) 421-2558*
*12443 Champlin Dr*
*Maplewood* ▪ *(651) 777-4500*
*1845 E County Rd*

## Romano's Macaroni Grill   ✪★📖
*Great Falls* ▪ *(406) 761-5900*
*1400 Market Place Dr*
*Helena* ▪ *(406) 495-1600*
*2790 N Washington*

### Sam & Louie's New York Pizzeria  ★▢

*Billings* ▪ *(406) 281-8333*
*1595 Grand Ave*

### Staggering Ox  ⊂LD

*Billings* ▪ *(406) 294-6969*
*2829 King Ave W*
*Helena* ▪ *(406) 443-1729*
*400 Euclid Ave*
*Missoula* ▪ *(406) 542-2206*
*1220 SW Higgins Ave*
*Great Falls* ▪ *(406) 315-2300*
*202 2nd Ave* ▪ *American* ▪ All 4 locations
offer GF potato/rice bowls and salads. The
Helena location also offers GF pizzas and
desserts. ▪ *www.staggeringox.com*

### Wrap Shack, The  ✪★⊂LD

*Big Sky* ▪ *(406) 995-3099*
*77 Aspen Dr #1* ▪ *Deli* ▪ Restaurant
states that all wraps can be made into
bowls, to accommodate all GF diners. ▪
*www.werollemfat.com*

### Zpizza  ✪▢

*Billings* ▪ *(406) 839-9333*
*1403 Country Manor Blvd*
*Billings* ▪ *(406) 281-8020*
*116 N Brdwy*

# NEBRASKA

## OMAHA

### 7M Grill  ✪$$D

*Omaha* ▪ *(402) 509-3225*
*15805 W Maple Rd* ▪ *Modern American* ▪
GF menu includes pomegranate hazelnut
scallops, bourbon mushroom steak, fish
tacos, carrot zucchini pesto, and more. For
dessert, there is vanilla crème brûlée and
"sin-viche", a dessert version of ceviche
made with 5 different kinds of chocolate. ▪
*www.restaurantomaha.net*

### Ahmad's Persian Cuisine  $$LD

*Omaha* ▪ *(402) 341-9616*
*1006 Howard St* ▪ *Middle Eastern* ▪
Owner Ahmad reports that GF diners
are welcome and that most dishes are
naturally GF. Alert a server upon arrival. ▪
*www.ahmadscuisine.com*

### Be'ne Pizza and Pasta  $LD

*Omaha* ▪ *(402) 498-0700*
*12301 W Maple Rd* ▪ *Pizza* ▪ GF pizza is available with any toppings. ▪
*benepizzaandpasta.com*

### Biaggi's  ✪★▢

*Omaha* ▪ *(402) 965-9800*
*13655 California St*

### Big Mama's Kitchen & Catering✪★$BLD

*Omaha* ▪ *(402) 455-6262*
*3223 N 45th St* ▪ *American* ▪ GF menu
includes breakfast, lunch, and dinner items.
Examples include omelets, grilled pork
chop, grilled shrimp, and stir fry cabbage. Some items require modification to
become GF, so be sure to alert the server.
GF pancakes and waffles are available.
The restaurant also does GF catering. ▪
*www.bigmamaskitchen.com*

### Blue Planet Natural Grill  ✪★⊂BLD

*Omaha* ▪ *(402) 218-4555*
*6307 Center St* ▪ *American* ▪ Extensive
GF menu includes burgers on GF buns, a
variety of pizzas including Thai chicken
and Hawaiian, and an assortment of GF
wraps, sandwiches, and curried soups. GF
macaroons and tarts available daily. Call
ahead of time to confirm availability of GF
options. ▪ *www.blueplanetnaturalgrill.com*

### Bonefish Grill  ✪▢

*Omaha* ▪ *(402) 391-3474*
*120 Regency Pkwy*

### Cantina Laredo  ▢

*Omaha* ▪ *(402) 345-6000*
*120 S 31st Ave*

### Carlos O'Kelly's  ✪

*Omaha* ▪ *(402) 445-2301*
*12930 W Maple Rd*

**Carrabba's Italian Grill** ✪📖
Omaha ▪ (402) 492-9500
14520 W Maple Rd

**Charleston's Restaurant** ✪📖
Omaha ▪ (402) 431-0023
13851 1st National Bank Pkwy

**Cheeseburger in Paradise** ✪★📖
Omaha ▪ (402) 289-4210
17304 Davenport St

**Crystal Jade** ✪$LD
Omaha ▪ (402) 398-1688
7255 Cedar St ▪ Asian ▪ Extensive GF
menu includes general chicken, red/yel-
low/green curry, chicken tikka masala,
and kung pao beef. Alert the manager
upon arrival to address CC concerns. ▪
jadedinners.com

**Firebirds Wood Fired Grill** ✪📖
Omaha ▪ (402) 359-1340
17415 Chicago St

**Fleming's Prime
Steakhouse & Wine Bar** ✪📖
Omaha ▪ (402) 393-0811
140 Regency Pkwy

**Fox and Hound Pub & Grille** 📖
Omaha ▪ (402) 964-9074
506 N 120th St

**Godfather's Pizza** ★📖
Omaha ▪ (402) 896-1177
17935 Welch Plaza
Omaha ▪ (402) 493-3833
3141 N 108th St
Omaha ▪ (402) 558-0110
2117 S 67th St
Omaha ▪ (402) 453-5533
7403 N 30th St
Omaha ▪ (402) 896-0555
14139 Q St

**HuHot Mongolian Grill** 📖
Omaha ▪ (402) 498-8890
710 N 114th St
Omaha ▪ (402) 408-3300
17660 Wright St
Omaha ▪ (402) 933-9550
990 S 72nd St

**Ingredient Restaurant** ✪★📖
Omaha ▪ (402) 715-4444
3201 Farnam St
Omaha ▪ (402) 932-2544
10317 Pacific St

**Jason's Deli** ✪📖
Omaha ▪ (402) 551-2233
7010 Dodge St
Omaha ▪ (402) 932-5544
12320 L St

**Jones Brothers Cupcakes** $LD
Omaha ▪ (402) 884-2253
2121 S 67th St ▪ Bakery & Café ▪ Non-
dedicated GF bakery and café offering
GF cupcakes and macaroons. GF bread
is available for sandwiches in the café. ▪
www.jonesbroscupcakes.com

**Lazlo's Brewery & Grill** ✪$$LD
Omaha ▪ (402) 289-5840
2425 S 192nd Ave ▪ American ▪ The res-
taurant reports that a complete GF menu is
available in house, which includes appetiz-
ers, salads, bunless burgers and sandwich-
es, a variety of entrées, desserts, and more.
▪ www.lazlosbreweryandgrill.com

**M's Pub** ✪★$LD
Omaha ▪ (402) 342-2550
422 S 11th St ▪ American ▪ Extensive GF
menu includes lettuce wraps, steamed
artichoke, a variety of burgers, steaks and
salads, and more. GF desserts include
crème brûlée and a mocha fudge torte. GF
pasta available. ▪ www.mspubomaha.com

**McFoster's Natural Kind Café** ✪$LD
Omaha ▪ (402) 557-6801
203 S 38th St ▪ American ▪ GF items
are marked on the menu. Included
is portabella mushroom cap, sautéed
brussels spouts, coconut curry na-
chos, honey-dijon chicken, and more. ▪
www.mcfosters.com/menu.html

**P.F. Chang's China Bistro** ✪★📖
Omaha ▪ (402) 390-6021
10150 California St

## Pizza Ranch  ✪▢
Omaha ▪ (402) 934-4888
3010 S 84th St

## Pizza Shoppe  ★▢
Omaha ▪ (402) 556-9090
6056 Maple St

## Pudgy's Pizza  ★$$D
Omaha ▪ (402) 884-7566
16919 Audry St ▪ Pizza ▪ GF pizza is available. ▪ pudgyville.com

## Roja Mexican Grill  ¢D
Omaha ▪ (402) 333-7652
17010 Wright Plz
Omaha ▪ (402) 346-9190
1212 Harney St ▪ Tex-Mex ▪ The restaurant reports that they have many items that are "GF in nature" and will "be sure to take all the precautions they are aware of" when preparing a meal for a GF diner. Alert a server upon arrival and they will go over the options or ask a manager. ▪ www.rojagrill.com

## Sam & Louie's New York Pizzeria  ★▢
Omaha ▪ (402) 884-7773
2418 Cuming St
Omaha ▪ (402) 390-2911
7641 Cass St
Omaha ▪ (402) 496-7900
2062 N 117th Ave
Omaha ▪ (402) 965-3858
541 N. 15th Plaza
Omaha ▪ (402) 895-2427
18010 R Plaza

## Spezia Restaurant  $$LD
Omaha ▪ (402) 391-2950
3125 S 72nd St ▪ Italian ▪ The restaurant reports that GF options on their menu include salads, steaks, seafood, and chicken. Confirm the timeliness of this information before dining in. Alert the server upon arrival. ▪ speziarestaurant.com

## Stokes Grill & Bar  $LD
Omaha ▪ (402) 408-9000
1122 Howard St
Omaha ▪ (402) 498-0804
13615 California St ▪ American ▪ The restaurant reports that many of their salads, soups, and meat entrées are GF or can be modified to be GF. Confirm the timeliness of this information before dining in, and alert the server upon arrival. ▪ www.restaurantsinc.netstokes/

## Upstream
## Brewing Company - Legacy  $$LD
Omaha ▪ (402) 778-0100
17070 Wright Plz ▪ American ▪ The restaurant reports that the chefs are "always ready to accommodate" dietary needs. Requesting to speak with a chef upon arrival is recommended. Hostess Carrie reports that an in-house GF menu is available and includes items like chicken, steaks, salads, and sandwiches with no bun. ▪ www.upstreambrewing.com

## Upstream
## Brewing Company - Old Market  $$LD
Omaha ▪ (402) 344-0200
514 S 11th St ▪ American ▪ The restaurant reports that the chefs are "always ready to accommodate" dietary needs. Requesting to speak with a chef upon arrival is recommended. Hostess Carrie reports that an in-house GF menu is available and includes items like chicken, steaks, salads, and sandwiches with no bun. ▪ www.upstreambrewing.com

## Valentino's  ★▢
Omaha ▪ (402) 596-0100
8417 Park Dr
Omaha ▪ (402) 333-5440
2606 S 132nd St
Omaha ▪ (402) 571-1400
10190 Maple St
Omaha ▪ (402) 331-0300
5022 S 108th St
Omaha ▪ (402) 345-5200
3540 Center St
Omaha ▪ (402) 553-8281
5070 Leavenworth St
Omaha ▪ (402) 895-0777
13805 P St

# NEBRASKA

## ALL OTHER CITIES

### Carlos O'Kelly's  ✪
Grand Island ▪ (308) 384-3045
1810 Diers Ave
Kearney ▪ (308) 238-0100
119 3rd Ave
Lincoln ▪ (402) 438-4455
4455 N 27th St
Lincoln ▪ (402) 423-2033
3130 Pine Lake Rd

### Cuppycakes  ★SS
Elkhorn ▪ (402) 618-7874
20902 Cumberland Dr ▪ Bakery ▪ This
non-dedicated GF bakery can make any
of their cupcakes flavors GF upon request.
The owner reports that GF cupcakes are
normally baked on Fridays and Saturdays,
but special orders can be placed for any day
of the week. ▪ www.cuppycakes.net

### DISH  ✪SSLD
Lincoln ▪ (402) 475-9475
1100 O St ▪ American ▪ Items "available
GF" are marked with an asterisk on the
menu and include hummus tahini, cream
of mushroom and wild rice soup, grilled
duck breast, pan roasted salmon, and more.
▪ www.dishdowntown.com

### FireWorks Restaurant  ✪SSLD
Lincoln ▪ (402) 434-5644
5750 S 86th Dr ▪ American ▪ GF menu
available in-house offers a wide variety of
appetizers, salads, and entrées, including
crab dip, steak salad, sandwiches without the bun, bourbon street chicken, fish
tacos, and more. Confirm the timeliness
of this information before dining in. ▪
www.telesis-inc.com

### Godfather's Pizza  ★▥
Lincoln ▪ (402) 483-4129
5220 S 48th St
Lavista ▪ (402) 592-7880
7920 S 84th St

Scottsbluff ▪ (308) 632-3644
2207 Broadway
N Platte ▪ (308) 534-8000
520 E Philip Ave
Wayne ▪ (402) 833-5077
106 S Main St

### HuHot Mongolian Grill  ▥
Lincoln ▪ (405) 464-1100
201 N 66th St

### Lazlo's Brewery & Grill  ✪SSLD
Lincoln ▪ (402) 323-8500
5900 Old Cheney Rd
Lincoln ▪ (402) 434-5636
210 N 7th St ▪ American ▪ The restaurant
reports that a complete GF menu is available in house, which includes appetizers,
salads, bunless burgers and sandwiches,
a variety of entrées, desserts, and more. ▪
www.lazlosbreweryandgrill.com

### Le Cupcake  ★SS
Lincoln ▪ (402) 202-5378
5563 S 48th St ▪ Bakery ▪ Non-dedicated
GF bakery offering a selection of GF
cupcakes "baked carefully and cleanly" to
avoid the risk of CC. ▪ www.lecupcakes.com

### Mazatlan  ✪SLD
Lincoln ▪ (402) 464-7201
211 N 70th St ▪ Mexican ▪ GF menu
includes standard Mexican fare such as
enchiladas, fajitas, and tacos, as well as
a variety of chicken, meat, and seafood
dishes.

### Oven, The  SSLD
Lincoln ▪ (402) 475-6118
201 N 8th St
Lincoln ▪ (402) 488-0650
4101 Pioneer Woods Dr ▪ Indian ▪ Both locations report that they can accommodate
GF customers, as many dishes are naturally
GF. They recommend alerting a server,
who will go over the options to ensure a
safe meal. ▪ www.theoven-lincoln.com

### Pizza Ranch  ✪▥
Columbus ▪ (402) 564-8131
2266 33rd Ave

## Romano's Macaroni Grill   ✪★📖
*Lincoln* ▪ *(402) 420-5577*
*6800 S 27th St*

## Sam & Louie's New York Pizzeria   ★📖
*Alliance* ▪ *(308) 761-1313*
*1313 W 3rd St*
*Beatrice* ▪ *(402) 806-4165*
*2205 N 6th St*
*Bellevue* ▪ *(402) 991-3400*
*3608 Twin Creek Dr*
*Blair* ▪ *(402) 426-9590*
*1995 Ridgeview Rd*
*Elkhorn* ▪ *(402) 575-5500*
*2949 N 204th St*
*Grand Island* ▪ *(308) 675-1512*
*928 Concord Ave*
*Lincoln* ▪ *(402) 475-0777*
*1332 P St*
*Lincoln* ▪ *(402) 420-0195*
*1501 Pine Lake Rd*
*Lincoln* ▪ *(402) 488-4144*
*4131 Pioneer Woods Dr*
*Seward* ▪ *(402) 643-3200*
*1519 W Hwy 34*
*Sidney* ▪ *(308) 203-1200*
*824 10th Ave*

## Skeeter Barnes   ✪$LD
*Kearney* ▪ *(308) 236-6400*
*516 S 2nd Ave*
*Columbus* ▪ *(402) 562-0030*
*510 E 23rd St*
*Lincoln* ▪ *(402) 421-3340*
*5800 S 58th St* ▪ *American* ▪ GF menu includes hickory grilled bacon-wrapped shrimp, Hawaiian grilled shrimp, a variety of steaks, burgers and sandwiches without buns, and more. The restaurant recommends speaking with a manager upon arrival. ▪ *www.skeeterbarnes.com*

## Valentino's   ★📖
*Lincoln* ▪ *(402) 437-9177*
*2701 S 70th St*
*Lincoln* ▪ *(402) 420-6800*
*3020 Pine Lake Rd*
*Lincoln* ▪ *(402) 464-2400*
*6401 Havelock Ave*
*Lincoln* ▪ *(402) 435-4500*

*1240 W O St*
*Lincoln* ▪ *(402) 467-3611*
*3457 Holdrege St*
*Lincoln* ▪ *(402) 434-9040*
*1702 South St*
*Lincoln* ▪ *(402) 423-3113*
*4200 S 27th St*
*Lincoln* ▪ *(402) 435-1800*
*4451 N 26th St*
*Lincoln* ▪ *(402) 476-7600*
*3310 A St*
*Lincoln* ▪ *(402) 421-2900*
*5240 S 48th St*
*Lincoln* ▪ *(402) 483-2811*
*2655 S 70th St*
*Lincoln* ▪ *(402) 489-2888*
*904 N 70th St*
*York* ▪ *(402) 362-2111*
*827 N Lincoln Ave*

## Wasabi Bistro   ★$LD
*Grand Island* ▪ *(308) 382-1722*
*2435 Diers Ave* ▪ *Asian* ▪ GF soy sauce is available. The restaurant reports that all sushi is GF. Most other dishes can be modified to be GF by alerting the chef not to use flour as a base for the sauce and to use GF soy sauce. They are "very careful" with GF orders and "know how to handle things" to minimize CC. Confirm the timeliness of this information before dining in. ▪ *www.wasabibistrous.com*

## Zpizza   ✪📖
*Reno* ▪ *(775) 828-6565*
*3600 Warren Wy*

# NEVADA

## LAS VEGAS

### Aurelio's Pizza                    ★ 🕮
Las Vegas ▪ (702) 399-3131
445 W Craig Rd

### B&B Ristorante              ★ $$$$LD
Las Vegas ▪ (702) 266-9977
3355 Las Vegas Blvd S ▪ Italian ▪ GF pasta
is available. ▪ www.bandbristorante.com

### BJ's Restaurant and Brewhouse ✪★🕮
Las Vegas ▪ (702) 851-8050
5881 Centennial Center Blvd
Las Vegas ▪ (702) 853-2300
10840 W Charleston

### Border Grill               ✪ $$$LD
Las Vegas ▪ (702) 632-7403
3950 Las Vegas Blvd S ▪ Mexican ▪
General manager Julie at the Los Angeles
location notes that they have "high sanitation practices" when it comes to preparing special dietary orders. Their extensive
GF menu includes plantain empanadas,
ceviche, chicken poblano enchiladas, chile
relleno, chicken mole verde, and more. ▪
www.bordergrill.com

### Buca di Beppo               ✪🕮
Las Vegas ▪ (702) 866-2867
412 E Flamingo Rd
Las Vegas ▪ (702) 363-6524
7690 W Lake Mead Blvd
Las Vegas ▪ (702) 795-1010
3850 Las Vegas Blvd S

### Café Rio Mexican Grill          🕮
Las Vegas ▪ (702) 953-3900
6575 N Decatur
Las Vegas ▪ (702) 967-8800
5675 Centennial Ctr Blvd
Las Vegas ▪ (702) 948-1500
9002 W Sahara Ave
Las Vegas ▪ (702) 987-3600
4680 S Maryland Pkwy
Las Vegas ▪ (702) 968-1300
4830 Blue Diamond Rd

### Capital Grille, The          ✪🕮
Las Vegas ▪ (702) 932-6631
3200 Las Vegas Blvd S

### Carrabba's Italian Grill      ✪🕮
Las Vegas ▪ (702) 304-2345
8771 W Charleston Blvd

### Culinary Dropout              $$LD
Las Vegas ▪ (702) 522-8100
4455 Paradise Rd ▪ Modern American ▪
Executive Chef Clint reports that there is
"plenty of stuff" on the menu that he can
prepare GF. Examples include salmon,
pork ribs, coq au vin, and bistro steak.
Confirm the timeliness of this information before dining in. Alert a server upon
arrival. Clint notes that they serve GF
diners "a couple times a week," and that the
servers are trained to ask him if they have
questions about GF items on the menu. ▪
www.foxrc.com

### Del Frisco's Double Eagle Steak House
🕮
Las Vegas ▪ (702) 796-0063
3925 Paradise Rd

### Eiffel Tower Restaurant       ✪$$$$LD
Las Vegas ▪ (702) 948-6937
3655 Las Vegas Blvd S ▪ French ▪ A
GF menu is available in-house and the
restaurant reports that they are "accustomed" to serving GF diners. Reservations noting GF are recommended,
as is alerting a server upon arrival. ▪
www.eiffeltowerrestaurant.com

### El Segundo Sol               ✪$$LD
Las Vegas ▪ (702) 258-1211
3200 Las Vegas Blvd S ▪ Mexican ▪ GF
menu is available upon request. Be sure to
alert a server, who will discuss GF requests
with the kitchen. ▪ www.elsegundosol.com

### Emeril's New Orleans Fish House$$$$LD
Las Vegas ▪ (702) 891-7374
3799 Las Vegas Blvd S ▪ Cajun & Creole
▪ The restaurant reports that they can
"absolutely" accommodate GF diners.
Reservations noting GF are recommended

so that the chef can be notified in advance. Located inside the MGM Grand Hotel.

### Fleming's Prime Steakhouse & Wine Bar ✪📖
Las Vegas ▪ (702) 838-4774
8721 W Charleston Blvd

### Fogo De Chao ★📖
Las Vegas ▪ (702) 431-4500
360 E Flamingo Rd

### Hard Rock Café ✪📖
Las Vegas ▪ (702) 733-7625
3771 S Las Vegas Blvd

### In-N-Out Burger 📖
Las Vegas ▪ (800) 786-1000
9240 S Eastern Ave
Las Vegas ▪ (800) 786-1000
4888 Dean Martin Dr
Las Vegas ▪ (800) 786-1000
4705 S Maryland Pkwy
Las Vegas ▪ (800) 786-1000
9610 W Tropicana Ave
Las Vegas ▪ (800) 786-1000
1960 Rock Springs
Las Vegas ▪ (800) 786-1000
3882 Blue Diamond Rd
Las Vegas ▪ (800) 786-1000
5690 Centennial Ctr
Las Vegas ▪ (800) 786-1000
51 N Nellis
Las Vegas ▪ (800) 786-1000
2900 W Sahara Ave
North Las Vegas ▪ (800) 786-1000
2765 E Craig Rd
North Las Vegas ▪ (800) 786-1000
6880N 5th St

### Islands Fine Burgers & Drinks 📖
Las Vegas ▪ (702) 360-3845
10810 W Charleston Blvd

### Jason's Deli ✪📖
Las Vegas ▪ (702) 270-0060
7305 Arroyo Crossing Pkwy
Las Vegas ▪ (702) 967-9008
1000 S Rampart Blvd
Las Vegas ▪ (702) 893-9799
3910 S Maryland Pkwy

Las Vegas ▪ (702) 366-0130
100 N City Pkwy

### Jersey Mike's 📖
Las Vegas ▪ (702) 693-5656
8680 W Warm Springs Rd
Las Vegas ▪ (702) 251-5656
1772 S Rainbow Blvd
North Las Vegas ▪ (702) 646-7827
5595 Simmons St
Las Vegas ▪ (702) 649-5656
3900 Paradise Rd
Las Vegas ▪ (702) 932-5656
8780 W Charleston Blvd #102

### Joe's Crab Shack ✪📖
Las Vegas ▪ (702) 646-3996
1991 N Rainbow Blvd

### Joe's Seafood, Prime Steak, and Stone Crab ✪$$$$LD
Las Vegas ▪ (702) 792-9222
3500 Las Vegas Blvd S ▪ Seafood & Steakhouse ▪ Full GF menu includes items such as maple glazed salmon, bacon-wrapped sea scallops, lamb chops, stone crabs, and a variety of salads and sides. GF desserts include vanilla ice cream, orange sherbet, and fresh berries with whipped cream. The restaurant reports that they safely handle GF orders "every day" and have "procedures in place" against CC. ▪ www.joes.net

### Julian Serrano $$$$LD
Las Vegas ▪ (877) 230-2742
3730 Las Vegas Blvd S ▪ Spanish ▪ A GF list is available upon request, but it is not a formal menu. Advance notice is not required, but alert a server upon arrival. Located inside the Aria Resort and Casino.

### Lawry's The Prime Rib $$$$D
Las Vegas ▪ (702) 893-2223
4043 Howard Hughes Pkwy ▪ Steakhouse ▪ Manager Christopher at Beverly Hills strongly recommends speaking to a manager prior to dining at any Lawry's restaurant to "ensure that they are aware of your situation and able to help you navigate through their individual menus." He notes

that plain prime rib (no gravy, no au jus) and lobster among items that are typically GF, but again stresses the importance of notifying the server and manager on duty so they can ensure safe preparation. ▪ *www.lawrysonline.com*

### Le Cirque   $$$$D
*Las Vegas* ▪ *(702) 693-8865*
*3600 Las Vegas Blvd S* ▪ *French* ▪ General manager Ivo reports that they receive GF requests "on a regular basis" and "will be happy to accommodate" GF diners. Reservations noting GF are strongly recommended so that the kitchen can be notified ahead of time. All dishes are made to order, however, so alert a server upon arrival. Located inside the Bellagio Resort. ▪ *www.bellagio.com*

### Maggiano's Little Italy   ★▢
*Las Vegas* ▪ *(702) 732-2550*
*3200 Las Vegas Blvd S Ste 2144*

### Margaritaville   ✪★▢
*Las Vegas* ▪ *(702) 733-3302*
*3555 Las Vegas Blvd S*

### Mark Rich's NY Pizza & Pasta   ✪★$$LD
*Las Vegas* ▪ *(702) 645-3337*
*7930 W Tropical Pkwy* ▪ *Pizza* ▪ GF pizza and pasta are available. A different screen is used for GF pizzas, to ensure that they don't come into contact with the regular pizzas. Confirm the timeliness of this information before dining in. ▪ *markrichsnypizza.com*

### Melting Pot, The   ✪▢
*Las Vegas* ▪ *(702) 384-6358*
*8704 W Charleston Blvd*

### Miller's Ale House Restaurants   ✪★▢
*Las Vegas* ▪ *(702) 616-3414*
*6683 Las Vegas Blvd S*

### Mint Indian Bistro   ✪★$$LD
*Las Vegas* ▪ *(702) 894-9334*
*730 E Flamingo Rd, # 9 & 10* ▪ *Indian* ▪ Manager notes that special precautions are taken when preparing GF dishes. Extensive GF menu and allergen information are available online. ▪ *mintbistro.com*

### Morton's Steakhouse   ✪▢
*Las Vegas* ▪ *(702) 893-0703*
*400 E Flamingo Rd*

### Mozen Bistro   ✪$$$BLD
*Las Vegas* ▪ *(888) 881-9367*
*3752 Las Vegas Blvd S* ▪ *Global* ▪ Mozen Bistro has a GF menu for all three meals. For breakfast they offer items suchs as waffles, smoked salmon bagel and French toast. The lunch menu consists of lasagnas and pastas in addition to a kobe beef burger. The dinner selections are Pad Thai and an angus beef tenderloin. ▪ *www.mandarinoriental.com*

### N9ne Steakhouse   $$$$D
*Las Vegas* ▪ *(702) 933-9900*
*4321 W Flamingo Rd* ▪ *Steakhouse* ▪ The restaurant reports that while they do not have specific GF items on the menu, they are always willing to accommodate. Reservations noting GF are recommended, as is speaking to a chef upon arrival. Located in The Palms Hotel. ▪ *www.n9negroup.com*

### Nine Fine Irishmen   ✪★$$$LD
*Las Vegas* ▪ *(702) 740-6463*
*3790 Las Vegas Blvd S* ▪ *Irish* ▪ There are separate GF menus for lunch and dinner. GF dinner menu includes shepherd's pie, potato crusted salmon, spice grilled pork porterhouse, and NY strip with au jus. GF beer & cider are available. Located inside New York New York Hotel and Casino. ▪ *www.ninefineirishmen.com*

### OTTO Enoteca Pizzeria   ★$LD
*Las Vegas* ▪ *(702) 677-3390*
*3355 Las Vegas Blvd S* ▪ *Italian* ▪ GF pasta is available. ▪ *www.ottopizzeria.com*

### P.F. Chang's China Bistro   ✪★▢
*Las Vegas* ▪ *(702) 836-0955*
*3667 Las Vegas Blvd S*
*Las Vegas* ▪ *(702) 968-8885*
*1095 S Rampart Blvd*
*Las Vegas* ▪ *(702) 792-2207*
*4165 Paradise Rd*

**Pampas Churrascaria**   ★$$$$**BLD**
*Las Vegas* ▪ *(702) 737-4748*
*3663 Las Vegas Blvd S* ▪ *Brazilian* ▪ General Manager Paul at the Las Vegas location reports that all meats and seafood are GF, and most items in the side/salad bar area are as well. GF bread is available. Paul adds that the Florida location will have the same GF options. Call either location before visting to ensure that GF options are available.
▪ *www.pampasusa.com*

**Pei Wei Asian Diner**   ✪📖
*Las Vegas* ▪ *(702) 233-4692*
*10830 W Charleston Blvd*
*Las Vegas* ▪
*McCarran Int Arpt Term 3*

**Romano's Macaroni Grill**   ✪★📖
*Las Vegas* ▪ *(702) 648-6688*
*2001 N Rainbow Blvd*
*Las Vegas* ▪ *(702) 248-9500*
*2400 W Sahara Ave*

**Rosati's Pizza**   ★📖
*Las Vegas* ▪ *(702) 294-1212*
*8001 N Durango Dr*
*Las Vegas* ▪ *(702) 478-5757*
*10030 W Cheyenne Ave*
*Las Vegas* ▪ *(702) 735-1122*
*430 E Silverado Ranch Blvd*
*North Las Vegas* ▪ *(702) 642-2121*
*5725 Losee Rd*

**Sammy's Woodfired Pizza**   ✪📖
*Las Vegas* ▪ *(702) 227-6000*
*6500 W Sahara Ave*
*Las Vegas* ▪ *(702) 365-7777*
*7160 N Durango Dr*
*Las Vegas* ▪ *(702) 263-7171*
*7345 Arroyo Crossing Pkwy*
*Las Vegas* ▪ *(702) 638-9500*
*9516 W Flamingo Rd*

**Saucy Tomato, The**   ✪★$$**LD**
*Las Vegas* ▪ *(702) 644-4000*
*3870 E Flamingo Rd* ▪ *Pizza* ▪ GF pizza is available in the 10-inch size only. GF pizzas are prepared in a dedicated area of the kitchen. ▪
*www.usmenuguide.com/thesaucytomato.html*

**Smith & Wollensky**   📖
*Las Vegas* ▪ *(702) 862-4100*
*3767 S Las Vegas Blvd*

**Stripburger**   ◁**LD**
*Las Vegas* ▪ *(702) 737-8747*
*3200 S Las Vegas Blvd* ▪ *American* ▪ The restaurant reports that GF diners can easily be accommodated. All burgers can be ordered with a lettuce wrap instead of the bun. Servers have a special form for dietary requests, which ensures that the kitchen separates GF food during preparation. ▪ *www.stripburger.com*

**Texas De Brazil Churrascaria**   ★📖
*Las Vegas* ▪ *(702) 614-0080*
*6533 Las Vegas Blvd S*

**Tony Roma's**   📖
*Las Vegas* ▪ *(702) 385-3232*
*200 E Fremont St*
*Las Vegas* ▪ *(702) 638-2100*
*2040 N Rainbow Blvd*
*Las Vegas* ▪ *(702) 733-9914*
*620 E Sahara Ave*

**Twist by Pierre Gagnaire**   $$$$**D**
*Las Vegas* ▪ *(702) 590-8888*
*3752 Las Vegas Blvd S* ▪ *French* ▪ No GF menu, however items can be prepared (if possible) GF upon request. Chefs and waiters are very cautious of CC and designate items to a separate preparation area using different utensils. ▪ *www.mandarinoriental.com/lasvegas/dining/*

**Verandah**   $$$$**BLD**
*Las Vegas* ▪ *(702) 632-5121*
*3960 Las Vegas Blvd S* ▪ *Italian* ▪ Team member Sanjiv reports that 80% of the menu is or can be prepared GF. Consult with your server, who will point out the best options. ▪ *www.fourseasons.com/lasvegas*

**Wolfgang Puck Bar & Grill**   ★$$$$**LD**
*Las Vegas* ▪ *(702) 891-3000*
*3799 Las Vegas Blvd S* ▪ *Modern American* ▪ GF pasta is available, as well as several other dishes that can be prepared GF.

Alert a server, who will communicate with the chef about how to modify menu items. Most meat and poultry dishes, like the organic half-chicken, can be easily modified to be GF. Confirm the timeliness of this information before dining in. Located inside the MGM Grand. ▪ *www.mgmgrand.com*

**Yard House**                    ✪📖
*Las Vegas* ▪ *(702) 734-9273*
*6593 Las Vegas Blvd S*

# NEVADA
## ALL OTHER CITIES

**Aurelio's Pizza**                ★📖
*Henderson* ▪ *(702) 685-6000*
*10960 S Eastern Ave*

**BJ's Restaurant and Brewhouse** ✪★📖
*Henderson* ▪ *(702) 473-2980*
*9520 S Eastern Ave*
*Reno* ▪ *(775) 853-7575*
*13999 S Virginia*
*Sparks* ▪ *(775) 398-3550*
*425 Sparks Blvd*

**Bonefish Grill**                ✪📖
*Henderson* ▪ *(702) 228-3474*
*10839 S Eastern Ave*

**Café Rio Mexican Grill**        📖
*Henderson* ▪ *(702) 953-2500*
*9595 S Eastern Ave*
*Henderson* ▪ *(702) 701-5100*
*509 N Stephanie St*

**Carino's Italian**              ✪📖
*Reno* ▪ *(775) 852-8875*
*13901 S Virginia St*

**Carrabba's Italian Grill**      ✪📖
*Henderson* ▪ *(702) 990-0650*
*10160 S Eastern Ave*

**Dandelion Deli**                ★℄L
*Reno* ▪ *(775) 322-6100*
*1170 S Wells Ave* ▪ *Deli* ▪ Non-dedicated bakery and deli with a variety of GF items available daily, including muffins and bread for their variety of deli sandwiches. Staff cautions that items are prepared in a shared environment, but that they are "very conscious" of CC concerns and are "as careful as they can be." ▪ *www.dandeliondelicafe.com*

**Genghis Grill**                 📖
*Henderson* ▪ *(702) 625-8289*
*550 N Stephanie St*
*Reno* ▪ *(775) 851-2695*
*191 Damonte Ranch Pkwy*
*Sparks* ▪ *(775) 354-2772*
*121 Los Altos Pkwy*

**Hard Rock Café**                ✪📖
*Stateline* ▪ *(775) 588-6200*
*18 Hwy 50*

**Haven on Earth Bread & Bakery Co** ℄BL
*Reno* ▪ *(775) 284-4200*
*10855 Double R Blvd Suite A* ▪ *Bakery* ▪ Dedicated GF bakery & café, serving soups, salads, sandwiches and hot entrées. Kathy reports that "no gluten has ever been inside" their doors. ▪ *www.havenonearthbakery.com*

**In-N-Out Burger**               📖
*Carson City* ▪ *(800) 786-1000*
*957 Topsy Ln*
*Henderson* ▪ *(800) 786-1000*
*1051 W Suset Rd*
*Laughlin* ▪ *(800) 786-1000*
*2085 Casino Dr*
*Reno* ▪ *(800) 786-1000*
*8215 S Virginia St*
*Sparks* ▪ *(800) 786-1000*
*280 Pyramid Wy*

**Jason's Deli**                  ✪📖
*Henderson* ▪ *(702) 898-0474*
*1281 W Warm Springs Rd*

**Joe's Crab Shack**　✪📖
Henderson ▪ (702) 990-2001
4250 E Sunset Blvd

**Ling & Louie's Asian Bar & Grill**　✪★📖
Reno ▪ (775) 826-5464
4965 S Virginia St

**Melting Pot, The**　✪📖
Reno ▪ (775) 827-6500
6950 S Mccarran Blvd

**P.F. Chang's China Bistro**　✪★📖
Henderson ▪ (702) 361-3065
101 S Green Valley Pkwy
Reno ▪ (775) 825-9800
5180 Kietzke Ln

**Pei Wei Asian Diner**　✪📖
Henderson ▪ (702) 898-6730
1311 W Sunset Rd
Henderson ▪ (702) 837-0861
10575 S Eastern Ave

**Pizza Fusion**　★📖
Henderson ▪ (702) 896-9669
10345 S Eastern Ave

**Romano's Macaroni Grill**　✪★📖
Henderson ▪ (702) 433-2788
573 N Stephanie St
Reno ▪ (775) 448-9994
5505 S Virginia St

**Rosati's Pizza**　★📖
Henderson ▪ (702) 568-6000
72 W Horizon Ridge Pkwy
Henderson ▪ (702) 897-8386
2555 Wigwan Pkwy

**Sammy's Woodfired Pizza**　✪📖
Henderson ▪ (702) 450-6664
4300 E Sunset Rd

**Tony Roma's**　📖
Henderson ▪ (702) 436-2227
555 N Stephanie

**Yard House**　✪📖
Summerlin ▪ (702) 363-9273
11011 W Charleston Blvd

**Zagol Ethiopian Restaurant**　★$LD
Reno ▪ (775) 786-9020
855 E 4th St ▪ Ethiopian ▪ Staff reports
that most of the menu is GF, including
the traditional Ethiopian injera bread,
which is made with teff flour. Alert your
server of your dietary requirements when
dining in or placing a telephone order. ▪
www.zagolofreno.com

# NEW HAMPSHIRE

**Amigos Mexican Cantina**　✪★$LD
Milford ▪ (603) 673-1500
20 South St
Merrimack ▪ (603) 578-9950
75 Daniel Webster Hwy ▪ Mexican ▪
Extensive GF menu includes appetizers,
salads, entrées, and even a GF kids menu.
Sample selections include: quesadillas, taco
salad, stuffed peppers, fajitas, and enchiladas. GF hamburger buns, pasta, and beer
are available. ▪ www.amigosmilford.com

**Andi's Gluten Free Desserts**　⊄S
Hampton ▪ (603) 601-2334
507 Ocean Blvd ▪ Bakery ▪ 100% GF
bakery serving breads, muffins, whoopie
pies, brownies, cakes, and cookies. ▪
www.andisglutenfree.com

**Au Bon Pain**　📖
Lebanon ▪ (603) 650-9228
1 Medical Center Dr
Salem ▪ (603) 894-6461
99 Rockingham Park Blvd

**Balducci's Wood Fired
Pizza & Wings**　✪$LD
Salem ▪ (603) 890-3344
419 S Broadway ▪ Pizza ▪ GF pizza is
available. Restaurant reports that most
toppings are GF EXCEPT meatball and
hamburger. Other GF options include

GF fries, GF wings, and a variety of salads. Alert the server upon arrival. ▪ *www.balduccispizza.com*

**Bertucci's**                    ✪▢
*Manchester* ▪ *(603) 668-6204*
*1500 S Willow St*
*Nashua* ▪ *(603) 595-7244*
*406 Amherst St*
*Salem* ▪ *(603) 890-3434*
*99 Rockingham Park Blvd*

**Blue Mermaid, The**          ✪$$$LD
*Portsmouth* ▪ *(603) 427-2583*
*409 The Hill* ▪ *Global* ▪ GF menu includes spinach salad, paella, seafood tagine, plantain-encrusted cod, Jamaican jerk chicken, and more. Some items marked as GF on the menu need to be modified in order to be GF. Alert a server upon arrival. Servers are trained to notify the kitchen staff, who will make the necessary modifications. Confirm the timeliness of this information before dining in. ▪ *www.bluemermaid.com*

**Boloco**                        ★▢
*Hanover* ▪ *(603) 643-0202*
*35 S Main St*
*Concord* ▪ *(603) 410-3089*
*10 Fort Eddy Rd*

**Brazo Restaurant**          ✪$$$LD
*Portsmouth* ▪ *(603) 431-0050*
*75 Pleasant St* ▪ *Latin American* ▪ Brazo features an entire GF menu which includes a jalapeno artichoke dip, Brazilian pork confit, seafood and chicken paella, and grilled vegetable pinon. Kitchen uses dedicated utensils and separate pots. ▪ *www.brazorestaurant.com*

**British Beer Company**
**Restaurant and Pub, The**    ✪★▢
*Manchester* ▪ *(603) 232-0677*
*1071 S Willow St*

**Brookstone Grille**            $$$LD
*Derry* ▪ *(603) 328-9250*
*14 Route 111* ▪ *Modern American* ▪ GF options available on request. ▪ *www.brookstone-park.com*

**Bugaboo Creek Steak House**   ✪▢
*Bedford* ▪ *(603) 625-2975*
*216 S River Rd*
*Nashua* ▪ *(603) 881-5816*
*16 Gusabel Ave*
*Newington* ▪ *(603) 422-0921*
*2024 Woodbury Ave*

**Burtons Grill**              ✪★▢
*Nashua* ▪ *(603) 888-4880*
*310 Daniel Webster Hwy*

**Café Momo**                    $$LD
*Manchester* ▪ *(603) 623-3733*
*1065 Hanover St* ▪ *Asian* ▪ Most of their menu items are GF. Be sure to confirm GF items before ordering. ▪ *www.cafemomonh.com*

**Carrabba's Italian Grill**    ✪▢
*Bedford* ▪ *(603) 641-0004*
*2 Upjohn St*

**Carriage House, The**        ✪$$D
*Rye* ▪ *(603) 964-8251*
*2263 Ocean Blvd* ▪ *American* ▪ GF menu includes haddock piccata, sea scallops florentine, gorgonzola club burger, NY sirloin, filet mignon, and more. Be sure to alert the server, as some items may require modification to become GF. ▪ *www.carriagehouserye.com*

**Chatila's Sugar-Free Bakery**   ★¢S
*Salem* ▪ *(603) 898-5459*
*254 N Broadway* ▪ *Bakery* ▪ GF items include sugar free jumbo chocolate chip and vanilla walnut cookies, macaroons, swiss rolls. GF New York style cheesecake available as well as mini cheesecakes. GF gift baskets available. ▪ *www.sugarfreebakery.net*

**Cornucopia Bakery & Catering**  ✪★¢BL
*Bristol* ▪ *(603) 568-8156*
*26 Central Sq* ▪ *Bakery & Café* ▪ Non-dedicated GF bakery menu complete with breakfast muffins and pastries and GF rolls for their sandwich menu. ▪ *www.thecornucopiabakery.com*

## Cotton
*Manchester* ▪ (603) 622-5488
*75 Arms St* ▪ *American* ▪ The restaurant reports that they accommodate GF diners "all the time", and recommends that GF customers "be careful of" their sauces. Alert the server upon arrival. ▪ *cottonfood.com*

## D's Delights                                    ⊄S
*Bethlehem* ▪ (603) 837-9027
*614 W Side Rd* ▪ *Bakery* ▪ Dedicated GF bakery where the owner and operator, Diane, has Celiac disease. They freshly bake bread, donuts, muffins, cakes, pies, english muffins, cookies and brownies. ▪ *www.dsdelights.com*

## Dining Room at the Bedford Village Inn, The                                    $$$BLD
*Bedford* ▪ (603) 472-2001
*2 Olde Bedford Wy* ▪ *Modern American* ▪ Manager Brie reports that the kitchen is "more than willing" to accommodate GF diners. She notes that the kitchen can modify items to be GF. Alert a server, who will relay requests to the kitchen. Reservations noting GF are recommended. ▪ *www.bedfordvillageinn.com*

## District, The                                    ✪$$LD
*Portsmouth* ▪ (603) 501-0586
*103 Congress St* ▪ *Modern American* ▪ The District features a GF menu with items such as fish tacos, salads, pan seared scallops, tofu fried koshihikari rice, and seared filet mignon. ▪ *www.thedistrictnh.comabout.cfm*

## Dover Natural Food & Café                                    ★⊄S
*Dover* ▪ (603) 749-9999
*7 Chestnut St* ▪ *Café* ▪ Fresh-baked GF bread for sandwiches, as well as GF soups, cookies, and muffins are available. Located inside the health food market.

## Elm City Bagels                                    ★⊄BL
*Keene* ▪ (603) 355-8255
*255 W St* ▪ *Deli* ▪ GF options include salads and sandwiches made with GF bread. There is always at least one GF soup available that comes with GF bread. Additionally, GF brownies, cookies and cinnamon rolls are available. The restaurant recommends calling ahead to confirm availability of GF items. ▪ *www.elmcitybagels.com*

## Fireworks Restaurant                                    ★$$D
*Keene* ▪ (603) 903-1410
*22 Main St* ▪ *Italian* ▪ Fireworks offers GF pizza and pasta for an additional charge of $2. ▪ *fireworksrestaurant.net*

## Flatbread Pizza Company                                    ★📖
*North Conway* ▪ (603) 356-4470
*2760 White Mountain Hwy*
*Portsmouth* ▪ (603) 436-7888
*138 Congress St*

## Fratello's Ristorante Italiano                                    ✪★$$$LD
*Laconia* ▪ (603) 528-2022
*799 Union Ave*
*Manchester* ▪ (603) 624-2022
*155 Dow St* ▪ *Italian* ▪ GF options include mussels fratello, carpaccio, Sicilian sausage soup, a variety of salads, grilled rib eye, chicken broccoli alfredo, pizzas, and a triple chocolate berry torte for dessert. ▪ *www.fratellos.com*

## Frontside Grind                                    ★⊄S
*North Conway Village* ▪ (603) 356-3603
*2697 White Mountain Hwy* ▪ *Café* ▪ GF muffins and whoopies are available in a variety of flavors. ▪ *www.frontsidecoffee.com*

## Garwoods Restaurant & Pub                                    ✪$$$LD
*Wolfeboro* ▪ (603) 569-7788
*6 N Main St* ▪ *Steakhouse* ▪ GF menu available. Denotations next to certain items indicate the product is GF. Inform server upon arrival. ▪ *www.garwoodsrestaurant.com*

## Gauchos Churrascaria Brazilian Steakhouse                                    $$$LD
*Manchester* ▪ (603) 669-9460
*62 Lowell St* ▪ *Brazilian* ▪ The restaurant reports that their entire menu of meats is GF, as well as the salad bar. Confirm the timeliness of this information before dining in. ▪ *www.gauchosbraziliansteakhouse.com*

## Gordi's Fish & Steakhouse ✪$$LD
*Lincoln* ■ *(603) 745-6635*
*260 Main St* ■ *Steakhouse* ■ Gordi's offers a wide variety of GF of entrées including all steaks, burgers, and prime rib, in addition to various chicken dishes. A potato vodka is offered along with dessert items such as ice cream and lava cake. ■ *www.gordisfishandsteak.com*

## Grammy Gordon's Bakery ✪★¢BLD
*Tamworth* ■ *(603) 323-2005*
*29 Tamworth Rd* ■ *Bakery* ■ GF specialty menu with baked goods and desserts, pie and pizza crusts, and various dinner entrées including scallops, meatballs, and several chicken options. Special orders for GF items should be placed 24 hours beforehand. ■ *www.dreamworks-antiques.com*

## Green Monkey, The ✪$$$D
*Portsmouth* ■ *(603) 427-1010*
*86 Pleasant St* ■ *Modern American* ■ The Green Monkey offers a wide variety of GF dining options including tuna carpaccio, brick grilled chicken, a citrus pork chop, sweet pea raviolis and a soused hanger steak. ■ *thegreenmonkey.net*

## Hagan's Grill ✪$$$D
*Hampton* ■ *(603) 926-5668*
*6 High St* ■ *Seafood* ■ Regular menu is labeled with GF options including entrées such as Atlantic salmon, scallops, fire grilled ahi tuna, griller ribeye steak and many others choices. ■ *www.hagansgrill.com*

## Italian Farmhouse ✪★$D
*Plymouth* ■ *(603) 536-4536*
*337 Daniel Webster Hwy* ■ *Italian* ■ GF pizza and pasta is available upon request. Alert server upon arrival.

## Juliano's Italian Pizzeria ✪★$LD
*Derry* ■ *(603) 425-7585*
*121 W Broadway* ■ *Italian* ■ GF menu includes chicken parmesan with ziti, ziti and broccoli in white wine sauce, lasagna, and cheese pizza. GF pasta and pizza are available. GF menu is often changed, call for a complete list. ■ *www.julianosnh.com*

## Just Like Mom's Pastries ★¢S
*Weare* ■ *(603) 529-6667*
*353 Riverdale Rd* ■ *Bakery* ■ Non-dedicated bakery offering GF pastries, cakes, and pies. GF items include several brownies and bars, cheesecake, apple blueberry pie, and more. The bakery won best GF brownie in a local newspaper's contest. ■ *www.justlikemomspastries.com*

## Kitchen Cravings ★¢BL
*Gilford* ■ *(603) 528-0001*
*15 Airport Rd* ■ *American* ■ Award winning Kitchen Cravings now offers GF pancakes, English muffins, benedicts, chowders, omelettes, soups, and corn pasta. ■ *www.kitchencravingsnh.com*

## Las Olas Taqueria ¢LD
*Exeter* ■ *(603) 418-8901*
*30 Portsmouth Ave*
*Hampton* ■ *(603) 967-4880*
*356 Lafayette Rd* ■ *Mexican* ■ Owner Matt reports that he is GF himself. He notes that the restaurant serves GF diners "without difficulty." Nearly the entire menu is naturally GF, and that the kitchen takes special precautions when dealing with GF diners. Alert a server upon arrival. ■ *www.lasolastaqueria.com*

## Local Grocer, The ★¢S
*North Conway* ■ *(603) 356-6068*
*3358 White Mountain Hwy* ■ *Café* ■ GF wraps and bread for sandwiches are available. GF soups are also available. ■ *www.nhlocalgrocer.com*

## Lou's Bakery ★¢BL
*Hanover* ■ *(603) 643-3321*
*30 S Main St* ■ *Bakery* ■ Although Lou's does not have marked GF options on their menu, several items are GF. Additionally, they bake GF cakes and cupcakes. ■ *lousrestaurant.net*

## Luca's Mediterranean Café ★$$LD
*Keene* ■ *(603) 358-3335*
*10 Central Sq* ■ *Mediterranean* ■ GF pasta is available and can be substituted into any pasta dish. Alert the server of GF needs

and they can indicate GF pasta sauces or other menu items. GF sauces are made to order so any that contain gluten can be made GF. ▪ *www.lucascafe.com*

### Lui Lui Pizza & Pasta   ✪★$LD
*Nashua* ▪ (603) 888-2588
*259 Daniel Webster Hwy*
*West Lebanon* ▪ (603) 298-7070
*8 Glen Rd* ▪ *Italian* ▪ GF pizza and pasta are available, as well as a small selection of other GF items such as mussels italiano and caprese salad. Menu also indicates which pasta and pizza options are available GF. ▪ *www.luilui.com*

### Maples Restaurant   $$$D
*Durham* ▪ (603) 868-7800
*17 Newmarket Rd* ▪ *Modern American*
▪ Several menu options are naturally GF which are marked on the menu. They also note that the chef will accommodate GF requests, as all dishes are made to order. Reservations noting GF are highly recommended. ▪ *www.threechimneysinn.com*

### Ninety Nine   ✪📖
*Tilton* ▪ (603) 286-4994
*154 Laconia Rd*
*West Lebanon* ▪ (603) 298-6991
*10 Benning St*
*North Conway* ▪ (603) 356-9909
*1920 White Mountain Hwy*
*Concord* ▪ (603) 224-7399
*60 D'Amante Dr*
*Littleton* ▪ (603) 444-7999
*687 Meadow St*
*Londonderry* ▪ (603) 421-9902
*41 Nashua Rd*
*Nashua* ▪ (603) 883-9998
*10 St. Laurent St*
*Salem* ▪ (603) 893-5596
*149 S Broadway*
*Manchester* ▪ (603) 641-5999
*1685 S Willow St*
*Portsmouth* ▪ (603) 422-9989
*2454 Lafayette Rd*
*Seabrook* ▪ (603) 474-5999
*831 Lafayette Rd*
*Dover* ▪ (603) 749-9992

*8 Hotel Dr*
*Hooksett* ▪ (603) 641-2999
*1308 Hooksett Rd*

### Nonni's Italian Eatery   ✪★$$D
*New London* ▪ (603) 526-2265
*225 Newport Rd* ▪ *Italian* ▪ GF menu includes GF pasta with any sauce, pizza (available only in 12" size), vegetable lasagna, and eggplant parmesan. ▪ *www.nonnisitalianeatery.com*

### Old Salt, The   ✪$$LD
*Hampton* ▪ (603) 926-8322
*490 Lafayette Rd* ▪ *American* ▪ GF menu includes the lobster salad plate, jumbo shrimp cocktail, broiled sea scallops, and seared steak with gorgonzola cheese. Restaurant reports that it gets at least a few GF customers each week. ▪ *www.oldsaltnh.com*

### Papagallos Restaurant   ✪★$$D
*Keene* ▪ (603) 352-9400
*9 Monadnock Hwy* ▪ *Italian* ▪ Limited GF menu includes chicken and sausage rustica, grilled chicken florentine, haddock dinner, and scallops. GF pizza and pasta are available. Alert the server upon arrival. ▪ *www.papagallos.com*

### Pizzico Pasta & Pizza   ✪$LD
*Merrimack* ▪ (603) 424-1000
*7 Continental Blvd*
*Nashua* ▪ (603) 897-0696
*7 Harold Dr* ▪ *Pizza* ▪ GF menu includes pasta options such as penne pasta with tomato sauce, penne pasta bolognese, and chicken broccoli. GF 10" pizza is also available. ▪ *www.pizzicorestaurant.com*

### Popovers on The Square   ✪★¢BD
*Portsmouth* ▪ (603) 431-1119
*8 Congress St* ▪ *Bakery* ▪ GF menu is simply a variation of their regular menu, as all items can be prepared GF using their GF pasta, bread, and flatbread. Owner Matthew states that they often serve GF customers and they are "well-versed" about how to prevent CC, and recommends that diners specify GF when placing an order. ▪ *popoversonthesquare.com*

## Portland Pie Company ★$LD
*Manchester* ▪ *(603) 622-7437*
*786 Elm St*
*Nashua* ▪ *(603) 882-7437*
*14 Railroad Sq* ▪ *Pizza* ▪ GF pizza is available. ▪ *www.portlandpie.com*

## Puritan Backroom, The ✪★$LD
*Manchester* ▪ *(603) 669-6890*
*245 Hooksett Rd* ▪ *American* ▪ Extensive GF menu includes a variety of salads, fresh vegetables with hummus or tzatziki, mashed or baked potatoes, fat free cottage cheese, charbroiled Atlantic swordfish, broiled filet of haddock, barbecued lamb, broiled chicken parmigiana and charbroiled ham steak. Kids menu available. Desserts include flourless chocolate torte, toffee brownie and rice pudding. ▪ *www.puritanbackroom.com*

## Rafferty's Restaurant & Pub ✪★$LD
*North Conway Village* ▪ *(603) 356-6460*
*36 Kearsarge Rd* ▪ *American* ▪ Their menu is reportedly "99% GF" and features extensive options for soups, salads, entrées, pasta dishes, burgers, and pizza. A GF kids' menu is also available. Owners John and Linda have 2 children with Celiac disease and take the preparation of safe GF meals very seriously. ▪ *www.raffspub.com*

## Republic Café $$BLD
*Manchester* ▪ *(603) 666-3723*
*1069 Elm St* ▪ *Mediterranean* ▪ GF items include chicken confit and quinoa-based pasta that can be substituted into any dish where applicable. ▪ *republiccafe.com*

## River House Restaurant ✪★$$LD
*Portsmouth* ▪ *(603) 431-2600*
*53 Bow St* ▪ *Seafood* ▪ GF food and beverage menu available upon request. Has items such as broiled scallops, pan seared salmon, a pan seared burger, and countless GF salad dressing choices. All GF entrées are prepared from start to finish by the same chef to ensure CC does not occur. ▪ *www.riverhouse53bow.com*

## Ron's Landing ✪$$$D
*Hampton* ▪ *(603) 929-2122*
*379 Ocean Blvd* ▪ *Seafood* ▪ Ron's Landing has a GF menu with options including sesame seared ahi tuna, twin grilled chicken and butter poached lobster. ▪ *www.ronslanding.com*

## Speaker's Corner Restaurant (Crowne Plaza Hotel) ✪★$$BLD
*Nashua* ▪ *(603) 695-4155*
*2 Somerset Pkwy* ▪ *American* ▪ Extensive GF menu includes buffalo chicken tenders, roasted beet & arugula salad, potato crusted salmon, chicken alforno, espresso dusted filet, a variety of burgers and sandwiches, and more. GF bread, hamburger buns, hot dog buns, pasta, and pizza are available. Flourless chocolate cake and other GF desserts are also available. Servers and kitchen staff are "well-versed in all dietary restrictions" and there is a specific button on the computer for GF orders to ensure proper preparation. ▪ *www.cpnashua.com*

## Stella Blu American Tapas ✪★$D
*Nashua* ▪ *(603) 578-5557*
*70 E Pearl St* ▪ *Spanish* ▪ Stella Blu offers a GF menu including items such as a pulled pork tapa, crab wrap tapas, fish tacos, and salad options including an apple fennel and roasted beef salad. ▪ *www.stellablu-nh.com*

## Sunflowers Restaurant ✪★$LD
*Jaffrey* ▪ *(603) 593-3303*
*21 Main St* ▪ *American* ▪ GF menu available. Items include chicken florentine, duck breast, New Zealand rack of lamb, grilled portabello tower, shrimp scampi made with GF pasta, burgers made with GF bun or no bun, and baked haddock made with no bread crumbs or GF bread crumbs. Dessert includes GF mini spice cupcakes. ▪ *www.sunflowerscatering.com*

**T-Bones Great American Eatery**   $$LD
*Derry ▪ (603) 434-3200*
*39 Crystal Ave*
*Hudson ▪ (603) 882-6677*
*77 Lowell Rd*
*Salem ▪ (603) 893-3444*
*311 S Broadway*
*Bedford ▪ (603) 641-6100*
*25 S River Rd*
*Laconia ▪ (603) 528-7800*
*1182 Union Ave ▪ American ▪* At all
locations, managers note that GF diners
should be specific about what they can eat.
All locations also note that many menu
items can be modified to be GF. At the
Bedford location, the kitchen has a list of
menu items that are GF. Alert a server,
who will notify the kitchen manager. ▪
*www.t-bones.com*

**Tavern 27**   ✪¢LD
*Laconia ▪ (603) 528-3057*
*2075 Parade Rd ▪ Spanish ▪* GF items
are marked on the menu and include
options such as seared scallops, grilled
chicken skewers and crispy crab cakes. ▪
*www.tavern27.com*

**Thai Smile**   ✪¢LD
*Plymouth ▪ (603) 536-1788*
*135 Main St*
*Durham ▪ (603) 868-2772*
*13 Jenkins Ct ▪ Thai ▪* GF menu items are
marked and include things such as summer
rolls, all types of curry, various rice noodle
dishes, and over 10 GF sushi dishes. ▪
*thaismilenh.com*

**Three Tomatoes Trattoria**   $$D
*Lebanon ▪ (603) 448-1711*
*1 Court St ▪ Italian ▪* GF dinner options include shrimp, salmon , chicken
alfredo, farm skirt steak, grilled rosemary chicken, and shrimp scampi. ▪
*www.threetomatoestrattoria.com*

**Uno Chicago Grill**   ✪★📖
*Concord ▪ (603) 226-8667*
*15 Fort Eddy Rd*
*Dover ▪ (603) 749-2200*

*238 Indian Brook Rd*
*Nashua ▪ (603) 888-6980*
*304 Daniel Webster Hwy*
*Nashua ▪ (603) 886-4132*
*593 Amherst St*
*Tilton ▪ (603) 286-4079*
*122 Laconia Rd*

**Vito Marcello's Italian Bistro**   ★$$$D
*North Conway ▪ (603) 356-7000*
*1857 White Mountain Hwy ▪ Italian ▪*
GF pasta and other GF items marked
on the regular menu. Other GF op-
tions include mussels, grilled salmon,
sirloin steak, and insalata caprese. ▪
*www.vitomarcellositalianbistro.com*

**Weeksie's Pizza**   ✪★$LD
*Dover ▪ (603) 742-5055*
*66 Third St ▪ Pizza ▪* GF pizza and rolls
for sandwiches are available. Separate GF
menu outlines which toppings are safe for
pizza orders. Restaurant reports that GF
pizzas are cooked in separate pans and
cut on separate cutting boards. Salads
can also be GF without the croutons. ▪
*www.weeksies.com*

**What A Crock Homemade Soup**   ✪¢LD
*Portsmouth ▪ (603) 766-0666*
*14 Manchester Sq*
*Durham ▪ (603) 590-9866*
*4 Jenkins Ct ▪ American ▪* GF soup
options are marked on their daily
menu located in store and online. Op-
tions include cream of broccoli, creamy
Mexican bean, spicy Indian, and more. ▪
*www.whatacrockhomemadesoups.com*

**White Mountain Hotel & Resort**
✪★$$$BLD
*N Conway ▪ (603) 356-7100*
*2560 W Side Rd ▪ American ▪* 95% of
the breakfast, lunch and dinner menu
is GF or can be made GF upon request.
Featured items on the GF menu include a hummus plate, Tullamore wings,
lobster roll, and lump crab cakes. ▪
*www.whitemountainhotel.com*

### Wild Willy's Burgers　★⊄LD
*Rochester* ▪ (603) 332-1193
*12 Gonic Rd* ▪ *American* ▪ GF buns are available and can be used to make almost any burger or sandwich GF. GF menus are available at all locations, and options differ slightly from restaurant to restaurant. The restaurant reports that all staff have been "trained in cross-contamination issues." ▪ *www.wildwillysburgers.com*

### Windham Deli　✪★⊄BL
*Windham* ▪ (603) 216-5106
*33 Indian Rock Rd* ▪ *Deli* ▪ GF menu items include homemade chili, various breads and bagels, hamburgers, all salad dressings, and homemade GF chocolate chip cookies are baked fresh daily. Owner Amy said they have regulars that are GF so they know a lot about CC and how to minimize the risks. ▪ *www.windhamdeli.com*

### Wolfe's Tavern　✪$$BLD
*Wolfeboro* ▪ (603) 569-3016
*90 N Main St* ▪ *American* ▪ GF menu options include a stuffed chicken breast, pan roasted asparagus, and several salad options. The restaurant also reports that most items that are not already GF can be prepared GF on request. ▪ *www.wolfestavern.com*

### Woodman's　✪$$LD
*Litchfield* ▪ (603) 424-2292
*454 Charles Bancroft Hwy Rt 3A* ▪ *Seafood* ▪ The few non-GF menu items are marked. GF options include fried plates and family style boxes. Examples are fried clams, fried scallops, boiled lobster, steamed clams, and clam chowder. All menu items are GF excluding the clamcakes, onion rings & sandwiches. ▪ *www.woodmans.com*

### Xo on Elm　$$$LD
*Manchester* ▪ (603) 206-5617
*827 Elm St* ▪ *American* ▪ They have GF items marked on the regular menu and online. ▪ *www.xoonelm.com*

### Yankee Smokehouse　✪★⊄LD
*West Ossipee* ▪ (603) 539-7427
*Junct of Rts 16 & 25* ▪ *Barbeque* ▪ GF menu includes ribs, BBQ chicken, sliced pork, corn on the cob, beans, chili and burgers and sandwiches served on a GF rolls. For dessert, they offer GF carrot cake. Other items on the menu can be modified as long as the meat is not fried. ▪ *www.yankeesmokehouse.com*

# NEW JERSEY

### Alfonso's 202　★$LD
*Flemington* ▪ (908) 237-2700
*482 US Hwy 202* ▪ *Italian* ▪ GF pizza and pasta are available. ▪ *alfonsos202.com*

### Aliperti's Ristorante　✪★$$LD
*Clark* ▪ (732) 381-2300
*1189 Raritan Rd* ▪ *Italian* ▪ GF items marked on the menu include grilled chicken parmagiana, chicken florentine, char grilled chicken and tilapia. GF pasta is available. ▪ *www.alipertisrestaurant.com*

### Artisan's Brewery & Italian Grill　✪$$$LD
*Toms River* ▪ (732) 244-7566
*1171 Hooper Ave* ▪ *American* ▪ GF menu includes split pea soup, buffalo wings, angus and chicken burgers served without buns, grilled chicken and vegetables and salmon with no rice or sauce. ▪ *www.artisanstomsriver.com*

### Atlantic Bar & Grill　$$$$D
*S Seaside Park* ▪ (732) 854-1588
*24th & Central Ave* ▪ *Seafood & Steakhouse* ▪ Chef Kristopher reports that serving GF diners is "part of the program" at the restaurant, as they do it many times each week. He adds that servers are "fully knowledgeable" about the GF diet, and

they can indicate which items can be prepared GF. ▪ *www.atlanticbarandgrillnj.com*

## Au Bon Pain 📖

*Jersey City* ▪ (201) 200-1867
101 Hudson St
*Warren* ▪ (732) 670-1892
15 Mountain View Rd
*Morristown* ▪ (973) 971-6899
111 Madison Ave
*Morristown* ▪ (973) 971-6506
100 Madison Ave
*Morristown* ▪ (973) 631-1524
100 Madison Ave
*Morristown* ▪ (973) 971-6797
100 Madison Ave
*Pomona* ▪ (609) 652-4364
Route 575 & Jimmie Leeds Rd
*Hackensack* ▪ (201) 488-6430
1 Riverside Square Mall
*New Brunswick* ▪ (732) 873-9845
126 College Ave
*Short Hills* ▪ (973) 379-7040
Short Hills Mall
*Short Hills* ▪ (973) 379-1848
1200 Morris Tpke
*Paterson* ▪ (973) 278-4162
703 Main St

## Bella Vida "Garden Café" ★ ¢BLD

*West Cape May* ▪ (609) 884-6332
406 Broadway ▪ American ▪ GF pancakes are available for breakfast, while GF bread, wraps, and pasta are available for lunch and dinner. Any sandwich can be prepared on GF bread, and any pasta dish can be made with GF pasta. Manager Jess reports that there are other items which can also be made GF, so discuss options with a server. ▪ *www.bellavidacafe.com*

## Bertucci's ✪📖

*Hazlet* ▪ (732) 264-2422
2847 Highway 35
*Jersey City* ▪ (201) 222-8088
560 Washington Blvd
*Marlton* ▪ (856) 988-8070
515 Route 73 N
*Mount Laurel* ▪ (856) 273-0400
1220 Nixon Dr

*Sicklerville* ▪ (856) 740-9960
625 Cross Keys Rd
*Woodbridge* ▪ (732) 636-8200
899 Saint George Ave
*North Brunswick* ▪ (732) 297-9800
2313 US 1 Commerce Center

## Blue Bottle Café, The ✪$$$LD

*Hopewell* ▪ (609) 333-1710
101 E Broad St ▪ Modern American ▪ GF items marked on the menu include sea scallops, pan-seared arctic char, wild mushroom risotto, and roasted duck breast. For dessert, they offer GF chocolate fudge cake. The restaurant recommends asking a server to notify the chef upon arrival. Confirm the timeliness of this information before dining in. ▪ *www.thebluebottlecafe.com*

## Bonefish Grill ✪📖

*Paramus* ▪ (201) 261-2355
601 From Rd
*Secaucus* ▪ (201) 864-3004
200 Mill Creek Dr
*Egg Harbor Township* ▪ (609) 646-2828
3121 Fire Rd
*East Brunswick* ▪ (732) 390-0838
335 State Route 18
*Iselin* ▪ (732) 634-7695
625 US Highway 1 S
*Brick* ▪ (732) 785-2725
179 Van Zile Rd
*Green Brook* ▪ (732) 926-8060
215 Rt 22 E
*Marlton* ▪ (856) 396-3122
500 Route 73 N
*Deptford* ▪ (856) 848-6261
1709 Deptford Center Rd
*Pine Brook* ▪ (973) 227-2443
28 US Highway 46
*Red Bank* ▪ (732) 530-4284
447 Route 35

## Boston's Restaurant & Sports Bar ✪★📖

*Toms River* ▪ (732) 608-0104
1356 Fischer Blvd

### Brothers Moon, The $$$LD
*Hopewell* ■ *(609) 333-1330*
*7 W Broad St* ■ *Modern American* ■
Hostess reports that accommodating
GF diners is "not a problem" and they
serve many GF customers daily. GF items
include salad, salmon dishes, scallops,
chicken breast, pork loin and lamb shank.
Be sure to alert server upon arrival. ■
*www.brothersmoon.com*

### Capital Grille, The ✪📖
*Cherry Hill* ■ *(856) 665-5252*
*2000 Route 38*
*Paramus* ■ *(201) 845-7040*
*1 Garden State Plaza*

### Carino's Italian ✪📖
*Clifton* ■ *(973) 662-0085*
*70 Kingsland Rd*
*Howell* ■ *(732) 730-0910*
*4731 Route 9 N*

### Carlo's Gourmet Pizzeria, Restaurant & Caterers ✪★$$LD
*Marlboro* ■ *(732) 536-6070*
*326 Route 9* ■ *Pizza* ■ GF menu includes
appetizers, GF rice rotini and penne,
ravioli, pizza, and meat entrées. GF items
available at the Marlboro location only. ■
*www.carlosgourmetpizza.com*

### Carmine's Restaurant ✪★$$$LD
*Atlantic City* ■ *(609) 572-9300*
*2801 Pacific Ave* ■ *Italian* ■ GF pasta is
available. An "allergy menu" with a GF
section can be requested. GF items include
all porterhouse steaks, chicken contadina,
lobster fra diavolo, and more. Several GF
desserts are available, including chocolate
torte, fresh fruit, or tartufo. Alert a server
upon arrival. ■ *www.carminesnyc.com*

### Carrabba's Italian Grill ✪📖
*Brick* ■ *(732) 262-3470*
*990 Cedarbridge Ave*
*East Brunswick* ■ *(732) 432-8054*
*335 Route 18*
*Egg Harbor Township* ■ *(609) 407-2580*
*6725 Black Horse Pike*
*Green Brook* ■ *(732) 424-1200*

*200 US Highway 22*
*Maple Shade* ■ *(856) 235-5525*
*500 Route 38 E*
*Marlton* ■ *(856) 988-0581*
*903 Route 73 S*
*Middletown* ■ *(732) 615-9061*
*1864 Highway 35*
*Turnersville* ■ *(856) 629-0100*
*4650 Route 42*
*Seacaucus* ■ *(201) 330-8497*
*485 Harmon Meadow Blvd*

### Chakra Restaurant $$D
*Paramus* ■ *(201) 556-1530*
*144 W State Rt 4* ■ *Modern American* ■ GF
accommodations can be made. Note when
making reservations and alert server upon
arrival who will then notify manager and
chef. ■ *www.chakrarestaurant.com*

### Chambers Walk $$$LD
*Lawrenceville* ■ *(609) 896-5995*
*2667 Main St* ■ *American* ■ The restaurant
reports that almost anything on the menu
can be made GF. Note GF when making
reservations, and alert a server upon
arrival. ■ *www.chamberswalk.com*

### Charlie Brown's Steakhouse ✪📖
*Chatham* ■ *(973) 822-1800*
*522 Southern Blvd*
*Denville* ■ *(973) 586-3095*
*167 W Main St*
*East Windsor* ■ *(609) 448-1765*
*60 Princeton-Hightstown Rd*
*Edison* ■ *(732) 494-6135*
*222 Plainfield Rd*
*Hamilton* ■ *(609) 584-0222*
*2110 Whitehorse-Mercerville Rd*
*Lakewood* ■ *(732) 367-4818*
*400 Route 70*
*Maple Shade* ■ *(856) 779-8003*
*114-116 E Main St*
*Millburn* ■ *(973) 376-1724*
*35 Main St*
*Old Tappan* ■ *(201) 767-6106*
*203 Old Tappan Rd*
*Oradell* ■ *(201) 265-0403*
*2 Kinderkamack Rd*
*Scotch Plains* ■ *(908) 232-3443*

2376 North Ave
*Silverton* ▪ (732) 279-0216
11 Kettle Creek Rd
*Washington Township* ▪ (201) 666-3080
95 Linwood Ave
*Wayne* ▪ (973) 686-1901
1207 Hamburg Tpke
*Westampton* ▪ (609) 265-1100
949 Route 541
*Woodbury* ▪ (856) 853-8505
111 N Broad St

### Cheeseburger in Paradise                    ✪★🕮
*Secaucus* ▪ (201) 392-0500
700 Plaza Dr

### Chimney Rock Inn                              ★$LD
*Bound Brook* ▪ (732) 469-4600
800 N Thompson Ave
*Gillette* ▪ (908) 580-1100
342 Valley Rd ▪ American ▪ GF menu is
available in Bridgewater every Tuesday
from 5pm-10pm and in Gillette every
Wednesday from 5pm-10pm. GF pasta and
pizza is available daily on the regular menu.
GF menu includes buffalo wings, chimney
rack ribs, burgers, chicken parmigiana
and GF beers. Confirm the timeliness
of this information before dining in. ▪
*www.chimneyrockinn.com*

### Cosi                                          ✪🕮
*Morristown* ▪ (973) 539-6664
29 Washington St
*Secaucus* ▪ (201) 330-1052
700 Plaza Dr
*Hackensack* ▪ (201) 343-1031
360 Essex St
*Livingston* ▪ (973) 994-2225
471 Mount Pleasant Rd
*Jersey City* ▪ (201) 369-7030
30 Hudson St
*Jersey City* ▪ (201) 963-0533
535 Washington Blvd
*Mt. Laurel* ▪ (856) 608-0800
4301 Dearborne Cir

### Court Street                                 $$$D
*Hoboken* ▪ (201) 795-4515
61 6th St ▪ American ▪ Management
reports that GF diners can be accommodated. Reservations noting GF are strongly
recommended. ▪ *www.courtstreet.com*

### DeLiteful Foods                              ★¢BL
*Lawrenceville* ▪ (609) 799-7756
4110 Quakerbridge Rd ▪ Bakery ▪ Dedicated GF market and bakery offering GF
items ranging from baguettes and english
muffins to cupcakes. Market contains two
adjacent stores, one of which is dedicated
GF. ▪ *www.delitefulfoods.com*

### Dinosaur Bar-B-Que                           🕮
*Newark* ▪ (862) 214-6100
224 Market St

### Don Pablo's                                  ✪🕮
*Deptford* ▪ (856) 374-3841
1860 Deptford Center Rd
*Moorestown* ▪ (856) 642-6160
1361 Nixon Dr

### Fallon's Gluten Free Bake Shop              ¢S
*Fords* ▪ (732) 710-3338
339 Crows Mill Rd ▪ Bakery ▪ Fallon's
offers 100% GF Italian cookies, pizza
crust, breads, buns (hot dog, hamburger),
cupcakes, muffins, brownies, and pies. ▪
*www.fallonsglutenfreebakeshop.com*

### Fleming's Prime Steakhouse & Wine
### Bar                                          ✪🕮
*Edgewater* ▪ (201) 313-9463
90 The Promenade
*Marlton* ▪ (856) 988-1351
500 Route 73 S

### Fontanarosa's Gourmet Specialty
### Foods                                        ★¢L
*Totowa* ▪ (973) 942-7784
86 Lincoln Ave ▪ Take-&-Bake ▪ GF pasta
available including spaghetti, gnocchi,
ravioli, linguini, spiralli and fettuccine. ▪
*www.fontanarosas.com*

### Fox and Hound Pub & Grille                   🕮
*Edison* ▪ (732) 452-9100
250 Menlo Park Dr

### Fresh City ★ □
*Livingston* ■ *(973) 322-2509*
*94 Old Short Hills Rd*

### Genteel's Trattoria & Pizzeria ★ $LD
*Skillman* ■ *(609) 252-0880*
*1378 Rte 206* ■ *Italian* ■ GF pizza is available, toppings are naturally GF except for the meatballs and eggplant. GF pasta is also available, with an advance notice of at least a week. ■ *www.montgomerynjpizza.com*

### Giuseppe's Pizza & Restaurant ★ $$LD
*Cedar Grove* ■ *(973) 857-1982*
*557 Pompton Ave* ■ *Pizza* ■ GF pizza is available.

### Gluten Free Gloriously ¢$
*Stirling* ■ *(908) 647-7337*
*267 Main Ave* ■ *Bakery* ■ Dedicated GF bakery offering pizza, muffins, bread, cupcakes, pies and more. ■ *www.glutenfreegloriously.com*

### Goodfellows Pizza & Italian ★ ¢LD
*Fords* ■ *(732) 738-7500*
*736 King George Post Rd*
*Parlin* ■ *(732) 707-4455*
*3 Johnson Ln* ■ *Pizza* ■ Personal size GF pizza is available at both locations. ■ *www.goodfellowstakeout.com*

### Greenhouse Café ★ $BLD
*Ship Bottom* ■ *(609) 494-7333*
*605 Long Beach Blvd* ■ *American* ■ GF options include egg, fruit and yogurt dishes, breakfast meats, pancakes, belgian waffles, selection of breads including 10" white sub roll and 4" whole grain round bun, 10" pizza crust, crab cakes, muscle and shrimp appetizers, grilled pork chops, strip steak, brown rice fusilli pasta. Any regular menu entrée can be made flourless. Desserts include GF chocolate brownies and cookies. ■ *www.greenhousecafelbi.com*

### Ground Round ✿ □
*Bradley Beach* ■ *(732) 774-5515*
*1217 Main St*

### Hard Rock Café ✿ □
*Atlantic City* ■ *(609) 441-0007*
*1000 Boardwalk*

### Iron Hill Brewery & Restaurant ✿ ★ □
*Maple Shade* ■ *(856) 273-0300*
*124 E Kings Hwy*
*Voorhees* ■ *(856) 545-9009*
*13107 Town Center Blvd*

### It's Greek To Me $$LD
*Westwood* ■ *(201) 722-3511*
*487 Broadway*
*Englewood* ■ *(201) 568-0440*
*36 E Palisade Ave*
*Fort Lee* ■ *(201) 947-2050*
*1611 Palisade Ave*
*Hoboken* ■ *(201) 216-1888*
*538 Washington St*
*Holmdel* ■ *(732) 275-0036*
*2128 State Route 35*
*Jersey City* ■ *(201) 222-0844*
*194 Newark Ave*
*Long Branch* ■ *(732) 571-0222*
*44 Centennial Dr*
*Ridgewood* ■ *(201) 612-2600*
*21 E Ridgewood Ave*
*Clifton* ■ *(973) 594-1777*
*852 State Route 3 W*
*Cliffside* ■ *(201) 945-5447*
*352 Anderson Ave* ■ *Greek* ■ Restaurant reports that many menu items, such as meats, salads, fish, and vegetables, are GF. Confirm the timeliness of this information before dining in. Ask for a manager, who will alert the servers and kitchen staff. ■ *www.itsgreektome.com*

### Jersey Mike's □
*Hamilton* ■ *(609) 585-6081*
*620 Marketplace Blvd*
*Whippany* ■ *(973) 599-1782*
*831 Route 10 E*
*Little Egg Harbor* ■ *(609) 294-5300*
*418 Route 9 S*
*Westfield* ■ *(908) 233-6002*
*144 E Broad St*
*Jackson* ■ *(732) 961-0600*
*2275 W County Line Rd*
*Manahawkin* ■ *(609) 597-9299*

25 S Main St
Howell ■ (732) 901-4348
3950 Route 9 & Aldrich Rd
Forked River ■ (609) 242-1100
1 Lacey Rd
Silverton ■ (732) 255-5400
1840 Hooper Ave
Middletown ■ (732) 671-1399
1209 Route 35
Brick ■ (732) 477-3400
602 Mantoloking Rd
Brick ■ (732) 892-7827
2085 Route 88
Point Pleasant ■ (732) 714-8878
2600 Bridge Ave
Manasquan ■ (732) 528-7878
2627 Highway 70
Shrewbury ■ (732) 542-3233
10 Shrewsbury Plaza
Wall ■ (732) 449-8383
1933 Highway 35 & Allaire Rd
Point Pleasant Beach ■ (732) 892-9546
901 Richmond Ave
West Long Branch ■ (732) 263-9749
175 Monmouth Rd
Lakewood ■ (732) 905-9520
1195 Route 70
Brick ■ (732) 477-5700
56 Chambers Bridge Rd
Parsippany ■ (973) 503-1800
317 Smith Rd
Bayville ■ (732) 269-1488
333 Atlantic Cuty Blvd
Cinnaminson ■ (856) 786-7827
195 Route 130
Moorestown ■ (856) 638-5041
1624 Nixon Dr
Morganville ■ (732) 972-4100
450 Union Hill Rd

## Joe's Crab Shack    ✪▥

Lawrenceville ■ (609) 896-0360
3191 US Route One
South Plainfield ■ (908) 753-4204
4901 Stelton Rd
Clifton ■ (973) 777-5114
405 Allwood Rd
Eatontown ■ (732) 389-2116
190 NJ State Hwy 35

## Joe's Pizzeria & Vittoria Ristorante   ★$$LD

Summit ■ (908) 522-0615
101 Springfield Ave ■ Pizza ■ GF pizza
and pasta are available. All GF dishes are
prepared using dedicated utensils and prep
areas. ■ www.joespizzasummit.com

## La Riviera Trattoria    ✪★$$LD

Clifton ■ (973) 478-4181
421 Piaget Ave ■ Italian ■ Chef Franco
and his daughter, who has Celiac, created an extensive GF menu that includes
appetizers, salads, pasta dishes, and
several entrées, plus the dessert of the
day. GF pasta is available. The restaurant
requires reservations for GF diners. ■
www.larivieratrattoria.com

## Lake Sea Restaurant    ★$LD

Wayne ■ (973) 616-5757
107 Terhune Dr ■ Asian ■ GF rice noodles
are available. Manager Jeff reports that a
GF white sauce can be substituted for soy
sauce. He also notes that "twenty percent
of the customers" who dine in are GF. He
recommends alerting the server, who will
accommodate GF requests.

## Legal Sea Foods    ✪▥

Paramus ■ (201) 843-8483
1 Garden State Plz
Short Hills ■ (973) 467-0089
1200 Morris Tpke

## Little Anthony's
## Pizzeria & Restaurant    ★$$LD

Vernon ■ (973) 764-9800
530 State Rte 515 ■ Pizza ■ GF pizza is
available. All GF pizza is baked in a separate
oven and prepared using dedicated utensils.

## Loving Hut    ▥

Ledgewood ■ (862) 251-4611
538 State Rte 10
Matawan ■ (732) 970-6129
952 Rte 34

### Maggiano's Little Italy ★ 📖
*Bridgewater* ■ *(908) 547-6045*
*600 Commons Wy*
*Cherry Hill* ■ *(856) 792-4470*
*2000 Route 38 Ste 1180*
*Hackensack* ■ *(201) 221-2030*
*390 Hackensack Ave Spc 70*

### Main Street Trattoria ✪★$LD
*Metuchen* ■ *(732) 205-9080*
*413 Main St* ■ *Italian* ■ GF menu includes pastas with a variety of sauces,
pizza with your choice of toppings and
chocolate chip cookies for dessert. ■
*www.mainsttrattoria.com*

### Mama's Restaurant & Café Baci
✪★$$LD
*Hackettstown* ■ *(908) 852-2820*
*260 Mountain Ave* ■ *Italian* ■ Mama's is
a member of the Gluten-Free Restaurant
Awareness Program (GFRAP) and has
an extensive GF menu. GF pizza, pasta,
bread, and soy sauce are available. For
dessert, a variety of GF cookies, cakes, and
other pastries are available. Be sure to alert
your server that your order must be GF. ■
*www.mamascafebaci.com*

### Market Restaurant & Bar $$$LD
*Morristown* ■ *(908) 502-5106*
*995 Mount Kemble Rd* ■ *American* ■ The
restaurant reports that there are many GF
options on the menu, either naturally GF
or easily modified to be. The staff is "always
willing to accommodate" GF diners and
modify any dish possible to meet their
needs. ■ *marketharding.com*

### Masina Trattoria ✪★$$BLD
*Weehawken* ■ *(201) 348-4444*
*500 Harbor Blvd* ■ *Italian* ■ Extensive
GF menu includes antipasti, pasta, soup,
meat, salad, fried bites, and seafood. GF
pasta and beer are available. The restaurant
reports that GF requests are prepared "with
meticulous attention" in the kitchen. ■
*www.masinatrattoria.com*

### Melting Pot, The ✪📖
*Atlantic City* ■ *(609) 441-1100*

*2112 Atlantic Ave*
*Hoboken* ■ *(201) 222-1440*
*100 Sinatra Dr*
*Red Bank* ■ *(732) 219-0090*
*2 Bridge Ave*
*Somerville* ■ *(908) 575-8010*
*190 W Main St*
*Westwood* ■ *(201) 664-8877*
*250 Center Ave*
*Whippany* ■ *(973) 428-5400*
*831 Route 10*

### Mileto Polish & Italian Restaurant ¢BLD
*Point Pleasant Beach* ■ *(732) 701-1400*
*718 Arnold Ave* ■ *Italian* ■ The restaurant
reports that they are always willing to
accommodate GF customers and have "a
couple dishes" on the menu that are suitable for GF diners. Alert the server upon
arrival. ■ *www.miletogourmet.com*

### Miller's Ale House Restaurants ✪★📖
*Mt. Laurel* ■ *(856) 722-5690*
*554 Fellowship Rd*
*Paramus* ■ *(201) 342-4800*
*270 RTE 4 E*

### Morton's Steakhouse ✪📖
*Hackensack* ■ *(201) 487-1303*
*1 Riverside Sq*
*Atlantic City* ■ *(609) 449-1044*
*2100 Pacific Ave*

### Nanoosh ¢LD
*Paramus* ■ *(201) 556-1300*
*1 Garden State Plz* ■ *Mediterranean* ■
The restaurant reports that most items on
the menu can be prepared GF, and recommends consulting a server to help make a
meal selection. They also recommend informing the staff that your requests are due
to an "allergy" as opposed to a preference
so they can take extra care when preparing
the meal. ■ *www.nanoosh.com*

### Natale's Pizzeria ★$LD
*Waldwick* ■ *(201) 445-2860*
*14 W Prospect St* ■ *Pizza* ■ GF pizza is
available and is prepared in a separate prep
area. ■ *www.natalespizzeria.com*

## Neil's Pizzeria                                    ★ $LD
*Wayne* ■ *(973) 305-0405*
*568 Valley Rd* ■ *Pizza* ■ GF pizza is available and baked over a screen to minimize CC. GF pasta is also available. Confirm availability of items before dining in.

## Organic4Life                                      $BLD
*Caldwell* ■ *(862) 210-8162*
*401 Bloomfield Ave* ■ *American* ■ Dedicated GF establishment serving a wide variety of selections, including waffles with guava preserves for breakfast, turkey meatball soup for lunch, and garlic stuffed chicken for dinner. Vegetarian and vegan options are also available. ■ *www.organic4life.com*

## P.F. Chang's China Bistro            ✪★▢
*Atlantic City* ■ *(609) 348-4600*
*2801 Pacific Ave Unit 101*
*Freehold* ■ *(732) 308-1840*
*3710 Route 9 Ste 2817*
*Hackensack* ■ *(201) 646-1565*
*390 Hackensack Ave Ste 50*
*Marlton* ■ *(856) 396-0818*
*500 Route 73 S Ste G1*
*Princeton* ■ *(609) 799-5163*
*3545 US Highway 1*
*West New York* ■ *(201) 866-7790*
*10 Port Imperial Blvd*

## Palermo's Restaurant and Pizzeria
✪★ $$LD
*Bordentown* ■ *(609) 298-6028*
*674 Rte 206 S*
*Roebling* ■ *(609) 499-8660*
*5th & Main St* ■ *Pizza* ■ GF menu includes ravioli, gnocchi, stuffed shells, pierogies, pencil points, pizza and tomato pie. GF menu available at listed locations only. ■ *www.palermostomatopie.com*

## Pantagis Diner, The                          ★ $BLD
*Edison* ■ *(732) 709-3555*
*3126 Woodbridge Ave* ■ *American* ■ Manager states that they "always do their best" to accommodate GF diners. All seafood items are GF. Alert a server and they can point out everything that is GF. Be sure to specify that your meal must be prepared

separately from any gluten items, as the restaurant seemed unsure about CC. ■ *pantagisdiner.com*

## Park & Orchard Restaurant        ✪★ $$$LD
*E Rutherford* ■ *(201) 939-9292*
*240 Hackensack St* ■ *Global* ■ Extensive GF menu includes pastrami smoked salmon with no sauce, peppered tuna carpaccio, smoked trout with no sauce, crab fingers with remoulade sauce, Tuscan salmon & cannelloni beans, and more. Some items on the menu are only served on certain days, so be sure to consult with the server. ■ *www.parkandorchard.com*

## Park Pizza                                          ★ $LD
*Park Ridge* ■ *(201) 391-9393*
*85 Park Ave* ■ *Pizza* ■ 12" GF pizza available. ■ *www.parkpizza.net*

## Pascarella Bros Delicatessen       ✪★ ¢BL
*Chatham* ■ *(973) 635-3354*
*34 Watchung Ave* ■ *Deli* ■ Restaurant reports that most sandwiches and salads can be made GF, and many GF specialty products are available. The owner's nephew has Celiac, so he takes CC very seriously, and all GF items are prepared in a separate area. ■ *www.pascarellabrosdeli.com*

## Pasta Pomodoro
## Ristorante Italiano & Catering     ✪★ $LD
*Voorhees* ■ *(856) 782-7430*
*700 County Route 561* ■ *Italian* ■ GF menu items include the blackened chicken sandwich, veal parmigiana, salmon Tribeca, and sautéed eggplant in wine sauce. GF pasta, pizza, garlic bread, and desserts are available. The restaurant reports that they have "a million customers" who are GF. Every staff member is well versed in the GF diet and dedicated prep areas and utensils are used to cook all GF dishes. ■ *www.pastapomodoronj.com*

## Pei Wei Asian Diner                            ✪▢
*Cherry Hill* ■ *(856) 792-9260*
*2050 Rte 70 W*
*Moorestown* ■ *(856) 778-0299*
*400 W Rte 38*

Maywood ■ (201) 556-1001
83 W Spring Valley Ave

## Peter Shields Inn & Restaurant $$$$D
Cape May ■ (609) 884-9090
1301 Beach Ave ■ Modern American ■
Innkeeper Bridget notes that GF diners
can "definitely" be accommodated. She
reports that the servers are all GF aware,
and she adds that because all meals are
made to order, GF requests are not a problem. Upon arrival, alert a server and ask
to speak with a chef about GF options. ■
www.petershieldsinn.com

## Pier House Restaurant $$$BLD
Cape May ■ (609) 898-0300
1327 Beach Ave ■ American ■ Chef George
reports that the restaurant serves GF
diners "often." He recommends noting
GF in reservations, and then alerting a
server upon arrival. He adds that most
fish dishes are naturally GF and that there
are many options for GF customers. ■
www.thepierhousecapemay.com

## Pizza and Sandwich Barn ★$LD
Caldwell ■ (973) 226-9020
323 Bloomfield Ave ■ Italian ■ GF pizza is
available in the 12-inch size. GF sub rolls
are also available to substitute into any of
the sandwiches.

## Pizza Fusion ★📖
Red Bank ■ (732) 345-1600
95 Broad St
Ridgewood ■ (201) 445-9010
33 Godwin Ave

## Plantation Restaurant & Bar ✪$$$LD
Harvey Cedars ■ (609) 494-8191
7908 Long Beach Blvd ■ Modern American ■ Items that are GF are indicated on
the regular menu. These items include several soups and salads, spicy ahi tunu potato
skins, root beer, glazed pork chop, and five
mushroom fettuccine. Reservations noting
GF are recommended. Alert a server, who
will discuss GF requests with the kitchen. ■
www.plantationrestaurant.com

## Portuguese Manor Restaurant $$LD
Perth Amboy ■ (732) 826-2233
310 Elm St ■ European ■ GF diners can be
accommodated. Alert server upon arrival
and note GF when making reservations. ■
www.portuguesemanorrestaurante.com

## Pure Tacos $LD
Ocean City ■ (609) 473-0710
1138 Boardwalk ■ Mexican ■ Dedicated GF
restaurant offering a variety of toppings
choices served in tacos, on nachos, or over
fresh greens. Options include cheeseburger,
orange-chili fish, chicken & bacon ranch,
BBQ pulled pork, seared mushrooms, and
more. ■ www.puretacos.com

## Romano's Macaroni Grill ✪★📖
East Hanover ■ (973) 515-1121
138 State Route 10
Edison ■ (732) 549-1177
1521 Route 1
Flanders ■ (973) 691-0932
51 International Dr S
Princetone ■ (609) 520-9700
3569 Route 1
Ramsey ■ (201) 327-7007
900 State Rt 17
Wayne ■ (973) 305-5858
1958 State Route 23

## Ruth's Chris Steak House ✪📖
Atlantic City ■ (609) 344-5833
2020 Atlantic Ave
Parsippany ■ (973) 889-1400
1 Hilton Ct
Princeton ■ (609) 452-0041
2 Village Blvd
Weehawken ■ (201) 863-5100
1000 Harbor Blvd

## Salt Creek Grille ✪$$LD
Princeton ■ (609) 419-4200
1 Rockingham Row
Rumson ■ (732) 933-9272
4 Bingham Ave ■ American ■ Corporate
executive chef Scott reports that there are
"several GF items" available, and they have
"specific protocols" in place to prevent
CC, including using clean utensils and

prep items when preparing a GF order. Scott recommends alerting the server of any dietary restrictions upon arrival. Since the Valencia location is franchised, he recommends calling ahead to ensure that they have GF options available. ▪ *www.saltcreekgrille.com*

### Shannon Rose, The                    ✪¢LD
*Clifton* ▪ *(973) 284-0200*
*98 Kingsland Rd*
*Woodbridge* ▪ *(732) 636-6100*
*855 St George's Ave*
*Ramsey* ▪ *(201) 962-7602*
*1200 Rte 17 N* ▪ *Pub Food* ▪ The Shannon Rose provides customers with a GF menu in the restaurant upon request however it can not be accessed online. ▪ *www.theshannonrose.com*

### Shelly's Vegetarian
### Café & Caterers                     ★$$LD
*Teaneck* ▪ *(201) 692-0001*
*482 Cedar Ln* ▪ *Vegetarian* ▪ GF pizza with any toppings and GF french fries are available. ▪ *www.shellyscafe.net*

### Smithville Inn, The                  $$$LD
*Smithville* ▪ *(609) 652-7777*
*1 N New York Rd* ▪ *American* ▪ Chef Chris reports that GF diners can be accommodated with "no problem." He notes that everything is "fresh and made to order," so he can modify any dish on the menu to be GF. ▪ *www.smithvilleinn.com*

### Stefano's Ristorante Italiano  ★$$$LD
*Mt Laurel* ▪ *(856) 778-3663*
*3815 Church Rd* ▪ *Italian* ▪ GF pasta, pizza, and cookies are available. Restaurant reports that almost all regular menu items can be modified to be GF. ▪ *www.stefanosristoranteitaliano.com*

### Stein's Bagels
### and Gourmet Deli               ✪★¢BL
*Montvale* ▪ *(201) 782-0087*
*106 Chestnut Ridge Rd* ▪ *Café* ▪ GF rolls and breads are available for sandwiches. Owner Jay also has a freezer of GF foods such as pizza, desserts, individual dinners, pasta, and bagels. He notes that with advance notice, he can bake pizzas, warm bagels, or cook a fresh GF pasta dish for GF customers who want to dine in. Confirm the timeliness of this information before dining in. ▪ *www.steinsbagels.com*

### Steve and Cookie's by the Bay  $$$$D
*Margate City* ▪ *(609) 823-1163*
*9700 Amherst Ave* ▪ *Modern American* ▪ Team member Brooke reports that there are many GF options on the menu, and the kitchen staff is familiar with GF preparation. She recommends reservations noting GF so that the chef can prepare in advance. Alert the server upon arrival. ▪ *www.steveandcookies.com*

### Sweet Avenue Bake Shop          ★¢S
*Rutherford* ▪ *(201) 935-2253*
*153 Park Ave* ▪ *Bakery* ▪ Bakery reports that at least one GF cupcake is available every day except for Mondays. Possible GF flavors include chocolate, vanilla, and red velvet. For special or large orders, advance notice of at least one week is required. ▪ *www.sweetavenuebakeshop.com*

### The Original Atilio's Pizza      ★$LD
*Tinton Falls* ▪ *(732) 922-6760*
*4057 Asbury Ave* ▪ *Pizza* ▪ GF pizza is available and cooked over a pan, so that no direct contact with the oven is made. ▪ *www.attiliospizzanj.com*

### Tony Roma's                          📖
*Newark* ▪ *(973) 547-7944*
*3 Newark Airport, Terminal A*

### Tortilla Press Cantina             ✪$$D
*Pennsauken* ▪ *(856) 356-2050*
*7716 Maple Ave* ▪ *Mexican* ▪ GF menu includes honey cholula wings, fried sweet plantains, calamari, chorizos muscles and clams, nachos, house salad, chile-crusted salmon, fire grilled jerk shrimp, coffee rubbed braised baby back ribs, maple roasted pork loin and arroz con pollo. All GF fried items are prepared in a dedicated GF fryer. ▪ *www.tortillapresscantina.com*

### Tortilla Press, The          ✪$$LD
*Collingswood* ▪ *(856) 869-3345*
*703 Haddon Ave* ▪ *Mexican* ▪ GF menu
includes fajitas, enchiladas, rainbow
shrimp, honey lime scallops, carne ran-
chero and rainbow shrimp, carne asada
with mushroom and rajas pablano and
ancho chile crusted tuna pineapple. ▪
*www.thetortillapress.com*

### Toscana's                    ★$$LD
*Bridgewater* ▪ *(908) 595-2000*
*474 Rte 28 (Villa Plaza)* ▪ *Italian* ▪ GF pizza is available and it's
baked over a dedicated GF screen. ▪
*www.toscanasnj.comtoscanas.htm*

### Uno Chicago Grill            ✪★📖
*Clifton* ▪ *(973) 574-1303*
*426 State Rt 3*
*Hamilton* ▪ *(609) 890-0864*
*225 Sloan Ave*
*Maple Shade* ▪ *(856) 722-5577*
*2803 Route 73 S*
*Metuchen* ▪ *(732) 548-7979*
*61 US Highway 1*
*Deptford* ▪ *(856) 853-7003*
*1162 Hurffville Rd*

### Vesuvio Pizza
### and Family Restaurant       ★$LD
*Perrineville* ▪ *(732) 446-1908*
*221 Millstone Rd* ▪ *Italian* ▪ GF menu available upon request. This menu includes GF
13" pizza, spaghetti marinara, shrimp marinara or scampi, grilled veal parmesan, seafood combo, chicken vesuvio and calamari
marinara. ▪ *www.vesuviosmillstone.com*

### Via 45                        $$$D
*Red Bank* ▪ *(732) 450-9945*
*45 Broad St* ▪ *Italian* ▪ The restaurant
reports that they have "a wide variety" of
GF options on their menu. Alert the server
upon arrival. ▪ *www.via45.com*

### Via Roma Pizza & Restaurant  ✪★$$LD
*Toms River* ▪ *(732) 364-1980*
*2360 Lakewood Rd* ▪ *Italian* ▪ The restaurant reports that they offer "the best
selection of GF menu items in NJ." Op-

tions include mozzarella sticks, garlic bread, chicken wings, crab cakes,
baked lasagna, and gnocchi ragu. GF
pizza and burger buns are available. ▪
*www.viaromatomsriver.com*

## NEW MEXICO

## ALBUQUERQUE

### 5 Star Burgers              ★¢LD
*Albuquerque* ▪ *(505) 821-1909*
*5901 Wyoming Blvd* ▪ *American* ▪ GF buns
are available for burgers and sandwiches. ▪
*www.5starburgers.com*

### Amadeo's Pizza              ★$LD
*Albuquerque* ▪ *(505) 873-2035*
*3109 Coors SW*
*Albuquerque* ▪ *(505) 831-9339*
*809 98th St SW*
*Albuquerque* ▪ *(505) 255-8888*
*5003 Lomas Blvd N* ▪ *Pizza* ▪ GF pizza in
the 10.5" size only. The restaurant recommends asking a server which toppings are
GF. ▪ *www.amadeospizza.com*

### Annapurna's
### World Vegetarian Café       ✪$BLD
*Albuquerque* ▪ *(505) 262-2424*
*2201 Silver Ave SE*
*Albuquerque* ▪ *(505) 254-2424*
*5939 4th St NW* ▪ *Vegetarian* ▪ All GF
items are indicated on the menu and
include assorted cakes, breakfast items,
Indian specialties, and sandwiches, among
other things. Alert the server upon arrival.
▪ *www.chaishoppe.com*

### Boston's Restaurant & Sports Bar
✪★📖
*Albuquerque* ▪ *(505) 890-8004*
*4300 25 Wy*

**Buca di Beppo**                              ✿📖
*Albuquerque* ▪ *(505) 872-2822*
*6520 Americas Pkwy NE*

**Carrabba's Italian Grill**                   ✿📖
*Albuquerque* ▪ *(505) 884-6040*
*4921 Jefferson*

**DaVinci's Gourmet Pizza**                    ★ $LD
*Albuquerque* ▪ *(505) 275-2722*
*5809 Juan Tabo NE* ▪ *Pizza* ▪ GF pizza is
available in the 10" and 12" sizes for an additional charge of $4.00. ▪ *www.dvgp.com*

**Desert Fish**                                $$$BD
*Albuquerque* ▪ *(505) 266-5544*
*4214 Central Ave SE* ▪ *Seafood* ▪ Ac-
cording to manager, 80% of menu can
be made GF and includes items such
as a mix fry, cooked with rice flour,
cioppino, and various fish dishes. ▪
*www.desertfishabq.com*

**Fox and Hound Pub & Grille**                 📖
*Albuquerque* ▪ *(505) 344-9430*
*4301 The Lane*

**Genghis Grill**                              📖
*Albuquerque* ▪ *(505) 344-9335*
*4410 The 25 Way NE*
*Albuquerque* ▪ *(505) 312-8333*
*2100 Louisiana Blvd NE*

**Jason's Deli**                               ✿📖
*Albuquerque* ▪ *(505) 897-2200*
*3410 State Hwy 528 NW*
*Albuquerque* ▪ *(505) 821-7100*
*5920 Holly Ave NE*
*Albuquerque* ▪ *(505) 881-6700*
*2105 Louisiana Blvd NE*

**JC's NYPD Pizza**                            ★ $LD
*Albuquerque* ▪ *(505) 766-6973*
*215 Central Ave NW* ▪ *Pizza* ▪ GF pizza is
available. ▪ *jcnypd.com*

**Just a Bite**                                ★ ¢S
*Albuquerque* ▪ *(505) 822-5001*
*7900 San Pedro Dr NE* ▪ *Bakery* ▪ GF
items available in bakery. Items include
brownies, pies, cinnamon rolls, and
pizza dough. Hummingbird and straw-
berry wine cakes, as well as other cakes,

can be made GF. Special orders require
advance notice of at least 48 hours. ▪
*www.justabitebakery.com*

**Lone Star Steakhouse & Saloon**             ✿📖
*Albuquerque* ▪ *(505) 899-7827*
*10019 Coors Rd NW*

**Melting Pot, The**                           ✿📖
*Albuquerque* ▪ *(505) 843-6358*
*2011 Mountain Rd NW*

**O'Niell's Irish Pub**                        ✿$LD
*Albuquerque* ▪ *(505) 255-6782*
*4310 Central SE*
*Albuquerque* ▪ *(505) 293-1122*
*3301 Juan Tabo Blvd NE* ▪ *Pub Food* ▪
Limited GF menu includes salads, chicken
kabobs, lemon basil salmon, rib-eye
steak, and a smothered chicken breast. ▪
*oniells.com*

**P.F. Chang's China Bistro**                  ✿★📖
*Albuquerque* ▪ *(505) 344-8282*
*4440 The 25 Way NE*

**Paisano's**                                  ★ $LD
*Albuquerque* ▪ *(505) 298-7541*
*1935 Eubank Blvd NE* ▪ *Italian* ▪ Manager
Iggy reports that the owner has Celiac and
GF items on regular menu include "just
about everything" and are marked accord-
ingly. GF garlic bread, pasta, and pizza are
available. For dessert, they offer GF molten
chocolate cake, GF tiramisu, chocolate
mousse, and more. ▪ *www.paisanosabq.com*

**Pars Cuisine**                               $$LD
*Albuquerque* ▪ *(505) 345-5156*
*4320 The 25 Way NE* ▪ *Middle Eastern* ▪
Most items on menu are GF. Items include
kebobs, vegetarian combos, vegetarian
plate, a variety of stews, lamb shank, and
a variety of salads. Alert the server upon
arrival. ▪ *www.parscuisine.us*

**Pei Wei Asian Diner**                        ✿📖
*Albuquerque* ▪ *(505) 897-4811*
*10420 Coors Bypass NW*
*Albuquerque* ▪ *(505) 883-1570*
*2201 Louisiana Blvd NE*

## Range Café                                    $BLD
*Albuquerque* ▪ *(505) 888-1660*
*2200 Menaul NE*
*Albuquerque* ▪ *(505) 293-2633*
*4401 Wyoming Blvd NE* ▪ *American* ▪
GF options available. Be sure to alert
server upon arrival. Manager Christie at
the Bernalillo location has made a list of
items that can be made GF. Servers are
familiar with GF requests and will be able
to have GF customers speak to chef. ▪
*www.rangecafe.com*

## Red Brick Pizza                              ✪★▥
*Alburqurque* ▪ *(505) 797-7848*
*8101 San Pedro NE*
*Alburqurque* ▪ *(505) 839-7333*
*2641 Coors Blvd*

## Romano's Macaroni Grill                      ✪★▥
*Albuquerque* ▪ *(505) 881-3400*
*2100 Louisiana Blvd NE*

## Slice Parlor                                  ★ ₵LD
*Albuquerque* ▪ *(505) 232-2808*
*3410 Central Ave SE* ▪ *Pizza* ▪ GF pizza
and beer are available. The restaurant reports that the GF pizza crusts are prepared
off site. ▪ *www.sliceparlor.com*

## Vinaigrette                                   $LD
*Albuquerque* ▪ *(505) 842-5507*
*1828 Central Ave SW* ▪ *Modern American* ▪ The restaurant reports that 95% of
the menu is GF or can be prepared GF.
They note that the possibility of CC is
very unlikely since most of the menu is
already GF. Alert the server upon arrival. ▪
*www.vinaigretteonline.com*

## Zio's                                         ✪▥
*Albuquerque* ▪ *(505) 792-9222*
*10041 Coors Blvd NW*

## NEW MEXICO
### ALL OTHER CITIES

## 5 Star Burgers                                ★₵LD
*Taos* ▪ *(575) 758-8484*
*1032 Paseo del Pueblo Sur*
*Santa Fe* ▪ *(505) 983-8977*
*604 N Guadalupe St* ▪ *American* ▪ GF
buns are available for burgers and sandwiches. ▪ *www.5starburgers.com*

## Annapurna's World
## Vegetarian Café                              ✪$BLD
*Santa Fe* ▪ *(505) 988-9688*
*1620 St Michael's Dr* ▪ *Vegetarian* ▪ All
GF items are indicated on the menu and
include assorted cakes, breakfast items,
Indian specialties, and sandwiches, among
other things. Alert the server upon arrival.
▪ *www.chaishoppe.com*

## Blue Corn Café                               $LD
*Santa Fe* ▪ *(505) 438-1800*
*4056 Cerrillos Rd*
*Santa Fe* ▪ *(505) 984-1800*
*133 W Water St* ▪ *Southwest* ▪ Both
locations report that many items on their
menus can be modified to be GF, including chili, meat plates, salads, soups,
and enchiladas. GF tortillas are available. Alert the server upon arrival. ▪
*www.bluecorncafe.com*

## Body Café                                    ✪★$BLD
*Santa Fe* ▪ *(505) 986-0362*
*333 W Cordova Rd* ▪ *American* ▪ GF
items marked on the menu include all the
appetizers, salads, soups, ginger chile stir
fry, soft tacos with rice and beans, south
east Asian curry, collard green burrito, raw
romaine tacos, raw pizza, raw enchiladas,
and more. GF bread, pastries, ice cream,
pies, cakes and chocolates available. ▪
*www.bodyofsantafe.com*

## Coyote Café                                  $$$$LD
*Santa Fe* ▪ *(505) 983-1615*
*132 W Water St* ▪ *Southwest* ▪ Reserva-

tions noting GF are recommended. Three dishes on menu are completely GF which are the elk tenderloin, Mexican white prawns and Hawaiian swordfish. All other items on the menu can be modified to be GF. Alert a server upon arrival. ▪ *www.coyotecafe.com*

### Dinner For Two                         $$$D
*Santa Fe* ▪ *(505) 820-2075*
*106 N Guadalupe St* ▪ *American* ▪ The restaurant reports that the majority of their main courses, such as the veal picatta and filet mignon, are GF, as well as all of their sauces. Alert the server upon arrival and they will help select a GF meal. ▪ *www.dinnerfortwonm.com*

### Graham's Grille                         ★ $BLD
*Taos* ▪ *(575) 751-1350*
*106 Paseo Del Pueblo Norte* ▪ *American* ▪ GF items indicated on menu. Items includes the Graham's granola, corn grits, blue corn blueberry pancake, huevos rancheros, corned beef hash, Spanish style mussels and Bilbao chorizo, tamale hecho a mano del dia, Mediterranean vegetable saganaki, crab, corn, bacon and potato chowder. The restaurant reports that all meat and seafood dishes can be made GF. GF sandwich buns are available. For dessert, there is mango cheesecake, hazelnut panna cotta, Udi's blueberry muffin, vanilla bean ice cream, and dairy free sorbet. ▪ *www.grahamstaos.com*

### Jason's Deli                           ✪ 📖
*Las Cruces* ▪ *(575) 521-0700*
*3845 E Lohman Ave*

### JC's NYPD Pizza                        ★ $LD
*Las Vegas* ▪ *(505) 454-4444*
*131 Bridge St* ▪ *Pizza* ▪ GF pizza is available. ▪ *jcnypd.com*

### Joe's Diner                            ✪ $BLD
*Santa Fe* ▪ *(505) 471-3800*
*2801 Rodeo Rd A-5* ▪ *American* ▪ Joe's has an extensive GF online menu with dishes including breakfast enchiladas, huevos rancheros, various salads and burgers, reuben,

BBQ beef brisket, eggplant parmesan and more. ▪ *joesdining.com*

### My Big Fat Greek Restaurant           ✪ 📖
*Farmington* ▪ *(505) 326-2000*
*3500 E Main St*

### Pranzo Italian Grill                   ★ $$$LD
*Santa Fe* ▪ *(505) 984-2645*
*540 Montezuma Ave* ▪ *Italian* ▪ GF brown rice pasta is available. General Manager Kate reports that several other dishes on the menu can be made GF using polenta or risotto. According to Kate, they serve about 20 GF customers a week so they are very knowledgeable about different GF options. Alert a server, who will discuss all GF options. ▪ *www.pranzo-italiangrill.com*

### Range Café                             $BLD
*Bernalillo* ▪ *(505) 867-1700*
*925 S Camino Del Pueblo* ▪ *American* ▪ GF options available. Be sure to alert server upon arrival. Manager Christie at the Bernalillo location has made a list of items that can be made GF. Servers are familiar with GF requests and will be able to have GF customers speak to chef. ▪ *www.rangecafe.com*

### Red Brick Pizza                        ✪ ★ 📖
*Roswell* ▪ *(575) 623-6300*
*625 N. Main St*
*Las Cruces* ▪ *(575) 521-7300*
*2808 #2 N*
*Farmington* ▪ *(505) 326-6222*
*5150 E Main*

### Rooftop Pizza                          ★ $$LD
*Santa Fe* ▪ *(505) 984-0008*
*60 E San Francisco St* ▪ *Pizza* ▪ GF 12" pizza crust is available for $2.00 extra. ▪ *www.rooftoppizzeria.comindex.php*

### Tree House Pastry Shop & Café          $BL
*Santa Fe* ▪ *(505) 474-5543*
*163 Pase de Peralta* ▪ *Bakery & Café* ▪ Tree House Pastry Shop has an in store GF menu which is available upon request. Manager designates separate preparation areas and utensils for the GF menu items. ▪ *www.treehousepastry.com*

### Tune-Up Café                    ✪$LD
*Santa Fe* ▪ *(505) 983-7060*
*1115 Hickox St* ▪ *Mexican* ▪ No GF menu
online, but entrées such as tamales and
enchiladas are GF, and the chefs and staff
are willing to modify other dishes upon
customer request. ▪ *tuneupsantafe.com*

### Uno Chicago Grill                ✪★📖
*Las Cruces* ▪ *(575) 522-8866*
*2102 Telshor Ct*

### Vinaigrette                      $⁇⁇
*Santa Fe* ▪ *(505) 820-9205*
*709 Don Cubero Alley* ▪ *Modern American* ▪ The restaurant reports that 95% of
the menu is GF or can be prepared GF.
They note that the possibility of CC is
very unlikely since most of the menu is
already GF. Alert the server upon arrival. ▪
*www.vinaigretteonline.com*

# NEW YORK

## NEW YORK

### 5 Napkin Burger                  $LD
*New York* ▪ *(212) 228-5500*
*150 E 14th St*
*New York* ▪ *(212) 757-2277*
*630 9th Ave @ 45th St*
*New York* ▪ *(212) 333-4488*
*2315 Broadway @ 84th St*
*Queens* ▪ *(718) 433-2727*
*35-01 36th St@ 35th Ave* ▪ *American*
▪ GF rolls are available for any burger.
*www.5napkinburger.com*

### Angelica Kitchen                 $LD
*New York* ▪ *(212) 228-2909*
*300 E 12th St* ▪ *Vegan* ▪ The restaurant
reports that they have many naturally GF
items on the menu, and each day they try
to have "at least one special" that is GF. A
GF recipe guide is available upon request.

Ask a server for help navigating the menu.
▪ *www.angelicakitchen.com*

### Angus' Café Bistro               ★$$$LD
*New York* ▪ *(212) 221-9222*
*258 W 44th St* ▪ *Modern American* ▪ GF
pasta is available. The restaurant reports
that most of the menu can be made GF
with "certain changes", such as "holding
the bun" on burgers and sandwiches. ▪
*www.anguscafebistro.com*

### Au Bon Pain                      📖
*New York* ▪ *(212) 246-6518*
*125 W 55th St*
*New York* ▪ *(212) 921-5908*
*1251 Ave of America*
*New York* ▪ *(212) 962-8453*
*222 Broadway*
*New York* ▪ *(212) 475-0453*
*6 Union Square E*
*New York* ▪ *(212) 668-8873*
*60 Broad St*
*New York* ▪ *(212) 952-9007*
*80 Pine St*
*New York* ▪ *(212) 481-5321*
*462 First Ave*
*New York* ▪ *(212) 994-4838*
*350 Fifth Ave*
*New York* ▪ *(212) 245-1170*
*One Intrepid Square Corner of W 46th St
& 12th Ave*
*New York* ▪ *(212) 244-5573*
*151 W 34th St*
*New York* ▪ *(212) 494-1091*
*151 W 34th St*
*New York* ▪ *(212) 475-8546*
*58 E 8th St*
*New York* ▪ *(212) 746-7642*
*525 E 68th St*
*New York* ▪ *(212) 742-7883*
*724 Whitehall St*
*New York* ▪ *(212) 502-5939*
*625 8th Ave*
*New York* ▪ *(212) 757-4628*
*30 Rockefeller Plaza, Concourse Level*
*New York* ▪ *(212) 962-9421*
*200 Liberty St*

**Aurora Ristorante**               $$$**BLD**
*Brooklyn* ▪ *(718) 388-5100*
*70 Grand St*
*New York* ▪ *(212) 334-9020*
*510 Broome St* ▪ *Italian* ▪ The restaurant
reports that many of their meat dishes are
naturally GF. Additionally, the chefs are
willing to modify any other dish pos-
sible to meet the needs of GF diners. ▪
*www.auroraristorante.com*

**BabyCakes NYC**                  ★¢**S**
*New York* ▪ *(212) 677-5047*
*248 Broome St* ▪ *Bakery* ▪ Non-dedicated
GF bakery offering only very few non-
GF products. GF items include cup-
cakes, muffins, crumb cakes, brownies,
scones, pies, and more. Bakery reports
that GF products are "always" in stock. ▪
*www.babycakesnyc.com*

**Basso 56**                      ★$$$**LD**
*New York* ▪ *(212) 265-2610*
*234 W 56th St* ▪ *Italian* ▪ GF pasta is
available and the restaurant reports that
all sauces are GF. Confirm the timeliness
of this information before dining in. ▪
*www.basso56.com*

**Bis.Co.Latte**                  ★¢**BL**
*New York* ▪ *(212) 581-3900*
*667 Tenth Ave* ▪ *Bakery & Café* ▪ Biscottis and other GF baked goods available. ▪
*www.biscolatte.com*

**Bistango**                      ★$$**LD**
*New York* ▪ *(212) 725-8484*
*415 3rd Ave* ▪ *Italian* ▪ GF pasta, pizza,
bread, desserts, and beer are available.
Restaurant reports that nearly all
menu items can be modified to be
GF. Selections include grilled salmon
with capers, prosciutto-wrapped veal
filet, and spinach & ricotta ravioli. ▪
*www.bistangonyc.com*

**Bloom's Delicatessen**          ✪★$**BLD**
*New York* ▪ *(212) 922-3663*
*350 Lexington Ave* ▪ *Deli* ▪ The GF menu
includes a variety of omelets, pancakes, and
French toast for breakfast. GF sandwiches

and salads are available, as are several
entrées such as the chopped steak and
the red snapper. GF desserts include NY
egg creams and creamy rice pudding. GF
bread and hamburger buns are available. ▪
*www.bloomsnewyorkdeli.com*

**Blue Smoke**                    ✪$$$**LD**
*New York* ▪ *(212) 447-7733*
*116 E 27th St*
*New York* ▪ *(212) 889-2005*
*255 Vesey St* ▪ *Barbeque* ▪ GF menu
includes oysters, deviled eggs, seared
Atlantic salmon, aged New York strip steak,
Kansas City spareribs, and more. Restaurant recommends reservations noting GF
so they can notify the kitchen in advance. ▪
*www.bluesmoke.com*

**Bread Tribeca**                 ✪$**BLD**
*New York* ▪ *(212) 334-0200*
*301 Church St* ▪ *Italian* ▪ Bread Tribeca has
a GF section on the regular lunch and dinner menu including items such as a quinoa
salad, no carb lasagna, and an arugula &
avocado entrée. ▪ *breadtribeca.com*

**Bubba Gump Shrimp Co.**         ✪📖
*New York* ▪ *(212) 391-7100*
*1501 Broadway*

**Café 82**                       ✪★$**BLD**
*New York* ▪ *(212) 875-8373*
*2282 Broadway* ▪ *Café* ▪ GF lasagna available. ▪ *www.cafe82ny.com*

**Café Viva Gourmet Pizza**       ★$**LD**
*New York* ▪ *(212) 663-8482*
*2578 Broadway* ▪ *Pizza* ▪ GF pizza is
available with various toppings such as
pesto, shitake mushrooms, tofu, vegan
cheese, tomatoes, mushrooms and marinara. The restaurant cautions that GF
pizzas are cooked in the same oven as
other pizzas.

**Candle Café**                   ✪$**LD**
*New York* ▪ *(212) 472-0970*
*1307 3rd Ave*
*New York* ▪ *(212) 769-8900*
*2427 Broadway*

*New York* ▪ *(212) 537-7179*
*154 E 79th St* ▪ *Vegetarian* ▪ Extensive new GF menu covers everything from starters to desserts. Examples include Moroccan spiced chickpea cake, vegetarian sushi, and salads. ▪ *www.candlecafe.com*

## Capital Grille, The ✪📖
*New York* ▪ *(212) 246-0154*
*120 W 51st St*
*New York* ▪ *(212) 953-2000*
*155 E 42nd St*

## Carmine's Restaurant ✪★$$$LD
*New York* ▪ *(212) 221-3800*
*200 W 44th St*
*New York* ▪ *(212) 362-2200*
*2450 Broadway* ▪ *Italian* ▪ GF pasta is available. An "allergy menu" with a GF section can be requested. GF items include all porterhouse steaks, chicken contadina, lobster fra diavolo, and more. Several GF desserts are available, including chocolate torte, fresh fruit, or tartufo. Alert a server upon arrival. ▪ *www.carminesnyc.com*

## Chloes's Soft Serve Fruit Co. ᏟS
*New York* ▪ *(212) 675-0550*
*25 E 17th St*
*New York* ▪ *(212) 794-2200*
*1371 Third Ave* ▪ *Ice Cream* ▪ Their soft serve fruit is 100% GF, but some of the toppings may not be. Alert a server and they will note which toppings are GF. The Watermill location is open from May-September. ▪ *www.chloesfruit.com*

## Chop't 📖
*New York* ▪ *(917) 338-4803*
*80 Pine St*
*New York* ▪ *(646) 336-5523*
*24 E 17th St*
*New York* ▪ *(646) 755-7837*
*18 E 23rd St*
*New York* ▪ *(212) 354-3284*
*1460 Broadway*
*New York* ▪ *(212) 974-8140*
*145 W 51st St*
*New York* ▪ *(212) 421-2300*
*165 E 52nd St*

*New York* ▪ *(212) 750-2467*
*60 E 56th St*
*New York* ▪ *(646) 783-1600*
*120 W 56th St*

## Corton ★$$$$D
*New York* ▪ *(212) 219-2777*
*239 W Broadway* ▪ *French* ▪ Chef Paul reports that they can easily accommodate GF diners. He recommends reservations noting GF, so that the staff knows to bring GF canapés instead of wheat flour canapés. He notes that all servers are educated on which menu items can be modified to be GF. ▪ *www.cortonnyc.com*

## Cosi ✪📖
*New York* ▪ *(212) 598-4070*
*257 Park Ave S*
*New York* ▪ *(212) 370-0705*
*38 E 45th St*
*New York* ▪ *(212) 344-5000*
*55 Broad St*
*New Yok* ▪ *(212) 588-1225*
*60 E 56th St*
*New York* ▪ *(212) 571-2001*
*200 Vesey-WFC*
*New York* ▪ *(212) 697-8329*
*685 Third Ave*
*New York* ▪ *(212) 397-9838*
*1633 Broadway*
*New York* ▪ *(212) 265-7579*
*61 W 48th St*
*New York* ▪ *(212) 614-8544*
*841 Broadway*
*New York* ▪ *(212) 634-3467*
*461 Park Ave S*
*New York* ▪ *(212) 947-1005*
*498 Seventh Ave*
*New York* ▪ *(212) 645-0223*
*700 Sixth Ave*
*New York* ▪ *(212) 260-1507*
*53 E 8th St*

## Del Frisco's Double Eagle Steak House 📖
*New York* ▪ *(212) 575-5129*
*1221 Ave Of The Americas*

## Dinosaur Bar-B-Que    📖
*New York* ▪ *(212) 694-1777*
*700 W 125th St*

## Friedman's Lunch    ✪ ★ $$**BLD**
*New York* ▪ *(212) 929-7100*
*75 9th Ave* ▪ *American* ▪ Items marked on
the menu can be prepared GF upon request. Sample items include chilaquiles for
breakfast, pulled pork sandwich for lunch,
and fish tacos for dinner, as well as many
other selections. GF bread is available. ▪
*www.friedmanslunch.com*

## Good Enough to Eat    $$**BLD**
*New York* ▪ *(212) 496-0163*
*483 Amsterdam Ave* ▪ *American* ▪
Hostess reports that GF options are
indicated on menu. Some items include
sweet potato fries, grilled salmon, salads, egg dishes, most vegetarian dishes.
Be sure to alert server upon arrival and
they will point out items on the menu. ▪
*www.goodenoughtoeat.com*

## Gradisca Ristorante    ★ $$$**D**
*New York* ▪ *(212) 691-4886*
*126 W 13th St* ▪ *Italian* ▪ GF pasta is available and can be substituted into most pasta
dishes. The restaurant also notes that many
of their meat dishes can be prepared GF.
Alert the server upon arrival and they will
go over the options. ▪ *www.gradiscanyc.com*

## GustOrganics Restaurant & Bar    ✪ $$**BLD**
*New York* ▪ *(212) 242-5800*
*519 Ave Of The Americas* ▪ *Organic* ▪
GF items marked on the menu include
watermelon gazpacho, mushroom risotto,
chicken lettuce wraps, and more. Several
GF desserts are available. Confirm the
timeliness of this information before dining in. ▪ *www.gustorganics.com*

## Hampton Chutney Co.    $**LD**
*New York* ▪ *(212) 226-9996*
*68 Prince St*
*New York* ▪ *(212) 362-5050*
*464 Amsterdam Ave* ▪ *Indian* ▪ The
restaurant reports that all of the dosas -
savory South Indian pancakes made from

rice and black lentils - are GF. She also
reports that the uttapams - like dosas, but
thicker - are GF. Fillings can be chosen a
la carte or from the many combinations
suggested on the menu. Dosas can also be
substituted for bread in the thali special. ▪
*www.hamptonchutney.com*

## Hard Rock Café    ✪ 📖
*New York* ▪ *(212) 343-3355*
*1501 Broadway*
*Niagara Falls* ▪ *(716) 282-0007*
*333 Prospect St*

## Hillstone Restaurants    📖
*New York* ▪ *(212) 689-1090*
*378 Park Ave S*
*New York* ▪ *(212) 888-3828*
*153 E 53rd St*

## Josie's Restaurant    ★ $$**LD**
*New York* ▪ *(212) 490-1558*
*565 3rd Ave*
*New York* ▪ *(212) 769-1212*
*300 Amsterdam Ave* ▪ *Asian Fusion*
▪ All items on menu are GF. Be sure to
stay away from the balsamic vinaigrette
because it contains gluten ingredients. ▪
*www.josiesnyc.com*

## Kuma Inn    $**D**
*New York* ▪ *(212) 353-8866*
*113 Ludlow St* ▪ *Asian Fusion* ▪ A list of GF
items is available in-house. This includes
steamed mussels in coconut curry, grilled
octopus with pickled bamboo shoots,
seared ahi tuna, oyster omelet, pork belly,
and more. Alert a server, who will go over
the GF options. ▪ *www.kumainn.com*

## L'Asso    ★ $**LD**
*New York* ▪ *(212) 219-2353*
*192 Mott St (at Kenmare)* ▪ *Italian* ▪ GF
pizza, pasta, and beer are available. Owner
Greg reports that though the GF desserts
change weekly, there is always one available. ▪ *www.lassonyc.com*

## Lili's 57                    ✪★$LD
*New York* ▪ *(212) 586-5333*
*200 W 57th St* ▪ *Asian Fusion* ▪ Extensive GF menu includes chicken satay, tom yum seafood, Saigon rolls, General Tso's chicken, spicy sweet chili shrimp, and cranberry teriyaki grilled chicken. GF soy sauce is available. ▪ *www.lilis57.com*

## Lilli and Loo                ✪★$LD
*New York* ▪ *(212) 421-8700*
*792 Lexington Ave* ▪ *Asian* ▪ GF menu includes rock shrimp tempura, pork dumplings, green papaya salad, Chilean bass, Manchurian beef, and more. GF soy sauce is available. Owner said they are constantly adding new GF dishes. ▪ *www.lilliandloo.com*

## Liquiteria                   ★¢BLD
*New York* ▪ *(212) 358-0300*
*170 2nd Ave* ▪ *Vegetarian* ▪ GF baked goods including cookies and brownies are available. Restaurant reports that most of its juices and smoothies are GF as well. Consult a server, who will point out which items to avoid. Confirm the timeliness of this information before dining in. ▪ *www.liquiteria.com*

## Loving Hut                   📖
*New York* ▪ *(217) 760-1900*
*348 7th Ave*

## Luigi's Pizzeria             ★$$LD
*New York* ▪ *(212) 410-1910*
*1701 1st Ave* ▪ *Pizza* ▪ GF pizza is available. ▪ *www.luigisnyc.com*

## Lumi                         ✪★$$$LD
*New York* ▪ *(212) 570-2335*
*963 Lexington Ave* ▪ *Italian* ▪ Extensive GF menu includes grilled salmon, rice-spaghetti marinara, and filet mignon. Manager Gent reports that the restaurant is "very accustomed" to GF diners. GF pasta is available. ▪ *www.lumirestaurant.com*

## Lupa Osteria Romana          ★$$$LD
*New York* ▪ *(212) 982-5089*
*170 Thompson St* ▪ *Italian* ▪ Menu is subject to change often so be sure to call ahead to see if GF entrées are available however GF pasta is always available. ▪ *www.luparestaurant.com*

## Market Café                  ✪$$$BLD
*New York* ▪ *(212) 967-3892*
*496 9th Ave* ▪ *American* ▪ The owner reports that the majority of the menu is naturally GF because it is all made from scratch. Every GF meal is prepared and cooked separately in its own pan and utensils. GF brunch, lunch and dinner menu available. Brunch is served on Saturdays and Sundays. ▪ *www.marketcafenyc.com*

## Mexican Radio                $LD
*New York* ▪ *(212) 343-0140*
*19 Cleveland Pl* ▪ *Mexican* ▪ The restaurant reports that the majority of the items on their menu can be modified to be GF. Alert the server upon arrival. ▪ *www.mexrad.com*

## Milk N' Honey NYC            ★$BLD
*New York* ▪ *(212) 764-4400*
*22 W 45th St* ▪ *Deli* ▪ GF pizza is available. ▪ *www.milknhoneykosher.com*

## Morton's Steakhouse          ✪📖
*New York* ▪ *(212) 972-3315*
*551 Fifth Ave*

## Mozzarelli's                 ★$$LD
*New York* ▪ *(212) 475-6777*
*38 E 23rd St* ▪ *Italian* ▪ GF pizza, bread crumbs, cookies and pasta available. Online ordering. ▪ *www.mozzarellis.com*

## Nanoosh                      ¢LD
*New York* ▪ *(212) 362-7922*
*2012 Broadway*
*New York* ▪ *(212) 387-0744*
*111 University Pl*
*New York* ▪ *(212) 447-4345*
*173 Madison Ave* ▪ *Mediterranean* ▪ The restaurant reports that most items on the menu can be prepared GF, and recommends consulting a server to help make a meal selection. They also recommend informing the staff that your requests are due to an "allergy" as opposed to a preference so they can take extra care when preparing the meal. ▪ *www.nanoosh.com*

## Nice Matin ✪$$$BLD
*New York* ▪ *(212) 873-6423*
*201 W 79th St* ▪ *French* ▪ GF menu is available for lunch and dinner. Manager Ashley reports that reservations noting GF are recommended. ▪ *www.nicematinnyc.com*

## Nizza Restaurant ✪★$LD
*New York* ▪ *(212) 956-1800*
*630 9th Ave* ▪ *Italian* ▪ GF menu includes pasta pesto, ziti pomodoro, grilled marinated tuna, branzino fillet, and more. GF sides are available and can be substituted in place of gluten items. GF bread, pasta, pizza, and beer are available. ▪ *www.nizzanyc.com*

## Nobu ★$$$$LD
*New York* ▪ *(212) 219-0500*
*105 Hudson St* ▪ *Fusion* ▪ The restaurant highly recommends alerting a server upon arrival. The server will then discuss GF options with the chefs, who are more familiar with GF items. All wait staff and cooks are familiar with GF requests. ▪ *www.myriadrestaurantgroup.com*

## Nobu Fifty Seven ★$$$$LD
*New York* ▪ *(212) 757-3000*
*40 W 57th St* ▪ *Fusion* ▪ The restaurant highly recommends alerting a server upon arrival. The server will then discuss GF options with the chefs, who are more familiar with GF items. All wait staff and cooks are familiar with GF requests. ▪ *www.myriadrestaurantgroup.com*

## Nobu Next Door $$$$D
*New York* ▪ *(212) 334-4445*
*105 Hudson St* ▪ *Fusion* ▪ The restaurant highly recommends alerting a server upon arrival. The server will then discuss GF options with the chefs, who are more familiar with GF items. All wait staff and cooks are familiar with GF requests. Restaurant shares the same kitchen and menu as the adjacent flagship Nobu restaurant. ▪ *www.myriadrestaurantgroup.com*

## Organique ₵BLD
*New York* ▪ *(212) 674-2229*
*110 E 23rd St* ▪ *American* ▪ GF bread is available, and GF pasta is available on occasion. Some of their soups are also GF. Online menu points out what is GF. ▪ *organiqueonline.com*

## OTTO Enoteca Pizzeria ★$LD
*New York* ▪ *(212) 995-9559*
*One 5th Ave* ▪ *Italian* ▪ GF pasta is available. ▪ *www.ottopizzeria.com*

## Palà ★$$LD
*New York* ▪ *(212) 614-7252*
*198 Allen St* ▪ *Pizza* ▪ GF menu available. ▪ *www.palapizza.com*

## Pappardella ✪★$$$BLD
*New York* ▪ *(212) 595-7996*
*316 Columbus Ave* ▪ *Italian* ▪ GF pizza, pasta, and bread are available. Extensive GF menu includes a wide variety of appetizers, pizza, paninis, salads, pasta dishes, pizza, fish dishes, and meat dishes. A variety of GF desserts, including flourless chocolate cake, gelato and sorbet is available. ▪ *www.pappardella.com*

## Peacefood Café ✪$LD
*New York* ▪ *(212) 362-2266*
*460 Amsterdam Ave* ▪ *Vegan* ▪ Items that are GF are marked on the regular menu with a flower symbol. Some of these items are chickpea fries, sushi, lasagna, pizza, fluffy quinoa, chef's potato salad, vegetable tamales and more. ▪ *www.peacefoodcafe.com*

## Per Se ★$$$$D
*New York* ▪ *(212) 823-9335*
*10 Columbus Cir* ▪ *American* ▪ Menu changes daily. Call ahead to restaurant to see what GF items are available for that day. ▪ *www.perseny.com*

## Prune $$$BLD
*New York* ▪ *(212) 677-6221*
*54 E 1st St* ▪ *Modern American* ▪ The restaurant reports that most items on the menu are naturally GF and recommends that GF diners consult with their server to arrange a GF meal. ▪ *www.prunerestaurant.com*

## Prêt A Manger

New York ▪ (212) 246-6944
*30 Rockefeller Ctr*
New York ▪ (212) 307-6100
*1350 6th Ave*
New York ▪ (212) 489-6458
*135 W 50th St*
New York ▪ (212) 825-8825
*60 Broad St*
New York ▪ (212) 867-0400
*287 Madison Ave*
New York ▪ (212) 867-1905
*205 E 42nd St*
New York ▪ (212) 871-6274
*380 Lexington Ave*
New York ▪ (212) 997-5520
*11 W 42nd St*
New York ▪ (646) 497-0510
*630 Lexington Ave*
New York ▪ (646) 728-0750
*530 7th Ave*
New York ▪ (212) 207-4101
*400 Park Ave*
New York ▪ (646) 360-1630
*2 Park Ave*
New York ▪ (212) 344-0105
*50 Broadway*
New York ▪ (212) 742-8563
*101 Maiden Ln 2*
New York ▪ (646) 572-8010
*857 Broadway*
New York ▪ (646) 688-1052
*485 Lexington Ave*
New York ▪ (646) 537-0020
*425 Madison Ave*
New York ▪ (212) 328-0015
*1 Astor Pl*
New York ▪ (212) 608-7501
*179 Broadway*
New York ▪ (212) 227-3108
*100 Church St*
New York ▪ (212) 847-0421
*350 Hudson St*
New York ▪ (212) 401-8686
*389 5th Ave*
New York ▪ (212) 292-3913
*425 Lexington Ave*
New York ▪ (646) 885-6330

*24 W 23rd St*
New York ▪ (646) 810-2422
*880 3rd Ave*
New York ▪ (212) 207-3503
*757 3rd Ave*
New York ▪ (646) 626-6477
*342 7th Ave*
New York ▪ (212) 847-0295
*62 W 45th St*
New York ▪ (646) 572-0490
*1410 Broadway*
New York ▪ (646) 688-1061
*1020 6th Ave*
New York ▪ (646) 360-1625
*485 7th Ave*
New York ▪ (646) 537-0030
*1200 Ave of Americas*
New York ▪ (212) 459-8971
*825 8th Ave*
New York ▪ (212) 255-2087
*655 6th Ave*

## Pure Food and Wine                    $$$D

New York ▪ (212) 477-1010
*54 Irving Pl* ▪ *Raw* ▪ Restaurant reports
that most of the menu is GF, but changes
frequently. A GF menu is available upon
request. Sample items include lasagna
made with zucchini instead of pasta and
sweet corn and cashew tamales. Confirm
the timeliness of this information before
dining in. ▪ *www.purefoodandwine.com*

## Rice to Riches                    ¢S

New York ▪ (212) 274-0008
*37 Spring St* ▪ *Dessert* ▪ Out of the 21
flavors offered only two of them contain gluten, the cookies and cream and
the honey graham. The rest are GF. ▪
*www.ricetoriches.com*

## Risotteria                    ✪★$LD

New York ▪ (212) 924-6664
*270 Bleecker St* ▪ *Italian* ▪ Extensive GF
menu includes a wide variety of GF pizza,
risotto and paninis. GF breadsticks, and
beer are also available. A wide variety of
GF desserts, including cupcakes, cookies,
tiramisu, and cakes are available from their
bakery. ▪ *www.risotteria.com*

**Rosa Mexicano**   ✪📖
*New York* ▪ *(212) 753-7407*
*1063 First Ave*
*New York* ▪ *(212) 977-7700*
*61 Columbus Ave*

**Rubirosa Ristorante**   ✪★$$$BLD
*New York* ▪ *(212) 965-0500*
*235 Mulberry St* ▪ *Italian* ▪ GF pizza and
pasta are available. Other GF options in-
clude brick pressed chicken, NY strip steak,
and risotto. Restaurant reports that GF
items are "kept separate" from possible CC.
▪ *rubirosanyc.com*

**Ruby Foo's**   ✪★$$LD
*New York* ▪ *(212) 489-5600*
*1626 Broadway* ▪ *Asian Fusion* ▪ GF menu
includes lettuce wraps, pad thai, orange
chicken, and chicken fried rice. For dessert, GF brownies and warm crumb cake
are available. GF beer is also available. ▪
*www.rubyfoos.com*

**Ruth's Chris Steak House**   ✪📖
*New York* ▪ *(212) 245-9600*
*148 W 51st St*

**S'MAC**   ★¢LD
*New York* ▪ *(212) 358-7912*
*345 E 12th St*
*New York* ▪ *(212) 683-3900*
*157 E 33rd St*
*New York* ▪ *(917) 580-0097*
*3 1st Ave* ▪ *American* ▪ Any macaroni and
cheese dish can be made with GF elbow
macaroni. The restaurant reports that their
béchamel contains no wheat and their
breadcrumbs are made from GF cornflakes.
More information about the restaurant's
GF practices can be found on their website.
▪ *www.smacnyc.com*

**Sacred Chow**   ★¢BLD
*New York* ▪ *(212) 337-0863*
*227 Sullivan St* ▪ *Vegetarian* ▪ GF items are
marked on the menu and include curried
steamed broccoli, Indonesian roasted tempeh, and Italian frittata. Several GF desserts
are also available. Some items may need

modification to become GF, so be sure to
alert your server. ▪ *sacredchow.com*

**Sambuca**   ✪★$D
*New York* ▪ *(212) 787-5656*
*20 W 72nd St* ▪ *Italian* ▪ Extensive GF
menu includes pasta dishes with many
different sauces. Examples are ricotta and
spinach ravioli, pasta primavera broccoli, and pasta with carbonara sauce.
GF pizza and beer are also available, as
are GF cakes and brownies for dessert. ▪
*www.sambucanyc.com*

**Slice**   ★$$LD
*New York* ▪ *(212) 929-2920*
*535 Hudson St* ▪ *Pizza* ▪ GF pizza and beer
are always available. Owner Miki advises
that customers looking for fast service
should order GF pizza in advance, as it
usually takes 20-30 minutes to prepare. ▪
*www.sliceperfect.com*

**Smith & Wollensky**   📖
*New York* ▪ *(212) 753-1530*
*49th St & 3rd Ave*

**Souen**   ✪$LD
*New York* ▪ *(212) 807-7421*
*210 Sixth Ave*
*New York* ▪ *(212) 627-7150*
*28 E 13th St*
*New York* ▪ *(212) 388-1155*
*326 E 6th St* ▪ *Japanese* ▪ Items that can
be prepared GF upon request are marked
on the menu. The East Village (6th Street)
location also points out naturally GF items
on the menu, and the staff at that location
report that they have "never had a prob-
lem" with CC. ▪ *www.souen.net*

**Ted's Montana Grill**   ✪📖
*New York* ▪ *(212) 245-5220*
*110 W 51st St & 6th Ave*

**Terri**   ★¢BLD
*New York* ▪ *(212) 647-8810*
*60 W 23rd St* ▪ *Vegan* ▪ GF bread and
tortillas are available. All sandwiches and
wraps can be modified to be GF, but all

their vegan "meat" contains gluten and must be substituted with tofu, avocado, or portobello. A GF cupcake is also available. ▪ *www.terrinyc.com*

### Tossed   ✪▢
*New York* ▪ *(212) 674-6700*
*295 Park Ave S*
*New York City* ▪ *(212) 674-6700*
*295 Park Ave*

### Tramonti Ristorante   ★$$**LD**
*New York* ▪ *(212) 245-2720*
*364 W 46th St* ▪ *Italian* ▪ GF pasta available.

### Tribeca Grill   $$$$**LD**
*New York* ▪ *(212) 941-3900*
*375 Greenwich St* ▪ *Modern American* ▪ Manager Kelly reports that many menu items can be prepared GF, including the swordfish barigoule, NY strip steak, herb roasted chicken, seared sea scallops with risotto, and more. Confirm the timeliness of this information before dining in. Servers are "very well-versed" in handling GF orders and will go over the menu with GF guests and notify the chefs.

### Tu-Lu's Gluten-Free Bakery   ℭ$
*New York* ▪ *(212) 777-2227*
*338 E 11th St* ▪ *Bakery* ▪ Dedicated GF bakery offering cupcakes, muffins, cookies, brownies, cheesecake bars, cornbread and many other baked goods. Full-sized GF cakes are also available with advance notice of 48 hours. ▪ *www.tu-lusbakery.com*

### Uno Chicago Grill   ✪★▢
*New York* ▪ *(212) 472-5656*
*220 E 86th St*
*New York* ▪ *(212) 595-4700*
*432 Columbus Ave*
*New York* ▪ *(212) 791-7999*
*89 South St*

### Zen Palate   ✪$$**LD**
*New York* ▪ *(212) 387-8885*
*115 E 18th St*
*New York* ▪ *(212) 582-1669*
*663 9th Ave*

*New York* ▪ *(212) 685-6888*
*515 3rd Ave* ▪ *Vegetarian* ▪ All locations offer a GF menu and accommodations. Alert the server that you are eating GF. ▪ *www.zenpalate.com*

### Zpizza   ✪▢
*New York* ▪ *(718) 244-4444*
*JFK Intl Airport*

## NEW YORK

### ROCHESTER

### Au Bon Pain   ▢
*Rochester* ▪ *(585) 276-1212*
*601 Elmwood Ave*

### Bugaboo Creek Steak House   ✪▢
*Rochester* ▪ *(585) 292-5800*
*935 Jefferson Rd*

### Dinosaur Bar-B-Que   ▢
*Rochester* ▪ *(585) 325-7090*
*99 Court St*

### Donna Marie's Gluten Free Bakery   ℭ$
*Rochester* ▪ *(585) 254-0706*
*164 Newbury St* ▪ *Bakery* ▪ Dedicated GF bakery offering a wide variety of breads, cookies, muffins, cinnamon rolls, cakes, various pound cakes, cupcakes and a pumpkin walnut mini loaf with cream cheese frosting. GF sandwich bread, sandwich rolls, pizza shells, croutons, and bread crumbs are also available. Specialty cakes are made to order in different flavors as well as custom cookie cakes. ▪ *www.donnamariesbakery.com*

### Keenan's   ✪$$**LD**
*Rochester* ▪ *(585) 266-2691*
*1010 E Ridge Rd* ▪ *American* ▪ Extensive 4 page GF menu includes instructions on how to make dishes GF, including which sauces to ask for and what not to include on dish. Chefs are report-

edly "very familiar" with GF requests. ▪ *www.keenansrestaurant.com*

### King and I ★ $LD
*Rochester* ▪ *(585) 427-8090*
*1455 E Henrietta Rd* ▪ *Thai* ▪ Any item on the menu can be made GF. Alert a server upon arrival. ▪ *www.thekingandithaicuisine.com*

### Mario's Authentic Italian Restaurant & Catering ✪★$$D
*Rochester* ▪ *(585) 271-1111*
*2740 Monroe Ave* ▪ *Italian* ▪ GF menu includes grilled calamari, salads, pasta including penne abruzzi, seafood cioppino cartoccio, sea bass and greens, rack of lamb and various cuts of steak with side dishes. All staff members are trained to handle GF requests. ▪ *www.mariosit.com*

### Natural Oasis Café ✪$LD
*Rochester* ▪ *(585) 325-1831*
*288 Monroe Ave* ▪ *Vegetarian* ▪ The restaurant reports that everything on the menu is GF EXCEPT the pizza▪ *www.naturaloasisny.com*

### Nick's Deli and Catering ✪★$LD
*Rochester* ▪ *(585) 247-6270*
*1098 Chili-Coldwater Rd* ▪ *Italian* ▪ GF menu available. Items include GF pizza, Italian style bread, dinner rolls, sandwich rolls, meatballs, chicken parmesan, pasta, cookies, bars, brownies and cream puffs. ▪ *www.nicksdeliandpizza.com*

### Owl House, The ✪$BLD
*Rochester* ▪ *(585) 360-2920*
*75 Marshall St* ▪ *American* ▪ GF menu includes smoked trout hummus with house made GF bread, Moroccan smoked beef jerky, baked nachos with GF tortilla chips, salads, sandwiches prepared on house made GF bread and entrées and desserts. Ask server about the GF entrées and desserts of the day. ▪ *www.owlhouserochester.com*

### Romano's Macaroni Grill ✪★📖
*Rochester* ▪ *(585) 427-8230*
*760 Jefferson Rd*

### Salena's Mexican Restaurant $$LD
*Rochester* ▪ *(585) 256-5980*
*302 N Goodman St* ▪ *Mexican* ▪ GF diners are commonly accommodated and many dishes can be prepared GF. Be sure to alert server upon arrival and they will list GF options. ▪ *www.salenas.com*

# NEW YORK
## ALL OTHER CITIES

### 97 Lake Sports Café & Restaurant ✪$LD
*West Harrison* ▪ *(914) 328-1414*
*97 Lake St* ▪ *American* ▪ Extensive GF menu includes appetizers, soups, salads, burgers & sandwiches on GF buns, several kinds of GF mac & cheese, and a variety of meat & seafood entrées. GF desserts include flourless chocolate cake, bread pudding, brownie sundae, rootbeer float, and more. Owner Alan has Celiac and reports that "we definitely know what we are doing" when it comes to preparing GF meals. ▪ *www.97lake.com*

### Airmont Eats ✪★$LD
*Airmont* ▪ *(845) 368-1973*
*211 Rt 59* ▪ *Pizza* ▪ GF pizza is available. The restaurant reports that many of the menu items are GF including salads, quinoa, and stuffed portobello mushroom. They can also make any of their sandwiches GF by substituting bread with pizza crust. All meats and cheeses are also GF. Confirm the timeliness of this information before dining in. ▪ *www.airmonteats.com*

### Aldente Pizzeria ★$LD
*Rye* ▪ *(914) 921-5300*
*7 Elm Pl* ▪ *Pizza* ▪ GF pizza is available.

## Amalfi Restaurant & Pizzeria    ★ $$ LD
Glen Cove ▪ (516) 801-6544
197 Forest Ave
Port Washington ▪ (516) 883-4191
49 Old Shore Rd ▪ Italian ▪ GF 15" pizza
and pasta available.

## Aroma Osteria    ★ $$$ LD
Wappingers Falls ▪ (845) 298-6790
114 Old Post Rd ▪ Italian ▪ GF pasta is
available. The restaurant reports that they
also have "a couple items" on the regular menu that can be prepared GF. Alert
a server, who will go over GF options. ▪
www.aromaosteriarestaurant.com

## Aroma Thyme Bistro    ★ $$ LD
Ellenville ▪ (845) 647-3000
165 Canal St ▪ Modern American ▪ GF
bread, pizza, beer, and soy sauce are
available. The restaurants reports that
90% of the menu "works for a GF diet."
GF entrées include shrimp with red Thai
curry, kobe beef skirt steak, wild Alaskan salmon, and more. For dessert, there
are GF brownies, chocolate torte and
maple pecan pie. Confirm the timeliness
of this information before dining in. ▪
www.aromathymebistro.com

## Artist's Palate, The    $$ LD
Poughkeepsie ▪ (845) 483-8074
307 Main St ▪ Fusion ▪ The restaurant
reports that most menu items are either
naturally GF or can easily be prepared
GF. Examples include the vegetable curry,
grilled swordfish, and organic salmon.
Alert a server, who will be able to point
out GF options. Confirm the timeliness
of this information before dining in. ▪
www.theartistspalate.biz

## Au Bon Pain    ▢
White Plains ▪ (914) 682-3306
125 Westchester Ave
Melville ▪ (631) 393-0212
300 Broadhollow Rd
Bronx ▪ (212) 994-4832
2155 University Ave
Brooklyn ▪ (718) 934-0539

2601 Ocean Pkwy
Elmhurst ▪ (718) 779-2033
79-01 Broadway
Glens Falls ▪ (518) 926-2646
100 Park St
Hempstead ▪ (516) 463-6539
116 California Ave
Jericho ▪ (516) 280-2494
2 Jericho Plaza
Bronx ▪ (718) 918-9309
1400 Pelham Pkwy S
Jamaica ▪ (718) 751-7488
JFK Int'l Airport- Departure Terminal 4
Jamaica ▪ (718) 751-4797
JFK Int'l Airport- American Airlines Ter-
minal
Jamaica ▪ (718) 751-7488
JFK Int'l Airport E Food Hall- Terminal 4
Jamaica ▪ (718) 751-4799
JFK Int'l Airport- Terminal 8, American
Airlines
Flushing ▪ (718) 639-2891
LaGuardia Airport- Central Terminal Bldg
Flushing ▪ (718) 639-2296
LaGuardia Airport- Terminal A
Flushing ▪ (718) 639-2476
LaGuardia Aiport- Terminal B
Flushing ▪ (718) 639-2516
LaGuardia Airport- Terminal C
Flushing ▪ (718) 334-0480
LaGuardia Airport- Terminal D- Ground Fl
Departure
Brooklyn ▪ (718) 246-4007
339 Hicks St
New Hyde Park ▪ (718) 343-3196
270-05 76th Ave
Manhasset ▪ (516) 365-7057
300 Community Dr
Woodbury ▪ (516) 802-5295
1000 Woodbury Rd
Brooklyn ▪ (718) 624-9598
70 Myrtle Ave
Staten Island ▪ (718) 420-0846
4 Ferry Terminal Dr
New Hyde Park ▪ (516) 502-4343
1981 Marcus Ave
Buffalo ▪ (716) 645-8880
146 Fargo Quad

*Valhalla* ▪ *(914) 347-2810*
*95 Grasslands Rd*
*Valhalla* ▪ *(914) 347-2810*
*19 Bradhurst Medical Bldg*
*Central Valley* ▪ *(845) 928-4516*
*498 Red Apple Ct*

### Azure Chocolat New York                                     ⟲S
*Greenlawn* ▪ *(631) 425-1885*
*72 Broadway* ▪ *Dessert* ▪ Entirely GF
environment that produces fresh truffles,
"chocolate comforts," and more. Check
timeliness of this information before dining in. ▪ *www.azurechocolate.com*

### B. Smith's                                                 $$$LD
*New York* ▪ *(212) 315-1100*
*320 W 46th St*
*Sag Harbor* ▪ *(631) 725-5858*
*Long Wharf at Bay St* ▪ *Modern American* ▪ Manager Mike reports that they
have "some items" which are GF or can be
prepared GF. He recommends making reservations noting GF and alerting a server
upon arrival. He notes that "the server will
be knowledgeable," and also that they have
an internal GF list which servers can consult. Some items that can be prepared GF
include their BBQ ribs, seared scallops, and
grilled catfish. ▪ *www.bsmith.com*

### Bartaco                                                    ✪SLD
*Port Chester* ▪ *(914) 937-8226*
*1 Willett Ave* ▪ *Mexican* ▪ Director of marketing Ria reports that they are "90% GF" and
use separate fryers as well as gloves when
preparing GF items. The menu features a
variety of specialty tacos, including lamb barbacoa, portobello with queso fresco, and Thai
shrimp, as well as salads, rice bowls, tamales,
ceviche, and more. The 3 non-GF items are
clearly marked on the menu. Alert server
upon arrival. ▪ *www.bartaco.com*

### Bellizzi                                            ✪★$$LD
*Mount Kisco* ▪ *(914) 241-1200*
*153 E Main St*
*Larchmont* ▪ *(914) 833-5800*
*1272 Boston Post Rd* ▪ *Italian* ▪ Extensive
GF menu includes a variety of pasta dishes

like truffle pasta and white clam sauce
pasta, an array of 9 or 12 inch personal
pizzas, chicken milanese, and chicken and
eggplant parmagiana. ▪ *www.bellizzi.us*

### Bertucci's                                          ✪▥
*Hauppauge* ▪ *(631) 952-2100*
*358 Vanderbilt Motor Pkwy*
*Melville* ▪ *(631) 427-9700*
*881 Walt Whitman Rd*
*Westbury* ▪ *(516) 683-8800*
*795 Merrick Ave*

### Biaggi's                                            ✪★▥
*Victor* ▪ *(585) 223-2290*
*818 Eastview Mall*

### Bocce Club Pizza                                    ★⟲LD
*Amherst* ▪ *(716) 833-1344*
*4174 N Bailey Ave*
*E Amherst* ▪ *(716) 689-2345*
*1614 Hopkins Rd* ▪ *Pizza* ▪ GF pizza
is available in the 10-inch size. ▪
*www.bocceclubpizza.com*

### Bonefish Grill                                      ✪▥
*Fayetteville* ▪ *(315) 637-0491*
*600 Towne Dr*
*Victor* ▪ *(585) 223-7059*
*1002 Eastview Mall*
*Amherst* ▪ *(716) 833-6106*
*1247 Niagara Falls Blvd*
*Poughkeepsie* ▪ *(845) 432-7507*
*2185 S Rd*
*Staten Island* ▪ *(718) 761-5628*
*280 Marsh Ave*

### Boulder Creek Steakhouse                            ✪$$$LD
*Hicksville* ▪ *(516) 942-7800*
*200 N Broadway*
*Brooklyn* ▪ *(718) 277-0222*
*355 Gateway Dr* ▪ *Steakhouse* ▪ GF menu
includes seared ahi tuna, center cut filet
mignon, ribeye, porterhouse, prime rib,
skirt steak, center cut top sirloin, Durango
chicken, steamboat spring baby back ribs,
cripple creek pork chops, rack of New Zealand lamb chops, catch of the day, salmon,
tilapia, garlic roasted mashed potatoes,
sweet potato and steamed vegetables. ▪
*www.bouldercreeksteakhouses.net*

### Broadway Pizzeria ✪★$LD
*Greenlawn ■ (631) 261-0828*
*60 Broadway ■ Pizza ■* GF pizza and pasta
are available. Restaurant recommends
calling 30 minutes ahead for pizza, but
pasta does not require advance notice.
A list of suitable GF pizza toppings and
pasta sauces is available on their website. ■
*www.broadwaycatering.com*

### Brooks' House of Bar-B-Q ✪$LD
*Oneonta ■ (607) 432-1782*
*5560 State Highway 7 ■ Barbeque ■*
Extensive GF menu includes chicken
wings, the St. Louis pork rib dinner, the
ribeye steak dinner, and more. For dessert,
there is GF tapioca pudding. Some items
may require modification to become GF.
The restaurant recommends speaking to
an owner or a manager upon arrival to
ensure that the meal is prepared properly.
■ *www.brooksbbq.com*

### Buca di Beppo ✪▢
*Colonie ■ (518) 459-2822*
*44 Wolf Rd*

### Bugaboo Creek Steak House ✪▢
*Poughkeepsie ■ (845) 297-2200*
*1955 S Rd*

### Buona Sera Ristorante Pizzeria ✪★$LD
*Smithtown ■ (631) 265-0625*
*88-90 E Main St ■ Italian ■* Dedicated
GF menu available. GF items include
appetizers, pizzas, pastas, chicken,
shrimp and steak entrées. There is
also a GF Children's menu, complete with GF brownies for dessert. ■
*www.serveyourfamily.com/buonasera*

### Burger Garage, The ★¢LD
*Long Island City ■ (718) 392-0424*
*25-36 Jackson Ave ■ American ■* GF burger
buns, hot dog buns, and beer are available.
The menu denotes which burger toppings
and other menu items GF diners should
avoid. ■ *www.theburgergarage.com*

### Café Pizzazz ★$LD
*Mohegan Lake ■ (914) 743-1055*
*1859 E Main St ■ Italian ■* GF pizza and
pasta are available. Be sure to inform the
server or manager of GF dietary needs so
that they can make the necessary arrangements. ■ *www.cafepizzapizzazz.com*

### Café Rustica ✪★$$LD
*Great Neck ■ (516) 829-6464*
*200 Middle Neck Rd ■ Italian ■* All GF
dishes are monitored closely and prepared
with clean/sanitized utensils in order to
prevent CC. ■ *caferusticarestaurant.com*

### Café Spiga Pizza & Pasta ★$$LD
*Mount Sinai ■ (631) 331-5554*
*176 N Country Rd ■ Pizza ■* GF pizza
(10" size only) and pasta are available.
The restaurant reports that they can
make "almost anything" on the menu
GF with the exception of pre-prepared
items like lasagna or stuffed shells. A
separate prep area is used for GF items. ■
*www.cafespigapizzapasta.com*

### Calabria Restaurant ✪★$$LD
*Orangeburg ■ (845) 365-2300*
*500 Route 303 ■ Italian ■* GF pizzas and
pastas are available. Restaurant recommends ordering GF pizzas at least 30 minutes in advance. ■ *www.calabriapizza.com*

### Cantina Laredo ▢
*Syracuse ■ (315) 476-1750*
*1 Destiny Ctr*

### Carrabba's Italian Grill ✪▢
*Amherst ■ (716) 833-5003*
*1645 Niagara Falls Blvd*
*Central Islip ■ (631) 232-1070*
*20 N Research Pl*
*Fayetteville ■ (315) 637-7400*
*550 Towne Dr*
*Latham ■ (518) 785-8886*
*675 Troy Schenectady Rd*
*Henrietta ■ (585) 292-6120*
*3340 W Henrietta Rd*
*Smithtown ■ (631) 265-1304*
*730 Smithtown Bypass*

**Charlie Brown's Steakhouse** ✪📖
*Fishkill* ▪ *(845) 896-2666*
*18 Westage Dr*
*Staten Island* ▪ *(718) 494-0179*
*1001 Goethals Rd N*

**Charlotte's
Restaurant & Catering** $$$D
*Millbrook* ▪ *(845) 677-5888*
*4258 Rte 44* ▪ *Modern American* ▪ The
restaurant reports that though the menu
changes daily, the chefs can always ac-
commodate GF diners with "tailor-made"
meals. Reservations noting GF are recom-
mended. Alert a server upon arrival. ▪
*www.charlottesny.com*

**Cheeseburger in Paradise** ✪★📖
*Middletown* ▪ *(845) 343-9252*
*340 Route 211 E*

**Chloes's Soft Serve Fruit Co.** ✄S
*Water Mill* ▪ *(631) 726-6166*
*869 Montauk Hwy* ▪ *Ice Cream* ▪ Their
soft serve fruit is 100% GF, but some of the
toppings may not be. Alert a server and
they will note which toppings are GF. The
Watermill location is open from May-Sep-
tember. ▪ *www.chloesfruit.com*

**Chop't** 📖
*Rye Brook* ▪ *(914) 908-4184*
*116 S Ridge St*
*New York* ▪ *(646) 439-0262*
*100 Park Ave*

**Chumley's BBQ** ✪$LD
*Florida* ▪ *(845) 651-3663*
*56 North Main St* ▪ *Barbeque* ▪ GF menu
items include famous ribs, rotisserie
chicken, salads, soups, chilis, sandwiches
made on GF rolls, BBQ platters, GF
sauces and sides, family and kids meals. ▪
*www.chumleysbbq.com*

**Circus Café** ✪★$LD
*Saratoga Springs* ▪ *(518) 583-1106*
*392 Broadway* ▪ *American* ▪ Extensive
GF menu includes starters, sandwiches,
salads, entrées, and signature dishes. Des-
serts on the GF menu include a chocolate
lava cake, cotton candy, and mango gelato.
GF bread, pasta, and beer are available. ▪
*www.circuscafe.com*

**Comfort** ★$LD
*Hastings On Hudson* ▪ *(914) 478-0666*
*583 Warburton Ave* ▪ *Global* ▪ The
restaurant manager reports that most of
the menu is GF. Examples include grilled
portobello, steak frites, sesame crusted
tuna, herb chicken, and grilled pork chop,
among other things. The manager notes
that all salads and sides are GF as well.
Alert a server, who will go over GF options.
Confirm the timeliness of this information
before dining in.

**Cosi** ✪📖
*Rye* ▪ *(914) 921-3322*
*50 Purchase St*
*New Rochelle* ▪ *(914) 637-8300*
*77 Quaker Ridge Rd*
*Mt. Kisco* ▪ *(914) 242-5408*
*12 S Moger Ave*
*Larchmont* ▪ *(914) 834-9797*
*1298 Boston Post Rd*
*Plainview* ▪ *(516) 937-0290*
*441 S Oyster Bay Rd*
*Flushing* ▪ *(613) 834-1525*
*LGA Central Terminal Concourse D*

**Cozymel's Coastel Mex** ✪📖
*Westbury* ▪ *(516) 222-7010*
*1177 Corporate Dr*

**Crabtree's Kittle House** $$$$LD
*Chappaqua* ▪ *(914) 666-8044*
*11 Kittle Rd* ▪ *Modern American* ▪ Res-
ervationist Heather reports that they are
"happy to tailor any dish" to meet the
dietary requirements of their guests, and
that many items on the menu are naturally
GF. She recommends reservations noting
GF so that the chef has time to prepare. ▪
*www.kittlehouse.com*

## Curly's Bar & Grill    ✪★$$$LD
*Lackawanna* ▪ *(716) 824-9716*
*647 Ridge Rd* ▪ *American* ▪ GF items indicated on menu include black bean soup, wild arugula salad, spinach salad, seafood linguini, angel hair pasta, Jamaican escovitche, cioppino, roasted fennel, scallops, NY strip steak, chicken mobay, and wood-fired tofu. GF desserts include chocolate mousse and Dominican gold chocolate chip cookies ▪ *www.curlysgrill.com*

## D'Cocco's    ★$LD
*Oceanside* ▪ *(516) 766-3938*
*3573 Long Beach Rd* ▪ *Italian* ▪ GF pasta and small pizza are available. ▪ *www.dcoccos.com*

## Davinci's    ★$$$LD
*Island Park* ▪ *(516) 889-3939*
*118 Long Beach Rd* ▪ *Italian* ▪ GF personal pizza available.

## Deanna's Pizzeria and Restaurant
★$$LD
*New Rochelle* ▪ *(914) 636-5960*
*1284 North Ave* ▪ *Pizza* ▪ GF pizza and pasta are available. ▪ *www.deannaspizza.com*

## Dinosaur Bar-B-Que    📖
*Syracuse* ▪ *(315) 476-4937*
*246 W Willow St*
*Troy* ▪ *(518) 308-0400*
*377 River St*

## El Loco Mexican Café    ✪$LD
*Albany* ▪ *(518) 436-1855*
*465 Madison Ave* ▪ *Tex-Mex* ▪ GF menu includes nachos, vegetarian black bean soup, meatless chili, quesadillas, fajitas, ancho-chipotle chicken and spinach enchiladas, pork tamales and soft tacos. Confirm the timeliness of this information before dining in. ▪ *www.ellocomexicancafe.com*

## Enzo's Antichi Sapori Restaurant    ★$LD
*Armonk* ▪ *(914) 273-4186*
*111 Bedford Rd* ▪ *Italian* ▪ A variety of items on the menu can be made to accommodate a GF diner. This restaurant carries GF spaghetti, rigatoni and penne pasta that can be substituted in any pasta dish. Chicken and veal dishes can also be made GF. Ask the server prior to ordering so that the necessary communication with the chef can be made. ▪ *www.enzosofarmonk.com*

## Epsteins Kosher Deli    ✪★$BLD
*Hartsdale* ▪ *(914) 428-5320*
*387 N Central Ave* ▪ *Deli* ▪ Extensive GF menu includes appetizers, salads, sandwiches, entrées, and desserts. Examples are the chopped steak, the roast turkey sandwich, and the pepper steak over rice. GF bread is available. ▪ *www.epsteinsdeli.com*

## Fifth Season    ✪★$$$D
*Port Jefferson* ▪ *(631) 477-8500*
*34 E Broadway* ▪ *Modern American* ▪ GF items indicated on menu. Options include omelet, frittata, chilled puree of corn soup, organic field greens, strawberry and goat cheese terrine, grilled salmon, pan seared long island sea scallops, cabernet braised short ribs, ginger-honey glazed long island duck breast, pan roasted all natural frenched chicken breast. Dessert includes a molten chocolate cake, mango crème brûlée, trio of sorbet and a trio of gelato. ▪ *www.thefifth-season.com*

## Frantoni's Pizzeria & Ristorante    ★$$LD
*East Meadow* ▪ *(516) 794-7878*
*1928 Hempstead Tpke*
*Williston Park* ▪ *(516) 747-3413*
*66 Hillside Ave* ▪ *Italian* ▪ GF pizza is available with any toppings. Both locations report that they have a variety of GF items on the in-house menu. Alert a server, who will go over the options. ▪ *www.frantonis.com*

## Gaudino's Brooklyn Pizza    ✪★$LD
*Ronkonkoma* ▪ *(631) 736-3957*
*1021 Portion Rd* ▪ *Pizza* ▪ GF 8" or 10" pizza is available. ▪ *gaudinospizza.com*

## Ghenet Brooklyn ★ $$D
*Brooklyn* ▪ *(718) 230-4475*
*348 Douglass St* ▪ *Ethiopian* ▪ All dishes
on the menu are GF. The restaurant can
make GF injera bread but you must call a
day in advance. ▪ *www.ghenet.com*

## Gianni Mazia's on Main ★ $LD
*Clarence* ▪ *(716) 759-2803*
*10325 Main St* ▪ *Italian* ▪ GF pizza and
chicken wings are available. Restaurant
reports that they use a separate fryer for GF
chicken wings. ▪ *giannimazias.com*

## Ginger Man $$$LD
*Albany* ▪ *(518) 427-5963*
*234 Western Ave* ▪ *Italian* ▪ The restaurant
reports that GF options include fruit &
cheese platter, mussels, tuna tartare, a variety of salads, strip steak, red snapper, tuna,
duck meatloaf and a vegetable tower. Confirm the timeliness of this information before dining in. ▪ *www.albanygingerman.com*

## Gino's Pizza ★ $$LD
*Flushing* ▪ *(718) 886-3411*
*2519 Parsons Blvd*
*Great Neck* ▪ *(516) 487-1122*
*60 Middle Neck Rd* ▪ *Pizza* ▪ GF
pizza is available in 12" size. ▪
*ginospizzaflushing.com*

## Golden Duck Restaurant ★ $LD
*Williamsville* ▪ *(716) 639-8888*
*1840 Maple Rd* ▪ *Chinese* ▪ GF soy sauce
is available. The restaurant notes that most
items can be made GF, with the exception
of appetizers, soups, and items coated in
flour. Alert a server, who will go over the
options. ▪ *www.goldenduckrestaurant.com*

## Golden Phoenix ✪★ $LD
*Fairport* ▪ *(585) 223-4539*
*7323 Pittsford-Palmyra Rd* ▪ *Asian* ▪
Extensive GF menu features chicken,
beef, shrimp, and eggplant curries, noodle
soups, fried rice, and more. GF soy sauce is
available. ▪ *www.goldenphoenixchinese.com*

## Gourmet Café $$LD
*Glens Falls* ▪ *(518) 761-0864*
*185 Glen St* ▪ *Deli* ▪ Restaurant reports
that GF diners are served quite frequently.
Any item on the menu can be made GF. ▪
*www.downtowngourmet.com*

## Ground Round ✪📖
*Brookhaven* ▪ *(631) 286-1512*
*2647 Montauk Hwy*
*Johnson City* ▪ *(607) 231-2020*
*214 Reynolds Rd*
*Plattsburgh* ▪ *(518) 561-2897*
*32 Smithfield Blvd*

## Halstead Avenue Bistro ★ $$LD
*Harrison* ▪ *(914) 777-1181*
*123 Halstead Ave* ▪ *American* ▪ GF items
are marked on the menu and include
forest mushroom soup, sesame seared
salmon filet, French-cut chicken breast,
grilled shrimp and seared sea scallops
risotto, and more. Confirm the timeliness
of this information before dining in. ▪
*www.halsteadbistro.com*

## Hampton Chutney Co. $LD
*Amagansett* ▪ *(631) 267-3131*
*6 Main St* ▪ *Indian* ▪ The restaurant reports
that all of the dosas - savory South Indian
pancakes made from rice and black lentils
- are GF. She also reports that the uttapams
- like dosas, but thicker - are GF. Fillings
can be chosen a la carte or from the many
combinations suggested on the menu. Dosas can also be substituted for bread in the
thali special. ▪ *www.hamptonchutney.com*

## Hard Rock Café ✪📖
*Bronx* ▪ *(646) 977-8888*
*1 E 161st St*

## Il Barilotto ★ $$$LD
*Fishkill* ▪ *(845) 897-4300*
*1113 Main St* ▪ *Italian* ▪ GF pasta is available. The restaurant notes that many
entrées are also GF or can easily be
made GF. Alert a server upon arrival,
and they will go over the GF options. ▪
*www.ilbarilottorestaurant.com*

## Il Capuccino　✪★$$$D
*Sag Harbor* ▪ *(631) 725-2747*
*30 Madison St* ▪ *Italian* ▪ GF pasta is available. GF menu includes calamari fra diavolo, steamed mussels, veal scaloppini piccata, grilled chicken parmagiana, shrimp fra diavolo, grilled salmon over greens, grilled chicken breast over greens, sautéed spinach in garlic & olive oil, and more. GF sorbet or gelato is available for dessert. ▪ *www.ilcapuccino.com*

## Ilio Dipaolo's Restaurant　✪★$$LD
*Blasdell* ▪ *(716) 825-3675*
*3785 S Park Ave* ▪ *Italian* ▪ GF menu includes sautéed scallops, chicken cacciatore, pork chops, and more. The "Friday Only" special is baked haddock in a white wine, lemon, and basil sauce. GF pasta and pizza are available, and sorbet or GF gelato are available for dessert. ▪ *www.iliodipaolos.com*

## Jackson Hall
## American Bar & Grille　✪★$$$LD
*East Islip* ▪ *(631) 277-7100*
*335 E Main St* ▪ *American* ▪ Limited GF menu but manager Jackie reports they are happy to modify any dish to be GF if possible. Alert the server upon arrival and ask to speak to a manager, who can assist in making a selection. ▪ *www.jacksonhallbarandgrille.com*

## Joan's GF Great Bakes　¢S
*Freeport* ▪ *(516) 804-5600*
*90 E Merrick Rd* ▪ *Bakery* ▪ Dedicated GF bakery offering pizza, bagels, corn bread, english muffins, rolls, and cookies. Owner Joan reports that many GF customers frequent the bakery. She also notes that menu items are frozen and available to take home. ▪ *www.gfgreatbakes.com*

## Joe and Pat's
## Pizzeria and Restaurant　✪★$$LD
*Staten Island* ▪ *(718) 981-0887*
*1758 Victory Blvd* ▪ *Pizza* ▪ GF pizza available. ▪ *joeandpatspizzany.com*

## Joe Willys Fish Shack　✪★$$$LD
*Fishkill* ▪ *(845) 765-0234*
*10 Old Route 9 W* ▪ *Seafood* ▪ GF menu available. Items on the regular menu can be modified to be GF as well EXCEPT for the crab cakes and stuffed clams. Alert a server upon arrival and they will inform the chef. ▪ *www.joewillysfishshack.com*

## Joe's Crab Shack　✪📖
*Henrietta* ▪ *(585) 272-9204*
*100 Marketplace Dr*
*Oceanside* ▪ *(516) 255-3705*
*3555 Long Beach Rd*
*Amherst* ▪ *(716) 836-4739*
*4125 Maple Rd*
*Latham* ▪ *(518) 785-0472*
*579 Troy Schenectady Rd #80*

## Joe's Pasta Garage　★$$LD
*Skaneateles* ▪ *(315) 685-6116*
*28 Jordan St* ▪ *Italian* ▪ GF pizza is available. ▪ *www.joespastagarage.com*

## Joey B's Restaurant　$$$D
*Fairport* ▪ *(585) 377-9030*
*400 Packetts Lndg* ▪ *American* ▪ GF diners can be accommodated. Any entrée on the menu can be made GF. Be sure to alert server upon arrival. ▪ *www.joeybsrestaurant.com*

## John Harvard's Brew House　$$LD
*Lake Grove* ▪ *(631) 979-2739*
*2093 Smithaven Plz*
*Ellicottville* ▪ *(617) 868-3585*
*6621 Holiday Valley Rd* ▪ *American* ▪ Manager Eric reports that the restaurant serves GF diners "sometimes." He notes that most salads can be made GF, but cautions that dressings are not made on site and may contain gluten. He also recommends ordering chicken or steak dishes without seasoning, as the seasoning is not GF. Confirm the timeliness of this information before dining in. ▪ *www.johnharvards.com*

## Karma Road　¢BLD
*New Paltz* ▪ *(845) 255-1099*
*11 Main St* ▪ *Vegetarian* ▪ The restaurant reports that most of the rotating menu is

GF and that servers are trained to help guide guests with "food sensitivities" to appropriate dishes. ▪ www.karmaroad.net

### Kilpatrick's Publick House          $$LD
*Ithaca* ▪ (607) 273-2632
*130 E Seneca St* ▪ *Irish* ▪ GF options include sandwiches and burgers without the buns. Alert the server upon arrival. ▪ www.kilpatrickspub.com

### La Bottega                          ★$$LD
*Huntington* ▪ (631) 271-3540
*9 Wall St* ▪ *Italian* ▪ GF pasta is available, as well as GF bread for paninis. The restaurant also reports that many of their entrées can be prepared GF. Alert the server upon arrival. ▪ labottegaofhuntington.com

### La Capannina Pizza               ✪★$$LD
*Holtsville* ▪ (631) 569-4524
*173 Morris Ave* ▪ *Pizza* ▪ GF pizza is available in the 12-inch size. GF pasta and beer are also available. The GF menu lists several other entrées and desserts as well. Only the listed location has GF items. ▪ www.lacapanninapizza.com

### La Fontanella                     ★$$$LD
*Tappan* ▪ (845) 398-3400
*52-54 Rt 303* ▪ *Italian* ▪ Most items on the menu can be made GF. GF items include GF pasta, pork chops, grilled chicken and a variety of steaks. Alert a server upon arrival and they will be more then happy to list items on the menu that can be made GF. ▪ www.lafontanella.webs.com

### La Pizzeria                        ★$$LD
*Great Neck* ▪ (516) 466-5114
*114 Middle Neck Rd* ▪ *Pizza* ▪ GF spaghetti including marinara, bolognese and a sausage red sauce. ▪ www.lapizzeriany.com

### La Tee Da                          ✪★$$D
*Buffalo* ▪ (716) 881-4500
*206 Allen St* ▪ *Italian* ▪ GF items indicated on menu. Items include spinach balls, hot banana peppers, fresh mussels, cauliflower croquettes, poached pear salad, autumn apple salad, ahi tuna and the New York

strip steak. GF pasta is available. Confirm the timeliness of this information before dining in. ▪ www.lateedacafe.net

### Legal Sea Foods                     ✪📖
*Garden City* ▪ (516) 248-4600
*630 Old Country Rd*
*Huntington Station* ▪ (631) 271-9777
*160 Walt Whitman Rd*
*White Plains* ▪ (914) 390-9600
*5 Mamaroneck Ave*

### Little Bake Shop, The               ★$$
*Valley Cottage* ▪ (845) 268-5511
*491 Kings Hwy* ▪ *Bakery* ▪ GF menu available. Items include New York style cheesecake available in 7" and 8", 8" pies including apple, apple-cranberry, seasonal fruit, pecan and fruit tart, GF breads including sandwich, focaccia, dinner rolls, dog, burger buns, scones, GF cakes in 7" and 8" sizes including chocolate, vanilla, strawberry shortcake, carrot, chocolate mousse and cappuccino mousse.

### Little Hen Specialties                 $$
*Binghamton* ▪ (607) 761-8561
*1217 Vestal Ave* ▪ *Bakery* ▪ GF dedicated bakery. Includes GF yeasted breads with daily specialty recipes, quick breads such as muffins and personal loafs, cookies, brownies, cannoli shells and cones, pies, cakes and cheesecake. GF cakes are customizable. Fresh handmade GF pasta can be made to order, call in advance. ▪ www.littlehenspecialties.com

### Lost Dog Café, The                 ✪★$$LD
*Binghamton* ▪ (607) 771-6063
*222 Water St* ▪ *American* ▪ GF items and options available on lunch and dinner menu. Items include spinach and artichoke dip, avocado goat cheese dip, mashed sweet potatoes, baby baked potato, sautéed mixed vegetables, Cajun beans and greens, key lime salmon, pineapple red curry, chicken chana masala and New York strip steak. Items are prepared and cooked separately in the kitchen. ▪ www.lostdogcafe.net

## Mama's Italian Restaurant  ✪★$$LD
*Oakdale* ▪ *(631) 567-0909*
*1352 Montauk Hwy* ▪ *Italian* ▪ Extensive
GF menu includes appetizers, soups, salads, and a kids' menu. GF pasta is available
and can be served with a wide variety of
sauces. Mini GF pizzas are also available.
Examples of GF entrées are veal piccata,
chicken marsala, and flounder parmigiana.
They also have GF specials, which change
weekly. ▪ *www.mamas-restaurant.com*

## Mangia Restaurant  ★$$LD
*Slingerlands* ▪ *(518) 439-5555*
*1562 New Scotland Rd* ▪ *Italian* ▪ GF
pasta is available. The restaurant notes
that most salads and some entrées, such
as chicken piccata and chicken marsala, can be prepared GF as well. Alert
a server, who will go over the options. ▪
*www.mangiarestaurant.com*

## Mangia Ristorante & Caffe  ★$$$LD
*Orchard Park* ▪ *(716) 662-9467*
*4264 N Buffalo Rd* ▪ *Italian* ▪ GF pasta can
be substituted in any pasta dish. Restaurant
cooks GF pasta separate from the regular
pasta. ▪ *www.mangiaristorante.com*

## Maria's Mexican Restaurant  $LD
*Webster* ▪ *(585) 872-1237*
*75 W Main St* ▪ *Mexican* ▪ GF options available on menu. Flour tortillas
and the white sauce are the two things
that cannot be made GF. Alert a server
upon arrival and they will list options. ▪
*www.mariasmexican.com*

## Maud's Tavern  ✪★$$LD
*Hastings-On-Hudson* ▪ *(914) 478-2326*
*149 Southside Ave* ▪ *Modern American*
▪ GF menu available. Items include soup
of the day, grilled portabello mushrooms,
smoked salmon, shrimp cocktail, roasted
half chicken, grilled black angus steak,
sautéed chicken breast, fish of the day
with GF sauce, rice and corn fusilli, grilled
marinated loin lamb chop, hamburger no
bun, sautéed shrimp, grilled salmon, grilled
chicken and chili. ▪ *www.maudstavern.com*

## Maxie's
## Supper Club and Oyster Bar  $$D
*Ithaca* ▪ *(607) 272-4136*
*635 W State St* ▪ *Modern American* ▪
The restaurant reports that many menu
items are GF or can easily be made GF. A
GF list is available in-house that denotes
all of these options, which include a
variety of salads, grilled shrimp skewers,
jambalaya, blackened catfish, sweet
potato fries, and more. Alert a server
upon arrival and they will go over the GF
list. ▪ *www.maxies.com*

## McKenzie's Bar & Grill  $$LD
*Hamburg* ▪ *(716) 627-9752*
*4151 Lake Shore Rd* ▪ *Modern*
*American* ▪ GF diners are common
in restaurant. Some GF items include
boiled fish, boiled chicken, brown rice,
broiled chicken and broiled scallops. ▪
*www.mckenziesbarandgrill.com*

## Melting Pot, The  ✪📖
*Albany* ▪ *(518) 862-1292*
*1 Crossgates Mall Rd*
*Farmingdale* ▪ *(631) 752-4242*
*2377 Broadhollow Rd*
*White Plains* ▪ *(914) 993-6358*
*30 Mamaroneck Ave*
*Buffalo* ▪ *(716) 685-6358*
*1 Walden Galleria*

## Merge  ✪★$$LD
*Buffalo* ▪ *(716) 842-0600*
*439 Delaware Ave* ▪ *American* ▪ GF items
are marked on the menu and include summer corn chowder, shrimp risotto, curried
quinoa bowl, coq au vin, and much more.
GF pasta is available. There is a $0.50 up
charge for GF options. Alert a server upon
arrival. ▪ *mergebuffalo.com*

## Mexican Radio  $LD
*Hudson* ▪ *(518) 828-7770*
*537 Warren St* ▪ *Mexican* ▪ The restaurant
reports that the majority of the items on
their menu can be modified to be GF. Alert
the server upon arrival. ▪ *www.mexrad.com*

### Miller's Ale House Restaurants ✪★📖
*Deer Park* ▪ **(631) 667-0228**
*1800 The Arches Cir*
*Levittown* ▪ **(516) 520-7000**
*3046 Hempstead Tpke*

### Moosewood Restaurant ✪★$$LD
*Ithaca* ▪ **(607) 273-9610**
*215 N Cayuga St* ▪ *Global* ▪ The menu changes every day, but the restaurant reports that they will always have GF options available. Sample menu items include roasted ratatouille and stuffed portobello mushroom. GF diners should alert a server and ask the server to communicate with the cooks. ▪ *www.moosewoodrestaurant.com*

### Morton's Steakhouse ✪📖
*Great Neck* ▪ **(516) 498-2950**
*777 Northern Blvd*

### Mr. Miceli
### Pizzeria & Italian Restaurant ★$$LD
*Rockville Centre* ▪ **(516) 764-7701**
*19 N Park Ave* ▪ *Italian* ▪ GF pasta, pizza, and several appetizers are available. Almost all the entrées can be made GF upon request. Owner Luca reports that he is GF, so his restaurant is dedicated to serving GF diners. ▪ *www.mrmiceli.com*

### Mr. P's Mountain Smokehouse ★$$LD
*Schroon Lake* ▪ **(518) 532-4300**
*1106 US Route 9* ▪ *Barbeque* ▪ All starters, sides, salads, meats, and desserts are GF. Additionally, GF sandwich rolls are always available, just be sure to specify GF when placing your order. The restaurant reports that they are "always happy to accommodate food allergies or sensitivities." ▪ *www.mrpsmountainsmokehouse.com*

### My Dad's Cookies $$$
*Nanuet* ▪ **(917) 653-0580**
*119 Rockland Ctr* ▪ *Bakery* ▪ Dedicated GF bakery offering brownies, cakes and cookies. Orders must be placed online only. ▪ *www.mydadscookies.com*

### New World Home Cooking ✪★$$D
*Saugerties* ▪ **(845) 246-0900**
*1411 Rt 212* ▪ *Bistro* ▪ GF menu includes a wide variety of appetizers, entrées, salads, burgers, and sides. GF pasta and sandwich buns are also available. The restaurant recommends alerting your server of any dietary restrictions upon arrival. Be sure to note that you are ordering from the GF menu, as some items require modification to become GF. ▪ *www.ricorlando.com*

### Ninety Nine ✪📖
*New Hartford* ▪ **(315) 736-9699**
*8675 Clinton St*
*Rotterdam* ▪ **(518) 374-7799**
*93 W Campbell Rd*
*Guilderland* ▪ **(518) 452-1999**
*1470 Western Ave*
*Colonie* ▪ **(518) 446-9909**
*107 Wolf Rd*
*Clifton Park* ▪ **(518) 348-1499**
*306 Clifton Park Center Rd*
*Kingston* ▪ **(845) 336-4399**
*53 Massa Dr*
*Plattsburgh* ▪ **(518) 798-0699**
*446 Route 3*
*Queensbury* ▪ **(518) 798-0699**
*578 Aviation Rd*
*Saratoga Springs* ▪ **(518) 584-9906**
*3073 Rte 50*

### Nirchi's Pizza ★₵LD
*Vestal* ▪ **(607) 729-5131**
*Vestal Parkway E*
*Conklin* ▪ **(607) 775-3822**
*1023 Conklin Rd*
*Binghamton* ▪ **(607) 723-8474**
*166 Water St*
*Binghamton* ▪ **(607) 722-6331**
*954 Upper Front St*
*Binghamton* ▪ **(607) 231-6561**
*219 Main St*
*Binghamton* ▪ **(607) 722-8756**
*907 Front St*
*Endicott* ▪ **(607) 786-9978**
*701 Taft Ave* ▪ *Pizza* ▪ GF personal pizza available. ▪ *www.nirchis.com*

## Noodle Pudding ★ $$D
*Brooklyn* ▪ *(718) 625-3737*
*38 Henry St* ▪ *Italian* ▪ GF penne pasta is available. Any item on the menu can be prepared GF. Alert server upon arrival.

## North Shore Grill ✪ $$LD
*Lakeville* ▪ *(585) 346-2200*
*5870 Big Tree Rd* ▪ *Seafood & Steakhouse* ▪ GF items are marked on the menu and include the hummus plate, appolo chili, grilled chicken caprese salad, steamed shellfish, surf & turf, and more. GF seasonings are noted on the menu and can be used for any grilled fish entrée. Alert a server upon arrival. ▪ *www.northshoregrillny.com*

## Nunzio's Pizza and Deli ★ $LD
*Saratoga Springs* ▪ *(518) 584-3840*
*119 Clinton St* ▪ *Pizza* ▪ GF 12" pizza available.

## Olives Greek Taverna ★ $LD
*Pittsford* ▪ *(585) 381-3990*
*50 State St* ▪ *Greek* ▪ The restaurant reports that they can easily make many menu items GF. Gyros can be served over greens instead of pita bread, and most of the souvlaki platters can be made GF as well. Various daily specials can also be prepared GF. Ask a server to go over the options when dining in. ▪ *www.olivespittsford.com*

## P.F. Chang's China Bistro ✪ ★ 📖
*Albany* ▪ *(518) 454-0040*
*131 Colonie Ctr Spc 305*
*Buffalo* ▪ *(716) 706-0791*
*1 Galleria Dr # Th131*
*Victor* ▪ *(585) 223-2410*
*820 Eastview Mall*
*Westbury* ▪ *(516) 222-9200*
*1504 Old Country Rd # B9A*
*White Plains* ▪ *(914) 997-6100*
*125 Westchester Ave Spc D315*

## P.S. Restaurant & Luxury Lounge ★ $$$D
*Vestal* ▪ *(607) 770-0056*
*100 Rano Blvd Suite 8* ▪ *Global* ▪ The chefs prepare all the dishes and sauces on site. If the chefs are informed ahead of time, any sauce and various menu items can be made GF. ▪ *www.psrestaurant.com*

## Pappardelle's ✪ ★
*Bethpage* ▪ *(516) 433-2463*
*554 Stewart Ave* ▪ *Pizza* ▪ GF 12" pizza and pasta available. Pizzas are prepared, cooked, and served using dedicated equipment. ▪ *www.pappardelles.com*

## Phuket Thai Cuisine ✪ $LD
*Webster* ▪ *(585) 671-8410*
*2014 Empire Blvd* ▪ *Thai* ▪ GF menu includes satay, grilled calamari salad, several curries, pad thai, and more. Owner Sim recommends alerting her upon arrival, so she can alert the chef and ensure the meal is prepared properly.

## Pizza 2000 ★ $LD
*Harrison* ▪ *(914) 835-8000*
*337 Halstead Ave* ▪ *Pizza* ▪ GF pizza is available in 9"and 12" sizes. GF pasta is also available. Meals are available for dining in, taking out, and delivery. ▪ *www.pizza2000.net*

## Pizza Bistro ✪ ★ $LD
*Massapequa Park* ▪ *(516) 797-4747*
*4952 Merrick Rd* ▪ *Italian* ▪ GF menu includes a variety of appetizers and salads, chicken parmigiana, eggplant rollatini, shrimp fra diavolo, grilled chicken, and more. A variety of pizza, pasta, and hero sandwich options can be made using GF alternatives. Examples include the meatball hero, the chicken & tomato pizza, and the penne ala vodka. The restaurant also offers nationwide delivery of their GF products and GF catering. ▪ *www.pizzabistrony.com*

## Pizza Gourmet ✪ ★ $LD
*Mamaroneck* ▪ *(914) 777-1056*
*597 E Boston Post Rd* ▪ *Pizza* ▪ GF pizza is available in the personal size, with any toppings. ▪ *www.pizzagourmetonline.com*

## Pizza Pizzazz ✪ ★ $$LD
*Shrub Oak* ▪ *(914) 245-6400*
*966 E Main St* ▪ *Pizza* ▪ GF 12" pizza is available. ▪ *www.cafepizzapizzazz.com*

## Pizza Plant Restaurant ✪★$D
*Williamsville* ▪ (716) 632-0800
*7770 Transit Rd*
*Williamsville* ▪ (716) 626-5566
*5110 Main St* ▪ *Pizza* ▪ GF menu available. Items include nachos, spinach and artichoke dip, chicken fingers, salads, medium pizza, lasagna, pasta, black angus burger, turkey burger and GF beer. ▪ *www.pizzaplant.com*

## Plum Tomatoes Pizzeria & Restaurant ★$LD
*Mineola* ▪ (516) 248-6390
*230-228 Old Country Rd*
*Belle Harbor* ▪ (718) 474-1775
*420 Beach 129th St* ▪ *Pizza* ▪ GF 14" inch pizza and pastas available. ▪ *www.plumtomatoespizzarest.com*

## Prince Umberto's Pizza ✪★$$LD
*Franklin Square* ▪ (516) 872-9049
*721 Franklin Ave* ▪ *Pizza* ▪ GF pasta and pizza (9" or 13") are available. ▪ *www.princeumberto.com*

## Ravenous $LD
*Saratoga Springs* ▪ (518) 581-0560
*21 Phila St* ▪ *French* ▪ GF crepes are now available for the savory crepe selections. The only two savory crepes that are not GF are the St. Tropez crepe and the Chicken Bechamel. Confirm the timeliness of this information before dining in. ▪ *www.ravenouscrepes.com*

## Red Bar & Restaurant ★$$$$LD
*Huntington* ▪ (631) 673-0304
*417 New York Ave* ▪ *Modern American* ▪ Reservations noting GF are recommended. GF menu options include sea scallops, shrimp, salmon, Tuscan chicken, steak, salads, fresh mozzarella, curried mussels, crab and avocado and carpaccio. Most items on menu are made with rice flour however the pasta and tuna cannot be made GF. ▪ *www.redrestaurantli.com*

## Red Mill Inn ★$$LD
*Williamsville* ▪ (716) 633-7878
*8326 Main St* ▪ *American* ▪ GF pasta, steak, most seafood dishes, as well as other various items on the menu can be prepared GF. Be sure to alert the server and they will supply a list of items that are or can be prepared GF. ▪ *www.redmillinn.com*

## Reel Seafood Co. ✪$$LD
*Albany* ▪ (518) 458-2068
*195 Wolf Rd* ▪ *Seafood* ▪ GF selections available. Includes fresh oysters, cherrystone clams, clams aliki, escargot, sea stew, Maine sea scallops, Tuscan salmon, blackened mahi, Lobster tail, Alaskan king crab legs, baked Maine lobster and aged New York strip steak. GF items prepared separately in kitchen. ▪ *www.reelseafoodco.com*

## Rocco's Pizzeria ★$$LD
*Mahopac* ▪ (845) 621-1215
*559 Route 6N* ▪ *Pizza* ▪ GF pizza is available. ▪ *www.mahopacrestaurants.com/roccos/*

## Rock Da Pasta ✪★$LD
*New Paltz* ▪ (845) 255-1144
*62 Main St* ▪ *Italian* ▪ GF bread, brown rice pasta, pizza, and beer are available. In addition to these options, the restaurant reports that 85% of the menu can be made GF. The dessert menu includes GF "alternatives" for most items, including apple crumble and brownies. Confirm the timeliness of this information before dining in. ▪ *www.rockdapasta.com*

## Roma Ristorante & Pizzeria ✪★$LD
*Sidney* ▪ (607) 563-8888
*25 Union St* ▪ *Italian* ▪ GF 12" pizza available. All toppings available except meatball and eggplant. ▪ *www.romaristorantepizzeria.com*

## Romano's Macaroni Grill ✪★📖
*Albany* ▪ (518) 446-9190
*1 Metro Oark Rd*

## Ruth's Chris Steak House ✪📖
*Garden City* ▪ (516) 222-0220
*600 Old Country Rd*
*Tarrytown* ▪ (914) 631-3311
*670 White Plains Rd*

### Santa Fe Restaurant ★ $D
*Tivoli* ▪ *(845) 757-4100*
*52 Broadway* ▪ *Mexican* ▪ Items that
can be prepared GF are indicated on the
menu. Alert a server and they will be
sure to inform the chef of request. Items
include quesadillas, dinner salad, pulled
pork tacos, spicy smoked sausage grilled
tacos, enchiladas, ribeye, pork tenderloin,
fish tacos, fire roasted poblano chiles,
roasted sweet potato tacos and chipotle ginger marinated steak skewers. ▪
*www.santafetivoli.com*

### Satelite Pizza ★ $$LD
*Bayport* ▪ *(631) 472-3800*
*799 Montauk Hwy* ▪ *Pizza* ▪ GF 12" pizza
is available. ▪ *www.satelitepizza.com*

### Scarsdale Pizza Station ✪★ $$LD
*Scarsdale* ▪ *(914) 723-4700*
*844 Scarsdale Ave* ▪ *Pizza* ▪ Mat-
teo's Special GF 12" Pizza is available. ▪
*www.scarsdalepizzastation.com*

### Season's Restaurant ✪ $$$LD
*Somers* ▪ *(914) 276-0600*
*289 Route 100* ▪ *Modern American* ▪ GF
menu includes skewered chicken sate,
bruschetta topped artichokes, New Zealand
mussels, grilled filet mignon, ribeye steak,
baked lemon salmon, pan seared sea bass
with a mango salsa, stuffed pork chop,
honey lime chicken and stuffed chicken. ▪
*www.seasonsatsomers.com*

### Shane's Rib Shack ✪📖
*Clifton Park* ▪ *(518) 615-0555*
*7 Southside Dr*

### Sherry Lynn's Gluten Free Bakery & Café $BLD
*Latham* ▪ *(518) 786-7700*
*836 Troy Schenectady Rd* ▪ *Café* ▪
Family-run, dedicated GF café offering a
wide variety of items, including French
toast, pizza, pasta, sandwiches, and baked
goods. Featured desserts include cherry
cheesecake with a graham cracker crust
and hot apple pie. There are extensive,
separate menus for breakfast and

sandwiches, as well as one for appetizers,
pizza, and pasta. There is also a kids' GF
menu. The bakery & café periodically
hosts all-you-can-eat GF buffets. ▪
*www.sherrylynnsglutenfree.net*

### Shogun Hibachi Steak & Seafood ★ $D
*Williamsville* ▪ *(716) 631-8899*
*7590 Transit Rd* ▪ *Japanese* ▪ All items on
the menu can be made GF. Alert a server
upon arrival for a list of items that are
naturally GF and the items that need to be
modified to be GF. ▪ *www.ichi-shogun.com*

### Simply Crepes Café ★ ¢BLD
*Pittsford* ▪ *(585) 383-8310*
*7 Schoen Pl*
*Canandaigua* ▪ *(585) 394-9090*
*101 S Main St* ▪ *French* ▪ GF buckwheat
crepes are available. Owner Pierre reports
that all staff members are GF aware, and
they can ensure a GF meal. He adds that
"approximately 70%" of the menu can be
prepared GF. Alert the server upon arrival
and they will specify which crepes can be
prepared GF. ▪ *www.simplycrepes.com*

### Smokey Bones 📖
*Cheektowaga* ▪ *(716) 683-0724*
*2007 Walden Ave*
*Syracuse* ▪ *(315) 652-7824*
*4036 State Route 31*
*Colonie* ▪ *(518) 464-9971*
*1557 Central Ave*
*Ronkonkoma* ▪ *(631) 580-2675*
*5012 Express Dr S*

### Soul Dog ★ ¢LD
*Poughkeepsie* ▪ *(845) 454-3254*
*107 Main St* ▪ *American* ▪ GF menu options available. Items include cookies, bars,
cupcakes, muffins, cakes, pies, bagels, sandwich loafs, jalapeno hush puppies, baked
mac and cheese, chicken fingers, fish and
chips, pizza and chicken pot pie.

### Spice of India Restaurant & Bar $$LD
*Nyack* ▪ *(845) 353-3663*
*125 Main St* ▪ *Indian* ▪ Restaurant reports
that the majority of the menu is GF, including tikka masala, korma, tandoori chicken,

and more. Confirm the timeliness of this information before dining in. Restaurant recommends alerting a server, who will guide GF diners through the menu. ▪ *www.spiceofindianyack.com*

### Stir Crazy                                    ★📖
*West Nyack* ▪ *(845) 727-2002*
*4422 Palisades Ctr Dr*

### Sun in Bloom                                  ¢BLD
*Brooklyn* ▪ *(718) 622-4303*
*460 Bergen St* ▪ *Bakery* ▪ Everything in the store is GF, dairy free, and egg free. Items on the menu include spring rolls, apple pie pancakes, tarts, and cheesecakes. A lot of options and special items baked daily. ▪ *suninbloom.wordpress.com*

### Sweet Karma Desserts              ✪★$$$$$
*East Meadow* ▪ *(516) 794-4478*
*550 E Meadow Ave* ▪ *Bakery* ▪ Non-dedicated bakery offering GF pastries, cookies, cupcakes, and cakes. Cookies are available in different flavors each day, and cakes can be ordered in advance. GF pizza crusts are also available. As with all specialty items, call ahead to confirm availability. ▪ *www.sweetkarmadesserts.com*

### Symeon's Greek Restaurant           ★$$LD
*Yorkville* ▪ *(315) 736-4074*
*4941 Commercial Dr* ▪ *Greek* ▪ Extensive GF options include dips, a gyro platter, a mixed grill, lamb chops, chicken florentine, strip steak, Greek chicken, lemon rosemary chicken, and more. ▪ *www.symeons.com*

### T & J Pizza and Pasta                    ★$LD
*Port Chester* ▪ *(914) 939-4134*
*227 Westchester Ave* ▪ *Pizza* ▪ GF pizza is available in the 12-inch size. GF pizza is served in the pizzeria only. T & J Villaggio Trattoria, which is located next door, does not serve GF items. ▪ *www.tandjs.net*

### Tantalus Restaurant / Bar / Café  ★$$LD
*East Aurora* ▪ *(716) 652-0341*
*634 Main St* ▪ *Global* ▪ The restaurant reports that many items on the menu can be prepared GF, such as seafood entrées,

meat entrées, pastas and salads. Confirm the timeliness of this information before dining in. Alert the staff on arrival. ▪ *www.tantaluseastaurora.com*

### Texas De Brazil Churrascaria        ★📖
*Yonkers* ▪ *(914) 652-9600*
*1 Ridge Hill Blvd*

### Three Dogs Gluten-Free Bakery        $$
*Briarcliff Manor* ▪ *(914) 762-2121*
*510 N State Rd* ▪ *Bakery* ▪ Dedicated GF bakery offering a wide variety of GF baked goods. Some items, like bread, muffins, scones, and cookies, are available every day, while others can be requested by calling ahead. Gluten is not allowed on the premises. ▪ *www.threedogsgfbakery.com*

### Tony Roma's                               📖
*Bayside* ▪ *(718) 224-8669*
*210-35 26th Ave*
*West Nyack* ▪ *(845) 353-8669*
*4304 Palisades Center Dr*

### Turiello's Pizza House & Restaurant
✪★$$LD
*Nyack* ▪ *(845) 358-5440*
*76 Main St* ▪ *Pizza* ▪ Regular Cheese, Arugula and Margherita pizzas are available GF, 12" size only. ▪ *www.turiellospizza.com*

### Uno Chicago Grill                     ✪★📖
*Albany* ▪ *(518) 869-3100*
*120 Washington Ave Ext*
*Bayside* ▪ *(718) 279-4900*
*3902 Bell Blvd*
*Bronx* ▪ *(718) 824-8667*
*71 Metropolitan Oval*
*Brooklyn* ▪ *(718) 748-8667*
*9201 4th Ave*
*Central Valley* ▪ *(845) 783-6560*
*20 Centre Dr*
*Fayetteville* ▪ *(315) 637-8667*
*520 Towne Dr*
*Forest Hills* ▪ *(718) 793-6700*
*10716 70th Rd*
*Latham* ▪ *(518) 782-7166*
*601 Troy Schenectady Rd*
*Liverpool* ▪ *(315) 622-0718*
*3974 State Route 31*

**Long Island City** ▪ *(718) 706-8800*
*3711 35th Ave*
**New Hartford** ▪ *(315) 736-8323*
*8645 Clinton St*
**Queensbury** ▪ *(518) 792-5399*
*880 State Route 9*
**Syracuse** ▪ *(315) 466-8667*
*9558 Carousel Ctr*
**Vestal** ▪ *(607) 770-7000*
*2503 Vestal Pkwy*
**Victor** ▪ *(585) 223-6100*
*7724 Victor Pittsford Rd*
**Plattsburgh** ▪ *(518) 561-7689*
*578 State Route 3*
**Webster** ▪ *(585) 872-4760*
*931 Holt Rd*
**White Plains** ▪ *(914) 684-7040*
*14 Martine Ave*
**Yonkers** ▪ *(914) 779-7515*
*2650 Central Park Ave*
**Saratoga Springs** ▪ *(518) 587-4270*
*3008 Route 50*
**Poughkeepsie** ▪ *(845) 452-4930*
*842A Main St*
**Henrietta** ▪ *(585) 272-8667*
*1000 Hylan Dr*

## Via Pizza                              ★ $$ LD
**East Setauket** ▪ *(631) 689-9540*
*205 Route 25 A* ▪ *Pizza* ▪ GF 12" pizza is
available.

## Victor's Pizza Restaurant             ★ $$ LD
**New City** ▪ *(845) 639-0454*
*68 N Main St* ▪ *Pizza* ▪ GF personal pizza
available.

## Villa Italian Specialties        ✪ ★ $ BLD
**East Hampton** ▪ *(631) 324-5110*
*7 Railroad Ave* ▪ *Italian* ▪ 12"
GF personal pizza available. ▪
*www.villaitalianspecialties.com*

## Villa Milano                           ★ $$ LD
**Manhasset** ▪ *(516) 365-3440*
*168 Plandome Rd* ▪ *Italian* ▪ GF 12" pizza
available. Most toppings are GF as well. Be
sure to stay away from the meats because
they are prepared with flour.

## Villa Monte Pizzeria                   ★ $$ LD
**Staten Island** ▪ *(718) 668-0490*
*170 New Dorp Ln* ▪ *Pizza* ▪ GF rigatoni available at location listed only. ▪
*www.villamontepizza.com*

## Village Pizzeria & Ristorante, The
★ $$ LD
**Middle Grove** ▪ *(518) 882-9431*
*2727 Route 29* ▪ *Italian* ▪ The Village offers
GF pasta with over ten sauce options avail-
able in addition to a 12" GF pizza crust. ▪
*www.villagepizzeria.com*

## Vin-Chet Pastry Shop                    ✪ ¢S
**Amherst** ▪ *(716) 839-0871*
*2178 Kensington Ave* ▪ *Bakery* ▪ Bakery
recognized by the Celiac Sprue Associa-
tion. GF items available Tuesday through
Saturdays. Items include cherry and apple
fruit rings, almond rings, sour cream cof-
fee cake, muffins, bread crumbs, signature
GF flour blend, breads, rolls, 12" pizza
crust, cookies, cakes, pies and donuts. ▪
*www.vinchet.com*

## Wheatfields Restaurant & Bar      ✪ $$$ LD
**Saratoga Springs** ▪ *(518) 587-0534*
*440 Broadway*
**Clifton Park** ▪ *(518) 383-4444*
*54 Crossing Blvd* ▪ *Italian* ▪ GF menu
includes pasta, pizza, steamed mussels, beet
and goat cheese salad, pan-seared scallops,
and Atlantic salmon. GF pasta and pizza
are available. Cheesecake, crème brûlée,
and chocolate mousse are available for dessert. ▪ *www.wheatfields.com*

## Whole in the Wall                     ✪ $$ LD
**Binghamton** ▪ *(607) 722-5138*
*43 S Washington St* ▪ *American* ▪ GF
options indicated on menu. Items include salad, creamy mushroom soup,
miso soup, stir fried vegetables, steamed
vegetables, Mexican platter, enchilada,
black bean chili, broiled fresh fish, shrimp
scampi, seafood platter, cheddar chicken
broil, tostada, organic brown rice, fried
rice, organic tofu and organic tempeh. ▪
*www.wholeinthewall.com*

**Wild Flours Bake Shop**                    ⊄S
*Huntington* ▪ *(631) 923-1090*
*11 New St* ▪ *Bakery & Café* ▪ Dedicated
GF bakery and café serving a variety of
sweet and savory items, including quiche,
scones, muffins, and fruit turnovers.
Shipping is now available if you are unable to pick up your order at the store. ▪
*wildfloursbakeshop.com*

**Yard House**                               ⊛▥
*West Nyack* ▪ *(845) 348-1528*
*4374 Paliades Center Dr*
*Yonkers* ▪ *(914) 375-9273*
*237 Market St*

# NORTH CAROLINA

## ASHEVILLE

**Bonefish Grill**                           ⊛▥
*Asheville* ▪ *(828) 298-6530*
*105 River Hills Rd*

**Brioso Fresh Pasta**                       ★$LD
*Asheville* ▪ *(828) 676-2260*
*33 Town Square Blvd* ▪ *Italian* ▪ GF penne
pasta and pizza are available. The GF
pizza is baked on top of a dedicated GF
wooden board to minimize the risk of CC.
▪ *www.briosopasta.com*

**Brixx Wood Fired Pizza**                   ⊛★▥
*Asheville* ▪ *(828) 654-0046*
*30 Town Sq Blvd*

**Carrabba's Italian Grill**                 ⊛▥
*Asheville* ▪ *(828) 281-2300*
*10 Buckstone Pl*

**Chai Pani Indian Street Food**            ⊛⊄LD
*Asheville* ▪ *(828) 254-4003*
*22 Battery Park Ave* ▪ *Indian* ▪ Most items
that are GF or can be prepared GF are
marked on the regular menu. These items
include the okra fries, uttapams, and chol-
les. ▪ *www.chaipani.net*

**Corner Kitchen, The**              ★$$$BLD
*Asheville* ▪ *(828) 274-2439*
*3 Boston Wy* ▪ *American* ▪ Manager Tracy
reports that GF diners are welcome. A vari-
ety of meat and fish dishes can be modified
to be GF. Alert the server and they will in-
form the kitchen. All kitchen staff has been
trained on GF food preparation. Confirm
the timeliness of this information before
dining in. ▪ *www.thecornerkitchen.com*

**Doc Chey's Noodle House**          ★⊄LD
*Asheville* ▪ *(828) 252-8220*
*37 Biltmore Ave* ▪ *Asian* ▪ GF menu in-
cludes Thai fried rice, Indian curry, tomato
ginger noodles, and Vietnamese prawn
salad. GF rice noodles and various other
items are also available. Manager Tyler rec-
ommends alerting a server, who can assure
that all GF meals are prepared properly. ▪
*www.doccheys.com*

**Fatz Eatz & Drinkz**                       ▥
*Asheville* ▪ *(828) 665-9950*
*5 Spartan Ave*

**Jason's Deli**                             ⊛▥
*Asheville* ▪ *(828) 252-7006*
*5 Westgate Pkwy*

**Jersey Mike's**                            ▥
*Asheville* ▪ *(828) 271-4612*
*1341 Parkwood Rd*
*Asheville* ▪ *(828) 255-5551*
*674 Merrimon Ave*
*Asheville* ▪ *(828) 277-1514*
*1550 Hendersonville Rd*
*Asheville* ▪ *(828) 298-6453*
*104A River Hills Rd*

**Mela Indian Restaurant**                  ★$LD
*Asheville* ▪ *(828) 225-8880*
*70 N Lexington Ave* ▪ *Indian* ▪ Manager
Amanda reports that GF diners are "pretty
safe" at the restaurant. She notes that all
servers are GF aware, and the restaurant
has an internal list of the few menu items
(mostly naan breads) that are not GF. ▪
*www.melaasheville.com*

### O'Charley's                    📖
*Asheville ▪ (828) 281-0540*
*2 Kenilworth Knoll*

### P.F. Chang's China Bistro      ✪★📖
*Asheville ▪ (828) 681-2975*
*26 Schenck Pkwy*

### Piazza                         ★$LD
*Asheville ▪ (828) 298-7224*
*4 Olde Eastwood Village Blvd ▪ Pizza ▪*
GF pasta and pizza are available. Owner
Reza notes that nearly all entrées on the
menu are GF. For dessert, they offer ice
cream and sorbet. ▪ *www.piazzaeast.com*

### Posana Café                    $BLD
*Asheville ▪ (828) 505-3969*
*1 Biltmore Ave ▪ American ▪* All menus
are entirely GF. Dishes include Vietnamese spring roll, Posana frittata, Carolina bison burger, sea scallop fettuccine,
Dulce de Leche cheesecake and more. ▪
*www.posanacafe.com*

### Ruth's Chris Steak House       ✪📖
*Asheville ▪ (828) 398-6200*
*26 All Souls Crescent*

### Travinia Italian Kitchen       ✪★📖
*Asheville ▪ (828) 684-8060*
*264 Thetford S*

### Vinnie's                       ★$$D
*Asheville ▪ (828) 253-1077*
*641 Merrimon Ave ▪ Italian ▪* GF pasta is
available. ▪ *www.vinniesitalian.com*

### West End Bakery                ★¢S
*Asheville ▪ (828) 252-9378*
*757 Haywood Rd ▪ Bakery & Café ▪*
Non-dedicated bakery offering GF bread,
muffins, cookies, cakes, and cupcakes.
Homemade GF sandwiches, soups and
salads are also available. Co-owner
Krista advises calling ahead to order GF
items, especially desserts. GF bread is
available to order every Wednesday. ▪
*www.westendbakery.com*

### World's Best Carrot Cake       ★$$$$$
*Asheville ▪ (828) 658-2738*
*175 Weaverville Hwy ▪ Bakery ▪* GF carrot cake and GF chocolate carrot cake are
available. Cakes for special occasions can
be ordered in advance. The bakery warns
that since they are not a dedicated GF facility, the chance of CC is "always present." ▪
*www.worldsbestcarrotcake.com*

## NORTH CAROLINA

## CHARLOTTE

### Aria Tuscan Grill              $$$LD
*Charlotte ▪ (704) 376-8880*
*100 N Tryon St ▪ Italian ▪* The manager
recommends alerting the staff upon arrival.
She reports that the entire staff is trained to
handle "allergies," and the chefs can always
"create something" special. Most items on
the regular menu can be modified to be GF
on request. ▪ *www.ariacharlotte.com*

### Blue Restaurant & Bar          ✪★$$$D
*Charlotte ▪ (704) 927-2583*
*206 N College St ▪ Mediterranean ▪* GF
items marked on the dinner menu include
yellow fin tuna, grilled ribeye, and the duo
of wild boar, among other various items.
GF beer and coconut flan are also available.
▪ *www.bluerestaurantandbar.com*

### Bonefish Grill                 ✪📖
*Charlotte ▪ (704) 541-6659*
*7520 Pineville Matthews Rd*

### BrickTop's                     ✪📖
*Charlotte ▪ (704) 364-6255*
*6401 Morrison Blvd*

### Brixx Wood Fired Pizza         ✪★📖
*Charlotte ▪ (704) 894-0044*
*16915 Birkdale Commons Pkwy*
*Charlotte ▪ (704) 347-2749*
*225 E 6th St*

*Charlotte* ▪ *(704) 295-0707*
*7814 Fairview Rd*
*Charlotte* ▪ *(704) 376-1000*
*1801 Scott Ave*
*Charlotte* ▪ *(704) 940-2011*
*9820 Rea Rd*

### Buona Vita Restaurant & Bar   ✪⟳LD
*Charlotte* ▪ *(704) 544-1011*
*3419 Toringdon Wy* ▪ *Italian* ▪ A full
GF menu is available on request, which
includes different pastas and appetizers. ▪
*www.buonavitacharlotte.com*

### Capital Grille, The   ✪📖
*Charlotte* ▪ *(704) 348-1400*
*201 N Tryon St*

### Carrabba's Italian Grill   ✪📖
*Charlotte* ▪ *(704) 377-2458*
*1520 S Blvd*

### Del Frisco's Double Eagle Steak House
📖
*Charlotte* ▪ *(704) 552-5502*
*4725 Piedmont Row Dr*

### Encore Bistro & Bar   ✪$$LD
*Charlotte* ▪ *(704) 341-3651*
*9824 Rea Rd* ▪ *Bistro* ▪ All items that can
be prepared GF are marked on the menu.
Alert the server upon arrival so they can
ensure your meal is prepared with GF
ingredients. ▪ *www.encorebistro.com*

### Fatz Eatz & Drinkz   📖
*Charlotte* ▪ *(704) 587-1772*
*10920 Winds Crossing Dr*

### Firebirds Wood Fired Grill   ✪📖
*Charlotte* ▪ *(704) 366-3655*
*3920 Sharon Rd*
*Charlotte* ▪ *(704) 752-7979*
*7716 Rhea Rd*
*Charlotte* ▪ *(704) 295-1919*
*6801 Northlake Mall Dr*

### Fleming's Prime Steakhouse & Wine Bar   ✪📖
*Charlotte* ▪ *(704) 333-4266*
*210 E Trade St*

### Fox and Hound Pub & Grille   📖
*Charlotte* ▪ *(704) 541-0794*
*8500 Pineville-Mathews Rd*
*Charlotte* ▪ *(704) 333-4113*
*330 N Tryon St*
*Charlotte* ▪ *(704) 544-8902*
*15235 John J Delaney Dr*
*Charlotte* ▪ *(704) 509-2853*
*9325 Ctr Lake Dr*

### FUEL Pizza   ✪★📖
*Charlotte* ▪ *(704) 376-3835*
*1501 Central Ave*
*Charlotte* ▪ *(704) 588-5333*
*14145 Rivergate Pkwy*
*Charlotte* ▪ *(704) 335-7375*
*1801 S Blvd*
*Charlotte* ▪ *(704) 370-2755*
*500 S College St*
*Charlotte* ▪ *(704) 350-1680*
*Corner of 6th & College*
*Charlotte* ▪ *(704) 525-3220*
*4267 Park Rd*

### Genghis Grill   📖
*Charlotte* ▪ *(980) 236-1427*
*11324 N Community House Rd*

### Harbor Inn Seafood Restaurant   ★📖
*Charlotte* ▪ *(704) 494-8901*
*8805 University E Dr*

### Harper's Restaurant   ✪$LD
*Charlotte* ▪ *(704) 366-6688*
*6518 Fairview Rd* ▪ *American* ▪ GF menu
varies slightly from location to location
but includes popular items such as steak,
chicken, BBQ, fish, and salads. GF flourless chocolate cake is also available. The
restaurant reports that they "take sanitation
very seriously" and "train all employees
about the hazard of cross-contamination."
Managers are reportedly Servsafe certified.
▪ *www.harpersrestaurants.com*

### Jason's Deli   ✪📖
*Charlotte* ▪ *(704) 921-1545*
*3509 David Cox Rd*
*Charlotte* ▪ *(704) 676-5858*

1600 E Woodlawn Rd
Charlotte ▪ (704) 688-1004
210 E Trade St

### Jersey Mike's   📖
Charlotte ▪ (704) 504-9343
11112-A S Tryon St
Charlotte ▪ (704) 543-3133
101110 Johnston Rd
Charlotte ▪ (704) 375-1985
2001 E 7th St
Charlotte ▪ (704) 540-1140
7828 Rea Rd
Charlotte ▪ (704) 549-9003
9211-12 N Tryon St
Charlotte ▪ (704) 536-9901
7309-21 E Independence Blvd
Charlotte ▪ (704) 343-0006
128 S Tryon St
Charlotte ▪ (704) 357-6453
2908 Oak Lake Blvd
Charlotte ▪ (704) 910-1717
1300 E Blvd

### Jim 'n Nick's Bar-B-Q   ✪★📖
Charlotte ▪ (704) 930-2290
13840 Steele Creek Rd

### Maggiano's Little Italy   ★📖
Charlotte ▪ (704) 916-2300
4400 Sharon Rd

### Mama Fu's Asian House   ✪📖
Charlotte ▪ (704) 714-7878
110 S Sharon Amity Rd

### Melting Pot, The   ✪📖
Charlotte ▪ (704) 548-2432
230 E W T Harris Blvd
Charlotte ▪ (704) 334-4400
901 S Kings Dr

### Morton's Steakhouse   ✪📖
Charlotte ▪ (704) 333-2602
227 W Trade St

### New South Kitchen & Bar   ★$$LD
Charlotte ▪ (704) 541-9990
8140 Providence Rd #300 ▪ Southern
▪ Owner and Chef Chris reports that
nearly all menu items are GF or can be
made GF. Alert the server upon arrival

and mention the word "allergy." All servers are trained to handle food "allergies,"
so they will provide menu guidance. ▪
*www.newsouthkitchen.com*

### O'Charley's   📖
Charlotte ▪ (704) 588-2737
8140 S Tryon St
Charlotte ▪ (704) 593-0106
8420 University City Blvd

### P.F. Chang's China Bistro   ✪★📖
Charlotte ▪ (704) 552-6644
6809 Phillips Place Ct Ste F
Charlotte ▪ (704) 598-1927
10325 Perimeter Pkwy

### Pei Wei Asian Diner   ✪📖
Charlotte ▪ (704) 543-1121
13855 Conlan Cir

### Pizza Fusion   ★📖
Charlotte ▪ (704) 370-0777
1055 Metropolitan Ave

### Romano's Macaroni Grill   ✪★📖
Charlotte ▪ (704) 595-9696
8620 Research Dr
Charlotte ▪ (704) 841-2511
10706 Providence Rd

### Ruth's Chris Steak House   ✪📖
Charlotte ▪ (704) 556-1115
6000 Fairview Rd
Charlotte ▪ (704) 338-9444
222 S Tryon St

### Shane's Rib Shack   ✪📖
Charlotte ▪ (704) 509-6553
9330 Center Lake Dr
Charlotte ▪ (704) 503-3113
440 Mccullough Dr

### Smokey Bones   📖
Charlotte ▪ (704) 549-8282
8760 JM Keynes Dr

### Sticky Fingers Smokehouse   ✪📖
Charlotte ▪ (704) 926-3441
12410 Johnston Rd

### Village Tavern   ✪📖
Charlotte ▪ (704) 552-9983
4201 Congress St

# NORTH CAROLINA

## RALEIGH/DURHAM

**Au Bon Pain**   &#x1F4D6;
*Raleigh* ▪ *(919) 250-9510*
*3000 New Bern Ave*

**Bella Monica Italian Restaurant** ✪★$LD
*Raleigh* ▪ *(919) 881-9778*
*3121-103 Edwards Mill Rd ▪ Italian ▪* GF
menu includes a variety of salads, stuffed
shells, and more. GF pizza and flatbreads
are also available, as are GF desserts such
as chocolate amore and mascarpone
panna cotta. Manager John notes that
they also have GF specials that are not
listed on the menu. Confirm the timeliness of this information before dining in. ▪
*www.bellamonica.com*

**Bonefish Grill**   ✪&#x1F4D6;
*Raleigh* ▪ *(919) 782-5127*
*4421 Six Forks Rd Ste 122*

**Brixx Wood Fired Pizza**   ✪★&#x1F4D6;
*Raleigh* ▪ *(919) 246-0640*
*8511 Brier Creek Pkwy*

**Carino's Italian**   ✪&#x1F4D6;
*Raleigh* ▪ *(919) 806-5524*
*8101 Brier Creek Pkwy*

**Carrabba's Italian Grill**   ✪&#x1F4D6;
*Raleigh* ▪ *(919) 871-0001*
*4821 Capital Blvd*
*Durham* ▪ *(919) 401-5950*
*5312 New Hope Commons Extension*

**Firebirds Wood Fired Grill**   ✪&#x1F4D6;
*Raleigh* ▪ *(919) 788-8778*
*4350 Lassiter At N Hills Ave*
*Durham* ▪ *(919) 544-6332*
*8030 Renaissance Pkwy*
*Raleigh* ▪ *(919) 788-8778*
*4350 Lassiter*

**Fleming's Prime Steakhouse & Wine
Bar**   ✪&#x1F4D6;
*Raleigh* ▪ *(919) 571-6200*
*4325 Glenwood Ave*

**Fox and Hound Pub & Grille**   &#x1F4D6;
*Raleigh* ▪ *(919) 781-4495*
*4158 Main*

**Jason's Deli**   ✪&#x1F4D6;
*Raleigh* ▪ *(919) 855-9898*
*909 Spring Forest Rd*
*Raleigh* ▪ *(919) 572-9996*
*8421 Brier Creek Pkwy*
*Raleigh* ▪ *(919) 840-4378*
*2400 Terminal Blvd Concourse D*

**Jersey Mike's**   &#x1F4D6;
*Raleigh* ▪ *(919) 787-2540*
*5910-119 Duraleigh Rd*
*Raleigh* ▪ *(919) 661-0111*
*7949 Fayetteville Rd*
*Raleigh* ▪ *(919) 870-6003*
*8111 Creedmoor Rd*
*Raleigh* ▪ *(919) 832-7972*
*200 W Peace St*
*Raleigh* ▪ *(919) 878-7827*
*3088 Wake Forest Rd*
*Raleigh* ▪ *(919) 848-4343*
*1121-105 Falls River Ave*
*Raleigh* ▪ *(919) 790-7827*
*4542 Capital Blvd*
*Raleigh* ▪ *(919) 231-0070*
*4121-101 New Bern Ave*
*Raleigh* ▪ *(919) 488-0262*
*14460-113 New Falls of the Neu*
*Raleigh* ▪ *(919) 870-7827*
*6176 Falls of Neuse Rd*

**Lone Star Steakhouse & Saloon**   ✪&#x1F4D6;
*Durham* ▪ *(919) 401-4800*
*5307 New Hope Commons Extension*

**Maggiano's Little Italy**   ★&#x1F4D6;
*Durham* ▪ *(919) 572-0070*
*8030 Renaissance Pkwy*

**Melting Pot, The**   ✪&#x1F4D6;
*Durham* ▪ *(919) 544-6358*
*7011 Fayetteville Rd*
*Raleigh* ▪ *(919) 878-0477*
*3100 Wake Forest Rd*

## Mo's Diner ★ $$D
*Raleigh* ▪ *(919) 856-9938*
*306 E Hargett St* ▪ *American* ▪ Owner Holly reports that nearly all menu items can be prepared GF. Examples include the rack of lamb, pork tenderloin, and spicy shrimp and scallops. Confirm the timeliness of this information before dining in. ▪ *www.mosdiner.net*

## O'Charley's 📖
*Raleigh* ▪ *(919) 484-4038*
*8115 Brier Creek Pkwy*

## P.F. Chang's China Bistro ✪★📖
*Durham* ▪ *(919) 294-3131*
*6801 Fayetteville Rd*
*Raleigh* ▪ *(919) 787-7754*
*4325 Glenwood Ave Ste 2089*

## Pei Wei Asian Diner ✪📖
*Raleigh* ▪ *(919) 484-4113*
*10251 Little Briar Creek Ln*
*Raleigh* ▪ *(919) 227-3810*
*4408 Falls Of Neuse Rd*

## Rockfish Seafood Grill ✪📖
*Durham* ▪ *(919) 544-9220*
*8030 Renaissance Pkwy*

## Romano's Macaroni Grill ✪★📖
*Raleigh* ▪ *(919) 792-2515*
*3421 Sumner Blvd*

## Ruth's Chris Steak House ✪📖
*Raleigh* ▪ *(919) 791-1103*
*4381 Lassiter Mill Rd*

## Shane's Rib Shack ✪📖
*Raleigh* ▪ *(919) 850-9900*
*5811 Poyner Village Pkwy*

## Simply Crepes Café ★ ¢BLD
*Raleigh* ▪ *(919) 322-2327*
*8470 Honeycutt Rd* ▪ *French* ▪ GF buckwheat crepes are available. Owner Pierre reports that all staff members are GF aware, and they can ensure a GF meal. He adds that "approximately 70%" of the menu can be prepared GF. Alert the server upon arrival and they will specify which crepes can be prepared GF. ▪ *www.simplycrepes.com*

## Yard House ✪📖
*Raleigh* ▪ *(919) 881-2590*
*4208 Six Forks Rd*

# NORTH CAROLINA
## ALL OTHER CITIES

## 32 Degrees Yogurt Bar 📖
*Knightdale* ▪ *(919) 266-4115*
*1018 Shoppes at Midway Dr*

## Angelina's Kitchen ✪★ ¢LD
*Pittsboro* ▪ *(919) 545-5505*
*23 Rectory St* ▪ *Greek* ▪ Manager Charlotte says they get "many Celiac customers every day" and therefore are knowledgeable about GF preparation and have many naturally GF or GF optional dishes. Alert the server upon arrival. ▪ *www.angelinaskitchenonline.com*

## Au Bon Pain 📖
*Durham* ▪ *(919) 613-4227*
*125 Science Dr Bryan Ctr*
*Greensboro* ▪ *(336) 334-5976*
*516 Stirling St*

## Bella Donna ★ $LD
*Pittsboro* ▪ *(919) 545-0900*
*87 Thompson St* ▪ *Italian* ▪ GF pizza available in small. All pizza are baked in the same oven so traces of flour are present in the oven. GF carrot cake is available for dessert. ▪ *www.belladonnaitalianrestaurant.com*

## Bento Box ★ $LD
*Wilmington* ▪ *(910) 509-0774*
*1121 L Military Cutoff Rd* ▪ *Japanese* ▪ GF soy sauce is available, as are GF soy sheets, which can be used instead of seaweed in the restaurant's "signature" rolls. Restaurant reports that it is one of the only establishments in North Carolina carrying GF soy sheets. ▪ *www.bentoboxsushi.com*

**Biaggi's**                           ✪★📖
Cary ▪ (919) 468-7229
1060 Darrington Dr

**Bonefish Grill**                       ✪📖
Winston Salem ▪ (336) 724-4518
300 S Stratford Rd
Greensboro ▪ (336) 851-8900
2100 Koury Blvd
Matthews ▪ (704) 845-8001
10056 E Independence Blvd
Wilmington ▪ (910) 313-1885
4719 New Centre Dr Ste K
Southern Pines ▪ (910) 692-1131
190 Partner Cir
Cary ▪ (919) 677-1347
2060 Renaissance Park Pl
Durham ▪ (919) 248-2906
7820 NC Hwy 751
Huntersville ▪ (704) 892-3385
8805 Townly Rd
Greenville ▪ (252) 754-0761
3616 S Memorial Dr

**Brixx Wood Fired Pizza**               ✪★📖
Burlington ▪ (336) 538-9770
1022 Boston Dr
Chapel Hill ▪ (919) 929-1942
501 Meadowmont Village Cr
Gastonia ▪ (704) 874-0404
501 Cox Rd
Greensboro ▪ (336) 235-2749
1424 Westover Terr
Wilmington ▪ (910) 256-9677
6801 Main St
Winston-Salem ▪ (336) 837-0664
1295 Creekshire Wy

**Bub O'Malley's**                       ★₵S
Chapel Hill ▪ (919) 942-6903
157 E Rosemary St ▪ Pub Food ▪ GF beer is
available.

**Buca di Beppo**                        ✪📖
Pineville ▪ (704) 542-5146
10915 Carolina Place Pkwy

**Carino's Italian**                     ✪📖
Durham ▪ (919) 405-1316
6709 Fayetteville Rd

Kannapolis ▪ (704) 782-9612
2235 Roxie St NE

**Carmine's Ristorante & Pizzeria**   ★$LD
Chapel Hill ▪ (919) 929-4300
18-16 E Franklin St ▪ Italian ▪ GF pasta,
spaghetti or penne, and GF pizza is available. Call ahead of time to confirm availability. ▪ www.carmineschapelhill.com

**Carolina Cupcakery**                   ✪★₵S
Manteo ▪ (252) 305-8501
205 Budleigh St ▪ Bakery ▪ Non-dedicated bakery offering a variety of sweets,
including cupcakes, cakes, lemon bars,
brownies, cookies, and more. Dinner
rolls and cheddar rolls are also available. Call ahead to confirm availability. ▪
www.carolinacupcakery.com

**Carrabba's Italian Grill**             ✪📖
Apex ▪ (919) 387-6336
1201 Haddon Hall Dr
Arden ▪ (828) 654-8411
332 Rockwood Rd
Cary ▪ (919) 467-9901
1148 Kildaire Farm Rd
Concord ▪ (704) 979-3224
7900 Lyles Ln NW
Fayetteville ▪ (910) 486-9300
4209 Sycamore Dairy Rd
Greensboro ▪ (336) 218-0623
1653 New Garden Rd
Greensboro ▪ (336) 323-6069
3200 High Point Rd
Hickory ▪ (828) 322-9032
1954 13Th Ave Dr SE
Huntersville ▪ (704) 895-3080
16408 Northcross Dr
Matthews ▪ (704) 844-0464
10400 E Independence Blvd
Wilmington ▪ (910) 794-9094
15 Van Campen Blvd
Winston Salem ▪ (336) 831-0580
587 S Stratford Rd

**Colington Café, The**                  $$$D
Kill Devil Hills ▪ (252) 480-1123
1029 Colington Rd ▪ American ▪ A GF
menu list is available in-house that "high-

lights" naturally GF menu items and lists modifications required for other items. Alert a server upon arrival, and they will present the list. ▪ *www.colingtoncafe.com*

### Fatz Eatz & Drinkz ⌂
Concord ▪ (704) 723-4044
6081 Bayfield Pkwy
Forest City ▪ (828) 286-8996
118 Hill Top Wy
Franklin ▪ (828) 524-5265
107 Sawmill Village Ln
Greensboro ▪ (336) 841-0081
619 S Regional Rd
Greensboro ▪ (336) 547-9221
3011 High Point Rd
Hendersonville ▪ (828) 696-9965
110 Henderson Crossing
Lenoir ▪ (828) 758-6190
975 Blowing Rock Blvd NW
Lincolnton ▪ (704) 732-7155
1430 E Main St
Marion ▪ (828) 659-1364
390 US 70 W
Morganton ▪ (828) 430-9766
2111 S Sterling
Rockingham ▪ (910) 582-4040
714 E US Hwy 74
Shelby ▪ (704) 482-8116
1235 E Dixon Blvd

### Firebirds Wood Fired Grill ✪⌂
Winston Salem ▪ (336) 659-3973
1215 Creekshire Wy
Winston Salem ▪ (336) 659-3973
1215 Creekshire Wy
Durham ▪ (919) 544-6332
8030 Renaissance Pkwy

### Fleming's Prime
### Steakhouse & Wine Bar ✪⌂
Greensboro ▪ (336) 294-7790
3342 W Friendly Ave

### Fox and Hound Pub & Grille ⌂
Huntersville ▪ (704) 895-4504
8711 Lindholm Dr
Winston-Salem ▪ (336) 722-6000

367 Lwr Thruway Mall
Chapel Hill ▪ (919) 918-1005
1722 N Fordham Blvd
Wilmington ▪ (910) 509-0805
920 Town Ctr Dr

### FUEL Pizza ✪★⌂
Davidson ▪ (704) 655-3835
402 S Main St

### Genghis Grill ⌂
Winston-Salem ▪ (336) 774-2154
3298 Silas Creek Pkwy SW

### Harbor Inn Seafood Restaurant ★⌂
Asheville ▪ (828) 665-9940
880 Brevard Rd
Morganton ▪ (828) 437-0294
2006 S Sterling St

### Harper's Restaurant ✪$LD
Greensboro ▪ (336) 299-8850
601 Friendly Center Rd
Pineville ▪ (704) 541-5255
11059 Carolina Place Pkwy ▪ American
▪ GF menu varies slightly from location to location but includes popular items such as steak, chicken, BBQ, fish, and salads. GF flourless chocolate cake is also available. The restaurant reports that they "take sanitation very seriously" and "train all employees about the hazard of cross-contamination." Managers are reportedly Servsafe certified. ▪ *www.harpersrestaurants.com*

### HuHot Mongolian Grill ⌂
Greenville ▪ (252) 758-4468
500 SW Greenville Blvd

### Irregardless
### Café & Catering, The ✪$$BLD
Raleigh ▪ (919) 833-8898
901 W Morgan St ▪ American ▪ GF items marked on the menu include Vietnamese spring rolls, soba tuna salad, lamb lollipops, chile rellenos, steak au poivre, shrimp & grits, and more. ▪ *www.irregardless.com*

## Jason's Deli ✿📖

Fayetteville ▪ (910) 860-0253
419 Cross Creek Mall
Huntersville ▪ (704) 895-2505
16639 Birkdale Commons Pkwy
Winston-Salem ▪ (336) 794-0015
1005 Hanes Mall Blvd
Durham ▪ (919) 493-3350
5408 New Hope Commons Dr
Pineville ▪ (704) 541-1228
10610 Centrum Pkwy
Hickory ▪ (828) 325-4938
2337 US 10
Greensboro ▪ (336) 297-9195
3326 W Friendly Ave
Cary ▪ (919) 233-6901
210 Crossroads Blvd
Wilmington ▪ (910) 795-4164
5301 Market St

## Jersey Mike's 📖

Morganton ▪ (828) 438-9889
108 Fiddler's Run Blvd
Boone ▪ (828) 264-4447
119 New Market Ctr
Gastonia ▪ (704) 823-7827
3754 E Franklin Blvd
Cornelius ▪ (704) 895-5559
20619 Torrence Chapel Rd
Huntersville ▪ (704) 948-7343
105 C S Statesville Rd
Mooresville ▪ (704) 663-7827
647 Brawley School Rd
Matthews ▪ (704) 847-0410
2332A Matthews Twp. Pkwy
Concord ▪ (704) 788-7725
300 Copperfield Blvd
Mocksville ▪ (336) 753-6453
1670 US Hwy 601 N
Monroe ▪ (704) 238-8855
2300-E W Roosevelt Blvd
Salisbury ▪ (704) 642-0111
850 Jake Alexander Blvd W
Winston-Salem ▪ (336) 765-1224
177 Jonestown Rd
Winston-Salem ▪ (336) 377-2700
5940 University Pkwy
Winston-Salem ▪ (336) 777-1122
2291 Cloverdale Ave

High Point ▪ (336) 885-3970
2200 N Main St
High Point ▪ (336) 889-2782
2620 S Main St
Jamestown ▪ (336) 856-0010
4835 W Wendover Ave
Greensboro ▪ (336) 286-6777
2939-B Battleground Ave
Stoney Creek ▪ (336) 446-1108
6307-L Burlington Rd
Laurinburg ▪ (910) 266-0013
12280 McColl Rd
Burlington ▪ (336) 226-8094
2138 S Church St
Aberdeen ▪ (910) 695-1110
1814B Sandhill Blvd
Mebane ▪ (919) 563-8800
102 Millstead Dr
Pembroke ▪ (910) 521-4055
409 W 3rd St
West Fayetteville ▪ (910) 867-4100
7711 Raeford Rd
Chapel Hill ▪ (919) 918-7827
245A S Elliot Rd
Fayetteville ▪ (910) 487-3388
5815 Yadkin Rd
Spring Lake ▪ (910) 436-9888
201 Spring Ave
Fayetteville ▪ (910) 860-9494
2043 Skibo Rd
Apex ▪ (919) 363-6453
1761 Hwy 55
Fayetteville ▪ (910) 232-5500
4225-B Ramsey St
Apex ▪ (919) 467-3900
922 Hwy 64
Durham ▪ (919) 484-7788
2945 S Miami Blvd
Cary ▪ (919) 461-0660
957 High Horse Rd
Morrisville ▪ (919) 319-0039
962D Airport Blvd
Fuquay-Varina ▪ (919) 557-3000
701-A N Main St
Cary ▪ (919) 363-7827
3490 Kildare Farm Rd
Greensboro ▪ (336) 333-0002
2104 Georgia St

*Durham* ▪ *(919) 620-7808*
*3600 N Duke St*
*Cary* ▪ *(919) 461-8100*
*701 Cary Towne Blvd*
*Garner* ▪ *(919) 779-7827*
*2345 Timber Dr*
*Garner* ▪ *(919) 662-9933*
*106-1 Bratton Dr*
*Goldsboro* ▪ *(919) 739-7200*
*2503 E Ash St*
*Wilson* ▪ *(252) 234-7400*
*2338 Forest Hills Rd*
*Wilmington* ▪ *(910) 452-9996*
*3905 G Independence Blvd*
*Wilmington* ▪ *(910) 799-6453*
*343-4 S College Rd*
*Wilmington* ▪ *(910) 256-2030*
*1968 Eastwood Rd*
*Rocky Mount* ▪ *(252) 937-6777*
*1469 Hunter Hill Rd*
*Wilmington* ▪ *(910) 686-4849*
*8207 Market St*
*Winterville* ▪ *(252) 321-7566*
*4054 S Memorial Dr*
*Greenville* ▪ *(252) 695-6161*
*796A Moye Blvd*
*Jacksonville* ▪ *(910) 353-8091*
*301 Western Blvd*
*Greenville* ▪ *(252) 758-8866*
*1915 S E Greenville Blvd*
*Greenville* ▪ *(252) 321-2220*
*310-D E Arlington Blvd*
*Washington* ▪ *(252) 975-0404*
*420 Pamlico Plaza*
*New Bern* ▪ *(252) 636-2566*
*2309 Hwy 70 E*
*Morehead City* ▪ *(252) 240-0202*
*4950 Arendell St*
*Denver* ▪ *(704) 827-9032*
*7260 Hwy 73*
*Arden* ▪ *(828) 684-4266*
*300 Airport Rd*
*Greenville* ▪ *(252) 321-1112*
*1908 E Firetower Rd*
*Cary* ▪ *(919) 233-0036*
*280 Meeting St*
*Concord* ▪ *(704) 792-0652*
*6028 Bayfield Pkwy*

*Leland* ▪ *(910) 523-5300*
*2029 Olde Regent Wy*

## Jim 'n Nick's Bar-B-Q               ✪★📖
*Concord* ▪ *(704) 453-2791*
*7791 Gateway Ln NW*

## Joe's Crab Shack                    ✪📖
*Fayetteville* ▪ *(910) 868-8422*
*155 S McPherson Chruch Rd*

## Johnny Brusco's
## New York Style Pizza                ★📖
*Concord* ▪ *(704) 788-3888*
*9900 Poplar Tent Rd*

## Kelly's Outer Banks
## Restaurant and Tavern               $$$D
*Nags Head* ▪ *(252) 441-4116*
*2316 S Croatan Hwy* ▪ *American* ▪
Restaurant reports that GF diners can be
accommodated. Reservations noting GF
are required. The chef will arrange for a
GF meal to be available at the time of the
reservation. ▪ *www.kellysrestaurant.com*

## Lone Star Steakhouse & Saloon       ✪📖
*Arden* ▪ *(828) 684-5506*
*341 Rockwood Rd*
*Clayton* ▪ *(919) 359-6201*
*13049 US 70 Business Hwy W*
*Fayetteville* ▪ *(910) 867-2222*
*1800 Skibo Rd*
*Greensboro* ▪ *(336) 855-1228*
*3025 High Point Rd*
*Knightdale* ▪ *(919) 217-7070*
*6601 Knightdale Blvd*
*Monroe* ▪ *(704) 291-2525*
*2841 W Highway 74*
*Mooresville* ▪ *(704) 799-3262*
*668 River Hwy*
*Mount Airy* ▪ *(336) 789-0142*
*1905 Woodland Dr*
*Statesville* ▪ *(704) 871-2929*
*700 Sullivan Rd*
*Winston-Salem* ▪ *(336) 760-9066*
*1110 Creekshire Wy*

## Melting Pot, The                    ✪📖
*Greensboro* ▪ *(336) 545-6233*
*2924 Battleground Ave*

*Wilmington* ▪ (910) 256-1187
*885 Town Center Dr*

**Morton's Steakhouse**                    ✪📖
*White Plains* ▪ (914) 683-6101
*100 Bloomingdale Rd*

**New Town Bistro and Bar**          ✪$$LD
*Winston Salem* ▪ (336) 659-8062
*420 Jonestown Rd* ▪ *American* ▪ Grilled
fish tacos, sautéed calamari, and creamy
pasta alfredo are a few dishes on the GF
menu. Restaurant notes that patrons
should allow extra time when a GF item is
being prepared. Shrimp grits may be made
GF, and GF pasta is available. Food on the
current menu can be prepared GF upon re-
quest, additional prep time may be added. ▪
*www.newtownbistro.com*

**Nicola's Italian Restaurant**          ✪$D
*Wilmington* ▪ (910) 798-2205
*5704 Oleander Dr* ▪ *Italian* ▪ GF menu
includes items such as chicken marsala,
veal picatta, filet mignon, fresh catch of the
day, and more. GF pasta is available with a
variety of sauces. ▪ *www.nicolasitalian.com*

**O'Charley's**                    📖
*Cary* ▪ (919) 851-9777
*101 Ashville Ave*
*Concord* ▪ (704) 785-9864
*1389 Concord Pkwy*
*Hickory* ▪ (828) 431-4777
*2360 US Hwy 70 SE*
*Hendersonville* ▪ (828) 692-4224
*65 Highland Square Dr*
*Jacksonville* ▪ (910) 455-8407
*1270 Western Blvd*
*Monroe* ▪ (704) 238-8554
*2412 W Roosevelt Blvd*
*Mooresville* ▪ (704) 799-8571
*604 River Hwy*
*Burlington* ▪ (336) 584-5652
*521 Huffman Mill Rd*
*Gastonia* ▪ (704) 865-6633
*1601 E Franklin Blvd*
*Greensboro* ▪ (336) 852-5758
*4505 Landover Rd*
*Salisbury* ▪ (704) 363-9445

*123 N Arlington St*
*Winston-Salem* ▪ (336) 377-2350
*300 E Hanes Mill Rd*

**P.F. Chang's China Bistro**          ✪★📖
*Greensboro* ▪ (336) 291-1302
*3338 W Friendly Ave*

**Pei Wei Asian Diner**                    ✪📖
*Cary* ▪ (919) 337-0050
*1107 Walnut St*

**Pure Taqueria**                    ✪¢LD
*Matthews* ▪ (704) 841-7873
*111 Matthews Stn St* ▪ *Latin American* ▪ GF
menu includes ceviche, fajitas with corn
tortillas, duck confit, pescado veracruz,
grilled shrimp, and more. The restaurant
reports that all salsas, rice, and beans are
GF, and adds that GF chips are available.
Since there is a common fryer for all items,
they recommend avoiding fried foods.
Confirm the timeliness of this information
before dining in. ▪ *www.puretaqueria.com*

**Romano's Macaroni Grill**          ✪★📖
*Cary* ▪ (919) 467-7727
*740 SE Maynard Rd*
*Greensboro* ▪ (336) 855-0676
*3120 Northline Ave*
*Wilmington* ▪ (910) 256-4550
*1035 International Dr*
*Winston Salem* ▪ (336) 765-6676
*1915 Hampton Inn Ct*

**Ruth's Chris Steak House**          ✪📖
*Cary* ▪ (919) 677-0033
*2010 Renaissance Park Pl*
*Cherokee* ▪ (828) 497-8577
*777 Casino Dr*
*Durham* ▪ (919) 361-0123
*7007 Fayetteville Rd*
*Greensboro* ▪ (336) 574-1515
*800 Green Valley Rd*
*Wilmington* ▪ (910) 343-1818
*301 N Water St*

**Shane's Rib Shack**                    ✪📖
*Greensboro* ▪ (336) 292-7272
*4217-A W Wendover Ave*
*Greensboro* ▪ (336) 272-4696
*1410 Westover Terrace*

**Smokey Bones**                                    📖
*Fayetteville* ▪ *(910) 864-1068*
*1891 Skibo Rd*
*Greensboro* ▪ *(336) 315-8755*
*3302 High Point Rd*

**Sticky Fingers Smokehouse**          ✪📖
*Concord* ▪ *(704) 979-7427*
*8021 Concord Mills Blvd*

**Stoney Knob Café**                      ★$LD
*Weaverville* ▪ *(828) 645-3309*
*337 Merrimon Ave* ▪ *Global* ▪ Restaurant
reports that they serve GF diners regularly.
Alert a server upon arrival. While not all
servers are equally trained on the GF diet,
they are trained to consult with the chef
about GF options. GF orders are sent to
the kitchen with an allergy flag so the chefs
know to use separate preparation utensils,
in an effort to reduce CC. Shrimp saganaki
and the paella are among the items that can
be modified to be GF. Confirm the timeliness of this information before dining in. ▪
*www.stoneyknobcafe.com*

**Sweet Cece's**                                   📖
*Wake Forest* ▪ *(919) 554-4030*
*3624 Rogers Rd*

**Ted's Montana Grill**                    ✪📖
*Durham* ▪ *(919) 572-1210*
*6911 Fayetteville Rd*

**Top of the Hill**                          ✪$$LD
*Chapel Hill* ▪ *(919) 929-8676*
*100 E Franklin St 3rd Floor* ▪ *American*
▪ GF menu includes NY strip steak,
buttermilk grilled chicken, and
jambalaya. Alert a server upon arrival.
The restaurant reports that servers
are knowledgeable about the GF diet
and can provide recommendations. ▪
*www.topofthehillrestaurant.com*

**Tossed**                                       ✪📖
*Morrisville* ▪ *(919) 460-4449*
*4117 Davis Dr*

**Travinia Italian Kitchen**         ✪★📖
*Morrisville* ▪ *(919) 467-1718*
*1301 Market Center Dr*

**Village Tavern**                           ✪📖
*Greensboro* ▪ *(336) 282-3063*
*1903 Westridge Rd*
*Winston-Salem* ▪ *(336) 748-0221*
*221 Reynolda Village*
*Winston-Salem* ▪ *(336) 760-8686*
*2000 Griffith Rd*

**Vimala's Curryblossom Café**      ✪$LD
*Chapel Hill* ▪ *(919) 929-3833*
*431 W Franklin St* ▪ *Indian* ▪ Manager
Shaun said that they "try their hardest"
to accommodate the dietary needs of all
diners, especially people with Celiac. Many
dishes are naturally GF or can be modified
to be GF. Alert the server upon arrival. ▪
*curryblossom.com*

**Weathervane**                            ★$$BLD
*Chapel Hill* ▪ *(919) 929-9466*
*201 S Estes Dr* ▪ *American* ▪ GF selections include pan-seared jumbo scallops, yellow tomato gazpacho, and brick
pressed chicken. Some items require
modification to become GF, so be sure to
alert the server. GF bread is available. ▪
*www.southernseason.com/cafe.asp*

**Zpizza**                                      ✪📖
*Cary* ▪ *(919) 465-9009*
*96 Cornerstone Dr*
*Raleigh* ▪ *(919) 844-0065*
*9630 Falls of the Neuse R*
*Raleigh* ▪ *(919) 838-0681*
*421 Fayetteville St*

# NORTH DAKOTA

**Carino's Italian**                         ✪📖
*Bismarck* ▪ *(701) 258-5655*
*1601 W Century Ave*
*Bismarck* ▪ *(701) 258-5655*
*1601 W Century Ave*

Bismarck ▪ (701) 258-5655
1601 W Century Ave
Fargo ▪ (701) 282-2922
4410 17th Ave SW

## Dempsey's Public House                              ★ ₵D
Fargo ▪ (701) 235-5913
226 Broadway ▪ Pub Food ▪ GF beer is
available. ▪ www.dempseyspublichouse.com

## Doolittles Woodfire Grill                    ✪ ★ $$LD
Fargo ▪ (701) 478-2200
2112 25th St S ▪ Fusion ▪ GF menu includes
scallops with red curry sauce, spit-roasted
chicken, smoked hanger steak, raspberry
& fresh pear salad, and more. Crème
brûlée and Italian custard are available for
dessert. Alexandria location also carries
GF beer and vodka. Confirm the timeliness of this information before dining in. ▪
www.doolittlesrestaurants.com

## Drunken Noodle                                     ✪₵LD
Fargo ▪ (701) 232-3380
623 NP Ave N ▪ Asian Fusion ▪ GF menu
available. Be sure to ask for GF soy sauce. ▪
www.drunkennoodle.com

## Godfather's Pizza                                    ★ 📖
Fargo ▪ (701) 277-1666
4340 13th Ave SW

## Green Market Kitchen                             ✪$LD
Fargo ▪ (701) 241-6000
69 4th St N ▪ Modern American ▪ Offers
a regular menu that uses asterisks to display which items are GF. Dishes without an
asterisk can also be prepared GF. Alert server
when ordering. Options include ricotta
stuffed peppers, seared halibut, braised beef
short ribs, spring chicken, and chocolate orbit
cake for dessert. The menu changes often, so
call ahead for the most current information.

## Green Mill Restaurant and Bar                  ✪📖
Fargo ▪ (701) 298-8000
3340 13th Ave S
Grand Forks ▪ (701) 780-9000
1930 Colombia Rd S

## Ground Round                                        ✪📖
Bismarck ▪ (701) 223-0000

526 S 3rd St
Fargo ▪ (701) 280-2288
2902 13Th Ave S
Grand Forks ▪ (701) 775-4646
2800 32nd Ave S
Minot ▪ (701) 838-3500
2110 Burdick Expwy E

## Happy Joe's Pizza & Ice Cream               📖
Bismarck ▪ (701) 355-1146
2921 N 11th St
Fargo ▪ (701) 293-5252
2511 S University
Fargo ▪ (701) 237-3801
3132 N Broadway
Grand Forks ▪ (701) 772-6655
2909 S Washington
Minot ▪ (701) 839-5637
420 20th Ave SE
West Fargo ▪ (701) 373-7000
1450 13th Ave E

## HoDo Restaurant                                  ★ $$$D
Fargo ▪ (701) 478-1000
101 Broadway N ▪ Fusion ▪ GF diners can
be accommodated. Note GF when making
reservations and alert server upon arrival. ▪
www.hoteldonaldson.com

## HuHot Mongolian Grill                             📖
Fargo ▪ (701) 478-4688
1801 45th St SW
Bismarck ▪ (701) 751-2800
409 S 3rd St

## Kic Bac Bar & Grill                               ★ ₵D
Cogswell ▪ (701) 724-3619
255 4th Ave ▪ American ▪ GF options
include a variety of salads, grilled chicken,
hamburgers with no buns and steak dishes.
GF beer is also available. Alert a server,
who will suggest GF options.

## Lone Star Steakhouse & Saloon              ✪📖
Fargo ▪ (701) 282-6642
4328 13th Ave SW

## Maxwell's Restaurant & Bar                    $$$$D
West Fargo ▪ (701) 277-9463
1380 9th St E ▪ Modern American ▪ GF
diners can be accommodated. Alert server

upon arrival and they will list items that can be made GF. ▪ *www.maxwellsnd.com*

### Minerva's ✪📖
*Bismarck* ▪ *(701) 222-1402*
*1800 N 12th*

### Nine Dragons Restaurant ✪★◖LD
*Fargo* ▪ *(701) 232-2411*
*4525 17th Ave S* ▪ Chinese ▪ GF items are clearly noted on the menu. Various beef, chicken, pork, shrimp and vegetables selections are available. ▪ *www.9dragonsrestaurant.com*

### Oakes American Legion ★$LD
*Oakes* ▪ *(701) 742-2411*
*22 N 5th St* ▪ American ▪ GF beer is available.

### Pizza Ranch ✪📖
*Dickinson* ▪ *(701) 483-0008*
*2184 2nd Ave W*
*Cooperstown* ▪ *(701) 797-2800*
*Hwy 45 & Main*
*Fargo* ▪ *(701) 356-4141*
*4480 23rd Ave S*
*Minot* ▪ *(701) 852-3663*
*305 37th Ave SW*
*Wahpeton* ▪ *(701) 672-7492*
*1110 3rd Ave N*
*Minot* ▪ *(701) 838-3500*
*2100 Burdick Expwy*
*Grand Forks* ▪ *(701) 775-2222*
*3750 2nd Ave S*
*Wahpeton* ▪ *(701) 672-7492*
*1110 3rd Ave*

### Rhombus Guys Pizza ✪📖
*Fargo* ▪ *(701) 540-4534*
*606 Main Ave*
*Grand Forks* ▪ *(701) 787-7317*
*312 Kittson Ave* ▪ GF pizza available in 8" size only.

### Smiling Moose Deli ✪📖
*Fargo* ▪ *(701) 277-8800*
*2877 45th St S*

### Spitfire Bar & Grill ★$$LD
*West Fargo* ▪ *(701) 478-8667*
*1660 13th Ave E* ▪ American ▪ GF op-

tions include steak, roast chicken, tuna and salmon dishes. Alert server upon arrival and they will point out what items on the menu can be made GF. ▪ *www.spitfirebarandgrillfargo.com*

### Xtreme Pizza Kitchen ★$LD
*Fargo* ▪ *(701) 298-0420*
*1404 33rd St SW Suite D* ▪ Pizza ▪ GF pizza is available for delivery, take out, and dining in. All toppings are GF EXCEPT: taco chips, crab meat, creamy garlic sauce, and cheddar cheese. Confirm the timeliness of this information before dining in. ▪ *www.xtremepizzakitchen.com*

# OHIO

## CINCINNATI

### Au Bon Pain 📖
*Cincinnati* ▪ *(513) 381-4034*
*2139 Auburn Ave*
*Cincinnati* ▪ *(513) 221-6789*
*234 Goodman St*

### BJ's Restaurant and Brewhouse ✪★📖
*Cincinnati* ▪ *(513) 671-1805*
*11700 Princeton Pike*

### Bonefish Grill ✪📖
*Cincinnati* ▪ *(513) 321-5222*
*2737 Madison Rd*

### Don Pablo's ✪📖
*Cincinnati* ▪ *(513) 631-1356*
*2692 Madison Rd*

### First Watch - The Daytime Café ✪📖
*Cincinnati* ▪ *(513) 489-6849*
*11301 Montgomery Rd*
*Cincinnati* ▪ *(513) 531-7430*
*2692 Madison Rd*
*Cincinnati* ▪ *(513) 721-4744*
*700 Walnut St*
*Cincinnati* ▪ *(513) 231-4620*
*7625 Beechmont Ave*

Cincinnati ▪ (513) 891-0088
8118 Montgomery Rd

**J. Gumbo's**                                             ★📖
Cincinnati ▪ (513) 407-6930
286 Ludlow Ave
Cincinnati ▪ (513) 429-4549
425 Walnut St
Cincinnati ▪ (513) 522-2695
879 W Galbraith

**Jersey Mike's**                                          📖
Cincinnati ▪ (513) 451-9400
5032 Geln Crossings Wy
Cincinnati ▪ (513) 923-2507
5624 Cheviot Rd
Cincinnati ▪ (513) 522-5774
8481 Winton Rd
Cincinnati ▪ (513) 871-8444
3770 Paxton Rd
Cincinnati ▪ (513) 984-5555
7346 Kenwood Rd
Cincinnati ▪ (513) 793-5225
9525 Kenwood Rd
Cincinnati ▪ (513) 583-1238
12133 Royal Point Dr

**LaRosa's Pizzeria**                                      ★📖
Cincinnati ▪ (513) 347-1111
7756 Beechmont Ave
Cincinnati ▪ (513) 347-1111
2411 Boudinot Ave
Cincinnati ▪ (513) 347-1111
7691 Montgomery Rd

**Loving Hut**                                             📖
Cincinnati ▪ (513) 731-2233
6227 Montgomery Rd

**Maggiano's Little Italy**                                ★📖
Cincinnati ▪ (513) 794-0670
7875 Montgomery Rd

**Melting Pot, The**                                       ✪📖
Cincinnati ▪ (513) 530-5501
11023 Montgomery Rd
Cleveland ▪ (440) 356-8900
3111 Westgate

**Morton's Steakhouse**                                    ✪📖
Cincinnati ▪ (513) 621-3111
441 Vine St

**O'Charley's**                                            📖
Cincinnati ▪ (513) 347-3200
5075 Crookshank Rd
Cincinnati ▪ (513) 753-6266
4531 Eastgate Blvd
Cincinnati ▪ (513) 469-0022
5262 Fields Ertel Rd

**P.F. Chang's China Bistro**                              ✪★📖
Cincinnati ▪ (513) 531-4567
2633 Edmondson Rd

**Palomino**                                               📖
Cincinnati ▪ (513) 381-1300
505 Vine St

**Romano's Macaroni Grill**                                ✪★📖
Cinicinnati ▪ (513) 671-2747
925 E Kemper Rd

**Ruth's Chris Steak House**                               ✪📖
Cincinnati ▪ (513) 381-0491
100 E Freedom Wy

**Smokey Bones**                                           📖
Cincinnati ▪ (513) 777-5360
9484 Civic Center Blvd

**Uno Chicago Grill**                                      ✪★📖
Cincinnati ▪ (513) 231-5357
7578 Beechmont Ave

# OHIO

## COLUMBUS

**Abuelo's**                                               ✪📖
Columbus ▪ (614) 337-9006
3950 Gramercy St

**Alana's Food and Wine**                                  ★$$$D
Columbus ▪ (614) 294-6783
2333 N High St ▪ Modern American ▪ The
restaurant reports that while the menu
changes often, they can always accommo-
date GF diners. Reservations noting GF are
recommended. ▪ www.alanas.com

### Au Bon Pain    📖
*Columbus* ▪ *(614) 224-1922*
*3rd and Broad St*

### Banana Leaf    ✪★¢LD
*Columbus* ▪ *(614) 459-4101*
*816 Bethel Rd* ▪ *Vegetarian* ▪ GF items
are marked on the menu and include a
variety of curries, rice dishes, and other
Indian specialties. The restaurant reports
that the majority of their menu is GF, as
they cater to diners with special needs. ▪
*www.bananaleafofcolumbus.com*

### BJ's Restaurant and Brewhouse ✪★📖
*Columbus* ▪ *(614) 885-1800*
*1414 Polaris Pkwy*

### Bon Vie    ★$$LD
*Columbus* ▪ *(614) 416-0463*
*4089 The Strand E* ▪ *French* ▪ Accommodations for GF diners can be made without
a problem. Alert the server, who will notify
the chef. ▪ *www.bon-vie.com*

### Bonefish Grill    ✪📖
*Columbus* ▪ *(614) 436-0286*
*1930 Polaris Pkwy*

### Boston's
### Restaurant & Sports Bar    ✪★📖
*Columbus* ▪ *(614) 229-4275*
*191 W Nationwide Blvd*

### Buca di Beppo    ✪📖
*Columbus* ▪ *(614) 621-3287*
*343 N Front St*

### Cameron's American Bistro    ✪$$$D
*Columbus* ▪ *(614) 885-3663*
*2185 W Dublin-Granville Rd* ▪ *Modern
American* ▪ GF menu available. Includes
sautéed portabello french fries, sautéed calamari, a variety of salads, shrimp and grits,
ponzu salmon, heritage farm pork chops,
pan roasted scallops, crispy moscovy duck
breast, roasted lamb loin, and grilled filet
mignon. Vanilla crème brûlée and meyer
lemon gratin are available for dessert.▪
*www.cameronsamericanbistro.com*

### Cantina Laredo    📖
*Columbus* ▪ *(614) 781-1139*
*8791 Lyra Dr*

### Cap City Fine Diner    ✪$$LD
*Columbus* ▪ *(614) 478-9999*
*1301 Stoneridge Dr*
*Columbus* ▪ *(614) 291-3663*
*1299 Olentangy River Rd* ▪ *American* ▪
GF menu includes salads and sandwiches,
as well as large plates such as pan seared
salmon and balsamic chicken. For dessert,
they offer crème brûlée and upside down
banana cream pie. Be sure to ask the server
for a copy of the GF menu upon arrival. ▪
*www.capcityfinediner.com*

### Claddagh Irish Pub    📖
*Columbus* ▪ *(614) 224-1560*
*585 S Front St*
*Columbus* ▪ *(614) 885-0100*
*8745 Sancus Blvd*

### Columbus Brewing Company    ★$$LD
*Columbus* ▪ *(614) 464-2739*
*525 Short St* ▪ *American* ▪ Any menu
item can be made GF. Alert the server
upon arrival and they will notify the
chef, who will then come out to discuss which items can be prepared GF. ▪
*www.columbusbrewingco.com*

### Columbus Fish Market    ✪$$$LD
*Columbus* ▪ *(614) 291-3474*
*1245 Olentangy River Rd*
*Columbus* ▪ *(614) 410-3474*
*40 Hutchinson Ave* ▪ *Seafood* ▪ Extensive
GF menu includes a selection of salads, fish
dishes, steaks, and shellfish. Mini crème
brûlée and sorbet of the day are available
for dessert. Be sure to notify your server
that you are ordering from the GF menu. ▪
*www.columbusfishmarket.com*

### Cosi    ✪📖
*Columbus* ▪ *(614) 472-2600*
*4074 The Strand W*
*Columbus* ▪ *(614) 459-5000*
*1478 Bethel Rd*
*Columbus* ▪ *(614) 431-6600*
*1310 Polaris Pkwy*

Columbus ▪ (614) 734-2674
6390 Sawmill Rd

### Dirty Frank's Hot Dog Palace          ★ ₵LD
Columbus ▪ (614) 824-4673
248 S 4th St ▪ American ▪ Dirty
Frank's offers a GF hot dog wrap
for an additional charge of $.50. ▪
www.dirtyfrankshotdogs.com

### First Watch - The Daytime Café    ✪▥
Columbus ▪ (614) 846-2738
2103 Polaris Pkwy
Columbus ▪ (614) 538-9866
3144 Kingsdale Ctr
Columbus ▪ (614) 475-8512
4770 Morse Rd
Columbus ▪ (614) 228-7554
496 S High St
Columbus ▪ (614) 876-4957
3800 Fishinger Blvd

### Giuseppe's Ritrovo               ★ $$LD
Columbus ▪ (614) 235-4300
2268 E Main St ▪ Italian ▪ GF pastas and
pizzas are available. Separate ovens and
toasters are used in order to prevent CC. ▪
www.giuseppesritrovo.com

### J. Gumbo's                          ★▥
Columbus ▪ (614) 469-9900
31 E Gay St
Columbus ▪ (614) 408-3100
1990 N High St
Columbus ▪ (614) 408-3100
8651 Sancus Blvd
Columbus ▪ (614) 471-1400
64 Granville St

### Jason's Deli                        ✪▥
Columbus ▪ (614) 785-0431
1122 Gemini Pl

### Jersey Mike's                        ▥
Columbus ▪ (614) 488-3660
1293 W Lane Ave
Columbus ▪ (614) 268-6909
4249 N High St
Columbus ▪ (614) 433-0333
1213 Polaris Pkwy

### Joe's Crab Shack                     ✪▥
Columbus ▪ (614) 799-6106
3720 W Dublin-Granville

### Lindey's Restaurant              ★ $$$LD
Columbus ▪ (614) 228-4343
169 E Beck St ▪ Bistro ▪ Restaurant offers
an in-house GF menu for their customers.
Alert server upon arrival and be sure to
note that it is an "allergy" and the server
will inform the kitchen. ▪ www.lindeys.com

### M                                  ✪$$$D
Columbus ▪ (614) 629-0000
2 Miranova Place Suite 100 ▪ Modern
American ▪ GF Menu available. Includes
items such as: salads, lobster mashed
potatoes, scallops, king crab, salmon, ahi
tuna, chicken, veal mignon, pork chop, filet
mignon and prime steak. Alert server upon
arrival so they can inform the kitchen. ▪
www.matmiranova.com

### Martini                           ✪$$$D
Columbus ▪ (614) 224-8259
445 N High St ▪ Italian ▪ GF menu
includes beef carpaccio, tuna crudo,
shrimp penne, short ribs, chicken carbonara, veal chop, veal martini and gamberi
divolo. Dessert includes vanilla brule. ▪
www.martinimodernitalian.com

### Melting Pot, The                    ✪▥
Columbus ▪ (614) 476-5500
4014 Townsfair Wy

### Mitchell's Ocean Club           ✪$$$$D
Columbus ▪ (614) 416-2582
4002 Easton Station ▪ Seafood & Steakhouse ▪ GF menu available. Includes appetizers and salads as well as sea scallops,
pork porterhouse, blackened snapper,
and chilean sea bass. A variety of steaks
and sides are also available GF. Dessert includes sorbet and crème brûlée. ▪
www.mitchellsoceanclub.com

### Mitchell's Steakhouse  ★$$$$LD
Columbus ▪ (614) 621-2333
45 N 3rd St
Columbus ▪ (614) 888-2467
1408 Polaris Pkwy ▪ Steakhouse ▪ Both
locations can accommodate GF customers. Alert server upon arrival. Most meat
and seafood dishes can be made GF.
Mention GF when making reservations ▪
www.mitchellssteakhouse.com

### O'Charley's  📖
Columbus ▪ (614) 895-7324
6285 Cleveland Ave
Columbus ▪ (614) 939-1889
4850 Morse Rd
Columbus ▪ (614) 846-9744
1425 Polars Pkwy
Columbus ▪ (614) 853-2748
1650 Georgesville Square Dr

### P.F. Chang's China Bistro  ✪★📖
Columbus ▪ (614) 416-4100
4040 Townsfair Wy

### Pei Wei Asian Diner  ✪📖
Columbus ▪ (614) 418-9825
4155 Morse Xing
Columbus ▪ (614) 985-4845
2050 Polaris Pkwy

### Pistacia Vera  ✪¢S
Columbus ▪ (614) 220-9070
541 S 3rd St ▪ Dessert ▪ GF menu is available. Items include preserves, cashew caramel, nougat, truffles, various pâtes de fruits,
a variety of macarons, pistachio cherry fig
dacquoise, and cassis berry flourless torte.
The patisserie notes that they are not a
100% GF facility. ▪ www.pistaciavera.com

### Rodizio Grill  ★📖
Columbus ▪ (614) 241-4400
125 W Nationwide Blvd

### Ruth's Chris Steak House  ✪📖
Columbus ▪ (614) 885-2910
7550 High Cross Blvd

### Shane's Rib Shack  ✪📖
Columbus ▪ (614) 436-9600
1522 Gemini Pl

### Smith & Wollensky  📖
Columbus ▪ (614) 416-2400
4145 The Strand

### Smokey Bones  📖
Columbus ▪ (614) 430-0572
1481 Polaris Pkwy

### Ted's Montana Grill  ✪📖
Columbus ▪ (614) 227-0013
191 W Nationwide Blvd

### Zpizza  ✪📖
Columbus ▪ (614) 885-0101
5060 N High St
Columbus ▪ (614) 299-3289
945 N High St

## OHIO

## ALL OTHER CITIES

### Abuelo's  ✪📖
Beaver Creek ▪ (937) 426-3070
2420 N Fairfield Rd
Mason ▪ (513) 336-7449
5010 Deerfield Blvd
Maumee ▪ (419) 866-4500
3415 Briarfield Blvd
Warrensville Heights ▪ (216) 360-9030
26100 Harvard Rd

### Altieri's Pizza  ✪★¢LD
Stow ▪ (330) 686-6860
3291 Kent Rd, Stow Plaza ▪ Pizza ▪ GF
items are marked on the menu. 9" GF pizza
and pastas are available. New GF Subs are
also available. All meals are available for
carry out only. GF pizzas have their own
designated area and cutting utensils. ▪
www.altierispizza.com

### Au Bon Pain  📖
Cleveland ▪ (216) 421-8672
2049 E 100th St
Cleveland ▪ (216) 771-1782

600 Superior Ave
Cleveland ▪ (216) 721-6473
9500 Euclid Ave

**Biaggi's**                                    ✪★📖
Perrysburg ▪ (419) 872-6100
1320 Levis Commons Blvd

**Bistro of Green**                    ✪★$$$**LD**
Uniontown ▪ (330) 896-1434
3459 Massillon Rd ▪ Modern American
▪ GF menu includes steamed mussels,
shrimp and feta, sandwiches, wraps, santa
fe chicken, catfish, a variety of salads,
salmon, mahi mahi steak, duck breast, pork
chops and GF pasta. Burgers can also be
served on a bed of lettuce rather than with
a bun. ▪ www.thebistroofgreen.com

**BJ's Restaurant and Brewhouse** ✪★📖
Dublin ▪ (614) 659-9400
5141 Tuttle Crossing

**Blue Point Grille**                    ★$$$**LD**
Cleveland ▪ (216) 875-7827
700 W Saint Clair Ave ▪ Seafood ▪
About half of the menu is naturally GF,
though it is not noted on the menu itself.
Other items can be prepared GF upon
request. Alert server upon arrival. ▪
www.bluepointgrille.com

**Bonefish Grill**                            ✪📖
West Chester ▪ (513) 755-2303
7710 Voice Of America Center Dr
Dublin ▪ (614) 789-3474
5712 Frantz Rd
Dayton ▪ (937) 428-0082
2818 Miamisburg Centerville Rd
Canton ▪ (330) 966-4853
6341 Strip Ave NW
Cleveland ▪ (216) 520-2606
6150 Rockside Pl

**Boston's Restaurant & Sports Bar**
✪★📖
Marysville ▪ (937) 642-0584
1099 Lydia Dr

**Buca di Beppo**                            ✪📖
Norwood ▪ (513) 396-7673
2635 Edmondson Rd
Strongsville ▪ (440) 846-6262
16677 Southpark Ctr
Westlake ▪ (440) 356-2276
23575 Detroit Rd
Worthington ▪ (614) 848-8466
60 E Wilson Bridge Rd

**Cheeseburger in Paradise**        ✪★📖
Hilliard ▪ (614) 876-3607
4081 Trueman Blvd

**Claddagh Irish Pub**                        📖
Lyndhurst ▪ (216) 691-0534
25389 Cedar Rd
Mason ▪ (513) 770-0999
5075 Deerfield Blvd
Toledo ▪ (419) 472-1414
5001 Monroe St

**Cooper's Hawk Winery & Restaurants**
✪★📖
Columbus ▪ (614) 428-6999
4230 The Strand

**Cosi**                                    ✪📖
Worthington ▪ (614) 844-4300
7166 N High St
Bexley ▪ (614) 238-2674
2212 E Main St

**Don Pablo's**                            ✪📖
Beavercreek ▪ (937) 320-1777
2745 Fairfield Commons
Maumee ▪ (419) 867-9979
6040 Knight's Inn Pl
North Canton ▪ (330) 966-3077
6476 Strip NW

**Eat 'n Park**                            ✪📖
Austintown ▪ (330) 779-0410
5451 Mahoning Ave
Cuyahoga Falls ▪ (330) 923-4111
200 Howe Ave
Elyria ▪ (440) 324-3286
1524 W River Rd N
Medina ▪ (330) 723-6390
1007 N Court St

Mentor ▪ (440) 255-5300
7061 Chillicothe Rd
Saint Clairsville ▪ (740) 695-5507
50620 Valley Frontage Rd
Warren ▪ (330) 372-6610
2057 Wal Mart Dr NE
Boardman ▪ (330) 758-1307
8051 Market St
Willoughby ▪ (440) 943-1050
6035 Som Center Rd
Parma ▪ (216) 459-1517
2075 Snow Rd
Steubenville ▪ (740) 266-6643
100 Mall Dr
Streetsboro ▪ (330) 422-1601
9436 State Route 14

### Ellen's Creative Cakes   ✪★$$$$
Maumee ▪ (419) 893-3543
512 W Dussel Dr ▪ Bakery ▪ Non-dedicated
bakery offering a variety of GF cakes.
Flavors include carrot, hummingbird,
and chocolate, and each is available in
a range of sizes. Owner Ellen suggests
placing an order in advance, but she
notes that she usually has some GF cake
stored in the freezer for fast pickup. ▪
*www.ellenscreativecakes.com*

### First Watch - The Daytime Café   ✪□
Dayton ▪ (937) 435-3127
2824 Miamisburg Centerville Rd
Dublin ▪ (614) 799-2774
6768 Perimeter Loop Rd
Fairlawn ▪ (330) 835-4076
3265 W Market St
Hilliard ▪ (614) 876-4957
3800 Fishinger Blvd
Kettering ▪ (937) 643-4077
4105 W Town And Country Rd
Rocky River ▪ (440) 333-3529
19340 Detroit Rd
Springdale ▪ (513) 671-1740
80 W Kemper Rd
University Heights ▪ (216) 321-1075
13950 Cedar Rd
West Chester ▪ (513) 942-5100
9233 Floer Dr
Westlake ▪ (440) 808-1082

168 Market St
Worthington ▪ (614) 431-9040
7227 N High St
Mayfield Heights ▪ (440) 684-1825
1431 Som Center Rd
Fairborn ▪ (937) 431-9150
2614A Colonel Glenn Hwy
Solon ▪ (440) 349-3447
6025 Kruse Dr
Reynoldsburg ▪ (614) 864-3447
2227 Baltimore-Reynolds Rd

### Fleming's Prime
### Steakhouse & Wine Bar   ✪□
Woodmere ▪ (216) 896-9000
28869 Chagrin Blvd
Akron ▪ (330) 670-5200
4000 Medina Rd
Dayton ▪ (937) 320-9548
4432 Walnut St

### Fox and Hound Pub & Grille   □
Mason ▪ (513) 229-7921
5113 Bowen Dr
Beavercreek ▪ (937) 426-4145
2661 Fairfield Commons Blvd
Canton ▪ (330) 497-2593
4834 Everhard Rd
Parma ▪ (440) 842-8840
8735 Day Dr
Mayfield Hgts ▪ (440) 646-9078
1479 SOM Center Rd

### Gluten-Free Bakeree, The   $$$
Bay Village ▪ (216) 408-3070
29261 Inverness Dr ▪ Bakery ▪ Dedicated
GF bakery offering cookies, cakes, breads,
pizza crust, sweet breads, pies and more.
Call 24 hours in advance for cake orders. ▪
*www.glutenfreebakeree.com*

### Godfather's Pizza   ★□
Marion ▪ (740) 387-3800
1204 Delaware Ave
Lima ▪ (419) 331-1900
2525 Elida Rd
Huber Hgts ▪ (937) 233-9900
4628 Brandt Pke
Centerville ▪ (937) 433-7777
5800 Wilmington Pke

## Gregory's Family Restaurant ✪★ⒸBL
Canton ▪ (330) 477-1296
2835 Whipple Ave NW ▪ American ▪ GF
menu features all day breakfast, including
pancakes. Owner Jean reports that they are
"ready to serve GF at any time." She notes
that many of the soups are GF, as are certain desserts such as rice pudding, peanut
butter cookies, and chocolate walnut cookies. ▪ www.jeanniescatering.com

## Ground Round ✪▱
Elyria ▪ (440) 324-5471
1550 W River Rd

## Hard Rock Café ✪▱
Cleveland ▪ (216) 830-7625
230 W Huron Rd

## Holiday Baking Company Gluten-Free
## Bakery Ⓢ
Worthington ▪ (614) 846-9300
1000 High St ▪ Bakery ▪ Dedicated GF
bakery offering breads including rolls
and buns, cookies, cupcakes, decorated
cakes, dessert bars, hand painted cookies,
mini muffins, pasta, pizza crust and quick
breads. All orders must be made a week in
advance. ▪ www.holidaybakingcompany.com

## J. Gumbo's ★▱
Baltimore ▪ (740) 862-2586
108 N Main St
Dayton ▪ (937) 522-0704
1822 Brown St
Delaware ▪ (740) 368-9494
12 S Sandusky St
Fairfield ▪ (513) 942-5486
5651-5 Boymel Dr

## Jason's Deli ✪▱
Dublin ▪ (614) 336-3853
225 W Bridge St
Grandview Heights ▪ (614) 291-7246
775 Yard St

## Jersey Mike's ▱
Springale ▪ (513) 671-5960
11409 Princeton Pike
West Chester ▪ (513) 755-8820
7240 Liberty Centre Dr

Blue Ash ▪ (513) 489-4969
4776 Cornell Rd
Mason ▪ (513) 336-7600
6651 Western Row Rd
Cincinnati ▪ (513) 474-4344
8138 Beechmont Ave
Centerville ▪ (937) 439-3840
6002 Far Hills Ave
Hillard ▪ (614) 876-8700
4664 Cemetery Rd
Dublin ▪ (614) 761-3800
5799 Karric Square Dr
Powell ▪ (614) 798-1724
3958 Powell Rd
Westerville ▪ (614) 899-7200
5957 Sunbury Rd
Gahanna ▪ (614) 337-1884
332 S Hamilton Rd
Gahanna ▪ (614) 536-0242
1340 N Hamilton Rd
Blacklick ▪ (614) 866-3080
7175 E Broad St
Pickerington ▪ (614) 863-3316
1213 Hill Rd N
Heath ▪ (740) 522-8540
609 Hebron Rd
Fairview Park ▪ (440) 333-6453
21875 Lorain Rd
Willoughby ▪ (440) 951-7827
36295 Euclid Ave
Chardon ▪ (440) 286-2030
209 Center St
Grove City ▪ (614) 594-0074
4114 Buckeye Pkwy
Dublin ▪ (614) 717-9235
6702 Perimeter Loop Rd

## Kathy's Creations Ⓢ
Alliance ▪ (330) 821-8183
2010 Crestview Ave ▪ Bakery ▪ Dedicated
GF bakery offering a wide selection of
baked goods, including a variety of cookies, graham crackers, biscotti, brownies,
muffins, bars and squares, pie crust, pies,
coffee cake, tarts, cupcakes, cakes, ginger-
bread, pound cake, shortbread, biscuits,
bear claws and cinnamon rolls. Special
orders should be placed 72 hours in advance. ▪ www.kathyscreationsbakery.com

## Kona Bistro                    ✪★$$LD
Oxford ▪ (513) 523-0686
31 W High St ▪ American ▪ GF menu available at restaurant. GF menu includes a variety of salads, burritos, pasta, burgers and sandwiches. Burgers and sandwiches are served on GF rolls and buns. ▪ www.konabistro.com

## LaRosa's Pizzeria              ★📖
Beavercreek ▪ (877) 347-1111
2453 Esquire Dr
Mason ▪ (513) 347-1111
6674 Tri Way Dr
Oxford ▪ (513) 347-1111
21 Lynn Ave
Centerville ▪ (877) 347-1111
291 E Alex-Bell Rd

## Lone Star Steakhouse & Saloon   ✪📖
Mason ▪ (513) 459-9191
9890 Escort Dr
Middletown ▪ (513) 424-7827
6780 Roosevelt Ave
Niles ▪ (330) 544-7000
5555 Youngstown Warren Rd
North Olmsted ▪ (440) 777-6522
24941 Country Club Blvd

## Loving Hut                     📖
Reynoldsburg ▪ (614) 863-0823
6569 E Livingston Ave

## Lucky's Taproom & Eatery       ★¢BLD
Dayton ▪ (937) 222-6800
520 E 5th St ▪ American ▪ Lucky's vegan menu items are all GF. Additionally, a separate grill and fryer is used to cook those items to ensure CC does not occur. ▪ www.luckystaproom.com

## Maggiano's Little Italy         ★📖
Beachwood ▪ (216) 755-3000
26300 Cedar Rd Ste 1103

## Melting Pot, The               ✪📖
Dayton ▪ (937) 567-8888
453 Miamisburg Centerville Rd
Lyndhurst ▪ (216) 381-2700
24741 Cedar Rd
Sylvania ▪ (419) 885-6358
5839 Monroe St

## Mitchell's Fish Market          ✪📖
West Chester ▪ (513) 779-5292
9456 Waterfront Dr
Woodmere ▪ (216) 765-3474
28601 Chagrin Blvd

## Momocho                        $$D
Cleveland ▪ (216) 694-2122
1835 Fulton Rd ▪ Mexican ▪ Note GF when making reservations so the restaurant can prepare. The chef will go through the menu and notify the server which dishes can be made GF. Alert the server upon arrival and they will go over the options. ▪ www.momocho.com

## Morton's Steakhouse            ✪📖
Cleveland ▪ (216) 621-6200
1600 W 2nd St

## Mustard Seed Market & Café     ✪★$$LD
Akron ▪ (330) 666-7333
3885 W Market St ▪ American ▪ GF items indicated on the lunch and dinner menu. Some items include quinoa nachos, salads, baked goat cheese, grilled marinated cauliflower steak, teriyaki brown rice bowl, grilled black pearl salmon and some sandwiches including grilled eggplant muffalatta wrap and salmon wrap. ▪ www.mustardseedmarket.com

## O'Charley's                    📖
Niles ▪ (330) 288-0066
5789 Mines Rd
Springfield ▪ (937) 342-1248
1830 N Bechtle
Springdale ▪ (513) 772-8830
11315 Princeton Pike
Reynoldsburg ▪ (614) 868-6963
2272 Baltimore-Reynoldsburg Rd
Boardman ▪ (330) 259-0207
930 Windham Ct
Canal Winchester ▪ (614) 834-0833
6224 Gender Rd
Cuyahoga Falls ▪ (330) 475-8444
283 Howe Ave
Dayton ▪ (937) 434-7639
2260 Miamisburg Centerville Rd
Dayton ▪ (937) 454-9780

7030 Miller Ln
Grove City ▪ (614) 801-1214
1657 Stringtown Rd
Harrison ▪ (513) 367-2444
616 Ring Rd
Mansfield ▪ (419) 747-6670
1335 Lexington Springmill Rd N
Middletown ▪ (513) 423-6394
3446 Village Dr
Milford ▪ (513) 722-3456
1088 State Route 28

### Old Spaghetti Factory, The   ✿★📖
Fairfield ▪ (513) 942-6620
6320 S Gilmore Rd

### Organic Bliss Gluten Free Bakery   ⊄S
Sylvania ▪ (419) 517-7799
3723 King Rd ▪ Bakery ▪ Dedicated
GF bakery offering a variety of breads,
cookies, sweet breads, brownies and
bars, scones, muffins, cakes and cupcakes, coffee cakes, pies and turnover.
GF Deli also available selling a variety
of GF breakfast wraps, salads and sandwiches. Allow 72 hours for special orders. ▪
www.organicblissmarket.com

### Original Gino's Pizza, The   ★$$LD
Toledo ▪ (419) 472-3567
3981 Monroe St
Perrysburg ▪ (419) 874-9170
26597 N Dixie Hwy
Toledo ▪ (419) 269-4466
1280 W Alexis Rd
Northwood ▪ (419) 690-4466
2670 Woodville Rd
Maumee ▪ (419) 897-4466
449 W Dussel Dr
Toledo ▪ (419) 843-3567
5307 Monroe St ▪ Pizza ▪ GF pizza is available at all locations. Customer service reports that GF prep and cooking is done "in
a manner to prevent cross-contamination."
▪ www.originalginos.com

### P.F. Chang's China Bistro   ✿★📖
Beachwood ▪ (216) 292-1411
26001 Chagrin Blvd
Dayton ▪ (937) 428-6085
2626 Miamisburg Centerville Rd
Dublin ▪ (614) 726-0070
6135 Parkcenter Cir
Fairlawn ▪ (330) 869-0560
3265 W Market St Ste 100A
Maumee ▪ (419) 878-8490
2300 Village Dr W Ste 140
West Chester ▪ (513) 779-5555
9435 Civic Centre Blvd

### Pei Wei Asian Diner   ✿📖
Dublin ▪ (614) 726-4190
7571 Sawmill Rd

### Pies & Pints   ★$$LD
Worthington ▪ (614) 885-7437
7227 N High St ▪ Pizza ▪ GF pizza is available, as well as several GF salads and soups.
▪ www.piesandpints.net

### Pizza Fusion   ★📖
Cleveland ▪ (216) 368-6274
10900 Euclid Ave

### Pizza Joe's   ★📖
Andover ▪ (440) 293-4778
310 E Main St
Boardman ▪ (330) 965-8888
6810 Market St
Campbell ▪ (330) 747-3164
196 McCartney Rd
Champion ▪ (330) 847-7244
4437 Mahoning Ave
Columbiana ▪ (330) 482-1781
1109 St Rt 14
Cornersburg ▪ (330) 799-6868
2000 Canfield Rd
Cortland ▪ (330) 638-1222
222 W Main St
E Palestine ▪ (330) 426-3223
96 Taggart St
Jefferson ▪ (440) 576-1111
51 N Chestnut St
Girard ▪ (330) 545-5550
621 N State St

Lordstown ▪ (330) 824-2020
6100 Todd Ave
Mineral Ridge ▪ (330) 544-5454
3971 Main St Ridge Crk Plaza
Salem ▪ (330) 337-5637
2440 SE Blvd
Struthers ▪ (330) 755-3636
1014 5th St
Youngstown ▪ (330) 744-0099
642 Gypsy Ln
Youngstown ▪ (330) 270-0116
3506 Mahoning Ave W
Youngstown ▪ (330) 746-4290
Fed Plaza Food Ct

**Real Seafood Co.**                     ✪$$$LD
Toledo ▪ (419) 697-5427
22 Main St ▪ Seafood ▪ GF pasta is
available. Other items can be modified
to be GF, just ask server beforehand and
they will list all the available options. ▪
www.realseafoodcorestaurant.com

**Romano's Macaroni Grill**          ✪★📖
Akron ▪ (330) 665-3881
41 Springside Dr
Canton ▪ (330) 492-0722
4721 Dressler Rd NW
Dublin ▪ (614) 792-3676
6115 Parkcenter Cir
North Olmsted ▪ (440) 734-9980
25001 Country Club Blvd
Strongsville ▪ (440) 878-3000
17095 Southpark Ctr

**Sandy Chanty Seafood Restaurant** ★$$LD
Geneva On The Lake ▪ (440) 415-1080
5457 Lake Ave ▪ Seafood ▪ Restaurant
caters to GF diets. Any pasta dishes can be
made GF, sauces are made with corn starch
instead of flour. Most fish and steak dishes
are GF and GF beer is also available. Alert
server that you would like to check out GF
options. ▪ www.sandychanty.com

**Sinfully Gluten-Free**                    ⊄S
Centerville ▪ (937) 433-1044
9146 Dayton-Lebanon Pike ▪ Bakery &
Café ▪ Dedicated GF restaurant and bak-

ery offering breads, brownies, cakes, short-
breads, cookies and gift baskets. Restaurant
menu includes pizza, sandwiches, salads,
chicken wings, french fries and chicken
strips. ▪ www.sinfullygf.com

**Smokey Bones**                            📖
Beechmont ▪ (513) 528-1725
509 Ohio Pike
Dayton ▪ (937) 415-0185
6744 Miller Ln
Grove City ▪ (614) 277-3270
1615 Stringtown Rd
Reynoldsburg ▪ (614) 577-0764
2200 Baltimore Reynoldsburg Rd
Boardman ▪ (330) 965-1554
6651 S Ave
N. Olmsted ▪ (440) 779-4384
257895 Brookpark Rd
Mentor ▪ (440) 942-0993
7725 Reynolds Rd

**Soup Pot, The**                        ✪★⊄S
Solon ▪ (440) 248-0996
34376 Aurora Rd ▪ American ▪ A wide variety of GF breads, muffins, scones and cookies
are available. Special ordered GF cake,
cheesecake, ganache, and lemon squares
must be ordered 3 days in advance. A GF
panini sandwich is also available as well as
a variety of soups including cabbage kielbasa, cheddar corn chowder, stuffed pepper,
chunky chicken vegetable, chicken paprikash,
garden vegetable, tomato basil, lentil and the
seasonal turkey chili. ▪ www.thesouppot.com

**Stir Crazy**                              ★📖
Lyndhurst ▪ (216) 381-7600
25385 Cedar Rd

**Sugar N Spice at the Carriage House**
★⊄S
Avon ▪ (440) 934-2998
36741 Detroit Rd ▪ Bakery ▪ GF items
include a variety of cookies such as snickerdoodle, cran orange and peanut butter, as
well as raspberry and mint brownies. GF
cakes, cupcakes, muffins and breads can be
are available by special order with at least
48 hours' notice. GF items are prepared

394 **OKLAHOMA** ▪ ▪ Oklahoma City

in a separate building to avoid CC. ▪ *www.chbakery.com*

**Sweet Shalom Tea Room**                    *$$$$*
*Sylvania* ▪ *(419) 297-9919*
*8216 Erie St* ▪ *Teahouse* ▪ Reservations noting GF are recommended so the kitchen will have time to prepare. They will look at the current menu, "work with it," and "adapt it" to accommodate the GF diet. None of the tea served contains gluten. ▪ *www.sweetshalomtearoom.com*

**Ted's Montana Grill**                    ✪📖
*Dublin* ▪ *(614) 760-7753*
*6195 Sawmill Rd*

**Tina's Sweet Treats**                    ¢S
*Franklin* ▪ *(513) 429-9428*
*4271 S Dixie Hwy* ▪ *Bakery* ▪ 100% dedicated GF sweet shop that bakes a variety of cookies, muffins, breads, and brownies. ▪ *www.tinassweettreats.com*

**Tommy's PCR**                    ✪★¢**BLD**
*North Ridgeville* ▪ *(440) 327-1212*
*34441 Ctr Ridge Rd* ▪ *American* ▪ GF menu includes box of nachos with a variety of toppings, potato skins, french fries, chicken fingers, cheesy bread, wings, pizza, calzones, pork chops, variety of sandwiches and tacos, ribs, fish fry and dessert including chocolate brownie, cinnamon stix and GF dessert pizza. ▪ *www.tommyspcr.com*

**Tommy's Pizza and Chicken**        ✪★$**LD**
*Strongsville* ▪ *(440) 878-9999*
*17664 Pearl Rd*
*Lakewood* ▪ *(216) 227-9999*
*16813 Madison Ave* ▪ *Italian* ▪ GF pizza is available in the 12-inch size, cooked or on a "take-&-bake" basis. GF breadsticks, cheesy garlic breadsticks, calzones, and chicken wings are also available. ▪ *www.tommyspizzaandchicken.com*

**Tree Huggers Café**                    ✪★¢**LD**
*Berea* ▪ *(440) 973-4277*
*1330 W Bagley Rd* ▪ *Organic* ▪ GF menu includes a cranberry walnut salad, "gi-

ant armadillo" fresh spinach salad, dandelion soup, rice bowls, grilled eggplant panini, lemon chicken panini, ground chicken burger, and more. An assortment of GF baked goods are also available. ▪ *www.treehuggerscafe.com*

**U Food Grill**                    📖
*Cleveland* ▪ *(216) 265-6000*
*5300 Riverside Dr*

**Uno Chicago Grill**                    ✪★📖
*Dayton* ▪ *(937) 910-8000*
*126 N Main St*
*Dublin* ▪ *(614) 793-8300*
*5930 Britton Pkwy*
*Pickerington* ▪ *(614) 501-1900*
*1720 Hill Rd N*
*West Chester* ▪ *(513) 942-6646*
*9246 Schulze Dr*
*Cleveland* ▪ *(216) 687-5490*
*2121 Euclid Ave*

# OKLAHOMA

## OKLAHOMA CITY

**Abuelo's**                    ✪📖
*Oklahoma City* ▪ *(405) 235-1422*
*17 E Sheridan*
*Oklahoma City* ▪ *(405) 755-2680*
*3001 W Memorial Rd*

**BJ's Restaurant and Brewhouse** ✪★📖
*Oklahoma City* ▪ *(405) 748-6770*
*2425 W Memorial Rd*

**Cafe do Brasil**                    ★¢**LD**
*Oklahoma City* ▪ *(405) 525-9779*
*440 NW 11Th St* ▪ *Brazilian* ▪ GF options include fruit salad, vegetable soup, black bean soup, avocado salad, spinach salad, orange almond salad and a chicken appetizer. ▪ *www.cafedobrazilokc.com*

**Cantina Laredo**    📖
*Oklahoma City* ▪ *(405) 840-1051*
*1901 NW Expwy*

**Carino's Italian**    ✪📖
*Oklahoma City* ▪ *(405) 752-0087*
*2905 W Memorial Rd*
*Oklahoma City* ▪ *(405) 632-4600*
*7900 S Walker Ave*

**Charleston's Restaurant**    ✪📖
*Oklahoma City* ▪ *(405) 721-0060*
*5907 NW Expwy*
*Oklahoma City* ▪ *(405) 681-6686*
*2000 S Meridian*
*Oklahoma City* ▪ *(405) 681-0055*
*1429 SW 74th St*

**Cheever's Café**    ✪$$$LD
*Oklahoma City* ▪ *(405) 525-7007*
*2409 N Hudson Ave* ▪ *Café* ▪ GF menu
available. Items include white bean hummus,
salads and soups, roasted chicken enchilada,
Cheever's chicken salad, angus filet, cherry-
pecan crusted salmon as well as some sides
and brunch items. ▪ *cheeverscafe.com*

**Chelino's Mexican Restaurant**    $LD
*Oklahoma City* ▪ *(405) 235-3533*
*15 E California*
*Oklahoma City* ▪ *(405) 947-5611*
*1605 N Meridian*
*Oklahoma City* ▪ *(405) 670-4600*
*115 S Sooner Rd*
*Oklahoma City* ▪ *(405) 636-1548*
*4221 S Robinson Ave*
*Oklahoma City* ▪ *(405) 631-3797*
*5804 S Western Ave*
*Oklahoma City* ▪ *(405) 842-4773*
*5900 N May Ave*
*Oklahoma City* ▪ *(405) 728-2770*
*9501 N Council Rd*
*Oklahoma City* ▪ *(405) 286-3112*
*10904 N May Ave*
*Oklahoma City* ▪ *(405) 636-1110*
*427 SW Grand Blvd* ▪ *Mexican* ▪ GF
items include chicken and rice dinner,
enchiladas and tacos. There are only
a few items on the menu that are GF,

be sure to alert server upon arrival. ▪
*www.chelinosmexicanrestaurant.com*

**Cool Greens**    ✪⊄LD
*Oklahoma City* ▪ *(405) 600-6444*
*204 N Robinson*
*Oklahome City* ▪ *(405) 841-2665*
*6475 Avondale*
*Oklahoma City* ▪ *(405) 286-9304*
*14201 N May Ave* ▪ *Deli* ▪ GF items
indicated on menu. Included are wild
sockeye salmon salad, southwest spicy
chicken, plaza skinny and Bahamian jerk. ▪
*mycoolgreens.com*

**Deep Fork Grill**    $$$$LD
*Oklahoma City* ▪ *(405) 848-7678*
*5418 N Western Ave* ▪ *Seafood & Steak-
house* ▪ Team member Wade reports that
the majority of the menu is GF, and that
GF items are prepared in a separate area
of the kitchen. Reservations noting GF
are recommended so that the kitchen has
time to prepare. Alert a server upon ar-
rival and they will go over the options. ▪
*www.deepforkgrill.com*

**First Watch - The Daytime Café**    ✪📖
*Oklahoma City* ▪ *(405) 748-3447*
*2328 W Memorial Rd*

**Fox and Hound Pub & Grille**    📖
*Oklahoma City* ▪ *(405) 751-7243*
*3031 W Mem Rd*

**Garbanzo**    📖
*Oklahoma City* ▪ *(405) 254-5055*
*4130 NW Exprswy*

**Genghis Grill**    📖
*Oklahoma City* ▪ *(405) 509-2695*
*2121 W Memorial Rd*

**Hefner Grill**    $$LD
*Oklahoma City* ▪ *(405) 748-6113*
*9201 Lake Hefner Pkwy* ▪ *American* ▪ GF
items include fish dishes, steaks, king crab
legs, seafood enchiladas and fish tacos
with grilled fish instead of beer battered. ▪
*hefnergrill.ehsrg.com*

**Hideaway Pizza**    ★
*Oklahoma City* ▪ *(405) 796-7777*

901 N Broadway Ave
*Oklahoma City* ▪ *(405) 470-4777*
5950 W Mem Rd
*Oklahoma City* ▪ *(405) 840-4777*
6616 N Western Ave
*Warr Acres* ▪ *(405) 603-7177*
5501 NW Expressway St
*Oklahoma City* ▪ *(405) 232-4776*
#2 Mickey Mantle Dr ▪ Hideaway was
voted Oklahoma's best pizza and has GF
crust available in a small size only.

### HuHot Mongolian Grill    ✪📖
*Oklahoma City* ▪ *(405) 748-3777*
2501 W Memorial Rd

### Jason's Deli    ✪📖
*Oklahoma City* ▪ *(405) 810-1800*
4236 NW Expwy

### Jersey Mike's    📖
*Oklahoma City* ▪ *(405) 753-9998*
2522 W Memorial Rd
*Oklahoma City* ▪ *(405) 524-1200*
1630 NW 23rd St
*Oklahoma City* ▪ *(405) 634-7300*
7500 S Santa Fe
*Oklahoma City* ▪ *(405) 787-7877*
6815 SW 3rd St
*Oklahoma City* ▪ *(405) 848-8900*
6719 N May Ave
*Oklahoma City* ▪ *(405) 721-8888*
6401 Northwest Expwy
*Oklahoma City* ▪ *(405) 600-7280*
3604 N May Ave

### Joe's Crab Shack    ✪📖
*Oklahoma City* ▪ *(405) 728-9906*
5940 NW Expwy
*Oklahoma City* ▪ *(405) 681-1200*
1508 SW 74th St

### Mantel Wine Bar & Bistro, The   $$$$**L D**
*Oklahoma City* ▪ *(405) 236-8040*
201 E Sheridan Ave ▪ Modern American
▪ Restaurant reports that they accommodate GF customers weekly. Both
servers and chefs are familiar with GF
requests and servers will be able to list
items on the menu that can be made GF. ▪
*www.themantelokc.com*

### Melting Pot, The    ✪📖
*Oklahoma City* ▪ *(405) 235-1000*
4 E Sheridan Ave

### P.F. Chang's China Bistro    ✪★📖
*Oklahoma City* ▪ *(405) 748-4003*
13700 N Pennsylvania Ave

### Paseo Grill    $$**L D**
*Oklahoma City* ▪ *(405) 601-1079*
2909 Paseo ▪ Modern American ▪ Every
item on the menu can be made GF with
the exception of the pasta dishes and
the meatloaf. Servers are reportedly
"very well versed" on GF selections. ▪
*www.paseogrill.com*

### Pei Wei Asian Diner    ✪📖
*Oklahoma City* ▪ *(405) 767-9001*
1841 Belle Isle Blvd

### Red Primesteak    ✪$$$$**D**
*Oklahoma City* ▪ *(405) 232-2626*
504 N Broadway Ave ▪ Steakhouse
▪ GF menu includes steak, tenderloin
tamales, salmon, halibut, tilapia, lobster
tail, pork chops and a number of sides. ▪
*www.redprimesteak.com*

### Romano's Macaroni Grill    ✪★📖
*Oklahoma City* ▪ *(405) 948-0055*
3510 NW Expwy

### Zio's    ✪📖
*Oklahoma City* ▪ *(405) 278-8888*
12 E California Ave
*Oklahoma City* ▪ *(405) 680-9999*
2035 S Meridian Ave

# OKLAHOMA

## TULSA

### Abuelo's ✪📖
*Tulsa* ▪ *(918) 249-1546*
*10909 E 71st St S*

### Bodean Seafood Restaurant $$$LD
*Tulsa* ▪ *(918) 749-1407*
*3376 E 51st St* ▪ Seafood ▪ Any item on the menu can be modified to be GF. Reservations noting GF are strongly recommended, as is alerting the server upon arrival. ▪ *www.bodean.net*

### Carino's Italian ✪📖
*Tulsa* ▪ *(918) 270-2000*
*6364 E 41st St*
*Tulsa* ▪ *(918) 298-7010*
*9718 Riverside Pkwy*

### Charleston's Restaurant ✪📖
*Tulsa* ▪ *(918) 495-3511*
*6839 S Yale Ave*
*Tulsa* ▪ *(918) 749-3287*
*3726 S Peoria*

### Cosmo Café ✪★¢LD
*Tulsa* ▪ *(918) 933-4848*
*3334 S Peoria Ave* ▪ Deli ▪ GF options include salads and sandwiches served on a GF bagel. For dessert, GF sundae options include hot fudge brownie, caramel cookie, and mint chocolate chip. ▪ *www.cosmo-cafe.com*

### First Watch - The Daytime Café ✪📖
*Tulsa* ▪ *(918) 296-9960*
*8178 S Lewis Ave #A*
*Tulsa* ▪ *(918) 610-3447*
*8104 E 68th St*

### Fleming's Prime Steakhouse & Wine Bar ✪📖
*Tulsa* ▪ *(918) 712-7500*
*1976 E 21st S Utica Sq*

### Freebirds on the Fly ✪📖
*Tulsa* ▪ *(918) 445-4113*
*7547B S Olympia Ave*

### Genghis Grill 📖
*Tulsa* ▪ *(918) 574-2695*
*1619 E 15th St*

### Hideaway Pizza ★
*Tulsa* ▪ *(918) 582-4777*
*1419 E 15th St*
*Tulsa* ▪ *(918) 270-4777*
*7877 E 51st St*
*Tulsa* ▪ *(918) 492-4777*
*8204 S Harvard Ave*
*Tulsa* ▪ *(918) 366-4777*
*8222 E 103rd St*
*Tulsa* ▪ *(918) 609-6777*
*7549 S Olympia Ave* ▪ Hideaway was voted Oklahoma's best pizza and has GF crust available in a small size only.

### HuHot Mongolian Grill 📖
*Tulsa* ▪ *(918) 459-5346*
*6746 S Memorial*

### Jason's Deli ✪📖
*Tulsa* ▪ *(918) 599-7777*
*1330 E 15th St*
*Tulsa* ▪ *(918) 252-9999*
*8321 E 61st St S*

### Joe Mamma's ★$LD
*Tulsa* ▪ *(918) 794-6563*
*112 S Elgin Ave* ▪ Pizza ▪ GF pizza crust is available in 10" size only. ▪ *joemommas.com*

### Joe's Crab Shack ✪📖
*Tulsa* ▪ *(918) 252-1010*
*7646 E 61st St*

### Kilkenny's Irish Pub ✪$$LD
*Tulsa* ▪ *(918) 582-8282*
*1413 E 15th St* ▪ Irish ▪ GF menu available. Some items include kabobs, steak, vegetables, potato soup, shrimp and burgers without the buns. GF beer is also available. ▪ *www.tulsairishpub.com*

### P.F. Chang's China Bistro ✪★📖
*Tulsa* ▪ *(918) 747-6555*
*1978 E 21st St*

### Pei Wei Asian Diner    ✪📖
*Tulsa* ▪ *(918) 749-6083*
*3535 S Peoria Ave*
*Tulsa* ▪ *(918) 497-1015*
*5954 S Yale Ave*

### Riverside Grill    ✪★$$$LD
*Tulsa* ▪ *(918) 394-2433*
*9912 Riverside Pkwy* ▪ *American* ▪
GF items available. Servers are well
versed on dishes that are naturally GF
as well as dishes that can be modified
to be GF. Alert a server upon arrival. ▪
*www.riversidegrilltulsa.com*

### Romano's Macaroni Grill    ✪★📖
*Tulsa* ▪ *(918) 254-7800*
*6603 S Memorial Dr*

### Zio's    ✪📖
*Tulsa* ▪ *(918) 250-5999*
*7111 S Mingo Rd*
*Tulsa* ▪ *(918) 298-9880*
*8112 S Lewis Ave*

# OKLAHOMA

## ALL OTHER CITIES

### BJ's Restaurant and Brewhouse    ✪★📖
*Norman* ▪ *(405) 360-4400*
*330 Ed Noble Pkwy*

### Blu Fine Wine & Food    ✪$LD
*Norman* ▪ *(405) 360-4258*
*201 S Crawford Ave* ▪ *Seafood* ▪ GF accommodations can be made to many items
on menu. Some GF items include shrimp
and grits, seared sea scallops, beef tenderloin and roasted quinoa with vegetables. ▪
*www.blufinewineandfood.com*

### Bonefish Grill    ✪📖
*Broken Arrow* ▪ *(918) 252-3474*
*4651 W Kenosha St*

### Carino's Italian    ✪📖
*Norman* ▪ *(405) 447-5000*
*970 Ed Noble Dr*
*Yukon* ▪ *(405) 350-0756*
*1608 Garth Brooks Blvd*

### Charleston's Restaurant    ✪📖
*Broken Arrow* ▪ *(918) 355-9177*
*251 Hillside Dr*
*Edmond* ▪ *(405) 478-4949*
*3409 S Broadway*
*Norman* ▪ *(405) 360-0900*
*300 Ed Noble Pkwy*

### Chelino's Mexican Restaurant    $LD
*Edmond* ▪ *(405) 340-3620*
*1612 S Blvd*
*Norman* ▪ *(405) 447-8050*
*1331 E Alameda St*
*Bethany* ▪ *(405) 440-9411*
*7000 NW 23rd St* ▪ *Mexican* ▪ GF
items include chicken and rice dinner,
enchiladas and tacos. There are only
a few items on the menu that are GF,
be sure to alert server upon arrival. ▪
*www.chelinosmexicanrestaurant.com*

### Cool Greens    ✪⊄LD
*Norman* ▪ *(405) 701-5000*
*3700 W Robinson*
*Edmond* ▪ *(405) 562-1020*
*1189 E 15th St* ▪ *Deli* ▪ GF items indicated on menu. Included are wild sockeye
salmon salad, southwest spicy chicken,
plaza skinny and Bahamian jerk. ▪
*mycoolgreens.com*

### Eischen's Bar    $LD
*Okarche* ▪ *(405) 263-9939*
*108 S 2Nd* ▪ *Pub Food* ▪ GF items include
roast beef without the bun and some bbq
items. Be sure to alert server and they will
be able to list GF options.

### Fox and Hound Pub & Grille    📖
*Broken Arrow* ▪ *(918) 307-2847*
*7001 S Garnett Rd*

### Frank and Lola's Neighborhood Res-
### taurant & Bar    ✪$LD
*Bartlesville* ▪ *(918) 336-5652*

200 E 2nd St ▪ American ▪ Frank and Lola's has a wide variety of GF foods located on their main menu. GF entrée options include catfish, pulled pork, salmon and ribeye steak ▪ www.frankandlolas.com

### Genghis Grill   📖
*Bixby* ▪ *(918) 364-2695*
*10438 S 82nd E Ave*
*Moore* ▪ *(405) 793-2695*
*2370 S I-35 Service Rd*

### Gina & Guiseppe's   ✪★$LD
*Jenks* ▪ *(918) 296-0111*
*400 Riverwalk Terrace* ▪ *Italian* ▪ All salads are available GF upon request. Other GF items include house GF pasta with choice of marinara, alfredo, pesto cream and white clam sauce as well as a number of meat options and an 8" GF pizza available. ▪ www.gngitalian.com

### Hideaway Pizza   ★
*Broken Arrow* ▪ *(918) 286-1777*
*1150 N 9th St*
*Edmond* ▪ *(405) 348-4777*
*116 E 5th St*
*Norman* ▪ *(405) 292-4777*
*577 Buchanan Ave*

### Jason's Deli   ✪📖
*Edmond* ▪ *(405) 330-1663*
*78 E 33rd St*
*Norman* ▪ *(405) 360-3600*
*950 Ed Noble Dr*

### Jersey Mike's   📖
*Midwest City* ▪ *(405) 741-2544*
*1940 S Air Depot Blvd*
*Edmond* ▪ *(405) 348-9520*
*1724 S Broadway Extension*
*Yukon* ▪ *(405) 265-2225*
*1600 Garth Brooks Blvd*
*Norman* ▪ *(405) 321-5100*
*1204 N Interstate Dr*
*Warr Acres* ▪ *(405) 603-3533*
*3800 N MacArthur Blvd*
*Edmond* ▪ *(405) 844-1988*
*1149 E 2nd St*
*Lawton* ▪ *(580) 699-8800*
*2504-A NW Cache Rd*

*Moore* ▪ *(405) 895-7478*
*660 SW 19th St*

### Lone Star Steakhouse & Saloon   ✪📖
*Broken Arrow* ▪ *(918) 355-1133*
*101 E Albany St*
*Lawton* ▪ *(580) 248-8785*
*5374 NW Cache Rd*
*Owasso* ▪ *(918) 274-3500*
*9013 N 121st E Ave*

### Melting Pot, The   ✪📖
*Jenks* ▪ *(918) 299-8000*
*300 Riverwalk Ter*

### On the Border
### Mexican Grill & Cantina   ✪📖
*Edmond* ▪ *(405) 359-5749*
*3233 S Broadway*
*Norman* ▪ *(405) 573-2022*
*3000 William Pereira* ▪ Allergen guide is available online and in restaurant upon request. They have a specific GF fryer and sanitizers at every station, as well as a comprehensive computer system that tells the kitchen staff exactly what to do per allergy order. Guest relations coordinator Robin recommends consulting with the manager on duty when dining in.

### Pei Wei Asian Diner   ✪📖
*Broken Arrow* ▪ *(918) 250-8557*
*4609 W Kenosha St*
*Edmond* ▪ *(405) 341-6850*
*1141 E 2nd St*
*Norman* ▪ *(405) 364-1690*
*1500 24th Ave NW*

### Pink Elephant Café   ★$LD
*Norman* ▪ *(405) 307-8449*
*301 E Main St* ▪ *American* ▪ GF quiche as well as some Spanish dishes are available. Be sure to alert server upon arrival and they will provide a list of items that can be made GF.

### Pizza Shoppe   ★📖
*Bixby* ▪ *(918) 369-2777*
*13161 S Memorial Dr*

### Rodney's Pizza Place   ★$LD
*Purcell* ▪ *(405) 527-7373*

2234 N Green Ave ▪ *Pizza* ▪ GF 10" pizza available. ▪ *www.rodneyspizzaplace.com*

### Shorty Smalls                                         📖
*Oklahoma City* ▪ *(405) 947-0779*
*2037 S Meridian*

### Zio's                                                 ✪📖
*Norman* ▪ *(405) 364-4650*
*1353 24th Ave NW*

# OREGON

## EUGENE

### BJ's Restaurant and Brewhouse ✪★📖
*Eugene* ▪ *(541) 342-6114*
*1600 Coburg Rd*

### Cozmic Pizza                                      ★$$$**LD**
*Eugene* ▪ *(541) 338-9333*
*199 W 8th St* ▪ *Pizza* ▪ GF pizza is available in slices and full pizzas. ▪ *www.cozmicpizza.com*

### Evergreen Indian Cuisine            $**LD**
*Eugene* ▪ *(541) 343-7944*
*1525 Franklin Blvd* ▪ *Indian* ▪ Owner Meeraali reports that everything except the bread is GF or can be prepared GF. She notes that many of the curries, soups, and other Indian dishes are GF. Confirm the timeliness of this information before dining in. ▪ *www.evergreenindianrestaurant.com*

### Go Healthy Café                          ✪★(**S**
*Eugene* ▪ *(541) 683-3164*
*3802 W 11th Ave* ▪ *American* ▪ GF menu includes a variety of sandwiches on GF focaccia bread, salads, burrito bowls, teriyaki chicken bowls, and more. Be sure to let your server know you are ordering off the GF menu. ▪ *www.gohealthycafe.com*

### Lok Yaun Restaurant                  ✪(**LD**
*Eugene* ▪ *(541) 345-7448*
*2360 W 11Th Ave* ▪ *Chinese* ▪ GF items

available. Alert server upon arrival. ▪ *www.lokyaunrestaurant.com*

### McGrath's Fish House                  ✪📖
*Eugene* ▪ *(541) 342-6404*
*1036 Valley River Wy*

### P.F. Chang's China Bistro        ✪★📖
*Eugene* ▪ *(541) 225-2015*
*124 Coburg Rd*

### Papa's Pizza Parlor                  ✪★$$**LD**
*Eugene* ▪ *(541) 485-5555*
*1577 Coburg Rd*
*Eugene* ▪ *(541) 485-5555*
*1700 W 11th Ave* ▪ *Pizza* ▪ GF menu includes an extensive list of GF pizzas. GF beer is also available. ▪ *www.papaspizza.net*

### Sweet Life Patisserie                    ★(**S**
*Eugene* ▪ *(541) 683-5676*
*755 Monroe St* ▪ *Bakery* ▪ Non-dedicated GF bakery offering GF cookies and brownies in assorted flavors. They always carry crème brûlée and chocolate mousse, which are naturally GF. GF cakes are available by special order only. ▪ *www.sweetlifedesserts.com*

### Tasty Thai Kitchen                    ✪$**BLD**
*Eugene* ▪ *(541) 302-6444*
*80 E 29th Ave* ▪ *Thai* ▪ Restaurant offers an extensive dedicated GF menu. Some items on the menu are naturally GF, while others can be prepared with alternative GF ingredients. Be sure to alert the server upon ordering with all GF requests. ▪ *tastythaikitchen.com*

# OREGON

## PORTLAND

### A Cena ★$$$LD
*Portland* ▪ (503) 206-3291
*7742 SE 13th Ave* ▪ *Italian* ▪ GF pasta available. Other items on the menu can also be modified to be GF. Alert the server upon arrival. ▪ *www.acenapdx.com*

### Andina Restaurant ✪$$LD
*Portland* ▪ (503) 228-9535
*1314 NW Glisan St* ▪ *Latin American* ▪ There are separate GF menus for lunch, dinner, and dessert. Various seafood dishes are available that include shrimp, fish, oysters and mussels as well as more familiar options such as chicken and beef plates. Some GF desserts include creamy goat cheese and lemon cake as well as a quinoa studded passion fruit mousse served with lemon sorbet and caramel. ▪ *www.andinarestaurant.com*

### Bellagios Pizza ✪★$$LD
*Portland* ▪ (503) 230-2900
*8112 SE 13th St*
*Portland* ▪ (503) 244-1737
*9059 SW Barbur Blvd*
*Portland* ▪ (503) 221-0110
*1742 SW Jefferson St* ▪ *Pizza* ▪ GF menu includes a variety of pizzas in either 10" or 14" inch with a "build your own pizza" option, salads, and appetizers. GF pizza dough is also available for "take-&-bake." Company President Julie Collins reports that they have "gone to great lengths to eliminate cross-contamination issues." ▪ *www.bellagiospizza.com*

### Besaws ✪★$$BLD
*Portland* ▪ (503) 228-2619
*2301 NW Savier St* ▪ *American* ▪ GF bread and pancakes are available for brunch. Alert server upon arrival and they will help select a meal. ▪ *www.besaws.com*

### BJ's Restaurant and Brewhouse ✪★📖
*Portland* ▪ (503) 289-5566
*12105 N Center Ave*

### Blossoming Lotus ★$BLD
*Portland* ▪ (503) 228-0048
*1713 NE 15th Ave* ▪ *Vegan* ▪ GF options for brunch, lunch, and dinner. Options include: tofu scrambles, buckwheat and oatmeal pancakes, crispy artichoke fritters, various salads, falafel wraps and more. ▪ *blpdx.com*

### Bluehour Restaurant ★$$$LD
*Portland* ▪ (503) 226-3394
*250 NW 13th Ave* ▪ *American* ▪ Restaurant reports that 75% of the menu is GF, though it is not noted on the menu. Ask the server for GF options when placing an order. ▪ *www.bluehouronline.com*

### Corbett Fish House ★$$LD
*Portland* ▪ (503) 246-4434
*5901 SW Corbett Ave* ▪ *Seafood* ▪ Restaurant reports that "almost the whole menu" is GF. All fish are breaded with rice flour, and corn tortillas are available for the fish tacos. GF sandwich buns are also available. ▪ *www.corbettfishhouse.com*

### Cravin' Raven Bakery ¢$
*Portland* ▪ (503) 234-0603
*8339 SE 13th Ave* ▪ *Bakery* ▪ Dedicated GF bakery offering muffins, cookies, cupcakes, and mini-loaves, as well as larger cakes by special order. All items are dairy-free as well as GF, and most are vegan and soy-free as well. ▪ *www.cravinraven.com*

### East India Co Grill & Bar ★$$LD
*Portland* ▪ (503) 227-8815
*821 SW 11th Ave* ▪ *Indian* ▪ Most of the items offered on the menu GF. Ask a server about GF options. Please note: Naan and Roti are NOT GF. ▪ *eastindiacopdx.com*

### Flying Pie Pizzeria ★
*Portland* ▪ (503) 254-2016
*7804 SE Stark St* ▪ *Pizza* ▪ GF pizza is available, and toppings that contain gluten

are marked on the menu for easy avoidance. ■ *www.flying-pie.com*

### Fratelli Cucina     $$D
*Portland* ■ *(503) 241-8800*
*1230 NW Hoyt St* ■ *Italian* ■ GF pasta available. ■ *www.fratellicucina.com*

### Fuel Café     ✪★₵BL
*Portland* ■ *(503) 335-3835*
*1452 NE Alberta St* ■ *American* ■ GF breads and English muffins can be substituted in any sandwich or breakfast order. GF cookies are also available. However, there is no dedicated prep area for the GF breads and pastries. ■ *www.fuelcafe.biz*

### Gluten Free Gem Bakery     ₵S
*Portland* ■ *(503) 288-1508*
*265 N Hancock St #105* ■ *Bakery* ■ Dedicated GF bakery offering a seasonally rotating variety of muffins, cookies, cakes, pies, breads and more. Some items may require advance orders depending on availability. ■ *www.glutenfreegem.com*

### Godfather's Pizza     ★📖
*Portland* ■ *(503) 646-1100*
*11140 SW Barnes Rd*

### Gustav's Pub & Grill     ✪★$LD
*Portland* ■ *(503) 288-5503*
GF menu includes mushroom schnitzel, Rhineland salmon, rotisserie chicken, sausage trio, and more. For dessert, there is GF flourless chocolate cake, Bavarian crème, and chocolate mousse. GF beer is available. Executive coordinator Hannah reports that all staff are GF aware, but cautions that all items are prepared using common equipment. *5035 NE Sandy Blvd* ■ *European* ■ *www.gustavs.net*

### Hawthorne Fish House     ★$$LD
*Portland* ■ *(503) 548-4434*
*4343 SE Hawthorne Blvd* ■ *Seafood* ■ Manager John reports that "almost the whole menu" is GF. All fish are breaded with rice flour, and corn tortillas are available for the fish tacos.

GF sandwich buns are also available. ■ *www.corbettfishhouse.com*

### Iorio Restaurant     ✪★$$D
*Portland* ■ *(503) 445-4716*
*912 SE Hawthorne Blvd* ■ *Italian* ■ The restaurant reports that they specialize in providing meals to satisfy all food allergies & dietary needs. They recommend mentioning GF needs when making reservations. The menu notes several items that are always GF or have GF alternatives available, including gnocchi, calamari with cornmeal crust and eggplant parmesan. ■ *www.ioriorestaurant.com*

### Keana's Candyland Restaurant & Bakery     ₵BL
*Portland* ■ *(503) 719-5131*
*5314 SE Milwaukie Ave* ■ *Bakery & Café* ■ Dedicated GF bakery and restaurant offering a variety of omelettes, crepes, pancakes, French toast, and more for breakfast. For lunch, they offer a wide variety of sandwiches and burgers, including BLT, mushroom burger, ham & cheese, and egg salad. The bakery offers cakes, cookies, danishes, muffins, pies, and more. ■ *www.keanascandyland.net*

### Le Pigeon     $$$D
*Portland* ■ *(503) 546-8796*
*738 E Burnside St* ■ *Fusion* ■ The restaurant reports that they can accommodate GF diners and recommends calling ahead to ask about the current GF options. ■ *lepigeon.com*

### Little Bird Bistro     $$$LD
*Portland* ■ *(503) 688-5952*
*219 SW 6th Ave* ■ *French* ■ The restaurant recommends cheking with the server for current GF options. They reportedly "cater to people with serious food allergies all the time" and take CC concerns "very seriously". Alert the server upon arrival. ■ *www.littlebirdbistro.com*

### Loving Hut     📖
*Portland* ■ *(503) 248-6715*
*1239 SW Jefferson St*

### Mama Mia Trattoria ☼★$$$D
*Portland* ▪ *(503) 295-6464*
*439 SW 2nd Ave* ▪ *Italian* ▪ GF pasta is
available, as well as many other appetizers, entrées, entrées, sides, and desserts. GF food
can be prepared in a separate area and
with dedicated cookware upon request.
Be sure to clarify with your server that
your meal must be completely GF. ▪
*www.mamamiatrattoria.com*

### Melting Pot, The ☼🕮
*Portland* ▪ *(503) 517-8960*
*Sw 6th Ave And Main St*

### Mi Mero Mole ☼¢LD
*Portland* ▪ *(503) 232-8226*
*5026 SE Division St* ▪ *Mexican* ▪ Restaurant menu has all items that contain gluten
marked with a "G", rather than listing items
that are GF. Consult a server before ordering to be sure the item selected is, in fact,
GF. ▪ *mmmtacospdx.com*

### Mississippi Pizza Pub, The ★$$$LD
*Portland* ▪ *(503) 288-3231*
*3552 N Mississippi Ave* ▪ *Pizza* ▪ GF pizza
is available. The restaurant reports that the
GF pizza is "very popular." GF pizza dough
is also available to take home. The company
also stated that they have a dedicated GF
oven and brush for their pizza sauces. ▪
*www.mississippipizza.com*

### Morton's Steakhouse ☼🕮
*Portland* ▪ *(503) 248-2100*
*213 S W Clay St*

### New Cascadia Traditional ¢S
*Portland* ▪ *(503) 546-4901*
*1700 SE 6th Ave* ▪ *Bakery* ▪ Bakery offering a large selection of GF baked goods
including, breads, cookies, pies, cakes, and
muffins. Lunch is also served daily from
11am-2pm. Lunch items include GF pizza,
sandwiches, and salads. Bakery's products
are also sold at the Portland Farmers Market. ▪ *www.newcascadiatraditional.com*

### Old Spaghetti Factory, The ☼★🕮
*Portland* ▪ *(503) 222-5375*
*0715 SW Bancroft St*

### Old Wives' Tale ☼★¢BLD
*Portland* ▪ *(503) 238-0470*
*1300 E Burnside* ▪ *Modern American* ▪
Much of the menu is GF and is indicated
on the menu in parentheses. There are
some GF dishes available, and the restaurant uses a separate prep area and utensils
for all the GF orders. GF items include,
grilled salmon cakes, tofu scrambles,
pumpkin pudding and various soups. ▪
*www.oldwivestalesrestaurant.com*

### P.F. Chang's China Bistro ☼★🕮
*Portland* ▪ *(503) 432-4000*
*1139 NW Couch St*
*Portland* ▪ *(503) 430-3020*
*7463 SW Bridgeport Rd*

### Papa G's ☼$LD
*Portland* ▪ *(503) 235-0244*
*2314 SE Division St* ▪ *Organic* ▪ GF
items are indicated with an asterisk on
the menu and include the curry bowl,
taco plate, BBQ tofu, raw collard roll and
nachos. GF beer and cider are available. ▪
*www.papagees.com*

### Papa Haydn $$LD
*Portland* ▪ *(503) 232-9440*
*5829 SE Milwaukie Ave*
*Portland* ▪ *(503) 228-7317*
*701 NW 23rd Ave* ▪ *American* ▪ GF dinner
and dessert items available. Alert server
upon arrival and they will list GF options. ▪
*www.papahaydn.com*

### Papa's Pizza Parlor ☼★$$LD
*Gresham* ▪ *(503) 251-5555*
*16321 SE Stark St* ▪ *Pizza* ▪ GF menu
includes an extensive list of GF pizzas. GF
beer is also available. *www.papaspizza.net*

### Park Kitchen $$D
*Portland* ▪ *(503) 223-7282*
*422 NW 8th Ave* ▪ *American* ▪ The restaurants reports that they are "very GF
friendly" Many menu items are natu-

rally GF, while others can be made GF. They recommend alerting a server, who can indicate appropriate menu items. ▪ www.parkkitchen.com

### Pastini Pastaria                          ★ ¢LD
*Portland* ▪ (503) 595-1205?
*1506 Northwest 23rd Ave*
*Portland* ▪ (503) 863-5188
*911 SW Taylor St*
*Portland* ▪ (503) 288-4300
*1426 NE Broadway*
*Portland* ▪ (503) 595-6400
*2027 SE Division St* ▪ *Italian* ▪ GF rice pasta is available and can be substituted in most pasta dishes. Carly at customer service also notes that they have a large selection of salads and a GF tiramisu available. Their meatballs contain bread crumbs and Manicotti and Cannelloni Frutti di Mare have beschamella sauce, which contains flour. All other cream sauces do not contain any flour. She recommends alerting a server upon arrival to help guide diners through the menu, and notes that an allergen guide is also available at all locations. ▪ www.pastini.com

### Piece of Cake Bakery              ✪★¢S
*Portland* ▪ (503) 234-9445
*8306 SE 17th Ave* ▪ *Bakery* ▪ Non-dedicated bakery offering GF cakes in a wide selection of flavors and sizes, including carrot, chocolate raspberry, and double chocolate. GF cookies, bundts, and mini loaves are also available. GF wedding cakes are available for order. GF items are made first thing in the morning before the wheat is brought out for the day. ▪ www.pieceofcakebakery.net

### Pudding on the Rice                    ★¢S
*Portland* ▪ (503) 427-1121
*1503 SW Park Ave* ▪ *Dessert* ▪ Restaurant reports they have many GF options available such as tart frozen yogurt and rice pudding. Upon arrival, ask for assistance. ▪ www.puddingontherice.com

### Rudy's Gourmet Pizza               ✪★$LD
*Portland* ▪ (503) 771-8008
*4716 SE Powell Blvd* ▪ *Pizza* ▪ All specialty pizzas can be made with GF pizza crust. You can also create your own pizza by selecting a variety of toppings from the menu and having them baked on GF crust. They use dedicated utensils, cutters, and pizza paddles, but the oven is shared. Consult the manager before placing an order to assess the risk of CC. ▪ www.rudysgourmetpizza.com

### Ruth's Chris Steak House          ✪ 📖
*Portland* ▪ (503) 221-4518
*850 SW Broadway*

### Saucebox Restaurant                 ✪$$$D
*Portland* ▪ (503) 241-3393
*214 SW Broadway* ▪ *Asian Fusion* ▪ GF menu includes organic white miso soup, roasted Javanese salmon, and tapioca dumplings with chicken. Confirm the timeliness of this information before dining in. The restaurant cautions that fried items are at risk for CC due to a common fryer being used. ▪ www.saucebox.com

### Seasons & Regions
### Seafood Grill                              ✪$$BLD
*Portland* ▪ (503) 244-6400
*6660 SW Capitol Hwy* ▪ *Global* ▪ GF menu includes honey ginger lime salmon salad, Thai red curry scallops and gulf shrimp, and soy ginger chicken stir fry, among many other things. Dining in and take out options are available.

### Sellwood Pizza Kitchen            ✪★$$LD
*Portland* ▪ (503) 238-7255
*8000 SE 13Th Ave* ▪ *Pizza* ▪ GF 12" pizza is available. Salads and dressings are GF without the croutons. All appetizers are GF or can be GF when GF bread is substituted. ▪ www.sellwoodpizzakitchen.com

### Slappy Cakes                            ★¢BL
*Portland* ▪ (503) 477-4805
*4246 SE Belmont St* ▪ *American* ▪ GF pancakes are available. They can be ordered off the menu or selected for the "make your

own pancakes" option. Ask the server what other menu items can be prepared GF. ▪ *www.slappycakes.com*

### TeaZone & Camellia Lounge, The ★ ⒞BLD
*Portland* ▪ *(503) 221-2130*
*510 NW 11Th Ave* ▪ *Teahouse* ▪ GF bread and hamburger buns are available, so any cold sandwich or panini can be prepared GF. Most soups are also GF, as are desserts like scones, earl grey truffles, cookies, and some of the bubble teas. Ask a server which items are GF, as sweets are GF on a rotational basis. ▪ *www.teazone.com*

### Tula Gluten Free Bakery Café　⒞BL
*Portland* ▪ *(503) 764-9727*
*4943 NE Martin Luther King Jr Blvd Suite 101* ▪ *Bakery & Café* ▪ A dedicated GF café that serves sweet and savory baked goods as well as sandwiches and salads. ▪ *www.tulabaking.com*

### Veggie Grill, The　✪★📖
*Portland* ▪ *(503) 841-6647*
*508 SW Taylor St*

### Vindalho　$$D
*Portland* ▪ *(503) 467-4550*
*2038 SE Clinton St* ▪ *Indian* ▪ Chef April reports that nearly everything on the menu is naturally GF. She notes that all of the sauces are thickened with coconut milk or yogurt rather than flour, and any dish can be served with rice instead of naan. Confirm the timeliness of this information before dining in. ▪ *www.vindalho.com*

### Ya Hala Lebanese Cuisine　⒞LD
*Portland* ▪ *(503) 256-4484*
*8005 SE Stark St* ▪ *Mediterranean* ▪ The restaurant reports that they have "quite a few" GF options, including kabob dishes served with rice, hummus served with cucumber, and baba ghanouj. In-house menus have GF items marked on them and the staff is aware of GF. Confirm the timeliness of this information before dining in. ▪ *www.yahalarestaurant.com*

### ¡Oba! Restaurante　✪$$$D
*Portland* ▪ *(503) 228-6161*
*555 NW 12th Ave* ▪ *Latin American* ▪ GF menu offers options such as pork tamales, grilled chicken with mango salsa, butternut squash enchiladas, and more. Confirm the timeliness of this information before dining in. ▪ *www.obarestaurant.com*

### ¿Por Que No? Taqueria　⒞LD
*Portland* ▪ *(503) 467-4149*
*3524 N Mississippi Ave*
*Portland* ▪ *(503) 954-3138*
*4635 SE Hawthorne Blvd* ▪ *Mexican* ▪ Both locations report that most of the menu is naturally GF. If servers have any questions about the GF status of a specific item, they will ask a manager. Confirm the timeliness of this information before dining in. ▪ *www.porquenotacos.com*

# OREGON

## ALL OTHER CITIES

### Angeline's Bakery　★⒞BL
*Sisters* ▪ *(541) 549-9122*
*121 W Main St* ▪ *Bakery & Café* ▪ GF items include lemon or lime bars, cookies, brownies, dairy free chocolate cupcakes, scones and GF loaves of bread. GF lunch options include polenta pizza, veggie enchiladas, spinach and mushroom quiche, and various soups and salads. ▪ *www.angelinesbakery.com*

### Bellagios Pizza　✪★$$LD
*Clackamas* ▪ *(503) 698-6699*
*12050 SE Sunnyside Rd*
*Gresham* ▪ *(503) 465-8000*
*862 NW Burnside Rd*
*Lake Oswego* ▪ *(503) 635-8700*
*1235 McVey Ave*
*Oregon City* ▪ *(503) 518-5000*
*19735 Trails End Hwy*

*Tigard* ▪ *(503) 639-1500*
*10115 SW Nimbus Ave*
*Tualatin* ▪ *(503) 691-7841*
*8835 SW Tualatin-Sherwood Rd*
*West Linn* ▪ *(503) 557-1406*
*1880 Willamette Falls Dr*
*Wilsonville* ▪ *(503) 682-3400*
*29702-G Town Center Loop W*
*Beaverton* ▪ *(503) 466-2070*
*16265 NW Cornell Rd*
*Portland* ▪ *(503) 954-3511*
*815 NE Weidler* ▪ *Pizza* ▪ GF menu
includes a variety of pizzas in either 10"
or 14" inch with a "build your own pizza"
option, salads, and appetizers. GF pizza
dough is also available for "take-&-bake."
Company President Julie Collins reports
that they have "gone to great lengths to
eliminate cross-contamination issues." ▪
*www.bellagiospizza.com*

## Bentley's Grill                              $$**LD**

*Salem* ▪ *(503) 779-1660*
*291 Liberty St SE* ▪ *American* ▪ Hostess
Haley reports that the kitchen will make
any dish GF upon request. She notes that
they have served GF customers in the past,
and recommends alerting a server, who
will ask the chef to discuss GF options. All
GF dishes are prepared in a separate area
with cleaned and sanitized prep items.. ▪
*www.bentleysgrill.com*

## Big River Restaurant and Bar    ✪$$$**LD**

*Corvallis* ▪ *(541) 757-0694*
*101 NW Jackson Ave* ▪ *American* ▪ GF
items are marked on the regular menu and
include pimiento de padron, grilled salmon
and the king salmon. Manager Grant says
that the kitchen is well-versed in preventing CC. ▪ *www.bigriverrest.com*

## BJ's Restaurant and Brewhouse ✪★▨

*Hillsboro* ▪ *(503) 615-2300*
*7390 NE Cornell Rd*

## Blue Moon Coffee                      ✪¢**BL**

*Lake Oswego* ▪ *(503) 805-1883*
*3975 Mercantile Dr* ▪ *Coffee Shop* ▪ GF
"jammer" cookies are available with either

blueberry or strawberry filling. The coffee
shop cautions that they usually run out of
cookies quickly. ▪ *www.bluemoonlo.com*

## Bombs Away Café                        ✪¢**LD**

*Corvallis* ▪ *(541) 757-7221*
*2527 NW Monroe* ▪ *American* ▪ GF menu
is located online. Separate preparation area
is used, in addition to different utensils. ▪
*www.bombsawaycafe.com*

## Boston's
## Restaurant & Sports Bar        ✪★▨

*Bend* ▪ *(541) 647-5050*
*61276 S Hwy 97*

## Bridgewater Bistro            ✪★$$$**LD**

*Astoria* ▪ *(503) 325-6777*
*20 Basin St Suite A* ▪ *Bistro* ▪ GF or GF
optional items are marked with an asterisk on the menu. Approximately 90% of
the menu is available GF. The owner of
the restaurant is GF so CC procedures are
followed, including separate fryers and cutting boards. Alert the server upon arrival. ▪
*bridgewaterbistro.com*

## Carino's Italian                        ✪▨

*Bend* ▪ *(541) 318-6300*
*63455 N Highway 97*

## Chan's Chinese Restaurant      ★¢**LD**

*Bend* ▪ *(541) 389-1725*
*1005 SE 3rd St* ▪ *Chinese* ▪ Restaurant
does not have a dedicated GF menu. However, they will do what they can to accommodate customers needs. They have no CC
policy and dishes are prepared in the same
area. Alert a manager prior to ordering. ▪
*www.chanschinese.com*

## Ciddici's                              ★$**LD**

*Albany* ▪ *(541) 928-2536*
*133 5th Ave SE*
*Albany* ▪ *(541) 928-1767*
*859 SW Belmont Ave* ▪ *Pizza* ▪ GF pizza
is available. The crust comes prepack-
aged and is cooked on a dedicated pan
to minimize cross-contamination risk. ▪
*www.ciddicipizza.com*

### Clarke's Restaurant　　　　$$$D
*Lake Oswego* ▪ *(503) 636-2667*
*455 2nd St* ▪ *Modern American* ▪ GF accommodations can be made to particular items on the menu. Alert a server, who will discuss GF options with the kitchen. Reservations noting GF are recommended. ▪ *www.clarkesrestaurant.net*

### Dundee Bistro　　　　$$LD
*Dundee* ▪ *(503) 554-1650*
*100-A SW 7th St* ▪ *Modern American* ▪ Team member Ashley reports that they usually serve GF diners 4-5 times a day. While they do not have a set GF menu, the kitchen is very accommodating of GF orders and diners are welcome to work with their waiter to design a dish to their liking with the ingredients on hand. ▪ *www.dundeebistro.com*

### Evergreen Indian Cuisine　　$LD
*Corvallis* ▪ *(541) 754-7944*
*136 SW 3rd St* ▪ *Indian* ▪ Owner Meeraali reports that everything except the bread is GF or can be prepared GF. She notes that many of the curries, soups, and other Indian dishes are GF. Confirm the timeliness of this information before dining in. ▪ *www.evergreenindianrestaurant.com*

### FireWorks Restaurant & Bar　★$$LD
*Corvallis* ▪ *(541) 754-6958*
*1115 SE 3rd St* ▪ *Modern American* ▪ GF pizza is available. Restaurant reports that many sauces are thickened with rice flour instead of wheat flour. They note that in addition to pizzas, there are many menu items that are or can be modified to be GF. Alert a server upon arrival. ▪ *www.fireworksvenue.com*

### Flying Pie Pizzeria　　　　★
*Gresham* ▪ *(503) 328-0018*
*1600 NW Fairview Dr*
*Milwaukie* ▪ *(503) 496-3170*
*16691 SW McLoughlin Blvd*
*Lake Oswego* ▪ *(503) 675-7377*
*3 Monroe Pkwy* ▪ *Pizza* ▪ GF pizza is available, and toppings that contain gluten are

marked on the menu for easy avoidance. ▪ *www.flying-pie.com*

### Fresh Thyme Soup Company　　✪★¢LD
*Beaverton* ▪ *(503) 466-9103*
*16155 NW Cornell Rd, Suite 500* ▪ *Deli* ▪ All soups are GF, but keep in mind that all garnishes may not be. GF sandwiches are also available. Be sure to ask about the options offered before ordering. ▪ *www.freshthymesoup.com*

### Garlic Jim's　　　　✪★📖
*Beaverton* ▪ *(503) 645-3400*
*12480 SW Walker Rd*
*Clackamas* ▪ *(503) 654-5467*
*10219 SE Sunnyside Rd*
*Beaverton* ▪ *(503) 601-5467*
*8410 SW Nimbus Ave*
*Keizer* ▪ *(503) 390-5516*
*5151 River Road N*
*Salem* ▪ *(503) 779-2722*
*4555 Liberty Rd S*

### Godfather's Pizza　　　　★📖
*Sherwood* ▪ *(503) 625-1600*
*15982 SW Tualatin-Sherwood Rd*
*Tigard* ▪ *(503) 590-0900*
*14200 SW Barrows Rd*
*Troutdale* ▪ *(503) 492-3300*
*2503 SW Cherry Park Rd*
*Clackamas* ▪ *(503) 658-2200*
*14682 SE Sunnyside Rd*

### Great Earth Natural Foods　✪★¢BL
*Madras* ▪ *(541) 475-1500*
*46 SW D St* ▪ *Bakery & Café* ▪ Most sandwiches on the menu can be prepared GF by substituting bread with a GF teff wrap. Various soups and salads are also available to GF diners. The restaurant reports that if GF diners are "extremely sensitive", they can request that a separate prep area be used to prepare their meal. ▪ *www.greatearth.biz*

### Greenleaf Restaurant　　✪★$BLD
*Ashland* ▪ *(541) 482-2808*
*49 N Main St* ▪ *Modern American* ▪ Extensive GF menu includes Greek salad, chicken marsala, coconut curry stir fry, and grilled wild salmon, as well

as various breakfast and lunch dishes. Items are prepared in a shared kitchen, but many precautions are taken for GF orders, including sanitizing utensils and surfaces, changing gloves, and putting butcher paper over the cutting boards. ▪ *www.greenleafrestaurant.com*

### Gustav's Pub & Grill   ✪★$LD
*Clackamas* ▪ *(503) 653-1391*
*12605 SE 97th Ave*
*Tigard* ▪ *(503) 639-4544*
*10350 SW Greenburg Rd*
*Portland* ▪ *(503) 284-4621*
*7000 NE Airport Wy* ▪ *European* ▪ GF menu includes mushroom schnitzel, Rhineland salmon, rotisserie chicken, sausage trio, and more. For dessert, there is GF flourless chocolate cake, Bavarian crème, and chocolate mousse. GF beer is available. Executive coordinator Hannah reports that all staff are GF aware, but cautions that all items are prepared using common equipment. ▪ *www.gustavs.net*

### Kam Meng Chinese Restaurant   ★¢LD
*Newport* ▪ *(541) 574-9450*
*4424 N Oregon Coast Hwy 101* ▪ *Chinese* ▪ The restaurant reports that most items on the regular menu are fried and not GF. Upon request the cooks can prepare items differently to accommodate GF customers. ▪ *kammengchineserestaurant.com*

### Kwan's Original Cuisine   ★$LD
*Salem* ▪ *(503) 362-7711*
*835 Commercial St SE* ▪ *Chinese* ▪ Manager said they are "very open to food allergies". Willing to accommodate and use rice flour and GF sauces on all of their main dishes upon request. ▪ *www.kwanscuisine.com*

### Marco Polo Global Restaurant   ✪$LD
*Salem* ▪ *(503) 364-4833*
*300 Liberty St SE* ▪ *Fusion* ▪ Extensive GF menu includes pesto and cream cheese filled mushrooms, garlic green beans with beef, sweet and sour salmon, and much more. The restaurant reports that they

regularly accommodate GF diners, and that all kitchen utensils are cleaned and oil/water changed before preparing a GF order. ▪ *www.mpologlobal.com*

### McGrath's Fish House   ✪📖
*Milwaukie* ▪ *(503) 653-8070*
*11050 SE Oak St*
*Bend* ▪ *(541) 388-4555*
*3118 N Hwy 97*
*Beaverton* ▪ *(503) 646-1881*
*3211 SW Cedar Hills Blvd*
*Salem* ▪ *(503) 362-0736*
*350 Chemeketa NE*
*Corvallis* ▪ *(541) 752-3474*
*350 Circle Blvd*
*Salem* ▪ *(503) 485-3086*
*3805 Center St NE*
*Medford* ▪ *(541) 732-1732*
*68 E Stewart Ave*

### Monteaux's Public House   ✪$LD
*Beaverton* ▪ *(503) 439-9942*
*16165 SW Regatta Ln* ▪ *American* ▪ Certain menu items can be "prepared without gluten on request" and include grilled oyster on the half shell, poached pear salad, grilled flat iron steak, grilled wild salmon, as well as GF buns for the burgers. Be sure to alert your server that your meal must be GF so it can be appropriately flagged for the kitchen. Confirm the timeliness of this information before dining in. ▪ *www.monteauxs.com*

### Nature's Corner Café & Market   ✪★$BLD
*Florence* ▪ *(541) 997-0900*
*185 Highway 101* ▪ *American* ▪ GF items are marked on the regular menu. GF bread and pancakes are available. Chef says there are "tons of GF options." The restaurant shares space with a food store offering many GF "take-&-bake" options. ▪ *www.naturescornercafe.com*

### Nearly Normal's   ✪★¢BLD
*Corvallis* ▪ *(541) 753-0791*
*109 NW 15th St* ▪ *Mexican* ▪ A GF menu is available in-house and includes selections for all three meals. GF bread is avail-

able for burgers and sandwiches. Some items may require modification to become GF, so be sure to alert your server. ▪ *www.nearlynormals.com*

### Oceana Natural Foods Cooperative   ₵L
*Newport* ▪ *(541) 265-8285*
*159 SE 2nd St* ▪ *Deli* ▪ Manager Linda reports that there are usually GF options available in the deli. She notes that all foods have "ingredient cards," so diners can easily read what does and does not contain gluten. Call ahead to ask about GF options of the day. ▪ *www.oceanafoods.org*

### Old Spaghetti Factory, The   ✪★📖
*Clackamas* ▪ *(503) 653-7949*
*12725 SE 93rd Ave*
*Hillsboro* ▪ *(503) 617-7614*
*18925 NW Tanasbourne Dr*

### P.F. Chang's China Bistro   ✪★📖
*Hillsboro* ▪ *(503) 533-4580*
*19320 NW Emma Wy*

### Papa's Pizza Parlor   ✪★$$LD
*Springfield* ▪ *(541) 485-5555*
*4011 Main St*
*Corvallis* ▪ *(541) 757-2727*
*1030 SW 3rd St*
*Beaverton* ▪ *(503) 531-7220*
*15700 NW Blueridge St* ▪ *Pizza* ▪ GF menu includes an extensive list of GF pizzas. GF beer is also available. ▪ *www.papaspizza.net*

### Pastini Pastaria   ★₵LD
*Beaverton* ▪ *(503) 619-2241*
*3487 SW Cedar Hills Blvd*
*Tigard* ▪ *(503) 718-2300*
*7307 SW Bridgeport Rd*
*Bend* ▪ *(541) 749-1060*
*375 SW Powerhouse Dr*
*Corvallis* ▪ *(541) 257-2579*
*1580 NW 9th St* ▪ *Italian* ▪ GF rice pasta is available and can be substituted in most pasta dishes. Carly at customer service also notes that they have a large selection of salads and a GF tiramisu available. Their meatballs contain bread crumbs and Manicotti and Cannelloni Frutti di Mare have beschamella sauce, which contains flour. All other

cream sauces do not contain any flour. She recommends alerting a server upon arrival to help guide diners through the menu, and notes that an allergen guide is also available at all locations. ▪ *www.pastini.com*

### R.R. Thompson House B&B   ★₵B
*Carlton* ▪ *(503) 852-6236*
*517 N Kutch St* ▪ *American* ▪ For guests at the bed and breakfast, GF breakfasts are available. They typically include pancakes or French toast, omelets, and fresh fruit. Reservations noting GF are required. ▪ *www.rrthompsonhouse.com*

### Ruby Cakes   ₵S
*McMinnville* ▪ *(503) 857-0636*
*920 NE 8th St* ▪ *Bakery* ▪ Dedicated GF bakery offering cupcakes, cookies, muffins, pies, brownies, bread, and more. ▪ *rubycakesbakeries.com*

### Savory Café & Pizzeria   ★$LD
*Newport* ▪ *(541) 574-9365*
*526 NW Coast St* ▪ *Global* ▪ GF pizza is available. The restaurant reports that many other menu items are or can be prepared GF as well, including the coconut shrimp, spicy fish tacos, chili orange prawns, and yellow curry. Alert a server, who will go over GF options. Confirm the timeliness of this information before dining in. ▪ *savorynyebeach.com*

### Stone Cliff Inn Restaurant & Bar ★$$$LD
*Oregon City* ▪ *(503) 631-7900*
*17900 S Clackamas River Dr* ▪ *American* ▪ Restaurant can accommodate GF diners, however they do not have a GF menu and no CC policies. Contact the restaurant ahead of time to ensure GF items can be prepared. ▪ *www.stonecliffinn.com*

### Tidal Raves   $$LD
*Depoe Bay* ▪ *(541) 765-2995*
*279 NW Hwy 101* ▪ *Seafood* ▪ Many menu items can be modified to be GF and include calamari, fish tacos, and green curry. The restaurant reports that they can "work around things" and that the kitchen is "very good about" taking dietary restrictions into

account. Be sure to alert a server that your meal must be GF, and confirm the timeliness of this information before dining in. ▪ *www.tidalraves.com*

### Veggie Grill, The          ✪★📖
*Beaverton* ▪ *(503) 350-2369*
*3435 SW Cedar Hills Blvd*
*Hillsboro* ▪ *(503) 466-0345*
*2065 NW 185th Ave*

### White Rabbit Bakery          ✪★¢$
*Aurora* ▪ *(503) 267-9044*
*21368 Highway 99E* ▪ *Bakery* ▪ A rotating variety of GF items are usually on hand, and special orders can be made if a specific item is desired. Options include GF cakes, muffins, cookies, pies, cheesecakes, brownies and scones. The owner, who is gluten sensitive herself, reports that items are prepared in the same kitchen but precautions are taken against CC. ▪ *www.whiterabbitbakery.com*

### Zeppo          ✪★$$**BLD**
*Lake Oswego* ▪ *(503) 675-2726*
*345 1st St, Suite 105* ▪ *Italian* ▪ The restaurant reports that they are open to accommodating all GF diners. GF pasta is available and noted on the menu. The chef also notes that they use dedicated utensils for GF orders and GF pasta is all made in one bowl from individually packaged pastas. ▪ *zepporestaurant.com*

### Zydeco Kitchen & Cocktails          ✪$$$**LD**
*Bend* ▪ *(541) 312-2899*
*919 Bond St* ▪ *Cajun & Creole* ▪ Extensive GF menu includes a large variety of starters, main courses, sides, and desserts. Examples include roasted clams, jambalaya, sesame encrusted ahi tuna, red beans and rice, and flourless chocolate cake. The chef reports that they use separate counter space and utensils for GF orders. Be sure to alert your server that you are ordering from the GF menu. ▪ *www.zydecokitchen.com*

### Amada          ✪$$**LD**
*Philadelphia* ▪ *(215) 625-2450*
*217-219 Chestnut St* ▪ *Spanish* ▪ Extensive GF menu includes meat and cheese dishes, traditional tapas, meat and seafood dishes such as the lobster, scallops and calamari, roasted pork, pork rib, chicken, chicken and chorizo paella and a lobster paella. Alert a server, who will present the GF menu. ▪ *www.amadarestaurant.com*

### Amis Trattoria          $$$**D**
*Philadelphia* ▪ *(215) 732-2647*
*412 S 13Th St* ▪ *Italian* ▪ GF menu includes salami, mussels, seared squid, pork belly, pork shoulder, steak, duck breast, roasted monk fish, chicken and, for dessert, rice pudding. ▪ *www.amisphilly.com*

### Au Bon Pain          📖
*Philadelphia* ▪ *(215) 567-8909*
*18th & Arch St*
*Philadelphia* ▪ *(215) 243-9897*
*2951 Market St*
*Philadelphia* ▪ *(215) 564-9705*
*2005 Market St*
*Philadelphia* ▪ *(215) 365-6160*
*Philadephia Airport- Terminals A, C, F*
*Philadelphia* ▪ *(215) 587-0458*
*1617 JFK Blvd*
*Philadelphia* ▪ *(215) 349-5783*
*3400 Spruce St*
*Philadelphia* ▪ *(215) 567-9005*
*1625 Chestnut St*
*Philadelphia* ▪ *(215) 413-5802*
*1101 Chestnut St*
*Philadelphia* ▪ *(215) 382-6160*
*421 Curie Blvd- Ground Floor*

### Barclay Prime          $$$$**D**
*Philadelphia* ▪ *(215) 732-7560*
*237 S 18th St* ▪ *Steakhouse* ▪ Many items on the menu can be made GF. Alert the

server, who will ask chef which dishes can be prepared GF. ▪ *www.barclayprime.com*

### Bistrot La Minette     $$LD
*Philadelphia* ▪ *(215) 925-8000*
*623 S 6th St* ▪ *French* ▪ The restaurant reports that they have "countless items" on the menu that can be made GF upon request. Alert the server upon arrival so the necessary changes can be made. ▪ *www.bistrotlaminette.com*

### Bliss     $$$LD
*Philadelphia* ▪ *(215) 731-1100*
*220 S Broad St* ▪ *Modern American* ▪ Almost all of the dishes on the menu can be made GF except for the sea bass, crab cakes and flatbread. Alert a server upon arrival. ▪ *www.bliss-restaurant.com*

### Buddakan     ✪$$$LD
*Philadelphia* ▪ *(215) 574-9440*
*325 Chestnut St* ▪ *Asian Fusion* ▪ Manager Jennessee reports that GF diners are welcome. She notes that servers are trained to indicate "many GF meal options." Reservations noting GF are recommended. ▪ *www.buddakan.com*

### Cantina Laredo     📖
*Philadelphia* ▪ *(215) 492-1160*
*8500 Essington Ave*

### Capital Grille, The     ✪📖
*Philadelphia* ▪ *(215) 545-9588*
*1338 Chestnut St*

### Chifa     ✪$$$D
*Philadelphia* ▪ *(215) 925-5555*
*707 Chestnut St* ▪ *Fusion* ▪ Extensive GF menu available in restaurant. Alert server upon arrival. ▪ *www.chifarestaurant.com*

### Cosi     ✪📖
*Philadelphia* ▪ *(215) 893-9696*
*235 S 15th St*
*Philadelphia* ▪ *(215) 399-0214*
*325 Chestnut St*
*Philadelphia* ▪ *(215) 569-2833*
*1700 Market St*
*Philadelphia* ▪ *(215) 222-4545*
*140 S 36th St*

*Philadelphia* ▪ *(215) 735-2004*
*1720 Walnut*
*Philadelphia* ▪ *(215) 922-6717*
*833 Chestnut St*
*Philadelphia* ▪ *(610) 660-3459*
*2461 N 54th St*
*Philadelphia* ▪ *(215) 222-0758*
*2955 Market St*
*Philadelphia* ▪ *(215) 413-1608*
*1128 Walnut St*

### Davio's Northern Italian Steakhouse     ✪📖
*Philadelphia* ▪ *(215) 563-4810*
*111 S 17th St*

### Del Frisco's Double Eagle Steak House   📖
*Philadelphia* ▪ *(215) 246-0533*
*1426 Chestnut St*

### Distrito Restaurant     ✪$LD
*Philadelphia* ▪ *(215) 222-1657*
*3945 Chestnut St* ▪ *Mexican* ▪ GF menu available. Alert the server upon arrival. ▪ *www.distritorestaurant.com*

### Fogo De Chao     ★📖
*Philadelphia* ▪ *(215) 636-9700*
*1337 Chestnut St*

### Fox and Hound Pub & Grille     📖
*Philadelphia* ▪ *(215) 732-8610*
*1501 Spruce St*

### Giorgio on Pine     ✪★$$LD
*Philadelphia* ▪ *(215) 545-6265*
*1328 Pine St* ▪ *Italian* ▪ Extensive list of GF items are listed on the Lunch and Dinner menus. Look for the "gf" next to the selected items. Restaurant also reports that they always try to have at least one GF dessert available for diners. ▪ *www.giorgioonpine.com*

### Hard Rock Café     ✪📖
*Philadelphia* ▪ *(215) 238-1000*
*1113-31 Market St*

### Iron Hill Brewery & Restaurant   ✪★📖
*Philadelphia* ▪ *(215) 948-5600*
*8400 Germantown Ave*

### Jersey Mike's                                           📖
*Philadelphia* ▪ *(215) 222-2133*
*2955 Market St*

### Lacroix                                                 $$LD
*Philadelphia* ▪ *(215) 790-2533*
*210 W Rittenhouse Sq* ▪ *Modern American*
▪ The restaurant reports that chef is "happy
to modify any dish possible" to accommodate GF diners. Alert the sever upon
arrival. ▪ *www.lacroixrestaurant.com*

### Legal Sea Foods                                         ✪📖
*Philadelphia* ▪ *(267) 295-9300*
*Philadelphia Int Arprt*

### Lolita                                                  $$$D
*Philadelphia* ▪ *(215) 546-7100*
*106 S 13th St* ▪ *Mexican* ▪ Entire menu is
GF. Items include carne asada, orange-
ginger glazed pork carnitas, and a flourless
chocolate cake. ▪ *www.lolitabyob.com*

### Maggiano's Little Italy                                 ★📖
*Philadelphia* ▪ *(215) 567-2020*
*1201 Filbert St*

### Marigold Kitchen                                        $$$D
*Philadelphia* ▪ *(215) 222-3699*
*501 S 45th St* ▪ *Modern American* ▪ The
restaurant reports that many items on the
menu are naturally GF and other can be
modified to be GF. Alert a server upon arrival. ▪ *www.marigoldkitchenbyob.com*

### Matyson                                                 $$$LD
*Philadelphia* ▪ *(215) 564-2925*
*37 S 19th St* ▪ *Modern American* ▪ GF
items include kombu cured kampachi,
heirloom tomatoes, shaved Tuscan kale,
golden tilefish, diver scallops, potato
crusted Alaskan halibut, aged black angus
hanger steak without the sourdough,
Lancaster county chicken breast without
corn bread stuffing, and any salads except
the sesame noodle salad. Chef reports
that some of their regulars are GF so she
is used to accommodating to GF diets. ▪
*www.matyson.com*

### Melting Pot, The                                        ✪📖
*Philadelphia* ▪ *(215) 922-7002*
*1219 Filbert St*

### Morimoto                                                $$$$LD
*Philadelphia* ▪ *(215) 413-9070*
*723 Chestnut St* ▪ *Japanese* ▪ The restaurant reports that restaurant "makes
GF accommodations all the time" and the
chef "would be happy to accommodate to
GF customers". For prime time reservations, call at least two weeks in advance. ▪
*www.morimotorestaurant.com*

### Morton's Steakhouse                                     ✪📖
*Philadelphia* ▪ *(215) 557-0724*
*1411 Walnut St*

### My Thai                                                 $$D
*Philadelphia* ▪ *(215) 985-1878*
*2200 South St* ▪ *Thai* ▪ Alert a server, who
will indicate "exactly" which menu items
are not GF.

### Osteria                                                 $$$D
*Philadelphia* ▪ *(215) 763-0920*
*640 N Broad St* ▪ *Italian* ▪ Hostess Jaclyn
reports that all servers are "extremely
familiar" with the GF diet. She notes that
"plenty of people" come in to request
GF meals, and she adds that they typically choose a slightly modified entrée off
the menu or bring their own pasta to be
prepared with any sauce on the menu. ▪
*www.osteriaphilly.com*

### Paesano's                                               ✪★dL
*Philadelphia* ▪ *(215) 440-0371*
*1017 S 9th St*
*Philadelphia* ▪ *(267) 886-9556*
*152 W Girard* ▪ *Deli* ▪ GF items are
marked on the regular menu, which
includes all of their sandwiches. ▪
*www.paesanosphillystyle.com*

### Paradiso Restaurant & Wine Bar      $$$LD
*Philadelphia* ▪ *(215) 271-2066*
*1627 E Passyunk Ave* ▪ *Italian* ▪ Chef
reports that 50% of the menu entrées are

GF. Items include the chicken, veal, duck, and pork chops, as well as the yellowfin and the halibut without the pasta. Confirm the timeliness of this information before dining in. Alert a server upon arrival. ▪ *www.paradisophilly.com*

### Pei Wei Asian Diner                    ✪📖
*Philadelphia* ▪ *(215) 594-8230*
*4040 City Ave*

### Pod                                    $$LD
*Philadelphia* ▪ *(215) 387-1803*
*3636 Sansom St* ▪ *Asian* ▪ The restaurant reports that many of the menu items can be modified to be GF, noting that the vegan and vegetarian dishes are GF as well as the sesame crusted tuna and the miso glazed sea bass. Confirm the timeliness of this information before dining in. Alert a server upon arrival. ▪ *www.podrestaurant.com*

### Pure Tacos                             $LD
*Philadelphia* ▪ *(215) 496-9393*
*1935 Chestnut St* ▪ *Mexican* ▪ Dedicated GF restaurant offering a variety of toppings choices served in tacos, on nachos, or over fresh greens. Options include cheeseburger, orange-chili fish, chicken & bacon ranch, BBQ pulled pork, seared mushrooms, and more. ▪ *www.puretacos.com*

### Ruth's Chris Steak House              ✪📖
*Philadelphia* ▪ *(215) 790-1515*
*260 S Broad St*

### Sazon Restaurant and Café            $$LD
*Philadelphia* ▪ *(215) 763-2500*
*941 Spring Garden St* ▪ *Latin American* ▪ Manager Robert reports that GF diners should alert the server upon arrival. The server will speak to Chef Judy, who is happy to prepare GF meals. Almost 90% of their menu is GF and manager Robert believes they are the best GF restaurant in Philadelphia. GF desserts include a variety of hot chocolates and truffles, egg custard, different flavors of flan, and a rice pudding drink. ▪ *sazonrestaurant.com*

### Smith & Wollensky                     📖
*Philadelphia* ▪ *(215) 545-1700*
*210 W Rittenhouse Sq*

### Supper                                $$$D
*Philadelphia* ▪ *(215) 592-8180*
*926 South St* ▪ *Global* ▪ Many menu items can be modified to be GF. Noting GF when making reservations is highly recommended so chefs and servers have the chance to prepare items. ▪ *www.supperphilly.com*

### Sweet Freedom Bakery                  ℃S
*Philadelphia* ▪ *(215) 545-1899*
*1424 South St* ▪ *Bakery* ▪ Dedicated GF bakery offering an extensive menu of cupcakes, cakes, cookies, loaves, brownies, blondies, coconut clusters, donuts, and more. Special orders should be placed 48 hours in advance. ▪ *www.sweetfreedombakery.com*

### Tinto                                 ✪$$$D
*Philadelphia* ▪ *(215) 665-9150*
*116 S 20th St* ▪ *Spanish* ▪ GF menu is a version of the regular menu that includes all charcuterie & cheeses, lobsters, scallops, mussels and chorizo, octopus, anchovies, green beans, potatoes, New York strip, organic chicken, lamb, pork loin, truffle chestnut soup. ▪ *www.tintorestaurant.com*

### Ugly Moose, The                       $$D
*Philadelphia* ▪ *(215) 482-2739*
*443 Shurs Ln* ▪ *Pub Food* ▪ The restaurant reports that GF diners can be accommodated and certain items on the menu can be modified to be GF. Alert the server, who will recommend dishes that can be prepared GF and notify the chef. ▪ *www.theuglymoose.com*

### Uno Chicago Grill                     ✪★📖
*Philadelphia* ▪ *(215) 632-5577*
*789 Franklin Mills Cir*

### Velvet Sky Bakery                     ★℃S
*Jenkintown* ▪ *(215) 884-0254*
*307 Leedom St* ▪ *Bakery* ▪ Owner Jordan reports that almost everything on the menu can be made GF, but since all items

are baked in the same oven, she notes that there is "always a chance" of CC. ▪ *www.velvetskybakery.com*

### Vetri Ristorante                                   $$$**LD**
*Philadelphia* ▪ (215) 732-3478
*1312 Spruce St* ▪ *Italian* ▪ The restaurant reports that the chef is "happy to work with any dietary needs" and can create an individual menu for each customer. Reservations noting GF are recommended. ▪ *www.vetriristorante.com*

### White Dog Café                                    $$$**LD**
*Philadelphia* ▪ (215) 386-9224
*3420 Sansom St* ▪ *Modern American* ▪ Reservations noting GF are recommended so that the chefs have time to prepare. GF items include apple bisque, garden salad, pear salad, chicken tempura, pork tenderloin, tofu, filet, pacific cod, grilled eggplant and heirloom tomatoes. Confirm the timeliness of this information before dining in. ▪ *www.whitedog.com*

# PENNSYLVANIA

## PITTSBURGH

### Au Bon Pain                                       📖
*Pittsburgh* ▪ (412) 566-1086
*625 Liberty Ave*
*Pittsburgh* ▪ (412) 471-6422
*Fifth Ave Place- Food Court- Upper Level*
*Pittsburgh* ▪ (412) 456-4309
*707 Grant St*
*Pittsburgh* ▪ (412) 263-2772
*535 Smithfield St*
*Pittsburgh* ▪ (412) 642-2187
*301 Grant St*
*Pittsburgh* ▪ (412) 456-2916
*2 PPG Place- Lower Level*
*Pittsburgh* ▪ (412) 456-2906
*600 Grant St*

### Buca di Beppo                                     ❂📖
*Pittsburgh* ▪ (412) 788-8444
*6600 Robinson Center Dr*
*Pittsburgh* ▪ (412) 471-9463
*3 E Station Square Dr*

### Calabria's Restaurant                             ★$$$**LD**
*Pittsburgh* ▪ (412) 885-1030
*3107 Library Rd Rte 88* ▪ *Italian* ▪ The restaurant reports that the entire menu can be modified to accommodate GF customers. Staff reports that they "get a lot of GF customers coming in" daily and ask that diners alert the server upon arrival. ▪ *www.calabrias.biz*

### Capital Grille, The                               ❂📖
*Pittsburgh* ▪ (412) 338-9100
*301 5th Ave*

### Carino's Italian                                  ❂📖
*Pittsburgh* ▪ (412) 788-8813
*1000 Sutherland Dr*

### Carlton, The                                      $$$**LD**
*Pittsburgh* ▪ (412) 391-4152
*500 Grant St* ▪ *American* ▪ Head chef Mark reports that "essentially any item on the menu" can modified to be GF. Reservations noting GF are recommended, as is alerting the server upon arrival. ▪ *www.thecarltonrestaurant.com*

### Claddagh Irish Pub                                📖
*Pittsburgh* ▪ (412) 381-4800
*407 Cinema Dr*

### Don Pablo's                                       ❂📖
*Pittsburgh* ▪ (412) 488-8222
*140 Andrew Dr*

### Double Wide Grill                                 $**LD**
*Pittsburgh* ▪ (412) 390-1111
*2339 E Carson St* ▪ *American* ▪ Menu indicates items that are wheat free. Items include blackened chicken salad, coconut chicken dinner, coconut rum tilapia, hot and sweet pineapple chicken, BBQ St. Louis ribs, tofu with chimichurri sauce, garlic and herb mash potatoes, caramelized onion and cilantro rice, NY

strip steak, and sirloin sizzler platter. ▪ *www.doublewidegrill.com*

### Eat 'n Park ✪ 📖
*Pittsburgh* ▪ *(412) 243-5530*
*1605 S Braddock Ave*
*Pittsburgh* ▪ *(412) 766-6764*
*1002 Ohio River Blvd*
*Pittsburgh* ▪ *(412) 366-6220*
*7370 Mcknight Rd*
*Pittsburgh* ▪ *(412) 561-4944*
*2874 W Liberty Ave*
*Pittsburgh* ▪ *(412) 882-0258*
*5100 Clairton Blvd*
*Pittsburgh* ▪ *(412) 422-7203*
*1816 Murray Ave*
*Pittsburgh* ▪ *(412) 364-1211*
*7671 Mcknight Rd*
*Pittsburgh* ▪ *(412) 561-7894*
*1300 Banksville Rd*
*Pittsburgh* ▪ *(412) 242-3700*
*11746 Frankstown Rd*
*Pittsburgh* ▪ *(412) 854-4855*
*301 S Hills Vlg*
*Pittsburgh* ▪ *(412) 787-8556*
*100 Park Manor Dr*

### Eleven $$$**LD**
*Pittsburgh* ▪ *(412) 201-5656*
*1150 Smallman St* ▪ *American* ▪ The restaurant reports that they have no problem accommodating GF diners and adds all of their proteins can be modified to be GF. Alert the server upon arrival. ▪ *www.elevenck.com*

### First Watch - The Daytime Café ✪ 📖
*Pittsburgh* ▪ *(412) 787-1049*
*215 Settlers Ridge Center Dr*

### Gluuteny ᴄꜱ
*Pittsburgh* ▪ *(412) 521-4890*
*1923 Murray Ave* ▪ *Bakery* ▪ Dedicated GF bakery offering fresh daily baked goods including cupcakes, cookies, brownies, tarts and pies, quickbreads, cakes, breads, and more. Special orders should be made at least one day in advance. Vegan and nut free options available. ▪ *www.gluuteny.com*

### Habitat ✪$$$$**LD**
*Pittsburgh* ▪ *(412) 773-8848*
*510 Market St* ▪ *Fusion* ▪ Restaurant reports that a GF menu is available in house. Additionally, they add that "if nothing on it satisfies your taste" the chef is "more than happy to accommodate" and alter any dish to make it GF if possible. Alert the server upon arrival. ▪ *habitatrestaurant.com*

### Hard Rock Café ✪ 📖
*Pittsburgh* ▪ *(412) 481-7625*
*230 W Station Sq Dr*

### Joe's Crab Shack ✪ 📖
*Pittsburgh* ▪ *(412) 690-2404*
*226 W Station Square Dr*
*Pittsburgh* ▪ *(412) 494-5444*
*6491 Robinson Center Dr*

### Kaya Ristorante $$$**LD**
*Pittsburgh* ▪ *(412) 261-6565*
*2000 Smallman St* ▪ *Seafood* ▪ Restaurant reports that many items on the menu are GF and the staff is very familiar with GF orders. The most popular GF dish is the tropical paella. Alert the server upon arrival. ▪ *bigburrito.com/kaya*

### Loving Hut 📖
*Pittsburgh* ▪ *(412) 787-2727*
*5474 Campbells Run Rd*

### Mandy's Pizza ★$**LD**
*Pittsburgh* ▪ *(412) 931-1120*
*512 Perry Hwy*
*Pittsburgh* ▪ *(412) 322-1102*
*3906 Perrysville Ave* ▪ *Pizza* ▪ GF pizza, jumbo chicken wings and flatbreads are available. The owners' son has severe food allergies, including gluten sensitivity, so the restaurant understands CC well. ▪ *www.mandyspizza.com*

### Melting Pot, The ✪ 📖
*Pittsburgh* ▪ *(412) 261-3477*
*125 W Station Square Dr*

### Mitchell's Fish Market ✪ 📖
*Pittsburgh* ▪ *(412) 571-3474*
*1500 Washington Rd*

### Monterey Bay Fish Grotto                $$$LD
*Pittsburgh* ▪ *(412) 481-4414*
*1411 Grandview Ave* ▪ *Seafood* ▪ GF
options available. Both locations have
different menus but both can accommodate GF diners. Reservations noting
GF made at least 2 days in advance are
recommended. Staff notes that chefs and
servers are familiar with GF requests and
will be happy to prepare GF dishes. ▪
*www.montereybayfishgrotto.com*

### Morton's Steakhouse                ✪📖
*Pittsburgh* ▪ *(412) 261-7141*
*625 Liberty Ave*

### Nine on Nine                $$$LD
*Pittsburgh* ▪ *(412) 338-6463*
*900 Penn Ave* ▪ *Modern American* ▪ The
restaurant reports that the chef is "very
familiar" with GF dishes and has "no issue"
modifying any dish to be GF, though many
dishes are naturally GF. Reservations noting GF are recommended. Alert the server
upon arrival. ▪ *nineonninepgh.com*

### P.F. Chang's China Bistro        ✪★📖
*Pittsburgh* ▪ *(412) 788-2901*
*1600 Settlers Ridge Center Dr*
*Pittsburgh* ▪ *(412) 464-0640*
*148 Bridge St*

### Ruth's Chris Steak House        ✪📖
*Pittsburgh* ▪ *(412) 391-4800*
*6 PPG Pl*

# PENNSYLVANIA

## ALL OTHER CITIES

### 1201 Kitchen                $$LD
*Erie* ▪ *(814) 464-8989*
*1201 State St* ▪ *Japanese* ▪ Restaurant
reports that most protein dishes are GF and
chefs and staff have "absolutely no issue"
accommodating GF diners. Alert the server
upon arrival. ▪ *www.1201restaurant.com*

### Alfredo's Pizza                ★$LD
*Broomall* ▪ *(610) 355-9424*
*2900 W Chester Pike* ▪ *Pizza* ▪ GF pizza is
available in the 12" size.

### Apollo Grill                $$$LD
*Bethlehem* ▪ *(610) 865-9600*
*85 W Broad St* ▪ *American* ▪ The restaurant reports that many items on the menu
are naturally GF or can be modified to be
GF. The restaurant recommends notifying
the server, who will highlight items that are
appropriate for GF diners. ▪ *apollogrill.com*

### Arpeggio                $$LD
*Spring House* ▪ *(215) 646-5055*
*542 Spring House Vlg Ctr* ▪ *Mediterranean* ▪ GF menu available. Some
items include pizza crust, penne pasta,
grilled veggies, red lentil soup, seared
calamari, kababs and filet medallion. ▪
*www.arpeggiobyob.com*

### Au Bon Pain                📖
*Tannersville* ▪ *(570) 688-0646*
*1000 Route 611*
*Hershey* ▪ *(717) 531-2655*
*500 University Dr*

### Austin's Restaurant & Bar    ✪★$$LD
*West Lawn* ▪ *(610) 678-5500*
*1101 Snyder Rd* ▪ *American* ▪ Extensive
GF menu includes soups, salads, burgers, sandwiches, pasta, and a variety of
chicken & steak dishes. GF brownies and
ice cream sundae are available for dessert. GF pasta, sandwich buns, and beer
are available. Confirm the timeliness
of this information before dining in. ▪
*www.austinsrestaurant.com*

### Baggataway Tavern            ★$$D
*West Conshohocken* ▪ *(610) 834-8085*
*31 N Front St* ▪ *Pub Food* ▪ The restaurant
reports that GF options include homemade
chili, baked wings, and burgers and sandwiches with no bun. GF beer is available.
Confirm the timeliness of this information
before dining in.

## Basically Burgers                    ★ ₵LD
*Doylestown* ▪ *(215) 345-8502*
*33 N Main St* ▪ *American* ▪ GF
hamburger buns are available. ▪
*www.basicallyburgers.com*

## Bella Tori at the Mansion          $$$D
*Langhorne* ▪ *(215) 702-9600*
*321 S Bellevue Ave* ▪ *Italian* ▪ Reservations noting GF are highly recommended. When making reservations, the restaurant advises that GF diners let them know what dishes they will be ordering so the kitchen and chefs can prepare them in advance and have them ready when guests arrive. The restaurant notes that many dishes on the menu can be prepared GF. Alert the server upon arrival. ▪ *www.bellatori.com*

## Bertrand's Bistro                   $$$D
*Erie* ▪ *(814) 871-6477*
*18 N Park Row* ▪ *Bistro* ▪ Restaurant reports that they have several entrées that are GF and are "more than willing" to modify others to make them GF if possible. Alert the server upon arrival. ▪
*www.bertrandsbistro.com*

## Bertucci's                          ✪ ▭
*Bryn Mawr* ▪ *(610) 519-1940*
*761 W Lancaster Ave # 763*
*Glen Mills* ▪ *(610) 358-0127*
*501 Byers Dr*
*Huntingdon Valley* ▪ *(215) 322-2200*
*2190 County Line Rd*
*Langhorne* ▪ *(215) 752-9200*
*675 Middletown Blvd*
*Norristown* ▪ *(610) 630-1890*
*711 S Trooper Rd*
*Plymouth Meeting* ▪ *(610) 397-0650*
*500 W Germantown Pike*
*Springfield* ▪ *(610) 543-8079*
*965 Baltimore Pike*
*Warrington* ▪ *(215) 918-1590*
*855 Easton Rd*
*Wayne* ▪ *(610) 293-1700*
*523 W Lancaster Ave*
*Trevose* ▪ *(267) 983-5416*
*3617 Horizon Blvd*

*North Wales* ▪ *(267) 498-5538*
*860 Bethlehem Pike*

## Blackfish Restaurant               $$$LD
*Conshohocken* ▪ *(610) 397-0888*
*119 Fayette St* ▪ *Seafood & Steakhouse* ▪ The restaurant reports that "almost the entire menu" is GF and recommends alerting the server upon arrival so they can go over the options. ▪ *blackfishrestaurant.com*

## Blue Sky Café                       ★ $BL
*Bethlehem* ▪ *(610) 867-9390*
*22 W 4th St* ▪ *Café* ▪ GF rolls are available for sandwiches and burgers, and GF tortillas can be substituted on wraps, paninis, and quesadillas. Alert the server upon arrival. ▪ *www.theblueskycafe.com*

## Bonefish Grill                      ✪ ▭
*Willow Grove* ▪ *(215) 659-5854*
*1015 Easton Rd*
*Whitehall* ▪ *(610) 264-3476*
*901 Lehigh Lifestyle Ctr*
*Newtown Square* ▪ *(610) 355-1784*
*4889 W Chester Pike*
*Exton* ▪ *(610) 524-1010*
*460 W Lincoln Hwy*
*Camp Hill* ▪ *(717) 737-6541*
*3505 Gettysburg Rd*
*Lancaster* ▪ *(717) 394-8414*
*970 Plaza Blvd*
*Langhorne* ▪ *(215) 702-1312*
*500 Oxford Valley Rd*
*Upper St. Clair* ▪ *(412) 835-3239*
*1835 Washington Rd*

## Boston's Restaurant & Sports Bar
✪ ★ ▭
*Allentown* ▪ *(610) 841-5900*
*327 Star Rd*
*Erie* ▪ *(814) 217-1140*
*8071 Peach St*

## Brothers Pizza West Chester        ✪ ★ $LD
*West Chester* ▪ *(610) 431-1000*
*670 Downingtown Pike* ▪ *Pizza* ▪ GF 12" pizza available. ▪
*www.brotherspizzawestchester.com*

## Buca di Beppo                    ⊙▢
*Exton* ▪ *(610) 524-9939*
*300 Main St*
*Whitehall* ▪ *(610) 264-3389*
*714 Grape St*
*Wyomissing* ▪ *(610) 374-3482*
*2745 Papermill Rd*
*Wynnewood* ▪ *(610) 642-9470*
*260 E Lancaster Ave*

## Café Monterosso                  ★$$LD
*Fairless Hills* ▪ *(215) 295-1311*
*530 Lincoln Hwy* ▪ *Italian* ▪ GF
pizza, pasta and desserts available. ▪
*www.cafemonterosso.com*

## Calabria's Restaurant            ★$$$LD
*Upper St Clair* ▪ *(724) 260-0760*
*2652 Hidden Valley Dr* ▪ *Italian* ▪ The
restaurant reports that the entire menu can
be modified to accommodate GF customers. Staff reports that they "get a lot of
GF customers coming in" daily and ask
that diners alert the server upon arrival. ▪
*www.calabrias.biz*

## Carino's Italian                 ⊙▢
*Monroeville* ▪ *(412) 856-1780*
*145 Mall Circle Dr*

## Carmen's Pizza                   ⊙★¢LD
*Milmont Park* ▪ *(610) 532-2300*
*MacDade Blvd & Milmont Ave* ▪
*Pizza* ▪ Limited GF menu that in-
cludes several pizzas and sandwiches. ▪
*originalcarmenspizza.com*

## Charlie Brown's Steakhouse       ⊙▢
*Springfield* ▪ *(610) 604-7410*
*1001 Baltimore Pike*

## Cosi                             ⊙▢
*Bryn Mawr* ▪ *(610) 520-5208*
*761 W Lancaster Ave*
*Elkins Park* ▪ *(215) 886-9000*
*50 Yorktown Plaza*
*Exton* ▪ *(610) 594-1928*
*295 Main St*
*Berwyn* ▪ *(610) 640-0151*
*424 W Swedesford Rd*
*Willow Grove* ▪ *(215) 659-4176*

*4025 Welsh Rd*
*Center Valley* ▪ *(610) 797-8801*
*2880 Center Valley Pkwy*
*Newtown* ▪ *(215) 968-2165*
*104 Pheasant Run*
*Wayne* ▪ *(610) 254-9400*
*223 E Lancaster Ave*
*Glen Mills* ▪ *(610) 459-9655*
*Route 1 & CR 322*

## Don Pablo's                      ⊙▢
*Monroeville* ▪ *(412) 380-0120*
*122 Mall Blvd*

## Double Wide Grill                $LD
*Mars* ▪ *(724) 553-5212*
*100 Adams Shoppes* ▪ *American* ▪ Menu
indicates items that are wheat free. Items
include blackened chicken salad, coconut chicken dinner, coconut rum tilapia,
hot and sweet pineapple chicken, BBQ
St. Louis ribs, tofu with chimichurri
sauce, garlic and herb mash potatoes,
caramelized onion and cilantro rice, NY
strip steak, and sirloin sizzler platter. ▪
*www.doublewidegrill.com*

## Eat 'n Park                      ⊙▢
*Altoona* ▪ *(814) 943-4070*
*Eatnpark*
*Belle Vernon* ▪ *(724) 930-7470*
*1675 Broad Ave*
*Clarion* ▪ *(814) 227-2188*
*35 Perkins Rd*
*Dubois* ▪ *(814) 375-8622*
*1355 Bee Line Hwy*
*Erie* ▪ *(814) 838-9125*
*2519 W 12Th St*
*Erie* ▪ *(814) 866-3970*
*7355 Peach St*
*Grove City* ▪ *(724) 748-5911*
*1911 Leesburg Rd*
*Harrisburg* ▪ *(717) 986-9194*
*4641 Lindle Rd*
*Hermitage* ▪ *(724) 342-1383*
*2270 E State St*
*Homestead* ▪ *(412) 464-7275*
*245 Waterfront Dr E*
*Indiana* ▪ *(724) 465-2301*
*2675 Oakland Ave*

*Irwin* ▪ *(724) 864-8031*
*8891 Route 30*
*Lancaster* ▪ *(717) 390-2212*
*1683 Oregon Pike*
*Latrobe* ▪ *(724) 532-1966*
*520 Mountain Laurel Plz*
*Mars* ▪ *(724) 776-4460*
*19085 Perry Hwy*
*Monaca* ▪ *(724) 770-0644*
*120 Wagner Rd*
*New Cumberland* ▪ *(717) 774-5004*
*146 Sheraton Dr*
*North Versailles* ▪ *(412) 816-2006*
*299 Lincoln Hwy*
*Somerset* ▪ *(814) 443-4579*
*926 N Center Ave*
*State College* ▪ *(814) 231-8558*
*1617 N Atherton St*
*Washington* ▪ *(724) 229-7333*
*320 Oak Spring Rd*
*York* ▪ *(717) 751-4891*
*145 Memory Ln*
*Mckeesport* ▪ *(412) 664-9148*
*805 Lysle Blvd*
*Bridgeville* ▪ *(412) 221-8800*
*1197 Washington Pike*
*Washington* ▪ *(724) 222-7110*
*875 W Chestnut St*
*Monongahela* ▪ *(724) 258-4654*
*1250 W Main St*
*Butler* ▪ *(724) 282-7674*
*114 Clearview Cir*
*Bethel Park* ▪ *(412) 835-4011*
*5220 Library Rd*
*Wexford* ▪ *(724) 940-3270*
*2650 Brandt School Rd*
*Canonsburg* ▪ *(724) 941-8261*
*3528 Washington Rd*
*Etna* ▪ *(412) 487-4870*
*930 Butler St*
*Natrona Hts* ▪ *(724) 224-2442*
*1626 Broadview Blvd*
*Johnstown* ▪ *(814) 255-7711*
*1900 Minno Dr*
*Beaver Falls* ▪ *(724) 847-7275*
*500 Chippewa Town Ctr*
*Uniontown* ▪ *(724) 439-0440*
*519 W Main St*

*Sewickley* ▪ *(412) 741-4650*
*201 Ohio River Blvd*
*Greensburg* ▪ *(724) 837-2759*
*5277 Route 30*
*Butler* ▪ *(724) 287-0153*
*214 New Castle Rd*
*New Kensington* ▪ *(724) 335-3361*
*380 Freeport St*
*Mc Kees Rocks* ▪ *(412) 331-2881*
*300 Chartiers Ave*
*Franklin* ▪ *(814) 432-3352*
*553 Allegheny Blvd*
*New Stanton* ▪ *(724) 925-1060*
*PO Box 223*
*New Castle* ▪ *(724) 654-2311*
*100 W Washington St*
*Monroeville* ▪ *(412) 373-8760*
*3987 Monroeville Blvd*
*Tarentum* ▪ *(724) 275-1014*
*3005 Pittsburgh Mills Blvd*
*Moon Twp* ▪ *(412) 264-7201*
*9516 University Blvd*
*Gibsonia* ▪ *(724) 443-7280*
*5143 Route 8*
*Murrysville* ▪ *(724) 327-7270*
*4584 William Penn Hwy*
*Johnstown* ▪ *(814) 266-5714*
*1461 Scalp Ave*

## Ferrara's                     ✪ ★ $LD
*Sharon* ▪ *(724) 347-1247*
*1208 Hall Ave* ▪ *Italian* ▪ GF pasta, pizza,
and bread are available. Extensive GF
menu includes appetizers, salads, pasta,
sandwiches, and pizza. As with all specialty
items, call ahead to confirm availability. ▪
*www.ferraraatasteofitaly.com*

## Firebirds Wood Fired Grill       ✪📖
*Chadds Ford* ▪ *(484) 785-6880*
*91 Wilmington W Chester Pke*
*Collegeville* ▪ *(484) 902-1850*
*51 Town Center*
*Erie* ▪ *(814) 864-1599*
*680 Millcreek Mall*

## First Watch - The Daytime Café   ✪📖
*Cranberry Township* ▪ *(724) 741-0581*
*20424 Route 19*

### Fleming's Prime Steakhouse & Wine Bar ✪📖
*Radnor* ▪ *(610) 688-9463*
*555 E Lancaster Ave*

### Fox and Hound Pub & Grille 📖
*Erie* ▪ *(814) 864-5589*
*250 Millcreek Pza*
*Pittsburgh* ▪ *(412) 364-1885*
*8000 McKnight Rd*
*Harrisburg E* ▪ *(717) 526-4415*
*2625 Brindle Dr*
*King Of Prussia* ▪ *(610) 962-0922*
*160 N Gulph Rd*

### Gamble Mill Restaurant $$$LD
*Bellefonte* ▪ *(814) 355-7764*
*160 Dunlap St* ▪ *Modern American* ▪
Restaurant reports that most entrées can be made GF. Confirm the timeliness of this information before dining in. Reservations noting GF are recommended. ▪
*www.gamblemill.com*

### Gluten Free Oven, The ¢S
*Mount Pleasant* ▪ *(724) 542-4457*
*125 W Main St* ▪ *Bakery* ▪ Dedicated GF bakery offering all the standards such as breads, buns, pizza crust, cookies and cakes, as well as specialty items such as pierogies, ravioli, and pepperoni rolls. Some items are also available casein-free. ▪
*theglutenfreeoven.net*

### Go Fish
### Bar and Seafood Restaurant $$LD
*West Reading* ▪ *(610) 376-6446*
*619 Penn Ave* ▪ *Seafood* ▪ The restaurant reports that a variety of GF options are available, and recommends notifying the server of any "food allergies" upon arrival. ▪ *www.gofishseafood.com*

### Good Eatz Green Café ✪★¢BLD
*West Reading* ▪ *(610) 670-4885*
*701 Penn Ave* ▪ *American* ▪ GF items marked on the menu include five bean vegan chili, potato pancakes, garlic/wine herb mussels, grilled caesar salad, avocado citrus salad, GF millet bread available for sandwiches, GF bread for wraps, 7"

GF pizza, vegan shepherd's pie, orange-rosemary wild caught salmon, seafood stir fry and GF cheese ravioli. Many of the items on the menu can be modified to be GF. Alert server upon arrival. ▪ *www.goodeatzgreencafe.com*

### Grandma's Grotto ✪★$$$LD
*Horsham* ▪ *(215) 675-4700*
*986 Easton Rd* ▪ *Italian* ▪ GF menu includes caprese salad, mussel soup, garlic bread, bruschetta, penne vodka, fettucine alfredo, chicken parmesan, veal with prosciutto and mushrooms, pizza, and more. Owner John reports that GF menu items are made fresh every day. GF pasta and bread are available. ▪ *www.grandmasgrotto.com*

### Ground Round ✪📖
*Coraopolis* ▪ *(412) 269-0644*
*5980 University Blvd*
*Greensburg* ▪ *(724) 836-1550*
*960 E Pittsburgh St*
*Langhorne* ▪ *(215) 757-2323*
*35 Middletown Blvd*
*Langhorne* ▪ *(215) 757-2323*
*735 Middletown Blvd*

### Gullifty's ✪★$LD
*Rosemont* ▪ *(610) 525-1851*
*1149 Lancaster Ave* ▪ *American* ▪ GF menu includes modifications that can be made to items on the menu. Alert server upon arrival and they will ask chef exactly what is in each dish if there are any questions. ▪ *www.gulliftys.com*

### Hershey Grill ★$$$LD
*Hershey* ▪ *(717) 534-8601*
*325 University Dr* ▪ *American* ▪ GF items can be found online under allergen information. Items include chicken cobb salad, filet mignon, grilled chicken breast, garlic fries, grilled salmon, corned beef hash, and mushroom & brie omelet. For dessert, there is crème brûlée and a nutella torte. GF pasta is available. Confirm the timeliness of this information before dining in. ▪ *www.hersheylodge.com*

## Iron Hill Brewery & Restaurant ✪★📖
*Lancaster* ▪ *(717) 291-9800*
*781 Harrisburg Pike*
*Media* ▪ *(610) 627-9000*
*30 E State St*
*North Wales* ▪ *(267) 708-2000*
*1460 Bethlehem Pike*
*Phoenixville* ▪ *(610) 983-9333*
*130 E Bridge St*
*West Chester* ▪ *(610) 738-9600*
*3 W Gay St*

## Isaac Newton's                      $LD
*Newtown* ▪ *(215) 860-5100*
*18 S State St* ▪ *American* ▪ The restaurant reports that a GF list is available upon request, and notes that the server "should be able to indicate" GF items. Alert server upon arrival. ▪ *www.isaacnewtons.com*

## Isaac's Famous Grilled Sandwiches
★ ¢LD
*Wyomissing* ▪ *(610) 376-1717*
*94 Commerce Dr*
*Exton* ▪ *(484) 875-5825*
*630 W Uwchlan Ave*
*Mechanicsburg* ▪ *(717) 795-1925*
*6520 Carlisle Pike*
*Mechanicsburg* ▪ *(717) 766-1111*
*4940 Ritter Rd*
*Lemoyne* ▪ *(717) 731-9545*
*1200 W Market St*
*Hummelstown* ▪ *(717) 533-9665*
*597 E Main St*
*Harrisburg* ▪ *(717) 920-5757*
*421 Friendship Rd*
*Harrisburg* ▪ *(717) 541-1111*
*2900 Linglestown Rd*
*Strasburg* ▪ *(717) 687-7699*
*226 Gap Rd*
*Lititz* ▪ *(717) 625-1181*
*4 Crosswinds Dr*
*Lancaster* ▪ *(717) 393-6067*
*565 Greenfield Rd*
*Lancaster* ▪ *(717) 560-7774*
*1559 Manheim Pike*
*Ephrata* ▪ *(717) 733-7777*
*120 N Reading Rd*
*Lancaster* ▪ *(717) 393-1199*
*245 Centerville Rd*
*Lancaster* ▪ *(717) 394-5544*
*25 N Queen St*
*York* ▪ *(717) 751-0515*
*2960 Whiteford Rd*
*York* ▪ *(717) 747-5564*
*235 Pauline Dr*
*York* ▪ *(717) 854-2292*
*2159 White St*
*Hanover* ▪ *(717) 646-0289*
*1412 Baltimore St*
*Mt Joy* ▪ *(717) 928-2130*
*919 E Main St* ▪ *Deli* ▪ GF flatbread is available for sandwiches at all locations. As with all specialty items, call ahead to confirm availability. ▪ *www.isaacsdeli.com*

## J.B. Dawson's Restaurant & Bar ✪★ $$LD
*Langhorne* ▪ *(215) 702-8119*
*92 N Flowers Mill Rd*
*Lancaster* ▪ *(717) 399-3996*
*491 Park City Ctr* ▪ *American* ▪ Extensive GF menu includes a variety of starters, soups, salads, burgers, and sandwiches, as well as pastas, fish dishes, meat dishes, and sides. Several GF desserts are available. GF beer, sandwich buns, and pasta are available. Necessary modifications are noted on the menu for applicable dishes. Director of Kitchens Steven notes that once a diner informs the server that they have Celiac, the floor manager and kitchen manager are immediately notified and oversee the preparation process from start to finish. ▪ *www.jbdawsons.com*

## Jersey Mike's                      📖
*Peters Township* ▪ *(724) 942-0202*
*4123 Washington Rd*
*Cranberry Township* ▪ *(724) 742-0200*
*20300 Route 19*
*Wexford* ▪ *(724) 933-0101*
*10640 Perry Hwy*
*State College* ▪ *(814) 954-7591*
*128 S Allen St*

## Joe's Crab Shack                   ✪📖
*King of Prussia* ▪ *(610) 265-2237*
*244 Mall Blvd*
*Bala Cynwyd* ▪ *(610) 949-0391*
*555 City Ave*

## Jules Thin Crust Pizza ★ $$LD
*Newtown* ▪ *(215) 579-0111*
*300 Sycamore St*
*Doylestown* ▪ *(215) 345-8565*
*78 S Main St*
*Jenkintown* ▪ *(215) 886-5555*
*817 Old York Rd*
*Wayne* ▪ *(484) 580-8003*
*114 E Lancaster Ave* ▪ *Pizza* ▪ GF pizza is available with any toppings. The restaurant reports that their staff has been "fully trained" on GF procedures, and notes that all their GF items are prepared with dedicated utensils and prep surfaces to avoid CC. ▪ *www.julesthincrust.com*

## La Bella $$D
*Erie* ▪ *(814) 456-2244*
*802 W 18th St* ▪ *Fusion* ▪ Owner reports that he personally created an "allergy guide" which denotes which items contain gluten and which ones do not. Alert server upon arrival.

## Lamberti's Cucina $LD
*Feasterville* ▪ *(215) 355-6266*
*1045 Bustleton Pike* ▪ *Italian* ▪ Restaurant reports that several items on the menu can be prepared GF. Alert the server upon arrival and they will help select a GF meal. ▪ *www.lambertis.com*

## Latinos Restaurant & Bar $LD
*Erie* ▪ *(814) 452-1966*
*1315 Parade St* ▪ *Mexican* ▪ Restaurant reports that 95% of their menu is GF and they strive to keep their kitchen as healthy as possible and are always willing to accommodate in any way possible. Alert server upon arrival. ▪ *www.latinosrb.com*

## Legal Sea Foods ✪▢
*King Of Prussia* ▪ *(610) 265-5566*
*690 W Dekalb Pke*

## Lisa's Gluten Free Bakery ¢S
*Dickerson Run* ▪ *(724) 529-2899*
*213 Hollow Rd* ▪ *Bakery* ▪ 100% GF bakery offering a variety of items such as cookies, cakes, muffins, pies, breads and rolls, and pizza dough.

## Little E's Pizzeria ★ $LD
*Greensburg* ▪ *(724) 834-7336*
*807 Highland Ave* ▪ *Pizza* ▪ GF pizza, hoagie buns, breadsticks, beer and desserts are available. GF items are prepared in a separate area to minimize CC. As with all specialty items, call ahead to confirm availability. ▪ *www.littleespizzeria.com*

## Lone Star Steakhouse & Saloon ✪▢
*Easton* ▪ *(610) 252-1180*
*20 Kunkle Dr*
*Johnstown* ▪ *(814) 262-0707*
*510 Galleria Dr*
*Mars* ▪ *(724) 779-4441*
*926 Sheraton Dr*
*West Mifflin* ▪ *(412) 655-1986*
*6111 Mountain View Rd*
*Wilkes Barre* ▪ *(570) 826-7080*
*805 Kidder St*

## Maggiano's Little Italy ★▢
*King Of Prussia* ▪ *(610) 992-3333*
*160 N Gulph Rd*

## Main Line Pizza ✪★$$LD
*Wayne* ▪ *(610) 687-4008*
*233 E Lancaster Ave* ▪ *Pizza* ▪ GF menu available. Items include GF pizza, baked chicken wings, GF ziti pasta with homemade GF meatballs, romaine turkey and tuna wraps, GF baked ziti, crab cake sandwich, crab cake dinner and GF flatbread. ▪ *www.mainlinepizza.com*

## Mamma D's Italian Restaurant ✪★$$$LD
*Pipersville* ▪ *(215) 766-9468*
*6637 Easton Rd* ▪ *Italian* ▪ GF options on menu include pasta marinara, chicken or eggplant parmigiana with rice pasta, New York strip steak with potato and vegetable and jumbo lumped crab cakes. Items on menu that can be prepared GF have an asterisks next to them. Alert server upon arrival. ▪ *www.mammadsitalianrestaurant.com*

## Margaret Kuo's   ★$$LD
*Wayne* ▪ *(610) 688-7200*
*175 E Lancaster Ave*
*Media* ▪ *(610) 892-0115*
*6 W State St*
*Malvern* ▪ *(610) 647-5488*
*190 Lancaster Ave* ▪ *Asian* ▪ Most of
the menu can be made GF, restaurant
offers many chicken, beef and seafood dishes. GF soy sauce is available. ▪
*www.margaretkuos.com*

## Melting Pot, The   ⊙🕮
*Bethlehem* ▪ *(484) 241-4939*
*1 E Broad St*
*Harrisburg* ▪ *(717) 564-6358*
*3350 Paxton St*
*King Of Prussia* ▪ *(610) 265-7195*
*150 Allendale Rd*
*Warrington* ▪ *(215) 343-0895*
*751 Easton Rd*

## Mi Scuzi   $$D
*Erie* ▪ *(814) 454-4533*
*2641 Myrtle St* ▪ *Italian* ▪ The restaurant reports that they have several GF
salad options as well as a variety of steak,
chicken, and pork entrées that are or can
be prepared GF. Confirm the timeliness
of this information before dining in. ▪
*www.miscuzirestaurant.com*

## Miller's Ale House Restaurants   ⊙★🕮
*Langhorne* ▪ *(267) 572-0750*
*2250 E Lincoln Hwy*
*Philadelphia* ▪ *(215) 464-8349*
*9495 E Roosevelt Blvd*
*Willow Grove* ▪ *(215) 657-0515*
*2300 Easton Rd*

## Miller's Smorgasbord   ⊙$$$BLD
*Ronks* ▪ *(717) 687-6621*
*2811 Lincoln Hwy E* ▪ *American* ▪ Note
GF when making reservations. GF items
include steamed or baked chicken ordered
prior to arrival, mixed veggies, Boston blue
fish, cottage cheese, fruit salad, vegetarian
chili, char grilled ham, beef or turkey, seasoned or plain shrimp. Confirm the timeli-

ness of this information before dining in. ▪
*www.millerssmorgasbord.com*

## Mitchell's Fish Market   ⊙🕮
*Homestead* ▪ *(412) 476-8844*
*185 Waterfront Dr W*

## Molinari's Restaurant   $$$D
*Bethlehem* ▪ *(610) 625-9222*
*322 E 3rd St* ▪ *Italian* ▪ The restaurant reports that several menu items are naturally
GF, and many more can be modifed to be
GF. It is recommended to call a day in advance to notify the chef so he can prepare
accordingly. ▪ *molinarimangia.com*

## Molto Pazzo   ★$$LD
*Bethlehem* ▪ *(610) 625-2733*
*553 Main St* ▪ *Italian* ▪ GF pasta is available. ▪ *moltopazzo.com*

## Mom's Bake At Home Pizza   ★¢BLD
*Glenmoore* ▪ *(610) 458-1022*
*2918 Conestoga Rd* ▪ *Take-&-Bake* ▪
GF "take-&-bake" pizza is available. ▪
*www.momsbakeathome.com*

## Monterey Bay Fish Grotto   $$$LD
*Monroeville* ▪ *(412) 374-8530*
*146 Mall Circle Dr* ▪ *Seafood* ▪ GF options
available. Both locations have different
menus but both can accommodate GF
diners. Reservations noting GF made
at least 2 days in advance are recommended. Staff notes that chefs and servers are familiar with GF requests and
will be happy to prepare GF dishes. ▪
*www.montereybayfishgrotto.com*

## Morton's Steakhouse   ⊙🕮
*King of Prussia* ▪ *(610) 491-1900*
*640 W Dekalb Pke*

## O'Charley's   🕮
*Erie* ▪ *(814) 464-2957*
*2077 Interchange Rd*

## Olive Branch   $LD
*Bethlehem* ▪ *(610) 814-0355*
*355 Broadway* ▪ *Middle Eastern* ▪ Restaurant reports that there are several options
for GF diners, including grilled proteins

served with veggies. Alert server upon arrival. ▪ *www.olivebranchbethlehem.com*

### P.F. Chang's China Bistro          ✪★📖
*Collegeville* ▪ *(610) 489-0110*
*10 Town Center Dr*
*Glen Mills* ▪ *(610) 545-3030*
*983 Baltimore Pike*
*Plymouth Meeting* ▪ *(610) 567-0226*
*510 W Germantown Pike*
*Warrington* ▪ *(215) 918-3340*
*721 Easton Rd*

### Pei Wei Asian Diner          ✪📖
*Springfield* ▪ *(610) 549-9060*
*950 Baltimore Pike*

### Piazza Sorrento          ✪★$$LD
*Hershey* ▪ *(717) 835-1919*
*16 Briarcrest Sq* ▪ *Italian* ▪ GF pizza, pasta, rolls, and beer are available. GF menu includes a variety of pasta dishes, salads, and sandwiches for lunch, and a selection of meat and seafood entrées and pizzas for dinner. For dessert, they offer GF tiramisu, ricotta cake and crème brûlée. ▪ *www.piazzasorrento.com*

### Pizza Joe's          ★📖
*Grove City* ▪ *(724) 458-0566*
*604 Main St*
*Beaver* ▪ *(724) 775-5655*
*606 3rd St*
*Beaver Falls* ▪ *(724) 846-4443*
*400 32nd St*
*Bessemer* ▪ *(724) 667-8500*
*Bessemer-Mt Jackson Rd*
*Butler* ▪ *(724) 284-0045*
*226 N Main St*
*Aliquippa* ▪ *(724) 728-0296*
*3403B Brodhead Rd*
*Chicora* ▪ *(724) 445-7200*
*501 N Main St*
*Conneaut Lake* ▪ *(814) 382-0222*
*Rte 18 E*
*Ellwood City* ▪ *(724) 752-9411*
*128 Spring Ave*
*Franklin* ▪ *(814) 432-8000*
*1145 Liberty St*
*Greenville* ▪ *(724) 588-4321*
*324 Main St*

*Grove City* ▪ *(724) 458-0566*
*604 Main St*
*Hermitage* ▪ *(724) 347-3844*
*4195 E State St*
*Hopewell* ▪ *(724) 857-0449*
*2296 Broadhead Rd*
*Leetsdale/Ambridge* ▪ *(724) 266-3066*
*192 Ohio River Blvd*
*Mercer* ▪ *(724) 662-2433*
*116 E Venango St*
*Monaca* ▪ *(724) 773-0100*
*815 Pennsylvania Ave*
*New Brighton* ▪ *(724) 847-3112*
*507 5th St*
*New Castle* ▪ *(724) 652-7355*
*1203 Croton Ave*
*New Castle* ▪ *(724) 652-4242*
*2700 Highland Ave*
*New Castle* ▪ *(724) 658-9090*
*2650 Ellwood Rd*
*New Wilmington* ▪ *(724) 946-2515*
*209 S Market St*
*Portersville* ▪ *(724) 368-8557*
*100 E St*
*Saegertown* ▪ *(814) 763-3222*
*538 Main St*
*Sharpsville* ▪ *(724) 962-2334*
*46 E Shenango St*
*Sharon* ▪ *(724) 342-2500*
*52 S Water Ave*
*New Castle* ▪ *(724) 654-1150*
*1815 W State St*

### Pop Pop's Pizza & Pasta          ★$$LD
*Warminster* ▪ *(215) 441-8217*
*216 W St Rd* ▪ *Pizza* ▪ GF 12" pizza is available.

### Prince Street Café          ★¢BLD
*Lancaster* ▪ *(717) 397-1505*
*15 N Prince St* ▪ *Café* ▪ GF muffins, cupcakes and biscotti are available. GF rolls are also available for sandwich orders. As with all specialty items, call ahead to confirm availability. ▪ *www.princestreetcafe.com*

## Roman Delight     ✪★$$LD
*Warminster* ▪ *(215) 957-6465*
*225 E St Rd* ▪ *Italian* ▪ GF personal pizza is on the menu. GF penne pasta is also available. ▪ *www.romandelightwarminster.com*

## Romano's Macaroni Grill     ✪★📖
*Fairless Hills* ▪ *(215) 949-9990*
*640 Commerce Blvd*
*Harrisburg* ▪ *(717) 371-4945*
*2531 Brindle Dr*
*Lancaster* ▪ *(717) 293-1090*
*925 Plaza Blvd*
*North Wales* ▪ *(215) 368-4210*
*29 Airport Sq*

## Ruth's Chris Steak House     ✪📖
*King of Prissia* ▪ *(610) 992-1818*
*220 N Gulph Rd*
*Wilkes-Barre* ▪ *(570) 208-2266*
*1280 Hwy 315*

## Smiler's Grill & Bar     $$LD
*Dickson City* ▪ *(570) 383-0041*
*600 Main St* ▪ *American* ▪ Restaurant reports that they have accommodated GF diners in the past. Upon arrival, alert server and they will speak to a chef, who can discuss GF options.

## Smokey Bones     📖
*Erie* ▪ *(814) 868-3388*
*2074 Interchange Rd*
*Robinson Township* ▪ *(412) 788-0123*
*6050 Robinson Ctr*
*Cranberry Township* ▪ *(724) 772-7000*
*1708 Route 228*
*Tarentum* ▪ *(724) 275-1240*
*1030 Pittsburgh Mills Blvd*
*Greensburg* ▪ *(724) 834-4871*
*100 Power Line Dr*
*Wilkes-Barre* ▪ *(570) 825-2540*
*265 Mundy St*
*Reading* ▪ *(610) 375-9580*
*2733 Pappermill Rd*
*York* ▪ *(717) 846-3760*
*1301 Kenneth Rd*

## Soba     $$$D
*Shadyside* ▪ *(412) 362-5656*
*5847 Ellsworth Ave* ▪ *Asian Fusion* ▪ The restaurant reports that their menu changes frequently, and recommends calling ahead to find out the current GF options. Alert the server upon arrival. ▪ *www.bigburrito.com/soba*

## Sunset Café     ✪$$D
*Greensburg* ▪ *(724) 834-9903*
*302 S Urania Ave* ▪ *Modern American* ▪ GF menu includes mussels, sausage and hot peppers, calamari, variety of soups and salads, strip steak, il pescatore ciopppino, north Atlantic salmon, pollo dicaprio, grilled chicken parmigiana, cod di napoli, polenta, shrimp or scallops scampi and, for dessert, flourless chocolate cake or crème brûlée. ▪ *www.sunsetcafepa.com*

## Susanna Foo Gourmet Kitchen     $$$LD
*Radnor* ▪ *(610) 688-8808*
*555 E Lancaster Ave* ▪ *Chinese* ▪ Hostess reports that "accommodations can be made" for GF diners. She recommends making reservations noting GF. Alert server upon arrival. ▪ *www.susannafoo.com*

## Sweet Cece's     📖
*Grove* ▪ *(724) 748-3755*
*1911 Leesburg Grove City Rd*

## Sweet Christine's
## Gluten Free Confections     ¢S
*Kennett Square* ▪ *(610) 444-5542*
*132 W State St* ▪ *Bakery & Café* ▪ Dedicated GF bakery offering GF muffins, donuts, cookies, breads, cakes, brownies, and pizza. Calling ahead for special requests is recommended. ▪ *www.sweetchristinesglutenfree.com*

## Tango     $$$LD
*Bryn Mawr* ▪ *(610) 526-9500*
*39 Morris Ave* ▪ *Modern American* ▪ The restaurant reports that almost the whole menu can be prepared GF upon request. Alert the server upon arrival. ▪ *www.tastetango.com*

**Ted's Montana Grill**                    ✪ 📖
*Warrington* ▪ *(215) 491-1170*
*1512 Main St*

**The Tom Cat Café**                       $BL
*Sinking Spring* ▪ *(610) 678-1098*
*3998 A Penn Ave* ▪ *Café* ▪ The breakfast menu is posted online and includes
a variety of omelets and meat items
which are GF. Alert server upon arrival. ▪
*www.tomcatcafe.com*

**Unique Desserts**                        ★$$$$
*West Reading* ▪ *(610) 372-7879*
*530 Grape St* ▪ *Bakery* ▪ GF items
available by special order. Orders must
be placed at least a week in advance. ▪
*www.uniquedesserts.biz*

**Uno Chicago Grill**                      ✪★📖
*Bensalem* ▪ *(215) 322-6003*
*801 Neshaminy Mall*
*Conshohocken* ▪ *(610) 825-3050*
*1009 Ridge Pike*
*Dickson City* ▪ *(570) 307-4200*
*3905 Commerce Blvd*
*Exton* ▪ *(610) 280-4555*
*8 N Pottstown Pike*
*Homestead* ▪ *(412) 462-8667*
*205 Waterfront Dr E*
*North Wales* ▪ *(215) 283-9760*
*1100 Bethlehem Pike*
*Warrington* ▪ *(215) 491-1212*
*1661 Easton Rd*

**Virago**                                 ✪★$
*Lansdale* ▪ *(215) 412-7071*
*322 1/2 W Main St* ▪ *Bakery* ▪ Non-dedicated bakery offering GF cupcakes, lunches,
"take-&-bake" pizzas, cakes, pastries, cookies, and rolls. Manager Joe reports that the
bakery is very careful to separate GF ingredients from non-GF ingredients. Notice of
at least 48hrs is required for special orders.
▪ *www.viragobakingcompany.com*

**White Dog Café**                         $$$LD
*Wayne* ▪ *(610) 225-3700*
*200 W Lancaster Ave* ▪ *Modern American*
▪ Reservations noting GF are recommend-
ed so that the chefs have time to prepare.

GF items include apple bisque, garden
salad, pear salad, chicken tempura, pork
tenderloin, tofu, filet, pacific cod, grilled
eggplant and heirloom tomatoes. Confirm
the timeliness of this information before
dining in. ▪ *www.whitedog.com*

**Wild Tomato, The**                       ✪★$LD
*Harrisburg* ▪ *(717) 545-6435*
*4315 Jonestown Rd Unit 2* ▪ *Pizza* ▪ Certi-
fied by the GIG and participants in the
GFRAP. Items available as GF are marked
on the menu and include a variety of hoa-
gies, pasta dishes, and pizzas. According to
the restaurant "97% of the menu is avail-
able GF." ▪ *www.pizzaharrisburgpa.com*

# RHODE ISLAND

## PROVIDENCE

**Au Bon Pain**                            📖
*Providence* ▪ *(401) 521-9092*
*100 Westminster St*
*Providence* ▪ *(401) 751-0472*
*223 Thayer St*
*Providence* ▪ *(401) 274-1451*
*593 Eddy St*
*Providence* ▪ *(401) 421-1532*
*101 Dudley St*

**Capital Grille, The**                    ✪📖
*Providence* ▪ *(401) 521-5600*
*1 Union Sta*

**Fire + Ice**                             ★📖
*Providence* ▪ *(401) 270-4040*
*48 Providence Pl*

**Fleming's Prime Steakhouse & Wine
Bar**                                      ✪📖
*Providence* ▪ *(401) 533-9000*
*1 W Exchange St*

## Il Fornello                    ✪ ★ $D
*No. Providence* ▪ *(401) 722-5599*
*16 Josephine St* ▪ *Italian* ▪ GF items are
identified by asterisks on menu. Items
include clams zuppa, stuffed eggplant rolls,
rabe and cannellini beans, tripe, bowtie
panna, gnocchi, shrimp fradiavlo, chicken
saltimbocca, chicken marsala, chicken
balsamic, salmon carolina, scrod arrabiata
and a sirloin steak. ▪ *ilfornellori.com*

## Jersey Mike's                    📖
*North Providence* ▪ *(401) 223-0251*
*1401 Douglas Ave*

## Kabob and Curry                 ✪$LD
*Providence* ▪ *(401) 273-8844*
*261 Thayer St* ▪ *Indian* ▪ GF items are
marked on the menu and include curries,
biryani, vindaloo, chicken, seafood, lamb,
and vegan entrées, and more. Be sure to
alert the server that you are ordering GF. ▪
*www.kabobandcurry.com*

## Melting Pot, The                 ✪📖
*Providence* ▪ *(401) 865-6670*
*199 Providence Pl*

## Pot Au Feu                       $$$D
*Providence* ▪ *(401) 273-8953*
*44 Custom House St* ▪ *French* ▪ The restaurant reports that GF diners are "always
welcome." Reservations noting GF are
strongly recommended. Alert the server
upon arrival and they will provide a list of
GF options. ▪ *www.potaufeuri.com*

## Ruth's Chris Steak House          ✪📖
*Providence* ▪ *(401) 272-2271*
*10 Memorial Blvd*

## Union Station Brewery             $$LD
*Providence* ▪ *(401) 274-2739*
*36 Exchange Ter* ▪ *American* ▪ GF
accommodations can be made. Note GF
when making reservations and alert server
upon arrival. Some items include bourbon
ale salmon, salads without croutons or
wontons, and burgers with no bun. GF salad
dressings include balsamic, sherry and basil
vinaigrette. ▪ *www.johnharvards.com*

## Uno Chicago Grill                 ✪ ★ 📖
*Providence* ▪ *(401) 270-4866*
*82 Providence Pl*

## Waterman Grille                   ✪ ★ $$LD
*Providence* ▪ *(401) 521-9229*
*4 Richmond Square* ▪ *Modern American* ▪
GF menu available. Items include steamed
PEI mussels, wood grilled chicken breast,
Atlantic salmon, wood grilled filet mignon,
penne and shrimp, and grilled vegetable
risotto. GF desserts include a chocolate
truffle cake, crème brûlée and a seasonal
fruit sorbet. GF beer is also offered. ▪
*www.watermangrille.com*

## Waterplace                        ✪ ★ $$LD
*Providence* ▪ *(401) 272-1040*
*1 Finance Wy* ▪ *Modern American* ▪ The
restaurant reports that all menu items can
be prepared GF. GF pizza dough and pasta
are available. Alert server upon arrival. ▪
*www.waterplaceri.com*

# RHODE ISLAND
## ALL OTHER CITIES

## Bertucci's                        ✪📖
*Warwick* ▪ *(401) 732-4343*
*1946 Post Rd*

## Bonefish Grill                    ✪📖
*Cranston* ▪ *(401) 275-4970*
*2000 Chapel View Blvd*

## Brick Alley Pub and Restaurant    ✪ ★ $$D
*Newport* ▪ *(401) 849-6334*
*140 Thames St* ▪ *American* ▪ GF menu available. Items include grilled chicken, broiled
salmon, baked native sea scallops, cheeseburger, New York sirloin, broiled native scrod
or sole and bone in cowboy ribeye. GF salad
dressings including blue cheese, parmesan
peppercorn, house made balsamic vinaigrette
and house made caesar. Dessert includes a
sorbet of the day. ▪ *www.brickalley.com*

## British Beer Company Restaurant and Pub, The ✪★📖
*Bristol* ▪ (401) 253-6700
*29 State St*

## Caffe Itri ★$$LD
*Cranston* ▪ (401) 942-1970
*1686 Cranston St* ▪ *Italian* ▪ GF pasta available. All food is made from scratch so any GF accommodations can be made. Alert server upon arrival and they will alert the chef. ▪ *www.caffeitri.com*

## Diego's ✪★$$LD
*Newport* ▪ (401) 619-2640
*11 Bowens Wharf* ▪ *Mexican* ▪ GF menu available. Some items include a variety of salads and appetizers, Diego's famous loaded fish tacos, mahi tacos, tequila lime hanger steak and tacos de pollo. ▪ *diegosnewport.com/index.php*

## Eva Ruth's Specialty Bakery $$
*Middletown* ▪ (401) 619-1924
*796 Aquidneck Ave Unit D* ▪ *Bakery* ▪ Dedicated GF bakery offering breads, cookies, brownies, muffins, cakes, and more. Many products are free of other common allergens as well. ▪ *stores.evaruths.com/storefront.bok*

## Fifth Element, The ✪★$$$D
*Newport* ▪ (401) 619-2552
*111 Broadway* ▪ *American* ▪ Notify server of GF diet. GF items are identified in main menu by asterisks. Items include mussels, baked chevre with herbs, tortilla de patatas, salads, grilled New York strip steak, marinated flat iron steak, pan seared duck breast, pan roasted cod, grilled Atlantic salmon and garlic mashed potatoes. ▪ *thefifthri.com*

## Fluke Wine Bar and Kitchen ★$$$$LD
*Newport* ▪ (401) 849-7778
*41 Bowens Wharf* ▪ *Modern American* ▪ Menu changes often. Note GF when making reservations and alert server upon arrival. ▪ *www.flukewinebar.com*

## Garden Grille Café, The ✪★$LD
*Pawtucket* ▪ (401) 726-2826
*727 E Ave* ▪ *Global* ▪ Hostess reports that dinner menu is the most accommodating for GF customers. Items include nachos, fried green tomatoes, all of the sides, risotto cakes, eggplant dish and mac & cheese. For the brunch and lunch menu, alert the server of GF diet and they will list items that can be modified to be GF. ▪ *www.gardengrillecafe.com*

## Jersey Mike's 📖
*Warwick* ▪ (401) 223-0427
*782 Warwick Ave*
*Warwick* ▪ (401) 921-4488
*1350 Greenwich Ave*

## Legal Sea Foods ✪📖
*Warwick* ▪ (401) 732-3663
*2099 Post Rd*

## Mamma Luisa Restaurant ★$LD
*Newport* ▪ (401) 848-5257
*673 Thames St* ▪ *Italian* ▪ GF menu available at restaurant. ▪ *www.mammaluisa.com/2002/*

## Ninety Nine ✪📖
*Cranston* ▪ (401) 463-9993
*1171 New London Ave*
*Newport* ▪ (401) 849-9969
*199 J.T. Connell Hwy*
*Westerly* ▪ (401) 348-8299
*7 Airport Rd*

## O'Brien's Pub ✪$$LD
*Newport* ▪ (401) 849-6623
*501 Thames St* ▪ *Pub Food* ▪ GF menu available. Menu includes rice cheese pizza, sunshine citrus chicken, pan seared salmon dinner and a jalapeno sirloin. ▪ *www.theobrienspub.com*

## Papa Razzi ★📖
*Cranston* ▪ (401) 942-2900
*1 Paparazzi Wy*

**Potenza** ✪$$$D
*Providence* ■ *(401) 273-2652*
*286 Atwells Ave* ■ *Italian* ■ Extensive GF
menu includes risotto with porcini mush-
rooms, seared scallops, pork tenderloin,
veal scaloppine, and much more. A GF des-
sert for 2 guests only can be ordered when
placing a reservation. ■ *www.chefwalter.com*

**Rasoi Restaurant** ✪★$LD
*Pawtucket* ■ *(401) 728-5500*
*727 E Ave* ■ *Indian* ■ GF items are marked
on the menu and include tawa shrimp, tan-
doori chicken, biryani, and vegetable man-
go curry, among other things. On Saturday
mornings, a dedicated GF buffet brunch is
available. ■ *www.rasoi-restaurant.com*

**Sardella's Restaurant** ★$$D
*Newport* ■ *(401) 849-6312*
*30 Memorial Blvd W* ■ *Italian* ■ GF pasta is
available. ■ *www.sardellas.com*

**Smokehouse Café, The** ★$$LD
*Newport* ■ *(401) 848-9800*
*31 Scotts Wharf* ■ *Barbeque* ■ No desig-
nated GF menu but most of the restau-
rants items are GF. Items include the ribs,
chicken, nachos hog wings and GF rolls are
available for the sandwiches and burgers.
No gluten contents in the BBQ sauce. ■
*www.smokehousecafe.com/index.php*

**Smokey Bones** 📖
*Warwick* ■ *(401) 821-2789*
*31B Universal Blvd*

**Tallulah on Thames** ★$$$$LD
*Newport* ■ *(401) 849-2433*
*464 Thames St* ■ *Modern American* ■
Note GF when making reservations and
servers will assist with GF options. ■
*www.tallulahonthames.com*

**Ted's Montana Grill** ✪📖
*Cranston* ■ *(401) 275-5070*
*2 Chapel Vw Blvd*

**Uno Chicago Grill** ✪★📖
*Smithfield* ■ *(401) 233-4570*
*371 Putnam Pike*

**Warwick** ■ *(401) 738-5610*
*399 Bald Hill Rd*

**White Horse Tavern, The** ★$$$D
*Newport* ■ *(401) 849-3600*
*26 Marlborough St* ■ *American* ■ Many
items on the regular menu can be
modified to be GF. Note GF when making reservations so that the server is
ready to point out options on menu. ■
*www.whitehorsetavern.us/index.htm*

**Wright's Farm Restaurant** $LD
*Harrisville* ■ *(401) 769-2856*
*84 Inman Rd* ■ *American* ■ GF items
include chicken, french fries and dry salad.
Confirm the timeliness of this information
before dining in. Alert the server upon arrival. ■ *www.wrightsfarm.com*

# SOUTH CAROLINA

**32 Degrees Yogurt Bar** 📖
*Charleston* ■ *(843) 937-9510*
*315 King St*
*Greenville* ■ *(864) 271-1490*
*2111 Augusta St*
*Columbia* ■ *(803) 787-1040*
*4840 Forest Dr*

**A.W. Shucks** ★$$LD
*Charleston* ■ *(843) 723-1151*
*70 State St* ■ *Seafood* ■ GF options
include any type of fish (not breaded),
burgers with no buns, vegetable plates,
and sirloin. Alert server upon arrival. ■
*a-w-shucks.com*

**Abuelo's** ✪📖
*Myrtle Beach* ■ *(843) 448-5533*
*740 Coastal Grand Cir*

**Alluette's Café** $$LD
*Charleston* ■ *(843) 577-6926*
*80 A Reid St* ■ *American* ■ Chef's diet is
GF, making GF menu accommodations

easy. GF offerings include breads, pasta, brown rice and tofu. ▪ *www.alluettes.com*

### Anna Bell's                    ¢BL
*North Charleston* ▪ *(843) 554-5333*
*2120 Noisette Blvd* ▪ *American* ▪ GF options include most of the salads as well as shrimp and grits plate without the corn fritters, grilled chicken and grilled shrimp.

### Au Bon Pain                    📖
*Greenville* ▪ *(864) 455-4817*
*701 Grove Rd*

### Barbeque Joint, The            ¢BL
*North Charleston* ▪ *(843) 747-4567*
*1083 E Montague Ave* ▪ *Barbeque*
▪ Most of the items on the menu are GF. Alert server upon arrival. ▪ *www.thebarbequejoint.com*

### Bats BBQ                       $LD
*Rock Hill* ▪ *(803) 980-2287*
*1912 Mt Gallant Rd* ▪ *Barbeque* ▪ According to a Bats employee, they do not add any form of wheat to their products and all items are prepared on the grill. They still recommend alerting the server upon arrival so they can be sure to take extra care with the meal. ▪ *www.batsbbq.com*

### Bella Luna Café              ★ $BLD
*Saint Helena Island* ▪ *(843) 838-3188*
*859 Sea Island Pkwy* ▪ *Italian* ▪ GF spaghetti is available. ▪ *bellalunacafesc.com*

### BIN112                       ✪$$$D
*Greer* ▪ *(864) 848-2112*
*112 Trade St* ▪ *American* ▪ Extensive GF menu online featuring items such as crab cakes, jumbo sea scallops, fresh mussels, duck breast, roasted chicken, grilled pork, and filet mignon. Modifications needed to make dishes GF are listed in the menu. Alert server upon arrival to ensure modifications are put in place. ▪ *www.bin112.com*

### Bistro 536                     $$LD
*Mt Pleasant* ▪ *(843) 971-6663*
*536 Belle Station Blvd* ▪ *American* ▪ Any item on the menu can be modified to be GF. Most of the salads are GF and any sandwich can be made over a bed of greens or wrapped in lettuce. ▪ *bistro536.com*

### Black Bean Co.                 ¢BLD
*Charleston* ▪ *(843) 277-0990*
*116 Spring St*
*Charleston* ▪ *(843) 277-2101*
*869 Folly Rd*
*Mt Pleasant* ▪ *(843) 416-8561*
*1600 Midtown Ave* ▪ *Organic* ▪ James Island location is the only location that serves dinner. GF items include salads, Mediterranean quinoa, pad thai and fajitas without the tortillas. All locations serve wraps that can be made into salads to accommodate GF customers. ▪ *www.blackbeanco.com*

### Black Marlin Bayside Grill, The   $$$LD
*Hilton Head Island* ▪ *(843) 785-4950*
*86 Helmsman Wy* ▪ *Seafood* ▪ Manager Jill reports that "plenty of seafood options" and steaks can be prepared GF. They can always provide rice pilaf on the side, as they have done "several times" for GF diners. Alert the server, who will act as a liaison to the chef. ▪ *www.blackmarlinhhi.com*

### Bluerose Café                  $BL
*Charleston* ▪ *(843) 225-2583*
*652 St Andrews Blvd* ▪ *American* ▪ All items on menu are made to order. Be sure to alert server upon arrival. ▪ *www.bluerosecafecharleston.com*

### Boathouse at Breach Inlet, The   $$$D
*Isle of Palms* ▪ *(843) 886-8000*
*101 Palm Blvd* ▪ *Seafood* ▪ GF items include sea scallops, spicy shrimp and grits, sirloin and lobster plate, and grilled local snapper. ▪ *www.boathouserestaurants.com*

### Bocci's Italian                $$LD
*Charleston* ▪ *(843) 720-2121*
*158 Church St* ▪ *Italian* ▪ GF items include chicken picatta, duck and veal or chicken marsala. ▪ *www.boccis.com/cms_pages/*

### Bonefish Grill                 ✪📖
*Columbia* ▪ *(803) 407-1599*
*1260 Bower Pkwy Ste A1*

Columbia ▪ (803) 787-6200
4708 Forest Dr
Surfside Beach ▪ (843) 215-4374
8703 Highway 17 Byp S Ste L
North Myrtle Beach ▪ (843) 280-6638
103 Highway 17 S
Hilton Head ▪ (843) 341-3772
890 William Hilton Pkwy Ste 74
Myrtle Beach ▪ (843) 497-5294
7401 N Kings Hwy
Greenville ▪ (864) 297-5142
1515 Woodruff Rd

### Boulevard Diner          $BLD
Mt Pleasant ▪ (843) 216-2611
409 W Coleman Blvd
James Island ▪ (843) 795-8983
1978 Maybank Hwy ▪ American ▪ GF
dishes available. Alert server upon arrival. ▪
dinewithsal.com

### Brioso Fresh Pasta          ★$LD
Clemson ▪ (864) 653-3800
360 College Ave ▪ Italian ▪ GF penne
pasta and pizza are available. The GF
pizza is baked on top of a dedicated GF
wooden board to minimize the risk of CC.
▪ www.briosopasta.com

### Brixx Wood Fired Pizza          ✪★📖
Greenville ▪ (864) 286-1070
1125 Woodruff Rd
Mnt Pleasant ▪ (843) 971-2120
656 Long Point Rd

### Bubba Gump Shrimp Co.          ✪📖
Charleston ▪ (843) 723-5665
99 S Market St

### Buddy Roe's Shrimp Shack          $LD
Mt Pleasant ▪ (843) 388-5270
1528 Ben Sawyer Blvd ▪ Seafood ▪ Any fried seafood can be
made GF with GF breading. ▪
www.buddyroesshrimpshack.com

### Burro Loco          ★$LD
Myrtle Beach ▪ (843) 626-1756
960 Jason Blvd ▪ Mexican ▪ Restaurant reports that several menu items
can be modified to be GF upon request,

including several enchiladas, fajitas,
and salads. Confirm the timeliness of
this information before dining in. ▪
www.centraarchy.com/burroloco.php

### Burtons Grill          ✪★📖
Mt Pleasant ▪ (843) 606-2590
1875 N Hwy 17

### Café at Williams Hardware, The          ★¢LD
Travelers Rest ▪ (864) 834-7888
13 S. Main St ▪ American ▪ Dinner only on
Friday & Saturday. Alert server upon arrival with any dietary needs. There is no GF
menu. ▪ www.cafeatwilliamshardware.com

### Café Kronic          ★¢BL
Charleston ▪ (843) 225-7574
915 Folly Rd ▪ Café ▪ GF bread and biscuits
are available and can be substituted into
sandwiches and other dishes where applicable. ▪ www.cafekronic.com

### Café Medley          ¢BLD
Sullivans Island ▪ (843) 793-4055
2213 Middle St ▪ Café ▪ Sandwiches can be
made without the bread. ▪ cafemedley.com

### Café on Main          ★$$$D
Sumter ▪ (803) 774-8287
5 S Main St ▪ American ▪ GF options such
as quinoa salad are available on menu. The
restaurant reports that they sometimes have
GF bread for sandwiches, and recommends
calling beforehand to make sure it is being
served. They also serve dinner on Fridays
featuring St. Louis ribs with potatoes, cod
with rice pilaf, and rotisserie chicken.

### Café Rivera's          $$$LD
Greer ▪ (864) 877-9600
117 E Poinsett St ▪ Seafood & Steakhouse
▪ Most items on menu can be made GF.
Ask server and they will go over the menu.
▪ caferivera.net

### California Dreaming Restaurant and Bar          ✪📖
Columbia ▪ (803) 254-6767
401 S Main St
Charleston ▪ (843) 766-1644
1 Ashley Pt Dr

**Greenville** ▪ **(964) 234-9000**
*40 Beacon Dr*
**Myrtle Beach** ▪ **(843) 663-2050**
*10429 N Kings Hwy*
**Surfside Beach** ▪ **(843) 215-5255**
*2657 Beaver Run Blvd*

### Carolina Roadhouse                    ✪★$LD
**Myrtle Beach** ▪ **(843) 497-9911**
*4617 N Kings Hwy* ▪ **American** ▪ A majority
of the menu is GF or can be prepared GF.
A few examples are the tilapia, the salmon,
most of the steaks, and all of the salads.
They use separate fryers and prep areas for
all GF meals. The manager is very aware of
GF needs and assures that they "can and
will do everything possible" to avoid CC. ▪
*www.centraarchy.com*

### Catch 22                              $$$D
**Hilton Head Island** ▪ **(843) 785-6261**
*37 New Orleans Rd* ▪ **Southern** ▪ GF menu
items are available in-house, upon request.
Call ahead for accommodations or alert
a server when ordering so they can speak
with the kitchen. ▪ *www.catch22hhi.com*

### Caviar & Bananas                      ¢BLD
**Charleston** ▪ **(843) 577-7757**
*51 George ST* ▪ **Deli** ▪ GF bakery items
and entrées available. Bakery items include
raspberry hazelnut bar, macaroon bar and a
GF muffin. Entrée items include a beet salad, white bean salad, tuna salad and a broccoli slaw. ▪ *www.caviarandbananas.com*

### Cellar on Greene                      ★$D
**Columbia** ▪ **(803) 343-3303**
*2001-D Greene St* ▪ **Modern American**
▪ The restaurant reports that there are
several GF options on the regular and
the staff is "perfectly happy" to accommodate the needs of GF customers. ▪
*www.cellarongreene.com*

### Cheeseburger in Paradise             ✪★📖
**Myrtle Beach** ▪ **(843) 497-3891**
*7211 N Kings Hwy*

### Chophouse 47 Steaks & Lobsters✪★$D
**Greenville** ▪ **(864) 286-8700**

*36 Beacon Dr* ▪ **Steakhouse** ▪ There is no
GF menu but all steak and chicken entrées
are GF. Some fish items are as well, with
the exception of anything with flour/bread
coating. Alert the server upon arrival and
they can direct GF diners to the safest options. ▪ *www.chophouse47.com*

### Circa 1886                           $$$$D
**Charleston** ▪ **(843) 853-7828**
*149 Wentworth St* ▪ **Southern** ▪ Any item
on menu can be made GF. Hostess has
reported that chef is very accommodating
to GF customers. Note GF when making
reservations. ▪ *circa1886.com*

### Co-Op, The                           ¢BLD
**Sullivan's Island** ▪ **(843) 882-8088**
*2019 Middle St* ▪ **Deli** ▪ GF
bread, bagels and beer available. ▪
*www.thecoopsullivans.com*

### Coffee To a Tea                       ★$BL
**Greenville** ▪ **(864) 373-9836**
*1 Augusta St* ▪ **Bakery & Café** ▪ Non-dedicated bakery and café offering GF versions
of all their cakes and cookies, as well as GF
bread in loaves and for sandwiches. They
are also willing to "try making GF" any of
their other desserts. ▪ *coffeetoatea.com*

### CQ's                                 ★$$$D
**Hilton Head Island** ▪ **(843) 671-2779**
*140 Lighthouse Rd* ▪ **American** ▪ There is
no GF menu available online but alert a
server upon arrival and they will provide a
list of GF items available. Be sure to specify
that your meal must be prepared separately from any items containing gluten. ▪
*cqsrestaurant.com*

### Crave it? Restaurant and Café   ★¢BLD
**Wade Hampton** ▪ **(864) 214-2792**
*2728 Wade Hampton Blvd* ▪ **Bakery &
Café** ▪ Many of the cakes and meals are
available GF and Vegan. GF products are
made with bean flour instead of wheat
flour, and 60% of bakery items are available
GF. ▪ *www.craveitbakery.com*

## Crave Kitchen & Cocktails ✪$$D
*Mount Pleasant* ■ *(843) 884-1177*
*1968 Riviera Dr* ■ *American* ■ GF menu includes seared bass, bouillabaisse, sirloin steak, and mussels. GF menu is not available for weekend brunches. Manager JC reports that they server GF diners "all the time." ■ *www.cravemtp.com*

## Delamater's Restaurant $LD
*Newberry* ■ *(803) 276-3555*
*1117 Boyce St* ■ *American* ■ GF options include soup and salad, several filets, blackened tilapia, and herbed chicken breast. Confirm the timeliness of this information before dining in. ■ *www.delamaters.com*

## Deveraux's $$$D
*Greenville* ■ *(864) 241-3030*
*25 E Court St* ■ *Southern* ■ GF options are available upon request only. Email or call ahead to speak with a staff member regarding menu options. ■ *www.devereauxsdining.com*

## Dianne's on Devine $$D
*Columbia* ■ *(803) 254-3535*
*2400 Devine St* ■ *Italian* ■ Staff reports that they have "a few GF items", most of which are proteins and seafood. Alert the server upon arrival. ■ *www.diannesondevine.com*

## Don Pablo's ✪📖
*Greenville* ■ *(864) 627-8550*
*741 Haywood Rd*

## Dragon Palace ✪$LD
*Daniel Island* ■ *(843) 388-8823*
*162 Seven Farms Dr* ■ *Chinese* ■ GF items are marked on the menu and include honey glazed roast pork, salt & pepper shrimp, garlic prawns, sautéed spinach, ginger chicken, and sweet & tangy pork loin. Confirm the timeliness of this information before dining in. ■ *www.dragonpalacesc.com*

## East Bay Meeting House ¢BLD
*Charleston* ■ *(843) 723-3446*
*160 E Bay St* ■ *Pub Food* ■ Variety of salads are GF. Dessert includes a flourless truffle cake. Alert server upon arrival. ■ *www.eastbaymeetinghouse.com*

## Ela's Blu Water Grille ✪★$$$LD
*Hilton Head Island* ■ *(843) 785-3030*
*1 Shelter Cove Ln* ■ *American* ■ The majority of their menu is GF, although it is not reflected online. Restaurant states that it is best to ask the server when ordering and they will point out the available items. ■ *www.elasgrille.com*

## Eli's Table $$$BLD
*Charleston* ■ *(843) 405-5115*
*129 Meeting* ■ *American* ■ Eli's Salads are naturally GF. Any of the wraps and sandwiches can be made GF without the bread, or into a salad. ■ *www.elischarleston.com*

## Erin's Restaurant $$LD
*Rock Hill* ■ *(803) 493-9428*
*129 Caldwell St* ■ *American* ■ Owner has Celiac, and reports that the staff are all very familiar with preparing GF food items and the care necessary to prevent CC from occurring. Most of the items on the menu are GF or can be prepared GF. Alert the server upon arrival. ■ *www.erinsrockhill.com*

## Everyday Organic $LD
*Greenville* ■ *(864) 498-9194*
*3225 N Pleasantburg Dr* ■ *Organic* ■ GF bread, soup, potato salads and dinner entrées available.

## Fat Hen Restaurant ✪$$D
*Johns Island* ■ *(843) 559-9090*
*3140 Maybank Hwy* ■ *French* ■ GF items marked on the menu include duck confit, coq au vin, flounder, and salmon béarnaise. Restaurant notes that they are "very GF friendly." ■ *www.thefathen.com*

## Fatz Eatz & Drinkz 📖
*Rock Hill* ■ *(803) 980-6500*
*478 S Herlong Ave*
*Aiken* ■ *(803) 641-4261*

996 Pine Log Rd
Anderson ▪ (864) 965-0055
105 Interstate Blvd
Camden ▪ (803) 432-3439
212 Wall St
Cheraw ▪ (843) 537-4205
973 Chesterfield Hwy
Clinton ▪ (864) 833-5280
179 E Corporate Center Dr
Columbia ▪ (803) 782-1183
5590 Forest Dr
Conway ▪ (843) 369-0591
2494 Church St
Easley ▪ (864) 859-9832
5051 Calhoun Memorial Hwy
Florence ▪ (843) 413-9186
2007 W Lucas St
Gaffney ▪ (864) 488-0310
294 Peachoid Rd
Greenwood ▪ (864) 229-3711
1302 Montague Ave
Greer ▪ (864) 801-9782
1361 W Wade Hampton Blvd
Irmo ▪ (803) 781-5036
7420 Broad River Rd
Lexington ▪ (803) 808-1905
942 E Main St
N. Charleston ▪ (843) 576-2680
4951 Centre Pointe Dr
Orangeburg ▪ (803) 534-8000
3575 St. Matthews Rd
Rock Hill ▪ (803) 980-6500
478 S Herlong Ave
Seneca ▪ (864) 888-1009
1615 Sandifer Blvd
Spartanburg ▪ (864) 574-4814
6750 Pottery Rd
Spartanburg ▪ (864) 599-7909
1925 Boiling Springs Rd
Spartanburg ▪ (864) 576-6228
100 Southport Rd

### Fiddlehead Pizza                     ★ $LD
Bluffton ▪ (843) 757-6466
142-A Burnt Church Rd ▪ Pizza ▪ GF 14"
pizza available. Restaurant reports that
all pizzas are cooked in the same oven. ▪
www.fiddleheadpizza.com

### Fig                                   $$$D
Charleston ▪ (843) 805-5900
232 Meeting St ▪ American ▪ Spoke with
an employee who stated that the menu
changes nightly. There is always a GF option on the menu which your server can
point out for you. Additionally other items
can be altered to be GF upon customer
request. ▪ www.eatfig.com

### Fish                                  $$$LD
Charleston ▪ (843) 722-3474
442 King St ▪ Asian Fusion ▪ GF items
include tuna tartar, mussels, oysters,
Carolina snapper, naked fish and sides. ▪
www.fishrestaurantcharleston.com

### Five Loaves Café                      $LD
Charleston ▪ (843) 937-4303
43 Cannon St
Mt Pleasant ▪ (843) 849-1043
1055 Johnnie Dodds Blvd ▪ Café ▪ GF
items indicated on menu. Some items
include arugula and marinated mushroom
salad, GF bread is available for sandwiches
at an extra charge, steamed mussels, grilled
eggplant, grilled rosemary pork loin, honey
mustard glazed salmon, all natural curried
chicken and marinated portabella mushrooms. ▪ www.fiveloavescafe.com

### Fox and Hound Pub & Grille           📖
Columbia ▪ (803) 407-3004
115 Afton Ct
Greenville ▪ (864) 281-9347
2409 Laurens Rd

### Frankie Bones                   ✪$$$BLD
Hilton Head Island ▪ (843) 682-4455
1301 Main St ▪ American ▪ Staff states
there is an entire GF menu featuring items such as filet mignon, lobster tail, grilled salmon, and various
salad options topped with chicken. ▪
www.facebook.comfrankieboneshhi

### Frodo's Pizza                         ★ $LD
Greenville ▪ (864) 232-1800
511 S Pleasantburg Dr ▪ Pizza ▪ GF
pizza crust available in 12" size. ▪
www.frodospizza.com

## FUEL Pizza ✪★📖
*Rock Hill* ■ (803) 327-2244
*1910 Cinema Dr*

## Fuji Sushi Bar & Grill $LD
*Mt Pleasant* ■ (843) 856-5798
*644 State Rd S-10-97* ■ *Japanese* ■ GF sushi rolls available. Alert server upon arrival. ■ *www.fujisushibarandgrill.com*

## Garibaldi's of Columbia $$D
*Columbia* ■ (803) 771-8888
*2013 Greene St* ■ *Italian* ■ The staff reports that they are "more than willing to accommodate to any dietary restrictions that they possibly can." Alert the server upon arrival and they will go over the options. ■ *www.garibaldicolumbia.com*

## Genghis Grill 📖
*Greenville Rd* ■ (864) 990-4560
*1140 Woodruff Rd*

## Gervais & Vine $$D
*Columbia* ■ (803) 799-8463
*620 A Gervais St* ■ *Mediterranean* ■ The restaurant reports that GF options include salads and protein dishes. The staff also adds that they are willing to "accommodate in any way possible" to meet the needs of GF diners. ■ *www.gervine.com*

## Gilligans Seafood ✪$$LD
*Mount Pleasant* ■ (843) 849-2244
*1475 Long Grove Dr*
*Ladson* ■ (843) 821-2244
*3852 Ladson Rd*
*Moncks* ■ (843) 761-2244
*582 Dock Rd*
*Lexington* ■ (803) 808-2244
*938 N Lake Dr*
*Johns Island* ■ (843) 766-2244
*160 Main Rd*
*Goose Creek* ■ (843) 818-2244
*219 St James Ave*
*Beaufort* ■ (843) 379-2244
*2601 Boundary St* ■ *Seafood* ■ GF menu includes grilled shrimp, crab legs, grilled sea scallops, grilled chicken breast, and more. The menu denotes the modifications required to make dishes GF, as well as which seasonings and sauces are GF. Be sure to notify the server that your meal must be GF. They will communicate with the kitchen staff to ensure all meals are cooked properly. ■ *www.gilligans.net*

## Gina's Pizza & Italian Gourmet ★¢LD
*Irmo* ■ (803) 781-7800
*107A N Royal Tower Dr* ■ *Italian* ■ GF pizza is available. ■ *ginaspizza.webs.com*

## Good Life Café ✪¢BLD
*West Columbia* ■ (803) 454-3516
*3681-D Leaphart Rd* ■ *Raw* ■ Online menu and in-house menu contains a key showing which items are GF and which are not. Some GF items include Lasagna made with zucchini noodles, a hummus sandwich made with onion bread, and a Mediterranean wrap. ■ *goodlifecafe.net*

## Graze $$$LD
*Mt Pleasant* ■ (843) 606-2493
*863 Houston Northcutt Blvd* ■ *Modern American* ■ GF items include black pepper seared scallops, blackened salmon salad, steamed mussels, spicy tuna tataki and a tandoori chicken breast. ■ *www.grazecharleston.com*

## Great Gardens Café ✪★$BLD
*Beaufort* ■ (843) 521-1900
*3669 Trask Pkwy* ■ *Global* ■ Restaurant states they offer a variety of GF items on their menu. There is no list available online. It is best to ask a staff member upon arrival. ■ *www.facebook.com/greatgardenscafe*

## Grover's Bar and Grill $LD
*Edisto Beach* ■ (843) 869-0345
*21 Fairway Dr* ■ *Southern* ■ Hostess reports that chef is very familiar with GF and would be happy to help select GF options on menu. Note GF when making reservations. ■ *www.groversbarandgrill.com*

## Gulfstream Café ★$$D
*Garden City* ■ (843) 651-8808
*1536 S Waccamaw Dr* ■ *Seafood* ■ While they do not have a GF menu they do offer a variety of GF options in-house.

Ask a server or manager upon arrival. ▪ *www.centraarchy.comgulfstream-cafe/*

### Halls Chophouse                    $$$$D
*Charleston* ▪ *(843) 727-0090*
*434 King St* ▪ *Steakhouse* ▪ Most of side dishes and some entrées are GF. Alert server upon arrival and note GF in reservations. ▪ *hallschophouse.com*

### Hamptons                           $$$LD
*Sumter* ▪ *(803) 774-4400*
*4 W Hampton Ave* ▪ *American* ▪ According to their extensive online menu Hamptons has a variety of GF entrées such as salads, maple glazed chicken breast, pan seared duck, roasted striped bass, and a grilled ribeye steak. ▪ *www.hamptonsfoods.com*

### Harbor Inn Seafood Restaurant    ★▢
*Greenville* ▪ *(864) 286-9047*
*321 Haywood Rd*
*Columbia* ▪ *(803) 462-3498*
*7375 Two Notch Rd*

### Hard Rock Café                     ✪▢
*Myrtle Beach* ▪ *(843) 946-0007*
*1322 Celebrity Cir*

### Harper's Restaurant                ✪SLD
*Columbia* ▪ *(803) 252-2222*
*700 Harden St* ▪ *American* ▪ GF menu varies slightly from location to location but includes popular items such as steak, chicken, BBQ, fish, and salads. GF flourless chocolate cake is also available. The restaurant reports that they "take sanitation very seriously" and "train all employees about the hazard of cross-contamination." Managers are reportedly Servsafe certified. ▪ *www.harpersrestaurants.com*

### High Cotton                        $$$LD
*Charleston* ▪ *(843) 724-3815*
*199 E Bay St* ▪ *Southern* ▪ Lunch only on weekends. No GF menu but most entrée items can be made GF. Alert server upon arrival. ▪ *www.mavericksouthernkitchens.com*

### Huck's Lowcountry Table            $$$LD
*Isle of Palms* ▪ *(843) 886-6772*
*1130 Ocean Blvd* ▪ *American* ▪ Most menu items can be modified to be GF. Alert server upon arrival. ▪ *www.huckslowcountrytable.com*

### HuHot Mongolian Grill              ▢
*Columbia* ▪ *(803) 407-3868*
*1260-A8 Bower Pkwy*

### Husk                               $$$LD
*Charleston* ▪ *(843) 577-2500*
*76 Queen St* ▪ *American* ▪ An employee stated that the menus are constantly changing, but there are always GF options available. Reservations noting GF are strongly recommended. They have a separate kitchen area to prevent CC. ▪ *www.huskrestaurant.com*

### Hyman's Seafood & Aaron's Deli   ✪$$LD
*Charleston* ▪ *(843) 723-6000*
*215 Meeting St* ▪ *Seafood* ▪ GF menu available for both Hyman's seafood and Aaron's deli. No GF alcohol available. ▪ *www.hymanseafood.com*

### Il Cortile Del Re                 ★$$$LD
*Charleston* ▪ *(843) 853-1888*
*193 King St* ▪ *Italian* ▪ GF penne pasta is available. Other items on the menu can be made GF. Alert server upon arrival. ▪ *www.ilcortiledelre.com*

### Irashiai Sushi
### Pub & Japanese Restaurant        ★SLD
*Greenville* ▪ *(864) 271-0900*
*115 Pelham Rd* ▪ *Japanese* ▪ Variety of GF items to choose from including cucumber sunomono, cucumber tornado roll, beef or shrimp carpaccio, beef tapaki, asparagus butter garlic yaki, edamame, steamed vegetables, spinach garlic butter yaki, fried rice, ahi Hawaiian, mussels yaki and a variety of rolls. Alert server upon arrival. ▪ *www.irashiai.com*

## J. Gumbo's ★📖
*Columbia* ▪ (803) 748-8878
*1401 Sumter St*

## Jason's Deli ✪📖
*Greenville* ▪ (864) 284-9870
*824 Woods Crossing Rd*
*Charleston* ▪ (843) 769-6900
*975 Savannah Hwy*
*Spartanburg* ▪ (864) 574-0202
*1450 W O Ezell Blvd*
*Charleston* ▪ (843) 764-0094
*2150 Northwoods Blvd*
*Columbia* ▪ (803) 540-1973
*823 Gervais St*

## Jersey Mike's 📖
*Columbia* ▪ (803) 865-8004
*136-3 Forum Dr*
*Conway* ▪ (843) 365-6453
*2676 Church St*
*Clemson* ▪ (864) 654-6544
*1067 Tiger Blvd*
*Greenville* ▪ (864) 242-2223
*233 N Main St*
*Greenville* ▪ (864) 233-0111
*215 Pelham Rd*
*Greenville* ▪ (864) 288-5782
*1507 Woodruff Rd*
*Simpsonville* ▪ (864) 963-2400
*325 Harrison Bridge Rd*
*Greer* ▪ (864) 877-1500
*1311-A W Wade Hampton Blvd*
*Irmo* ▪ (803) 749-3022
*7241 Broad River Rd*
*West Columbia* ▪ (803) 796-1126
*1720 Sunset Blvd*
*Rock Hill* ▪ (803) 980-6453
*735 Cherry Rd*
*Rock Hill* ▪ (803) 909-6453
*2748 Celanese Rd*
*Fort Mill* ▪ (803) 548-6453
*1710 Gold Hill Rd*
*Columbus* ▪ (803) 787-0945
*4717 Devine St*
*Okatie* ▪ (843) 705-6453
*101-F Commerce Place W*
*Sumter* ▪ (803) 905-7827
*1222 Alice Dr*

*Goose Creek* ▪ (843) 569-2800
*217-A St. James Ave*
*Charleston* ▪ (843) 766-2999
*65A Sycamore Ave*
*Mt. Pleasant* ▪ (843) 881-7996
*280D W Coleman Blvd*
*Mt. Pleasant* ▪ (843) 388-6300
*1909 Hwy 17 N*
*Murrells Inlet* ▪ (843) 357-6545
*4390 Hwy 17 Bypass*
*North Myrtle Beach* ▪ (843) 361-2636
*4031 Hwy 17 S*
*Indian Land* ▪ (803) 578-4142
*8431 Charlotte Hwy*
*Beaufort* ▪ (843) 379-8820
*272 Robert Smalls Pkwy*
*Myrtle Beach* ▪ (843) 497-4949
*9713 N Kings Hwy*
*Mount Pleasant* ▪ (843) 388-7456
*3010 S Morgans Point Rd*
*North Charleston* ▪ (843) 793-2483
*8983 University Blvd*
*Lexington* ▪ (803) 356-0033
*5594 Sunset Blvd*
*Charleston* ▪ (843) 718-1606
*52 Folly Rd*
*Bluffton* ▪ (843) 815-2536
*1019 Fording Island rd*
*Summerville* ▪ (843) 875-3480
*310 Azalea Square Blvd*
*North Myrtle Beach* ▪ (843) 663-9003
*515 Hwy 17 N*
*Columbia* ▪ (803) 407-5200
*7001 St. Andrews Rd*
*Lake Wylie* ▪ (803) 831-0912
*604 Nautical Dr*
*Easley* ▪ (864) 855-9444
*125 Rolling Hills Cir*
*North Charleston* ▪ (843) 414-7371
*7225 Rivers Ave*

## Jim 'n Nick's Bar-B-Q ✪★📖
*Bluffton* ▪ (843) 706-9741
*872 Fording Island Rd*
*North Charleston* ▪ (843) 747-3800
*4964 Center Pointe Dr*
*Charleston* ▪ (843) 577-0406
*288 King St*

## Joe's Crab Shack ✪📖
Greenville ▪ (864) 987-0009
102 E Beacon Dr
North Myrtle Beach ▪ (843) 272-5900
4846 Hwy 17 S
Myrtle Beach ▪ (843) 626-4490
1219 Celebrity Circle Broadway at the
Beach

## Joe's New York Pizza $LD
Seneca ▪ (864) 888-0009
685 By Pass 123 ▪ Pizza ▪ GF pizza available in the small size. ▪
www.joespizzaseneca.com

## Juniper ★ $$BLD
Ridge Spring ▪ (803) 685-7547
640 E Main St ▪ American ▪ GF bread,
flour, and crackers are available and can
be substituted to make many dishes GF.
The restaurant reports that they "try to
be as GF as possible" and are "happy to
accommodate their customers needs." ▪
www.yelp.com/biz/juniper-ridge-spring

## Kannicka's Thai Kitchen ★ $LD
Greenville ▪ (864) 297-4557
599 Haywood Rd ▪ Asian Fusion ▪ Restaurant reports that most items on the menu
are either naturally GF or can be prepared
so. Alert server upon arrival and accommodations will be made.

## Ladles Homemade Soups ¢LD
Charleston ▪ (843) 769-9800
3125 Bees Ferry Rd
Mt Pleasant ▪ (843) 606-2711
1164 Basketweave Dr
Johns Island ▪ (843) 243-9881
190 Gardners Cir
Summerville ▪ (843) 875-3770
100 W Richardson Ave
N Charleston ▪ (843) 266-9772
8600 Dorchester Rd ▪ Deli
Only GF item available is the turkey chili.
www.ladlessoups.com

## Lana Restaurant $$$LD
Charleston ▪ (843) 720-8899
210 Rutledge Ave ▪ Mediterranean ▪ GF
options available. Alert server upon arrival.
▪ www.lanarestaurant.com/home

## Laura Alberts Tasteful Options ✪$LD
Daniel Island ▪ (843) 881-4711
891 Island Park Dr ▪ American ▪ GF lunch
menu available that includes pan-seared
salmon, shrimp creole, and roasted vegetables napoleon. Dinner is only served on
Wednesdays and server Caroll said they
usually have at least 2 GF options available.
▪ www.lauraalberts.com

## Lazy Goat, The $$LD
Greenville ▪ (864) 679-5299
170 River Pl ▪ Mediterranean ▪ GF options are available upon request only.
Email or call ahead to speak with a staff
member regarding menu options. ▪
thelazygoat.typepad.com

## Leaf Café & Bar $$LD
Charleston ▪ (843) 793-2230
15 Beaufain St ▪ American ▪ The restaurant reports that while they do not
have a GF menu, they can accommodate
GF diners. Alert server upon arrival. ▪
www.leafcharleston.com

## Lemongrass Thai Cuisine ★$LD
Greenville ▪ (864) 241-9988
106 N. Main St ▪ Thai ▪ Restaurant reports
that GF diners are always welcome. Alert
servers upon arrival and they will provide
a list of the items that can be made GF. ▪
www.lemongrassthai.net

## Lizard's Thicket ★ ¢BLD
Columbia ▪ (803) 419-5662
10170 Two Notch Rd
Blythewood ▪ (803) 451-8400
711-1 University Village Dr
Columbia ▪ (803) 787-8781
3147 Forest Dr
Columbia ▪ (803) 779-6407
818 Elmwood Ave
Columbia ▪ (803) 647-0095
7938 Garners Ferry Rd
Columbia ▪ (803) 738-0006

402 Beltline Blvd
Cayce ▪ (803) 791-0314
501 Know Abbott Dr
Columbia ▪ (803) 788-3088
7620 2 Notch Rd
West Columbia ▪ (803) 796-7820
2240 Airport Blvd
West Columbia ▪ (803) 794-0923
2234 Sunset Blvd
Columbia ▪ (803) 798-6427
1824 Broad River Rd
Irmo ▪ (803) 732-1225
7569 St Andrews Rd
Lexington ▪ (803) 951-3555
621 W Main St
Lexington ▪ (803) 785-5560
4616 Augusta Rd
Florence ▪ (843) 519-1083
1712 W Palmetto St ▪ Southern ▪ GF
options available on menu. Some items
include coleslaw, vegetable soup, different types of vegetables with the exception of the fried veggies, broiled flounder,
baked chicken and grilled chicken. ▪
lizardsthicket.com

### Long Point Grill $$LD
Mt Pleasant ▪ (843) 884-3101
479 Long Point Rd ▪ American ▪ Entire
GF menu available. Items include mussels,
butternut squash, all salads, all sandwiches
without bread, scallops, short ribs, New
York strip steaks and a blackened or macadamia nut crusted fish. ▪ dinewithsal.com

### Macintosh, The $$D
Charleston ▪ (843) 789-4299
479 B King St ▪ American ▪ According to
an employee all of the meat entrées can be
altered or prepared GF upon customer request. The chef and staff "have no problem
accommodating customer needs" and recommend alerting the server upon arrival. ▪
themacintoshcharleston.com

### Maggie's Pub ✪★$$D
Beaufort ▪ (843) 379-1719
17 Market ▪ Pub Food ▪ Reservations noting GF are strongly recommended. During
call make a request for a GF menu and they

will have one prepared for when you come
in. ▪ www.maggiespub.net

### Magnolia Natural Market and Café $L
Aiken ▪ (803) 649-3339
210 York St SE ▪ American ▪ An abun-
dance of GF options available. All soups
and salads are GF as well as lettuce
wraps and burgers come with GF buns.
GF bakery items are also available. ▪
www.magnolianaturalmarket.com

### Magnolias $$$LD
Charleston ▪ (843) 577-7771
185 E Bay St ▪ Seafood ▪ Magnolias
does not have a specific GF menu. However, various entrées and dishes on their
regular menu are GF or can be made
GF. Blackened catfish, bourbon glazed
porterhouse pork chop, grilled filet, and
chili rubbed ahi tuna are just a few. ▪
magnolias-blossom-cypress.com

### Main Squeeze, The ¢S
Mt Pleasant ▪ (843) 856-7399
656-C Long Pt Rd ▪ American ▪ GF
smoothies and fruit juices are available. ▪
www.charlestonsmoothies.com

### Malia's $$$LD
Aiken ▪ (803) 643-3086
120 Laurens St SW ▪ American ▪ GF
options available on menu. Alert server
upon arrival and they will inform the chef.
Note GF when making reservations. ▪
www.maliasrestaurant.com

### Margaritaville ✪★▢
Myrtle Beach ▪ (843) 448-5455
1114 Celebrity Cir

### Melting Pot, The ✪▢
Columbia ▪ (803) 731-8500
1410 Colonial Life Blvd W
Greenville ▪ (864) 297-5035
475 Haywood Rd Ste 5
Myrtle Beach ▪ (843) 692-9003
5001 N Kings Hwy Ste 104

### Mezza Vista Lebanese Bistro & Hookah Lounge ✪$LD
Columbia ▪ (803) 708-0236

701 Gervais St ▪ Mediterranean ▪ GF items are noted on the regular menu with a "G". ▪ mezzavista.com

### Michael's Rock Hill Grille          ★ $$LD
*Rock Hill* ▪ (803) 985-3663
*1039 Charlotte Ave* ▪ American ▪ The restaurant reports that all of their salads are GF and most of their chicken and protein entrées can be made GF upon customer request. ▪ www.michaelsrockhillgrille.com

### Miyo's                               ★ $LD
*Columbia* ▪ (803) 255-8878
*701 Lady St, suite C*
*Columbia* ▪ (803) 779-5788
*1417 Sumter St*
*Columbia* ▪ (803) 788-8878
*715 Fashion Dr Suite 1*
*Columbia* ▪ (803) 743-9996
*3250 Forest Dr Suite B*
*Columbia* ▪ (803) 781-7788
*1220 E-2 Bower Pkwy Suite E-2*
*Lexington* ▪ (803) 957-9888
*5594 Sunset Blvd Suite D & E*
*Columbia* ▪ (803) 779-6496
*922 S Main St* ▪ Asian Fusion ▪ Several items on menu are GF. Restaurant recommends notifying server prior to ordering so special precautionary steps can be taken to prevent CC. ▪ miyos.com

### Mr. Friendly's New Southern Café   $$LD
*Columbia* ▪ (803) 254-7828
*2001 Greene St* ▪ American ▪ The restaurant reports that the staff has no problem modifying any dish on the menu to be GF, and also notes that there are several items and proteins on the menu that are naturally GF. ▪ www.mrfriendlys.com

### Mustard Seed, The                   ✪ ★ $LD
*Summerville* ▪ (843) 821-7101
*101 N Main St*
*Charleston* ▪ (843) 762-0072
*1970 Maybank Hwy*
*Mount Pleasant* ▪ (843) 849-0500
*1036 Chuck Dawley Blvd* ▪ American ▪ GF menu includes hummus, mussels, gazpacho, scallop salad, mushroom risotto, and

pasta dishes with GF rice noodles. All three locations have the same GF menu. Confirm the timeliness of this information before dining in. ▪ www.dinewithsal.com

### New York Prime                      ✪ ★ $$$D
*Myrtle Beach* ▪ (843) 448-8081
*405 28th Ave N* ▪ Steakhouse ▪ All steak and chicken entrées are GF. Most fish entrées are too, with the exception of anything covered with flour/bread. If a customer likes something on the menu that is usually not GF, the restaurant is willing to alter the recipe if possible. Alert the server upon arrival. ▪ www.newyorkprime.com

### Nose Dive A Gastropub               ★ $$LD
*Greenville* ▪ (864) 373-7300
*116 S Main St* ▪ Pub Food ▪ Restaurant states they have a separate fryer for GF items. Be sure to alert server upon arrival of any dietary needs. ▪ www.thenosedive.com

### O'Charley's                          📖
*Aiken* ▪ (803) 644-8874
*168 S Aiken Ln*
*Anderson* ▪ (864) 224-1417
*3723 Clemson Blvd*
*Charleston* ▪ (843) 763-9568
*2126 Henry Tecklenburg Dr*
*Columbia* ▪ (803) 699-1192
*10136 Two Notch Rd*
*Greenwood* ▪ (864) 227-0272
*452 Bypass 72 NW*
*Lexington* ▪ (803) 356-4220
*5595 Sunset Blvd*
*North Charleston* ▪ (843) 824-2365
*21500 Northwoods Blvd*
*Rock Hill* ▪ (803) 329-4530
*2265 Cross Pointe Dr*
*Simpsonville* ▪ (864) 228-3681
*671 Fairview Rd*
*Spartanburg* ▪ (864) 595-4011
*106 Blackstock Rd*
*Summerville* ▪ (843) 832-0825
*315 Azalea Square Blvd*

## O-Ku Sushi                                         $$$LD
*Charleston* ■ (843) 737-0112
*463 King St* ■ *Sushi* ■ No GF menu but many
items are naturally GF. Their sashimi taco,
edamame, all hand rolls, and miso soup are
GF. ■ www.o-kusushi.com

## Oak Steakhouse                                    $$$$D
*Charleston* ■ (843) 722-4220
*17 Broad St* ■ *Steakhouse* ■ Restaurant
reports that they are "100% able to accommodate" GF diners. The kitchen can prepare several dishes GF. Restaurant has ac-
commoded entire GF parties in the past.
Reservations noting GF are recommended.
■ www.oaksteakhouserestaurant.com

## Odyssey                                           $LD
*Charleston* ■ (843) 225-9933
*915 Folly Rd* ■ *Greek* ■ GF items include
falafels, dosa, lentil soup and hummus. ■
www.odysseygreek.com

## Old Firehouse Restaurant                          $$D
*Hollywood* ■ (843) 889-9512
*6350 Hwy 162* ■ *Southern* ■ The restaurant
reports that GF diners can be accommodated, and recommends alerting the server
upon arrival to find out GF options. ■
www.oldfirehouserestaurant.com

## Old Fort Pub                                      ★$$$D
*Hilton Head Island* ■ (843) 681-2386
*65 Skull Creek Dr* ■ *Southern* ■ Notify
an employee upon arrival so they can
point out the items which are not GF. ■
oldfortpub.com

## Old Oyster Factory, The                           ✪$$$LD
*Hilton Head Island* ■ (843) 681-6040
*101 Marshland Rd.* ■ *Seafood* ■ GF
menu available online and in-house.
Items include cold king shellfish sampler, seafood medley, brick chicken,
mahi mahi, and a New York strip steak. ■
www.oldoysterfactory.com

## Old Post Office Restaurant                        $$$D
*Edisto Island* ■ (843) 869-2339
*1442 Hwy 174* ■ *Southern* ■ GF items
include shrimp and grits, scallops, broiled

flounder (chef needs to be informed of
request before hand), ribeye, filet mignon,
pork tenderloin and a porterhouse pork
chop. Mention GF when making reservations. ■ www.theoldpostofficerestaurant.com

## Old Village Post House                            $$$D
*Mt Pleasant* ■ (843) 388-8935
*101 Pitt St* ■ *American* ■ Restaurant reports
that everything on menu can be made
GF, but cautions that grits may have a
risk of CC. Alert server upon arrival. ■
www.mavericksouthernkitchens.com

## One Hot Mama's American Grille ✪$$LD
*Hilton Head Island* ■ (843) 682-6262
*7B Greenwood Dr* ■ *Barbeque* ■ GF items
are marked with a "GF" on the regular
menu. Most of them are meat and protein
based entrées, however salads and other
sides are also available. ■ onehotmamas.com

## Original Pancake House, The      ★CBL
*Hilton Head Island* ■ (843) 815-3452
*1532 Fording Island Rd* ■ *American* ■ GF pancakes are available. ■
eatpancakesnow.com

## P. Simpson's Hometown Grille      ★$$D
*Simpsonville* ■ (864) 757-9691
*111 N Main St* ■ *American* ■ Restaurant
reports that half of the menu is GF. Inform
server of GF needs and they will offer recommendations. ■ www.psimpsons.com

## P.F. Chang's China Bistro          ✪★▥
*Greenville* ■ (864) 297-0589
*1127 Woodruff Rd*
*Myrtle Beach* ■ (843) 839-9470
*1190 Farrow Pkwy*

## Paolo's Gelato Italiano            CS
*Charleston* ■ (843) 577-0099
*41 John St* ■ *Ice Cream* ■ All gelatos are GF.
■ www.paolosgelato.com

## Patat Spot Friet & Falafel         ★CLD
*Charleston* ■ (843) 723-7438
*41B George St* ■ *American* ■ All their
falafels and black bean potato cakes are
GF. They have two types of GF beer, and

over 20 GF options in their salad bar. ▪ *patatspot.com*

### Pattya Thai Restaurant                    $LD
*Mt Pleasant* ▪ (843) 856-1808
*607 Johnnie Dodds Blvd* ▪ *Thai* ▪ Many items on the menu can be made GF. Alert server upon arrival.

### Peninsula Grill                           $$$D
*Charleston* ▪ (843) 723-0700
*112 N Market St* ▪ *American* ▪ The restaurant reports that they can alter various dishes on the menu to make them suitable for GF diners. They also add that their white chocolate mousse is GF. Alert the server upon arrival and they will note current GF options. ▪ *peninsulagrill.com*

### Pomegranate on Main            ★$$$LD
*Greenville* ▪ (864) 241-3012
*618 S Main St* ▪ *Middle Eastern* ▪ The restaurant reports that the entire menu is GF. Bread is served with spreads but can be replaced with a side of cucumber instead.▪ *www.pomegranateonmain.com*

### Porta Via Bistro & Bar          ✪★$LD
*Okatie* ▪ (843) 645-0606
*149 Riverwalk Blvd* ▪ *Italian* ▪ Chef is very open to accommodating GF diners. The online menu is only part of what they offer. They also serve entrées such as steak, chicken and shrimp. He said that GF diners should come in and he will work with their dietary needs. ▪ *www.portaviabistroandbar.com*

### Puree                                     ✪$BL
*Mt Pleasant* ▪ (864) 320-5526
*1034 Chuck Dawley Blvd* ▪ *Café* ▪ GF items indicated on menu. Some breakfast items include homemade baked granola, organic fruit bowl and any of the baby bowls. Lunch items include mixed green goodness salad. GF options available for sandwiches and wraps as well as the baby bowls. GF dessert is also available with items such as Kelli's decadent chocolate pudding and a chocolate pecan truffle. ▪ *www.thinkpuree.com*

### Rainbow Garden
### Chinese Restaurant                        $LD
*Seneca* ▪ (864) 654-6868
*1085 Old Clemson Hwy* ▪ *Chinese* ▪ GF options available. Items include steamed mixed vegetables, chicken with mixed vegetables and shrimp with mixed vegetables. Alert server upon arrival. ▪ *www.rainbowgarden88.com*

### Rascal's                                  ¢LD
*Sumter* ▪ (803) 418-0151
*1075 Alice Dr* ▪ *American* ▪ GF options include grilled chicken, burgers with no buns, Philly cheese steak with no bun and chicken salad. Alert server upon arrival and they will notify the chef. ▪ *www.rascalssc.com*

### Rays Café                                 ★¢BL
*Hilton Head Island* ▪ (843) 342-7297
*40 Palmetto Pkwy* ▪ *Café* ▪ GF 12" pizza available.

### Red Bowl Asian Bistro                    ✪$LD
*Fort Mill* ▪ (803) 802-5666
*845 Stockbridge Dr* ▪ *Asian* ▪ Extensive GF menu includes the shrimp summer roll, egg drop soup, red curry chicken, and beef with spinach in white sauce, among other things. Confirm the timeliness of this information before dining in. ▪ *www.redbowltegacay.com*

### Red Drum Gastropub                        $$$D
*Mt Pleasant* ▪ (843) 849-0313
*803 Coleman Blvd* ▪ *American* ▪ Manager reports that 90% of the menu is GF. Note GF when making reservations. ▪ *www.reddrumrestaurant.com*

### Red Fish                                  ★$$$LD
*Hilton Head Island* ▪ (843) 686-3388
*8 Archer Rd* ▪ *Southern* ▪ According to a staff member the mahi mahi is naturally GF. All of the servers are very well informed regarding which items are GF and which are not. They are more than happy to accommodate and inform customers of what can be altered to make any entrée GF. ▪ *www.redfishofhiltonhead.com*

### Red Orchid China Bistro                          $LD
*Charleston* ▪ (843) 573-8787
*1401 Sam Rittenberg Blvd* ▪ *Chinese* ▪
Dinner only on Sundays. Can make any
dish with white sauce and no soy sauce. ▪
*www.redorchidsmenu.com*

### Red Pepper, The                                  $$LD
*Summerville* ▪ (843) 873-8600
*709 N Main St* ▪ *Italian* ▪ GF penne pasta
available. ▪ *www.theredpepper.com*

### Restaurant at the Willcox, The          $$$LD
*Aiken* ▪ (803) 648-1898
*100 Colleton Ave SW* ▪ *American* ▪ GF
options include edamame, baby sausage,
New Zealand lamb chop pops, steaks
and risotto. Other items on the menu
can be made GF, be sure to alert server. ▪
*www.thewillcox.comrestaurant*

### Roastfish & Cornbread                       ★$$LD
*Hilton Head Island* ▪ (843) 342-2996
*70 Marshland Rd* ▪ *Southern* ▪ Restaurant states the entire vegetarian menu
is GF and the rest of the menu can be
altered to be GF. For example: leaving the bread off of the fish and grill-
ing or pan roasting it versus frying. ▪
*www.roastfishandcornbread.com*

### Robert Irvine's Eat!                         ✪$$$$D
*Hilton Head Island* ▪ (843) 785-4850
*1000 William Hilton Pkwy Ste B6* ▪ *Modern American* ▪ Restaurant offers a wide
variety of GF entrées such as a pan roasted
chicken, filet mignon, and diver scallops. ▪
*www.eathhi.com*

### Romano's Macaroni Grill                  ✪★▢
*Columbia* ▪ (803) 781-2313
*148 Harbison Blvd*
*Greenville* ▪ (864) 675-6676
*105 E Beacon Dr*

### Ruan Thai Hut                                   $$LD
*Hilton Head Island* ▪ (843) 681-3700
*1107 Main St* ▪ *Thai* ▪ The restaurant reports that most veggie meals can be made
GF. Ask a server when deciding on your

meal and they will let you know if GF is
possible. ▪ *www.ruanthaihut.com*

### Ruth's Chris Steak House                   ✪▢
*Columbia* ▪ (803) 212-6666
*924-A Senate St*
*Greenville* ▪ (864) 248-1700
*851-A Congaree Rd*
*Myrtle Beach* ▪ (843) 839-9500
*8761 Marina Pkwy*

### Sake House                                        $LD
*Beaufort* ▪ (843) 379-5888
*274 Robert Small Pkwy* ▪ *Sushi* ▪ GF
items are not listed on the menu but
the staff states they "do their best" to
accommodate GF diners. Ask a server
upon arrival for a list of GF options. ▪
*www.sakehousesc.com*

### San Miguel's                                ✪★$$LD
*Hilton Head Island* ▪ (843) 842-4555
*9 Shelter Cove Ln* ▪ *Mexican* ▪ GF items
include fajitas with corn tortillas, refried
beans, and black beans. Be sure to ask a
server for all GF alternatives when placing
an order. ▪ *www.sanmiguels.com*

### Sea Grass Grille                            ★$$$LD
*Hilton Head Island* ▪ (843) 785-9990
*807 William Hilton Pkwy* ▪ *Seafood* ▪
The restaurant reports that they regularly serve GF diners. Kitchen staff and
chef are well versed in GF dietary needs
and know how to avoid CC. Call ahead
for dining in, as they are a small place
and fill up quickly. Alert the server upon
arrival of your dietary needs and they
will direct you to the GF friendly items. ▪
*www.seagrassgrille.com*

### Sermet's Courtyard                          $$D
*Daniel Is* ▪ (843) 471-1777
*115 River Landing Dr* ▪ *Mediterranean* ▪ GF
options include basil salmon and shrimp
polenta. ▪ *www.sermetscourtyard.com*

### Sesame Burgers and Beer                ★$LD
*Charleston* ▪ (843) 554-4903
*4726 Spruill Ave*
*Charleston* ▪ (843) 766-7770
*2070 Sam Rittenburg Blvd*

**Mt Pleasant** ▪ (843) 884-5553
*675 E Johnny Dodds Blvd* ▪ *American* ▪ GF
buns available. Alert server upon arrival. ▪
*www.sesameburgersandbeer.com*

### Sette                                                         $LD
*Mt Pleasant* ▪ (843) 388-8808
*201 Coleman Blvd* ▪ *Italian* ▪ The restaurant reports that they can "adjust" many
items on the menu for GF customers. ▪
*dinewithsal.com*

### Shane's Rib Shack                                      ✪📖
*Florence* ▪ (843) 679-3503
*1940 Hoffmeyer Rd Ste B*
*Indian Land* ▪ (803) 548-9227
*10092 Charlotte Hwy*

### Sigler's Rotisserie & Seafood          ✪$$$D
*Bluffton* ▪ (843) 815-5030
*12 Sheridan Park Cir* ▪ *American* ▪ Restaurant has a wide variety of GF dining
options such as rotisserie half chicken,
Prince Edward Island mussels, pan roasted
scallops, grilled salmon, and stuffed flounder. The menu changes regularly so it is not
always noted on the menu itself. Be sure to
alert a server upon placing an order to ensure the meal is cooked and labeled properly. ▪ *www.siglersrotisserieofhiltonhead.com*

### Skull Creek Boathouse                   ✪★$$$LD
*Hilton Head Island* ▪ (843) 681-3663
*397 Squire Pope Rd* ▪ *Seafood* ▪ Restaurant reports many GF seafood and protein
options, in addition to a variety of salad
and side options for their GF diners.

### Slightly North of Broad                    ✪$$$LD
*Charleston* ▪ (843) 723-3424
*192 E Bay St* ▪ *American* ▪ GF Menu
available. Some items include BBQ tuna,
maverick shrimp and grits, Carolina
flounder, sautéed duck breast, roasted lamb
rack, grilled pork chop, maverick beef
tenderloin, Prince Edward Island mussels,
local beef carpaccio and a vegetable plate. ▪
*www.mavericksouthernkitchens.com*

### Smoke on the Water                          ★$$LD
*Greenville* ▪ (864) 232-9091
*1 Augusta St* ▪ *Barbeque* ▪ Regular menu
items can be modified to be GF. Alert server upon arrival. ▪ *www.saucytavern.com*

### Smokehouse, The                             ✪$$LD
*Hilton Head Island* ▪ (843) 842-4227
*34 Palmetto Bay Rd* ▪ *Barbeque* ▪ Recently created GF menu available in-house.
Additionally any regular menu item that
can be altered to be GF has been marked. ▪
*smokehousehhi.com*

### Smokey Bones                                       📖
*North Charleston* ▪ (843) 572-3420
*7250 Rivers Ave*

### Soby's                                                 ★$$$D
*Greenville* ▪ (864) 232-7007
*207 S Main St* ▪ *Southern* ▪ GF options are
available upon request only. Email or call
ahead to speak with a staff member regarding menu options. ▪ *www.sobys.com*

### Sole Sushi Bar and Grill                          $LD
*Seneca* ▪ (864) 822-9463
*700 Bypass 123* ▪ *Asian* ▪ GF accommodations can be made. Alert server upon
arrival. ▪ *www.solesushi.com*

### Square Onion                                          ₵LD
*Mt Pleasant* ▪ (843) 856-4246
*18 Resolute Ln* ▪ *American* ▪ GF options include salads and all sandwiches
can be made into a lettuce wrap. ▪
*squareonion.com*

### Stax Omega Diner                                ₵BLD
*Greenville* ▪ (864) 297-6639
*72 Orchard Park Dr* ▪ *American* ▪ GF options available. Alert server upon arrival. ▪
*www.staxs.net*

### Stella's Southern Bistro                      $$$LD
*Simpsonville* ▪ (864) 757-1212
*684-C Fairview Rd* ▪ *Southern* ▪ GF menu
items are indicated with an asterisk, and
include shrimp & grits, seared trout, grilled
pork chop, hanger steak, and more. ▪
*www.stellasbistro.com*

## Steven W's Downtown Restaurant $$$D
*Newberry* ■ (803) 276-7700
*1100 Main St* ■ *American* ■ Note GF when making reservations so that restaurant has time to prepare items. ■ *www.stevenws.com*

## Sticky Fingers Smokehouse ✪🕮
*Mt. Pleasant* ■ (843) 856-7427
*341 Johnnie Dodds Blvd*
*Summerville* ■ (843) 871-7427
*1200 N Main St*
*Charleston* ■ (843) 853-7427
*235 Meeting St*
*Greenville* ■ (864) 458-7427
*3 Market Point Dr*
*Myrtle Beach* ■ (843) 839-7427
*2461 Coastal Grand Cir*
*Greenville* ■ (864) 331-7427
*1 S Main St*
*North Myrtle Beach* ■ (843) 663-7675
*4200 Highway 17 S*

## Stono Market & Tomato Shed Café ℄L
*Johns Island* ■ (843) 559-9999
*842 Main Rd* ■ *American* ■ Menu changes daily. Alert server upon arrival and they will be sure to accommodate GF needs.

## Sweet Carolina Cupcakes ★℄S
*Hilton Head Island* ■ (843) 342-2611
*1 N Forest Beach Dr* ■ *Dessert* ■ GF & vegan cupcakes made every Monday and Thursday. ■ *sweetcarolinacupcakes.com*

## Sweet Cece's 🕮
*Charleston* ■ (843) 277-2108
*99 S Market St*

## Sweetgrass Restaurant and Bar $$LD
*St Helena Island* ■ (843) 838-2151
*100 Marina Dr* ■ *Seafood* ■ GF menu available. Some items include deviled eggs, vegetable plates, cut of the day, catch of the day, salmon BLT no bun, burgers with no buns, variety of salads, french and sweet potato fries, sirloins, flounder and shrimp. ■ *sweetgrassdataw.com*

## Taco Mamacita ℄LD
*Sullivan's Island* ■ (843) 789-4107
*2213 Middle St* ■ *Mexican* ■ GF items include guacamole, tacos with soft corn tortilla. Soups and salads are served with no tortilla strips. Alert server upon arrival. ■ *tacomamacita.com*

## Taco Spot, The ★℄LD
*Charleston* ■ (843) 225-7426
*1301 Ashley River Rd*
*Charleston* ■ (843) 720-1888
*221 1/2 Coming St* ■ *Mexican* ■ Everything on the menu can be made GF using corn tortillas and shells. ■ *www.thetacospot.com*

## Terra $$LD
*W Columbia* ■ (803) 791-3443
*100 State St* ■ *American* ■ Terra does not have a GF menu. However, several regular menu items can be prepared GF. They include shrimp remoulade, seared yellow fin tuna, salads, and pork pastor crepes. ■ *www.terrasc.com*

## Thai Wasabi ★℄LD
*Lexington* ■ (803) 957-9849
*5454 Sunset Blvd Ste. E* ■ *Asian Fusion* ■ GF dishes available. Manager recommends alerting a server upon ordering to ensure CC does not occur. ■ *www.thaiwasabi.net*

## Trattoria Divina ✪★$$$D
*Hilton Head Island* ■ (843) 686-4442
*33 Office Park Rd* ■ *Italian* ■ GF pasta is available. The restaurant also recommends that GF diners ask about other options that the chef might be able to prepare specially. ■ *www.trattoriadivina.com*

## Trattoria Lucca $$$D
*Charleston* ■ (843) 973-3323
*41-A Bogard St* ■ *Italian* ■ GF items available, mostly protein dishes. Alert server upon arrival. ■ *luccacharleston.com*

## Travinia Italian Kitchen ✪★🕮
*Greenville* ■ (864) 458-8188
*1625 Woodruff Rd*
*Columbia* ■ (803) 419-9313
*101 Sparkleberry Crossing Rd*
*Myrtle Beach* ■ (843) 233-8500
*4011 Deville St*
*Lexington* ■ (803) 957-2422

*5074 Sunset Blvd*
*Aiken* ▪ *(803) 642-9642*
*470 Fabian Dr*

### Triangle Char & Bar     ¢**LD**
*Charleston* ▪ *(843) 377-1300*
*828 Savannah Hwy*
*Mt Pleasant* ▪ *(843) 606-2900*
*1440 Ben Sawyer Blvd* ▪ *American* ▪ GF
items include tacos, variety of salads,
grilled salmon and ribs. Alert server upon
arrival. ▪ *trianglecharandbar.com*

### Trio Café     ✪**SLD**
*Greenville* ▪ *(864) 467-1000*
*22 N Main St* ▪ *American* ▪ Manager Joe
reports that they have several GF customers that come on a regular basis, so they are
"very educated" about GF options. They
have an extensive GF menu with items
such as a grilled chicken parmesan and a
crème brûlée. ▪ *www.triocafe.com*

### Tropical Escape Café     $**SLD**
*Rock Hill* ▪ *(803) 366-3888*
*590 N Anderson Rd* ▪ *American* ▪ The
entire "Fire Grilled" section of the menu
is GF, including items such as BBQ grilled
chicken, teriyaki beef, skewered shrimp,
Cajun chicken breast. Additionally, vegetable stir frys are available with various types
of meats. ▪ *www.tropicalescapecafe.net*

### Twenty-Six Divine     $$**LD**
*Charleston* ▪ *(843) 297-8118*
*682 King St* ▪ *American* ▪ GF options include a variety of salad, a tomato and lentil
soup and for dessert a flourless chocolate
torte. ▪ *www.twentysixdivine.com*

### Uno Chicago Grill     ✪★📖
*Lexington* ▪ *(803) 359-3888*
*5304 Sunset Blvd*

### Uno Mas     $**LD**
*Mt Pleasant* ▪ *(843) 856-4868*
*880 Allbritton Blvd* ▪ *Mexican* ▪ GF
options available. Some items include
tacos and enchiladas with corn tortillas. ▪
*www.dinewithsal.com*

### Verde     ¢**LD**
*Charleston* ▪ *(843) 579-2884*
*347 King St* ▪ *American* ▪ GF tomato basil,
black bean and corn soup available. A
detailed list of items that can be made GF
is available. Alert server upon arrival. ▪
*eatatverde.com*

### Wise Guys     ✪$$$$**D**
*Hilton Head Island* ▪ *(843) 842-8866*
*1513 Main St.* ▪ *American* ▪ Extensive
GF menu online. Menu items include
spicy shrimp and calamari, a variety of
salads, sides, steaks and surf and turfs. ▪
*www.wiseguyshhi.com*

### Yo Burrito     ¢**LD**
*Charleston* ▪ *(843) 853-3287*
*77 Wentworth St* ▪ *Mexican* ▪ Most burritos can be made GF and in a bowl instead
of a tortilla. Tacos can be made with corn
tortillas. ▪ *yoburrito.com*

### Zpizza     ✪📖
*Columbia* ▪ *(803) 736-5118*
*4760 Hardscrabble Rd*

## SOUTH DAKOTA

### Beau Jo's Colorado Style Pizza   ✪★$**LD**
*Rapid City* ▪ *(605) 716-1033*
*2520 W Main St* ▪ *Pizza* ▪ GF pizza is
available at all locations. GF menu includes
GF appetizers, pizzas, and sandwiches and
notes which pizza sauces and toppings are
safe for GF diners. ▪ *www.beaujos.com*

### Boss' Pizza & Chicken     ★$$**LD**
*Sioux Falls* ▪ *(605) 217-2677*
*2111 S Minnesota Ave*
*Brookings* ▪ *(605) 692-4949*
*420 N Main Ave*
*Harrisburg* ▪ *(605) 767-2677*
*300 Cliff St*
*Sioux Falls* ▪ *(605) 271-9378*

5330 W 26th St ▪ Pizza ▪ GF pizza is available in the medium size. ▪ www.bosspizzaandchicken.com

### Boston's Restaurant & Sports Bar
✪★📖
*Rapid City* ▪ *(605) 348-7200*
*620 E Disk Dr*

### Buffaloberries                                   ★🗚L
*Sioux Falls* ▪ *(605) 271-8280*
*309 S Phillips Ave* ▪ *Café* ▪ GF pizza, bread, pumpkin muffins, brownies, and more are available. Owner Karen notes that with very few exceptions, items on the menu are GF or can be modified to be GF. ▪ www.buffaloberries.com

### Bully Blends Coffee & Tea Shop   ★🗚BLD
*Rapid City* ▪ *(605) 342-3559*
*908 Main St* ▪ *Café* ▪ GF beer is available from 11am to close. GF cheesecake brownies and soups are sometimes available. ▪ www.bullyblends.com

### Carino's Italian                                 ✪📖
*Sioux Falls* ▪ *(605) 361-7222*
*2310 S Louise Ave*

### Cattleman's Club Steakhouse   $$$LD
*Pierre* ▪ *(605) 224-9774*
*29608 S D Hwy 34* ▪ *Steakhouse* ▪ Cattleman's offers a wide variety of GF meat options. Available are prime rib, USDA choice sirloin steaks, a jumbo shrimp dinner, and several bone in steaks. ▪ www.cattlemansclublodge.com

### Colonial House Restaurant & Bar   $$LD
*Rapid City* ▪ *(605) 342-4640*
*2501 Mt Rushmore Rd* ▪ *Pub Food* ▪ The Colonial House offers a variety of GF menu items such as salads. Also available are entrées such as grilled cod, countless steaks, ocean salmon, and BBQ ribs. ▪ www.colonialhousernb.com

### Corn Exchange, The                       $$$LD
*Rapid City* ▪ *(605) 343-5070*
*727 Main St* ▪ *Bistro* ▪ The restaurant reports that they have "a ton" of GF options, including wild Alaskan salmon,

all of their steaks, Thai curry, and sides such as seasonal vegetables. Confirm the timeliness of this information before dining in. Alert the server upon arrival. ▪ www.cornexchange.com

### Dakotah Steakhouse                       $$$LD
*Rapid City* ▪ *(605) 791-1800*
*1325 N Elk Vale Rd* ▪ *Steakhouse* ▪ Dakotah Steakhouse has a variety of meat options which are all GF. Menu items include top sirloin steak, lamb chops, ribeye steak, sockeye salmon, and wild shrimp skewers. ▪ www.dakotahsteakhouse.com

### Delmonico Grill                             $$$LD
*Rapid City* ▪ *(605) 791-1664*
*609 Main St* ▪ *Steakhouse* ▪ The restaurant reports that many of their steak, seafood, and other protein options are GF or can be made GF. Alert the server upon arrival. ▪ www.delmonicogrill.biz

### Gator's Pizza                               ★$$LD
*Pierre* ▪ *(605) 224-6262*
*1615 N Harrison Ave* ▪ *Pizza* ▪ GF pizza is available in the 12" size.

### Godfather's Pizza                           ★📖
*Sioux Falls* ▪ *(605) 338-5225*
*2331 E 10th St*
*Sioux Falls* ▪ *(605) 361-8029*
*5107 W 41st St*
*Huron* ▪ *(605) 352-6925*
*195 21St St SW*
*Watertown* ▪ *(605) 882-1232*
*Watertown Mall*
*Yankton* ▪ *(605) 665-2525*
*2101 Broadway*

### Gregg's Substation                         ★🗚D
*Sioux Falls* ▪ *(605) 332-5454*
*1000 W 41st St* ▪ *American* ▪ GF bread is available and can be substituted into any sandwich.

### Ground Round                               ✪📖
*Brookings* ▪ *(605) 697-5357*
*2500 E 6th St*

### HuHot Mongolian Grill  📖
*Sioux Falls* ▪ *(605) 221-1200*
*5430 Arrowhead Pkwy*
*Sioux Falls* ▪ *(605) 334-7400*
*2101 W 41st St*

### Jim's Tap  ★ ⊄S
*Brookings* ▪ *(605) 692-2833*
*309 Main Ave* ▪ *Pub Food* ▪ GF beer is available.

### La Minestra  $$LD
*Pierre* ▪ *(605) 224-8090*
*106 E Dakota Ave* ▪ *Italian* ▪ La Minestra offers a variety of GF options such as salads, pepper steak, steak and mushrooms, and a grilled salmon. ▪ *www.laminestra.comwww.laminestra.com*

### Lintz Brother's Pizza  ★ ⊄D
*Hermosa* ▪ *(605) 255-4808*
*14287 SD Highway 36* ▪ *Pizza* ▪ GF pizza is available in the 10-inch size. Any available toppings can be put on the GF crust including pepperoni, Canadian bacon, ground beef, Italian sausage and a variety of veggies. ▪ *lintzbrospizza.com*

### Lone Star Steakhouse & Saloon  ✪📖
*Sioux Falls* ▪ *(605) 331-3648*
*1801 W 41st St*

### Mad Mary's Steakhouse & Saloon  $$D
*Pierre* ▪ *(605) 224-6469*
*110 E Dakota Ave*
*Flandreau* ▪ *(605) 997-9901*
*306 N Veterans St* ▪ *Steakhouse* ▪ The restaurant reports that most of their meat entrées can be modified to be GF by "omitting certain sauces and marinades". Alert the server upon arrival and ask to speak to a manager or chef about which seasonings are suitable for GF diners. ▪ *www.madmarysflandreau.com*

### Meadowood Lanes  ★ ⊄D
*Rapid City* ▪ *(605) 343-0923*
*3809 Sturgis Rd* ▪ *American* ▪ GF beer is available. ▪ *www.meadowoodlanes.com*

### Minerva's  ✪📖
*Sioux Falls* ▪ *(605) 334-0386*
*301 S Phillips Ave*
*Rapid City* ▪ *(605) 394-9505*
*111 N LaCrosse St*
*Aberdeen* ▪ *(605) 226-2988*
*1400 8th Ave NW*
*Watertown* ▪ *(605) 882-1777*
*1901 9th Ave SW*
*Yankton* ▪ *(605) 664-2244*
*1607 E Hwy 50*

### Monkey's Bar & Grill  ★ ⊄S
*Dell Rapids* ▪ *(605) 428-6000*
*313 N Garfield Ave* ▪ *Pub Food* ▪ GF beer is available.

### Nucci's Italian Bistro & Gelato  ✪★⊄LD
*Sioux Falls* ▪ *(605) 362-1444*
*5005 S. Western Ave* ▪ *Italian* ▪ Nucci's offers a full GF menu including items and entrées such as GF pasta and wraps made with brown rice in addition to various soup, salad and dessert options. ▪ *www.nuccisbistro.com*

### Pizza Ranch  ✪📖
*Aberdeen* ▪ *(605) 725-2525*
*1010 6th Ave SE*
*Brandon* ▪ *(605) 582-6322*
*202 Splitrock Blvd*
*Brookings* ▪ *(605) 692-3663*
*1815 6th St*
*Canton* ▪ *(605) 987-0099*
*719 E 5th St*
*Del Rapids* ▪ *(605) 428-5967*
*500 W 4th St*
*Hartford* ▪ *(605) 528-3663*
*120 W Hwy 38*
*Lennox* ▪ *(605) 647-2828*
*112 E 1st St*
*Madison* ▪ *(605) 256-3333*
*1111 NW 2nd St*
*Mitchell* ▪ *(605) 996-8009*
*502 E Norway*
*Mobridge* ▪ *(605) 845-2700*
*1209 10th St W*
*Platte* ▪ *(605) 337-3250*
*801 E 7th St*
*Rapid City* ▪ *(605) 348-9114*

1556 Luna Ave
*Sioux Falls* ▪ *(605) 271-8648*
2712 W 41st St
*Sioux Falls* ▪ *(605) 275-9777*
3890 E 10th St
*Spearfish* ▪ *(605) 642-4422*
2625 E Colorado Blvd
*Sturgis* ▪ *(605) 347-3400*
2711 Lazelle St

### Sam & Louie's New York Pizzeria   ★▣
*Rapid City* ▪ *(605) 721-4102*
2101 Mount Rushmore Rd
*Spearfish* ▪ *(605) 559-2100*
1420 North Ave

### Sanaa's Gourmet                    ✪★⑁D
*Sioux Falls* ▪ *(605) 275-2516*
401 E 8th St ▪ *Mediterranean* ▪ GF menu
includes Mediterranean calzones, kufta
kabob, and chicken with saffron rice. GF
bread and pizza are available. Confirm the
timeliness of this information before dining in. ▪ *www.sanaasgourmet.com*

### Shahi Palace                        $LD
*Sioux Falls* ▪ *(605) 361-5050*
2527 S Shirley Ave ▪ *Indian* ▪ The
restaurant reports that all of their entrées
are GF. The only non-GF menu items are
the appetizers and complimentary bread
received upon being seated. Alert server
upon arrival to ensure proper preparation.
▪ *www.shahipalaceinc.com*

### Spezia Restaurant                   $$LD
*Sioux Falls* ▪ *(605) 334-7491*
4801 S Louise Ave ▪ *Italian* ▪ The restaurant reports that GF options on their
menu include salads, steaks, seafood, and
chicken. Confirm the timeliness of this information before dining in. Alert the server
upon arrival. ▪ *speziarestaurant.com*

### Tally's Silver Spoon Restaurant    $$$D
*Rapid City* ▪ *(605) 342-7621*
530 6th St ▪ *American* ▪ The Silver Spoon
offers a GF rice pasta which can be made
with a variety of sauces. Additionally available are entrées such as a hanger steak, pan

seared coalfish, seared duck breast, and
bison skirt. ▪ *tallyssilverspoon.com*

### Taste of The Big Apple, A          ★$LD
*Sioux Falls* ▪ *(605) 339-2400*
600 N Maine Ave ▪ *Pizza* ▪ GF
pizza is available in the 10" size. ▪
*www.atasteofthebigapple.com*

### View 34                             $$LD
*Pierre* ▪ *(605) 224-7537*
4251 E Hwy 34 ▪ *American* ▪ View 34 offers
a variety of GF options such as chicken cor-
don, cedar plank salmon, and several prime
cuts of steak. ▪ *www.viewthirtyfour.com*

### Wooly Mammoth Family Fun          ★$$BLD
*Hot Springs* ▪ *(605) 745-6414*
1648 County Hwy 18 ▪ *American* ▪ GF beer
is available. The only other GF options are
sandwiches without a bun and burritos
without a tortilla.

# TENNESSEE

## KNOXVILLE

### Abuelo's                            ✪▣
*Knoxville* ▪ *(865) 966-0075*
11299 Parkside Dr

### Bistro At The Bijou                 $LD
*Knoxville* ▪ *(865) 544-0537*
807 S Gay St ▪ *American* ▪ The restaurant reports that the majority of dinner
entrées are GF, including items such as
fried catfish, Jamaican jerk chicken, and
a ribeye steak. Confirm the timeliness
of this information before dining in. ▪
*www.thebistroatthebijou.com*

### Bistro By The Tracks               $$$LD
*Knoxville* ▪ *(865) 558-9500*
215 Brookview Ctr Wy ▪ *Bistro* ▪ Bistro by
the Tracks offers a wide variety of GF entrées such as pan seared duck, grilled salm-

on, filet mignon, grilled pork chops, and bistro chicken. ▪ *www.bistrobythetracks.com*

### Bonefish Grill   ✪▢
*Knoxville* ▪ *(865) 558-5743*
*6604 Kingston Pike*
*Knoxville* ▪ *(865) 966-9777*
*11395 Parkside Dr*

### Brazeiro's   $$$D
*Knoxville* ▪ *(865) 247-0295*
*6901 Kingston Pke* ▪ *Brazilian* ▪ The restaurant reports that since they are a steakhouse serving mostly meats and proteins, a vast majority of their dinner entrées are GF. Alert the server upon arrival to ensure a GF meal. ▪ *www.brazeiros.com*

### Brixx Wood Fired Pizza   ✪★▢
*Knoxville* ▪ *(865) 288-4186*
*10978 Parkside Dr*
*Knoxville* ▪ *(865) 474-9971*
*7403 Kingston Pike*

### Carino's Italian   ✪▢
*Knoxville* ▪ *(865) 671-1900*
*210 Lovell Rd*

### Don Pablo's   ✪▢
*Knoxville* ▪ *(865) 633-4978*
*2916 Knoxville Center Dr*
*Knoxville* ▪ *(865) 633-4978*
*2916 Knoxville Center Dr*

### Fleming's Prime Steakhouse & Wine Bar   ✪▢
*Knoxville* ▪ *(865) 675-9463*
*11287 Parkside Dr*

### Fox and Hound Pub & Grille   ▢
*Knoxville* ▪ *(865) 531-2644*
*250 N 7 Oaks Dr*

### Genghis Grill   ▢
*Knoxville* ▪ *(865) 951-7208*
*11316 Parkside Dr*

### Jason's Deli   ✪▢
*Knoxville* ▪ *(865) 357-3354*
*133 N Peters Rd*
*Knoxville* ▪ *(865) 247-5222*
*2120 Cumberland Ave*

### Melting Pot, The   ✪▢
*Knoxville* ▪ *(865) 971-5400*
*111 N Central St*

### Nama Sushi Bar   $LD
*Knoxville* ▪ *(865) 633-8593*
*506 S Gay St*
*Knoxville* ▪ *(865) 588-9811*
*5130 Kingston Pke* ▪ *Sushi* ▪ The restaurant reports that many items on the menu are naturally GF or can easily be altered to be GF. Alert the server so they can omit sauces such as soy and teriyaki if necessary. ▪ *www.namasushibar.com*

### O'Charley's   ▢
*Knoxville* ▪ *(865) 691-5885*
*8077 Kingston Pike*
*Knoxville* ▪ *(865) 689-2870*
*117 Cedar Ln*
*Knoxville* ▪ *(865) 524-9114*
*3050 S Mall Rd*
*Knoxville* ▪ *(865) 675-4244*
*11036 Parkside Dr*

### P.F. Chang's China Bistro   ✪★▢
*Knoxville* ▪ *(865) 212-5514*
*6741 Kingston Pike*

### Pei Wei Asian Diner   ✪▢
*Knoxville* ▪ *(865) 966-1610*
*11301 Parkside Dr*

### Pizza Kitchen, The   ★¢LD
*Knoxville* ▪ *(865) 531-1422*
*9411 S Northshore Dr* ▪ *Pizza* ▪ GF 10" pizza and beer are available. Ask server about GF options available. ▪ *www.thepizzakitchen.net*

### Roman's Pizza   ✪★$$LD
*Knoxville* ▪ *(865) 539-1784*
*179 N Seven Oaks Dr* ▪ *Pizza* ▪ The restaurant recommends calling ahead for GF items because they have a longer prep time. GF items include garlic knots, cheesebread, pizza, calzones, stramboli, spinach ravioli alfredo, cheese ravioli, stuffed shells, gnocchi, and lasagna. GF desserts include carrot, chocolate and red velvet cake, tiramisu, and shortcake. The restaurant also offers a

GF buffet on certain days. Call ahead for schedule. ▪ *www.romans-pizza.com*

### Romano's Macaroni Grill ✪★📖
*Knoxville* ▪ *(865) 691-0809*
*7723 Kingston Pike*

### Ruth's Chris Steak House ✪📖
*Knoxville* ▪ *(865) 546-4696*
*950 Volunteer Landing Ln*

### Surin of Thailand 📖
*Knoxville* ▪ *(865) 330-0007*
*6213 Kingston Pike*

### Tomato Head ★$$LD
*Knoxville* ▪ *(865) 637-4067*
*12 Market Sq*
*Knoxville* ▪ *(865) 584-1077*
*7240 Kingston Pke* ▪ *Pizza* ▪ GF pizza crust is available. Also available are burritos and tacos, both of which can be made with corn tortillas. ▪ *thetomatohead.com*

# TENNESSEE

## NASHVILLE

### Amerigo Italian Restaurant ✪$$LD
*Nashville* ▪ *(615) 320-1740*
*1920 W End Ave* ▪ *Italian* ▪ GF menu features a variety of salads such as tomato and mozzarella, as well as GF entrées such as flame grilled salmon acuto, prime sirloin, and wild mushroom pasta. ▪ *amerigo.net*

### Aquarium Restaurant $$LD
*Nashville* ▪ *(615) 514-3474*
*516 Opry Mills Dr* ▪ *Seafood* ▪ Upon arrival, alert the manager, who will alert the chef. The chef will come to the table and recommend some dishes that can be made GF. ▪ *www.aquariumrestaurants.com*

### Au Bon Pain 📖
*Nashville* ▪ *(615) 320-0164*
*2215 Garland Ave*

### BrickTop's ✪📖
*Nashville* ▪ *(615) 298-1000*
*3000 W End Ave*
*Franklin* ▪ *(615) 771-8760*
*1576 W McEwen Dr*

### Calypso Café ✪$LD
*Nashville* ▪ *(615) 227-6133*
*1101 Gartland Ave*
*Nashville* ▪ *(615) 321-3878*
*2424 Elliston Pl*
*Nashville* ▪ *(615) 297-3888*
*5101 Harding Pike*
*Nashville* ▪ *(615) 771-5665*
*700 Thompson Ln* ▪ *Vegetarian* ▪ The restaurant reports that they are "a popular destination for GF diners" and have many GF options on the menu. The GF section on the website denotes items that are NOT GF. Alert the server when dining in and they can help choose a suitable meal. ▪ *www.calypsocafe.com*

### Cantina Laredo 📖
*Nashville* ▪ *(615) 259-9282*
*592 12Th Ave S*

### Demos' Restaurant ✪$LD
*Nashville* ▪ *(615) 256-4655*
*300 Commerce St* ▪ *Italian* ▪ GF menu includes shrimp cocktail, steak and feta salad, stuffed potatoes, steaks, catfish, shrimp scampi, mozzarella chicken, and more. The restaurant recommends notifying your server prior to ordering to ensure CC does not occur. ▪ *www.demosrestaurants.com*

### Fleming's Prime Steakhouse & Wine Bar ✪📖
*Nashville* ▪ *(615) 342-0131*
*2525 W End Ave*

### Fox and Hound Pub & Grille 📖
*Nashville* ▪ *(615) 254-5452*
*408 Broadway*

### Hard Rock Café ✪📖
*Nashville* ▪ *(615) 742-9900*
*100 Broadway*

### Italia Pizza and Pasta ★¢LD
*Nashville* ▪ *(615) 262-5001*

1600 Woodland St ▪ *Italian* ▪ GF pizza is available. ▪ *www.italiapizza37206.com*

### J. Gumbo's ★📖
*Nashville* ▪ *(615) 687-7979*
*2 Arcade*

### Jason's Deli ✪📖
*Nashville* ▪ *(615) 340-9991*
*2028 W End Ave*

### Jersey Mike's 📖
*Nashville* ▪ *(615) 673-1099*
*7114 US Hwy 70 S*
*Nashville* ▪ *(615) 352-3004*
*73 White Bridge Rd*
*Nashville* ▪ *(615) 329-4304*
*2311 Elliston Pl*
*Nashville* ▪ *(615) 255-7760*
*2050 Rosa Parks Blvd*
*Nashville* ▪ *(615) 315-5555*
*5527 Edmondson Pike*
*Nashville* ▪ *(615) 360-6600*
*2280 Murfreesboro Pike*
*Nashville* ▪ *(615) 891-3750*
*211 Union St*
*Nashville* ▪ *(615) 942-9372*
*2184 Bandywood Dr* ▪ *Deli*

### Jim 'n Nick's Bar-B-Q ✪★📖
*Nashville* ▪ *(615) 352-5777*
*7004 Charlotte Pike*

### Joe's Crab Shack ✪📖
*Nashville* ▪ *(615) 242-2722*
*123 2nd Ave S*

### Maggiano's Little Italy ★📖
*Nashville* ▪ *(615) 514-0270*
*3106 W End Ave*

### Margaritaville ✪★📖
*Nashville* ▪ *(615) 208-9080*
*322 Broadway*

### Margot Café $$$D
*Nashville* ▪ *(615) 227-4668*
*1017 Woodland St* ▪ *Café* ▪ GF options include grilled pork tenderloin, pan roasted chicken, and a seafood steampot. Alert the server upon arrival and ask about any modifications necessary to make the dishes GF. ▪ *www.margotcafe.com*

### Matter of Taste, A ₵L
*Nashville* ▪ *(615) 866-8144*
*2401 B Franklin Rd* ▪ *American* ▪ The owner is gluten-intolerant and the entire menu is GF (they do carry gluten-full bread, but it is not made in house). Selections include sandwiches, soups, and salads as well as a frequently changing variety of GF sweets. ▪ *amatteroftastetakeout.com*

### Melting Pot, The ✪📖
*Nashville* ▪ *(615) 742-4970*
*166 2nd Ave N*

### Mitchell Delicatessen ★$LD
*Nashville* ▪ *(615) 262-9862*
*1402 McGavock Pike* ▪ *Deli* ▪ GF bread is available for any sandwich. ▪ *mitchelldeli.com*

### Morton's Steakhouse ✪📖
*Nashville* ▪ *(615) 259-4558*
*618 Church St*

### O'Charley's 📖
*Nashville* ▪ *(615) 356-1344*
*17 White Bridge Rd*
*Nashville* ▪ *(615) 662-4026*
*110 Coley Davis Ct*

### Old Spaghetti Factory, The ✪★📖
*Nashville* ▪ *(615) 254-9010*
*160 2nd Ave N*

### P.F. Chang's China Bistro ✪★📖
*Nashville* ▪ *(615) 329-8901*
*2525 W End Ave Ste 2535*

### Pei Wei Asian Diner ✪📖
*Nashville* ▪ *(615) 514-3230*
*4017 Hillsboro Pike*

### Prime 108 $$LD
*Nashville* ▪ *(615) 726-1001*
*1001 Broadway* ▪ *American* ▪ The restaurant reports that nearly all of their dishes can be prepared GF, with the omission of sauces in some cases. Alert the server upon arrival and they will go over the options. ▪ *www.prime108.com*

### Romano's Macaroni Grill ✪★📖
*Nashville* ▪ *(615) 686-2861*
*517 Opry Mills Dr*

**Ruth's Chris Steak House**    ☉🕮
*Nashville* ▪ *(615) 320-0163*
*2100 W End Ave*

**Silly Goose**    ★ $$$LD
*Nashville* ▪ *(615) 915-0757*
*1888 Eastland Ave* ▪ *American* ▪ GF bread
is available for sandwiches. Other GF op-
tions include salads topped with meat and
various protein based entrées like pork
ribs, cast iron flank steak and pan roasted
salmon. ▪ *sillygoosenashville.com*

**Sole Mio**    ★ $$$LD
*Nashville* ▪ *(615) 256-4013*
*311 3rd Ave S* ▪ *Italian* ▪ GF menu items
include bruschetta, caesar salad, chicken
dishes, chicken and vegetable dishes and
GF pasta with a red pomodoro sauce. Confirm the timeliness of this information before dining in. ▪ *www.solemionashville.com*

**Sunset Grill**    $$$LD
*Nashville* ▪ *(615) 386-3663*
*2001 Belcourt Ave* ▪ *Modern American* ▪
GF items indicated on menu. Items include
seared sea scallops, chicken breast, Sonoma
salad, grilled hanger steak, grilled filet
mignon, and vegetable stir fry. Confirm the
timeliness of this information before din-
ing in. ▪ *www.sunsetgrill.com*

**Sweet Cece's**    🕮
*Nashville* ▪ *(615) 383-1711*
*4322 Harding Pike*
*Nashville* ▪ *(615) 678-7239*
*7114 Hwy 70 S*
*Nashville* ▪ *(615) 750-5523*
*4031 Hillsboro Pke*
*Nashville* ▪ *(615) 891-2534*
*311 12th Ave S*
*Nashville* ▪ *(615) 942-8908*
*1708 21st Ave S*
*Nashville* ▪ *(615) 457-1925*
*5545 Edmondson Pke*
*Nashville* ▪ *(615) 819-0001*
*6688 Nolensville Pke*
*Nashville* ▪
*433 Opry Mills Dr*

**Ted's Montana Grill**    ☉🕮
*Nashville* ▪ *(615) 329-3415*
*2817 W End Ave*

**Wild Cow, The**    ☉★ ⊄LD
*Nashville* ▪ *(615) 262-2717*
*1896 Eastland Ave* ▪ *Vegetarian* ▪ GF
menu features sandwiches made with in-
house prepared GF bread, entrées such as
sweet potato and black bean tacos, and var-
ious salad options. ▪ *www.thewildcow.com*

# TENNESSEE

## ALL OTHER CITIES

**32 Degrees Yogurt Bar**    🕮
*Franklin* ▪ *(615) 771-0793*
*1556 W McEwen Dr*

**Abuelo's**    ☉🕮
*Bartlett* ▪ *(901) 672-0769*
*8274 Hwy 64*
*Chattanooga* ▪ *(423) 855-7400*
*2102 Hamilton Place Blvd*

**Amerigo Italian Restaurant**    ☉$$LD
*Brentwood* ▪ *(615) 377-7070*
*1656 Westgate Cir*
*Memphis* ▪ *(901) 761-4000*
*1239 Ridgeway Rd* ▪ *Italian* ▪ GF menu features a variety of salads such as tomato and
mozzarella, as well as GF entrées such as
flame grilled salmon acuto, prime sirloin,
and wild mushroom pasta. *amerigo.net*

**Au Bon Pain**    🕮
*Cookeville* ▪ *(931) 372-3221*
*1000 N Dixie*

**Bonefish Grill**    ☉🕮
*Chattanooga* ▪ *(423) 892-3175*
*2115 Gunbarrel Rd*
*Murfreesboro* ▪ *(615) 217-1883*
*505 N Thompson Ln*
*Franklin* ▪ *(615) 771-1025*
*3010A Mallory Ln*

Cordova ▪ (901) 753-2220
1250 N Germantown Pkwy Ste 118
Collierville ▪ (901) 854-5822
4680 Merchants Park Cir Ste 200
Johnson City ▪ (423) 434-0247
1902 N Roan St

### Brixx Wood Fired Pizza   ✪★📖
Franklin ▪ (615) 771-7797
1550 W McEwen Dr
Hendersonville ▪ (615) 826-5907
300 Indian Lake Blvd

### Bubba Gump Shrimp Co.   ✪📖
Gatlinburg ▪ (865) 430-3034
900 Pkwy

### Buca di Beppo   ✪📖
Franklin ▪ (615) 778-1321
1722 Galleria Blvd

### Café 1912   $$$D
Memphis ▪ (901) 722-2700
243 S Cooper St ▪ Bistro ▪ GF options include salads and soups, as well as proteins such as baked lemon chicken, steak filets, and seared salmon. ▪ www.cafe1912.com

### Calypso Café   ✪SLD
Franklin ▪ (615) 356-1678
600 Frazier Dr ▪ Vegetarian ▪ The restaurant reports that they are "a popular destination for GF diners" and have many GF options on the menu. The GF section on the website denotes items that are NOT GF. Alert the server when dining in and they can help choose a suitable meal. ▪ www.calypsocafe.com

### Carino's Italian   ✪📖
Johnson City ▪ (423) 952-0790
1902 N Roan St
Pigeon Forge ▪ (865) 868-0790
2425 Pkwy

### Cido's Pizza   ★ĊLD
Powell ▪ (865) 859-0214
7215 Clinton Hwy ▪ Pizza ▪ GF pizza is available. Ask your server which pizza toppings are safe from CC, as some may come in contact with gluten. ▪ www.cidospizza.net

### Couture Cakes & Confections by Bountiful Harvest   ★$$$$$
Hixson ▪ (423) 876-1922
5228 Hixson Pike ▪ Bakery ▪ GF cookies, cupcakes, brownies, bundt cakes, cheesecakes, coffee cakes, loaves, doughnuts, muffins, scones, pizza crust, bread, multi-layered cakes, birthday cakes and gift baskets available. ▪ www.customcouturecakes.com

### Cozy Corner Restaurant   $$LD
Memphis ▪ (901) 527-9158
745 N Pkwy ▪ Barbeque ▪ The Cozy Corner has a variety of meat only BBQ options which are GF. Additionally, the sandwich buns can be omitted upon request in order to make their sandwich menu GF. ▪ www.cozycornerbbq.com

### Demos' Restaurant   ✪SLD
Murfreesboro ▪ (615) 895-3701
1115 NW Broad St
Lebanon ▪ (615) 443-4600
130 Legends Dr
Hendersonville ▪ (615) 824-9097
161 Indian Lake Blvd ▪ Italian ▪ GF menu includes shrimp cocktail, steak and feta salad, stuffed potatoes, steaks, catfish, shrimp scampi, mozzarella chicken, and more. The restaurant recommends notifying your server prior to ordering to ensure CC does not occur. ▪ www.demosrestaurants.com

### Easy Bistro & Bar   $$$D
Chattanooga ▪ (423) 266-1121
203 Broad St ▪ American ▪ Some items on the menu can be prepared GF. Alert server upon arrival and they will guide you through the different GF options on the menu. ▪ easybistro.com

### Erlin Jensen Restaurant   $D
Memphis ▪ (901) 763-3700
1044 S Yates Rd ▪ French ▪ The manager reports that they will "make it happen" for GF diners by omitting ingredients on several main entrées, making them "deliciously GF". Alert the manager upon arrival and they will go over the options. ▪ www.ejensen.com

## Fatz Eatz & Drinkz  📖

*Bristol* ▪ *(423) 968-4498*
*1175 Volunteer Pkwy*
*Elizabethton* ▪ *(423) 547-0001*
*980 Over Mountain Dr*
*Greeneville* ▪ *(423) 787-9090*
*3140 E Andrew Johnson Fwy*
*Johnson City* ▪ *(423) 926-3289*
*3101 W Market St*
*Kingsport* ▪ *(423) 392-9885*
*2610 W Stone Dr*

## Firebirds Wood Fired Grill  ✪📖

*Memphis* ▪ *(901) 379-1300*
*8470 US Hwy 64*
*Collierville* ▪ *(901) 850-1603*
*4600 Merchants Pk Cir*

## First Watch - The Daytime Café  ✪📖

*Brentwood* ▪ *(615) 376-6161*
*210 Franlin Rd*

## Fleming's Prime
## Steakhouse & Wine Bar  ✪📖

*Memphis* ▪ *(901) 761-6200*
*6245 Poplar Ave*

## Folk's Folly  $$$$D

*Memphis* ▪ *(901) 762-8200*
*551 S Mendenhall Rd* ▪ *Steakhouse* ▪ The restaurant reports that most of their steaks are GF, and recommends alerting the server upon arrival to ensure that "proper precautions are taken" when preparing your meal. ▪ *www.folksfolly.com*

## Fox and Hound Pub & Grille  📖

*Cordova* ▪ *(901) 624-9060*
*819 Exocet Dr*
*Memphis* ▪ *(901) 763-2013*
*5101 Sanderlin Rd*
*Antioch* ▪ *(615) 731-4999*
*5316 Mt View Rd*
*Goodlettsville* ▪ *(615) 851-9509*
*786 2 Mile Pkwy*
*Chattanooga* ▪ *(423) 490-1200*
*2040 Hamilton Pl Blvd*
*Johnson City* ▪ *(423) 929-1370*
*2102 N Roan St*

## Fresh 2 Order  ✪$LD

*Chattanooga* ▪ *(423) 826-5000*
*1919 Gunbarrel Rd* ▪ *Café* ▪
*www.fresh2order.com*

## Genghis Grill  📖

*Chattanooga* ▪ *(423) 634-1188*
*138 Market St*
*Memphis* ▪ *(901) 584-0412*
*2362 N Germantown Pkwy*
*Franklin* ▪ *(615) 771-0111*
*600B Frazier Dr*
*Hendersonville* ▪ *(615) 824-9901*
*1050 Glenbrook Wy*
*Jackson* ▪ *(731) 736-0166*
*1231 Vann Dr*
*Memphis* ▪ *(901) 308-4040*
*5849 US Hwy 72*
*Memphis* ▪ *(901) 522-5048*
*7706 Winchester Rd*
*Murfreesboro* ▪ *(615) 494-1181*
*2615 Medical Center Pkwy*
GF menu includes a variety of salads, as well as brown sugar roasted pork loin, salmon entrée without sauce or seasoning, and un-marinated grilled chicken breast. The GF menu also notes which salad dressings, add-ons, sauces, and sides are GF. Area director Craig recommends asking for a manager upon arrival.

## Gondola Pizza House  ✪★$LD

*Cookeville* ▪ *(931) 854-1466*
*1156 S Jefferson Ave* ▪ *Pizza* ▪ GF small pizza and pasta are available. Pasta choices are spaghetti and lasagna. Dedicated equipment for all GF menu items. ▪ *www.theoriginalgondola.com*

## Hard Rock Café  ✪📖

*Gatlinburg* ▪ *(865) 430-7625*
*515 Pkwy*
*Memphis* ▪ *(901) 529-0007*
*315 Beale St*

## Jason's Deli  ✪📖

*Memphis* ▪ *(901) 324-3181*
*3473 Poplar Ave*
*Memphis* ▪ *(901) 844-1840*
*1585 Chickering Ln*

Memphis ▪ (901) 685-3333
1199 Ridgeway Rd
Chattanooga ▪ (423) 296-1096
2115 Gunbarel Rd
Franklin ▪ (615) 771-2626
3065 Mallory Ln
Murfreesboro ▪ (615) 217-3617
452 N Thompson Ln
Jackson ▪ (731) 660-0594
6 Stonebridge Blvd
Johnson City ▪ (423) 467-3354
1091 Hamilton Pl

## Jersey Mike's                                    📖

Clarksville ▪ (931) 906-5001
1960 L Madison St
Spring Hill ▪ (615) 302-8200
5018 Spedale Ct
Franklin ▪ (615) 591-3268
1010 Murfreesboro Rd
Franklin ▪ (615) 435-8812
2000 Mallory Ln
Brentwood ▪ (615) 370-5557
214 Ward Cir
Nashville ▪ (615) 460-9933
736 Thompson Ln
Madison ▪ (615) 868-2246
1706 Gallatin Pike N
Hendersonville ▪ (615) 826-6800
247 W Main St
Hermitage ▪ (615) 885-6080
5506 Old Hickory Blvd
Smyrna ▪ (615) 220-8525
479 Sam Ridley Pkwy W
Murfreesboro ▪ (615) 890-8065
2705 A Old Fort Pkwy
Murfreesboro ▪ (615) 494-1311
2932 S Church St
Lebanon ▪ (615) 444-9886
1315 W Main St
Cookeville ▪ (931) 528-9224
447 S Jefferson Ave
Kingsport ▪ (423) 378-4533
1127-B N Eastman Rd
Kingsport ▪ (423) 239-2600
4260 Fort Henry Dr
Johnson City ▪ (423) 929-1221
1805 W State of Franklin Rd
Johnson City ▪ (423) 282-6019

2106 Mount Castle Dr
Bristol ▪ (423) 968-2838
1430 Volunteer Pkwy S Gate
Franklin ▪ (615) 472-1741
1175 Meridian Blvd
Clarksville ▪ (931) 245-0961
2808 Wilma Rudolph Blvd
Kingsport ▪ (423) 378-7827
2637 E Stone Dr

## Jim 'n Nick's Bar-B-Q                          ✪★📖

Crodova ▪ (901) 388-0998
2359 N Germantown Pkwy
Murfreesboro ▪ (615) 893-1001
436 N Thompson Ln
Smyrna ▪ (615) 220-8508
523 Sam Ridley Pkwy W

## Joe's Crab Shack                               ✪📖

Memphis ▪ (901) 384-7478
7990 Horizon Center Blvd
Sevierville ▪ (865) 774-3023
1605 Pkwy

## Johnny Brusco's
## New York Style Pizza                           ★📖

Johnson City ▪ (423) 477-4992
2111 N Roan St
Kingsport ▪ (423) 247-5646
1700 n Eastman Rd

## Lone Star Steakhouse & Saloon                  ✪📖

Elizabethton ▪ (423) 543-1313
1361 Hwy 19 E Bypass

## Matteo's Pizzeria                              ★$LD

Brentwood ▪ (615) 661-5811
1800 Carothers Pkwy ▪ Pizza ▪ GF pizza
crust is made in-house. According to
the restaurant, they take many precautions against CC and their GF prep room
is designed "like a surgical suite." They
also ship their GF crusts nationwide. ▪
www.matteospizza.com

## Mauricio's                                     ★$$LD

Cookeville ▪ (931) 528-2456
232 N Peachtree Ave ▪ Italian ▪ GF spaghetti is available. ▪ mauricioscookeville.com

## Melting Pot, The    ✪⬚

*Chattanooga* ▪ *(423) 893-5237*
*2553 Lifestyle Wy*
*Memphis* ▪ *(901) 380-9500*
*2828 Wolfcreek Pkwy*

## O'Charley's    ⬚

*Alcoa* ▪ *(865) 379-9424*
*364 Fountainview Cir*
*Antioch* ▪ *(615) 731-7606*
*923 Bell Rd*
*Bartlett* ▪ *(901) 373-5602*
*6045 Stage Rd*
*Brentwood* ▪ *(615) 370-0274*
*100 E Park Dr*
*Chattanooga* ▪ *(423) 892-3343*
*2340 Shallowford Village Dr*
*Chattanooga* ▪ *(423) 877-8966*
*5031 Hixson Pike*
*Clarksville* ▪ *(931) 552-7800*
*674 N Riverside Dr*
*Clarksville* ▪ *(931) 552-6335*
*2792 Wilma Rudolph Blvd*
*Cleveland* ▪ *(423) 472-2192*
*148 Sgt Paul Huff Pkwy NW*
*Collierville* ▪ *(901) 861-5811*
*656 W Poplar Ave*
*Columbia* ▪ *(931) 840-4353*
*202 S James Campbell Blvd*
*Cookeville* ▪ *(931) 520-1898*
*1401 Interstate Dr*
*Cordova* ▪ *(901) 754-6201*
*1040 N Germantown Pkwy*
*Dickson* ▪ *(615) 446-8085*
*2409 Hwy 46 S*
*Franklin* ▪ *(615) 794-9438*
*1202 Murfreesboro Rd*
*Gallatin* ▪ *(615) 230-8103*
*1009 Village Green Crossing*
*Goodlettsville* ▪ *(615) 859-4704*
*912 Rivergate Pkwy*
*Hendersonville* ▪ *(615) 826-9543*
*212 Indian Lake Blvd*
*Hermitage* ▪ *(615) 883-6993*
*5500 Old Hickory Blvd*
*Jackson* ▪ *(731) 661-0840*
*644 Carriage House Rd*
*Johnson City* ▪ *(423) 854-9110*
*112 Broyels Dr*

*Kingsport* ▪ *(423) 246-8868*
*1920 N Eastman Rd*
*Lebanon* ▪ *(615) 453-1185*
*902 Murfreesboro Rd*
*Manchester* ▪ *(931) 728-6336*
*2367 Hillsboro Blvd*
*Memphis* ▪ *(901) 388-8022*
*2844 New Brunswick Rd*
*Morristown* ▪ *(423) 587-0175*
*3412 W Andrew Johnson Hwy*
*Mt. Juliet* ▪ *(615) 773-3619*
*401 S Mt Juiet Rd*
*Murfreesboro* ▪ *(615) 895-4441*
*2450 Old Fort Pkwy*
*Murfreesboro* ▪ *(615) 898-0390*
*1006 Memorial Blvd*
*Pigeon Forge* ▪ *(865) 429-2201*
*2167 Pkwy*
*Smyrna* ▪ *(615) 220-1772*
*820 Expo Dr*
*Spring Hill* ▪ *(931) 486-3822*
*2000 Crossings Cir*
*Springfield* ▪ *(615) 382-3321*
*3535 Tom Austin Hwy*

## P.F. Chang's China Bistro    ✪★⬚

*Chattanooga* ▪ *(423) 242-0045*
*2110 Hamilton Place Blvd*
*Franklin* ▪ *(615) 503-9640*
*439 Cool Springs Blvd*
*Memphis* ▪ *(901) 818-3889*
*1181 Ridgeway Rd*

## Pei Wei Asian Diner    ✪⬚

*Brentwood* ▪ *(615) 514-4990*
*101 Creekside Xing*
*Cordova* ▪ *(901) 382-1822*
*2257 N Germantown Pkwy*
*Memphis* ▪ *(901) 722-3780*
*1680 Union Ave*
*Murfreesboro* ▪ *(615) 896-3886*
*1911 Medical Ctr Pkwy*
*Franklin* ▪ *(615) 778-1676*
*1560 W McEwen Dr*

## Restaurant Iris    $$**LD**

*Memphis* ▪ *(901) 590-2828*
*2146 Monroe Ave* ▪ *French* ▪ The restaurant reports that the staff is "very familiar
with accommodating GF diners". They are

"more than happy" to alter ingredients and sides to make dishes suitable for GF guests. Alert the server upon arrival. ▪ *www.restaurantiris.com*

### Romano's Macaroni Grill ✪★📖
*Chattanooga* ▪ *(423) 894-2221*
*2271 Gunbarel Rd*
*Franklin* ▪ *(615) 771-7002*
*1712 Galleria Blvd*
*Germantown* ▪ *(901) 753-6588*
*6705 Poplar Ave*
*Memphis* ▪ *(901) 266-4565*
*2859 N Germantown Pkwy*
*Murfreesboro* ▪ *(615) 893-6670*
*2535 Medical Center Pkwy*

### Ruth's Chris Steak House ✪📖
*Memphis* ▪ *(901) 761-0055*
*6120 Poplar Ave*

### Shane's Rib Shack ✪📖
*Cleveland* ▪ *(423) 476-5970*
*4484 Frontage Rd NW*
*Franklin* ▪ *(615) 591-8626*
*3046 Columbia Ave*
*Hendersonville* ▪ *(615) 264-2597*
*203 N Anderson Ln*

### Smokey Bones 📖
*Chattanooga* ▪ *(423) 893-7850*
*2225 Ginbarrel Rd*
*Johnson City* ▪ *(423) 979-1706*
*1905 N Roan St*

### St. John's Restaurant & Meeting Place $$$D
*Chattanooga* ▪ *(423) 266-4400*
*1278 Market St* ▪ *Modern American* ▪ GF options include vegan goods plate, burger without the bun, beef filet, tilefish, and steak frites. Confirm the timeliness of this information before dining in. Alert the server upon arrival. ▪ *www.stjohnsrestaurant.com*

### Sticky Fingers Smokehouse ✪📖
*Chattanooga* ▪ *(423) 265-7427*
*420 Broad St*
*Chattanooga* ▪ *(423) 899-7427*
*2031 Hamilton Place Blvd*

### Sweet Cece's 📖
*Brentwood* ▪ *(615) 760-5599*
*269 Franklin Rd*
*Chattanooga* ▪ *(423) 710-1633*
*330 Frazier Ave*
*Franklin* ▪ *(615) 472-8260*
*3021 Mallory Ln*
*Farragut* ▪ *(865) 671-0070*
*161 Brooklawn St*
*Franklin* ▪ *(615) 807-1412*
*500 W Main St*
*Gallatin* ▪ *(615) 989-1431*
*1101 Nashville Pike*
*Goodlettsville* ▪ *(615) 239-8267*
*919 Conference Dr*
*Greenville* ▪ *(423) 639-2323*
*1337 Tusculum Blvd*
*Hendersonville* ▪ *(615) 265-8014*
*162 E. Main St*
*Jackson* ▪ *(731) 661-9860*
*1142 Vann Dr*
*Kingsport* ▪ *(423) 230-0565*
*1880 N Eastman Rd*
*Memphis* ▪ *(901) 767-1422*
*4615 Poplar Ave*
*Murfreesboro* ▪ *(615) 849-1060*
*2615 Medical Ctr Pkwy*
*Murfreesboro* ▪ *(615) 900-3383*
*2658 New Salem Hwy*
*Smyrna* ▪ *(615) 267-0828*
*315 Sam Ridley Pkwy*
*Spring Hill* ▪ *(931) 489-6000*
*1005 Crossings Blvd*

### Taco Mamacita ⊄LD
*Chattanooga* ▪ *(423) 648-6262*
*109 N Market St*
*Nashville* ▪ *(615) 730-8552*
*1200 Villa Pl* ▪ *Mexican* ▪ GF items include guacamole, tacos with soft corn tortilla. Soups and salads are served with no tortilla strips. Alert server upon arrival. ▪ *tacomamacita.com*

### Texas De Brazil Churrascaria ★📖
*Memphis* ▪ *(901) 526-7600*
*150 Peabody Pl*

**Tony Roma's**                               📖
*Pigeon Forge* ▪ (865) 908-8777
*2050 Pkwy*

# TEXAS

## AUSTIN

**Abuelo's**                                  ✪📖
*Austin* ▪ (512) 306-0857
*2901 S Capital of Texas Hwy*

**Austin's Pizza**                            ★$LD
*Austin* ▪ (512) 795-8888
*2324 Guadalupe St*
*Austin* ▪ (512) 795-8888
*3637 Far W Blvd*
*Austin* ▪ (512) 795-8888
*1600 W 35th St*
*Austin* ▪ (512) 795-8888
*3638 Bee Cave Rd*
*Austin* ▪ (512) 795-8888
*10900 Research Blvd*
*Austin* ▪ (512) 795-8888
*7301 Ranch Rd 620 N*
*Austin* ▪ (512) 795-8888
*1817 S Lamar Blvd*
*Austin* ▪ (512) 795-8888
*3601 W William Cannon Dr*
*Austin* ▪ (512) 795-8888
*9900 S IH-35* ▪ *Pizza* ▪ GF pizza is available
in the 10-inch size. A YouTube video detailing their entire GF preparation process
is available online. YouTube channel: OfficialAustinsPizza. ▪ *www.austinspizza.com*

**Beets Living Food Café**                    $BLD
*Austin* ▪ (512) 477-2338
*1611 W 5th St* ▪ *Café* ▪ Staff reports that
everything on the menu is GF. Selections
include a taco plate, curried carrot soup,
and rainbow salad. Confirm the timeliness of this information before dining in. ▪
*www.beetscafe.com*

**BJ's Restaurant and Brewhouse** ✪★📖
*Austin* ▪ (512) 349-9000
*10515 Mopac Expwy*

**Brick Oven Restaurant**                     ✪★$LD
*Austin* ▪ (512) 292-3939
*9911 Brodie Ln*
*Austin* ▪ (512) 477-7006
*1209 Red River St*
*Austin* ▪ (512) 345-6181
*10710 Research Blvd* ▪ *Italian* ▪ GF options
available at all three locations. All locations
offer GF pizza, in the medium size and
GF pasta. The Research Boulevard location offers GF carrot cake and beer and
the Brodie lane location offers a GF menu
with the medium pizza and pasta as well
as GF bread for appetizers, carrot cake and
brownies. ▪ *brickovenaustin.com*

**Buca di Beppo**                             ✪📖
*Austin* ▪ (512) 342-8462
*3612 Tudor Blvd*

**Cantina Laredo**                            📖
*Austin* ▪ (512) 542-9670
*201 W 3rd St*

**Carino's Italian**                          ✪📖
*Austin* ▪ (512) 506-8181
*11620 N Fm 620*
*Austin* ▪ (512) 292-1658
*9500 S Ih 35 Ste B*
*Austin* ▪ (512) 989-6464
*12901 N I-35 Service Rd*

**Casa de Luz**                               ✪$BLD
*Austin* ▪ (512) 476-2535
*1701 Toomey Rd* ▪ *Organic* ▪ Menu changes
daily and is almost always 100% GF. Call
ahead to confirm GF status of the daily
menu. ▪ *www.casadeluz.org*

**Clay Pit, The**                             $$LD
*Austin* ▪ (512) 322-5131
*1601 Guadalupe St* ▪ *Indian* ▪ Staff reports
that almost all items on the menu are
naturally GF and are marked as such on the
menu. Since the menu is primarily GF, the
restaurant reports that the chance of CC is
low. ▪ *www.claypit.com*

### Conscious Cravings ⟨LD
*Austin* ▪ *(512) 782-0546*
*1901 Rio Grande St*
*Austin* ▪ *(512) 582-9182*
*1311 S 1st St* ▪ *Vegetarian* ▪ Restaurant reports that everything on their menu is GF except for tortillas/wraps, seitan and couscous. Quinoa-rice pilaf may be substituted for the tortilla in any of their wraps, and several salads are also available. ▪ *www.consciouscravingsaustin.com*

### CraigO's Pizza and Pasta ★$LD
*Austin* ▪ *(512) 891-7200*
*4970 Hwy 290 W*
*Austin* ▪ *(512) 282-7499*
*11215 S IH 35*
*Austin* ▪ *(512) 323-0660*
*5501 Balcones Dr* ▪ *Pizza* ▪ GF pizza is available in 10" and 14" sizes. ▪ *www.craigospizzaandpasta.com*

### Eastside Café ✪$$LD
*Austin* ▪ *(512) 476-5858*
*2113 Manor Rd* ▪ *American* ▪ GF menu includes Greek chicken salad, poblano chicken sandwich without a bun, skewered pork tenderloin, and eggs benedict without the english muffin. Confirm the timeliness of this information before dining in. ▪ *www.eastsidecafeaustin.com*

### Eddie V's ✪📖
*Austin* ▪ *(512) 472-1860*
*301 E 5th St*
*Austin* ▪ *(512) 342-2642*
*9400 B Arboretum Blvd*

### Fire Bowl Café ✪📖
*Austin* ▪ *(512) 795-8998*
*9828 Great Hills*
*Austin* ▪ *(512) 899-8998*
*5601 Brodie Ln*

### Fleming's Prime Steakhouse & Wine Bar ✪📖
*Austin* ▪ *(512) 457-1500*
*320 E 2nd St*
*Austin* ▪ *(512) 835-9463*
*11600 Century Oaks Ter*

### Food 4 Fitness Café ⟨BLD
*Austin* ▪ *(512) 472-1674*
*1112 N Lamar Blvd* ▪ *Organic* ▪ Manager Sarah reports that the café has several GF options, including kale salads, quinoa salads, meat entrées with quinoa on the side, and raw desserts. She recommends asking for a manager upon arrival, but she also notes that all ingredients are marked in the deli cases. Located in Castle Hill Specialized Fitness. ▪ *www.food4fitness.com*

### Freebirds on the Fly ✪📖
*Austin* ▪ *(512) 836-9700*
*11101 Burnet Rd*
*Austin* ▪ *(512) 326-4100*
*4032 S Lamar Blvd*
*Austin* ▪ *(512) 451-5514*
*1000 E 41st St*
*Austin* ▪ *(512) 462-3512*
*515 S Congress Ave*
*Austin* ▪ *(512) 251-9701*
*1100 Ctr Ridge Dr*

### Garrido's ✪$$LD
*Austin* ▪ *(512) 320-8226*
*360 Nueces St* ▪ *Mexican* ▪ "95% GF" menu includes include a selection of tacos, enchiladas, chile rellenos, and gulf red snapper. Vanilla bean crème brûlée is available for dessert. Confirm the timeliness of this information before dining in. ▪ *www.garridosaustin.com*

### Genghis Grill 📖
*Austin* ▪ *(512) 891-0152*
*4477 S Lamar*

### Grove Wine Bar & Kitchen, The ★$$LD
*Austin* ▪ *(512) 327-8822*
*6317 Bee Cave Rd* ▪ *American* ▪ GF bread, pizza crust, and pasta available on request, just alert server beforehand. Call and make a reservation in order to confirm availability before dining in restaurant. ▪ *grovewinebar.com*

### Guero's Taco Bar                    ✪₵LD
*Austin* ▪ *(512) 447-7688*
*1412 S Congress Ave* ▪ *Mexican* ▪ GF
menu includes huevos rancheros, black
bean & cheese tamales, enchiladas, tacos,
and several soups and salads. The rice
has trace elements of gluten, so all GF
entrées must be ordered without rice. ▪
*www.guerostacobar.com*

### Hula Hut                           ✪$LD
*Austin* ▪ *(512) 476-4852*
*3825 Lake Austin Blvd* ▪ *Hawaiian* ▪
GF menu includes guacamole salad,
black beans, the Hula Hut burger with
no bun, grilled salmon, the Hula Hut
chop salad, and flan for dessert. ▪
*www.hulahut.com/Our_Food.pdf*

### Iron Cactus                        ✪$LD
*Austin* ▪ *(512) 472-9240*
*606 Trinity St*
*Austin* ▪ *(512) 794-8778*
*10001 Stonelake Blvd* ▪ *Mexican* ▪ GF
menu available. GF items include steak
fajita nachos, taco salad, chipotle smoked
pork chops, Yucatan fish tacos, vanilla bean
flan, Mexican chocolate mousse and more.
▪ *www.ironcactus.com*

### Jason's Deli                       ✪📖
*Austin* ▪ *(512) 345-9586*
*10225 Research Blvd*
*Austin* ▪ *(512) 328-0200*
*3300 Bee Cave Rd*
*Austin* ▪ *(512) 258-7888*
*13729 Research Blvd*
*Austin* ▪ *(512) 453-8666*
*1000 E 41st St*
*Austin* ▪ *(512) 280-0990*
*9600 S Interstate 35*

### Jasper's                           $$$LD
*Austin* ▪ *(512) 834-4111*
*11506 Century Oaks Terrace* ▪ *American* ▪
Any item on the menu can be made GF except for the pizza, soup, crab cakes or blue
cheese chips. Alert server upon arrival. ▪
*www.kentrathbun.com*

### Java Dive Organic Café             ✪★₵BL
*Austin* ▪ *(512) 266-5885*
*1607 Ranch Road 620 N* ▪ *Organic* ▪
Extensive GF menu includes quesadillas, falafel, paninis, bagels, and more. For
weekend brunch, it offers banana bread
French toast, waffles, and pancakes, among
other options. A wide variety of GF specialty items, including bread, is available. They
have dedicated fryers and other utensils
when dealing with GF items. Alert server
upon arrival. ▪ *www.javadivecafe.com*

### Jersey Mike's                      📖
*Austin* ▪ *(512) 250-8700*
*11521 FM 620 N*
*Austin* ▪ *(512) 338-4200*
*10001 Research Blvd*
*Austin* ▪ *(512) 233-6333*
*9500 S IH-35*
*Austin* ▪ *(512) 891-0222*
*4404 W William Cannon*

### Joe's Crab Shack                   ✪📖
*Austin* ▪ *(512) 441-1010*
*600 E Riverside Dr*

### Ka-Prow Pan Asian Bistro          ✪$LD
*Austin* ▪ *(512) 990-2111*
*1200 W Howard Ln* ▪ *Asian* ▪ GF items
indicated on menu. Items include satey,
edamame, crystal noodle soup, ka-prow
fried rice, Burmese chicken, pad thai,
lettuce wrap, papaya salad, seaweed
salad, ginger tilapia, spicy grilled duck,
and all curries. Confirm the timeliness
of this information before dining in. ▪
*www.kaprowleaf.com*

### Kobe Japanese Steakhouse         $$$LD
*Austin* ▪ *(512) 288-7333*
*13492 Research Blvd* ▪ *Japanese* ▪ The
restaurant reports that every item on
the menu can be made GF and can be
prepared separately from items that
may contain gluten. Alert a server upon
arrival and they will notify the chefs. ▪
*www.kobeaustin.com*

### Koriente ✪₵LD
Austin ▪ (512) 275-0852
621 E 7th St ▪ Asian ▪ Several menu items can be modified to be GF, including the obake bowl with shrimp or tofu, smoked salmon tapioca wrap, and pan-seared ahi tuna. Be sure to alert your server that your meal must be GF. ▪ www.koriente.com

### Maggiano's Little Italy ★📖
Austin ▪ (512) 501-7870
10910 Domain Dr

### Mama Fu's Asian House ✪📖
Austin ▪ (512) 637-6774
100 Colorado St
Austin ▪ (512) 637-6771
11301 Lakeline Blvd
Austin ▪ (512) 637-6772
9600 S I-35
Austin ▪ (512) 637-6773
4615 M Lamar Blvd

### Matt's El Rancho
### Mexican Restaurant $$LD
Austin ▪ (512) 462-9333
2613 S Lamar Blvd ▪ Mexican ▪ Manager Billy reports that the restaurant is very familiar with the GF diet and that most items on the menu can be prepared GF. He recommends asking for a manager upon arrival so they can go over the menu and help guests make a decision on a GF meal. ▪ www.mattselrancho.com

### Maudie's Tex-Mex ✪$$BLD
Austin ▪ (512) 832-0900
10205 N Lamar Blvd
Austin ▪ (512) 473-3740
2608 W 7th St
Austin ▪ (512) 306-8080
3801 N Capital Of Texas Hwy
Austin ▪ (512) 280-8700
9911 Brodie Ln
Austin ▪ (512) 440-8088
1212 S Lamar
Austin ▪ (512) 263-1116
12506 Shops Pkwy ▪ Tex-Mex ▪ GF menu includes guacamole salad, tortilla bean dip, fajita salad, beef, chicken, or shrimp fajitas, enchilada platters, and more. Restaurant notes that they are "very conscious" of the GF diet. ▪ www.maudies.com

### Melting Pot, The ✪📖
Austin ▪ (512) 401-2424
13343 Research Blvd
Austin ▪ (512) 401-2424
305 E 3rd St

### Mother's Café & Garden ₵LD
Austin ▪ (512) 451-3994
4215 Duval St ▪ Vegetarian ▪ GF items include enchiladas, stir fry, salads and salad dressings, tofu, southwest stuffed peppers as well as some brunch items. ▪ www.motherscafeaustin.com

### Mr. Natural ★₵BLD
Austin ▪ (512) 916-9223
2414A S Lamar Blvd
Austin ▪ (512) 477-5228
1901 E Cesar Chavez St
Austin ▪ (512) 234-8543
205 E Rundberg Ln ▪ Vegetarian ▪ GF items marked on the menu include tamales, several omelets, crispy tacos, and various types of migas. GF bread, pies, cakes, muffins, brownies, and cookies are available, though they may have to be specially ordered. ▪ www.mrnatural-austin.com

### New India Cuisine ✪$LD
Austin ▪ (512) 445-9727
2304 S Congress Ave ▪ Indian ▪ GF items are marked on the menu and include vindaloo, coconut chicken curry, channa masala, and much more. GF bhakri (multi grain unleavened bread) is available. Confirm the timeliness of this information before dining in. ▪ www.newindia.us

### North by Northwest Restaurant & Brewery ✪$$LD
Austin ▪ (512) 467-6969
10010 Capital Of Texas Hwy N ▪ American ▪ GF menu includes jumbo shrimp cocktail, salads, NXNW chicken, grilled duck breast, fresh vegetable grille, At-

lantic salmon, smoked pork tenderloin and grilled center cut sirloin. ▪
*www.nxnwbrew.com*

### P.F. Chang's China Bistro          ✪★▢
*Austin ▪ (512) 457-8300*
*201 San Jacinto Blvd*
*Austin ▪ (512) 231-0208*
*10114 Jollyville Rd*

### Pappasito's Cantina                 ▢
*Austin ▪ (512) 459-9214*
*6513 I-35 N*

### Pei Wei Asian Diner                 ✪▢
*Austin ▪ (512) 996-0095*
*13429 N Hwy 183*
*Austin ▪ (512) 382-2990*
*4200 S Lamar Blvd*
*Austin ▪ (512) 382-3860*
*1000 E 41st St*
*Austin ▪ (512) 691-3060*
*12901 N I-35*

### People's RX                         ★¢BLD
*Austin ▪ (512) 459-9090*
*4018 N Lamar Blvd*
*Austin ▪ (512) 219-9499*
*13860 US 183 N*
*Austin ▪ (512) 444-8866*
*3801 S Lamar Blvd*
*Austin ▪ (512) 327-8877*
*4201 Westbank Dr ▪ Bakery & Café ▪*
Health food store and pharmacy offering various GF items like burritos, bread,
donuts, and muffins. Selection varies by
location. ▪ *www.peoplesrx.com*

### Promise Pizza                       ★$LD
*Austin ▪ (512) 345-7492*
*10225 Research Blvd Suite #110 ▪ Pizza ▪*
A GF pizza is available in the 10 inch and
12 inch sizes and all the toppings are GF.
Manager said they take severe precautions to prevent CC such as using completely separate prep areas and utensils. ▪
*www.promisepizza.com*

### Red Brick Pizza                     ✪★▢
*Austin ▪ (512) 345-6060*
*10515 N Mopac*

### Rio's Brazilian                     ✪★$BLD
*Austin ▪ (512) 828-6617*
*408 N Pleasant Valley Rd ▪ Brazilian ▪* GF
menu selections include caldo verde soup,
stuffed yucca root pastries, and Brazilian
chicken stroganoff served over rice. GF
Brazilian pão de queijo (cheese bread) is
available, along with several GF desserts.
Confirm the timeliness of this information
before dining in. ▪ *www.riosofaustin.com*

### Romano's Macaroni Grill             ✪★▢
*Austin ▪ (512) 795-0460*
*9828 Great Hills Trl*
*Austin ▪ (512) 693-9076*
*701 E Stassney Ln*

### Ruth's Chris Steak House            ✪▢
*Austin ▪ (512) 477-7884*
*107 W 6th St*

### Snack Bar                           ✪★$BLD
*Austin ▪ (512) 445-2626*
*1224 S Congress Ave ▪ American ▪* GF
items are marked on the menu, and include
tomato lemongrass curry, rock shrimp
ceviche, steak & frites, and much more.
GF bread is available, as well as several GF
desserts. Restaurant cautions that they "do
their best" but that CC may be a possibility.
A server will be able to advise which items
are the safest. ▪ *www.snackbaraustin.com*

### Snap Kitchen                        ✪$BLD
*Austin ▪ (512) 459-9000*
*4616 Triangle Ave*
*Austin ▪ (512) 479-5959*
*1014 W 6th St*
*Austin ▪ (512) 459-9000*
*501 Congress*
*Austin ▪ (512) 346-5959*
*10001 Research Blvd ▪ American ▪*
Specialty order foods made fresh daily.
GF menu online. Menu includes protein
shakes, spinach and goat cheese scramble
and baked vegetable quiche for breakfast.
GF Lunch includes grass-fed bison quinoa
hash, chicken sweet potatoes with green
beans and chicken with butternut squash
spaghetti; Dinner includes crispy chicken,

Santa Fe pork and crispy Scottish salmon. GF snack items and dessert are also prepared. ▪ *www.snapkitchen.com*

### Steeping Room, The    ✪¢**BLD**
*Austin* ▪ (512) 977-8337
*11410 Century Oaks Terrace Suite 112*
*Austin* ▪ (512) 467-2663
*4400 N Lamar Blvd* ▪ *Teahouse* ▪ The restaurant reports that everything from their entrées to their pastries can be made GF. They recommend indicating to the server that it is an "allergy" as opposed to a preference, and note that the staff will "try their hardest" to suit the needs of their customers. ▪ *www.thesteepingroom.com*

### Tam Deli & Café    ¢**LD**
*Austin* ▪ (512) 834-6458
*8222 N Lamar Blvd* ▪ *Vietnamese* ▪ GF options available. Ask for manager upon arrival.

### Wild Wood Bake House & Café    $**BLD**
*Austin* ▪ (512) 327-9660
*3016 Guadalupe St* ▪ *Bakery & Café* ▪ GF bakery offering breads, muffins, cookies, cupcakes, pies, cakes, granola, pizza & pie crust, lasagna, tamales, tiramisu, cheesecake, and more. Breakfast and lunch menu available as well offering salads, soups, pizza, variety of baked goods, French toast, breakfast tacos, GF sandwiches and enchiladas. ▪ *www.wildwoodartcafe.com*

### Z'Tejas Southwestern Grill    ✪★▣
*Austin* ▪ (512) 346-3506
*9400 A Arboretum Blvd*
*Austin* ▪ (512) 388-7772
*10525 W Parmer Ln*
*Austin* ▪ (512) 478-5355
*1110 W 6th St*

### Zen Japanese Food Fast    ★¢**LD**
*Austin* ▪ (512) 451-4811
*2900 W Anderson Ln*
*Austin*
*2201 Speedway*
*Austin* ▪ (512) 300-2633
*3423 Guadalupe St* ▪ *Japanese* ▪ Eight GF sauces available and a wide range of sides and salads to choose from. These can be substituted into any dish on the menu, and the fully trained kitchen staff will use clean woks and utensils to cook GF meals. Confirm the timeliness of this information before dining in. GF rice noodles are available. ▪ *www.eatzen.com*

### Zio's    ✪▣
*Arlington* ▪ (817) 468-1411
*5005 S Cooper St*

### Zpizza    ✪▣
*Austin* ▪ (512) 394-9331
*5701 W Slaughter Ln*

# TEXAS

## DALLAS

### Asian Mint    ✪$$**LD**
*Dallas* ▪ (214) 219-6468
*4246 Oak Lawn Ave*
*Dallas* ▪ (214) 363-6655
*11617 N Central Expwy Suite 135* ▪ *Asian* ▪ The restaurant reports that bold items on the menu can be made GF. Separate GF sauces are provided for certain dishes and proper cleaning procedures are used. Alert the server upon arrival. ▪ *asianmint.com*

### Au Bon Pain    ▣
*Dallas* ▪ (214) 661-7466
*200 Crescent Ct*
*Dallas* ▪ (972) 574-1562
*Dallas/Ft. Worth Int'l Airport- Terminal C Gate 33*
*Dallas* ▪ (972) 574-6342
*Dallas/Ft. Worth Int'l Airport- Terminal A Gate 14*
*Dallas* ▪ (972) 574-6341
*Dallas/Ft. Worth Int'l Airport- Terminal A Gate 37*
*Dallas* ▪ (972) 574-6340
*Dallas/Ft. Worth Int'l Airport- Terminal A Gate 37*

*Dallas* ■ *(972) 574-7600*
*Dallas/Ft. Worth Int'l Airport- Terminal B*
*Gate 20*
*Dallas* ■ *(972) 574-1533*
*Dallas/Ft. Worth Int'l Airport- Terminal C*
*Gate 21*
*Dallas* ■ *(972) 973-4338*
*Dallas/Ft. Worth Int'l Airport- Terminal D*
*Dallas* ■ *(214) 220-9027*
*1445 Ross Ave*
*Dallas* ■ *(972) 566-6880*
*7777 Forest Ln*
*Dallas* ■ *(214) 345-5076*
*8198 Walnut Hill Rd*

**Banana Leaf Thai Cuisine**            **$LD**
*Dallas* ■ *(972) 713-0123*
*17370 Preston Rd* ■ *Thai* ■ Every item on
the menu can be made GF. Alert a server
upon arrival. ■ *www.thaibananaleaf.com*

**BJ's Restaurant and Brewhouse** ✪★⌂
*Dallas* ■ *(972) 392-4600*
*4901 Belt Line Rd*

**Blue Mesa Grill**                      ✪**$LD**
*Dallas* ■ *(214) 378-8686*
*7700 W Northwest Hwy* ■ *Southwest* ■
Ask for the "Nutritional Brochure," which
contains a list of GF items and advice on
GF ordering. This information is also available online. GF options include red chili
crusted salmon, free range chicken with
roasted serrano pesto, carne asada, Baja
shrimp, and more. For dessert, they offer
flan. ■ *www.bluemesagrill.com*

**Bob's Steak & Chop House**            ⌂
*Dallas* ■ *(214) 528-9446*
*4300 Lemmon Ave*
*Dallas* ■ *(214) 652-4800*
*555 S Lamar St*

**Buca di Beppo**                       ✪⌂
*Dallas* ■ *(214) 361-8462*
*7843 Park Ln*

**Cantina Laredo**                      ⌂
*Dallas* ■ *(214) 350-5227*
*165 Inwood Vlge*
*Dallas* ■ *(469) 828-4818*
*17808 Dallas Pkwy*

*Dallas* ■ *(214) 821-5785*
*2031 Abrams Rd*
*Dallas* ■ *(214) 265-1610*
*6025 Royal Ln*

**Capital Grille, The**                 ✪⌂
*Dallas* ■ *(214) 303-0500*
*500 Crescent Ct*

**Del Frisco's**
**Double Eagle Steak House**            ⌂
*Dallas* ■ *(972) 490-9000*
*5251 Spring Valley Rd*

**Eddie V's**                           ✪⌂
*Dallas* ■ *(214) 890-1500*
*4023 Oak Lawn Ave*

**Freebirds on the Fly**                ✪⌂
*Dallas* ■ *(972) 788-1828*
*5000 Belt Line Rd*
*Dallas* ■ *(214) 265-9992*
*5500 Greenville Ave*

**Genghis Grill**                       ⌂
*Dallas* ■ *(972) 490-0300*
*13350 Dallas Pkwy*
*Dallas* ■ *(214) 987-3330*
*5500 Greenville Ave*
*Dallas* ■ *(214) 350-4554*
*10220 Technology Blvd E*
*Dallas* ■ *(214) 219-5426*
*4140 Lemmon Ave*

**Hard Rock Café**                      ✪⌂
*Dallas* ■ *(469) 341-7625*
*2211 N Houston St*

**Hillstone Restaurants**               ⌂
*Dallas* ■ *(214) 691-8991*
*8300 A Preston Rd*

**In-N-Out Burger**                     ⌂
*Dallas* ■ *(800) 786-1000*
*12909 Midway Rd*
*Dallas* ■ *(800) 786-1000*
*15260 Dallas Pkwy*
*Dallas* ■ *(800) 786-1000*
*7909 Lyndon B Johnson Fwy*
*Dallas* ■ *(800) 786-1000*
*7940 N Central Expwy*

## Iron Cactus                              ✪$LD
*Dallas* ▪ *(214) 749-4766*
*1520 Main St* ▪ *Mexican* ▪ GF menu available.
GF items include steak fajita nachos, taco
salad, chipotle smoked pork chops, Yucatan
fish tacos, vanilla bean flan, Mexican chocolate mousse and more. ▪ *www.ironcactus.com*

## Jason's Deli                            ✪📖
*Dallas* ▪ *(214) 904-8200*
*10220 Technology Blvd E*
*Dallas* ▪ *(214) 739-1800*
*7412 Greenville Ave*
*Dallas* ▪ *(972) 818-3354*
*18111 Dallas Pkwy*
*Dallas* ▪ *(214) 672-9340*
*1409 Main St*

## Jersey Mike's                           📖
*Dallas* ▪ *(214) 350-7611*
*5301 W Lovers Ln*
*Dallas* ▪ *(214) 692-6981*
*5521 Greenville Ave*
*Dallas* ▪ *(972) 387-1900*
*14060 Dallas Pkwy*
*Dallas* ▪ *(214) 691-7827*
*8411 Preston Rd*
*Dallas* ▪ *(214) 520-7827*
*3001 Knox St*

## Joe's Crab Shack                        ✪📖
*Dallas* ▪ *(214) 654-0909*
*10250 E Technology Blvd*

## Kozy Kitchen, The                       ★$$$BL
*Dallas* ▪ *(214) 219-5044*
*4433 Mckinney Ave* ▪ *Café* ▪ 99% of the
menu is GF. Anything with an asterisk
on the menu is not GF. GF foods include
breakfast tacos, pancakes and French
toast, buffalo and fish tacos, chicken
marsala, buffalo bolognese, wild salmon
and all burgers can be made GF. Dessert
includes GF cookies and cakes including
the German chocolate, chocolate chip
brownie and cookie monster cake. ▪
*www.thekozy.net*

## Lawry's The Prime Rib                    $$$$D
*Dallas* ▪ *(972) 503-6688*
*14655 Dallas Pkwy* ▪ *Steakhouse* ▪ Manager Christopher at Beverly Hills strongly
recommends speaking to a manager
prior to dining at any Lawry's restaurant
to "ensure that they are aware of your
situation and able to help you navigate
through their individual menus." He notes
that plain prime rib (no gravy, no au jus)
and lobster among items that are typically
GF, but again stresses the importance of
notifying the server and manager on duty
so they can ensure safe preparation. ▪
*www.lawrysonline.com*

## Maggiano's Little Italy                  ★📖
*Dallas* ▪ *(214) 360-0707*
*8687 N Central Expy Ste 205*

## Mansion Restaurant                       $$$$BLD
*Dallas* ▪ *(214) 559-2100*
*2821 Turtle Creek Blvd* ▪ *American* ▪ The
restaurant reports that the chef and restaurant staff will "do everything they can" to
accommodate GF diners. They note that
the meat and seafood dishes are "the safest
bet" for GF guests. Alert the server upon
arrival. ▪ *www.mansiononturtlecreek.com*

## Melting Pot, The                        ✪📖
*Dallas* ▪ *(972) 960-7027*
*4900 Belt Line Rd*

## Morton's Steakhouse                      ✪📖
*Dallas* ▪ *(214) 741-2277*
*2222 McKinney Ave*

## P.F. Chang's China Bistro                ✪★📖
*Dallas* ▪ *(214) 265-8669*
*225 Northpark Ctr*
*Dallas* ▪ *(972) 818-3336*
*18323 Dallas Pkwy*

## Palomino                                 📖
*Dallas* ▪ *(214) 999-1222*
*500 Crescent Ct*

## Pappas Bros. Steakhouse                  $$$$D
*Dallas* ▪ *(214) 366-2000*
*10477 Lombardy Ln* ▪ *Steakhouse* ▪
Manager Pete reports that GF diners are

"absolutely" welcome and advises making reservations noting GF. He notes that the staff's GF knowledge is "extensive" and that there is a special label servers use to notify the kitchen. ▪ *www.pappasbros.com*

### Pappasito's Cantina   📖
*Dallas* ▪ *(214) 350-1970*
*10433 Lombardy Ln*
*Dallas* ▪ *(972) 615-3219*
*DFW Airport, Terminal A, Gate A28*
*Dallas* ▪ *(972) 480-8595*
*723 S. Central Expwy*

### Pei Wei Asian Diner   ✪📖
*Dallas* ▪ *(972) 985-0090*
*18204 Preston Rd*
*Dallas* ▪ *(214) 219-0000*
*3001 Knox St*
*Dallas* ▪ *(214) 765-9911*
*8305 Westchester Dr*
*Dallas* ▪ *(214) 965-0007*
*2222 Mckinney Ave*
*Dallas* ▪ *(214) 765-0030*
*11700 Preston Rd*

### Rex's Seafood   $LD
*Dallas* ▪ *(214) 351-6363*
*5200 W Lovers Ln* ▪ *Seafood* ▪ The restaurant reports that most of the menu is naturally GF and the rest can be modified to be GF upon customer request. Alert the server upon arrival. ▪ *www.rexsseafood.com*

### Rockfish Seafood Grill   ✪📖
*Dallas* ▪ *(214) 823-8444*
*5331 E Mockingbird Ln*
*Dallas* ▪ *(214) 363-7722*
*11661 Preston Rd*

### Romano's Macaroni Grill   ✪★📖
*Dallas* ▪ *(214) 265-0770*
*5858 W Northwest Hwy*

### Ruth's Chris Steak House   ✪📖
*Dallas* ▪ *(972) 250-2244*
*17840 Dallas Pkwy*

### Sundown At Granada   $$D
*Dallas* ▪ *(214) 823-8305*
*3520 Greenville Ave* ▪ *American* ▪ Sundown at Granada offers seared free range chicken, sundown surf and turf, and spicy BBQ Atlantic salmon. All are GF in addition to various salad, soup, and GF vegan options. ▪ *sundownatgranada.com*

### Texas De Brazil Churrascaria   ★📖
*Dallas* ▪ *(214) 720-1414*
*2727 Cedar Springs Rd*

### Tin Star Taco Bar   ✪¢LD
*Dallas* ▪ *(972) 458-2000*
*13710 Dallas Pkwy*
*Dallas* ▪ *(214) 363-6629*
*NorthPark Ctr*
*Dallas* ▪ *(214) 965-0812*
*2101 Cedar Springs* ▪ *Mexican* ▪ GF menu includes salads, soups, burrito bowls and over ten types of tacos, all served on corn tortillas. ▪ *tinstartacobar.com*

### Tu-Lu's Gluten-Free Bakery   ¢S
*Dallas* ▪ *(214) 730-0049*
*6055 Sherry Ln*
*Dallas* ▪ *(214) 780-0188*
*3699 McKinney Ave* ▪ *Bakery* ▪ Dedicated GF bakery offering cupcakes, muffins, cookies, brownies, cheesecake bars, cornbread and many other baked goods. Full-sized GF cakes are also available with advance notice of 48 hours. ▪ *www.tu-lusbakery.com*

### U Food Grill   📖
*Dallas* ▪ *(214) 879-1450*
*5201 Harry Hines Blvd*
*Dallas* ▪ *(972) 586-0380*
*3200 E Airfield Dr*

### Wholesome Foods Bakery   ★¢S
*Dallas* ▪ *(214) 414-2414*
*718 N Buckner Blvd #154* ▪ *Bakery* ▪ 100% GF facility. GF foodbars, muffins, brownies, cakes and sweet and savory breads are available. ▪ *www.unrefinedbakery.com*

# TEXAS

## HOUSTON

### Aquarium Restaurant    $$LD
*Houston* ▪ *(713) 223-3474*
*410 Bagby St* ▪ Seafood ▪ Alert manager who will alert chef. Chef will come to the table and recommend some dishes that can be made GF. ▪ *www.aquariumrestaurants.com*

### Au Bon Pain    📖
*Houston* ▪ *(713) 795-0144*
*6400 Fannin St*
*Houston* ▪ *(713) 464-2525*
*929 S Gessner St*
*Houston* ▪ *(713) 659-2525*
*1200 McKinney*

### BJ's Restaurant and Brewhouse ✪★📖
*Houston* ▪ *(281) 477-8777*
*7637 FM 1960 W*

### Bonefish Grill    ✪📖
*Houston* ▪ *(281) 807-3892*
*7877 Willow Chase Blvd*

### Buca di Beppo    ✪📖
*Houston* ▪ *(713) 665-2822*
*5192 Buffalo Speedway*

### Cantina Laredo    📖
*Houston* ▪ *(713) 952-3287*
*11129 Westheimer Rd*

### Capital Grille, The    ✪📖
*Houston* ▪ *(713) 623-4600*
*5365 Westheimer Rd*

### Carino's Italian    ✪📖
*Houston* ▪ *(281) 458-4424*
*5921 E Sam Houston Pkwy N*

### Chama Gaucha
### Brazilian Steakhouse    $$$LD
*Houston* ▪ *(713) 244-9500*
*5865 Westheimer Rd* ▪ Steakhouse ▪ Chama Gaucha offers a variety of GF entrées including filet mignon, ribeye, chicken, and pork ribs. ▪ *chamagaucha.com*

### Del Frisco's
### Double Eagle Steak House    📖
*Houston* ▪ *(713) 355-2600*
*5061 Westheimer Rd*

### Dessert Gallery    ★$$$$LD
*Houston* ▪ *(713) 522-9999*
*3600 Kirby Dr Ste D* ▪ Dessert ▪ GF mousse cake, lemon vacherin, chocolate and white chocolate concorde cakes, peanut butter truffles and French macarons. ▪ *www.dessertgallery.com*

### Eddie V's    ✪📖
*Houston* ▪ *(832) 200-2380*
*12848 Queensbury Ln*
*Houston* ▪ *(713) 874-1800*
*2800 Kirby Dr*

### Fleming's Prime
### Steakhouse & Wine Bar    ✪📖
*Houston* ▪ *(713) 520-5959*
*2405 W Alabama St*
*Houston* ▪ *(713) 827-1120*
*788 W Sam Houston Pkwy N*

### Fogo De Chao    ★📖
*Houston* ▪ *(713) 978-6500*
*8250 Westheimer Rd*

### Fox and Hound Pub & Grille    📖
*Houston* ▪ *(281) 589-2122*
*11470 Westheimer Rd*
*Houston* ▪ *(281) 481-0068*
*12802 Gulf Frwy*
*Houston* ▪ *(281) 894-6100*
*17575 Tomball Pkwy*

### Fred's Italian Corner Restaurant ★$$LD
*Houston* ▪ *(713) 665-7506*
*2278 W Holcombe Blvd* ▪ Italian ▪ GF pasta, salad, ribeye steak, chicken fresco, shrimp scampi, salmon and garlic pork ribeye. GF pasta is cooked and prepared separately in the kitchen. Ask server to see GF menu. ▪ *www.eatatfreds.com*

### Freebirds on the Fly    ✪📖
*Houston* ▪ *(832) 358-0300*
*9774 Katy Fwy*
*Houston* ▪ *(281) 444-3336*
*6940 FM 1960 W*

*Houston* ▪ *(281) 531-4004*
*11700 B Westheimer Rd*
*Houston* ▪ *(713) 690-3116*
*13280 Northwest Fwy*
*Houston* ▪ *(713) 862-0080*
*1923 Taylor St*
*Houston* ▪ *(713) 524-0621*
*3745 Greenbriar St*
*Houston* ▪ *(713) 383-0700*
*8057 Kirby Dr*

**Genghis Grill**　　　　　　　　　📖
*Houston* ▪ *(713) 461-9975*
*9766 Katy Fwy*
*Houston* ▪ *(281) 890-5942*
*19710 Northwest Fwy*
*Houston* ▪ *(713) 960-1100*
*3879 Southwest Fwy*

**Gluten Free Houston**　　　　　★♁
*Houston* ▪ *(713) 784-7122*
*1014 Wirt Rd* ▪ *Bakery* ▪ Dedicated GF
facility. GF breads such as sandwich,
hamburger and hot dog buns, muffins, cookies, biscotti, cakes, lemon
pound cake, pumpkin bread and custom
made special occasion cakes and pies. ▪
*glutenfreehouston.com*

**Goode Company Seafood**　　✪$$$🄻🄳
*Houston* ▪ *(713) 523-7154*
*2621 Westpark Dr*
*Houston* ▪ *(713) 464-7933*
*10211 Katy Fwy* ▪ *Seafood* ▪ GF menu
available. Items include oysters, boiled
shrimp, a variety of salads, red beans,
roasted garlic mashed potatoes, swordfish,
halibut, catfish con salsa, filet mignon,
chicken breast, and more. All meats and
seafood must be ordered pan-fried or
broiled with no marinade. Alert the server
upon arrival. ▪ *www.goodecompany.com*

**Goode Company Texas BBQ**　　✪★$🄻🄳
*Houston* ▪ *(713) 522-2530*
*5109 Kirby Dr*
*Houston* ▪ *(713) 464-1901*
*8911 Katy Fwy*
*Houston* ▪ *(832) 678-3562*
*20102 NW Fwy* ▪ *Barbeque* ▪ GF menu

available. Items include beef brisket, Czech
sausage, jalapeno pork sausage, pork ribs,
honey smoked ham, chicken, sweet water
duck, spicy pork, turkey breast, turkey
sausage, bbq sauce, baked potatoes, jala-
peno pinto beans, potato salad, cole slaw,
ketchup, sour cream, mustard and dessert
includes blue bell vanilla ice cream. All
rubs and seasonings are GF; avoid any-
thing that has rice because it is made with
chicken stock. This restaurant is certified
by GF restaurant awareness program of the
gluten intolerance group. GF beer is also
available. ▪ *www.goodecompany.com*

**Hard Rock Café**　　　　　　✪📖
*Houston* ▪ *(713) 227-1392*
*502 Texas Ave*

**Jason's Deli**　　　　　　　　✪📖
*Houston* ▪ *(713) 975-0357*
*11081 Westheimer Rd*
*Houston* ▪ *(713) 739-1200*
*1200 Smith St*
*Houston* ▪ *(713) 650-1500*
*901 Mckinney St*
*Houston* ▪ *(281) 358-2603*
*1275 Kingwood Dr*
*Houston* ▪ *(713) 956-0122*
*5215 W 34th St*
*Houston* ▪ *(281) 531-1999*
*14604 Memorial Dr*
*Houston* ▪ *(713) 975-7878*
*5860 Westheimer Rd*
*Houston* ▪ *(281) 444-7515*
*5403 Farm to Market 1960 W*
*Houston* ▪ *(713) 520-6728*
*2611 S Shepard Dr*
*Houston* ▪ *(713) 522-2660*
*2400 University Blvd*
*Houston* ▪ *(713) 467-2007*
*10321 Katy Fwy*
*Houston* ▪ *(281) 858-7500*
*7010 Hwy 6*
*Houston* ▪ *(281) 970-5044*
*10915 Farm to Market 1960 W*

**Jersey Mike's**　　　　　　　📖
*Houston* ▪ *(281) 589-6453*
*1635 Eldridge Pkwy*

Houston ▪ (713) 960-9992
5393-B Westheimer St
Houston ▪ (713) 523-3151
5819 Kirby Dr

### Joe's Crab Shack    ✪▥
Houston ▪ (281) 875-5400
14901 N Fwy I-45
Houston ▪ (713) 666-2150
2621 S Loop W
Houston ▪ (713) 910-3232
12400 Gulf Fwy
Houston ▪ (281) 558-7111
2120 S Hwy 6
Houston ▪ (832) 912-1094
17111 Tomball Pkwy

### Loving Hut    ▥
Houston ▪ (281) 531-8882
2825 S Kirkwood Rd

### Maggiano's Little Italy    ★▥
Houston ▪ (713) 961-2700
2019 Post Oak Blvd

### Masraff's    $$$LD
Houston ▪ (713) 355-1975
1753 Post Oak Blvd ▪ Seafood ▪ According to an employee, the chef and staff are "more than happy" to accommodate their customers' needs. They will alter any dish requested to the best of their ability in order to make it GF. ▪ www.masraffs.com

### Melting Pot, The    ✪▥
Houston ▪ (713) 532-5011
6100 Westheimer Rd

### Mockingbird Bistro    $$$$LD
Houston ▪ (713) 533-0200
1985 Welch St ▪ Modern American ▪ Reservationist Monica reports that they accommodate GF diners "every day." She notes that several seafood, meat, and poultry items are naturally GF or can be modified to be GF. Confirm the timeliness of this information before dining in. Alert a server, who will discuss GF options with the kitchen. Reservations noting GF are recommended. ▪ www.mockingbirdbistro.com

### Morton's Steakhouse    ✪▥
Houston ▪ (713) 659-3700
1001 McKinney St
Houston ▪ (713) 629-1946
5000 Westheimer

### P.F. Chang's China Bistro    ✪★▥
Houston ▪ (713) 627-7220
4094 Westheimer Rd
Houston ▪ (281) 571-4050
18250 Tomball Pkwy
Houston ▪ (281) 920-3553
11685 Westheimer Rd

### Pappas Bros. Steakhouse    $$$$D
Houston ▪ (713) 780-7352
5839 Westheimer Rd ▪ Steakhouse ▪ Manager Pete reports that GF diners are "absolutely" welcome and advises making reservations noting GF. He notes that the staff's GF knowledge is "extensive" and that there is a special label servers use to notify the kitchen. ▪ www.pappasbros.com

### Pappas Seafood House    $$$LD
Houston ▪ (281) 999-9928
11301 I-45 N @ Aldine Bender
Houston ▪ (713) 453-3265
12010 I-10 E
Houston ▪ (713) 641-0318
6945 I-45 S @ Woodridge
Houston ▪ (713) 522-4595
3001 S Shepherd Dr @ Alabama ▪ Seafood ▪ The restaurant reports that accommodating dietary requirements is "part of their service." They recommend consulting a server or manager upon arrival, who will help guide diners through the menu and select appropriate options. ▪ www.pappasseafood.com

### Pappasito's Cantina    ▥
Houston ▪ (713) 455-8378
11831 I-10 E At Federal Rd
Houston ▪ (713) 468-1913
10409 I-10 W At Sam Houston Tollway
Houston ▪ (713) 520-5066
2536 Richmond Ave
Houston ▪ (713) 668-5756
2515 S Loop W At S Main

Houston ■ *(713) 784-5253*
*6445 Richmond Ave*
Houston ■ *(281) 821-4500*
*15280 I-45 N At Airtex*
Houston ■ *(713) 462-0245*
*13070 Hwy 290*
Houston ■ *(281) 657-6157*
*7800 Airport Blvd*
Houston ■ *(281) 821-2266*
*3950 S Terminal Rd*
Houston ■ *(281) 565-9797*
*13750 Hwy 59 S*
Houston ■ *(281) 893-5030*
*7050 Fm 1960 Rd W*

### Pei Wei Asian Diner                    ✪ 📖

Houston ■ *(281) 885-5430*
*5203 Fm 1960 Rd W*
Houston ■ *(281) 506-3500*
*14008 Memorial Dr*
Houston ■ *(713) 661-0900*
*5110 Buffalo Speedway*
Houston ■ *(713) 785-1620*
*1413 S Voss Rd*
Houston ■ *(281) 571-4990*
*12020 Fm 1960 Rd W*
Houston ■ *(713) 353-7366*
*1005 Waugh Dr*

### Post Oak Grill                          $$LD

Houston ■ *(713) 993-9966*
*1415 S Post Oak Ln*
Houston ■ *(713) 650-1700*
*1111 Louisiana* ■ *American* ■ The Post Oak Grill does not offer a GF menu. However, several items from their regular menu are naturally GF or can be prepared GF such as the grilled salmon, grilled rainbow trout, and various premium cuts of meat. ■ *www.postoakgrill.com*

### Rioja Tapas                         ✪$$$LD

Houston ■ *(281) 531-5569*
*11920 J Westheimer Rd* ■ *Spanish* ■ GF menu includes paellas, lamb dishes, chicken dishes, and other items. Manager Luis notes that they accommodate "a bunch" of GF diners on a regular basis. ■ *www.riojarestaurant.com*

### Rockfish Seafood Grill               ✪📖

Houston ■ *(281) 558-7380*
*11805 Westheimer Rd*
Houston ■ *(281) 587-2900*
*5500 FM 1960 Rd W*

### Romano's Macaroni Grill           ✪★📖

Houston ■ *(713) 789-5515*
*5802 Westheimer Rd*
Houston ■ *(281) 955-1388*
*7607 FM 1960 Rd W*

### Ruggles Green                       ✪★$LD

Houston ■ *(713) 533-0777*
*2311 W Alabama St*
Houston ■ *(713) 464-5557*
*801 Town & Country Blvd* ■ *Organic* ■ GF menu includes pizzas, quinoa spaghetti, and several salads. Hostess Dakota reports that they have "tons" of GF customers. ■ *www.rugglesgreen.com*

### Ruth's Chris Steak House            ✪📖

Houston ■ *(713) 789-2333*
*6213 Richmond Ave*

### Smith & Wollensky                    📖

Houston ■ *(713) 621-7555*
*4007 Westheimer*

### Snap Kitchen                       ✪$BLD

Houston ■ *(713) 526-5700*
*3600 Kirby Dr*
Houston ■ *(713) 426-4700*
*5710 Memorial Dr* ■ *American* ■ Specialty order foods made fresh daily. GF menu online. Menu includes protein shakes, spinach and goat cheese scramble and baked vegetable quiche for breakfast. GF Lunch includes grass-fed bison quinoa hash, chicken sweet potatoes with green beans and chicken with butternut squash spaghetti; Dinner includes crispy chicken, Santa Fe pork and crispy Scottish salmon. GF snack items and dessert are also prepared. ■ *www.snapkitchen.com*

## Sparrow Bar & Cookshop          $$LD
*Houston* ▪ *(713) 524-6922*
*3701 Travis St* ▪ *Modern American* ▪
Manager Tino reports that the restaurant
serves GF diners "all the time." He recommends making reservations noting GF, and
then alerting a server, who will speak to the
chef about GF options. He notes that the
menu changes daily, but there are always
dishes that can be modified to be GF. ▪
*sparrowhouston.com*

## Taco Milagro
## Restaurant & Beach Bar          ✪¢LD
*Houston* ▪ *(713) 522-1999*
*2555 Kirby Dr* ▪ *Mexican* ▪ Most items on
the menu are GF. Be sure to stay away from
the flour tortillas, french fries and salsa.
Owner's wife has Celiac, so the restaurant
"definitely prepared" to accommodate GF
diners. ▪ *www.taco-milagro.com*

## Tossed          ✪📖
*Houston* ▪ *(281) 556-8677*
*13410 Briar Forest Dr Suite 200*

## Yard House          ✪📖
*Houston* ▪ *(713) 461-9273*
*800 W Sam Houston Pkwy N*

## Zio's          ✪📖
*Houston* ▪ *(281) 872-5333*
*14915 North Fwy*

## Zpizza          ✪📖
*Houston* ▪ *(713) 432-7219*
*4010 Bissonnet St*
*Houston* ▪ *(281) 230-3000*
*GB Airport/IAH*

# TEXAS
## SAN ANTONIO

## Aldaco's Mexican Cuisine          ✪★$LD
*San Antonio* ▪ *(210) 222-0561*
*100 Hoefgen Ave* ▪ *Mexican* ▪ GF menu
features chips and salsa, fajitas, steak mari-
sol, caldito de pollo and more. Restaurant
makes sure that all GF items are dedicated
GF. ▪ *www.aldacos.net*

## Asia Kitchen          ★$LD
*San Antonio* ▪ *(210) 673-0662*
*1739 SW Loop 410* ▪ *Thai* ▪ GF items indicated on menu. Items include pad woon-
sen, pad thai, thai basil, thai basil with
vegetables, sweet and sour (pork, beef or
chicken), cashew (pork, beef or chicken),
ginger (pork, beef or chicken), red curry,
green curry, yellow curry and much more.
▪ *www.asia-kitchen.com*

## Auden's Kitchen          $LD
*San Antonio* ▪ *(210) 494-0070*
*700 E Sonterra Blvd* ▪ *American* ▪ Chef
reports that anything on the menu can be
made GF. Alert server upon arrival and
chef will come out and list GF options. ▪
*www.audenskitchen.com*

## Beto's on Broadway          ¢LD
*San Antonio* ▪ *(210) 930-9393*
*8142 Broadway St* ▪ *Latin American* ▪ GF
options include quesadillas on corn tortillas, rice and beans, soups and salads and
tacos. Alert a server upon arrival and they
will provide GF options. ▪ *betosinfo.com*

## Biga on the Banks          $$$$D
*San Antonio* ▪ *(210) 225-0722*
*203 S Saint Marys St* ▪ *Modern American* ▪ The menu changes daily, but the
restaurant reports that they can always
accommodate GF diners. Alert server upon
arrival. ▪ *www.biga.com*

## Bistro Vatel          $$$LD
*San Antonio* ▪ *(210) 828-3141*
*218 E Olmos Dr* ▪ *French* ▪ The restaurant

reports that any item on the menu can be modified to be GF. Alert server and they will go through menu of items that can be made GF as well as inform the chef of all dietary needs. ▪ *www.bistrovatel.com*

### BJ's Restaurant and Brewhouse ✪★📖
*San Antonio* ▪ *(210) 497-6070*
*22410 US Hwy 281 N*
*San Antonio* ▪ *(210) 690-2600*
*17503 IH-10 W*
*San Antonio* ▪ *(210) 523-5700*
*5447 W Loop 1604 N*

### Carino's Italian                        ✪📖
*San Antonio* ▪ *(210) 493-9998*
*1301 N Fm 1604 W*

### Chama Gaucha
### Brazilian Steakhouse                    $$$**LD**
*San Antonio* ▪ *(210) 564-9400*
*18318 Sonterra Pl* ▪ *Steakhouse* ▪ Chama Gaucha offers a variety of GF entrées including filet mignon, ribeye, chicken, and pork ribs. ▪ *chamagaucha.com*

### Cosi                                     ✪📖
*San Antonio* ▪ *(210) 558-1040*
*17503 La Cantera Pkwy*

### Cove, The                              ✪★◖**LD**
*San Antonio* ▪ *(210) 227-2683*
*606 W Cypress St* ▪ *American* ▪ GF items include appetizers, organic salads, sustainable organic local burgers with little aussie bakery GF buns, tacos and desserts. GF kids menu available. The chefs are trained to treat GF requests with care. Alert a server upon arrival. ▪ *www.thecove.us*

### Fire Bowl Café                          ✪📖
*San Antonio* ▪ *(210) 829-0887*
*255 E Basse Rd*

### Fleming's Prime
### Steakhouse & Wine Bar                    ✪📖
*San Antonio* ▪ *(210) 824-9463*
*255 E Basse Rd*

### Fox and Hound Pub & Grille              📖
*San Antonio* ▪ *(210) 696-1356*
*12651 Vance Jackson Rd*

### Freebirds on the Fly                    ✪📖
*San Antonio* ▪ *(210) 684-1300*
*5519 W Loop 1604*
*San Antonio* ▪ *(210) 877-9606*
*11224 Huebner Rd*
*San Antonio* ▪ *(210) 525-9990*
*125 NW Loop 410*
*San Antonio* ▪ *(210) 495-0101*
*20811 N Hwy 281*
*San Antonio* ▪ *(210) 267-1062*
*8603 State Hwy 151*

### Garbanzo                                 📖
*San Antonio* ▪ *(210) 572-4382*
*11075 Huebner Oaks*

### Genghis Grill                            📖
*San Antonio* ▪ *(210) 853-2695*
*11745 I.H. 10 W*
*San Antonio* ▪ *(210) 496-5426*
*1903 N Loop 1604E*
*San Antonio* ▪ *(210) 647-5426*
*8603 State Hwy 151*

### Hard Rock Café                          ✪📖
*San Antonio* ▪ *(210) 224-7625*
*111 W Crockett St*

### HuHot Mongolian Grill                    📖
*San Antonio* ▪ *(210) 641-1288*
*12710 IH 10 W*

### Iron Cactus                            ✪$**LD**
*San Antonio* ▪ *(210) 224-9835*
*200 River Walk* ▪ *Mexican* ▪ GF menu available. GF items include steak fajita nachos, taco salad, chipotle smoked pork chops, Yucatan fish tacos, vanilla bean flan, Mexican chocolate mousse and more. ▪ *www.ironcactus.com*

### Jason's Deli                            ✪📖
*San Antonio* ▪ *(210) 524-9288*
*25 NE Loop 410*
*San Antonio* ▪ *(210) 690-3354*
*9933 W Interstate 10*
*San Antonio* ▪ *(210) 647-5000*
*5819 NW Interstate 410 Loop Frontage Rd*
*San Antonio* ▪ *(210) 545-6888*
*1141 N Loop 1604 E*

### Jersey Mike's 📖
San Antonio ▪ (210) 236-9351
8603 State Hwy 151
San Antonio ▪ (210) 254-9618
7970 Fredricksburg Rd
San Antonio ▪ (210) 290-9533
20323 Huebner Rd

### Joe's Crab Shack ✪📖
San Antonio ▪ (210) 523-1010
4711 NW Loop 410
San Antonio ▪ (210) 699-9779
12485 IH 10 W
San Antonio ▪ (210) 930-1736
255 E Basse Rd
San Antonio ▪ (210) 271-9981
212 College St

### Little Aussie Bakery & Café, The ¢BL
San Antonio ▪ (210) 826-7877
3610 Ave B ▪ Bakery & Café ▪ Dedicated
GF bakery and café offering garlic bread,
pasta, sandwiches, quiches, pizzas, and
soup and salads. They have a kids' menu
and various types of desserts including cookies, brownies and cake slices. ▪
www.thelittleaussiebakery.com

### Maggiano's Little Italy ★📖
San Antonio ▪ (210) 451-6000
17603 Ih 10 W

### Melting Pot, The ✪📖
San Antonio ▪ (210) 479-6358
14855 Blanco Rd

### Mi Tierra Café & Bakery ¢BLD
San Antonio ▪ (210) 225-1262
218 Produce Row ▪ Mexican ▪ The restaurant reports that they will modify "any dish
possible" to accommodate GF diners. Alert
server upon arrival. ▪ mitierracafe.com

### Morton's Steakhouse ✪📖
San Antonio ▪ (210) 228-0700
300 E Crockett St

### P.F. Chang's China Bistro ✪★📖
San Antonio ▪ (210) 507-1000
255 E Basse Rd Ste 1200
San Antonio ▪ (210) 507-6500
15900 La Cantera Pkwy Ste 1100 Bldg #

### Paloma Blanca Mexican Cuisine ✪$$LD
San Antonio ▪ (210) 822-6151
5800 Broadway St ▪ Mexican ▪ Extensive
GF menu includes a variety of enchiladas,
tacos, chicken, and squab dishes. Ask the
hostess for the "Celiac menu." Make sure
to inform the server that you are GF. ▪
www.palomablanca.net

### Pam's Patio Kitchen ★$LD
San Antonio ▪ (210) 492-1359
11826 Wurzbach Rd ▪ Deli ▪ GF items
indicated on menu. Items include hop sing's
lettuce wrap, campeche shrimp cocktail, tacos, nachos, salads, Thai panang beef curry,
pad thai, stacked chicken enchiladas, serious
black ribeye, tenderloin fillets with roquefort
and GF pizza crust. ▪ www.pamspatio.com

### Pappasito's Cantina 📖
San Antonio ▪ (210) 691-8974
10501 I-10 W

### Pei Wei Asian Diner ✪📖
San Antonio ▪ (210) 523-0040
11398 Bandera Rd
San Antonio ▪ (210) 561-5600
11267 Huebner Rd
San Antonio ▪ (210) 507-3600
999 E Basse Rd
San Antonio ▪ (210) 507-9160
1802 N Loop 1604 E
San Antonio ▪ (210) 507-5520
430 W Loop 1604 N

### Piatti Ristorante & Bar ★$$LD
San Antonio ▪ (210) 832-0300
255 E Basse Rd ▪ Italian ▪ GF pasta is
available. The restaurant reports that staff
is trained on GF preparation and GF diners
are accommodated "all the time." They note
that the risotto is GF and that many menu
items can be modified to be GF. Alert a
server upon arrival. ▪ www.piatti.com

### Romano's Macaroni Grill ✪★📖
San Antonio ▪ (210) 402-3019
1011 N Loop 1604 E
San Antonio ▪ (210) 691-1360
11745 W IH 10

### Ruth's Chris Steak House    ✪📖
San Antonio ▪ (210) 227-8847
1170 E Commerce St
San Antonio ▪ (210) 821-5051
7720 Jones Maltsberger

### Sweet Cece's    📖
San Antonio ▪ (210) 493-0022
1150 Loop 1604

### Texas De Brazil Churrascaria    ★📖
San Antonio ▪ (210) 299-1600
313 E Houston St

### Tony Roma's    📖
San Antonio ▪ (210) 225-7662
849 E Commerce St

### Yard House    ✪📖
San Antonio ▪ (210) 691-0033
15900 La Cantera Pkwy

### Z'Tejas Southwestern Grill    ✪★📖
San Antonio ▪ (210) 690-3334
15900 La Cantera Pkwy

### Zio's    ✪📖
San Antonio ▪ (210) 697-7222
12858 W Interstate 10
San Antonio ▪ (210) 495-7722
18030 N US Hwy 281
San Antonio ▪
2747 SE Military Dr

# TEXAS

## ALL OTHER CITIES

### Abuelo's    ✪📖
Abilene ▪ (325) 692-4776
4782 S 14th St
Amarillo ▪ (806) 354-8294
3501 W 45th Ave
Arlington ▪ (817) 468-2622
1041 W I-20
College Station ▪ (979) 260-3400
840 University Dr
Fort Worth ▪ (817) 386-5600

4740 S Hulen St
Hurst ▪ (817) 514-9355
824 Airport Fwy
Lewisville ▪ (972) 315-6057
2520 S Stemmons Fwy
Lubbock ▪ (806) 794-1762
4401 82nd St
Midland ▪ (432) 685-3335
4610 N Garfield
Plano ▪ (972) 423-9290
3420 N Central Expwy
Plano ▪ (972) 781-1613
3701 Dallas Pkwy

### Aquarium Restaurant    $$LD
Kemah ▪ (281) 334-9010
11 Kemah Boardwalk ▪ Seafood ▪ Upon arrival, alert the manager, who will alert the chef. The chef will come to the table and recommend some dishes that can be made GF. ▪ www.aquariumrestaurants.com

### Au Bon Pain    📖
Plano ▪ (972) 943-9205
7300 Lonestar Dr

### Auntie Pasto's    ★$$LD
Bellaire ▪ (713) 669-8658
5101 Bellaire Blvd ▪ Italian ▪ GF spaghetti or penne is available. GF pizza is available in 10" size only at the Waipahu location. ▪ www.auntiepastos.com

### Austin's Pizza    ★$LD
Pflugerville ▪ (512) 795-8888
15424 Farm-To-Market 1825 Rd
Cedar Park ▪ (512) 795-8888
2800 E Whitestone Blvd
Round Rock ▪ (512) 795-8888
3750 Gattis School Rd ▪ Pizza ▪ GF pizza is available in the 10-inch size. A YouTube video detailing their entire GF preparation process is available online. YouTube channel: OfficialAustinsPizza. ▪ www.austinspizza.com

### Bavarian Grill    ✪$$LD
Plano ▪ (972) 881-0705
221 W Parker Rd ▪ European ▪ GF menu available. ▪ www.bavariangrill.com

## Bees Knees Bakeshop                                    ★ CS
*Cedar Park* ▪ (512) 931-4323
*109 Cypress Creek* ▪ *Bakery* ▪ Dedicated
GF facility offering gourmet cupcake, pies,
brownies, bars, cookies, cookie sandwiches, cake balls, quiche, muffins, scones,
breakfast and lunch menu available as
well as a kids menu. Custom cake orders
must be made 48 hours in advance. ▪
*www.beeskneesbakeshop.com*

## BJ's Restaurant and Brewhouse ✪★📖
*Allen* ▪ (972) 678-4050
*190 E Stacy Rd*
*Arlington* ▪ (817) 465-5225
*201 E Interstate 20*
*College Station* ▪ (979) 696-5700
*1520 Harvey Rd*
*El Paso* ▪ (915) 633-8300
*11905 Gateway Blvd*
*Fort Worth* ▪ (817) 750-0005
*9401 Sage Meadow Trl*
*Fort Worth* ▪ (817) 292-9200
*4720 S Hulen St*
*Hurst* ▪ (817) 595-3705
*952 N E Loop 820*
*Lewisville* ▪ (972) 459-9700
*2609 S Stemmons Fwy*
*Lubbock* ▪ (806) 783-8600
*4805 S Loop 289*
*McAllen* ▪ (956) 687-2005
*3200 Expwy 83*
*Mesquite* ▪ (972) 682-5800
*1106 Town E Mall*
*New Braunfels* ▪ (830) 620-1400
*2951 Cold Springs Dr*
*Pearland* ▪ (713) 436-7805
*11200 Broadway St*
*Plano* ▪ (972) 424-4262
*1101 N Central Expwy*
*Round Rock* ▪ (512) 868-5705
*4201 N IH-35*
*Shenandoah* ▪ (936) 273-7100
*19075 IH-45 S*
*Sugar Land* ▪ (281) 242-0400
*2231 State Hwy 6*
*Sunset Valley* ▪ (512) 892-3800
*5207 Brodie Ln*
*Temple* ▪ (254) 778-3300

*3550 S General Bruce Dr*
*Tyler* ▪ (903) 939-2840
*210 W Southwest Loop 323*
*Waco* ▪ (254) 776-0200
*5929 W Waco Dr*
*Webster* ▪ (281) 316-3037
*515 W Bay Area Blvd*

## Blue Mesa Grill                                    ✪$LD
*Fort Worth* ▪ (817) 332-6372
*1600 S University Dr*
*Plano* ▪ (214) 387-4407
*8200 Dallas Pkwy*
*Southlake* ▪ (817) 416-0055
*1586 E Southlake Blvd*
*Addison* ▪ (972) 934-0165
*5100 Beltline Rd*
*Lubbock* ▪ (806) 368-0751
*2522 Marsha Sharp Fwy* ▪ *Southwest* ▪
Ask for the "Nutritional Brochure," which
contains a list of GF items and advice on GF
ordering. This information is also available
online. GF options include red chili crusted
salmon, free range chicken with roasted
serrano pesto, carne asada, Baja shrimp,
and more. For dessert, they offer flan. ▪
*www.bluemesagrill.com*

## Bob's Steak & Chop House                                    📖
*Grapevine* ▪ (817) 481-5555
*1255 S Main St*
*Fort Worth* ▪ (817) 350-4100
*1300 Houston St*
*Plano* ▪ (972) 608-2627
*5760 Legacy Dr*

## Bonefish Grill                                    ✪📖
*Southlake* ▪ (817) 421-3263
*1201 E Southlake Blvd*
*Webster* ▪ (281) 332-0430
*19325 Gulf Fwy*

## Boston's Restaurant & Sports Bar
✪★📖
*McKinney* ▪ (214) 585-0900
*6800 State Hwy 121*
*Killeen* ▪ (254) 501-9690
*2800 E Central TX Exp*
*Irving* ▪ (972) 869-2210
*1100 Market Pl Blvd*

**College Station** ▪ (979) 260-8646
820 University Dr E
**Grapevine** ▪ (817) 481-1117
1713 Crossroads Rd
**Fort Worth** ▪ (817) 232-3400
6501 N Fwy
**Arlington** ▪ (817) 633-7773
2501 E Lamar Blvd

**Bubba Gump Shrimp Co.**　　　✪▥
**Galveston** ▪ (409) 766-4952
2501 Seawall Blvd

**Buca di Beppo**　　　　　　　✪▥
**Frisco** ▪ (972) 668-3287
8580 State Highway 121
**Southlake** ▪ (817) 749-6262
2701 E State Highway 114
**Conroe** ▪ (936) 321-6262
19075 I-45 S
**Mesquite** ▪ (972) 279-2822
1104 Town E Mall

**Cakes by Monica**　　　　　　$$$$$
**Pasadena** ▪ (281) 998-1658
5005 Anthony Ln ▪ Bakery ▪ Dedicated GF bakery offering cakes, cookies,
pies and more. Items are available by
phone or email order only. Orders must
be placed at least 4 days in advance. ▪
*www.monicasgfcakes.com*

**Cantina Laredo**　　　　　　　▥
**Addison** ▪ (972) 458-0962
4546 Belt Line Rd
**Frisco** ▪ (214) 618-9860
1125 Legacy Dr
**Ft Worth** ▪ (817) 810-0773
530 Throckmorton St
**Grapevine** ▪ (817) 358-0505
4020 William D Tate Ave
**Lewisville** ▪ (972) 315-8100
2225 S Stemmons Fwy
**DFW Airport** ▪ (972) 973-4267
3200 E Airfield Dr

**Carino's Italian**　　　　　　✪▥
**Abilene** ▪ (325) 698-4950
4157 Buffalo Gap Rd
**Amarillo** ▪ (806) 468-9375
8400 I-40 W

**Baytown** ▪ (281) 421-7077
7017 Garth Rd
**Beaumont** ▪ (409) 842-1919
3805 Interstate 10 S
**El Paso** ▪ (915) 778-7771
1201 Airway Blvd
**El Paso** ▪ (915) 581-7042
675 Sunland Park Dr
**Ft Worth** ▪ (817) 346-4456
5900 S Hulen St
**Humble** ▪ (281) 812-6127
7069 Fm 1960 Rd E
**Hurst** ▪ (817) 503-8917
2175 Precinct Line Rd
**Jersey Village** ▪ (281) 970-1554
19820 Northwest Fwy
**Katy** ▪ (281) 398-5646
21875 Katy Fwy
**Longview** ▪ (903) 236-9654
411 E Loop 281 Ste B
**Lubbock** ▪ (806) 798-0944
6821 Slide Rd
**Midland** ▪ (432) 520-7600
4711 W Loop 250 N
**Missouri City** ▪ (281) 261-2630
5750 Highway 6
**New Braunfels** ▪ (830) 609-1141
1304 E Common St
**Odessa** ▪ (432) 362-4426
5111 E 42nd St
**Pearland** ▪ (713) 436-0090
3050 Silverlake Village Dr
**Round Rock** ▪ (512) 238-8288
2600 Ih 35 N
**San Angelo** ▪ (325) 655-8744
1407 Knickerbocker Rd
**San Marcos** ▪ (512) 393-5060
1207 Ih 35 S
**Sherman** ▪ (903) 813-8595
306 W US Highway 82
**Sunset Valley** ▪ (512) 899-0572
5601 Brodie Ln
**Texarkana** ▪ (903) 223-8655
3402 Saint Michael Dr
**Tyler** ▪ (903) 534-8280
1723 W Southwest Loop 323
**Wichita Falls** ▪ (940) 691-8900
4330 Kell Blvd

## Charleston's Restaurant ✪📖
*Fort Worth* ▪ *(817) 735-8900*
*3020 S Hulen*

## Classic Café at Roanoke, The $$$LD
*Roanoke* ▪ *(817) 430-8185*
*504 N Oak St* ▪ *American* ▪ Several menu items can be made GF as well as many items on the menu are naturally GF. Items include salads, fish dishes, steak dishes, lamb dishes and pork dishes. ▪ *www.theclassiccafe.com*

## Coconut Thai Grill ✪$LD
*Carrollton* ▪ *(972) 418-8424*
*2512 E Belt Line* ▪ *Thai* ▪ Naturally GF items are indicated on the menu and include peanut chicken, pad thai, citrus salmon, several curries, and much more. The restaurant states that most of the other dishes can be prepared GF upon request. ▪ *www.menuaid.com*

## Cozymel's Coastel Mex ✪📖
*Grapevine* ▪ *(972) 724-0277*
*2655 Grapevine Mills Cir*
*Brentwood* ▪ *(615) 377-6363*
*1654 Westgate Cir*

## CraigO's Pizza and Pasta ★$LD
*Round Rock* ▪ *(512) 671-9900*
*603 Louis Henna Blvd*
*Lakeway* ▪ *(512) 402-1600*
*2501 Ranch Road 620 S* ▪ *Pizza* ▪ GF pizza is available in 10" and 14" sizes. ▪ *www.craigospizzaandpasta.com*

## Del Frisco's
## Double Eagle Steak House 📖
*Fort Worth* ▪ *(817) 877-3999*
*812 Main St*

## Don Pablo's ✪📖
*Fort Worth* ▪ *(817) 731-0497*
*7050 Ridgmar Meadow Rd*
*Grand Prairie* ▪ *(972) 642-9595*
*444 W I-20*
*N. Richland Hills* ▪ *(817) 485-4499*
*5121 Rufe Snow*

## Eddie V's ✪📖
*Fort Worth* ▪ *(817) 336-8000*
*3100 W 7th St*

## Essence Cakery ★$$
*Plano* ▪ *(972) 422-5141*
*1717 E Spring Creek Pkwy* ▪ *Bakery* ▪ The bakery offers GF cupcakes daily and special order cakes in a variety of flavors, including vanilla, chocolate, Mexican chocolate, strawberry, lemon, mimosa, carrot, and pumpkin spice. The bakery reports that they "work under the assumption that every GF customer has Celiac disease" and take precautions accordingly. GF policies include cleaning and sanitizing all surfaces and utensils, storing GF products separately, and preparing GF items before any other items. ▪ *essencecakery.com*

## Fire Bowl Café ✪📖
*Round Rock* ▪ *(512) 248-2695*
*150 Sundance Pkwy*

## Fleming's Prime Steakhouse & Wine Bar ✪📖
*The Woodlands* ▪ *(281) 362-0103*
*1201 Lake Woodlands Dr*

## Fogo De Chao ★📖
*Addison* ▪ *(972) 503-7300*
*4300 Belt Line Rd*

## Fox and Hound Pub & Grille 📖
*Lubbock* ▪ *(806) 791-1526*
*4210 82nd St*
*Arlington* ▪ *(817) 277-3591*
*1001 NE Green Oaks Blvd*
*Dallas* ▪ *(972) 732-0804*
*18918 Midway Rd*
*Fort Worth* ▪ *(817) 423-3600*
*6051 SW Loop 820*
*Fort Worth* ▪ *(817) 338-9200*
*603 Houston St*
*Lewisville* ▪ *(972) 221-8346*
*1640 S Stemmons Frwy*
*Richardson* ▪ *(972) 437-4225*
*112 W Campbell Rd*
*College Station* ▪ *(979) 846-0211*
*505 University Dr*
*Shenandoah* ▪ *(832) 813-0102*
*19189 Interstate 45 S*

### Freebirds on the Fly    ✪📖

*Allen* ▪ (918) 445-4113
190 E Stacy Rd
*Arlington* ▪ (817) 795-1608
300 E Abram S
*Baytown* ▪ (281) 422-9570
4555 Garth Rd
*Beaumont* ▪ (409) 898-2900
4438 Dowlen Rd
*College Station* ▪ (979) 260-9086
700 Earl Rudder Fwy
*College Station* ▪ (979) 846-9298
319 University Dr
*College Station* ▪ (979) 485-8829
3525 D Longmire Dr
*College Station* ▪ (979) 695-0151
2050 Texas Ave S
*Conroe* ▪ (936) 756-1830
1188 W Dallas St
*Corpus Christi* ▪ (361) 906-0970
5425 S Padre Island Dr
*Denton* ▪ (940) 565-5400
2700 W University
*Fort Worth* ▪ (817) 348-0820
2736 W 7th St
*Fort Worth* ▪ (817) 750-1331
9501 Sage Meadow Trl
*Fort Worth* ▪ (817) 294-7241
4965 Overton Ridge Blvd
*Grapevine* ▪ (817) 488-7100
1501 William D Tate Ave
*Humble* ▪ (281) 446-0279
9490 FM 1960 W
*Hurst* ▪ (817) 282-8100
1301 W Pipeline Rd
*Irving* ▪ (972) 869-3500
7601 N MacArthur Pk Blvd
*Katy* ▪ (281) 574-3704
21923 Katy Fwy
*Killeen* ▪ (254) 833-8383
2511 Trimmier Rd
*League City* ▪ (281) 534-9291
1615 W FM 646
*Lewisville* ▪ (972) 315-2452
565 E Highway 3040
*Lubbock* ▪ (806) 741-0900
1201 University Ave
*Lubbock* ▪ (806) 791-0101

*4930 S Loop 289*
*Midland* ▪ (432) 689-9100
3322 N Loop 250 W
*Mission* ▪ (956) 928-1531
2521 E Exprswy 83
*Nederland* ▪ (409) 729-9022
1629 Hwy 69
*Pasadena* ▪ (281) 991-1977
5718 Fairmont Pkwy
*Pearland* ▪ (281) 741-3337
11302 Broadway
*Plano* ▪ (214) 705-6808
8240 Preston Rd
*Richardson* ▪ (972) 907-9999
238 W Campbell Rd
*Rockwall* ▪ (214) 771-4448
1067 E IH 30
*Rosenberg* ▪ (281) 232-4432
24401 Southwest Fwy
*Round Rock* ▪ (512) 904-0070
200 University Blvd
*San Angelo* ▪ (325) 942-5690
3204 Sherwood Wy
*San Marcos* ▪ (512) 392-2072
909 State Hwy 80
*Selma* ▪ (210) 590-6800
14975 IH 35 N
*Sugar Land* ▪ (281) 565-8740
15285 SW Fwy
*The Woodlands* ▪ (281) 419-8011
1640 Lake Woodlands Dr
*Waco* ▪ (254) 741-0060
120 N New Rd
*Webster* ▪ (281) 557-2300
528 W Bay Area Blvd

### Fresco's Cocina Mexicana    ✪$$**LD**

*Watauga* ▪ (817) 498-6370
7432 Denton Hwy
*Burleson* ▪ (817) 426-9990
112 S Main St ▪ Mexican ▪ GF menu
includes cheese and guacamole appetizers, Mexican salad, ribeye and brisket
fajitas, tamales, and more. Restaurant
recommends calling 48 hours in advance
if you want GF chips or taco shells. ▪
*www.frescosmexicanfood.com*

## Genghis Grill    📖

Abilene ▪ (325) 480-1802
4438 S Clack St
El Paso ▪ (915) 600-2822
1318 George Dieter Dr
Lubbock ▪ (806) 797-5426
6201 Slide Rd
Midland ▪ (432) 520-5426
4517 Midkiff
Odessa ▪ (432) 362-5426
4301 E 42nd St
Wichita Falls ▪ (940) 691-5426
3210 Midwestern Pkwy
Addison ▪ (972) 503-5426
4201 Beltline Rd
Arlington ▪ (817) 465-7847
4000 Five Points Blvd
Carrollton ▪ (972) 267-5426
3450 E Hebron Pkwy
Denton ▪ (940) 381-0150
2416 Lillian Miller Pkwy
Duncanville ▪ (972) 296-5426
150 E Hwy 67
Frisco ▪ (972) 668-5426
3211 Preston Rd
Ft. Worth ▪ (817) 737-5800
4469 Bryant Irvin Rd
Ft. Worth ▪ (817) 306-7560
6600 N Fwy
Garland ▪ (972) 496-0193
215 Coneflower Dr
Hurst ▪ (817) 284-7999
1101 Melbourne Rd
Mansfield ▪ (817) 453-2695
1718 Hwy 287 N
McKinney ▪ (214) 585-4745
1920 Eldorado Pkwy
Mesquite ▪ (972) 270-5426
1765 N Town E Blvd
Plano ▪ (972) 422-4745
921 N Central Expwy
Rockwall ▪ (972) 771-5426
1699 Laguna Dr
Longview ▪ (903) 686-0083
310 E Loop 281
Texarkana ▪ (430) 200-2301
4270 Saint Michael Dr
Tyler ▪ (903) 920-0783

3709 Troup Hwy
Webster ▪ (281) 332-0970
510 W Bay Area Blvd
East College Station ▪ (979) 260-6800
700 University Dr
Humble ▪ (281) 964-4000
9490 FM 1960 Bypass W
Katy ▪ (281) 394-2445
23501 Cinco Ranch Blvd
Sugar Land ▪ (281) 277-0233
1531 S Hwy 6
The Woodlands ▪ (281) 363-4745
9300 Six Pines Dr
Corpus Christi ▪ (361) 400-2330
5633 S Padre Island Dr
Harker Heights ▪ (254) 953-1150
201 E Central Texas Expwy
McAllen ▪ (856) 686-0094
1304 E Expwy 83
Mission ▪ (956) 205-1310
2521 E Expwy 83
Live Oak ▪ (210) 658-5426
8214 Agora Pkwy

## Gristmill River Restaurant & Bar   $$$LD

New Braunfels ▪ (830) 625-0684
1287 Gruene Rd ▪ American ▪ Manager
Tim reports that the restaurant serves "a
few GF diners each week." He notes that
the restaurant has an internal, electronic
list of items that are or can be modified to
be GF, and he recommends asking for that
list and alerting a manager upon arrival.
He cites steaks, salads, and ribs as popular
dishes among the restaurant's GF clientele.
▪ www.gristmillrestaurant.com

## In-N-Out Burger    📖

Allen ▪ (800) 786-1000
190 E Stacy Rd
Arlington ▪ (800) 786-1000
1075 W I-20
Fort Worth ▪ (800) 786-1000
2900 W 7th St
Fort Worth ▪ (800) 786-1000
2916 Quebec St
Frisco ▪ (800) 786-1000
2800 Preston Rd
Garland ▪ (800) 786-1000

150 Town Center Blvd
**Hurst** ▪ (800) 786-1000
780 Airport Fwy
**Irving** ▪ (800) 786-1000
6501 N MacArthur Blvd
**Lancaster** ▪ (800) 786-1000
740 N I-35 E
**Plano** ▪ (800) 786-1000
2740 N Central Expwy
**Rockwall** ▪ (800) 786-1000
1106 E I-30

### Iron Cactus                    ✪$LD
**Bee Cave** ▪ (512) 263-7636
13420 Galleria Circle Suite A128 ▪ Mexican ▪ GF menu available. GF items include steak fajita nachos, taco salad, chipotle smoked pork chops, Yucatan fish tacos, vanilla bean flan, Mexican chocolate mousse and more. ▪ *www.ironcactus.com*

### Jason's Deli                   ✪📖
**Beaumont** ▪ (409) 866-9015
535 Dowlen Rd
**Odessa** ▪ (432) 362-3135
3167 E Univeristy Blvd
**Flower Mound** ▪ (972) 355-3867
60220 Long Prairie Rd
**Frisco** ▪ (972) 377-8625
8250 State Hwy 121
**Round Rock** ▪ (512) 238-9023
117 Louis Henna Blvd
**College Station** ▪ (979) 764-2929
1404 S Texas Ave
**Addison** ▪ (972) 239-0074
5000 Belt Line Rd
**Arlington** ▪ (817) 860-2888
780 Road to 6 Flags W
**Fort Worth** ▪ (817) 738-7144
6244 Camp Bowie Blvd
**Richardson** ▪ (972) 437-9156
101 S Coit Rd
**Bedford** ▪ (817) 354-1511
2200 Airport Fwy
**Tyler** ▪ (903) 561-5380
4913 S Broadway Ave
**Irving** ▪ (972) 432-0555
7707 N MacArthur Blvd
**Beaumont** ▪ (409) 833-5914

112 Gateway St
**Webster** ▪ (281) 338-8000
541 W Bay Area Blvd
**Sugar Land** ▪ (281) 565-3737
15275 Southeast Fwy
**Katy** ▪ (281) 693-3354
21953 Katy Fwy
**Humble** ▪ (281) 540-2551
19755 US 59 Frontage Rd N
**McKinney** ▪ (972) 542-9393
1681 N Central Expwy
**Port Arthur** ▪ (409) 727-6420
170 Central Mall Dr
**Allen** ▪ (972) 727-3440
906 W McDermott Dr
**Plano** ▪ (972) 519-0022
4801 W Parker Rd
**Plano** ▪ (972) 578-2520
925 N Central Expwy
**Grapevine** ▪ (817) 421-0566
1270 William D Tate Ave
**Fort Worth** ▪ (817) 370-9187
5100 Overton Ridge Blvd
**Lewisville** ▪ (972) 459-2905
500 E Round Grove Rd
**Mesquite** ▪ (972) 681-7878
1725 N Town E Blvd
**Waco** ▪ (254) 772-6611
4302 W Waco Dr
**Pasadena** ▪ (713) 946-3354
3905 Spencer Hwy
**The Woodlands** ▪ (281) 419-0100
1340 Lake Woodlands Dr
**Killeen** ▪ (254) 690-7888
3213 E Central Texas Expwy
**Denton** ▪ (940) 484-1234
2219 Hwy 288 Loop
**Abilene** ▪ (325) 692-1975
3490 Catclaw Dr
**Amarillo** ▪ (806) 353-4440
7406 W 34th Ave
**San Marcos** ▪ (512) 393-3354
901 State Highway 80
**Harlingen** ▪ (956) 428-3354
2224 S 77 Sunshine Strip
**McAllen** ▪ (956) 664-2199
4100 N 2nd St
**McAllen** ▪ (956) 664-1700

1308 US 83 Frontage Rd S
**Longview** ▪ (903) 663-5161
103 Route 281 Loop
**Midland** ▪ (432) 682-2200
4610 N Garfield St
**Corpus Christi** ▪ (361) 992-4649
1416 Airline Rd
**Corpus Christi** ▪ (361) 980-8300
5325 Saratoga Blvd
**Victoria** ▪ (361) 575-3354
5301 N Navarro St
**Arlington** ▪ (817) 557-3311
951 Interstate 20 W
**Lubbock** ▪ (806) 799-8660
4001 S Loop 289
**Brownsville** ▪ (956) 350-2400
4365 Route 77
**Rowlett** ▪ (972) 475-0088
5601 President George Bush Tpke
**Fort Worth** ▪ (817) 750-0151
9517 Sage Meadow Trl
**Baytown** ▪ (281) 422-5434
4555 Garth Rd
**Abilene** ▪ (325) 672-4232
1772 State Hwy 351
**Temple** ▪ (254) 771-1948
3034 S 31st St
**Texarkana** ▪ (903) 255-0480
2700 Richmond Rd
**Wichita Falls** ▪ (940) 761-5313
2907 Garnett Ave
**New Braunfels** ▪ (830) 620-4901
280 Interstate 35 Business

### Jasper's　　　　　　　　$$$LD
**Plano** ▪ (512) 832-8012
7161 Bishop Rd
**The Woodlands** ▪ (281) 298-6600
9595 Six Pines Dr ▪ American ▪ Any item
on the menu can be made GF except
for the pizza, soup, crab cakes or blue
cheese chips. Alert server upon arrival. ▪
*www.kentrathbun.com*

### Jersey Mike's　　　　　📖
**Fort Worth** ▪ (817) 358-1807
14113 Trinity Blvd
**Watauga** ▪ (817) 788-2100
7608 Denton Hwy

**Plano** ▪ (972) 509-1881
1881 N Central Expwy
**Irving** ▪ (972) 556-0900
6550 N MacArthur Blvd
**Tyler** ▪ (903) 561-4955
4754 S Broadway
**Southlake** ▪ (817) 488-9090
410 W Southlake Blvd
**Wichita Falls** ▪ (940) 696-8072
3801 Call Field Rd
**Flower Mound** ▪ (972) 906-1066
2701 Cross Timbers Rd
**Richardson** ▪ (972) 994-9900
700 E Campbell Rd
**Plano** ▪ (214) 436-5100
8100 Dallas Pkwy
**Fort Worth** ▪ (817) 294-2460
4833 S Hulen St
**Denton** ▪ (940) 383-8848
1800 S Loop 288
**Tyler** ▪ (903) 747-3437
1690 S Beckham Ave
**Fort Worth** ▪ (817) 570-5875
6318 Camp Bowie Blvd
**Hurst** ▪ (817) 590-8383
1308 W Pipeline Rd
**Richardson** ▪ (972) 792-7100
1920 N Coit Rd
**Longview** ▪ (903) 297-4962
2199 Gilmer Rd
**Frisco** ▪ (972) 668-6003
5110 Eldorado Pkwy
**Longview** ▪ (903) 663-3362
3312 N Fourth St

### Joe's Crab Shack　　　　✪📖
**Arlington** ▪ (817) 261-4696
1520 Nolan Ryan Expwy
**Grapevine** ▪ (817) 251-1515
201 W State Hwy 114
**Galveston** ▪ (409) 766-1515
3502 Seawall Blvd
**McAllen** ▪ (956) 668-9922
711 E Expwy 83
**Lubbock** ▪ (806) 797-8600
5802 W Loopp S 289

*Beaumont* ▪ (409) 842-4433
3825 I-10 S
*Round Rock* ▪ (512) 246-8500
2401 S IH 35
*Plano* ▪ (972) 423-2800
3320 Central Expwy
*Corpus Christi* ▪ (361) 980-0023
5025 S Padre Island Dr
*Mesquite* ▪ (972) 329-7111
1340 N Peachtree Rd
*Humble* ▪ (281) 540-7509
20100 US Hwy 59
*Corpus Christi* ▪ (361) 904-0227
444 N Shoreline
*Galveston* ▪ (409) 763-6888
2000 Harborside Dr on Pier 19
*Fort Worth* ▪ (682) 286-1000
3040 Western Center Blvd
*Lewisville* ▪ (972) 459-9955
2066 S Stemmons
*Cedar Hill* ▪ (972) 293-9612
735 N Hwy 67
*Sugar Land* ▪ (281) 344-2100
19740 Southwest Fwy
*Pearland* ▪ (713) 436-8880
3239 Silverlake Village Dr

### Johnny Brusco's New York Style Pizza
★📖

*Flower Mound* ▪ (972) 691-4900
6050 Long Prairie Rd

### La Trattoria　　　　　　★$$BLD
*Alpine* ▪ (432) 837-2200
901 E Holland Ave ▪ *Italian* ▪ GF items
include medium pizza, linguine or penne
pasta, GF sauces, steaks, chicken and
shrimp dishes. ▪ *www.latrattoriacafe.com*

### Loving Hut　　　　　　　📖
*Addison* ▪ (972) 980-1840
14925 Midway Rd
*Arlington* ▪ (817) 472-0550
4515 Matlock Rd

### Maggiano's Little Italy　　★📖
*Plano* ▪ (972) 781-0776
6001 W Park Blvd

### Mama Fu's Asian House　　✪📖
*Sunset Valley* ▪ (512) 637-6778

5400 Brodie Ln
*Georgetown* ▪ (512) 686-1955
1003 W University Ave
*New Braunfels* ▪ (830) 515-5614
140 S State Hwy 46
*Lubbock* ▪ (806) 500-2336
2531 82nd St

### Melting Pot, The　　　　✪📖
*Arlington* ▪ (817) 469-1444
4000 Five Points Dr
*Shenandoah* ▪ (936) 271-7416
19075 Interstate 45 S

### Nature's Garden Market Café　ɕBLD
*Friendswood* ▪ (281) 996-9596
400 W Parkwood Suite 112 ▪ *Vegetarian*
▪ Sandwiches except for the tuna and the
reuben can be made GF, all of the salads
are GF. ▪ *www.nagamaca.com*

### P.F. Chang's China Bistro　✪★📖
*Allen* ▪ (972) 390-1040
915 W Bethany Dr
*Arlington* ▪ (817) 375-8690
215 E I-20 Hwy
*El Paso* ▪ (915) 845-0166
760 Sunland Park Dr
*Ft Worth* ▪ (817) 840-2450
400 Throckmorton St
*Grapevine* ▪ (817) 421-6658
650 W Highway 114
*Mcallen* ▪ (956) 664-1516
3100 E Expwy 83
*Sugar Land* ▪ (281) 313-8650
2120 Lone Star Dr
*The Woodlands* ▪ (281) 203-6350
1201 Lake Woodlands Dr Ste 301

### Palio's Pizza Café　　　　★ɕLD
*Fort Worth* ▪ (817) 294-7254
4855 Bryant Irvin Rd
*Mansfield* ▪ (817) 453-4992
2200 N Hwy 157 Suite 232 ▪ *Pizza* ▪ GF
pizza is available with homemade pizza
sauce, pesto, or olive oil and with any
toppings except for meatballs. The restaurant reports that they understand the
importance of preventing CC and "work
diligently with their staff to maintain a safe

environment." GF desserts are "coming soon." ▪ *palioscafe.com*

## Pappas Seafood House                    $$$**LD**
*Humble* ▪ *(281) 446-7707*
*20410 Hwy 59 N*
*Webster* ▪ *(281) 332-7546*
*19991 I-45 S* ▪ *Seafood* ▪ The restaurant reports that accommodating dietary requirements is "part of their service" They recommend consulting a server or manager upon arrival, who will help guide diners through the menu and select appropriate options. ▪ *www.pappasseafood.com*

## Pappasito's Cantina                    📖
*Humble* ▪ *(281) 540-8664*
*10005 FM 1960*
*Webster* ▪ *(281) 338-2885*
*20099 Gulf Fwy*
*Arlington* ▪ *(817) 795-3535*
*321 W Road to Six Flags*
*Fort Worth* ▪ *(817) 877-5546*
*2704 W Fwy*

## Pei Wei Asian Diner                    ✪📖
*Allen* ▪ *(469) 675-2266*
*1008 W Mcdermott Dr*
*Amarillo* ▪ *(806) 352-5632*
*3350 S Soncy Rd*
*Arlington* ▪ *(817) 299-8687*
*2100 N Collins St*
*Arlington* ▪ *(817) 466-4545*
*4133 S Cooper St*
*Beaumont* ▪ *(409) 866-0620*
*3050 Dowlen Rd*
*Bee Cave* ▪ *(512) 263-8565*
*12913 Galleria Cir*
*Carrollton* ▪ *(972) 407-0056*
*3412 E Hebron Pkwy*
*College Station* ▪ *(979) 260-1209*
*980A University Dr E*
*Denton* ▪ *(940) 380-9303*
*1931 S Loop 288*
*El Paso* ▪ *(915) 591-2006*
*1325 George Dieter Dr*
*El Paso* ▪ *(915) 581-8540*
*7500 N Mesa St*
*Fort Worth* ▪ *(817) 294-0808*
*5900 Overton Ridge Blvd*

*Fort Worth* ▪ *(817) 806-9950*
*2600 W 7th St*
*Garland* ▪ *(972) 202-5490*
*4170 Lavon Dr*
*Highland Village* ▪ *(972) 317-8809*
*3090 Fm 407*
*Irving* ▪ *(972) 373-8000*
*7600 N MacArthur Blvd*
*Katy* ▪ *(281) 392-1410*
*1590 S Mason Rd*
*Kingwood* ▪ *(281) 318-2877*
*702 Kingwood Dr*
*Lewisville* ▪ *(469) 948-9000*
*713 Hebron Pkwy*
*Lubbock* ▪ *(806) 792-4896*
*4210 82nd St*
*Mckinney* ▪ *(972) 548-9843*
*3000 S Central Expy*
*Pasadena* ▪ *(281) 487-2226*
*5932 Fairmont Pkwy*
*Pearland* ▪ *(713) 436-3840*
*11302 Broadway St*
*Plano* ▪ *(469) 362-8288*
*8412 Preston Rd*
*Plano* ▪ *(972) 202-5380*
*601 W 15th St*
*Round Rock* ▪ *(512) 863-4087*
*200 University Blvd*
*Shenandoah* ▪ *(936) 271-9217*
*19075 I H 45 S*
*Southlake* ▪ *(817) 722-0070*
*1582 E Southlake Blvd*
*Sugar Land* ▪ *(281) 240-1931*
*16101 Kensington Dr*
*Waco* ▪ *(254) 772-0190*
*4300A W Waco Dr*
*Watauga* ▪ *(817) 605-0145*
*7620 Denton Hwy*
*Webster* ▪ *(281) 554-9876*
*19411 Gulf Fwy*
*Addison* ▪ *(972) 764-0844*
*4801 Beltline Rd*

## Post Oak Grill                    $$**LD**
*Sugar Land* ▪ *(281) 491-2901*
*1550 Lake Pointe Pkwy* ▪ *American* ▪ The Post Oak Grill does not offer a GF menu. However, several items from their regular menu are naturally GF or can be prepared

GF such as the grilled salmon, grilled rainbow trout, and various premium cuts of meat. ▪ *www.postoakgrill.com*

### Promise Pizza ★ $LD
*Round Rock* ▪ (512) 674-2642
*1500 A W Grimes Blvd Suite #410* ▪ *Pizza*
▪ A GF pizza is available in the 10 inch and 12 inch sizes and all the toppings are GF. Manager said they take severe precautions to prevent CC such as using completely separate prep areas and utensils. ▪ *www.promisepizza.com*

### RC's Pizza ★ $LD
*Kingwood* ▪ (281) 358-4663
*1202 Kingwood Dr Suite A* ▪ *Pizza* ▪ 12"
GF pizza available. ▪ *www.rcspizza.com*

### Reata Restaurant ✪ $$$$LD
*Alpine* ▪ (432) 837-9232
*203 N 5th St*
*Fort Worth* ▪ (817) 336-1009
*310 Houston St* ▪ *American* ▪ GF menu is available at both locations. The Alpine location does not have as many items on the GF menu as the Fort Worth location does. Items include bacon wrapped shrimp, tamales, elk sausage, smoked quail, salads, ribeye, steak & lobster, grilled chicken, mahi mahi, and salmon. ▪ *www.reata.net*

### Red Brick Pizza ✪★📖
*Colleyville* ▪ (817) 503-7979
*5615 Colleyville Blvd*

### Rio Mamba ✪ $$LD
*Colleyville* ▪ (817) 354-3124
*5150 Hwy 121*
*Fort Worth* ▪ (817) 423-3124
*6125 SW Loop 820*
*Arlington* ▪ (817) 465-3122
*6407 S Cooper St*
*Weatherford* ▪ (817) 598-5944
*1302 S Main St* ▪ *Tex-Mex* ▪ Extensive GF menu available. ▪ *www.riomambo.com*

### Riviera Bistro $$LD
*Bee Cave* ▪ (512) 263-2960
*12801 Shops Pkwy Suite 200* ▪ *European*
▪ Everything in the restaurant is 100% GF.

Dishes include chicken parmesan goujon, seafood and ricotta crepe, macaroni and crab, wild mushroom risotto and more. GF desserts also available, including crepe with chantilly cream and berries, vanilla bean creme brûlée, cheesecake du jour, beignets and more. ▪ *www.rivierabistro.com*

### Rockfish Seafood Grill ✪📖
*Arlington* ▪ (817) 419-9988
*3785 S Cooper St*
*Ft Worth* ▪ (817) 738-3474
*3050 S Hulen St*
*Highland Village* ▪ (972) 317-7744
*4061 Barton Creek*
*Las Colinas* ▪ (214) 574-4111
*7400 N Macarthur Blvd*
*Lubbock* ▪ (806) 780-7625
*6253 Slide Rd*
*Mckinney* ▪ (972) 542-2223
*2780 S Central Expy*
*Plano* ▪ (972) 599-2190
*4701 W Park Blvd*
*Richardson* ▪ (972) 267-8979
*7639 Campbell Rd*
*Southlake* ▪ (817) 442-0131
*228 State St*

### Romano's Macaroni Grill ✪★📖
*Addison* ▪ (972) 386-3831
*4535 Belt Line Rd*
*Arlington* ▪ (817) 784-1197
*1670 W Interstate 20*
*Cedar Hill* ▪ (469) 272-0272
*388 N Highway 67*
*Corpus Christi* ▪ (361) 993-6466
*5133 S Padre Island Dr*
*El Paso* ▪ (915) 594-3979
*11885 Gateway Blvd W*
*Frisco* ▪ (972) 668-6688
*3111 Preston Rd*
*Fort Worth* ▪ (817) 306-9722
*6300 North Fwy*
*Fort Worth* ▪ (817) 336-6676
*1505 S University Dr*
*Grapevine* ▪ (817) 481-1339
*700 W State Highway 114*
*Lewisville* ▪ (972) 459-7700
*2437 S Stemmons Fwy*

McAllen ▪ (756) 687-3500
3500 W Expwy 83
Plano ▪ (972) 527-8829
7205 N Central Expwy
Plano ▪ (972) 964-6676
5005 W Park Blvd
Round Rock ▪ (512) 341-7979
2501 S IH 35
Selma ▪ (210) 566-6055
8355 Agora Pkwy
Spring ▪ (281) 367-3773
1155 Lake Woodlands Dr

### Rosati's Pizza                                 ★ 📖
Garland ▪ (972) 496-9000
5255 N President George Bush Hwy
Waco ▪ (254) 666-6066
824 Hewitt Dr

### Ruggles Green                               ✪★$LD
Sugar Land ▪ (281) 565-1175
15903 City Walk ▪ Organic ▪ GF menu
includes pizzas, quinoa spaghetti, and
several salads. Hostess Dakota reports
that they have "tons" of GF customers. ▪
www.rugglesgreen.com

### Ruth's Chris Steak House              ✪📖
Fort Worth ▪ (817) 348-0080
813 Main St

### Smiling Moose Deli                        ✪📖
Midland ▪ (432) 697-3354
3322 N Loop 250 W
San Angelo ▪ (325) 227-6786
3204 Sherwood
Arlington ▪ (855) 307-3354
441 S Pecan St

### Sugarless DeLite                          ✪★ȼS
Richardson ▪ (972) 644-2000
1389 W Campbell Rd ▪ Bakery ▪ Non-
dedicated bakery with extensive GF offerings. They offer GF cheesecake, chocolate
chip cookies, brownies, and crackers.
All GF items are baked fresh every day. ▪
www.sugarlessdelite.com

### Taste of Ethiopia                           $$$LD
Pflugerville ▪ (512) 251-4053
1100 Grand Ave Pkwy ▪ Ethiopian ▪ GF
options available on request, but the restaurant recommends calling 2 days ahead of
time to ensure timeliness and availability. ▪
www.tasteofethiopiaaustin.com

### Texas De Brazil Churrascaria        ★📖
Fort Worth ▪ (817) 882-9500
101 N Houston St
Addison ▪ (972) 385-1000
15101 Addison Rd

### Thai Thippawan                             ȼLD
Hurst ▪ (469) 454-8424
461 W Harwood Rd ▪ Thai ▪ Restaurant reports that many items on the
menu are GF or can be prepared GF. A
server will be able to advise which options are safe. GF soy sauce is available. ▪
www.thaithippawan.com

### Tin Star Taco Bar                         ✪ȼLD
Arlington ▪ (817) 466-3900
3811 S Cooper St
Frisco ▪ (972) 668-4610
3301 Preston Rd
Frisco ▪ (214) 387-0315
2601 Preston Rd
Plano ▪ (972) 312-8040
340 Coit Rd
Plano ▪ (972) 403-1765
2208 Dallas Pkwy ▪ Mexican ▪ GF menu
includes salads, soups, burrito bowls and
over ten types of tacos, all served on corn
tortillas. ▪ tinstartacobar.com

### Tony Roma's                                   📖
Brownsville ▪ (956) 986-2884
1805 North Expwy
Laredo ▪ (956) 722-7427
5300 San Dario Ave
McAllen ▪ (956) 631-2121
2121 10th St
McAllen ▪ (956) 682-4400
4400 N 10th St

### Uno Chicago Grill                          ✪★📖
Fort Worth ▪ (817) 885-8667
300 Houston St

## Wildfire　$$$LD
**Georgetown** ■ *(512) 869-3473*
*812 S Austin Ave* ■ *American* ■ Manager
Billy reports the restaurant serves GF diners "all the time." He recommends alerting
a server upon arrival, as most servers are
well versed in the GF diet. If, however, a
server seems not to know about the GF
diet, ask for Billy, who will be happy to discuss GF options. ■ *www.wildfiretexas.com*

## Yao Fuzi　★$$D
**Plano** ■ *(214) 473-9267*
*4757 W Park Blvd* ■ *Asian Fusion* ■ GF
soy sauce is available. Restaurant reports
that most of the menu can be modified
to be GF. Alert a server upon arrival. ■
*www.yaofuzi.com*

## Zio's　✪📖
**Ft Worth** ■ *(817) 232-3632*
*6631 Fossil Bluff Dr*
**Georgetown** ■ *(512) 869-6600*
*1007 W University Ave*
**Humble** ■ *(281) 540-7787*
*20380 Hwy 59 N*
**Live Oak** ■ *(210) 637-7787*
*7824 Pat Booker Rd*
**Webster** ■ *(281) 338-7800*
*820 W Bay Area Blvd*
**Lubbock** ■ *(806) 780-6003*
*4414 82nd St*

## Zpizza　✪📖
**Flower Mound** ■ *(972) 355-8585*
*2911 Cross Timbers Rd*
**Round Rock** ■ *(512) 863-8118*
*200 University Blvd*
**San Antonio** ■ *(210) 402-1500*
*700 E Sonterra Blvd*
**West Lake Hills** ■ *(512) 520-8051*
*3300 Bee Caves Rd*

# UTAH

## SALT LAKE CITY

## Bayou　$LD
*Salt Lake City* ■ *(801) 961-8400*
*645 S State St* ■ *Cajun & Creole* ■ The
Bayou features an in restaurant GF menu
with countless options including various protein dishes, salads, and soups. ■
*www.utahbayou.com*

## Biaggi's　✪★📖
*Salt Lake City* ■ *(801) 596-7222*
*194 S 400 W*

## Blossom Fine Foods - Gluten Free
## Bakery　★$S
*Salt Lake City* ■ *(801) 746-4405*
*902 E Logan Ave* ■ *Bakery* ■ Non-dedicated bakery that is primarily wholesale,
but opens to the public on Thursdays
and Fridays. GF cookies, cakes, muffins,
brownies, and more are available. The
signature chocolate torte is GF, as are some
of the carrot cakes, cheesecakes, marble
cream cheese brownies, and other items. ■
*www.blossomfinefoods.com*

## Bombay House　★$D
*Salt Lake City* ■ *(801) 581-0222*
*2731 Parleys Wy* ■ *Indian* ■ Manager
Singh reports that "lots of people" who
are GF dine in. He notes that with the
exception of the samosas and naan bread,
almost everything is naturally GF. Confirm the timeliness of this information
before dining in. Alert a server, and if the
server is not GF aware, ask him or her
to speak to Singh about GF options. ■
*www.bombayhouse.com*

## Buca di Beppo　✪📖
*Salt Lake City* ■ *(801) 575-6262*
*202 W 300 S*

## Café Rio Mexican Grill　📖
*Salt Lake City* ■ *(801) 463-7250*
*3025 E 3300 S*
*Salt Lake City* ■ *(801) 924-3800*

532 E 400 S
*Salt Lake City* ■ (801) 562-4431
6985 S Park Ctr
*Salt Lake City* ■ (385) 282-5400
776 Terminal Dr

### Café Trio $$LD
*Salt Lake City* ■ (801) 533-8746
680 S 900 E ■ *Italian* ■ Café Trio has a
menu that is constantly changing however
they always have a GF dish available in
addition to GF pasta which can be topped
with a majority of their pasta sauces. ■
*www.triodining.com*

### Cakewalk Baking Company ★ $$
*Salt Lake City* ■ (801) 953-0804
434 S 900 E Salt Lake City ■ *Bakery* ■
Various GF baked goods available upon request. ■ *www.cakewalkbakingcompany.com*

### Dodo Restaurant, The ✪$$LD
*Salt Lake City* ■ (801) 486-2473
1355 E 2100 S ■ *Fusion* ■ GF menu available. Items include wings, hummus and
polenta cakes, honey salmon, ahi steak and
Cuban pork as well as a variety of salads. ■
*www.thedodo.net*

### Fleming's Prime
### Steakhouse & Wine Bar ✪▥
*Salt Lake City* ■ (801) 355-3704
20 S 400 W

### Jason's Deli ✪▥
*Salt Lake City* ■ (801) 456-8989
178 S Rio Grande St

### Mazza ✪★$$LD
*Salt Lake City* ■ (801) 521-4572
912 E 900 S
*Salt Lake City* ■ (801) 484-9259
1515 S 1500 E ■ *Middle Eastern* ■ GF menu
available online and in restaurant. Items
include appetizers, soups, salad, falafel,
chicken kabob, shwarma, kafta, baked
eggplant, beef and okra, lamb and spinach,
lamb and rice dolaa, baked kafta, seafood
platter, kebab platter, vegetarian and chick-
en and cauliflower kabseh and a chicken
and eggplant dish. ■ *www.mazzacafe.com*

### Melting Pot, The ✪▥
*Salt Lake City* ■ (801) 521-6358
340 S Main St

### Oh Mai ¢LD
*Salt Lake City* ■ (801) 467-6882
3425 S State St ■ *Vietnamese* ■ GF options
are marked with an asterisk on the online
menu. Dishes include all of the pho noodle
soups, vermicelli noodles "bun", veggie
roll, lemongrass bean curd and more. ■
*www.ohmaisandwich.com*

### Old Spaghetti Factory, The ✪★▥
*Salt Lake City* ■ (801) 521-0424
189 Trolley Sq

### P.F. Chang's China Bistro ✪★▥
*Salt Lake City* ■ (801) 539-0500
174 W 300 S

### Pei Wei Asian Diner ✪▥
*Salt Lake City* ■ (801) 907-2030
1028 E 2100 S
*Salt Lake City* ■ (801) 907-2030
1028 E 2100
*Salt Lake City* ■ (801) 907-2030
1028 E 2100 S

### Penny Ann's Café $$LD
*Salt Lake City* ■ (801) 935-4760
1810 S Main St ■ *Café* ■ Penny Ann's offers
a GF pasta topped with marinara sauce in
addition to various salad and soup options.

### Red Iguana $LD
*Salt Lake City* ■ (801) 322-1489
736 W North Temple ■ *Mexican* ■ GF
items are marked on the menu and include
enchiladas, fish tacos, steak a la ranchera,
chile colorado, tacos, and more. Alert
server upon arrival. ■ *www.rediguana.com*

### Red Rock Brewery $$LD
*Salt Lake City* ■ (801) 521-7446
254 S 200 W ■ *American* ■ Manager
Chantel reports that the staff is "absolutely"
trained on the GF diet. She recommends
alerting the server upon arrival, as they
accommodate GF diners "a lot" and can
help choose a GF meal. GF options include
steak, rice, mashed potatoes, and salads.

Seafood dishes can be made GF without breading. Confirm the timeliness of this information before dining in. Alert a server, who will notify the kitchen. ▪ *www.redrockbrewing.com*

### Rodizio Grill                    ★ 📖
*Salt Lake City* ▪ *(801) 220-0500*
*600 S 700 E Trolley Sq*

### Romano's Macaroni Grill          ✪★📖
*Salt Lake City* ▪ *(801) 293-9003*
*102 E Winchester St*
*Salt Lake City* ▪ *(801) 521-3133*
*110 W Broadway*

### Ruth's Chris Steak House         ✪📖
*Salt Lake City* ▪ *(801) 363-2000*
*275 S W Temple*

### Sage's Café                      ★ $LD
*Salt Lake City* ▪ *(801) 322-3790*
*473 E 300 S* ▪ *Vegetarian* ▪ The "Sensitivity Menu" lists "GF alternative" menu items, including tacos vegetarianos, pesto brown rice risotto, and mushroom stroganoff. For dessert, it lists rum-infused bananas, as well as shakes, floats, and smoothies. GF soy sauce, beer, and cookies are available. ▪ *www.sagescafe.com*

### Sweet Cake Bake Shop             $$$
*Salt Lake City* ▪ *(801) 478-6830*
*457 E 300 S* ▪ *Bakery* ▪ Bakery is 100% GF. From cupcakes to breads, they have an impressive GF menu available to all customers. ▪ *www.sweetcakebakeshop.com*

### U Food Grill                     📖
*Salt Lake City* ▪ *(801) 575-2401*
*776 N Terminal Dr*

### Vertical Diner                   ★ ₵LD
*Salt Lake City* ▪ *(801) 484-8378*
*2280 S W Temple* ▪ *American* ▪ Server David reports that all staff members are "pretty dialed in" to the GF diet, as they serve GF customers "daily." The sunshine burger on a corn tortilla is naturally GF. GF pancakes, biscuits, and gravy are available all day. ▪ *www.verticaldiner.com*

### Vinto                            ✪★₵LD
*Salt Lake City* ▪ *(801) 539-9999*
*418 E 200 S* ▪ *Pizza* ▪ GF pizza and pasta are available. ▪ *www.vinto.com*

### Wing Nutz                        $LD
*Salt Lake City* ▪ *(801) 474-9464*
*3163 E 3300*
*Salt Lake City* ▪ *(801) 456-4255*
*188 Rio Grande* ▪ *American* ▪ The restaurant reports that their wings are neither breaded nor deep fried, making them naturally GF. However, some sauces may contain gluten, so the restaurant recommends asking the server to check ingredients upon dining in. ▪ *www.bakedwingsarebetter.com*

### Z'Tejas Southwestern Grill       ✪★📖
*Salt Lake City* ▪ *(801) 456-0450*
*191 S Rio Grande*

## UTAH

## ALL OTHER CITIES

### 350 Main New American Brasserie
✪$$$D
*Park City* ▪ *(435) 649-3140*
*350 Main St* ▪ *Global* ▪ GF menu includes garlic roasted fingerling potatoes, spinach and warm brie, lobster bisque siam, black pepper crusted venison medallions, New York steak, grilled rocky mountain red trout, basil roasted natural chicken breast, coffee rubbed pork tenderloin and a variety of sides. ▪ *www.350main.com*

### Anasazi Steakhouse & Gallery     $$D
*St. George* ▪ *(435) 674-0095*
*1234 W Sunset Blvd* ▪ *Steakhouse* ▪ GF options include salads topped with chicken, NY strip steak, filet mignon, top sirloin, and sides such as baked potatoes and in season vegetables. ▪ *www.anasazisteakhouse.com*

## Bangkok Garden ★ ₵LD
*Ogden* ▪ *(801) 621-4049*
*2426 Grant Ave* ▪ *Asian Fusion* ▪ Everything on the menu can be made GF upon request. Alert a server, who will inform the chef.

## Black Sheep Café $LD
*Provo* ▪ *(801) 607-2485*
*19 N University Ave* ▪ *Café* ▪ GF options include cheese enchiladas, several salads, proteins, and vegetables. Alert the server upon arrival. ▪ *blacksheepmenu.com*

## Blind Dog Restaurant ★ $$D
*Park City* ▪ *(435) 655-0800*
*1251 Kearns Blvd* ▪ *Modern American* ▪ GF pasta is available with advance notice. Make reservations noting GF, as GF items may take longer to prepare. ▪ *blinddogpc.com*

## Blossom Fine Foods - Gluten Free Bakery ★ ₵S
*West Valley* ▪ *(801) 746-4454*
*3403 S 1400 W* ▪ *Bakery* ▪ Non-dedicated bakery that is primarily wholesale, but opens to the public on Thursdays and Fridays. GF cookies, cakes, muffins, brownies, and more are available. The signature chocolate torte is GF, as are some of the carrot cakes, cheesecakes, marble cream cheese brownies, and other items. ▪ *www.blossomfinefoods.com*

## Blu Pig, The ★ $D
*Moab* ▪ *(435) 259-3333*
*811 S Main St* ▪ *Barbeque* ▪ The manager states that almost 95% of their menu is GF, and recommends alerting the server to assist in selecting a GF meal. ▪ *www.blupigbbq.com*

## Bombay House ★ $D
*Provo* ▪ *(801) 373-6677*
*463 N University Ave*
*West Jordan* ▪ *(801) 282-0777*
*7726 Campus View Dr* ▪ *Indian* ▪ Manager Singh reports that "lots of people" who are GF dine in. He notes that with the exception of the samosas and naan bread, almost everything is naturally GF.

Confirm the timeliness of this information before dining in. Alert a server, and if the server is not GF aware, ask him or her to speak to Singh about GF options. ▪ *www.bombayhouse.com*

## Boston's Restaurant & Sports Bar ✪ ★ 📖
*Layton* ▪ *(801) 779-9088*
*694 W Antelope Dr*

## Buca di Beppo ✪📖
*Midvale* ▪ *(801) 561-9463*
*935 Fort Union Blvd*
*St. George* ▪ *(435) 627-6832*
*1812 E Red Cliffs Dr*

## Café Rio Mexican Grill 📖
*St. George* ▪ *(435) 656-0200*
*471 E St George Blvd*
*American Fork* ▪ *(801) 756-9088*
*821 W State St*
*Bountiful* ▪ *(801) 383-6500*
*234 S 500 W*
*Draper* ▪ *(801) 572-3125*
*62 E 12300 S*
*W Valley City* ▪ *(801) 613-4000*
*2885 S 5600 W*
*Layton* ▪ *(801) 991-1800*
*2065 N Harris Blvd*
*Logan* ▪ *(435) 774-8300*
*1460 N Main St*
*Ogden* ▪ *(801) 409-9800*
*4015 S Riverdale Rd*
*Orem* ▪ *(801) 822-5700*
*147 N State St*
*Snyderville* ▪ *(435) 200-6200*
*1456 W Newpark Blvd*
*Provo* ▪ *(801) 375-5133*
*2250 N University Pkwy*
*Sandy* ▪ *(801) 316-1000*
*9320 S Village Shop Dr*
*S Jordan* ▪ *(801) 495-4340*
*1664 W Town Ctr Dr*
*Taylorsville* ▪ *(801) 327-9050*
*1856 W 5400 S*
*Cedar City* ▪ *(435) 867-3800*
*1243 S Sage Dr*
*Vernal* ▪ *(435) 781-8100*
*1205 W Hwy 40*
*Toole* ▪ *(435) 228-9800*

1205 N Main St
*Spanish Fork* ▪ *(801) 210-5200*
*782 N 800 E*

### Carino's Italian                    ✿ 📖
*Sandy* ▪ *(801) 553-2580*
*10585 S State St*
*West Jordan* ▪ *(801) 282-8591*
*7191 Plaza Center Dr*

### Center Street Deli                ★ ₵L
*Provo* ▪ *(801) 607-5783*
*434 W Center St* ▪ *Deli* ▪ GF bread
and bagels are available and can be
used to make any sandwich GF. ▪
*www.centerstreetdeliprovo.com*

### Chimayo                          $$$$D
*Park City* ▪ *(435) 649-6222*
*368 Main St* ▪ *Southwest* ▪ Restaurant
reports that 90% of the menu is GF. ▪
*www.chimayorestaurant.com*

### David's Pizza                    ★ $LD
*Kaysville* ▪ *(801) 593-0897*
*253 W 200 N* ▪ *Pizza* ▪ GF pizza is available. ▪ *www.davidspizzakaysville.com*

### Diego's Taco Shop                ₵LD
*Provo* ▪ *(801) 377-4710*
*45 W 300 N* ▪ *Mexican* ▪ The restaurant reports that any of their tacos are GF if made
with corn tortillas. Confirm the timeliness
of this information before dining in.

### Eddie McStiff's                  ✿★ ₵LD
*Moab* ▪ *(435) 259-2337*
*57 S Main St* ▪ *American* ▪ GF pizza and
beer is available ▪ *www.eddiemcstiffs.com*

### Eleanor's                        ₵BLD
*Sandy* ▪ *(801) 563-7466*
*9495 S 560 W Building D* ▪ *Bakery & Café*
▪ Owner said because all of their cooks
have Celiac, they understand the importance of creating delicious and healthy GF
foods. Their menu is updated daily with
items such as fruit cake pops, mini loaves,
and cinnamon with raisin sweet rolls. ▪
*www.eleanorsbakeshop.com*

### Freebirds on the Fly             ✿ 📖
*Arlington* ▪ *(817) 468-5300*
*4000 Arlington Highlands Blvd*

### Gecko's Mexican Grill            $LD
*S Jordan* ▪ *(801) 253-8668*
*781 W 10600 S Jordan Pkwy* ▪ *Mexican*
▪ Many dishes on the menu can be modified to be GF. Avoid enchilada sauce and
chimichangas. Most dishes can be made
with a corn tortilla and the enchilada
sauce can be replaced with a salsa verde.
Restaurant has a separate fryer for GF
foods, but GF diners must request that
items are cooked in the separate fryer. ▪
*www.geckosmexicangrill.com*

### Goodwood Barbecue Company        $LD
*Orem* ▪ *(801) 224-1962*
*777 E University Pkwy*
*Draper* ▪ *(801) 495-4840*
*133 E 12300 S*
*Riverdale* ▪ *(801) 393-0426*
*4237 S Riverdale Rd* ▪ *Barbeque* ▪ Most
menu items except for sandwiches are
GF, manager will assist with GF orders. ▪
*goodwoodbbq.com*

### Grub Steak Restaurant           ✿$$$$LD
*Park City* ▪ *(435) 649-8060*
*2200 Sidewinder Dr* ▪ *Steakhouse* ▪ GF
menu available. Items include king crab
and shrimp martini, fresh grilled artichoke, roasted chicken, baked Idaho ruby
trout, black tiger jumbo prawns, northwestern salmon filet, Maine cold water
lobster tail, Alaskan halibut, Kansas city
steak, elk sirloin, aged rocky mountain
natural lamb chops, filet of fresh salmon
and dessert includes a flourless chocolate
cake, crème brûlée and fresh berries. ▪
*www.grubsteakrestaurant.com*

### In-N-Out Burger                  📖
*American Fork* ▪ *(800) 786-1000*
*601 W Main St*
*Centerville* ▪ *(800) 786-1000*
*475 North 700 W*
*Draper* ▪ *(800) 786-1000*

*12191 S State St*
*Midvale ▪ (800) 786-1000*
*7206 S Union Park Ave*
*Orem ▪ (800) 786-1000*
*350 E University Pkwy*
*Riverton ▪ (800) 786-1000*
*12569 S Crossing Dr*
*Washington City ▪ (800) 786-1000*
*832 W Telegraph St*
*West Jordan ▪ (800) 786-1000*
*7785 Jordan Landing Blvd*
*West Valley City ▪ (800) 786-1000*
*3715 S Constitution Blvd*

**Jason's Deli**    ✪📖
*Murray ▪ (801) 263-1000*
*184 E Winchester St*
*Orem ▪ (801) 655-1150*
*771 E University Pkwy*

**Joe's Crab Shack**    ✪📖
*Sandy ▪ (801) 225-9571*
*9400 S State St*
*West Jordan ▪ (801) 282-8802*
*7277 S Plaza Center Dr*

**Loco Lizard Cantina**    ✪$LD
*Park City ▪ (435) 645-7000*
*1612 Ute Blvd Suite 101 ▪ Mexican ▪* Manager Steve says that almost everything on their menu is GF or can be requested to be GF. ▪ *www.locolizardcantina.com*

**Lone Star Steakhouse & Saloon**    ✪📖
*Midvale ▪ (801) 568-2600*
*7176 S 900 E*

**Los Hermanos**
**Mexican Restaurant**    ★$LD
*Provo ▪ (801) 375-5732*
*71 E Center St*
*Lindon ▪ (801) 785-1715*
*295 N State St ▪ Mexican ▪* Manager states they always make a special effort to accommodate any needs of their customers, especially people who are gluten intolerant. Be sure to ask the server about GF alternatives before ordering. ▪ *www.loshermanosutah.com*

**Maddox Ranch House**    $$$LD
*Perry ▪ (435) 723-8545*
*1900 S Highway 89 ▪ Steakhouse ▪* Alert server upon arrival, and they will provide a list of items that are NOT GF and help select a GF meal. ▪ *www.maddoxfinefood.com*

**Madeline's Steakhouse & Grill**    $$$LD
*Sandy ▪ (801) 446-6639*
*10290 S State ST ▪ Steakhouse ▪* GF options specified on menu. Items include fire roasted artichokes, Italian stuffed mushroom caps, pineapple chicken, slow roasted prime rib, ribeye, New York strip steak, filet mignon, grilled halibut, broiled Maine lobster tail and Alaskan snow crab. ▪ *www.madelinessteakhouse.com*

**Mandarin**    ✪★$D
*Bountiful ▪ (801) 298-2406*
*348 E 900 N ▪ Chinese ▪* GF menu includes cashew chicken or vegetable, curry chicken or beef, Mongolian beef, and tropical Thai chicken, halibut, or tofu, among other selections. GF soy sauce is available. Among the GF desserts are ginger ice cream and raspberry vanilla bean crème brûlée. ▪ *www.mandarinutah.com*

**McGrath's Fish House**    ✪📖
*Sandy ▪ (801) 571-1905*
*10590 S State St*
*Layton ▪ (801) 771-3474*
*908 N Main St*

**Mountain West Burrito**    ¢LD
*Provo ▪ (801) 805-1870*
*1796 N 950 W*
*Provo ▪ (801) 607-1766*
*815 N 700 E ▪ Mexican ▪* The restaurant offers GF salads as well as tacos made with corn tortillas, which are available with a variety of meats such as chicken, beef, and shrimp. Confirm the timeliness of this information before dining in. Alert the server upon arrival. ▪ *mountainwestburrito.com*

## Old Spaghetti Factory, The   ✪★📖
*Orem ▪ (801) 224-6199*
*575 E University Pkwy*
*Taylorsville ▪ (801) 966-2765*
*5718 S 1900 W*

## P.F. Chang's China Bistro   ✪★📖
*Orem ▪ (801) 426-0900*
*575 E University Pkwy*

## Painted Pony Restaurant, The   $LD
*St. George ▪ (435) 634-1700*
*2 W St George Blvd ▪ Seafood & Steak-*
house ▪ The staff reports that they are always willing to accommodate GF diners and have many dishes on the menu that can be prepared GF. Alert server upon arrival. ▪ *www.painted-pony.com*

## Park City Pizza Co.   ✪★$$LD
*Park City ▪ (435) 649-1591*
*1612 Ute Blvd #111 ▪ Pizza ▪* GF pizza, pasta, and sandwiches are available upon request. ▪ *www.parkcitypizzaco.com*

## Pasta Jays   ★
*Moab ▪ (435) 259-2900*
*4 S Main St ▪ Italian ▪* GF pizza is available in the small size, as well as GF pasta. Staff reports that GF pizzas are prepared in a separate area and cooked on a separate stone to reduce the chance of CC. Selection changes daily so be sure to call ahead to confirm availability. ▪ *www.pastajays.com*

## Pei Wei Asian Diner   ✪📖
*Midvale ▪ (801) 601-3170*
*1148 E Fort Union Blvd*
*Sandy ▪ (801) 601-1990*
*10373 S State St*
*W Bountiful ▪ (801) 294-0929*
*71 N 500 W*

## Pizza Pie Café   ✪★$LD
*Provo ▪ (801) 373-5561*
*2235 N University Pkwy*
*Highland ▪ (801) 763-5530*
*5435 W 11000 N*
*Logan ▪ (435) 753-5590*
*25 E 1400 N*
*Bountiful ▪ (801) 683-8735*

*370 W 500 S ▪ Pizza ▪* GF pizza and pasta are available. Any pizza can be made with GF crust; however, pasta sauce options are somewhat limited. ▪ *www.pizzapiecafe.co/*

## Red Rock Brewery   $$LD
*Park City ▪ (435) 575-0295*
*1640 Redstone Ctr Dr*
*Murray ▪ (801) 262-2337*
*Fashion Pl Mall ▪ American ▪* Manager Chantel reports that the staff is "absolutely" trained on the GF diet. She recommends alerting the server upon arrival, as they accommodate GF diners "a lot" and can help choose a GF meal. GF options include steak, rice, mashed potatoes, and salads. Seafood dishes can be made GF without breading. Confirm the timeliness of this information before dining in. Alert a server, who will notify the kitchen. ▪ *www.redrockbrewing.com*

## Riverwalk Grill   $LD
*St. George ▪ (435) 773-4111*
*4210 Bluegrass Wy ▪ American ▪* The restaurant reports that many items on the menu can be prepared GF. Options include grilled chicken and salmon, fresh trout, and a roasted pork tenderloin. Some items require the omission of a certain ingredient or side, so be sure to alert the server upon arrival. ▪ *www.theriverwalkgrill.com*

## Rodizio Grill   ★📖
*American Fork ▪ (801) 763-4946*
*749 W 100 N*

## Romano's Macaroni Grill   ✪★📖
*Provo ▪ (801) 765-1688*
*4801 N University Ave*

## Roosters Brewing Company   ★$$LD
*Ogden ▪ (801) 627-6171*
*253 Historic 25th St*
*Layton ▪ (801) 774-9330*
*748 W Heritage Pk Blvd ▪ American ▪* The GF menu items include pepperjack shrimp, fish tacos, enchiladas, Atlantic salmon and a GF 10" pizza with three flavor options. ▪ *www.roostersbrewingco.com*

## Ruth's Chris Steak House ✪📖
*Park City* ▪ *(435) 940-5070*
*2001 Park Ave*

## Sakura Japanese Steak House & Sushi
★$$LD
*St. George* ▪ *(435) 275-2888*
*939 E St George Blvd* ▪ *Steakhouse* ▪ GF
soy sauce can be used to prepare most
dishes, making almost every menu item
available GF. Alert the server upon arrival.
▪ *www.sakuraut.com*

## Smoky Mountain Pizzeria Grill ✪★$LD
*Sandy* ▪ *(801) 523-7070*
*1850 E 9400 S* ▪ *Pizza* ▪ GF pizza is
available in the 10.5 inch size, as well as
GF penne pasta and several grilled meat
and fish items. Food & beverage director
Tom reports that they have procedures
in place to prevent CC, and recommends
consulting with a manager upon arrival to
ensure that your meal is handled safely. ▪
*www.smokymountainpizza.com*

## Sweet Cake Bake Shop $$$
*Kaysville* ▪ *(801) 444-3288*
*237 W 200 N* ▪ *Bakery* ▪ Bakery is 100%
GF. From cupcakes to breads, they have an
impressive GF menu available to all customers. ▪ *www.sweetcakebakeshop.com*

## Taste of India ★$LD
*Layton* ▪ *(801) 614-0107*
*1664 N Woodland Park Dr*
*West Jordan* ▪ *(801) 618-2200*
*9200 S Redwood Rd*
*Bountiful* ▪ *(801) 683-7393*
*282 S 500 W* ▪ *Indian* ▪ There is no
GF menu but the manager states most
items on the menu are GF. They do not
use any gluten in their food except for
their samosas, which is an appetizer. ▪
*www.tasteofindiautah.com*

## Texas De Brazil Churrascaria ★📖
*Salt Lake City* ▪ *(385) 232-8070*
*50 S Main St*

## Union Grill $LD
*Ogden* ▪ *(801) 621-2830*
*2501 Wall Ave* ▪ *American* ▪ Manager
Annette reports that most items must be
modified to be GF. For example, GF diners can order fajitas with no tortilla, or
filet mignon without sauce. BBQ ribs are
naturally GF. Confirm the timeliness of
this information before dining in. Annette
notes that servers have lists of GF items
at all service stations. Alert a server upon
arrival. Located in the south end of Union
Station. ▪ *www.uniongrillogden.com*

## Vinto ✪★¢LD
*Park City* ▪ *(435) 615-9990*
*900 Main St* ▪ *Pizza* ▪ GF pizza and pasta
are available. ▪ *www.vinto.com*

## Wahso Asian Grill $$$$D
*Park City* ▪ *(435) 615-0300*
*577 Main St* ▪ *Asian* ▪ Almost everything
on the menu can be made GF or is naturally
GF. Alert a server upon arrival and they will
list a selection of items. ▪ *www.wahso.com*

## Wallabys Smokehouse ✪¢LD
*Lindon* ▪ *(801) 785-4447*
*131 S State St* ▪ *Barbecue* ▪ Menu states
that 95% of the menu is GF. The kitchen
staff takes extra care in preventing CC
because of the large volume of gluten intolerant customers that they have on a daily
basis. ▪ *www.wallabyssmokehouse.com*

## Windy's Sukiyaki ✪$D
*Ogden* ▪ *(801) 621-4505*
*3809 Riverdale Rd* ▪ *Japanese* ▪ Extensive
GF menu that includes miso soup, suki-
yaki, and many other options. Confirm
the timeliness of this information before
dining in. ▪ *windyssukiyaki.com*

## Wing Nutz $LD
*St George* ▪ *(435) 231-4492*
*1091 N Bluff St*
*S Jordan* ▪ *(801) 495-4623*
*11580 S District Main Dr*
*Ogden* ▪ *(801) 528-5698*
*2332 Kiesel Ave*
*Draper* ▪ *(801) 727-7813*

12300 S 121 E
Orem ■ (801) 655-1433
1054 S 750 E
Sandy ■ (801) 727-7850
9260 S Village Shop Dr
W Valley City ■ (801) 965-9464
2843 S 5600 W
Murray ■ (801) 268-9464
5967 S State St
St George ■ (435) 628-6889
15 S River Rd
Taylorsville ■ (801) 955-9644
1899 W 5400 S ■ American ■ The restaurant reports that their wings are neither breaded nor deep fried, making them naturally GF. However, some sauces may contain gluten, so the restaurant recommends asking the server to check ingredients upon dining in. ■ www.bakedwingsarebetter.com

## Xetava Gardens Restaurant    $$BLD
Ivins ■ (435) 656-0165
815 Coyote Gulch Cir ■ American ■ GF options include seared tenderloin, wild salmon, and chili garlic lamb in addition to sides such as salad, fried avocado, and artichokes. Alert the server upon arrival. ■ sites.google.comsite/xetava/home/

## Zoom    $$$$D
Park City ■ (435) 649-9108
660 Main St ■ American ■ GF items include steamed mussels, ceviche with avocado and corn chips, tomato soup, salads, rotisserie chicken with Spanish rice, grilled steelhead, filet mignon and ribeye steak. ■ www.zoomparkcity.com

# VERMONT

## 1846 Tavern & Restaurant at the West Dover Inn    $$$D
W Dover ■ (802) 464-5207
108 Rte 100 ■ American ■ The restaurant reports that they have "a few items" that can be prepared GF. Examples include seafood, filet mignon without sauce, and salads. Ask to speak with a manager upon arrival and they will go over the options. ■ www.mountsnowrestaurant.com

## American Flatbread    ★$D
Waitsfield ■ (802) 496-8856
46 Lareau Rd
Burlington ■ (802) 861-2999
115 Saint Paul St
Middlebury ■ (802) 388-3300
137 Maple St ■ American ■ GF flatbread pizza is available at all Vermont locations. George at customer service reports that they use a new cutter and peel for each GF order, but since there is "flour everywhere", CC is still a possibility. ■ www.americanflatbread.com

## Amuse Restaurant    $$$$D
Essex Junction ■ (802) 764-1489
70 Essex Wy ■ American ■ Head chef reports that they can always accommodate GF diners, and adds that the majority of salads and meat dishes are naturally prepared GF. Reservations noting GF are highly recommended.

## Angkor Wat    $D
Woodstock ■ (802) 457-9029
61 Pleasant St ■ Asian Fusion ■ The restaurant reports that all dishes can be prepared GF by "removing certain sauces". Alert the server upon arrival and they will make recommendations for GF options and notify the chef. ■ www.angkorwatrestaurant.com

### Asiana Noodle Shop $LD
*Burlington* ■ *(802) 862-8828*
*88 Church St* ■ *Asian* ■ Manager Lynn
says they occasionally have a few GF
options but recommends calling ahead
before visiting to confirm availability. ■
*www.asiananoodleshop.com*

### Bagitos ★ ¢BLD
*Montpelier* ■ *(802) 229-9212*
*28 Main St* ■ *Global* ■ GF items vary
daily. Some sample items include cookies,
brownies, and other baked goods. Call before visiting to find out current GF options.
■ *www.bagitos.com*

### Barkeaters Restaurant ✪$$LD
*Shelburne* ■ *(802) 985-2830*
*97 Falls Rd* ■ *American* ■ Barkeaters offers
a GF menu featuring items such as various
garden salads, cedar planked salmon, lemon garlic & herb roasted chicken and filet
mignon. ■ *www.barkeatersrestaurant.com*

### Bee's Knees ✪$$BLD
*Morrisville* ■ *(802) 888-7889*
*82 Lwr Main St* ■ *American* ■ GF items
are marked on the menu and include
dishes such as steamed mussels, nachos
with black bean dip, grilled salmon, and
spicy fries. Alert the server upon arrival
and note that your meal must be GF. ■
*www.thebeesknees-vt.com*

### Benner's Bagels Pizza 'N What Nosh
¢BLD
*Bennington* ■ *(802) 753-7772*
*604 Main St* ■ *American* ■ GF pizza is
available daily in the 12". Pizza is made
on separate surfaces and then baked
on top of dedicated GF pan in order to
minimize CC.

### Bennington Station Restaurant $$LD
*Bennington* ■ *(802) 442-7900*
*150 Depot St* ■ *American* ■ No GF menu
but some items on the regular menu can
be made GF. Alert server of any dietary
restrictions and they will inform kitchen
staff. Kitchen staff reports that prep items

are cleaned before being used to prepare
GF meals. ■ *www.benningtonstation.com*

### Birchgrove Baking ¢BL
*Montpelier* ■ *(802) 223-0200*
*279 Elm St* ■ *Bakery & Café* ■ Various "flourless" baked goods and cakes
are available if ordered in advance. ■
*www.birchgrovebaking.com*

### Bistro Henry $$$D
*Manchester Ctr* ■ *(802) 362-4982*
*1942 Depot St* ■ *French* ■ The restaurant reports a variety of entrées which
are GF or can be prepared GF. Options
include rabbit, chicken breast, duck, and
seafood items like lobster and tuna. ■
*www.bistrohenry.com*

### Boho Café ¢L
*White River Jct* ■ *(802) 296-2227*
*39 Main St* ■ *Deli* ■ GF bread is available
for sandwiches. Some of their soups and
salads are also GF. Ask a server for details. ■
*bohocafe.co*

### Boloco ★📖
*Burlington* ■ *(802) 658-9771*
*92 Church St*

### Café & Bakery at Healthy Living ★¢S
*S Burlington* ■ *(802) 863-2569*
*222 Dorset St* ■ *American* ■ GF options available daily. Some items include
quinoa black bean and cheddar stuffed
peppers, red lentil dhal, and sautéed
vegetable medley. Call ahead of time
to confirm timeliness of information. ■
*www.healthylivingmarket.com*

### Café Provence ✪$$$LD
*Brandon* ■ *(802) 247-9997*
*11 Center St* ■ *Mediterranean* ■ GF menu
available online and in-house. Items included are rustic tomato soup, caesar salad,
various appetizers, entrees and dessert. ■
*cafeprovencevt.com*

### Cai's Dim Sum Teahouse ✪¢D
*Brattleboro* ■ *(802) 257-7898*
*814 Western Ave* ■ *Chinese* ■ GF and GF
optional items are marked on the regular

menu and include Vietnamese spring rolls, eight treasure rice, stir-fried greens with tofu, ginger shrimp, stir-fried beef, and more. Alert server upon arrival. ■ *dimsumvt.com*

### Cantina di Gerardo                          $$LD
*St Johnsbury* ■ *(802) 748-0598*
*378 Railroad St* ■ *Italian* ■ The restaurant reports that almost anything on the menu can be altered to be GF. Alert the server upon arrival.

### Chubby Muffin, The                          ¢BL
*Burlington* ■ *(802) 540-0050*
*88 Oak St* ■ *Deli* ■ GF muffins are prepared on a daily basis and are baked first to prevent CC. The restaurant recommends calling beforehand to confirm that GF items are in stock. ■ *www.thechubbymuffin.com*

### Church & Main                               $$LD
*Burlington* ■ *(802) 540-3040*
*156 Church St* ■ *Modern American* ■ The restaurant reports that a GF dish is prepared every night in addition to the variety of naturally GF chicken, steak, and seafood items on the menu. Alert the server upon arrival. ■ *www.churchandmainvt.com*

### Cilantro                                     ¢LD
*Manchester* ■ *(802) 768-8141*
*5036 Main St* ■ *Mexican* ■ A Cilantro employee said they have corn tacos which are GF and are prepared in a separate area to prevent CC from occurring. ■ *cilantrorestaurantvt.com*

### Cloudland Farm Restaurant                    $$$$D
*N Pomfret* ■ *(802) 457-2599*
*1101 Cloudland Rd* ■ *American* ■ The restaurant reports that they are willing to accommodate GF diners and have a variety of items on the menu that can easily be made GF. ■ *www.cloudlandfarm.com*

### Cockadoodle Pizza & Café            ★ ¢LD
*Bethel* ■ *(802) 234-9666*
*235 Main St* ■ *Pizza* ■ GF pizza crust is available. ■ *cockadoodlepizza.com*

### Das Bierhaus                                 ★ $$LD
*Burlington* ■ *(802) 881-0600*
*175 Church St* ■ *European* ■ Several GF beers available daily, which include Green's Endevour and Bard's gold lager. All their sausages, red cabbage, and kebobs are GF too. Alert server and the server will discuss all the GF options available for that night. ■ *www.dasbierhausvt.com*

### Dover Forge Restaurant                       $$$LD
*W Dover* ■ *(802) 464-5320*
*183 Rte 100* ■ *American* ■ Dover Forge does not have a GF menu, however they offer several options which can be prepared GF such as filet mignon, chicken, salmon, and various soups and salads. ■ *www.doverforge.com*

### El Cortijo                                   ¢LD
*Burlington* ■ *(802) 497-1668*
*189 Bank St* ■ *Mexican* ■ The restaurant reports that most items on the regular menu are naturally GF, but recommends avoiding fried items, as there is no dedicated fryer. Alert server upon arrival. ■ *www.cortijovt.com*

### El Zorro                                     $$LD
*Cambridge* ■ *(802) 644-1499*
*87 Edwards Rd* ■ *Mexican* ■ The restaurant reports that many items on the menu can be prepared GF. Be sure to alert server upon arrival and they will list items that can be made GF. ■ *elzorrovt.com*

### Elixir Restaurant                            $$D
*White River Jct* ■ *(802) 281-7009*
*188 S Main St* ■ *American* ■ Several dishes and entrées are or can be prepared GF. Owners are "big on hospitality" and will make the necessary accommodations for any dietary needs possible. ■ *www.elixirrestaurant.com*

### Farmhouse Tap & Grill                        $$LD
*Burlington* ■ *(802) 859-0888*
*160 Bank St* ■ *Modern American* ■ According to server Sherry, many items on the menu can be modified to be GF. Their house burgers can be made GF

by substituting their buns with lettuce. They do not have dedicated fryers, so they recommend avoiding fried foods. ▪ *www.farmhousetg.com*

### Fiddle Heads Café   ¢LD
*Worcester* ▪ *(802) 223-2111*
*18 Worcester Village Rd* ▪ *Vegan* ▪ Owner Linda reports that everything on the menu is GF. ▪ *www.vt-fiddle.com*

### Fifty-Six Main Street Restaurant   $$LD
*Springfield* ▪ *(802) 885-6987*
*56 Main St* ▪ *American* ▪ GF pizza is available, as well as a nightly GF en-trée. Call ahead for availability. ▪ *www.fiftysixmainstreet.com*

### Firebird Café, The   ★¢BL
*Essex Junction* ▪ *(802) 316-4265*
*163 Pearl St* ▪ *American* ▪ All wraps and paninis can be made with GF bread upon request. Call ahead to confirm availability. ▪ *www.thefirebirdcafe.com*

### Fireworks Restaurant   ★$$D
*Brattleboro* ▪ *(802) 254-2073*
*69-73 Main St* ▪ *Italian* ▪ Fireworks offers GF pizza and pasta for an additional charge of $2. ▪ *fireworksrestaurant.net*

### Garlic John's Restaurant   ✿$$D
*Manchester Ctr* ▪ *(802) 362-9843*
*1610 Depot St* ▪ *Italian* ▪ GF items in-dicated on menu. Items include Prince Edward Island mussels, baby hard-shell clams, grilled shrimp, mixed baby greens, arugula salad, caprese, wedge salad, GF fusilli pasta and grilled salmon. ▪ *www.garlicjohnsrestaurant.com*

### Green Goddess Café   ¢BL
*Stowe* ▪ *(802) 253-5255*
*618 S Main St* ▪ *American* ▪ Several items on the regular menu are naturally GF, including the build your own salad section and sandwiches and wraps without the bun or tortilla. ▪ *www.greengoddessvt.com*

### Gringo Jacks   ✿$LD
*Manchester Ctr* ▪ *(802) 362-0836*
*5103 Main St* ▪ *Southwest* ▪ GF menu

includes several tacos, enchiladas, fajitas, and several BBQ options. For dessert, Mexican flan and sorbet are available. ▪ *www.gringojacks.com*

### Handy's Lunch   ¢BL
*Burlington* ▪ *(802) 864-5963*
*74 Maple St* ▪ *American* ▪ GF breakfast items are available, as well as sandwiches that can be wrapped in lettuce. Call ahead before visiting to order potatoes, as they are fried in a shared fryer but can be pan fried with advance notice. ▪ *www.handyslunch.com*

### Harrison's Restaurant   $$$D
*Stowe* ▪ *(802) 253-7773*
*25 Main St* ▪ *American* ▪ The restau-rant reports that most of their menu is naturally GF. Options include Prince Edward Island mussels, filet mignon, grilled ribeye, pan seared trout, and chicken piccata. Alert server upon arrival. ▪ *www.harrisonsstowe.com*

### Healthy Living Market and Café   ✪$BLD
*S Burlington* ▪ *(802) 853-2569*
*222 Dorset St* ▪ *Café* ▪ Menu changes daily, but the restaurant reports that GF options are always available. Examples include teri-yaki tofu, tortilla soup, and paprika roasted chicken. ▪ *healthylivingmarket.com*

### Hearth & Candle   $$$D
*Jeffersonville* ▪ *(802) 644-8090*
*4323 Vt Rte 108 S* ▪ *American* ▪ No GF menu but manager said they can "cer-tainly" modify a few dishes to be GF upon request. There is also a flourless chocolate cake for dessert. Confirm the timeliness of this information before dining in. ▪ *www.hearthandcandle.com*

### Hen of the Wood   $$$D
*Waterbury* ▪ *(802) 244-7300*
*92 Stowe St* ▪ *Modern American* ▪ Execu-tive Chef Eric reports that while they do not have any specific CC policies, they can "definitely provide GF alternatives." ▪ *www.henofthewood.com*

## Hunger Mountain Coop ★ ¢BLD
*Montpelier ■ (802) 223-8000*
*623 Stone Cutters Wy ■ Café ■* Menu
changes periodically. However, they always
offer some form of GF baked good such
as a Currant Cinnamon GF muffin. ■
*www.hungermountain.coop/*

## India House, The $LD
*Burlington ■ (802) 862-7800*
*207 Colchester Ave ■ Indian ■* Does not
feature a GF menu. However, they offer
several soups, salads, and curries all of
which are GF.

## Istanbul Kebab House $LD
*Essex Junction ■ (802) 857-5091*
*10 Kellogg Rd ■ Mediterranean ■* The
restaurant reports that they have many
naturally GF dishes on the menu, and recommends asking a server to help select a
GF meal. ■ *www.istanbulkebabhousevt.com*

## J Morgan's Steakhouse $$D
*Montpelier ■ (802) 223-5222*
*100 State St ■ Steakhouse ■* J Morgan's has a wide variety of GF protein
items such as chicken Vermont, mint
lamp lollipops, blackened jumbo scallops, and teriyaki chicken skewers. ■
*www.capitolplaza.com/jMorgans.php*

## Jeff's Restaurant ★ $$$LD
*Saint Albans ■ (802) 524-6135*
*65 N Main St ■ Seafood ■* GF pasta is "usually" available. Call ahead to confirm availability, and alert the server upon arrival. ■
*www.jeffsmaineseafoodrestaurant.com*

## Julio's Cantina $LD
*Montpelier ■ (802) 229-9348*
*54 State St ■ Mexican ■* The restaurant reports that most menu items can
be made GF if served with corn tortillas. Alert the server upon arrival. ■
*www.julioscantina.com*

## Juniper's at the Wildflower Inn ✪ ★ $$$LD
*Lyndonville ■ (802) 626-8310*
*2059 Darling Hill Rd ■ American ■* Full GF
menu includes maple bacon wrapped scallops, grilled NY sirloin, baked stuffed trout,
polenta au gratin, and more. GF hamburger buns and pasta are available. The chef reports that they are "very conscious" about
CC, as one of owner's children is gluten
sensitive. ■ *www.junipersrestaurant.com*

## Kismet ★ ¢D
*Montpelier ■ (802) 223-8646*
*52 State St ■ American ■* GF buckwheat crepes and bread are available.
Ask about other GF options, as the
restaurant may offer other things. Call
beforehand to confirm availability of GF
options and timeliness of information. ■
*www.kismetkitchen.blogspot.com*

## Leonardo's Fresh Quality Pizza ★ $LD
*Burlington ■ (802) 862-7700*
*83 Pearl St*
*South Burlington ■ (802) 951-9000*
*1160 Williston Rd ■ Pizza ■* GF pizza
is available in size medium only
with an additional charge of $3. ■
*www.leonardosonline.com*

## Leunig's Bistro ✪$$LD
*Burlington ■ (802) 863-3759*
*115 Church St ■ American ■* Extensive
GF lunch and dinner menu. Items on
their menu include salade nicoise, peach
and balsamic braised duck, and escargot
maison. Alert server of GF needs and the
manager will come out personally to go
over any concerns. ■ *www.leunigsbistro.com*

## Little Harry's $$$D
*Rutland ■ (802) 747-4848*
*121 W St Suite 101 ■ American ■* GF options include grilled duck breast, grilled
scallops, poached cod, NY sirloin and pan
blackened fish of the day. Several soups and
salads are also available GF. Alert server
upon arrival. ■ *littleharrys.com*

### Loretta's Fine Italian Cuisine    $$$LD
*Essex Junction* ▪ *(802) 879-7777*
*44 Park St* ▪ *Italian* ▪ The restaurant reports that several items on the menu are naturally GF, including chicken lenora and shrimp scampi. Confirm the timeliness of this information before dining in. Alert the server upon arrival and ask about additional GF options that might be available. ▪ *www.lorettas.net*

### Lucy's Tavern    $$D
*Perkinsville* ▪ *(802) 263-9217*
*1342 Rte 106* ▪ *American* ▪ Lucy's Tavern offers a GF chicken entrée and appetizers such as marinated olives. ▪ *www.weathersfieldinn.com*

### Madera's Restaurante Mexicano & Cantina    ✪$LD
*Burlington* ▪ *(802) 657-3377*
*180 Battery St* ▪ *Mexican* ▪ Manager Jenna reports that the WF menu is GF "to the best of our knowledge." It includes ceviches and salads, as well as house specials like fajitas, enchiladas, and various fish and meat dishes. Manager Josh reports that servers "know all about" the GF diet, and they accommodate GF diners "pretty often." All fried items are prepared in shared oil. ▪ *maderasvermont.com*

### Magnolia Bistro    ✪¢BL
*Burlington* ▪ *(802) 846-7446*
*1 Lawson Ln* ▪ *Modern American* ▪ GF items are marked on the regular menu and include potato pancakes, house cured salmon, and a veggie burger. Confirm the timeliness of this information before dining in. ▪ *www.magnoliabistro.com*

### Mangowood Restaurant at Lincoln Inn    ✪$$D
*Woodstock* ▪ *(802) 457-3312*
*530 Woodstock Rd* ▪ *Modern American* ▪ GF options include creamy coconut risotto cakes, tandoori spiced chicken breast, and a mint glazed rack of lamb. Several appetizers are also available GF. Alert server upon arrival. ▪ *www.mangowood.com*

### Marigold Kitchen    ★$LD
*N Bennington* ▪ *(802) 445-4545*
*25 Main St* ▪ *Pizza* ▪ GF pizza is available. Each GF pizza is made with a clean screen but Manager David recommends that customers who are "highly sensitive to gluten" take caution, as their kitchen is not a GF environment. ▪ *www.marigoldkitchen.info*

### Michael's on the Hill    $$$D
*Waterbury Center* ▪ *(802) 244-7476*
*4182 Waterbury-Stowe Rd RTE 100 N* ▪ *European* ▪ Owner Laura reports that they are accustomed to serving GF diners, as they do so every day. She notes that all staff members are trained on the GF diet, and she recommends making reservations noting GF. For dessert, they serve a GF chocolate torte and chocolate fondue. ▪ *www.michaelsonthehill.com*

### Mint    $LD
*Waitsfield* ▪ *(802) 496-5514*
*4403 Main St* ▪ *Vegetarian* ▪ Mint offers a GF menu containing items such as mint salad, cardamom rice and okra and red pepper stew. ▪ *www.mintvermont.com*

### Mio Bistro    ★$$$D
*Dorset* ▪ *(802) 231-2530*
*3239 Rte 30* ▪ *Global* ▪ Many items on the menu are naturally GF except for the bread crumbs on the salmon and the pasta. Alert a server upon arrival. A GF penne pasta is available if requested in advance. ▪ *www.miobistro.net*

### Mirabelles    ★¢L
*Burlington* ▪ *(802) 658-3074*
*198 Main St* ▪ *Bakery* ▪ Non-dedicated GF bakery offering GF cakes and other dessert items. According to an employee, GF items on the lunch menu include various soups and salads topped with chicken. Alert the server upon arrival. ▪ *www.mirabellescafe.com*

## Ninety Nine                                    ✿ 📖
*Rutland* ▪ *(802) 775-9288*
*288 S Main St*
*Brattleboro* ▪ *(802) 251-0899*
*1184 Putney Rd*
*Rutland* ▪ *(802) 775-9288*
*315 S Main St*
*Williston* ▪ *(802) 879-9901*
*11 Taft Corners Shopping Ctr*

## NiteJars                                       ★ ¢S
*N Bennington* ▪ *(802) 445-4545*
*25 Main St* ▪ *Coffee Shop* ▪ GF pizza is
available; however, Manager Joe recommends caution on the part of GF diners,
since GF pizzas are prepared in a non-GF
environment. ▪ *www.nitejars.com*

## Nova Mae Café                                  ¢BL
*Bennington* ▪ *(802) 447-9790*
*512 Main St* ▪ *Café* ▪ Bake GF items daily
including several lunch items and desserts.
▪ *novamaecafe.wordpress.com*

## On the Rise Bakery                             ✿¢BLD
*Richmond* ▪ *(802) 434-7787*
*39 Esplanade* ▪ *Bakery & Café* ▪ Non-
dedicated bakery and café offering a changing variety of GF baked goods, including
bagels, cookies, and macaroons. The bakery
reports that they bake all their GF goods at
a designated time to minimize the possibility of CC. ▪ *ontherisebakery.net*

## One Federal                                    $$LD
*St Albans* ▪ *(802) 524-0330*
*1 Federal St* ▪ *American* ▪ GF menu
is available in stores. Manager Jaime
advises GF diners to avoid fried foods
because they do not have dedicated
fryers. She also advises GF customers
to make sure to tell servers that it is an
"allergy" as opposed to a preference. ▪
*www.onefederalrestaurant.com*

## Penny Cluse Café                               $BL
*Burlington* ▪ *(802) 651-8834*
*169 Cherry St* ▪ *American* ▪ The restaurant reports that GF diners can "mix and
match" ingredients to create a variety of GF
omelets for breakfast. For lunch, GF salads

are available. Alert the server upon arrival.
▪ *pennycluse.com*

## Piecasso Pizzeria & Lounge                     ★ $LD
*Stowe* ▪ *(802) 253-4411*
*1899 Mountain Rd* ▪ *Pizza* ▪ GF pizza is
available. The restaurant reports that they
are "really careful about using separate
equipment" to prepare their GF pizzas. In
addition to the GF pizza they also offer GF
salads without the croutons, roasted portobello panini, turkey panini, piatto di oliva
and more. ▪ *piecasso.com*

## Pizzeria Verita                                ★ $D
*Burlington* ▪ *(802) 489-5644*
*156 Saint Paul St* ▪ *Pizza* ▪ Features a GF
specialty menu section with various pizza
options in addition to a few GF desserts. ▪
*www.pizzeriaverita.com*

## Ponce Bistro                                   $BLD
*Manchester* ▪ *(802) 768-8095*
*4659 Main St* ▪ *American* ▪ Ponce Bistro
offers several salads and vegetable based
appetizers which are GF. Entrées such as
Prince Edward Island mussels, steak, and
chicken can also be prepared GF upon
request. ▪ *www.poncebistro.com*

## Positive Pie                                   ★ $$LD
*Montpelier* ▪ *(802) 229-0453*
*22 State St*
*Plainfield* ▪ *(802) 454-0133*
*69 Main St*
*Hardwick* ▪ *(802) 472-7126*
*87 S Main St* ▪ *Italian* ▪ GF pizza and pasta
are available, as well as various salads and
soups that are GF. ▪ *www.positivepie.com*

## Pub at Grey Fox Inn, The                       $$D
*Stowe* ▪ *(802) 253-8921*
*990 Mountain Rd* ▪ *Pub Food* ▪ The restaurant offers several dishes that can be altered
to be GF. Examples include slow roasted
prime rib, orange glazed salmon, and several chicken dishes. ▪ *greyfoxinn.com/dining*

### Pulcinella's Italian Restaurant $$$LD
*S Burlington* ▪ *(802) 863-1000*
*100 Dorset St* ▪ *Italian* ▪ The restaurant reports a wide variety of GF appetizers, salads, and entrées. Alert server upon arrival and they will help select a GF meal. ▪ *www.pulcinellas.us*

### Putney Inn, The $$BLD
*Putney* ▪ *(802) 387-5517*
*57 Putney Ldg Rd* ▪ *Modern American* ▪ Putney Inn offers a variety of GF options including salads, a veggie patty sandwich, and entrées such as pan seared scallops, roaster turkey, and grilled beef sirloin. ▪ *www.putneyinn.com*

### Restaurant Verterra ✪$$$D
*Perkinsville* ▪ *(802) 263-9217*
*1342 Route 106* ▪ *Modern American* ▪ The main chef reports that they have a variety of GF options, including a 3 course GF specialty dinner experience. Also, most of their meat items can be prepared GF. Reservations noting GF are strongly recommended, as is alerting the server upon arrival. ▪ *www.weathersfieldinn.com*

### Roots The Restaurant ✪$$LD
*Rutland* ▪ *(802) 747-7414*
*51 Wales St* ▪ *Italian* ▪ Roots offers a marked menu displaying their GF options. Including entrées such as tomatillo scallops, smoked chicken, pecan salmon, and desserts like blueberry cobbler. ▪ *www.rootsrutland.com*

### Salt $$$D
*Montpelier* ▪ *(802) 229-6678*
*207 Barre St* ▪ *American* ▪ The restaurant reports that the menu changes frequently but there will be always GF options available, either naturally GF dishes or dishes that can be altered to be GF. Alert server upon arrival to find out current options. ▪ *www.saltcafevt.com*

### San Sai Japanese Restaurant ★$$LD
*Burlington* ▪ *(802) 862-2777*
*112 Lake St* ▪ *Japanese* ▪ Many items on their regular menu can be modified to be GF upon request. Items such as their edamame, sashimi, sushi pizza, and tofu skewers are naturally GF. For customers craving sushi, GF soy sauce is available for substitution. Confirm the timeliness of this information before dining in.

### Sarducci's ✪★$$LD
*Montpelier* ▪ *(802) 223-0229*
*3 Main St* ▪ *Italian* ▪ Extensive lunch and dinner GF menu available everyday. GF pasta is available daily and they have GF bread occasionally. GF items include their pasta verdure, gauzetto, and mista. Restaurant advises to make reservations noting GF so the kitchen can make any other needed preparations. ▪ *www.sarduccis.com*

### Silver Fork, The $$$$LD
*Manchester* ▪ *(802) 768-8444*
*4201 Main St* ▪ *Global* ▪ Owner reports that they have "many GF options", though their menu changes often. The chef reportedly uses "a variety of alternatives to wheat in his cooking" and is "happy to serve" GF diners.

### Silver Palace $$LD
*S Burlington* ▪ *(802) 864-0125*
*1216 Williston Rd* ▪ *Chinese* ▪ No GF menu but several GF options available on request. Most of their sauces, like their oyster sauce, are GF. Alert the server that your meal must be GF and they will list the available options.

### Simon Pearce Restaurant $$$LD
*Quechee* ▪ *(802) 295-1470*
*1760 Main St* ▪ *Modern American* ▪ Manager Deanna reports that the kitchen is "very accommodating." The beef carpaccio, arugula salad, strawberry and spinach salad, venison meatloaf, and mascarpone polenta are possible GF options. Servers are given sheets detailing GF foods, and they will indicate GF options upon request. Reservations noting GF are recommended. ▪ *www.simonpearce.com*

## Single Pebble, A ★$$LD
*Burlington* ■ *(802) 865-5200*
*133 Bank St* ■ *Chinese* ■ GF soy sauce
is available. GF items are marked on
their regular menu with a GF indica-
tion. Restaurant reports that most dishes
can be prepared GF. Servers are well
trained in accommodating GF diners. ■
*www.asinglepebble.com*

## Skinny Pancake, The ★¢BLD
*Montpelier* ■ *(802) 262-2253*
*89 Main St* ■ *French* ■ All GF crepes use
a vegan batter made of chickpea flour, oil
and water. According to Manager Mike, the
kitchen staff wipes down the crepe griddle
thoroughly and uses fresh utensils to help
minimize CC. They have other options
beside crepes, just call ahead of time to
confirm the other options available for that
day. ■ *www.skinnypancake.com*

## Solstice $$$$BD
*Stowe* ■ *(802) 760-4735*
*7412 Mountain Rd* ■ *Modern American* ■
Solstice does not have a GF menu. However, a majority of their dinner entrées are GF
such as spiced halibut, pan seared scallops,
chicken and lobster.

## Spooner's Bar & Grille $$D
*Woodstock* ■ *(802) 457-4066*
*21710 Maxham Meadow Wy* ■ *American* ■
The restaurant reports that they will "alter
any dish possible" to accommodate GF diners. Alert server upon arrival.

## Spot, The ✪¢BLD
*Burlington* ■ *(802) 540-1778*
*210 Shelburne Rd* ■ *American* ■ Several
GF options available daily. Alert the server
upon arrival. ■ *www.thespotvt.com*

## Square Biscuit, The ¢BLD
*Northfield* ■ *(802) 485-7392*
*40 Depot Sq* ■ *Southern* ■ The Square Bis-
cuit offers GF dinner options such as several stir frys, and grilled teriyaki chicken. ■
*www.squarebiscuitrestaurant.com*

## Stowe Meadows Bakery ✪¢S
*Stowe* ■ *(802) 888-0002*
*3233 Elmore Mtn Rd* ■ *Bakery* ■ GF products and menus are offered year around
at Stowe Meadows and a full GF menu is
available. ■ *www.skipthegluten.com*

## Sugarsnap ★¢BL
*Burlington* ■ *(802) 652-5922*
*1 College St*
*S Burlington* ■ *(802) 861-2718*
*30 Community Dr*
*Burlington* ■ *(802) 652-5922*
*505 Riverside Ave* ■ *American* ■ GF options available. Items include salads and
bean salads, GF bread for sandwiches as
well as a curried chick pea, spinach and
brown rice casserole. ■ *thesnapvt.com*

## Sweetwaters ✪$$LD
*Burlington* ■ *(802) 864-9800*
*120 Church St* ■ *American* ■ GF menu includes bacon wrapped scallops, several salads, burgers and sandwiches with GF buns,
NY strip steak, and more. Alert server
upon arrival. ■ *www.sweetwatersvt.com*

## Table 24 $$LD
*Rutland* ■ *(802) 775-2424*
*24 Wales St* ■ *American* ■ The restaurant reports that all servers have a list
of GF options which can be shown
to customers upon request. They also
add that they are willing to alter any
other dish possible to accommodate GF
guests. Alert the server upon arrival. ■
*www.table24.netwww.table24.net*

## Three Tomatoes Trattoria $$D
*Rutland* ■ *(802) 747-7747*
*88 Merchants Row*
*Burlington* ■ *(802) 660-9533*
*83 Church St*
*Williston* ■ *(802) 857-2200*
*Maple Tree Pl* ■ *Italian* ■ Three Tomatoes
offers GF dinner options such as shrimp,
salmon , chicken alfredo, farm skirt steak,
grilled rosemary chicken and shrimp
scampi. ■ *www.threetomatoestrattoria.com*

### Toscano Café Bistro          $$LD
*Richmond* ▪ *(802) 434-3148*
*27 Bridge St* ▪ *Mediterranean* ▪ No GF
menu but has several dishes that can be
modified to be GF. Their chicken piccata,
steak, and toscano Italian sausage and
julienned chicken breast are some of the
options. According to server Lucia, they
serve GF customers every day and are well
informed about how to address their needs.
▪ *www.toscanocafe.com*

### Trattoria Delia          $$$D
*Burlington* ▪ *(802) 864-5253*
*152 Saint Paul St* ▪ *Italian* ▪ The restaurant
reports that several of their dinner entrées
can be prepared GF, including the wood
grilled boneless ribeye, pan seared tenderloin, and wood grilled fish of the day. ▪
*www.trattoriadelia.com*

### Twilight Tea Lounge          ★$$
*Brattleboro* ▪ *(802) 254-8887*
*41 Main St* ▪ *Teahouse* ▪ Pastry selection includes various GF choices. ▪
*www.twilighttealounge.com*

### Uno Chicago Grill          ✪★📖
*S Burlington* ▪ *(802) 865-4000*
*1330 Shelburne Rd*

### Upper Crust          ★$LD
*Essex Junction* ▪ *(802) 871-5647*
*118 Pearl S* ▪ *Pizza* ▪ Upper Crust has a 12"
GF pizza in addition to GF chicken wings/
tenders. ▪ *www.uppercrustvermont.com*

### West Meadow Farm Bakery          ⚙$
*Essex Junction* ▪ *(802) 878-1646*
*34 Park St* ▪ *Bakery* ▪ Dedicated GF
bakery offering several types of GF
bread, as well as a wide variety of baked
goods such as cookies, brownies, and
biscotti. They also offer GF flour blends
to take home and "groovy GF granola". ▪
*www.westmeadowfarmbakery.com*

### Whip Bar & Grill          ✪$$$LD
*Stowe* ▪ *(802) 253-7301*
*18 Main St* ▪ *American* ▪ Limited GF menu
includes mussels, angus filet, and a crispy

chicken salad. Alert sever upon arrival and
request that special care be taken with the
meal, as no CC policy is normally in place.
▪ *www.thewhip.com*

### White Rock Pizza & Pub          ★$D
*Woodbury* ▪ *(802) 225-5915*
*848 Vt Hwy 14* ▪ *Pizza* ▪ White Rock Offers
a GF pizza crust. ▪ *www.whiterockpizza.com*

### Windjammer, The          ✪$$$LD
*S Burlington* ▪ *(802) 862-6585*
*1076 Williston Rd* ▪ *Seafood & Steakhouse*
▪ Manager Mike reports that "a lot" of GF
diners come in and their own employees,
some of whom have Celiac, are accommodated. A lunch and dinner GF menu is
available in stores and online. He notes that
there are many options for GF diners, and
the staff is very well educated on the GF
diet. While there are no dedicated utensils/
prep surface areas, Manager Mike says they
do take a lot of precautions to minimize
CC. ▪ *www.windjammerrestaurant.com*

### Ye Olde Tavern          $$$D
*Manchester Center* ▪ *(802) 362-0611*
*5183 Main St* ▪ *American* ▪ The restaurant
reports that most of the steak and fish
is GF along with their veggie cakes, but
cautions that since they do not operate
a GF kitchen, there is a chance of CC. ▪
*www.yeoldetavern.net*

### Zabby & Elf's Stone Soup          ★$BLD
*Burlington* ▪ *(802) 862-7616*
*211 College St* ▪ *American* ▪ GF soups,
stews, rices, and salads are available, and
the restaurant bakes GF muffins fresh on
Saturdays. ▪ *www.stonesoupvt.com*

### iDuino! (Duende)          ✪¢BLD
*Burlington* ▪ *(802) 660-9346*
*10 N Winooski Ave* ▪ *Global* ▪ GF menu
includes items such as carnitas tacos,
dancing noodles, and beef yakitori. Several
dishes that are not marked GF can also be
prepared GF. Alert the server upon arrival
for further details. ▪ *duinoduende.com*

# VIRGINIA

## ARLINGTON/ALEXANDRIA

### 219, The                                    $$$LD
*Alexandria* ▪ *(703) 549-1141*
*219 King St* ▪ *French* ▪ Chef Ryan reports
that GF diners are "very welcome" at the
restaurant. He notes that the sole, ribs,
salmon, cassoulet, seafood au gratin,
chicken breast with shrimp scampi, steak,
and lamb can be modified to be GF. Alert
a server, who will notify the kitchen and
Chef Ryan will personally come out to
list out available options for that night. ▪
*www.219restaurant.com*

### Au Bon Pain
*Arlington* ▪ *(703) 418-0715*
*2102 Crystal Plaza*
*Arlington* ▪ *(703) 415-0973*
*1100 S Hayes St*

### Austin Grill                              ✪$LD
*Alexandria* ▪ *(703) 684-8969*
*801 King St* ▪ *Tex-Mex* ▪ GF menu includes
grilled salmon salad, carnitas fajitas, huevos rancheros, grilled vegetable enchiladas, and more. Regional manager Robert
stresses the importance of noting GF when
placing an order so that the server can
notify the manager and start the appropriate procedures for GF preparation. ▪
*www.austingrill.com*

### Bertucci's                               ✪
*Alexandria* ▪ *(703) 548-8500*
*725 King St*
*Arlington* ▪ *(703) 528-9177*
*2800 Clarendon Blvd*

### Bonefish Grill                            ✪
*Alexandria* ▪ *(703) 971-3202*
*5920 Kingstowne Towne Ctr Ste 110*

### Busboys and Poets                      ✪$$BLD
*Arlington* ▪ *(703) 379-9756*
*4251 S Campbell Ave* ▪ *American* ▪ Offer countless GF options for all three
meals of the day including but not limited to nachos, pizza, salmon, pan fried
chicken, and pan seared basil tofu. ▪
*www.busboysandpoets.com*

### Buzz                                    ★ ¢S
*Alexandria* ▪ *(703) 600-2899*
*901 Slaters Ln*
*Arlington* ▪ *(703) 650-9676*
*818 N Quincy St* ▪ *Bakery & Café* ▪
Non-dedicated bakery offering GF cupcakes, brownies, muffins, crème brûlée,
and ice cream. All items are freshly made
every day. Bakery recommends calling in
advance, as they sometimes sell out of particular items. ▪ *www.buzzonslaters.com*

### CakeLove                                 ★
*Arlington* ▪ *(703) 933-0099*
*4150 Campbell Ave*

### Carlyle                                ✪$$LD
*Arlington* ▪ *(703) 931-0777*
*4000 Campbell Ave* ▪ *American* ▪ The
"low-gluten" menu features the chicken
grill, New Orleans shrimp, and roast
pork tenderloin. For dessert, there is
a flourless chocolate macadamia nut
waffle. The menu is "low-gluten" rather
than GF because the items are prepared
in the same kitchen as non-GF items. ▪
*www.greatamericanrestaurants.com*

### Cava Mezze                             ✪$LD
*Arlington* ▪ *(703) 276-9090*
*2940 Clarendon Blvd* ▪ *Greek* ▪ Restaurant reports frequently accommodating
GF diners. Alert a server upon arrival.
Many menu items are naturally GF, such
as salads, dips, omelets and saffron risotto.
Confirm the timeliness of this information before dining in. They have a GF
list of menu items online and instores. ▪
*www.cavamezze.com*

### Clyde's
*Alexandria* ▪ *(703) 820-8300*
*1700 N Beauregard St*

## Cosi                                    ✪📖
*Arlington* ▪ (703) 522-0300
*2050 Wilson Blvd*
*Alexandria* ▪ (703) 299-9833
*700 King St*
*Arlington* ▪ (703) 527-9717
*4250 Fairfax Dr*
*Arlington* ▪ (703) 248-9408
*3503 Fairfax Dr*
*Arlington* ▪ (703) 521-1904
*2011 Crystal Dr*
*Arlington* ▪ (703) 294-6750
*1801 N Lynn St*

## Dairy Godmother, The              ¢S
*Alexandria* ▪ (703) 683-7767
*2310 Mount Vernon Ave* ▪ *Dessert* ▪
Restaurant reports that most custards
and sorbets are GF. Always check with
a staff member to ensure that the flavor is GF and a clean spoon is used. ▪
*www.thedairygodmother.com*

## Evening Star                         $$$D
*Alexandria* ▪ (703) 549-5051
*2000 Mt Vernon Ave* ▪ *American* ▪ The
Evening Star features an online menu offering GF items such as seared beef tenderloin, chargrilled swordfish, and pan seared
halibut. ▪ *www.eveningstarcafe.net*

## Fireworks Pizza                    ★$LD
*Arlington* ▪ (703) 527-8700
*2350 Clarendon Blvd* ▪ *Pizza* ▪ GF pizza is
available. Restaurant reports that GF pizza
is available with any topping except meatballs, which are not GF. Many of the soups
and several beers and drinks are also GF.
Confirm the timeliness of this information
before dining in. ▪ *www.fireworkspizza.com*

## Fontaine Caffe & Creperie        ★$BLD
*Alexandria* ▪ (703) 535-8151
*119 S Royal St* ▪ *French* ▪ The restaurant
reports that their savory crepes are made
using 100% buckwheat flour, and they can
make the sweet crepes with the same mix
on request. However, they note that the
crepe irons are cast iron and attached to
a gas line, and therefore are not washed

between cooking, making the chance of CC
very high. ▪ *www.fontainecaffe.com*

## Fox and Hound Pub & Grille         📖
*Arlington* ▪ (703) 465-1300
*4238 Wilson Blvd*
*Arlington* ▪ (703) 416-0452
*2010-A Crystal Dr*

## Gadsby's Tavern                    $$$LD
*Alexandria* ▪ (703) 548-1288
*138 N Royal St* ▪ *American* ▪ Chef Frank
reports that they can accommodate GF
diners, as they have a scratch kitchen
and everything can be modified. He
notes, however, that most sauces are
premade and are not GF. Alert a server,
and be specific about GF restrictions.
The server will notify the kitchen. ▪
*www.gadsbystavernrestaurant.com*

## Genghis Grill                        📖
*Alexandria* ▪ (703) 313-4781
*7001F Manchester Blvd*

## Greene Turtle
## Sports Bar & Grill, The           ✪📖
*Arlington* ▪ (703) 741-0901
*900 N Glebe Rd*

## Jaleo Crystal City               ✪$$$LD
*Arlington* ▪ (703) 413-8181
*2250 A Crystal Dr* ▪ *Spanish* ▪ GF menu
items include paellas, grilled hangar steak
tapas, duck confit tapas, and a traditional
chorizo tapas, and more. General Manager
Joseph recommends speaking to a manager
upon arrival. ▪ *www.jaleo.com*

## Jersey Mike's                        📖
*Alexandria* ▪ (571) 481-4445
*7732 D Richmond Hwy*

## La Bergerie                      ★$$$$LD
*Alexandria* ▪ (703) 683-1007
*218 N Lee St* ▪ *French* ▪ Owner Laurent
reports that they accommodate GF diners.
The menu changes seasonally, but the fresh
fish of the day and the baby rack of lamb
can be prepared GF. Confirm the timeliness
of this information before dining in. GF
bread, pasta, soy sauce, pies, and cakes are

available. Located on the 2nd floor of the Crilley Warehouse. ■ *www.labergerie.com*

### Legal Sea Foods ✪📖
*Arlington* ■ *(703) 415-1200*
*2301 Jefferson Davis Hwy*

### Lone Star Steakhouse & Saloon ✪📖
*Alexandria* ■ *(703) 823-7827*
*3141 Duke St*

### Lost Dog Café, The ★$LD
*Arlington* ■ *(703) 237-1552*
*5876 Washington Blvd*
*Arlington* ■ *(703) 553-7770*
*2920 Columbia Pike* ■ *Deli* ■ GF pizza and beer are available. Restaurant cautions that all pizzas are baked in the same oven without a screen. ■ *www.lostdogcafe.com*

### Melting Pot, The ✪📖
*Arlington* ■ *(703) 243-4490*
*1110 N Glebe Rd*

### Morton's Steakhouse ✪📖
*Arlington* ■ *(703) 418-1444*
*1750 Crystal Dr*

### P.F. Chang's China Bistro ✪★📖
*Arlington* ■ *(703) 527-0955*
*901 N Glebe Rd*

### Peking Duck Restaurant ★$LD
*Alexandria* ■ *(703) 768-2774*
*7531 Richmond Hwy* ■ *Chinese* ■ Owner Peter reports that GF items include curry chicken, shrimp pepperada, and moo goo gai pan. GF soy sauce is available, so many other menu items can be modified to be GF. For dessert, they offer lychee nuts and taffy strawberries. ■ *www.pekingduck.com*

### Pete's New Haven Style Apizza ★¢LD
*Arlington* ■ *(703) 527-7383*
*3017 Clarendon Blvd* ■ *Pizza* ■ GF pizza is available, as are GF pasta and GF beer. Customers can add toppings of their choice to the GF pizza. The restaurant reports that they "take special dietary needs very seriously," and recommends asking for a manager, chef, or owner when placing a GF order. ■ *www.petesapizza.com*

### Red Velvet Cupcakery ★¢S
*Arlington* ■ *(703) 243-5660*
*3035 Clarendon Blvd* ■ *Bakery* ■ The Red Velvet Cupcakery offers GF "Black and White Velvet" cupcakes in GF options. ■ *www.redvelvetcupcakery.com*

### Romano's Macaroni Grill ✪★📖
*Alexandria* ■ *(703) 719-9082*
*5925 Kingstowne Towne Ctr*

### Rustico ★$$$LD
*Alexandria* ■ *(703) 224-5051*
*827 Slaters Ln*
*Arlington* ■ *(571) 384-1820*
*4075 Wilson Blvd* ■ *Modern American* ■ GF pizza, made with chickpea dough, is available. Manager Jason reports that salads, eggplant, and chicken dishes can also be made GF. He cautions that the kitchen works with a lot of flour, and CC is always a risk but they get a lot of GF customers daily so they try their hardest to suit the needs of their customers. ■ *www.rusticorestaurant.com*

### Ruth's Chris Steak House ✪📖
*Arlington* ■ *(703) 979-7275*
*2231 Crystal Dr*

### Shane's Rib Shack ✪📖
*Alexandria* ■ *(703) 660-6288*
*7698 Richmond Hwy*

### Ted's Montana Grill ✪📖
*Arlington* ■ *(703) 416-8337*
*2200 Crystal Dr*
*Arlington* ■ *(703) 741-0661*
*4300 Wilson Blvd*
*Alexandria* ■ *(703) 960-0500*
*2451 Eisenhower Ave*

### Zpizza ✪📖
*Arlington* ■ *(703) 647-9005*
*1100 Wilson Blvd*
*Arlington* ■ *(703) 528-2828*
*2710-B Washington Blvd*

# VIRGINIA

## RICHMOND

### Acacia Midtown                          $$LD
Richmond ▪ (804) 562-0138
2601 W Cary St ▪ Seafood ▪ The restaurant
reports that many items on the menu can
be prepared GF, particularly proteins, many
of which are naturally GF. Alert the server
upon arrival. ▪ www.acaciarestaurant.com

### Au Bon Pain                            📖
Richmond ▪ (804) 644-0296
1250 E Marshall St

### Balliceaux                             $$LD
Richmond ▪ (804) 355-3008
203 N Lombardy St ▪ Southern ▪ GF options are marked on the online menu. ▪
www.balliceauxrva.com

### Bertucci's                             ✪📖
Richmond ▪ (804) 360-1252
11721 W Broad St

### Café Rustica                          $$LD
Richmond ▪ (804) 225-8811
414 E Main St ▪ Fusion ▪ The restaurant reports that GF dishes include salads, Prince
Edward Island mussels, whole trout, and
roast chicken. Confirm the timeliness of
this information before dining in. Alert the
server upon arrival. ▪ caferusticarva.com

### Can Can Brasserie                     $$$LD
Richmond ▪ (804) 358-7274
3120 W Cary St ▪ French ▪ Owner Chris
reports that the restaurant serves GF diners frequently, and that servers are "very
well trained" on the GF diet. He notes that
the menu contains all fresh and seasonal
foods, making it easy to modify items to be
GF. Alert the hostess and server, who will
notify the kitchen. Items that can be prepared GF include cranberry stuffed trout
and hanger steak. Confirm the timeliness
of this information before dining in. Mint

chocolate crème brûlée is available for dessert. ▪ www.cancanbrasserie.com

### Empress, The                          ✪$$BLD
Richmond ▪ (804) 592-4000
2043 W Broad St ▪ American ▪ Owner
Melissa, who has Celiac, says they take
all necessary precautions to prevent
CC. Almost everything on their menu
can be made GF or is already GF. ▪
theempressrva.com

### Firebirds Wood Fired Grill           ✪📖
Richmond ▪ (804) 440-0000
11448 Belvedere Vista Ln
Richmond ▪ (804) 364-9744
11800 W Broad St

### Fleming's Prime
### Steakhouse & Wine Bar                 ✪📖
Richmond ▪ (804) 272-7755
9200 Stony Point Pkwy

### Fox and Hound Pub & Grille           📖
Richmond ▪ (804) 755-6800
7502 W Broad St
Richmond ▪ (804) 560-4600
11581 Robious Rd

### Genghis Grill                         📖
Richmond ▪ (804) 420-8888
11500 Midlothian Tpke

### Glory Days Grill                      ✪📖
Richmond ▪ (804) 754-3710
10466 Ridgefield Pkwy

### Ichiban                               ★$LD
Richmond ▪ (804) 750-2380
10490 Ridgefield Pkwy ▪ Japanese ▪
Manager Jerry reports that they have "a
lot of customers who are GF." He adds that
GF soy sauce is available, and "soy paper"
can be substituted for the "seaweed paper",
which may contain gluten. Alert a server
upon arrival and they will see to your
needs. ▪ www.ichibanjapanesecuisine.com

### Jason's Deli                          ✪📖
Richmond ▪ (804) 323-9390
7115 Forest Hill Ave
Richmond ▪ (804) 673-5290
1700 Willow Lawn Dr

## Jersey Mike's   📖
*Richmond* ▪ *(804) 320-8805*
*2709 Buford Rd*
*Richmond* ▪ *(804) 627-0507*
*8654 Staples Mill Rd*
*Richmond* ▪ *(804) 340-5563*
*927 W Broad St*

## Lemaire Restaurant   $$$LD
*Richmond* ▪ *(804) 649-4629*
*101 W Franklin St* ▪ *Seafood* ▪ Staff
reports that since everything is made
to order, GF requests are easily accommodated. Alert server upon arrival and
they will help make a GF selection. ▪
*www.lemairerestaurant.com*

## Maggiano's Little Italy   ★📖
*Richmond* ▪ *(804) 253-0900*
*11800 W Broad St*

## Melting Pot, The   ✪📖
*Richmond* ▪ *(804) 741-3120*
*9704 Gayton Rd*

## Morton's Steakhouse   ✪📖
*Richmond* ▪ *(804) 648-1662*
*111 Virginia St*

## Nile Ethiopian Restaurant   ★$$LD
*Richmond* ▪ *(804) 225-5544*
*309 N Laurel St* ▪ *Ethiopian* ▪ Manager
Benyam reports that everything on the
menu is GF, except for desserts because
the restaurant uses Teff flour in substitution for regular flour. He recommends any
meat or vegetarian dish. GF diners can ask
servers about GF options, just to confirm. ▪
*www.nilerichmond.com*

## O'Charley's   📖
*Richmond* ▪ *(804) 323-3030*
*7131 Forest Hill Ave*
*Richmond* ▪ *(804) 747-9999*
*9927 Maryland Dr*
*Richmond* ▪ *(804) 673-8233*
*6291 W Broad St*

## Old Original Bookbinder's   $$$D
*Richmond* ▪ *(804) 643-6900*
*2306 E Cary St* ▪ *Seafood & Steakhouse* ▪ The majority of the items on the
menu are GF, according to the restaurant. Reservations noting GF are recommended. Alert the server upon arrival. ▪
*www.bookbindersrichmond.com*

## P.F. Chang's China Bistro   ✪★📖
*Richmond* ▪ *(804) 253-0492*
*9212 Stony Point Pkwy*

## Ruth's Chris Steak House   ✪📖
*Richmond* ▪ *(804) 378-0600*
*11500 W Huguenot Rd*

## Texas De Brazil Churrascaria   ★📖
*Richmond* ▪ *(804) 750-2003*
*11800 W Broad St*

## Thai Diner Too   ✪$LD
*Richmond* ▪ *(804) 353-9514*
*3028 W Cary St* ▪ *Thai* ▪ GF menu
includes pad ping curry, chicken satay
with peanut sauce, masaman curry, rama,
and sticky rice with mango for dessert. ▪
*tdtoo.webs.com*

# VIRGINIA

## VIRGINIA BEACH

## Bonefish Grill   ✪📖
*Virginia Beach* ▪ *(757) 306-3323*
*3333 Virginia Blvd Suite 41*

## Burtons Grill   ✪★📖
*Virginia Beach* ▪ *(757) 442-8970*
*741 First Colonial Rd*

## Cheeseburger in Paradise   ✪★📖
*Virginia Beach* ▪ *(757) 498-1518*
*739 Lynnhaven Pkwy*

## Jason's Deli   ✪📖
*Virginia Beach* ▪ *(757) 456-5481*
*4554 Virginia Beach Blvd*

## Jersey Mike's   📖
*Virginia Beach* ▪ *(757) 631-0233*
*4224 Virginia Beach Blvd*
*Virginia Beach* ▪ *(757) 333-6006*

5832 Northampton Blvd
*Virginia Beach* ▪ *(757) 333-5010*
*1047 Independence Blvd*

**Melting Pot, The**                    ✪▱
*Virginia Beach* ▪ *(757) 425-3463*
*1564 Laskin Rd*

**One Fish, Two Fish**              $$$**LD**
*Virginia Beach* ▪ *(757) 496-4350*
*2109 W Great Neck Rd* ▪ *Seafood* ▪
The restaurant reports that also any
items on the menu can be prepared
GF. Alert the server upon arrival. ▪
*www.onefish-twofish.com*

**P.F. Chang's China Bistro**      ✪★▱
*Virginia Beach* ▪ *(757) 473-9028*
*4551 Virginia Beach Blvd*

**Reginella's Italian Ristorante**  ★$**LD**
*Virginia Beach* ▪ *(757) 498-9770*
*4000 Virginia Beach Blvd* ▪ *Italian* ▪ GF
pasta is available and can be substituted
into most pasta dishes. Additional GF
options may be available. Alert the server
upon arrival and ask about current GF op-
tions. ▪ *www.reginellas.com*

**Romano's Macaroni Grill**       ✪★▱
*Virginia Beach* ▪ *(757) 518-9901*
*4574 Virginia Beach Blvd*

**Ruth's Chris Steak House**       ✪▱
*Virginia Beach* ▪ *(757) 213-0747*
*205 Central Park Ave*

**Smokey Bones**                         ▱
*Virginia Beach* ▪ *(757) 671-1622*
*4590 Virginia Beach Blvd*

**Tautog's**                             $$**LD**
*Virginia Beach* ▪ *(757) 422-0081*
*205 23rd St* ▪ *Seafood* ▪ Tautog's offers a
variety of GF menu entrées such as blackened tuna, Thai baked chicken, salmon
salad, shrimp scampi, and a flat iron steak.
▪ *www.tautogs.com*

**Uno Chicago Grill**                ✪★▱
*Virginia Beach* ▪ *(757) 306-9101*
*1005 Lynnhaven Mall Loop*

**Waterman's Surfside Grille**     $$$**LD**
*Virginia Beach* ▪ *(757) 428-3644*
*5th St & Atlantic Ave* ▪ *Seafood* ▪ Accord-
ing to the hostess they have a variety of GF
options on their regular menu including
items such as salads, chicken, seafood and
steak. ▪ *www.watermans.com*

**Y-Not Pizza & Italian Cuisine**   ★$**LD**
*Virginia Beach* ▪ *(757) 496-9111*
*2102 Great Neck Sq Shpg Ctr*
*Virginia Beach* ▪ *(757) 474-6000*
*5257 Providence Rd* ▪ *Pizza* ▪ GF pasta
and pizza available upon request ▪
*www.ynotpizza.com*

**Yard House**                          ✪▱
*Virginia Beach* ▪ *(757) 490-9273*
*4549 Commerce St*

**Zoe's Restaurant**                $$$**D**
*Virginia Beach* ▪ *(757) 437-3636*
*713 19th St* ▪ *Seafood & Steakhouse* ▪ GF
entrées include porterhouse steak, filet
mignon, herb grilled Hawaiian ahi, charred
scallops, and seared Hawaiian snapper.
Confirm the timeliness of this information
before dining in. ▪ *www.zoesvb.com*

# VIRGINIA

## ALL OTHER CITIES

**456 FISH**                          $$$**D**
*Norfolk* ▪ *(757) 625-4444*
*456 Granby St* ▪ *Seafood* ▪ Manager
Ronnie reports that most menu items are
naturally GF. GF items like pan-seared
grouper in spicy Creole sauce, blackened
tuna, and stuffed baked squash topped with
mozzarella are included. Confirm the time-
liness of this information before dining in.
▪ *www.456fish.com*

### 99 Main Restaurant $$$D
*Newport News* ▪ *(757) 599-9885*
*99 Main St* ▪ *European* ▪ No separate GF menu but many items on the regular menu are either naturally GF or can be modified to be GF. Examples are roasted oysters, beef tenderloin, a rack of lamb, and NY strip rossini. For dessert, they offer pomegranate crème brûlée. ▪ *www.99mainrestaurant.com*

### Abuelo's ✪ 📖
*Chesepeake* ▪ *(757) 961-7610*
*1712 Ring Rd*
*Hampton* ▪ *(757) 224-5340*
*2423 McMenamin*
*Roanoke* ▪ *(540) 265-3555*
*4802 Valley View Blvd*

### Alexander's Restaurant $$$D
*Roanoke* ▪ *(540) 982-6983*
*105 S Jefferson St* ▪ *American* ▪ The restaurant reports that most items on the menu can be prepared GF. They have rice flour that they can substitute where applicable. Alert a server, who will indicate menu items that are GF or can be modified to be GF. Reservations noting GF are recommended. ▪ *www.alexandersva.com*

### AnnaB's Gluten Free Bakery $$
*Richmond* ▪ *(804) 740-6659*
*9033 Quioccasin Rd* ▪ *Bakery* ▪ Dedicated GF bakery offering bagels, hamburger buns, breads, pies, cakes, cookies, donuts, muffins, brownies, and more. All items are made to order, in small batches. Items not listed on the menu may be available upon request. Orders can be placed online only. ▪ *www.annabglutenfree.com*

### Argia's ★ $$LD
*Falls Church* ▪ *(703) 534-1033*
*124 N Washington St* ▪ *Italian* ▪ GF pasta and beer are available. Owner and Chef Amy recommends "emphasizing" to the server that the meal must be GF. There is no strict cross-contamination policy in effect. ▪ *www.argias.com*

### Artie's $LD
*Fairfax* ▪ *(703) 273-7600*
*3260 Old Lee Hwy* ▪ *American* ▪ Reservationist Chelsea reports that the "low-gluten" menu includes a variety of salads, cheddar cheeseburgers without buns, and hickory barbeque burgers without buns. The menu is "low-gluten" rather than GF because the items are prepared in the same kitchen as non-GF items. Chelsea notes, however, that "at least two or three people per day" come to the restaurant for its "low-gluten" menu. ▪ *www.greatamericanrestaurants.com/arties*

### Au Bon Pain 📖
*McLean* ▪ *(703) 448-6875*
*1676 International Dr*
*Norfolk* ▪ *(757) 446-8582*
*300 Monticello Ave*
*Radford* ▪ *(540) 831-5810*
*Radford University- E Main St*
*Blacksburg* ▪ *(540) 231-9421*
*125 College Ave*
*Blacksburg* ▪ *(540) 231-5859*
*Virginia Tech- Otey & College Ave*
*Williamsburg* ▪ *(757) 585-2900*
*6692 D Richmond Rd*

### Austin Grill ✪$LD
*Springfield* ▪ *(703) 644-3111*
*8430A Old Keene Mill Rd* ▪ *Tex-Mex* ▪ GF menu includes grilled salmon salad, carnitas fajitas, huevos rancheros, grilled vegetable enchiladas, and more. Regional manager Robert stresses the importance of noting GF when placing an order so that the server can notify the manager and start the appropriate procedures for GF preparation. ▪ *www.austingrill.com*

### Bertucci's ✪📖
*Gainesville* ▪ *(571) 248-6397*
*8114 Stonewall Shops Sq*
*Herndon* ▪ *(703) 787-6500*
*13195 Parcher Ave*
*Springfield* ▪ *(703) 313-6700*
*6525 Frontier Dr*
*Vienna* ▪ *(703) 893-5200*
*1934 Old Gallows Rd*

## Big Bowl Restaurant    ✪$LD
*Reston* ▪ *(703) 787-8852*
*11915 Democracy Dr* ▪ *Asian* ▪ GF menu includes Thai chicken lettuce wraps as an appetizer, various pad thai dishes and chicken kung pao as entrées, and two GF desserts, including the trio of tastes. ▪ *www.bigbowl.com*

## Bizou    $LD
*Charlottesville* ▪ *(434) 977-1818*
*119 W Main St* ▪ *American* ▪ Manager Mundo reports that they have "a couple of regular customers" who are GF. The staff is very educated and can accommodate GF diners. Mundo emphasizes that there are GF meals on both the lunch and dinner menus. They have an open kitchen, so GF diners can speak to the chef directly.

## Blackstone Grill    $$D
*Christiansburg* ▪ *(540) 381-0303*
*420 Peppers Ferry Rd NW* ▪ *Seafood & Steakhouse* ▪ The restaurant notes that GF diners come in "frequently." GF diners can be easily accommodated. Alert a server upon arrival. Reservations noting GF are recommended. ▪ *www.blackstonegrillva.com*

## Blue Iguana    $$LD
*Fairfax* ▪ *(703) 502-8108*
*12727 Shoppes Ln* ▪ *American* ▪ Manager David reports that all food is made to order, and accommodating GF diners is "relatively common." He notes that all kitchen staff members are certified to produce GF meals. He further reports that GF diners should "pick their protein" and the kitchen will prepare a suitable dish. ▪ *www.blueiguana.net*

## Boardwalk Café    ✪★¢LD
*Waynesboro* ▪ *(540) 941-8224*
*2556 Jefferson Hwy* ▪ *American* ▪ Manager reports that the restaurant "makes great efforts to makes customers with Celiac feel welcome" and adds that his own wife, who has Celiac, frequents the restaurant. Alert the server upon arrival and they will provide the current selection of GF options.

## Bonefish Grill    ✪📖
*Charlottesville* ▪ *(434) 975-3474*
*269 Connor Dr*
*Fredericksburg* ▪ *(540) 548-1984*
*1779 Carl D Silver Pkwy*
*Fairfax* ▪ *(703) 378-4970*
*13005 Lee Jackson Hwy Ste J*
*Ashburn* ▪ *(703) 723-8246*
*43135 Broadlands Center Plz Ste 137*
*Centreville* ▪ *(703) 815-7427*
*6315 Multiplex Dr*
*Williamsburg* ▪ *(757) 229-3474*
*5212 Monticello Ave*
*Newport News* ▪ *(757) 269-0002*
*340 Oyster Point Rd Ste 106*
*Midlothian* ▪ *(804) 639-2747*
*6081 Harbour Park Dr*
*Gainesville* ▪ *(703) 753-2597*
*7611 Somerset Crossing Dr*
*Glen Allen* ▪ *(804) 360-3740*
*11251 W Broad St*

## Bray Bistro    $$$B
*Williamsburg* ▪ *(757) 253-1703*
*1010 Kingsmill Rd* ▪ *American* ▪ Chef Justin reports that GF diners are becoming more common at the restaurant. He recommends noting GF in reservations and asking to speak with the chef, who will go over the menu with GF customers. Located at Kingsmill Resort & Spa, the restaurant is open only for Friday buffet-style dinners and Sunday brunches. ▪ *www.kingsmill.com/braydiningroom/*

## Brick House Kitchen    $$D
*Charleston* ▪ *(843) 406-4655*
*1575 Folly Rd* ▪ *Seafood* ▪ Menu changes often, but the restaurant reports that they can always accommodate GF diners. Examples of GF dishes include seared tuna, BBQ mahi-mahi, and pan fried flounder in addition to several salad and vegetable options. Alert server upon arrival. ▪ *www.brickhousecharleston.com*

## Brixx Wood Fired Pizza   ✪★📖
*Charlottesville* ▪ *(434) 245-4050*
*1133 Emmet St N*
*Woodbridge* ▪ *(703) 878-3152*
*14900 Potomac Town Pl*

## C&O Restaurant   $$$D
*Charlottesville* ▪ *(434) 971-7044*
*515 E Water St* ▪ *French* ▪ Chef Eric
reports that GF diners are accommodated
regularly and "all of the staff is very knowledgeable." The menu changes regularly, so
calling ahead is recommended. Dishes that
can be modified to be GF include squash
and tomato soups, smoked dates stuffed
with mascarpone cheese, and a three bird
roast with root vegetable gratin. Confirm
the timeliness of this information before
dining in. ▪ *www.candorestaurant.com*

## Café Rio Mexican Grill   📖
*Manassas* ▪ *(571) 358-3500*
*7803 Sudley Rd*
*Falls Church* ▪ *(703) 962-9100*
*6108 Arlington Blvd*
*Burke* ▪ *(571) 522-2200*
*6003 Burke Ctr Pkwy*
*Fairfax* ▪ *(703) 774-1400*
*13057 Lee Jackson Mem Hwy*

## CakeLove   ★📖
*Fairfax* ▪ *(703) 359-2972*
*11750 Fair Oaks Mall*
*Tysons Corner* ▪ *(703) 442-4880*
*1961 Chain Bridge Rd*

## Capital Grille, The   ✪📖
*McLean* ▪ *(703) 448-3900*
*1861 International Dr*

## Carlos O'Kelly's   ✪
*Fredericksburg* ▪ *(540) 373-5436*
*2306 Plank Rd*
*Stafford* ▪ *(540) 659-9982*
*2860 Jefferson Davis Hwy*

## Carolina Cupcakery   ✪★C$
*Chesapeake* ▪ *(757) 204-4773*
*1200 N. Battlefield*
*Ghent* ▪ *(757) 609-9304*
*2019 Colley Ave, Suite 102* ▪ *Bakery* ▪

Non-dedicated bakery offering a variety of
sweets, including cupcakes, cakes, lemon
bars, brownies, cookies, and more. Dinner rolls and cheddar rolls are also available. Call ahead to confirm availability. ▪
*www.carolinacupcakery.com*

## Cheeseburger in Paradise   ✪★📖
*Woodbridge* ▪ *(703) 580-0214*
*14000 Foulger Sq*
*Fredericksburg* ▪ *(540) 548-3092*
*1811 Carl D Silver Pkwy*
*Newport News* ▪ *(757) 269-4940*
*12361 Hornsby Ln*

## Chef Geoff's   ✪$$$LD
*Vienna* ▪ *(571) 282-6003*
*8045 Leesburg Pike* ▪ *American* ▪ Manager Benjamin reports that every location
is very happy to adjust their menu to fit the
needs of their gluten intolerant customers.
He notes that if customers have a specific
dish they want prepared GF, they should
call ahead a day ahead of time to inform
the chef. ▪ *www.chefgeoff.com*

## Choices by Shawn   ✪★$BLD
*Fairfax* ▪ *(703) 385-5433*
*3950 Chain Bridge Rd* ▪ *American* ▪ GF
items marked on the menu include mussels
in white wine, crab cakes, and NY strip
steak with Cajun spice rub. For dessert,
they offer GF carrot cake, flourless chocolate cake, and more. GF bread and pasta
are available. GF meals are prepared in a
separate kitchen and served on special red
plates so the server knows the meal is GF. ▪
*choicesbyshawn.com*

## Chop't   📖
*Rosslyn* ▪ *(703) 875-2888*
*1735 N Lynn St*

## Clyde's   📖
*Reston* ▪ *(703) 787-6601*
*11905 Market St*
*Vienna* ▪ *(703) 734-1901*
*8332 Leesburg Pike*
*Broadlands* ▪ *(571) 209-1200*
*42920 Broadlands Blvd*

## Coastal Flats                    $$LD
*McLean* ▪ *(703) 356-1440*
*7860 Tysons Blvd*
*Fairfax* ▪ *(571) 522-6300*
*11946 Grand Commons Ave* ▪ American
▪ The "low-gluten" menu includes warm
goat cheese and spiced pecan salad,
sautéed shrimp and creamy grit cakes, as
well as other seafood and steak options.
For dessert, there is a warm flourless
chocolate waffle. Management reports
that the menu is "low-gluten" instead
of GF because items are prepared in
the same kitchen as non-GF items. ▪
*www.greatamericanrestaurants.com*

## Cooking and Company Restaurant
★ $$$D
*Fairfax* ▪ *(703) 352-0331*
*10579 Fairfax Blvd* ▪ Italian ▪ GF pasta and
bread is available. Chef Raymond reports
that they are "absolutely" able to serve GF
customers. He adds that all servers are
"very well educated" about the GF diet,
and that Chef Anna is an expert on it. ▪
*www.vespuccirestaurant.com*

## Cosi                              ✪ 📖
*Reston* ▪ *(703) 435-7600*
*11909 Democracy Dr*
*Falls Church* ▪ *(703) 237-7766*
*513 W Broad St*

## Cranberry's Grocery & Eatery    ✪ ★ ₡S
*Staunton* ▪ *(540) 885-4755*
*7 S New St* ▪ Café ▪ GF items marked
on the menu include the Mediterranean
wrap, the grilled tempeh sandwich, the
turkey reuben, the taj mahal salad, bagels,
and scrambles. Owner Kathleen reports
that diners should specify GF requests,
and the kitchen will modify items to be
GF. GF bread and wraps are available. ▪
*www.gocranberrys.com*

## Dixie Bones BBQ                  $LD
*Woodbridge* ▪ *(703) 492-2205*
*13440 Occoquan Rd* ▪ Barbeque ▪ CEO
Nelson reports that the restaurant is ac-
customed to serving GF diners, as they do

it on a weekly basis. He notes that over half
the menu is naturally GF or can be pre-
pared GF. Managers are trained on the GF
diet, so ask to speak with one upon arrival.
▪ *www.dixiebones.com*

## Dogfish Head Alehouse           ✪$$LD
*Falls Church* ▪ *(703) 534-3342*
*6220 Leesburg Pike*
*Fairfax* ▪ *(703) 961-1140*
*13041 Lee Jackson Memorial Hwy* ▪ American ▪ Full GF menu includes several salads, burgers and sandwiches without buns,
NY strip, wood grilled salmon, and more.
Modifications necessary to make dishes GF
are also noted on the menu. Alert server
upon arrival. ▪ *www.dogfishalehouse.com*

## Don Pablo's                      ✪📖
*Alexandria* ▪ *(703) 548-4129*
*3525 Jefferson Davis Hwy*
*Manassas* ▪ *(703) 257-7884*
*10691 Davidson Pl*
*Sterling* ▪ *(703) 421-9524*
*46280 Potomac Run Plaza*

## Don's Woodfired Pizza, The       ★$$LD
*Sterling* ▪ *(703) 444-4959*
*21018 Southbank St* ▪ Pizza ▪ GF pizza
is available in the medium size only. ▪
*www.thedonspizza.com*

## Duck Chang's Restaurant          ★$LD
*Annandale* ▪ *(703) 941-9400*
*4427 John Marr Dr* ▪ Chinese ▪ Owner
Peter reports that GF items include curry
chicken, shrimp pepperada, and moo
goo gai pan. GF soy sauce is available,
and other dishes may be modified for GF
customers. The only thing that should be
avoided is fried foods because they do not
have dedicated fryers. For dessert, they
offer lychee nuts and taffy strawberries. ▪
*www.duckchangs.com*

## Fatz Eatz & Drinkz               📖
*Dublin* ▪ *(540) 674-8046*
*4586 Alexander Farm Rd*

### Firebirds Wood Fired Grill ✪🕮
*Fredericksburg* ▪ *(540) 548-5100*
*1 Towne Ctr Blvd*
*Woodbridge* ▪ *(703) 763-5022*
*15100 Potomac Twn Pl*
*Leesburg* ▪ *(703) 804-0443*
*1607 Vlg Mrkt Blvd*

### Fireworks Pizza    ★ $LD
*Leesburg* ▪ *(703) 779-8400*
*201 Harrison St SE* ▪ *Pizza* ▪ GF pizza is available. Restaurant reports that GF pizza is available with any topping except meatballs, which are not GF. Many of the soups and several beers and drinks are also GF. Confirm the timeliness of this information before dining in. ▪ *www.fireworkspizza.com*

### First Watch - The Daytime Café ✪🕮
*Fairfax* ▪ *(703) 978-3421*
*9600 Main St*
*Chantilly* ▪ *(703) 263-2344*
*13027 Lee Jackson Memorial Hwy*

### Fleming's Prime
### Steakhouse & Wine Bar ✪🕮
*McLean* ▪ *(703) 442-8384*
*1960A Chain Bridge Rd*

### Fox and Hound Pub & Grille 🕮
*Fredericksburg* ▪ *(540) 548-4105*
*1861 Carl D Silver Pkwy*
*Newport News* ▪ *(757) 881-9180*
*12300 Jefferson Ave*

### Frostings    ★ ¢S
*Glen Allen* ▪ *(804) 360-2712*
*11331 W Broad St* ▪ *Bakery* ▪ Non-dedicated bakery offering GF chocolate and vanilla cupcakes every day. There is usually one more flavor available as the "weekly special." Possible special flavors include carrot cake, hummingbird cake, and coconut. Advance notice of 48 hours is needed for special orders of a dozen or more. ▪ *www.frostingsva.com*

### Gabriel Archer Tavern, The    $L
*Williamsburg* ▪ *(757) 229-0999*
*5800 Wessex Hundred* ▪ *American* ▪ Restaurant reports that GF diners

are welcome. Alert a server upon arrival, and be specific about dietary needs. Limited GF offerings include salads, along with a meat and cheese platter. ▪ *www.williamsburgwinery.com/gat*

### Genghis Grill 🕮
*Chantilly* ▪ *(703) 961-1825*
*14412 Chantilly Crossing Ln*
*Henrico* ▪ *(804) 360-4206*
*11849 W Broad St*
*Sterling* ▪ *(703) 651-2000*
*46300 Potomac Run Plaza*

### Glory Days Grill ✪🕮
*Burke* ▪ *(703) 866-1911*
*9526 Old Keene Mill Rd*
*Centreville* ▪ *(703) 266-4100*
*13850 Braddock Rd*
*Culpepper* ▪ *(540) 829-7133*
*15295 Montanus Dr*
*Fairfax* ▪ *(703) 204-0900*
*3059 Nutley St*
*Gainesville* ▪ *(571) 261-1500*
*7581 Somerset Crossing Dr*
*Lorton* ▪ *(703) 372-1770*
*9459 Lorton Market St*
*Manassas* ▪ *(703) 361-9040*
*9516 Liberia Ave*
*Herndon* ▪ *(703) 390-5555*
*2567 John Milton Dr*
*Midlothian* ▪ *(804) 608-8350*
*6151 Harbourside Ctr Loop*
*Sterling* ▪ *(703) 430-3456*
*21800 Towncenter Plz*
*Stone Ridge* ▪ *(703) 327-8811*
*42010 Village Center Plz*
*Winchester* ▪ *(540) 662-9922*
*130 Featherbed Ln*
*Woodbridge* ▪ *(703) 730-3663*
*13800 Smoketown Rd*

### Greene Turtle
### Sports Bar & Grill, The ✪🕮
*Fredericksburg* ▪ *(540) 785-4832*
*1 Towne Centre Blvd*
*Leesburg* ▪ *(703) 777-5511*
*603 Potomac Station Dr NE*
*Chesapeake* ▪ *(757) 361-6854*

*1401 Greenbrier Pkwy S #2260*
*Fairfax* ▪ *(703) 934-5550*
*3950 University Dr Suite 209*
*Hampton* ▪ *(757) 838-3854*
*3610 Von Schilling Dr*
*Sterling* ▪ *(703) 421-0676*
*21035 Dulles Town Cir*

## Jackson's ✪$$**LD**
*Reston* ▪ *(703) 437-0800*
*11927 Democracy Dr* ▪ *American* ▪ The
"low-gluten" menu includes the hickory
grilled fish of the day, Hong Kong style
sea bass, filet mignon, steak frites, a
variety of salads, and more. For dessert, there is a warm flourless chocolate
waffle. The menu is "low-gluten" rather
than GF because items are prepared in
the same kitchen as non-GF items. ▪
*www.greatamericanrestaurants.com/jacksons*

## Jason's Deli ✪📖
*Chesapeake* ▪ *(757) 382-0889*
*717 Eden Way N*
*Hampton* ▪ *(757) 825-1501*
*39 Coliseum Crossing*
*Henrico* ▪ *(804) 364-9016*
*11740 W Broad St*
*Falls Church* ▪ *(703) 448-5514*
*7505 Leesburg Pike*
*Fairfax* ▪ *(703) 449-0924*
*12955 Fair Lakes Shopping Center*
*Newport News* ▪ *(757) 898-3978*
*12515 Jefferson Ave*
*Charlottesville* ▪ *(434) 566-0147*
*900 Shoppers World Ct*

## Java Java ★C$
*Charlottesville* ▪ *(434) 245-0020*
*421 E Main St* ▪ *Coffee Shop* ▪ GF muffins
and biscotti are available. The restaurant
recommends calling early in the day to
reserve muffins and biscotti, as they only
make a few per day.

## Jersey Mike's 📖
*Chesterfield* ▪ *(804) 739-2200*
*7317 Hancock Village Dr*
*Bristol* ▪ *(276) 466-2517*
*102 Bonham Rd*

*Ashland* ▪ *(804) 550-9457*
*10180 Lakeridge Pkwy*
*Charlottesville* ▪ *(434) 975-3511*
*3440 Seminole Trl*
*Midlothian* ▪ *(804) 763-4400*
*4500 Commonwealth Centre Pkwy*
*Midlothian* ▪ *(804) 379-5363*
*100 Heaths Way Rd*
*Glen Allen* ▪ *(804) 364-3711*
*11444 W Broad St*
*Chesterfield* ▪ *(804) 706-1970*
*6945 Commons Plaza*
*Ashland* ▪ *(804) 798-6290*
*708 England St*
*Colonial Heights* ▪ *(804) 520-6080*
*2011 Blvd*
*Mechanicsville* ▪ *(804) 730-8555*
*7262 Mechanicsville Tpke*
*Lynchburg* ▪ *(434) 582-1300*
*3919 Wards Rd*
*Norfolk* ▪ *(757) 216-5555*
*1211 N Military Hwy*
*Leesburg* ▪ *(703) 777-3880*
*522 Fort Evans Rd*
*Chesapeake* ▪ *(757) 819-7766*
*733 Eden Way N*
*Sterling* ▪ *(703) 433-1929*
*21031 Tripleseven Rd*
*Fairfax* ▪ *(703) 865-7722*
*11199 Lee Hwy*
*Fairfax* ▪ *(703) 293-6293*
*10394 Willard Wy*
*Chantilly* ▪ *(571) 299-4980*
*5005 Westone Plaza Blvd*
*Ashburn* ▪ *(571) 223-0112*
*20070 Ashbrook Commons Plaza*
*Stafford* ▪ *(540) 288-5443*
*1495 Stafford Market Pl*
*Fairfax* ▪ *(703) 502-3036*
*12703 Shoppes Ln*

## Joe's Crab Shack ✪📖
*Fairfax* ▪ *(703) 968-7260*
*12831 Fair Lakes Pkwy*
*Norfolk* ▪ *(757) 625-0655*
*333 Water Side Dr*
*Chesapeake* ▪ *(757) 420-8330*
*1568 Crossways Blvd*
*Fredrickburg* ▪ *(540) 548-3844*

*2805 Plank Rd*
*Hampton* ▪ *(757) 262-1560*
*1974 Power Plant Pkwy*

### Kasha's Kitchen                    ★ ₵LD
*Falls Church* ▪ *(703) 533-8484*
*1053 W Broad St* ▪ *Deli* ▪ GF bread is
available. Manager Elise reports that many
soups are also GF, and all sandwiches can
be made with GF bread. GF items are
marked with a smiley face on the regular
menu ▪ *www.nourishmarket.com*

### Kincaid's                    📖
*Norfolk* ▪ *(757) 622-8000*
*300 Monticello Ave*

### La Sandia                    $$LD
*McLean* ▪ *(703) 893-2222*
*7852 Tysons Corner Ctr* ▪ *Mexican* ▪ Restaurant reports 90% of their menu is GF. ▪
*www.modernmexican.com*

### Legal Sea Foods                    ✪📖
*McLean* ▪ *(703) 827-8900*
*2001 International Dr*

### Lone Star Steakhouse & Saloon    ✪📖
*Chesapeake* ▪ *(757) 424-6917*
*1570 Crossways Blvd*
*Colonial Heights* ▪ *(804) 520-1009*
*2001 Southpark Rd*
*Danville* ▪ *(434) 791-4428*
*255 Lowes Dr*
*Fredericksburg* ▪ *(540) 374-1565*
*2051 Plank Rd*
*Hampton* ▪ *(757) 262-0013*
*1940 Power Plant Pkwy*
*Norfolk* ▪ *(757) 466-0124*
*450 N Military Hwy*

### Lost Dog Café, The                    ★ $LD
*McLean* ▪ *(703) 356-5678*
*1690 Anderson Rd*
*Fairfax* ▪ *(703) 205-9001*
*2729 Merrilee Dr* ▪ *Deli* ▪ GF pizza and
beer are available. Restaurant cautions that
all pizzas are baked in the same oven without a screen. ▪ *www.lostdogcafe.com*

### Loving Hut                    📖
*Falls Church* ▪ *(703) 942-5622*
*2842 Rogers Dr*

### Maggiano's Little Italy                    ★📖
*McLean* ▪ *(703) 356-9000*
*2001 International Dr*

### Magnolia at the Mill                    ✪$LD
*Purcellville* ▪ *(540) 338-9800*
*198 N 21st St* ▪ *American* ▪ GF pizza is
available. GF menu is only available in
stores and is quite extensive according
to the head server. Servers are reportedly well-trained on the GF diet and
know which dishes can be prepared GF ▪
*www.magnoliasmill.com*

### Majestic Café                    $$$LD
*Alexandria* ▪ *(703) 837-9117*
*911 King St* ▪ *American* ▪ The restaurant
reports that several menu items are naturally GF and others can be made GF upon
request. Alert the server upon arrival. ▪
*www.majesticcafe.com*

### Mamma's of Reston                    ✪★$$LD
*Reston* ▪ *(703) 689-4894*
*1428 North Point Village Center* ▪ *Ital-*
*ian* ▪ Over half of the items on the menu
are GF or can be prepared that way. ▪
*www.mammaluciareston.com*

### Melting Pot, The                    ✪📖
*Charlottesville* ▪ *(434) 244-3463*
*501 E Water St*
*Fredericksburg* ▪ *(540) 785-9690*
*1618 Carl D Silver Pkwy*
*Newport News* ▪ *(757) 369-9500*
*12233 Jefferson Ave*
*Reston* ▪ *(703) 264-0900*
*11400 Commerce Park Dr*

### Mike's American                    $$LD
*Springfield* ▪ *(703) 644-7100*
*6210 Backlick Rd* ▪ *American* ▪ The
"low-gluten" menu includes a variety
of salads, prime rib, filet mignon, and
the fresh fish of the day. For dessert,
there is a warm flourless chocolate
waffle. The menu is "low-gluten" instead

of GF because items are prepared in the same kitchen as non-GF items. ▪ *www.greatamericanrestaurants.com*

### Morton's Steakhouse   ✪▯
*Reston* ▪ *(703) 796-0128*
*11956 Market St*

### Natalia's Elegant Creations Pastry Shop and Café   ✪★¢S
*Falls Church* ▪ *(703) 241-8040*
*230 W Broad St* ▪ *Bakery & Café*
▪ Non-dedicated bakery offering several GF desserts and cookies. GF pies, cakes, and muffins are available. For lunch, they offer different GF options every day, including soups. GF cakes are listed online and can be ordered in advance. Most GF items are prepared using dedicated utensils. ▪ *www.nataliaselegantcreations.com*

### Not Your Average Joe's   ✪▯
*Leesburg* ▪ *(571) 333-5637*
*19307 Promenade Dr*

### O'Charley's   ▯
*Bristol* ▪ *(276) 642-0113*
*3173 Linden Dr*
*Chester* ▪ *(804) 751-9250*
*12301 Bermuda Crossroad Ln*
*Christiansburg* ▪ *(540) 382-5651*
*150 Laurel St NE*
*Fredericksburg* ▪ *(540) 786-9370*
*1791 Carl D. Silver Pkwy*
*Glen Allen* ▪ *(804) 261-0882*
*9990 Brook Rd*
*Harrisonburg* ▪ *(540) 432-6662*
*101 Burgess Rd*
*Lynchburg* ▪ *(434) 832-8282*
*4042 Wards Rd*
*Midlothian* ▪ *(804) 763-0616*
*12401 Tennessee Plaza*
*Roanoke* ▪ *(540) 563-9870*
*4765 Valley View Blvd NW*

### P.F. Chang's China Bistro   ✪★▯
*Fairfax* ▪ *(703) 266-2414*
*4250 Fairfax Corner Ave*
*Mc Lean* ▪ *(703) 734-8996*
*1716M International Dr*

### Pasha Mezze   ✪★$$**BLD**
*Norfolk* ▪ *(757) 627-1317*
*340 W 22nd St* ▪ *Mediterranean* ▪ Manager Ashley reports that many of their dishes are naturally GF and they are "more than happy to answer any questions about the menu". Alert server upon arrival. ▪ *www.pashamezze.com*

### Pei Wei Asian Diner   ✪▯
*Dulles* ▪ *(703) 421-5590*
*22000 Dulles Retail Plz*
*Fairfax* ▪ *(703) 803-4466*
*4461 Market Commons Dr*
*Gainesville* ▪ *(703) 753-3880*
*5035 Wellington Rd*
*Herndon* ▪ *(703) 251-0090*
*2338 Woodland Crossing Dr*
*Leesburg* ▪ *(703) 443-2411*
*528A E Market St*

### Pizza NY Margherita   ★$**LD**
*Gainesville* ▪ *(703) 753-0744*
*5115 Wellington Rd* ▪ *Pizza* ▪ GF pasta and pizza crust in available. The GF pizza crust in only available in the 9" and 12". According to kitchen staff, GF pizza is prepared in a separate oven and cut with a dedicated cutting knife. ▪ *www.pizzanymargherita.com*

### Red Velvet Cupcakery   ★¢S
*Reston* ▪ *(703) 464-7075*
*11939 Democracy Dr* ▪ *Bakery* ▪ The Red Velvet Cupcakery offers GF "Black and White Velvet" cupcakes in GF options. ▪ *www.redvelvetcupcakery.com*

### Renatos   $$$**LD**
*Fredericksburg* ▪ *(540) 371-8228*
*422 William St* ▪ *Italian* ▪ Manager reports that GF diners are frequent. Everything is made to order, which lowers the risk of CC. Alert a server upon arrival. GF pasta is available with advance notice. ▪ *rrenato.com*

### Restaurant Eve   $$$**LD**
*Alexandria* ▪ *(703) 706-0450*
*110 S Pitt St* ▪ *American* ▪ The restaurant

reports that they have many naturally GF items on the menu as well as several items that can be modified to GF. The staff is "more than happy" to accommodate GF diners and requests that they alert the server upon arrival to ensure proper preparation. ▪ *www.restauranteve.com*

### Revolutionary Soup                    ★ ⊄LD
*Charlottesville* ▪ *(434) 296-7687*
*108 2nd St SW*
*Charlottesville* ▪ *(434) 979-9988*
*104 14th St NW* ▪ *Deli* ▪ Manager Alfonso reports that GF soups such as tomato basil, carrot and ginger, and lamb curry are always available. Ask a server for the current GF soup options. ▪ *www.revolutionarysoup.com*

### Romano's Macaroni Grill             ✪★▥
*Fairfax* ▪ *(703) 273-6676*
*12169 Fair Lakes Promenade Dr*
*Reston* ▪ *(703) 471-4474*
*1845 Fountain Dr*
*Sterling* ▪ *(571) 434-0771*
*21055 Dulles Town Cir*
*Woodbridge* ▪ *(703) 491-3434*
*2641 Prince William Pkwy*

### Ruth's Chris Steak House            ✪▥
*Fairfax* ▪ *(703) 266-1004*
*4100 Monument Corner Dr*
*Vienna* ▪ *(703) 848-4290*
*8521 Leesburg Pike*

### Second St                           ✪$$LD
*Williamsburg* ▪ *(757) 220-2286*
*140 2nd St* ▪ *American* ▪ Extensive GF menu from shrimp kabobs to their signature wagyu kobe burger. All fried items are fried in dedicated GF fryers to help prevent CC. ▪ *www.secondst.com*

### Shane's Rib Shack                   ✪▥
*Fredricksburg* ▪ *(540) 785-4234*
*1150 Carl D Silver Pkwy*

### Silverado                          $$LD
*Annandale* ▪ *(703) 354-4560*
*7052 Columbia Pike* ▪ *American* ▪ The "low-gluten" menu includes a variety of

salads, as well as smoked BBQ pulled pork, baby back ribs, hickory smoked black angus ribeye, and more. For dessert, there is a warm flourless chocolate waffle. The menu is "low-gluten" instead of GF because items are prepared in the same kitchen as non-GF items. ▪ *www.greatamericanrestaurants.com*

### Smokey Bones                        ▥
*Woodbridge* ▪ *(703) 491-0390*
*2601 Prince William Pkwy*
*Fredricksburg* ▪ *(540) 548-1201*
*1801 Carl D Silver Pkwy*
*Newport News* ▪ *(757) 988-0028*
*12541 Jefferson Ave*
*Chesapeake* ▪ *(757) 361-6843*
*1405 Greenbrier Pkwy*

### Southern Inn                        ★$$LD
*Lexington* ▪ *(540) 463-3612*
*37 S Main St* ▪ *American* ▪ Bookkeeper Mandy reports that they serve GF diners "pretty regularly," and that all servers are trained to accommodate "dietary modifications." Menu items that can be prepared GF include spinach and artichoke dip, rigatoni bolognaise, and blackened chicken penne. GF pasta is not listed on the menu, but it is available. ▪ *www.southerninn.com*

### SweetWater Tavern                   $$LD
*Falls Church* ▪ *(703) 645-8100*
*3066 Gatehouse Plz*
*Sterling* ▪ *(571) 434-6500*
*45980 Waterview Plz*
*Centreville* ▪ *(703) 449-1100*
*14250 Sweetwater Ln* ▪ *American* ▪ The "low-gluten" menu includes black angus prime rib (dinner only), wood-grilled filet mignon, hickory grilled pork chops, roasted chicken and more. For dessert, there is a warm flourless chocolate waffle. The menu is "low-gluten" instead of GF because items are prepared in the same kitchen as non-GF items. ▪ *www.greatamericanrestaurants.com*

### Teddy's Pizza & Subs                ★$LD
*Middleburg* ▪ *(540) 687-8880*

*9 E Federal St* ▪ *Pizza* ▪ GF pizza is available but it is "baked in the same oven since it saves time and space" according to manager. ▪ *www.teddyspizzaandsubs.com*

## Texas De Brazil Churrascaria   ★ 📖
*Fairfax* ▪ *(703) 352-4111*
*11720U Lee Jackson Mem Hwy*

## Tony's NY Pizza   ★ $$ LD
*Fairfax* ▪ *(703) 502-0808*
*13087 Fair Lakes Shopping Ctr* ▪ *Pizza* ▪ GF pizza and GF beer are available along with a few other entrées, which include gnocchi and shrimp scampi. Restaurant notes that GF diners are "common." GF spaghetti and cheese ravioli are available. Alert the counter attendant, who will discuss GF options in detail. ▪ *www.tonysnypizza.com*

## Travinia Italian Kitchen   ✪ ★ 📖
*Leesburg* ▪ *(703) 777-6511*
*1605 Village Market Blvd SE*
*Woodbridge* ▪ *(703) 670-6663*
*Potomac Town Center*

## Triple Oak Bakery   $$$$$
*Sperryville* ▪ *(540) 987-9122*
*11692 Lee Hwy* ▪ *Bakery* ▪ Dedicated GF bakery offering cakes, cupcakes, lemon curd tarts, cream puffs, apple turnovers, and more. Pumpkin, apple, and sweet potato pies are available. Cakes are sold by the slice or whole. Owner Brooke recommends calling beforehand because she sometimes steps out to deliver orders. ▪ *www.tripleoakbakery.com*

## Uno Chicago Grill   ✪ ★ 📖
*Falls Church* ▪ *(703) 645-9590*
*3058 Gate House Plz*
*Kingstowne* ▪ *(703) 822-0957*
*5935 Kingstowne Towne Ctr*
*Manassas* ▪ *(703) 365-0056*
*10701 Bulloch Dr*
*Norfolk* ▪ *(757) 466-0923*
*5900 E Virginia Beach Blvd*
*Reston* ▪ *(703) 742-8667*
*11948 Market St*
*Tabb* ▪ *(757) 886-9050*
*5007 Victory Blvd*

*Williamsburg* ▪ *(757) 220-5454*
*205 Bypass Rd*
*Woodbridge* ▪ *(703) 490-4883*
*2680 Prince William Pkwy*

## Wildfire Restaurant   ✪ ★ 📖
*McLean* ▪ *(703) 442-9110*
*1714 Intl Dr*

## Y-Not Pizza & Italian Cuisine   ★ $ LD
*Norfolk* ▪ *(757) 624-9111*
*1517 Colley Ave*
*Chesapeake* ▪ *(757) 382-9111*
*1036 Volvo Pkwy*
*Norfolk* ▪ *(757) 502-8211*
*4412 Monarch Wy* ▪ *Pizza* ▪ GF pasta and pizza available upon request ▪ *www.ynotpizza.com*

## Zpizza   ✪ 📖
*Alexandria* ▪ *(703) 660-8443*
*6328-C Richmond Hwy*
*Alexandria* ▪ *(703) 600-1193*
*3217 Duke St*
*Falls Church* ▪ *(703) 536-6969*
*1051 W Broad St*
*Gainesville* ▪ *(703) 753-7492*
*7929 Heritage Village Plaza*
*Lorton* ▪ *(703) 372-1538*
*9451 Lorton Market St*
*Manassas* ▪ *(703) 580-8100*
*12817 Galveston Ct*
*Fairfax* ▪ *(703) 207-2380*
*8442 Lee Hwy*
*Springfield* ▪ *(703) 313-8181*
*6699-B Frontier Dr*
*Virginia Beach* ▪ *(757) 368-9090*
*3376 Princess Anne Rd*
*Williamsburg* ▪ *(757) 645-3303*
*4902 Courthouse St*

# WASHINGTON

## SEATTLE

### 50 North                    ✪ $BLD
*Seattle* ▪ *(206) 397-3939*
*5001 25th Ave NE Suite 100* ▪ *American*
▪ Extensive GF menu includes cioppino,
seared sea scallops, and pomegranate short
ribs. Staff reports that the kitchen uses a
designated fryer for GF items and keeps GF
meals as separate as possible from gluten-
full items. ▪ *50northrestaurant.com*

### Andaluca Restaurant            ✪ $$$BD
*Seattle* ▪ *(206) 382-6999*
*407 Olive Wy* ▪ *Spanish* ▪ Extensive
GF menu includes breakfast and dinner
selections. Examples are spinach frittata, a ratatouille omelet, roasted mussels,
beef tenderloin skewer, and paella . The
restaurant recommends alerting your
server of any "food allergies" upon arrival.
▪ *www.andaluca.com*

### Blue C Sushi                   ✪ ★ ¢LD
*Seattle* ▪ *(206) 633-3411*
*3411 Fremont Ave N*
*Seattle* ▪ *(206) 525-4601*
*4601 26th Ave NE*
*Seattle* ▪ *(206) 467-4022*
*1510 7th Ave* ▪ *Sushi* ▪ GF soy sauce is
available. A GF menu is available in-house
upon request, and includes selections for
rolls, nigiri, sashimi, and more. The restaurant recommends alerting a server upon
arrival so they can speak with the manager,
who will ensure that GF items are properly
prepared. ▪ *www.bluecsushi.com*

### Blue Dog Kitchen               ★ ¢BLD
*Seattle* ▪ *(206) 462-6083*
*5905 15th Ave NW* ▪ *Café* ▪ GF buttermilk,
banana, banana chocolate chip, and blueberry pancakes are available for breakfast
only. These pancakes are labeled WF on the
menu, but the restaurant confirms that they
are GF. ▪ *www.bluedogkitchen.com*

### Buca di Beppo                  ✪ 📖
*Seattle* ▪ *(206) 244-2288*
*701 9th Ave N*

### Buckley's on Queen Anne        ★ $$LD
*Seattle* ▪ *(206) 691-0232*
*232 1st Ave W* ▪ *American* ▪ GF beer is
available. ▪ *www.buckleysseattle.com*

### Café Flora                     ✪ ★ $$BLD
*Seattle* ▪ *(206) 325-9100*
*2901 E Madison St* ▪ *Vegetarian* ▪ GF
items are marked on the menu and include
the quesadilla verde, Oaxaca tacos, and
asparagus basil pizza. A variety of GF
desserts are also available. GF diners are
welcome, but should alert a server upon
arrival. ▪ *www.cafeflora.com*

### Capital Grille, The            ✪ 📖
*Seattle* ▪ *(206) 382-0900*
*1301 4th Ave*

### Cedars Restaurant              ★ $LD
*Seattle* ▪ *(206) 527-4000*
*4759 Brooklyn Ave NE*
*Seattle* ▪ *(206) 325-3988*
*500 Broadway* ▪ *Vegetarian* ▪ Staff reports
that the entire menu, which features both
Indian and Mediterranean cuisine, is
GF except for items made with bread. ▪
*www.cedarsseattle.com*

### Chaco Canyon Organic Café      ★ $BLD
*Seattle* ▪ *(206) 522-6966*
*4757 12th Ave NE*
*Seattle* ▪ *(206) 937-8732*
*3770 SW Alaska St* ▪ *Organic* ▪ GF items
are noted on the menu and include "grain
bowls" made with rice or quinoa, GF
French toast, select sandwiches, all salads,
and all soups. Be sure to mention GF when
placing your order. Confirm the timeliness of this information before dining in. ▪
*www.chacocanyoncafe.com*

### Chandler's Crab House          $$$$LD
*Seattle* ▪ *(206) 223-2722*
*901 Fairview Ave N* ▪ *Seafood* ▪ The
restaurant reports that servers are trained
to help diners select GF items from the

menu. Some menu items can also be modi-fied to be GF. Confirm the timeliness of this information before dining in. Reservations noting GF are recommended. ▪ *www.schwartzbros.com/chandlers-crabhouse*

### Cinnamon Works                                ★ⒸⓈ
*Seattle* ▪ *(206) 583-0085*
*1536 Pike Pl* ▪ *Bakery* ▪ Non-dedicated bakery offering a variety of GF breads and other baked goods, as well as take-home mixes. *www.cinnamonworks.com*

### Coffee And... A Specialty Bakery         ⒸⓈ
*Seattle* ▪ *(206) 280-7946*
*1500 Western Ave* ▪ *Coffee Shop* ▪ Dedicated GF bakery offering breads, tarts, cakes, cookies, cinnamon rolls, and more. A different sandwich special is available each day, as well as soup and seasonal house salad. ▪ *www.coffeeandpikeplace.com*

### Flying Apron                                 ⒸBL
*Seattle* ▪ *(206) 442-1115*
*3510 Fremont Ave N* ▪ *Bakery* ▪ Dedicated GF bakery offering cookies, pies, cakes, and other sweets, as well as a rotating variety of savory items and breads. The lunch menu includes soups, salads, pizzas, and more. ▪ *www.flyingapron.net*

### Flying Fish                                  $$$LD
*Seattle* ▪ *(206) 728-8595*
*300 Westlake Ave N* ▪ *Seafood* ▪ The restaurant reports that they can easily accommodate GF diners. Many menu items are naturally GF or easily adapted. Reservations noting GF are recommended, but not required. All servers are very knowledgeable about the GF diet. ▪ *www.flyingfishseattle.com*

### Garlic Jim's                                ✪★📖
*Seattle* ▪ *(206) 524-5467*
*2400 NE 65th St*

### Hard Rock Café                              ✪📖
*Seattle* ▪ *(206) 204-2233*
*116 Pike St*

### Hotwire Online Coffeehouse           ★ⒸⓈ
*Seattle* ▪ *(206) 935-1510*
*4410 California Ave SW* ▪ *Coffee Shop* ▪ GF baked goods arrive on Wednesdays and usually sell out, but some may still be available on Thursdays. The coffee shop reports that GF selections vary each week, but standard fare includes cookies, loaf cakes, and bars. ▪ *www.hotwirecoffee.com*

### Jodee's Desserts                            ⒸⓈ
*Seattle* ▪ *(206) 525-2900*
*7214 Woodlawn Ave NE* ▪ *Dessert* ▪ Dedicated GF establishment offering a wide variety of desserts, smoothies, sweets, and savory items. The restaurant is 95% organic, and most items are raw and vegan. ▪ *jodeesdesserts.com*

### Juliano's Pizza                             ✪★$LD
*Seattle* ▪ *(206) 782-9000*
*8335 15th Ave NW* ▪ *Pizza* ▪ GF pizza is available. When ordering be sure to consult with the staff member as to which toppings would best suit their GF crust. ▪ *www.julianos-pizza.com*

### Loving Hut                                  📖
*Seattle* ▪ *(206) 299-2219*
*1226 S Jackson St*

### Melting Pot, The                           ✪📖
*Seattle* ▪ *(206) 378-1208*
*14 Mercer St*

### Morton's Steakhouse                        ✪📖
*Seattle* ▪ *(206) 223-0550*
*1511 6th Ave*

### Old Spaghetti Factory, The                 ✪★📖
*Seattle* ▪ *(206) 441-7724*
*2801 Elliott Ave*

### P.F. Chang's China Bistro                  ✪★📖
*Seattle* ▪ *(206) 393-0070*
*400 Pine St Ste 136*

### Palomino                                    📖
*Seattle* ▪ *(206) 623-1300*
*1420 Fifth Ave*

### Piatti Ristorante & Bar          ★ $$**LD**
*Seattle* ▪ *(206) 524-9088*
*2695 NE Village Ln* ▪ *Italian* ▪ GF pasta is
available. The restaurant reports that staff
is trained on GF preparation and GF diners
are accommodated "all the time." They note
that the risotto is GF and that many menu
items can be modified to be GF. Alert a
server upon arrival. ▪ *www.piatti.com*

### Pink Door, The          ✪ ★ $$**LD**
*Seattle* ▪ *(206) 443-3241*
*1919 Post Alley, Pike Place Market* ▪
*Italian* ▪ Bionaturae GF pasta and Udi's
GF bread are available. There are several
other menu items that are either naturally GF or can be made GF. Precautions
are taken in the kitchen but items are not
prepared in a GF environment. Restaurant
states they do all they can to prevent CC. ▪
*www.thepinkdoor.net*

### Pizza Pi          ★ $**D**
*Seattle* ▪ *(206) 343-1415*
*5500 University Way NE* ▪ *Pizza* ▪ GF
pizza is available in the 9-inch size. All toppings except for the "fake meat" are GF. ▪
*www.pizza-pi.net*

### Plum Bistro          ✪ ★ $$**BLD**
*Seattle* ▪ *(206) 838-5333*
*1429 12th Ave* ▪ *Vegan* ▪ Menu features a
variety of GF selections, including crepes,
pancakes, grilled pesto eggplant, curry
yam fries, and orange roasted beet salad.
Staff reports that they clean the grill and
change cutting boards for GF orders, but
use a common fryer. A server will be able
to direct GF diners to the safest options. ▪
*www.plumbistro.com*

### Portage Bay Café          ★ $**BL**
*Seattle* ▪ *(206) 547-8230*
*4130 Roosevelt Way NE*
*Seattle* ▪ *(206) 462-6400*
*391 Terry Ave N*
*Seattle* ▪ *(206) 783-1547*
*2821 NW Market* ▪ *American* ▪ Several GF
pancake selections are available for breakfast, as well as GF French toast and sweet

rice porridge. Sandwiches for lunch can
be made on GF bread, and several of their
salads can be modified to be GF as well. ▪
*www.portagebaycafe.com*

### Razzi's Pizza          ✪ ★ $$**LD**
*Seattle* ▪ *(206) 782-9005*
*8523 Greenwood Ave N* ▪ *Pizza* ▪ Extensive GF menu includes GF paninis,
sandwiches, gyros, calzones, soups, and
salads. GF pizza and pasta are available. ▪
*www.razzispizza.com*

### Ruth's Chris Steak House          ✪📖
*Seattle* ▪ *(206) 624-8524*
*727 Pine St*

### Seastar Restaurant & Raw Bar   ★ $$$$**LD**
*Seattle* ▪ *(206) 462-4364*
*2121 Terry Ave* ▪ *Seafood* ▪ GF soy sauce
is available. Front-desk manager Joel notes
that all servers are "very well-versed" on
GF dining. He also notes that all dishes
are made to order, so most menu items
can be modified to be GF. Alert a server,
who will indicate GF options. Reservations noting GF are recommended. ▪
*www.seastarrestaurant.com*

### Sunlight Café          $**BLD**
*Seattle* ▪ *(206) 522-9060*
*6403 Roosevelt Way NE* ▪ *Vegetarian* ▪
The restaurant reports that they can make
menu of their menu items GF by "leaving out particular ingredients." A server
will be able to specify the best options. ▪
*sunlightcafevegetarian.com*

### Ten Mercer          ✪$$**D**
*Seattle* ▪ *(206) 691-3723*
*10 Mercer St* ▪ *Modern American* ▪ Full
GF menu includes several options for
each course, including applewood smoked
sturgeon, grilled flat iron steak salad, artichoke and spring pea risotto, and vanilla
bean custard. Kitchen staff reports that
new utensils and cookware will be used
for GF orders, so make sure to let your
server know that your meal must be GF. ▪
*www.tenmercer.com*

### Thrive ⊄BLD
*Seattle* ▪ *(206) 525-0300*
*1026 NE 65th St #A102* ▪ *Vegetarian* ▪
Dedicated GF, vegan/vegetarian restaurant.
Menu items include warm grain bowls
made with quinoa and rice, soups, salads,
and a vegan burger. ▪ *generationthrive.com*

### Tulio Ristorante ✪★$$$BLD
*Seattle* ▪ *(206) 624-5500*
*1100 Fifth Ave* ▪ *Italian* ▪ Extensive GF
menus available for both lunch and dinner. Entrées include roasted chicken with
lemon risotto, lamb sirloin, and duck breast
with crispy confit. GF pasta is also available. ▪ *www.tulio.com*

### Veggie Grill, The ✪★📖
*Seattle* ▪ *(206) 623-0336*
*446 Terry Ave N*
*Seattle* ▪ *(206) 523-1961*
*2681 NE University Village St*

### Village Sushi ★$LD
*Seattle* ▪ *(206) 985-6870*
*4741 12th Ave NE* ▪ *Japanese* ▪ Staff reports
that most menu items can be prepared GF.
Ask a server for details. GF soy sauce is
available. ▪ *www.villagesushiseattle.com*

### Wheatless in Seattle ⊄S
*Seattle* ▪ *(206) 782-5735*
*10003 Greenwood Ave N* ▪ *Bakery & Café*
▪ Dedicated GF bakery and café offering a
rotating variety of sweets and savory items,
including specialty breads, pizza crust,
muffins, loaf cakes, and cookies. All items
are available by special order on their website. ▪ *www.wheatlessinseattle.net*

### Wild Ginger Thai Restaurant ★$$LD
*Seattle* ▪ *(206) 623-4450*
*1401 3rd Ave* ▪ *Thai* ▪ Anything on the
menu can be prepared GF except the egg
rolls, calamari and wonton soup. GF dishes
include Thai spicy clams, Panang beef
curry and seabass. Alert the server upon
arrival. ▪ *www.wildginger.net*

### Zaw Artisan Bake at Home Pizza ★$D
*Seattle* ▪ *(206) 325-5528*
*1424 E Pine St*
*Seattle* ▪ *(206) 623-0299*
*434 Yale Ave N*
*Seattle* ▪ *(206) 787-1198*
*1635 Queen Anne Ave N*
*Seattle* ▪ *(206) 232-0515*
*7635 SE 27th St*
*Seattle* ▪ *(206) 297-1334*
*4612 Stone Way N*
*Seattle* ▪ *(206) 658-2929*
*7320 35th Ave NE* ▪ *Pizza* ▪ *www.zaw.com*

### Zpizza ✪📖
*Seattle* ▪ *(206) 432-9158*
*1620 Brdway Ave*

## WASHINGTON

## ALL OTHER CITIES

### Adriatic Grill Italian Cuisine & Wine Bar ★$$$LD
*Tacoma* ▪ *(253) 475-6000*
*4201 S Steele St* ▪ *Italian* ▪ A variety of
items on the menu can be prepared GF.
Consult with the server as to what is available. All GF foods are prepared separately.
▪ *www.adriaticgrill.com*

### Avellino ★⊄S
*Bellingham* ▪ *(360) 715-1005*
*1329 Railroad Ave*
*Bellingham* ▪ *(360) 922-0933*
*4260 Cordata Pkwy* ▪ *Coffee Shop* ▪
GF baked goods such as muffins, scones,
and cookies are available. GF items are
prepared every morning before anything else to minimize CC risk. Barista
Zach reports that the GF options rotate
daily and that they usually run out before
close. Special orders for specific items
can be placed one day ahead of time. ▪
*www.espressoavellino.com*

### Bellagios Pizza   ✪★$$LD
*Vancouver* ▪ (360) 567-1007
*322 SE 192nd Ave* ▪ *Pizza* ▪ GF menu
includes a variety of pizzas in either 10"
or 14" inch with a "build your own pizza"
option, salads, and appetizers. GF pizza
dough is also available for "take-&-bake."
Company President Julie Collins reports
that they have "gone to great lengths to
eliminate cross-contamination issues." ▪
*www.bellagiospizza.com*

### Billy's Bar & Grill   ★$$BLD
*Aberdeen* ▪ (360) 533-7144
*322 E Heron & G St* ▪ *American* ▪ GF buns
are available for sandwiches and burgers,
and some other menu options can be modified to be GF. Team member Robin reports
that "some" servers are aware of the GF
diet, but all of the servers will communicate with the kitchen when alerted by a GF
diner. ▪ *www.techline.com/banners/billys/*

### Bin on the Lake   $$$D
*Kirkland* ▪ (425) 803-5595
*1270 Carillon Pt* ▪ *American* ▪ Restaurant
notes that servers are trained on the GF diet,
and they know which menu items are or can
be modified to be GF. GF items on the menu
include salads, seafood dishes, and steak.
Confirm the timeliness of this information
before dining in. Reservations noting GF are
recommended. ▪ *www.thewoodmark.com*

### Bison Creek Pizza & Pub   ★¢LD
*Burien* ▪ (206) 244-8825
*630 SW 153rd St* ▪ *Pizza* ▪ GF pizza is
available in the 8-inch, 12-inch, and
14-inch sizes. GF crust can be prepared
with any toppings except for the chicken
or meatballs, which are not GF. Confirm
the timeliness of this information before
dining in. GF beer is also available. ▪
*www.bisoncreekpizza.com*

### BJ's Restaurant and Brewhouse ✪★📖
*Tacoma* ▪ (253) 472-1220
*4502 S Steele St*
*Tukwila* ▪ (206) 439-7500
*1159 Southcenter Mall*

### Black Pearl   ✪★$LD
*Bellingham* ▪ (360) 756-5003
*1255 Barkley Blvd*
*Bellingham* ▪ (360) 318-7655
*202 E Holly St #117* ▪ *Vietnamese* ▪ GF
menu available with a wide variety of
items, including spring rolls, pho made
with GF rice noodles, teriyaki dishes with
house-made GF teriyaki sauce, vermicelli bowls, and Thai curries. Owner Laila
recommends alerting a server upon arrival,
and says she will "make sure everything
is GF for you." Confirm the timeliness
of this information before dining in. ▪
*www.blackpearlbellingham.com*

### Blackbird Bakery   ★¢S
*Bainbridge Island* ▪ (206) 780-1322
*210 Winslow Way E* ▪ *Bakery* ▪ Non-
dedicated bakery offering GF rolls topped
with either vegetables or gruyere, along
with an assortment of cakes and desserts
such as GF lemon poppyseed muffins and
chocolate chip cookies. Breads and pie
shells are available by special order only. ▪
*blackbirdbakery.com*

### Blue C Sushi   ✪★¢LD
*Lynnwood* ▪ (425) 329-3596
*3000 184th St SW*
*Bellevue* ▪ (425) 454-8288
*503 Bellevue Sq*
*Tukwila* ▪ (206) 277-8744
*468 Southcenter Mall* ▪ *Sushi* ▪ GF soy
sauce is available. A GF menu is available in-house upon request, and includes
selections for rolls, nigiri, sashimi, and
more. The restaurant recommends alerting a server upon arrival so they can
speak with the manager, who will ensure
that GF items are properly prepared. ▪
*www.bluecsushi.com*

### Bonefish Grill   ✪📖
*Bothell* ▪ (425) 485-0305
*22616 Bothell Everett Hwy*
*Richland* ▪ (509) 628-9296
*133 Gage Blvd*

## Boston's
### Restaurant & Sports Bar   ✪★📖
Spokane ▪ (509) 927-4284
14004 E Indiana
Bellingham ▪ (360) 676-5111
70 Bellis Fair Pky
Mill Creek ▪ (425) 338-4900
15310 Main St
Smokey Point ▪ (360) 652-9999
16918 Twin Lakes Ave

## Breadline Café   ✪★$BLD
Omak ▪ (509) 826-5836
102 S Ash Ave ▪ Café ▪ GF menu available
in-house is mostly comprised of items such
as salads and meat entrées. GF pasta is
available. Alert a server, who will note the
gluten "allergy" on the ticket that goes to
the kitchen. ▪ www.breadlinecafe.com

## Buca di Beppo   ✪📖
Lynnwood ▪ (425) 744-7272
4301 Alderwood Mall Blvd

## Café Juanita   ✪★$$$$D
Kirkland ▪ (425) 823-1505
9702 NE 120th Pl ▪ Italian ▪ Restaurant
states that many of their dishes are GF.
Those that are not are easily modified to fit
dietary restrictions. Call ahead to request a
special GF menu. Be sure to alert a server
upon arrival and they will help select the
best GF options. ▪ cafejuanita.com

## Canyons Restaurant   ✪$$LD
Redmond ▪ (425) 556-1390
15740 Redmond Wy
Bothell ▪ (425) 485-3288
22010 17th Ave SE ▪ American ▪ GF menu
includes Smoked BBQ ribs, Chianti braised
pork chops and a sizzling fajita platter.
GF dessert includes the Canyon sundae.
Alert a server, who will notify the kitchen.
Safe handling procedures are followed to
ensure no CC of during preparation. ▪
www.canyonsrestaurant.com

## Carino's Italian   ✪📖
Burlington ▪ (360) 757-4535
150 Cascade Mall Dr

## Charlie's Safari   $LD
Lacey ▪ (360) 292-1600
5400 Martin Way E ▪ American ▪ Operations manager Laura reports that accommodations can be made for GF guests. She
recommends indicating any "allergies"
when making reservations. GF options
include chicken nachos made with corn
chips, vegetables trays, and fruit trays.
Outside food is not permitted, with the
exception of cake and ice cream for parties.
▪ www.charliessafari.com

## Churchill's Steakhouse   $$$LD
Spokane ▪ (509) 474-9888
165 S Post St ▪ Steakhouse ▪ The restaurant reports that they offer a wide variety
of GF steaks and sides such as soup and
salad. Alert the server upon arrival. ▪
www.churchillssteakhouse.com

## Coho Café   $LD
Issaquah ▪ (425) 391-4040
6130 E Lake Sammamish Pkwy SE, Suite A
Redmond ▪ (425) 885-2646
8976 161st Ave NE ▪ American ▪ The
restaurant reports that several items are
naturally GF or can easily be modified
to be GF, including coconut green curry,
ginger chicken lettuce wraps, and pit
roasted salmon. They also note that the
kitchen references a list of GF items, and
a special note is attached to GF orders
to prevent CC. Confirm the timeliness
of this information before dining in. ▪
www.cohocafe.com

## Colophon Café   ★¢BLD
Bellingham ▪ (360) 647-0092
1208 11th St ▪ American ▪ GF items are
marked on the menu and include quiche
made with potato crust, Mexican corn &
bean sopa, split pea soup, and a salsa platter. A GF version of their signature peanut
butter pie is available for dessert. Be sure
to specify GF when placing your order.
Confirm the timeliness of this information
before dining in. ▪ www.colophoncafe.com

## Country Cousin Restaurant $BLD
*Centralia* ▪ (360) 736-2200
*1054 Harrison Ave* ▪ *American* ▪ The restaurant reports that most menu items can be adapted to be GF, including steaks, chicken, and salads. Ask your server for details and they will consult with the kitchen if necessary. ▪ *countrycousinrestaurant.com*

## Daddy D's BBQ $LD
*Vancouver* ▪ (360) 892-4418
*7204 4th Plain Blvd*
*Vancouver* ▪ (360) 573-4393
*4409 78th St* ▪ *Barbeque* ▪ According to the owner, everything on their menu is GF. This includes items such as pork ribs, hot links, and grilled chicken. ▪ *www.daddydsbbq.com*

## Earls Kitchen & Bar ✪$LD
*Bellevue* ▪ (425) 452-3275
*700 Bellevue Way NE* ▪ *Global* ▪ Each location has a "Gluten Aware" menu with a variety of salads, entrées, and sides available. Marketing coordinator Melissa reports that all chefs are trained to "be aware of allergy needs" and will "happily accommodate" dietary restrictions. Alert server upon arrival. ▪ *www.earls.ca*

## Fairhaven Pizza ★$$LD
*Bellingham* ▪ (360) 756-7561
*1307 11th St* ▪ *Pizza* ▪ 12-inch GF pizza is available with any toppings except BBQ sauce, which has trace amounts of wheat. The restaurant reports that all of its other menu items are GF or can be prepared GF. Ask a server for more details. ▪ *www.fairhavenpizza.com*

## Flat Iron Grill $$$LD
*Issaquah* ▪ (425) 657-0373
*317 NW Gilman Blvd Ste 28* ▪ *Modern American* ▪ Many items on the menu are GF or can be easily modified. Alert a server upon arrival. All servers are trained on the GF diet and will be able to assist in choosing a GF meal. ▪ *www.theflatirongrill.com*

## Flying Apron ¢BL
*Redmond* ▪ (206) 442-1115
*16541 Redmond Way Suite E* ▪ *Bakery* ▪ Dedicated GF bakery offering cookies, pies, cakes, and other sweets, as well as a rotating variety of savory items and breads. The lunch menu includes soups, salads, pizzas, and more. ▪ *www.flyingapron.net*

## Frankie's Pizza & Pasta ✪$LD
*Redmond* ▪ (425) 883-8407
*16630 Redmond Wy* ▪ *Pizza* ▪ GF pizza is available. "Low-Carb/Gluten-Free" menu includes a chicken Italian sausage bake, chicken parmesan, shrimp sauté with gorgonzola cream sauce, and several "crustless" pizzas, along with other items. Not all items on this menu are entirely GF, so check with the server before ordering. ▪ *www.frankiesredmond.com*

## Friesenburgers ✪★¢BLD
*Tacoma* ▪ (253) 203-6753
*308 E 26th St* ▪ *American* ▪ GF menu includes burgers, cheeseburgers, bison burgers, and salmon burgers. GF hamburger and hotdog buns are available. Sometimes, they also have GF desserts like carrot cake and brownies. The restaurant reports that they have a dedicated fryer for GF french fries, and the entire staff is educated on the GF diet. ▪ *www.friesenburgers.com*

## Full Moon Thai Cuisine ★¢LD
*Shoreline* ▪ (206) 542-5777
*1441 NW Richmond Beach Rd* ▪ *Thai* ▪ RRestaurant reports that GF tamari sauce is available, and that most dishes can be modified to be GF upon request. Confirm the timeliness of this information before dining in. ▪ *www.fullmoonthaicuisine.com*

## Garlic Jim's ✪★📖
*Bellevue* ▪ (425) 455-5467
*1105 Bellevue Wy NE*
*Bothell* ▪ (425) 483-5555
*18404 120th Ave NE*
*Edmonds* ▪ (425) 771-5467

*9796 Edmonds Wy*
*Federal Way* ▪ *(253) 838-7744*
*34024 Hoyt Rd SW*
*Kirkland* ▪ *(425) 307-1122*
*9758 NE 119th Wy*
*Lacey* ▪ *(360) 456-8100*
*5730 Ruddell Rd SE*
*Lakewood* ▪ *(253) 588-5467*
*6030 Main St SW*
*Lynnwood* ▪ *(425) 787-5800*
*5031 168th St SW*
*Maple Valley* ▪ *(425) 433-2525*
*23330 Maple Valley Black Diamond Hwy*
*Mill Creek* ▪ *(425) 379-8900*
*3922 148th St SE*
*Mukilteo* ▪ *(425) 493-8646*
*10924 Mukilteo Speedway*
*Redmond* ▪ *(425) 861-9000*
*11523 Avondale Rd NE*
*Kirkland* ▪ *(425) 822-8881*
*8431 122nd Ave NE*
*Vancouver* ▪ *(360) 573-8400*
*13317 NE 12th Ave*

### Giggles Gluten-Free Bakery                     ⊂S
*Pasco* ▪ *(509) 521-3572*
*350 Tracie Rd* ▪ *Bakery* ▪ Dedicated GF
bakery offering bread, hamburger buns,
muffins, cookies, pies, cakes, brownies, and
more. GF dry mixes for at home baking are
also available. Special orders can also be
placed for pickup, delivery, or shipping. ▪
*gigglesglutenfree.com*

### Godfather's Pizza                             ★⌨
*Vancouver* ▪ *(360) 256-0000*
*2100 SE 164th Ave*

### Gustav's Pub & Grill                          ✪★$LD
*Vancouver* ▪ *(360) 883-0222*
*1705 SE 164th Ave* ▪ *European* ▪ GF menu
includes mushroom schnitzel, Rhineland
salmon, rotisserie chicken, sausage trio,
and more. For dessert, there is GF flourless chocolate cake, Bavarian crème, and
chocolate mousse. GF beer is available.
Executive coordinator Hannah reports
that all staff are GF aware, but cautions
that all items are prepared using common
equipment. ▪ *www.gustavs.net*

### Haley's Corner Bakery                         ⊂S
*Kent* ▪ *(253) 852-4486*
*10216 SE 256th St* ▪ *Bakery* ▪ Dedicated GF
bakery offering a large menu with varieties of pizzas (which are available to bake
at home), breads, and baked goods. Baked
goods include cakes, cheesecakes, coffee
cakes, pies, cookies, muffins, scones, and
more. ▪ *www.haleyscorner.com*

### HuHot Mongolian Grill                         ⌨
*Spokane Valley* ▪ *(509) 891-8711*
*11703 E Sprague*

### i.talia pizzeria                              ★⊂LD
*Olympia* ▪ *(360) 754-3393*
*2505 4th Ave W* ▪ *Pizza* ▪ GF pizza and
beer are available. GF pizza is available
with any toppings for an additional $1.
The restaurant reports that it GF pizzas are
prepared on separate pans using dedicated
utensils. ▪ *www.ramblinrestaurants.com*

### Il Lucano Ristorante Italiano     ✪★$$$LD
*Gig Harbor* ▪ *(253) 514-8945*
*3119 Judson St* ▪ *Italian* ▪ Restaurant offers
GF foods on a separate menu, in-house
only. GF pasta is packaged separately
but cooked on shared equipment. The
restaurant reports that "sanitization and
cleanliness take high importance", but they
"cannot guarantee" CC will not occur. ▪
*www.illucanoristorante.com*

### J J Hills Fresh Grill                         ✪$$D
*Leavenworth* ▪ *(509) 548-8000*
*505 Highway 2* ▪ *American* ▪ GF items
are marked on the menu and include
grilled top sirloin steak, quinoa topped
with grilled chicken, and vegetables. GF
desserts include chocolate decadence cake
made with GF cake mix and a Ghirardelli
chocolate mousse. Alert the manager
upon arrival to address CC concerns. ▪
*www.jjhillsfreshgrill.com*

### Jeckyl and Hyde Deli & Ale House ★⊂BL
*Bellingham* ▪ *(360) 715-9100*
*709 W Orchard Dr*
*Bellingham* ▪ *(360) 656-5303*
*794 Kentucky St* ▪ *Deli* ▪ GF pizza is

available at the Orchard Drive location only. Any toppings can be put on the GF pizza crust, which comes in 7 and 10-inch sizes. GF bread is available for sandwiches at both locations can be made to order with any available fillings. GF beer is also available. ▪ *www.jhdeli.com*

### Jersey Mike's　　　　　　　　¢**BLD**📖
*Shoreline* ▪ *(206) 546-9050*
*1289 N 205th St*
*Mukilteo* ▪ *(425) 348-5480*
*11815 Mukilteo Speedway*
*Lynnwood* ▪ *(425) 774-4466*
*2701 184th St SW*
*Kent* ▪ *(425) 251-8055*
*18119 E Valley Hwy S*
*Bonney Lake* ▪ *(253) 862-5111*
*21180 SR 410 E*
*Redmond* ▪ *(425) 641-3969*
*15230 NE 24th St #1-G*
*Covington* ▪ *(253) 639-3700*
*17309 SE 270th Pl*
*Arlington* ▪ *(360) 548-3979*
*3704 172nd St NE*

### Joe's Crab Shack　　　　　　　✪📖
*Vancouver* ▪ *(360) 693-9211*
*101 E Columbia Wy*

### Juliano's Pizzeria　　　　　✪★$**LD**
*Vancouver* ▪ *(360) 254-1286*
*15606 SE Mill Plain Blvd* ▪ *Pizza* ▪ GF pizza available in 10" and 14". Pizzas are prepared in an entirely separate area but baked in a common oven. ▪ *www.julianospizza.com*

### La Fiamma Wood Fire Pizza　　★$$**LD**
*Bellingham* ▪ *(360) 647-0060*
*200 E Chestnut St* ▪ *Pizza* ▪ GF pizza is available. Also, corn chips can be substituted for pita chips for some of their appetizers. ▪ *www.lafiamma.com*

### Little Pine Tree, A　　　　　　　$**LD**
*Vancouver* ▪ *(360) 597-4266*
*585 W 8th St* ▪ *Thai* ▪ The restaurant reports that "several GF dishes" are available. Staff recommends asking a server for options upon arrival. ▪ *www.alittlepinetree.com*

### Lombardi's　　　　　　　　✪★$**LD**
*Issaquah* ▪ *(425) 391-9097*
*695 NW Gilman Blvd*
*Everett* ▪ *(425) 252-1886*
*1620 W Marine View Dr.*
*Issaquah* ▪ *(425) 391-9097*
*695 NW Gilman Blvd*
*Everett* ▪ *(425) 252-1886*
*1620 W Marine View Dr*
*Bothell* ▪ *(425) 892-2931*
*19409 Bothell Everett Hwy* ▪ *Italian* ▪ GF menu offers small plates and salads, as well as meat and seafood entrées. Examples include Tuscan prawns, spinach chicken salad, salmon picatta, and chicken marsala. GF pasta is available. Alert a server upon arrival. ▪ *www.lombardisitalian.com*

### Maggiano's Little Italy　　　　★📖
*Bellevue* ▪ *(425) 519-6476*
*10455 NE 8th St*

### Main Event Sports Grill
*Vancouver* ▪ *(360) 448-7146*
*800 Main St* ▪ *American* ▪ The restaurant keeps a list of around 30 GF items, some of which are naturally GF and others that can be easily modified upon request. Alert the server upon arrival. ▪ *www.mesportsgrill.com*

### McGrath's Fish House　　　　✪📖
*Vancouver* ▪ *(360) 514-9555*
*12501 SE 2nd Cir*
*Federal Way* ▪ *(253) 839-5000*
*1911 S 320th St*

### Melting Pot, The　　　　　　✪📖
*Bellevue* ▪ *(425) 646-2744*
*302 108th Ave NE*
*Tacoma* ▪ *(253) 535-3939*
*2121 Pacific Ave*
*Spokane* ▪ *(509) 926-8000*
*707 W Main Ave*

### Mercato Ristorante　　　　★$$**LD**
*Olympia* ▪ *(360) 528-3663*
*111 Market St NW* ▪ *Italian* ▪ GF pasta is available, and the restaurant reports that many menu items can be modified to be GF. As with all specialty items, call ahead

to confirm availability. Alert a server, who will discuss GF options with the kitchen. ▪ *www.ramblinrestaurants.com*

### Mike's Four Star BBQ                    ¢LD
*Port Gamble* ▪ (360) 297-4227
*4719 NE State Hwy 104* ▪ *Barbeque* ▪ Owner Mike reports that nearly everything is GF, and they have a dedicated GF fryer. All of the seasonings and most of the sauces are GF, as they are made from scratch. Mike recommends alerting the cashier upon ordering, and the cashier will know exactly what is and what is not GF, as all staff members are thoroughly trained. ▪ *www.mikesfourstarbbq.com*

### Milford's Fish House                    $$D
*Spokane* ▪ (509) 326-7251
*719 N Monroe St* ▪ *Seafood* ▪ Milford's offers a variety of GF seafood options including fresh Alaskan cod filets, wild Brazilian lobster tail, and fresh planked wild Alaskan salmon filets. ▪ *www.milfordsfishhouse.com*

### Mora Iced Creamery                    ★¢S
*Bainbridge Island* ▪ (206) 855-1112
*139 Madrone Ln N*
*Kingston* ▪ (206) 855-1112
*11250 State Hwy 104*
*Poulsbo* ▪ (206) 855-1112
*18801 Front St* ▪ *Ice Cream* ▪ GF ice cream cones are available. Manager Jerry at Bainbridge Island reports that most ice cream and sorbet flavors are GF, and recommends asking a server for more details. Ingredients for each ice cream flavor are listed on the website. ▪ *www.moraicecream.com*

### Mustard Seed Asian Café                    ✿★$LD
*Spokane* ▪ (509) 483-1500
*4750 N Division* ▪ *Asian* ▪ The Missoula location has a GF menu, and the Spokane location expects to have one soon. Missoula's GF menu includes several halibut dishes, the Singapore beef, and a few tilapia entrées. GF soy sauce is available at both locations. ▪ *www.mustardseedweb.com*

### Old Spaghetti Factory, The                    ✿★📖
*Lynnwood* ▪ (425) 672-7006
*2509 196th St SW*
*Spokane* ▪ (509) 624-8916
*152 S Monroe St*
*Tacoma* ▪ (253) 383-2214
*1735 Jefferson Ave*
*Tukwila* ▪ (206) 664-6800
*17100 Southcenter Pkwy Ste 160*
*Vancouver* ▪ (360) 253-9030
*730 SE 160th Ave*

### P.F. Chang's China Bistro                    ✿★📖
*Bellevue* ▪ (425) 637-3582
*525 Bellevue Sq*
*Kennewick* ▪ (509) 735-3270
*8108 W Gage Blvd*
*Lynnwood* ▪ (425) 921-2100
*3000 184th St SW Ste 912*

### Pacific Grill                    ✿$$$LD
*Tacoma* ▪ (253) 627-3535
*1502 Pacific Ave* ▪ *American* ▪ GF menu includes Hawaiian ahi tuna, sautéed scallops, arctic char, grilled NY steak, lobster, pork tenderloin, filet mignon, and duck breast, as well as a variety of sides, salads, and appetizers. ▪ *www.pacificgrilltacoma.com*

### Palomino                    📖
*Bellevue* ▪ (425) 455-7600
*610 Bellevue Wy NE*

### Ramblin Jacks                    $$LD
*Olympia* ▪ (360) 754-8909
*520 4th Ave E* ▪ *American* ▪ The restaurant reports that while they do not have a GF menu, they are willing to "work with" customers to modify menu items. Team member Melissa recommends consulting your server, who will know which items can be made GF and alert the kitchen. Avoid fried items, as a common fryer is used. ▪ *www.ramblinrestaurants.com*

### Romano's Macaroni Grill                    ✿★📖
*Lynnwood* ▪ (425) 368-2875
*3000 184th St SW*

## Ruth's Chris Steak House  ✪📖
*Bellevue* ▪ *(425) 451-1550*
*565 Bellevue Sq*

## Sages Restaurant  ✪$$LD
*Redmond* ▪ *(425) 881-5004*
*15916 NE 83rd St* ▪ *Italian* ▪ There are separate GF menus for lunch and dinner. GF dinner menu includes cioppino, lemon herb chicken, and wild salmon picatta, among other things. For dessert, they offer GF chocolate decadence. GF beer is available. The restaurant notes that they "take extreme caution" when handling GF orders. Be sure to alert your server that you are ordering from the GF menu. ▪
*www.sagesrestaurant.com*

## Saigon Restaurant  ₵LD
*Vancouver* ▪ *(360) 944-8338*
*3021 NE 72nd Dr* ▪ *Vietnamese* ▪ The restaurant reports that the majority of the menu is naturally GF, as most items are rice-based. Alert the server upon arrival to ask about specific GF options and to ensure proper preparation.

## Seastar Restaurant & Raw Bar  ★$$$$LD
*Bellevue* ▪ *(425) 456-0010*
*205 108th Ave NE* ▪ *Seafood* ▪ GF soy sauce is available. Front-desk manager Joel notes that all servers are "very well-versed" on GF dining. He also notes that all dishes are made to order, so most menu items can be modified to be GF. Alert a server, who will indicate GF options. Reservations noting GF are recommended. ▪
*www.seastarrestaurant.com*

## Solstice Wood Fire Café  ✪★$$LD
*Bingen* ▪ *(509) 493-4006*
*415 W Steuben St (Hwy 14)* ▪ *Pizza* ▪ GF 10" pizzas and pastas are available. The restaurant reports that most meat entrées are or can be prepared GF as well. GF flourless chocolate cake is available for dessert. Confirm the timeliness of this information before dining in. ▪
*www.solsticewoodfirecafe.com*

## Spazzo Italian Grill & Wine Bar  ★$$$LD
*Redmond* ▪ *(425) 881-4400*
*16499 NE 74th St* ▪ *Italian* ▪ General manager Cory reports that they serve GF diners "on a regular basis." GF pasta is available, as well as a variety of GF side dishes. Alert the server upon arrival. ▪
*www.schwartzbros.com*

## Sushi I  ★
*Spokane* ▪ *(509) 703-7053*
*4314 S Regal* ▪ *Sushi* ▪ GF soy sauce is available and can be substituted to make most sushi dishes GF. Alert the server upon arrival.

## SweetCakes Bakery  ★₵S
*Kirkland* ▪ *(425) 822-6565*
*128 Park Ln* ▪ *Bakery* ▪ Non-dedicated bakery carrying GF cakes, cupcakes, cookies, dessert bars, and cheesecakes. Most items are available every day, but some items may require special order. Call for availability. ▪
*www.sweetcakeskirkland.com*

## Taste of Amazing  ★₵S
*Redmond* ▪ *(425) 867-1516*
*18005 NE 68th St* ▪ *Take-&-Bake* ▪ They offer a huge number of GF "take-&-bake" options, including chicken cacciatore, teriyaki chicken, chiles rellenos, macaroni and cheese, and many more. GF pasta, bread, crackers, donuts, cookies, and more are available. ▪ *www.savorymoment.com*

## Thai Little Home  ★₵LD
*Vancouver* ▪ *(360) 693-4061*
*3214 E Fourth Plain Blvd* ▪ *Thai* ▪ Restaurant can prepare GF stir-fry and noodle dishes, using rice noodles. Consult with the server to arrange for a GF meal. ▪
*thailittletogo.com*

## The Flying Goat  $$LD
*Spokane* ▪ *(509) 327-8277*
*3318 W NW Blvd* ▪ *Pizza* ▪ GF pizza is available. Additionally, the restaurant reports that all of their salad dressings are GF. ▪ *www.theflyinggoat.com*

### Tony Roma's                                    📖
*Kennewick* ■ *(509) 783-7002*
*8551 Gage Blvd*

### Trumpeter Public House          ✪★$$LD
*Mount Vernon* ■ *(360) 588-4515*
*416 Myrtle St* ■ *Modern American* ■
GF items marked on the menu include
crispy artichoke hearts, Thai chicken
skewers, stuffed roasted crimini, crab
cakes, pita and toppers, antipasti platter, hot crab dip, calamari, garlic bread,
clams and mussels, margarita flat bread,
soups and salads, variety of sandwiches
and burgers, shepard's pie, fish and
chips, cedar plank wild Alaskan sockeye, Spanish seafood guisado, smokey
tuscan linguini, chicken marsala, crab
mac and cheese, Moroccan spiced pork
stew, beef tenderloin, lentil croquette and
a petite New York steak and blackened
prawns. GF beers are also available. ■
*www.trumpeterpublichouse.com*

### Twigs Bistro & Martini Bar     ✪★$$$LD
*Spokane* ■ *(509) 232-3376*
*808 W Main Ave*
*Spokane* ■ *(509) 443-8000*
*4320 S Regal St*
*Spokane* ■ *(509) 465-8794*
*401 E Farwell Rd*
*Kennewick* ■ *(509) 735-3411*
*1321 N Columbia Center Blvd*
*Spokane Valley* ■ *(509) 290-5636*
*14728 E Indiana Ave*
*Union Gap* ■ *(509) 469-9327*
*2529 Main St*
*Spokane* ■ *(509) 468-9820*
*9820 N Nevada St* ■ *Modern American*
■ GF menu includes Moroccan beef,
pesto margherita chicken, crab mac and
cheese, pepper salmon, and more. GF
pizza and sandwich buns are available,
and all pizza and sandwich options are
listed on the menu. For dessert, there is
crème brûlée, strawberry rhubarb crisp,
and a flourless chocolate torte. Corporate
chef Jonathan reports that they "take every precaution to reduce the risk of cross

contamination", including training the
staff to handle GF items and using dedicated equipment to prepare GF meals. ■
*www.twigsbistro.com*

### Twilight Pizza Bistro          ✪★$LD
*Camas* ■ *(360) 833-9222*
*224 NE 4th Ave* ■ *Pizza* ■ Dedicated
utensils as well as surfaces are used to
prepare GF 10" pizza, pastas and desserts. ■
*www.twilightpizzabistro.com*

### Vancouver Pizza Company         ★$$LD
*Vancouver* ■ *(360) 750-1176*
*2219 Main St* ■ *Pizza* ■ GF pizza is available
■ *www.vancouverpizza.net*

### Wild Ginger Asian Restaurant      $$LD
*Bellevue* ■ *(425) 495-8889*
*11020 NE 6th St* ■ *Thai* ■ The two locations
have slightly different menus but both have
GF items marked with a "G". Examples
include Thai chicken satay, squash & sweet
potato stew, and panang beef curry. Reservations noting GF are recommended. ■
*www.wildginger.net*

### Wild Sage American Bistro       ✪★$$LD
*Spokane* ■ *(509) 456-7575*
*916 W 2nd Ave* ■ *Bistro* ■ GF menu
includes soup and salad combinations,
entrées such as seafood, steaks, pastas, and
desserts like coconut cream layer cake and
house churned ice cream. GF items are
prepared in a kitchen with products that
contain gluten. ■ *www.wildsagebistro.com*

### Windmill, The                 ★$$$$D
*Wenatchee* ■ *(509) 665-9529*
*1501 N Wenatchee Ave* ■ *Steakhouse* ■
The restaurant reports that certain menu
items can be prepared GF upon request.
Alert the server upon placing an order
and they will consult with the kitchen. ■
*www.thewindmillrestaurant.com*

## Woodman Lodge Steakhouse & Saloon
★$$$$**BD**

*Snoqualmie* ▪ *(425) 888-4441*
*38601 SE King St* ▪ *Steakhouse* ▪ GF items
include fish, steak, eggplant and bunless
burgers. Ask a server for GF accommodations. ▪ *www.woodmanlodge.com*

## Z'Tejas Southwestern Grill      ✪★📖
*Bellevue* ▪ *(425) 467-5911*
*535 Bellevue Sq*

## Zaw Artisan Bake at Home Pizza   ★$D
*Redmond* ▪ *(425) 952-4420*
*8145 161st Ave NE* ▪ *Pizza* ▪ GF pizza is
available. The restaurant reports that they
are "extremely sensitive to the difference
between Celiac and gluten intolerant" and
recommends mentioning that you have
Celiac and need extra care taken with your
order. Keep in mind that while they take
every precaution, their kitchen is not a GF
environment. ▪ *www.zaw.com*

# WEST VIRGINIA

## Chop House, The      ✪$$$$D
*Charleston* ▪ *(304) 344-3950*
*1003 Charleston Town Center* ▪ *Steakhouse* ▪ District manager Sue reports
that all locations offer GF items, which
are marked on the regular menu. She
notes that GF diners should always alert
a manager about GF requirements. ▪
*www.thechophouserestaurant.com*

## CJ's Italian Kitchen      ✪★$LD
*Vienna* ▪ *(304) 916-1852*
*75 Covington Wy* ▪ *Italian* ▪ GF pasta
is available, as well a GF crust for any
pizza. GF menu lists all pasta and pizza
options as well as a variety of salads. The
restaurant recommends calling ahead to
confirm individual suitability, as their

pizzas are cooked in a common oven. ▪
*www.cjsitaliankitchen.commenu.html*

## da Vinci's Italian Restaurant      ★$LD
*Williamstown* ▪ *(304) 375-3633*
*215 Highland Ave* ▪ *Italian* ▪ GF spaghetti
is available. ▪ *www.villadavinci.com*

## Eat 'n Park      ✪📖
*Bridgeport* ▪ *(304) 842-7668*
*100 Tolley Dr*
*Morgantown* ▪ *(304) 598-0020*
*353 Patterson Dr*
*Triadelphia* ▪ *(304) 547-9500*
*80 Fort Henry Rd*
*Weirton* ▪ *(304) 723-5179*
*226 Three Springs Dr*

## First Watch - The Daytime Café      ✪📖
*Charleston* ▪ *(304) 343-3447*
*164 Summers St*

## Glory Days Grill      ✪📖
*Ranson* ▪ *(304) 728-9000*
*190 Oak Lee Dr*

## Husson's Pizza      ★$LD
*Charleston* ▪ *(304) 345-7717*
*611 Ohio Ave*
*Charleston* ▪ *(304) 925-0382*
*301 36th St SE*
*Charleston* ▪ *(304) 342-2388*
*1008 Bridge Rd*
*Scott Depot* ▪ *(304) 757-7775*
*4040 Teays Valley Rd*
*St Albans* ▪ *(304) 722-2135*
*2415 Kanawha Ter*
*Cross Lanes* ▪ *(304) 776-4989*
*822 Cross Lanes Dr*
*Sissonville* ▪ *(304) 984-0053*
*6826 Sissonville Dr*
*Spring Hill* ▪ *(304) 768-4440*
*4010 Maccorkle Ave SW*
*Pinch* ▪ *(304) 965-0955*
*4 Quick Rd*
*Huntington* ▪ *(304) 781-2488*
*335 Hal Greer Blvd* ▪ *Pizza* ▪
*hussonspizza.com*

### Jersey Mike's ¢BLD
*Charles Town* ■ (304) 725-0070
*71-C Jefferson Crossing Wy*

### Later Alligator ¢BL
*Wheeling* ■ (304) 233-1606
*2145 Market St* ■ Modern American ■
Manager Amanda reports that although
the restaurant does not offer any GF specialty items, many of the salads, such as the
spinach salad with berries and walnuts, can
be modified to be GF. They also have GF
chips available daily and often times their
soup of the day is GF. Confirm the timeliness of this information before dining in.
She suggests that GF diners bring their
own bread for sandwiches, and she notes
that if enough demand arises for GF bread,
they would be open to carrying it. Ask for
Amanda or another manager upon arrival,
and he or she will confer with the kitchen
staff. ■ *www.lateralligator.net*

### Little India $LD
*Charleston* ■ (304) 720-3616
*1604 Washington St E* ■ Indian ■ GF
options include soups and salads, various types of curry, several meat kebab options, and sides of vegetables. ■
*www.littleindiawv.com*

### Lone Star Steakhouse & Saloon ✪▥
*Beckley* ■ (304) 255-7827
*4288 Robert C Byrd Dr*
*Charleston* ■ (304) 926-8459
*6515 Maccorkle Ave SE*

### O'Charley's ▥
*Barboursville* ■ (304) 733-9301
*3060 Champion Dr*
*South Charleston* ■ (304) 746-0920
*70 RHL Blvd*

### Panorama at the Peak $$$LD
*Berkeley Springs* ■ (304) 258-0050
*3299 Cacapon Rd* ■ American ■ GF
items are always marked on the menu,
which changes frequently. The restaurant recommends alerting the server
of your needs so they can "input the
information" to the chef, who is "the

expert on gluten and Celiacs", according to co-owner Patti. Reservations noting GF are recommended. ■
*www.panoramaatthepeak.com*

### Pies & Pints ★$$LD
*Charleston* ■ (304) 342-7437
*222 Capitol St*
*Fayetteville* ■ (304) 574-2200
*219 W Maple Ave* ■ Pizza ■ GF pizza is
available, as well as several GF salads and
soups. ■ *www.piesandpints.net*

### Pretty Penny Cafe $LD
*Hillsboro* ■ (304) 653-2646
*Rte 219* ■ Café ■ The restaurant reports that
they have "several" GF options. Most of
their sandwiches and burgers can be made
GF by replacing the bread with a salad and
their french fries can be fried in a separate fryer. Alert the server upon arrival. ■
*prettypennyfood.com*

### River City Ale Works $LD
*Wheeling* ■ (304) 233-4555
*1400 Main St* ■ American ■ The kitchen
can modify most things to be GF upon
request but only the baked potatoes and
chicken breast are naturally GF. Confirm
the timeliness of this information before
dining in. Upon arrival, alert a server,
who will go over GF options in detail. ■
*www.rivercitybanquets.com*

### Secret Sandwich Society ✪★$LD
*Fayetteville* ■ (304) 574-4777
*103 1/2 Keller Ave* ■ Deli ■ GF
menu available in restaurant. ■
*www.secretsandwichsociety.com*

### South Mountain Grille $$LD
*Snowshoe* ■ (304) 572-2990
*1 Soaring Eagle Lodge Blvd* ■ Modern
American ■ Manager reports that they are
"experienced with GF customers" and they
"always leave happy." Alert a server upon
arrival and they will discuss GF options. ■
*www.southmountaingrille.com*

## Sushi Atlantic　$LD
*Charleston* ▪ *(304) 342-0021*
*422 Shrewsbury St* ▪ *Sushi* ▪ The restaurant reports that many of their sushi and seafood items can be prepared GF. Alert the server upon arrival and request that any sauces containing gluten be omitted from the meal.

## Tidewater Grill　✪$$$LD
*Charleston* ▪ *(304) 345-2620*
*1060 Charleston Town Ctr* ▪ *Seafood* ▪ GF menu, only available in stores, includes coconut crusted fried shrimp, barbequed salmon, chicken artichoke pasta, and char grilled chicken salad julienne. GF pasta is available. Restaurant recommends alerting the server upon arrival. Store does not enforce a CC policy but manager says all chefs are trained to minimize CC to its lowest degree. ▪ *www.tidewatergrillrestaurant.com*

## Tricky Fish　¢LD
*Charleston* ▪ *(304) 344-3474*
*1611 E Washington St* ▪ *Seafood* ▪ The Tricky Fish has a variety of GF tacos. Options are made with an organic corn tortilla including mahi-mahi, shrimp, chicken, pulled pork and catfish. ▪ *www.trickyfish.net*

## Uno Chicago Grill　✪★📖
*Huntington* ▪ *(304) 697-8667*
*279 9th St*

## Venerable Bean Bakery, The　★$$
*Morgantown* ▪ *(304) 685-5524*
*1400 University Ave* ▪ *Bakery* ▪ Nondedicated bakery offering GF items by special order. Items include double chocolate brownies with walnuts, cherry coconut cookies, brownie cakes, chocolate cake, vanilla cream and ganache. ▪ *venerablebean.blogspot.com*

## Ye Olde Alpha　$LD
*Wheeling* ▪ *(304) 242-1090*
*50 Carmel Rd* ▪ *American* ▪ The restaurant reports that they can modify certain dishes to be GF. They recommend bringing a dining card, as the kitchen staff may not educated about gluten. Alert the server upon arrival. ▪ *www.yeoldealpha.com/eat.html*

# WISCONSIN
## MADISON

## Benvenuto's Italian Grill　✪★$LD
*Madison* ▪ *(608) 241-1144*
*1849 Northport Dr* ▪ *Italian* ▪ GF menu includes 10" pizzas, a variety of salads, baked haddock, flame grilled steak, bruschetta chicken pasta, cajun grilled pasta and more. ▪ *www.benvenutos.com*

## Biaggi's　✪★📖
*Madison* ▪ *(608) 664-9288*
*601 Junction Rd*

## Bluephies
## Restaurant and Vodkatorium　✪★$LD
*Madison* ▪ *(608) 231-3663*
*2701 Monroe St* ▪ *American* ▪ Items that can be made GF are marked on the regular menu. Options include cobb salad, artichoke & olive crusted salmon, a variety of sandwiches and burgers made on GF buns, and several pasta dishes made with GF pasta. ▪ *www.foodfightinc.com*

## Bunky's Café　✪★$LD
*Madison* ▪ *(608) 204-7004*
*2425 Atwood Ave* ▪ *Mediterranean* ▪ Italian and Mediterranean café offering extensive GF options. GF bread, pasta, and beer are available. GF pizza is available for dinner only. For dessert, they offer GF chocolate mousse pie, chocolate or caramel toffee cheesecake, and lemon mousse with ginger crust, among other things. ▪ *www.bunkyscafe.net*

### Chautara                                                    $$LD
Madison ▪ (608) 251-3626
334 State St ▪ Asian ▪ The restaurant
reports that many items on their menu can
be prepared GF, and recommends asking a
server about GF options.

### Coopers Tavern, The                                         ★$LD
Madison ▪ (608) 256-1600
20 W Mifflin St ▪ Pub Food ▪ GF modifications can be made to many items on
the menu. Alert a server upon arrival.
Four types of GF beer are available. ▪
www.thecooperstavern.com

### Cosi                                                        ✪📖
Madison ▪ (608) 257-2140
250 State St

### Eldorado Grill                                              ✪$$D
Madison ▪ (608) 280-9378
744 Williamson St ▪ Southwest ▪ GF
items marked on the regular menu
include enchiladas, chalupas, fajitas,
tacos, and quesadillas, among other
things. Alert a server upon arrival. ▪
www.eldoradogrillmadison.com

### Flat Top Grill                                              📖
Madison ▪ (608) 236-0500
538 N Midvale Blvd

### Fleming's Prime
### Steakhouse & Wine Bar                                       ✪📖
Madison ▪ (608) 233-9550
750 N Midvale Blvd

### Fresco Rooftop
### Restaurant & Lounge                                         ✪$$$D
Madison ▪ (608) 663-7374
227 State St ▪ American ▪ GF menu
includes seared sashimi grade scallops,
shrimp diablo, Prince Edward Island mussels, soups and salads, seared tuna and wild
mushroom salad, chicken fresco, grilled
salmon, seared Alaskan halibut, ciopinno,
lamb lollipop chops and a dry aged New
York strip steak. ▪ www.frescomadison.com

### Great Dane Pub & Brewing Co., The
✪★$$LD
Madison ▪ (608) 284-0000
123 E Doty St
Madison ▪ (608) 661-9400
357 Price Pl
Madison ▪ (608) 442-1333
876 Jupiter Dr ▪ American ▪ GF menu in-
cludes Thai pasta, Japanese tuna roll salad,
peanut stew, petite-cut sirloin, mango
mahi mahi, and more. Chocolate nut torte
is available for dessert. Executive chef
Matthew cautions that while they do their
best to ensure GF meals, there is "no way
to guarantee" that CC has not occurred. ▪
www.greatdanepub.com

### HuHot Mongolian Grill                                       📖
Madison ▪ (608) 827-7110
610 Junction Rd

### Johnny Delmonico's Steakhouse   $$$LD
Madison ▪ (608) 257-8325
130 S Pinckney St ▪ Steakhouse ▪ GF items
include steaks and seafood dishes. Alert
server upon arrival and they will help select
a GF meal. ▪ www.johnnydelmonicos.com

### L'Etoile Restaurant                                         $$$$D
Madison ▪ (608) 251-0500
1 S Pinckney St ▪ Modern American ▪
Hostess notes that they accommodate "dietary needs fairly regularly," so all servers
are able to help and are familiar with GF
options on the menu. Menu does change
daily, so calling ahead to find out current
GF options is recommended. Reservations noting GF are also recommended. ▪
www.letoile-restaurant.com

### Macha Teahouse                                              ⌐L
Madison ▪ (608) 442-0500
1934 Monroe St ▪ Teahouse ▪ Co-owner
Anthony reports that they "try to offer GF"
on Fridays, but it is not guaranteed to be
available. He adds that they offer a light
lunch that has "some GF options." Call
ahead to find out what options are available. ▪ www.machateahouse.com

## Melting Pot, The ◎▥
*Madison* ▪ *(608) 833-5676*
*6816 Odana Rd*

## Monty's Blue Plate Diner ◎¢BLD
*Madison* ▪ *(608) 244-8505*
*2089 Atwood Ave* ▪ *American* ▪ GF menu
includes corned beef hash, Wisconsin
salmon hash, sweet potato hash, huevos
rancheros, tofu scramble, pesto and mushroom omelette, spinach and feta omelette,
hamburgers and sandwiches served on
GF bread as well as a variety of soups and
salads. ▪ *www.montysblueplatediner.com*

## Nitty Gritty, The ◎★¢LD
*Madison* ▪ *(608) 251-2521*
*223 N Frances St* ▪ *American* ▪ GF beer,
cider, and sandwich buns are available.
GF menu is available online and includes
a variety of burgers, sandwiches, and hot
dogs, as well as denoting which sauces and
dressings are GF. The downtown location
has a WF fryer, but the Middleton location does not. Be sure to note GF when
making a reservation or placing an order. ▪
*www.nittygrittybirthdayplace.com*

## Otto's Restaurant & Bar $$$D
*Madison* ▪ *(608) 274-4044*
*6405 Mineral Point Rd* ▪ *Mediterranean*
▪ Restaurant reports that 90% of their
entrées are GF. Restaurant notes that it is
important to alert the server upon arrival. ▪
*www.ottosrestaurant.com*

## Rosati's Pizza ★▥
*Madison* ▪ *(608) 833-9300*
*6644 Mineral Point Rd*

## Samba Brazilian Grill $$$$D
*Madison* ▪ *(608) 257-1111*
*240 W Gilman St* ▪ *Brazilian* ▪ The restaurant reports that most of the menu is
naturally GF, and any staff member can indicate which items are GF and which must
be modified. A list of GF items is available
in-house. Examples of GF items include the
top sirloin, flank steak, pork tenderloin, leg
of lamb, and linguiça. Alert a server upon
arrival. ▪ *www.sambabraziliangrill.com*

## Silly Yak Bakery ¢S
*Madison* ▪ *(608) 833-5965*
*7866 Mineral Point Rd* ▪ *Bakery* ▪ This
dedicated GF bakery shares a building
with its sister store, The Bread Barn, which
makes non-GF goods. However, the two
facilities have completely separate kitchens.
Silly Yak carries a wide selection of GF
baked goods, including a variety of breads,
cinnamon rolls, brownies, cookies, and
cakes. ▪ *www.sillyyakbakery.com*

## Tex Tubb's Taco Palace $LD
*Madison* ▪ *(608) 242-1800*
*2009 Atwood Ave* ▪ *Tex-Mex* ▪ Items on
the menu can be modified to be GF. Most
items are naturally GF such as the enchiladas and tacos made with corn tortillas.
Alert a server upon arrival and they will
list items as well as any sauces that can be
made GF. ▪ *www.textubbstacos.com*

## Uno Chicago Grill ◎★▥
*Madison* ▪ *(608) 244-3266*
*3010 Crossroads Dr*
*Madison* ▪ *(608) 833-7200*
*7601 Mineral Point Rd*

# WISCONSIN
## ALL OTHER CITIES

## Abuelo's ◎▥
*Middleton* ▪ *(608) 831-0739*
*2229 Deming Wy*

## Au Bon Pain ▥
*Waukesha* ▪ *(262) 650-4989*
*210 N Grand Ave*

## Beans & Barley Deli, Market, Café ★¢BLD
*Milwaukee* ▪ *(414) 278-7878*
*1901 E North Ave* ▪ *Café* ▪ GF bread is
available. Most items on the menu can be
made GF. Consult with server for GF options. ▪ *www.beansandbarley.com*

**Benvenuto's Italian Grill**  ✪★$LD
*Beaver Dam* ▪ *(920) 887-7994*
*831 Park Ave*
*Fitchburg* ▪ *(608) 278-7800*
*2949 Triverton Pike Dr*
*Oshkosh* ▪ *(920) 230-2300*
*300 S Koeller St*
*Middleton* ▪ *(608) 826-0555*
*1109 Fourier Dr* ▪ *Italian* ▪ GF menu includes 10" pizzas, a variety of salads, baked haddock, flame grilled steak, bruschetta chicken pasta, cajun grilled pasta and more. ▪ *www.benvenutos.com*

**Bonefish Grill**  ✪▢
*Brookfield* ▪ *(262) 797-0166*
*18355 W Bluemound Rd*

**Buca di Beppo**  ✪▢
*Milwaukee* ▪ *(414) 224-8672*
*1233 N Van Buren St*
*Appleton* ▪ *(920) 739-3745*
*1190 N Casaloma Dr*

**Café Calamari**  ★$$$D
*Williams Bay* ▪ *(262) 245-9665*
*8th E Geneva St* ▪ *Italian* ▪ GF options include calamari, caprese salad, raw oysters, oysters rockefeller, bolognese, pomodoro cremosa, chicken and shrimp gambaretti, NY strip steak (blackened or Sicilian encrusted), grilled pork chops, pittine seared scallops, and chicken victoria. Chef Bryan reports that he can "tailor his ingredients from his original recipes to provide you with a GF option." Note GF when making reservations. ▪ *www.cafecalamari.com*

**Capital Grille, The**  ✪▢
*Milwaukee* ▪ *(414) 223-0600*
*310 W Wisconsin Ave*

**Carlos O'Kelly's**  ✪
*Onalaska* ▪ *(608) 783-1782*
*9396 State Rd 16*

**Charcoal Grill**  ✪$$LD
*Grafton* ▪ *(262) 375-1700*
*1200 N Port Washington Rd*
*Burlington* ▪ *(262) 767-0000*
*580 Milwaukee Ave*

*Kenosha* ▪ *(262) 942-9896*
*5745 75th St*
*Manitowoc* ▪ *(920) 682-1000*
*4101 Harbor Town Ln*
*New Berlin* ▪ *(262) 432-3000*
*15375 W Greenfield Ave*
*Racine* ▪ *(262) 639-2050*
*3839 Douglas Ave*
*Racine* ▪ *(262) 884-9400*
*8300 Washington Ave*
*Plover* ▪ *(715) 295-0200*
*190 Crossroads Dr* ▪ *Barbeque* ▪ GF menu available online and in-house. Items include chiles, spinach dip with tortilla chips, nachos, salads, and sandwiches without buns. Alert a server upon arrival. The staff cautions that they "do their best" to accommodate GF diners but "cannot guarantee" no CC. ▪ *www.charcoalgrill.com*

**Cheese Corner, The**  ✪¢LD
*Viroqua* ▪ *(608) 637-7779*
*323 S Main St* ▪ *Deli* ▪ Offers GF bread baked by Udi's and other GF options. ▪ *www.cheese-corner.com*

**Cheese Factory Restaurant, The** ✪★$BLD
*Wisconsin Dells* ▪ *(608) 253-6065*
*521 Wisconsin Dells Pkwy S* ▪ *Vegetarian* ▪ GF items marked on the vegan menu include the grilled "chicken" tofu salad, spicy Thai lomein, Malaysian coconut noodles, hummus, and more. Some items require modification to become GF, so be sure to alert a server upon arrival. GF pizza and pasta are available. ▪ *www.cookingvegetarian.com*

**Cheeseburger in Paradise**  ✪★▢
*Middleton* ▪ *(608) 831-2413*
*1601 Aspen Cmns*

**Claddagh Irish Pub**  ▢
*Middleton* ▪ *(608) 833-5070*
*1611 Aspen Cmns*

**Cooper's Hawk
Winery & Restaurants**  ✪★▢
*Brookfield* ▪ *(847) 836-9463*
*15 S Moorland Rd*

## Cosi ⊕▢

*Fox Point* ▪ *(414) 228-6930*
*8775 N Port Washington Rd*
*Middleton* ▪ *(608) 836-3180*
*8310 Greenway Blvd*

## Crawdaddy's Restaurant ⊕$$$LD

*West Allis* ▪ *(414) 778-2228*
*6414 W Greenfield Ave* ▪ *Cajun & Creole*
▪ GF menu includes appetizers, soups,
salads, fish and seafood entrées, as well
as meat dishes. Examples are the shrimp
Creole, ribeye steak, and BBQ ribs. The restaurant cautions that many of the GF menu
items are modified from regular menu
items, so it is important to specify GF when
ordering. ▪ *www.crawdaddysrestaurant.com*

## Fiesta Café ⊕★$$LD

*Hudson* ▪ *(715) 377-7533*
*1801 Ward Ave*
*La Crosse* ▪ *(608) 788-3268*
*5200 Mormon Coulee Rd* ▪ *Mexican* ▪ GF
menu includes fajitas, enchiladas, tortilla
soup, and seafood. Other items on the
regular menu can also be modified to be
GF. Restaurant recommends asking for
manager Victorino, who can discuss GF
options. ▪ *www.fiestacafeandbar.com*

## Fifth Ave Restaurant & Lounge ⊕★⊄LD

*Antigo* ▪ *(715) 623-2893*
*714 5th Ave* ▪ *American* ▪ The restaurant
reports that almost anything on the menu
can be made GF. Alert a server upon arrival
and they will help select the best option.

## Fireside Theater, The $$$$D

*Fort Atkinson* ▪ *(920) 563-9505*
*1131 Janesville Ave* ▪ *American* ▪ GF
diners can be accommodated. Baked
chicken or baked fish is generally available
for GF diners, and the chefs are accustomed to modifying dishes to be GF. ▪
*www.firesidetheatre.com*

## First Watch - The Daytime Café ⊕▢

*Brookfield* ▪ *(262) 754-5900*
*17550 W Bluemound Rd*
*Mequon* ▪ *(236) 518-0028*
*11032 N Port Washington Rd*

## Flat Top Grill ▢

*Wauwatosa* ▪ *(414) 258-7676*
*2751 N Mayfair Rd*

## Fleming's Prime Steakhouse & Wine Bar ⊕▢

*Brookfield* ▪ *(262) 782-9463*
*15665 W Bluemound Rd*

## Fontana Grill $$$$$

*Fontana* ▪ *(262) 275-1433*
*269 Fontana Blvd* ▪ *Seafood & Steakhouse* ▪ The restaurant reports that GF
accommodations can be made for "pretty
much any items on the menu". Be sure to
note GF when making reservations so that
the kitchen has time to prepare dishes.
Server will then go over the GF options
created by chef. ▪ *www.theabbeyresort.com*

## GingeRootz Asian Grille ★$LD

*Appleton* ▪ *(920) 738-9688*
*2920 N Ballard Rd* ▪ *Asian* ▪ The restaurant
recommends informing a team member of
"any special dietary needs" and they will
"do their best to accommodate." GF soy
sauce is available so any dish that is stir
fried can be made GF. Hawaiian sweet and
sour dishes are GF as well. Confirm the
timeliness of this information before dining in. ▪ *www.gingerootz.com*

## Gluten Free Frenzy, A ★⊄S

*Brookfield* ▪ *(262) 785-7020*
*19555 W Bluemound Rd* ▪ *Bakery & Café*
▪ Everything in the store is GF. Café inside
store offers GF pizza, sandwiches, desserts
and pies. ▪ *www.aglutenfreefrenzy.com*

## Godfather's Pizza ★▢

*Weston* ▪ *(715) 355-1118*
*2106 Schofield*

## Great Dane Pub & Brewing Co., The ⊕★$$LD

*Fitchburg* ▪ *(608) 442-9000*
*2980 Cahill Main*
*Wausau* ▪ *(715) 845-3000*
*2305 Sherman St* ▪ *American* ▪ GF menu
includes Thai pasta, Japanese tuna roll
salad, peanut stew, petite-cut sirloin, man-

go mahi mahi, and more. Chocolate nut torte is available for dessert. Executive chef Matthew cautions that while they do their best to ensure GF meals, there is "no way to guarantee" that CC has not occurred. *www.greatdanepub.com*

### Green Mill Restaurant and Bar ✪📖
*Eau Claire* ▪ *(715) 839-8687*
*2703 Craig Rd*
*Hudson* ▪ *(715) 386-9900*
*2410 Gateway Ct*
*Rothschild* ▪ *(715) 355-9200*
*1000 Imerpial Ave*

### Ground Round ✪📖
*Janesville* ▪ *(608) 314-8540*
*2753 Milton Ave*
*Neenah* ▪ *(920) 725-1010*
*1010 Cameron Wy*
*Tomah* ▪ *(608) 372-4000*
*201 Helen Walton Dr*

### Hackberry's Bistro ★$$BL
*La Crosse* ▪ *(608) 784-5798*
*315 5th Ave S* ▪ *American* ▪ GF pancakes and toast are available for brunch and lunch entrées. GF bread is also available for sandwiches. Alert server upon arrival. ▪ *www.pfc.coop*

### Happy Joe's Pizza & Ice Cream 📖
*Appleton* ▪ *(920) 954-6000*
*3401 E Evergreen Dr*
*Green Bay* ▪ *(920) 465-0690*
*1675 E Mason St*
*Lancaster* ▪ *(608) 723-4101*
*105 Alona Ln*
*Medford* ▪ *(715) 748-6778*
*909 Casement Ct*

### Hubbard Avenue Diner and Bakery ✪¢BLD
*Middleton* ▪ *(608) 831-6800*
*7445 Hubbard Ave* ▪ *American* ▪ Gluten sensitive menus are available upon request. Extensive GF menu includes a variety of breakfast items including eggs, omelettes, frittatas and skillets, sides, soups and salads, Santa Fe chicken bowl, blackened catfish salad, burgers with no

bun, oven roasted turkey dinner, ham and scalloped potato casserole and meatloaf of the gods. GF specials of the week include baked cod and Sunday pot roast. ▪ *www.hubbardavenuediner.com*

### HuHot Mongolian Grill 📖
*Appleton* ▪ *(920) 257-2555*
*3456 College Ave*
*Kenosha* ▪ *(262) 697-8522*
*7214 Green Bay Rd*
*Ashwaubenon* ▪ *(920) 405-8888*
*2621 S Oneida St*
*La Crosse* ▪ *(608) 781-2636*
*3800 State Hwy 16*
*Eau Claire* ▪ *(715) 834-2222*
*3805 S Oakwood Mall Dr*

### Imperial Garden West ★$LD
*Middleton* ▪ *(608) 238-6445*
*2039 Allen Blvd* ▪ *Chinese* ▪ GF soy sauce is available. Restaurant notes that most dishes can be made GF. Alert a server, who will notify the kitchen. ▪ *www.imperialgarden.com*

### Jersey Mike's ¢BLD
*Brookfield* ▪ *(262) 641-7827*
*17550-C W Bluemound Rd*
*Waukesha* ▪ *(262) 278-4070*
*1190 W Sunrise Dr*

### Key Westconsin ✪$LD
*Waukesha* ▪ *(262) 446-2346*
*331 Riverfront Plz* ▪ *Seafood & Steakhouse* ▪ The restaurant reports that 95% of their menu is GF and they use dedicated fryers to help prevent CC. Items that can be prepared GF are marked on the menu. Alert the server upon arrival. ▪ *keywestconsin.com*

### King's Noodle House ✪¢LD
*Delavan* ▪ *(262) 728-3289*
*322 S 7th St* ▪ *Vietnamese* ▪ Owner Dusty reports that the entire menu is GF with the exception of the French bread used for their Banh Mi sandwich. Menu selections include pho, clay pot dishes, fried rice dishes, and rice vermicelli dishes. ▪ *www.kingsnoodlehouse.com*

## Lakefront Brewery Palm Garden  ★ ¢D
*Milwaukee* ▪ **(414) 372-8800**
*1872 N Commerce St* ▪ *Modern American*
▪ Open on Friday evenings only. The brewery's own GF beer, New Grist, is available. ▪
*www.lakefrontbrewery.com*

## Libby Montana Bar & Grill  ★ $LD
*Mequon* ▪ **(262) 242-2232**
*5616 W Donges Bay Rd* ▪ *American* ▪ GF
pizza is available. The restaurant notes
that "a number of items" on the regular
menu can be prepared GF as well. GF
"chocolate bomb" (a chocolate soufflé with
vanilla ice cream) is available for dessert. ▪
*www.libby-montana.com*

## Market Street Diner & Bakery  ✪ ¢BLD
*Sun Prairie* ▪ **(608) 825-3377**
*110 Market St* ▪ *American* ▪ GF menu
includes Denver omelette, eggs to order,
popeye omelette, corned beef hash, skinny
scrambler, bacon or turkey sausage links,
mashed potatoes, cole slaw, a variety of
salads, burgers with no buns, oven roasted
turkey breast, market chicken and seared
salmon. ▪ *www.marketstreetdiner.com*

## Maxie's Southern Comfort  ✪ ★ $$D
*Milwaukee* ▪ **(414) 292-3969**
*6732 W Fairview Ave* ▪ *American* ▪ Restaurant reports they serve GF diners daily.
Almost all of their dishes are GF naturally
or can be modified. The chef prepares everything from scratch so substitutions are
easy to make. Alert your server upon being
seated and they will go over the options
with you. ▪ *www.maxies.com*

## Melting Pot, The  ✪ ▭
*Appleton* ▪ **(920) 739-3533**
*2295 W College Ave*
*Brookfield* ▪ **(262) 782-6358**
*19850 W Bluemound Rd*

## Mitchell's Fish Market  ✪ ▭
*Brookfield* ▪ **(262) 789-2426**
*275 N Moorland Rd*

## Molly's Gluten Free Bakery  ¢S
*Pewaukee* ▪ **(262) 369-1404**

*N47 W28270 Lynndale Rd* ▪ *Bakery* ▪
Dedicated GF bakery carrying cakes,
pie crusts, muffins, bread, bagels, mock
rye bread, rolls, cookies and brownies. Everything is made fresh to order.
The restaurant reports that bread needs
to be ordered two days in advance. ▪
*www.mollysglutenfreebakery.com*

## Monical's Pizza Restaurant  ★ ▭
*Arbor Vitae* ▪ **(715) 358-9959**
*360 US Highway 51 N*

## Nick-N-Willy's  ★ ▭
*Fond du Lac* ▪ **(920) 322-6425**
*1143 E Johnson St*
*Kenosha* ▪ **(262) 857-8039**
*7435 117th Ave*

## Nitty Gritty, The  ✪ ★ ¢LD
*Middleton* ▪ **(608) 833-6489**
*1021 N Gammon Rd* ▪ *American* ▪ GF beer,
cider, and sandwich buns are available.
GF menu is available online and includes
a variety of burgers, sandwiches, and hot
dogs, as well as denoting which sauces and
dressings are GF. The downtown location
has a WF fryer, but the Middleton location does not. Be sure to note GF when
making a reservation or placing an order. ▪
*www.nittygrittybirthdayplace.com*

## Outdoorsman Restaurant, The  
✪ ★ $$$BLD
*Boulder Junction* ▪ **(715) 385-2826**
*10383 Main St* ▪ *American* ▪ GF menu
includes sundried tomato shrimp, rib-eye
steak, and orange ginger-glazed Cornish
game hen. GF beer is available. Staff is educated on the GF diet, as one of the chefs is
GF. ▪ *www.outdoorsmanrestaurant.com*

## Outpost Natural Foods  ★ ¢S
*Wauwatosa* ▪ **(414) 778-2012**
*7000 W State St*
*Milwaukee* ▪ **(414) 961-2597**
*100 E Capitol Dr*
*Milwaukee* ▪ **(414) 755-3202**
*2826 S Kinnickinnic Ave* ▪ *Bakery* ▪
All locations report that although the
deli and bakery menus rotate weekly,

there are always GF options available. They also report that most sandwiches can be made using GF breads. Located in the Outpost Natural Foods market. ▪ *www.outpostnaturalfoods.coop*

### Phoenix Bar and Grill                ★$LD
*Baldwin* ▪ *(715) 688-3473*
*2570 Gracie Dr* ▪ *American* ▪ GF pizza is available, as well as GF bread for sandwiches. ▪ *www.phoenixbarandgrill.com*

### Pizza Ranch                ✪📖
*Baraboo* ▪ *(608) 448-2215*
*1000 Log Lodge Ct*
*Elkhorn* ▪ *(262) 723-7880*
*28 W Hidden Trl*
*Fond Du Lac* ▪ *(920) 929-8800*
*1235 W Johnson*
*Oostburg* ▪ *(920) 564-6333*
*944 Center Ave*
*Sheboygan* ▪ *(920) 395-2506*
*3518 Kohler Mem Dr*
*Waupun* ▪ *(920) 324-9000*
*900 W Main*
*Portage* ▪ *(608) 566-1750*
*2905 New Pinery*
*Greenbay* ▪ *(920) 468-3555*
*2206 Main St*
*Manitowoc* ▪ *(920) 769-0015*
*3212 Calumet Ave*
*Reedsburg* ▪ *(608) 768-5555*
*2670 E Main St*

### River Room, The                ✪$$BLD
*Green Bay* ▪ *(920) 437-5900*
*200 Main St* ▪ *American* ▪ GF menu contains regular menu items that can be modified to be GF. It includes breakfast, lunch, and dinner options. A salad bar as well as fresh cut fruit are also available for GF patrons. ▪ *www.greatlakesinn.com/dining/*

### Rosati's Pizza                ★📖
*Brookfield* ▪ *(262) 797-6466*
*17565 W North Ave*
*Fox Point* ▪ *(414) 228-8585*
*6900 N Santa Monica Blvd*
*Franklin* ▪ *(414) 529-1400*
*6558 S Lovers Lane Rd*

*Kenosha* ▪ *(262) 697-0123*
*6804 Green Bay Rd*
*Menomonee Falls* ▪ *(262) 250-3333*
*15086 Appleton Ave*
*New Berlin* ▪ *(262) 784-5700*
*14260 W National Ave*
*Waukesha* ▪ *(262) 574-1111*
*310 W Saint Paul Ave*

### Rustico Pizzeria                ★$LD
*Milwaukee* ▪ *(414) 220-9933*
*223 N Water St* ▪ *Pizza* ▪ GF pizza and pasta are available. Be sure to alert the server when placing your order. ▪ *www.rusticopizzeria.com*

### Ruth's Chris Steak House                ✪📖
*Middleton* ▪ *(608) 828-7884*
*2137 Deming Wy*

### Saz's State House                ✪$$LD
*Milwaukee* ▪ *(414) 453-2410*
*5539 W State St* ▪ *American* ▪ Limited GF menu includes shredded BBQ pork, BBQ pan seared chicken, filet mignon, and broiled haddock, among other things. The restaurant notes that all BBQ sauce products are naturally GF. ▪ *www.sazs.com*

### Slow Pokes Local Food                ★(LD
*Grafton* ▪ *(262) 375-5522*
*1229 12Th Ave* ▪ *Take-&-Bake* ▪ Dedicated GF store that carries a variety of GF bakery and deli items, including pizzas, sandwiches, soups, pies, granola, and more. ▪ *www.slowpokeslocalfood.com*

### Smiling Moose Deli                ✪📖
*Eau Claire* ▪ *(715) 838-9999*
*329 Riverfront Terr*

### Smokey's Bar-B-Que House                ✪★$BLD
*Lake Geneva* ▪ *(262) 249-3411*
*7020 Grand Geneva Wy* ▪ *Global* ▪ Extensive GF menu includes, among other things, French toast for breakfast, white chicken chili for lunch, and a variety of BBQ sandwiches. GF sandwich buns are available, as are GF pizza crusts and GF bread. The restaurant recommends having the server advise the kitchen that

you are GF so they can properly prepare. Located in the Timber Ridge Lodge. ■ *www.timberridgeresort.com*

### Stack'd ★ $LD
*Milwaukee* ■ *(414) 273-7800*
*170 S 1st St* ■ *American* ■ GF buns are available for burgers, as well as GF beer and cider. French fries can be made in a separate GF fryer upon request. The restaurant reports GF meals are prepared using dedicated GF utensils and prep area, and all staff are knowledgeable about which items are safe for GF diners. Alert the server upon arrival. ■ *www.stackedbar.com*

### Stir Crazy ★ 📖
*Brookfield* ■ *(262) 786-3100*
*15795 Bluemound Rd*

### Taste of Africa Restaurant $$LD
*Port Washington* ■ *(262) 268-1007*
*117 E Main St* ■ *African* ■ Dedicated GF restaurant serves chicken, pork, beef, catfish, tilapia, shrimp, rice dishes, a variety of sauces, and more. A selection of GF beer is available. ■ *tasteofafrica.us*

### Tess Restaurant ✪★$$D
*Milwaukee* ■ *(414) 964-8377*
*2499 N Bartlett Ave* ■ *Modern American* ■ GF items are marked clearly on the menu. GF bread is always available, and GF pasta is usually available. All desserts, including a flourless chocolate cake and two flavors of crème brûlée, are GF. All GF dishes are prepared separately and with dedicated GF utensils. ■ *hstrial-tess0.intuitwebsites.com*

### Tony Roma's 📖
*Green Bay* ■ *(920) 499-9070*
*2581 S Packerland Dr*

### Uno Chicago Grill ✪★📖
*Menomonee Falls* ■ *(262) 255-1440*
*W 180 N 9455 Premier Land*
*Lake Delton* ■ *(608) 253-2111*
*1000 S Wisconsin Dells Pwy*
*Appleton* ■ *(920) 731-2111*
*W 3254 Van Roy Rd*

### Urban Frog, The ★ ¢BL
*Green Bay* ■ *(920) 490-1170*
*163 N Broadway* ■ *Deli* ■ Restaurant reports that the entire menu is available GF, and staff members are trained to "take all the necessary steps to meet your dietary and allergy needs." GF bread, pizza, and hamburger buns are available, as well as GF wraps for sandwiches. ■ *www.urbanfrogdeli.com*

# WYOMING

### Altitude Chophouse & Brewery ✪$$LD
*Laramie* ■ *(307) 721-4031*
*320 S 2nd St* ■ *Steakhouse* ■ GF menu available upon request when dining in. Various chicken and steak entrées are available. No CC policy, however surfaces are wiped down thoroughly before preparing a GF dishes. ■ *www.altitudechophouse.com*

### Betty Rock ✪¢LD
*Jackson* ■ *(307) 733-0747*
*325 W Pearl Ave* ■ *American* ■ GF burger buns, hot dog buns and restaurant size bread available. GF turkey chili, salads and house roasted turkey are also on the menu. Alert server upon arrival. ■ *www.bettyrock.com*

### Blue Lion, The $$$D
*Jackson Hole* ■ *(307) 733-3912*
*160 N Millward St* ■ *Global* ■ "Allergy sheet" available upon request includes GF items. Some GF items include grilled chicken, elk, beef tenderloin, salmon, trout, shrimp, green curry prawns and a risotto dish. Confirm the timeliness of this information before dining in. ■ *www.bluelionrestaurant.com*

## Bosco's Italian Restaurant ★$$LD
*Casper* ▪ *(307) 265-9658*
*847 E A St* ▪ *Italian* ▪ GF pasta is available.
Other GF menu items include chicken
parmigiana, shrimp scampi, shrimp diablo
and the shrimp and scallops dish.

## Botticelli Ristorante Italiano ✪$$LD
*Casper* ▪ *(307) 266-2700*
*129 Wet Second St* ▪ *Italian* ▪ GF pasta
available. ▪ *www.botticelli-casper.com*

## Café Rio Mexican Grill 📖
*Rock Springs* ▪ *(307) 212-4300*
*1453 Dewar Dr*

## Chophouse Restaurant $$$LD
*Gillette* ▪ *(307) 682-6805*
*113 S Gillette Ave* ▪ *Steakhouse* ▪ GF
menu available. Items include cilantro lime
tilapia, beef stir-fry, chicken and shrimp
lettuce wrap, grilled halibut and a grilled
sirloin salad. ▪ *www.gillettechophouse.com*

## Dsasumo ✪★$LD
*Casper* ▪ *(307) 237-7874*
*320 W First St* ▪ *Thai* ▪ GF menu available
in house. Items include fresh garden rolls,
5 different soups, 3 salads, pad thai, fried
rice, 4 different types of curry including
red, green, panang and yellow, and for dessert a sticky rice cake with either custard or
mango. ▪ *www.dsasumo.com*

## Elevated Grounds Coffeehouse ✪★¢BL
*Wilson* ▪ *(307) 734-1343*
*3445 N Pines Way Suite #102* ▪ *Café* ▪ GF
blended frappes with flavors such as chocolate, java, vanilla bean, cookies and cream,
peanut butter cookie dough, fudge brownie
and spiced chai. GF bakery items are also
available such as GF florentina cookies. ▪
*elevatedgroundscoffeehouse.com*

## Jeffrey's Bistro $LD
*Laramie* ▪ *(307) 742-7046*
*123 E Ivinson Ave* ▪ *Fusion* ▪ All staff
members are used to GF requests, many
GF customers come in frequently. GF
options include Jeffrey's stir fry, Szechwan
chicken and shitake mushrooms, dopiazah,

Thai curried chicken with bananas and
marsala chicken with apples and sage. ▪
*www.jeffreysbistro.com*

## JH Organics ★¢BL
*Jackson* ▪ *(307) 733-0365*
*365 W Broadway Ave* ▪ *Bakery & Café*
▪ GF bread, wraps and oatmeal available.
Everything on the menu can be modified
to be GF. ▪ *www.jhorganics.com*

## La Cocina ✪¢LD
*Casper* ▪ *(307) 266-1414*
*1040 N Center St* ▪ *Mexican* ▪ GF menu
includes fajitas, quesadillas, tacos, and burritos. Majority of items on the menu can be
modified to be GF. The restaurant advises
avoiding the chili and anything fried due to
high risk of CC. ▪ *www.lacocinacasper.com*

## Los Agaves ¢LD
*Sheridan* ▪ *(307) 674-0900*
*922 Coffeen Ave* ▪ *Mexican* ▪ Most items
on the menu can be prepared GF. Enchiladas, tacos, etc. can be made with corn
tortillas. Alert server upon arrival and they
will point out GF options.

## Lulu's Café ★$BLD
*Sheridan* ▪ *(307) 763-4644*
*118 N Brooks* ▪ *Bakery & Café* ▪ Restaurant states that most breakfast
and lunch items can be prepared GF
upon request. GF crepes, bread, wraps
and rigatoni pasta also available. ▪
*www.luluscafewyo.com/welcome.html*

## Million Dollar Cowboy Steakhouse, The $$$D
*Jackson Hole* ▪ *(307) 733-4790*
*25 N Cache Dr* ▪ *Steakhouse* ▪ Alert server
upon arrival and they will notify chef, who
can make any of the options on the menu
GF. ▪ *www.cowboysteakhouse.net*

## Nikai Sushi ★$D
*Jackson* ▪ *(307) 734-6490*
*225 N Cache* ▪ *Sushi* ▪ GF Items on menu
are highlighted. ▪ *www.nikaisushi.com*

### Ole's Pizz & Spaghetti House ✪$LD
*Sheridan* ▪ (307) 672-3636
*927 Coffeen Ave* ▪ *Pizza* ▪ GF menu includes 10.5" pizza crust, salads and bunless burgers. ▪ *www.oles-pizza.com*

### Pearl St. Meat & Fish Company ★¢BLD
*Jackson* ▪ (307) 733-1300
*260 W Pearl St* ▪ *Deli* ▪ GF bread, vegetarian chili, cookies and crackers available. ▪ *www.pearlstmarketjh.com*

### Rendezvous Bistro $$D
*Jackson* ▪ (307) 739-1100
*380 S. Broadway* ▪ *Bistro* ▪ Many dishes can be modified to be GF. A few items on the menu include the chipotle pork chops, smoked salmon omelet, organic chicken dish and the Idaho rainbow trout. ▪ *www.rendezvousbistro.net*

### Smiling Moose Deli ✪📖
*Gillette* ▪ (307) 363-4104
*2711 S Douglas Hwy*

### Snake River Grill $$$D
*Jackson Hole* ▪ (307) 733-0557
*84 E Broadway* ▪ *Modern American* ▪ GF items include tomato soup, variety of salads, hibachi tartare, and grilled swordfish. The trout and halibut can also be made GF. Alert server upon arrival and they will notify chef. ▪ *www.snakerivergrill.com*

# SECTION 3: CHAIN RESTAURANTS

## User's Guide

In this section, you will find gluten-free information for more than 80 chain restaurants across the United States, many of which have locations listed in Section II. While some chains are listed for their extensive gluten-free selections, others are listed simply because of their ubiquity. We know you can't always choose a restaurant with a great gluten-free menu. Sometimes, you just have to settle for your child's favorite, but not so Celiac friendly, fast food restaurant.

In a departure from previous editions, we have chosen not to include gluten-free lists and menus from these restaurants, but rather an overview of what each restaurant offers. Lists and menus change frequently, and rather than list information that will quickly become outdated, we have provided website addresses for each chain so that customers can easily view their gluten-free options online. Section III chains are laid out in much the same format as the restaurants in Section II. As such, the same rules apply to these restaurants as the ones in Section II. Do not take any of the information for granted. Always double check before dining in and/or upon arrival in the restaurant. Some of the restaurants have sample dishes listed here in the guide; do not order directly from the guide. Instead ask the server or manager for the most current gluten-free options.

### Do Not Order Directly From These Lists

Unfortunately, there's no such thing as worry-free gluten-free dining. By its nature, ordering a gluten-free meal will almost always take more time and effort than ordering a "regular" one. Our guide is meant to help you save time by honing in on the restaurants or dishes that are most likely to be suitable for a gluten-free diet. We aim to prevent you from spending hours chasing dead ends, to provide you more time to engage with the restaurant staff and make sure you have updated information. To that end, we have provided the information in this section as a starting point for your research. We have not independently confirmed that any sample dishes described are gluten-free, nor have we confirmed the ability of each chain restaurant location to prepare gluten-free foods.

Finally, please use common sense when reviewing the information we've compiled from restaurants. For example, if a restaurant tells you that the hamburger is gluten-free, assume that only the patty is gluten-free. That is, unless you've independently confirmed that they have gluten-free hamburger buns. In general, if something seems unusual or not quite right, use your own good judgment and double-check the information. Also, keep in mind that the creators of these lists may or may not be familiar with all the nuances of the gluten-free diet. For example, if you see French fries on the gluten-free list, don't assume they have a dedicated fryer without confirmation from the restaurant.

## Not All Restaurants are Created Equal

We do not endorse or recommend any of the restaurants listed in this book. Just because a restaurant has a gluten-free list or menu doesn't mean you should eat there. Certain types of restaurants (e.g., buffets, sandwich or burrito shops) naturally present higher risk factors than others, and management responsiveness can vary or be otherwise hard to predict. Before you eat at any restaurant, you should independently assess the likelihood for cross-contamination, expected responsiveness of the service, and other factors that may impact your ability to get a gluten-free meal. (Please see the Section II User's Guide for more details.) Reasonable people will differ in the amount they want to risk in pursuit of restaurant dining. This Guide is designed to help you make intelligent, informed choices, but those choices are ultimately your own to make.

## Always Get the Most Recent Information

We obtained the information listed here in the winter of 2012-2013. Please note, however, that the restaurant industry is dynamic: Menus, suppliers, supplier ingredients, management, etc. are always changing.

We've provided websites and, when possible, phone numbers for the corporate headquarters of listed restaurants. Please use this information to get up-to-date lists!

## A Note About Ingredient Lists

Many restaurants release complete ingredient lists that enumerate the contents of every dish on their menu. We have not provided these resources here, but you may find them useful in evaluating the safety of a restaurant's offerings. For ingredient information, please contact a restaurant's corporate headquarters directly.

## Always Individually Verify Information

Even if you've received the most up-to-date gluten-free information from the restaurant's corporate office, don't stop there. It's important to realize the limitations inherent in a gluten-free list from a large chain restaurant. There is no way for any restaurant, especially a large chain, to guarantee a gluten-free meal. For starters, large chains may use different suppliers in different regions, meaning that the same ingredient may have a different composition in the Midwest than it does on the East Coast, for example. A supplier can also change the composition of ingredients. Moreover, a restaurant may change suppliers at any time. And some restaurant locations may not follow corporate procedures or recipes as closely as others; this is especially true of smaller franchise operations without far-reaching quality assurance departments. In addition, the staff of certain restaurants may not be specifically trained about Celiac disease or versed in the appropriate food handling techniques necessary to prepare a gluten-free meal. For example, some large fast food chains have gluten-free lists, but their average employees aren't trained to understand the gluten-free diet or to avoid cross-contamination. Until a particular restaurant has established a good track record, always assume that this will be the case. Use a gluten-free list or menu as a starting point only. It's up to you to order the correct food and ask for it to be prepared in a manner that will avoid cross-contamination (be specific – ask for clean gloves, clean utensils, etc.). In addition, preparation techniques for certain dishes may vary by region or even by restaurant location. Menu items and their ingredients can change over time. And, no matter how careful the restaurant staff is, there's always a chance of cross-contamination, because there are almost always gluten-containing items in a restaurant's kitchen.

## Don't Expect Any Guarantees

As we discussed, no restaurant can guarantee a gluten-free meal. And no restaurant will accept any liability for damages that result from your use of their gluten-free lists or menus. It's unfortunate, but today's reality is that you're on your own out there. Therefore, please always be alert and use your own good judgment in choosing where and what to eat. Be careful, cautious and deliberate. Ask questions, collect up-to-date information, use common sense and make intelligent, informed decisions.

# Chain Restaurants Organized Alphabetically by Restaurant Name

## Stop!

Before you visit any restaurant listed in this guide, review this Summary Checklist and the User's Guides in Sections 2 and 3.

### Before You Leave the House

- ☑ Research the restaurant. Is it a buffet, sandwich shop, or other type of cuisine that increases the risk of cross-contamination? If so, will you feel safe eating there?
- ☑ If dining at a chain restaurant, call the corporate office to request the most recent gluten-free menu or list. (See Section III for contact information.)
- ☑ Regardless of the type of restaurant, call the location you plan to visit in advance. Does the restaurant still have a gluten-free menu? (If not, can they accommodate you tonight?)
- ☑ Also, confirm that gluten-free specialty items are in stock. (E.g., if you're going for the gluten-free pasta, do they have it tonight?)

### When You Get There

- ☑ Introduce yourself to the maitre d', and mention your dietary needs.
- ☑ Ask for the gluten-free menu, if applicable.
- ☑ Never make any assumptions. Present your dining card, even if they have a gluten-free menu. Ask a few questions. Confirm that they understand the diet, even if they have a gluten-free menu.
- ☑ Also, review and use the tips and strategies for safe restaurant dining presented in the previous sections of this book.
- ☑ And remember, there is no way any restaurant (or restaurant guide) can guarantee a gluten-free meal. Always independently verify information and be vigilant when eating out. A bit of caution goes a long way in getting a safe and delicious gluten-free meal.

# Symbols Summary

 **Gluten-free menu is available on site.** See the Section 2 User's Guide for more information about what constitutes a gluten-free menu.

 **Gluten-free specialty items, such as bread, beer, pasta, etc., are available.** Always call ahead to confirm the availability of gluten-free specialty items. Restaurants may sell out and deliveries can arrive late.

 **This chain restaurant does not have locations listed in Section 2.**

**No Icon.** None of the above apply. See the restaurant's description for information about its gluten-free accommodations.

**B** = Breakfast     **L** = Lunch     **D** = Dinner     **S** = Snack

**¢** = under $10     **$** = $10 to $15     **$$** = $15 to $20     **$$$** = $21 to $29     **$$$$** = $30+

## 32 Degrees Yogurt Bar ¢S
*Dessert*

Amanda at customer service reports that "the majority of" their yogurts are GF. She notes that every location has nutritional information available in-store, but cautions that the toppings bars are self-serve and therefore at high risk for CC.
*www.32yogurt.com*

## Abo's Pizza ★ $LD
*Pizza*

According to owner Steve, GF pizza is available at "most" locations. He recommends calling individual locations to find out if they carry GF pizza. Sizes and toppings vary by location.
*www.abospizza.com*

## Abuelo's ✪$LD
*Mexican*

GF menu includes salads, tacos, tamales, and, house specialties like ribeye steak, pork tenderloin, and salmon. Flan is available for dessert.
*www.abuelos.com*

## Applebee's ☎$$LD
*American*

Guest relations specialist Elizabeth reports that a list of GF items is available under the Allergen Info link on their webpage. Selections include fiesta lime chicken, NY strip steak, and blackened tilapia. Elizabeth recommends alerting the server upon arrival and asking to speak to a manager if necessary.
*www.applebees.com*

## Aurelio's Pizza ★ ¢LD
*Pizza*

GF pizza is available in the 6-inch personal size and small 9-inch size. Call ahead to confirm availability.
*www.aureliospizza.com*

## Backyard Burgers $LD
*American*

Allergen guide online denotes items containing gluten, which are generally limited to burger buns. Alert the server upon arrival.
*www.backyardburgers.com*

## Bertucci's ✪ $ LD
*Italian*

GF menu includes grilled shrimp, roasted butternut squash, pesto grilled salmon, filet mignon with chianti sauce, and more. Chocolate mousse is available for dessert. The restaurant reports that GF orders go under a separate section that tells employees to use all separate supplies, and are prepared in a separate area to minimize the risk of CC.
*www.bertuccis.com*

## Biaggi's ✪ ★ $LD
*Italian*

GF pasta and pizza are available. GF menu includes a variety of pasta and pizza options, as well as appetizers, salads, and meat & seafood entrées. The restaurant reports that they take precautions and have separate prep area for GF items.
*www.biaggis.com*

## BJ's Restaurant and Brewhouse ✪ ★ $$LD
*American*

GF menu includes salads, thin crust pizza, soups, stuffed potatoes, New York strip steak, and fresh Atlantic salmon. A GF chocolate chip pizookie is available for dessert. Area VP of Operations Mel reports that team members are trained in CC procedures, and recommends speaking with a manager when dining in. Confirm the timeliness of this information before dining in.
*www.bjsbrewhouse.com*

## Bob's Steak & Chophouse    $$$$D
*Steakhouse*

The restaurant reports that GF entrées include prime ribeye, New York strip steak, a veal rib chop, oven roasted duck, and pork chops. Confirm the timeliness of this information before dining in.
*www.bobs-steakandchop.com*

## Boloco    ★ ¢LD
*Mexican*

A GF items list is available in every store, and GF tortillas are available. When they receive a GF request, a staff member trained in GF preparation makes the order on a separate tray.
*www.boloco.com*

## Bonefish Grill    ✪ ★ $$LD
*American*

Full GF menu includes appetizers, wood-grilled specialties, and desserts. GF beer is available at some locations. Call ahead for availability. Managers report that staff thoroughly cleans all surfaces and utensils before they are used to make a GF meal.
*www.bonefishgrill.com*

## Boston Market    ☎$LD
*American*

GF information is available online under Special Dietary Information. Allergen list denotes GF items. Staff reports that they have dedicated GF utensils at 3 food stations, with only one station containing GF items. Alert the manager upon arrival to help make a safe selection.
*www.bostonmarket.com*

## Boston's Restaurant & Sports Bar    ★ $$LD
*Pizza*

GF pizza crusts are available for all pizzas except those with breaded chicken, which is not GF. As with all specialty items, call ahead to confirm availability.
*www.bostons.com*

## Bricktop's    ✪$$$LD
*Seafood & Steakhouse*

GF menu includes a variety of salads, rotisserie chicken, BBQ chicken, grilled salmon, grilled trout, prime rib, filet mignon, and more. Modifications required to make items GF are included on the menu. Be sure to specify GF when placing your order, and ask to speak to a manager if anything is unclear.
*www.bricktops.com*

## British Beer Company    ✪ ★ $LD
*American*

Extensive GF menu includes lettuce wraps, bourbon BBQ ribs, a variety of salads, flat iron steak, sweet plum salmon, and more. GF rolls and wraps are available for sandwiches and burgers, as well as GF pizza and beer. Corporate chef Karl reports that they "work very hard to make sure all of their customers are safe."
*www.britishbeer.com*

## Brixx Wood Fired Pizza    ✪ ★ $LD
*Pizza*

GF pizza and beer are available. Tim of the Charlotte location reports that their kitchen teams have been "trained on all procedures to prevent cross-contamination." GF pizzas are prepared using separate ingredients, utensils, and cooking pans.
*www.brixxpizza.com*

## Bubba Gump Shrimp Co.    ✪$$LD
*American*

GF menu in stores. For GF guests, the entire process from order to serving is supervised and carried out by the manager and head chef. GF meals are made in a separate area with dedicated utensils and served by the manager. Confirm the timeliness of this information before dining in.
*www.bubbagump.com*

## Buca di Beppo ✪$$LD
*Italian*

GF menu includes chicken marsala, salmon limone, sausage & peppers, mozzarella caprese salad, and more. Dedicated utensils are used for GF orders, and employees also change gloves and prepare the meal on a designated tray. Alert the server upon arrival and ask to speak to a manager if necessary.

www.bucadibeppo.com

## Bucceto's Smiling Teeth ★$LD
*Italian*

GF pizza crust is available in medium size only, though some toppings are not GF. Ask your server which ones are safe. GF spaghetti is also available. Regional manager Adam reports that many entrées can be made GF as well, and all of their salad dressings are GF. Confirm the timeliness of this information before dining in.

buccetos.com

## Buffalo Wild Wings ☎$LD
*American*

Online allergen list denotes which items are GF. CC policy includes washing all utensils and surfaces before preparing GF items. Alert the server upon arrival.

www.buffalowildwings.com

## Bugaboo Creek Steak House ✪$$LD
*Steakhouse*

GF menu includes smoked baby back ribs, grilled rainbow trout, black magic steak, burgers without buns, several salads, and more. To ensure that your meal is prepared GF, ask to speak with the manager on duty and "request that all items are prepared in separate containers and on clean food contact surfaces."

www.bugaboocreek.com

## Burtons Grill ✪★$$$LD
*American*

GF sandwich buns, pasta, and beer are available. Extensive GF lunch and dinner menus are offered, including a wide variety of appetizers, sandwiches, salads, and entrées. GF desserts are available as well. Mary at North Andover reports that they take dietary restrictions "very seriously" and are "extremely careful" when preparing GF orders. A manager will personally deliver GF orders on a special plate.

www.burtonsgrill.com

## Café Rio Mexican Grill $LD
*Mexican*

GF options include salads served with your choice of meat and toppings, as well as tacos and enchiladas made with corn tortillas. Alert the server upon arrival and ask to speak to a manager if necessary.

www.caferio.com

## CakeLove ★$$
*Bakery*

Non-dedicated GF bakery offering GF cakes and cupcakes. All are available to order with advance notice of at least 4 days. Orders can be placed online for quick and easy pick-up.

www.cakelove.com

## California Dreaming Restaurant ✪$$LD
*American*

GF menu is available on request and includes items such as baby back ribs, BBQ chicken, nachos, and several salads.

www.californiadreaming.co

## Cantina Laredo ✪$LD
*Mexican*

GF items are marked on the menu and include chicken and mango salad, fish tacos, and avocado enchilada. Flan is available for dessert. Managers reports

that preparation items and surfaces are thoroughly cleaned before GF orders are prepared.
*www.cantinalaredo.com*

## Capital Grille     ✪$$$$LD
*Seafood & Steakhouse*
GF menu in stores. The restaurant reports that GF orders are handled exclusively by the head chef and served only by the manager. Alert the server upon arrival to start the GF process.
*www.thecapitalgrille.com*

## Captain D's
## Seafood Kitchen     ☎$LD
*Seafood*
GF items include catfish, wild Alaskan salmon, seasoned tilapia, scampi shrimp, shrimp skewers, wild Alaskan salmon salad, plain baked potato, side salad, roasted red potatoes, corn on the cob, broccoli and a variety of condiments including the sweet chili sauce, tartar sauce, cocktail sauce, ranch dressing, blue cheese dressing and the honey mustard dressing.
*www.captainds.com*

## Carino's Italian     ☎✪$$LD
*Italian*
GF items are marked on the menu and include chicken scaloppini, jalapeno garlic tilapia, chicken marsala, lemon rosemary chicken, and more. Corporate reports that they use dedicated prep items and cleaned surfaces for GF orders.
*www.carinos.com*

## Carlos O'Kelly's     $LD
*Mexican*
The restaurant reports that there are many options for GF diners. Alert the server and they will be able to list all available options.
*www.carlosokellys.com*

## Carrabba's Italian Grill     ✪$LD
*Italian*
GF menu includes Sicilian chicken soup, steamed mussels, chicken Bryan, and more. The menu also denotes any modifications required to make the items GF. Managers note that there is no GF grill, but reports that all other preparation items are thoroughly cleaned before being used for a GF order.
*www.carrabbas.com*

## Ceviche     $$LD
*Spanish*
The restaurant reports that "a little over twenty" menu items can be modified to be GF. Managers recommend to interface with the server and make sure they are aware of your needs, and also to be "extra careful" of the sauces, as some contain gluten.
*www.ceviche.com*

## Charleston's Restaurant     ✪$LD
*American*
Full GF menu includes items such as chicken picatta, salmon, grilled pork chops, and sides such as garlic mashed potatoes and various salad options.
*www.charlestons.ehsrg.com*

## Charlie Brown's
## Steakhouse     ✪$$$LD
*Steakhouse*
GF menu was created in cooperation with the GIG. Items include balsamic chicken, Mediterranean salmon, cioppino, barbecue ribs, several steaks, and more. The menu also specifies which sauces and condiments are GF. Confirm the timeliness of this information before dining in.
*www.charliebrowns.com*

## Cheeseburger in Paradise     ✪★¢LD
*American*
GF hamburger buns are available. Tia at customer service reports that they use separate fryers and skillets as well as separate utensils for GF orders. She

recommends alerting a manager upon arrival. Extensive GF menu is available online and in stores, and includes salads, burgers, sandwiches, entrées, desserts, as well as a selection of GF cocktails and other beverages. *www.cheeseburgerinparadise.com*

## Chick-fil-A ☎ ¢LD
*American*

A GF list is available upon request, listing each item that they "strive to make GF" and all of its ingredients. The restaurant reports that while they do not have a GF prep area, their procedures "have been written to avoid cross-contamination." *www.chick-fil-a.com*

## Chili's Grill & Bar ☎ $LD
*Global*

Allergen list available online and in stores denotes GF items and modifications needed. Alert server upon arrival and ask for a manager if necessary. *www.chilis.com*

## Chipotle Mexican Grill ☎ ¢LD
*Mexican*

Customer service reports that everything is GF except for tortillas, so the restaurant recommends that GF customers order the bowl option. Alert the employee who is assembling the meal to ensure that they take precautions against CC. *www.chipotle.com*

## Chop't ¢LD
*Deli*

Online Allergen Chart notes which items are GF, and CC prevention procedures are in place at all locations. Alert a manager upon arrival to initiate the allergy protocol. Sarah at customer service also recommends alerting the "Assembler" and "Chop'r" preparing your order of your dietary needs. *www.choptsalad.com*

## Claddagh Irish Pub ✪ $LD
*Irish*

GF menu includes corned beef & cabbage, balsamic chicken, grilled salmon, a variety of salads, and more. Corportate chef Joe reports that their chefs are trained in handling "allergens" and recommends alerting a server upon arrival so they can inform the kitchen to take precautions. *www.claddaghirishpubs.com*

## Clyde's $LD
*American*

Operations manager Claude reports that their servers, chefs and managers are "very familiar with gluten intolerances and allergies" and are "fully prepared" handle GF orders. They do not have a GF menu, but can "customize" most dishes to meet the needs of their customers. Alerting the manager is very important and will help ensure that your meal is handled properly. *www.clydes.com*

## Cooper's Hawk
## Winery & Restaurants ✪ ★ $$LD
*American*

Extensive GF menu includes appetizers, salads, burgers, sandwiches, entrées, sides, and desserts. GF sandwich buns and beer are available. Alert your server upon arrival to ensure proper protocols are put in place. The manager and chef sign off on GF orders before they are placed, and the head chef oversees production. *www.coopershawkwinery.com*

## Cosi ✪ ¢BLD
*American*

Staff member Alicia reports that there is a small GF menu as well as a list of GF items from which you can build your own meal. *www.getcosi.com*

## Costa Vida Mexican Grill          $LD
*Mexican*

The restaurant reports that they have "oceans of GF options" including all enchiladas, all tacos, all salads, all nachos, and the chicken tortilla soup. Be sure to alert the server and request corn tortillas where applicable.

*www.costavida.net*

## Cozymel's Coastal Mex          ✪$$LD
*Mexican*

GF menu includes baked tortilla chips, ahi tuna spinach salad with cilantro-lime vinaigrette, enchiladas with corn tortillas, chipotle honey glazed salmon, and more.

*www.cozymels.com*

## Chuck E. Cheese's          ☎ ★ ¢LD
*American*

GF personal cheese pizza and GF chocolate cupcakes are available. Pizzas are prepared in a GF facility and prepared in a sealed Bake In Bag, which is not opened until it reaches your table and comes with its own pizza cutter. The GF cupcake is also sealed until it reaches the table.

*www.chuckecheese.com*

## Davio's Northern Italian Steakhouse          ✪$$$LD
*Italian*

Extensive GF menu available. According to several managers, each restaurant has a strict CC prevention policy because of the high number of Celiac customers they have.

*www.davios.com*

## Del Frisco's Double Eagle Steak House          $$$$LD
*Steakhouse*

The restaurant reports that they can "definitely accommodate" GF diners. Store administrator Leslie stresses the imporance of notifying the chef when making a reservation as well as notifying the server upon arrival.

*www.delfriscos.com*

## Dinosaur Bar-B-Que          $$LD
*Barbeque*

An Allergen Sheet denoting items that contain gluten is available. GF options include most sandwiches without the bun, skirt steak, bronzed catfish, and more. Confirm the timeliness of this information before dining in.

*www.dinosaurbarbque.com*

## Donatos          ☎ ★ $LD
*Pizza*

GF "No Dough" pizza is available. No Dough pizza is made on a soy cracker crust that comes individually packaged with its own baking tray to limit CC. Salads are also available.

*www.donatos.com*

## Don Pablo's          ✪$LD
*Tex-Mex*

GF menu includes fajitas, tacos, grilled tilapia, enchiladas, and more. The menu also denotes which sauces and sides are GF. The restaurant requests that patrons alert their server of their "allergy" before placing an order.

*www.donpablos.com*

## Duffy's Sports Grill          ✪$$LD
*American*

GF menu includes Duffy's chili, steak salad with arugula, burgers without buns, NY strip steak, baby back ribs, mahi mahi, broiled bay scallops, and more. Confirm the timeliness of this information before dining in.

*www.duffyssportsgrill.com*

## Eat 'N Park          ✪¢BLD
*American*

Celiac menu is available online and in stores and includes breakfast, lunch, and dinner items. They have a special "GF kit" that contains, knives, cutting boards, etc. only used for GF.

*www.eatnpark.com*

## Eddie V's                    ✿$$D

*Seafood & Steakhouse*

GF menu includes items such as a seafood chopped salad, north Atlantic scallops, filet mignon, ahi tuna, and cold water lobster.
*www.eddiev.com*

## Fatz Eatz & Drinks                    ✿$$LD

*American*

GF options are identified by asterisks on the menu. The restaurant also reports that all of their proteins can be prepared GF. Staff recommends that GF diners alert the server upon arrival and note specifically any precautions they would like taken during preparation of their meals.
*www.fatz.com*

## Fire + Ice                    ★$$LD

*Asian*

GF sauces are available. Restaurant notes that servers have access to an internal list of GF ingredients. They add that GF meals can be prepared separately in the kitchen on request, instead of on common cooking surfaces. Alert the server, who will make arrangements.
*www.fire-ice.com*

## Fire Bowl Café                    ✿¢LD

*Asian*

GF menu includes spicy coconut soup, Thai tom kha noodle soup, a variety of salads, and more. It features "Stir Fry Your Way," so diners choose their own meats, sauces, and starches. The GF sauce options are ginger white wine, coconut curry, and lemongrass basil. The restaurant recommends consulting a manager to ensure that your meal is properly prepared. Confirm the timeliness of this information before dining in.
*www.firebowlcafe.com*

## Firebirds Wood Fired Grill  ✿$$$LD

*American*

GF menu includes a variety of salads, steaks, and seafood, as well as several sides and a kids menu. General manager Max at the Raleigh location reports that they have "many procedures in place to prevent cross-contamination", and recommends consulting with a manger when dining in.
*www.firebirdsrockymountaingrill.com*

## First Watch - The Daytime Café                    ✿¢BL

*American*

Gluten-Free Guide and "Allergen Chart" on their website point guests to possible GF options, including items such as omelets and skillet hashes. Most items require modification to become GF, so be sure to consult your server before placing your order. Marketing manager Jessica reports that they "take food safety very seriously" and they "welcome special orders and modifications."
*www.firstwatch.com*

## Flat Top Grill                    $LD

*Asian*

The restaurant reports that their self-serve style "lends itself to being GF." An "allergen list" that includes gluten is available online and in stores. The restaurant notes that their servers are "trained to be sensitive to allergy restrictions."
*www.flattopgrill.com*

## Flatbread Pizza Company      ★$LD

*Pizza*

GF pizza/flat breads are available in the 8-inch size. GF beer and desserts like brownies are also available.
*www.flatbreadcompany.com*

## Fleming's Prime Steakhouse & Wine Bar                    ✪$$$LD
*Steakhouse*
Extensive GF menu includes Cajun barbecue shrimp, porcini rubbed filet mignon, pork chop, Alaskan king crab legs, and more. For dessert, they offer crème brûlée, mixed berries with whipped cream, or vanilla ice cream. The restaurant reports that all kitchen staff is required to take classes on preventing CC of all allergens during preparation.
*www.flemingssteakhouse.com*

## Fogo De Chao                    ★$$$$LD
*Brazilian*
Jennifer from management reports that they can "accommodate many of their guests' dietary concerns because of the variety of choices they offer." She notes that they do not have a CC policy currently in place, and recommends speaking to the manager upon arrival at the restaurant. GF cheese bread made with yucca flour is available.
*www.fogodechao.com*

## Fox and Hound Pub & Grill                    $LD
*Pub Food*
The restaurant reports that while they do not have a GF menu, there are several items on the regular menu that can be modified to be GF. Alert server upon arrival and they will list the options. There is a completely separate prep area and grill for GF orders.
*www.foxandhound.com*

## Freebirds on the Fly                    ✪¢LD
*Latin American*
GF menu available upon request. Items include GF sauces, produce, meat selections as well as rice and beans. GF items are made with corn tortillas.
*www.freebirds.com*

## Fresh City                    ★¢BLD
*Deli*
Menu includes a section where GF suggested items are listed. They include stir fry served over rice instead of noodles, classic burritos served in a bowl instead of flour tortilla, soups such as organic tomato basil, and salads. Alert server that your meal must be GF and they will inform kitchen staff to "be more careful."
*www.freshcity.com*

## FUEL Pizza                    ✪★$LD
*Pizza*
GF 12" Pizza crust available. Note: all 35 toppings are GF, except for their meatballs. Red Bridge GF beer is also on the menu.
*www.fuelpizza.com*

## Garbanzo                    ¢LD
*Mediterranean*
Staff member Theresa reports that almost everything on the menu is GF, and servers will be able to note which items are not. Nutritional information, including a list of ingredients for each item, is available online.
*www.eatgarbanzo.com*

## Garlic Jim's                    ✪★$$LD
*Pizza*
GF menu includes GF pizza, salads, and wings. An FAQ section detailing their CC policies and other concerns can be found on the Garlic Jim's website.
*www.garlicjims.com*

## Genghis Grill                    ¢LD
*Asian*
Director of Culinary Research and Development Jax reports that the dragon, sweet & sour, and tomato sauces are all GF, as well as the brown and white rice. He recommends letting the "grill master" know of your "allergy" when dining in. Confirm the timeliness of this information before dining in.
*www.genghisgrill.com*

## Glory Days Grill ✪ $$LD
*American*
GF menu available. Items include chicken wings, bun-less burgers and sandwiches, grilled shrimp platter, BBQ ribs and fresh grilled salmon. Kids menu is also available.
*www.glorydaysgrill.com*

## Godfather's Pizza ★ $$LD
*Pizza*
GF pizza is available at the listed locations only. VP David reports that GF pizzas arrive pre-topped and individually wrapped. Some locations bake pizzas in-store, which requires a training program and strict procedures against CC. Others sell the pizzas as take-and-bake only.
*www.godfathers.com*

## Green Mill Restaurant ✪ $LD
*Pub Food*
GF menu includes items such as chicken wings, grilled salads, and bunless hamburgers.
*www.greenmill.com*

## Greene Turtle Sports Bar & Grill ✪ ¢LD
*American*
GF menu includes baby back ribs, blackened tilapia, mozzarella caprese, Maryland crab soup, and more. General manager Dan of Annapolis recommends speaking to a manager upon arrival, who will put the appropriate CC procedures into place.
*www.greeneturtle.com*

## Ground Round ✪ $LD
*American*
Limited GF menu includes wings, salads, and bunless burgers. Restaurant reports that they always use fresh gloves and separate utensils for GF orders.
*www.groundround.com*

## Guapo's Fine Mexican Cuisine ✪ $LD
*Mexican*
GF menu available in stores and available on request. Each store has different CC policies, some stores have dedicated utensils for the preparation of GF items and some do not have a policy.
*www.guaposrestaurant.com*

## Happy Joe's Pizza & Ice Cream ★ $$LD
*Pizza*
GF pizza is available in the small size only.
*www.happyjoes.com*

## Harbor Inn Seafood $LD
*Seafood*
GF options are available upon request. Alert the server upon arrival.
*www.harborinnseafood.com*

## Hard Rock Café $$LD
*American*
Manager Anthony reports that they have a reference book in the kitchen that informs chefs of the necessary steps to prevent CC of each major allergen, including gluten. Alert server upon arrival and they will list GF options or ask a manager.
*www.hardrock.com*

## Hillstone $$$LD
*American*
The restaurant reports that many menu items that can be modified to be GF. Alert the server upon arrival to find out the current options.
*www.hillstone.com*

## HuHot Mongolian Grill ¢LD
*Asian*
The restaurant reports that they are an "allergy friendly restaurant" where customers "create their own dinners and watch them cook on a large grill." Host Ryan notes that GF noodles are available,

as well as several GF sauces, and "tons of vegetables and meats." The grills are thoroughly cleaned and they have GF dedicated spatulas.
*www.huhot.com*

## Ingredient Restaurant    ✪ ★ $LD
*Pizza*

GF menu includes salads with GF dressings and pizzas with a variety of toppings. GF pizza and GF breadsticks are available. Operations director Nick reports that they "strive to meet all dietary and food restrictions" but recommends keeping in mind that they are not a GF environment.
*www.ingredientrestaurant.com*

## In-N-Out Burger    ¢LD
*American*

The only menu item containing gluten is their bun, and customers can order "protein style" for the same burger wrapped in lettuce. Alert the staff so they can change gloves and keep the buns away from your burger.
*www.in-n-out.com*

## Iron Hill
## Brewery & Restaurant    ✪ ★ $$LD
*American*

GF menu is available at all locations and includes salads, burgers and sandwiches without buns, steaks, chicken, and seafood. GF beer is available.
*www.ironhillbrewery.com*

## Islands Fine Burgers
## & Drinks    ¢LD
*American*

Manager Mark reports that they have a small GF menu. When preparing GF orders, they change their gloves, use separate utensils, and put foil down on the grill to cook GF items. All nutritional information, including a list of GF items, is available on their website.
*www.islandsrestaurants.com*

## J. Gumbo's    ✪ ¢BLD
*Cajun & Creole*

GF items are marked on the menu and include jambalaya, red beans & rice, voodoo chicken, white chili, creole ratatouille, and more. President of operations Ronnie reports that they are "dedicated to customer safety" and that all nutrition information can be found online and in stores. Confirm the timeliness of this information before dining in.
*www.jgumbos.com*

## Jamba Juice    ☎ ¢S
*American*

Greg in guest services reports that none of their sherbets, frozen yogurt, sorbet, fruits, or juice concentrates contain gluten, and all boosts are "non-gluten." However, since they do serve non-GF items in their stores, they cannot guarantee no CC. A Nutritional Analysis Guide that lists ingredients in detail is located in each store.
*www.jambajuice.com*

## Jason's Deli    ✪ ★ ¢BLD
*Deli*

GF menu includes soups, salads, potatoes, and sandwiches made on Udi's GF bread. Director of Testing & Research Kim cautions that the risk of CC is high, and does not recommend the menu for Celiac patients.
*www.jasonsdeli.com*

## Jersey Mike's    ¢BLD
*Deli*

GF option is "Sub in a Tub". Food allergy & sensitivity chart available online denotes which items contain gluten. Alert the server that your meal must be GF.
*www.jerseymikes.com*

## Jim 'n Nick's Bar-B-Que ✪ ★ $$LD

*Barbeque*

Restaurant states they have an in-house listing of GF options and restrictions. Some of the available items include chicken, pork, chicken and ribs and sides such as baked and mashed potatoes and french fries.
*www.jimnnicks.com*

## Jimmy John ☎ ¢LD

*Deli*

Customer service reports that any sandwich can be made into an "unwich", wrapped in lettuce instead of bread. They note that the avocado, bacon, ham, capicola, salami, turkey, cheese, mayo, and chips are all GF. Note that the beef is NOT GF.
*www.jimmyjohns.com*

## Joe's Crab Shack ✪$LD

*Seafood*

GF menu includes items such as sunset fire-grilled crab steampot, snow crab bucket, lobster daddy feast, Aruba chicken salad, and more. The restaurant strongly recommends that guests with "special dietary needs" speak with a manager before placing an order.
*www.joescrabshack.com*

## Johnny Brusco's New York Style Pizza ★ $$LD

*Pizza*

GF pizza is available in the 10.5-inch size with any toppings. Call ahead to confirm availability.
*www.johnnyspizza.com*

## Kincaid's ✪$$LD

*American*

Gluten Sensitive menu includes a variety of appetizers, salads, entrées, sides, and desserts. Sample items include steamed fresh clams, iceberg lettuce wedge, rock salt roasted prime rib, smoked mushrooms with truffle, and seasonal sorbet.
*www.kincaids.com*

## Larkburger ★ $LD

*American*

GF hamburger buns are available. Burgers are also available wrapped in lettuce instead of a bun.
*www.larkburger.com*

## LaRosa's Pizzeria ★ $LD

*Pizza*

GF pizza is available at the listed locations only. Supervisor Kim reports that they follow "very strict cleaning and preparation procedures", including changing gloves, using separate utensils and toppings, and cleaning the prep area.
*www.larosas.com*

## Legal Sea Foods ✪$$$LD

*Seafood*

GF menu available at all locations. Sample items include surf & turf, shrimp & garlic, steamed lobster, and a variety of wood grilled seafood options. Items may vary by location, availability, and season. Ask for the GF menu and alert a manager when dining in.
*www.legalseafoods.com*

## Ling & Louie's Asian Bar & Grill ✪ ★ $LD

*Asian*

Extensive GF menu includes chicken and seafood, rice and noodle dishes, as well as "not-so-sizzling" platters. Examples include sweet and sour chicken, salmon, and edamame. For dessert, there is a chocolate volcano cake. GF beer is available.
*www.lingandlouies.com*

## Lone Star Steakhouse & Saloon ✪$$LD

*Steakhouse*

The restaurant offers a "GF recommendations" list that denotes the safest menu options as well as the recommended preparation. Items include mesquite grilled steaks, sweet bourbon salmon, chicken, shrimp,

and more. Holly at guest relations strongly recommends alerting a manager upon arrival so that he or she "may ensure that the food is safely prepared."
*www.lonestarsteakhouse.com*

## LongHorn Steakhouse ☎ ✪ $$LD
*Steakhouse*

GF menu includes a wide variety of steaks and seafood dishes, as well as salads, vegetables, and potatoes. CC policy includes using tinfoil on the grill when cooking GF items, and staff also notes that everything that they have in the store is received separately packaged and is only combined at the time the order is placed so it is "very easy for them to be GF."
*www.longhornsteakhouse.com*

## Lou Malnati's $$LD
*Pizza*

Marketing director Mindy reports that all locations have a "crustless" pizza available upon request.
*www.loumalnatis.com*

## Loving Hut ✪ ¢LD
*Asian*

GF optional items are marked on the menu and range from salads to soups, noodle dishes, and tofu entrees. Alert the server upon arrival.
*www.lovinghut.us*

## Maggiano's Little Italy $$$LD
*Italian*

Though they do not have a GF menu, their chefs can create "customized dishes" that will meet any dietary needs. The restaurants recommends alerting your server and asking to speak directly with a chef, who will "suggest and prepare a meal that will meet your dietary requirements."
*www.maggianos.com*

## Mama Fu's Asian House ✪ $LD
*Asian Fusion*

Restaurant offers a full GF menu with items such as shrimp salad, seared ahi tuna, rice noodle bowls, and a seared steak.
*www.mamafus.com*

## Margaritaville ✪ ★ $$LD
*American*

GF sandwich buns and beer are available. GF menu includes items such as nachos, sirloin steak, jerk salmon, several burgers & sandwiches, and more. A GF "chocolate hurricane" brownie is available for dessert. Executive chef Craig of Myrtle Beach notes that the company-wide policy for preparing GF items includes washing hands, changing gloves, using fresh utensils, and cleaning the cooking space. Be sure to notify your server that you are ordering from the GF menu.
*www.margaritaville.com*

## McAlister's Deli ☎ ¢BL
*Deli*

An "allergen guide" is available, which lists all menu items and any "allergens", including gluten, that they contain. General manager Dave of Aurora reports that they are "well-versed" in CC procedures.
*www.mcalistersdeli.com*

## McGrath's Fish House ✪ $LD
*Seafood*

GF menu features a large selection of seafood entrées and appetizers, as well as salads and steaks.
*www.mcgrathsfishhouse.com*

## Mellow Mushroom ☎ ✪ ★ $LD
*Pizza*

GF pizza is available. General manager Travis at the Chattanooga location reports that all restaurants have a strict CC policy, including using separate utensils and baking pizzas in a separate oven.
*www.mellowmushroom.com*

## Melting Pot, The ✪ $LD

*European*

Operating partner Frankie reports that all Melting Pot locations have GF options, and all staff is "highly trained in food sensitivities/preventing cross-contamination." However, since they are individually franchised, he recommends speaking with a manager at the location you wish to visit to ensure a safe dining experience.
www.meltingpot.com

## Miller's Ale House ✪ ★ $LD

*American*

GF menu includes steamed oysters, several salads, NY strip steak, filet mignon, catch of the day, burgers without buns, and GF cheese pizza, among other things. The restaurant reports that kitchens are inspected on GF cleanliness twice daily by managers, and a ll GF items are individually wrapped or portioned to go directly into the pot/pan.
www.millersalehouse.com

## Minerva's ✪ $$LD

*American*

The restaurant reports that they have a GF menu in-house which features "countless delicious GF options". Alert the server upon arrival.
www.minervas.net

## Mitchell's Fish Market ✪ $$$LD

*Seafood*

Extensive GF menu includes a selection of salads, fish dishes, steaks, and shellfish. Mini crème brûlée and sorbet of the day are available for dessert. Be sure to notify your server that you are ordering from the GF menu.
www.mitchellsfishmarket.com

## Monical's Pizza ★ $$LD

*Pizza*

GF pizza is available at "most, but not all" restaurants according to their corporate office. They were unable to provide a complete list of locations serving GF pizza, so Triumph recommends calling ahead to the specific location you would like to visit.
www.monicalspizza.com

## Morton's Steakhouse $$LD

*Steakhouse*

The restaurant reports that meals are cooked on a made to order basis, and GF is fairly easy to ensure if one person is handling the entire transaction. Alert a manager upon arrival to ensure a GF meal. Lunch availability varies by location.
www.mortons.com

## My Big Fat Greek Restaurant ✪ $$LD

*Greek*

GF items are marked on the menu and include souvlaki, lamb chops, stuffed peppers, fresh salmon, chicken caprese, and more. The restaurant recommends alerting the manager upon arrival to ensure proper GF preparation.
www.eatmoregreek.com

## Nick-N-Willy's ★ $LD

*Pizza*

GF pizza is available.
www.nicknwillys.com

## Ninety Nine Restaurant ✪ $$LD

*American*

GF menu features items such as broiled sirloin tips, herbed salmon & vegetables, balsamic grilled chicken, a variety of salads, and more.
www.99restaurants.com

## Noodles & Company   ☎ ★ ¢LD
*Global*

GF pasta is available. Online allergen guide denotes GF items and sauces. The restaurant recommends alerting both the server and manager upon arrival.
www.noodles.com

## Not Your Average Joe's   ✪$$LD
*American*

GF menu includes Vietnamese flounder, Mediterranean chicken, grilled turkey kabob, several salads, and more. GF bread and beer are available, as well as a GF kid's menu. Food and beverage director Kristin reports that all GF orders are overseen by a manager to ensure proper preparation.
www.notyouraveragejoes.com

## O'Charley's   $$LD
*American*

Online "allergen information" sheet denotes which items do not contain gluten. The restaurant recommends notifying a manager upon arrival to "assist with your selection."
www.ocharleys.com

## Old Spaghetti Factory   ✪★$LD
*Italian*

GF pasta is available. GF menu denotes which pasta sauces are GF as well as which other selections may be prepared GF. All GF items are stored in their own area in the walk in fridge and are prepped for the day before all items containing gluten are even brought out of their containers. All GF items are stored in blue containers, and when handling them employees must be wearing the designated blue gloves and corresponding blue utensils that are not to be used on anything else.
www.osf.com

## Olive Garden   ✪ ★ ☎ ¢LD
*Italian*

GF pasta is available. GF menu includes several pasta dishes as well as steak toscano, herb-grilled salmon, chicken skewers, and salads. The restaurant stresses the importance of notifying the server of all dietary requirements.
www.olivegarden.com
www.ontheborder.com

## On the Border
## Mexican Grill & Cantina   ☎ ¢LD
*Mexican*

Allergen guide is available online and in restaurant and includes a section for GF items. They have a specific GF fryer and sanitizers at every station, as well as a comprehensive computer system that tells the kitchen staff exactly what to do per allergy order. Guest relations coordinator Robin recommends consulting with the manager on duty when dining in.
www.ontheborder.com

## Original Pancake House   ★ ☎ ¢BL
*American*

GF pancakes are available at "most locations" according to corporate chef Jon. He notes that each location is franchised and therefore can choose whether or not to serve GF pancakes. He recommends calling the location you wish to visit beforehand to find out whether they carry them.
www.originalpancakehouse.com

## Outback Steakhouse   ✪☎$LD
*Steakhouse*

GF menu was developed in partnership with the GIG and items are "continuously renewed" by their registered dietitian and nutrition team. Restaurant recommends "discussing GF needs with a manager" before placing an order.
www.outback.com

## P.F. Chang's China Bistro ✪★$LD
*Chinese*

Extensive GF menu includes chicken lettuce wraps, egg drop soup, fried rice, caramel mango chicken, Mongolian beef, moo goo gai pan, and more. Be sure to alert the server that your meal must be GF, as some items require modification. GF soy sauce is available upon request.
*www.pfchangs.com*

## Palomino $$$LD
*Modern American*

Manager Justin at Indianapolis reports that there are "quite a few GF options to choose from" and that "the service staff is well-versed" in handling GF orders. He notes that there are "safety guidelines in place to prevent cross-contamination", and adds that all of this information is valid for all locations. Reservations noting GF are recommended, as is alerting a server upon arrival.
*www.palomino.com*

## Papa Razzi ★$$LD
*Italian*

GF pasta and pizza are available. Andrea at corporate reports that anything on the menu can be made GF, and that the chefs use separate utensils as well as fresh water when preparing GF meals.
*www.paparazzitrattoria.com*

## Pappasito's Cantina $$LD
*Tex-Mex*

Triumph spoke with a manager at each location, and all reported having served GF diners before. All locations recommend alerting a server upon arrival. All servers are trained to alert a manager, who will communicate with the kitchen staff. Recommend alerting the cashier upon arrival.
*www.pappasitos.com*

## Pasta House Co., The ✪★$LD
*Italian*

GF menu available in stores. Ask for a manager when dining in, and they will put the kitchen "on alert" for a GF order. Separate pots, pans, and utensils are used to prepare GF meals.
*www.pastahouse.com*

## Pei Wei Asian Diner ✪¢LD
*Asian*

GF menu includes Vietnamese rolls, spicy shrimp, sweet & sour chicken, Asian chopped chicken salad, and more. Be sure to specify to the server that you are ordering from the GF menu.
*www.peiwei.com*

## Piatti ★$$LD
*Italian*

GF pasta is available. The restaurant reports that staff is trained on GF preparation and GF diners are accommodated "all the time." They note that the risotto is GF and that many menu items can be modified to be GF. Alert a server upon arrival.
*www.piatti.com*

## Piccadilly $LD
*American*

GF options include baked fish with crab meat, baked chicken, roast beef, chop steak and liver and onion dish.
*www.piccadilly.com*

## Pizza Fusion ★$$$LD
*Pizza*

GF pizza is available. The NFCA training program is used to instruct employees on proper GF preparation. All GF foods are prepared with "sanitized equipment, special utensils, and on a separate, designated surface."
*www.pizzafusion.com*

## Pizza Joe's ★ $LD
*Pizza*

GF pizza is available. Call ahead to confirm that the store you wish to visit has GF pizza in stock.

www.pizzajoes.com

## Pizza Ranch ✪ $$LD
*Pizza*

GF pizza is available. Corporate reports that GF pizza is an optional product and restaurants may decide to serve it on an individual basis. They recommend contacting the location you are interested in to see if they carry GF pizza. Director of operations Al reports that locations with GF pizza have a thorough CC policy that includes sanitizing all cookware and surfaces and cooking the pizzas in an aluminum pan with an additional pan beneath for added protection.

www.pizzaranch.com

## Pizza Shoppe ★ $LD
*Pizza*

GF pizza is available in the 8" size.

www.pizzashoppe.com

## Prêt A Manger ¢BL
*Deli*

GF soups, chilis, and salads are sometimes available. All locations report that most things are pre-made. Calling ahead to discuss the day's GF options is strongly recommended. Triumph notes that some locations seem more aware than others.

www.pret.com

## Puccini's Smiling Teeth ★ $LD
*Italian*

GF pizza and pasta are available.

www.puccinissmilingteeth.com

## Red Brick Pizza ✪ ★ ¢LD
*Pizza*

GF menu features a "build your own pizza" section listing GF toppings and sauces, as well as a "gourmet favorites" section listing established pizza options. GF flatbread is also available for their signature Fhazani sandwiches.

www.redbrickpizza.com

## Red Robin Gourmet Burgers ☎ ✪ $LD
*American*

Wheat/gluten allergy menu is available online, and includes salads and burgers served "protein-style" wrapped in lettuce. Quality assurance manager Eric reports that all "allergy" orders are immediately flagged for the kitchen and prepared using "clean utensils and a clean workspace to ensure cross-contamination is controlled."

www.redrobin.com

## Rockfish Seafood Grill ✪ $LD
*Seafood*

Extensive GF menu includes soups, salads, a variety of seafood dishes, steaks, and more.

www.rockfish.com

## Rodizio Grill $$$LD
*Brazilian*

The restaurant offers a printed description of which items on the menu contain gluten, and reports that people come in specifically for the GF options. Alert a server, who will discuss GF options and notify the chef.

www.rodiziogrill.com

## Romano's Macaroni Grill ✪ ★ $LD
*Italian*

Online GF menu and allergen guide features dishes such as lentil soup, caprese salad, fettuccine alfredo and shrimp portofino all of which are GF without a side of bread. The restaurant reports that there is a specific pot of water for GF pasta.

www.macaronigrill.com

## Rosa Mexicano ✪$$$BLD
*Mexican*

Manager George at the West Hollywood location recommends alerting a manager upon arrival to ensure that your meal is prepared safely. They have a dedicated GF fryer and clean and sanitize all items used for GF orders. The 1st Avenue location in Manhattan offers only GF dinner. Examples of GF dishes offered are tortilla soup, crab turnovers, pork belly and scallop tacos, enchiladas suizas, chicken tortilla pie and more.
*www.rosamexicano.com*

## Rosati's Pizza ★$LD
*Pizza*

GF pizza is available. Call ahead to confirm that the store you wish to visit has GF pizza in stock.
*www.myrosatis.com*

## Roy's $$$D
*Hawaiian*

Laura at the corporate office reports that they do not have a set GF menu but their chefs are "more than willing and able to meet your dietary needs." Reservations noting GF are recommended, and a server should be alerted upon arrival.
*www.roysrestaurant.com*

## Ruby Tuesday ☎$LD
*American*

Allergen guide available displaying GF entrée options. Manager Kevin says they pride themselves on not only their GF standards but their overall cleanliness and allergy free standards. Even for non allergen orders there are specific fryers, cutting boards, utensils, etc. for each food group and separate protein, which "prevents CC in the first place."
*www.rubytuesday.com*

## Ruth's Chris Steak House ✪$$$$D
*Steakhouse*

GF menu includes barbequed shrimp, spinach & pear salad, jumbo sea scallops with Cajun béarnaise, all signature steak entrées, and more. General manager Stephen at the Huntsville location reports that they "do their best to take care of folks with special dietary needs" and they are "happy to prepare any items to your specifications."
*www.ruthschris.com*

## Sam & Louie's New York Pizzeria ★$$LD
*Pizza*

GF pizza is available. Jessica at the Elkhorn location reports that they "take great precautions" when preparing GF meals and "enforce these regulations at each location." GF pizzas are prepared in a designated area using toppings set aside specifically for that purpose.
*www.samandlouiespizza.com*

## Sammy's Woodfired Pizza ✪$LD
*Pizza*

GF items are marked on the menu and include a variety of artisan thin crust and woodfired pizzas, oak roasted chicken breast, shrimp & grits, several salads, and more. Operations coordinator Luz recommends alerting the server upon arrival, and reports that the kitchen "will take the necessary precautions" against CC.
*www.sammyspizza.com*

## Shane's Rib Shack ✪¢LD
*Barbeque*

Almost all plated meat options are GF as well as most of their sides except for their Texas toast. They have designated fryers and prep areas for items containing gluten.
*www.shanesribshack.com*

## Shorty Smalls                    $LD
*American*

The restaurant reports that they do not have a GF menu, but are "willing and able" to modify certain dishes to meet their customers' needs. Staff notes that meat and seafood dishes are usually the safest options, and recommends alerting a manager upon arrival.
*www.shortysmalls.com*

## Smiling Moose Deli          ★ $BLD
*Deli*

GF bread is available for sandwiches. The restaurant reports that they have "procedures that they follow" when preparing GF items. While they are not a 100% GF environment, they "do make an effort to make sure there is no cross-contamination."
*www.smilingmoosedeli.com*

## Smith & Wollensky          $$$$LD
*Steakhouse*

Regional director of operations Kim reports that they have many GF items on the menu. Included are seared scallops, split pea soup, sirloin steak, free-range chicken, red snapper, and more. She recommends alerting the server to indicate GF options. This will ensure that "extra attention is paid" when preparing a GF meal.
*www.smithandwollensky.com*

## Smokey Bones                    $LD
*Barbeque*

GF options and menu available. Alert hostess and server of GF request.
*www.smokeybones.com*

## Sticky Fingers Smokehouse    $LD
*Barbeque*

GF items indicated on the Allergen Guide include wings, all ribs, pulled pork, smoked chicken, baked beans, coleslaw, mashed potatoes without the gravy, loaded baked and mashed potatoes.
*www.stickyfingers.com*

## Stir Crazy                    ★ $$LD
*Asian*

Triumph spoke with a manager at each location. All report that servers are educated about GF and able to indicate the three GF sauce options: teriyaki, classic Chinese, and Szechuan. Any of these sauces can be used on a menu item or at the stir fry market bar. GF rice noodles are available. Confirm the timeliness of this information before dining in.
*www.stircrazy.com*

## Surin of Thailand              $LD
*Thai*

Team member Thanes reports that there are several items on the menu that can be prepared without gluten ingredients, and recommends consulting the server or manager to assist with choosing an appropriate dish.
*www.surinofthailand.com*

## Sweet Cece's                      ¢S
*Dessert*

Staff reports that all frozen yogurt flavors EXCEPT Cake Batter, Cookies n' Cream, Red Velvet Cake, and Heath Bar, are GF. Confirm the timeliness of this information before dining in.
*www.sweetceces.com*

## Taco Del Mar                  ☎ ¢LD
*Mexican*

A chart that shows which items are GF and which contain gluten is available online under Nutritional Information. Most items can be made GF by using a corn tortillas.
*www.tacodelmar.com*

## TacoTime                      ☎ ¢LD
*Mexican*

The restaurant reports they have a GF enchilada made with corn tortillas, as well as soft tacos that can be made GF. Confirm this information before dining in.
*www.tacotime.com*

## Ted's Montana Grill    ✪ $LD
*American*

GF menu includes cedar plank salmon, beef tenderloin filet, bison strip steak, a variety of burgers without buns, and more. The menu also lists GF sides and specifies the modifications that must be made to make certain dishes GF. Director of operations Chris reports that they "take their GF practices seriously" and "deal with GF diners daily." Confirm the timeliness of this information before dining in.
*www.tedsmontanagrill.com*

## Texas De Brazil Churrascaria    $$$$D
*Brazilian*

GF list available in-house. Alert the server upon arrival and they will provide the list.
*www.texasdebrazil.com*

## Tin Drum AsiaCafé    ✪ ¢LD
*Asian*

GF menu includes sweet 'n sour stir-fry, egg drop soup, mandarin fried rice, Thai basil roll, and several curry dishes, among other things. Modifications needed in order to make some dishes GF are included on the menu. Alert the server upon arrival.
*www.tindrumcafe.com*

## Tokyo Joe's    ★ $LD
*Asian*

GF teriyaki sauce and soy sauce are available. Online ingredients list denotes which menu items are GF. Customer service agent Betsy recommends consulting with your server to ensure that your meal is prepared safely.
*www.tokyojoes.com*

## Tony Roma's    $$LD
*Seafood & Steakhouse*

Martha in guest relations reports that their barbeque sauce, ribs, steaks, chicken, and fish are GF. Sauce toppings and fried items should be avoided as these are NOT GF. She recommends speaking with a manager for additional information when dining in.
*www.tonyromas.com*

## Tossed    ✪ ¢ BLD
*American*

GF menu includes various salad selections such as southwest blackened chicken salad, cayenne shrimp salad, Asian chicken salad and apple walnut salad. GF guests can also opt for the "Design your own salad" option, as the menu denotes which salad toppings are GF. Alert the server when ordering to ensure that proper precautions are taken.
*www.tossed.com*

## Travinia Italian Kitchen    ★ $$LD
*Italian*

GF menu is available at all locations and includes seared scallops, chicken scaloppine, NY strip steak, wild mushroom carbonara, pine nut encrusted salmon, and more. GF pasta is available, and all GF pasta options are listed on the menu. For dessert, there is crème brûlée and zabaglione.
*www.traviniaitaliankitchen.com*

## True Food Kitchen    ✪ ★ $BLD
*Fusion*

GF items marked on the menu include local vegetable crudités with tzatziki dipping sauce, curry with rice noodles, and turkey bolognese, among other things. GF brown rice pasta is available.    www
*www.foxrc.com*

## U Food Grill    ¢LD
*American*

Nutrition Guide on website lists GF items. These include several bunless burgers and salads, as well as a variety of side dishes like sweet potato mash, seasoned black beans, and brown rice. Alert server upon arrival to ensure proper preparation of GF items.
*www.ufoodgrill.com*

## Uno Chicago Grill ✪ ★ $LD
*Global*

GF menu includes herb rubbed chicken breast, lemon basil salmon, beef chili, grilled shrimp & sirloin, burgers on GF buns, and more. GF pizza and burger buns are available. For dessert, an ice cream sundae is available. Procedures to mitigate CC include training staff to handle special dietary requirements and using dedicated equipment and separate areas to prepare GF items.
*www.unos.com*

## Valentino's ★ $LD
*Pizza*

GF pizza is confirmed available at listed locations only. All other locations are independently owned and have the option of offering GF pizza based on local demand. Contact each individual location to enquire.
*www.valentinos.com*

## Veggie Grill, The ✪ ★ ¢LD
*American*

GF menu includes quinoa pilaf, kale salad, several soups, sandwiches without buns, and more. GF pasta is available, as well as chocolate pudding for dessert. Specific items on GF menu may vary by location.
*www.veggiegrill.com*

## Village Tavern ✪ $$LD
*Fusion*

Extensive GF brunch and dinner menu featuring items such as GF pizzas, fresh market fish , steaks and prime rib, and specialties such as pork chops, seared scallops, and shrimp scampi.
*www.villagetavern.com*

## Wildfire ✪ ★ $$$LD
*Steakhouse*

CC policy is very thorough and begins as soon as you sit at your table. Alert your server of your dietary needs and they will inform the manager and the chef. GF menu includes a wide variety of items, including salads, burgers, steaks, and seafood. GF pizza, buns, and beer are available, as well as several GF dessert options.
*www.wildfirerestaurant.com*

## Yard House ✪ $LD
*American*

Gluten sensitive menu includes "protein style" burgers and sandwiches, several salads, pan seared ahi, ginger crusted Norwegian salmon, pepper crusted filet, and more. Guest services manager Kristi reports that the kitchen is notified and "all precautions are taken" for every GF order, but since they are not a GF environment, they cannot guarantee no CC.
*www.yardhouse.com*

## Zio's ✪ $LD
*Italian*

GF menu includes salmon caesar salad, chicken piccata, Greek pasta, lemon chicken primavera, shrimp with marinara, ribeye tuscano, grilled sirloin, and more. Confirm the timeliness of this information before dining in.
*www.zios.com*

## Zpizza ✪ ★ $LD
*Pizza*

GF pizza crust is available with a list of safe toppings and sauces on their website in the FAQ section.
*www.zpizza.com*

## Z'Tejas Southwestern Grill ✪ ★ $LD
*Southwest*

GF menu includes wild mushroom enchiladas, pesto rubbed salmon, grilled fish salad, and more. Frozen margaritas and GF beer are also available. R&D chef Matthew reports that they "have policies in place" for the preparation of GF items, but cautions that their kitchens are not totally GF.
*www.ztejas.com*